WHO'S WHO OF PULITZER PRIZE WINNERS

WHO'S WHO OF PULITZER PRIZE WINNERS

Elizabeth A. Brennan and
Elizabeth C. Clarage

Foreword by Seymour Topping

Oryx Press
1999

The rare Arabian Oryx is believed to have inspired the myth of the unicorn. This desert antelope became virtually extinct in the early 1960s. At that time, several groups of international conservationists arranged to have nine animals sent to the Phoenix Zoo to be the nucleus of a captive breeding herd. Today, the Oryx population is over 1,000, and over 500 have been returned to the Middle East.

© 1999 by The Oryx Press
4041 North Central at Indian School Road
Phoenix, Arizona 85012-3397

Published simultaneously in Canada
Printed and bound in the United States of America

The paper used in this publication meets the minimum requirements of American National Standard for Information Science—Permanence of Paper for Printed Library Materials, ANSI Z39.48, 1984.

Cover photos clockwise from upper left are Russell Baker, Gwendolyn Brooks, Edna St. Vincent Millay, Sheryl WuDunn, Gian-Carlo Menotti, Willa Cather, Caro Brown, Robert Frost, Aaron Copland, Carlos Romulo, and Marya Zaturenska (Center).

Photo of Sheryl WuDunn printed with permission of NYT Pictures.
Other cover photos are from the National Archives and Records Administration (NARA), Washington, D.C.

Photos for the following entries in the book were reprinted with the permission of Columbia University, New York: 1, 5, 9, 94, 98, 99, 100, 101, 106, 107, 110, 112, 114, 115, 116, 117, 118, 144, 147, 157, 163, 252, 263, 265, 270, 276, 281, 282, 340, 349, 353, 385, 417, 426, 429, 484, 488, 614, 620, 622, 627, 628, 630, 641, 644, 651, 664, 668, 672, 714, 716, 786, 897, 900, 906, 908, 1001, 1002, 1116, 1136, 1144, 1155, 1166. All of the other photos are from NARA.

Library of Congress Cataloging-in-Publication Data
Brennan, Elizabeth A.
    Who's who of Pulitzer Prize winners / by Elizabeth A. Brennan,
Elizabeth Clarage.
      p. cm.
    Includes bibliographical references and index.
    ISBN 1-57356-111-8
    1. Pulitzer Prizes. 2. Biography—20th century. I. Clarage,
Elizabeth. II. Title.
AS911.P8B74 1999
071'.3'092273—dc21   98-44979
                                    CIP

Contents

Foreword

Joseph Pulitzer and the Pulitzer Prizes

by Seymour Topping

HISTORY OF THE PRIZE

In the latter years of the 19th century, Joseph Pulitzer stood out as the very embodiment of American journalism. Hungarian-born, an intense indomitable figure, Pulitzer was the most skillful of newspaper publishers, a passionate crusader against dishonest government, a fierce, hawk-like competitor who did not shrink from sensationalism in circulation struggles, and a visionary who richly endowed his profession. His innovative *New York World* and *St. Louis Post-Dispatch* reshaped newspaper journalism. Pulitzer was the first to call for the training of journalists at the university level in a school of journalism. And certainly, the lasting influence of the Pulitzer Prizes on journalism, literature, music, and drama is to be attributed to his visionary acumen. In writing his 1904 will, which made provision for the establishment of the Pulitzer Prizes as an incentive to excellence, Pulitzer specified solely four awards in journalism, four in letters and drama, one for education, and four traveling scholarships. In letters, prizes were to go to an American novel, an original American play performed in New York, a book on the history of the United States, an American biography, and a history of public service by the press. But, sensitive to the dynamic progression of his society Pulitzer made provision for broad changes in the system of awards. He established an overseer advisory board and willed it "power in its discretion to suspend or to change any subject or subjects, substituting, however, others in their places, if in the judgment of the board such suspension, changes, or substitutions shall be conducive to the public good or rendered advisable by public necessities, or by reason of change of time." He also empowered the board to withhold any award where entries fell below its standards of excellence. The assignment of power to the board was such that it could also overrule the recommendations for awards made by the juries subsequently set up in each of the categories. Since the inception of the prizes in 1917, the board, later renamed the Pulitzer Prize Board, has increased the number of awards to 21 and introduced poetry, music, and photography as subjects, while adhering to the spirit of the founder's will and its intent.

The board typically exercised its broad discretion in 1997, the 150th anniversary of Pulitzer's birth, in two fundamental respects. It took a significant step in recognition of the growing importance of work

Seymour Topping was appointed Administrator of the Pulitzer Prizes and Professor of International Journalism at the Graduate School of Journalism of Columbia University in 1993. After serving in World War II, Professor Topping worked for 10 years for The Associated Press as a correspondent in China, Indochina, London, and Berlin. He left the Associated Press in 1959 to join the *New York Times,* where he remained for 34 years, serving as a foreign correspondent, foreign editor, managing editor, and editorial director of the company's 32 regional newspapers. He is a graduate of the School of Journalism at the University of Missouri and is the author of *Journey Between Two Chinas* (New York: Harper & Row, 1972) and *The Peking Letter, A Novel of the Chinese Civil War* (New York, Public Affairs, to be published in 1999).

being done by newspapers in online journalism. Beginning with the 1999 competition, the board sanctioned the submission by newspapers of online presentations as supplements to print exhibits in the Public Service category. The board left open the distinct possibility of further inclusions in the Pulitzer process of online journalism as the electronic medium developed. The other major change was in music, a category that was added to the Plan of Award for prizes in 1943. The prize always had gone to composers of classical music. The definition and entry requirements of the music category beginning with the 1998 competition were broadened to attract a wider range of American music. In an indication of the trend toward bringing mainstream music into the Pulitzer process, the 1997 prize went to Wynton Marsalis's "Blood on the Fields, which has strong jazz elements, the first such award. In music, the board also took tacit note of the criticism leveled at its predecessors for failure to cite two of the country's foremost jazz composers. It bestowed Special Awards on George Gershwin marking the 1998 centennial celebration of his birth and Duke Ellington on his 1999 centennial year.

Over the years the Pulitzer board has at times been targeted by critics for awards made or not made. Controversies also have arisen over decisions made by the board counter to the advice of juries. Given the subjective nature of the award process, this was inevitable. The board has not been captive to popular inclinations. Many, if not most, of the honored books have not been on bestseller lists, and many of the winning plays have been staged off-Broadway or in regional theaters. In journalism the major newspapers, such as *The New York Times, The Wall Street Journal,* and *The Washington Post,* have harvested many of the awards, but the board also has often reached out to work done by small, little-known papers. The Public Service award in 1995 went to *The Virgin Islands Daily News,* St.

Thomas, for its disclosure of the links between the region's rampant crime rate and corruption in the local criminal justice system. In letters, the board has grown less conservative over the years in matters of taste. In 1963 the drama jury nominated Edward Albee's *Who's Afraid of Virginia Woolf?,* but the board found the script insufficiently "uplifting," a complaint that related to arguments over sexual permissiveness and rough dialogue. In 1993 the prize went to Tony Kushner's *Angels in America: Millennium Approaches,* a play that dealt with problems of homosexuality and AIDS and whose script was replete with obscenities. On the same debated issue of taste, the board in 1941 denied the fiction prize to Ernest Hemingway's *For Whom the Bells Tolls,* but gave him the award in 1953 for *The Old Man and the Sea,* a lesser work. Notwithstanding these contretemps, from its earliest days, the board has in general stood firmly by a policy of secrecy in its deliberations and refusal to publicly debate or defend its decisions. The challenges have not lessened the reputation of the Pulitzer Prizes as the country's most prestigious awards and as the most sought-after accolades in journalism, letters, and music. The prizes are perceived as a major incentive for high-quality journalism and have focused worldwide attention on American achievements in letters and music.

The formal announcement of the prizes, made each April, states that the awards are made by the president of Columbia University on the recommendation of the Pulitzer Prize board. This formulation is derived from the Pulitzer will, which established Columbia as the seat of the administration of the prizes. Today, in fact, the independent board makes all the decisions relative to the prizes. In his will Pulitzer bestowed an endowment on Columbia of $2,000,000 for the establishment of a School of Journalism, one-fourth of which was to be "applied to prizes or scholarships for the encouragement of public, service, public morals,

American literature, and the advancement of education." In doing so, he stated: "I am deeply interested in the progress and elevation of journalism, having spent my life in that profession, regarding it as a noble profession and one of unequaled importance for its influence upon the minds and morals of the people. I desire to assist in attracting to this profession young men of character and ability, also to help those already engaged in the profession to acquire the highest moral and intellectual training." In his ascent to the summit of American journalism, Pulitzer himself received little or no assistance. He prided himself on being a self-made man, but it may have been his struggles as a young journalist that imbued him with the desire to foster professional training.

JOSEPH PULITZER, 1847–1911

Joseph Pulitzer was born in Mako, Hungary on April 10, 1847, the son of a wealthy grain merchant of Magyar-Jewish origin and a German mother who was a devout Roman Catholic. His younger brother, Albert, was trained for the priesthood but never attained it. The elder Pulitzer retired in Budapest and Joseph grew up and was educated there in private schools and by tutors. Restive at the age of seventeen, the gangling 6'2" youth decided to become a soldier and tried in turn to enlist in the Austrian Army, Napoleon's Foreign Legion for duty in Mexico, and the British Army for service in India. He was rebuffed because of weak eyesight and frail health, which were to plague him for the rest of his life. However, in Hamburg, Germany, he encountered a bounty recruiter for the U.S. Union Army and contracted to enlist as a substitute for a draftee, a procedure permitted under the Civil War draft system. At Boston he jumped ship and, as the legend goes, swam to shore, determined to keep the enlistment bounty for himself rather than leave it to the agent. Pulitzer collected the bounty by enlisting for a year in the Lincoln Cavalry, which suited him since there were

many Germans in the unit. He was fluent in German and French but spoke very little English. Later, he worked his way to St. Louis. While doing odd jobs there, such as muleteer, baggage handler, and waiter, he immersed himself in the city's Mercantile Library, studying English and the law. His great career opportunity came in a unique manner in the library's chess room. Observing the game of two habitués, he astutely critiqued a move and the players, impressed, engaged Pulitzer in conversation. The players were editors of the leading German language daily, *Westliche Post,* and a job offer followed. Four years later, in 1862, the young Pulitzer, who had built a reputation as a tireless enterprising journalist, was offered a controlling interest in the paper by the nearly bankrupt owners. At age 25, Pulitzer became a publisher and there followed a series of shrewd business deals from which he emerged in 1878 as the owner of the *St. Louis Post-Dispatch,* and a rising figure on the journalistic scene.

Earlier in the same year, he and Kate Davis, a socially prominent Washingtonian woman, were married in the Protestant Episcopal Church. The Hungarian immigrant youth— once a vagrant on the slum streets of St. Louis and taunted as "Joey the Jew"— had been transformed. Now he was a American citizen and as speaker, writer, and editor had mastered English extraordinarily well. Elegantly dressed, wearing a handsome, reddish-brown beard and pince-nez glasses, he mixed easily with the social elite of St. Louis, enjoying dancing at fancy parties and horseback riding in the park. This lifestyle was abandoned abruptly when he came into the ownership of the *St. Louis Post-Dispatch.* James Wyman Barrett, the last city editor of *The New York World*, records in his biography *Joseph Pulitzer and His World* how Pulitzer, in taking hold of the *Post-Dispatch,* "worked at his desk from early morning until midnight or later, interesting himself in every detail of the paper." Appealing to the public to accept that his paper was their champion, Pulitzer splashed investigative articles and editorials assailing government corruption, wealthy tax-dodgers, and gamblers. This populist appeal was effective, circulation mounted, and the paper prospered. Pulitzer would have been pleased to know that in the conduct of the Pulitzer Prize system which he later established, more awards in journalism would go to exposure of corruption than to any other subject.

Pulitzer paid a price for his unsparingly rigorous work at his newspaper. His health was undermined and, with his eyes failing, Pulitzer and his wife set out in 1883 for New York to board a ship on a doctor-ordered European vacation. Stubbornly, instead of boarding the steamer in New York, he met with Jay Gould, the financier, and negotiated the purchase of *The New York World,* which was in financial straits. Putting aside his serious health concerns, Pulitzer immersed himself in its direction, bringing about what Barrett describes as a "one-man revolution" in the editorial policy, content, and format of *The World*. He employed some of the same techniques that had built up the circulation of the *Post-Dispatch*. He crusaded against public and private corruption, filled the news columns with a spate of sensationalized features, made the first extensive use of illustrations, and staged news stunts. In one of the most successful promotions, *The World* raised public subscriptions for the building of a pedestal at the entrance to the New York harbor so that the Statue of Liberty, which was stranded in France awaiting shipment, could be emplaced.

The formula worked so well that in the next decade the circulation of *The World* in all its editions climbed to more than 600,000, and it reigned as the largest circulating newspaper in the country. But unexpectedly Pulitzer himself became a victim of the battle for circulation when Charles Anderson Dana, publisher of *The Sun*, frustrated by the success of *The World*, launched vicious personal attacks on him as "the Jew

who had denied his race and religion." The unrelenting campaign was designed to alienate New York's Jewish community from *The World*. Pulitzer's health was fractured further during this ordeal and in 1890, at the age of 43, he withdrew from the editorship of *The World* and never returned to its newsroom. Virtually blind, having in his severe depression succumbed also to an illness that made him excruciatingly sensitive to noise, Pulitzer went abroad frantically seeking cures. He failed to find them, and the next two decades of his life he spent largely in soundproofed "vaults," as he referred to them, aboard his yacht, Liberty, in the "Tower of Silence" at his vacation retreat in Bar Harbor Maine, and at his New York mansion. During those years, although he traveled very frequently, Pulitzer managed, nevertheless, to maintain the closest editorial and business direction of his newspapers. To ensure secrecy in his communications he relied on a code that filled a book containing some 20,000 names and terms. During the years 1896 to 1898 Pulitzer was drawn into a bitter circulation battle with William Randolph Hearst's *Journal* in which there were no apparent restraints on sensationalism or fabrication of news. When the Cubans rebelled against Spanish rule, Pulitzer and Hearst sought to outdo each other in whipping up outrage against the Spanish. Both called for war against Spain after the U.S. battleship *Maine* mysteriously blew up and sank in Havana harbor on February 16, 1898. Congress reacted to the outcry with a war resolution. After the four-month war, Pulitzer withdrew from what had become known as "yellow journalism." *The World* became more restrained and served as the influential editorial voice on many issues of the Democratic Party. In the view of historians, Pulitzer's lapse into "yellow journalism" was outweighed by his public service achievements. He waged courageous and often successful crusades against corrupt practices in government and business. He was responsible to a large extent for passage of antitrust legislation and regulation of the insurance industry. In 1909, *The World* exposed a fraudulent payment of $40 million by the United States to the French Panama Canal Company. The federal government lashed back at *The World* by indicting Pulitzer for criminally libeling President Theodore Roosevelt and the banker J.P. Morgan, among others. Pulitzer refused to retreat, and *The World* persisted in its investigation. When the courts dismissed the indictments, Pulitzer was applauded for a crucial victory on behalf of freedom of the press. In May 1904, writing in *The North American Review* in support of his proposal for the founding of a school of journalism, Pulitzer summarized his credo: "Our Republic and its press will rise or fall together. An able, disinterested, public-spirited press, with trained intelligence to know the right and courage to do it, can preserve that public virtue without which popular government is a sham and a mockery. A cynical, mercenary, demagogic press will produce in time a people as base as itself. The power to mould the future of the Republic will be in the hands of the journalists of future generations."

In 1912, one year after Pulitzer's death aboard his yacht, the Columbia School of Journalism was founded, and the first Pulitzer Prizes were awarded in 1917 under the supervision of the advisory board to which he had entrusted his mandate. Pulitzer envisioned an advisory board composed principally of newspaper publishers. Others would include the president of Columbia University and scholars, and "persons of distinction who are not journalists or editors." In 1998 the board was composed of five publishers, six editors, six academics including the president of Columbia University and the dean of the Columbia Graduate School of Journalism, one columnist, and the administrator of the prizes. The dean and the administrator are nonvoting members. The chair rotates annually to the most senior member. The board is self-perpetuating in the election of members. Voting members may serve three terms of three years. In the selection of the members of the board and of the juries, close attention is given to professional excellence and affiliation, as well as diversity in terms of gender, ethnic background, geographical distribution, and in the choice of journalists and size of newspaper.

THE ADMINISTRATION OF THE PULITZER PRIZES

More than 2,000 entries are submitted each year in the Pulitzer Prize competitions, and only 21 awards are normally made. The awards are the culmination of a year-long process that begins early in the year with the appointment of 90 distinguished judges who serve on 20 separate juries and are asked to make three nominations in each of the 21 categories. By February 1, the Administrator's office in the Columbia School of Journalism has received the journalism entries—in 1997, typically 1,470. Entries for journalism awards may be submitted by any individual from material appearing in a United States newspaper published daily, Sunday, or at least once a week during the calendar year. In early March, 65 editors, publishers, writers, and educators gather in the School of Journalism to judge the entries in the 14 journalism categories. The juries of five persons each, working intensively for three days, examine every entry before making their nominations. Exhibits in the public service, cartoon, and photography categories are limited to 20 articles, cartoons, or pictures, and in the remaining categories, to 10 articles or editorials— except for feature writing, which is limited to three articles of more than 1500 words or five articles of 1500 words or less. In photography, a single jury judges both the spot news and the feature categories. Since the inception of the prizes the journalism categories have been expanded and repeatedly redefined by the board to keep abreast of the evolution of American journalism. The cartoons prize was created in 1922. The prize for photography was established in 1942, and in 1968 the category was divided into spot and feature. With the development of computer-altered photos, the board stipulated in 1995 that "no entry whose content is manipulated or altered, apart from standard newspaper cropping and editing, will be deemed acceptable."

These were the Pulitzer Prize category definitions in the 1998 competition:

1. For a distinguished example of meritorious public service by a newspaper through the use of its journalistic resources which may include editorials, cartoons, and photographs, as well as reporting.
2. For a distinguished example of local reporting of breaking news.
3. For a distinguished example of investigative reporting by an individual or team, presented as a single article or series.
4. For a distinguished example of explanatory reporting that illuminates a significant and complex subject, demonstrating mastery of the subject, lucid writing and clear presentation.
5. For a distinguished example of beat reporting.
6. For a distinguished example of reporting on national affairs.
7. For a distinguished example of reporting on international affairs, including United Nations correspondence.
8. For a distinguished example of feature writing giving prime consideration to high literary quality and originality.
9. For distinguished commentary.
10. For distinguished criticism.
11. For distinguished editorial writing, the test of excellence being clearness of style, moral purpose, sound reasoning, and power to influence public opinion in what the writer conceives to be the right direction.
12. For a distinguished cartoon or portfolio of cartoons published during the year, characterized by originality, editorial effectiveness, quality of drawing, and pictorial effect.
13. For a distinguished example of spot news photography in black and white or color, which may consist of a photograph or photographs, a sequence or an album.
14. For a distinguished example of feature photography in black and white or color, which may consist of a photograph or photographs, a sequence or an album.

While the journalism process goes forward, shipments of books totaling some 800 titles are being sent to five letters juries for their judging in these categories:

1. For distinguished fiction by an American author, preferably dealing with American life.
2. For a distinguished play by an American author, preferably original in its source and dealing with American life.
3. For a distinguished book upon the history of the United States.
4. For a distinguished biography or autobiography by an American author.
5. For a distinguished volume of original verse by an American author.
6. For a distinguished book of non-fiction by an American author that is not eligible for consideration in any other category.

The award in poetry was established in 1922 and that for non-fiction in 1962. Unlike the other awards which are made for works in the calendar year, eligibility in drama and music extends from March 2 to March 1. The drama jury of five critics attend plays both in New York and the regional theaters. The award in drama goes to a playwright but production of the play as well as script are taken into account.

The music jury, usually made up of four composers and one newspaper critic, meet in New York to listen to recordings and study the scores of pieces, which in 1997 numbered 87. The category definition states:

> For distinguished musical composition of significant dimension by an American that has had its first performance in the United States during the year.

The final act of the annual competition is enacted in early April when the board assembles in the Pulitzer World Room of the Columbia School of Journalism. In prior weeks, the board had read the texts of the journalism entries and the 15 nominated books, listened to music cassettes, read the scripts of the nominated plays, and attended the performances or seen videos where possible. By custom, it is incumbent on board members not to vote on any award under consideration in drama or letters if they have not seen the play or read the book. There are subcommittees for letters and music whose members usually give a lead to discussions. Beginning with letters and music, the board, in turn, reviews the nominations of each jury for two days. Each jury is required to offer three nominations but in no order of preference, although the jury chair in a letter accompanying the submission can broadly reflect the views of the members. Board discussions are animated and often hotly debated. Work done by individuals tends to be favored. In journalism, if more than three individuals are cited in an entry, any prize goes to the newspaper. Awards are usually made by majority vote, but the board is also empowered to vote 'no award,' or by three-fourths vote to select an entry that has not been nominated or to switch nominations among the categories. If the board is dissatisfied with the nominations of any jury, it can ask the Administrator to consult with the chair by telephone to ascertain if there are other worthy entries. Meanwhile, the deliberations continue.

Both the jury nominations and the awards voted by the board are held in strict confidence until the announcement of the prizes, which takes place about a week after the meeting in the World Room. Towards three o'clock p.m. (Eastern Time) of the day of the announcement, in hundreds of newsrooms across the United States, journalists gather about news agency tickers to wait for the bulletins that bring explosions of joy and celebrations to some and disappointment to others. The announcement is made precisely at three o'clock after a news conference held by the administrator in the World Room. Apart from accounts carried prominently by newspapers, television, and radio, the details appear on the Pulitzer Web site http\\: www.pulitzer.org. The announcement includes the name of the winner in each category as well as the names of the other two finalists. The three finalists in each category are the only entries in the competition that are recognized by the Pulitzer office as nominees. The announcement also lists the board members and the names of the jurors (which have previously been kept confidential to avoid lobbying).

A gold medal is awarded to the winner in Public Service. Along with the certificates in the other categories, there are cash awards of $5,000, raised in 1997 from $3,000. Four Pulitzer fellowships of $5,000 each are also awarded annually on the recommendation of the faculty of the School of Journalism. They enable three of its outstanding graduates to travel, report, and study abroad and one fellowship is awarded to a graduate who wishes to specialize in drama, music, literary, film, or television criticism. For most recipients of the Pulitzer prizes, the cash award is only incidental to the prestige accruing to them and their works. There are numerous competitions that bestow far larger cash awards, yet which do not rank in public perception on a level with the Pulitzers. The Pulitzer accolade on the cover of a book or on the marquee of a theater where a prize-winning play is being staged usually does translate into commercial gain.

The Pulitzer process initially was funded by investment income from the original endowment. But by the 1970s the program was suffering a loss each year. In 1978 the advisory board established a foundation for the creation of a supplementary endowment, and fund raising on its behalf continued through the 1980s. The program is now comfortably funded with investment income from the two endowments and the $50 fee charged for each entry into the competitions. The investment portfolios are administered by Columbia University. Members of the Pulitzer Prize Board and journalism jurors receive no compensation. The jurors in letters, music, and drama, in appreciation of their year-long work, receive honoraria, raised to $2,000, effective in 1999.

Unlike the elaborate ceremonies and royal banquets attendant upon the presentation of the Nobel Prizes in Stockholm and Oslo, Pulitzer winners receive their prizes from the president of Columbia University at a modest luncheon in May in the rotunda of the Low Library in the presence of family members, professional associates, board members, and the faculty of the School of Journalism. The board has declined offers to transform the occasion into a television extravaganza.

The Who's Who of Pulitzer Prize Winners is more than simply a roster of names and biographical data. It is a list of people in journalism, letters, and music whose accomplishments enable researchers to trace the historical evolution of their respective fields and the development of American society. We are indebted to Joseph Pulitzer for this and an array of other contributions to the quality of our lives.

Preface

SCOPE

Who's Who of Pulitzer Prize Winners was inspired by the difficulty we had as librarians when attempting to answer questions from students and library patrons about the people who won the award. We believe that the winners of the Pulitzer Prize, one of the pre-eminent awards given in journalism, letters, and music, deserve coverage in a source that includes information on their lives, careers, and accomplishments.

The first edition of this work includes 1175 entries for 1334 awards presented. The discrepancy exists where some prizes were awarded to groups of individuals, each of whom is profiled, or where winners won multiple prizes. All prize winners from 1917, when the prizes were established, through 1998 are included. The authors researched each entry by using traditional biographical sources as well as information from the Pulitzer Prize archive at Columbia University Office of Public Affairs, and from information supplied by the individual winners.

ARRANGEMENT

The main body of this book is arranged alphabetically by prize category. Within each category, entries are arranged chronologically, and in the case of multiple winners in a given year, alphabetically. For winners who have received more than one award, a full entry is provided the first time one of their prize categories appears according to the alphabetical arrangement of this book, and cross-references to that full entry appear thereafter under each prize category and year that the winners have received the award. If no award was given in a particular year for a certain category, "No award" is noted under the year for that category.

The Prize Categories

- **Beat Reporting:** Awarded 1991 to the present. This category was previously called Specialized Reporting.
- **Biography or Autobiography:** Awarded 1917 to the present.
- **Breaking News Reporting:** Awarded in 1998. This category was previously called Spot News Reporting.
- **Commentary:** Awarded 1970 to the present. This category was officially Criticism or Commentary in 1970 and 1971; however, awards were given in both categories and in 1972, the categories were divided into two separate awards.
- **Correspondence:** Awarded 1929 to 1947 for Washington and foreign correspondence. In 1942, Telegraphic Reporting (International) and Telegraphic Reporting (National) were created. In 1948, these were shortened to the titles of International Reporting and National Reporting.
- **Criticism**: Awarded 1970 to the present. This category was officially Criticism or Commentary in 1970 and 1971; however, awards were given in both categories and in 1972, the categories were divided into two separate awards.
- **Drama:** Awarded 1917 to the present.
- **Editorial Cartooning:** Awarded 1922 to the present.

- **Editorial Writing:** Awarded 1917 to the present.
- **Explanatory Journalism:** Awarded 1985 to the present.
- **Feature Photography:** Awarded 1968 to the present. Prior to 1968, awards were given in the Photography category.
- **Feature Writing:** Awarded 1979 to the present.
- **Fiction:** Awarded 1948 to the present.
- **General News Reporting:** Awarded 1985 to 1990. This category was previously known as Local General Spot News Reporting. The category changed to Spot News Reporting in 1991.
- **General Non-Fiction:** Awarded 1962 to the present.
- **History:** Awarded 1917 to the present.
- **International Reporting:** Awarded 1948 to the present. This category was previously known as Telegraphic Reporting (International).
- **Investigative Reporting:** Awarded 1985 to the present. This category was previously known as Local Investigative Specialized Reporting.
- **Local General Spot News Reporting:** Awarded 1964 to 1984. This category was previously known as Local Reporting, Edition Time. It changed to General News Reporting in 1985.
- **Local Investigative Specialized Reporting:** Awarded 1964 to 1984. This category was previously known as Local Reporting, No Edition Time. It changed to Investigative Reporting in 1985.
- **Local Reporting:** Awarded 1948 to 1952. This category was divided into Local Reporting, Edition Time and Local Reporting, No Edition Time in 1953.
- **Local Reporting, Edition Time:** Awarded 1953 to 1963. This category was previously known as Local Reporting. It changed to Local General Spot News Reporting in 1964.
- **Local Reporting, No Edition Time:** Awarded 1953 to 1963. This category was previously known as Local Report-

ing. It changed to Local Investigative Specialized Reporting in 1964.
- **Meritorious Public Service:** Awarded 1917 to the present.
- **Music:** Awarded 1943 to the present.
- **National Reporting:** Awarded 1948 to the present. This category was previously known as Telegraphic Reporting (National).
- **Newspaper History Award:** Awarded in 1918, the only year in which this award was given.
- **Novel:** Awarded 1918 to 1947. The Fiction category began in 1948 and subsumed Novel.
- **Photography:** Awarded 1942 to 1967. This category was divided into Feature Photography and Spot News Photography in 1968.
- **Poetry:** Awarded from 1918 to the present. The prize for this category was not officially established until 1922. Prizes in 1918 and 1919 were made from gifts provided by the Poetry Society.
- **Reporting:** Awarded 1917 to 1947. In 1929, the Correspondence category was created. In 1942, Telegraphic Reporting (International) and Telegraphic Reporting (National) were created. In 1948, the four reporting categories were combined into Local Reporting, National Reporting, and International Reporting.
- **Special Awards and Citations: Journalism:** Awarded periodically from 1930 to the present.
- **Special Awards and Citations: Letters:** Awarded periodically from 1944 to the present.
- **Special Awards and Citations: Music:** Awarded periodically from 1974 to the present.
- **Specialized Reporting:** Awarded 1985 to 1990. This category changed to Beat Reporting in 1991.
- **Spot News Photography:** Awarded 1968 to the present. Prior to 1968, awards were given in the Photography category.

- **Spot News Reporting:** Awarded 1991 to 1997. This category changed to Breaking News Reporting in 1998.
- **Telegraphic Reporting (International):** Awarded 1942 to 1947. This category changed to International Reporting in 1948.
- **Telegraphic Reporting (National):** Awarded 1942 to 1947. This category changed to National Reporting in 1948.

ENTRIES

Each entry includes up to 15 fields of biographical and bibliographic information. (See "Using This Book.") Information has been included in each field when available and verifiable. The dates of winning newspaper articles were provided whenever such information was readily available from sources such as the Pulitzer Prize archive, newspaper articles about the prizes, or from the winning newspaper. Unfortunately, many newspaper companies cited in the entries are no longer in existence. We have often tried to keep the exact wording used by the Pulitzer Committees when they awarded these prizes. We've also included other information about the winners in the Commentary field.

INDEXES

Four indexes have been developed to assist users of *Who's Who in Pulitzer Prize Winners*: (1) Newspaper and Organization Winners—an alphabetical listing of these winners; (2) Individual Winners—an alphabetical listing of individual winners; (3) Education Institutions—a listing of all postsecondary educational institutions and the winners who attended those schools; and (4) Chronology of Prizes Awarded—a listing arranged by year of all the awards and their recipients.

ACKNOWLEDGMENTS

A special note of thanks goes to Seymour Topping for writing the foreword for this book and to Bud Kliment, both administrators of the prizes. We are particularly indebted to the late Fred Knubel, director of public information at Columbia University, who helped us enormously. We gratefully thank each winner who supplied information in reply to our more than 400 letters of inquiry. We also wish to thank the many librarians and publisher, newspaper, and wire service staff members who aided our research efforts.

The authors gratefully acknowledge the Research and Publication Committee of the University of Illinois at Urbana-Champaign library for its support in the completion of our research. We also express our appreciation to C.B. Hayden and all the staff of the ABC News Research Center, the Photo Collection staff at the National Archives and Record Administration, and Maura Danahy and Patti Rosen for their assistance with this project.

We would like to thank our editor at Oryx Press, Magon Kinzie, who has been a great help in our first venture into creating a reference book. She and the staff at Oryx Press have worked hard to help us create a useful product. Finally, the authors would like to thank Matthew E. Clarage and Markku Ripatti for their help, patience, and understanding during the creation of this book.

We have tried to make this volume as complete and as accurate as possible. However, while every effort has been made to ensure that all information is both accurate and current within the confines of format and scope, the authors cannot assume any responsibility for errors or omissions in the *Who's Who of Pulitzer Prize Winners,* whether such errors or omissions result from accident, negligence, or any other cause. In the event of publication error or omission, the sole responsibility of the authors will be the entry of corrected information in succeeding editions. Please direct all such information to Elizabeth A. Brennan and Elizabeth C. Clarage, in care of The Oryx Press, 4041 North Central at Indian School Road, Phoenix, AZ 85012.

We hope that *Who's Who of Pulitzer Prize Winners* will prove to be a useful and valued resource.

Elizabeth A. Brennan
Information Specialist

Elizabeth C. Clarage
Assistant Professor University of Illinois
at Urbana-Champaign

Using This Book

Each entry in the "Profiles of the Winners" section contains up to 15 fields of information. The format of each field and an explanation of the fields are offered here. There are two types of entries—those for individuals who have been awarded Pulitzer Prizes and those for newspapers or publishers that have won the award. The entries are numbered consecutively throughout the book and the indexes reference the entries by number.

Names

For individuals, the names used in this book are those that the Pulitzer Committee chose in awarding the prizes. If, during the research process, a pseudonym or nickname was discovered, it is included in the commentary section of the entry.

Birth Date, Birthplace and Death Date

The birth and death dates (when available and applicable) of each winner are listed, along with the birthplace. For birthplace information, states within the United States of America are given in abbreviated form, using the standard two-letter postal codes. In each case, the fullest information available is presented. Example:

> **Birth:** October 6, 1862; Border of Adams and Highland Counties, OH. **Death:** April 27, 1927

Founded, Location, Founders, and Date of Cessation

This field applies only to newspapers and publishing establishments. Where such information could be obtained, the founding date and founder names are included. Cessation refers to date or year in which a newspaper was no longer published. Where such information could be obtained, the date on which the publication ceased to operate is included.

Parents

The names of each winner's father and mother are included in the fullest form available. The mother's name is assumed to contain the surname of the father unless otherwise noted. The mother's maiden name is included in parentheses. Mothers' names may be incomplete due to the difficulty in finding the full information. If the information cannot be found, the field has been left out. Depending upon the source of the information, two different styles of presentation have been used. Examples of both are:

> **Parents:** Thomas H. and Frances (Parkinson) Beveridge

or

> **Parents:** Thomas H. Beveridge and Frances (Parkinson)

Education

The name of the university attended by each winner is presented, and if the institution has changed its name, that information is also included in this field. When the name of the university does not contain the state in which it is located, a two-letter state code follows the name of the university. If the degree granted to the winner is known, the abbreviation for the degree follows the name of the institution.

Religion

In the cases of individuals for whom a definitive reference to a religious affiliation could be found, that information is included. In many cases, this information was difficult or impossible to locate in published resources. In those cases, this field will not be included in the entry.

Spouse

When possible, the full name of spouse(s) of each winner is included, followed by the year of the marriage if that information was available (preceded by m.). If the full name of the spouse could not be determined, the most complete information available is included.

If a marriage ended, the year of the death or divorce of the spouse has been included after the spouse's name. If it could not be determined whether a spouse had died or the marriage ended in divorce, a notation "d." precedes the year that the marriage ended. If it is known how the marriage ended, either the word "died" or the abbreviation "div." precedes the year. An example of each is:

Spouse: Jane Smith (m. 1887; died 1900)

Spouse: Mary Young (m. 1954; div. 1990)

Spouse: Jean Jones (m. 1872; d. 1885)

Children

When names of the children were found, the names have been included. If specific names of children could not be determined, but it is known that children existed, a note to indicate the number of offspring has been included in the entry. In cases of multiple marriages, when known, the initials of the spouse who was the biological father/mother have been included after the names of the children.

Prize

The prizes awarded are identified along with the year that the prize was conferred. The name of the winning publication is identified, and publishing information on the winning entry is included after the prize name and year.

For each year that a Pulitzer Prize was offered, information on the winner is given. If the Pulitzer Prize Board did not award a prize, the phrase "No award" follows the year. If an individual or organization has won more than one Pulitzer Prize, the full entry for the winner is given only once, with "see" references that easily lead the user back to the full entry, if the user so chooses, from each additional prize entry. An example of the abbreviated, additional prize entry is as follows:

Russell Wayne Baker
Full entry appears as #75 under "Biography or Autobiography," 1983.

Career

The information in the career field in its most complete form is presented as:

Name of Position, Place of Employment, Years of Employment

The information in this category usually begins with the first professional position held by the winner. In cases for which the winner held concurrent positions, the years of employment will reflect the overlapping time periods. The information in this category runs from earliest time period to the most recent. If specific and accurate years of employment could not be determined, that information has been left open-ended or has been omitted.

Other Awards

The information in this field is taken from the resources consulted and is as complete as could be determined by the authors; however, not all awards, and especially those from state associations, are included in each entry. The information is presented in chronological order. The year of the award has been included if that information could be identified.

Selected Works

For all entries, the information in this category is not comprehensive, but it attempts to be representative of the winners' works. For journalism entries, this field includes only the full-length books that were authored by the winners, and not the many hundreds, or even thousands of articles that were authored by the winners at various newspapers. Information in this category is arranged chronologically.

For More Information

If a published biography or biographical article could be identified, that information is included in this field. Information in this category is arranged chronologically. For newspaper articles on the individual and the award, article titles are not included.

Commentary

The commentary field gives a brief explanation on each piece winning the Pulitzer Prize and in some cases additional information on the individual winner. In this field, individuals are often referred to by their full names or by their familiar names, rather than by the name that appears at the beginning of the entry. If the language of the citation from the Pulitzer Prize Board was available (either from information in the Pulitzer Prize archive, the press release from the Office of Public Affairs at Columbia University, or in a reputable source such as the *New York Times*), it has been included verbatim in the commentary. If the individual winner offered a comment on the award in reply to queries from the authors of this book, this information is also noted in the commentary field.

PROFILES OF THE WINNERS

Beat Reporting

1991

Natalie Angier 1

Birth: February 16, 1958; New York, NY. **Parents:** Keith Angier and Adele Bernice (Rosenthal). **Education:** University of Michigan. Barnard College, NY: BA, magna cum laude. **Spouse:** Richard Steven Weiss (m. 1991).

Prize: *Beat Reporting,* 1991: *New York Times,* New York: New York Times, 1990.

Career: Staff Writer, *Discover Magazine,* 1980-83; Editor, *Savvy Magazine,* 1983-84; Staff Writer, *Time* magazine, 1984-86; Freelance science writer; Adjunct Professor, New York University; Science Correspondent, *New York Times,* 1990-.

Selected Works: *Natural Obsessions: The Search for the Oncogene,* 1988. *The Beauty of the Beastly: New Views on the Nature of Life,* 1995.

Other Awards: Lewis Thomas Award, Marine Biology Labs, 1990. Journalism Award, General Motors Industrial Board, 1991. Journalism Award, American Association for the Advancement of Science, 1992. Distinguished Alumni Award, Barnard College, NY, 1993.

Commentary: Natalie Angier has reported on science since the mid-1980s. She tries "to give the readers the feeling that they are right there in the middle of the scientific process." Her vivid and readable style explains a scientific topic to her readers in language appropriate for a scientist but also understandable to a lay person.

Angier has degrees in English and physics from Barnard College.

1992

Deborah Leigh Blum 2
Birth: October 19, 1954; Urbana, IL. **Parents:** Murray Blum and Ann (Hilpp). **Education:** University of Georgia: BA, magna cum laude with general honors, Phi Beta Kappa. University of Wisconsin: MA. **Spouse:** Peter Haugen (m. 1982). **Children:** Marcus, Lucas.

Prize: *Beat Reporting,* 1992: *Sacramento Bee,* "Monkey Wars," Sacramento, CA: The Sacramento Bee, 1991.

Career: General Assignment Reporter, *Gainesville (FL) Times,* 1976-77; General Assignment Reporter, *Macon (GA) Telegraph,* 1977-78; General Assignment Reporter, *St. Petersburg (FL) Times,* 1979-80; Environmental Reporter, *Fresno (CA) Bee,* 1982-84; Part-Time Journalism Instructor, California State University, Fresno, 1984; Science Writer, *Sacramento (CA) Bee,* 1984-; Corporate Trainer, McClatchy Newspapers, 1989-; Scientific Writer-in-Residence, University of Wisconsin, Madison, 1994; Freelance writer.

Selected Works: *Bad Karma* (with others), 1986. *The Monkey Wars,* 1994. *Sex on the Brain: The Biological Differences between Men and Women,* 1997. *A Field Guide for Science Writers: The Official Guide of the National Association of Science Writers* (with Mary Knudson), 1997.

Other Awards: Livingston Award for Young Journalists, University of Michigan Department of Communications, 1987. Summer Fellow, University of California, Santa Barbara, 1988. Westinghouse Award, American Academy of Arts and Sciences, 1992. Clarion Award for Investigative Reporting, 1992. Ralph O. Nafziger Award, University of Wisconsin, Madison, School of Journalism and Mass Communication, 1993. Honorary Member, Sigma Xi, 1993.

For More Information: *Contemporary Authors, Volume 150,* Detroit: Gale Research Company, 1996; *Sacramento Bee,* 19 December (1992): B3.

Commentary: Deborah Blum's four-part series "The Monkey Wars" was published in November 1991. It covered the ethical questions that arise from conducting scientific experiments on primates and the growing fight over animal research.

1993

Paul Joseph Ingrassia 3

Birth: August 18, 1950; Laurel, MS. **Parents:** Angelo Paul Ingrassia and Regina (Iacono). **Religion:** Roman Catholic. **Education:** University of Illinois: BS. University of Wisconsin: MA. **Spouse:** Susan Rougeau (m. 1973). **Children:** Adam, Charles, Daniel.

Prize: *Beat Reporting,* 1993: *Wall Street Journal,* New York: Dow Jones, 1992.

Career: Editor-in-Chief, college paper, *Daily Illini;* Editorial Writer, *Decatur (IL) Lindsay-Schaub Newspaper,* 1973-76; Reporter, Chicago (IL) Bureau, *Wall Street Journal,* 1977-80; News Editor, Chicago (IL) Bureau, *Wall Street Journal,* 1980-81; Cleveland (OH) Bureau Chief, *Wall Street Journal,* 1981-85; Detroit (MI) Bureau Chief, *Wall Street Journal,* 1985-93; Senior Editor, *Wall Street Journal,* 1993-94; Assistant Vice-President, New Product Development, Dow Jones Telerate, 1994-95; Vice-President of News Service, Dow Jones, 1995; Executive Editor, Dow Jones Newswires, 1995-; Chief Operating Officer, Dow Jones Newswires, 1996-; Vice-President, Dow Jones and Company, Incorporated, 1995-; President, Dow Jones Newswires, 1998-.

Selected Works: *Comeback: The Fall and Rise of the American Automobile Industry* (with Joseph B. White), 1994.

Other Awards: Gerald Loeb Award, Anderson Graduate School of Management, University of California, Los Angeles, 1993.

For More Information: *Wall Street Journal,* 14 April (1993): A2.

Commentary: Paul Ingrassia and Joseph B. White's coverage of the upheaval within the management of General Motors was "authoritative, comprehensive, and unfailingly accurate." They consistently were first to report many of the developments of the corporate shake-up, including naming the next chairman of the company.

Ingrassia has since climbed the corporate ladder at Dow Jones and is now president of its Newswires.

Joseph B. White 4

Birth: July 7, 1958; New York, NY. **Parents:** Thomas R. White and Mary C. **Education:** Harvard University, MA: BA. **Spouse:** Laurie Mayers (m. 1985). **Children:** Catherine, Anna.

Prize: *Beat Reporting,* 1993: *Wall Street Journal,* New York: Dow Jones, 1992.

Career: Reporter, *Edgartown (MA) Vineyard Gazette,* 1979-82; Reporter, *St. Petersburg (FL) Times,* 1982-86; Reporter, *Connecticut Law Tribune,* 1986-87; Reporter, Detroit (MI), *Wall Street Journal,* 1987-90; Detroit (MI) Deputy Bureau Chief, *Wall Street Journal,* 1990-94; News Editor, *Wall Street Journal,* 1994-.

Selected Works: *Comeback: The Fall and Rise of the America Automobile Industry* (with Paul Ingrassia), 1994.

Other Awards: Gerald Loeb Award, Anderson Graduate School of Management, University of California, Los Angeles, 1993.

For More Information: *Wall Street Journal,* 14 April (1993): A2.

Commentary: Joseph B. White and Paul Ingrassia's reporting of the management turmoil within General Motors was highly detailed and accurate. They wrote about corporate governance and the board of directors. During 1992, General Motors went through factory closings, financial losses, and the removal of its chairman, Robert C. Stempel.

1994

Eric Freedman 5

Birth: November 6, 1949; Brookline, MA. **Parents:** Morris Freedman and Charlotte (Nadler). **Education:** Lansing Community College, MI. State University of New York, Albany. Cornell University, NY: BA. New York University: JD. **Spouse:** Mary Ann Sipher (m. 1974). **Children:** Ian, Cara.

Prize: *Beat Reporting,* 1994: *Detroit News,* Detroit, MI: Detroit News, 1993.

Career: Aide, U.S. Representative Charles Rangel, 1971-76; Reporter, *Albany (NY) Knickerbocker News,* 1976-84; Journalist-in-Residence, Colorado State University, 1983; Reporter, Lansing Bureau, *Detroit News,* 1984-95; Visiting Assistant Professor of Journalism, Michigan State University, 1996-.

Selected Works: *On the Water, Michigan: Your Comprehensive Guide to Water Recreation in the Great Lakes State,* 1992. *Pioneering Michigan,* 1992. *Michigan Free: A Comprehensive Guide to Free Travel, Recreation, and Entertainment Opportunities,* 1993. *Great Lakes, Great National Forests,* 1995.

Other Awards: O'Leary Award, University of Michigan, Department of Communication Studies, 1994.

Commentary: Eric Freedman and Jim Mitzelfeld's investigation of the Michigan House Fiscal Agency led to felony convictions of four people, one a state representative.

Jim Mitzelfeld   6

Birth: April 26, 1961; Royal Oak, MI. **Education:** Michigan State University. University of Michigan: JD.

Prize: *Beat Reporting,* 1994: *Detroit News,* Detroit, MI: Detroit News, 1993.

Career: Reporter, *Flint (MI) Journal, Oakland (CA) Press,* United Press International, Associated Press; City Desk Reporter, *Detroit News,* 1988-90; Investigative Reporter, *Detroit News,* 1990-93; Law Clerk, Judge David McKeague, Lansing, MI.

Other Awards: O'Leary Award, University of Michigan, Department of Communication Studies, 1994.

Commentary: Jim Mitzelfeld and Eric Freedman's series of articles about spending abuse within the Michigan state legislature won a Pulitzer Prize for Beat Reporting. Mitzelfeld received a tip that someone was writing out checks to cash. Their story led to four convictions, including that of a state representative.

1995

David M. Shribman   7

Birth: March 2, 1954; Salem, MA. **Education:** Dartmouth College, NH, summa cum laude, Phi Beta Kappa. Cambridge University, England: Postgraduate, James Reynolds Scholar. **Spouse:** Cindy Skrzycki. **Children:** Elizabeth, Natalie.

Prize: *Beat Reporting,* 1995: *Boston Globe,* Boston: Boston Globe, 1994.

Career: City Staff member, *Buffalo (NY) Evening News,* Staff member, Washington (DC) Bureau *Buffalo (NY) Evening News;* National Staff member, *Washington (DC) Star;* Congress and National Political Correspondent, *New York Times;* National Political Correspondent, *Wall Street Journal;* Assisting Managing Editor, Columnist, Washington (DC) Bureau Chief, *Boston Globe.*

Selected Works: *One Hundred Years of Dartmouth Football,* 1980.

Commentary: David Shribman's analytical coverage of national developments within Washington won him a Pulitzer Prize. He wrote, among other things, about President Clinton, Newt Gingrich, the House of Representatives, the deaths of former President Nixon and former First Lady Jacqueline Kennedy Onassis, and voter rebellion.

1996

Robert F. Keeler   8

Birth: February 1944; Brooklyn, NY. **Parents:** Robert D. Keeler and June (Blanch). **Religion:** Roman Catholic. **Education:** Fordham University, NY. **Spouse:** Judith Ann Dempsey. **Children:** Rebekah, Rachel.

Prize: *Beat Reporting,* 1996: *Newsday,* Long Island, NY: Newsday, 1995.

Career: Copyboy, *New York Herald-Tribune,* 1965; Editorial Assistant, *New York Herald-Tribune;* Reporter, U.S. Army, Monthly Newsletter, *Missile Command News;* Reporter, *Waterbury (CT) Republican;* Reporter, *Staten Island (NY) Advance;* Brookhaven Beat Reporter, *Newsday (NY),* 1971; Albany (NY) Bureau Chief, National Correspondent, Editor, *Newsday (NY);* Editor, *Newsday Magazine (NY),* 1982-84; State News Editor, *Newsday (NY),* 1984-; Religion Writer, *Newsday (NY),* 1993-; Journalism Instructor, State University of New York, Stony Brook.

Selected Works: *Newsday: A Candid History of the Respectable Tabloid,* 1990. *Parish! The Pulitzer Prize-Winning Story of One Vibrant Catholic Community,* 1997.

For More Information: *Newsday,* April 11, 1996: A11; *Newsday,* April 16, 1996: 5; *America,* 174 (May 25 and June 1, 1996): 8-9.

Commentary: Robert F. Keeler's series on St. Brigid's, a progressive Roman Catholic parish, examined the life of the church and its members. Keeler is the first person covering the religion beat to win a Pulitzer Prize. His winning series was published occasionally throughout 1995. Keeler, who has been with *Newsday* since 1971, wrote the history of the paper in 1990.

1997

Byron Acohido   9

Birth: July 3, 1955; Wahiawa, HI. **Parents:** Ben V. Acohido and Caroline (Flores). **Religion:** Christian. **Education:** University of Oregon: BS. **Spouse:** Robin Cassady (m. 1977). **Children:** Blake, Justin, Kyle, Landon.

Prize: *Beat Reporting,* 1997: *Seattle Times,* Seattle, WA: Seattle Times, 1996.

Career: General Assignment Reporter, *Everett (WA) Herald;* Business Editor/Reporter, *Dallas (TX) Times-Herald,* 1985-87; Business Reporter, *The Seattle (WA) Times,* 1987-88; Aerospace Reporter, *Seattle (WA) Times,* 1988-.

Other Awards: Bosch Award, Society of Professional Journalists, Western Washington Chapter, 1997. Edgar A. Poe Award, White House Correspondents Association, 1997. George Polk Memorial Award, Long Island University, NY, 1997. Investigative Reporters and Editors Award, 1997. Journalism Award, Washington Society of Professional Engineers, 1997. National Headliners Club Award, 1997. Seldon Ring Award, 1997. Worth Bingham Prize, 1997.

For More Information: Chespesiuk, Ron, Haney Howell, and Edward Lee, *Raising Hell: Straight Talk with Investigative Journalists,* Jefferson, NC: McFarland & Company, Inc., 1997: 103-116.

Commentary: Byron Acohido has covered the aerospace beat since 1988 for the *Seattle Times.* His story on rudder problems on Boeing 737s captured many of the major journalism awards for 1997. His series led to an agreement between Boeing and the Federal Aviation Administration for rudder modifications to those airplanes still in service, roughly 2700

worldwide.

"The most gratifying response to my series on 737 rudder problems was the expressions of gratitude from people who lost loved ones on United Flight 585 and USAir Flight 427. It is my firm belief that my research over two years was buttressed by their prayers that something positive come from the deaths of the 132 passengers and crew killed in those two crashes. I'm grateful for the prayers and loyal support of my wife, Robin, and our sons Blake, Justin, Kyle and Landon. And I would not have gotten very far without the dedication of my colleagues and supervisors at the *Seattle Times,* whose commitment to serving our readers is a daily inspiration." —B. Acohido

1998

Linda Joyce Greenhouse   10

Birth: January 9, 1947; New York, NY. **Parents:** H. Robert Greenhouse and Dorothy (Greenlick). **Religion:** Jewish. **Education:** Radcliffe College, MA: BA, magna cum laude, Phi Beta Kappa. Yale University, CT: MSL. **Spouse:** Eugene R. Fidell (m. 1981). **Children:** Hannah Margalit.

Prize: *Beat Reporting,* 1998: *New York Times,* "High Court Hears 2 Cases Involving Assisted Suicide," January 9; "What Level of Protection for Internet Speech?" March 24; "High Court Voids a Law Expanding Religious Rights," June 26; "Court 9-0, Upholds State Laws Prohibiting Assisted Suicide; Protects Speech on Internet," June 27; "Justices Limit Brady Gun Law As Intrusion on States' Rights," June 28; "William Brennan, 91, Dies: Gave Court Liberal Vision," July 25; "A Case on Race Puts Justice O'Connor in a Familiar Pivotal Role," August 4; "Why Bork Is Still a Verb in Politics, 10 Years Later," October 5; "Settlement Ends High Court Case on Preferences: Tactical Retreat," November 22, New York: *New York Times,* 1997.

Career: Editor, college paper, *Harvard Crimson;* Assistant to James Reston, *New York Times,* 1968-69; Metropolitan Staff Reporter, *New York Times,* 1969-74; Correspondent, Albany (NY), *New York Times,* 1974-75; Albany (NY) Bureau Chief, *New York Times,* 1976-77; Supreme Court Correspondent, *New York Times,* 1978-; Congressional Correspondent, *New York Times,* 1986-87; Senior Writer, *New York Times,* 1990-.

Selected Works: *Yale Law Journal,* "Telling the Court's Story: Justice and Journalism at the Supreme Court," April 1996.

Other Awards: Ford Foundation Fellow, Yale University, CT, 1977-78. Honorary Degree, Brown University, RI, 1991. Honorary Degree, Colgate University, NY, 1993. John Peter Zenger Special Media Award, New York State Bar Association, 1993. Chief

Alumni Marshall, Harvard University Commencement, 1993. Fellow, American Academy of Arts and Sciences, 1994. Honorary Degree, City University of New York, 1997. Honorary Degree, Northeastern University, MA, 1997.

For More Information: *Contemporary Authors, Volumes 77-80,* Detroit, MI: Gale Research Company, 1979: 195; *American Journalism Review,* 20:4 (May 1998): 7.

Commentary: Linda Greenhouse was awarded a Pulitzer Prize for her "consistently illuminating coverage of the United States Supreme Court." Greenhouse had been a finalist in the Explanatory Reporting category but was moved into the Beat Reporting category by the Pulitzer Prize Board. Her winning entry included the Supreme Court's treatment of free speech on the Internet, the Court's opinion on assisted suicide, and an in-depth review of Justice William Brennan's impact on the Court, as well as other coverage on the activities of the Court. She has written about the Supreme Court since 1978, after receiving a Master of Studies in Law from Yale University.

Biography or Autobiography

1917

Maud Howe Elliott — 11

Birth: 1854; Boston, MA. **Death:** 1948. **Parents:** Dr. Samuel Gridley and Julia (Ward) Howe. **Education:** University of California.

Prize: *Biography or Autobiography,* 1917: *Julia Ward Howe, 1819-1910,* Boston: Houghton Mifflin, 1915.

Selected Works: *A Newport Aquarelle,* 1883. *The San Rosario Ranch,* 1884. *Atlanta in the South: A Romance,* 1886. *Art and Handicraft in the Woman's Building of the World's Columbian Exposition, Chicago, 1893* (Elliott, Maude Howe, ed.), 1893. *Laura Bridgman: Dr. Howe's Famous Pupil and What He Taught Her,* 1903. *Roma Beata: Letters from the Eternal City,* 1904. *Two in Italy,* 1905. *Sun and Shadow in Spain,* 1908. *Sicily in Shadow and in Sun: The Earthquake and the American Relief Work,* 1910. *Three Generations,* 1923. *Lord Byron's Helmet,* 1927. *My Cousin, F. Marion Crawford,* 1934. *Uncle Sam Ward and His Circle,* 1938. *This Was My Newport,* 1944.

For More Information: *American Women,* Detroit: Gale, 1973; *Feminist Companion to Literature in English,* New Haven, CT: Yale, 1990.

Commentary: Laura Richards, Maud Howe Elliott, and Florence Howe Hall were awarded the 1917 Pulitzer Prize for their two-volume biography of their mother, *Julia Ward Howe.* Julia was an American social reformer, author, suffragist, and penner of the "Battle Hymn of the Republic." Her husband Samuel Gridley Howe was also a reformer and a philanthropist. Together they published the abolitionist paper *The Commonwealth.*

Elliott, sister to Laura E. Richards and Florence Howe Hall, was born in Boston, Massachusetts. Primarily a historian and a biographer, Elliot also wrote travel pieces. She was, like her mother, a campaigner for women's rights. She also worked for the election of Theodore Roosevelt. Her other works include *Uncle Sam Ward and His Circle* and *This Was My Newport.*

Florence Marion Howe Hall — 12

Birth: 1845. **Death:** 1922. **Parents:** Dr. Samuel Gridley and Julia (Ward) Howe.

Prize: *Biography or Autobiography,* 1917: *Julia Ward Howe, 1819-1910,* Boston: Houghton Mifflin, 1915.

Selected Works: *The Story of the Battle Hymn of the Republic,* 1916.

For More Information: *Childhood in Poetry,* Detroit: Gale, 1972; *American Women Writers,* New York: Unger, 1979-1982.

Commentary: Laura Richards, Maud Howe Elliott, and Florence Howe Hall were awarded the 1917 Pulitzer Prize for their two-volume biography of their mother, *Julia Ward Howe.* Julia was an American social reformer, author, suffragist, and penner of the "Battle Hymn of the Republic." Her husband Samuel Gridley Howe was also a reformer and a philanthropist. Together they published the abolitionist paper *The Commonwealth.*

Hall, sister to Laura E. Richards and Maud Howe Elliott, was born in Boston, Massachusetts. She collaborated with her sister Maud on a biography of Laura Bridgman. Her other works include *Memories Grave and Gay.*

Laura E. Richards — 13

Birth: February 27, 1850; Boston, MA. **Death:** January 14, 1943. **Parents:** Dr. Samuel Gridley and Julia (Ward) Howe. **Spouse:** Henry Richards (m. 1871). **Children:** Seven children.

Prize: *Biography or Autobiography,* 1917: *Julia Ward Howe, 1819-1910,* Boston: Houghton Mifflin, 1915.

Career: Children's author, poet and biographer; Founder and President, Woman's Philanthropic Union, 1895-1921; Founder and Director, Camp Merryweather, Lake Cobbosseecontee, ME, 1900-1930; President, Maine Consumers League, 1905-1911; Associated, District Nurse Association; Associated, National Child Labor Committee.

Selected Works: *Baby's Rhyme Book: With Pretty Pictures, for Our Little Ones,* 1878. *In My Nursery,* 1890. *Hildegarde's Holiday: A Sequel to Queen Hildegarde,* 1891. *Captain January,* 1892. *Hildegarde's Home,* 1892. *Glimpses of the French Court: Sketches from French History,* 1893. *Melody,* 1893. *Marie,* 1894. *Narcissa,* 1894. *When I Was Your Age,* 1894. *Five Minute Stories,* 1895. *Nautilus,* 1895. *Jim of Hellas,* 1896. *"Some Say" Neighbours in Cyrus,* 1896. *Three Margarets,* 1897. *Love and Rocks,* 1898. *Margaret Montfort,* 1898. *Rosin the Beau: A Sequel to "Melody" and "Marie,"* 1898. *Sundown Songs,* 1899. *Rita,* 1900. *For Tommy, and Other Stories,* 1900. *Geoffrey Strong,* 1901. *Mrs. Tree,* 1902. *The Golden Windows: A Book of Fables for Young and Old,* 1903. *The Armstrongs,* 1905. *Mrs. Tree's*

Will, 1905. *The Piccolo,* 1906. *The Silver Crown: Another Book of Fables,* 1906. *Grandmother: The Story of a Life That Never Was Lived,* 1907. *The Wooing of Calvin Parks,* 1908. *Letters and Journals of Samuel Gridley Howe,* 1909. *"Up to Calvin's,"* 1910. *Miss Jimmy,* 1913. *The Golden Windows: A Book of Fables for Young and Old,* 1913. *Elizabeth Fry: The Angel of the Prisons,* 1916. *Abigail Adams and Her Times,* 1917. *Pippin: A Wandering Flame,* 1917. *The Joyous Story of Toto,* 1917. *A Daughter of Jehu,* 1918. *To Arms! Songs of the Great War,* 1918. *Joan of Arc,* 1919. *The Squire,* 1923. *Laura Bridgman: The Story of an Opened Door,* 1928. *Stepping Westward,* 1931. *Tirra Lirra: Rhymes Old and New,* 1932. *Merry-Go-Round: New Rhymes and Old,* 1935. *Samuel Gridley Howe,* 1935. *E.A.R.,* 1936. *Harry in England: Being the Partly True Adventures of H.R. in the Year 1857,* 1937. *I Have a Song to Sing You,* 1938.

Other Awards: Junior Literary Guild Selection, 1932: *Tirra Lirra: Rhymes Old and New,* New York: Junior Literary Guild, 1932. Honorary DHL, University of Maine, 1936.

For More Information: *Laura E. Richards and Gardiner,* Augusta, ME: Gannett, 1940; Smith, Danny D., *The Yellow House Papers: The Laura E. Richards Collection,* Gardiner, ME: Smith, 1991.

Commentary: Laura Richards, Maud Howe Elliott, and Florence Howe Hall were awarded the 1917 Pulitzer Prize for their two-volume biography of their mother, *Julia Ward Howe.* Julia was an American social reformer, author, suffragist, and penner of the "Battle Hymn of the Republic." Her husband Samuel Gridley Howe was also a reformer and a philanthropist. Together they published the abolitionist paper *The Commonwealth.*

Laura Elizabeth Howe Richards, sister to Maud Howe Elliott and Florence Howe Hall, was born in Boston. She made a career writing children's books, nursery rhymes, and biographies. She is perhaps best known for the children's story *Captain January.* Her biographies include *Samuel Gridley Howe* and *E.A.R.,* the life of the Pulitzer Prize-winning poet Edward Arlington Robinson.

1918

William Cabell Bruce   14
Birth: March 12, 1860; Staunton Hall, VA. **Death:** May 6, 1946. **Education:** University of Maryland. **Spouse:** Louise Este Fisher. **Children:** Three sons.

Prize: *Biography or Autobiography,* 1918: *Benjamin Franklin, Self-Revealed,* New York: Putnam's, 1917.

Career: President, Maryland State Senate, 1893; Editor, University of Virginia magazine; Head, City of Baltimore Law Department, 1903; Chief Counsel,

Public Service Commission of Maryland, 1910; Maryland Senator, U.S. Senate, 1923.

Selected Works: *The Negro Problem,* 1891. *Below the James: A Plantation Sketch,* 1918. *John Randolph of Roanoke, 1773-1833,* 1922. *Imaginary Conversations with Franklin,* 1933. *Recollections,* 1936.

For More Information: *Encyclopedia of American Biography,* New York: American Historical Society, 1936.

Commentary: William Cabell Bruce was awarded the 1918 Pulitzer Prize in Biography for *Benjamin Franklin, Self-Revealed,* a two-volume study based on Franklin's own writings.

Bruce was born in Staunton Hall, Charlotte County, Virginia. Trained as a lawyer, Bruce wrote a revised city charter for Baltimore, Maryland. He also served on the Maryland Public Service Commission for many years before being elected to the United States Senate in 1923 as the Democratic senator from Maryland. As senator, he fought for the rights of individuals against the Ku Klux Klan, prohibition, and anti-Catholic bigotry. His other works include *John Randolph of Roanoke.*

1919

Henry Adams   15
Birth: February 16, 1838; Boston, MA. **Death:** March 27, 1918. **Parents:** Charles Francis and Abigail (Brooks) Adams. **Education:** Harvard University, MA: BA. University of Berlin, Germany. **Spouse:** Marian Hooper (m. 1872; died 1885).

Prize: *Biography or Autobiography,* 1919: *The Education of Henry Adams,* Boston: Houghton Mifflin, 1918.

Career: Private Secretary to his father in Washington, DC, and London, England, 1861-1868; Freelance journalist, 1868-1870; Assistant Professor of Medieval History, Harvard University, MA, 1870-1877; Historian and Writer, 1877-1918; President, American Historical Association, 1894.

Selected Works: *Documents Relating to New-England Federalism, 1800-1815* (Adams, Henry, ed.), 1877. *The Writings of Albert Gallatin* (Adams, Henry, ed.), 1879. *John Randolph,* 1882. *Democracy: An American Novel,* 1883. *History of the United States of America,* 1889-1891. *Historical Essays,* 1891. *John Randolph,* 1898. *Documents Relating to New-England Federalism* (Adams, Henry, ed.), 1905. *John Randolph,* 1908. *A Letter to American Teachers of History,* 1910. *The Life of George Cabot Lodge,* 1911. *Mont-Saint-Michel and Chartres,* 1913. *Letters to a Niece and Prayer to the Virgin of Chartres,* 1920. *The Tendency of History,* 1928. *History of the United States of America,* 1930. *Letters of Henry Adams*

(Ford, Worthington Chauncey, ed.), 1930-1938. *Esther,* 1938. *The War of 1812,* 1944. *The Degradation of the Democratic Dogma,* 1947. *Tahiti,* 1947. *The Letters of Henry Adams* (Levenson, J.C., ed.), 1982-1988. *Sketches for the North American Review,* 1986. *The Correspondence of Henry James and Henry Adams, 1877-1914* (Monteiro, George, ed.), 1992. *Henry Adams, Selected Letters* (Samuels, Ernest, ed.), 1992.

Other Awards: Loubat Prize, Columbia University, 1894: *History of the United States of America during the Administrations of Thomas Jefferson and James Madison.*

For More Information: Samuels, Ernest, *Henry Adams,* Cambridge, MA: Harvard University, 1989; Decker, William Merrill, *The Literary Vocation of Henry Adams,* Chapel Hill: University of North Carolina, 1990; Bush, Clive, *Halfway to Revolution: Investigation and Crisis in the Work of Henry Adams, William James, and Gertrude Stein,* New Haven, CT: Yale University, 1991; Jacobson, Joanne, *Authority and Alliance in the Letters of Henry Adams,* Madison: University of Wisconsin, 1992; James, Henry, *The Correspondence of Henry James and Henry Adams, 1877-1914,* Baton Rouge: Louisiana State University, 1992; Rowe, John Carlos, *New Essays on the Education of Henry Adams,* Cambridge, England: Cambridge University, 1996; Simpson, Brooks D., *The Political Education of Henry Adams,* Columbia: University of South Carolina, 1996.

Commentary: *The Education of Henry Adams* won the 1919 Pulitzer Prize in Autobiography for Henry Brooks Adams. Descended from a long line of American statesmen, Adams was uniquely familiar with American politics.

Adams was born in Boston, Massachusetts. He was the grandson of John Quincy Adams, the sixth president of the United States. His father, Charles Francis Adams, was a congressman and ambassador to Great Britain during the Civil War. Adams considered a career as a statesman, but instead took up a professorship of history at Harvard University. His other works include a novel, *Democracy, History of the United States,* and *Documents Related to New England Federalism.*

1920

Albert Jeremiah Beveridge   16

Birth: October 6, 1862; Border of Adams and Highland Counties, OH. **Death:** April 27, 1927. **Parents:** Thomas H. and Frances (Parkinson) Beveridge. **Education:** Asbury College, IN. **Spouse:** Katherine Langsdale (m. 1887; died 1900); Catherine Eddy (m. 1907). **Children:** Two children.

Prize: *Biography or Autobiography,* 1920: *The Life of John Marshall,* Boston: Houghton Mifflin, 1916-1919.

Career: Railroad laborer, logger and teamster; Lawyer, Indiana; U.S. Senator, Indiana, 1899-1922.

Selected Works: *The Russian Advance,* 1901. *The Young Man and the World,* 1905. *The Bible as Good Reading,* 1907. *Work and Habits,* 1908. *Americans of To-day and To-morrow,* 1908. *The Meaning of the Times, and Other Speeches,* 1908. *What Is Back of the War,* 1915. *The Art of Public Speaking,* 1924. *The State of the Nation,* 1924. *Abraham Lincoln, 1809-1858,* 1928.

For More Information: Bowers, Claude Gernade, *Beveridge and the Progressive Era,* Boston: Houghton Mifflin, 1932; Braeman, John, *Albert J. Beveridge: American Nationalist,* Chicago: University of Chicago, 1971.

Commentary: Albert J. Beveridge won the 1920 Pulitzer Prize in Biography for *The Life of John Marshall,* a four-volume work on the fourth chief justice and one of the most influential jurists of the United States Supreme Court.

Beveridge was born in Highland County, Ohio. He was elected United States Senator from Indiana in 1899 and served until 1911. He was an organizer of the Progressive Party in 1912 and supported Theodore Roosevelt. He died before completing a biography of Abraham Lincoln.

1921

Edward Bok   17

Birth: October 9, 1863; Helder, The Netherlands. **Death:** 1930. **Spouse:** Mary Louise Curtis.

Prize: *Biography or Autobiography,* 1921: *The Americanization of Edward Bok,* New York: Scribners, 1920.

Career: Night office boy, *Brooklyn Eagle;* Stenographer, Head, advertising department, *Scribners* magazine; Founder, *Brooklyn* magazine (it later became *Cosmopolitan*), 1882-1884; Founder, Bok Syndicate Press, 1886; Managing Editor, *Ladies Home Journal,* 1889-1919.

Selected Works: *Beecher Memorial,* 1887. *Real Opponents to the Suffrage Movement* (Pamphlets in American History. Women, WO 200), 1909. *A Man from Maine,* 1923. *Twice Thirty: Some Short and Simple Annals of the Road,* 1925.

For More Information: *Edward W. Bok, October 9, 1863-January 9, 1930,* Pamphlets in American History, Biography: B221. Philadelphia, PA: American Foundation, 1930; Steinberg, Salme Harju, *Reformer in the Marketplace: Edward W. Bok and the Ladies Home Journal,* Baton Rouge: Louisiana State University, 1979.

Commentary: Edward Bok won the 1921 Pulitzer Prize in Autobiography for *The Americanization of Edward Bok,* his remarkable life story, which began with his boyhood in Holland and followed his journey to becoming the editor of one of America's most successful magazines, the *Ladies Home Journal.*

Bok was born in Helder, The Netherlands. He immigrated to the United States at the age of six. He was educated in Brooklyn public schools and at 13 took a job at the *Brooklyn Eagle,* the first in a series of editorial positions. He founded the Bok Syndicate Press in 1886, which he ran until becoming editor of the *Ladies Home Journal* in 1889. As the *Journal's* editor, he instituted the women's page, which included articles on infant care and decorating. Bok advocated increased roles for women in civic and cultural activities and also advocated peace. He offered a $100,000 American Peace Award for the best plan to promote peace between the United States and other countries. His other works include *Dollar's Worth.*

1922

Hamlin Garland 18

Birth: September 14, 1860; West Salem, WI. **Death:** March 4, 1940. **Parents:** Richard Hayes and Isabelle Charlotte (McClintock) Garland. **Spouse:** Zulime Taft. **Children:** Two daughters.

Prize: *Biography or Autobiography,* 1922: *A Daughter of the Middle Border,* New York: Macmillan, 1921.

Career: Novelist and biographer.

Selected Works: *A Little Norsk,* 1892. *A Member of the Third House: A Dramatic Story,* 1892. *A Spoil of Office: A Story of the Modern West,* 1892. *Jason Edwards: An Average Man,* 1892. *Prairie Folks,* 1892. *Prairie Songs,* 1893. *Wayside Courtships,* 1897. *The Spirit of Sweetwater,* 1898. *The Trail of the Goldseekers,* 1899. *Main-Travelled Roads,* 1899. *Boy Life on the Prairie,* 1899. *The Eagle's Heart,* 1900. *Her Mountain Lover,* 1901. *The Captain of the Gray-Horse Troop,* 1902. *The Light of the Star: A Novel,* 1904. *The Tyranny of the Dark,* 1905. *Witch's Gold,* 1906. *Money Magic: A Novel,* 1907. *The Long Trail: A Story of the Northwest Wilderness,* 1907. *The Shadow World,* 1908. *The Moccasin Ranch: A Story of Dakota,* 1909. *Other Main-Travelled Roads,* 1910. *Cavanagh, Forest Ranger: A Romance of the Mountain West,* 1910. *Victor Ollnee's Discipline,* 1911. *The Forester's Daughter: A Romance of the Bear-Tooth Range,* 1914. *They of the High Trails,* 1916. *A Son of the Middle Order,* 1917. *The Book of the American Indian,* 1923. *Trail-Makers of the Middle Border,* 1926. *The Westward March of American Settlement,* 1927. *Back-Trailers from the Middle Border,* 1928. *Companions on the Trail: A Literary Chronicle,* 1931. *My Friendly Contemporaries: A Literary Log,* 1932. *Afternoon Neighbors,* 1934. *Forty Years of Psychic Research,* 1936. *The Mystery of the Buried Crosses: A Narrative of Psychic Exploration,* 1939. *Crumbling Idols,* 1960. *The Rose of Dutcher's Coolly,* 1969.

Other Awards: Honorary LHDs: University of Wisconsin; Beloit College, WI; University of Southern California.

For More Information: Holloway, Jean, *Hamlin Garland: A Biography,* Austin: University of Texas, 1960; McCullough, Joseph B., *Hamlin Garland,* Boston: Twayne, 1978; Nagel, James, ed., *Critical Essays on Hamlin Garland,* Boston: G.K. Hall, 1982; Silet, Charles L.P., ed., *The Critical Reception of Hamlin Garland, 1891-1978,* Troy, NY: Whitston, 1985; Hagan, William Thomas, *Theodore Roosevelt and Six Friends of the Indian,* Norman: University of Oklahoma, 1997.

Commentary: *A Daughter of the Middle Border* won the 1922 Pulitzer Prize in Biography for Hamlin Garland. This was a sequel to his autobiography, *Son of the Middle Border,* which was about farm life in the Middle West.

Garland was born in West Salem, Wisconsin. His family moved to different states while Garland was growing up. He moved to Boston when he was in his early 20s and he became friends with several writers. He was encouraged to write about his experiences and the result was the Middle Border series, first serialized in *Collier's Weekly.* His first book of stories, *Main-Travelled Roads,* was hailed for its realism. He was referred to as the "dean of American novels."

1923

Burton Jesse Hendrick   19

Birth: December 8, 1870; New Haven, CT. **Death:** March 24, 1949. **Parents:** Charles B. and Mary Elizabeth (Johnson) Hendrick. **Education:** Yale University, CT: BA, MA. **Spouse:** Bertha Jane Ives (m. 1896). **Children:** Ives, Hobart.

Prize: *History,* 1921: *The Victory at Sea,* Garden City, NY: Doubleday, Page, 1920. *Biography or Autobiography,* 1923: *The Life and Letters of Walter H. Page,* Garden City, NY: Doubleday, Page, 1922-25. *Biography or Autobiography,* 1929: *The Training of an American: The Earlier Life and Letters of Walter H. Page,* Garden City, NY: Doubleday, Page, 1922-25.

Career: Journalist, author; Editor, *New Haven Morning News;* Writer, *McClure's.*

Selected Works: *The Astor Fortune,* 1905. *The Story of Life Insurance,* 1907. *The Jews in America,* 1923. *William Crawford Gorgas, His Life and Work* (with Marie D. Gorgas), 1924. *The Life of Andrew Carnegie,* 1932. *Bulwark of the Republic: A Biography of the Constitution,* 1937. *Statesmen of the Lost Cause: Jefferson Davis and His Cabinet,* 1939. *Lincoln's War Cabinet,* 1946. *Louise Whitfield Carnegie: The Life of Mrs. Andrew Carnegie,* 1950.

For More Information: *Who Was Who in Literature, 1906-1934,* Detroit: Gale, 1979.

Commentary: Burton Jesse Hendrick was awarded three Pulitzer Prizes. The first was in History in 1920 for *The Victory at Sea,* which he co-authored with William Sowden Sims (see entry for Sims). In 1923, Hendrick won a second Pulitzer, this time in Biography for *The Life and Letters of Walter H. Page.* Walter Hines Page (1855-1918) was the Ambassador to the Court of St. James (Great Britain) during the war years of 1914 to 1918. The history explores the foreign relations between the United States and Great Britain.

He won a third Pulitzer Prize for Biography in 1929 for *The Training of an American: The Earlier Life and Letters of Walter H. Page.* This volume recorded Page's life in the United States during and after the Civil War.

Hendrick was born in New Haven, Connecticut. He worked as a journalist for the New York *Evening Post* and *McClure's Magazine.*

1924

Michael Idvorsky Pupin   20

Birth: 1858; Serbia, Austria-Hungary. **Death:** 1935. **Education:** Columbia University, NY.

Prize: *Biography or Autobiography,* 1924: *From Immigrant to Inventor,* New York: Scribners, 1923.

Career: President, American Association for the Advancement of Science; President, American Institute of Electrical Engineers; President, New York Academy of Sciences; President, Radio Institute of America.

Selected Works: *Serbian Orthodox Church,* 1918. *The New Reformation, from Physical to Spiritual Realities,* 1927. *Romance of the Machine,* 1930.

Other Awards: Elliot Cresson Medal, Franklin Institute, 1902. Hobort Prize, French Academy, 1916. Edison Medal, American Institute of Electrical Engineers, 1920. Medal of Honor, Radio Institute of America. Gold Medal, American Institute of Social Sciences. Washington Award, Western Society of Engineers, 1928.

For More Information: *Dictionary of American Immigration History,* Metuchen, NJ: Scarecrow, 1990.

Commentary: Michael Idvorsky Pupin won the 1924 Pulitzer Prize in Autobiography for *From Immigrant to Inventor,* the story of his life and inventions, chiefly "pupinisation," which made the first long-distance phone calls possible.

Pupin was born in Idvor, Banat, Yugoslavia. A poor Serbian immigrant, Pupin came to the United States at the age of 15. He attended Columbia University, Cambridge University in England, and the University of Berlin, where he earned a PhD degree. He taught engineering at Columbia from 1889 until 1935. His discoveries of the overload coil for communications transmission, X-ray radiation, and a method of X-ray photography were enormous advances in their respective fields. He patented 24 inventions in the fields of telephony, telegraphy, and radio. He was instrumental in bringing the Italian nuclear physicist Enrico Fermi and Dr. John Dunning to Columbia University, where they conducted their first successful demonstration of uranium fission.

1925

Mark Antony Dewolfe Howe   21

Birth: August 28, 1864; Bristol, RI. **Death:** December 6, 1960. **Education:** Lehigh University, PA: BA. Harvard University, MA: BA, MA. **Spouse:** Fanny Huntington Quincy (m. 1899; died 1933). **Children:** One daughter, two sons.

Prize: *Biography or Autobiography,* 1925: *Barrett Wendell and His Letters,* Boston: Atlantic Monthly, 1924.

Career: Associate Editor, *Atlantic Monthly,* 1893-1905; Associate Editor, *Youth Companion,* 1899-1913; Vice President, *Atlantic Monthly* Company 1911-1929; Editor, *Harvard Graduate* magazine, 1917, 1918; Consultant in Biography, Library of Congress, 1929-1931; Trustee and Director, Boston Athenaeum, 1933-1937; Overseer, Harvard University, 1933-1939.

Selected Works: *Memoirs of the Life and Services of the Rt. Rev. Alonzo Potter, D.D., LL.D. Bishop of the Protestant Episcopal Church in the Diocese of Pennsylvania,* 1870. *American Bookmen,* 1898. *Boston: The Place and the People,* 1903. *Boston Common: Scenes from Four Centuries,* 1910. *The Atlantic Monthly and Its Makers,* 1919. *Causes and Their Champions,* 1926. *Bristol, Rhode Island: A Town Biography,* 1930. *The Boston Symphony Orchestra, 1881-1931,* 1931. *The Children's Judge Frederick Pickering Cabot,* 1932. *The Articulate Sisters: Passages from Journals and Letters of the Daughters of President Josiah Quincy of Harvard University,* 1946. *Boston Landmarks,* 1946.

Other Awards: Honorary LittD, Lehigh University, PA.

For More Information: *Time,* April 19, 1939; Howe, Helen Huntington, *The Gentle Americans, 1864-1960: Biography of a Breed,* New York: Harper & Row, 1965.

Commentary: Mark Antony Dewolfe Howe was awarded the 1925 Pulitzer Prize in Biography for *Barrett Wendell and His Letters,* about the educator and historian who taught the first American literature class at Harvard University.

Howe wrote biographies, histories, and poetry. He was on the staff of *Youth's Companion* and the *Atlantic Monthly,* where he served as vice-president. His other biographies include *James Ford Rhodes* and *Oliver Wendell Holmes.* His last volume of verse, *Sundown,* was published when Howe was 92. It has been suggested that Howe was the person *The Late George Apley* was based upon.

1926

Harvey Williams Cushing 22
Birth: 1869. **Death:** 1939.

Prize: *Biography or Autobiography,* 1926: *The Life of Sir William Osler,* Oxford, England: Clarendon, 1925.

Career: Author and neurosurgeon.

Selected Works: *Dr. Garth, the Kit-Kat Poet 1661-1718,* 1906. *Consecratio Medici, and Other Papers,* 1928. *The Personality of a Hospital,* 1930. *The Medical Career,* 1930. *From a Surgeon's Journal, 1915-1918,* 1936. *Harvey Cushing: Selected Papers on Neurosurgery* (Matson, Donald D., and William J. German, eds.), 1969.

For More Information: Harvey Cushing Society, *Harvey Cushing's Seventieth Birthday Party, April 8, 1939*; *Speeches, Letters, and Tributes,* Spring-

field, IL: Thomas, 1939; Fulton, John F., *Dedication Address: The Harvey Cushing General Hospital,* Framingham, MA: Colish, 1944; Fulton, John F., *Harvey Cushing: A Biography,* Oxford, England: Blackwell Scientific, 1946; Thomson, Elizabeth Harriet, *Harvey Cushing: Surgeon, Author, Artist,* New York: Schuman, 1950.

Commentary: Harvey Williams Cushing was awarded the 1926 Pulitzer Prize in Biography for *The Life of Sir William Osler,* a two-volume biography of Osler, who was a physician and professor of medicine and the author of *The Principles and Practice of Medicine,* a popular textbook in the field.

Cushing was born in Cleveland, Ohio, and he was educated at Johns Hopkins, Yale, and Harvard universities. He became a surgeon and taught medicine at Harvard from 1912 until 1932, when he became a professor at Yale. His teaching specialty was the brain and the pituitary gland. Cushing's disease of the pituitary is named for him. He also wrote *The Pituitary Body and Its Disorders.*

1927

Emory Holloway 23
Birth: March 16, 1885; Marshall, MO. **Death:** 1977. **Education:** Hendrix College, AR: BA. University of Texas: MA, LLD. Columbia University, NY. **Spouse:** Ella Brooks (m. 1915). **Children:** Two sons, one daughter.

Prize: *Biography or Autobiography,* 1927: *Whitman: An Interpretation in Narrative,* New York: Knopf, 1926.

Career: English Teacher, Amity, AR, 1906-1908; English Teacher, Morrisville College, MO, 1910-1911; English Instructor, University of Texas, 1912; Professor of English, Adelphi College, NY, 1914-1937; Transport Secretary, YMCA, France, 1918; Chairman, Walt Whitman Memorial Committee, 1925; Professor of English, Queens College, NY, beginning in 1937; Editor, *American Literature,* beginning in 1940.

Selected Works: *The Uncollected Poetry and Prose of Walt Whitman* (Holloway, Emory, ed.), 1921. *I Sit and Look Out: Editorials from the Brooklyn Daily Times, by Walt Whitman* (Holloway, Emory, ed.), 1932. *Janice in Tomorrow-Land,* 1936. *"Leaves of Grass" by Walt Whitman* (Holloway, Emory, ed.), 1947. *Free and Lonesome Heart: The Secret of Walt Whitman,* 1960. *Complete Poetry & Selected Prose and Letters* (Holloway, Emory, ed.), 1971.

For More Information: *Dictionary of Literary Biography,* Detroit: Gale, 1991.

Commentary: Emory Holloway won the 1927 Pulitzer Prize in Biography for *Whitman, An Interpretation in Narrative,* the life story of the poet Walt

Whitman. Holloway was an expert on Whitman. His many years of researching and writing about the poet helped others in their scholarship.

Holloway was born in Marshall, Missouri and attended Hendrix College, the University of Texas, and Columbia University. He taught English at Queens College of the City University of New York from 1937 until his retirement. He was the editor for many years of *American Literature*. His other works include *The Uncollected Poetry and Prose of Walt Whitman*.

1928

Charles Russell   24
Birth: September 25, 1860; Davenport, IA. **Death:** April 23, 1941. **Spouse:** Abby Osborn. **Children:** John.

Prize: *Biography or Autobiography,* 1928: *The American Orchestra and Theodore Thomas,* Garden City, NY: Doubleday, Page, 1927.

Career: City Editor, *New York World,* 1894-1897; Managing Editor, *New York American,* 1897-1902; Publisher, *Chicago American,* 1900-1902; Candidate, Governor of NY, NY State Senator, Mayor of New York City; Nominated as a presidential candidate, Socialist Party, 1916; Expelled from party for advocating war; Delegate to Russia, U.S. Committee on Public Information, 1917; President, U.S. Civil Legion, 1922; Honorary President, American Association for Recognition of the Irish Republic.

Selected Works: *Such Stuff as Dreams,* 1901. *The Twin Immortalities and Other Poems,* 1904. *The Uprising of the Many,* 1907. *Thomas Chatterton, the Marvelous Boy: The Story of a Strange Life 1752-1770,* 1908. *Songs of Democracy and on Other Themes,* 1909. *Why I Am a Socialist,* 1910. *The Story of Wendell Phillips: Soldier of the Common Good,* 1914. *These Shifting Scenes,* 1914. *Unchained Russia,* 1918. *After the Whirlwind: A Book of Reconstruction and Profitable Thanksgiving,* 1919. *Bolshevism and the United States,* 1919. *The Hero of the Filipinos: The Story of Jos Rizal, Poet, Patriot and Martyr* (with E.B. Rodriguez), 1923. *Julia Marlowe, Her Life and Art,* 1926. *A-Rafting on the Mississip',* 1928. *An Hour of American Poetry,* 1929. *From Sandy Hook to 62,* 1929. *Charlemagne, First of the Moderns,* 1930. *Haym Salomon and the Revolution,* 1930. *Bare Hands and Stone Walls: Some Recollections of a Side-Line Reformer,* 1933. *A Pioneer Editor in Early Iowa: A Sketch of the Life of Edward Russell,* 1941.

Other Awards: Honorary LLD, Howard University, Washington, DC.

For More Information: Miraldi, Robert, *Charles Edward Russell: "Chief of the Muckrakers,"* Co-lumbia, SC: Association for Education in Journalism and Mass Communication, 1995.

Commentary: Charles Edward Russell was awarded the 1928 Pulitzer Prize in Biography for *The American Orchestra and Theodore Thomas,* about the 19th-century German-American conductor.

Russell was born in Iowa. He was a journalist known for muckraking articles on the railroads and the meatpacking industry. He traveled to Russia at the request of President Woodrow Wilson in 1917. He wrote about his experiences there in *Unchained Russia*. His other works include *Such Stuff as Dreams* and *Stories of the Great Railroads.*

1929

Burton Jesse Hendrick
Full entry appears as **#19** under "Biography or Autobiography," 1923.

1930

Marquis James   25
Birth: August 29, 1891; Springfield, MO. **Death:** November 19, 1955. **Parents:** Houshin and Rachel (Marquis) James. **Education:** Oklahoma Christian University (now Phillips University). **Spouse:** Bessie Williams Rowland (m. 1914); Jacqueline Mary Parsons (m. 1954). **Children:** Cynthia (BWR).

Prize: *Biography or Autobiography,* 1930: *The Raven: A Biography of Sam Houston,* Indianapolis, IN: Bobbs-Merrill, 1929. *Biography or Autobiography,* 1938: *The Life of Andrew Jackson: Portrait of a President,* New York: Garden City, 1937.

Career: Reporter: *Enid Eagle,* Enid, OK, *Kansas City Journal,* Kansas City, MO, *Globe-Democrat,* St. Louis, MO, *St. Louis Republic,* St. Louis, *New Orleans Item,* New Orleans, LA, 1909-1913; Copy Reader, *Chicago Tribune,* Chicago, 1914; Assistant City Editor, *Chicago Daily Journal,* Chicago, 1915; Rewrite Person, *New York Tribune,* NY, 1916; Captain, U.S. Army, France, 1917-1919; National Director of Publicity, American Legion, 1919-1923; Editorial Staff member, *American Legion Monthly,* 1923-1932; Editorial Staff member, *New Yorker,* NY, 1925; Member: American Yacht Club, National Institute of Arts and Letters, National Press Club, Society of American Historians.

Selected Works: *A History of the American Legion,* 1923. *Andrew Jackson: The Border Captain,* 1933. *They Had Their Hour,* 1934. *Mr. Garner of Texas,* 1939. *Alfred I. DuPont: The Family Rebel,* 1941. *Biography of a Business, 1792-1942: Insurance Company of North America,* 1942. *The Cherokee Strip: A Tale of an Oklahoma Boyhood,* 1945. *The*

Metropolitan Life: A Study in Business Growth, 1947. *Merchant Adventurer: The Story of W.R. Grace,* 1993.

For More Information: *Newsweek,* October 4, 1937; *Saturday Revue of Literature,* May 7, 1938.

Commentary: Marquis James won two Pulitzer Prizes, both in Biography. He was awarded the 1930 Pulitzer Prize for *The Raven,* the combined story of Sam Houston and the history of the state of Texas up to the Civil War. He was a co-winner of the 1938 prize for *Andrew Jackson,* a two-volume work on Jackson as the border captain and a portrait of a president.

James was born in Springfield, Missouri. He grew up near the town of Enid, Oklahoma. He briefly attended university, choosing instead to become a reporter. He wrote for the Chicago *Evening Journal,* the New York *Tribune,* and the *New Yorker,* continually trying to get longer works published. He finally succeeded with *The Raven,* which sold 100,000 copies. His second work, *Andrew Jackson,* took seven years to complete and sold 250,000 copies.

1931

Henry James   26

Birth: 1879; Boston, MA. **Death:** 1947. **Parents:** William and Alice H. (Gibbons) James. **Education:** Harvard University, MA: BA. Harvard Law School, MA: LLB. **Spouse:** Olivia Cutting (m. 1917; div. 1930); Dorothea Blogden (m. 1938).

Prize: *Biography or Autobiography,* 1931: *Charles W. Eliot, President of Harvard University, 1869-1909,* Boston: Houghton Mifflin, 1930.

Career: Lawyer, 1906-1912; Manager, Rockefeller Institute for Medical Research, 1912; Manager, War Relief Commission, Rockefeller Foundation, 1914-1916; American Expeditionary Forces, France, WWI; Member of Versailles Peace Conference, 1918-1919.

Selected Works: *The Letters of William James* (James, Henry, ed.), 1920. *Richard Olney and His Public Service,* 1923.

For More Information: Harvard University Class of 1899, Secretary's Fortieth Anniversary Report, 1939.

Commentary: Henry James was awarded the 1931 Pulitzer Prize in Biography for *Charles W. Eliot,* the story of Harvard University's president and educational reformer from 1869 to 1909.

James was born in Boston, Massachusetts. He was the son of William James, the psychologist and philosopher, and the nephew of the noted writer Henry James. Trained in law, he managed the Rockefeller Institute for Medical Research and the War Relief Commission for the Rockefeller Foundation. His other works include *The Letters of William James.* He

was referred to as Harry in the letters of his famous uncle, Henry.

1932

Henry F. Pringle   27

Birth: August 23, 1897; New York, NY. **Death:** April 7, 1958. **Parents:** James Maxwell and Marie (Juergens) Pringle. **Education:** Cornell University, NY: BA. **Spouse:** Helena Huntington Smith (m. 1926). **Children:** Two sons, one daughter.

Prize: *Biography or Autobiography,* 1932: *Theodore Roosevelt, A Biography,* New York: Harcourt, Brace, 1931.

Career: Journalist and Writer: *Evening Sun,* 1916, *Boston Globe,* 1922, *New York World,* 1924-1927, *American Mercury.*

Selected Works: *Big Frogs,* 1928. *The Life and Times of William Howard Taft; A Biography,* 1939. *The Color Line in Medicine* (with Katherine Pringle), 1948.

For More Information: *Dictionary of American Biography,* New York: Scribners, 1980.

Commentary: Henry Fowles Pringle won the 1932 Pulitzer Prize in Biography for *Theodore Roosevelt,* a work praised by some critics for its truthfulness.

Pringle was born in New York City. He was educated at Cornell University and pursued a career as a journalist. He worked for the *Boston Globe,* the New York *Evening Sun,* the New York *World,* and the *American Mercury.* His other works include *Alfred E. Smith: A Critical Study* and *The Life and Times of William Howard Taft.*

1933

Allan Nevins   28

Birth: May 20, 1890; Camp Point, IL. **Death:** March 15, 1971. **Parents:** Allan and Emma (Smith) Nevins. **Education:** University of Illinois: BA, MA. **Spouse:** May Fleming Richardson (m. 1916). **Children:** Ann, Elizabeth, Meredith.

Prize: *Biography or Autobiography,* 1933: *Grover Cleveland: A Study in Courage,* New York: Dodd, Mead, 1933. *Biography or Autobiography,* 1937: *Hamilton Fish: The Inner History of the Grant Administration,* New York: Dodd, Mead, 1936.

Career: Editorial Writer, *New York Evening Post,* 1917-1927; Contributor, *Nation* and *Evening Post,* 1913-1918; Literary Editor, *New York Sun,* 1924-1925; Writer, biography and history.

Selected Works: *Illinois,* 1917. *American Social History as Recorded by British Travellers* (Nevins, Allan, ed.), 1923. *The Diary of Philip Hone, 1828-*

1851 (Nevins, Allan, ed.), 1927. *American Press Opinion, Washington to Coolidge,* 1928. *Fremont, the West's Greatest Adventurer,* 1928. *Polk: The Diary of a President, 1845-1849* (Nevins, Allan, ed.), 1929. *Henry White: Thirty Years of American Diplomacy,* 1930. *Letters of Grover Cleveland, 1850-1908* (Nevins, Allan, ed.), 1933. *History of the Bank of New York and Trust Company, 1784 to 1934,* 1934. *Abram S. Hewitt: With Some Account of Peter Cooper,* 1935. *Fremont, Pathmaker of the West,* 1939. *John D. Rockefeller: The Heroic Age of American Enterprise,* 1940. *This Is England Today,* 1941. *America in World Affairs,* 1942. *America: The Story of a Free People* (with Henry Steele Commager), 1942. *The United States and Its Place in World Affairs, 1918-1943* (Nevins, Allan, and Louis M. Hacker, eds.), 1943. *A Century of Political Cartoons: Caricature in the United States from 1800 to 1900* (with Frank Weitenkampf), 1944. *The Greater City: New York, 1898-1948* (Nevins, Allan, and John A. Krout, eds.), 1948. *America through British Eyes,* 1948. *The Chronicles of America Series* (Nevins, Allan, ed.), 1951. *The Diary of John Quincy Adams, 1794-1845* (Nevins, Allan, ed.), 1951. *Polk: The Diary of a President, 1845-1849,* 1952. *Study in Power: John D. Rockefeller, Industrialist and Philanthropist,* 1953. *The Statesmanship of the Civil War,* 1953. *Ford: The Times, the Man, the Company,* 1954. *Times of Trial* (Nevins, Allan, ed.), 1958. *The War for the Union,* 1959-1960. *The Strategy of Peace* (Nevins, Allan, ed.), 1960. *The Origins of the Land-Grant Colleges and State Universities,* 1962. *The State Universities and Democracy,* 1962. *A Diary of Battle: The Personal Journals of Colonel Charles S. Wainwright, 1861-1865,* 1962. *The State Universities and Democracy,* 1962. *The Statesmanship of the Civil War,* 1962. *Lincoln: A Contemporary Portrait* (Nevins, Allan, and Irving Stone, eds.), 1962. *Herbert H. Lehman and His Era,* 1963. *Timber and Men: The Weyerhaeuser Story* (with Ralph W. Hidy and Frank E. Hill), 1963. *The Place of Franklin D. Roosevelt in History,* 1965. *The Price of Survival,* 1967. *James Truslow Adams: Historian of the American Dream,* 1968. *The American States during and after the Revolution, 1775-1789,* 1969. *Allan Nevins on History* (Billington, Ray A., ed.), 1975. *A Short History of the United States* (with Henry Steele Commager), 1976. *The Gateway to History,* 1984. *The Diary of George Templeton Strong* (Nevins, Allan, ed.), 1988. *Civil War Books: A Critical Bibliography* (Nevins, Allan, ed.), 1996.

For More Information: Sheehan, Donald Henry and Harold C. Syrett, eds., *Essays in American Historiography: Papers Presented in Honor of Allan Nevins,* New York: Columbia University, 1960.

Commentary: Allan Nevins won two Pulitzer Prizes, both in Biography. He was awarded the 1933 prize for his biography of *Grover Cleveland,* the 22nd

and 24th President of the United States. He won the 1937 prize for *Hamilton Fish: The Inner History of the Grant Administration,* a portrait of Grant's secretary of state, the diplomat responsible for settling the *Alabama* claims.

Nevins was born in Camp Point, Illinois and educated at the University of Illinois. He worked as an editor and contributor to the New York *Evening Post,* the *Nation,* and the New York *Evening Sun.* He had a long career as author and editor of voluminous history and biography books. He also advised and encouraged other authors. His other works include *American Press Opinion: From Washington to Coolidge* and *Study in Power: John D. Rockefeller, Industrialist and Philanthropist.*

1934

Tyler Dennett   29

Birth: June 13, 1883; Spencer, WI. **Death:** December 29, 1949. **Parents:** Rev. William Eugene and Roxie (Tyler) Dennett. **Religion:** Congregationalist. **Education:** Bates College, ME. Williams College, MA. Johns Hopkins University, MD: PhD. **Spouse:** Maybelle Raymond (m. 1911). **Children:** George Raymond, Tyler Eugene, Audrey, Laurence.

Prize: *Biography or Autobiography,* 1934: *John Hay: From Poetry to Politics,* American Political Leaders, New York: Dodd, Mead, 1933.

Career: Associate Editor, *World Outlook,* a Methodist magazine, 1914-1916; Director of Publicity, Methodist Centenary; Editor-in-Chief, Division of Publications, U.S. Department of State, 1924-1929; Historical Advisor, 1929-1931; Lecturer, American History; Professor, International Relations, Princeton University, 1932-1934; President of Williams College.

Selected Works: *The Democratic Movement in Asia,* 1918. *Americans in Eastern Asia,* 1922. *Roosevelt and the Russo-Japanese War,* 1925. *Lincoln and the Civil War in the Diaries and Letters of John Hay* (Dennet, Tyler, ed.), 1939. *Americans in Eastern Asia: A Critical Study of United States' Policy in the Far East in the Nineteenth Century,* 1963.

Other Awards: Honorary Degrees: Wesleyan University, CT; Harvard University, MA; Amherst College, MA; Columbia University, NY; Beloit College, WI; Lafayette College, PA; Clark University, NY; Princeton University, NJ; Williams College, MA.

For More Information: *Dictionary of American Biography,* New York: Scribners, 1980.

Commentary: *John Hay: From Poetry to Politics* won the 1934 Pulitzer Prize in Biography for Tyler Dennett. Hay was secretary to Abraham Lincoln, an ambassador and secretary of state, and also a writer.

Dennett was born in Spencer, Wisconsin. He was educated at Williams College, Union Theological, and Johns Hopkins University. As a Congregationalist minister, he traveled to Asia as a member of the board of the Church World Movement. He became a leading expert on United States Far East diplomatic history and also served as president of Williams College. His other works include *Americans in Eastern Asia.*

1935

Douglas Southall Freeman   30

Birth: May 16, 1886; Lynchburg, VA. **Death:** June 13, 1953. **Parents:** Walker Burford and Bettie (Allen) Freeman. **Education:** Richmond College, VA: BA. Johns Hopkins University, MD: PhD. **Spouse:** Inez Virginia Goddin (m. 1914). **Children:** Two daughters, one son.

Prize: *Biography or Autobiography,* 1935: *R. E. Lee: A Biography,* New York: Scribners, 1934-1936. *Biography or Autobiography,* 1958: *George Washington, A Biography,* New York: Scribners, 1948-57.

Career: Writer, *Richmond Times Dispatch,* 1909; Secretary, Virginia Commonwealth Tax Commission, 1910-1912; Editorial Writer, Richmond *Times Dispatch & News Leader,* 1913; Editorial Writer, *New Leader,* 1914; Editor, *New Leader,* 1915; Visiting Professor of Journalism, 1934; Lecturer, Columbia University, 1935; President: Poe Foundation, Southern Historical Society, Confederate Memorial Institute, Society of American Historians.

Selected Works: *Lee's Dispatches,* 1915. *The Last Parade,* 1932. *The South to Posterity,* 1939. *Lee's Lieutenants: A Study in Command,* 1942-1944. *Lee of Virginia,* 1958.

Other Awards: Parchment of Distinction, New York Southern Society.

For More Information: *Life,* May 13 and June 3, 1940; *Time,* April 1, 1940; *Douglas Southall Freeman: A Register of His Papers in the Library of Congress, Manuscript Division,* Washington, DC: Library of Congress, 1960.

Commentary: Douglas S. Freeman won two Pulitzer Prizes, both in Biography. He was awarded the 1935 prize for *R. E. Lee,* the four-volume story of the Confederate general and college president. Freeman was posthumously named as a co-winner of the 1958 prize for *George Washington, Volumes I-VI.* Volume VII was completed after Freeman's death by John A. Carroll and Mary Wells Ashworth, who were also awarded prizes.

Freeman was born in Lynchburg, Virginia. He was educated at Richmond College and Johns Hopkins University. He became a reporter for Richmond's *Times-Dispatch* and *News-Leader.* When asked to write a brief biography of Lee, Freeman found that many already existed. He unearthed a wealth of new material which resulted in the prize-winning biography. He served as president of the Southern Historical Foundation and the Society of American Historians.

1936

Ralph Barton Perry   31

Birth: July 3, 1876; Poultney, VT. **Death:** July 19, 1957. **Education:** Princeton University, NJ: BA. Harvard University, MA: MA, PhD. **Spouse:** Rachel Berenson (m. 1905; died 1933). **Children:** Two sons.

Prize: *Biography or Autobiography,* 1936: *The Thought and Character of William James,* Boston: Little, Brown, 1935.

Career: Philosophy Instructor, Williams College, MA, 1899-1902; Philosophy Instructor, Smith College, MA, 1900-1902; Professor, Harvard University, MA, beginning in 1913; Major and Secretary, Committee on Special Training and Education, War Department, WWI; Hyde Lecturer, French universities, 1921-1922; President, American Historical Society.

Selected Works: *The Approach to Philosophy,* 1905. *The Moral Economy,* 1909. *The Free Man and the Soldier: Essays on the Reconciliation of Liberty and Discipline,* 1916. *Present Philosophical Tendencies: A Critical Survey of Naturalism, Idealism, Pragmatism and Realism, Together with a Synopsis of the Philosophy of William James,* 1916. *The Present Conflict of Ideals: A Study of the Philosophical Background of the World War,* 1918. *Collected Essays and Reviews,* 1920. *General Theory of Value: Its Meaning and Basic Principles Construed in Terms of Interest,* 1926. *Philosophy of the Recent Past: An Outline of European and American Philosophy Since 1860,* 1926. *A Defense of Philosophy,* 1931. *In the Spirit of William James,* 1938. *Shall Not Perish from the Earth,* 1940. *On All Fronts,* 1941. *Plea for an Age Movement,* 1942. *Our Side Is Right,* 1942. *Puritanism and Democracy,* 1944. *The Hope for Immortality,* 1945. *Characteristically American,* 1949. *The Citizen Decides: A Guide to Responsible Thinking in Time of Crisis,* 1951. *Freedom—For What?,* 1954. *Realms of Value: A Critique of Human Civilization,* 1954. *The Ethics of War: Bertrand Russell and Ralph Barton Perry on World War I* (Chatfield, Charles, ed.), 1972.

Other Awards: Chevalier Legion of Honor, France, 1936.

For More Information: Aspell, Patrick J., *Thomistic Critique of Transsubjectivity in Recent American Realism,* Washington, Catholic University of America Press, 1959; Soper, William Wayne, *The Self and Its World in Ralph Barton Perry, Edgar Sheffield Brightman, Jean-Paul Sartre, and Soren Kierkegaard,* Boston: Boston University Graduate School, 1962; Steinberg, Ira S., *Ralph Barton Perry on Education for Democracy,* Columbus: Ohio State University, 1970.

Commentary: Ralph Barton Perry was awarded the 1936 Pulitzer Prize in Biography for *The Thought and Character of William James,* a work derived from the unpublished writings of the philosopher and father of American psychology.

Perry was born in Vermont. He was a professor of philosophy at Harvard and a biographer. As both a student and friend of James, Perry is best known as the expert on him. Perry's other works include *The New Realism* and *Characteristically American.*

1937

Allan Nevins
Full entry appears as **#28** under "Biography or Autobiography," 1933.

1938

Marquis James
Full entry appears as **#25** under "Biography or Autobiography," 1930.

Odell Shepard   32
Birth: July 22, 1884; Sterling, IL. **Death:** 1967. **Parents:** Bishop William Orville and Emily (Odell) Shepard. **Education:** Northwestern School of Music, IL. Northwestern University, IL. University of Chicago, IL: PhB, PhM. Harvard University, MA: PhD. **Spouse:** Mary Farwell Record (m. 1908). **Children:** Willard.

Prize: *Biography or Autobiography,* 1938: *Pedlar's Progress: The Life of Bronson Alcott,* Boston: Little, Brown, 1937.

Career: Organist, Chicago churches, 1905-1907; Reporter, Chicago and St. Louis, MO, 1906-1909; Instructor, Smith Academy, St. Louis, 1908-1909; Professor of English, University of Southern California, Los Angeles, 1909-1914; Instructor of English, Harvard University and Radcliffe College, Cambridge, MA, 1916-1917; Goodwin Professor of English, Trinity College, Hartford, CT, 1917-1946; Visiting Professor, University of California, 1920; Lieutenant Governor of Connecticut, 1940-1943; Lecturer, Trinity College, Hartford, CT, 1946-1966; Visiting Professor, Bread Loaf School, VT, 1947; Visiting Professor, Bard College, 1950-1951; Co-Founder, Thoreau Society of America; Co-Founder and President, College English Association; Correspondent, Connecticut, Civil Liberties Union; Member: Connecticut Academy of Fine Arts, Delta Tau Delta, Phi Beta Kappa Member, Society of American Historians.

Selected Works: *A Lonely Flute,* 1917. *Bliss Carman,* 1923. *The Harvest of a Quiet Eye: A Book of Digressions,* 1927. *The Heart of Thoreau's Journals,* 1927. *The Joys of Forgetting: A Book of Bagtalles,* 1928. *Contemporary Essays, 1929. Representative Selections,* 1934. *The Journals of Bronson Alcott* (Shepard, Odell, ed.), 1938. *Connecticut, Past and Present,* 1939. *Irving Babbitt, Man and Teacher* (Shepard, Odell, and Frederick Manchester, eds.), 1941. *Holdfast Gaines* (with Odell Shepard and Willard Shepard), 1946. *The Best of W. H. Hudson* (Shepard, Odell, ed.), 1949. *Jenkins' Ear: A Narrative*

Attributed to Horace Walpole, Esq., 1951. *The Lore of the Unicorn,* 1967.

Other Awards: Guggenheim Fellowship, 1927-1928. Huntington Library International Research Fellow, 1934-1935. Little, Brown Centennial Contest Prize, 1939: *Pedlar's Progress,* Boston: Little, Brown, 1937. Honorary LittDs: Northwest University, IL, 1932; Wesleyan University, CT, 1939. Honorary LHD, Boston University, MA, 1941.

For More Information: *Saturday Review of Literature,* May 7, 1938; *Twentieth-Century Authors,* New York: Wilson, 1942; *Oxford Companion to American Literature,* New York: Oxford, 1983.

Commentary: Odell Shepard was a co-winner of the 1938 Pulitzer Prize in Biography for *Pedlar's Progress: The Life of Bronson Alcott,* philosopher, educator, utopian, and father of Louisa May Alcott.

Shepard was born in Illinois. He attended Northwestern University, the University of Chicago, and Harvard University. He held a variety of jobs and served as lieutenant governor of Connecticut from 1940 to 1943. In addition to writing essays, poetry, and novels, he was an editor of the works of Thoreau, Alcott, and Longfellow. His other works include *Connecticut, Past and Present.*

1939

Carl Van Doren   33

Birth: September 10, 1885; Hope, IL. **Death:** July 18, 1950. **Parents:** Charles Lucius and Dora Ann (Butz) Van Doren. **Religion:** Atheist. **Education:** University of Illinois: BA. Columbia University, NY: PhD. **Spouse:** Irita Bedford (m. 1912; div. 1939); Jean Wright Gorman (div. 1945). **Children:** Three daughters.

Prize: *Biography or Autobiography,* 1939: *Benjamin Franklin,* New York: Viking, 1938.

Career: Rhetoric Assistant, University of Illinois, 1907-1908; English Instructor, Columbia University, 1911-1930; Headmaster, Brearley School, 1916-1919; Literary Editor, the *Nation,* 1919-1922; Roving Critic, *Century,* 1922-1925; Co-Founder, Literary Guild; Managing Editor, *Cambridge History of American Literature,* 1917-1921; Member, Committee on Management, *Dictionary of American Biography,* 1926-1936.

Selected Works: *The Life of Thomas Love Peacock,* 1911. *The American Novel,* 1921. *Contemporary American Novelists, 1900-1920,* 1922. *Cambridge History of American Literature* (Van Doren, Carl, ed.), 1922. *Selections from the Writings of Thomas Paine* (Van Doren, Carl, ed.), 1922. *The Roving Critic,* 1923. *Many Minds,* 1924. *James Branch Cabell,* 1925. *American and British Literature Since 1890* (with Mark Van Doren), 1925. *Other*

Provinces, 1925. *The Ninth Wave,* 1926. *Swift,* 1930. *American Literature: An Introduction,* 1933. *An American Omnibus,* 1933. *Sinclair Lewis, A Biographical Sketch,* 1933. *What Is American Literature?,* 1935. *An Anthology of World Prose* (Van Doren, Carl, ed.), 1935. *Modern American Prose,* 1934. *The Borzoi Reader,* 1936. *Three Worlds,* 1936. *The American Novel, 1789-1939,* 1940. *Twenty Stories: Selected,* 1940. *Secret History of the American Revolution,* 1941. *The Literary Works of Abraham Lincoln* (Van Doren, Carl, ed.), 1942. *The Three Readers,* 1943. *Benjamin Franklin's Autobiographical Writings,* 1945. *Carl Van Doren, Selected by Himself,* 1945. *American Scriptures* (with Carl Carmer), 1946. *Letters and Papers of Benjamin Franklin and Richard Jackson, 1753-1785* (Van Doren, Carl, ed.), 1947. *The Great Rehearsal: The Story of the Making and Ratifying of the Constitution of the United States,* 1948. *The Letters of Benjamin Franklin & Jane Mecom* (Van Doren, Carl, ed.), 1950. *Jane Mecom: The Favorite Sister of Benjamin Franklin,* 1950. *The Life of Thomas Love Peacock,* 1966. *Many Minds: Critical Essays on American Writers,* 1966.

For More Information: *Newsweek,* February 17, 1941; *New York Times Book Review,* March 9, 1941; *Twentieth-Century Literary Criticism,* Detroit: Gale, 1985.

Commentary: *Benjamin Franklin* won the 1939 Pulitzer Prize in Biography for Carl Clinton Van Doren.

Van Doren was born in Hope, Illinois. He was the brother of the Pulitzer Prize-winning poet Mark Van Doren. He was educated at the University of Illinois and Columbia University. He was editor of the the the *Nation* from 1919 to 1922, where he became known for his insightful opinion pieces. He was also literary editor of the *Cambridge History of American Literature* from 1917 to 1921. In addition to the biography, Van Doren edited Franklin's papers, published in *Letters and Papers.*

1940

Ray Stannard Baker   34

Birth: April 17, 1870; Lansing, MI. **Death:** July 12, 1946. **Parents:** Joseph and Alice (Potter) Baker. **Education:** Michigan Agricultural College: BS. **Spouse:** Jessie I. Beal. **Children:** Two sons, one daughter.

Prize: *Biography or Autobiography,* 1940: *Woodrow Wilson, Life and Letters,* Garden City, NY: Doubleday, Page, 1927-1939.

Career: Reporter and Editor, *Chicago Record,* 1872-1897; Contributor, *Century, Youth Companion;* Manager, *McClure's* Syndicate, 1898; Owner and Editor, *American Magazine,* 1906-1915; Editor, Woodrow Wilson's papers.

Selected Works: _Seen in Germany,_ 1901. _What Is a Lynching? A Study of Mob Justice, South and North,_ 1905. _The Negro in Southern City Life,_ 1907. _Adventures in Contentment_ (Grayson, David, pseudonym), 1907. _Following the Color Line: An Account of Negro Citizenship in the American Democracy,_ 1908. _New Ideals in Healing,_ 1909. _Adventures in Friendship_ (Grayson, David, pseudonym), 1910. _The Spiritual Unrest,_ 1910. _Hempfield: An American Novel_ (Grayson, David, pseudonym), 1915. _What Wilson Did at Paris,_ 1919. _Woodrow Wilson and World Settlement,_ 1922. _Adventures in Understanding,_ 1925. _The Public Papers of Woodrow Wilson_ (Baker, Stannard, and William E. Dodd, eds.), 1925-1927. _An American Pioneer in Science: The Life and Service of William James Beal,_ 1925. _Native American: The Book of My Youth_ (Grayson, David, pseudonym), 1941. _American Chronicle: The Autobiography of Ray Stannard Baker_ (Grayson, David, pseudonym), 1945.

Other Awards: Honorary LLD, Michigan State University, 1917.

For More Information: Rand, Frank Prentice, _The Story of David Grayson,_ Amherst, MA: Jones Library, 1963; Bannister, Robert C., _Ray Stannard Baker: The Mind and Thought of a Progressive,_ New Haven, CT: Yale University, 1966; Semonche, John E., _Ray Stannard Baker: A Quest for Democracy in Modern America, 1870-1918,_ Chapel Hill: University of North Carolina, 1969.

Commentary: Ray Stannard Baker was awarded the 1940 Pulitzer Prize in Biography for _Woodrow Wilson, Life and Letters, Volumes VII and VIII,_ of eight volumes. Baker was a supporter of and enjoyed a close relationship with Wilson, who appointed him director of the American press bureau at the Paris Peace Conference. Wilson later made Baker his official biographer.

Baker was born in Lansing, Michigan and he was educated at Michigan Agricultural College. He began his writing career as a reporter for the Chicago _News-Record._ He later was on the staff of _McClure's,_ as "muckraker." Perhaps as a counterbalance to the muckraking, he produced nine volumes of essays under the pseudonym David Grayson, which sang the praises of country life. He is noted for _Following the Color Line,_ a report on race relations which, at the time it was published (1908), was considered extremely liberal.

1941

Ola Elizabeth Winslow   35

Birth: 1885; Grant City, MO. **Death:** September 27, 1977. **Parents:** William Delas and Hattie Elizabeth (Colby) Winslow. **Education:** Stanford University,

CA: AB, AM. University of Chicago, IL: PhD. Johns Hopkins University, MD.

Prize: _Biography or Autobiography,_ 1941: _Jonathan Edwards, 1703-1758,_ New York: Collier, 1940.

Career: Instructor, College of the Pacific (now University of the Pacific), San Jose, CA, 1909-1914; Professor of English and Head of Department, Goucher College, Baltimore, MD, 1914-1944; Assistant Dean, Goucher College, Baltimore, MD, 1919-1921; Professor, Wellesley College, MA, 1944-1950; Professor of English, Radcliffe College, MA, 1950-1962; Professor Emeritus, Wellesley College, MA, 1950-1977.

Selected Works: _Low Comedy as a Structural Element in English Drama From the Beginnings of 1642,_ 1926. _Harper's Literary Museum,_ 1927. _American Broadside Verse From Imprints of the 17th & 18th Centuries,_ 1930. _Meetinghouse Hill, 1630-1783,_ 1952. _Master Roger Williams: A Biography,_ 1957. _John Bunyan,_ 1961. _Samuel Sewall of Boston,_ 1964. _Portsmouth: The Life of a Town,_ 1966. _John Eliot, Apostle to the Indians,_ 1968.

Other Awards: Honorary DLitt, Goucher College, MD, 1951.

For More Information: _Saturday Review of Literature,_ May 10, 1941; _Twentieth Century Authors,_ New York: Wilson, 1942.

Commentary: Ola Elizabeth Winslow won the 1941 Pulitzer Prize in Biography for _Jonathan Edwards,_ the story of the Puritan philosopher and theologian who lived from 1703 to 1758.

Winslow was born in Grant City, Missouri. She was educated at Stanford University, the University of Chicago, and Johns Hopkins University. She taught English and history at Goucher College in Baltimore, Maryland, becoming chairperson of the English department. Her other works include _John Bunyan_ and _John Eliot, Apostle to the Indians._

1942

Robert Forrest Wilson   36

Birth: January 20, 1883; Warren, OH. **Death:** May 9, 1942. **Parents:** James Forrest and Harriet Rose (Larned) Wilson. **Education:** California School of Fine Arts, San Francisco: 1939. Atelier Sculpture Moderne. Pratt Institute, NY. Union Graduate School: PhD. **Spouse:** Katherine Denniston Dewey (m. 1907); Marie Humphreys. **Children:** One daughter.

Prize: _Biography or Autobiography,_ 1942: _Crusader in Crinoline: The Life of Harriet Beecher Stowe,_ Philadelphia, PA: Lippincott, 1941.

Career: Reporter, Scripps Newspapers, Washington, DC, 1910-1916; Captain, Chemical Warfare Division, U.S. Army, WWI; Researcher, Secretary of

War, War Department; European Correspondent, *McCall's*, 1923-1927.

Selected Works: *Demobilization: Our Industrial and Military Demobilization after the Armistice, 1918-1920* (with Benedict Crowell), 1921. *The Armies of Industry: Our Nation's Manufacture of Munitions for a World in Arms, 1917-1918* (with Benedict Crowell), 1921. *The Giant Hand: Our Mobilization and Control of Industry and Natural Resources, 1917-1918* (with Benedict Crowell), 1921. *The Road to France: The Transportation of Troops and Military Supplies, 1917-1918* (with Benedict Crowell), 1921. *The Living Pageant of the Nile,* 1924. *Paris on Parade,* 1925. *Rich Brat: A Novel of Paris,* 1929. *How to Wine and Dine in Paris,* 1930.

For More Information: *New York Times,* May 5 and 11, 1942; *Twentieth-Century Authors,* New York: H.W. Wilson, 1942; *Oxford Companion to American Literature,* New York: Oxford University, 1965.

Commentary: *Crusader in Crinoline: The Life of Harriet Beecher Stowe* won the 1942 Pulitzer Prize in Biography for Robert Forrest Wilson. Stowe was the author of *Uncle Tom's Cabin,* the strongly abolitionist classic.

Wilson was born in Warren, Ohio. He pursued a career as a reporter, working for the Scripps newspapers in Cleveland, Washington, DC, and South America. He was co-author with Benedict Crowell of *How America Went to War,* a six-volume work on World War I. He later worked as European correspondent for *McCall's* and wrote about life in Paris. He also studied art in Paris and at Pratt Insitute. His other works include *Paris on Parade.*

1943

Samuel Eliot Morison   37

Birth: July 9, 1887; Boston, MA. **Death:** May 15, 1976. **Parents:** John Holmes and Emily (Marshall) Morison. **Education:** Harvard University, MA: BA, PhD. Ecole des Sciences Politiques, France. Oxford University, England: MA. **Spouse:** Elizabeth S. Greene (m. 1910; died 1945); Priscilla Barton (m. 1949; died 1975). **Children:** Elizabeth Gray, Emily Marshall, Peter Green, Catharine.

Prize: *Biography or Autobiography,* 1943: *Admiral of the Ocean Sea, A Life of Christopher Columbus,* Boston: Little, Brown, 1942. *Biography or Autobiography,* 1960: *John Paul Jones: A Sailor's Biography,* Boston: Little, Brown, 1959.

Career: Instructor, History, University of California, 1914; Instructor, History, Harvard University, MA, 1915-1918, 1919-1922; Served in Infantry, U.S. Army, 1918-1919; Harold Vyvyan Harmsworth Professor of American History, Oxford University, Oxford, England, 1922-1925; Professor, Jonathan

Trumbull Professor of American History, Jonathan Trumbull Professor of American History Emeritus, Harvard University, 1925-1976, 1955-1976; Anson G. Phelps Lecturer, New York University, 1934; Naval Historian, U.S. Naval Reserve, 1942-1951; Dunning Lecturer, Queen's University, Kingston, Ontario, 1956; Fellow: American Academy of Arts and Letters, American Academy of Arts and Sciences, American Philosophical Society, British Academy, Real Academia de la Historia, Madrid, Society of Antiquarians; Member: Charitable Irish Society, St. Botolph Club, Cruising Club, Tavern Club; President: American Antiquarian Society, American Historical Association, Colonial Society of Massachusetts, Massachusetts Historical Society; Trustee, Franklin D. Roosevelt Library; Vice-President, Naval Historical Foundation.

Selected Works: *The Oxford History of the United States, 1783-1917,* 1927. *An Hour of American History: From Columbus to Coolidge,* 1929. *Builders of the Bay Colony,* 1930. *The Proprietors of Peterborough, New Hampshire, with Some Considerations on the Origin of the Name,* 1930. *The Founding of Harvard College,* 1935. *Harvard College in the Seventeenth Century,* 1936. *The Puritan Pronaos: Studies in the Intellectual Life of New England in the Seventeenth Century,* 1936. *Three Centuries of Harvard, 1636-1936,* 1936. *The Second Voyage of Christopher Columbus from Cadiz to Hispaniola and the Discovery of the Lesser Antilles,* 1939. *Portuguese Voyages to America in the Fifteenth Century,* 1940. *By Land and by Sea: Essays and Addresses,* 1953. *Christopher Columbus, Mariner,* 1955. *The Parkman Reader: From the Works of Francis Parkman,* 1955. *Freedom in Contemporary Society,* 1956. *The Intellectual Life of Colonial New England,* 1956. *The Story of the "Old Colony" of New Plymouth, 1620-1692,* 1956. *Nathaniel Holmes Morison, 1815-1890: Provost of the Peabody Institute of Baltimore, 1867-1890,* 1957. *American Contributions to the Strategy of World War II,* 1958. *William Hickling Prescott, 1796-1859,* 1958. *The Story of Mount Desert Island, Maine,* 1960. *The Scholar in America: Past, Present, and Future,* 1961. *One Boy's Boston, 1887-1901,* 1962. *Sources and Documents Illustrating the American Revolution, 1764-1788, and the Formation of the Federal Constitution,* 1962. *The Growth of the American Republic* (with Henry Steele Commager), 1962. *The Two-Ocean War: A Short History of the United States Navy in the Second World War,* 1963. *Vistas of History,* 1964. *The Caribbean as Columbus Saw It* (with Mauricio Obregon), 1964. *The Oxford History of the American People,* 1965. *"Old Bruin": Commodore Matthew C. Perry, 1794-1858,* 1967. *Harrison Gray Otis, 1765-1848: The Urbane Federalist,* 1969. *Admiral of the Ocean Sea: A Life of Christopher Columbus,* 1970. *The European Discovery of America,*

1971-1974. *Samuel de Champlain, Father of New France,* 1972. *The Conservative American Revolution,* 1976. *Sailor Historian: The Best of Samuel Eliot Morison* (Morison, Emily, ed.), 1977. *A Concise History of the American Republic* (with Henry Steele Commager and William E. Leuchtenburg), 1977. *The Great Explorers: The European Discovery of America,* 1978.

Other Awards: Seven Battle Stars, World War I. Loubat Prize, Columbia University. Jusserand Medal: *The Tercentennial History of Harvard University, 1636-1936.* Bancroft Prize, Columbia University, 1949: *The Rising Sun in the Pacific,* 1972. Theodore Roosevelt Distinguished Service Medal, 1956. Thomas Alva Edison Foundation National Mass Media Award, 1957: *The Story of the "Old Colony" of New Plymouth 1620-1692,* New York: Knopf, 1956. Christopher Award, 1960. St. Thomas More Award, Rockhurst College, 1960. Alfred Thayer Mayan Award, Navy League, 1961. Emerson-Thoreau Medal, American Association for the Advancement of Science, 1961. Gold Medal, History and Biography, National Institute of Arts and Letters, 1962. Balzan Foundation Award, History, 1963. Presidential Medal of Freedom, 1964. Honorary LHDs: Trinity College, 1935; Amherst College, MA, 1936. Honorary LittDs: Harvard University, MA, 1936; Columbia University, NY, 1942; Yale University, CT, 1949; Williams College, MA, 1950; Oxford University, England, 1951; University of Notre Dame, IN, 1954; College of the Holy Cross, MA, 1962. Honorary LLDs: Union College, MA, 1939; Boston College, MA, 1960; Bucknell College (now University), PA, 1960; University of Maine, 1968.

For More Information: *Current Biography,* New York: Wilson, 1942, 1955; Pfitzer, Gregory M., *Samuel Eliot Morison's Historical World: In Quest of a New Parkman,* Boston: Northeastern University, 1991.

Commentary: Samuel Eliot Morison won two Pulitzer Prizes, both in Biography. He was awarded the 1943 prize for *Admiral of the Ocean Sea: A Life of Christopher Columbus,* a two-volume work. He was awarded the 1960 prize for *John Paul Jones: A Sailor's Biography.*

Morison was born in Boston and educated at Harvard University and at the School of Political Science (Ecole des Sciences Politiques) in France. He became a maritime historian as well as the official biographer at Harvard where he taught from 1915 to 1955. Morison retired as a rear admiral. His other works included *History of United States Naval Operations in World War II* in 15 volumes and *The Oxford History of the American People.*

1944

Carleton Mabee 38

Birth: December 25, 1914; Shanghai, China. **Parents:** Fred Carleton and Miriam (Bentley) Mabee. **Education:** Bates College, ME: AB. Columbia University, NY: PhD. **Spouse:** Norma Dicking (m. 1945). **Children:** Timothy Irving, Susan Mabee Newhouse.

Prize: *Biography or Autobiography,* 1944: *The American Leonardo: The Life of Samuel F.B. Morse,* New York: Knopf, 1943.

Career: Civilian Public Service Worker, 1941-1945; Relief Worker, American Friends Service Committee, Vienna, Austria, 1946-1947; Tutor, Olivet College, Olivet, MI, 1947-1949; Assistant Professor and Professor, Clarkson College of Technology, Potsdam, NY, 1949-1961; Professor of American Civilization, Keio University, Tokyo, Japan, 1953-1954; Delta College, University Center, MI, Director of Social Studies Division, 1961-1964; Chairman, Department of Humanities and Social Sciences, Rose Polytechnic Institute (now Rose-Hulman Institute of Technology), Terre Haute, IN, 1964-1965; Professor of History, State University of New York College at New Paltz, 1965-1980; Professor Emeritus, State University of New York College at New Paltz, beginning in 1980; Member: Delta Sigma Rho, Long Island Historical Society, New York Historical Society, New York State Historical Association, Phi Beta Kappa.

Selected Works: *The Seaway Story,* 1961. *Black Freedom: The Nonviolent Abolitionists from 1830 through the Civil War,* 1970. *Charity in Travail: Two Orphan Asylums for Blacks,* 1974. *Black Education in New York State: From Colonial to Modern Times,* 1979. *Sojourner Truth: Slave, Prophet, Legend,* 1993. *Listen to the Whistle: An Anecdotal History of the Wallkill Valley Railroad in Ulster and Orange Counties, New York,* 1995.

Other Awards: Bergstein Award, Excellence in Teaching, Delta College, 1963. Anisfield-Wolf Award, Cleveland Foundation, 1971: *Black Freedom: The Nonviolent Abolitionists from 1830 through the Civil War,* New York: Macmillan, 1970. Gustavus Myers Award for Outstanding Book on Human Rights, 1994: *Sojourner Truth: Slave, Prophet, Legend,* New York: New York University, 1993.

For More Information: *Saturday Review of Literature,* May 6, 1944; *Oxford Companion to American Literature,* New York: Oxford, 1965.

Commentary: *The American Leonardo: The Life of Samuel F. B. Morse* won the 1944 Pulitzer Prize in Biography for Carleton Mabee. This was Mabee's doctoral thesis, presented in 1942 at Columbia University.

Mabee was born in Shanghai, China, where his parents were teachers at an American church college.

He was educated at Bates College in Maine and at Columbia University. He has taught history at the State University of New York at New Paltz, where he is the Professor Emeritus of History. His most recent work is *Sojourner Truth: Slave, Prophet, Legend,* published in 1993.

1945

Russell Blaine Nye   39
Birth: February 17, 1913. **Death:** 1993. **Parents:** Charles H. and Zelma (Schimmeyer) Nye. **Education:** Oberlin College, OH: AB. University of Wisconsin: MA, PhD. **Spouse:** Kathryn Charey (m. 1938). **Children:** Peter William.

Prize: *Biography or Autobiography,* 1945: *George Bancroft: Brahmin Rebel,* New York: Knopf, 1944.

Career: Instructor, Adelphi College (now University), Garden City, NY, 1939-1940; Instructor, Professor, Michigan State University, East Lansing, beginning in 1941; Professor Emeritus, Michigan State University, East Lansing, beginning in 1963; President, American Studies Association, 1965-1967; Member, Board of Control, Ferris State College, 1950-1967; Member, American Historical Association, Modern Language Association of America.

Selected Works: *Fettered Freedom: Civil Liberties and the Slavery Controversy, 1830-1860,* 1949. *Midwestern Progressive Politics: A Historical Study of Its Origins and Development, 1870-1950,* 1951. *William Lloyd Garrison and the Humanitarian Reformers,* 1955. *A Baker's Dozen: Thirteen Unusual Americans,* 1956. *Midwestern Progressive Politics: A Historical Study of Its Origins and Development, 1870-1958,* 1959. *The Cultural Life of the New Nation, 1776-1830,* 1960. *Fettered Freedom: Civil Liberties and the Slavery Controversy, 1830-1860 (Revised),* 1963. *Michigan,* 1966. *This Almost Chosen People: Essays in the History of American Ideas,* 1966. *The Unembarrassed Muse: The Popular Arts in America,* 1970. *A History of the United States* (with J.E. Morpurgo), 1970. *Crises on Campus* (Nye, Russell Blaine, ed.), 1971. *New Dimensions in Popular Culture* (Nye, Russell Blaine, ed.), 1972. *Society and Culture in America, 1830-1860,* 1974.

Other Awards: Donner Medal, Association for Canadian Studies, 1977. Honorary LHD, Northern Michigan University, 1968. Honorary LLDs: Ferris State College, MI, 1969; Bowling Green State University, OH, 1976.

For More Information: *Blue Book,* New York: St. Martins, 1976; Waldmeir, Joseph ed., *Essays in Honor of Russel B. Nye,* East Lansing: Michigan State University, 1978; *Current Biography,* New York: Wilson, 1993.

Commentary: Russell Blaine Nye was awarded the 1945 Pulitzer Prize in Biography for *George Bancroft: Brahmin Rebel,* the story of President James K. Polk's Secretary of the Navy and the planner of the U.S. Naval Academy at Annapolis.

Nye was born in Viola, Wisconsin. He was educated at Oberlin College and the University of Wisconsin. He taught English and history at various colleges and universities including Michigan State University. His other works include *A Baker's Dozen: Thirteen Unusual Americans* and *The Cultural Life of the New Nation, 1776-1830.*

1946

Linnie Marsh Wolfe   40
Birth: 1881; Michigan. **Death:** September 25, 1945. **Education:** Whitman College, WA. Radcliffe College, MA.

Prize: *Biography or Autobiography,* 1946: *Son of the Wilderness: The Life of John Muir,* New York: Knopf, 1945.

Career: Librarian; Muir biographer.

Selected Works: *John of the Mountains: The Unpublished Journals of John Muir* (Wolfe, Linnie Marsh, ed.), 1938.

Commentary: Linnie Marsh Wolfe won the 1946 Pulitzer Prize in Biography for *Son of the Wilderness: The Life of John Muir,* about the Scottish-born American naturalist who greatly expanded the national park system in the United States.

Wolfe was born in Michigan. She was educated at Whitman College in Walla Walla, Washington. She was a high school teacher and a librarian who, while working in Los Angeles, developed an interest in Muir. She befriended some of Muir's family and friends and also organized outings for schoolchildren to a Muir estate. She had published *John of the Mountains* in 1938.

1947

William Allen White   41
Birth: February 10, 1868; Emporia, KS. **Death:** January 29, 1944. **Parents:** Dr. Allen White and Mary (Hatton). **Education:** University of Kansas. **Spouse:** Sallie Lindsay (m. 1893). **Children:** William L., Mary.

Prize: *Editorial Writing,* 1923: *Emporia Gazette,* "To an Anxious Friend," July 27, Emporia, KS: *Emporia Gazette,* 1922. **Special Awards and Citations: Journalism,** 1944. **Biography or Autobiography,** 1947: *The Autobiography of William Allen White,* New York: Macmillan Company, 1946.

Career: Staff member, *Kansas City (MO) Star,* 1892-95; Proprietor and Editor, *Emporia (KS) Daily and Weekly Gazette,* 1895-; Observer, France, American Red Cross, 1917; Delegate, Russian Conference at Prinkipo, 1919.

Selected Works: *The Real Issue,* 1896. *The Court of Boyville,* 1899. *Stratagems and Spoils: Stories of Love and Politics,* 1901. *In Our Town,* 1906. *A Certain Rich Man,* 1909. *The Old Order Changeth: A View of American Democracy,* 1910. *God's Puppets,* 1918. *The Martial Adventures of Henry and Me,* 1918. *Woodrow Wilson: The Man, His Times, and His Task,* 1924. *Calvin Coolidge: The Man Who Is President,* 1925. *Masks in a Pageant,* 1928. *Forty Years on Main Street,* 1937. *A Puritan in Babylon,* 1938. *The Changing West and Economic Theory about Our Golden Age,* 1939. *The Autobiography of William Allen White,* 1946.

Other Awards: Honorary President, Sigma Delta Chi, 1925-26. Awarded Gold Medal for Citizenship, Theodore Roosevelt Memorial Association, 1933. Honorary Degrees: Baker University, MI; Beloit College, WI; Brown University, RI; Columbia University, NY; Knox College, IL; Harvard University, MA; Northwestern University, IL; Oberlin College, OH; Washburn College, KS.

For More Information: *National Cyclopaedia of American Biography, Volume 11,* New York: James T. White & Company, 1901; Rich, Everett, *William Allen White, The Man From Emporia,* New York: Farrar & Rinehart, 1941; Johnson, Walter, *William Allen White Defends America,* Chicago: The University of Chicago Press, 1945; *Dictionary of American Biography, Supplement 3,* New York: Charles Scribner's Sons, 1973; McKee, John DeWitt, *William Allen White: Maverick on Main Street,* Westport, CT: Greenwood Press, 1975; *Dictionary of Literary Biography, Volume 9,* Detroit: Gale Research Company, 1981; *Dictionary of Literary Biography, Volume 25,* Detroit: Gale Research Company, 1984; Griffith, Sally Foreman, *Home Town News: William Allen White and The Emporia Gazette,* New York: Oxford University Press, 1989; McKerns, Joseph P., *Biographical Dictionary of American Journalism,* New York: Greenwood Press, 1989.

Commentary: William Allen White's winning editorial was actually a reply to a friend about White's defiance of the governor of Kansas. White had displayed a placard for striking railroad workers against the governor's orders. It was an editorial for the freedom of expression and against suppression of that fundamental right. In 1944, his widow was given a scroll in appreciation of White's interest and service of seven years on the Pulitzer Prize advisory board. His autobiography, published after his death, was awarded a Pulitzer Prize in 1947.

1948

Margaret Antoinette Clapp   42
Birth: April 11, 1910; East Orange, NJ. **Death:** 1974. **Parents:** Alfred Chapin and Anna (Roth) Clapp. **Education:** Wellesley College, MA: BA. Columbia University, NY: MA, PhD.

Prize: *Biography or Autobiography,* 1948: *Forgotten First Citizen: John Bigelow,* Boston: Little, Brown, 1947.

Career: Teacher, Todhunter School, 1937-1939; Teacher, Dalton School, New Jersey College for Women, Columbia University; Researcher, British Broadcasting Company, 1942-1943; President, Wellesley College, 1949; Trustee, Walnut Hill School, Natick, MA.

Selected Works: *The Modern University,* 1950.

For More Information: *Current Biography,* New York: Wilson, 1948; *Time,* October 10, 1949.

Commentary: *Forgotten First Citizen: John Bigelow* won the 1948 Pulitzer Prize in Biography for Margaret Clapp. Bigelow, who lived from 1817 to 1911, was a history and biographical writer as well as a diplomat who worked with William Cullen Bryant on the New York *Evening Post.*

Clapp was born in East Orange, New Jersey. She was educated at Wellesley College and Columbia University. Under Allan Nevins's tutelage at Columbia, she set forth to write the biography of Bigelow. She later was a professor of history at Brooklyn College of the City University of New York. She also published *The Modern University.*

1949

Robert E. Sherwood   43
Birth: April 4, 1896; New Rochelle, NY. **Death:** November 14, 1955. **Parents:** Arthur Murray and Rosina Ernest (Emmet) Sherwood. **Education:** Harvard University, MA: BA. **Spouse:** Mary Brandon (m. 1922; div. 1934); Madeline Hurlock Connelly (m. 1935).

Prize: *Drama,* 1936: *Idiot's Delight,* New York: Scribners, 1936. *Drama,* 1939: *Abe Lincoln in Illinois, A Play in Twelve Scenes,* New York: Scribners, 1939. *Drama,* 1941: *There Shall Be No Night,* New York, Scribners, 1940. *Biography or Autobiography,* 1949: *Roosevelt and Hopkins, An Intimate History,* New York: Harper, 1948.

Career: Playwright and screenwriter; Served in Canadian Black Watch Regiment, 1918-19, WWI and wounded in action; Drama Critic, *Vanity Fair,* 1919-1920; Movie Critic, *Life,* 1920-28; Editor, *Life,* 1924-28; Literary Editor, Scribners, 1928; Speechwriter and Adviser to President Franklin Roosevelt; Special

Assistant to the Secretary of War, WWII; Special Assistant to the Secretary of the Navy, WWII; Director of the Overseas Branch, Office of War Information, WWII; Co-Founder, Playwrights' Producing Company, 1938; Co-Founder, Committee to Defend America by Aiding the Allies; President, Dramatists Guild.

Selected Works: *The Road to Rome,* 1927. *The Queen's Husband,* 1928. *Waterloo Bridge,* 1930. *This Is New York,* 1931. *The Virtuous Knight,* 1931. *Reunion in Vienna: A Play in Three Acts,* 1932. *Unending Crusade,* 1932. *The Petrified Forest,* 1935. *Tovarich* (Adaptation), 1937. *Second Threshold,* 1951. *Small War on Murray Hill,* 1957. **Films:** *Idiot's Delight,* MGM, 1939; *Abe Lincoln in Illinois,* MGM, 1940.

Other Awards: Megrue Prize for Comedy, 1932: *Reunion in Vienna,* New York: Scribners, 1932. Drama Study Club Award, 1936: *Idiot's Delight.* Academy Award, 1946: *The Best Years of Our Lives.*

For More Information: Shuman, R. Baird, *Robert E. Sherwood,* New York: Twayne, 1964; Brown, John Mason, *The Worlds of Robert E. Sherwood: Mirror to His Times, 1896-1939,* New York: Harper & Row, 1965.

Commentary: Robert Emmet Sherwood won four Pulitzer Prizes, three in Drama and one in Biography. His first prize came in 1936 for *Idiot's Delight,* a drama set in an Alpine hotel, whose guests represent the opposing views of Western nations in a prelude to World War II; it premiered on March 24, 1936 at New York's Shubert Theater. His second prize was awarded in 1939 for the dramatization *Abe Lincoln in Illinois,* which premiered on October 15, 1938 at New York's Plymouth Theater. His drama about a Finnish pacifist who sacrifices his life to fight against the Nazis, *There Shall Be No Night,* won Sherwood his third Pulitzer in 1941. It premiered on April 29, 1940 at New York's Booth Theater. Sherwood's fourth Pulitzer was awarded in 1949 for his biography, *Roosevelt and Hopkins,* about President Franklin D. Roosevelt and his advisor, Harry L. Hopkins.

Sherwood was born in New Rochelle, New York. He attended Harvard University, but left to serve in World War I. He was gassed and wounded, and he left with the belief that war was futility. He harbored strong pacifist feelings which came through in his writing. His writing career began as drama critic at *Vanity Fair.* He moved on to *Life* magazine and became editor. He was a member of the Algonquin Roundtable. Sherwood was a speechwriter for President Roosevelt during World War II, which helped immensely in his writing of the prize-winning biography. He is also remembered for his screenplay of MacKinlay Kantor's *The Best Years of Our Lives.*

1950

Samuel Flagg Bemis 44

Birth: October 20, 1891; Worcester, MA. **Death:** September 26, 1973. **Parents:** Charles Harris and Flora Bemis. **Religion:** Unitarian. **Education:** Clark University, MA: AB, AM. Harvard University, MA: AM, PhD. **Spouse:** Ruth M. Steele (m. 1919). **Children:** Barbara.

Prize: *History,* 1927: *Pinckney's Treaty: A Study of America's Advantage from Europe's Distress, 1783-1800,* Baltimore, MD: Johns Hopkins, 1926. ***Biography or Autobiography,*** 1950: *John Quincy Adams and the Foundations of American Foreign Policy.*

Career: Instructor, History, Colorado College, 1917-1918; Associate Professor, Colorado College, 1918-1920; Professor of History, Whitman College, WA, 1920-1923; Professor of History, Carnegie Institution of Washington University, DC, 1924-1934; Director of European Mission, Library of Congress, Washington, DC, 1927-29; Lecturer, Harvard University, MA, 1934-1935; Professor of Diplomatic History and Inter-American Relations, 1935-1960; Carnegie Visiting Professor to Latin American Universities, 1937-1938; Carnegie Visiting Professor to Cuba, 1945, 1956; Professor Emeritus, Yale University, CT, 1960-1973; President, American Historical Association, 1961; Member: American Antiquarian Society, Massachusetts Historical Society.

Selected Works: *Jay's Treaty: A Study in Commerce and Diplomacy,* 1923. *The Hussey-Cumberland Mission and American Independence: An Essay in the Diplomacy of the American Revolution,* 1931. *The Diplomacy of the American Revolution,* 1935. *Guide to the Diplomatic History of the United States, 1775-1921* (with Grace Gardner Griffin), 1935. *A Diplomatic History of the United States,* 1942. *The Latin American Policy of the United States,* 1943. *The United States as a World Power: A Diplomatic History, 1900-1950,* 1950. *John Quincy Adams and the Union,* 1956. *The Diplomacy of the American Revolution,* 1957. *The American Secretaries of State and Their Diplomacy,* 1958-1980. *A Short History of American Foreign Policy and Diplomacy,* 1959. *American Foreign Policy and the Blessings of Liberty, and Other Essays,* 1962. *John Quincy Adams and the Foundations of American Foreign Policy,* 1969.

Other Awards: Knights of Columbus Award, Best Book on American History by a College Teacher, 1923: *Jay's Treaty, A Study in Commerce and Diplomacy,* New York: Macmillan, 1923. Honorary DHLs: Clark University, MA; Yale University, CT. Honorary Doctor of Letters, Williams College, MA.

For More Information: *Benet's Reader's Encyclopedia of American Literature,* New York: Harper-Collins, 1991.

Commentary: Samuel Flagg Bemis was awarded two Pulitzer Prizes. He was the winner of the 1927 Pulitzer Prize in History for *Pinckney's Treaty.* It was an examination of the foreign relations between the United States and Spain from 1783 to 1803, and of the San Lorenzo Treaty which governed the Mississippi River Valley. Charles Pinckney was a South Carolina soldier and statesman involved in the mediations. Bemis won a second Pulitzer Prize in 1950, this time in Biography for *John Quincy Adams and the Foundations of American Foreign Policy.*

Bemis was born in Worcester, Massachusetts. He was considered the leading authority on the history of American foreign policy. He is also known for *The Diplomacy of the American Revolution,* and a standard reference text, *A Diplomatic History of the United States.* He was the Sterling Professor of Diplomatic History and Inter-American Relations at Yale University until his retirement in 1960.

1951

Margaret Louise Coit   45

Birth: May 30, 1919; Norwich, CT. **Parents:** Archa Willoughby and Grace (Leland) Coit. **Religion:** Episcopalian. **Education:** University of North Carolina: AB. **Spouse:** Albert E. Ewell (m. 1968).

Prize: *Biography or Autobiography,* 1951: *John C. Calhoun: American Portrait,* Great Lives Observed, Englewood Cliffs, NJ: Prentice Hall, 1970.

Career: Correspondent, *Lawrence (MA) Daily Eagle,* 1941-1955; Instructor, Fairleigh Dickinson University, Rutherford, NJ, 1956-1960; Assistant Professor, Fairleigh Dickinson University, 1960-1962; Associate Professor, Fairleigh Dickinson University, 1962-1971; Professor of History, Fairleigh Dickinson University, beginning in 1971; Lecturer, Writers' Conferences; Member, American Association of University Professors, American Historical Association, Authors Guild, Laurel Grange, National Platform Association, Phi Beta Kappa, Society of American Historians, Theta Sigma Phi.

Selected Works: *Mr. Baruch,* 1957.

Other Awards: National Book Award, Council of Women of the United States, 1958. Thomas Edison Award, 1962. Honorary DLitt, University of North Carolina, 1958.

For More Information: *New York Times,* Page 28, May 8, 1951; *Current Biography,* New York: Wilson, 1951.

Commentary: Margaret Louise Coit won the 1951 Pulitzer Prize in Biography for *John C. Calhoun: American Portrait.* Calhoun served as a member of Congress at the time of the War of 1812. He was Secretary of War under United States President James Monroe, Vice-President with John Quincy Adams and Andrew Jackson, and Secretary of State under President John Tyler, and then for many years a senator from South Carolina.

Coit was born in Norwich, Connecticut. She was educated at Woman's College of the University of North Carolina. She worked as a journalist, book reviewer and contributor to history journals. She spent ten years researching and writing the Calhoun biography.

1952

Merlo John Pusey   46

Birth: February 3, 1902; Woodruff, UT. **Death:** 1985. **Parents:** John Sidney and Nellie (Quibell) Pusey. **Education:** University of Utah: AB. **Spouse:** Dorothy Richards (m. 1928). **Children:** C. Richards, David R., John R.

Prize: *Biography or Autobiography,* 1952: *Charles Evans Hughes,* New York: Macmillan, 1951.

Career: Reporter and Assistant Editor, *Deseret News,* Salt Lake City, UT, 1922-1928; Editorial Writer, *Washington Post,* Washington, DC, beginning in 1928; Part-time Journalism Instructor, George Washington University, 1939-1942; Occasional Expert, U.S. Senate Finance Committee, 1931-1933; Associate Editor, *Washington Post,* Washington, DC, 1946; Member: American Association for the Advancement of Science, American Political Science Association.

Selected Works: *Big Government: Can We Control It?,* 1945. *Eisenhower, the President,* 1956. *The Way We Go to War,* 1969. *The U.S.A. Astride the Globe,* 1971. *Eugene Meyer,* 1974. *Builders of the Kingdom: George A. Smith, John Henry Smith, George Albert Smith,* 1981.

Other Awards: Bancroft Award, 1952. Tamiment Institute Award, 1952. Distinguished Alumni Award, University of Utah, 1958. American Bar Association Gavel Award, 1960. Honorary DLitt, Brigham Young University, UT.

For More Information: *New York Times,* May 6, 1952; *Current Biography,* New York: Wilson, 1952.

Commentary: Merlo J. Pusey was awarded the 1952 Pulitzer Prize in Biography for *Charles Evans Hughes,* story of the 11th chief justice of the United States, Secretary of State, governor of the state of New York, and judge of the World Court.

Pusey was born in Woodruff, Utah, a Mormon community. He was educated at the University of Utah. He worked as a reporter and editor on several newspapers including the Washington *Daily News* and the *Washington Post.* He grew concerned at the diminishment of power of the judicial branch during the administration of President Franklin D. Roosevelt, which he first wrote about in *The Supreme Court Crisis,* published in 1937. His concerns led him to write about Charles Evans Hughes. His other works include *Big Government: Can We Control It?*

1953

David John Mays   47
Birth: 1896. **Death:** 1971.
 Prize: *Biography or Autobiography,* 1953: *Edmund Pendleton, 1721-1803,* Cambridge, MA: Harvard University, 1952.
 Selected Works: *The Letters and Papers of Edmund Pendleton, 1734-1803,* 1967.
 For More Information: *Oxford Companion to American Literature,* New York: Oxford University, 1965.
 Commentary: *Edmund Pendleton 1721-1803* won the 1953 Pulitzer Prize in Biography for David J. Mays. This was a two-volume study of Pendleton, a colonial statesman who served as governor of the state of Virginia and president of Virginia's Supreme Court of Appeals.
 Mays made many addresses on the subject of the Constitution. *A Question of Intent: The States, Their Schools and the 14th Amendment,* was given before a subcommittee of the United States Senate on May 14, 1959. *What the Constitution Means to the State of Virginia* was an address presented at Independence Hall, Philadelphia, March 6, 1962.

1954

Charles A. Lindbergh   48
Birth: February 4, 1902; Detroit, MI. **Death:** August 26, 1974. **Parents:** Charles Augustus and Evangeline Lodge (Land) Lindbergh. **Education:** University of Wisconsin. Nebraska Aircraft Corporation Flying School. **Spouse:** Anne Spencer Morrow (m. 1929). **Children:** Charles Augustus, Jon Morrow, Land Morrow, Anne Spencer, Reave, Scott.
 Prize: *Biography or Autobiography,* 1954: *The Spirit of St. Louis,* New York: Scribners, 1953.
 Career: Stunt flier, barnstormer, and mechanic, American Midwest, 1922-1924; Brigadier General, U.S. Army Air Service Reserve, 1924-1941, 1954-1974; Airmail Pilot, Chicago to St. Louis and back, Robertson Aircraft Corporation, 1926; Solo Pilot, first successful transcontinental flight, New York to Paris, 1927; Goodwill Ambassador, U.S. to Central America, West Indies, and Cuba, 1927-1928; Inventor and Designer, Rockefeller Institute, 1930-1935; Re-

searcher and Inventor with Alexis Carrel in France, 1935-1939; Consultant, Ford Motor Company, Detroit, MI, and U.S. War Department, 1939-1944; Civilian Consultant, United Aircraft Corporation, both Connecticut and the Pacific Theater, 1943-1944; Consultant and Writer, 1944-1974; Conservationist, 1964-1974; Consultant and Technical Adviser, Pan American Airways; Chairman, Technical Committee, Transcontinental Air Transport Company; Consultant to Secretary, U.S. Air Force; Member, CHORE Project for Army Ordinance, University of Chicago; Member, Scientific Ballistic-Missile Committee, Air Force and Defense Department; Reorganizer, Strategic Air Command (SAC).
 Selected Works: *We,* 1927. *Of Flight and Life,* 1948. *The Wartime Journals of Charles A. Lindbergh,* 1970. *Boyhood on the Upper Mississippi: A Reminiscent Letter,* 1972. *Banana River,* 1976. *Autobiography of Values,* 1978.
 Other Awards: Distinguished Flying Cross and Congressional Medal of Honor, United States Congress, 1927: Transcontinental Flight. Chevalier of the Legion of Honor, France, 1927: Transcontinental Flight. Order of Leopold, Belgium, 1927: Transcontinental Flight. Royal Air Cross from Great Britain, 1927: Transcontinental Flight. Orteig Prize, Raymond B. Orteig, 1927: Transcontinental Flight. Woodrow Wilson Medal, and Stipend, 1927: Goodwill Flight to Mexico, Central America, and the West Indies. Service Cross of the German Eagle, Germany, 1938. Wright Brothers Memorial Trophy, 1949. Daniel Guggenheim International Aviation Award, 1953. Cross of Honor, U.S. Flying Association. Hubbard Medal, National Geographical Society. Langley Medal, Smithsonian Institution. Medal of Valor, State of New York. Honorary Master of Aeronautics, New York University, 1928. Honorary Doctor of Laws: Northwestern University, IL, 1928; University of Wisconsin, 1928. Honorary Master of Science, Princeton University, NJ, 1931.
 For More Information: Gill, Brendan, *Lindbergh Alone,* New York: Harcourt Brace Jovanovich, 1977; Alhgren, Gregory and Stephen Monier, *Crime of the Century: The Lindbergh Kidnapping Hoax,* Boston: Branden, 1993; Milton, Joyce, *Loss of Eden: A Biography of Charles and Anne Morrow Lindbergh,* New York: HarperCollins, 1993; Behn, Noel, *Lindbergh: The Crime,* New York: Atlantic Monthly, 1994.
 Commentary: Charles Augustus Lindbergh was awarded the 1954 Pulitzer Prize in Autobiography for *The Spirit of St. Louis,* his inspiring account of the nonstop transatlantic solo flight that made him internationally famous.
 Lindbergh was born in Detroit and educated at the University of Wisconsin. He learned to fly at the Nebraska Aircraft Corporation Flying School. He was

an air reserve officer. He landed his airplane, *The Spirit of St. Louis,* in Paris on May 21, 1927. Lindbergh was the first *Man of the Year* to grace the cover of *Time* magazine. He and his wife, Anne Morrow Lindbergh, suffered greatly due to the kidnapping and murder of their infant son in 1932. He was unpopular for his support of the Nazis and his opposition to the United States joining World War II.

1955

William S. White   49

Birth: May 20, 1907; De Leon, Texas. **Death:** April 30, 1994. **Education:** University of Texas, Austin. **Spouse:** Irene Mason (div. 1945); June McConnell (m. 1946). **Children:** Lucia Stanton, Ann Victoria (JM).

Prize: *Biography or Autobiography,* 1955: *The Taft Story,* New York: Harper, 1954.

Career: Correspondent, Associated Press; Senate Correspondent, *New York Times;* Contributing Editor, *Harper's* magazine.

Selected Works: *Citadel, the Story of the U.S. Senate,* 1957. *Majesty & Mischief: A Mixed Tribute to F.D.R.,* 1961. *The Professional: Lyndon B. Johnson,* 1964. *Home Place: The Story of the U.S. House of Representatives,* 1965. *The Responsibles,* 1971. *The Making of a Journalist,* 1986.

For More Information: *Current Biography,* New York: Wilson, 1955; *American Bench,* Minneapolis, MN: Forster, 1979; Obituary, *New York Times,* May 29, 1994.

Commentary: William S. White won the 1955 Pulitzer Prize in Biography for *The Taft Story,* the story of Robert A. Taft, the eldest child of United States President William Howard Taft and senator (1938-1953) from the state of Ohio. Known as Mister Conservative, Taft was author of the Taft-Hartley Labor Relations Act of 1947, which restricted organized labor's collective bargaining rights.

White was born in De Leon, Texas. He was educated at the University of Texas in Austin. He worked for the Associated Press, beginning as a legislative correspondent, later as editor of its photo service, and he covered World War II as the war editor. After the war, he worked for the *New York Times* covering Capitol Hill in Washington, DC.

1956

Talbot Faulkner Hamlin   50

Birth: 1889; New York, NY. **Death:** 1956. **Education:** Amherst College, MA: BA. Columbia University, NY: BArch. **Spouse:** Jessica H.

Prize: *Biography or Autobiography,* 1956: *Benjamin Henry Latrobe,* New York: Oxford University, 1955.

Career: Architecture Instructor, Columbia University, NY, 1916-1946; Professor of Architecture, beginning in 1947; Avery Architecture Librarian, Columbia University, NY.

Selected Works: *Some European Architectural Libraries,* 1939. *We Took to Cruising: From Maine to Florida Afloat* (with Jessica Talbot), 1951.

For More Information: *Current Biography,* New York: Wilson, 1954, 1955, 1957; *Dictionary of Biography,* 1980; Vance, Mary A., *Talbot F. Hamlin: A Bibliography,* Monticello, IL: Vance Bibliographies, 1983.

Commentary: *Benjamin Henry Latrobe* won the 1956 Pulitzer Prize in Biography for Talbot Faulkner Hamlin. Latrobe was the surveyor of public buildings in Washington, DC, and the architect and engineer charged with rebuilding the Capitol building. He and Dolley Madison decorated the White House from 1809 to 1811.

Hamlin was born in in New York City and educated at Amherst College and Columbia University. He taught architecture at Columbia from 1916 to 1954 and was the Avery architecture librarian from 1934-1945. His other works included *Architecture Through the Ages* and *Greek Revival Architecture in America.*

1957

John Fitzgerald Kennedy   51

Birth: May 29, 1917; Brookline, MA. **Death:** November 22, 1963. **Parents:** Joseph D. and Rose (Fitzgerald) Kennedy. **Religion:** Roman Catholic. **Education:** London School of Economics, England.

Harvard University, MA: BA, with honors. Stanford University, CA. **Spouse:** Jacqueline Bouvier (m. 1953). **Children:** Caroline, John Jr., Patrick Bouvier.

Prize: *Biography or Autobiography,* 1957: *Profiles in Courage,* New York: Harper, 1956.

Career: Commander, PT Boat, U.S. Navy, 1941-1945; Correspondent, San Francisco United Nations Conference, Potsdam Conference, and British elections, *Chicago Herald-American* and International News Service, 1945; Congressman, 11th Congressional District of Massachusetts, U.S. House of Representatives, Washington, DC, 1946-1952; U.S. Senator, Massachusetts, Washington, DC, 1952-1960; Member, Board of Overseers, Harvard University, 1957; President of the U.S., 1961-1963.

Selected Works: *Let the Lady Hold up Her Head: Reflections on American Immigration Policy,* 1957. *The Strategy of Peace* (Nevins, Allan, ed.), 1960. *Why England Slept,* 1961. *The Quotable Mr. Kennedy,* 1962. *The Kennedy Wit* (Adler, Bill, ed.), 1964. *A Nation of Immigrants,* 1964. *The Burden and the Glory* (Nevins, Allan, ed.), 1964. *Memorable Quotations of John F. Kennedy* (Meyersohn, Maxwell, ed.), 1965. *The Wisdom of JFK* (Setel, T.S., ed.), 1965.

Other Awards: Navy and Marine Corps Medal. Purple Heart, WWII. National Conference of Christians and Jews Annual Brotherhood Award. University of Notre Dame Patriotism Award, 1956. Italian Star of Solidarity of the First Order. Grande Official, Italian Government. Greek Cross of the Commander of the Royal Order of the Phoenix. American Library Association Notable Book Award, 1956: *Profiles in Courage,* New York: Harper, 1956. Christopher Book Award, 1956: *Profiles in Courage.* Secondary Education Board Award: *Profiles in Courage.* Honorary DSc, Lowell Technological Institute, 1956. Honorary LLDs: University of Notre Dame, IN, 1950; Tufts College, MA, 1950; Boston University, MA, 1955; Harvard University, MA, 1956; Boston College, MA; Loras College, IA; Northeastern University, MA; Rockhurst College, MO.

For More Information: White, Theodore Harold, *The Making of A President,* New York: Atheneum, 1961; Tregaskis, Richard, *John F. Kennedy and PT-109,* New York: Random, 1962; Schlesinger, Arthur Meier, *A Thousand Days: John F. Kennedy in the White House,* Boston: Houghton Mifflin, 1965; Sorensen, Theodore C., *Kennedy,* New York: Harper & Row, 1965; Sorenson, ed., *"Let the Word Go Forth": The Speeches, Statements, and Writings of John F. Kennedy,* New York: Delacorte, 1988; Thompson, Robert Smith, *The Missiles of October: The Declassified Story of John F. Kennedy and the Cuban Missile Crisis,* New York: Simon & Schuster, 1992; Lowe, Jacques, *JFK Remembered,* New York: Random, 1993; Reeves, Richard, *President Kennedy: Profile of Power,* New York: Simon &

Schuster, 1993; Andersen, Christopher P., *Jack and Jackie: Portrait of An American Marriage,* New York: Morrow, 1996; Brogan, Hugh, *Kennedy,* New York: Longman, 1996; Hellmann, John, *The Kennedy Obsession: The American Myth of JFK,* New York: Columbia University, 1997; Hersh, Seymour M., *The Dark Side of Camelot,* Boston: Little, Brown, 1997; Salinger, Pierre, *John F. Kennedy, Commander in Chief: A Profile in Leadership,* New York: Penguin Studio, 1997.

Commentary: John F. Kennedy was awarded the 1957 Pulitzer Prize in Biography for *Profiles in Courage,* a portrait of prominent American statesmen who in difficult times exhibited great courage.

John F. Kennedy was born in Brookline, Massachusetts. He came from a prominent Irish-American family active in Boston and national politics, as well as Wall Street finance. He was educated at Harvard University and the London School of Economics. In a close election race, he was the elected 35th president of the United States in 1960. He was assassinated in Dallas, Texas, on November 22, 1963, before completing the third year of his term in office, leaving behind a widow and two small children and a nation deep in grief. His was a legacy of unfulfilled promise.

1958

Mary Wells Ashworth 52

Birth: May 28, 1903; Plant City, FL. **Death:** September 12, 1992. **Parents:** John Clarence and Mary Jane (Wells) Knight. **Religion:** Episcopalian. **Education:** Hollins College, VA: AB. **Spouse:** Osbourne O. Ashworth. **Children:** Osbourne O. Jr., John Sheriden.

Prize: *Biography or Autobiography,* 1958: *George Washington, Volume 7: First in Peace,* New York: Scribners, 1948-1957.

Career: History Associate, Douglas Southall Freeman, Richmond, VA, 1945-1953; Writer, Charles Scribner's Sons, NY, 1954-1957; Board Member, English-Speaking Union, 1957-1959; Board Member, Richmond Woman's Club, 1957-1960; President, Richmond Woman's Club, 1959-1960; Vice-President, Friends of the Library, VA, 1960-1963; Trustee, Hollins College, 1962-1967; Member: Gamma Phi Beta, Garden Club of Virginia, Phi Beta Kappa, Virginia Historical Society.

Other Awards: Guggenheim Fellow, 1955.

Commentary: Douglas Southall Freeman, John Alexander Carroll, and Mary Wells Ashworth won the 1958 Pulitzer Prize in Biography for *George Washington,* a seven-volume work on the life of the Revolutionary War general and America's first president. Freeman died after completion of volumes I through VI. Carroll and Ashworth completed volume VII.

Mary Wells Knight Ashworth was born in Plant

City, Florida and educated at Hollins College in Virginia. She was a staff member and history associate of Freeman's from 1945 to 1953. She worked with Carroll for Scribners to complete Freeman's series on George Washington.

John Alexander Carroll   53

Death: 1958.

Prize: *Biography or Autobiography,* 1958: *George Washington, Volume 7: First in Peace,* New York: Scribners, 1948-1957.

Selected Works: *Current Biography,* 1959.

For More Information: Carroll, John and Faulk, Odie B., *Home of the Brave: A Patriot's Guide to American History,* New Rochelle, NY: Arlington House, 1976.

Commentary: Douglas S. Freeman, John Alexander Carroll, and Mary Wells Ashworth won the 1958 Pulitzer Prize in Biography for *George Washington,* a seven-volume work on the life of the Revolutionary War general and America's first president. Freeman died after completion of volumes I through VI. Carroll and Ashworth completed volume VII.

Carroll's other works include *Home of the Brave: A Patriot's Guide to American History.*

Douglas Southall Freeman

Full entry appears as #30 under "Biography or Autobiography," 1935.

1959

Arthur Clarence Walworth   54

Birth: July 9, 1903; Newton, MA. **Parents:** Arthur Clarence Jr. and Ruth Richardson (Lippincott) Walworth. **Religion:** Baptist. **Education:** Yale University, CT: AB.

Prize: *Biography or Autobiography,* 1959: *Woodrow Wilson, American Prophet,* New York: Longman's Green, 1958.

Career: Author, Editor, Houghton Mifflin, 1927-1943; Staff member, Office of War Information, 1943; Staff member (summers), Medomak Camp, ME, 1943-1967; Member: Cosmos Club, Graduate Club.

Selected Works: *School Histories at War: A Study of the Treatment of Our Wars in the Secondary School History Books of the United States and in Those of Its Former Enemies,* 1938. *Black Ships off Japan: The Story of Commodore Perry's Expedition,* 1946. *Cape Breton, Isle of Romance,* 1948. *America's Moment, 1918: American Diplomacy at the End of World War I,* 1977. *Wilson and His Peacemakers: American Diplomacy at the Paris Peace Conference, 1919,* 1986.

For More Information: *Current Biography,* New York: 1959.

Commentary: Arthur Walworth was awarded the 1959 Pulitzer Prize in Biography for *Woodrow Wilson, American Prophet,* the first of two volumes on the 28th president of the United States.

Walworth was born in Newton, Massachusetts. He was educated at Yale University. The paperback of the 1978 edition of the Wilson biography is still available from W. W. Norton. His other works include *School Histories at War* and *Black Ships Off Japan.*

1960

Samuel Eliot Morison

Full entry appears as #37 under "Biography or Autobiography," 1943.

1961

David Herbert Donald   55

Birth: October 1, 1920; Goodman, MS. **Parents:** Ira Unger and Sue Ella (Belford) Donald. **Religion:** Episcopalian. **Education:** Holmes Junior College, MS. Millsaps College, MS: AB. University of Illinois: AM, PhD. **Spouse:** Aida Di Pace (m. 1955). **Children:** Bruce Randall.

Prize: *Biography or Autobiography,* 1961: *Charles Sumner and the Coming of the Civil War,* New York: Knopf, 1960. *Biography or Autobiography,* 1988: *Look Homeward: A Life of Thomas Wolfe,* Boston: Little, Brown, 1987.

Career: Teaching Fellow, University of North Carolina, Chapel Hill, 1942; Research Assistant, University of Illinois, Urbana-Champaign, 1943-1946; Research Associate, University of Illinois, Urbana-Champaign, 1946-1947; Instructor, Columbia University, NY, 1947-1949; Associate Professor of History, Smith College, MA, 1949-51; Visiting Associate Professor of History, Amherst College, 1950; Assistant Professor, Columbia University, NY, 1951-1952; Associate Professor, Columbia University, NY, 1952-1957; Fulbright Lecturer, American History, University College of North Wales, 1953-1954; Professor of History, Columbia University, NY, 1957-1959; Member, Institute for Advanced Study, Princeton, NJ, 1957-1958; Professor of History, Princeton University, NJ, 1959-1962; Harmsworth Professor of American History, Oxford University, 1959-1960; Professor of History, Johns Hopkins University, MD, 1962-1973; Harry C. Black Professor of American History, Johns Hopkins University, MD, 1963-1973; John P. Young Lecturer, Memphis State University, 1963; Walter Lynwood Fleming Lecturer, Louisiana State University, 1965; Director, Institute of Southern History, Johns Hopkins University, MD, 1966-1972; Visiting Professor, Center for Advanced Study in the Behavioral Sciences, 1969-1970; President, Southern Historical Association, 1969-1970; Benjamin Rush Lecturer, American Psychiatric Association, 1972; Charles Warren Professor of American History, Harvard University, MA, 1973-1991; Commonwealth Lecturer, University College, University of London, 1975; Chair, Graduate Program in American Civilization, Harvard University, MA, 1979-1985; Professor Emeritus, Harvard University, MA, 1991-; Samuel Paley Lecturer, Hebrew University, Jerusalem, Israel, 1991; Member: American Historical Association, Omicron Delta Kappa, Organization of American Historians, Phi Beta Kappa, Phi Kappa Phi, Pi Kappa Alpha, Pi Kappa Delta, Society of American Historians.

Selected Works: *Lincoln's Herndon,* 1948. *Lincoln Reconsidered: Essays on the Civil War Era,* 1956. *The Divided Union* (with J.G.Randall), 1961. *The Politics of Reconstruction, 1863-1867,* 1965. *Charles Sumner and the Rights of Man,* 1970. *Liberty and Union,* 1978. *Lincoln,* 1995.

Other Awards: Social Science Research Council Fellowship, 1945-1946. George A. and Eliza G. Howard Fellowship, 1957-1958. Guggenheim Fellowship, 1964-1965, 1985-1986. American Council of Learned Societies Fellowship, 1969-1970. National Endowment for the Humanities Senior Fellow, 1971-1972. C. Hugh Holman Prize, Modern Language Association, 1988. Benjamin L. C. Wailes Award, Mississippi Historical Society, 1994. Lincoln Prize, Gettysburg College, 1996: *Lincoln,* New York: Simon & Schuster, 1995. Jefferson Davis Award, Museum of the Confederacy, 1996: *Lincoln.* Christopher Award, 1996: *Lincoln.*

For More Information: *Current Biography,* New York: Wilson, 1961; Cooper, William J. and Holt, Michael F. and McCardell, John, eds., *A Master's Due: Essays in Honor of David Herbert Donald,* Baton Rouge: Louisiana State University, 1985.

Commentary: David Herbert Donald won two Pulitzer Prizes, both in Biography. He was awarded the 1961 prize for *Charles Sumner and the Coming of the Civil War,* the biography of the senator from Massachusetts who was an outspoken opponent of slavery. Donald won the 1988 prize for *Look Homeward: A Life of Thomas Wolfe,* a biography of the novelist and author of *Look Homeward, Angel.*

Donald was born in Goodman, Mississippi. He was educated at Holmes Junior College, Millsap College, and the University of Illinois. He is a member of the executive committee of the Department of Afro-American studies at Harvard University. His other works include *Lincoln Reconsidered: Essays on the Civil War Era* and *Charles Sumner and the Rights of Man.*

1962
No award

1963

Leon Edel   56
Birth: September 9, 1907; Pittsburgh, PA. **Death:** September 5, 1997. **Parents:** Simon and Fannie (Malamud) Edel. **Education:** McGill University, Montreal, Canada: BA: MA, with honors. University of Paris, France: Docteur des Lettres. **Spouse:** Bertha Cohen (m. 1935; div. 1950); Roberta Roberts (m. 1950; div. 1979); Marjorie Sinclair (m. 1980).

Prize: *Biography or Autobiography,* 1963: *Henry James,* A Spectrum Book: Twentieth Century Views, Englewood Cliffs, NJ: Prentice Hall, 1963.

Career: Assistant Professor of English, Sir George Williams University, Canada, 1932-1934; Writer, 1934-1943; First Lieutenant, U.S. Army, 1943-1947; Visiting Professor, New York University, 1950-1952; Associate Professor, New York University, NY, 1953-1955; Visiting Professor, Indiana University, 1954-1955; Visiting Professor, University of Hawaii, 1955, 1969-1970; Professor of English, New York University, NY, 1955-1966; Christian Gauss Lecturer in Criticism, Princeton University, NJ, 1952-1953; Alexander Lecturer, University of Toronto, Canada, 1955-1956; President, U.S. Center, PEN, 1957-1959; Visiting Professor, Harvard University, 1959-1960; Secretary, National Institute of Arts and Letters, 1964-65; Visiting Professor, Center for Advanced Study, Wesleyan University, 1965; Henry James Professor of English and American Letters, New York University, NY, 1966-1972; Visiting Professor, University of Toronto, 1967; President, Authors' Guild, 1969-1970; Professor Emeritus, New York University, NY, 1972-; Citizens Professor of English, University of Hawaii, Honolulu, 1972-1978; Visiting Fellow, Australian National University, 1976; Vernon Visiting Professor in Biography, Dartmouth College, 1977; Professor Emeritus, University of Hawaii, Honolulu, beginning in 1978; President, Hawaii Literary Arts Council, 1979; Fellow, American Academy of Arts and Sciences; Fellow, Royal Society of Literature; Member: American Association of University Professors, International Association of University Professors of English, Modern Humanities Research Association, Athenaeum Club, Century Club.

Selected Works: *The Prefaces of Henry James,* 1931. *James Joyce: The Last Journey,* 1947. *The Complete Plays of Henry James* (Edel, Leon, ed.), 1949. *Henry James,* 1953-1972. *The Future of the Novel: Essays on the Art of Fiction,* 1956. *The Diary of Alice James* (Edel, Leon, ed.), 1964. *Henry James,* *the Master: 1901-1916,* 1972. *Literary Biography,* 1973. *Letters: Henry James* (Edel, Leon, ed.), 1974-1984. *Bloomsbury: A House of Lions,* 1979. *Telling Lives: The Biographer's Art,* 1979. *Writing Lives: Principia Biographica,* 1984. *Henry James: A Life,* 1985. *The Complete Notebooks of Henry James* (Edel, Leon, and Lyall H. Powers, eds.), 1987.

Other Awards: Bronze Star Medal. Guggenheim Fellow, 1936-1938, 1966. Bollingen Foundation Fellow, 1958-1960. National Institute of Arts and Letters Award, 1959. National Book Award, Non-Fiction, 1963: *Henry James, Volumes II and III.* American Academy of Arts and Letters Grant, 1972. Gold Medal for Biography, American Academy and Institute of Arts and Letters, 1976. Hawaii Writers Award, 1977. National Arts Club Gold Medal for Literature, 1981. National Book Critics Circle Award, Biography, 1985: *Henry James: A Life.* Honorary LittDs: Union College, NY, 1963; McGill University, Canada, 1963; University of Saskatchewan, 1982.

For More Information: *Current Biography,* New York: Wilson, 1967; *Contemporary Literary Criticism,* Detroit: Gale, 1984; Fromm, Georgia, ed., *Essaying Biography: A Celebration for Leon Edel,* Honolulu: Biographical Research Center, University of Hawaii, 1987; Powers, Lyall H., ed., *Leon Edel and Literary Art,* Ann Arbor: UMI Research, 1988. *Series Studies in Modern Literature,* No. 84; *Dictionary of Literary Biography,* Detroit: Gale, 1991; Obituary, *New York Times,* September 8, 1997.

Commentary: Leon Joseph Edel won the 1963 Pulitzer Prize in Biography for volumes II and III of *Henry James, A Collection of Critical Essays,* from the series, *Twentieth Century Views.* A five-volume work when completed, it is still considered an excellent biographical analysis and a perfect example of a literary biography. The first volume was written by Edel in French, published in France, and translated by him into English.

Edel was born in Pittsburgh, Pennsylvania. He was educated at McGill University in Canada and at the University of Paris in France. He was a former Henry James Professor of English and American Letters at New York University. His other works included *Bloomsbury: A House of Lions.*

1964

Walter Jackson Bate 57

Birth: May 23, 1918; Mankato, MN. **Parents:** William G. and Isabel (Melick) Bate. **Education:** Harvard University, MA: AB, MA, PhD.

Prize: *Biography or Autobiography,* 1964: *John Keats,* Cambridge, MA: Belknap, 1963. *Biography or Autobiography,* 1978: *Samuel Johnson,* New York: Harcourt Brace Jovanovich, 1977.

Career: Assistant Professor of English, Harvard University, MA, 1946-1949; Associate Professor, Harvard University, 1949-1956; Chairman, Department of History and Literature, Harvard University, 1955-1956; Professor of English and Chairman of Department of English, Harvard University, 1956-1962; Abbott Lawrence Lowell Professor of the Humanities, Harvard University, 1962-1979; Kingsley Porter University Professor, Harvard University, 1979-present; Member, American Academy of Arts and Sciences.

Selected Works: *Criticism: The Major Texts,* 1952. *The Achievement of Samuel Johnson,* 1955. *The Stylistic Development of Keats,* 1962. *Keats: A Collection of Critical Essays* (Bate, Walter Jackson, ed.), 1964. *Essays from the Rambler, Adventurer, and Idler,* 1968. *The Burden of the Past and the English Poet,* 1970. *Criticism: The Major Texts,* 1970. *Biographia Literaria, or, Biographical Sketches of My Literary Life and Opinions, Samuel Taylor Coleridge* (Bate, Walter Jackson, and James Engell, eds.), 1983.

Other Awards: Christian Gauss Prize for Literary History and Criticism, 1955: *The Achievement of Samuel Johnson,* New York: Oxford University, 1955. Guggenheim Fellow, 1956. Christian Gauss Prize, 1954: *John Keats,* Cambridge, MA: Belknap, 1963. Harvard Faculty Prize, 1964: *John Keats.* National Book Award, 1978: *John Keats.* Book Critics Circle Award, 1978: *John Keats.*

For More Information: *Current Biography,* New York: Wilson, 1981; Barth, J. Robert and Mahoney, John L., eds., *Coleridge, Keats, and the Imagination: Romanticism and Adam's Dream: Essays in Honor of Walter Jackson Bate,* Columbia: University of Missouri, 1990.

Commentary: Walter Jackson Bate won two Pulitzer Prizes, both in Biography. He was awarded the 1964 prize for *John Keats,* the story of one of the greatest poets of the English language. Bate won his second prize for *Samuel Johnson,* the biography of the 18th-century British lexicographer, poet, and critic.

Bate was born in Mankato, Minnesota. He was educated at Harvard University. He taught English at Harvard University from 1946 to 1979. His other works include *From Classic to Romantic* and *The Burden of the Past and the English Poet.*

1965

Ernest Samuels 58

Birth: May 19, 1903; Chicago, IL. **Death:** February 12, 1996. **Parents:** Albert and Mary (Kaplan) Samuels. **Education:** University of Chicago, IL: PhB, JD, MA, PhD. **Spouse:** Jayne Newcomer (m. 1938). **Children:** Susanna, Jonathan, Elizabeth.

Prize: *Biography or Autobiography,* 1965: *Henry Adams: The Major Phase,* Cambridge, MA: Belknap, 1964.

Career: Member, Texas Bar Association, 1938; Franklin Bliss Snyder, Professor of English, Northwestern University, 1942-1971; Chairman, English Department, 1964-1966; Fulbright Lecturer; Inter-University Chair in American Studies, Belgium, 1958-1959; Director, Memorial National Council of Teachers of English, 1956-1957; President, College English Association, Chicago area, 1957; President, American Studies Association, Wisconsin-Northern Illinois chapter, 1960-1961; Member, Editorial Board, *American Literature,* 1964-71; Leo S. Bing Visiting Professor, University of Southern California, 1966-1967; Member, Council of Scholars, Library of Congress; Member, Witter Brynner Foundation, 1979-1980.

Selected Works: *Henry Adams: The Middle Years,* 1958. *History of the United States of America during the Administrations of Jefferson and Madison, by Henry Adams* (Samuels, Ernest, ed.), 1967. *Bernard Berenson: The Making of a Connoisseur,* 1979. *Bernard Berenson: The Making of a Legend,* 1987. *Henry Adams,* 1989. *Henry Adams: Selected Letters* (Samuels, Ernest, ed.), 1992.

Other Awards: Guggenheim Fellow, 1955-1956, 1971-1972. Bancroft Prize, 1965: *Henry Adams,* Cambridge, MA: Belknap, 1964. Francis Parkman Prize, 1965: *Henry Adams.* Friends of American Literature Award, 1965: *Henry Adams.*

For More Information: *Dictionary of Literary Biography,* Detroit: Gale, 1981.

Commentary: *Henry Adams* won the 1965 Pulitzer Prize in Biography for Ernest Samuels. A three-volume work, it tells the story of Henry Adams, the historian who was the son and grandson of two American presidents.

Samuels was born in Chicago and educated at the University of Chicago. He was trained in law and was admitted to the Texas and Illinois bars. He taught English at Northwestern University from 1942 until his retirement in 1971. He served on several Pulitzer juries for biography. His other works include *Bernard Berenson: The Making of a Connoisseur* and as editor, *History of the United States of America during the Administrations of Jefferson and Madison.*

1966

Arthur Meier Schlesinger Jr.   59

Birth: October 15, 1917; Columbus, OH. **Parents:** Arthur and Elizabeth (Bancroft) Schlesinger. **Religion:** Unitarian. **Education:** Harvard University, MA: AB, summa cum laude. Cambridge University, England: Henry Fellow. **Spouse:** Marion Cannon (m.

1940, div. 1970); Alexandra Emmet (m. 1970). **Children:** Katherine Bancroft, Stephen Cannon, Christina, Andrew Bancroft (MC); Robert Emmet Kennedy (AE).

Prize: *History,* 1946: *The Age of Jackson,* Boston: Little Brown, 1945. *Biography or Autobiography,* 1966: *A Thousand Days,* Boston: Houghton-Mifflin, 1965.

Career: Office of War Information, Washington, DC, 1942-1943; Office of Strategic Services, Washington, DC, London, England, and Paris, France, 1943-1945; Served in Europe, U.S. Army, 1945; Freelance writer, Washington, DC, 1945-1946; Associate Professor, Harvard University, MA, 1946-1954; Consultant, Economic Cooperation Administration, 1948; Consultant, Mutual Security Administration, 1951-1952; Staff member, Adlai Stevenson presidential campaign, 1952, 1956; National Chairman, Americans for Democratic Action, 1953-1954; Professor of History, Harvard University, MA, 1954-1962; Special Assistant to President John F. Kennedy, 1961-1963, Special Assistant to President Lyndon B. Johnson, 1963-1964; Albert Schweitzer Professor in the Humanities, City University of New York, 1966-Present; President, American Academy and Institute of Arts and Letters, 1981-1984; Chairman, Franklin Delano Roosevelt Four Freedoms Foundation, 1983-Present; Chancellor of the Academy, American Academy and Institute of Arts and Letters, 1985-1988; President, Society of American Historians, 1989-1992; Advisor, Arthur and Elizabeth Schlesinger Library on the History of Women in America; Advisor, Library of America; Board Member: Harry S. Truman Library Institute, John Fitzgerald Kennedy Library, Harriman Institute of Russian Studies, Ralph Bunche Institute; Member: American Historical Association, Association for the Study of Afro-American Life and History, Center for Inter-American Relations, Colonial Society of Massachusetts, Council on Foreign Relations, Library of Congress Council of Scholars, Massachusetts Historical Society, National Council, American Civil Liberties, Organization of American Historians, Phi Beta Kappa, Society for Historians of American Foreign Relations; Trustee: Robert F. Kennedy Memorial, Recorded Anthology of American Music, Twentieth Century Fund.

Selected Works: *The Vital Center: The Politics of Freedom,* 1949. *The Rise of Modern America, 1865-1951,* 1951. *The General and the President, and the Future of American Foreign Policy* (with Richard H. Rovere), 1951. *The Age of Roosevelt,* 1957. *Kennedy or Nixon: Does It Make Any Difference?,* 1960. *The Politics of Hope,* 1962. *The Vital Center: The Politics of Freedom,* 1962. *Congress and the Presidency: Their Role in Modern Times* (with Alfred De Grazia), 1967. *Violence: America in the Sixties,* 1968. *The Crisis of Confidence: Ideas, Power, and Violence* *in America,* 1969. *Nothing Stands Still: Essays,* 1969. *The Best and the Last of Edwin O'Connor* (Schlesinger, Arthur, Jr., ed.), 1970. *The Origins of the Cold War* (with Lloyd C. Gardner and Hans J. Morgenthau), 1970. *The Coming to Power: Critical Presidential Elections in American History* (Schlesinger, Arthur, Jr., ed.), 1972. *The Imperial Presidency,* 1973. *The Dynamics of World Power: A Documentary History of United States Foreign Policy, 1945-1973* (Schlesinger, Arthur, Jr., ed.), 1973. *History of U.S. Political Parties* (Schlesinger, Arthur, Jr., ed.), 1973. *Congress Investigates: A Documented History, 1792-1974* (Schlesinger, Arthur, Jr. and Burns, Roger, eds.), 1975. *Robert Kennedy and His Times,* 1978. *Detente: Prospects for Democracy and Dictatorship* (with Aleksandr Solzhenitsyn), 1980. *The Almanac of American History* (Schlesinger, Arthur, Jr., ed.), 1983. *The Cycles of American History,* 1986. *History of American Presidential Elections, 1789-1984* (Schlesinger, Arthur, Jr., ed.), 1986. *The Disuniting of America,* 1991. *Running for President: The Candidates and Their Images* (Schlesinger, Arthur, Jr., ed.), 1994. *A History of American Life* (Carnes, Mark C. and Schlesinger, Arthur, Jr., eds.), 1996.

Other Awards: Henry Fellow, Cambridge University, 1938-1939. Harvard Fellow, 1939-1942. Guggenheim Fellow, 1946. American Academy of Arts and Letters Grant, 1946. Francis Parkman Prize, Society of American Historians, 1957: *The Age of Roosevelt, Volume 1: The Crisis of the Old Order,* Boston: Houghton Mifflin, 1957. Bancroft Prize, Columbia University, 1958: *The Age of Roosevelt, Volume 1: The Crisis of the Old Order.* National Book Award, 1966: *A Thousand Days: John F. Kennedy in the White House,* Boston: Houghton Mifflin, 1965. Gold Medal in History and Biography, National Institute and American Academy of Arts and Letters, 1967. Ohio Governor's Award for History, 1973. Sidney Hillman Foundation Award, 1973: *The Imperial Presidency,* Boston: Houghton Mifflin, 1973. Eugene V. Debs Award in Education, 1974. National Book Award, 1979: *Robert Kennedy and His Times,* Boston: Houghton Mifflin, 1978. Fregene Prize for Literature, Italy, 1983.

For More Information: Depoe, Stephen P., *Arthur M. Schlesinger, Jr., and the Ideological History of American Liberalism,* Tuscaloosa: University of Alabama, 1994; Diggins, John Patrick, ed., *The Liberal Persuasion: Arthur Schlesinger, Jr., and the Challenge of the American Past,* Princeton, NJ: Princeton University, 1997.

Commentary: Arthur Meier Schlesinger Jr. won two Pulitzer Prizes. He was selected as the winner of the 1946 History prize for *The Age of Jackson.* Schlesinger interpreted this period in American history not as one of Westward expansion, but as a democracy seeking to keep in check the power of

business. Schlesinger was awarded the 1966 Biography award for *A Thousand Days,* his account of the Kennedy presidency based on the journal he kept during his time as Special Advisor to the President.

Schlesinger was born in Columbus, Ohio, the son of the noted historian Arthur Meier Schlesinger Sr. Schlesinger has enjoyed a long and distinguished career, beginning at the Office of War Information during World War II. He was an advisor to Presidents Kennedy and Johnson and the author of numerous works covering the history of government, politics, and foreign relations. He is the editor of the *Almanac of American History* and is currently Albert Schweitzer Professor of the Humanities at City College of the City University of New York.

1967

Justin Kaplan   60

Birth: September 5, 1925; New York, NY. **Parents:** Tobias D. and Anna (Rudman) Kaplan. **Religion:** Jewish. **Education:** Harvard University, MA: BS. **Spouse:** Anne Bernays (m. 1954). **Children:** Susanna, Hester, Polly.

Prize: *Biography or Autobiography,* 1967: *Mr. Clemens and Mark Twain,* New York: Simon and Schuster, 1966.

Career: Freelancer, publishing, NY, 1946-1954; Editor, Simon & Schuster, NY, 1954-1959; Full-time writer, 1959-; Lecturer, Harvard University, 1969, 1973, 1976, 1978; Editor, Bartlett's *Familiar Quotations,* Little, Brown, Boston; Member: American Academy of Arts and Sciences, Society of American Historians, Phi Beta Kappa.

Selected Works: *With Malice toward Women: A Handbook for Women-Haters Drawn from the Best Minds of All Time* (Kaplan, Justin, ed.), 1952. *Mark Twain and His World,* 1974. *Lincoln Steffens: A Biography,* 1974. *Walt Whitman: A Life,* 1980. *Familiar Quotations, by John Bartlett* (Kaplan, Justin, ed.), 1992. *The Language of Names* (with Anne Bernays), 1997.

Other Awards: National Book Award, 1967: *Mr. Clemens and Mark Twain,* New York: Simon and Schuster, 1966. Guggenheim Fellow, 1975-1976. American Book Award for Biography, 1981: *Walt Whitman: A Life,* New York: Simon and Schuster, 1980.

For More Information: *Dictionary of Literary Biography,* Detroit: Gale, 1991; Kaufman, Joanne, "You Know a Good Quote When You See It," *Wall Street Journal,* November 12, 1992.

Commentary: Justin Kaplan was awarded the 1967 Pulitzer Prize in Biography for *Mr. Clemens and Mark Twain,* a critically acclaimed portrait of Samuel Langhorne Clemens, also known as Mark Twain, humorist, journalist, and novelist. Twain (1835-1910) is perhaps best known for his stories of life on the Mississippi, told in his novels *The Adventures of Tom Sawyer* and *The Adventures of Huckleberry Finn.*

Kaplan was born in New York City and educated at Harvard University. He has lectured extensively and taught at Harvard and at Griffith University in Brisbane, Australia. He was most recently the Jenks Professor of Contemporary Letters at the College of the Holy Cross in Worchester, Massachusetts. He was the general editor of the 1992 edition of *Bartlett's Familiar Quotations.*

1968

George F. Kennan 61

Birth: February 16, 1904; Milwaukee, WI. **Parents:** Kossuth Kent and Florence (James) Kennan. **Education:** Princeton University, NJ: AB. Berlin Seminary for Oriental Languages. **Spouse:** Annalise Sorenson (m. 1931). **Children:** Grace Kennan Warneke, Joan Kennan Delany, Christopher, Wendy Kennan Pfaeffli.

Prize: *History,* 1957: *Russia Leaves the War: Soviet-American Relations, 1917-1920,* Princeton, NJ: Princeton University, 1956-58. *Biography or Autobiography,* 1968: *Memoirs, 1925-1950,* 2 Volumes, Boston: Little, Brown, 1967-72.

Career: Officer, U.S. Foreign Service, 1926-1927; Vice-Consul, Geneva, Switzerland and Hamburg, Germany, 1927; Vice-Consul, Berlin, Germany and Tallinn, Estonia, 1928; Language Officer, Berlin, 1929; Third Secretary, Riga, Latvia, 1929, 1931; Assistant to U.S. Ambassador William C. Bullitt to Moscow, to reopen American Embassy, 1933; Third Secretary, Moscow, USSR, 1934; Consul, Vienna, Austria, 1935; Second Secretary, Prague, 1935; Second Secretary, Czechoslovakia, 1938; Second Secretary, Berlin, 1939; First Secretary, 1940; Counselor of Legation, Lisbon, Portugal, 1942; Counselor, American Delegation to European Advisory Commission, London, England, 1943; Minister-Counselor, Moscow, 1944; Deputy for Foreign Affairs, National War College, Washington, DC, 1946; Director, Policy Planning Staff, U.S. Department of State, Washington, DC, 1947; Counselor, 1949-50; Charles R. Walgreen Foundation Lecturer, University of Chicago, 1951; U.S. Ambassador to USSR, 1952; Stafford Little Lecturer, Princeton University, 1954; Professor, Institute for Advanced Study, 1956-1974; George Eastman Visiting Professor, Balliol College, Oxford, England, 1957-1958; Visiting Lecturer, Harvard University, 1960; U.S. Ambassador to Yugoslavia, 1961-1963; Professor, Princeton University, 1963-1964; University Fellow, Harvard University, 1965-1969; President, National Institute of Arts and Letters, 1965-1967; President, American Academy of Arts and Letters, 1968-1972; Benjamin Franklin Fellow, Manufactures and Commerce, 1968-present; Visiting Fellow, All Souls College, Oxford, England, 1969; Professor Emeritus, Institute for Advanced Study, 1974-Present; Founder, Kennan Institute for Advanced Russian Studies, Washington, DC, 1975; Member Emeritus, American Academy of Diplomacy, 1985-Present; Member: American Philosophical Society, British Academy for the Promotion of Historical, Philosophical, and Philological Studies, Century Association, Council on Foreign Relations, Order of Pour le Merite for Arts and Sciences (Germany), Royal Society for the Encouragement of Arts Member of National Advisory Council, W. Averell Harriman Institute for Advanced Study of the Soviet Union, Columbia University.

Selected Works: *American Diplomacy, 1900-1950,* 1951. *Realities of American Foreign Policy,* 1954. *International Exchange in the Arts,* 1956. *Russia, the Atom and the West,* 1958. *Soviet Foreign Policy, 1917-1941,* 1960. *Russia and the West under Lenin and Stalin,* 1961. *On Dealing with the Communist World,* 1964. *Memoirs: 1925-1950,* 1967. *From Prague after Munich: Diplomatic Papers, 1938-1940,* 1968. *The Marquis de Custine and His Russia in 1839,* 1971. *The Cloud of Danger: Current Realities of American Foreign Policy,* 1977. *The Decline of Bismarck's European Order: Franco-Russian Relations, 1875-1890,* 1979. *Memoirs: 1925-1950,* 1967. *The Nuclear Delusion: Soviet-American Relations in the Atomic Age,* 1982. *The Fateful Alliance: France, Russia, and the Coming of the First World War,* 1984. *George F. Kennan on Russian Diplomacy in the 19th Century and the Origins of World War I,* 1986. *Sketches from a Life,* 1989. *Around the Cragged Hill: A Personal and Political Philosophy,* 1993. *At a Century's Ending: Reflections, 1982-1995,* 1996.

Other Awards: Freedom House Award, 1951: *American Diplomacy, 1900-1950,* Chicago: University of Chicago, 1951. National Book Award, 1957: *Russia Leaves the War,* Princeton, NJ: Princeton University, 1956-58. Bancroft Prize, Columbia University, 1957: *Russia Leaves the War.* Francis Parkman Prize, 1957: *Russia Leaves the War.* National Book Award, 1968: *Memoirs, 1925-1950,* Boston: Little, Brown, 1967-72. Overseas Press Club of America Award, 1968: *Memoirs, 1925-1950.* Director General's Cup, American Foreign Service Association. Emory Buckner Medal, Federal Bar Council of New York. Knight Commander's Cross, Federal Republic of Germany, 1973. John F. Lewis Prize, American Philosophical Society, 1974. Fellow, Woodrow Wilson International Center for Scholars, 1974-1975. Woodrow Wilson Award, Princeton University, 1976. Albert Einstein Peace Prize, 1981. Grenville Clark Prize, 1981. Pacem in Terris Peace and Freedom

Award, 1982. Quad City Peace and Justice Coalition, 1982. Boersenverein Peace Prize, Frankfurt, Germany, 1982. Peace Prize, German Book Trade, 1982. Charles E. Merriam Award, American Political Science Association, 1984. Gold Medal for History, American Academy and Institute of Arts and Letters, 1984. Creative Arts Award for Nonfiction, Brandeis University, 1986. Freedom from Fear Award, Four Freedoms Foundation of the Franklin and Eleanor Roosevelt Institute, 1987. Physicians for Social Responsibility Award, 1988. Toynbee Prize, 1988. Encyclopaedia Britannica Award, 1989. Presidential Medal of Freedom, 1989. Woodrow Wilson Public Service Award, 1990. Coalition for Nuclear Disarmament Tribute, 1990. Honored by City of Milwaukee with "George F. Kennan Week," May 7 to 12, 1990. Outstanding Achievement Award, Wisconsin Library Association, 1990. Honorary LLDs: Yale University, CT, 1950; Dartmouth College, NH, 1950; Colgate University, NY, 1951; University of Notre Dame, IN, 1953; Kenyon College, OH, 1954; New School for Social Research, NY, 1955; Princeton University, NJ, 1956; University of Michigan, 1957; Northwestern University, IL, 1957; Brandeis University, MA, 1958; Harvard University, MA, 1963; Duke University, NC, 1977; Brown University, RI, 1983; New York University, 1985; Columbia University, NY, 1986. Honorary DPol, University of Helsinki, 1986. Honorary DCLS: Oxford University, 1969, University of Wisconsin, Milwaukee, 1990.

For More Information: Isaacson, Walter and Evan Thomas, *The Wise Men,* New York: Simon & Schuster, 1986; Mayers, David, *George Kennan and the Dilemmas of U.S. Foreign Policy,* Oxford, England: Oxford University, 1988; Hixson, Walter L., *George F. Kennan Cold War Iconoclast,* New York: Columbia University, 1989; Stephanson, Anders, *Kennan and the Art of Foreign Policy,* Cambridge, MA: Harvard University, 1989; Miscambe, Wilson D., *George F. Kennan and the Making of American Foreign Policy, 1947-1950,* Princeton, NJ: Princeton University, 1992.

Commentary: George Frost Kennan won two Pulitzers. He was awarded the 1957 Pulitzer Prize in History for *Russia Leaves the War: Soviet-American Relations, 1917-1920,* a work in three volumes. He also won the 1968 Pulitzer Prize in Autobiography for his *Memoirs.*

Kennan was born in Milwaukee, Wisconsin. He was educated at Princeton University and at the Berlin Seminary for Oriental Languages. He had a distinguished career in the United States Foreign Service, holding diplomatic posts in Central and Eastern Europe from the 1920s to the 1950s. He was the director of policy planning at the Department of State in 1947. He initially advocated a policy of "containment" toward the Soviet Union, but reversed his view

in the late 1950s to encourage peaceful coexistence. He is at the top of required reading lists for all students of foreign policy. His counsel is sought after on issues of international security. He has been Professor Emeritus at the Institute of Advanced Studies at Princeton University since 1974 and is the Honorary Chairman of the American Committee on United States/Soviet Relations.

1969

Benjamin Lawrence Reid   62

Birth: May 3, 1918; Louisville, KY. **Death:** November 30, 1990. **Parents:** Isaac Errett and Margaret (Lawrence) Reid. **Religion:** Episcopalian. **Education:** University of Louisville, KY: AB. Columbia University, NY: AM. University of Virginia: PhD. **Spouse:** Joan Davidson (m. 1942). **Children:** Jane Lawrence, Colin Way.

Prize: *Biography or Autobiography,* 1969: *The Man From New York: John Quinn and His Friends,* New York: Oxford University, 1968.

Career: English Instructor, Iowa State College of Science and Technology (now University), Ames, 1946-1948; English Instructor, Smith College, Northampton, MA, 1948-1951; Instructor, Sweet Briar College, Sweet Briar, VA, 1951-1956; Assistant Professor of English, Sweet Briar College, 1956-1957; Assistant Professor, Mount Holyoke College, South Hadley, MA, 1957-1959; Associate Professor, Mount Holyoke College, 1959-1963; Professor, Mount Holyoke College, 1963-1970; Visiting Professor, Amherst College, 1965-1966; Andrew W. Mellon Professor of English, beginning in 1970; Member: Modern Language Association of America, American Association of University Professors.

Selected Works: *Art by Subtraction: A Dissenting Opinion of Gertrude Stein,* 1958. *William Butler Yeats: The Lyric of Tragedy,* 1961. *The Lives of Roger Casement,* 1976. *First Acts: A Memoir,* 1988. *Necessary Lives: Biographical Reflections,* 1990.

Other Awards: Fulbright Grant, England, 1963-1964. Fellowship, American Council of Learned Societies, 1966-1967. Senior Fellowship, National Endowment for the Humanities, 1971-1972. Honorary DHL, University of Louisville, KY, 1970.

For More Information: "Benjamin L. Reid, 72," *St. Louis Post-Dispatch,* December 6, 1990.

Commentary: Benjamin Lawrence Reid won the 1969 Pulitzer Prize in Biography for *The Man From New York: John Quinn and His Friends,* about a corporation lawyer in New York City who left behind a private collection of paintings, drawings, and sculpture as well as books and manuscripts of contemporary authors. Quinn promoted avant-garde and modern art in all forms, and was a supporter of the

Irish Literary Revival writers, the artists of the Paris School, and English and American writers of his time.

Reid was born in Louisville, Kentucky. He was educated at the University of Louisville, Columbia University, and the University of Virginia. His wife Mary was a critic. Reid was the Andrew W. Mellon Professor of English at Mount Holyoke College in South Hadley, Massachusetts.

1970

T. Harry Williams   63
Birth: May 19, 1909; Vinegar Hill, IL. **Death:** 1979. **Parents:** William Dwight and Emeline Louisa (Collins) Williams. **Education:** Platteville State Teachers College (now University of Wisconsin—Platteville): EdB. University of Wisconsin: PhM, PhD. **Spouse:** Estelle Skofield (m.1952). **Children:** May Frances.

Prize: *Biography or Autobiography*, 1970: *Huey Long*, New York: Knopf, 1969.

Career: Instructor, University of Wisconsin Extension Division, 1936-1938; Instructor and Assistant Professor, Municipal University of Omaha (now University of Nebraska at Omaha), NE, 1938-1941; Professor of History, Louisiana State University, Baton Rouge, 1941-1979; Boyd Professor of History, Louisiana State University, Baton Rouge, 1953-1979; Member, History Advisory Committee, Department of the Army, 1955-1960; Vice-President, Southern Historical Association, 1957-1958; President, Southern Historical Association, 1958-1959; Vice-Chairman, Louisiana Civil War Centennial Commission, 1961-1965; Harmsworth Professor of American History, Queen's College, Oxford University, England, 1966-1967; Vice-President, Organization of American Historians, 1971-1972; President, Organization of American Historians, 1972-1973; Visiting Director, Civil War Centennial Association; Member: American Association of University Professors, American Historical Association, American Military Institute, Society of American Historians.

Selected Works: *Lincoln and the Radicals*, 1941. *Selected Writings and Speeches of Abraham Lincoln* (Williams, T. Harry, ed.), 1943. *Lincoln and His Generals*, 1952. *P.G.T. Beauregard: Napoleon in Gray*, 1954. *With Beauregard in Mexico: The Mexican War Reminiscences of P.G.T. Beauregard* (Williams, T. Harry, ed.), 1956. *A History of the United States* (with Richard N. Current and Frank Freidel), 1959. *Americans at War: The Development of the American Military System*, 1960. *McClellan, Sherman, and Grant*, 1962. *Hayes: The Diary of a President 1875-1881, Covering the Disputed Election, the End of Reconstruction, and the Beginning of Civil Service* (Williams, T. Harry, ed.), 1964. *Hayes of the Twenty-Third: The Civil War Volunteer Officer*, 1965.

The History of American Wars from 1745 to 1918, 1981.

Other Awards: Lincoln Diploma of Honor, Lincoln Memorial University, 1956. Guggenheim Fellow, 1957. Harry S. Truman Award, Civil War History, 1963. National Book Award, 1970: *Huey Long* New York: Knopf, 1969. Honorary LLD, Northland College, WI, 1953. Honorary Doctor of Letters, Bradley University, IL, 1959.

For More Information: *Blue Book,* New York: St. Martin's, 1979; *Dictionary of Literary Biography,* Detroit: Gale, 1983; Heleniak, Roman J. and Lawrence L. Hewitt, *Leadership During the Civil War: The 1989 Deep Delta Civil War Symposium: Themes in Honor of T. Harry Williams,* Shippensburg, PA: White Mane, 1992.

Commentary: *Huey Long* won the 1970 Pulitzer Prize in Biography for T. Harry Williams. Huey Long (1893-1935) was both governor of the state of Louisiana and a United States senator whose social reforms and radical welfare proposals were ultimately overshadowed by his demagoguery. His slogan, "every man a king," gained him the nickname "Kingfish."

Williams was born in Vinegar Hill, Illinois. He was educated at Platteville State Teachers College and the University of Wisconsin. Williams was the Boyd Professor of History at Louisiana State University in Baton Rouge. He served as president of both the Southern Historical Association and the Organization of American Historians. His other works include *Lincoln and His Generals* and *Americans at War: The Development of the American Military System.*

1971

Lawrance Thompson   64
Birth: April 3, 1906. **Death:** 1973. **Parents:** Roger Everett and Magdalena (Keller) Thompson. **Education:** Wesleyan University, CT: BA. Columbia University, NY: PhD. **Spouse:** Janet McLeod Arnold (m. 1945).

Prize: *Biography or Autobiography,* 1971: *Robert Frost: The Years of Triumph, 1915-1938,* New York: Holt, Rinehart and Winston, 1970.

Career: English Instructor, Wesleyan University, CT, 1934-1935; Instructor, English and Comparative Literature, Columbia University, NY, 1935-1936; Research Fellow, Columbia University, NY 1936-1937; Curator of Rare Books and Manuscripts, University Library, Princeton University, NJ, 1937-1942; Assistant Professor, English, 1939-1947; Associate Professor, 1947-1951; Professor of English, 1951-1968; Guest Lecturer, Salzburg Seminar in American Studies, 1954; Guest Lecturer, University of Oslo, 1954; Trustee, Princeton University, Press, 1955-1960; Guest Lecturer, University of Puerto

Rico, 1959; Member, Princeton Township Board of Education, 1960-1963; Guest Lecturer, Hebrew University of Jerusalem, 1961-1962; Holmes Professor of Belles Lettres, 1968-1973, Princeton University.

Selected Works: _Young Longfellow (1807-1843),_ 1938. _Emerson and Frost: Critics of Their Times,_ 1940. _Fire and Ice: The Art and Thought of Robert Frost,_ 1942. _Melville's Quarrel with God,_ 1952. _William Faulkner: An Introduction and Interpretation,_ 1963. _Robert Frost: Poetry and Prose_ (Thompson, Lawrance, and Connery Lathem, eds.), 1972. _Robert Frost: A Biography_ (with R.H. Winnick), 1981.

For More Information: _New Statesman,_ February 19, 1971; Obituary, _New York Times,_ April 16, 1973; _New Yorker,_ April 11, 1977.

Commentary: Lawrance "Roger" Thompson won the 1971 Pulitzer Prize in Biography for _Robert Frost: The Years of Triumph, 1915-1938._ Thompson's biography uncovered the dark side of one of the 20th century's major poets.

Thompson took ill after completeing the third volume of the Frost biography. He died in 1973. Since the publication of these three volumes, there has been much debate on the negative descriptions contained there.

1972

Joseph P. Lash   65

Birth: December 2, 1909; New York, NY. **Death:** October 1987. **Parents:** Samuel and Mary (Duchin) Lash. **Religion:** Jewish. **Education:** City College, NY: AB. Columbia University, NY: MA. **Spouse:** Trude Wenzel (m. 1944).

Prize: _Biography or Autobiography,_ 1972: _Eleanor and Franklin,_ New York: Norton, 1971.

Career: Second Lieutenant, U.S. Army, WWII; Director, Americans for Democratic Action, NY, 1946-1949; United Nations Correspondent, _New York Post,_ NY, 1950-1961; Assistant Editor, Editorial Page, _New York Post,_ NY, 1961-1966; Freelance writer, beginning in 1966.

Selected Works: _War: Our Heritage_ (with James A. Wechsler), 1936. _Dag Hammarskjold,_ 1961. _Eleanor Roosevelt: A Friend's Memoir,_ 1964. _Eleanor: The Years Alone,_ 1972. _From the Diaries of Felix Frankfurter: With a Biographical Essay and Notes,_ 1975. _Roosevelt and Churchill, 1939-1941: The Partnership That Saved the West,_ 1976. _Helen and Teacher: The Story of Helen Keller and Anne Sullivan Macy,_ 1980. _Love, Eleanor: Eleanor Roosevelt and Her Friends,_ 1982. _A World of Love: Eleanor Roosevelt and Her Friends, 1943-1962,_ 1984. _Life Was Meant to Be Lived: A Centenary_

Portrait of Eleanor Roosevelt, 1984. _Dealers and Dreamers: A New Look at the New Deal,_ 1988.

Other Awards: Air Medal, WWII. National Book Award, Biography, 1972: _Eleanor and Franklin: The Story of Their Relationship Based on Eleanor Roosevelt's Private Papers,_ New York: Norton, 1971. Samuel E. Morison Award for History, 1978: _Roosevelt and Churchill: A Study of Their Relationship,_ New York: Norton, 1976. American Library Association Notable Book Citation, 1981: _Helen and Teacher: The Story of Helen Keller and Anne Sullivan Macy,_ New York: Delacorte, 1980.

For More Information: _Current Biography,_ New York: Wilson, 1972; _Something About the Author,_ Detroit: Gale, 1986.

Commentary: Joseph P. Lash won the 1972 Pulitzer Prize in Biography for _Eleanor and Franklin,_ a two-volume story of their relationship based on the private papers of Eleanor Roosevelt. He was a close friend of Eleanor Roosevelt and the official biographer of the Roosevelts.

Lash was born in New York City. He was educated at City College of the City University of New York and at Columbia University. Lash became a journalist, covering the United Nations beat for the _New York Post_ from 1950 to 1961, and an assistant editor of the editorial page. He left to devote all his time to writing. His other works included _Helen and Teacher: The Story of Helen Keller and Anne Sullivan Macy_ and _Dealers and Dreamers: A New Look at the New Deal._

1973

W.A. Swanberg   66

Birth: November 23, 1907; St. Paul, MN. **Death:** September 17, 1992. **Parents:** Charles Henning and Valborg (Larsen) Swanberg. **Education:** University of Minnesota: BA. New York University. **Spouse:** Dorothy Upham Green (m. 1936). **Children:** John William, Sara Valborg.

Prize: _Biography or Autobiography,_ 1973: _Luce and His Empire,_ New York: Scribners, 1972.

Career: Various jobs, 1931-1935; Assistant Editor, Dell Publishing, NY, 1935-1936; Editor, Dell Publishing, NY, 1936-1944; Writer in Europe, U.S. Office of War Information, 1944-1945; Freelance writer, 1945-; Fellow, Society of American Historians; Member: Authors League of America, International PEN, New York Historical Society, Newtown, Connecticut Library Board.

Selected Works: _Sickles the Incredible,_ 1956. _First Blood: The Story of Fort Sumter,_ 1957. _Jim Fisk: The Career of an Improbable Rascal,_ 1959. _Citizen Hearst: A Biography of William Randolph Hearst,_ 1961. _Pulitzer,_ 1967. _The Rector and the Rogue,_ 1968.

Norman Thomas, the Last Idealist, 1976. *Whitney Father, Whitney Heiress,* 1980.

Other Awards: Christopher Award: *First Blood,* New York: Scribners, 1957. Minnesota Centennial Award: *First Blood.* Guggenheim Fellow, 1960. Frank Luther Mott-Kappa Tau Alpha Award, 1961: *Citizen Hearst,* New York: Scribners, 1961. Van Wyck Brooks Award, Nonfiction, 1967. National Book Award, Biography, 1977: *Norman Thomas: The Last Idealist.* New York: Scribners, 1976.

For More Information: Saxon, Wolfgang, "William A. Swanberg Dies at 84: A Pulitzer-Winning Biographer," *New York Times* Current Events Edition, September 19, 1992; "W. A. Swanberg Dies at 84: Prize-Winning Biographer," *Washington Post,* September 20, 1992.

Commentary: *Luce and His Empire* won the 1973 Pulitzer Prize in Biography for W.A. Swanberg. Henry Robinson Luce, the son of American missionaries in China, was an American editor and publisher, born in Shantung Province, China. His wife was Clare Boothe Luce. He was a co-founder and editor-in-chief of Time, Incorporated.

William Andrew Swanberg was born in St. Paul, Minnesota and educated at the University of Minnesota and New York University. He was an editor for publishing houses before World War II. During the war he wrote for the Office of War Information. Afterward, he was a freelance writer.

1974

Louis Sheaffer   67

Birth: October 18, 1912; Louisville, KY. **Death:** August 7, 1993.

Prize: *Biography or Autobiography,* 1974: *O'Neill, Son and Artist,* Boston: Little, Brown, 1973.

Career: Journalist and Critic, *Brooklyn Eagle,* 1930s-1950s; Freelance journalist.

Selected Works: *O'Neill: Son and Playwright,* 1968.

Other Awards: Three Guggenheim Fellowships. Grants, National Endowment for the Humanities. Grants, American Council of Learned Societies. George Freedley Award, Theater Library Association, 1969: *O'Neill, Son and Playwright,* Boston: Little, Brown, 1968.

For More Information: *Dictionary of Literary Biography,* Detroit: Gale, 1991.

Commentary: Louis Sheaffer was awarded the 1974 Pulitzer Prize in Biography for *O'Neill, Son and Artist,* the second volume of a two-volume set on the life of Eugene O'Neill, one of the premiere dramatists of American theatre in the 20th century. The first volume was titled *O'Neill, Son and Playwright.*

Sheaffer was born Louis Sheaffer Slung in Lou-

isville, Kentucky. He had a career as a reporter, columnist, and film and theatre critic for the *Brooklyn Eagle,* but he is best known for his critically acclaimed O'Neill biography.

.

1975

Robert Caro   68

Birth: October 30, 1935; New York, NY. **Parents:** Benjamin and Cele (Mendelow) Caro. **Religion:** Jewish. **Education:** Princeton University, NJ: BA. Harvard University, MA: Nieman Fellow. **Spouse:** Ina Joan Sloshberg (m. 1957). **Children:** Chase A.

Prize: *Biography or Autobiography,* 1975: *The Power Broker: Robert Moses and the Fall of New York,* New York: Knopf, 1974.

Career: Writer; Reporter, *New Brunswick Home News,* New Brunswick, NJ, 1957-1959; Investigative Reporter, *Newsday,* Garden City, NY, 1959-1966; President, Authors Guild.

Selected Works: *The Path to Power: The Years of Lyndon Johnson,* 1982. *Extraordinary Lives: The Art and Craft of American Biography,* 1986. *Means of Ascent: The Years of Lyndon Johnson,* 1990.

Other Awards: Society of Silurians Award for Public Service Writing, 1965. Nieman Fellow, Harvard University, 1965-66. Carnegie Foundation Fellow, 1967. Francis Parkman Prize, Society of American Historians, 1975: *The Power Broker: Robert Moses and the Fall of New York,* New York: Knopf, 1974. Washington Monthly Political Book Award, 1975: *The Power Broker: Robert Moses and the Fall of New York.* National Book Critics Circle Award, Best Nonfiction Book, 1983: *The Path to Power: The Years of Lyndon Johnson,* New York: Knopf, 1982. Texas Institute of Letters Award, Best Nonfiction Book, 1983: *The Path to Power: The Years of Lyndon Johnson.* Washington Monthly Political Book Award, 1983: *The Path to Power: The Years of Lyndon Johnson.* H. L. Mencken Prize, 1983: *The Path to Power: The Years of Lyndon Johnson.* American Academy and Institute of Arts and Letters Award in Literature, 1986. National Book Critics Circle Award, Best Biography, 1991: *Means of Ascent: The Years of Lyndon Johnson,* New York: Knopf, 1990. Washington Monthly Political Book Award, 1991: *Means of Ascent: The Years of Lyndon Johnson.*

For More Information: *Current Biography,* New York: Wilson, January, 1984; Von Hoffman, Nicolas, "Robert Caro's Holy Fire," *Vanity Fair,* April, 1990; Busby, Horace, "Robert Caro's L.B.J.: There Was Such a Man, Warts, and All," *Los Angeles Times,* March 31, 1991.

Commentary: Robert Caro won the 1975 Pulitzer Prize in Biography for *The Power Broker: Robert Moses and the Fall of New York,* the masterful telling of the political maneuvers of New York state public servant Robert Moses, the man behind many monumental state public works projects. Moses lived from 1888 to 1981. _The Power Broker_ was also awarded the Francis Parkman Prize from the Society of American Historians for the book which "exemplifies the union of historian and artist."

Caro was born in New York City and educated at Princeton and Harvard Universities. He was an investigative reporter for _Newsday,_ before writing biography and history. His dramatic and masterful storytelling makes for absorbing reading. He has also written, in two-volumes, _The Years of Lyndon Johnson._

1976

R.W.B. (Richard Warrington Baldwin) Lewis   69

Birth: November 1, 1917; Chicago, IL. **Parents:** Leichester Crosby and Beatrix Elizabeth (Baldwin) Lewis. **Education:** Harvard University, MA: AB. University of Chicago, IL. **Spouse:** Nancy Landau (m. 1950). **Children:** Nathaniel Landau, Sophia Baldwin.

Prize: _Biography or Autobiography,_ 1976: _Edith Wharton: A Biography,_ New York: Harper & Row, 1975.

Career: Major, U.S. Army, 1942-1946; Teacher, Bennington College, Bennington, VT, 1948-1950; Dean of Salzburg Seminar in American Studies, 1950-1951; Visiting Lecturer of English, Smith College, Northampton, MA, 1951-1952; Hodder Fellow in the Humanities, Princeton University, NJ, 1952-1953; Resident Fellow in Creative Writing, Princeton University, NJ, 1953-1954; Associate Professor and Professor of English, Rutgers University, NJ, 1954-1959; Kenyon Fellow in Criticism, Florence, Italy, 1954-1955; Fellow of School of Letters, Indiana University, 1957-; Fulbright Lecturer, American Literature, University of Munich, 1957-1958; Professor of English and American Studies, Yale University, CT, 1960-; Fellow, Calhoun College, 1960; Fellow, American Council of Learned Societies, 1962-1963; Senior Fellow, Indiana University, 1964-; Chairman of English Institute, Indiana University, 1965; Literary Consultant, Universal Pictures, beginning in 1966.

Selected Works: _The Picaresque Saint: Representative Figures in Contemporary Fiction,_ 1958. _The Presence of Walt Whitman: Selected Papers from the English Institute_ (Lewis, R.W.B., ed.), 1962. _Trials of the Word: Essays in American Literature and the Humanistic Tradition,_ 1965. _The Letters of Edith Wharton_ (Lewis, R.W.B., and Nancy Lewis, eds.), 1988. _The Selected Short Stories of Edith Wharton_ (Lewis, R.W.B, ed.), 1991. _The Jameses: A Family Narrative,_ 1991. _Literary Reflections: A Shoring of Images, 1960-1993,_ 1993. _The City of Florence: Historical Vistas and Personal Sightings,_ 1995.

Other Awards: National Institute of Arts and Letters Award, 1958. Friends of Literature Award, 1976: _Edith Wharton: A Biography,_ New York: Harper & Row, 1975. National Book Critics Circle Award, 1976: _Edith Wharton: A Biography._ Bancroft Prize, 1976: _Edith Wharton: A Biography._ Honorary LittD, Wesleyan University, CT, 1961.

For More Information: _Dictionary of Literary Biography,_ Detroit: Gale, 1991.

Commentary: _Edith Wharton: A Biography_ won the 1976 Pulitzer Prize in Biography for R.W.B. Lewis. Edith Wharton (1862-1937) was an American novelist of manners and a Pulitzer Prize winner who was noted for her depictions of New York's elite and their social restrictions at the end of the 19th century.

Richard Warrington Baldwin Lewis was born in Chicago and educated at Harvard University and the University of Chicago. Lewis was professor of English and American studies at Yale University and a Senior Fellow at Indiana University. His other works include _The Jameses: A Family Narrative_ and _The City of Florence: Historical Vistas and Personal Sightings._

1977

John E. Mack   70

Birth: October 4, 1929; New York, NY. **Parents:** Edward Clarence and Ruth (Prince) Mack. **Education:** Oberlin College, OH: AB. Harvard University, MA: MD. **Spouse:** Sally Stahl (m. 1959). **Children:** Daniel, Kenneth, David Anthony.

Prize: _Biography or Autobiography,_ 1977: _A Prince of Our Disorder: The Life of T.E. Lawrence,_ Boston: Little, Brown, 1976.

Career: Intern, Massachusetts General Hospital, Boston, 1955-1956; Resident in Psychiatry, Massachusetts Mental Health Center, Boston, 1956-1959; Teaching Fellow and Research Fellow, Harvard University Medical School, MA, 1956-1959; Chief Resident, Day and Night Hospitals, Massachusetts Mental Health Center, Boston, 1957-1959; Captain, U.S. Air Force, 1959-1961; Psychiatry Specialist, Cambridge and Brookline, MA, 1961; Candidate in Training, Boston Psychoanalytic Society and Institute, MA, 1961-1967; Senior Physician, Massachusetts Mental Health Center, 1961; Fellow, Child Psychiatry of the Children's Unit, Massachusetts Mental Health Center, 1961-1963; Member, Legal Medicine Division, Roxbury Court Clinic, MA, 1962-1963; Assistant in Psychiatry, Harvard University Medical School, 1963-1964; Staff Psychiatrist, Massachusetts Mental

Health Center, 1963-1967; Visiting Staff, Massachusetts Mental Health Center, 1963-1965; Faculty member, Harvard University Medical School, 1964-; Principal Psychiatrist, Massachusetts Mental Health Center, 1965; Associate Director of Psychiatry, Massachusetts Mental Health Center, 1965-1967; Director of Research, Children's Unit, Massachusetts Mental Health Center, 1967-1970; Head, Department of Psychiatry, Cambridge Hospital at Harvard University, MA, 1967-1977; Junior Visiting Physician, Cambridge City Hospital, MA, 1967; Coordinator, Children's Unit, Harvard University Medical Teaching School, 1968-1970; Senior Visiting Physician, Cambridge City Hospital, MA, 1968-1969; Chief, Department of Psychiatry, Cambridge City Hospital, MA, 1969-1977; Faculty member, Boston Psychoanalytic Society and Institute, beginning in 1969; Professor of Psychiatry, Harvard University Medical School, 1972-; Professor of Psychiatry, Cambridge Hospital at Harvard University, MA, 1972-; Consultant, University Health Services, Harvard University, 1972-1975; Department Head, Harvard University Medical School, 1973-1977; Cambridge-Somerville Mental Health and Retardation Center, MA, beginning in 1975; Director of Education, Education Committee Member, Boston Psychoanalytic Society and Institute, beginning in 1975; Chairman, Executive Committee, Harvard Department of Psychiatry, beginning in 1980; Editorial Board, *Journal of the American Psychoanalytic Association;* Fellow, American Psychiatric Association; Lecturer, psychological aspects of the Arab-Israeli Conflict; Member: Alpha Omega Alpha, American Academy of Child Psychiatry, American Board of Psychology, American Group Psychotherapy Association, Association for the Psychophysiological Study of Sleep, Boylston Society, Group for the Advancement of Psychiatry, Massachusetts Medical Society, Norfolk County Medical Society, New England Council of Child Psychiatry.

Selected Works: *Nightmares and Human Conflict,* 1970. *The Development and Sustenance of Self-Esteem in Childhood: From the Study Group of the Division of Child Psychiatry of the Cambridge Hospital, Department of Psychiatry, Harvard Medical School, and the Cambridge-Somerville Mental Health and Retardation Center* (Mack, John E., Steven L. Ablon, eds.), 1983. *Abduction: Human Encounters with Aliens,* 1994.

Other Awards: Felix and Helene Deutsch Science Prize, Boston Psychoanalytic Society and Institute, 1964: *Heterosexual Impass in the Precipitation of Schizophrenia.* Harry S. Solomon Award, Massachusetts Mental Health Center, 1967.

For More Information: Daly, Christopher B., "Alien Book Carries Scholar from Harvard to 'Oprah,'" *Washington Post,* May 27, 1995.

Commentary: John E. Mack was awarded the 1977 Pulitzer Prize in Biography for *A Prince of Our Disorder: The Life of T.E. Lawrence,* about the man called Lawrence of Arabia, who led an Arab insurgency against the Turks from 1916 to 1918.

Dr. John E. Mack was born in New York City. He was educated at Oberlin College and at Harvard University. He is a child psychoanalyst and was head of the department of psychiatry at Cambridge City Hospital at Harvard from 1967-1977. His other works include *Close Encounters of the Fourth Kind, Alien Abduction, U.F.O.s and the Conference at M.I.T.*

1978

Walter Jackson Bate

Full entry appears as **#57** under "Biography or Autobiography," 1964.

1979

Leonard Baker   71
Birth: January 24, 1931; Pittsburgh, PA. **Parents:** Charles and Bess Baker. **Religion:** Jewish. **Education:** University of Pittsburgh, PA: BA. Columbia University, NY: MS. **Spouse:** Liva B. (m. 1958). **Children:** David, Sara.

Prize: *Biography or Autobiography,* 1979: *Days of Sorrow: Leo Baeck and the Berlin Jews,* New York: Macmillan, 1978.

Career: Newspaper reporter, 1955-1965; Washington (DC) Correspondent, 1958-1965.

Selected Works: *The Johnson Eclipse: A President's Vice Presidency,* 1966. *The Guaranteed Society,* 1968. *Brahmin in Revolt: A Biography of Herbert C. Pell,* 1972. *John Marshall: A Life in Law,* 1974. *Brandeis and Frankfurter: A Dual Biography,* 1984.

Commentary: Leonard Baker won the 1979 Pulitzer Prize in Biography for *Days of Sorrow: Leo Baeck and the Berlin Jews.* Leo Baeck was the leading rabbi in Berlin when Hitler came to power, and he assumed a main role as head of the Jewish "self-administration" in Germany from 1933 to 1945. He was the last Jewish leader in Germany helping the Berlin Jews to emigrate, and when that was no longer possible, to resist through underground activities. He refused to leave Germany; he eventually was sent to Theresienstadt concentration camp.

Baker was born in Pittsburgh, Pennsylvania. He was educated at the University of Pittsburgh and at Columbia University. Baker was a newspaper reporter before he began writing biographies. He is also the author of *Brandeis and Frankfurter, Roosevelt and Pearl Harbor,* and *John Marshall: A Life in Law.*

1980

Edmund Morris 72

Birth: May 27, 1940; Nairobi, Kenya. **Parents:** Eric Edmund and May (Dowling) Morris. **Education:** Rhodes University, Grahamstown, South Africa. **Spouse:** Sylvia Jukes (m. 1966).

Prize: *Biography or Autobiography,* 1980: *The Rise of Theodore Roosevelt,* New York: Coward, McCann & Geoghegan, 1979.

Career: Copywriter, advertising, London, England, 1964-1968; Copywriter, advertising, NY, 1968-1971; Writer, 1971-.

Selected Works: *National Geographic Traveler,* "Romance of Cornwall," May 1, 1989. *Time,* "Ronald Reagan: At His Prime," August 1996. *New Yorker,* "Reporter at Large," February 16, 1998. *Time,* "Theodore Roosevelt," April 13, 1998.

For More Information: *Contemporary Biography,* Detroit: Gale, 1990.

Commentary: *The Rise of Theodore Roosevelt* won the 1980 Pulitzer Prize in Biography for Edmund Morris. It covers Roosevelt's rise in politics before he was elected the 26th president of the United States.

Morris was born in Nairobi, Kenya and educated at Rhodes University. He worked in advertising as a copywriter before devoting himself full time to writing. He immigrated to the United States in 1969 and was naturalized in 1979.

1981

Robert K. Massie 73

Birth: January 5, 1929; Lexington, KY. **Parents:** Robert K. and Mary (Kimball) Massie. **Education:** Yale University, CT: BA. Oxford University, England: BA, Rhodes Scholar, BA. **Spouse:** Suzanne Rohrbach (m. 1954; div. 1990). **Children:** Robert Kinlock, Susanna, Elizabeth.

Prize: *Biography or Autobiography,* 1981: *Peter the Great: His Life and World,* New York: Knopf, 1980.

Career: Lieutenant, U.S. Naval Reserves, 1952-1955; Reporter, *Collier's,* NY, 1955-1956; Writer and Correspondent, *Newsweek,* NY, 1956-1962; Writer, USA-1, NY, 1962; Writer, *Saturday Evening Post,* NY, 1962-1965; Freelance writer, 1965; Ferris Professor of Journalism, Princeton University, NJ, 1977, 1985; Mellon Professor of Humanities, Tulane University, 1981; Vice President, Authors Guild, 1985-1987; President, Authors Guild, beginning in 1987; Member: Authors League of America, PEN, Society of American Historians.

Selected Works: *Nicholas and Alexandra,* 1967. *Journey* (with Suzanne Massie), 1975. *Dreadnought:*

Britain, Germany, and the Coming of the Great War, 1991. *The Romanovs: The Final Chapter,* 1995. *Loosing the Bonds: The United States and South Africa in the Apartheid Years,* 1997.

Other Awards: Christopher Award, 1976: *Journey,* New York: Knopf, 1975. American Library Association Notable Book Citation, 1981: *Peter the Great: His Life and World,* New York: Knopf, 1980.

For More Information: *World Authors,* New York: Wilson, 1985.

Commentary: Robert K. Massie was awarded the 1981 Pulitzer Prize in Biography for *Peter the Great: His Life and World,* the story of Peter I, Tsar of Russia who lived from 1672 to 1725 and was the founder of the Russian Empire.

Massie was born in Lexington, Kentucky. He was educated at Yale University and he was a Rhodes Scholar at Oxford University in England. Massie was a writer and correspondent for *Collier's, Newsweek,* and the *Saturday Evening Post.* He has taught journalism at Princeton. His other works include *Nicholas and Alexandra* and *The Romanovs.*

1982

William Shield McFeely 74

Birth: September 25, 1930; New York, NY. **Parents:** William Clarance and Marguerite (Shield) McFeely. **Education:** Amherst College, MA: BA. Yale University, CT: MA, PhD. **Spouse:** Mary Drake (m. 1952). **Children:** William Drake, Eliza, Jennifer.

Prize: *Biography or Autobiography,* 1982: *Grant: A Biography,* New York: Norton, 1981.

Career: Assistant Cashier, First National City Bank, NY, 1952-1961; Assistant Professor, Yale University, CT, 1966-1969; Teacher, Yale / Harvard / Columbia Intensive Summer Studies Program, 1967-1969; Associate Professor of History, Yale University, CT, 1969-1970; Professor of History, Mount Holyoke College, MA, 1970-1980; Consultant to Committee on the Judiciary, U.S. House of Representatives, 1974; Affiliation, Huntington Library, Harvard University, MA, 1976, 1983; Visiting Professor of History, University College, London, England, 1978-1979; Rodman Professor of History, Mount Holyoke College, MA, 1980-1982; Visiting Professor of History, Amherst College, 1980-1981; Andrew W. Mellon Professor in the Humanities, Mount Holyoke College, MA, 1982-1986; Visiting Professor, University of Massachusetts, 1984-1985; Richard B. Russell Professor of American History, University of Georgia, Athens, 1986-1994; John J. McCloy Professor, University of Massachusetts, 1988-1989; Associate Fellow, Charles Warren Center, Harvard University, MA, 1991-1992; Visiting Scholar, W. E. B. DuBois Institute, Harvard University, MA, 1992-; Franklin Professor of History, University of Georgia, Athens, 1994-present; Member: American Historical Association, Association for the Study of Afro-American Life and History, Authors Guild, Century Association, Organization of American Historians, PEN, Southern Historical Association.

Selected Works: *The Freedmen's Bureau: A Study in Betrayal,* 1966. *Yankee Stepfather: General O. O. Howard and the Freedmen,* 1968. *The Black Man in the Land of Equality* (with Thomas J.Ladenburg), 1969. *Frederick Douglass,* 1991. *Sapelo's People: A Long Walk into Freedom,* 1994.

Other Awards: Morse Fellow, 1968-1969. American Council of Learned Societies Fellow, 1974-1975. Francis Parkman Prize, 1982: *Grant: A Biography,* New York: Norton, 1981. Guggenheim Fellow, 1982-1983. National Endowment for the Humanities Grant, 1986-1987. New York Public Library "Literary Lion" Award, 1991. Lincoln Prize, 1992. Avery O. Craven Award, 1992. Christopher Award, 1992. Honorary LHD, Amherst College, MA, 1982. Honorary Doctor of Humane Letters, Washington, College, 1992.

For More Information: Jenkins, McKay, "New England Scholar Thinks South," *Atlanta Journal-Constitution,* April 12, 1992.

Commentary: William McFeely won the 1982 Pulitzer Prize in Biography for *Grant: A Biography,* the story of Ulysses S. Grant, the 18th president of the United States and Union Army general during the Civil War. The book was also awarded the Francis Parkman Prize from the Society of American Historians.

McFeely was born in New York City. He was educated at Amherst College and at Yale University. He was Dean of the faculty at Mount Holyoke College from 1970 to 1973 and Andrew W. Mellon Professor of Humanities. He is currently the Abraham Baldwin Professor of the Humanities at the University of Georgia. His other works include *Yankee Stepfather: Gen. O.O. Howard and the Freedmen, Frederick Douglass,* and *Failure and Success.*

1983

Russell Wayne Baker 75

Birth: August 14, 1925; Loudoun County, VA. **Parents:** Benjamin Rex Baker and Lucy Elizabeth (Robinson). **Education:** Johns Hopkins University, MD: BA. **Spouse:** Miriam Emily Nash (m. 1950). **Children:** Kathleen, Allen, Michael.

Prize: *Commentary,* 1979: *New York Times,* "Observer," New York: New York Times, 1978. *Biography or Autobiography,* 1983: *Growing Up,* New York: Signet, 1982.

Career: Served in U.S. Navy, 1943-45; Police Reporter, *Baltimore (MD) Sun* 1947-49; Rewriteman, *Baltimore (MD) Sun;* London Bureau Chief, *Baltimore (MD) Sun,* 1952; White House Correspondent, *Baltimore (MD) Sun,* 1954; Washington Bureau Staff, *New York Times,* 1954-62; Columnist, *New York Times,* 1962-; Host, PBS *Masterpiece Theater,* 1993-.

Selected Works: *An American in Washington,* 1961. *No Cause for Panic,* 1964. *Baker's Dozen,* 1964. *All Things Considered,* 1965. *Our Next President,* 1968. *Poor Russell's Almanac,* 1972. *Better Times* (with John Albright), 1975. *The Upside Down Man* (with Gahan Wilson), 1977. *So This Is Depravity,* 1980. *Growing Up,* 1982. *The Rescue of Miss Yaskell and Other Pipe Dreams,* 1983. *Inventing the Truth: The Art and Craft of Memoir* (with William Zinsser), 1987. *The Good Times,* 1989. *There's a Country in the Cellar,* 1990. *Russell Baker's Book of American Humor,* 1993.

Other Awards: Fellow, American Academy of Arts and Sciences. Frank Sullivan Memorial Award, 1976. George Polk Memorial Award, Long Island University, NY, 1979. Elmer Holmes Bobst Prize, 1983: *Growing Up.* American Academy and Institute of Arts and Letters, 1984. Howland Memorial Prize,

1989. Fourth Estate Award, 1989. National Press Club Award, 1989. Honorary Degrees: Hamilton College, NY; Princeton University, NJ; John Hopkins University, MD; Franklin Pierce College, NH; Hood College, MD; Columbia University, NY; Yale University, CT; Long Island University, NY; Connecticut College; Union College, NY; Wake Forest University, NC; University of Miami, FL; Rutgers University, NJ.

For More Information: *Esquire,* 85 (April 1976): 22+; *Current Biography Yearbook, 1980,* New York: H.W. Wilson Company, 1980: 4-7; Grauer, Neil A., *Wits and Sages,* Baltimore, MD: Johns Hopkins University Press, 1984: 37-53; *Contemporary Authors, New Revision Series, Volume 11,* Detroit: Gale Research Company, 1984 Taft, William H., *Encyclopedia of Twentieth-Century Journalists,* New York: Garland Publishing Incorporated, 1986.

Commentary: Russell Baker won his first Pulitzer Prize for his column "Observer." He began the column in 1962. In it he employed humor and satire to make observations on life in America.

He won a second award for his autobiography, *Growing Up,* in which he wrote of his youth and young adulthood. It is also a chronicle of America's recent past. He wrote a second book, *The Good Times,* which continued his memoirs into his journalistic career.

1984

Louis R. Harlan   76

Birth: July 13, 1922; West Point, MS. **Parents:** Allen Dorset and Isabel (Knoffl) Harlan. **Education:** Emory University, GA: BA. Vanderbilt University, TN: MA. Johns Hopkins University, MD: PhD. **Spouse:** Sadie Morton (m.1947). **Children:** Louis Knoffl, Benjamin Wailes.

Prize: *Biography or Autobiography,* 1984: *Booker T. Washington,* New York: Oxford University, 1983.

Career: Lieutenant, U.S. Navy, 1943-1946; Instructor, East Texas State University, Commerce, 1950-1959; Associate Professor of History, East Texas State University, Commerce, 1955-1959; Associate Professor and Professor of History, University of Cincinnati, OH, 1959-1965; Professor of History, University of Maryland, College Park, 1966-1984; Member, Executive Council, Association for the Study of Negro Life and History, 1968-1975; University Distinguished Professor, University of Maryland, 1985-1992; President, American Historical Association, 1988; President, Organization of American Historians, 1989; Professor Emeritus, University of Maryland, 1992-; Fellow, Society of American Historians; Member: American Association of University

Professors, American Civil Liberties Union, Phi Beta Kappa, Phi Kappa Phi.

Selected Works: *The Booker T. Washington Papers* (Harlan, Louis R., ed.), 1972. *Separate and Unequal: Public School Campaigns and Racism in the Southern Seaboard States, 1901-1915,* 1958. *The Negro in American History,* 1965. *Booker T. Washington: The Making of a Black Leader, 1856-1901,* 1972. *Booker T. Washington and the "Atlanta Compromise,"* 1987. *Booker T. Washington in Perspective: Essays of Louis R. Harlan* (Smock, Raymond W., ed.), 1988. *All at Sea: Coming of Age in World War II,* 1996.

Other Awards: American Philosophical Society Grants-in-Aid, Summers, 1961-1964. American Council of Learned Societies Fellowship, 1963. Academic Freedom Award, University of Cincinnati Chapter, American Association of University Professors, 1964. Bancroft Prize in American History, 1973: *Booker T. Washington: The Making of a Black Leader, 1856-1901,* New York: Oxford University Press, 1972. Guggenheim Fellowship, 1974. Bancroft Prize in American History, 1984: *Booker T. Washington: The Wizard of Tuskegee, 1901-1915,* New York: Oxford University Press, 1983. Beveridge Award, 1984: *Booker T. Washington: The Wizard of Tuskegee, 1901-1915,* Julian P. Boyd Award, Association for Documentary Editing, 1989. B.L.C. Wailes Award, Mississippi Historical Society.

For More Information: Turk, Richard W., "All at Sea: Coming of Age in World War II," *Journal of Military History,* April, 1997.

Commentary: *Booker T. Washington: The Wizard of Tuskegee, 1901-1915* won the 1984 Pulitzer Prize in Biography for Louis Rudolph Harlan. Booker Taliaferro Washington (1856-1915) was the last African-American leader who was born in slavery. He secured an education for himself and founded the Tuskegee Institute. He was the author of many books, including *The Story of the Negro.*

Harlan was born in West Point, Mississippi and educated at Emory, Vanderbilt, and Johns Hopkins universities. He has taught history at the University of Maryland, where he is professor emeritus. He served as president of both the American Historical Association and the Organization of American Historians. He edited and published the papers of Washington and authored *Booker T. Washington: The Making of a Black Leader, 1856-1901.*

1985

Kenneth Silverman   77

Birth: February 5, 1936; New York, NY. **Parents:** Gustave and Bessie Silverman. **Education:** Columbia

University, NY: BA, MA, PhD. **Spouse:** Sharon Medjuck (m. 1957; div. 1976). **Children:** Willa, Ethan.

Prize: *Biography or Autobiography,* 1985: *The Life and Times of Cotton Mather,* New York: Columbia University, 1984.

Career: Instructor of English, University of Wyoming, Laramie, 1958-1959; Instructor, Professor of English and Co-Director, Program in American Civilization, New York University, NY, beginning in 1964; Executive Council Member, Institute of Early American History and Culture; Chairman of Bicentennial Committee, Modern Language Association of America, 1973-1976; Honorary Member, Society of American Historians; Member: American Antiquarian Society, PEN American Center, Phi Beta Kappa.

Selected Works: *Timothy Dwight,* 1969. *Selected Letters of Cotton Mather* (Silverman, Kenneth, ed.), 1971. *A Cultural History of the American Revolution: Painting, Music, Literature, and the Theatre in the Colonies and the United States from the Treaty of Paris to the Inauguration of George Washington, 1763-1789,* 1976. *Autobiography and Other Writings, Benjamin Franklin* (Silverman, Kenneth, ed.), 1986. *Edgar A. Poe: Mournful and Never-Ending Remembrance,* 1991. *New Essays on Poe's Major Tales* (Silverman, Kenneth, ed.), 1993. *Houdini!: The Career of Ehrich Weiss: American Self-Liberator, Europe's Eclipsing Sensation, World's Handcuff King & Prison Breaker,* 1996.

Other Awards: Danforth Associate, 1968-1971. Bicentennial Grant from National Endowment for the Humanities, 1973-1976: *A Cultural History of the American Revolution,* New York: Crowell, 1976. Bancroft Prize, American History, 1985: *The Life and Times of Cotton Mather.*

For More Information: Lears, Jackson, "Now You See Him, Now You Don't: Houdini!!!," *New Republic,* February 17, 1997.

Commentary: Kenneth Silverman won the 1985 Pulitzer Prize in Biography for *The Life and Times of Cotton Mather,* about the American clergyman and author of over 400 books covering medicine, science, and theology.

Silverman was born in New York City and educated at Columbia University. Silverman specializes in colonial history and is a professor of English at New York University. He was chairman of the Bicentennial Commission of the Modern Language Association of America. His other works include *A Cultural History of the American Revolution* and *Edgar A. Poe: Mournful and Never-Ending Remembrance.*

1986

Elizabeth Frank   78

Birth: September 14, 1945; Los Angeles, CA. **Parents:** Melvin G. and Anne (Ray) Frank. **Education:** Bennington College, VT. University of California, Berkeley: BA, MA, PhD. **Spouse:** Howard Buchwald (m. 1984). **Children:** Anne Louise.

Prize: *Biography or Autobiography,* 1986: *Louise Bogan: A Portrait,* New York: Knopf, 1985.

Career: Instructor, Mills College, Temple University, Williams College, University of California, Irvine, Bard College; Freelance writer.

Selected Works: *Margot Fonteyn,* 1958. *Jackson Pollock,* 1983. *Esteban Vicente,* 1995.

For More Information: Breslin, James E.B., "Book Reviews: Louise Bogan," *American Literature,* March 1986; Delatiner, Barbara, "Days of Reckoning for 2 Important Artists," *New York Times,* January 28, 1996.

Commentary: Elizabeth Frank won the 1986 Pulitzer Prize in Biography for *Louise Bogan: A Portrait,* the life story of the 20th century poet and poetry reviewer for the *New Yorker.*

Frank was born in Los Angeles, California and grew up in Hollywood. Her father, Melvin Frank, was a director, producer, and screenwriter. She was educated at Bennington College and the University of California at Berkeley. Her other works include *Jackson Pollock* and *Eva Hesse Gouaches.*

1987

David J. Garrow   79

Birth: May 11, 1953; New Bedford, MA. **Parents:** Walter and Barbara (Fassett) Garrow. **Education:** Wesleyan University, CT: BA. Duke University, NC: MA, PhD.

Prize: *Biography or Autobiography,* 1987: *Bearing the Cross, Martin Luther King, Jr. and the Southern Christian Leadership Conference,* New York: Morrow, 1986.

Career: Instructor of Political Science, Duke University, NC, beginning in 1978; Visiting Member, School of Social Sciences, Institute for Advanced Study, Princeton, NJ, 1979-1980.

Selected Works: *The FBI and Martin Luther King, Jr.,* 1981. *The Montgomery Bus Boycott and the Women Who Started It: The Memoir of Jo Ann Gibson Robinson* (Garrow, David J., ed.), 1987. *St. Augustine, Florida, 1963-1964: Mass Protest and Racial Violence* (Garrow, David J., ed.), 1989. *Atlanta, Georgia, 1960-1961: Sit-Ins and Student Activism* (Garrow, David J., ed.), 1989. *Birmingham, Alabama, 1956-1963: The Black Struggle for Civil Rights* (Garrow,

David J., ed.), 1989. *We Shall Overcome: The Civil Rights Movement in the United States in the 1950s and 1960s* (Garrow, David J., ed.), 1989. *Martin Luther King, Jr.: Civil Rights Leader, Theologian, Orator* (Garrow, David J., ed.), 1989. *Chicago 1966: Open Housing Marches, Summit Negotiations, and Operation Breadbasket,* 1989. *Liberty and Sexuality: The Right to Privacy and the Making of Roe v. Wade,* 1994.

For More Information: Devins, Neal, "Garrow: Liberty And Sexuality: The Right to Privacy and the Making of Roe v. Wade," *Michigan Law Review,* May 1, 1995; Glenn, Gwendolyn, "Bringing King to the Classroom," *Black Issues in Higher Education,* June 27, 1996.

Commentary: *Bearing the Cross: Martin Luther King, Jr. and the Southern Christian Leadership Conference* won the 1987 Pulitzer Prize in Biography for David J. Garrow. As a result of extensive research through interviews and archives and the use of FBI documents, Garrow provides exacting detail on Dr. King's activities.

Garrow was born in New Bedford, Massachusetts and he was educated at Wesleyan and Duke universities. He has taught history at the University of North Carolina at Chapel Hill and at City College of the City University of New York. He is a board member of the Martin Luther King Jr. Papers Project. He is currently the Presidential Distinguished Professor at Emory University.

1988

David Herbert Donald

Full entry appears as #55 under "Biography or Autobiography," 1961.

1989

Richard Ellmann   80
Birth: March 15, 1918; Highland Park, MI. **Death:** May 13, 1987. **Parents:** James I. and Jeanette (Barsook) Ellmann. **Education:** Yale University, CT: BA, MA, PhD. Trinity College, Ireland: BLitt. Oxford University, England: MA. **Spouse:** Mary Donohue (m. 1949). **Children:** Stephan, Maud, Lucy.

Prize: *Biography or Autobiography,* 1989: *Oscar Wilde,* New York: Knopf, 1988.

Career: Instructor, Harvard University, MA, 1942-1943; Served in U.S. Navy and Office of Strategic Services (OSS), 1943-1946; Instructor, Harvard University, MA, 1947-1948; Briggs-Copeland Assistant Professor of English Composition, Harvard University, MA, 1948-1951; Professor of English, Northwestern University, IL, 1951-1963; School of Letters Fellow, Indiana University, 1956, 1960;

Frederick Ives Carpenter Visiting Professor, University of Chicago, 1959, 1967, and 1975-1977; Chairman of English Institute, Modern Language Association of America, 1961-1962; Member of Executive Council, Modern Language Association of America, 1961-1965; Franklin Bliss Snyder Professor, Northwestern University, IL, 1963-1968; Senior Fellow, Indiana University, 1966-1972; Professor of English, Yale University, CT, 1968-1970; Goldsmiths' Professor of English Literature, Oxford University, England, 1970-1984; Fellow, New College, Oxford University, England, 1970-1984; Member, U.S. / U.K. Educational Commission, 1970-1985; Visiting Professor, Emory University, GA, 1978-1981; Woodruff Professor of English, Emory University, 1982-1987; Consultant, "The World of James Joyce," PBS, 1983; Honorary Fellow, Oxford University, England, 1984-1987; Extraordinary Fellow, Wolfson College, Oxford University, England, 1984-1987; Fellow, American Academy and Institute of Arts and Letters; Fellow, British Academy; Fellow, Royal Society of Literature; Member: Athenaeum, Chi Delta Theta, Elizabethan Club, Phi Beta Kappa, Signet.

Selected Works: *James Joyce,* 1959. *Critical Writings* (Ellmann, Richard, and Mason, Ellsworth, eds.), 1959. *Joyce in Love,* 1959. *Joyce,* 1959. *The Identity of Yeats,* 1964. *The Modern Tradition: Backgrounds of Modern Literature* (Ellmann, Richard, and Feidelson, Charles, Jr., eds.), 1965. *Eminent Domain: Yeats among Wilde, Joyce, Pound, Eliot and Auden,* 1967. *The Artist as Critic: Critical Writings of Oscar Wilde* (Ellmann, Richard, ed.), 1969. *Oscar Wilde: A Collection of Critical Essays,* 1969. *Literary Biography (An Inaugural Lecture Delivered before the University of Oxford on 4 May 1971),* 1971. *Ulysses on the Liffey,* 1972. *Golden Codgers: Biographical Speculations,* 1973. *The New Oxford Book of American Verse* (Ellmann, Richard, ed.), 1976. *The Consciousness of Joyce,* 1977. *James Joyce,* 1982. *Along the Riverrun: Selected Essays,* 1988. *The Norton Anthology of Modern Poetry* (Ellmann, Richard, and O'Clair, Robert, eds.), 1988.

Other Awards: Rockefeller Foundation Fellow in Humanities, 1946-1947. Guggenheim Fellow, 1950, 1957-1958, 1970. American Philosophical Society Grant, 1953. Modern Language Association of America Grant, 1953. *Kenyon Review*: Fellowship in Criticism, 1955-1956. National Book Award for Nonfiction, 1960: *James Joyce,* New York: Oxford University Press, 1959. Friends of Literature Award in Biography, 1960: *James Joyce,* Thormond Monson Award, Society of Midland Authors, 1960: *James Joyce.* George Polk Memorial Award, 1970: *The Artist as Critic: Critical Writings of Oscar Wilde,* New York: Random House, 1969. National Endowment for the Humanities Research Grant, 1977. Duff Cooper

Prize, 1982: *James Joyce.* James Tair Black Prize, New and Revised Edition, 1982: *James Joyce.* National Book Critics Circle Award, Best Biography / Autobiography, 1989: *Oscar Wilde,* Englewood Cliffs, NJ: Prentice Hall, 1969. Honorary DLitts: National University of Ireland, 1975; Emory University, GA, 1979; Northwestern University, IL, 1980; McGill University, Canada, 1986. Honorary PhD, University of Gothenburg, Sweden, 1978. Honorary DHLs: Boston College, MA, 1979; University of Rochester, NY, 1979.

For More Information: *Essays for Richard Ellmann: Omnium Gatherum,* Kingston, Ontario, Canada: McGill-Queen's University, 1989.

Commentary: Richard Ellmann was awarded the 1989 Pulitzer Prize in Biography posthumously for *Oscar Wilde.* Written about the Irish poet and dramatist best known for his plays, including *The Importance of Being Earnest,* and for his extravagant lifestyle, Ellman's work was 20 years in the making.

Ellmann was born in Highland Park, Michigan. He was educated at Yale University and at Trinity College in Ireland and Oxford University in England. He was a distinguished critic and biographer. He won the National Book Award in 1960 for his biography of *James Joyce.* Ellmann was editor of the *Norton Anthology of Modern Poetry* and *The New Oxford Book of American Verse.* His other works included *Four Dubliners* and *Yeats, the Man and the Masks.*

1990

Sebastian De Grazia   81

Birth: August 11, 1917; Chicago, IL. **Parents:** Alfred Joseph and Catherine Cardinale (Lupo) de Grazia. **Education:** University of Chicago, IL: AB, PhD. **Spouse:** Miriam Lund Carlson; Anna Maria D'Annunzio di Montenevoso; Lucia Peavey Heffelfinge. **Children:** Alfred Joseph III, Margreta, Sebastian Jr. (MLC); Marco, Tancredi (ADM).

Prize: *Biography or Autobiography,* 1990: *Machiavelli in Hell,* Princeton, NJ: Princeton University, 1989.

Career: Research Staff, Federal Communications Commission, Washington, DC, 1941-1943; Staff member, Office of Strategic Services (OSS), 1943-1945; Assistant Professor of Political Science, University of Chicago, 1945-1950; Consultant to businesses, state and federal governments, beginning in 1947; Visiting Research Professor, University of Florence, Italy, 1950-1952; Visiting Professor, University of Florence, 1950-1952; Senior Research Scientist, George Washington University, Washington, DC, 1952-1955; Visiting Professor, Princeton University, NJ, 1957; Director of Research, Twentieth Century Fund, NY, 1957-1962; Professor of Political

Philosophy at Eagleton Institute, Rutgers University, NJ, 1962-1985; Visiting Professor, University of Madrid, Spain, 1963; Visiting Professor, John Jay College of Criminal Justice of the City University of New York, 1967-1973; Visiting Professor, Institute for Advanced Study, Princeton, NJ, 1982-1983; Visiting Professor, Princeton University, NJ, 1991-1992; Member: American Political Science Association, American Society for Political and Legal Philosophy, Century Club, Cosmos Club, Association Internationale de Science Politique, Institut International de Philosophie Politique, Nassau Club, Prettybook Club, Quadrangle Club.

Selected Works: *The Political Community: A Study of Anomie,* 1948. *Errors of Psychotherapy,* 1952. *Of Time, Work, and Leisure,* 1962. *Time and the Machine,* 1963. *Masters of Chinese Political Thought: From the Beginnings to the Han Dynasty,* 1973. *A Country with No Name: Tales from the Constitution,* 1997.

Other Awards: American Philosophical Society Research Grant. Social Science Research Council Grant. American Council of Learned Societies.

For More Information: Rubinstein, Nicolai, "New, Radical — And Moral: Machiavelli in Hell," *TLS, Times Literary Supplement,* January 19, 1990; Baker-Smith, Dominic, "Ends and Means: Machiavelli in Hell," *History Today,* July 1990.

Commentary: Sebastian De Grazia won the 1990 Pulitzer Prize in Biography for *Machiavelli in Hell,* about the Florentine Renaissance statesman and author of *On the Art of War,* a work which formed the foundations of modern military tactics.

De Grazia was born in Chicago. He was educated at the University of Chicago where he was an assistant professor of political science after World War II. During the war, he was a staff member of the Office of Strategic Services (OSS). He taught political philosophy at Rutgers University for many years. His other works include *Of Time, Work and Leisure* and *Masters in Chinese Political Thought.*

1991

Steven Woodward Naifeh   82

Birth: June 19, 1952; Tehran, Iran. **Parents:** George Amel and Marion (Lamphear) Naifeh. **Education:** Princeton University, NJ: AB, summa cum laude. Harvard University, MA: JD, MA.

Prize: *Biography or Autobiography,* 1991: *Jackson Pollock, Making Miracles Happen, an American Saga,* New York: Potter, 1989.

Career: Artist, Lecturer; Lieutenant, U.S. Marine Corps, Vietnam, 1968; Summer Staff Lecturer, National Gallery of Art, Washington, DC, 1976; Summer Associate, Milbank, Tweed, Hadley & McCloy, NY,

1976; Vice President, Sabbagh, Naifeh & Associates, Washington, DC, beginning in 1980; Chairman and CEO, Woodward/White, Incorporated, 1985-present; Member, Phi Beta Kappa.

Selected Works: *Culture Making: Money, Success, and the New York Art World,* 1976. *How to Make Love to a Woman* (with Michael Morgenstern and Gregory White Smith), 1982. *Gene Davis,* 1982. *Why Can't Men Open Up? Overcoming Men's Fear of Intimacy,* 1984. *The Mormon Murders: A True Story of Greed, Forgery, Deceit, and Death,* 1988. *The Best Lawyers in America: Directory of Experts,* 1992-Present. *The Best Doctors in America,* 1992. *Final Justice: The True Story of the Richest Man Ever Tried for Murder,* 1993. *A Stranger in the Family: A True Story of Murder, Madness, and Unconditional Love,* 1995. *On a Street Called Easy, In a Cottage Called Joye,* 1996.

For More Information: "Pages," *People,* September 30, 1996; "PW Interview," *Publishers Weekly,* August 25, 1997 V. 244 No. 35, p. 40.

Commentary: Stephen Woodward Naifeh and Gregory White Smith won the 1991 Pulitzer Prize in Biography for *Jackson Pollock: Making Miracles Happen, an American Saga.* Pollock (1912-1956) was an abstract painter of huge canvases who was the first advocate of "action painting."

Steven Woodward Naifeh was born in Tehran, Iran. He was educated at Colby College and at Harvard University. He is an artist as well as a writer, and has exhibited in solo shows in the United States, United Arab Emirates, Nigeria, and Pakistan, and has lectured in art. He was vice president of Sabbagh, Naifeh, and Associates in Washington, DC and is currently the Chairman and CEO of Woodward / White, a company that markets and publishes professional and trade books, and is the publisher of the *Best Doctors in America* series. His other works, coauthored with Smith, include *What Every Client Needs to Know About Using a Lawyer* and *Best Lawyers in America.*

Gregory White Smith   83

Birth: October 4, 1951; Ithaca, NY. **Parents:** William R. and Kathryn (White) Smith. **Education:** Colby College, ME: AB. Harvard University, MA: JD, MEd.

Prize: *Biography or Autobiography,* 1991: *Jackson Pollock: Making Miracles Happen, an American Saga,* New York: Potter, 1989.

Career: Author; Attorney, Morrison & Foerster, San Francisco, CA, 1976; Assistant Instructor, Harvard Law School and Harvard Graduate School of Education, 1976-1978; Attorney, private legal practice, 1978-1978; Senior Editor, Free Press, division of Macmillan Publishing Company, 1979-1981; Associate Producer, Adrian Malone Productions, Incorpo-

rated, for PBS, 1981-1982; President, Woodward / White, Incorporated, SC, 1981; Scriptwriter, Multimedia Entertainment,NBC, 1985-1986; Vice President, Best Doctors, Incorporated, SC, 1985; Adjunct Professor, University of South Carolina; Chairman, Aiken Historical Commission; Member: American Bar Association, Massachusetts Bar Association, Boston Bar Association, Author's Guild, Board of Overseers, Colby College, ME, Board of Trustees, The Columbus Academy.

Selected Works: *How to Make Love to a Woman* (with Michael Morgenstern and Stephen Woodward Naifeh), 1982. *Gene Davis,* 1982. *Why Can't Men Open Up? Overcoming Men's Fear of Intimacy,* 1984. *The Mormon Murders: A True Story of Greed, Forgery, Deceit, and Death,* 1988. *The Best Lawyers in America: Directory of Experts,* 1992. *The Best Doctors in America,* 1992. *Final Justice: The True Story of the Richest Man Ever Tried for Murder,* 1993. *A Stranger in the Family: A True Story of Murder, Madness, and Unconditional Love,* 1995. *On a Street Called Easy, in a Cottage Called Joye,* 1996.

For More Information: "Pages," *People,* September 30, 1996; "PW Interview," *Publishers Weekly,* August 25, 1997 V. 244 n 35, p. 40.

Commentary: Stephen Woodward Naifeh and Gregory White Smith won the 1991 Pulitzer Prize in Biography for *Jackson Pollock: Making Miracles Happen, an American Saga.* Pollock (1912-1956) was an abstract painter of huge canvases who was the first advocate of "action painting."

Smith was born in Ithaca, New York. He was educated at Princeton University, where he graduated summa cum laude, and at Harvard University. He is the president of Woodward / White, a company that markets and publishes professional and trade books, and is the publisher of the *Best Doctors in America* series. His other works, co-authored with Naifeh, include *What Every Client Needs to Know About Using a Lawyer* and *Best Lawyers in America.*

1992

Lewis B. Puller Jr.   84

Birth: 1945; Camp Lejeune, NC. **Death:** 1994. **Parents:** Lewis B. Puller. **Education:** College of William and Mary, VA: BA, Law Degree. **Spouse:** Linda Ford Todd (m. 1968). **Children:** Lewis III, Maggie.

Prize: *Biography or Autobiography,* 1992: *Fortunate Son: The Healing of a Vietnam Vet,* New York: Grove Weidenfeld, 1991.

Career: Affiliated with Veteran's Administration, 1974; Member of President Gerald Ford's Clemency Board during 1970s; Service Director, Paralyzed Veterans of America; Democratic congressional candidate, 1978; U.S. Department of Defense, Washington, DC, Senior Attorney in Office of General Council, 1980-1994.

Other Awards: Silver Star, World War II. Two Purple Hearts, World War II.

For More Information: "Tribute," *People,* May 30, 1994; Kerrey, Bob, "For Lew," *New Republic,* June 6, 1994.

Commentary: *Fortunate Son: The Healing of a Vietnam Vet* won the 1992 Pulitzer Prize in Biography for Lewis B. Puller Jr. This is the chronicle of a Vietnam veteran's experience going into and coming out of the war. Puller stepped on a booby trap during routine rounds in Vietnam. This cost him both legs and resulted in massive internal injuries. His autobiography is devastating in its reality.

Puller was born in Camp Lejeune, North Carolina, the "fortunate son" of "Chesty" Puller, a World War II hero and Marine who embodied strength, determination, and courage. Puller made an unsuccessful bid for Congress in 1978. He worked as the Senior Attorney for the Department of Defense's Office of General Counsel until he committed suicide in 1994, leaving behind a widow and two children.

1993

David McCullough 85

Birth: July 7, 1933; Pittsburgh, PA. **Parents:** Christian Hox and Ruth (Rankin) McCullough. **Education:** Yale University, CT: BA. **Spouse:** Rosalee Ingram Barnes (m. 1954). **Children:** Melissa, David Jr., William Barnes, Geoffrey Barnes, Doreen Kane.

Prize: *Biography or Autobiography,* 1993: *Truman,* New York: Simon & Schuster, 1992.

Career: Writer and Editor, *Time,* NY, 1956-1961; Writer and Editor, U.S. Information Agency, Washington, DC, 1961-1964; Writer and Editor, American Heritage Publishing, NY, 1964-1970; Freelance writer, beginning in 1970; Member, Bennington College Writers Workshop, 1978-1979; Scholar-in-Residence, University of New Mexico, 1979; Scholar-in-Residence, Wesleyan University Writers Conference, 1982-1983; Host, *Smithsonian World* television series, PBS, 1984-1988; Host, *The American Experience* televison series, PBS, beginning in 1988; Newman Visiting Professor of American Civilization, Cornell University, 1989; Documentary Narrator; President, Society of American Historians, beginning in 1991; Honorary Member, American Society of Civil Engineers; Member, Advisory Board, Center for the Book, Library of Congress; Member, Harry S. Truman Centennial Commission; Trustee, Shady Side Academy, Pittsburgh, PA.

Selected Works: *The American Heritage Picture History of World War II,* by C. L. Sulzberger and the Editors of American Heritage (McCullough, David,

ed.), 1966. *The Johnstown Flood,* 1968. *The Great Bridge,* 1972. *The Path between the Seas: The Creation of the Panama Canal, 1870-1914,* 1977. *Mornings on Horseback,* 1981. *Brave Companions: Portraits in History,* 1992.

Other Awards: Special Citation for Excellence, Society of American Historians, 1973. Diamond Jubilee Medal for Excellence, City of New York, 1973. Certificate of Merit, Municipal Art Society of New York, 1974: *The Great Bridge,* New York: Simon and Schuster, 1972. National Book Award for History, 1978: *The Path between the Seas: The Creation of the Panama Canal, 1870-1914,* New York: Simon and Schuster, 1977. Francis Parkman Award, Society of American Historians. Samuel Eliot Morison Award, 1978: *The Path between the Seas: The Creation of the Panama Canal, 1870-1914.* Cornelius Ryan Award, 1978: *The Path between the Seas: The Creation of the Panama Canal, 1870-1914.* Civil Engineering History and Heritage Award, 1978. *Los Angeles Times* Award for Biography, 1981. American Book Award for Biography, 1982: *Mornings on Horseback,* New York: Simon and Schuster, 1981. Emmy Award, 1987. Interview with Anne Morrow Lindbergh on Smithsonian World. Guggenheim Fellowship, 1987. Harry S. Truman Public Service Award, 1993. St. Louis Literary Award, 1993. Honorary HLD, Rensselaer Polytechnic Institute, NY, 1983. Honorary DEng, Villanova University, PA, 1984. Honorary LittDs: Allegheny College, PA, 1984; Middlebury College, VT, 1986. Honorary LHD, Wesleyan University, CT, 1984.

For More Information: "David McCullough, Public Historian," *U.S. News & World Report,* June 22, 1992; "'The Old Water Pull': An Interview with David McCullough," *Naval History,* January 1, 1994.

Commentary: David McCullough was awarded the 1993 Pulitzer Prize in Biography for *Truman,* about the 33rd president of the United States.

McCullough was born in Pittsburgh, Pennsylvania and educated at Yale University. McCullough has hosted the Public Television series *Smithsonian World* and *The American Experience.* He has been president of the American Society of Historians. His other works include *The Great Bridge,* the story of the building of the Brooklyn Bridge, and *The Path between the Seas,* about the building of the Panama Canal. McCullough is an honorary member of the American Society of Civil Engineers. He is also the author of *Mornings on Horseback,* a biography of the young Theodore Roosevelt.

1994

David Levering Lewis   86

Birth: May 25, 1936; Little Rock, AR. **Parents:** John H. and Urnestine (Bell) Lewis. **Education:** Fisk University, TN: BA. Columbia University, NY: MA. London School of Economics, England: PhD. **Spouse:** Sharon Siskino (m. 1956; div. 1988); Ruth Ann Stewart (m. 1994). **Children:** Eric Levering, Allison Lillian, Jason Bradwell (SS); Allegra (RAS).

Prize: *Biography or Autobiography,* 1994: *W.E.B. Du Bois: Biography of a Race 1868-1919,* New York: Holt, 1993.

Career: Served in Medical Corps, Army, 1961-1963; Lecturer of Modern French History, University of Ghana, Accra, 1963-1964; Lecturer of Modern French History, Howard University, Washington, DC, 1964-1965; Assistant Professor of Modern French History, University of Notre Dame, IN, 1965-1966; Associate Professor of Modern French History, Morgan State College, MD, 1966-1970; Associate Professor of Modern French History, Federal City College, Washington, DC, 1970-1974; Professor of History, University of the District of Columbia, Washington, DC, 1974-1980; Professor of History, University of California at San Diego, La Jolla, 1981-1985; Martin Luther King Jr. Professor of History, Rutgers University, New Brunswick, NJ, beginning in 1985; Member: African Studies Association, American Historical Association, American Association of University Professors, Authors Guild, Phi Beta Kappa, Organization of American Historians, Society for French Historical Studies, Southern Historical Association.

Selected Works: *King: A Critical Biography,* 1970. *Prisoners of Honor: The Dreyfus Affair,* 1973. *District of Columbia: A Bicentennial History,* 1976. *King: A Biography,* 1978. *When Harlem Was in Vogue,* 1981. *The Civil Rights Movement in America: Essays* (Eagles, Charles W., ed.), 1986. *The Race to Fashoda: European Colonialism and African Resistance in the Scramble for Africa,* 1987. *The Portable Harlem Renaissance Reader* (Lewis, David Levering, ed.), 1994. *W.E.B. Du Bois: A Reader,* 1995.

Other Awards: Grants from American Philosophical Society, 1967. Social Science Research Council, 1971. National Endowment for the Humanities, 1975. Woodrow Wilson International Center for Scholars Fellow, 1977-1978. Bancroft Prize, Columbia University, 1994. Francis Parkman Prize, Society of American Historians, 1994: *W. E. B. Du Bois: Biography of a Race, 1868-1919.*

For More Information: Appiah, K. Anthony, "A Black Man's Burden," *Boston Globe,* November 7, 1993; Gonzales, Prizgar, "Lewis Explains Du Bois's Vision," *Chicago Defender,* February 5, 1994; "Four Blacks Win Pulitzer, Record High Say Officials," *Jet,* May 2, 1994.

Commentary: David Levering Lewis won the 1994 Pulitzer Prize in Biography for *W.E.B. Du Bois: Biography of a Race 1868-1919,* about the African American editor, historian, sociologist, and civil rights activist who helped found the National Association for the Advancement of Colored People (NAACP).

Lewis was born in Little Rock, Arkansas. He was educated at Fisk and Columbia Universities. He has lectured on modern French history at the University of Ghana, taught history at the University of California at San Diego, and is currently the Martin Luther King Jr. Professor of History at Rutgers University. He has received numerous grants and fellowships to advance his studies and writings. His other works include *The Race to Fashoda: European Colonialism and African Resistance in the Scramble for Africa, Black Reconstruction in America: 1860-1880,* and *When Harlem Was in Vogue.*

1995

Joan D. Hedrick   87

Birth: May 1, 1944; Baltimore, MD. **Parents:** Paul Thomas and Jane (Connorton) Doran. **Education:** Vassar College, NY: AB. Brown University, RI: PhD. **Spouse:** Travis D. Hedrick (m. 1967). **Children:** Jessica, Rachel.

Prize: *Biography or Autobiography,* 1995: *Harriet Beecher Stowe: A Life,* New York: Oxford University Press, 1994.

Career: Instructor, Wesleyan University, CT, 1972-1974; Assistant Professor of English, Wesleyan University, CT, 1974-1980; Visiting Assistant Professor, Trinity College, CT, 1980-1981; Visiting Associate Professor, History and American Studies, Trinity College, CT, 1981; Associate Professor of History and Director of Women's Studies, Trinity College, CT, Present; Member: American Studies Association, Modern Language Association of America.

Selected Works: *Solitary Comrade, Jack London and His Work,* 1982.

For More Information: Arkin, Marc M., "Joan D. Hedrick, Harriet Beecher Stowe: A Life," *New Criterion,* March 1, 1994.

Commentary: Joan Doran Hedrick was awarded the 1995 Pulitzer Prize in Biography for *Harriet Beecher Stowe,* the story of the abolitionist who wrote *Uncle Tom's Cabin,* a vivid depiction of slavery which was a force in bringing about the American Civil War.

Hedrick was born in Baltimore, Maryland. She was educated at Vassar College and Brown University. She is currently the director of women's studies and a professor of history at Trinity College in Hartford, Connecticut. She has also written *Solitary Comrade: Jack London and His Work.*

1996

Jack Miles   88

Birth: July 30, 1942; Chicago, IL. **Religion:** Roman Catholic. **Education:** Pontifical Gregorian College, Italy. Hebrew University, Israel. Harvard University, MA: PhD. **Spouse:** Married. **Children:** One daughter.

Prize: *Biography or Autobiography,* 1996: *God: A Biography,* New York: Alfred A. Knopf, 1995.

Career: Instructor, Loyola University of Chicago and the University of Montana, early 1970s; Executive Editor, University of California Press; Editor, Doubleday & Company, NY; Assistant Director, Scholars Press; Book Editor, Editorial Board Member, and Director, Times Book Prize Program, *Los Angeles Times,* CA, 1985-1995; Director, Graduate Humanities Center, Claremont Graduate School, CA; Contributor, magazines, 1995.

For More Information: Feeney, Mark, "Looking at the Lord as a Literary Character," *Boston Globe,* April 16, 1995; Lanham, Fritz, "He Wrote the Book on God," *Houston Chronicle,* April 21, 1996.

Commentary: Jack Miles won the 1996 Pulitzer Prize in Biography for *God: A Biography,* a portrait of the higher being taken from biblical descriptions that seem to be conflicting.

Miles was born in Chicago and was educated at the Pontifical Gregorian College in Italy where he became a Jesuit, at Harvard University, where he studied Near East languages, and at Hebrew University in Jerusalem. (He later left the Jesuits.) He has been an editor for Doubleday and the University of California at Berkeley Press and was book editor for the *Los Angeles Times.* He is currently the director of the Graduate Humanities Center at Claremont Graduate School. He is also a freelance writer for such publications as the *Atlantic Monthly, Harvard Theological Review, Washington Post,* and *Boston Globe.*

1997

Frank McCourt   89

Birth: August 19, 1930; Brooklyn, NY. **Parents:** Malachy and Angela (Sheehan) McCourt. **Education:** New York University.

Prize: *Biography or Autobiography,* 1997: *Angela's Ashes: A Memoir,* New York: Scribners, 1996.

Career: Writing Teacher, Stuyvesant High School, NY, 1985 to Present.

Other Awards: Anne Rea Jewell Non-Fiction Prize, 1996: *Angela's Ashes,* New York: Scribners, 1995. *Los Angeles Times* Book Award, 1996: *Angela's Ashes.* Salon Book Award, 1996: *Angela's Ashes,* Top Nonfiction Book, *Time Magazine,* 1996: *Angela's Ashes.* Book of the Year, *The Orange County Register,* 1996: *Angela's Ashes.* Favorite Book, FanFare, *Newsday,* 1996: *Angela's Ashes.* Best Nonfiction Book, *Detroit Free Press,* 1996: *Angela's Ashes.* Best Book, *Milwaukee Journal Sentinel,* 1996: *Angela's Ashes.*

For More Information: *Current Biography,* New York: Wilson, February 1998; Walter Goodman, "Memories, Most Bitter, Of a Lane In Limerick," Review, *New York Times,* March 16, 1998.

Commentary: Frank McCourt won the 1997 Pulitzer Prize in Biography for *Angela's Ashes,* the true tale supporting McCourt's statement that "worse than the ordinary miserable childhood is the miserable Irish childhood, and worse yet is the miserable Irish Catholic childhood."

McCourt was born in Brooklyn, New York. Hard times forced his parents to leave the United States and return to Ireland when he was still a small boy. These early years made an indelible impression on McCourt and are the basis for his book. McCourt was a literature teacher at Stuyvesant High School in Manhattan, New York. *Angela's Ashes* has been at the top of bestseller lists and is already in its 23rd printing.

1998

Katharine Graham   90

Birth: June 16, 1917; New York, NY. **Parents:** Eugene and Agnes (Ernst) Meyer. **Education:** Vassar College, NY. University of Chicago, IL: BA. **Spouse:** Philip L. Graham (m. 1940). **Children:** Elizabeth Morris Graham Weymouth, Donald Edward, William Welsh, Stephen Meyer.

Prize: *Biography or Autobiography,* 1998: *Personal History,* New York: Knopf, 1996.

Career: Reporter, *San Francisco News,* CA, 1938-1939; Member, Editorial Staff, *Washington Post,* 1939-1945; President, *Washington Post* Company, 1963-1973, 1977; Member, Sunday Circulation and Editorial Departments, 1969-1979; Chairman, *Washington Post* Company, 1973-1993; CEO, *Washington Post* Company, 1973-1991; Chairman, Executive Committee, *Washington Post* Company, 1993-present; Co-Chairman, *International Herald Tribune*; Trustee, Reuters Founders Share Company Limited; Vice-Chair, Board of Directors, Urban Institute; Member, Council on Foreign Relations; Member, Overseas Development Council; Past Chair, New York Publishers Association; Life Trustee, University of Chicago; Honorary Trustee, George Washington

University, DC; Member, Collection Conservation Committee, National Gallery of Art; Active, District of Columbia Committee for Public Education; Fellow, American Academy of Arts and Sciences; Past President and Member, American Society of Newspaper Editors; Member: National Press Club, Council on Foreign Relations, Overseas Development Council, National Campaign to Reduce Teenage Pregnancy, Metropolitan Club, Cosmo Club.

Other Awards: Fellow, National Academy of Arts and Sciences.

For More Information: Jennings, Charles and Lisa Jennings, "Dynasties: A History of Power and Heritage in Local Families," *Washington Business Journal,* December 9, 1985; Felsenthal, Carol, *Power, Privilege, and the Post: The Katharine Graham Story,* New York: Putnam's, 1993; Field, David, "Katharine Graham Steps Down at Post," *Washington Times,* September 10, 1993; Taylor, Martin, Jurek, "Self-Por-trait of a Lady: Woman in the News, Katharine Graham," *Financial Times,* February 1, 1997.

Commentary: The 1998 Pulitzer Prize in Autobiography was awarded to *Personal History,* written by Katharine M. Graham. It is a full account of Mrs. Graham's life and how she found herself at the helm of the *Washington Post.*

Katharine Meyer Graham was born in New York City, the daughter of Eugene Meyer, the owner of the *Washington Post.* She married Philip Graham, who took over the helm of the newspaper from her father. After her husband committed suicide in 1963, Katharine surprised herself and others by assuming the role of managing this national newspaper. She grew into this role quite successfully, proving her abilities especially through labor disputes and the Watergate era. Though she is no longer the manager, she is still active in the affairs of the *Washington Post.*

Breaking News Reporting

1998

Los Angeles Times 91

Founded: 1881; Los Angeles, CA. **Founder(s):** Harrison Gray Otis.

Prize: *Meritorious Public Service*, 1942. *Meritorious Public Service*, 1960. *Local General Spot News Reporting*, 1966. *Meritorious Public Service*, 1969. *Meritorious Public Service*, 1984. *Spot News Reporting*, 1993. *Spot News Reporting*, 1995. *Breaking News Reporting*, 1998.

Selected Works: *America's First Newspaper in the Nation's Second Market, Los Angeles Times Presents Los Angeles: The Market, Its Newspaper, 1958. Images of Our Times: Sixty Years of Photography from the Los Angeles Times, 1987.*

Other Awards: The *Los Angeles Times*'s staff, editors, and reporters have won 24 Pulitzer Prizes, in addition to other journalism and public service awards.

For More Information: Ainsworth, Ed, *Recording the Exciting Growth and Experience of the Los Angeles Times,* Los Angeles: 1949; Bonelli, William G., *Billion Dollar Blackjack,* Beverly Hills, CA: Civic Research Press, 1954; Hart, Jack R., *The Information Empire: The Rise of the Los Angeles Times and the Times Mirror Corporation,* Washington, DC: University Press of America, 1981; Berges, Marshall, *The Life and Times of Los Angeles: A Newspaper, A Family, and a City,* New York: Atheneum, 1984; Contact the Offices of the California Newspaper Project, University of California, Berkeley, telephone: (510) 643-7680.

Commentary: The Los Angeles Times has won four Meritorious Public Service awards. The first award came in 1942 for its successful campaign which resulted in the clarification and confirmation for all American newspapers of the free press as guaranteed under the Constitution. The second prize awarded was in 1960 for its thorough, sustained, and well-conceived attack on narcotics traffic and the enterprising reporting of Gene Sherman, which led to the opening of negotiations between the United States and Mexico to halt the flow of illegal drugs into southern California and other border states. The *Times* won the Local General Spot News Reporting prize in 1966 for its coverage of the Watts riots. The third Meritorious Public Service prize came in 1969 for its expose of wrongdoing within the Los Angeles City Government Commissions, resulting in resignations or criminal convictions of certain members, as well as widespread reforms. It won the 1984 Meritorious Public Service prize for an in-depth examination of southern California's growing Latino community by a team of editors and reporters. The 1993 Spot News Reporting prize went to the *Times* for balanced, comprehensive, penetrating coverage — under deadline pressure — of the second and most destructive day of the Los Angeles riots. It won the Spot News Reporting prize again in 1995 for its reporting on January 17, 1994, of the chaos and devastation in the aftermath of the Northridge earthquake. A new category, Breaking News Reporting, found the *Times* the winner in 1998 for its comprehensive coverage of a botched bank robbery and subsequent police shoot-out in North Hollywood.

The *Los Angeles Times* was founded in 1881 and purchased in 1884 by Harrison Gray Otis. He incorporated the paper into the Times Mirror Company. Otis's son-in-law, Harry Chandler, took on the management in 1917 and it has remained in the Chandler family. The *Times* established the United States' first newspaper-owned radio station in 1922 and it began delivery of papers to other cities in 1928 via airplane. Norman Chandler took over from his father in 1944. Norman passed the reins on to his son Otis in 1958 and a change in editorial policy was evident, with less conservativism and more balanced journalism.

Commentary

1970

Marquis William Childs 92

Birth: March 17, 1903; Clinton, IA. **Death:** June 30, 1990. **Parents:** William Henry Childs and Lilian Malissa (Marquis). **Education:** University of Wisconsin: BA. University of Iowa: MA. **Spouse:** Lue Prentiss (m. 1926, died 1969); Jane Neylan McBain (m. 1969). **Children:** Henry, Malissa (LP).

Prize: *Commentary,* 1970: *St. Louis Post-Dispatch,* St. Louis: St. Louis Post-Dispatch, 1969.

Career: Reporter, United Press International, 1923-24; English Composition Instructor, University of Iowa, 1924-25; Reporter, United Press International, 1925; Feature Writer, *St. Louis (MO) Post-Dispatch,* 1926-30; Special Correspondent, Washington, DC Staff, *St. Louis (MO) Post-Dispatch,* 1934-44; Syndicated Columnist, United Features Syndicate, 1944-54; Columnist, *St. Louis (MO) Post-Dispatch,* 1954-62; Washington Bureau Chief, *St. Louis (MO) Post-Dispatch,* 1962-69; Contributing Editor, *St. Louis (MO) Post-Dispatch,* 1969-74; Contributor, *St. Louis (MO) Post-Dispatch,* ?-1989; Visiting Professor, University of Texas.

Selected Works: *Sweden the Middle Way,* 1936. *They Hate Roosevelt,* 1936. *Washington Calling,* 1937. *This Is Democracy,* 1938. *This Is Your War: An Atlantic Monthly Press Book,* 1942. *I Write from Washington,* 1942. *The Cabin,* 1944. *The Farmer Takes a Hand,* 1952. *The Ragged Edge,* 1955. *Eisenhower, Captive Hero,* 1958. *The Peacemakers,* 1961.

Taint of Innocence, 1967. *Witness to Power,* 1975. *Ethics in Business Society* (with Douglass Cater), 1954. *Walter Lippmann and His Times* (with others), 1959. *Mighty Mississippi: Biography of a River,* 1982.

Other Awards: Best Washington Correspondent, Sigma Delta Chi, 1944. Order of the North Star, Sweden, 1945. Journalism Award, University of Missouri, 1951. Honorary Degrees: Upsala College, NJ, 1943; University of Wisconsin, 1966; University of Iowa, 1969.

For More Information: *Current Biography Yearbook, 1943,* New York: H.W. Wilson, 1943: 126-128; *The Reminiscences of Marquis William Childs, Columbia University Oral History Collection, Part 1,* 1962; Taft, William H., *Encyclopedia of Twentieth-Century Journalists,* New York: Garland Publishing Incorporated, 1986; *St. Louis Post-Dispatch,* 1 July (1990): A1; *New York Times,* 2 July (1990): 10; *San Francisco Chronicle,* 2 July (1990): B6.

Commentary: Marquis W. Childs won the first Pulitzer Prize given in the Commentary category. He wrote on themes that are still relevant today, such as the gun lobby and the condition of mental institutions.

Childs had decided at age 13 that he wanted to be a reporter. He wrote firsthand accounts of the Spanish Civil War and World War II, as well as articles about political and diplomatic developments from 1945 until his retirement in 1974. He had private interviews with several presidents of the United States. During his tenure at the *St. Louis Post-Dispatch,* he wrote 6,380 articles.

1971

William Anthony Caldwell 93

Birth: December 5, 1906; Butler, PA. **Death:** April 11, 1986. **Parents:** William Arthur Caldwell and Johanna Marie (DeLeuw). **Religion:** Presbyterian. **Spouse:** Dorothy C. Alexander (m. 1938, died 1988). **Children:** Tonia, Alix, William.

Prize: *Commentary,* 1971: *Record,* Hackensack, NJ: Record, 1970.

Career: Reporter, Editor, *The Record (NJ),* 1926-72; Editorial Page Columnist, *Vineyard Gazette (MA),* 1972-86.

Selected Works: *In the Record: The Simeon Stylites Columns of William A. Caldwell,* 1972.

Other Awards: Bronze Medal, American Cancer Society, 1961. Editorial Writing Medal, Society of Silurians, 1964. Honorary Degrees: Rutgers, NJ,

1970; William Paterson College, NJ, 1972; Fairleigh Dickinson University, 1973.

For More Information: *New York Times,* 12 April (1986): 32; *Bergen Record,* 13 April (1986): A1; *Bergen Record,* 4 June (1995): Special Section, 83; *Bergen Record,* 4 January (1998): N7.

Commentary: William A. Caldwell won a Pulitzer Prize the year before he retired. He had written his daily column "Simeon Stylites" for 41 years. The column was named after the fifth-century saint who spent 36 years preaching from the top of a pillar. After retiring, he contributed a weekly column to his local paper in Martha's Vineyard.

1972

Michael Royko   94

Birth: September 19, 1932; Chicago, IL. **Death:** April 29, 1997. **Parents:** Michael Royko and Helen (Zak). **Education:** Wright Junior College, IL. **Spouse:** Carol Joyce Duckman (m. 1954, died 1979); Judith Arndt (m. 1985). **Children:** David, Robert (CD); Sam, Kate (JA).

Prize: *Commentary,* 1972: *Chicago Daily News,* Chicago: Chicago Daily News, 1971.

Career: Usher, Chicago Theater; Merchandise Collector, Marshall Field and Co.; Served in U.S. Air Force, 3 Years in Korea, 1 Year at O'Hare Field in Chicago; Reporter, *Lincoln-Belmont Booster,* 1956; Reporter, *Chicago's City News Bureau,* 1956; Assistant Editor, *Chicago's City News Bureau,* 1957; Night Police Reporter, *Chicago Daily News,* 1959-; Phone salesman of tombstones, 1959; Columnist, two times per week *Chicago Daily News,* 1963; Columnist, five times per week *Chicago Daily News,* 1964-78; Col-

umnist, *Chicago Sun-Times,* 1978-84; Columnist, *Chicago Tribune,* 1984-97.

Selected Works: *Up Against It,* 1967. *I May Be Wrong but I Doubt It,* 1968. *Boss: Richard J. Daley of Chicago,* 1971. *Slats Grobnik and Some Other Friends,* 1973. *Sez Who? Sez Me,* 1982. *Like I Was Sayin',* 1984. *Dr. Kookie, You're Right!,* 1989. *Otoko No Koramu* (with Kazuma Inoue), 1992.

Other Awards: Heywood Broun Award, American Newspaper Guild, 1969. National Headliners Club Award, 1971. Service to Journalism Medal, University of Missouri School of Journalism, 1979. Chicago Journalism Hall of Fame, Chicago Press Club, 1980. H.L. Mencken Award, 1981. Ernie Pyle Award, 1982. "Best Newspaper Columnist in America" Award, *Washington Journalism Review* Reader's Poll, 1985, 1987-88, 1990. Lifetime Achievement Award, National Press Club, 1990. Damon Runyon Award, Denver Press Club, 1995.

For More Information: Grauer, Neil A., *Wits and Sages,* Baltimore, MD: Johns Hopkins University Press, 1984: 215-236; *Chicago,* 39:3 (March 1990): 94+; *Chicago Tribune,* April 30, 1997: 1+.

Commentary: Mike Royko was a columnist in Chicago newspapers for 34 years, and for most of his career he wrote five days a week. He expressed what he thought, using his dry wit. In his column he had many conversations with Slats Grobnik, "a fictitious blue-collar alter ego," who provided analysis on life. His column was syndicated in over 600 newspapers.

1973

David Salzer Broder   95

Birth: September 11, 1929; Chicago Heights, IL. **Parents:** Albert Broder and Nina M. (Salzer). **Education:** University of Chicago, IL: BA, MA. **Spouse:** Ann Creighton Collar (m. 1951). **Children:** George, Joshua, Matthew, Michael.

Prize: *Commentary,* 1973: *Washington Post,* Washington, DC: Washington Post, 1972.

Career: Served in U.S. Army, 1951-53; *Bloomington (IL) Pantagraph,* 1953-55; Staff Reporter, *Congressional Quarterly,* 1955-60; Reporter, *Washington (DC) Star,* 1960-65; Washington Bureau, *New York Times,* 1965-66; Reporter, Columnist, *Washington (DC) Post,* 1966-; Associate Editor, *Washington (DC) Post,* 1975-.

Selected Works: *The Republican Establishment* (with Stephen Hess), 1967. *The Party's Over: The Failure of Politics in America,* 1971. *Politics, Parties, and Media: Maxwell Summer Lecture Series, 1972,* 1972. *Changing of the Guard and Power and Leadership in America,* 1980. *The Pursuit of the Presidency,* 1980. *Behind the Front Page: A Candid Look at How the News Is Made,* 1987. *The Man Who Would*

Be President: Dan Quayle (with Bob Woodward), 1992. *The System: The American Way of Politics at the Breaking Point* (with Haynes Bonner Johnson), 1996.

Other Awards: Newspaper Guild Award, 1961, 1973-74. Fellow, John F. Kennedy School of Government, Harvard University, MA, 1969-70. Poynter Fellow, Yale University, CT and Indiana University, 1973. Fellow, Institute of Policy Science and Public Affairs, Duke University, NC. White Burkett Miller Presidential Award, 1989. Lovejoy Fellow, Colby College, ME. Fourth Estate Award, National Press Foundation, 1990. Recognition Award, National Press Foundation, 1992. Lifetime Achievement Award, National Society of Newspaper Columnists, 1997. National Citation, William Allen White Foundation, 1997.

For More Information: Grauer, Neil A., *Wits & Sages,* Baltimore, MD: Johns Hopkins University Press, 1984: 97-118; Taft, William H., *Encyclopedia of Twentieth-Century Journalists,* New York: Garland Publishing Incorporated, 1986; *Editor & Publisher,* 130: 27 (1997): 32.

Commentary: David S. Broder has been a political commentator for nearly 40 years. In 1972, he was chosen as the most respected political writer in the nation in a poll of political correspondents. He makes regular appearances on CNN's *Inside Politics,* NBC's *Meet the Press,* and PBS's *Washington in Review.*

1974

Edwin Albert Roberts Jr. 96

Birth: November 14, 1932; Weehawken, NJ. **Parents:** Edwin Albert Roberts and Agnes (Seuferling). **Religion:** Roman Catholic. **Education:** College of William and Mary, VA. New York University. St. Petersburg Junior College, FL: AA. **Spouse:** Barbara Anne Collins (m. 1958). **Children:** Elizabeth, Leslie, Amy, Jacqueline.

Prize: *Commentary,* 1974: *National Observer,* Silver Spring, MD: Dow Jones & Co., 1973.

Career: General Assignment Reporter, *Asbury Park (NJ) Press;* Editorial Writer, *Wall Street Journal,* 1957-63; Washington Correspondent, *Wall Street Journal,* 1963-64; Writer, *National Observer (MD),* 1963-69; Columnist, *National Observer (MD),* 1969-1977; Editorial Writer, Columnist, *Detroit News,* 1977-78; Editorial Page Editor, *Detroit News,* 1978-83; Columnist, *Tampa (FL) Tribune,* 1983-.

Selected Works: *Elections 1964: National Observer Newsbook,* 1964. *Latin America: National Observer Newsbook,* 1964. *The Stock Market: National Observer Newsbook,* 1965. *The Smut Rakers; a Report in Depth on Obscenity and the Censors: National Observer Newsbook,* 1966. *America Outdoors: Na-*

tional Observer Newsbook, 1966. *The Busy Rich: National Observer Newsbook,* 1967. *Russia Today: National Observer Newsbook,* 1967.

Other Awards: Distinguished Reporting Award, University of Missouri, 1969.

For More Information: *New York Times,* 7 May (1974): 40.

Commentary: Edwin A. Roberts Jr. began writing his column "Mainstreams" in 1969. His writings covered many different topics, such as gardening, the administration, abortion, and self-interviews.

1975

Mary McGrory 97

Birth: August 22, 1918; Boston, MA. **Parents:** Edward Patrick McGrory and Mary (Jacobs). **Education:** Emmanuel College, MA: AB.

Prize: *Commentary,* 1975: *Washington Star,* Washington, DC: Washington Star, 1974.

Career: Picture Cropper, Houghton Mifflin Company, 1939-42; Secretary to the Book Review Editor, *Boston Herald Traveler,* 1942-47; Reviewer, *Washington (DC) Evening Star,* 1947-54; National Commentator, Columnist, *Washington (DC) Evening Star,* 1954-81; Columnist, *Washington (DC) Post,* 1981-.

Selected Works: *In Memoriam: John Fitzgerald Kennedy,* 1963. *Interviews with Mary McGrory, Women in Journalism Oral History Project,* 1993.

Other Awards: George Polk Memorial Award, Long Island University, NY, 1963. Sigma Delta Chi Fellow, 1973. Elijah Parish Lovejoy Fellow, 1985. Franklin D. Roosevelt Four Freedoms Award for Freedom of Speech, 1995. Lifetime Achievement Award, John F. Kennedy Journalism Awards, 1995.

For More Information: *Contemporary Authors, Volume 106,* Detroit: Gale Research Company, 1982; Belford, Barbara, *Brilliant Bylines: A Biographical Anthology of Notable Newspaperwomen in America,* New York: Columbia University Press, 1986: 270-283; Braden, Marie, *She Said What? Interviews With Women Newspaper Columnists,* Lexington: University Press of Kentucky, 1993: 25-34; Riley, Sam G., *Biographical Dictionary of American Newspaper Columnists,* Westport, CT: Greenwood Press, 1995.

Commentary: Mary McGrory, a Washington columnist who does all her own legwork for her columns, is known for diligently producing her column even though she does not like to write. She started her career as a secretary, worked her way up to book reviewer, and now appears frequently on the weekly television show *Meet the Press.* She was awarded a Pulitzer Prize for her commentary on public affairs in 1974.

1976

Walter Wellesley Smith 98

Birth: September 25, 1905; Green Bay, WI. **Death:** January 15, 1982. **Parents:** Walter Philip Smith and Ida (Richardson). **Religion:** Roman Catholic. **Education:** University of Notre Dame, IN: AB, cum laude. **Spouse:** Catherine M. Cody (m. 1933, died 1967); Phyllis Warner Weiss (m. 1968). **Children:** Catherine, Terence (CC).

Prize: *Commentary,* 1976: *New York Times,* New York: New York Times, 1975.

Career: Editor, *The Dome,* Notre Dame University annual publication, 1925-26; General Assignment Reporter, *Milwaukee (WI) Sentinel,* 1927-28; Copyreader, Sportswriter, *St. Louis (MO) Star,* 1928-32; Sportswriter, Rewriteman, *St. Louis (MO) Star-Times,* 1932-36; Sportswriter, Sports Columnist, *Philadelphia (PA) Record,* 1936-45; Sportswriter, *New York Herald-Tribune,* 1945; Sports Columnist, *New York Herald-Tribune,* 1954-66; Syndicated columnist, 1966-71; Sports Columnist, *New York Times,* 1971-82.

Selected Works: *Terry and Bunky Play Football* (with Richard Mark Fischel), 1945. *Selected Sports Stories,* 1949. *Out of the Red,* 1950. *How to Get to First Base: A Picture Book of Baseball* (with Marc Simont), 1952. *Views of Sports,* 1954. *Red Smith's Sports Annual,* 1961. *The Best of Red Smith* (with Verna Reamer), 1963. *Red Smith on Fishing around the World,* 1963. *Strawberries in the Wintertime: The Sporting World of Red Smith,* 1974. *Red Smith's Favorite Sports Stories,* 1976. *The Red Smith Reader* (with Dave Anderson), 1982. *To Absent Friends from Red Smith,* 1982. *Press Boys: Red Smith's Favorite Sports Stories,* 1983.

Other Awards: National Headliners Club Award, 1946. Grantland Rice Memorial Award, Sportsmanship Brotherhood of New York, 1956. Honorary Degrees: University of Notre Dame, IN, 1968; Brown University, RI, 1981.

For More Information: *Current Biography Yearbook, 1959,* New York: H.W. Wilson Company, 1959; *Contemporary Authors, Volumes 77-80,* Detroit: Gale Research Company, 1979; *New York Times,* 16 January (1982): 1; Berkow, Ida, *Red: A Biography of Red Smith,* New York: Times Books, 1986.

Commentary: When Walter "Red" Smith won for his sports commentary in 1976, he was the third sportswriter to win a Pulitzer Prize. He once said, "Writing is easy. I just open a vein and bleed." He had an exceptional command of English and was a consultant for several dictionaries and encyclopedias. However, his skills were not always as valued; when he graduated from college, he wrote to about 100 newspapers for a job. One paper, the *New York Times,* wrote back, saying "No." (That paper did hire him in 1971.)

1977

George Frederick Will 99

Birth: May 21, 1941; Champaign, IL. **Parents:** Frederick L. Will and Louise. **Education:** Trinity College, CT: BA. Magdalen College, Oxford University, England. Princeton University, NJ: PhD. **Spouse:** Madeleine Marion (m. 1967, div. 1989). **Children:** Jonathan, Geoffrey, Victoria.

Prize: *Commentary,* 1977: *Washington Post,* Washington, DC: Washington Post, 1976.

Career: Sports Editor, college newspaper; Political Science Instructor, Michigan State University, 1967-68; Political Science Instructor, University of

Toronto, 1968-69; Staff member, Senator Alcott of Colorado, 1970-72; Washington Editor, *National Review,* 1972-76; Occasional Columnist, *Washington (DC) Post,* 1973; Syndicated Columnist, *Washington (DC) Post* Writers Group, 1974-; Panelist, *Agronsky and Company,* 1979-84; Participant, *This Week With David Brinkley,* ABC-TV, 1981-; Commentator, *World News Tonight,* ABC-TV, 1984-; Writer.

Selected Works: (Thesis), Beyond the Reach of Majorities: Closed Questions in the Open Society, 1968. *The Pursuit of Happiness, and Other Sobering Thoughts,* 1978. *Solzhenitsyn and American Democracy: Ethics and Public Policy Reprint, 29,* 1980. *The Pursuit of Virtue and Other Tory Notions,* 1982. *Statecraft as Soulcraft: What Government Does,* 1983. *The Morning After: American Successes and Excesses, 1981-1986,* 1986. *The New Season: A Spectator's Guide to the 1988 Election,* 1987. *Men at Work: The Craft of Baseball,* 1990. *Suddenly: The American Idea Abroad and at Home, 1986-1990,* 1992. *Restoration: Congress, Term Limits, and the Recovery of Deliberative Democracy,* 1992. *The Leveling Wind: Politics, the Culture, and Other News, 1990-1994,* 1994. *The Woven Figure: Conservatism and America's Fabric, 1994-1997,* 1997.

Other Awards: Young Leader of America Award, *Time Magazine,* 1974. Honorary Degrees: University of San Diego, 1977; Dickinson College, PA, 1978; Georgetown University, Washington, DC, 1978; University of Illinois, 1988.

For More Information: *People,* 19 September (1983): 104; Grauer, Neil A., *Wits & Sages,* Baltimore, MD: Johns Hopkins University Press, 1984: 239-261; *Washington Post,* 26 September (1986): B1; Burner, David, *Column Right: Conservative Journalists in the Service to Nationalism,* New York: New York University Press, 1988; *Contemporary Authors, New Revision Series, Volume 32,* Detroit: Gale Research Company, 1991; Chappell, Larry W., *George F. Will, Twayne's United States Authors Series, No. 675,* New York: Twayne, 1997.

Commentary: George F. Will won a Pulitzer Prize in Commentary in 1977. His citation acknowledged that he "is at home with a wide range of topics, from international relations, campaigns, and urban problems to the history of machine guns and the vagaries of the press." His column has been syndicated since 1974.

1978

William L. Safire 100

Birth: December 17, 1929; New York, NY. **Parents:** Oliver C. Safir and Ida (Panish). **Education:** Syracuse University, NY. **Spouse:** Helene Belmar Julius (m. 1962). **Children:** Mark, Annabel.

Prize: *Commentary,* 1978: *New York Times,* New York: New York Times, 1977.

Career: Reporter, *New York Herald-Tribune* Syndicate, 1949-51; Europe and Middle East Correspondent, WNBC-WNBT, 1951; U.S. Army Correspondent, 1952-54; Chief of Staff, Madison Square Garden Rally for Dwight D. Eisenhower, 1952; Radio, Television Producer, WNBC (NY), 1954-55; Vice-President, Tex McCrary Incorporated, 1955-60; President, Safire Public Relations Incorporated, 1961-68; Worked on 5 Political Campaigns for Nixon; Director of Advertising for Republican City Committee in New York, 1961; Deputy Campaign Manager, 1962; Director of Public Relations, New York City for Rockefeller, Governor Campaign, 1964; Speechwriter, Vice President Spiro Agnew, 1968-73; Senior White House Speechwriter, Nixon Administration; Columnist, *New York Times,* 1973-.

Selected Works: *The Relations Explosion: A Diagram of the Coming Boom and Shakeout in Corporate Relations,* 1963. *Plunging into Politics: How to Become or Support a Candidate on the National, State or Local Level* (with Marshall Loeb), 1964. *The New Language of Politics: An Anecdotal Dictionary of Catchwords, Slogans, and Political Usage,* 1968. *Before the Fall: An Inside View of the Pre-Watergate White House,* 1975. *Full Disclosure: A Novel,* 1977. *Big Government, Myth or Might? The M.L. Siedman Memorial Town Hall Lecture Series, 11* (with others), 1977. *Safire's Political Dictionary,* 1978. *Safire's*

Washington, 1980. *On Language*, 1980. *What's the Good Word?*, 1982. *Good Advice* (with Leonard Safir), 1982. *I Stand Corrected: More on Language*, 1984. *Take My Word for It: More on Language*, 1986. *Freedom*, 1987. *You Could Look It Up: More on Language from William Safire*, 1988. *Words of Wisdom: More Good Advice* (with Leonard Safir), 1989. *Language Maven Strikes Again*, 1990. *Fumblerules: A Lighthearted Guide to Grammar and Good Usage*, 1990. *Coming to Terms*, 1991. *Lend Me Your Ears: Great Speeches in History*, 1992. *The First Dissident: The Book of Job in Today's Politics*, 1992. *Good Advice on Writing: Past and Present on How to Write Well* (with Leonard Safir), 1992. *Quoth the Maven*, 1993. *Safire's New Political Dictionary: The Definitive Guide to the New Language of Politics*, 1993. *Old Books Have a Future*, 1993. *In Love with Norma Loquendi*, 1994. *Sleeper Spy*, 1995. *Pictures of the Times: A Century of Photography from the New York Times* (with others), 1996. *Watching My Language: Adventures in the World Trade*, 1997.

For More Information: *Current Biography Yearbook, 1973,* New York: H.W. Wilson Company, 1973; *New York Times,* 18 April (1978): 28; *Contemporary Authors, New Revision Series, Volume 31,* Detroit: Gale Research Company, 1990; Riley, Sam G., *Biographical Dictionary of American Newspaper Columnists,* Westport, CT: Greenwood Press, 1995.

Commentary: William Safire, a jack of all trades, has been a reporter, public relations executive, columnist, speechwriter, and novelist. His column has been syndicated in more than 100 newspapers.

1979

Russell Wayne Baker

Full entry appears as **#75** under "Biography or Autobiography," 1983.

1980

Ellen Holtz Goodman   101

Birth: April 11, 1941; Boston, MA. **Parents:** Jackson Jacob Holtz and Edith (Weinstein). **Education:** Radcliffe College, MA: BA, cum laude. **Spouse:** Anthony Goodman (m. 1963, div. 1971); Robert Levey (m. 1982). **Children:** Katherine Anne (AG).

Prize: *Commentary,* 1980: *Boston Globe,* Boston: Boston Globe, 1979.

Career: Reporter and Researcher, *Newsweek,* 1963-65; Freelance writer, *Patriot Ledger,* 1965; General Assignment Reporter, *Detroit Free Press,* 1965-67; Staff member, *Boston Globe,* 1967-; Columnist, *Boston Globe,* 1974-; Associate Editor, *Boston Globe,* 1987-; Lorry I. Lokey Visiting Professor in Professional Journalism, Stanford University, 1996.

Selected Works: *Turning Points,* 1979. *Close to Home,* 1979. *At Large,* 1981. *Keeping in Touch,* 1985. *Making Sense,* 1989. *Value Judgments,* 1993. *Interviews with Ellen Goodman, Women in Journalism Oral History Project,* 1994.

Other Awards: Woman of the Year Award, New England Women's Press Association, 1968. Catherine L. O'Brien Award, 1971. Media Award, Massachusetts Commission on the Status of Women, 1973. Nieman Fellow, Harvard University, MA, 1973-74. Columnist of the Year, New England Women's Press Association, 1974. Distinguished Writing Award, American Society of Newspapers Editors, 1980. Hubert H. Humphrey Civil Rights Award, 1988. Presidents' Award, National Women's Political Caucus, 1993. American Woman Award, Women's Research and Education Institute, 1994.

For More Information: *Contemporary Authors, Volume 104,* Detroit: Gale Research Company, 1982; Grauer, Neil A., *Wits & Sages,* Baltimore, MD: Johns

Hopkins University Press, 1984: 163-177; Taft William H., *Encyclopedia of Twentieth-Century Journalists,* New York: Garland Publishing Incorporated, 1986; Belford, Barbara, *Brilliant Bylines: A Biographical Anthology of Notable Newspaperwomen in America,* New York: Columbia University Press, 1986: 337-349; Braden, Maria, *She Said What? Interviews with Women Newspaper Columnists,* Lexington: University Press of Kentucky, 1993: 77-88.

Commentary: Ellen Goodman gives readers a historical background for the current ideas and situations that she writes about in her column. She writes two columns a week and uses humor as well as insight to bring her columns to life.

1981

David Poole Anderson   102

Birth: May 6, 1929; Troy, NY. **Parents:** Robert P. Anderson and Josephine (David). **Religion:** Roman Catholic. **Education:** College of the Holy Cross, MA: BA. **Spouse:** Maureen Ann Young (m. 1953). **Children:** Stephen, Mark, Mary Jo, Jean Marie.

Prize: *Commentary,* 1981: *New York Times,* New York: New York Times, 1980.

Career: Sports Editor, college newspaper; Sportswriter, *Brooklyn (NY) Eagle,* 1951-55; Sportswriter, *New York Journal-American,* 1955-66; Sportswriter, *New York Times,* 1966-71; Sports Columnist, *New York Times,* 1971-.

Selected Works: *Great Quarterbacks of the NFL: The Punt, the Pass and Kick Library, 2,* 1966. *Great Pass Receivers of the NFL: The Punt, the Pass and Kick Library, 6,* 1966. *Great Defensive Players of the NFL: The Punt, the Pass and Kick Library, 7,* 1967. *Upset: The Unexpected in the World of Sports* (with Milton Lancelot), 1967. *Countdown to Super Bowl,* 1969. *Sugar Ray* (with Sugar Ray Robinson), 1970. *Always on the Run* (with others), 1973. *Frank: The First Year* (with Frank Robinson), 1976. *Sports of Our Times,* 1979. *The Yankees,* 1979. *Miracle on Ice* (with Gerald Eskenazi), 1980. *The Red Smith Reader,* 1982. *Hey, Wait a Minute, I Wrote a Book* (with John Madden), 1984. *Shooting for the Gold* (with Walter Iooss), 1984. *One Knee Equals Two Feet* (with John Madden), 1986. *One Size Doesn't Fit All* (with John Madden), 1988. *In the Corner: Great Boxing Trainers Talk about Their Act,* 1991. *Sugar Ray Robinson: Autobiography* (with Sugar Ray Robinson), 1992. *Pennant Races: Baseball at Its Best,* 1994. *All Madden: Hey, I'm Talking Pro Football* (with John Madden), 1996.

Other Awards: E.P. Dutton Award, Best Magazine Sports Story, 1965. Page One Award, New York Newspaper Guild, 1972. E.P. Dutton Award, Best Sports Feature Story of the Year, 1972. Grand Prize,

Pro-Football Writers Contest, 1973. Nat Fleischer Award for Excellence in Boxing Journalism, 1974. Hall of Fame, National Sportswriters and Sportscasters, 1990. Xavier High School Hall of Fame, 1991. New York Sports Hall of Fame, 1991. Red Smith Award, 1994.

For More Information: *Contemporary Authors, Volumes 89-92,* Detroit: Gale Research Company, 1980.

Commentary: Dave Anderson won a Pulitzer Prize for his sports reporting. His colleague "Red" Smith, with whom he worked for many years, won the award in 1976. Anderson writes the "Sports of The Times" column for his paper.

1982

Arthur Buchwald   103

Birth: October 20, 1925; Mount Vernon, NY. **Parents:** Joseph Buchwald and Helen (Kleinberger). **Religion:** Jewish. **Education:** University of Southern California. **Spouse:** Ann McGarry (m. 1952, died 1994). **Children:** Joel, Conchita Mathilda, Marie Jennifer.

Prize: *Commentary,* 1982: *Los Angeles Times Syndicate,* Los Angeles, CA: Los Angeles Times Syndicate, 1981.

Career: Served in U.S. Marine Corps, 1942-45; Managing Editor, *Campus Humor* Magazine, University of Southern California; Staff member, *Variety Magazine,* Paris, France 1948; Nightlife Correspondent, *International Herald-Tribune,* 1949-52; Syndicated columnist, 1952-.

Selected Works: *Art Buchwald's Paris,* 1954. *A Gift for the Boys,* 1955. *The Brave Coward,* 1957. *More Carrier,* 1959. *Don't Forget to Write,* 1960.

How Much Is That in Dollars, 1961. *Is It Safe to Drink the Water?,* 1962. *I Chose Capitol Punishment,* 1963. *And Then I Told the President: The Secret Papers of Art Buchwald,* 1965. *Son of the Great Society,* 1966. *Have I Ever Lied to You?,* 1968. *The Establishment Is Alive and Well in Washington,* 1969. *Counting Sheep,* 1970. *Getting High in Government Circles,* 1971. *I Never Danced at the White House,* 1973. *I Am Not a Crook,* 1974. *Washington Is Leaking,* 1976. *Down the Seine and up the Potomac,* 1977. *The Buchwald Stops Here,* 1978. *Seems Like Yesterday* (with Ann Buchwald), 1980. *Laid Back in Washington,* 1981. *While Reagan Slept,* 1983. *You Can Fool All the People All the Time,* 1985. *I Think I Don't Remember,* 1987. *Whose Rose Garden Is It Anyway?,* 1989. *Lighten up, George,* 1991. *Leaving Home: A Memoir,* 1993. *I'll Always Have Paris: A Memoir,* 1996.

Other Awards: Prix de la Bonne Humeur, 1958: French Translation of *A Gift For the Boys,* New York: Harper, 1957. Horatio Alger Award, Horatio Alger Association of Distinguished Americans. Hall of Fame, Society of Professional Journalists, Washington, DC Chapter, 1993. Honorary Degree, Yale University, CT, 1970.

For More Information: *Current Biography Yearbook, 1960,* New York: H.W. Wilson, 1960; Grauer, Neil A., *Wits & Sages,* Baltimore, MD: Johns Hopkins University Press, 1984: 121-139; Taft, William, H., *Encyclopedia of Twentieth-Century Journalists,* New York: Garland Publishing Incorporated, 1986; *Contemporary Authors, New Revision Series, Volume 21,* Detroit: Gale Research Company, 1987.

Commentary: Art Buchwald, who grew up in a variety of foster homes, quit school at the age of 17 to join the Marines. He worked in Paris for a number of years writing the column "Paris After Dark." Well known for his humor, he has been syndicated in over 550 newspapers.

1983

Claude Fox Sitton   104

Birth: December 4, 1925; Atlanta, GA. **Parents:** Claude B. Sitton and Pauline (Fox). **Education:** Emory University, GA: AB. **Spouse:** Eva McLaurin Whetstone (m. 1953). **Children:** Lea, Clinton, Suzanna, McLaurin.

Prize: *Commentary,* 1983: *Raleigh News and Observer,* Raleigh, NC: Raleigh News and Observer, 1982.

Career: Served in U.S. Naval Reserve, 1943-46; Georgia, Florida, Alabama, International News Service, 1949-51; Correspondent, Nashville (TN), Atlanta (GA), Miami (FL), and New York (NY), United Press International, 1951-55; U.S. Information Officer and Press Attache, U.S. Embassy in Accra, Ghana, 1955-

57; Chief Southern Correspondent, *New York Times,* 1957-64; National News Director, *New York Times,* 1964-68; Editorial Director, *Raleigh (NC) News and Observer,* 1968-90; Editor, *Raleigh (NC) News and Observer,* 1970-90; Editorial Director and Vice-President, News and Observer Publishing Company, 1970-90; Senior Lecturer, Emory University (GA), 1991-94.

Selected Works: *News in Our Time; a Problem of Perception: Ralph McGill Lecture, XII,* 1990.

Other Awards: Neely Young Award, Georgia Press Association, 1988. George Polk Memorial Award, Long Island University, NY, 1992. Honorary Degree, Emory University, GA, 1984.

Commentary: Claude Sitton won a Pulitzer Prize for his weekly Sunday column that analyzed "national and international issues and politics for a regional audience." His topics during 1982 ranged from civil rights to the Environmental Protection Agency to public education. On learning that he had won the award, he acknowledged the staff at the *News and Observer,* by saying that "without excellent reporting there can be no good commentary." He was a member of the Pulitzer Prize Board from 1985 to 1994.

1984

Vermont Connecticut Royster   105

Birth: April 30, 1914; Raleigh, NC. **Death:** July 22, 1996. **Parents:** Wilbur Hugh Royster and Olivette (Broadway). **Religion:** Episcopalian. **Education:** University of North Carolina: BA, Phi Beta Kappa. **Spouse:** Frances Claypoole (m. 1937). **Children:** Frances, Sara.

Prize: *Editorial Writing,* 1953: *Wall Street Journal,* New York: Dow Jones, 1952. *Commentary,* 1984: *Wall Street Journal,* New York: Dow Jones, 1983.

Career: Reporter, *New York City News Bureau,* 1935-36; Correspondent, Washington (DC), *Wall Street Journal,* 1936-40; Lieutenant Commander, U.S. Navy Reserves, 1940-45; Correspondent, Washington (DC), *Wall Street Journal,* 1945-46; Washington (DC) Bureau Chief, *Wall Street Journal,* 1946-49; Associate Editor, *Wall Street Journal,* 1949-58; Editor, *Wall Street Journal,* 1958-71; Editor Emeritus, Columnist, *Wall Street Journal,* ?-1986; Director, Dow Jones and Company; William Rand Professor of Journalism and Public Affairs, University of North Carolina, Chapel Hill, 1971-86.

Selected Works: *Journey through the Soviet Union,* 1962. *A Pride of Prejudices,* 1967. *My Own, My Country's Time: A Journalist's Journey,* 1983. *The Essential Royster: A Vermont Royster Reader* (with Edmund Fuller), 1985.

Other Awards: Distinguished Service Award, Sigma Delta Chi, 1958. William Allen White Award, University of Kansas, 1971. Fourth Estate Award, 1971, 1978. Gerald Loeb Award for Distinguished Business and Financial Journalism, Anderson Graduate School of Management, University of California, Los Angeles, 1975. North Carolina Journalism Hall of Fame, 1980. Presidential Medal of Freedom, 1986. Honorary Degrees: University of North Carolina, 1959; Temple University, PA, 1964; Elon College, NC, 1968; Colby College, ME, 1976; Williams College, MA, 1979.

For More Information: *Christian Science Monitor,* 2 February (1984): 22; Riley, Sam G., *Biographical Dictionary of American Newspaper Columnists,* Westport, CT: Greenwood Press, 1995; *New York Times,* 23 July (1996): B6; *Wall Street Journal,* 23 July (1996): B5.

Commentary: Vermont Connecticut Royster, whose name was a family tradition, won his first Pulitzer Prize for his work in general. The citation presented to him on the subject of his editorials said they showed, "an ability to discern the underlying moral issue, illuminated by a deep faith and confidence in the people of our country." With his second Pulitzer Prize, which came more than 30 years after the first, he was cited for his compassion and for placing current events into an historical context.

1985

James Murray Kempton   106

Birth: December 16, 1917; Baltimore, MD. **Death:** May 5, 1997. **Parents:** James Branson Kempton and Sally (Ambler). **Education:** Johns Hopkins University, MD: BA. **Spouse:** Mina Bluethenthal (m. 1942,

div.); Beverly Gary (m., died 1996). **Children:** Sally, James, Arthur, David (MN); Christopher (BG).

Prize: *Commentary,* 1985: *Newsday,* Garden City, NY: Newsday, 1984.

Career: Welfare Investigator, 1939; Labor organizer; Writer, Young People's Socialist League and American Labor Party; Staff member, *New York Post,* 1942; Served in U.S. Army, 1942-45; Writer, *Wilmington (NC) Star,* 1946-47; Assistant Labor Editor, *New York Post,* 1947-49; Labor Editor, *New York Post,* 1949-63; Editor, *New Republic,* 1963-64; Columnist, *New York World-Telegram and Sun,* 1964-66; Columnist, *New York Post,* 1966-69; Columnist, *National Review of Books,* 1969-71; Journalism Instructor, Hunter College, NY; Political Journalism Instructor, Eagleton Institute, Rutgers University, NJ; News Commentator, CBS-Radio, 1970-77; Columnist, *New York Post,* 1977-81; Columnist, *Newsday (NY),* 1981-97; Contributor to *Esquire, Playboy, Commonwealth, Life, Harper's, Atlantic Monthly* magazines.

Selected Works: *Part of Our Time,* 1955. *America Comes of Middle Age: Columns, 1950-62,* 1972. *The Briar Patch,* 1973. *Finding an Authentic Voice, Red Smith Lecture in Journalism* (with Robert Schmuhl), 1984. *Rebellions, Perversities, and Main Events,* 1994.

Other Awards: Sydney Hillman Foundation Award, 1950. Page One Award, Newspaper Guild of New York, 1955, 1960, 1982. Fulbright Foundation Grant, 1958. George Polk Memorial Award, Long Island University, NY, 1967, 1988. National Book Award for Contemporary Affairs, 1974: *The Briar Patch,* New York: E.P. Dutton Company, 1973. Society of Silurians Award, 1978. Distinguished Writing Award, American Society of Newspaper Editors, 1985. Grammy Award, National Academy of Recording Arts, 1987. Lifetime Achievement, George Polk Memorial Award, Long Island University, NY, 1988. Inducted into American Academy of Fine Arts and Letters, 1995. Honorary Degrees: Grinnell College, IA, 1973; Long Island University, NY, 1987; Hofstra University, 1994; Lewis and Clark College, OR, 1994; Colby College, ME, 1995.

For More Information: *Current Biography Yearbook, 1973,* New York: H.W. Wilson, 1973: 215-218; *Contemporary Authors, Volumes 97-100,* Detroit: Gale Research Company, 1981; *New York Times,* 6 May (1997): 24; *Newsday,* 6 May (1997): A5.

Commentary: Murray Kempton, a liberal columnist, won a Pulitzer Prize for his "witty and insightful reflection on public issues in 1984 and throughout a distinguished career." During the 1950s, Kempton earned a reputation for his defense of civil liberties of suspected Communists. He was a product of New York and his writings reflected the city. His writing was also in intricate prose that sometimes took a second reading to be truly appreciated. But as George Will once wrote about Kempton's writing and reading it twice, "Why complain about a second sip of vintage claret?"

1986

Jimmy Breslin 107

Birth: October 17, 1930; Ozone Park, NY. **Parents:** James Earl Breslin and Frances (Curtin). **Religion:** Roman Catholic. **Education:** Long Island University, NY. **Spouse:** Rosemary Dattolico (m. 1954, died 1981); Ronnie Myers Eldridge (m. 1982). **Children:** James, Kevin, Rosemary, Patrick, Kelly, Christopher (RD); Stepchildren: Daniel, Emily, Lucy (RE).

Prize: *Commentary,* 1986: *New York Daily News,* New York: New York Daily News, 1985.

Career: Sportswriter, *Long Island (NY) Press,* 1948; Copyreader, *Boston Globe;* Feature Writer, Sportswriter, Scripps-Howard Newspaper Enterprise Association; Sportswriter, *New York Journal-American;* Columnist, *New York Herald-Tribune,* 1963-65; Columnist, *New York World Journal-Tribune,* 1965-67; Columnist, *New York Post,* 1968-69; Commentator, WABC-TV (NY), 1968-69; Contributor, *New York Magazine,* 1968-71; News Commentator, WNBC-TV (NY), 1973; Columnist, *New York Daily News,* 1978-88; Columnist, *Newsday* (NY), 1988.

Selected Works: *Sunny Jim: The Life of America's Most Beloved Horseman, James Fitzsimmons,* 1962. *Can't Anybody Here Play This Game? The Improbable Saga of the New York Mets, First Year,* 1967. *The World of Jimmy Breslin,* 1967. *The Gang That Couldn't Shoot Straight,* 1969. *World without End, Amen,* 1973. *How the Good Guys Finally Won,*

1975. *.44* (with Dick Schaap), 1978. *Forsaking All Others,* 1982. *Table Money,* 1986. *He Got Hungry and Forgot His Manners: A Fable,* 1988. *Damon Runyon,* 1991. *I Want to Thank My Brain for Remembering Me: A Memoir,* 1996.

Other Awards: Best Sports Stories Award, E.P. Dutton and Company, 1961. Sigma Delta Chi Award, 1964. New York Reporters Association Award, 1964. Meyer Berger Award, Columbia University, NY, 1964. George Polk Memorial Award, Long Island University, NY, 1986. American Society of Newspaper Editors Award, 1988.

For More Information: Manso, Peter, *Running Against the Machine: The Mailer-Breslin Campaign,* Garden City, NY: Doubleday, 1969; *Current Biography Yearbook, 1973,* New York: H.W. Wilson Company, 1973: 62-64; *Christian Science Monitor,* 14 April (1988); *Contemporary Authors, New Revision Series, Volume 31,* Detroit: Gale Research Company, 1990; *Publisher's Weekly,* 243:36 (1996): 96.

Commentary: Jimmy Breslin won the Commentary Pulitzer Prize for his columns, which "consistently champion ordinary citizens."

He began his career as a sportswriter, but has spent over 30 years as a columnist. His columns cover any number of subjects, from politics to murder. In his very liberal style, he tells it as he sees it.

1987

Charles Krauthammer 108

Birth: March 13, 1950; New York, NY. **Parents:** Shulim Krauthammer and Thea. **Education:** McGill University, Montreal, Canada: BA, First Class Honors. Oxford University, England. Harvard University, MA: MD. **Spouse:** Robyn Trethewey (m. 1974). **Children:** Daniel.

Prize: *Commentary,* 1987: *Washington Post,* Washington, DC: Washington Post, 1986.

Career: Resident, Massachusetts General Hospital, 1975-78; Director, Planning in Psychiatric Research, Carter Administration, 1978; Contributor, *New Republic,* 1981; Speech Writer, Vice-Presidential candidate Walter Mondale, Presidential Campaign, 1980; Writer, Editor, *New Republic,* 1981-88; Contributor, Monthly Essay, *Time* magazine, 1985-; Columnist, *Washington Post,* 1985-.

Selected Works: *Cutting Edges,* 1985. *After the Cold War and the Gulf War: A New Moment in America* (with Penn Kemble), 1991.

Other Awards: Commonwealth Scholar in Politics, Oxford University, England, 1970-71. Woodrow Wilson Fellowship, 1970. DuPont-Warren Fellowship, 1975-78. Edwin Dunlop Prize (Top Psychiatric Resident), 1978. Champion Media Award for Economic Understanding, Amos Tuck School of Business Administration, Dartmouth College, NH, 1984. National Magazine Award, Columbia University, NY, 1984. First Amendment Award, People For the American Way, 1985. Honorary Degree, McGill University, Canada, 1993.

For More Information: Burner, David, with Thomas R. West, *Column Right: Conservative Journalists in the Service of Nationalism,* New York: New York University Press, 1988; *Contemporary Authors, Volume 121,* Detroit: Gale Research Company, 1987.

Commentary: Charles Krauthammer has changed careers three times in his life. First he was a doctor, next he wrote speeches for Vice-Presidential candidate Walter Mondale, then he turned to journalism. He won a Pulitzer Prize "for his witty, insightful columns on national issues." Topics he covered during the year included the Reykjavik Summit, affirmative action, AIDS in the workplace, and Iran-Contra. He was a finalist for a Pulitzer Prize in 1986.

1988

David M. Barry 109

Birth: July 3, 1947; Armonk, NY. **Parents:** David W. Barry and Marion (MacAllister). **Education:** Haverford College, PA: BA. **Spouse:** Elizabeth Lenox Pyle (m. 1975, div. 1994); Michelle Kaufman (m. 1996). **Children:** Robert (EP).

Prize: *Commentary,* 1988: *Miami Herald,* Miami, FL: Miami Herald, 1987.

Career: Reporter, Editor, *West Chester (PA) Daily Local News,* 1971-75; Reporter, Associated Press, 1975-76; Writing Instructor, Burger Associates, 1976-83; National syndicated humor columnist, 1980-; Columnist, *Miami (FL) Herald,* 1983-.

Selected Works: *The Taming of the Screw: Several Million Homeowners' Problems* (with Jerry O'Brien), 1983. *Babies and Other Hazards of Sex: How to Make a Tiny Person in Only 9 Months, with Tools You Probably Have around the Home,* 1984. *Bad Habits: A 100% Fact Free Book,* 1985. *Stay Fit & Healthy Until You're Dead,* 1985. *Claw Your Way to the Top: How to Become the Head of a Major Corporation in Roughly a Week,* 1986. *Dave Barry's Guide to Marriage and/or Sex,* 1987. *Dave Barry's Greatest Hits,* 1988. *Homes and Other Black Holes* (with Jeff MacNelly), 1988. *Dave Barry Slept Here,* 1989. *Dave Barry Turns 40,* 1990. *Dave Barry Talks Back* (with Jeff MacNelly), 1991. *Dave Barry's Only Travel Guide You'll Ever Need,* 1991. *Dave Barry Does Japan,* 1992. *Dave Barry Is Not Making This Up* (with Jeff MacNelly), 1994. *Dave Barry's Gift Guide to End All Gift Guides,* 1994. *Dave Barry's Complete Guide to Guys: A Fairly Short Book,* 1995. *Dave Barry in Cyberspace,* 1996. *Dave Barry's Book of Bad Songs,* 1997. *Dave Barry Is from Mars and Venus,* 1997.

Other Awards: Distinguished Writing Award for Commentary, American Society of Newspaper Editors, 1987.

For More Information: *Miami Herald,* 1 April (1988): A1; *Contemporary Authors, Volume 134,* Detroit: Gale Research Company, 1992.

Commentary: Dave Barry, whose weekly humor column is syndicated nationally, was awarded a Pulitzer Prize for his "consistently effective use of humor as a device for presenting fresh insights into serious concerns." Barry, upon whose life a television show, *Dave's World,* was loosely based, has been writing his column since 1980. He has written on many different topics, adding his own humorous twist to them.

1989

Clarence Eugene Page 110

Birth: June 2, 1947; Dayton, OH. **Parents:** Clarence Hannibal Page and Maggie (Williams). **Education:** Ohio University: BS. **Spouse:** Leanita McClain (div. 1981); Lisa Johnson Cole (m. 1987). **Children:** Grady Johnson (LC).

Prize: *Commentary,* 1989: *Chicago Tribune,* Chicago: Chicago Tribune, 1988.

Career: Freelance writer, Photographer, *Middletown Journal* and *Cincinnati (OH) Enquirer,* 1964; Freelance writer, *Chicago Magazine, Chicago Reader, Playboy, Washington Monthly;* Reporter and Assistant City Editor, *Chicago Tribune,* 1970-80; Director of the Community Affairs Department, On Air Reporter, and Planning Editor, WBBM-TV, 1980-84; Editorial Board Member and Columnist, *Chicago Tribune,* 1984-91; Columnist, Washington (DC), *Chicago Tribune,* 1991-.

Selected Works: *A Foot in Each World: Essays and Articles by Leanita McClain,* 1987. *Showing My Color: Impolite Essays on Race and Identity,* 1996.

Other Awards: Best Feature Article of 1965 Award, Southeast Ohio High School Journalism Association. Edward Scott Beck Award for Foreign Reporting, *Chicago Tribune,* 1976. Illinois United Press International Award, 1980. Commentary Award, National Association of Black Journalists, 1989. Chicago Journalism Hall of Fame, 1992. Honorary Degrees: Columbia College, IL; Lake Forest College, IL.

For More Information: *Contemporary Black Biography, Volume 4,* Detroit: Gale Research Company, 1993; *Contemporary Authors, Volume 145,* Detroit: Gale Research Company, 1995; Riley, Sam G., *Biographical Dictionary of American Newspaper Columnists,* Westport, CT: Greenwood Press, 1995.

Commentary: Clarence Page's "provocative and eclectic set of commentaries" won him a Pulitzer Prize. Some of the topics he wrote about in 1986 included television's ignorance about black life, Martin Luther King Jr., violence in schools, and Jimmy "The Greek" Snyder. While others were calling Snyder to task for his comments about black athletes, Page commented on Snyder's lack of hypocrisy and his "oddball notions about black athletes."

1990

James Patrick Murray 111

Birth: December 29, 1919; Hartford, CT. **Death:** August 16, 1998. **Parents:** James Patrick Murray and Molly (O'Connell). **Religion:** Roman Catholic. **Education:** Trinity College, CT: BA. **Spouse:** Geraldine Norma Brown (m. 1945, died 1984); Linda McCoy (m. 1996). **Children:** Theodore, Anthony, Pamela, Eric (GB).

Prize: *Commentary,* 1990: *Los Angeles Times,* Los Angeles, CA: Los Angeles Times, 1989.

Career: Campus Correspondent, *Hartford (CT) Times,* 1943; Police and Federal Beat Reporter, *New Haven (CT) Register,* 1943-44; General Assignment Reporter and Rewriteman, *Los Angeles Examiner,* 1944-48; Los Angeles Correspondent, *Time* Magazine, 1948-54; Writer, *Sports Illustrated,* 1953-61; Columnist, *Los Angeles Times,* 1961-.

Selected Works: *The Best of Jim Murray,* 1965. *The Sporting World of Jim Murray,* 1968. *The Jim Murray Collection,* 1988. *Jim Murray: An Autobiography,* 1993.

Other Awards: America's Best Sportswriter, National Association of Sportscasters and Sportswriters, 1964, 1966-74. National Headliners Club Award, 1965, 1976. Alumni Medal, Trinity College, CT, 1972. Hall of Fame, National Sportscasters and

Sportswriters, 1977. Victor Award, 1982. Red Smith Award for Sportswriting, 1982. Best Column Writing Award, Associated Press Sports Editors Association Award, 1984. J.G. Taylor Spink Award for Meritorious Contributions to Baseball Writing, Baseball Writers Association of America, 1987. Inducted Writer's Wing, Baseball Hall of Fame, 1988. Washington, DC Journalism Award. Lifetime Achievement Award, Professional Golfers Association, 1993. Lincoln Werden Memorial Award, Metropolitan Golf Writers Association, 1997. Honorary Degrees: Trinity College, CT, 1981; Pepperdine University, CA, 1987.

For More Information: *The Pulitzer Prizes 1990,* New York: Simon & Schuster, 1990: 353-377; *Los Angeles Times,* 18 February (1996): C3; *Los Angeles Times,* 18 August (1998): 1+.

Commentary: Jim Murray started out in Los Angeles covering Hollywood and its various celebrities. He went on to help found the West Coast edition of *Sports Illustrated* and then settled into reporting sports in his unique way for the *Los Angeles Times.* He won the Commentary Pulitzer Prize for the body of his work during 1989. He was the fourth sportswriter to be honored with a Pulitzer Prize. (The three previous honorees were writers for the *New York Times.*)

1991

Jimmie Lee Hoagland 112

Birth: January 22, 1940; Rock Hill, SC. **Parents:** Lee Roy Hoagland Jr. and Edith Irene (Sullivan). **Education:** University of South Carolina: AB, Phi Beta Kappa. University of Aix-en-Provence, France. **Spouse:** Elizabeth Hue Becker (m. 1979, d.); Jane

Stanton Hitchcock (m. 1995). **Children:** Laura Lee, Lily Hue, Lee Clayton (EB).

Prize: *International Reporting,* 1971: *Washington Post,* Washington, DC: Washington Post, 1970. *Commentary,* 1991: *Washington Post,* March 29; April 10; April 23; July 5, Washington, DC: Washington Post, 1990.

Career: Part-Time Summer Reporter, *Rock Hill (SC) Evening Herald,* 1958-60; Reporter, *Rock Hill (SC) Evening Herald,* 1960-62; Served in U.S. Air Force, 1962-64; Copy Editor, Paris (France), *New York Times,* 1964-66; City Reporter, *Washington (DC) Post,* 1966-68; Correspondent, Africa, *Washington (DC) Post,* 1969-72; Correspondent, Middle East, *Washington (DC) Post,* 1972-75; Foreign Editor, *Washington (DC) Post,* 1979-81; Assistant Managing Editor, Foreign News, *Washington (DC) Post,* 1981-86; Associate Editor and Chief Foreign Correspondent, *Washington (DC) Post,* 1986-; Columnist, *Washington (DC) Post,* 1990-.

Selected Works: *Apartheid,* 1970. *South Africa: Civilizations in Conflict,* 1972.

Other Awards: Ford Foundation Fellow, Advanced International Reporting Program, Columbia University, NY, 1968-69. Overseas Press Club Award, 1977. Eugene Meyer Career Achievement Award, 1994.

For More Information: *Washington Post,* 10 April (1991): A1; *Rock Hill Herald,* December 16, 1995: 1A.

Commentary: Jim Hoagland's first Pulitzer Prize was for his coverage of apartheid in South Africa. Between April 12 and May 25, 1970, he studied the institution in South Africa. He produced a series of articles which included a description of how apartheid worked, the economic and political pressures it produced, and the effects of the policy both inside and outside South Africa.

For his 1991 award, his column delved into the events leading up to the Persian Gulf War and the problems of Soviet President Mikhail Gorbachev. During the year, he interviewed both President Gorbachev and Saddam Hussein. His column has been syndicated since 1988.

1992

Anna Quindlen   113

Birth: July 8, 1953; Philadelphia, PA. **Parents:** Robert V. Quindlen and Prudence Q. **Religion:** Roman Catholic. **Education:** Barnard College, NY: BA. **Spouse:** Gerald Krovatin (m. 1978). **Children:** Quindlen, Christopher, Maria.

Prize: *Commentary,* 1992: *New York Times,* New York: New York Times, 1991.

Career: Reporter, *New York (NY) Post,* 1974-77; General Assignment Reporter, *New York Times,* 1977-81; Columnist, "About New York," *New York Times,* 1981-83; Deputy Metropolitan Editor, *New York Times,* 1983-85; Columnist, "Life in the 30's," *New York Times,* 1986-88; Columnist, "Public and Private," *New York Times,* 1989-94; Writer.

Selected Works: *Living Out Loud,* 1988. *Object Lessons,* 1991. *The Tree That Came to Stay* (with Nancy Carpenter), 1992. *Thinking Out Loud,* 1993. *One True Thing,* 1994. *Naked Babies* (with Nick Kelsh), 1996. *Happily Ever After* (with James Stevenson), 1997. *Black and Blue,* 1998.

Other Awards: Meyer Berger Award, Columbia University, NY, 1983. Outstanding Mother of America, National Mother's Day Committee, 1988.

For More Information: Ricchiardi, Sherry, *Women on Deadline: A Collection of America's Best,* Ames: Iowa State University Press, 1991: 117-134; *Buffalo News Magazine,* 1 November (1992): 6; Braden, Maria, *She Said What? Interviews With Women Newspaper Columnists,* Lexington: University Press of Kentucky, 1993: 175-187; *New York Times,* 10 September (1994): Section 1: 15; *Chicago Tribune,* 11 December (1994): Woman News: 1; *Houston Chronicle,* 10 November (1995): 6.

Commentary: Anna Quindlen's career began as a general assignment reporter; she then became a columnist at the *New York Times,* an editor, and then a columnist once again, all while raising a family. She left the *New York Times* in 1994 to pursue writing novels full time. Her column "Public and Private" and its comments and observations on life won her a Pulitzer Prize in 1992.

1993

Elizabeth R. Balmaseda   114

Birth: January 17, 1959; Puerto Padre, Cuba. **Parents:** Eduardo Balmaseda and Ada. **Education:** Miami-Dade Community College, FL: AA. Florida

International University: BS. **Spouse:** Pedro R. Sevcec (m. 1987).

Prize: *Commentary,* 1993: *Miami Herald,* Miami, FL: Miami Herald, 1992.

Career: Editor, college paper; Reporter, WINZ News Radio, 1979-80; Intern, *Miami (FL) Herald,* 1980; Staff Reporter, *Miami (FL) Herald,* 1981; General Assignment Reporter, *Miami Herald,* ?-1985; Central America Bureau Chief, *Newsweek,* 1985; Field Producer, NBC-News, Honduras, ?-1987; Feature Writer, *Miami Herald,* 1987-90; Staff, *Miami Herald Sunday Magazine,* 1990-91; Columnist, *Miami Herald,* 1991-.

Other Awards: National Association of Hispanic Journalists Award, 1989.

For More Information: Riley, Sam G., *Biographical Dictionary of American Newspaper Columnists,* Westport, CT: Greenwood Press, 1995.

Commentary: Liz Balmaseda left Cuba at the age of 10 months in 1959. She has said that she tries to reflect "the real" Miami in her column, to capture the "ever-changing, multiethnic, and multiracial" aspects of the city. She was cited by the Pulitzer Board for her writing from Haiti, on its crumbling political and social conditions and for her columns on the lives of Cuban Americans in Miami. She was a finalist for a Pulitzer Prize in 1992.

1994

William James Raspberry   115

Birth: October 12, 1935; Okolona, MS. **Parents:** James Lee Raspberry and Willie Mae (Tucker). **Education:** Indiana Central College: BS. **Spouse:** Sondra Patricia Dodson (m. 1966). **Children:** Patricia, Angela, Mark.

Prize: *Commentary,* 1994: *Washington Post,* Washington, DC: Washington Post, 1993.

Career: Reporter, Photographer, Proofreader, Editorial Writer, Associate Managing Editor, *Indianapolis (IN) Recorder,* 1956-60; Public Information Officer, U.S. Army, 1960-62; Teletypist, *Washington (DC) Post,* 1962; Reporter, *Washington (DC) Post,* 1962-64; Assistant City Editor, *Washington (DC) Post,* 1965; Columnist, *Washington (DC) Post,* 1966-; Journalism Instructor, Howard University, 1971-73; Commentator, Washington, DC, WTTG-TV, 1973-75; Discussion Panelist, Washington, DC WRC-TV, 1974-75.

Selected Works: *Looking Back at Us,* 1991. *Crisis at Community: Alfred M. Landon Lectures on Public Issues,* 1995.

Other Awards: Journalist of the Year, Capital Press Club, 1965. Liberty Bell Award, Federal Bar Association. Silver Em Award, University of Mississippi. Hall of Fame, Society of Professional Journalists, 1992. Lifetime Achievement Award, National Society of Newspaper Columnists, 1995. Honorary Degrees: Georgetown University, Washington, DC; University of Maryland; University of Indianapolis; Virginia State University.

For More Information: *Contemporary Black Biography, Volume 2,* Detroit: Gale Research Company, 1992; *Contemporary Authors, Volume 110,* Detroit: Gale Research Company, 1984; *American Journalism Review,* 16 (May 1994): 28-33; Riley, Sam G., *Biographical Dictionary of American Newspaper Columnists,* Westport, CT: Greenwood Press, 1995.

Commentary: William Raspberry, a longtime columnist for the *Washington Post,* won a Pulitzer Prize "for his compelling commentaries on social and political subjects."

1995

James Dwyer   116

Birth: March 4, 1957; New York, NY. **Parents:** Philip Dwyer and Mary (Molloy). **Religion:** Roman Catholic. **Education:** Fordham University, NY: BS. Columbia University, NY: MS. **Spouse:** Catherine Muir. **Children:** Maura Jean, Catherine Elizabeth.

Prize: *Commentary,* 1995: *Newsday,* Garden City, NY: Newsday, 1994.

Career: Reporter, *Hudson (NY) Dispatch,* 1980-81; Reporter, *Elizabeth (NJ) Daily Journal,* 1982; Reporter, *Hackensack (NJ) Record,* 1983-84; Queens Court Reporter, *Newsday (NY),* 1984; Subway Beat Reporter, *Newsday (NY),* 1986-90; Columnist, *Newsday (NY)* 1990-95; Columnist, *New York Daily News,* 1995-.

Selected Works: *Subway Lives: 24 Hours in the Life of the New York City Subway,* 1991. *Two Seconds under the World: Terror Comes to America; the Conspiracy behind the World Trade Center Bombing* (with others), 1994.

Other Awards: Full Presidential Scholarship, Fordham University, NY, 1979. Meyer Berger Award, Columbia University, NY, 1988. National Headliners Club Award, 1989-90. Distinguished Writing Award, American Society of Newspaper Editors, 1991.

For More Information: Bates, J. Douglas, *The Pulitzer Prize: The Inside Story of America's Most Prestigious Award,* New York: Carol Publishing Group, 1991; *Newsday,* 19 April (1995): A3; *New York Daily News,* 17 September (1995): 3.

Commentary: Jim Dwyer, a 1990 finalist for a Specialized Reporting Pulitzer Prize, won the Commentary award for his "compelling and compassionate columns about New York City." He became the second writer of the "In the Subway" column, and after taking a break to write a book, he returned to *Newsday* to write a general interest column. In 1995 he moved to the *New York Daily News.*

1996

E.R. Shipp   117

Birth: June 6, 1955; Conyers, GA. **Parents:** Johnnie Will Shipp Sr. and Minnie Ola (Moore). **Education:** Georgia State University: BA. Columbia University, NY: MS. Columbia University, NY: JD. Columbia University, NY: MA.

Prize: *Commentary,* 1996: *New York Daily News,* New York: New York Daily News, 1995.

Career: Intern, *Atlanta (GA) Journal;* Reporter, Editor, *New York Times,* 1980-93; Columnist, *New York Daily News,* 1994-; Assistant Professor of Journalism, Columbia University (NY), 1994-.

Selected Works: *Outrage: The Story behind the Tawana Brawley Hoax* (with others), 1990.

For More Information: *Editor & Publisher,* 129 (9 November 1996): 38-39.

Commentary: E.R. Shipp said in *Editor & Publisher,* "If you feel passionate about a subject, the columns almost write themselves." She won a Pulitzer Prize for her commentary on race, welfare, and other social issues. A few topics she covered in 1995 were Johnnie Cochran's use of race as a tactic in the O.J. Simpson trial, affirmative action, and the Million Man March.

Shipp, who grew up in the South, the oldest of six children, went north for graduate school and stayed there.

1997

Eileen McNamara 118

Birth: May 30, 1952; Cambridge, MA. **Education:** Barnard College, NY. Columbia University, NY. **Spouse:** Peter May. **Children:** Timothy Daniel, Patrick, Katie.

Prize: *Commentary,* 1997: *Boston Globe,* Boston: Boston Globe, 1996.

Career: Copy Writer, United Press International; Secretary, *Boston Globe,* 1976; Reporter, *Boston Globe,* ?-1994; Columnist, *Boston Globe,* 1995-; Journalism Lecturer, Brandeis University (MA); Freelance writer.

Selected Works: *Breakdown: Sex, Suicide, and the Harvard Psychiatrist,* 1994.

Other Awards: Robert F. Kennedy Journalism Award. Best Reporter in Boston, *Boston Magazine,* 1987. Year's Most Promising Young Americans, *Esquire Magazine,* 1987. Nieman Fellow, Harvard University, MA, 1988. Sigma Delta Chi Award, 1993. Feature Writing Award, New England Associated Press News Executive Association, 1993. Distinguished Writing Award, American Society of Newspaper Editors, 1997.

For More Information: *Boston Globe,* 8 April (1997): A1.

Commentary: Eileen McNamara says that her column "is about the ordinary people of Boston who open their lives to us and tell us their stories." She was named a columnist in 1995 after 20 years as a reporter. Her column in 1996 covered such topics as the story of a newlywed who had been widowed by a drunk driver, and the New England Patriots professional football team, who extended a job offer to a college player convicted of sexual assault. (The Patriots backed away after McNamara wrote her column.)

1998

Michael McAlary 119

Birth Place: Brooklyn, NY. **Parents:** Jack McAlary and Ellen. **Education:** Syracuse University, NY. **Spouse:** Alice Argento. **Children:** Ryan, Carla, Mickey, Quinn.

Prize: *Commentary,* 1998: *New York Daily News,* "Frightful Whisperings From a Coney Island Hospital Bed," August 13; "Victim and City Deeply Scarred," August 14; "Gal Pal: He Couldn't Do It," August 18; "'It Wasn't Me,' Cop Maintains," August 22; "Rudy & Brass Reap Harvest of Hate," August 29; "They Saw Louima's Terror," September 5; "Home Sweet Heartache," October 10, New York: *New York Daily News,* 1997.

Career: Sportswriter, *Boston Herald-American,* 1979; *ABC Sports; New York Post; New York Newsday;* Columnist, *New York Daily News;* Columnist, *New York Post;* Columnist, *New York Daily News,* 1993-94; Columnist, *New York Post,* 1994-; Columnist, *New York Daily News,.*

Selected Works: *Buddy Boys: When Good Cops Turn Bad,* 1987. *Cop Shot: The Murder of Edward Byrne,* 1990. *Good Cop, Bad Cop: Detective Joe Trimboli's Heroic Pursuit of NYPD Officer Michael Dowd,* 1994. *Cop Land: Based on the Screenplay by James Mangold* (with James Mangold), 1997. *Sore Loser: A Mickey Donovan Mystery.*

Other Awards: Society of Professional Journalists Award, New York Chapter, 1998.

For More Information: *Washington Times,* February 2, 1989: E2; *New York Daily News* April 15, 1998: 2, 3; *American Journalism Review,* 20:5 (June 1998): 14-15.

Commentary: Mike McAlary was awarded a Pulitzer Prize "for his coverage of the brutalization of a Haitian immigrant by police officers at a Brooklyn stationhouse." McAlary had been a finalist in the Breaking News Reporting category but was moved into the Commentary category by the Pulitzer Prize Board. His column covers issues in the metropolitan New York region and has broken many stories, including a few on police corruption.

Correspondence

1929

Paul Scott Mowrer 120

Birth: July 14, 1887; Bloomington, IL. **Death:** April 4, 1971. **Parents:** Rufus Mowrer and Nell (Scott). **Religion:** Protestant. **Education:** University of Michigan. **Spouse:** Winifred Adams (m. 1909, died); Hadley Hemingway (m. 1933). **Children:** Richard Scott, David Adams (WA).

Prize: *Correspondence,* 1929: *Chicago Daily News,* Chicago: Chicago Daily News, 1928.

Career: Picture Chaser, *Chicago Daily News,* 1905; Reporter, *Chicago Daily News,* 1905-06; Paris Correspondent, *Chicago Daily News,* 1908-10; Correspondent, Allied Armies, First Balkan War, 1912-13; Paris (France) Bureau Director, *Chicago Daily News,* 1914-18; Official War Correspondent to French Armies, 1917; Peace Conference Bureau Director, *Chicago Daily News,* 1918-19; War Correspondent, Morocco, *Chicago Daily News,* 1924-25; Associate Editor and Chief Editorial Writer, *Chicago Daily News,* 1934-35; Editor, *Chicago Daily News,* 1935-44; European Editor, *New York (NY) Post,* 1945-46; Editor, *New York (NY) Post,* 1946-48; Free-lance writer.

Selected Works: *Hours of France,* 1918. *Balkanized Europe: A Study in Political Analysis and Reconstruction,* 1921. *The Good Comrade and Fairies,* 1923. *Our Foreign Affairs,* 1924. *Steadfast France* (with others), 1924. *Red Russia's Menace: Chicago Daily News Reprints, 21,* 1925. *1938 A.D.* (with Vaughn Shoemaker), 1938. *Poems between Wars: Hail Illinois! France Farewell,* 1941. *The House of Europe,* 1945. *On Going to Live in New Hampshire,* 1953. *And Let the Glory Go,* 1955. *Twenty-One and Sixty-Five,* 1958. *The Mothering Land, Selected Poems, 1918-1958,* 1960. *High Mountain Pond,* 1962. *School for Diplomats,* 1964. *This Teeming Earth,* 1965. *The Island Ireland,* 1966. *Six Plays,* 1967. *The Poems of Paul Scott Mowrer, 1918-1966,* 1968.

Other Awards: Legion of Honor, French General Headquarters, 1918. Sigma Delta Chi National Scholarship Award for Foreign Correspondent, 1932. Lyric Poetry Award, 1961-62. Honorary Degree, University of Michigan, 1941.

For More Information: *Chicago Daily News,* 13 May (1929): 1, 7; *Contemporary Authors, First Revision Series, Volumes 5-8,* Detroit: Gale Research Company, 1969; *Chicago Daily News,* 6 April (1971): 3; *Dictionary of Literary Biography, Volume 29,* Detroit: Gale Research Company, 1984; McKerns,

Joseph P., *Biographical Dictionary of American Journalism,* New York: Greenwood Press, 1989.

Commentary: Paul Scott Mowrer won the first Pulitzer Prize given in the Correspondence category. It was for his work from Paris. Mowrer covered every European battlefront during World War I. His brother, Edgar Ansel Mowrer, would win the same prize four years later.

1930

Leland Stowe 121

Birth: November 10, 1899; Southbury, CT. **Death:** January 16, 1994. **Parents:** Frank Philip Stowe and Eva Sarah (Noe). **Religion:** Methodist. **Education:** Wesleyan University, CT: BA. **Spouse:** Ruth F. Bernot (m. 1924, div.); Theodora F. Calauz (m. 1952). **Children:** Bruce, Alan (RB).

Prize: *Correspondence,* 1930: *New York Herald-Tribune,* New York: New York Herald-Tribune, 1929.

Career: Campus Correspondent, *Springfield (MA) Republican;* Reporter, *Worchester (MA) Telegram,* 1921; Reporter, *New York Herald and Pathe News,* 1922-26; Paris Correspondent, *New York Herald-Tribune,* 1926-35; Reporter, League of Nations Councils and Assemblies, *New York Herald-Tribune,* 1927; War Correspondent, *Chicago (IL) Daily News,* 1939-43; War Correspondent, *New York Post,* 1939-43; Freelance war correspondent, 1944-45; Radio Commentator, American Broadcasting Company, 1944-46; Radio Commentator, Mutual Broadcasting System, 1945-46; Foreign Editor, *Reporter Magazine,* 1949-50; Director, Radio Free Europe News Service, 1952-54; Roving Editor, *Reader's Digest,* 1955-76; Professor of Journalism, University of Michigan, 1956-69; Journalist, Freelance writer, Radio commentator.

Selected Works: *No Other Road to Freedom,* 1941. *Nazi Mean War,* 1943. *Are You Voting for a Third World War?,* 1944. *They Shall Not Sleep,* 1944. *Challenge to Freedom* (with Constantine Poulos), 1945. *While Time Remains,* 1946. *Target: You. Conquest by Terror: The Story of Satellite Europe,* 1952. *Crusoe of Lonesome Lake,* 1957. *The Last Great Frontiersman,* 1982.

Other Awards: French Legion d'Honneur Award. Distinguished Service Award, Sigma Delta Chi, 1941. Distinguished Service Award, Overseas Press Club, 1941. Distinguished Service Award, University of Missouri School of Journalism, 1941. Military Cross, Greece, 1945. James L. McConaughty Award, Wesleyan University, CT, 1963. Honorary Degrees: Wesleyan University, CT, 1936, 1944; Harvard University, MA, 1945; Hobart College, NY, 1946.

For More Information: *Current Biography Yearbook, 1940,* New York: H.W. Wilson, 1940: 372-373; *Dictionary of Literary Biography, Volume 29,* Detroit: Gale Research Company, 1984; McKerns, Joseph P., *Biographical Dictionary of American Journalism,* New York: Greenwood Press, 1989; *Detroit News,* 17 January (1994): D9; *New York Times,* 18 January (1994): D23.

Commentary: Leland Stowe won a Pulitzer Prize for his coverage of the 1929 Paris reparations conference. It was at this conference that the Young Plan for reducing and extending Germany's World War I reparations was made. The conference also created the Bank for International Settlements.

1931

Hubert Renfro Knickerbocker 122

Birth: January 31, 1898; Yoakum, TX. **Death:** July 12, 1949. **Parents:** Rev. Hubert Delancey Knickerbocker and Julia Catherine (Opdenweyer). **Education:** Southwestern University, TX: AB. Columbia University, NY. Munich University, Germany. University of Vienna, Austria. University of Berlin, Germany. **Spouse:** Laura Patrick (m. 1918, div.); Agnes Schjoldager. **Children:** One son (LP); Three daughters (AS).

Prize: *Correspondence,* 1931: *Philadelphia Public Ledger* and *New York Evening Post,* 1930.

Career: Signal Corps member, U.S. Army, WWI; Reporter, *Newark (NJ) Morning Ledger,* 1920-22; Reporter, *New York Sun,* 1922; Reporter, *New York Evening Post,* 1922; Head of the Journalism Department, Southern Methodist University (TX), 1922-23; Occasional Correspondent, United Press International, 1923; Assistant Correspondent, Berlin (Germany), *New York Evening Post* and *Philadelphia (PA) Public Ledger,* 1924-25; Correspondent, Moscow (Russia) International News Service, 1925-27; Correspondent, Berlin (Germany), International News Service, 1928-33; Traveling Correspondent, International News Service, 1933-41; Reporter, Italo-Abyssinian War, 1935-36, Spanish Civil War, 1936-37, Sino-Japanese War, 1937, Battle of France, 1939-40, Battle of Britain, London Blitz, 1940; Chief Foreign Service, Southwest Pacific, Java, Australia, New Guinea, North Africa, Sicily, Italy, Normandy, France, Belgium, Germany, Middle East, Palestine, Turkey, *Chicago Sun,* 1941-45.

Selected Works: *Fighting the Red Trade Menace,* 1931. *The Red Menace: Progress of the Soviet Five Year Plan,* 1931. *The German Crisis,* 1932. *Can Europe Recover?,* 1932. *The Boiling Point: Will War Come in Europe?,* 1934. *Siege of the Alcazar: A Warlog of the Spanish Revolution,* 1937. *Is Tomorrow Hitler's: 200 Questions on the Battle of Mankind,* 1941. *Danger Forward: The Story of the First Division in World War II,* 1947.

Other Awards: Honorary Degree, Southwestern University, TX, 1941.

For More Information: *Current Biography Yearbook, 1940,* New York: H.W. Wilson Company, (1940): 460-61; *New York Times,* 13 July (1949): 3; Sloan, William David, et al., *The Great Reporters: An Anthology of News Writing at its Best,* Northport, AL: Vision Press, 1992.

Commentary: H.R. Knickerbocker's 24 stories in his series titled "The Red Trade Menace," won a Pulitzer Prize for correspondence in 1930. The series was one of the first looks at the Soviet Union's five-year plan and the background and the history of Joseph Stalin. Knickerbocker died in an airplane crash that killed several journalists returning from India.

1932

Walter Duranty 123

Birth: May 25, 1884; Liverpool, England. **Death:** October 3, 1957. **Parents:** William Steel Duranty and Emmeline (Hutchins). **Education:** Harrow and Bedford College. Emanuel College of Cambridge University, England, First Class Honors. **Spouse:** Anna Enwright (m. 1957).

Prize: *Correspondence,* 1932: *New York Times,* "The Russian Looks at the World," "Stalin's Russia

Is an Echo of Iron Ivan's," "Red Russia of Today Ruled by Stalinism," New York: New York Times, 1931.

Career: Foreign Correspondent, *New York Times,* 1913-39; Correspondent with French Armies, 1917-18; Head of Paris Bureau, *New York Times,* 1920-22; Roving Correspondent, *New York Times,* 1934-39; Correspondent, Europe, U.S.S.R, Japan, North American Newspaper Alliance, 1939-41; Writer.

Selected Works: *The Curious Lottery and Other Tales of Russian Justice,* 1929. *Red Economics* (with Gerherd Dobbert), 1932. *Duranty Reports Russia* (with others), 1934. *Europe: War or Peace? World Affairs Pamphlets, No. 7,* 1935. *I Write as I Please,* 1935. *One Life, One Kopeck: A Novel,* 1937. *Soloman's Cat,* 1937. *Babies without Tails: Stories; Modern Age Books, Blue Seal Books, No. 1,* 1937. *The Kremlin and the People,* 1941. *Search for a Key,* 1943. *USSR: The Story of Soviet Russia,* 1944. *Return to the Vineyard* (with Mary Loos), 1945. *Stalin & Co.: The Politburo, the Men Who Run Russia,* 1949.

Other Awards: O. Henry Short Story Prize, 1929.

For More Information: Scheffer, Paul, *Seven Years in Soviet Russia,* New York: MacMillan, 1932; Berger, Meyer, *The Story of the New York Times,* New York: Simon & Schuster, 1951; *New York Times,* 4 October (1957): 23; Filene, Peter G., *Americans and the Soviet Experiment, 1917-1933,* Cambridge, MA: Harvard University Press, 1967; *Dictionary of American Biography, Supplement 6,* New York: Charles Scribner's Sons, 1980; *Dictionary of Literary Biography, Volume 29,* Detroit: Gale Research Company, 1984; McKerns, Joseph P., *Biographical Dictionary of American Journalism,* New York: Greenwood Press, 1989; Taylor, S.J., *Stalin's Apologist: Walter Duranty, the New York Time's Man in Moscow,* New York: Oxford University Press, 1990.

Commentary: There were two awards given in the Correspondence category in 1932, one to Charles G. Ross and another to Walter Duranty. Duranty's award was for his coverage of Russia, which showed his "profound and intimate comprehension of conditions in Russia."

Duranty had a very descriptive writing style and he could translate easily into French, Russian, Latin, or Greek. His reporting from Russia has created some controversy in recent years, as he did not portray many of the harsher aspects of the Soviet Union in the dispatches he sent to the *New York Times.*

Charles Griffith Ross   124

Birth: November 9, 1885; Independence, MO. **Death:** December 5, 1950. **Parents:** James Bruce Ross and Ella (Thomas). **Education:** University of

Missouri: AB, Phi Beta Kappa. **Spouse:** Florence Griffin (m. 1913). **Children:** John, Walter.

Prize: *Correspondence,* 1932: *St. Louis Post-Dispatch,* "The Country's Plight—What Can Be Done About It?" St. Louis: St. Louis Post-Dispatch, 1931.

Career: Staff member *Columbia (MO) Herald,* 1904-06; Staff member *Victor (CO) Record,* 1906; Staff member *St. Louis (MO) Post-Dispatch,* 1906-07; Staff member *St. Louis (MO) Republic,* 1907-08; Faculty member, School of Journalism, University of Missouri, 1908-18; Faculty member, sabbatical leave, 1916-17; Sub-Editor, *Melbourne (Australia) Herald* 1916-17; Chief Correspondent, Washington (DC), *St. Louis (MO) Post-Dispatch,* 1918-34; Editorial Page Editor, *St. Louis (MO) Post-Dispatch,* 1934-39; Contributing Editor, *St. Louis (MO) Post-Dispatch,* 1939-45; Presidential Press Secretary, Harry S Truman, 1945.

Selected Works: *The Writing of News,* 1911. *The Country's Plight—What Can Be Done about It? An Exposition of What President Hoover Has Characterized as the "Greatest Crisis the World Has Ever Known,"* 1931. *The Story of the St. Louis Post-Dispatch,* 1940.

Other Awards: Medal of Honor, University of Missouri, 1933. Honorary National President, Sigma Delta Chi, 1935. Honorary Degrees: George Washington University, DC, 1935; University of Missouri, 1936.

For More Information: *St. Louis Post-Dispatch,* 20 April (1945): 1+; *New York Times,* 6 December (1950): 1+; *National Cyclopaedia of American Biography, Volume 42,* New York: James T. White & Company, 1958: 199; Farrar, Ronald T., *Reluctant Servant, The Story of Charles G. Ross,* Columbia: University of Missouri Press, 1969; *Dictionary of American Biography, Supplement 4,* New York: Charles Scribner's Sons, 1974.

Commentary: In a rare occurrence, there were two Prizes given in the Correspondence category in 1932, one to Walter Duranty and another to Charles G. Ross. Ross's winning article discussed the economic condition of the United States. He wrote the article while head of the Washington bureau of the *St. Louis Post-Dispatch.* He later was appointed press secretary to Harry S. Truman.

1933

Edgar Ansel Mowrer   125

Birth: March 8, 1892; Bloomington, IL. **Death:** March 2, 1977. **Parents:** Rufus Mowrer and Nell (Scott). **Religion:** Deist. **Education:** University of Michigan: BA. University of Chicago. Sorbonne University, Paris, France. **Spouse:** Lilian May Thomson (m. 1916, died 1990). **Children:** Diane.

Prize: *Correspondence,* 1933: *Chicago Daily News,* Chicago: Chicago Daily News, 1932.

Career: Contributor to American and English magazines, 1914-77; War Correspondent, France, Belgium, Italy, *Chicago Daily News,* 1914-15; Correspondent, Rome (Italy), *Chicago Daily News,* ?-1924; Berlin (Germany) Bureau Chief, *Chicago Daily News,* 1924-33; Paris (France) Bureau Chief, *Chicago Daily News,* 1934-39; Correspondent, Washington (DC), *Chicago Daily News,* 1940-41; Staff member, Office of Facts and Figures and Office of War Information, ?-1943; Columnist of foreign affairs, broadcaster; Editor, *Western World,* 1957-60.

Selected Works: *Immortal Italy,* 1922. *This American World,* 1928. *Germany Puts the Clock Back,* 1933. *The Dragon Wakes: A Report from China,* 1939. *Fifth Column Lessons for America* (with William J. Donovan), 1941. *Global War: An Atlas of World Strategy* (with Marthe Rajchman), 1942. *Our State Department and North Africa,* 1943. *The Nightmare of American Foreign Policy,* 1948. *Challenge and Decision,* 1950. *A Good Time to Be Alive,* 1959. *An End to Make-Believe,* 1961. *Triumph and Turmoil: A Personal History of Our Time,* 1968. *Umano and the Price of Lasting Peace* (with Lilian T. Mowrer), 1973.

Other Awards: Officer, Legion of Honor.

For More Information: *Chicago Daily News,* 2 May (1933): 4; Mowrer, Lilian T., *Journalist's Wife,* New York: W. Morrow and Company, 1937; *Current Biography Yearbook, 1941,* New York: H.W. Wilson Company, 1941; *Chicago Daily News,* 3 March (1977): 6; *New York Times,* 4 March (1977): 12; *Dictionary of Literary Biography, Volume 29,* Detroit: Gale Research Company, 1984; McKerns, Joseph P., *Biographical Dictionary of American Journalism,* New York: Greenwood Press, 1989; *Dictionary of American Biography, Supplement 10,* New York: Charles Scribner's Sons, 1995; Riley, Sam G., *Biographical Dictionary of American Newspaper Columnists,* Westport, CT: Greenwood Press, 1995.

Commentary: Edgar Ansel Mowrer was the second member of his family to win a Pulitzer Prize in the Correspondence category. His brother Paul Scott Mowrer won in 1929. Edgar Mowrer won for his day-to-day coverage of events in Europe. Also noted in his citation was "his interpretation ... of the German political crises in 1932." He was a war correspondent during World War I and was arrested several times for entering military zones where journalists were forbidden. He also covered the rise of Mussolini and the Fascists in Italy.

1934

Frederick T. Birchall   126

Birth: 1871; Warrington, England. **Death:** March 7, 1955. **Parents:** Thomas Birchall and Elizabeth (King). **Spouse:** Annie Hood (m. 1895, died 1955).

Prize: *Correspondence,* 1934: *New York Times,* New York: New York Times, 1933.

Career: Volunteer Reporter, Local Newspaper Staff member; *Pall Mall Gazette;* Editor, small weekly newspaper in Philadelphia; Police Headquarters Reporter for News Bureau, 2 years; Copyreader, *New York Tribune,* 2 Years; Copy Editor, *Morning Sun;* Night City Editor, *New York Times,* 1905; Employee of British Government in London During WWI; Assistant Managing Editor, *New York Times,* 1920-26; Acting Managing Editor, *New York Times,* 1926-31; European News Service, *New York Times,* 1932-1941; Ottawa (Canada) Bureau Chief, *New York Times,* ?-1943.

Selected Works: *The Storm Breaks: A Panorama of Europe and the Forces That Have Wrecked Its Peace,* 1940.

For More Information: *New York Times,* 8 May (1934): 20; *New York Times,* 7 March (1955): 27; *Dictionary of American Biography, Supplement 5,* New York: Charles Scribner's Sons, 1977; McKerns, Joseph P., *Biographical Dictionary of American Journalism,* New York: Greenwood Press, 1989.

Commentary: Frederick T. Birchall did not retire when he had the opportunity; instead, he left an editorial job for a reporting position. It was his writing from Europe that won him a Pulitzer Prize.

Birchall immigrated to the United States in 1893. After little success in the Philadelphia news business, he moved to New York City. He covered the police beat and police headquarters when Theodore Roosevelt was the police commissioner of New York.

1935

Arthur Krock   127

Birth: November 16, 1886; Glasgow, KY. **Death:** April 12, 1974. **Parents:** Joseph Krock and Caroline (Morris). **Education:** Lewis Institute, IL: AA. Princeton University, NJ. **Spouse:** Marguerite Polleys (m. 1911, died 1938); Martha McCullock Granger Blair (m. 1939). **Children:** Thomas (MP).

Prize: *Correspondence,* 1935: *New York Times,* New York: *New York Times,* 1934. *Correspondence,* 1938: *New York Times,* New York: *New York Times,* 1937. *Special Awards and Citations: Journalism,* 1951: *New York Times,* New York: New York Times, 1950.

Career: Police Reporter, *Louisville (KY) Herald,* 1906-08; Assistant Kentucky Correspondent, *Cincinnati (OH) Enquirer,* 1907; Chief Deputy Sheriff, Jefferson County (KY); Night Editor, Associated Press, 1908; Correspondent, Washington (DC), *Louisville (KY) Times,* 1909-; Correspondent, Washington (DC), *Louisville (KY) Courier-Journal,* 1910-; Managing Editor, *Louisville (KY) Courier-Journal,* and *Louisville (KY) Times,* 1915-1919; Editor-in-Chief, *Louisville (KY) Times,* 1919-23; Assistant to Chairman, Democratic National Committee, New York, 1920; Assistant to President, *New York (NY) World,* 1923-27; Editorial Staff, *New York Times,* 1927-; Correspondent, Washington (DC), *New York Times,* 1932-53; Columnist, *New York Times,* 1932-67; Washington (DC) commentator, 1953-67.

Selected Works: *The Editorials of Henry Watterson,* 1923. *We Saw It Happen: The News behind the News That's Fit to Print* (with others), 1938. *In the Nation,* 1966. *Memoirs: Sixty Years on the Firing Lane,* 1968. *The Consent of the Governed and Other Deceits,* 1971. *Myself When Young: Growing up in*

the *1890s,* 1973. *Reminiscences of Arthur Krock,* 1950.

Other Awards: Decorated Commander, Legion D'Honneur, France, 1937. Officer's Cross, Polonia Restituta, 1950. Knights' Cross, Order of St. Olav, Norway, 1950. John Peter Zenger Award, University of Arizona, 1967. Presidential Medal of Honor, 1970. Valley Forge Award, Freedoms Foundation, 1971. Honorary Degrees: Princeton University, NJ, 1937; University of Louisville, KY, 1939; University of Kentucky, 1956; Northwestern University, IL, 1967; Hamilton College, NY, 1967.

For More Information: *Quill,* 31:5 May (1943): 6-8+; *New York Times,* 13 April (1974): 13; *Dictionary of Literary Biography, Volume 29,* Detroit: Gale Research Company, 1984; McKerns, Joseph P., *Biographical Dictionary of American Journalism,* New York: Greenwood Press, 1989; *Louisville Courier-Journal,* 19 September (1993): 6M-Extra; *Dictionary of American Biography, Supplement 9,* New York: Charles Scribner's Sons, 1994; Riley, Sam G., *Biographical Dictionary of American Newspaper Columnists,* Westport, CT: Greenwood Press, 1995.

Commentary: Arthur Krock won Pulitzer Prizes for his excellent correspondence from Washington, DC. His award in 1935 was for his dispatches describing the city under Roosevelt's New Deal. The prize in 1938 was for his exclusive interview with the United States president on February 27, 1937.

The Pulitzer Prize board has a policy of not awarding prizes to individual members of the board; as Krock was a member of the Pulitzer Prize advisory board in 1951, the board did not give him a prize in National Reporting; instead, he was given a special citation.

1936

Wilfred Courtenay Barber   128

Birth: September 15, 1903; New York, NY. **Death:** October 6, 1935. **Parents:** Frederick Courtenay Barber and Clara Marie (Gabler). **Education:** Columbia University, NY. **Spouse:** Josephine Dorothy Sibbald (m. 1934).

Prize: *Correspondence,* 1936: *Chicago Tribune,* Chicago: Chicago Tribune, 14 July 1935: 11.

Career: Junior Partner, Frederick Courtenay Barber and Associates; Associate Editor, *Citizen-Bulletin;* Staff member, *New York Herald-Tribune;* Reporter and Editor, Paris Edition *Chicago Tribune;* Reporter and Editor, London Office, *Chicago Tribune,* 1934; Correspondent, Ethiopia, *Chicago Tribune,* 1935.

Selected Works: *Chicago Daily Tribune,* July 14, 1935.

For More Information: *Chicago Tribune,* 7 October (1935).

Commentary: Wilfred C. Barber, the son, grandson, great grandson, and great-great grandson of war correspondents, was awarded a Pulitzer Prize posthumously. He was the first United States journalist to enter Ethiopia. In September 1935, he went on a 10-day desert trip to the Ogaden front, the only United States correspondent permitted to do so. After returning to Addis Ababa, the capital, he fell ill and died of malaria.

1937

Anne Elizabeth O'Hare McCormick   129

Birth: May 16, 1880; Wakefield, Yorkshire, England. **Death:** May 29, 1954. **Parents:** Thomas J. O'Hare and Teresa Beatrice (Berry). **Religion:** Roman Catholic. **Education:** St. Mary's College, OH: BA. **Spouse:** Francis J. McCormick (m. 1910, died 1954).

Prize: *Correspondence,* 1937: *New York Times,* New York: New York Times, 1936.

Career: Associate Editor, *Catholic Universe Bulletin,* 1898-1910; Freelance writer, 1910-20; Correspondent, *New York Times,* 1922-; Editorial Staff, *New York Times,* 1936-.

Selected Works: *St. Agnes Church, Cleveland, Ohio: An Interpretation,* 1920. *The Hammer and Scythe: Communist Russia Enters the Second Decade,* 1928. *Story of St. Agnes Parish, Cleveland, Ohio, 1893-1937* (with Gilbert P. Jennings), 1937. *The World at Home: Selections from the Writings of Anne O'Hare McCormick,* 1956. *Vatican Journal, 1921-1954,* 1957.

Other Awards: *New York Evening Post,* 1934, Medal for Eminent Achievement, American Women's Association, 1939. Theodore Roosevelt's Association Women's Medal, 1941. Siena Medal, Theta Phi Alpha, 1941. Gold Medal, National Institute of Social Sciences, 1942. Laetare Medal of University of Notre Dame, 1944. Distinguished Service Award of International Altrusa, 1945. Women's National Press Club Achievement Award, 1945. National Achievement Award, Chi Omega, 1946. Theodore Roosevelt D.S.M., 1950. William the Silent Award for Journalism, 1952. Chevalier, National Order of the Legion of Honor. Member, National Institute of Arts and Letters. Honorary Degrees: College of St. Mary of the Spring, 1928; Smith College, MA; University of Dayton, OH; Villanova College, PA; Middlebury College, VT; Elmira College, NY; Columbia University, NY; New York University; Wilson College, PA; New Jersey College for Women; Lafayette College, PA; Fordham University, NY; Manhattan College, NY; Rollins College, FL; Ohio State University; College of Mount St. Vincent, NY; Wellesley College, MA.

For More Information: *New York Times,* 4 May (1937): 20; Hoehn, Matthew, *Catholic Authors: Contemporary Biographical Sketches, 1930-1947,* Newark, NJ: St. Mary's Abbey, 1948; *New York Times,* 30 May (1954): 1; *Notable American Women, The Modern Period: A Biographical Dictionary,* Cambridge, MA: Harvard University Press, 1980; Belford, Barbara, *Brilliant Bylines: A Biographical Anthology of Notable Newspaperwomen in America,* New York: Columbia University Press, 1986: 165-174.

Commentary: Anne O'Hare McCormick was the first woman to win a Pulitzer Prize in a journalism category. Her dispatches and feature articles during 1936 won her the award.

Her husband's career included extensive travel and she took advantage of the opportunity to write about the events and conditions of those places. She interviewed many of the world's leaders of her day, including Mussolini, Hitler, Stalin, Benes, Eden, Dollfuss, Schuschnigg, Stresemann, de Valera, and Roosevelt.

1938

Arthur Krock

Full entry appears as **#127** under "Correspondence," 1935.

1939

Louis Paul Lochner   130

Birth: February 22, 1887; Springfield, IL. **Death:** January 8, 1975. **Parents:** Frederick Lochner and Maria (von Haugwitz). **Education:** Wisconsin Conservatory of Music. University of Wisconsin: AB, Phi Beta Kappa, With Honors. **Spouse:** Emmy Hoyer (m. 1910, died 1920); Hilde De Terra (m. 1922). **Children:** Elsbeth, Robert (EH); Rosemarie (HS).

Prize: *Correspondence,* 1939: Associated Press, 1938.

Career: Editor, student and alumni magazines, Education News Service, 1909-14; Director, Central West Department, American Peace Society, 1913; Secretary, Henry Ford, 1915-16; Secretary, Neutral Conference for Continuous Mediation, 1916; Editor, International Labor News Service, 1918; Foreign Correspondent, 1919-42; European Director, *Federated Press,* 1921-24; Reporter, *Milwaukee (WI) Free Press and Madison (WI) Democrat,* ?-1924; Berlin (Germany) Bureau Chief, Associated Press, 1924-42; War Correspondent, German Western Front, Yugoslavia, Greece, Finland, and Russia, Associated Press, 1941; News Analyst, Commentator, NBC-TV, 1942-44; War Correspondent, Associated Press, 1944-46; Journalist, Germany, 1946-52; German Affairs Consultant, U.S. Department of State, 1952-58; German Affairs Consultant, United Nations, 1958-60; Radio commentator, 1960-63; Writer, 1963-75.

Selected Works: *Mexico: Whose War?,* 1919. *Henry Ford, American's Don Quixote,* 1925. *What about Germany,* 1943. *Fritz Kreisler,* 1950. *Herbert Hoover and Germany,* 1960.

Other Awards: Honorary Degrees: Muhlenberg College, PA, 1942; University of Wisconsin, 1961.

For More Information: *New York Times,* 2 May (1939): 20; Schaleben-Lewis, Joy, *Getting the Story Out of Nazi Germany: Louis P. Lochner, Journalism Monographs, No. 11,* Austin, TX: Association for Education in Journalism, 1969; Rigsby, Gwendolyn Gezelle, A History of Associated Press Pulitzer Prizes (thesis), University of South Carolina, 1993; *New York Times,* 9 January (1975): 38; *Contemporary Authors, Volumes 53-56,* Detroit: Gale Research Company, 1976.

Commentary: Louis P. Lochner won a 1939 Pulitzer Prize for his outstanding correspondence from Germany. Lochner was a pacifist who had served as secretary of the Chicago Peace Society for three years. His skill as a reporter soon overshadowed that portion of his life. Lochner covered many of the major events leading up to World War II as well as the war itself. He interviewed Hitler in 1925 and again in 1932. He also covered the Olympic Games, diplo-

matic conferences, and the first trip of the Hindenburg in Spring 1936.

1940

Otto David Tolischus   131

Birth: November 20, 1890; Russ, Memel Territory, Germany. **Death:** February 24, 1967. **Parents:** David Tolischus and Marie (Kubillus). **Education:** Columbia University, NY: BLitt. **Spouse:** Naya Grecia Zavoyanni (m. 1949).

Prize: *Correspondence,* 1940: *New York Times,* New York: New York Times, 1939.

Career: Reporter, City Editor, Managing Editor, *Cleveland (OH) Press,* 1916-23; Served in U.S. Army, 1918; Correspondent, Berlin (Germany), Universal Service and International News Service, 1923-31; London (England) Bureau Chief, International News Service, 1931-32; Freelance magazine writer, 1932-33; Staff member, Berlin (Germany) Bureau *New York Times,* 1933-40; Correspondent, Stockholm (Sweden), *New York Times,* 1940; Correspondent, Tokyo (Japan), *New York Times* and *London (England) Times,* 1941; Prisoner of War, 1941-42; Editorial Writer, *New York Times,* 1942-64.

Selected Works: *They Wanted War,* 1940. *How Hitler Prepared,* 1940. *Tokyo Record,* 1943. *Through Japanese Eyes,* 1945.

Other Awards: Medal for Excellence, Columbia University, 1941.

For More Information: *Current Biography Yearbook, 1940,* New York: H.W. Wilson Company, 1940; *New York Times,* 7 May (1940): 20; *New York Times,* 25 February (1967): 27; *Contemporary Authors, Volumes 93-96,* Detroit: Gale Research Company, 1980.

Commentary: Otto D. Tolischus's writings on Germany and its economic and ideological background won him a Pulitzer Prize in 1940. Tolischus immigrated to the United States in 1907 and became a naturalized citizen in 1913. He returned to Europe in 1923 and while there, he decided to become a foreign correspondent. He covered the rise of the National Socialist (Nazi) Party and traveled extensively in Poland and Czechoslovakia. He was requested to leave Germany in 1940 and granted an eight-day visa to retrieve his belongings.

1941

Group award   132

Prize: *Correspondence,* 1941.
Commentary: Instead of an individual Pulitzer Prize, a group prize was awarded to the American

news reporters in the war zones of Europe, Asia, and Africa for their distinguished public service and individual achievements.

1942

Carlos Pena Romulo 133

Birth: January 14, 1899; Manila, Philippines. **Death:** December 15, 1985. **Parents:** Gregorio Romulo and Maria (Pena). **Religion:** Catholic. **Education:** University of the Philippines: BA. Columbia University, NY: MA. **Spouse:** Virginia Llamas (m. 1924, died 1968); Beth Day (m. 1979). **Children:** Carlos, Gregorio, Ricardo, Roberto (VL).

Prize: *Correspondence,* 1942: *Philippines Herald,* Philippines: Philippines Herald, 1941.

Career: Editor, Several Philippines Island newspapers, 1919-41; Member, Philippine Independence Mission to U.S., 1921, 1924, 1929, 1933; Faculty member, University of Philippines, 1923-28; Member, Board of Regents, University of Philippines, 1929-45; Editor, *Manila Tribune,* 1930; Editor, *Tribune-Vanguardia-Taliba,* 1931; Publisher of Newspaper Group, *Philippine Herald,* 1933-41; Managing Director of Radio Stations, KZRM and KZRF, Manila, 1939-41; Major, Philippine Army Reserve, U.S. Army, 1941-44; Secretary of Information and Public Relations, President Quezon's War Cabinet, 1943; Secretary of Public Instruction, 1944; Resident Commissioner Of Philippines to U.S., 1944; Permanent Delegate, Republic of Philippines to the United Nations, 1945-54; President of United Nations General Assembly, 1949; Secretary of Foreign Affairs, Philippines, 1950-52, 1969-85; Special and Personal Envoy of the President of the Philippines to U.S., 1954-55; President, University of the Philippines,

1962-68; Secretary of Education, Philippines, 1962-65, 1966-68; Advisor on Foreign Affairs, 1963-85.

Selected Works: *I Saw the Fall of the Philippines,* 1942. *Mother America: A Living Story of Democracy,* 1943. *My Brother Americans,* 1945. *I See the Philippines Rise,* 1946. *The United: A Novel,* 1951. *Crusade in Asia: Philippine Victory,* 1955. *The Meaning of Bandung: Weil Lectures on American Citizenship,* 1956. *The Maysaysay Story* (with Marvin Gray), 1956. *Friend to Friend* (with Pearl S. Buck), 1958. *I Walked with Heroes,* 1961. *Mission to Asia: The Dialogue Begins,* 1964. *Contemporary Nationalism, and the World Order: Azad Memorial Lectures, 1964,* 1964. *Identity and Change towards a Definition,* 1965. *Evasions and Response: Lectures on the American Novel, 1890-1930,* 1966. *Rejoining Our Asian Family,* 1969. *Agenda for the Seventies,* 1969. *The Diplomacy of Consent,* 1976. *Economic Decolonization: The New Imperative of Our Time,* 1977. *The Philippines in the World Today,* 1978. *A Sense of World Community,* 1983. *Forty Years: A Third World Soldier at the UN; Studies in Freedom, No. 3* (with Beth Day Romulo), 1986. *The Philippine Presidents: Memoirs Of* (with Beth Day Romulo), 1988.

Other Awards: Gold Medal Award, Woodrow Wilson Memorial Fund, 1947. Gold Medal, International Benjamin Franklin Society, 1948. Philippine Congressional Gold Medal of Honor, 1950. Grand Cross of the Order of the Phoenix, Greece, 1950. Commander, United States Legion of Merit, 1950. Grand Cross of Order of Queen Isabella, Spain, 1950. Cardinal Gibbons Gold Medal, Catholic University of America, 1950. Order of Sikatuna, Philippines, 1953. Golden Heart Presidential Award, Philippines, 1954. Gran Cordon of La Orden del Libertador, Venezuela, 1955. Christopher Literary Award, 1955. Four Freedoms Award, 1958. Munha Medal, Republic of Korea, 1961. Grand Cordon of Order of the Brilliant Star, Republic of China, 1962. Grand Cross of the Military Order of Christ, Portugal, 1962. Medallion of Valor, Israel, 1962. Honorary Degrees: University of Notre Dame, IN, 1935; University of Athens, 1948; University of the Philippines, 1949; Harvard University, MA, 1950; University of Hawaii, 1955; Georgetown University, Washington, DC, 1960; Nihon University, Japan, 1963; Sophia University, 1963; Delhi University, India, 1964; University of Indonesia, 1964.

For More Information: Hoehn, Matthew, *Catholic Authors, First Volume 1930-1947,* Newark, NJ: St. Mary's Abbey, 1948; Spencer, Cornelia, *Romulo: Voice of Freedom,* New York: J. Day Company, 1953; Wells, Evelyn, *Carlos P. Romulo: Voice of Freedom,* New York: Funk and Wagnalls, 1964; Joaquin, Nick, *The Seven Ages of Romulo,* Makati, Metro Manila: Filipinas Foundation, 1979; *The New York Times,* 16 December (1985): B18; Andrade, Pio,

The Fooling of America: The Untold Story of Carlos P. Romulo, Philippines: P. Andrade, 1990; Ancell, R. Manning, *Biographical Dictionary of World War II Generals and Flag Officers,* Westport, CT: Greenwood Press, 1996.

Commentary: Carlos P. Romulo, a Philippine national, won a Pulitzer Prize for his correspondence from Southeast Asia. He traveled through Hong Kong, China, French Indo-China (Vietnam), Burma, Thailand, Singapore, and the Dutch East Indies on a six-week fact-finding trip. He was the first Filipino journalist to make such a trip and convey his impressions of historic developments in the area.

Romulo was one of the original signers of the United Nations Charter. He had succeeded in having the charter explicitly endorse the independence of colonial countries. A longtime diplomat, he became the first Asian President of the General Assembly of the United Nations. He was elected three times to one-month terms as head of the Security Council.

1943

Hanson Weightman Baldwin   134

Birth: March 22, 1903; Baltimore, MD. **Death:** November 13, 1991. **Parents:** Oliver Perry Baldwin and Caroline (Sutton). **Education:** United States Naval Academy, MD: BS. **Spouse:** Helen Bruce (m. 1931). **Children:** Barbara, Elizabeth.

Prize: *Correspondence,* 1943: *New York Times,* New York: New York Times, 1942.

Career: Served in U.S. Navy, 1920-27; Police Reporter, *Baltimore (MD) Sun,* 1928; Reporter, *New York Times,* 1929-37; Military and Naval Correspondent, *New York Times,* 1937; Military Editor, *New York Times,* 1942-68; Roving Editor, *Reader's Digest.*

Selected Works: *Men and Ships of Steel* (with Wayne Francis Palmer), 1935. *The Caissons Roll: A Military Survey of Europe,* 1938. *We Saw It Happen: The News behind the News That's Fit to Print* (with others), 1938. *Admiral Death: Twelve Adventures of Men against the Sea,* 1939. *United We Stand! Defense of the Western Hemisphere,* 1941. *What the Citizen Should Know about the Navy,* 1941. *Strategy for Victory,* 1942. *The Navy at War: Paintings and Drawings by Combat Artists,* 1943. *The Price of Power,* 1948. *Power and Politics: The Price of Security in the Atomic Age,* 1950. *Great Mistakes of the War,* 1950. *Sea Fights, and Shipwrecks: True Tales of the Seven Seas,* 1955. *Middle East in Turmoil: Headline Series, No. 123,* 1957. *The Great Arms Race,* 1958. *World War I: An Outline History,* 1962. *The New Navy,* 1964. *Battles Lost and Won: Great Campaigns of World War II,* 1966. *Strategy for Tomorrow,* 1970.

The Crucial Years: 1939-1941, 1976. *Tiger Jack,* 1979.

Other Awards: Distinguished Service Medal, Syracuse University School of Journalism, NY, 1944. Honorary Degrees: Drake University, IA, 1945; Clarkson Institute of Technology, NY.

For More Information: *Current Biography Yearbook, 1942,* New York: H.W. Wilson Company, 1942; *Reminiscences of Hanson Weightman Baldwin, U.S. Navy (Retired), Oral History Program (Navy),* Annapolis, MD: U.S. Naval Institute, 1976; *New York Times,* 14 November (1991): 24; *Washington Post,* 14 November (1991): D11; Rothmeyer, Karen, *Winning Pulitzers: The Stories Behind Some of the Best News Coverage of Our Times,* New York: Columbia University Press, 1991: 45-50.

Commentary: Hanson W. Baldwin won a Pulitzer Prize for his series of eight articles dating from October 23, 1942 that covered the war in the Pacific. More than half the work for a reporter at the time was getting articles past the censors. Baldwin obtained approval from the United States Navy to have his articles published, and even though his articles were critical in tone, they were praised by top officials in the war department.

1944

Ernest Taylor Pyle   135

Birth: August 3, 1900; Dana, IN. **Death:** April 18, 1945. **Parents:** William Clyde Pyle and Maria (Taylor). **Education:** Indiana University. **Spouse:** Geraldine Siebolds (m. 1925, div. 1942); Geraldine Siebolds (m. 1943, died 1945).

Prize: *Correspondence,* 1944: *Scripps-Howard Newspaper Alliance,* 1943.

Career: Served in U.S. Navy, 1923; Cub Reporter, *LaPorte (IN) Herald,* 1923; Reporter, Deskman, *Washington (DC) Daily News,* 1923-26; Deskman, *New York (NY) Evening World* and *New York (NY) Evening Post,* 1926-27; Aviation Editor, Scripps-Howard Newspaper Alliance, 1928-32; Managing Editor, *Washington (DC) Daily News,* 1932-35; Roving Reporter, Scripps-Howard Newspaper Alliance, 1935-45; War Correspondent, Scripps-Howard Newspaper Alliance, 1942-45.

Selected Works: *Ernie Pyle in England,* 1941. *Here Is Your War,* 1943. *Brave Men,* 1944. *Reprinting of the "Fifteenth Previously Unpublished" Articles of World War II by Ernie Pyle* (with Howard Skidmore), 1987. *Ernie's America: The Best of Ernie Pyle's 1930's Travel Dispatches* (with David Nichols), 1989. *On a Wing and a Prayer: The Aviation Columns of Ernie Pyle* (with others), 1995.

Other Awards: Raymond Clapper Memorial Award, 1945. Honorary Degrees: Indiana University, 1944; University of New Mexico, 1944.

For More Information: *New York Times,* 19 April (1945): 1; *National Cyclopaedia of American Biography, Volume 33,* New York: James T. White & Company, 1947 Miller, Lee Graham, *Ernie Pyle,* New York: Bantam Books, 1953; Jakes, John, *Great War Correspondents,* New York: G.P. Putnam's Sons, 1967; *Dictionary of American Biography, Supplement 3,* New York: Charles Scribner's Sons, 1973; *Dictionary of Literary Biography, Volume 29,* Detroit: Gale Research Company, 1984; *Contemporary Authors, Volume 115,* Detroit: Gale Research Company, 1985; McKerns, Joseph P., *Biographical Dictionary of American Journalism,* New York: Greenwood Press, 1989; Riley, Sam G., *Biographical Dictionary of American Newspaper Columnists,* Westport, CT: Greenwood Press, 1995; Melzer, Richard, *Ernie Pyle in the American Southwest,* Santa Fe, NM: Sunstone Press, 1996; Tobin, James, *Ernie Pyle's War: America's Eyewitness to World War II,* New York: Free Press, 1997.

Commentary: Ernest Pyle's combat correspondence told the story of the average G.I. in the war. His daily column appeared in approximately 200 Scripps-Howard newspapers. It was also published in the United States military paper, the *Stars and Stripes,* Algiers edition. His dispatches described the war for the people back in the United States from a soldier's perspective. He was killed by Japanese machine gun fire at Ie Shima.

1945

Harold Vincent Boyle 136

Birth: February 21, 1911; Kansas City, MO. **Death:** April 1, 1974. **Parents:** Peter Edward Boyle and Margaret (Gavaghan). **Education:** University of Missouri: BS. University of Missouri: BJ. **Spouse:** Mary Frances Young (m. 1937).

Prize: *Correspondence,* 1945: Associated Press, 1944.

Career: Night office boy, Kansas City (MO), Associated Press, 1928-30; Sports and College News writer, Columbia (MO), Associated Press, 1931-32; Staff member, Columbia (MO), Associated Press, 1933-35; Staff member, St. Louis (MO), Associated Press, 1935; Night Editor, St. Louis (MO), Associated Press, 1935; Feature Editor, Kansas City (MO), Associated Press, 1936; Reporter and Editor, New York (NY), Associated Press, 1937-41; Night City Editor, New York (NY), Associated Press, 1942; War Correspondent, Allied Campaigns in Mediterranean and Europe Associated Press, 1942-1950s; Columnist, Associated Press, 1950s-74.

Selected Works: *Help, Help, Another Day! The World of Hal Boyle,* 1969. *The Best of Boyle,* 1980.

Other Awards: Distinguished Service Cross. Overseas Press Club, 1951.

For More Information: *Current Biography Yearbook, 1945,* New York: H.W. Wilson Company, 1945; *New York Times,* 2 April (1974): 42; *New York Times,* 4 April (1974): 42; *Contemporary Authors, Volume 101,* Detroit: Gale Research Company, 1981; Taft, William A., *Encyclopedia of Twentieth-Century Journalists,* New York: Garland Publishing, Incorporated, 1986; Rigsby, Gwendolyn Gezelle, "A History of Associated Press Pulitzer Prizes" (thesis), University of South Carolina, 1993; *Dictionary of American Biography, Supplement 9,* New York: Charles Scribner's Sons, 1994.

Commentary: Harold V. "Hal" Boyle told the tale of the American foot soldier. He worked in the same period as the columnist Ernie Pyle. One day on the North African front, Boyle of the Associated Press met Ernie Pyle. Boyle quipped, "So you're Ernie Pyle? Well, shake hands with Boyle, the poor man's Ernie Pyle."

Boyle's column, "Leaves from a War Correspondent's Notebook," was distributed by the Associated Press and published by 400 newspapers. His Pulitzer Prize was for "distinguished war correspondence during the year 1944."

1946

Arnaldo Cortesi 137

Birth: September 21, 1897; Rome, Italy. **Death:** November 26, 1966. **Parents:** Salvatore Cortesi and Isabelle Laudeur (Cochrane). **Education:** Birmingham University, England: BS.

Prize: *Correspondence,* 1946: *New York Times,* "All Freedom Found Ended in Argentina," June 1;

"Buenos Aires Decided Not to Act Against Writer Who Bared Terror," June 4; "Argentina is Seen in Debt to Braden," August 27; "250,000 Argentines Rally for Liberty," September 20, New York: New York Times, 1945.

Career: Westinghouse Electric Plant worker; Staff member, Rome *New York Times,* 1922; Correspondent, Rome (Italy), *New York Times,* 1922-39; Correspondent, Mexico City (Mexico), *New York Times,* 1939-41; Chief South America Correspondent, Buenos Aires (Argentina), *New York Times,* 1941-46; Head of Rome (Italy) Bureau, *New York Times,* 1946-63.

Selected Works: *Industrial Control: Italy's Experience; Pamphlet, The Italian Historical Society, No. 14,* 1933.

Other Awards: Sigma Delta Chi Award, 1946.

For More Information: *New York Times,* November 27, 1966: 86.

Commentary: Arnaldo Cortesi immigrated to the United States in 1922. His first position with the *New York Times* was in Rome. Seventeen years after he took up that post, Mussolini decreed that Italian citizens could not represent foreign news agencies in Italy. He was then sent to South America. His dispatches from South America won him a Pulitzer Prize in 1946. He became a naturalized United States citizen that same year. He returned to Rome for the *New York Times,* taking over the reins of that bureau from his sister.

1947

Justin Brooks Atkinson   138

Birth: November 28, 1894; Melrose, MA. **Death:** January 13, 1984. **Parents:** Jonathan H. Atkinson and Narafella (Taylor). **Education:** Harvard University, MA: AB. **Spouse:** Oriana T. MacIlveen (m. 1926). **Children:** Stepson: Bruce.

Prize: *Correspondence,* 1947: *New York Times,* New York: New York Times, 1946.

Career: Served in U.S. Army, WWI; District Reporter, *Springfield (MA) Daily News,* 1917-19; English Instructor, Dartmouth College; Reporter and Assistant to the Drama Critic, *Boston Evening Transcript,* 1919-22; Associate Editor, *Harvard Alumni Bulletin;* Reporter, *New York Times;* Editor, *New York Times Book Review,* 1922-25; Drama Critic, *New York Times,* 1925-42; Correspondent, China, Moscow, *New York Times,* 1942-46; Drama Critic, *New York Times,* 1946-60; Critic-at-Large, *New York Times,* 1960-65.

Selected Works: *Skyline Promenades: A Potpourri,* 1925. *Henry Thoreau: The Cosmic Yankee,* 1927. *East of the Hudson,* 1931. *The Cingalese Prince,* 1934. *Cleo for Short,* 1940. *Broadway Scrapbook,* 1947. *Once around the Sun,* 1951. *Harvard Men* (with David Aloian), 1957. *A Memorial Tribute to Moss Hart, January 9, 1962* (with others), 1962. *Tuesdays and Fridays,* 1963. *Brief Chronicles,* 1966. *Broadway,* 1970. *The Lively Years, 1920-73* (with Al Hirschfeld), 1973. *This Bright Land: A Personal View,* 1972. *New England's White Mountains: At Home in the Wild* (with others), 1978. *Sean O'Casey, from Times Past* (with Robert G. Lowery), 1982.

Other Awards: Theatre Hall of Fame and Museum, 1972. Honorary Degrees: Williams College, MA, 1941; Adelphi College, NY, 1960; Brandeis University, MA, 1965; Pace College, NY, 1965; Franklin and Marshall College, PA, 1965; Clark University, MA, 1965; Washington College, MD, 1966; Long Island University, NY, 1967; Dartmouth College, NH, 1975.

For More Information: *Contemporary Authors, Volumes 61-64,* Detroit: Gale Research Company, 1976; Comtois, M.E. and Lynn F. Miller, *Contemporary American Theater Critics,* Metuchen, NJ: Scarecrow Press, 1977; *New York Times,* 15 January (1984): 1; Taft, William A., *Encyclopedia of Twentieth-Century Journalists,* New York: Garland Publishing Inc., 1986.

Commentary: Brooks Atkinson left the *New York Times Book Review* to be a foreign correspondent in 1942. His study of Soviet Russia detailed the nature of the regime and its domestic and foreign policies.

In 1946, he returned to his main field of journalism, criticism. A Broadway theater was named after him in 1960.

Criticism

1970

Ada Louise Huxtable   139

Birth: March 14, 1921; New York, NY. **Parents:** Michael Louis Landman and Leah (Rosenthal). **Education:** Hunter College, NY: BA, magna cum laude, Phi Beta Kappa. Institute of Fine Arts, New York University. **Spouse:** L. Garth Huxtable (m. 1942).

Prize: *Criticism,* 1970: *New York Times,* New York: New York Times, 1969.

Career: Editor, high school newspaper; Assistant Curator, Department of Architecture and Design, Museum of Modern Art, 1946-50; Freelance writer, magazines, 1952-63; Contributing Editor, *Progressive Architecture;* Contributor, *New York Times Magazine;* Architecture Critic, *New York Times,* 1963-82; Member of Editorial Board, *New York Times,* 1973-82; Cook Lecturer, University of Michigan, 1977; Hitchcock Lecturer, University of California, Berkeley, 1982.

Selected Works: *Pier Luigi Nervi: The Masters of World Architecture Series,* 1960. *Four Walking Tours of Modern Architecture in New York City,* 1961. *The Architecture of New York: A History and a Guide,* 1964. *Will They Ever Finish Bruckner Boulevard?,* 1970. *Kicked a Building Lately?,* 1976. *The Tall Building Artistically Reconsidered: The Search for a Skyscraper Style,* 1984. *Goodbye History, Hello Hamburger: An Anthology of Architectural Delights and Disasters,* 1986. *Architecture, Anyone?,* 1986.

Other Awards: Fulbright Scholarship, 1950, 1952. Fellow, American Academy of Arts and Sciences. Honorary Member, American Institute of British Architects. Honorary Member, Royal Institute of British Architects. Guggenheim Fellowship, 1958. Front Page Award, Newspaper Women's Club of New York, 1965. Kaufmann International Design Award, Institute of International Education, 1965. Frank Jewett Mather Award, College Art Association, 1967. New York State Council on the Arts, 1967. Elsie de Wolfe Award, American Institute of Interior Designers, 1969. Medal, American Institute of Architects, 1969. Strauss Memorial Award, New York Society of Architects, 1970. Special Award, National Trust for Historic Preservation, 1971. National Arts Club Medal, 1971. Press Award, National Society of Interior Designers, 1972. Diamond Jubilee Medallion, City of New York, NY, 1973. Secretary's Award, Conservation, United States Department of the Interior, 1976. Thomas Jefferson Medal, University of Virginia, 1977. Genius Grant, MacArthur Foundation, 1981. MacArthur Prize Fellowship, 1981-86. Honorary Degree, Bard College, NY; Cleveland State University, OH; Emerson College, MA; Finch College, NY; Fordham University, NY; Hamilton College, NY; Long Island University, NY Maryland Institute and College of Art; Miami University, FL; Oberlin College, OH; Pace University, NY; Pratt Institute, NY; Radcliffe University, MA; Rhode Island School of Design; Rutgers University, NJ; Skidmore College, NY; Smith College, MA; Trinity College, CT; University of Massachusetts; University of Pennsylvania; Washington University, MO; Williams College, MA; Yale University, CT.

For More Information: *Contemporary Authors, Volume 120,* Detroit: Gale Research Company, 1987; *New Yorker,* 10 August (1970); *Christian Science Monitor,* 3 May (1985); Belford, Barbara, *Brilliant Bylines: A Biographical Anthology of Notable Newspaperwomen in America,* New York: Columbia University Press, 1986: 296-309.

Commentary: Ada Louise Huxtable won the first Pulitzer Prize given in the Criticism category. She has studied art and architectural history and incorporates the historical significance of buildings for culture into her reviews. Besides commenting on architectural design, she has written on skylines, the "themed environment" of development, and many other topics.

1971

Harold Charles Schonberg   140

Birth: November 29, 1915; New York, NY. **Parents:** David Schonberg and Minnie (Kirsch). **Education:** Brooklyn College, NY: BA, cum laude. New York University: MA. **Spouse:** Rosalyn Krokover (m. 1942, died 1973); Helene Cornell (m. 1975).

Prize: *Criticism,* 1971: *New York Times,* New York: New York Times, 1970.

Career: Columnist, *Musical Advance,* 1937; Associate Editor, *American Music Lover,* 1939-42; Served in U.S. Army Air Forces, 1942-46; Contributing Editor, *Music Digest,* 1946-48; Assistant Music Critic, *New York Sun,* 1946-50; Contributing Editor, *Musical Courier,* 1948-52; Columnist, *Gramophone Magazine* London, 1948; Music and Record Critic, *New York Times,* 1950-60; Chief Music Critic, *New York Times,* 1960-80; Cultural Correspondent, *New York Times,* 1980-.

Selected Works: *Chamber and Solo Instrument Music: The Guide to Long-Playing Records, v. 3,* 1955. *The Collector's Chopin and Schumann; Keystone Books, KB-8,* 1959. *The Great Pianists,* 1963. *The Great Conductors,* 1967. *The Lives of the Great Composers,* 1970. *Fischer-Spassky: Le Super-Match du Siecle* (with Richard Roberts), 1972. *Grandmasters of Chess,* 1973. *How to Play Double Bogey Golf* (with others), 1975. *Facing the Music,* 1981. *The Glorious Ones: Classical Music's Legendary Performers,* 1985. *Horowitz: His Life and Music,* 1992.

Other Awards: Ambassador of Honor Books Award, English-Speaking Union Books-Across-the-Sea, 1982: *Facing the Music,* New York: Summit Books, 1981. Honorary Degrees: Temple University, PA, 1964; Grinnell College, IA, 1967.

For More Information: *New York Times,* 8 February (1981): section 6, 38; *Contemporary Authors, Volume 112,* Detroit: Gale Research Company, 1985.

Commentary: Harold C. Schonberg was the first music critic to win a Pulitzer Prize. He resolved to be a music critic when he was 12 years old and figured out that he could get paid for doing the things he loved best, "listening to music and comparing performances." When he was young, he recognized that a musician "had everything to do with how the music sounded."

1972

Frank Lewis Peters Jr.   141

Birth: October 19, 1930; Springfield, MO. **Parents:** Frank Lewis Peters and Mary (Frissel). **Religion:** Episcopalian. **Education:** Drury College, MO: BA. Iowa State University. **Spouse:** Alba Manciani. **Children:** Carl, Adrian.

Prize: *Criticism,* 1972: *St. Louis Post-Dispatch,* St. Louis: St. Louis Post-Dispatch, 1971.

Career: Served in U.S. Army, 1951-53; News Writer and Editor, Radio Stations, KGBX and KWTO, Springfield, MO, 1954-57; Copy Editor, *Arkansas Gazette,* 1957-59; Feature Writer, *Springfield (MO) Leader and Press,* 1959-62; Managing Editor, *Rome (Italy) Daily American,* 1962-64; Copy Editor, *St. Louis (MO) Post-Dispatch,* 1964-67; Music Critic, *St. Louis (MO) Post-Dispatch,* 1967-84; Arts Editor, *St. Louis (MO) Post-Dispatch,* 1984-88.

Selected Works: *A Guide to the Architecture of St. Louis* (with George McCue), 1989.

For More Information: *St. Louis Post-Dispatch,* 2 May (1972): B1, B4.

Commentary: Frank Peters won a Pulitzer Prize for his music criticism. His citation for the award read that Peters's "clearly written criticism elucidated music in a manner useful to both the musician and the lay reader." Peters had "functional" music training while

growing up, but never considered becoming a musician. His goal when writing was to make people want to hear good music. He wrote about 150 music reviews a year as well as articles on music for the Sunday issue of his paper.

1973

Ronald D. Powers   142

Birth: November 18, 1941; Hannibal, MO. **Parents:** Paul Sidney Powers and Elvadine (Toalson). **Education:** University of Missouri: BA. **Spouse:** Honoree Fleming (m. 1978). **Children:** Two sons.

Prize: *Criticism,* 1973: *Chicago Sun-Times,* Chicago: Chicago Sun-Times, 1972.

Career: Sportswriter, Suburban News Reporter, *St. Louis (MO) Post-Dispatch,* 1963-68; Columnist, local teenage magazine; Writer, satirical radio show, local station; General Assignment Reporter, *Chicago Sun-Times,* 1968-69; Television and Radio Critic, *Chicago Sun-Times,* 1969-77; Critic-at-Large, WMAQ-TV, Chicago, IL, 1977-79; Critic, WNET-TV, NY, 1979; Media Critic, CBS News Sunday Morning, 1983-88; Television Columnist, *GQ* magazine, 1983-90; Creative Writing Instructor, Middlebury College (VT), 1989; Writer.

Selected Works: *The Newscasters: The News Business as Show Business,* 1977. *Face Value,* 1979. *Toot-Toot-Tootsie, Goodbye,* 1981. *Supertube: The Rise of Television Sports,* 1983. *White Town Drowsing,* 1986. *The Beast, the Eunuch, and the Glass-Eyed Child: Television in the 80s,* 1990. *Far from Home: Life and Loss in Two American Towns,* 1991. *The Cruel Radiance: Notes of a Prosewriter in a Visual Age,* 1994.

Other Awards: Emmy Award, National Academy of Television Arts and Sciences, 1978, 1985.

For More Information: *Contemporary Authors, Volumes 97-100,* Detroit: Gale Research Company, 1981; Taft, William H., *Encyclopedia of Twentieth-Century Journalists,* New York: Garland Publishing, 1986; *Vermont Business Magazine,* 23:2 (February 1995): section 1, 9.

Commentary: Ronald Powers won a Pulitzer Prize for his criticism of radio and television. He wrote on media until 1990. He currently teaches and is a writer. A native of Mark Twain's Hannibal, Missouri, he has written about his hometown as well as about television.

1974

Emily Genauer   143

Birth: July 19, 1910; New York, NY. **Parents:** Joseph Genauer and Rose (Milch). **Education:**

Hunter College, NY. Columbia University, NY: BLitt. **Spouse:** Frederick Gash (m. 1935, died 1993). **Children:** Constance Lee.

Prize: *Criticism,* 1974: *Newsday Syndicate,* New York: Newsday, 1973.

Career: Reporter and Art Feature Writer, *New York World,* 1929-31; Art Critic and Editor, *New York World-Telegram,* 1931-48; Chief Art Critic and Editor, *New York Herald-Tribune,* 1949-66; Chief Art Critic, *New York World-Journal-Tribune,* 1966-67; Art Critic, *Newsday (NY)* Syndicate, 1967-78; Art Commentator, Education Television System of NY, 1967-80; Art Reviewer, *New York Post;* Art Commentator, NBC and ABC Networks.

Selected Works: *Modern Interiors Today and Tomorrow,* 1939. *Best of Art,* 1948. *Marc Chagall,* 1956. *Chagall at the Met,* 1971. *Rufino Tamayo,* 1974.

Other Awards: Outstanding Writing in a Specialized Field, New York Newspaper Women's Club, 1937. New York Newspaper Women's Club Annual Award for the Year's Outstanding Column, 1949, 1956, 1958, 1960, 1969. Journalism Alumni Award, Columbia University, NY, 1960.

For More Information: *New York Times,* 7 May (1974): 40; *Contemporary Authors,* Detroit: Gale Research Company.

Commentary: Emily Genauer covered the art world for over 50 years. Her once-a-week column on art won her a Pulitzer Prize in Criticism in 1974.

1975

Roger Joseph Ebert   144

Birth: June 18, 1942; Urbana, IL. **Parents:** Walter H. Ebert and Annabel (Stumm). **Education:** University of Illinois: BA. University of Cape Town, South Af-

rica. University of Chicago, IL: Postgraduate. **Spouse:** Chaz Hammelsmith (m. 1992).

Prize: *Criticism,* 1975: *Chicago Sun-Times,* Chicago: Chicago Sun-Times, 1974.

Career: Editor, college paper, *Daily Illini;* Staff Writer, *News Gazette (IL),* 1958-66; President, U.S. Student Press Association, 1963-64; Film Critic, *Chicago Sun-Times,* 1967-; Instructor, Chicago City College, IL, 1967-68; Film Lecturer, University of Chicago's Division of Continuing Education, 1969; Host, Co-Producer of "The World of Ingmar Bergman," 1973-74; Lecturer, Columbia College, NY, 1973-74; Co-Host, *Sneak Previews,* 1978-82; Co-Host, *At the Movies,* 1982-86; Co-Host, *Siskel and Ebert at the Movies,* 1986-.

Selected Works: *An Illini Century,* 1967. *A Kiss Is Still a Kiss,* 1984. *Roger Ebert's Movie Home Companion,* 1985. *The Perfect London Walk* (with Daniel Curley), 1986. *Two Weeks in the Midday Sun,* 1987. *The Future of the Movies,* 1991. *Behind the Phantom's Mask,* 1993. *Ebert's Little Movie Glossary,* 1994. *Questions for the Movie Answer Man.*

Other Awards: Overseas Press Club Award, 1963. Chicago Headline Club Award, 1963. Rotary Fellow, 1965. Stick-o-Type Award, Chicago Newspaper Guild, 1973. Chicago Emmy Award, 1979. Kluge Fellow in Film Studies, University of Virginia, 1995-96. Honorary Degree, University of Colorado, 1993.

For More Information: *Contemporary Authors, Volumes 69-72,* Detroit: Gale Research Company, (1978): 202-203.

Commentary: Roger Ebert, a film critic at the *Chicago Sun-Times,* and his crosstown colleague Gene Siskel, who writes for the *Chicago Tribune,* are best known for being partners on the syndicated movie review show, *Siskel and Ebert at the Movies.* Ebert has been a film critic since the late 1960s. He has taught criticism and is acknowledged as truly knowing his subject, the history of film and movie criticism.

1976

Alan Mortimer Kriegsman   145

Birth: February 28, 1928; Brooklyn, NY. **Parents:** Harry P. Kriegsman and May (John). **Religion:** Jewish. **Education:** Massachusetts Institute of Technology. Columbia University, NY: BS. Columbia University, NY: ABD. **Spouse:** Sali Ann Ribakove (m. 1957).

Prize: *Criticism,* 1976: *Washington Post,* Washington, DC: Washington Post, 1975.

Career: Served in U.S. Army, 1949-50; Music Lecturer, Columbia University (NY), 1954; Lecturer, Barnard College (NY); Lecturer, Hunter College (NY); Contributing Editor, *Musical Courier,* 1957-

60; Instructor, University of California, San Diego, 1960-65; Music and Drama Critic, *San Diego (CA) Union,* 1960-65; President, Juilliard School of Music, (NY), 1965-66; Music and Performing Arts Critic and Columnist, *Washington (DC) Post,* 1966-74; Dance Critic, *Washington (DC) Post,* 1974-96; Critic Emeritus, *Washington (DC) Post,* 1996-; Lecturer, Instructor, Columbia University (NY), Barnard College (NY), Harvard University (MA), Juilliard School of Music (NY), Temple University (PA), George Washington University (DC).

Selected Works: *Suzanne Farrell: Dance Horizons Spotlight Series,* 1975. *Writing in Style,* 1975.

Other Awards: Fulbright Scholar, University of Vienna, Austria, 1956-57.

For More Information: Williams, Carolyn, *The Washington Post: Views from the Inside,* Englewood Cliffs, NJ: Prentice Hall, 1976; Roberts, Chalmers M., *The Washington Post: The First 100 Years,* Boston: Houghton Mifflin, 1977; English, John W., *Criticizing the Critics, Humanistic Studies in the Communication Arts Communication Arts Books.* New York: Hastings House, 1979; *DCA News,* Autumn (1996): 4-5, 7.

Commentary: Alan M. Kriegsman's writings on dance won him a Pulitzer Prize in 1976.

"My award in the Criticism category (1976) was the first, and still to date, the only such given for writings in the field of dance." —A. Kriegsman

1977

William Alexander McPherson   146
Birth: March 16, 1933; Sault Sainte Marie, MI. **Parents:** Harold Agnew McPherson and Ruth (Brubaker). **Education:** University of Michigan. Michigan State University. George Washington University, Washington, DC. **Spouse:** Elizabeth Mosher (m. 1959, div. 1979). **Children:** Jane Elizabeth.

Prize: *Criticism,* 1977: *Washington Post,* Washington, DC: Washington Post, 1976.

Career: Copyperson, *Washington (DC) Post,* 1958; Staff Writer and Editor, *Washington (DC) Post,* 1959-63; Travel Editor, *Washington (DC) Post,* 1963-67; Senior Editor, William Morrow and Company, Incorporated, 1967-69; Contributing Editor, Book World Section, *Washington (DC) Post,* 1969-72; Lecturer, American University in Washington, 1971; Editor of The Book World, *Washington (DC) Post,* 1972; Adjunct Professor, American University, 1975; Book Critic, *Washington (DC) Post,* 1978-79; Editorial Page Staff member, *Washington (DC) Post,* 1981-85; Columnist, *Washington (DC) Post,* 1983-85; Writer.

Selected Works: *Testing the Current: A Novel,* 1984. *To the Sargasso Sea: A Novel,* 1987.

For More Information: *Contemporary Authors, New Revision Series, Volume 28,* Detroit: Gale Research Company, 1990.

Commentary: William McPherson's book reviews throughout 1976 won him the 1977 Criticism Pulitzer Prize. He brought a literary and historic perspective to his reviews on works by authors ranging from E.B. White to Saul Bellow.

1978

Walter Francis Kerr   147

Birth: July 8, 1913; Evanston, IL. **Death:** October 9, 1996. **Parents:** Walter Sylvester Kerr and Esther M. (Daugherty). **Religion:** Roman Catholic. **Education:** DePaul University, IL. Northwestern University, IL: BS. Northwestern University, IL: MA. **Spouse:** Jean Collins (m. 1943). **Children:** Christopher, Colin, John, Gilbert, Gregory, Katharine.

Prize: *Criticism,* 1978: *New York Times,* New York: New York Times, 1977.

Career: Editor of Fine Arts Page, college paper, *Daily Northwestern;* Assistant Editor, *Drama Magazine;* Reviewing Films, Junior Section of Weekly *Evanston (IL) Review;* Editor, school newspapers; Movie Critic, *Evanston (IL) Daily News-Index;* Speech and Drama Instructor, Catholic University, Washington (DC), 1938-45; Associate Professor of Drama, Catholic University, Washington (DC), 1945-49; Drama Critic, *Commonweal Magazine,* 1949-52; Drama Critic, *New York Herald-Tribune,* 1951-66; Drama Critic, *New York Times,* 1966-67; Author, Round-up Column of Drama Events, Sunday Arts and Leisure Section, *New York Times,* 1967-79; Chief Drama Critic, *New York Times,* 1979-83; Film Director.

Selected Works: *Murder in Reverse,* 1935. *Denison's Variety Review,* 1935. *Harmony Minstrel First-Part,* 1936. *Mystery Minstrel First-Part,* 1937. *Movie Minstrel First-Part,* 1938. *Hyacinth on Wheels,* 1939. *Christmas, Incorporated,* 1939. *Stardust,* 1946. *Sing Out, Sweet Land: A Musical Biography of American Song,* 1949. *Criticism and Censorship: The Gabriel Richard Lecture, No. 5,* 1954. *How Not to Write a Play,* 1955. *Pieces at Eight,* 1957. *Goldilocks* (with J. Kerr), 1958. *The Decline of Pleasure,* 1962. *The Theater in Spite of Itself,* 1963. *Harold Pinter: Columbia Essays on Modern Writers, No. 27,* 1967. *Tragedy and Comedy,* 1967. *Thirty Plays Hath November,* 1969. *God on the Gymnasium Floor and Other Theatrical Adventures,* 1971. *Silent Clowns,* 1975. *Journey to the Center of the Theater,* 1979.

Other Awards: George Jean Nathan Award, 1964. Dinean Award, National Catholic Theater Conference, 1965: *The Theater in Spite of Itself.* Iona Award, 1970. Campion Award, 1971. Laetare Medal, University of Notre Dame, IN, 1971. National Institute of Arts and Letters Award, 1972. Honorary Degrees: St. Mary's College, IN, 1956; LaSalle College, PA, 1956; Northwestern University, IL, 1962; Fordham University, NY, 1965; University of Notre Dame, IN, 1968; University of Michigan, 1972.

For More Information: Bladel, Roderick, *Walter Kerr: An Analysis of His Criticism,* Metuchen, NJ: Scarecrow Press, 1976; Comtois, M.E. and Lynn F. Miller, *Contemporary American Theater Critics,* Metuchen, NJ: Scarecrow Press, 1977; *New York Times,* 18 April (1978): 28; *American Catholic Who's Who, Volume 23, 1980-1981,* Washington, DC: National Catholic News Service, 1979; *Contemporary Authors, New Revision Series, Volume 7,* Detroit: Gale Research Company, 1982; *New York Times,* 10 October (1996): 22; *Los Angeles Times,* 11 October (1996): A22.

Commentary: Walter Kerr, a reviewer and critic from the age of 13, started his career on his hometown weekly, moved on to his college paper, and then to the New York dailies. In 1990, the restored Ritz Theater in Manhattan was renamed the Walter Kerr Theater in his honor.

1979

Paul John Gapp 148

Birth: June 26, 1928; Cleveland, OH. **Death:** July 30, 1992. **Parents:** Bernard Leonard Gapp and Florence (Ganley). **Religion:** Roman Catholic. **Education:** Ohio University: BS. **Spouse:** Mary Jo Finch (m. 1970). **Children:** Steve, Leslie.

Prize: *Criticism,* 1979: *Chicago Tribune,* Chicago: Chicago Tribune, 1978.

Career: Reporter and Editor, *Dispatch (OH),* 1950-56; Reporter, Editorial Page Writer, Feature Editor, *Chicago Daily News,* 1956-66; Executive Director, Chicago Chapter and Illinois Council of the American Institute of Architects; Executive, Chicago public relations firm; Coordinator, Urban Fellowship Program of the University of Chicago, IL, 1969-76; Assistant City Editor for Urban Affairs, *Chicago Tribune,* 1972-74; Architecture Critic, *Chicago Tribune,* 1974; Contributing Editor, *Inland Architecture* magazine.

Other Awards: Illinois Associated Press Award for Best Spot News Reporting. Honorary Member, Architects Club of Chicago. Orchid Award, American Institute of Architects, 1980. Distinguished Alumnus Medal, Ohio University, 1980. L.J. Horton Distinguished Alumnus Award, Ohio University, 1988. Chicago Journalism Hall of Fame, 1993.

For More Information: *Chicago Tribune,* 31 July (1992): 8; *San Francisco Chronicle,* 1 August (1992): C10.

Commentary: Paul Gapp won a Pulitzer Prize for his architecture criticism. He was "evenhanded in his judgements," praising good architecture while denouncing "bad architecture and 'technocratic' planning." He once had a $500 million lawsuit filed against him and the Tribune by Donald Trump after he criticized the developer's plan for a 150-story building off the tip of Manhattan. The case was dismissed in United States District Court in 1985.

1980

William Alfred Henry III 149

Birth: January 24, 1950; South Orange, NJ. **Death:** June 28, 1994. **Parents:** William Alfred Henry and Catherine A (Elliot). **Education:** Yale University, CT: BA. Boston University, MA. **Spouse:** Gail L. Manyam (m. 1981).

Prize: *Criticism,* 1980: *Boston Globe,* Boston: Boston Globe, 1979.

Career: Education Writer, *Boston Globe,* 1971-72; Arts Critic, *Boston Globe,* 1972-74; State House Political Reporter, *Boston Globe,* 1974-75; Editorial Writer, *Boston Globe,* 1975-77; Television Editor and Columnist, *Boston Globe,* 1977-80; Member of Theater Panel, Massachusetts Council on the Arts, 1977-80; Faculty member, Tufts University (MA), 1979; Faculty member, Yale University (CT), 1980; Weekly book reviewer and occasional national and foreign political reporter; Critic-at-Large, *New York Daily News,* 1980-81; Associate Editor, *Time* magazine, 1981-89; Press Critic, *Time* magazine, 1982-85; Theater Critic, Book Reviewer, *Time* magazine, 1985-94; Senior Writer, *Time* magazine, 1989-94; Lecturer,

Harvard University (MA), Massachusetts Institute of Technology, Columbia University (NY).

Selected Works: *The Blue Football Book* (with C. Vizas), 1971. *Visions of America: How We Saw the 1984 Elections,* 1985. *American Institutions and the Media: Inquiry on the Mass Media and the Public Trust, No. 1,* 1985. *The Great One: The Life and Legend of Jackie Gleason,* 1992. *In Defense of Elitism,* 1994. **Films:** *Bob Fosse: Steam Heat,* PBS Great Performances, 1990.

Other Awards: Story of the Year Award, 1976. Best Feature of the Year Award, 1976. New England Editorial Prize, 1977. Young American Leader Traveling Fellow, European Economic Community, 1977. Poynter Fellow, Yale University, CT, 1980. Co-Finalist in National Magazine Award, 1982, 1989, 1994. Lowell Mellett Citation in Press Criticism, 1984. William Allen White Award, 1989. Overseas Press Club Award, 1990. Emmy Award, 1990. Gay and Lesbian Alliance Against Defamation, 1990-91. Liberty-Unity in Media Award, Lincoln University, PA, 1991.

For More Information: Taft, William H., *Encyclopedia of Twentieth-Century Journalists,* New York: Garland Publishing, 1986; *Boston Globe,* 29 (1994): 33, 81.

Commentary: William A. Henry III won a Pulitzer Prize for his "critical writing about television." At 30, he was the youngest person to win the Criticism award. He also contributed to the *Boston Globe*'s coverage of racial integration that won the Meritorious Public Service award in 1975.

He moved on from the *Boston Globe* to become a theater critic and served as president of the New York Drama Critics Circle for two terms. He died after a heart attack at age 44.

1981

Jonathan Yardley   150
Birth: October 27, 1939; Pittsburgh, PA. **Parents:** William Woolsey Yardley and Helen (Gregory). **Religion:** Episcopalian. **Education:** University of North Carolina: AB. **Spouse:** Rosemary Roberts (m. 1961, div. 1975); Susan Hartt (m. 1975). **Children:** James Barrett, William Woolsey II.

Prize: *Criticism,* 1981: *Washington Star,* Washington, DC: Washington Star, 1980.

Career: Editor, college paper, *Daily Tar Heel;* Assistant to Washington Correspondent James Reston, 1961-62; Writer, *New York Times,* 1961-64; Writer of "News of the Week in Review," 1962-64; Editorial Writer, Book Editor, *Greensboro (NC) Daily News,* 1964-74; Lecturer, University of North Carolina, Greensboro, 1972-73; Book and Viewpoint Editor, *Miami (FL) Herald,* 1974-78; Weekly syndicated book review columnist, Knight Newspapers;

Book Editor and Columnist, *Washington (DC) Star,* 1978-; Contributing Editor, *Sports Illustrated;* Book Critic and Columnist, *Washington (DC) Post,* 1981-.

Selected Works: *Ring: A Biography of Ring Lardner,* 1977. *Our Kind of People: The Story of an American Family,* 1989. *Out of Step: Notes from a Purple Decade,* 1991. *My Life as an Author and Editor* (with H.L. Mencken), 1993. *States of Mind: A Personal Journey through the Mid-Atlantic,* 1993. *Misfit: The Strange Life of Frederick Exley,* 1997.

Other Awards: Nieman Fellow, Harvard University, MA, 1968-69. Chairman of the Fiction Jury for the 1973 National Book Awards. Distinguished Alumnus Award, University of North Carolina, Chapel Hill, 1989.

For More Information: *Publishers Weekly,* 235:11 (17 March 1989): 75-76.

Commentary: Jonathan Yardley wrote more than 50 book reviews in 1980 covering all areas of fiction and nonfiction. For the 1981 awards, he happened to be chairman of a Pulitzer Prize jury for fiction.

After he had heard that he won the prize, he quoted a friend saying, "it's quite extraordinary to be paid to read books." He also commented that it is a pleasure to discover new writers. His particular area of interest is contemporary American fiction, but he covers all styles of writing.

1982

Martin Bernheimer   151
Birth: September 28, 1936; Munich, Germany. **Parents:** Paul Ernst Bernheimer and Louise (Nassauer). **Education:** Brown University, RI: BA. New York University: MA. Munich Conservatory, Germany. **Spouse:** Lucinda Pearson (m. 1961, div. 1989); Linda Winer (m. 1992). **Children:** Mark, Nora, Erika, Marina (LP).

Prize: *Criticism,* 1982: *Los Angeles Times,* Los Angeles, CA: Los Angeles Times, 1981.

Career: Music Staff member, *New York Herald-Tribune,* 1959-62; Part-Time Music Lecturer, New York University, 1959-62; Contributing Editor, *Musical Courier,* 1961-64; Temporary Music Critic, *New York Post,* 1961-65; Managing Editor, *Philharmonic Hall Program Magazine,* 1962-65; Assistant Music Critic, *Saturday Review,* 1962-65; Contributed to many music publications; Music Editor and Chief Critic, *Los Angeles Times,* 1965-96; Faculty member, Rockefeller Program for the Training of Music Critics, University of Southern California, 1966; Music Faculty member, University of Southern California, 1966-71; Music Faculty member, University of California, Los Angeles, 1969-75; Faculty member, California Institute of Arts, 1975-82; Faculty member,

California State University, Northridge, 1978-81; Critic, writer, lecturer.

Other Awards: Deems Taylor Award, American Society of Composers, Authors, and Publishers for Outstanding Service to Music and Journalism, 1974, 78. National Headliners Club Award, 1979. Honorary Member, Chapter of Pi Kappa Lambda, the National Music Honor Society, 1982. Lifetime Achievement Award in Music, California Association of Professional Music Teachers, 1990.

For More Information: *Contemporary Authors, Volume 69-72,* Detroit: Gale Research Company, (1978): 69; *Los Angeles Times,* 15 February (1996): F1.

Commentary: Martin Bernheimer wrote on music and dance for the *Los Angeles Times* for over 30 years. He won a 1982 Pulitzer Prize for his classical music criticism.

His personality and insights along with his "strong opinions" evoke reactions both for and against his reviews. He taught at a variety of institutions and has been a lecturer on the Metropolitan Opera radio broadcasts.

1983

Manuela Vali Hoelterhoff   152

Birth: April 6, 1949; Hamburg, West Germany. **Parents:** Heinz Alfons Hoelterhoff and Olga Christine (Goertz). **Education:** Hofstra University, NY: BA, magna cum laude. Institute of Fine Arts, New York University: MA.

Prize: *Criticism,* 1983: *Wall Street Journal,* New York: Dow Jones, 1982.

Career: Editorial Page Staff member, 1975; Associate Editor, Arete Publishing Company, *Academic Encyclopedia,* 1977-80; Editor-in-Chief, *Art and Auction* Magazine, 1979-81; Associate Editor, *Portfolio* Magazine; Arts Editor, *Wall Street Journal,* 1981-89; Book Editor, *Wall Street Journal,* 1989-; Senior Consulting Editor, *Smart Money* Magazine, 1989-.

Other Awards: American Society of Newspaper Editors for Distinguished Commentary, 1982-83.

For More Information: *New York Times,* 19 April (1983): B4; *Contemporary Authors, Volume 120,* Detroit: Gale Research Company, 1987.

Commentary: Manuela Hoelterhoff won a Pulitzer Prize for her "wide-ranging criticism on the arts and other subjects." The *Wall Street Journal* nominated her for her "keen critical eye with distinctive, lively writing." She wrote on such topics as the public television series "Life on Earth" and the Giorgio de Chirico exhibit at the Museum of Modern Art in 1982.

1984

Paul J. Goldberger   153

Birth: December 4, 1950; Passaic, NJ. **Parents:** Morris Goldberger and Edna (Kronman). **Education:** Yale University, CT: BA. **Spouse:** Susan Lynn Solomon (m. 1980). **Children:** Stepchild: Adam Hirsh; Benjamin, Alexander.

Prize: *Criticism,* 1984: *New York Times,* New York: New York Times, 1983.

Career: Staff member, *New York Times Sunday Magazine,* 1972-73; Daily Architecture Critic, *New York Times,* 1973-81; Senior Architecture Critic, *New York Times,* 1981-90; Visiting Lecturer, Yale University, CT, 1984; Lecturer at other institutions; Cultural News Editor, *New York Times,* 1990-93; Chief Cultural Correspondent, *New York Times,* 1994-.

Selected Works: *The Visible City,* New York, 1979. *The City Observed, New York: A Guide to the Architecture of Manhattan,* 1979. *The Skyscraper,* 1981. *On the Rise: Architecture and Design in the Post Modern Age,* 1983. *The House of the Hamptons,* 1986. *Above New York: A Collection of Historical and Original Aerial Photographs of New York City,* 1988. *How to Look at a Building,* 1998.

Other Awards: Medal for his Architecture Criticism, American Institute of Architects, 1981. President's Medal of the Municipal Art Society of New York City, NY, 1984. Roger Starr Journalism Award, 1987. Medal of Honor, Landmarks Preservation Foundation of New York, 1991. Award of Merit of the Lotus Club. Literary Lion, The New York Public Library, 1993. Honorary Degree, Pratt Institute, NY, 1992.

For More Information: *A Talk With Architectural Critic Paul Goldberger: A Video,* Tucson: University of Arizona College of Architecture, 1985; *Contemporary Authors, Volume 122,* Detroit: Gale Research Company, 1988.

Commentary: Paul Goldberger won a Pulitzer Prize for his judgments on architectural developments across the country. He has commented on the various styles and structures as well as urban development and the redevelopment of downtown areas; what works and what does not.

1985

Howard Rosenberg   154

Birth: June 10, 1942; Kansas City, MO. **Parents:** Sherman Rosenberg and Claire (Kanchuk) Rosenberg Magadey. **Education:** University of Oklahoma: BA. University of Minnesota: MA. **Spouse:** Carol Finkel. **Children:** Kirsten.

Prize: *Criticism,* 1985: *Los Angeles Times,* Los Angeles, CA: Los Angeles Times, 1984.

Career: Editor, *White Bear Weekly Press (MN),* 1965-66; General Assignment Reporter, *Moline (KS) Dispatch,* 1966-68; General Assignment and Political Reporter, *Louisville (KY) Times,* 1968-70; Television Critic, *Louisville (KY) Times,* 1970-78; Published Articles in *American Film, Emmy, Washington (DC) Journalism Press;* Television Critic and Columnist, *Los Angeles Times,* 1978-; Syndicated columnist; Adjunct Professor of Critical Studies, California State University, Northridge, and University of Southern California.

Other Awards: Times Editorial Award for Sustained Excellence, 1982. National Headliners Club Award, 1983. Windwalker Award, 1983. Print Journalist of the Year, Society of Professional Journalists. Murrow Award. Genesis Award, Los Angeles Press Club. Distinguished Achievement in Journalism Award, University of Southern California Journalism Alumni Association, 1995.

For More Information: *Los Angeles Times,* 26 April (1985): part 6, 1; *Los Angeles Times,* 22 May (1985): part 6, 1.

Commentary: Howard Rosenberg, a critic of film and television, won a Pulitzer Prize for his columns that ranged in topics from the media coverage of the presidential campaign to the treatment of death to the coverage of the Olympics. He was also a finalist for the award in 1981.

1986

Donal Joseph Henahan   155
Birth: February 28, 1921; Cleveland, OH. **Parents:** William Anthony Henahan and Mildred (Doyle). **Education:** Kent State University, OH. Ohio University. Northwestern University, IL. University of Chicago, IL: Postgraduate. Chicago School of Music, IL.

Prize: *Criticism,* 1986: *New York Times,* New York: New York Times, 1985.

Career: Served in U.S. Air Force, 1942-45; Staff member, *Chicago Daily News,* 1947-57; Chief Music Critic, *Chicago Daily News,* 1957-67; Music Critic, *New York Times,* 1967-91; Chief Music Critic, *New York Times,* 1980-91.

Other Awards: Page One Award, Chicago Newspaper Guild. Poynter Fellow, Yale University, CT, 1983. Honorary Degree, Providence College, RI, 1990.

For More Information: *New York Times,* 10 July (1991): C17.

Commentary: Donal J. Henahan was appointed chief music critic for the *New York Times* in 1980. He succeeded Harold C. Schonberg, who won a Pulitzer Prize in 1971 for his criticism.

Henahan's background includes training as a pianist, singer, and classical guitarist. He retired in 1991.

1987

Richard Gray Eder   156
Birth: August 16, 1932; Washington, DC. **Parents:** George Jackson Eder and Marceline (Gray). **Religion:** Roman Catholic. **Education:** Harvard University, MA: BA. **Spouse:** Esther Garcia Aguirre (m. 1955). **Children:** Maria Eder Lavitas, Ann Alicia Eder-Mulhane, Claire Marceline, Michael, Luke, Benjamin, James.

Prize: *Criticism,* 1987: *Los Angeles Times,* Los Angeles, CA: Los Angeles Times, 1986.

Career: News Clerk and Copyboy, Police Reporter, General Assignment Writer and Rewriter,*New York Times,* 1954-82, 1954-62; South America and Caribbean Correspondent, *New York Times,* 1962-65; Correspondent, State Department, Washington (DC), *New York Times,* 1965-67; Correspondent, Eastern Europe, *New York Times;* Correspondent, Spain, Portugal, and other parts of the Mediterranean, *New York Times,* 1968-72; Correspondent, London (England), *New York Times,* 1972; Deputy Film Critic, *New York Times,* 1975-77; Drama Critic, *New York Times,* 1977-79; Cultural Correspondent, *New York Times,* 1979-80; Paris (France) Chief, *New York Times,* 1980-82; New York Arts Critic, *Los Angeles Times,* 1982; Specialized in book criticism reviews that appeared twice weekly; Instructor, Princeton University, 1983; Instructor, Bard College, NY, 1983; Instructor, Boston University, 1989.

Other Awards: Excellence in Reviewing, National Book Critics Circle, 1987.

For More Information: *Contemporary Authors,* Detroit: Gale Research Company; *New York Times,* 17 April (1987).

Commentary: Richard Eder is the book critic for the *Los Angeles Times.* He writes two book reviews each week and reviews more fiction than nonfiction. His reviews are never reworked, borrowed opinions. He tries to identify and review books by talented unknowns as well as those by the most established writers. He was a finalist for a Pulitzer Prize in 1986.

1988

Thomas W. Shales   157

Birth: November 3, 1944; Elgin, IL. **Parents:** Clyde LeRoy Shales and Hulda Louise (Reko). **Education:** Elgin Community College, IL. American University, Washington, DC: BA.

Prize: *Criticism,* 1988: *Washington Post,* Washington, DC: Washington Post, 1987.

Career: Entertainment Editor, *Washington (DC) Examiner,* 1968-71; Writer, Style Section, *Washington (DC) Post,* 1972-77; Film Critic, Morning Edition, National Public Radio, 1977; Chief Television Critic, *Washington (DC) Post,* 1977-79; Occasional film critic on radio and television; Contributor to national magazines; Part-Time Instructor of Film, American University; Adjunct Professor, American University, 1978; Television Editor, *Washington (DC) Post,* 1979; Syndicated Columnist, Washington Post Writers Group, 1979; Critic, *The Progressive Review.*

Selected Works: *The American Film Heritage* (with Kevin Brownlow), 1972. *On the Air,* 1982. *Legends: Remembering America's Greatest Stars,* 1989.

Other Awards: Distinguished Alumnus Award, American University, Washington, DC. American Society of Newspaper Editors Writing Award.

For More Information: *Contemporary Authors, Volume 110,* Detroit: Gale Research Company, 1984.

Commentary: Tom Shales has been a television critic for over 20 years. He won a Pulitzer Prize for his reviews and articles on the public's perception of news events. One of his articles examined how the major networks handled the Reagan-Gorbachev summit. His syndicated column is published twice a week.

1989

Michael Skube   158

Birth: December 6, 1943; Springfield, IL. **Parents:** John Skube. **Education:** Louisiana State University. **Spouse:** Married. **Children:** Noah, Alex.

Prize: *Criticism,* 1989: *News and Observer,* Raleigh, NC: News and Observer, 1988.

Career: Sports Reporter, *Illinois State Journal;* Mathematics and science teacher, Louisiana; U.S. Customs Service staff member; Book Reviewer, *Miami (FL) Herald,* 1974; Contributor, book reviews, articles, *Washington (DC) Post, St. Louis (MO) Post-Dispatch, New Republic;* Raleigh (NC) Bureau Chief Covering State Politics, *Winston-Salem (NC) Journal,* 1978; Sunday Columnist, *Atlanta (GA) Journal-Constitution;* Editorial Writer, *Raleigh (NC) News and Observer,* 1982-86; Book Editor, *Raleigh (NC) News and Observer,* 1986-93; Book Editor, Columnist, *Atlanta (GA) Journal and Constitution,* 1993-.

Other Awards: Distinguished Journalism Award, Duke University, NC, 1981. First Place Award for Columns, North Carolina Press Association, 1989. Distinguished Writing Award for Commentary and Column Writing, American Society of Newspaper Editors, 1989.

Commentary: Michael Skube submitted nine columns for consideration for a Pulitzer Prize. One piece was on Robert Penn Warren's memoirs, *Portrait of a Father,* with the theme of fathers and sons. Claude Sitton, the editor of the *Raleigh News and Observer,* who has also won a Pulitzer Prize, said that Skube's "got a beautiful writing touch. He has a knowledge of literature unequaled, I think, in North Carolina." Sitton also noted that Skube is not afraid to write what he thinks. Skube was a finalist for a Pulitzer Prize in 1988.

1990

Allan Bernard Temko   159

Birth: February 4, 1924; New York, NY. **Parents:** Emanuel Temko and Betty (Alderman). **Education:** Columbia University, NY: AB. University of California, Berkeley: Postgraduate. Sorbonne University, Paris, France. **Spouse:** Elizabeth Ostroff (m. 1950, died 1996). **Children:** Susannah, Alexander.

Prize: *Criticism,* 1990: *San Francisco Chronicle,* San Francisco: San Francisco Chronicle, 1989.

Career: Served in U.S. Naval Reserve, 1943-46; Lecturer, Sorbonne, France, 1953-54; Lecturer, Ecole des Arts et Metiers, Paris (France), 1954-55; Assistant Professor of Journalism, University of California, Berkeley, 1956-62; Architecture Critic, *San Francisco Chronicle,* 1961-93; Lecturer, University of

California, Berkeley, 1966-70; Professor of Art, California State University, Hayward, 1971-80; Art Editor, *San Francisco Chronicle,* 1979-82; Lecturer of Art, Stanford University, CA, 1981-82; Architecture West Coast Editor and Principal Contributor, *Architectural Forum;* Advisor, President John F. Kennedy; Advisor, Governor Edmund G. Brown, California.

Selected Works: *Notre-Dame of Paris,* 1955. *Eero Saarinen: Makers of Contemporary Architecture,* 1962. *No Way to Build a Ballpark, and Other Irreverent Essays on Architecture,* 1993.

Other Awards: Gold Medal, Commonwealth Club of California, 1956. Guggenheim Fellow, 1956-57. First Prize for Criticism, American Institute of Architects, 1961. Rockefeller Foundation Grant, 1962-63. Twentieth Century Fund Grant, 1963-66. Silver Spur Award, San Francisco Planning and Urban Renewal Association, 1985. First Prize for Architectural Criticism, Manufacturers Hanover, 1986-87. National Endowment for the Arts Grant, 1988. Lifetime Achievement Award, Society of Professional Journalists, 1988. First Prize for Architectural Criticism, 1986-87. American Institute of Architects Honor, 1991.

For More Information: *A Talk With Architecture Critic Allan Temko, a Video,* Tucson: University of Arizona College of Architecture, 1986; *The Pulitzer Prizes 1990,* New York: Simon & Schuster, 1990: 319-351; *Contemporary Authors, Volume 136,* Detroit: 1992.

Commentary: Allan Temko, a literary wordsmith, opened up architecture to everyone. He "blends social commentary with analysis of building and the environment." Some of the topics he touched upon in 1989 were preservation of a historic rail station, proposals for the Presidio, and "the Great Building Inspector in the sky." He was a finalist for a Pulitzer Prize in 1981 and 1988.

1991

David Lyle Shaw   160
Birth: January 4, 1943; Dayton, OH. **Parents:** Harry Shaw and Lillian (Walton). **Religion:** Jewish. **Education:** University of California, Los Angeles: BA. **Spouse:** Alice L. Eck (m. 1965, div. 1974); Ellen Torgerson (m. 1977, died 1983); Lucy Stille (m. 1988). **Children:** Lucas Michael (LS).

Prize: *Criticism,* 1991: *Los Angeles Times,* Los Angeles, CA: Los Angeles Times, 1990.

Career: *Huntington Park Signa,* 1963-66; Reporter, Feature Writer, *Long Beach (CA) Independent,* 1966-68; Reporter, *Los Angeles Times,* 1968-74; Media Reporter and Critic, *Los Angeles Times,* 1974.

Selected Works: *Wilt: Just Like Any Other 7-Foot Black Millionaire Who Lives Next Door* (with

Wilt Chamberlain), 1973. *The Levy Caper,* 1974. *Journalism Today: A Changing Press for a Changing America,* 1977. *Press Watch: A Provocative Look at How Newspapers Report the News,* 1984. *Luring the Young: For Papers, Generation Is Missing; Young People Read, but Papers Aren't No. 1 Choice,* 1989. *The Pleasure Police: How Bluenose Busybodies and Lily-Livered Alarmists Are Taking All the Fun out of Life,* 1996. *The Cheapskate's Guide to Weddings and Honeymoons,* 1996.

Other Awards: American Political Science Association, 1969. Education Writers Association, 1969. Los Angeles Press Club, 1969-77, 1983. American Bar Association Award, 1972. Lowell Mellet Award, 1982. PEN Center West Annual Literary Award for Journalism, 1990.

For More Information: *Contemporary Authors, Volumes 49-52,* Detroit: Gale Research Company, 1975; Bacon, Mark S., David Shaw in the Continuum of Press Self-Criticism (thesis), University of Nevada, Las Vegas, 1993.

Commentary: David Shaw's four-part series detailed how the news media covered the McMartin Preschool molestation case. In his analysis, he noted that his own paper, the *Los Angeles Times,* provided the worst coverage of any newspaper. He has reported on the news media since 1974. He was a finalist for a Pulitzer Prize in 1989 and 1991.

"When I began work on this series, examining media coverage of the McMartin Preschool molestation case, one of the top editors at my paper ordered the reporter who had covered the case since its inception not to speak to me. I had no idea why. But by the time I'd finished my reporting, I could understand his concern (but not his action): The *L.A. Times* in general and this reporter in particular had done a poor, biased job on the case—and so I wrote." —D. Shaw

1992
No award

1993

Michael Dirda   161
Birth: November 6, 1948; Lorain, OH. **Education:** Oberlin College, OH: BA, Highest Honors. Cornell University, NY: MA. Cornell University, NY: PhD. **Spouse:** Marian Peck. **Children:** Christopher, Michael, Nathaniel.

Prize: *Criticism,* 1993: *Washington Post,* Washington, DC: Washington Post, 1992.

Career: English Instructor, Marseilles, France, 1971; Literature Instructor, American University (DC) and George Mason University; Freelance writer, translator, editor; Editor, *Washington (DC) Post Book World,* 1978-.

Selected Works: *Caring for Your Books.*

For More Information: *Washington Post,* 1 November (1992): R16; *Washington Post,* 14 April (1993): A1.

Commentary: Michael Dirda's literary reviews range "from history and biography to science fiction and children's literature." Dirda describes himself as "a writer and appreciator of books." He won a Pulitzer Prize for his book reviews, covering a wide variety of subjects.

1994

Lloyd Schwartz 162

Birth: November 29, 1941; Brooklyn, NY. **Parents:** Sam Schwartz and Ida (Singer). **Education:** Queens College, NY: BA, magna cum laude, Phi Beta Kappa. Harvard University, MA: MA. Harvard University, MA: PhD.

Prize: *Criticism,* 1994: *Boston Phoenix,* Boston: Boston Phoenix, 1993.

Career: Co-Director, Creative Writing Program, University of Massachusetts, Boston; Lecturer, Queens College of the City of New York, 1964-65; Assistant Professor of English, Hellenic College, MA, 1968-71; Associate Professor of English, Boston State College, MA 1971-82; Associate Editor, *Ploughshares,* 1975-76; Music Critic, *Boston Herald American,* 1975-78; Classical Music Editor, *Boston Phoenix,* 1977; Classical Music Critic, *Boston Phoenix,* 1978; Visiting Professor, Harvard University, MA, 1978-79, 82-83; Coordinating Editor, *Ploughshares,* 1979; Associate Professor of English, University of Massachusetts, Boston, 1982; Director of Creative Writing Program, University of Massachusetts, Boston, 1982-83; Feature Writer, *Vanity Fair,* 1983; Classical Music Critic, National Public Radio, *Fresh Air,* 1987-.

Selected Works: *These People: Wesleyan Poetry Program, vol. 103,* 1981. *Elizabeth Bishop and Her Art* (with Sybil Estess), 1982. *That Sense of Constant Re-Adjustment: Elizabeth Bishop's North and South; Harvard Dissertations in American and English Literature,* 1987. *Goodnight, Gracie,* 1992.

Other Awards: Woodrow Wilson Fellowship, 1962. Outstanding Poet Award, Pushcart Press, 1978: *Song of the Self-Stimulator.* Outstanding Poet Award, Pushcart Press, 1979: *Swimming.* New York Music Critics Institute Fellowship, Music Critics Association, 1980. Deems Taylor Award, American Society of Composers, Authors, and Publishers, 1980. Creative Writing Fellowship Grant, National Endowment for the Arts, 1990.

For More Information: *Boston Globe,* 13 April (1994): 14.

Commentary: Lloyd Schwartz, the classical music critic for the *Boston Phoenix,* won a Pulitzer Prize for his "skillful and resonant" critiques. Schwartz has also published literary criticism. Some of his work during 1993 included pieces on Seiji Ozawa and the Boston Symphony Orchestra, as well as various artists.

1995

Margo L. Jefferson 163

Birth: October 17, 1947; Chicago, IL. **Parents:** Ron Jefferson and Irma. **Education:** Brandeis University, MA: BA, cum laude. Columbia University, NY: MS.

Prize: *Criticism,* 1995: *New York Times,* "Fear of the Puritans: The Appeal of the Indians," April 6; "One Disney Character's Real Life," May 11; "Art and Business of Courting the Camera," July 6, New York: New York Times, 1994.

Career: Associate Editor, *Newsweek* magazine, 1973-78; Assistant Professor of Journalism, New York University, 1979-83; Contributing Editor for Arts Criticism, *Vogue* magazine, 1984-89; Contributing Editor, *7 Days* magazine, 1988-89; Assistant Professor of Journalism, New York University, 1989-91; Lecturer, Columbia University, NY, 1991-93; Book Critic, *New York Times,* 1993-95; Sunday Theater Critic, *New York Times,* 1995-96; Cultural Critic, *New York Times,* 1996-.

Selected Works: *Roots of Time: A Portrait of African Life and Culture* (with Elliott Skinner), 1974.

For More Information: *Jet,* 87:26 (May 8, 1995): 22-23; *New York Times,* January 5, 1995: C16; *Columbus Dispatch,* May 22, 1996: 8E.

Commentary: Margo Jefferson won a Pulitzer Prize for her "book reviews and other cultural criticism." Her citation noted that she wrote "forcefully and originally without ever muscling out the author in question." She wrote on a variety of subjects including modeling, the French and Indian War, and Annette Funicello.

1996

Robert Campbell   164

Birth: March 31, 1937; Buffalo, NY. **Parents:** R. Douglas Campbell and Amy (Armitage). **Education:** Harvard University, MA: AB, magna cum laude, Highest Honors, Phi Beta Kappa. Harvard University, MA: MArch. Columbia University, NY: MS. **Spouse:** Janice Jaye Gold (m. 1963, div. 1990). **Children:** Nicholas.

Prize: *Criticism,* 1996: *Boston Globe,* Boston: Boston Globe, 1995.

Career: Associate Editor, *Parade Magazine,* 1960-63; Earl R. Flansburgh and Associates, Cambridge, MA, 1966; Waterhouse and Ripley, London, England, 1966-67; Benjamin Thompson and Associates, Cambridge, MA, 1968-69; Sert, Jackson, and Associates, Incorporated, 1967-68, 1969-76; Member of Graham Foundation, 1968; Architecture Critic, *Boston Globe,* 1973; Architect, private practice, 1976; Lecturer, Harvard University, MA, 1976; Instructor, Harvard University, MA, 1977-78; Visiting Critic, University of North Carolina, Charlotte, 1979-94; Contributing Editor, *Architecture* magazine, 1983-89; Contributing Editor, *Architecture Record* magazine, 1990; Instructor, Harvard University, MA, 1990; Visiting Scholar, Massachusetts Institute of Technology, 1991-94; Sam Gibbons Eminent Scholar in Architecture and Urban Planning, University of South Florida, 1993.

Selected Works: *Artists and Architects Collaborate: Design of the Wiesner Building* (with others), 1985. *American Architecture of the 1980s,* 1990. *Cityscapes of Boston: An American City through Time* (with Peter Vander Warker), 1992.

Other Awards: Francis Kelley Prize for Best Thesis Project, 1967. Julia Amory Appleton Traveling Fellowship, 1968. Design Fellowship, National Endowment for the Arts, 1976. Award of Excellence, Art Museum Association of America: *Artists and Architects Collaborate: Design of the Wiesner Building.* Cambridge, MA: MIT Press, 1985. Architectural Criticism Medal, American Institute of Architects, 1980. Newspaper Criticism Award, *Art World Magazine* and Manufacturers Hanover Trust, 1984. Historic Neighborhoods Foundations Award, 1986. Graham Foundation for Advanced Studies in the Visual Arts Grant, 1991. Bostonian Society History Award, 1996.

Artist-in-Residence, American Academy in Rome, 1997.

Commentary: Robert Campbell has been an architecture critic for the *Boston Globe* since 1973. He has written on all aspects of buildings. He also writes a monthly column, "Cityscapes," for the *Boston Globe Magazine.* Some of the places he has written about include the Boston Holocaust Memorial, the Rock and Roll Hall of Fame in Cleveland, and the Charles River Park.

1997

Tim Page   165

Birth: October 11, 1954; San Diego, CA. **Parents:** Ellis Batten Page and Elizabeth Latimer (Thaxton). **Education:** Columbia University, NY: BA. Tanglewood Music Center, MA. Mannes College of Music, NY. **Spouse:** Vanessa Marie Weeks (m. 1984). **Children:** William, Robert, Jack.

Prize: *Criticism,* 1997: *Washington Post,* Washington, DC: Washington Post, 1996.

Career: Founder, Catalyst-Contemporary Music Label BMG Classics; Writer, *Soho Weekly News and Car Stereo;* Contributor, *New York Times,* 1982-87; Chief Music Critic, *Newsday (NY) and New York Newsday,* 1987-95; Chief Classical Music Critic, *Washington (DC) Post,* 1995-.

Selected Works: *The Glenn Gould Reader,* 1984. *Selected Letters of Virgil Thomson* (with Vanessa Weeks Page), 1988. *William Kapell: A Documentary Life History of the American Pianist,* 1992. *Music from the Road: Views and Reviews, 1978-1992,* 1992. *Dawn Powell at Her Best* (with Dawn Powell), 1994. *The Diaries of Dawn Powell, 1931-1965* (with Dawn Powell), 1995.

Other Awards: Deems Taylor Award, American Society of Composers, Authors, and Publishers, 1983.

For More Information: *Washington Post,* 8 April (1997): A1; *Hartford Courant,* 9 May (1997): B1; *Cleveland Plain Dealer,* 24 August (1997): 8.

Commentary: After only one year at the *Washington Post,* Tim Page won a Pulitzer Prize for his critical writing on music. His citation notes that his writing was "lucid and illuminating." Among his articles for the year was an exploration of the decline of the classical music recording industry. He also wrote about "radical music that will remain radical."

1998

Michiko Kakutani   166

Birth: January 9, 1955; New Haven, CT. **Parents:** Shizuo Kakutani and Keiko. **Education:** Yale University, CT: BA, magna cum laude.

Prize: *Criticism,* 1998: *New York Times,* "Coping With the Idea of Representing One's Race," January 28; "From Salinger, A New Dash of Mystery," February 20; "Bickering with Mom and Making His Boxes," March 18; "Norman Mailer's Perception of Jesus," April 14; "A Postwar Paradise Shattered From Within," April 15; "Pynchon Hits the Road With Mason and Dixon," April 29; "Master of Magic Realism Works in Real Realism," June 19; "Of America as a Splendid Junk Heap," September 16; "On Sex, Death and the Self: An Old Man's Sour Grapes," September 30; "Woe is Me: Rewards and Perils of Memoirs," October 21, New York: *New York Times,* 1997.

Career: Editor, college paper, *Yale Daily News Magazine;* Reporter, *Washington (DC) Post;* Staff Writer, *Time* magazine, 1977-79; Cultural News Reporter, *New York Times,* 1979-83; Book Critic, *New York Times,* 1983-; Senior Book Critic, *New York Times;*.

Selected Works: *New Haven Blues. The Poet at the Piano: Portraits of Writers, Filmmakers, Playwrights, and Other Artists at Work,* 1988.

For More Information: *New York Times,* April 15, 1998: A22; *American Journalism Review,* 20:4 (May 1998): 7.

Commentary: Michiko Kakutani was awarded a Pulitzer Prize for her "passionate, intelligent writing on books and contemporary literature." A graduate in English, Kakutani has been with the *New York Times* since 1979. Included in her winning entry was a review of Philip Roth's *American Pastoral,* which was awarded the 1998 Pulitzer Prize in Fiction.

Drama

1917
No award

1918

Jesse Lynch Williams   167
Birth: August 17, 1871; Sterling, IL. **Death:** 1929.
Parents: Meade Creighton and Elizabeth (Riddle)
Williams. **Education:** Princeton University, NJ: BA.
Spouse: Alise Laidlaw. **Children:** Three children.

    Prize: *Drama,* 1918: *Why Marry?,* New York:
Scribners, 1918.

    Career: Novelist, playwright, and editor.

    Selected Works: *Princeton Stories,* 1895. *The
Adventures of a Freshman,* 1899. *The Stolen Story and
Other Newspaper Stories,* 1899. *New York Sketches,*
1902. *The Day-Dreamer,* 1906. *My Lost Duchess,*
1908. *The Girl and the Game,* 1908. *Mr. Cleveland:
A Personal Impression,* 1909. *The Married Life of the
Frederic Carrolls,* 1911. *"And So They Were Mar-
ried,"* 1914. *Remating Time,* 1916. *Not Wanted,* 1923.
They Still Fall in Love, 1929. *She Knew She Was
Right,* 1930.

    For More Information: *Twentieth Century
Authors,* New York: Wilson, 1942.

    Commentary: Jesse Lynch Williams was
awarded the 1918 Pulitzer Prize in Drama for *Why
Marry?,* a play based on his short story, *And So They
Were Married.* It premiered on December 25, 1917 at
New York's Astor Theater.

    Williams was born in Illinois. He attended
Princeton University and was a member of its Triangle
Club along with Booth Tarkington. He worked as a
journalist for the *New York Sun,* and also began pub-
lishing short stories. His other works include *The
Married Life of the Frederic Carrolls.*

1919
No award

1920

Eugene O'Neill   168

Birth: October 16, 1888; New York, NY. **Death:**
November 27, 1953. **Parents:** James O'Neill and
Mary Ellen (Quinlan). **Education:** Princeton Univer-
sity, NJ. Harvard University, MA. **Spouse:** Kathleen
Jenkins (m. 1909; div. 1912); Agnes Boulton (m.
1918; div. 1929); Carlotta Monterey (m. 1929). **Chil-
dren:** Eugene Gladston Jr. (KJ); Shane Rudraighe,
Oona (AB).

    Prize: *Drama,* 1920: *Beyond the Horizon,* New
York: Boni and Liveright, 1920. *Drama,* 1922: *Anna
Christie,* New York: Boni and Liveright, 1922.
Drama, 1928: *Strange Interlude,* New York: Boni and
Liveright, 1928. *Drama,* 1957: *Long Day's Journey
into Night,* New Haven, CT: Yale University, 1955.

    Career: Playwright; Secretary, New York-Chi-
cago Supply Company, NY, 1907-1908; Prospector,
Honduras, 1909-1910; Assistant stage manager and
actor, his father's theater company, 1910, 1912; Sailor
and laborer, Buenos Aires, Argentina, 1910-1911;
Reporter, *New London Telegraph,* New London, CT,
1912; Co-Manager, Provincetown Players, 1923;
Member: American Academy of Arts and Letters,
American Philosophical Society, Authors League of
America, Dramatists Guild, Irish Academy of Letters,
National Institute of Arts and Letters.

    Selected Works: *Thirst, and Other One Act
Plays,* 1914. *Gold: A Play in Four Acts,* 1920. *The
Emperor Jones, Diff'rent, The Straw,* 1921. *All God's*

Chillun Got Wings, and Welded, 1924. *Desire under the Elms,* 1925. *The Great God Brown; The Fountain; The Moon of the Caribbees; and Other Plays,* 1926. *Marco Millions,* 1927. *Lazarus Laughed,* 1927. *Dynamo,* 1929. *Mourning Becomes Electra: A Trilogy,* 1931. *Ah, Wilderness!,* 1933. *Days without End,* 1934. *The Iceman Cometh,* 1946. *A Moon for the Misbegotten,* 1952. *A Touch of the Poet,* 1957. *Hughie,* 1959. *Inscriptions: Eugene O'Neill to Carlotta Monterey O'Neill,* 1960. *Ten "Lost" Plays,* 1964. **Films:** *Anna Christie,* MGM, 1930; *Strange Interlude,* MGM, 1932; *Long Day's Journey into Night,* USA, 1962.

Other Awards: Gold Medal from National Institute of Arts and Letters, 1923. Nobel Prize in Literature, 1936. New York Drama Critics Circle Award, 1957: *Long Day's Journey Into Night.* Honorary LittD, Yale University, CT, 1923.

For More Information: Floyd, Virginia, *The Plays of Eugene O'Neill: A New Assessment,* New York: Ungar, 1985; Bogard, Travis, *Contour in Time: The Plays of Eugene O'Neill,* New York: Oxford University, 1988; Moorton, Richard F. Jr., ed., *Eugene O'Neill's Century: Centennial Views on America's Foremost Tragic Dramatist,* New York: Greenwood, 1991; Houchin, John H., *The Critical Response to Eugene O'Neill,* Westport, CT: Greenwood, 1993; Berlin, Normand, *O'Neill's Shakespeare,* Ann Arbor: University of Michigan, 1993; Bryan, George B. and Wolfgang Miedereds, eds., *The Proverbial Eugene O'Neill: An Index to Proverbs in the Works of Eugene Gladstone O'Neill,* Westport, CT: Greenwood, 1995.

Commentary: Eugene O'Neill won four Pulitzer Prizes, all in Drama. He was awarded the 1920 prize for *Beyond the Horizon,* about two Irish brothers in love with the same girl, which premiered on February 2, 1920 at New York's Morosco Theater. His second prize came in 1922 for *Anna Christie,* a tale of a barge captain's daughter, which premiered on November 2, 1922 at New York's Vanderbilt Theater. *Strange Interlude,* the story of the loves of Nina Leeds, premiered on January 30, 1928 at New York's John Golden Theater, and won the 1928 prize for O'Neill. O'Neill won his fourth Pulitzer Drama prize in 1957 for *Long Day's Journey Into Night,* an autobiographical tale, which premiered on November 28, 1957 at New York's Ethel Barrymore Theater.

O'Neill, whose father was an actor, was born in a hotel room in the Broadway district of New York City. After attending Princeton University without graduating, O'Neill worked as a gold prospector in Honduras and as a merchant seaman. These experiences, and the people he met, laid the groundwork for his plays and characters. O'Neill would write 33 plays between 1913 and 1919. He stopped writing in 1943, due to an illness that caused his hands to tremble so much that he could not hold a pen. He wrote 49 plays

in his lifetime, mostly serious dramas. He is considered by many to be the most significant playwright in America's history.

1921

Zona Gale   169
Birth: 1874; Portage, WI. **Death:** 1938. **Parents:** Charles Franklin and Elizabeth (Beers) Gale. **Education:** University of Wisconsin: BL, MA. **Spouse:** William Llewelyn Breese. **Children:** Leslyn.

Prize: *Drama,* 1921: *Miss Lulu Bett,* New York: D. Appleton, 1920.

Career: Writer; Reporter, *Milwaukee Evening Wisconsin,* 1895-1896; Reporter, *Milwaukee Journal,* 1896-1901; Reporter, *New York Evening World,* 1901-1903; Member, Wisconsin Library Commission, 1920-1932; Member, Wisconsin Board of Regents, 1923-29; Member, Board of Visitors, University of Wisconsin, 1936-1938; Wisconsin Delegate, International Congress for Women, Chicago, 1933.

Selected Works: *Romance Island,* 1906. *The Loves of Pelleas and Etarre,* 1907. *Friendship Village,* 1908. *Friendship Village Love Stories,* 1909. *Mothers to Men,* 1911. *Christmas,* 1912. *Neighborhood Stories,* 1914. *Heart's Kindred,* 1915. *A Daughter of the Morning,* 1917. *Peace in Friendship Village,* 1919. *The Secret Way,* 1921. *Friendship Village,* 1922. *Birth,* 1923. *Faint Perfume,* 1923. *When I Was a Little Girl,* 1925. *Mister Pitt,* 1925. *Preface to a Life,* 1926. *Yellow Gentians and Blue,* 1927. *Portage, Wisconsin, and Other Essays,* 1928. *Borgia,* 1929. *Bridal Pond,* 1930. *Papa La Fleur,* 1933. *Old-Fashioned Tales,* 1933. *Faint Perfume: A Play with a Prologue and Three Acts,* 1934. *Light Woman,* 1937. *Frank Miller of Mission Inn,* 1938. *Magna,* 1939. **Films:** *Miss Lulu Bett,* Famous Players—Lasky, 1921.

Other Awards: Butterick Prize, 1911. Honorary DLitts: Ripon College, 1922; University of Wisconsin, 1929; Rollins College, FL, 1930.

For More Information: Derleth, August William, *Elegy: On a Flake of Snow for Zona Gale,* Muscatine, IA: Prairie, 1939; Derleth, August William, *Still Small Voice: The Biography of Zona Gale,* New York: D. Appleton-Century, 1940; Simonson, Harold Peter, *Zona Gale,* New York: Twayne, 1962.

Commentary: Zona Gale won the 1920 Pulitzer Prize in Drama for *Miss Lulu Betts,* a dramatization of Gale's novel of the same title about a spinster who prevails over attempts by her family to misuse her. It premiered on December 27, 1921 at New York's Belmont Theater.

Gale was born in Portage, Wisconsin and educated at the University of Wisconsin. She worked as a reporter before turning to freelance writing. She was successful at getting short stories published. Her first novel, *Romance Island,* was published in 1906. She was a vocal pacifist during World War I and later was active in the Progressive Party, led by Senator Robert M. LaFollette. Her other works include *Faint Perfume, Papa La Fleur,* and her autobiography, *When I Was a Little Girl.*

1922

Eugene O'Neill
Full entry appears as #**168** under "Drama," 1920.

1923

Owen Davis   170
Birth: January 29, 1874; Bangor, ME. **Death:** 1956. **Parents:** Warren and Abby (Gould) Davis. **Education:** Harvard University, MA. **Spouse:** Elizabeth Breyer. **Children:** Owen Jr.

Prize: *Drama,* 1923: *Icebound,* Boston, NY: Little, Brown, 1923.

Career: Playwright.

Selected Works: *The Detour,* 1922. *I'd Like to Do It Again,* 1931. *Just to Remind You,* 1931. *Ethan Frome* (Adaptation) (with Donald Davis), 1936. *Mr. and Mrs. North* (Adaptation), 1941. *No Way Out,* 1945. *My First Fifty Years in the Theatre,* 1950. **Films:** *Icebound,* Famous Players—Lasky, 1924.

For More Information: Middleton, George, *Owen Davis, January 29, 1874-October 14, 1956,* New York: Dramatist Guild of the Authors League of America, 1957.

Commentary: *Icebound,* the story of a family waiting for an inheritance, won the 1923 Pulitzer Prize in Drama for Owen Davis. It premiered on February 10, 1923 at New York's Sam H. Harris Theater.

Davis was born in Maine. He attended Harvard University and was a mining engineer before beginning his writing career. His work consisted of mostly melodramas, which included *The Nervous Wreck* and *The Detour.* He wrote two autobiographies; the second, entitled *My First 50 Years in the Theatre,* was published in 1950.

1924

Hatcher Hughes   171
Birth: 1881; Polkville, NC. **Death:** 1945. **Parents:** Andrew Jackson and Martha (Hold) Hughes. **Education:** University of North Carolina: BA. Columbia University, NY: MA. **Spouse:** Jane Ranney Cool (m. 1930).

Prize: *Drama,* 1924: *Hell-Bent fer Heaven,* New York: Harper, 1924.

Career: Teacher, Columbia University; U.S. Army Captain.

Selected Works: *Ruint,* 1925. *Wake Up, Jonathan,* 1928. **Films:** *Hell-Bent fer Heaven,* Warner Bros., 1926.

For More Information: *Twentieth-Century Authors,* New York: Wilson, 1942.

Commentary: Hatcher Hughes was awarded the 1924 Pulitzer Prize in Drama for *Hell-Bent fer Heaven,* a tale about a religious fanatic living in the hills of North Carolina who employs various means to get his message across. It premiered on January 4, 1924 at New York's Klaw Theater.

Hughes was born in Polkville, North Carolina. He taught English at Columbia University. He collaborated with Elmer Rice on the play *Wake Up, Jonathan,* which was successful. His other works include *A Marriage Made in Heaven* and *The Lord Blesses the Bishop.*

1925

Sidney Howard   172
Birth: June 26, 1891; Oakland, CA. **Death:** August 23, 1939. **Parents:** John L. and Helen (Coe) Howard. **Education:** University of California, Berkeley. **Spouse:** Claire Eames (m. 1921; div. 1930); Leopoldine Blaine Damrosch (m. 1931). **Children:** Clare Jenness (CE); One daughter, one son (LBD).

Prize: *Drama,* 1925: *They Knew What They Wanted,* Garden City, NY: Doubleday, Page, 1925.

Career: Dramatist.

Selected Works: *The Late Christopher Bean,* 1933. *Swords,* 1921. *Casanova* (Adaptation), 1924. *Three Flights Up,* 1924. *Lucky Sam McCarver,* 1926. *Half Gods,* 1930. *One Heavenly Night,* 1931. *Alien Corn,* 1933. *Thames to Tahiti,* 1933. *Yellow Jack,* 1934. *Sinclair Lewis's Dodsworth,* 1934. *Paths of Glory,* 1935. *Gone with the Wind* (Screenplay), 1937. *The Ghost of Yankee Doodle,* 1938. **Films:** *Gone with the Wind,* Selznick, 1939; *They Knew What They Wanted,* RKO, 1940.

For More Information: White, Sidney Howard, *Sidney Howard,* Boston: Twayne, 1977.

Commentary: Sidney Coe Howard won the 1925 Pulitzer Prize in Drama for *They Knew What They Wanted,* a melodrama about a Napa vintner who lures a mail-order bride by using a photograph of a vineyard worker. It premiered on November 24, 1924 at New York's Garrick Theater. It was later made into a musical film by Frank Loesser, titled *The Most Happy Fella.*

Howard was born in Oakland, California and attended the University of California at Berkeley.

Howard was a student of George Pierce Baker's Harvard 47 Workshop, a popular playwriting course which also attracted Eugene O'Neill, George Abbott, and Thomas Wolfe, among others. Howard became a successful original playwright as well as a screen adaptor, most notably adapting two Pulitzer Prize-winning novels, Sinclair Lewis's *Arrowsmith* and Margaret Mitchell's *Gone With the Wind.* His other works include *The Silver Cord* and *Yellow Jack,* a documentary about the Army's battle with yellow fever.

1926

George Kelly   173
Birth: January 16, 1887; Bryn Mawr, PA. **Death:** June 18, 1974. **Parents:** John Henry and Mary (Costello) Kelly.

Prize: *Drama,* 1926: *Craig's Wife,* Boston: Little, Brown, 1926.

Career: Playwright.

Selected Works: *The Torch-Bearers,* 1924. *The Flattering Word, and Other One-Act Plays,* 1925. *The Show-Off,* 1925. *Daisy Mayme,* 1927. *Behold, the Bridegroom,* 1928. *Philip Goes Forth,* 1931. *Reflected Glory,* 1937. *The Deep Mrs. Sykes,* 1946. *The Fatal Weakness,* 1947. **Films:** *Craig's Wife,* Pathe Exchange, 1928.

For More Information: Hirsch, Foster, *George Kelly,* Boston: Twayne, 1975.

Commentary: *Craig's Wife,* a drama about a woman who is a cold, dissatisfied complainer, won the 1926 Pulitzer Prize in Drama for George Kelly. It premiered on October 12, 1925 at New York's Morosco Theater.

Kelly began his career writing sketches for vaudeville and moved on to full-length plays. He was an actor and scriptwriter as well as a playwright. He is best remembered for his play, *The Show-Off,* a comedy classic that was adapted to the screen three times.

1927

Paul Green   174
Birth: March 17, 1894; Lillington, NC. **Death:** 1981. **Parents:** William Archibald and Betty (Byrd) Green. **Education:** Buie's Creek Academy, NC. University of North Carolina, NC: AB. Cornell University, NY. **Spouse:** Elizabeth Atkinson Lay (m. 1922). **Children:** Paul E. Jr., Byrd Green Cornwell, Betsy Green Moyer, Janet Green Catlin.

Prize: *Drama,* 1927: *In Abraham's Bosom,* London, England: Allen & Unwin, 1929.

Career: Second Lieutenant, Belgium and France, U.S. Army Engineers, 1918-1919; Instructor in Philosophy, University of North Carolina at Chapel Hill, 1923-1938; President, American Folk Festival, 1934-1945; Professor of Dramatic Art, University of North Carolina at Chapel Hill, 1939-1944; Member, National Theatre Conference, 1940-1942; President, North Carolina State Literary and Historical Association, 1942-1943; Member, Executive Commission, U.S. National Committee for UNESCO, 1950-1952; Delegate, UNESCO Conference, Paris, France, 1951; Rockefeller Foundation Lecturer, in Asia, on Arts (music, drama, and literature) in the American Theater, 1951; Director, American National Theater Academy, 1959-1961; Delegate, International Conference on the Performing Arts, Athens, Greece, 1962; Professor of Radio, Television, and Motion Pictures, University of North Carolina at Chapel Hill, 1962-1963; Member: American Educational Theater Association, American Society of Composers, Authors and Publishers, National Institute of Arts and Letters, Phi Beta Kappa, Southern Regional Council, Southeastern Theatre Conference.

Selected Works: *In Aunt Mahaly's Cabin,* 1925. *The Lord's Will, and Other Carolina Plays,* 1925. *Lonesome Road,* 1926. *The Field God,* 1927. *The Man Who Died at Twelve O'Clock,* 1927. *In the Valley, and Other Carolina Plays,* 1928. *Wide Fields,* 1928. *The House of Connelly,* 1931. *The Laughing Pioneer,* 1932. *Roll Sweet Chariot,* 1935. *Shroud My Body Down,* 1935. *This Body the Earth,* 1935. *Hymn to the Rising Sun,* 1936. *The Lost Colony,* 1937. *The Enchanted Maze,* 1939. *Out of the South, the Life of a People in Dramatic Form,* 1939. *The Highland Call,* 1941. *Native Son: The Biography of a Young American* (with Richard Wright), 1941. *The Hawthorn Tree,* 1943. *Forever Growing,* 1945. *Salvation on a String, and Other Tales of the South,* 1946. *The Common Glory,* 1948. *Dog on the Sun,* 1949. *The Last of the Lowries,* 1950. *The Common Glory,* 1951. *Peer Gynt* (Adaptation), 1951. *Dramatic Heritage,* 1953. *Wilderness Road,* 1956. *The Founders,* 1957. *Drama and the Weather,* 1958. *The Confederacy,* 1959. *Wings for to Fly,* 1959. *The Stephen Foster Story,* 1960. *Plough and Furrow,* 1963. *Five Plays of the South,* 1963. *Hymn to the Rising Sun: A Drama in One Act,* 1963. *The Sheltering Plaid,* 1965. *Cross and Sword,* 1966. *Texas,* 1967. *Rassie,* 1968. *Home to My Valley,* 1970. *Johnny Johnson: The Biography of a Common Man,* 1971. *Trumpet in the Land,* 1972. *Land of Nod,* 1976. **Films:** *The Cabin in the Cotton,* Warner Bros., 1932.

Other Awards: Belasco Cup, 1925: *The No 'Count Boy.* Guggenheim Fellow, 1928-1930. Claire M. Senie Drama Study Award, 1937: *Johnny Johnson,* New York: French, 1937. Freedom Foundation Medal, 1951: *Faith of Our Fathers.* Freedom Foundation Medal, 1956: *Wilderness Road.* Paul

Green Year Declared, Southeastern Theatre Conference, 1956-1957. Fortieth Anniversary Award, Yale Drama School, 1965. Theta Alpha Phi Medallion of Honor, 1965. North Carolina Achievement Award, 1965. Freedom Foundation Medal, 1967: *Texas.* Distinguished Alumnus Award, University of North Carolina, 1973. Distinguished Alumnus Award, Campbell College, 1975. National Theatre Conference Citation, 1974. Distinguished Citizen Award, State of North Carolina, 1976. First North Caroliniana Award, 1978. Dedication, Paul Green Theatre, University of North Carolina at Chapel Hill, 1978. Award for Distinguished Service to Theatre, American Theatre Association, 1978. Dramatist Laureate of North Carolina, 1979. Honorary LittDs: Western Reserve University, OH, 1941; Davidson College, NC, 1948; University of North Carolina at Chapel Hill, 1956; Berea College, KY, 1957; University of Louisville, KY, 1957; Campbell College, NC, 1969; North Carolina School of the Arts, 1976; Moravian College, PA, 1976; Duke University, NC, 1980.

For More Information: Clark, Barrett Harper, *Paul Green,* New York: McBride, 1928; Lazenby, Walter, *Paul Green,* Austin, TX: Steck-Vaughn, 1970; Kenny, Vincent S., *Paul Green,* New York: Twayne, 1971; Avery, Lawrence, ed., *A Southern Life: Letters of Paul Green, 1916-1981,* Chapel Hill: University of North Carolina, 1994.

Commentary: Paul Green was awarded the 1927 Pulitzer Prize in Drama for *In Abraham's Bosom,* a tragedy about a mulatto who wants to start a school for African Americans but cannot secure all the funds needed. It premiered on December 30, 1926 at New York's Provincetown Theater.

Green was born in Lillington, North Carolina. He attended the University of North Carolina at Chapel Hill and Cornell University. His first plays were produced by the Carolina Playmakers. He was the first white writer to bring to focus the plight of African Americans in America with plays like *Lonesome Road: Six Plays for Negro Theatre.* Later in his career he wrote "symphonic dramas," usually folk tales which were to be performed in outdoor amphitheaters. These included *The Common Glory, Faith of Our Fathers,* and *Stephen Foster.*

1928

Eugene O'Neill

Full entry appears as #**168** under "Drama," 1920.

1929

Elmer L. Rice   175
Birth: September 28, 1892; New York, NY. **Death:** May 8, 1967. **Parents:** Jacob and Fanny (Lion) Reizenstein. **Education:** New York Law School: LLB, cum laude. Columbia University, NY. **Spouse:** Hazel Levy (m. 1915; div. 1942); Betty Field (m. 1942; div. 1955); Barbara A. Marshall. **Children:** Robert, Margaret (HL); John, Judith, Paul (BF).

Prize: *Drama,* 1929: *Street Scene,* New York: French, 1929.

Career: Playwright, novelist, and writer.

Selected Works: *The Subway,* 1929. *See Naples and Die,* 1930. *Counsellor-at-Law,* 1931. *The Left Bank,* 1931. *We, the People,* 1933. *Not for Children and between Two Worlds,* 1935. *American Landscape,* 1939. *A New Life,* 1944. *Dream Girl,* 1946. *The Grand Tour,* 1952. *The Winner,* 1954. **Films:** *Street Scene,* UA/MGM, 1931.

For More Information: Durham, Frank, *Elmer Rice,* New York: Twayne, 1970; Palmieri, Anthony F. R., *Elmer Rice: A Playwright's Vision of America,* Rutherford, NJ: Fairleigh Dickinson University, 1980; Vanden Heuvel, Michael, *Elmer Rice: A Research and Production Sourcebook,* Westport, CT: Greenwood, 1996.

Commentary: Elmer Rice won the 1929 Pulitzer Prize in Drama for *Street Scene,* an urban drama set in a slum tenement that culminates in a double murder. It premiered on January 10, 1929 at New York's Playhouse Theater and was innovative for its special effects in the sound department.

"Elmer Reizenstein" was born in New York City. He was trained in law, which he practiced before turning to a writing career. He became noted for using the German Expressionistic technique, employed in his satire, *The Adding Machine,* about the increasingly machine-oriented society. His other works include *American Landscape* and his autobiography, *Minority Report.*

1930

Marc Connelly 176

Birth: December 13, 1890; McKeesport, PA. **Death:** December 21, 1980. **Parents:** Patrick Joseph and Mabel Louise (Cook) Connelly. **Spouse:** Madeleine Hulock (m. 1930; div. 1935).

Prize: *Drama,* 1930: *The Green Pastures,* New York: Farrar & Rinehart, 1929.

Career: Playwright, actor, director, producer, lecturer and educator; Reporter, *Pittsburgh Press* and *Gazette Times,* Pittsburgh, PA, 1908-16; Reporter, *New York Morning Telegraph,* NY, 1916-21; Director of Broadway plays, some his own, beginning with "The Wisdom Tooth," 1926; Professor of Playwriting, Yale University, New Haven, CT, 1946-50; President, National Institute of Arts and Letters, 1953-1956; Founding Member, Actors Equity Association, Dramatists Guild; Member: American Federation of TV & Radio Artists, Dutch Treat Club (New York), Players Club, NY, Savage Club, London, England, Screen Actors Guild; President, Authors League of America.

Selected Works: *Dulcy* (with George S. Kaufman), 1921. *Beggar on Horseback* (with George S. Kaufman), 1924. *A Souvenir from Qam,* 1965. *Voices Offstage: A Book of Memoirs,* 1968. **Films:** *Green Pastures,* Warner Bros., 1936.

Other Awards: O. Henry Short Story Prize, 1930: "Coroner's Inquest." Best One-Act Plays, 1937: "Little David: An Unproduced Scene from *The Green Pastures.* Certificate of Appreciation on the Occasion of His 90th Birthday, City Hall, New York City, NY, 1980. Honorary Degrees: Bowdoin College, ME, 1952; Baldwin-Wallace College, OH, 1962.

For More Information: Nolan, Paul T., *Marc Connelly,* New York: Twayne, 1969.

Commentary: *The Green Pastures,* stories of African Americans derived from Roark Bradford's book *Ol' Man Adam an' His Chillun,* won the 1930 Pulitzer Prize in Drama for Marc Connelly. It premiered on February 26, 1930 at New York's Mansfield Theater. A 1951 revival of the play was criticized for promoting stereotypical African American characters.

Marcus Cook Connelly was born in McKeesport, Pennsylvania, the son of actor parents. He began his career as a journalist. While working for New York's *Morning Telegraph,* he began a successful collaboration with the *New York Times*'s drama reporter, George S. Kaufman. Together, they wrote the Broadway hits, *Dulcy* and *Beggar on Horseback.* Both were members of the literary gathering known as the Algonquin Roundtable, and Connelly wrote about those days in his memoir, *Voices Offstage: A Book of Memoirs.*

1931

Susan Glaspell 177

Birth: July 1, 1882; Davenport, IA. **Death:** July 27, 1948. **Parents:** Elmer S. and Alice (Keating) Glaspell. **Education:** University of Chicago, IL. Drake University, IA: PhD. **Spouse:** George Gram Cook (m. 1913; died 1924); Norman Matson (m. 1925; div. 1932).

Prize: *Drama,* 1931: *Alison's House,* New York: French, 1930.

Career: Writer, Reporter, *Des Moines Daily News* and *Des Moines Capital,* Des Moines, IA, 1899-1901; Freelance writer, Davenport, IA, 1900-1911; Co-Founder and Writer, Provincetown Players, Provincetown, MA, 1915-1922; Federal Theater Project's Midwest Play Bureau, 1936-1938.

Selected Works: *The Glory of the Conquered,* 1909. *The Visioning,* 1911. *Lifted Masks,* 1912. *The Anarchist—His Dog,* 1914. *According to His Lights,* 1914. *Fidelity: A Novel,* 1915. *Plays,* 1920. *Inheritors,* 1921. *The Road to the Temple,* 1926. *Brook Evans,* 1928. *The Verge,* 1922. *Fugitive's Return,* 1929. *Ambrose Holt and Family,* 1931. *Cherished and Shared of Old,* 1940. *The Morning Is Near Us,* 1940. *Norma Ashe,* 1942. *Judd Rankin's Daughter,* 1945.

For More Information: Waterman, Arthur E., *Susan Glaspell,* New York: Twayne, 1966; Papke, Mary E., *Susan Glaspell: A Research and Production Sourcebook,* Westport, CT: Greenwood, 1993; Makowsky, Veronica A., *Susan Glaspell's Century of American Women: A Critical Interpretation of Her Work,* New York: Oxford University, 1993; Ben-Zvi, Linda, ed., *Susan Glaspell: Essays on Her Theater and Fiction,* Ann Arbor: University of Michigan, 1995.

Commentary: Susan Glaspell was awarded the 1931 Pulitzer Prize in Drama for *Alison's House,* a story based on the poet Emily Dickinson and her sister's preservation of Dickinson's love poems to a married man.

Glaspell was born in Davenport, Iowa and educated at Drake University. She worked as a journalist briefly before devoting all her time to writing short stories. Her first novel, *The Glory of the Conquered,* was published in 1909. In 1913, she married George Cram Cook and together they founded the Provincetown Players in 1915 to launch their one-act play, *Suppressed Desires.* The Players produced some of the early works of Eugene O'Neill before the theatre moved to New York. Her other works include the play *The Verge,* the novel *The Fugitive's Return,* and a biography of her husband, *The Road to the Temple.*

1932

Ira Gershwin   178

Birth: December 6, 1896; New York, NY. **Death:** August 17, 1983. **Parents:** Morris and Rose Gershwin. **Education:** City College, NY. **Spouse:** Leonore Stunsky (m. 1926).

Prize: *Drama,* 1932: *Of Thee I Sing,* New York: Knopf, 1932.

Career: Lyricist.

Selected Works: *Let 'Em Eat Cake,* 1933. *Porgy and Bess (Music by George Gershwin),* 1935. *Lady in the Dark,* 1941. *Girl Crazy,* 1954. *The Complete Lyrics of Ira Gershwin* (Kimball, Robert, ed.), 1993.

For More Information: Jablonski, Edward, *The Gershwin Years,* Garden City, NY: Doubleday, 1958; Kimball, Robert, *The Gershwins,* New York: Atheneum, 1973; Rosenberg, Deena, *Fascinating Rhythm: The Collaboration of George and Ira Gershwin,* New York: Dutton, 1991; Furia, Philip, *Ira Gershwin: The Art of the Lyricist,* New York: Oxford University, 1996.

Commentary: Ira Gershwin, together with George S. Kaufman and Morrie Ryskind, won the 1932 Pulitzer Prize in Drama for *Of Thee I Sing,* a political satire-set-to-music of a presidential campaign. It premiered on December 26, 1931 at New York's Music Box Theater.

Israel (Ira) Gershwin was born in New York City, the son of Russian-Jewish immigrant parents and older brother of Pulitzer Prize-winner George Gershwin. He was educated at City College of the City University of New York. The Gershwin brothers collaborated on many of the best-loved musicals in American theatre and film, Ira writing the lyrics (at first under the pseudonym Arthur Francis) and George composing the music. Among their works were the musicals *An American in Paris* and *Porgy and Bess,*

and the popular songs *Embraceable You, A Foggy Day,* and *S'Wonderful.* Ira continued writing lyrics after his brother's death, finishing some of his brother's compositions and also collaborating with other composers like Moss Hart and Kurt Weill. He and Howard Arlen produced *A Star Is Born.* He was busy rewriting the lyrics to his brother's *My One and Only* before he passed away in 1983.

George S. Kaufman   179

Birth: November 16, 1889; Pittsburgh, PA. **Death:** 1961. **Parents:** Joseph S. and Nettie Schaumberg (Myers) Kaufman. **Education:** Columbia University, NY. **Spouse:** Beatrice Bakrow (m. 1917; died 1945); Leueen MacGrath (m. 1949; div. 1957). **Children:** Anne Scheider (BB).

Prize: *Drama,* 1932: *Of Thee I Sing,* New York: Knopf, 1932. *Drama,* 1937: *You Can't Take It with You,* New York: Farrar & Rinehart, 1937.

Career: Journalist, playwright, actor and director; Stenographer, coal company; Chain man, Transit man, and Surveyor, City of Pittsburgh, PA; Traveling shoelace and hatband salesman, Columbia Ribbon Company; Window Clerk, Tax Office, Allegheny County, PA; Humor Columnist, "This and That and a Little of the Other," *Washington Times,* 1912-1913; Humor Columnist, "Be That as It May," *New York Evening Mail,* New York City, 1914-1915; Theatre Reporter, *New York Tribune,* New York City, 1915-1917; Theatre Reporter, Critic, and Editor of Drama Page, *New York Times,* New York City, 1917-1930; Playwright, 1918-1961; Member, Lambs and Players Clubs.

Selected Works: *Dulcy* (with Marcus C. Connelly), 1921. *Beggar on Horseback* (with Marcus C. Connelly), 1924. *The Cocoanuts: A Musical Comedy in Two Acts* (with Irving Berlin), 1925. *The Butter and*

Egg Man, 1926. *The Royal Family* (with Edna Ferber), 1928. *Animal Crackers* (with Morrie Ryskind), 1930. *June Moon* (with Ring Lardner), 1930. *Once in a Lifetime* (with Moss Hart), 1930. *Dinner at Eight* (with Edna Ferber), 1932. *Let 'Em Eat Cake* (with Morrie Ryskind and Ira Gershwin), 1933. *The Dark Tower* (with Alexander Woollcott), 1934. *Merrily We Roll Along* (with Moss Hart), 1934. *Bring on the Girls: An American Farce* (with Morrie Ryskind), 1934. *First Lady* (with Katherine Dayton), 1935. *A Night at the Opera* (with Morrie Ryskind), 1935. *Stage Door* (with Edna Ferber), 1936. *I'd Rather Be Right* (with Moss Hart), 1937. *The Fabulous Invalid* (with Moss Hart), 1938. *The Man Who Came to Dinner* (with Moss Hart), 1939. *The American Way* (with Moss Hart), 1939. *George Washington Slept Here* (with Edna Ferber), 1940. *The Land Is Bright* (with Howard Teichmann), 1941. *The Solid Gold Cadillac* (with Leueen MacGrath), 1954. *Amicable Parting* (with Edna Ferber), 1957. *Dinner at Eight: A Play in Three Acts,* 1959. *By George: A Kaufman Collection* (with Moss Hart), 1979. *Three Plays,* 1980. **Films:** *You Can't Take It with You,* Columbia, 1938.

Other Awards: Megrue Prize for Comedy, 1931: *Once in a Lifetime.* New York: Farrar & Rinehart, 1930. Elected to Theatre Hall of Fame, 1972.

For More Information: Teichmann, Howard, *George S. Kaufman, An Intimate Portrait,* New York: Atheneum, 1972; Meredith, Scott, *George S. Kaufman and His Friends,* Garden City, NY: Doubleday, 1974; Goldstein, Malcolm, *George S. Kaufman: His Life, His Theater,* New York: Oxford University, 1979; Pollack, Rhoda-Gale, *George S. Kaufman,* Boston: Twayne, 1988.

Commentary: George Simon Kaufman won two Pulitzer Prizes, both in Drama. He won his first prize, together with Morrie Ryskind and Ira Gershwin, in 1932 for *Of Thee I Sing,* a political satire-set-to-music of a presidential campaign. It premiered on December 26, 1931 at New York's Music Box Theater. He won his second prize, along with Moss Hart, in 1939 for *You Can't Take It With You,* a romantic comedy of two families, the eccentric Vanderhofs and the stodgy Kirbys, which premiered on December 14, 1936, at New York's Booth Theater.

Kaufman was born in Pittsburgh, Pennsylvania. He began his career as a journalist and was writing drama reviews for the *New York Times* when he began a collaboration with Marc Connelly. Together they wrote *Dulcy* and *Beggar on Horseback,* two Broadway hits. Kaufman's collaboration with Moss Hart also produced *The Man Who Came to Dinner.* He also collaborated with Pulitzer Prize winner Edna Ferber on *Dinner at Eight* and directed plays such as *The Front Page, My Sister Eileen,* and *Of Mice and Men.*

Morrie Ryskind 180

Birth: October 20, 1895; New York, NY. **Death:** 1985. **Parents:** Abraham and Ida (Etelson) Ryskind. **Education:** Columbia University, NY: BLitt. **Spouse:** Mary House (m. 1929). **Children:** One son, one daughter.

Prize: *Drama,* 1932: *Of Thee I Sing,* New York: Knopf, 1932.

Career: Playwright, columnist.

Selected Works: *Unaccustomed As I Am,* 1921. *Animal Crackers* (with George S. Kaufman), 1928. *Let 'Em Eat Cake* (with George S. Kaufman), 1933. *Bring on the Girls: An American Farce* (with George S. Kaufman), 1934. *A Night at the Opera* (with George S. Kaufman), 1935. *I Shot an Elephant in My Pajamas,* 1994. **Films:** *A Night at the Opera,* MGM, 1935.

For More Information: Meredith, Scott, *George S. Kaufman and His Friends,* Garden City, NY: Doubleday, 1974.

Commentary: Morrie Ryskind, together with George S. Kaufman and Ira Gershwin, won the 1932 Pulitzer Prize in Drama for *Of Thee I Sing,* a political satire-set-to-music of a presidential campaign. It premiered on December 26, 1931 at New York's Music Box Theater.

1933

Maxwell Anderson 181

Birth: December 15, 1888; Atlantic, PA. **Death:** February 28, 1959. **Parents:** William Lincoln Anderson and Premerly (Stevenson) Anderson. **Education:** University of North Dakota: BA. Stanford University, CA: MA. **Spouse:** Margaret Haskett (m. 1911; died

1931); Gerthrude Maynard (m. 1933). **Children:** One daughter (GM).

Prize: *Drama,* 1933: *Both Your Houses,* New York: French, 1933.

Career: Playwright, high school English teacher and school principal, Minnewauken, ND, 1911-13; High school English teacher, San Francisco, CA, 1914-17; Head of English Department, Whittier College, Whittier, CA, 1917-18; Staff member, several San Francisco newspapers, 1918; Staff member, *New Republic,* New York City, 1918-1919; Staff member, *Globe and Commercial Advertiser,* New York City, 1919-1921; Staff member, *New York World,* New York City, 1921-1924; Founder and Editor, *Measure,* 1921-1926; Member, American Academy of Arts and Letters.

Selected Works: *You Who Have Dreams,* 1925. *Saturday's Children,* 1927. *Outside Looking In* (Adaptation), 1928. *Elizabeth the Queen,* 1932. *Night over Taos,* 1932. *Valley Forge,* 1934. *Mary of Scotland,* 1934. *Winterset,* 1935. *The Wingless Victory,* 1936. *The Star-Wagon,* 1937. *The Masque of Kings,* 1937. *High Tor,* 1937. *Key Largo,* 1939. *Journey to Jerusalem,* 1940. *Candle in the Wind,* 1941. *The Eve of St. Mark,* 1942. *Storm Operation,* 1944. *Joan of Lorraine,* 1946. *Winterset,* 1946. *Anne of the Thousand Days,* 1948. *Lost in the Stars* (Adaptation), 1950. *Barefoot in Athens,* 1951. *Bad Seed,* 1955. *Julius Caesar,* 1958. **Films:** *Key Largo,* Warner Bros., 1948.

Other Awards: Drama Critics' Circle Award, 1936: *Winterset.* Drama Critics' Circle Award, 1937: *High Tor.* Brotherhood Award, National Conference of Christians and Jews, 1950: *Lost in the Stars.* Gold Medal for Drama, American Academy and National Institute of Arts and Letters, 1954. Honorary LittDs: Columbia University, NY, 1946; University of North Dakota, 1958.

For More Information: Avery, Laurence G., ed., *Dramatist in America: Letters of Maxwell Anderson, 1912-1958,* Chapel Hill, NC: University of North Carolina Press, 1977; Shivers, Alfred S., *The Life of Maxwell Anderson,* New York: Stein and Day, 1983; Adam, Julie, *Versions of Heroism in Modern American Drama: Redefinitions by Miller, O'Neill, and Anderson,* New York: St. Martin's Press, 1991.

Commentary: Maxwell Anderson was awarded the 1933 Pulitzer Prize in Drama for *Both Your Houses,* a story of political corruption in Congress and one congressman's unsuccessful attempt to fight it. It premiered on March 6, 1933, at New York's Royale Theater.

Anderson was born in Atlantic, Pennsylvania and attended the University of North Dakota and Stanford University. He was a high school English teacher before becoming a journalist. His first play, *White Desert,* was produced while he was writing for the *New York World.* He popularized the use of poetry in contemporary drama. He was a prolific writer who produced a new play almost every season for over 30 years. He is most noted for *Winterset, Key Largo,* and the musical *Lost in the Stars,* a collaboration with Kurt Weill.

1934

Sidney Kingsley   182

Birth: October 18, 1906; New York, NY. **Death:** March 20, 1995. **Parents:** Robert and Sonia (Smolcuff) Kirchner. **Education:** Cornell University, NY: BA. **Spouse:** Madge Evans (m. 1939).

Prize: *Drama,* 1934: *Men in White,* New York: Covici Friede, 1933.

Career: Actor, director, producer, and playwright; Lieutenant, U.S. Army, 1939-1943.

Selected Works: *Dead End,* 1936. *The Patriots,* 1943. *Detective Story,* 1949. *Darkness at Noon* (Adaptation), 1951. *Night Life,* 1966. *Sidney Kingsley: Five Prizewinning Plays* (Couch, Nina ed.), 1995. **Films:** *Men in White,* MGM, 1934.

Other Awards: Theatre Club Award, Best Play, 1934: *Men in White,* New York: Covici Friede, 1933. Theatre Club Award, Best Play, 1936: *Dead End,* New York: Random House, 1936. New York Drama Critics Circle Award, Best Play, 1943: *The Patriots,* New York: Random House, 1943. Newspaper Guild Page One Award, 1943: *The Patriots.* Theatre Club Award, Best Play, 1943: *The Patriots.* Edgar Allan Poe Award, 1949: *Detective Story,* New York: Random House, 1949. New York Drama Critics Circle Award, 1951: *Darkness at Noon,* New York: Random House, 1951. Donaldson Award for Outstanding Achievement in Theatre, 1951: *Darkness at Noon.* Medal of Merit for Outstanding Drama, American Academy of Arts and Letters, 1951.

For More Information: *Legends in Their Own Time,* New York: Prentice Hall, 1994.

Commentary: Sidney Kingsley won the 1931 Pulitzer Prize in Drama for *Men In White,* a story highlighting the conflict of love and duty for a surgeon and touching on the issue of abortion. Originally titled *Crisis,* it premiered under its new name on September 26, 1933 at New York's Broadhurst Theater.

Kingsley was born Sidney Kirchner in New York City. He was educated at Cornell University. He tried acting before writing. His plays typically explored social issues, which were plentiful during the Depression. His most noted works were *Dead End* and *Detective Story.*

1935

Zoe Akins 183

Birth: October 30, 1886; Humansville, MO. **Death:** 1958. **Parents:** Thomas J. and Elizabeth (Green) Akins. **Spouse:** Hugo Cecil Levinge Rumbold (m. 1932; dec).

Prize: *Drama,* 1935: *The Old Maid,* New York: Appleton-Century, 1935.

Career: Playwright.

Selected Works: *Interpretations: A Book of First Poems,* 1912. *Papa: An Amorality in Three Acts,* 1913. *Cake upon the Waters,* 1919. *Declasse; Daddy's Gone-A-Hunting; and Greatness—A Comedy,* 1923. *The Little Miracle,* 1936. *The Hills Grow Smaller: Poems by Zoe Akins,* 1937. *In the Shadow of Parnassus: Zoe Akins's Essays on American Poetry* (Parke, Catherine N., ed.), 1994. **Films:** *The Old Maid,* Warner Bros., 1939.

For More Information: Narda, Schwartz L., *Articles on Women Writers, Volume 2,* Santa Barbara, CA: ABC-Clio, 1986.

Commentary: *The Old Maid,* an adaptation of the Edith Wharton novel by the same title, won the 1935 Pulitzer Prize in Drama for Zoe Akins. The "old maid" is actually the mother of the illegitimate Tina, who is raised by an aunt, not knowing her true parentage. It premiered on January 7, 1935 at New York's Empire Theater.

Akins was born in Missouri. She began her career as a journalist. She wrote plays for the Washington Square Players, and in 1919, *Declasse* was greeted with critical acclaim. Her other works included *Daddy's Gone-A-Hunting,* an adaptation of Edna Ferber's *Showboat,* and the novel *Forever Young.*

1936

Robert E. Sherwood

Full entry appears as **#43** under "Biography or Autobiography," 1949.

1937

Moss Hart 184

Birth: October 24, 1904; New York, NY. **Death:** December 20, 1961. **Parents:** Barnett and Lillian (Solomon) Hart. **Education:** Columbia University, NY. **Spouse:** Kitty Carlisle (m. 1946). **Children:** Christopher, Cathy Carlisle.

Prize: *Drama,* 1937: *You Can't Take It with You,* New York: Farrar & Rinehart, 1937.

Career: Playwright, librettist, and director; Staff member, A. L. Newberger Furs, Incorporated, New York City, 1918-1921; Travelling Secretary, Augustus Pitou, Jr., Theatrical Manager, 1921-1923; Social Director and Entertainer, Catskill Mountains, summers, 1923-1929; Director of Little Theatre in New York and New Jersey, winters, 1923-1929; Actor, *The Emperor Jones,* Mayfair Theatre, New York City, 1926; Director of stage productions, 1931-1961.

Selected Works: *Once in a Lifetime* (with George Kaufman), 1930. *Merrily We Roll Along* (with George Kaufman), 1934. *I'd Rather Be Right* (with George Kaufman), 1937. *The Fabulous Invalid* (with George Kaufman), 1938. *The Man Who Came to Dinner* (with George Kaufman), 1939. *The American Way* (with George Kaufman), 1939. *George Washington Slept Here* (with George Kaufman), 1940. *Lady in the Dark,* 1941. *Six Plays* (with George Kaufman), 1942. *Winged Victory: The Army Air Forces Play,* 1943. *Christopher Blake,* 1947. *Light up the Sky,* 1949. *Hans Christian Andersen* (Screenplay), 1952. *The Climate of Eden,* 1953. **Films:** *You Can't Take It With You,* Columbia, 1938.

Other Awards: Roi Cooper McGrue Prize, 1930: *Once in a Life Time.* New York: Farrar & Rinehart, 1930. New York Drama Critics Award, Best Director,

1955. Antoinette F. Perry Award, Best Director, 1956: *My Fair Lady.* Elected, Theatre Hall of Fame, 1972.

For More Information: *Kitty: An Autobiography,* New York: Doubleday, 1988.

Commentary: Moss Hart and George S. Kaufman won the 1937 Pulitzer Prize in Drama for *You Can't Take It With You,* a romantic comedy of two families, the eccentric Vanderhofs and the stodgy Kirbys. It premiered on December 14, 1936 at New York's Booth Theater.

Hart was born in New York City. He was 21 when he began his career in theatre with the drama, *The Hold-Up Man.* His collaboration with George S. Kaufman produced such successful plays as *Merrily We Roll Along, The Man Who Came to Dinner,* and *George Washington Slept Here.* His other works include *Light Up the Sky* and his autobiography, *Act One.* He won a Tony award for direction in 1957 for the musical *My Fair Lady.*

George S. Kaufman

Full entry appears as **#179** under "Drama," 1932.

1938

Thornton Wilder   185

Birth: April 17, 1897; Madison, WI. **Death:** December 7, 1975. **Parents:** Amos Parker and Isabella Thornton (Niven) Wilder. **Religion:** Congregationalist. **Education:** Oberlin College, OH. Yale University, CT.

Prize: *Novel,* 1928: *The Bridge of San Luis Rey,* New York: Boni, 1928. *Drama,* 1938: *Our Town,* New York: Coward McCann, 1938. *Drama,* 1943: *The Skin of Our Teeth,* New York: Harper, 1942.

Career: Teacher, Lawrenceville School, Princeton, NJ; Teacher and Assistant Master, Davis House, 1921-1925; Tutor and writer, 1925-1927; Master, Davis House, 1927-1928; Writer and Lecturer, 1928-1929; Lecturer, Comparative Literature, University of Chicago, 1930-1936; Writer, 1930-1936; Visiting Professor, University of Hawaii, 1935; American Delegate, Institut de Cooperation Intellectuelle, Paris, France, 1937; Goodwill Representative to Latin America, U.S. Department of State, 1941; Delegate, International PEN Club Congress, 1941; Charles Eliot Norton Professor of Poetry, Harvard University, MA, 1950-1951; Chief, U.S. Delegation, UNESCO Conference of Arts, Venice, Italy, 1952.

Selected Works: *The Cabala,* 1926. *The Angel That Troubled the Waters: And Other Plays* (Play), 1928. *The Woman of Andros,* 1930. *The Long Christmas Dinner, & Other Plays in One Act* (Play), 1931. *Queens of France: A Satiric Comedy in One Act* (Play), 1931. *Heaven's My Destination,* 1935. *The Geographical History of America; or, The Relation of*

Human Nature to the Human Mind (Play), 1936. *The Merchant of Yonkers: A Farce in Four Acts* (Play), 1939. *The Skin of Our Teeth: Play in Three Acts* (Play), 1942. *The Ides of March,* 1948. *The Eighth Day,* 1967. *Theophilus North,* 1973. *The Alcestiad: or, A Life in the Sun: A Play in Three Acts, with a Satyr Play, The Drunken Sisters* (Play), 1977. **Films:** *Our Town,* United Artists, 1940; *The Bridge of San Luis Rey,* United Artists, 1944; *The Matchmaker,* Paramount, 1958; *The Skin of Our Teeth,* Granada (TV, GB), 1959; *Hello Dolly,* Fox, 1969; *Theophilus North* (based on *Mr. North*), Goldwyn, 1988.

Other Awards: Chevalier, Legion of Honor, France, 1951. Gold Medal for Fiction, American Academy of Arts and Letters, 1952. Brandeis University Creative Arts Award, 1959-60. Presidential Medal of Freedom, 1963. National Medal for Literature, National Book Committee, 1965. National Book Award, 1968: *The Eighth Day,* New York: Harper & Row, 1967. Honorary Degrees: College of Worchester, MA; Harvard University, MA; Kenyon College, OH; New York University; Northeastern University, MA; Oberlin College, OH; University of New Hampshire; University of Zurich, Switzerland; Yale University, CT.

For More Information: Simon, Linda, *Thornton Wilder, His World,* Garden City, NY: Doubleday, 1979; Harrison, Gilbert A., *The Enthusiast: A Life of Thornton Wilder,* New Haven, CT: Ticknor & Fields, 1983; Castronovo, David, *Thornton Wilder,* New York: Ungar, 1986; Walsh, Claudette, *Thornton Wilder: A Reference Guide, 1926-1990,* New York: Hall, 1993.

Commentary: Wilder's first Pulitzer Prize was won for the novel *The Bridge of San Luis Rey.* Set in 18th-century Peru, it concerns the deaths of five individuals and a subsequent theological inquiry into the deeper meaning, when a bridge expected to last an eternity disintegrates. Wilder won his second Pulitzer Prize in 1938 for the play *Our Town,* a drama about a typical American town. His third Pulitzer Prize was won for the play *The Skin of Our Teeth,* in 1943.

A successful novelist and playwright, Wilder once said he would like to be the poet laureate of Coney Island. He excelled at presenting the comic side of human drama. He was awarded the first National Medal for Literature in 1965.

1939

Robert E. Sherwood

Full entry appears as **#43** under "Biography or Autobiography," 1949.

1940

William Saroyan   186

Birth: August 31, 1908; Fresno, CA. **Death:** May 18, 1981. **Spouse:** Carol Marcus (m. 1943; div. 1949; rem. 1951; div. 1952). **Children:** Aram, Lucy.

Prize: *Drama,* 1940: *The Time of Your Life,* New York: Harcourt, Brace, 1939.

Career: Short story writer, playwright, novelist; Newspaper boy, *Fresno Evening Herald;* Telegraph messenger boy; Clerk in uncle's law office; Grocery clerk; Vineyard worker; Postal employee; Office Manager, San Francisco Postal Telegraph Company; Co-Founder, Conference Press, 1936; Founder and Director, The Saroyan Theatre, August, 1942; Served in U.S. Army, 1942-1945; Writer-in-Residence, Purdue University, IN, 1961.

Selected Works: *The Daring Young Man on the Flying Trapeze and Other Stories,* 1934. *Inhale & Exhale,* 1936. *Little Children,* 1937. *Love, Here Is My Hat,* 1938. *The Trouble with Tigers,* 1938. *My Heart's in the Highlands,* 1939. *Peace, It's Wonderful,* 1939. *My Name Is Aram,* 1940. *Love's Old Sweet Song,* 1941. *Three Plays by William Saroyan: The Beautiful People, Sweeney in the Trees, and Across the Board on Tomorrow Morning,* 1941. *Razzle Dazzle,* 1942. *The Human Comedy,* 1943. *Dear Baby,* 1944. *Get Away, Old Man: A Play in Two Acts,* 1944. *The Adventures of Wesley Jackson,* 1946. *Jim Dandy, Fat Man in a Famine: A Play,* 1947. *The Saroyan Special: Selected Short Stories,* 1948. *The Assyrian, and Other Stories,* 1950. *Rock Wagram: A Novel,* 1951. *Tracy's Tiger,* 1951. *The Bicycle Rider in Beverly Hills,* 1952. *The Laughing Matter: A Novel,* 1953. *Mama, I Love You,* 1956. *Opera, Opera: One-Act Opera Goofo,* 1956. *The Whole Voyald, and Other Stories,* 1956. *Papa, You're Crazy,* 1957. *The Cave Dwellers: A Play,* 1958. *The William Saroyan Reader,* 1958. *Once around the Block: A Play in One Act,* 1959. *Here Comes, There Goes, You Know Who,* 1961. *Sam, the Highest Jumper of Them All; or, The London Comedy,* 1961. *Not Dying,* 1963. *Boys and Girls Together,* 1963. *Me,* 1963. *One Day in the Afternoon of the World,* 1964. *Short Drive, Sweet Chariot,* 1966. *I Used to Believe I Had Forever, Now I'm Not So Sure,* 1968. *Letters from 74 rue Taitbout; or, Don't Go, but If You Must, Say Hello to Everybody,* 1969. *Days of Life and Death and Escape to the Moon,* 1970. *Places Where I've Done Time,* 1972. *Sons Come and Go, Mothers Hang in Forever,* 1976. *Chance Meetings,* 1978. *Obituaries,* 1979. *My Name Is Saroyan,* 1983. *An Armenian Trilogy,* 1986. *Madness in the Family,* 1988. *The Man with the Heart in the Highlands & Other Early Stories,* 1989. **Films:** *The Time of Your Life,* United Artists, 1948.

Other Awards: O. Henry Award, 1934: *The Daring Young Man on the Flying Trapeze,* New York: Random House, 1934. Drama Critics Circle Award, 1940: *The Time of Your Life,* New York: Harcourt, Brace, 1939. Academy Award, 1943: *The Human Comedy,* New York: Harcourt, Brace, 1943. California Literature Gold Medal, 1952: *Tracy's Tiger,* Garden City, NY: Doubleday, 1951.

For More Information: Saroyan, Aram, *Last Rites: The Death of William Saroyan,* New York: W. Morrow, 1982; Lee, Lawrence and Barry Gifford, *Saroyan: A Biography,* New York: Harper & Row, 1984; Samuelian, Varaz, *Willie and Varaz: Memories of My Friend William Saroyan,* Fresno, CA: Panorama West, 1985; Hamalian, Leo, *William Saroyan: The Man and the Writer Remembered,* Rutherford, NJ: Fairleigh Dickinson University, 1987; Foster, Edward Halsey, *William Saroyan: A Study of the Short Fiction,* New York: Twayne, 1991; Whitmore, Jon, *William Saroyan: A Research and Production Sourcebook,* Westport, CT: Greenwood, 1994; *Critical Essays on William Saroyan, Critical Essays on American Literature,* New York: G.K. Hall, 1995.

Commentary: William Saroyan was awarded the 1940 Pulitzer Prize in Drama for *The Time of Your Life,* a play about the importance of empathy and compassion for those less fortunate. It premiered on October 25, 1939 at New York's Plymouth Theater. Saroyan refused the Pulitzer on the grounds that artists should not be judged.

Saroyan was born in Fresno, California, the son of Armenian immigrants. His first collection of stories, *The Daring Young Man on the Flying Trapeze,* was published in 1934. His first play was produced in 1939, *My Heart's in the Highlands.* Most of his writings were strongly autobiographical. Saroyan would eventually move to Paris. His other works included *The Human Comedy* and *Here Comes, There Goes You Know Who.*

1941

Robert E. Sherwood

Full entry appears as #**43** under "Biography or Autobiography," 1949.

1942
No award

1943

Thornton Wilder

Full entry appears as #**185** under "Drama," 1938.

1944
No award

1945

Mary Coyle Chase   187

Birth: February 25, 1907; Denver, CO. **Death:** 1981. **Parents:** Frank Denard and Mary (McDonough) Coyle. **Education:** Denver University, CO. University of Colorado. **Spouse:** Robert Lamont Chase (m. 1928). **Children:** Michael Lamont, Colin Robert, Barry Jerome.

Prize: *Drama,* 1945: *Harvey,* New York: Oxford University, 1953.

Career: Playwright and children's author; Reporter, *Rocky Mountain News,* Denver, CO, 1928-1931; Freelance Correspondent, International News Service and United Press, 1932-1936; Publicity Director, National Youth Administration, Denver, CO, 1941-1942; Member of Teamsters Union, 1942-1944; Member, Dramatists Guild.

Selected Works: *Mrs. McThing,* 1952. *Bernardine,* 1953. *Midgie Purvis,* 1963. **Films:** *Harvey,* Universal, 1950.

Other Awards: William MacLeod Raine Award, Colorado Authors League, 1944. Honorary LittD, University of Denver, CO, 1947.

For More Information: *Current Biography,* New York: Wilson, 1982.

Commentary: *Harvey,* a comedy about an eccentric drunkard who sees and talks to a six-foot tall rabbit that is invisible to everyone else, won the 1945 Pulitzer Prize in Drama for Mary Coyle Chase. It premiered on November 1, 1944 at New York's 48th Street Theater. It was made into a film starring James Stewart as the drunkard. The story is under the copyright title, *The White Rabbit.*

Chase was born in Denver, Colorado. She wrote several plays, none meeting with much success until *Harvey.*

1946

Russel Crouse   188
Birth: February 20, 1893; Findlay, OH. **Death:** April 3, 1966. **Parents:** Hiram Powers and Sarah (Schumacher) Crouse. **Spouse:** Alison Smith (m. 1923). **Children:** Lindsay.

Prize: *Drama,* 1946: *State of the Union: A Comedy,* New York: Random House, 1946.

Career: Playwright and producer.

Selected Works: *It Seems Like Yesterday,* 1931. *The American Keepsake,* 1932. *Murder Won't Out,* 1932. *Clarence Day's Life with Father* (Adaptation) (with Howard Lindsay), 1940. *Strip for Action* (with Howard Lindsay), 1943. *Clarence Day's Life with Mother* (Adaptation) (with Howard Lindsay), 1949. *Remains to Be Seen* (with Howard Lindsay), 1951. *Call Me Madam* (with Howard Lindsay), 1952. *Peter Stuyvesant of Old New York* (with Ana E. Crouse), 1954. *The Prescott Proposals* (with Howard Lindsay), 1954. *The Great Sebastians* (with Howard Lindsay), 1956. *Tall Story* (with Howard Lindsay), 1959. **Films:** *State of the Union,* MGM, 1948.

For More Information: Skinner, Cornelia Otis, *Life with Lindsay & Crouse,* Boston: Houghton Mifflin, 1976.

Commentary: Russel Crouse and Howard Lindsay were awarded the 1946 Pulitzer Prize in Drama for *State of the Union,* a satire on American politics which changed daily to reflect current events. It premiered on November 14, 1945 at New York's Hudson Theater.

Crouse was born in Findlay, Ohio. He was a journalist for 20 years before writing for the theatre. He formed a successful partnership with Howard Lindsay and the works they produced together included *Life With Father* and *Life With Mother* based on the Clarence Day books of the same titles. Crouse wrote the book upon which *The Sound of Music* is based. He and Lindsay wrote the libretto for the musical. They are also remembered for the production of *Arsenic and Old Lace.*

Howard Lindsay   189

Birth: March 29, 1889; Saratoga, NY. **Death:** February 11, 1968. **Education:** Harvard University, MA. **Spouse:** Dorothy Stickney (m. 1927).

Prize: *Drama,* 1946: *State of the Union: A Comedy,* New York: Random House, 1946.

Career: Actor, director, and playwright.

Selected Works: *A Slight Case of Murder* (with Damon Runyon), 1935. *Clarence Day's Life with Father (Adaptation)* (with Russel Crouse), 1940. *Strip for Action* (with Russel Crouse), 1943. *Clarence Day's Life with Mother (Adapation)* (with Russel Crouse), 1949. *Call Me Madam* (with Russel Crouse), 1950. *Remains To Be Seen* (with Russel Crouse), 1951. *The Prescott Proposals* (with Russel Crouse), 1954. *The Great Sebastians: A Melodramatic Comedy* (with Russel Crouse), 1956. *Tall Story: A Comedy in Three Acts* (with Russel Crouse), 1959. **Films:** *State of the Union,* MGM, 1948.

For More Information: Skinner, Cornelia Otis *Life with Lindsay & Crouse,* Boston: Houghton Mifflin, 1976.

Commentary: Howard Lindsay and Russel Crouse were awarded the 1946 Pulitzer Prize in Drama for *State of the Union,* a satire on American politics which changed daily to reflect current events. It premiered on November 14, 1945 at New York's Hudson Theater.

Lindsay was born in Waterford, New York. He was an actor, director, and playwright before teaming up with Russel Crouse. Their successful partnership produced such favorites as *Life With Father* and *Life With Mother,* based on the Clarence Day books of the same titles. He and Crouse wrote the libretto for the musical *The Sound of Music.* They are also remembered for the production of *Arsenic and Old Lace.*

1947
No award

1948

Tennessee Williams   190

Birth: March 26, 1911; Columbus, MS. **Death:** February 25, 1983. **Parents:** Cornelius Coffin and Edwina (Dakin) Williams. **Religion:** Roman Catholic. **Education:** University of Missouri. Washington University, MO. University of Iowa: AB.

Prize: *Drama,* 1948: *A Streetcar Named Desire,* New York: New Directions, 1947. *Drama,* 1955: *Cat on a Hot Tin Roof,* New York: New Directions, 1955.

Career: Playwright, novelist, short story writer, and poet; Essayist, first published and awarded Third Prize, Essay Contest sponsored by *Smart Set* magazine, 1927; Author, first story published in *Weird Tales,* August, 1928; Clerical worker and manual laborer, International Shoe Company, St. Louis, MO, 1934-36; Author, first published under name Tennessee Williams in *Story,* summer, 1939; Waiter and hotel elevator operator, New Orleans, LA, 1939; Teletype operator, Jacksonville, FL, 1940; Waiter and theatre usher, NY, 1942; Screenwriter for Metro-Goldwyn-Mayer, 1943; Full-time writer, 1944-83; President, American Automatic Control Council, 1965-67; Member: Alpha Tau Omega, American Society of Composers, Authors, and Publishers (AS-CAP), Dramatists Guild, National Institute of Arts and Letters.

Selected Works: *The Glass Menagerie,* 1945. *27 Wagons Full of Cotton and Other One-Act Plays,* 1945. *You Touched Me!* (with Donald Windham), 1947. *Summer and Smoke,* 1948. *The Roman Spring of Mrs. Stone,* 1950. *The Rose Tattoo,* 1951. *Camino Real,* 1953. *Hard Candy,* 1954. *In the Winter of Cities,* 1956. *The Dark at the Top of the Stairs,* 1958. *Orpheus Descending, with Battle of Angels,* 1958. *Suddenly Last Summer,* 1958. *Garden District: Two Plays; Something Unspoken and Suddenly Last Summer,* 1959. *Sweet Bird of Youth,* 1959. *Period of Adjustment: High Point over a Cavern, a Serious Comedy,* 1960. *The Night of the Iguana,* 1961. *The Milk Train Doesn't Stop Here Anymore,* 1964. *The Knightly Quest: A Novella and Four Short Stories,* 1966. *One Arm,* 1967. *Kingdom of Earth: The Seven Descents of Myrtle,* 1968. *Dragon Country, a Book of Plays,* 1970. *The Theatre of Tennessee Williams,* 1971-1992. *Small Craft Warnings,* 1972. *Moise and the World of Reason,* 1975. *Memoirs,* 1976. *Androgyne, Mon Amour: Poems,* 1977. *Where I Live: Selected Essays* (with Christine R. Day and Bob Woods), 1978. *Vieux Carre,* 1979. *A Lovely Sunday for Creve Coeur,* 1980. *Clothes for a Summer Hotel: A Ghost Play,* 1981. *The*

Remarkable Rooming-House of Mme. Le Monde, 1984. *Collected Stories,* 1985. *The Red Devil Battery Sign,* 1988. *Baby Doll & Tiger Tail: A Screenplay and Play, 1991,* 1991. *Something Cloudy, Something Clear,* 1995. **Films:** *A Streetcar Named Desire,* Warner Bros., 1951; *Cat on a Hot Tin Roof,* MGM, 1958.

Other Awards: Rockefeller Foundation Fellowship, 1940. American Academy and National Institute of Arts and Letters Grant, 1943. New York Drama Critics Circle Award, 1945: *The Glass Menagerie,* New York: Random House, 1945. Donaldson Award, 1945: *The Glass Menagerie,* Sidney Howard Memorial Award, 1945: *The Glass Menagerie.* New York Drama Critics Circle Award, 1948: *A Streetcar Named Desire,* New York: New Directions, 1947. Donaldson Award, 1948: *A Streetcar Named Desire.* Elected to National Institute of Arts and Letters, 1952: *Cat on a Hot Tin Roof,* New York: New Directions, 1955. New York Drama Critics Circle Award, 1955: *Cat on a Hot Tin Roof.* London Evening Standard Award, 1958: *Cat on a Hot Tin Roof.* New York Drama Critics Circle Award, 1962: *The Night of the Iguana,* New York: New Directions, 1961. First Place, Best New Foreign Play, London Critics' Poll, 1964-1965: *The Night of the Iguana.* Creative Arts Medal, Brandeis University, 1964-1965. National Institute of Arts and Letters Gold Medal, 1969. First Centennial Medal of Cathedral of St. John the Divine, 1973. Elected to Theatre Hall of Fame, 1979. Kennedy Honors Award, 1979. Common Wealth Award for Distinguished Service in Dramatic Arts, 1981.

For More Information: Bloom, Harold, ed., *Tennessee Williams,* New York: Chelsea House, 1987; Boxill, Roger, *Tennessee Williams,* London, England: Macmillan, 1987; Hayman, Ronald, *Tennessee Williams: Everyone Else Is An Audience,* New Haven, CT: Yale University, 1993; Kolin, Philip C., ed., *Confronting Tennessee William's 'A Streetcar Named Desire': Essays in Critical Pluralism,* Westport, CT: Greenwood, 1993; Leverich, Lyle, *Tom: The Unknown Tennessee Williams,* New York: Crown Publishers, 1995; Griffin, Alice, *Understanding Tennessee Williams,* Columbia: University of South Carolina, 1995; Crandell, George W., *The Critical Response to Tennessee Williams,* Westport, CT: Greenwood, 1996.

Commentary: Tennessee Williams won two Pulitzer Prizes in Drama. He won the 1948 Pulitzer for *A Streetcar Named Desire,* a drama set in New Orleans about Blanche DuBois, an aging beauty whose hopes for marriage are shattered by her brother-in-law, Stanley Kowalski. It premiered on December 3, 1947 at New York's Barrymore Theater. Williams won his second prize in 1955 for *Cat on a Hot Tin Roof. Cat,* the story of the Pollitt family's maneuverings for Big Daddy's plantation and money when he is diagnosed

with cancer, premiered on March 24, 1955 at New York's Morosco Theatre.

Thomas Lanier Williams was born in Mississippi, but spent most of his early years in St. Louis. He received a typewriter for his 11th birthday and began his lifelong occupation. He won awards for his writing while attending the University of Missouri, but lost his father's financial support after he failed at ROTC. Williams eventually completed a degree in playwriting at the University of Iowa. His first big success came in 1945 with *The Glass Menagerie.* Williams would publish two collections of poetry and four of short fiction, two novels, and over 60 plays during his career. His other works include *The Night of the Iguana, The Rose Tatoo,* and *Suddenly Last Summer.* He won four New York Drama Critics Circle Awards. Toward the end of his life, critics were less receptive to his work.

1949

Arthur Miller   191

Birth: October 17, 1915; New York, NY. **Parents:** Isadore and Augusta (Barnett) Miller. **Education:** University of Michigan: AB. **Spouse:** Mary Grace Slattery (m. 1940; div. 1952); Marilyn Monroe (m. 1956; div. 1961); Ingeborg Morath (m. 1962). **Children:** Jane Ellen, Robert Arthur (MGS); Rebecca Augusta, Daniel (IM).

Prize: *Drama,* 1949: *Death of a Salesman: Certain Private Conversations in Two Acts and a Requiem,* New York: Viking, 1949.

Career: Writer; Worker, automobile parts warehouse; Worker, Brooklyn Navy Yard; Worker, box factory; Associate, Federal Theater Project, 1938; Writer, 1938-present; Author of radio plays, 1939-

1944; Dramatist and essayist, 1944-present; Resident Lecturer, University of Michigan, 1973-1974; Member: Authors League of America, Dramatists Guild, National Institute of Arts and Letters.

Selected Works: *Situation Normal,* 1944. *Focus,* 1945. *All My Sons,* 1947. *The Crucible,* 1953. *A View from the Bridge,* 1955. *A Memory of Two Mondays,* 1956. *The Misfits,* 1961. *After the Fall,* 1964. *Incident at Vichy,* 1965. *I Don't Need You Anymore,* 1967. *The Price,* 1968. *In Russia* (with Inge Morath), 1969. *The Creation of the World and Other Business,* 1973. *Chinese Encounters* (with Inge Morath), 1979. *Elegy for a Lady,* 1982. *The American Clock,* 1982. *Salesman in Beijing,* 1984. *Arthur Miller's Playing for Time* (Adaptation), 1985. *Timebends: A Life,* 1987. *The Archbishop's Ceiling: The American Clock; Two Plays,* 1989. *Everybody Wins: A Screenplay,* 1990. *Homely Girl, a Life* (with Louise Bourgeois), 1992. *The Ride down Mt. Morgan,* 1992. **Films:** *Death of a Salesman,* Columbia, 1951.

Other Awards: Avery Hopwood Award, University of Michigan, 1936: *Honors at Dawn.* Avery Hopwood Award, University of Michigan, 1937: *No Villain: They Too Arise.* Bureau of New Plays Prize, Theatre Guild of New York, 1938. Theatre Guild National Prize, 1944: *The Man Who Had All the Luck.* Antoinette Perry Award, 1947: *All My Sons,* New York: Reynal & Hitchcock, 1947. Donaldson Award, 1947: *All My Sons.* Drama Critics Circle Award, 1947: *All My Sons.* Antoinette Perry Award, 1949: *Death of a Salesman,* New York: Viking, 1949. Donaldson Award, 1949: *Death of a Salesman.* Drama Critics Circle Award, 1949: *Death of a Salesman.* Antoinette Perry Award, 1953: *The Crucible,* New York: Viking, 1953. Donaldson Award, 1953: *The Crucible.* National Association of Independent Schools Award, 1954. Obie Award from Village Voice, 1958: *The Crucible.* American Academy of Arts and Letters Gold Medal, 1959. Anglo-American Award, 1966. Emmy Award, National Academy of Television Arts and Sciences, 1967: *Death of a Salesman.* Brandeis University Creative Arts Award, 1969. George Foster Peabody Award, 1981: *Playing for Time.* John F. Kennedy Award for Lifetime Achievement, 1984. National Medal of the Arts, 1993. Olivier Award, London, 1995: *Broken Glass.* Honorary LHDs: University of Michigan, 1956; Carnegie-Mellon University, PA, 1970.

For More Information: Evans, Richard I., *Psychology and Arthur Miller,* New York: Dutton, 1969; Carson, Neil, *Arthur Miller,* New York: St. Martin's, 1982; Bloom, Harold, ed., *Willy Loman,* New York: Chelsea House, 1991; Centola, Steve, *Arthur Miller in Conversation,* Dallas, TX: Northouse & Northouse, 1993; Murphy, Brenda, *Miller: Death of a Salesman,* New York: Cambridge University, 1995; Bigsby,

Christopher, ed., *The Cambridge Companion to Arthur Miller,* New York: Cambridge University, 1997.

Commentary: *Death of a Salesman,* the story of Willy Loman, whose career is ending along with his identity, won the 1949 Pulitzer Prize in Drama for Arthur Miller. It premiered on February 10, 1949 at New York's Morosco Theater.

Miller was born in New York City. He was educated at the University of Michigan, where he won the Avery Hopwood Prize for his first play. His first Broadway production in 1944, *The Man Who Had All the Luck,* was not a critical success. His next outing, *All My Sons,* however, drew unanimous praise and a Drama Critics Circle Award. After winning the Pulitzer Prize, he went on to write *The Crucible, A View From the Bridge,* and *After the Fall.* His *Salesman* has been hailed as the best American drama ever written.

1950

Oscar Hammerstein II   192

Birth: July 12, 1895; New York, NY. **Death:** August 23, 1960. **Parents:** William and Alicia Vivian (Nimmo) Hammerstein. **Education:** Columbia University, NY: AB, Law Degree. **Spouse:** Myra Finn (m. 1917); Dorothy Blanchard (m. 1929). **Children:** William, Alice (MF); James (DB).

Prize: *Drama,* 1950: *South Pacific,* New York: Random House, 1949.

Career: Clerk in law office; Stage manager, 1918-1919; Composer, 1919-1960; Co-Founder and Partner, Williamson Music, Inc., 1945; Producer of own plays; Member of War Music Committee, 1943; Sponsor, American Youth Orchestra.

Selected Works: *Show Boat: Screenplay* (with Edna Ferber), 1935. *The Castles: Screenplay,* 1938. *Oklahoma!* (Adaptation) (with Richard Rodgers), 1943. *Carousel* (Adaptation) (with Richard Rodgers), 1946. *Allegro* (with Richard Rodgers), 1948. *The King and I* (with Richard Rodgers), 1951. *Me and Juliet* (with Richard Rodgers), 1953. *Flower Drum Song* (Adaptation) (with Richard Rodgers), 1959. *The Sound of Music* (with Richard Rodgers, Russel Crouse, and Howard Lindsay), 1960. **Films:** *South Pacific,* 20th Century Fox, 1958.

Other Awards: Academy Award, Academy of Motion Picture Arts and Sciences, 1945: *The Last Time I Saw Paris.* Donaldson Award, 1944: *Oklahoma,* New York: Random House, 1943. Donaldson Award, 1945: *Carousel,* New York: Knopf, 1946. New York Drama Critics Circle Award, 1945: *Carousel.* Academy Award, Academy of Motion Picture Arts and Sciences, 1946: *It Might as Well Be Spring.* Donaldson Award, 1946: *Show Boat,* Universal City, CA: Universal Pictures. Medal of Excellence, Columbia University, 1949. New York Drama Critics Circle

Award, 1949: *South Pacific,* New York: Random House, 1949. Antoinette Perry Award, 1950: *South Pacific.* Antoinette Perry Award, 1952: *The King and I,* New York: Random House, 1951. Antoinette Perry Award, 1960: *The Sound of Music,* New York: Random House, 1960. Grammy Award, 1960: *The Sound of Music.* Alexander Hamilton Award, Columbia College Alumni Association. Honorary LLD, Drury College, MO, 1949. Honorary DHLs: Dartmouth College, NH, 1952; Boston University; Columbia University, MA; University of Massachusetts; Knox College, IL.

For More Information: *Rodgers and Hammerstein Fact Book,* New York: R. Rodgers and O. Hammerstein, II, 1955; Skouras, Thana, ed., *The Tale of Rodgers and Hammerstein's South Pacific,* New York: Lehmann, 1958.

Commentary: Oscar Hammerstein II, Richard Rodgers, and Joshua Logan won the 1950 Pulitzer Prize in Drama for *South Pacific,* a musical adaption of James Michener's Pulitzer Prize-winning novel, *Tales of the South Pacific.* It premiered on April 7, 1949 at New York's Majestic Theater. Hammerstein also won a special award in 1944 with Richard Rodgers for the musical *Oklahoma!*

Hammerstein was born in New York City and educated at Columbia University. After college, he began his career as a librettist. Among his early works were *The Desert Song,* with music by Sigmund Romberg, and *Show Boat,* with music by Jerome Kern including the song "Old Man River." His collaboration with Richard Rodgers began in 1942 with *Oklahoma,* a musical adaptation of the Lynn Riggs play *Green Grow the Lilacs.* A string of musical Broadway hits would follow, including *Carousel, The King and I,* and *The Sound of Music.*

Joshua Logan 193
Birth: October 5, 1908; Texarkana, TX. **Death:** August 23, 1960. **Parents:** Joshua Lockwood and Susan (Nabors) Logan. **Education:** Princeton University, NJ. Moscow Art Theatre, USSR. **Spouse:** Barbara O'Neill (m. 1940; div. 1941); Nedda Harrigan (m. 1945). **Children:** Thomas Heggars, Susan Harrigan (NH).

Prize: *Drama,* 1950: *South Pacific,* New York: Random House, 1949.

Career: Director and producer of numerous plays and films, beginning in 1936; Captain, Combat Intelligence, U.S. Air Force, 1942-1945; Co-Founder, University Players, Falmouth, Massachusetts.

Selected Works: *Mister Roberts* (with Thomas Heggen), 1948. *The Wisteria Trees (Adaptation),* 1950. *Fanny: A Musical Play (Adaptation) (with S. N. Behrman),* (with S. N. Behrman), 1955. *Josh, My Up and Down, In and Out Life,* 1976. *Movie Stars, Real People, and Me,* 1978. **Films:** *South Pacific,* 20th Century Fox, 1958.

Other Awards: Honorary MA, Princeton University, 1953.

For More Information: Skouras, Thana, ed., *The Tale of Rodgers and Hammerstein's South Pacific,* New York: Lehmann, 1958.

Commentary: Joshua Logan, Richard Rodgers, and Oscar Hammerstein II won the 1950 Pulitzer Prize in Drama for *South Pacific,* a musical adaption of James Michener's Pulitzer Prize-winning novel, *Tales of the South Pacific.* It premiered on April 7, 1949 at New York's Majestic Theater.

Joshua Lockwood Logan was born in Texarkana, Texas. He attended Princeton University and then studied acting at the Moscow Art Theatre under Konstantin Stanislavsky. He directed, coauthored, and coproduced *South Pacific.* He began his career as an actor, but turned to writing and directing. His many successful works included *Annie Get Your Gun, Mr. Roberts,* and *Fanny.* The films he directed include *South Pacific* and *Camelot.*

Richard Rodgers 194

Birth: June 28, 1902; New York, NY. **Death:** December 30, 1979. **Parents:** William Abraham and Marie (Levy) Rodgers. **Education:** Columbia University, NY. Institute of Musical Art (now Juilliard School of Music). **Spouse:** Dorothey Feiner (m. 1930). **Children:** Mary, Linda.

Prize: *Special Awards and Citations: Letters,* 1944: *Oklahoma! Drama,* 1950: *South Pacific,* New York: Random House, 1949.

Career: Composer, producer, lyricist; Associated with Music Theatre of Lincoln Center, Barnard College, Actors Fund of America and New York Philharmonic; Former Member, Board of Directors,

Juilliard School of Music; Member: Authors League of America, National Institute of Arts and Letters, National Association of American Composers and Conductors, and Former President, Dramatists Guild.

Selected Works: *Oklahoma!* (with Oscar Hammerstein), 1943. *Carousel* (Adaptation) (with Oscar Hammerstein), 1946. *Allegro* (with Oscar Hammerstein), 1948. *The King and I* (with Oscar Hammerstein), 1951. *Pal Joey* (with Lorenz Hart and John O'Hara), 1952. *Me and Juliet* (with Oscar Hammerstein), 1953. *Flower Drum Song* (Adaptation) (with Oscar Hammerstein), 1959. *The Sound of Music* (with Oscar Hammerstein, Russel Crouse, and Howard Lindsay), 1960. *No Strings* (with Samuel Taylor), 1962. *Two by Two* (Adaptation) (with Martin Charnin and Peter Stone), 1970. *Musical Stages: An Autobiography,* 1975. **Films:** *South Pacific,* 20th Century Fox, 1958.

Other Awards: Donaldson Award, 1945: *Carousel,* New York: Knopf, 1946. University Medal for Excellence, Columbia University, NY, 1949. Donaldson Award, 1949. Antoinette Perry Award, 1950: *South Pacific,* New York: Random House, 1949. Donaldson Award, 1952: *Pal Joey,* New York: Random House, 1952. Antoinette Perry Award, 1952. Christopher Award, 1956: *The King and I,* New York: Random House, 1951. Columbia College Award, 1952. U.S. Navy Distinguished Public Service Award, 1953. Alexander Hamilton Medal, Columbia College Alumni Association, 1956. Emmy Award, National Academy of Television Arts and Sciences, 1962: *The Valiant Years.* Antoinette Perry Award, 1962: *No Strings,* New York: Random House, 1962. Creative Arts Award, Brandeis University, 1968. Honorary Degrees: Drury College, MO, 1949; Columbia University, NY, 1954; University of Massachusetts, 1954; University of Bridgeport, CT, 1962; University of Maryland, 1962; Hamilton College, NY, 1965; Brandeis University, MA, 1965; Fairfield University, CT, 1968; New York University, 1971; New England Conservatory of Music, MA, 1976.

For More Information: *Rodgers and Hammerstein Fact Book,* New York: R. Rodgers and O. Hammerstein, II, 1955; Skouras, Thana, ed., *The Tale of Rodgers and Hammerstein's South Pacific,* New York: Lehmann, 1958; Nolan, Frederick W., *The Sound of Their Music: The Story of Rodgers & Hammerstein,* London, England: Dent, 1978.

Commentary: Richard Rodgers, Oscar Hammerstein II, and Joshua Logan won the 1950 Pulitzer Prize in Drama for *South Pacific,* a musical adaption of James Michener's Pulitzer Prize-winning novel, *Tales of the South Pacific.* It premiered on April 7, 1949 at New York's Majestic Theater. Rodgers also won a special award in 1944, with Oscar Hammerstein II, for the musical *Oklahoma!*

Rodgers was born in New York City. He attended Columbia University, where he met Lorenz Hart, with whom he would collaborate on several musical outings. He continued his studies at what is now the Juilliard School. Among the musicals Rodgers and Hart would produce were *Babes in Arms* and *Pal Joey.* Rodgers's collaboration with Oscar Hammerstein II began in 1942 with *Oklahoma!,* a musical adaptation of the Lynn Riggs play *Green Grow the Lilacs.* A string of musical Broadway hits would follow, including *Carousel, The King and I,* and *The Sound of Music.*

1951
No award

1952

Joseph Kramm   195
Birth: September 30, 1908; Philadelphia, PA. **Parents:** Samuel and Cecelia Kramm. **Education:** University of Kansas: AB. George Peabody College for Teachers: AM. **Spouse:** Anna Marie Loevner (m. 1932; div. 1932); Isabel Bonner (m. 1940; died 1955).

Prize: *Drama,* 1952: *The Shrike,* New York: Random House, 1952.

Career: Actor and playwright.

Films: *The Shrike,* Universal, 1955.

For More Information: *Current Biography,* New York: Wilson, 1952.

Commentary: Joseph Kramm was awarded the 1952 Pulitzer Prize in Drama for *The Shrike,* about a mentally ill man released from an institution into the custody of his possessive wife. It premiered on January 15, 1952 at New York's Cort Theater.

Kramm was born in South Philadelphia, Pennsylvania and educated at the University of Pennsylvania. He began his career working for the Philadelphia Inquirer as a rewrite man and acting for a local repertory company. He secured many roles and managed to build a reputation on Broadway, but his acting career was interrupted by World War II. When the war ended, he ventured into directing and writing. His first play to be produced was *The Shrike.*

1953

William Inge   196

Birth: May 3, 1913; Independence, KS. **Death:** June 10, 1973. **Parents:** Luther Clayton and Maude Sarah (Gibson) Inge. **Education:** University of Kansas: AB. Teachers College, MA. Yale University, CT.

Prize: *Drama,* 1953: *Picnic,* New York: Random House, 1953.

Career: Playwright; High School Teacher, Columbus, KS, 1937-1938; Instructor, Stephens College, Columbia, MO, 1938-1943; Drama, Music, and Film Critic, *St. Louis Star-Times,* St. Louis, MO, 1943-1946; Instructor, Washington University, St. Louis, MO, 1946-1949; Instructor, University of North Carolina, NC, 1969; Instructor, University of California, Irvine, CA, 1970.

Selected Works: *Come Back, Little Sheba,* 1950. *Bus Stop,* 1955. *The Dark at the Top of the Stairs,* 1958. *A Loss of Roses,* 1960. *Summer Brave, and Eleven Short Plays,* 1962. *Natural Affection,* 1963. *Where's Daddy?,* 1966. *Good Luck, Miss Wyckoff,* 1970. *My Son Is a Splendid Driver,* 1971. **Films:** *Picnic,* Columbia, 1955.

Other Awards: George Jean Nathan Award, 1950. Theatre Time Award, 1950: *Come Back, Little Sheba,* New York: Random House, 1950. Donaldson Award, 1953: *Picnic.* New York Drama Critics Circle Award, 1953: *Picnic.* Outer Circle Award, 1953: *Picnic.* Academy Award, Academy of Motion Picture Arts and Sciences, 1961: *Splendor in the Grass.*

For More Information: McClure, Arthur F., *Memories of Splendor: The Midwestern World of William Inge,* Topeka: Kansas State Historical Society, 1989; Shuman, R. Baird, *William Inge,* Boston: Twayne, 1989; Voss, Ralph F., *A Life of William Inge: The Strains of Triumph,* Lawrence, KS: University

Press of Kansas, 1989; Leeson, Richard M., *William Inge: A Research and Production Sourcebook,* Westport, CT: Greenwood, 1994.

Commentary: *Picnic,* set in a small Kansas town among a group of lonely women, won the 1953 Pulitzer Prize in Drama for William Inge. It premiered on February 19, 1953 at New York's Martin Beck Theater.

William Motter Inge was born in Independence, Kansas. He was given encouragement by Tennessee Williams after sending Williams his first play, *Farther off from Heaven.* He was a teacher until the age of 37, when his first Broadway play, *Come Back, Little Sheba,* was produced in 1950. This was the beginning of a string of plays and films which would make Inge a popular writer of the 1950s. His other works include *Bus Stop, Dark at the Top of the Stairs,* and *Splendor in the Grass,* all of which take place in small Midwestern towns.

1954

John Patrick   197

Birth: May 17, 1907; Louisville, KY. **Parents:** John Frances and Myrtle (Osborn) Patrick. **Education:** Holy Cross College, MA. Harvard University, MA. Columbia University, NY.

Prize: *Drama,* 1954: *The Teahouse of the August Moon (Adaptation),* New York: Putnam, 1952.

Career: Playwright and screenwriter; Writer, NBC Radio, San Francisco, CA, 1933-1936; Freelance writer, Hollywood, CA, 1936-1938; Ambulance driver and Captain, American Field Service, 1942-44; Member, Dramatists Guild.

Selected Works: *The Hasty Heart,* 1945. *The Story of Mary Surratt,* 1947. *Everybody Loves Opal,* 1962. *Inapatua,* 1966. *Everybody's Girl,* 1968. *The Dancing Mice,* 1972. *The Enigma,* 1974. *Opal's Baby,* 1974. *It's Been Wonderful: A Play in Three Acts,* 1976. *Suicide—Anyone?,* 1976. *Opal's Million Dollar Duck,* 1980. *The Girls of the Garden Club,* 1980. *It's a Dog's Life: Three One-Act Plays,* 1984. *The Gay Deceiver,* 1988. **Films:** *The Teahouse of the August Moon,* MGM, 1956.

Other Awards: Aegis Club Award, 1954: *The Teahouse of the August Moon,* New York: Putnam, 1952. Antoinette Perry Award, 1954: *The Teahouse of the August Moon.* Donaldson Award, 1954: *The Teahouse of the August Moon.* New York Drama Critics Circle Award, Best American Play, 1954: *The Teahouse of the August Moon.* Foreign Correspondents Award, 1957: *Les Girls.* Screenwriters Guild Award, 1957: *Les Girls.* Patrick Film Festival in his honor, Virgin Islands, 1979. Honorary DFA, Baldwin-Wallace College, 1972.

For More Information: *Dictionary of Literary Biography,* Detroit: Gale, 1981.

Commentary: John Patrick was awarded the 1954 Pulitzer Prize in Drama for *The Teahouse of the August Moon,* an adaptation of a Vern Schneider novel about a teahouse built as a gift to the Okinawans by American soldiers occupying Okinawa Island just after World War II. It premiered on October 15, 1953, at New York's Morosco Theater.

Patrick was born "John Patrick Goggan" in Louisville, Kentucky. He was raised in foster homes and boarding schools. As soon as he was old enough, he moved to the West Coast to start a writing career. He began with radio scripts, later writing plays and film scripts. His other works include *Three Coins in a Fountain, Love Is a Many Splendored Thing,* and *High Society.*

1955

Tennessee Williams

Full entry appears as **#190** under "Drama," 1948.

1956

Frances Goodrich 198

Birth: 1891; Belleville, NJ. **Death:** January 29, 1984. **Parents:** Henry W. and Madeleine Christie (Lloyd) Goodrich. **Education:** Vassar College, NY. **Spouse:** Robert Ames (m. 1917; div. 1923); Henrik Willem van Loon (m. 1927; div. 1929); Albert Hackett (m. 1931).

Prize: *Drama,* 1956: *The Diary of Anne Frank,* New York: Random House, 1956.

Career: Playwright, scenarist.

Selected Works: *It's a Wonderful Life* (Screenplay) (with Albert Hackett), 1946. *Summer Holiday* (Screenplay) (with Albert Hackett), 1948. *Give a Girl a Break* (Screenplay) (with Albert Hackett), 1953. **Films:** *The Diary of Anne Frank,* 20th Century Fox, 1959.

For More Information: Levin, Meyer *The Obsession,* New York: Simon & Schuster, 1973.

Commentary: Albert Hackett and Frances Goodrich won the 1956 Pulitzer Prize in Drama for *The Diary of Anne Frank,* an adaptation of the nonfiction bestselling book about a Jewish girl who hid with her family in a sealed-off flat in Amsterdam, The Netherlands, for over a year before being betrayed and sent to the Belsen concentration camp, where she died. It premiered on October 5, 1955 at New York's Cort Theater.

Goodrich married Albert Hackett and together they authored popular screenplays which included

The Thin Man, It's a Wonderful Life, and *Seven Brides for Seven Brothers.*

Albert Hackett 199

Birth: February 16, 1900; New York, NY. **Death:** March 16, 1995. **Parents:** Maurice and Florence (Spreen) Hackett. **Spouse:** Frances Goodrich (m. 1931).

Prize: *Drama,* 1956: *The Diary of Anne Frank,* New York: Random House, 1956.

Career: Playwright, scenarist.

Selected Works: *It's a Wonderful Life* (Screenplay) (with Frances Goodrich), 1946. *Summer Holiday* (with Frances Goodrich), 1948. *Give a Girl a Break* (Screenplay) (with Frances Goodrich), 1953. **Films:** *The Diary of Anne Frank,* 20th Century Fox, 1959.

For More Information: *Twentieth-Century Authors,* New York: Wilson, 1955.

Commentary: Albert Hackett and Frances Goodrich won the 1956 Pulitzer Prize in Drama for *The Diary of Anne Frank,* an adaptation of the nonfiction bestselling book about a Jewish girl who hid with her family in a sealed-off flat in Amsterdam, The Netherlands for over a year before being betrayed and sent to the Belsen concentration camp, where she died. It premiered on October 5, 1955 at New York's Cort Theater.

Hackett was born in New York City. He married Goodrich and together they authored popular screenplays which included *The Thin Man, It's a Wonderful Life,* and *Seven Brides for Seven Brothers.*

1957

Eugene O'Neill

Full entry appears as **#168** under "Drama," 1920.

1958

Ketti Frings 200

Birth: 1915; Columbus, OH. **Death:** 1981. **Parents:** Guy Herbert and Pauline (Sparks) Hartley. **Education:** Principia College, MO. **Spouse:** Kurt Frings (m. 1938). **Children:** Kathie, Peter.

Prize: *Drama,* 1958: *Look Homeward, Angel,* New York: French, 1958.

Career: Writer, Advertising Copywriter, L. Bamberger & Company, Newark, NJ; Copywriter, advertising agencies, NY; Columnist, script writer, and ghost writer; Feature Writer, United Press International (UPI), 1950; Member: Dramatists Guild, League of New York Theatres, Screen Writers Guild.

Selected Works: *Hold Back the Dawn,* 1940. *God's Front Porch,* 1944.

Other Awards: New York Drama Critics Circle Award, 1958: *Look Homeward, Angel,* New York: French, 1958. Martha Kinney Cooper Ohioana Award. Woman of the Year, *Los Angeles Times,* 1958. Distinguished Achievement Award, Theta Sigma Phi.

For More Information: *Current Biography,* New York: Wilson, 1960.

Commentary: *Look Homeward, Angel,* a dramatization of Thomas Wolfe's novel about a young man coming of age in North Carolina, won the 1958 Pulitzer Prize in Drama for Ketti Frings. It premiered on November 28, 1957 at New York's Ethel Barrymore Theater.

Frings was born "Katherine Hartley" in Columbus, Ohio and she attended Principia College in St. Louis, Missouri. She married a former lightweight boxer, Kurt Frings, in 1938. She is noted for her screen adaptations of the plays *Come Back, Little Sheba* and *The Shrike.* Her other works include *Mr. Sycamore* and *God's Front Porch.*

1959

Archibald MacLeish   201

Birth: May 7, 1892; Glencoe, IL. **Death:** April 20, 1982. **Parents:** Andrew and Martha (Hillard) MacLeish. **Education:** Yale University, CT: AB. Harvard University, MA: LLB. **Spouse:** Ada Hitchcock (m. 1916). **Children:** Kenneth, Brewster Hitchcock, Mary Hillard, William Hitchcock.

Prize: *Poetry,* 1933: *Conquistador,* Boston: Houghton Mifflin, 1932. *Poetry,* 1953: *Collected Poems, 1917-1952,* Boston: Houghton Mifflin, 1952.

Drama, 1959: *J.B.: A Play in Verse,* New York: French, 1958.

Career: Poet, dramatist, lawyer, and statesman; Captain, Field Artillery, U.S. Army, France, 1917-18; U.S. Supreme Court Bar Association member, 1942; Instructor, Constitutional Law, Harvard University, MA, 1919; Staff member, Choate, Hall & Stewart, Boston, MA, 1920-23; Freelance writer, France, 1923-1928; Staff member, *Fortune,* NY, 1929-1938; Chairman, League of American Writers, 1937; First Curator, Niemann Collection of Contemporary Journalism, Harvard University, MA, 1938; Adviser to Niemann Fellows, Harvard University, MA, 1938; Librarian of Congress, U.S. Government, Washington, DC, 1939-1944; Trustee, Museum of Modern Art, NY, beginning in 1940; Director, Office of Facts and Figures, 1941-1942; Assistant Director, Office of War Information, 1942-1943; Assistant Secretary of State, 1944-1945; American Delegate, Conference of Allied Ministers of Education in London, 1944; Chairman, U.S. Delegation to London Conference for draft of UNESCO constitution, 1945; First U.S. Delegate, General Conference of UNESCO, 1946; First U.S. Member, Executive Council of UNESCO; Trustee, Sara Lawrence College, Bronxville, NY, beginning in 1949; Boylston Professor of Rhetoric and Oratory, Harvard University, 1949-1962; President, American Academy of Arts and Letters, 1953-1956; Lecturer in Europe, U.S. Department of State, 1957; Boylston Professor Emeritus, Harvard University, 1962-1982; Simpson Lecturer, Amherst College, 1963-1967; Fellow, Academy of American Poets, 1966; Member: Century Club (New York), National Committee for an Effective Congress Commission on Freedom of the Press, National Institute of Arts and Letters, Phi Beta Kappa, Somerset Club (Boston), Tavern Club.

Selected Works: *Tower of Ivory,* 1917. *The Happy Marriage, and Other Poems,* 1924. *The Pot of Earth,* 1925. *Streets in the Moon,* 1926. *The Hamlet of A. MacLeish,* 1928. *New Found Land: Fourteen Poems,* 1930. *Panic: A Play in Verse,* 1935. *Public Speech, Poems by Archibald MacLeish,* 1936. *The Fall of the City: A Verse Play for Radio,* 1937. *Air Raid: A Verse for Radio,* 1938. *Land of the Free,* 1938. *Law and Politics: Occasional Papers of Felix Frankfurter, 1913-1938* (MacLeish, Archibald and Prichard, E.F., eds.), 1939. *America Was Promises,* 1939. *The Irresponsibles: A Declaration,* 1940. *A Time to Speak: The Selected Prose of Archibald MacLeish,* 1940. *The Next Harvard, as Seen by Archibald MacLeish,* 1941. *The American Cause,* 1941. *A Free Man's Books: An Address,* 1942. *American Opinion and the War,* 1942. *A Time to Act: Selected Addresses,* 1943. *The American Story: Ten Broadcasts by Archibald MacLeish,* 1944. *Actfive, and Other Poems,* 1948. *Freedom is the Right to Choose:*

An Inquiry into the Battle for the American Future, 1951. *This Music Crept by Me upon the Waters,* 1953. *Songs for Eve,* 1954. *Poetry and Experience,* 1960. *Three Short Plays: The Secret of Freedom; Air Raid; The Fall of the City,* 1961. *The Dialogues of Archibald MacLeish and Mark Van Doren* (Bush, Warren E., ed.), 1964. *A Continuing Journey,* 1967. *Herakles: A Play in Verse,* 1967. *The Wild Old Wicked Man, & Other Poems,* 1968. *The Great American Frustration,* 1968. *Scratch (A Play Suggested by Stephen Vincent Bent's Short Story The Devil and Daniel Webster),* 1970. *The Human Season: Selected Poems, 1926-1972,* 1972. *The Great American Fourth of July Parade: A Verse Play for Radio,* 1975. *Riders on the Earth: Essays and Recollections,* 1978. *Six Plays,* 1980. *Letters of Archibald MacLeish, 1907 to 1982* (Winnick, R.H., ed.), 1983. *Archibald MacLeish: Reflections* (Drabeck, Bernard A. and Ellis, Helen E., eds.), 1986.

Other Awards: John Reed Memorial Prize, 1929. Shelley Memorial Award for Poetry, 1932. Golden Rose Trophy of New England Poetry Club, 1934. Levinson Prize, 1941. Commander, Legion of Honor, France, 1946. Commander, el Sol del Peru, 1947. Bollingen Prize, Poetry, Yale University Library, 1952. National Book Award in Poetry, 1953: *Collected Poems: 1917-1952.* Boston Arts Festival Poetry Award, 1956. Sarah Josepha Hale Award, 1958. Chicago Poetry Day Poet, 1958. Antoinette Perry, Best Drama, 1959: *J. B.: A Play in Verse.* Academy Award, Best Screenplay, 1966: *The Eleanor Roosevelt Story.* Presidential Medal of Freedom, 1977. National Medal for Literature, 1978. Gold Medal for Poetry, American Academy of Arts and Letters, 1979. Honorary MA, Tufts University, MA, 1932. Honorary LittDs: Colby College, ME, 1938; Wesleyan University, CT, 1938; Yale University, CT, 1939; University of Pennsylvania, 1941; University of Illinois, 1946; Washington University, MO, 1948; Rockford College, IL, 1953; Columbia University, NY, 1954; Harvard University, MA, 1955; University of Pittsburgh, 1959; Princeton University, NJ, 1965; University of Massachusetts, 1969; Hampshire College, MA, 1970. Honorary LHDs: Dartmouth University, NH, 1940; Williams College, MA, 1942. Honorary DCLs: Union College, 1941; University of Puerto Rico, 1953. Honorary LLDs: Johns Hopkins University, MD, 1941; University of California, 1943; Queen's University at Kingston, 1948; Carleton College, 1956; Amherst College, MA, 1963.

For More Information: Falk, Signi Lenea, *Archibald MacLeish,* New York: Twayne, 1965; Smith, Grover Cleveland, *Archibald MacLeish,* Minneapolis: University of Minnesota, 1971; Mullaly, Edward J. *Archibald MacLeish: A Checklist,* Kent, OH: Kent State University, 1973; Donaldson, Scott, *Archibald*

MacLeish: An American Life, Boston: Houghton Mifflin, 1992.

Commentary: Archibald MacLeish won three Pulitzer Prizes, two in Poetry and one in Drama. He won his first Poetry prize in 1933 for *Conquistador,* a collection about the Spanish conquest of Mexico. He won again in 1953 for *Collected Poems: 1917-1952.* He was awarded the Drama prize in 1959 for *J.B.,* a philosophical verse drama contrasting different attitudes toward faith and how they hold up in a catastrophe.

MacLeish was born in Glencoe, Illinois. He was educated at Yale University and at Harvard Law School. A modern renaissance man, his many accomplishments in a variety of areas are quite remarkable. He was trained in law, published poetry while promoting New Deal public policy, administered the flow of public information during World War II, and wrote stage and radio plays, prose, and commentary. He was both an editor of *Fortune* magazine and the Boylston Professor of Rhetoric and Oratory at Harvard University.

1960

George Abbott 202

Birth: June 25, 1887; Forestville, NY. **Death:** January 31, 1995. **Parents:** George Burwell and Mary (McLaury) Abbott. **Education:** University of Rochester, NY: BA. Harvard University, MA. **Spouse:** Edna Lewis (m. 1914; died 1930); Mary Sinclair (m. 1946; div. 1957). **Children:** Judith Ann (EL).

Prize: *Drama,* 1960: *Fiorello!,* New York: Random House, 1960.

Career: Actor, playwright, director, producer; Co-Founder, Abbott-Dunning, Inc., 1931-1934.

Selected Works: *Broadway* (with Philip Dunning), 1927. *Coquette* (with Ann Preston Bridgers), 1928. *Where's Charley?,* 1948. *The Pajama Game* (with Richard Bissell), 1954. *Damn Yankees,* 1955. *Tenderloin* (with Jerome Weidman), 1961. *Tryout,* 1979.

Other Awards: Award, *Boston Globe,* 1912: *Man in the Manhole.* Donaldson Award, 1946: *Billion Dollar Baby.* Donaldson Award, 1948: *High Button Shoes.* New York Drama Critics Circle Award, Best Musical, 1953: *Wonderful Town.* Antoinette Perry Award, 1953: *Wonderful Town.* Donaldson Award, 1953: *Wonderful Town.* Antoinette Perry Award, 1955: *The Pajama Game,* New York: Random House, 1954. Donaldson Award, 1955: *The Pajama Game.* Antoinette Perry Award, 1956: *Damn Yankees,* New York: Frank Music, 1955. Antoinette Perry Award, 1960: *Fiorello!,* New York: Random House, 1960. New York Drama Critics Circle Award, 1961: *Fiorello!,* Outer Circle Award, Most Effective Individual Contribution, 1962: *A Funny Thing Happened on the Way to the Forum.* Antoinette Perry Award, Best Director, 1963: *A Funny Thing Happened on the Way to the Forum.* Society of Stage Directors Award of Merit, 1968. Theater Hall of Fame and Museum, NY, 1972. Honorary PhD, University of Rochester, 1961.

For More Information: *George Abbott, Director,* videocassette, VHS, 58 minutes, Graduate School, CUNY, City University Television in Association with the Center for Advanced Study in Theater Arts and the Harold Clurman Endowment, 1989.

Commentary: George Abbott, Jerome Weidman, Jerry Bock, and Sheldon Harnick won the 1952 Pulitzer Prize in Drama for *Fiorello!* A musical drama about the mayor of New York City, Fiorello LaGuardia, it premiered on November 23, 1959 at New York's Broadhurst Theater.

Abbott was born in Forestville, New York. He attended the University of Rochester. Afterward, he pursued an acting career on Broadway which evolved into directing, writing, and producing. His many works included *Pal Joey, Damn Yankees,* and *A Funny Thing Happened on the Way to the Forum.* He wrote an autobiography, *Mister Abbott,* which was published in 1963. He was active in New York theatre into the 1990s. He died at the age of 107.

Jerry Bock   203

Birth: November, 1928; New Haven, CT. **Parents:** Geroge Joseph and Rebecca (Albert) Bock. **Education:** University of Wisconsin. **Spouse:** Patti Fagen (m. 1950). **Children:** One son, one daughter.

Prize: *Drama,* 1960: *Fiorello!,* New York: Random House, 1960.

Career: Composer.

Selected Works: *Mr. Wonderful* (Libretto), 1956. *She Loves Me* (Libretto), 1963. *Fiddler on the Roof* (Libretto), 1964. *The Apple Tree* (Libretto), 1967.

Other Awards: Antoinette Perry Award, 1960: *Fiorello!,* New York: Random House, 1960. New York Drama Critics Circle Award, 1961: *Fiorello!*

For More Information: Altman, Richard, *The Making of a Musical: Fiddler on the Roof,* New York: Crown, 1971.

Commentary: Jerry Bock, Jerome Weidman, George Abbott, and Sheldon Harnick won the 1952 Pulitzer Prize in Drama for *Fiorello!* A musical drama about the mayor of New York City, Fiorello LaGuardia, it premiered on November 23, 1959 at New York's Broadhurst Theater.

Bock was born Jerrold Lewis Bock in New Haven, Connecticut. In addition to co-authoring *Fiorello,* Bock also composed *Fiddler on the Roof* with Sheldon Harnick and Joseph Stein; it was adapted from stories by Shalom Aleichem.

Sheldon Harnick   204

Birth: April 30, 1924; Chicago, IL. **Parents:** Harry M. and Ester (Kanter) Harnick. **Education:** Northwestern University, IL: BMus. **Spouse:** Mary Boatner (m. 1950; div. 1957); Elaine May (m. 1962; div. 1963); Margery Gray (m. 1965). **Children:** Beth, Matthew.

Prize: *Drama,* 1960: *Fiorello!,* New York: Random House, 1960.

Career: Lyricist, songwriter.

Selected Works: *Body Beautiful,* 1958. *Fiddler on the Roof,* 1964. *Apple Tree,* 1967. *Dr. Heidegger's Fountain of Youth,* 1998.

Other Awards: Antoinette Perry Award, 1960: *Fiorello!,* New York: Random House, 1960. New York Drama Critics Circle Award, 1961: *Fiorello!* Grammy Award, 1963: "She Loves Me." Tony Award, 1964: *Apple Tree,* New York: Random House, 1967.

For More Information: Altman, Richard, *The Making of a Musical: Fiddler on the Roof,* New York: Crown, 1971.

Commentary: Sheldon Harnick, Jerome Weidman, George Abbott, and Jerry Bock won the 1952 Pulitzer Prize in Drama for *Fiorello!* A musical about the mayor of New York City, Fiorello LaGuardia, it premiered on November 23, 1959 at New York's Broadhurst Theater.

Harnick was born in Chicago. He is best known for the 1964 Broadway hit, *Fiddler on the Roof,* written with Jerry Bock and Joseph Stein, which was adapted from stories by Shalom Aleichem (pseudonym for Sholem Rabinowitz).

Jerome Weidman   205

Birth: April 4, 1913; New York, NY. **Parents:** Joseph and Annie (Falkowitch) Weidman. **Education:** City College, NY. Washington Square College, NY. New York University Law School. **Spouse:** Elizabeth Ann Payne. **Children:** Jeffrey, John Whitney.

Prize: *Drama,* 1960: *Fiorello!,* New York: Random House, 1960.

Career: Novelist, playwright, short story writer, and essayist; Clerk, New York City, NY, 1930s; Staff member, U.S. Office of War Information, 1942-1945; President, Authors Guild and Dramatists Guild, Authors League of America, 1969-1974; Member, Writers Guild of America East.

Selected Works: *I Can Get It for You Wholesale,* 1937. *What's in It for Me?,* 1938. *The Horse That Could Whistle "Dixie" and Other Stories,* 1939. *Letter of Credit,* 1940. *I'll Never Go There Any More,* 1941. *The Lights around the Shore,* 1943. *Too Early to Tell,* 1946. *The Captain's Tiger,* 1947. *The Price Is Right,* 1949. *The Hand of the Hunter,* 1951. *The Third Angel,* 1953. *Before You Go,* 1960. *My Father Sits in the Dark, and Other Selected Stories,* 1961. *Tenderloin* (with George Abbott), 1961. *The Sound of Bow Bells,* 1962. *Word of Mouth,* 1964. *The Death of Dickie Draper, and Nine Other Stories,* 1965. *Other People's Money,* 1967. *The Center of the Action,* 1969. *Ivory Tower* (with James Yaffe), 1969. *Asterisk! A Comedy of Terrors,* 1969. *Fourth Street East,* 1970. *Last Respects,* 1971. *Tiffany Street,* 1974. *A Family Fortune,* 1978. *Praying for Rain,* 1986.

Other Awards: Antoinette Perry Award, 1960: *Fiorello!,* New York: Random House, 1960. New York Drama Critics Circle Award, 1960: *Fiorello!*

For More Information: *Contemporary Dramatists,* Chicago: St. James, 1988.

Commentary: Jerome Weidman, George Abbott, Jerry Bock, and Sheldon Harnick won the 1952 Pulitzer Prize in Drama for *Fiorello!* A musical drama about the mayor of New York City, Fiorello LaGuardia, it premiered on November 23, 1959 at New York's Broadhurst Theater.

Weidman was born in New York City and attended City College and New York University. He began his career on Simon and Schuster's editorial staff. His first novel, *I Can Get It for You Wholesale,* was published in 1937. He used his World War II experiences for several other novels including *Lights Around the Shore.* His other plays include *Tenderloin.*

1961

Tad Mosel   206

Birth: May 1, 1922; Steubenville, Ohio. **Parents:** George Ault and Margaret (Norman) Mosel. **Religion:** Presbyterian. **Education:** Amherst College, MA: BA. Yale University, CT. Columbia University, NY: MA.

Prize: *Drama,* 1961: *All the Way Home,* New York: French, 1961.

Career: Sergeant, U.S. Air Force Weather Service, 1943-1946; Playwright, television dramatist, beginning in 1949; Clerk, Northwest Airlines, 1951-1953; Visiting Critic, television writing, Yale University, CT, 1957-1958; Member of Executive Council, Writers Guild; Member, Theta Delta Chi.

Selected Works: *Other People's Houses, Six Television Plays,* 1956. *That's Where the Town's Going,* 1962. *Leading Lady: The World and Theatre of Katharine Cornell,* 1978. **Films:** *All the Way Home,* Paramount, 1963.

Other Awards: New York Drama Critics Circle Award, 1961: *All the Way Home,* New York: French, 1961. Honorary LittD, College of Wooster, OH, 1963.

For More Information: *Current Biography,* New York: Wilson, 1961.

Commentary: Tad Mosel was awarded the 1961 Pulitzer Prize in Drama for *All the Way Home,* a dramatization of James Agee's *A Death in the Family.* It premiered on November 30, 1960 at New York's Belasco Theater.

Mosel was born in Ohio. He attended Amherst College and the Yale School of Drama. He struggled to get his own plays produced and was a television scriptwriter. He garnered critical acclaim for his adaptation of Agee's novel. His own works include *The Lawn Party* and *Other People's Houses.*

1962

Abe Burrows   207

Birth: December 10, 1910; New York, NY. **Death:** May 17, 1985. **Parents:** Louis and Julia (Salzberg) Burrows. **Education:** City College, NY. New York University. **Spouse:** Ruth (Carin Smith Kinzel) (m. 1950). **Children:** Jimmie, Laura.

Prize: *Drama,* 1962: *How to Succeed in Business Without Really Trying,* New York: Meyerson, 1961.

Career: Playwright, performer, writer, and stage director; Writer and Director, *The Abe Burrows Show,* radio show, 1946-47; *Breakfast With Burrows,* radio show on CBS, 1949; *Abe Burrows Almanac,* televison show on CBS, 1950; Member: American Federation of Television and Radio Artists, Musicians Union,

American Society of Composers, Authors, and Publishers, Writers Guild of America.

Selected Works: *Guys and Dolls* (Adaptation), 1950. *Can-Can,* 1953. **Films:** *How to Succeed in Business without Really Trying,* Mirisch, 1967.

Other Awards: Radio Critics Award, 1947. The Abe Burrows Show. New York Drama Critics Circle Award, 1951: *Guys and Dolls,* New York: Frank Music, 1950. Antoinette Perry Award, League of New York Theatres and Producers, 1951: *Guys and Dolls.* Antoinette Perry Award, Best Writer, 1961: *How to Succeed in Business without Really Trying,* New York: Meyerson, 1961. Antoinette Perry Award, Best Director, 1961: *How to Succeed in Business without Really Trying.*

For More Information: *Current Biography,* New York: Wilson, 1951.

Commentary: Abe Burrows and Frank Loesser won the 1962 Pulitzer Prize in Drama for *How to Succeed in Business without Really Trying,* based on the book by Shepherd Mead. It was a musical satire about climbing the corporate ladder. It premiered on October 14, 1961 at New York's 46th Street Theater.

Burrows was born in New York City. He developed a talent for witticism early and used it to create humorous characters for radio, television, and Broadway shows. One of his early characters, Archie, was the central figure in the Columbia Broadcasting System's *Duffy's Tavern.* In 1949, he had a radio show, *Breakfast With Burrows,* and his own television show in 1950, *Abe Burrows's Almanac.* He went on to work with Frank Loesser on *Guys and Dolls.*

Frank Loesser   208

Birth: June 29, 1910; New York, NY. **Death:** July 28, 1969. **Parents:** Henry and Julia (Ehrlich) Loesser. **Education:** City College, NY. **Spouse:** Mary Alice Blankenbaker (m. 1935). **Children:** Susan.

Prize: *Drama,* 1962: *How to Succeed in Business Without Really Trying,* New York: Meyerson, 1961.

Career: Editor, lyricist.

Selected Works: *Where's Charley?,* 1948. *Guys and Dolls* (Adaptation), 1950. **Films:** *How to Succeed in Business without Really Trying,* Mirisch, 1967.

For More Information: Loesser, Susan, *A Most Remarkable Fella: Frank Loesser and the Guys and Dolls in His Life,* New York: Fine, 1993.

Commentary: Frank Loesser and Abe Burrows won the 1962 Pulitzer Prize in Drama for *How to Succeed in Business without Really Trying,* based on the book by Shepherd Mead. It was a musical satire about climbing the corporate ladder. It premiered on October 14, 1961 at New York's 46th Street Theater.

Loesser was born in New York City. He was a City College dropout who pursued a career as composer and lyricist. Some of his earliest lyrics were written for his friend and Pulitzer Prize-winning com-

poser, William Schuman. His first success was the song "Praise the Lord and Pass the Ammunition," which he wrote just after the Pearl Harbor attack. It became a hit during World War II. Loesser is well-known for such works as *Guys and Dolls* and *The Most Happy Fella.* He won an Academy Award in 1948 for Best Song with "Baby It's Cold Outside."

1963
No award

1964
No award

1965

Frank D. Gilroy   209

Birth: October 13, 1925; Bronx, NY. **Parents:** Frank B. and Bettina (Vasti) Gilroy. **Education:** Dartmouth College, NH: BA, magna cum laude. Yale University, CT: 1967. **Spouse:** Ruth Dorothy Gaydos (m. 1954). **Children:** Anthony, Daniel, John.

Prize: *Drama,* 1965: *The Subject Was Roses,* New York: French, 1962.

Career: Served in U.S. Army, Infantry, Europe, 1943-46; Messenger, Young and Rubicam, NY; Cabana rental clerk, Atlantic City, NJ; Playwright, scriptwriter, screenwriter and director, beginning in 1952; President, Writers Guild of America, Dramatists Guild, 1969-1971; Member: Authors League of America, Directors Guild of America.

Selected Works: *Who'll Save the Plowboy?,* 1962. *About Those Roses; or, How Not to Do a Play and Succeed, and the Text of the Subject Was Roses,* 1965. *That Summer, That Fall, & Far Rockaway,* 1967. *The Only Game in Town,* 1968. *Private,* 1970. *From Noon Till Three: The Possibly True and Certainly Tragic Story of an Outlaw and a Lady Whose Love Knew No Bounds,* 1973. *Last Licks: A Play,* 1979. **Films:** *The Subject Was Roses,* MGM, 1968.

Other Awards: Obie Award, Best Play Produced Off-Broadway, *Village Voice,* 1962: *Who'll Save the Plowboy?,* London, England: S. French, 1962. Outer Circle Award, Outstanding New Playwright, 1964. New York Drama Critics Circle Award, 1964: *The Subject Was Roses,* New York: Random House, 1965. New York Theatre Club Award, 1965: *The Subject Was Roses.* Antoinette Perry Award, League of New York Theatres and Producers, 1965: *The Subject Was Roses.* Grant, Dartmouth College, NH, 1967. Silver Bear Award, Berlin Film Festival, 1971: *Desperate Characters.* Honorary DLitt, Dartmouth College, NH, 1966.

For More Information: *Current Biography,* New York, NY: Wilson, 1965.

Commentary: Frank D. Gilroy was awarded the 1964 Pulitzer Prize in Drama for *The Subject Was Roses,* a story about an Irish family living in the Bronx. It premiered on May 25, 1964 at New York's Royale Theater.

Gilroy was born in the Bronx, New York City. He was educated at Dartmouth College and at the Yale School of Drama. His first play, *Who'll Save the Plowboy?,* was published in 1962. His other works include *The Only Game In Town* and *Dreams of Glory.*

1966
No award

1967

Edward Franklin Albee   210
Birth: March 12, 1928; Virginia. **Parents:** Reed A. and Frances (Cotter) Albee. **Religion:** Christian. **Education:** Trinity College, CT.

Prize: *Drama,* 1967: *A Delicate Balance,* New York: Atheneum, 1966. *Drama,* 1975: *Seascape,* New York: Atheneum, 1975. *Drama,* 1994: *Three Tall Women,* New York: Dutton, 1995.

Career: Writer, producer, and director of plays; Continuity writer, WNYC-Radio; Office boy, Warwick & Legler Advertising; Record salesman for G. Schirmer, Inc., Music Publishers; Luncheonette counterman, Manhattan Towers Hotel; Messenger, Western Union, 1955-1958; Co-Producer, New Playwrights Unit Workshop, 1963-; Director, touring retrospective of his one-act plays; Founder, William Flanagan Center for Creative Persons, Montauk, NY, 1971; Co-Director, Vivian Beaumont Theatre, Lincoln Center for the Performing Arts, NY, 1979-1981; Lecturer, Brandeis University; Lecturer, Johns Hopkins University; Lecturer, Webster University cultural exchange visit to USSR and Latin American countries for U.S. State Department; President, Edward F. Albee Foundation; Instructor and Artist-in-Residence, University of Houston; Member: Dramatists Guild Council, Governing Commission, New York State Council for the Arts, National Academy of Arts and Letters, National Endowment Grant-Giving Council, PEN American Center.

Selected Works: *The Zoo Story; The Death of Bessie Smith; The Sandbox: Three Plays,* 1960. *The American Dream: A Play,* 1961. *Who's Afraid of Virginia Woolf? A Play,* 1962. *The Play: The Ballad of the Sad Cafe* (Adaptation), 1963. *Tiny Alice: A Play,* 1965. *Malcolm* (Adaptation of a novel by James Purdy), 1966. *Everything in the Garden: A Play* (Ad-

aptation), 1968. *All Over: A Play,* 1971. *Counting the Ways; and Listening: Two Plays,* 1977. *The Lady from Dubuque: A Play,* 1980. *Conversations with Edward Albee* (Kolin, Philip C., ed.), 1988. **Films:** *Who's Afraid of Virginia Woolf?* Warner Bros., 1966; *A Delicate Balance,* USA, 1973.

Other Awards: Berlin Festival Award, 1959: *The Zoo Story,* New York: Coward, McCann & Geoghegan, 1960. Berlin Festival Award, 1961: *The Death of Bessie Smith,* New York: Coward, McCann & Geoghegan, 1960. Best Plays of the 1960-1961 Season, Foreign Press Association, 1961: *The Death of Bessie Smith,* and *The American Dream.* Obie Award, 1960: *The Zoo Story.* Vernon Rice Memorial Award, 1960: *The Zoo Story.* Argentine Critics Circle Award, 1961: *The Zoo Story.* Lola D'Annunzio Award, 1961: *The American Dream,* New York: Coward-McCann, 1961. Most Promising Playwright of 1962-63 Season, New York Drama Critics, 1963. New York Drama Critics Circle Award, 1963: *Who's Afraid of Virginia Woolf?,* New York: Dramatists Play Service, 1962. Foreign Press Association Award, 1963: *Who's Afraid of Virginia Woolf?* Antoinette Perry Award, 1963: *Who's Afraid of Virginia Woolf?* Outer Circle Award, 1963: *Who's Afraid of Virginia Woolf?* Saturday Review Drama Critics Award, 1963: *Who's Afraid of Virginia Woolf? Variety* Drama Critics' Poll Award, 1963: *Who's Afraid of Virginia Woolf? Evening Standard* Award, 1964: *Who's Afraid of Virginia Woolf?* Margo Jones Award for Encouraging New Playwrights, 1965. American Academy and Institute of Arts and Letters Gold Medal, 1980. Theater Hall of Fame Inductee, 1985. New York Drama Critics Circle Award, 1994: *Three Tall Women,* New York: Dutton, 1995. Honorary DLitts: Emerson College, MA, 1967; Trinity College, 1974.

For More Information: Giantvalley, Scott, *Edward Albee: A Reference Guide,* Boston: G.K. Hall, 1987; Parker, Dorothy, *Essays on Modern American Drama: Williams, Miller, Albee, and Shepard,* Toronto, Canada: University of Toronto, 1987; Roudan, Matthew Charles, *Understanding Edward Albee,* Columbia: University of South Carolina, 1987; Mayberry, Bob, *Theatre of Discord: Dissonance in Beckett, Albee, and Pinter,* Rutherford, NJ: Fairleigh Dickinson University, 1989.

Commentary: Edward Albee won three Pulitzer Prizes, all for Drama. He won the 1967 prize for *A Delicate Balance,* a drama about a troubled middle-aged couple whose relationship has changed. It premiered on September 22, 1966 at New York's Martin Beck Theater. His second prize was awarded in 1975 for *Seascape,* a play in which a middle-aged couple meet up with two sea creatures while at the beach and the foursome discuss the meaning of existence. It premiered on January 26, 1975 at New York's Shubert Theater. In 1994, Albee won a third prize for *Three*

Women, which premiered Off-Broadway on February 13, 1994 at New York's Vineyard Theater.

Albee was born in Virginia and adopted into the wealthy family that owned the Reed-Albee Theatre Circuit. Raised in Larchmont, New York, he was provided with all the amenities offered by wealth. He attended Trinity College in Connecticut and then headed for Greenwich Village. His first play, *Zoo Story,* was published in 1958 and its premier in 1960 received exceptional reviews. His produced several more plays and in 1962, *Who's Afraid of Virginia Woolf* was pronounced an unqualified success. His other works include *The Ballad of the Sad Cafe* and *Box and Quotations from Mao Tse-Tung.* Albee is among the leading dramatists of the 20th century.

1968
No award

1969

Howard Sackler   211
Birth: December 19, 1929; New York, NY. **Death:** October 14, 1982. **Parents:** Martin and Ida Sackler. **Education:** Brooklyn College, NY: BA. **Spouse:** Greata Lynn Lungren (m. 1963). **Children:** Molly, Daniel.

Prize: *Drama,* 1969: *The Great White Hope,* New York, Dial Press, 1968.

Career: Playwright and screenwriter, 1950-1982; Director, Caedmon Records, NY, and London, England, 1953-1968; Director of plays, New York, London, Dublin, and Los Angeles, including *The Family Reunion,* 1954-1964.

Selected Works: *A Few Enquiries,* 1970. **Films:** *The Great White Hope,* 20th Century Fox, 1970.

Other Awards: Rockefeller Foundation Grant, 1953. Littauer Foundation Grant, 1954. Maxwell Anderson Award, 1954. Sergel Award, 1959. New York Drama Critics Circle Award, 1969: *The Great White Hope,* New York: Dial Press, 1968. Antoinette Perry Award, 1969: *The Great White Hope.*

For More Information: *Contemporary Dramatists,* London, England: Berney, 1993.

Commentary: Howard Sackler was awarded the 1969 Pulitzer Prize in Drama for *The Great White Hope,* a dramatization of the life of African American world heavyweight boxing champion Jack Johnson. It premiered on December 12, 1967 at New York's Arena Theater.

Sackler was born in New York City. He attended Brooklyn College. His first play, *Uriel Acosta,* was published in 1954. His other works include *Mr. Welk and Jersey Jim* and *The Nine O'Clock Mail.*

1970

Charles Gordone   212
Birth: October 12, 1925; Cleveland, OH. **Death:** November 17, 1995. **Parents:** William and Camille (Morgan) Gordone. **Education:** Los Angeles State College of Applied Arts and Sciences (now California State University), Los Angeles: BA. University of California, Los Angeles. **Spouse:** Jeanne Warner (m. 1959); Susan Kouyomjian. **Children:** Stephen, Judy, Leah, Carla, David (JW).

Prize: *Drama,* 1970: *No Place to Be Somebody,* Indianapolis, IN: Bobbs-Merrill, 1969.

Career: Playwright, actor, and director; Served in U.S. Air Force; Stage actor, 1952-1979; Co-Founder and Chair, Committee for the Employment of Negro Performers, 1962; Member, Commission on Civil Disorders, 1967; Instructor, Cell Block Theatre, Yardville and Bordontown Detention Centers, New Jersey, 1977-1978; Judge, Missouri Arts Council Playwriting Competition, 1978; Instructor, New School for Social Research, 1978-1979; Instructor of English and Theater, Texas A & M University, College Station, 1986-1995; Member, Ensemble Studio Theatre and Actors Studio.

Selected Works: *Under the Boardwalk,* 1976. *The Last Chord: A Black-Black Drama in Three Acts,* 1976.

Other Awards: Obie Award, Best Actor, 1953: *Of Mice and Men.* Vernon Rice Award, 1970. Los Angeles Critics Circle Award, 1970: *No Place to Be Somebody,* Indianapolis, IN: Bobbs-Merrill, 1969. Drama Desk Award, 1970: *No Place to Be Somebody.* American Academy Award, 1971. National Institute of Arts and Letters Grant, 1971. National Endowment for the Humanities Grant, 1978. D. H. Lawrence Fellow, 1987.

For More Information: *Oxford Companion to American Theatre,* New York: Oxford University, 1984.

Commentary: Charles Gordone was awarded the 1970 Pulitzer Prize in Drama for *No Place to Be Somebody: A Black Comedy,* based on Gordone's experiences as a bartender in New York's Greenwich Village. It premiered on May 4, 1970 at New York's Public Theater.

Gordone was born in Cleveland, Ohio. He was also the co-founder (with Godfrey Cambridge) and chairman of the Committee for the Employment of Negro Actors in 1962. He was appointed by President Lyndon Johnson to the research team of the Commission on Civil Disorders in 1967. He is the co-founder, with Susan Kouyomjian, of American Stage in Berkeley, California. In the 1980s he wrote several screenplays for Paramount Pictures. In addition to playwriting, he has acted, notably in an all-black production of *Of Mice and Men,* and he has directed. He is the first African American playwright to win a Pulitzer Prize in Drama. His other works include the monologue *Gordone Is a Muthah.*

1971

Paul Zindel   213

Birth: May 15, 1936; Staten Island, NY. **Parents:** Paul and Beatrice Mary (Frank) Zindel. **Education:** Wagner College, NY: BS, MSc. **Spouse:** Bonnie Hildebrand (m. 1973). **Children:** David Jack, Lizabeth Claire.

Prize: *Drama,* 1971: *The Effect of Gamma Rays on Man-in-the-Moon Marigolds,* New York: Bantam Books, 1970.

Career: Technical Writer, Allied Chemical, NY, 1958-1959; Chemistry Teacher, Tottenville High School, Staten Island, NY, 1959-1969; Playwright; Author of children's books, beginning in 1969; Playwright-in-Residence, Alley Theatre, Houston, TX, 1967; Member, Actors Studio.

Selected Works: *My Darling, My Hamburger,* 1969. *I Never Loved Your Mind,* 1970. *And Miss Reardon Drinks a Little,* 1971. *Let Me Hear You Whisper: A Play,* 1974. *I Love My Mother,* 1975. *Pardon Me, You're Stepping on My Eyeball!,* 1976. *Confessions of a Teenage Baboon,* 1977. *When a Darkness Falls,* 1984. *The Pigman & Me,* 1992. **Films:** *The Effect of Gamma Rays on Man-in-the-Moon Marigolds,* 20th Century Fox, 1972.

Other Awards: Ford Foundation Grant for Drama, 1967. Child Study Association of America's Children's Books of the Year, 1968: *The Pigman. Boston Globe-Horn Book* Award for Text, 1969: *The Pigman.* Outstanding Children's Book of the Year, *New York Times,* 1969: *My Darling, My Hamburger,* New York: Harper & Row, 1969. Outstanding Children's Book of the Year, *New York Times,* 1970: *I Never Loved Your Mind,* New York: Harper & Row, 1970. Obie Award, Best American Play, *Village Voice,* 1970: *The Effect of Gamma Rays on Man-in-the-Moon Marigolds,* New York: Bantam Books, 1970. Vernon Rice Drama Desk Award, New York Drama Critics, Most Promising Playwright, 1970. New York Drama Critics Circle Award, Best American Play of the Year, 1970: *The Effect of Gamma Rays on Man-in-the-Moon Marigolds,* New York Critics Award, 1971: *The Effect of Gamma Rays on Man-in-the-Moon Marigolds.* American Library Association's Best Young Adult Books Citation, 1971: *The Effect of Gamma Rays on Man-in-the-Moon Marigolds.* Media & Methods Maxi Award, 1973: *The Pigman.* American Library Association's Best Young Adult Books Citation, 1975: *The Pigman.* Outstanding Children's Book of the Year, *New York Times,*

1976: *Pardon Me, You're Stepping on My Eyeball!,* New York: Harper & Row, 1976. American Library Association's Best Young Adult Books Citation, 1976: *Pardon Me, You're Stepping on My Eyeball!,* American Library Association's Best Young Adult Books Citation, 1977: *Confessions of a Teenage Baboon,* New York: Harper & Row, 1977. Outstanding Children's Book of the Year, *New York Times,* 1978: *The Undertaker's Gone Bananas.* Outstanding Children's Book of the Year, *New York Times,* 1980: *The Pigman's Legacy.* New York Public Library, Books for the Teens Citation, 1980: *Confessions of a Teenage Baboon.* American Library Association's Best Young Adult Books Citation, 1980: *The Pigman's Legacy.* New York Public Library, Books for the Teens Citation, 1980, 1981, 1982: *The Effect of Gamma Rays on Man-in-the-Moon Marigolds.* New York Public Library, Books for the Teens Citation, 1980, 1981: *A Star for the Latecomer.* New York Public Library, Books for the Teens Citation, 1980, 1981, 1982: *The Pigman's Legacy.* American Library Association's Best Young Adult Books Citation, 1982: *To Take a Dare.* Honorary Doctorate of Humanities, Wagner College, 1971.

For More Information: Forman, Jack Jacob, *Presenting Paul Zindel,* Boston: Twayne, 1988.

Commentary: *The Effect of Gamma Rays on Man-in-the-Moon Marigolds,* a play about a young girl preparing her experiment for the school science fair, won the 1971 Pulitzer Prize in Drama for Paul Zindel. It premiered on April 7, 1970 at New York's Mercer Theater.

Zindel was born in New York City, where he taught high school prior to winning the Pulitzer Prize. His other works include a novel, *The Pigman,* and two plays, *And Miss Reardon Drinks a Little* and *Pardon Me, You're Stepping on My Eyeball.*

1972
No award

1973

Jason Miller   214

Birth: 1939; Long Island City, NY. **Parents:** John and Mary Miller. **Education:** University of Scranton, PA: BA. Catholic University of America, Washington, DC. **Spouse:** Linda Gleason (m. 1963; sep. 1975). **Children:** Jennifer, Jason, Jordan.

Prize: *Drama,* 1973: *That Championship Season,* New York: Atheneum, 1972.

Career: Messenger, waiter, truck driver, welfare investigator, and actor in New York City; Film and television actor appearing in such films as *The Exor-*

cist, 1973, and *Nickel Ride,* 1975; Actor on television in the *Bell System Family Theater,* 1975; Playwright.

Selected Works: *Lou Gehrig Did Not Die of Cancer,* 1970. *Nobody Hears a Broken Drum,* 1970.

Other Awards: New York Drama Critics Circle Award, 1972: *That Championship Season,* New York: Atheneum, 1972. Best Play Citation, 1972: *That Championship Season,* Antoinette Perry Award, 1973: *That Championship Season.*

For More Information: *Current Biography,* New York: Wilson, 1974.

Commentary: Jason Miller was awarded the 1973 Pulitzer Prize in Drama for *That Championship Season,* a story about basketball players looking back at their glory days. It premiered on May 2, 1972 at New York's Public Theater, moving in September of that year to Broadway's Booth Theater.

Miller was born in Long Island City, New York. He attended the University of Scranton in Pennsylvania. He got his start as an actor in Joseph Papp's Shakespeare Festival and wrote plays in his spare time. He was appearing as an actor in dinner theatre when he wrote *That Championship Season.* Papp decided to produce it.

1974
No award

1975

Edward Franklin Albee
Full entry appears as #**210** under "Drama," 1967.

1976

Michael Bennett   215
Birth: April 8, 1943; Buffalo, NY. **Death:** July 2, 1987. **Parents:** Salvatore Joseph and Helen (Ternoff) Bennett.

Prize: *Drama,* 1976: *A Chorus Line,* New York: Studio Duplicating Service, 1975.

Career: Professional dancer in stage plays, 1959-1964; Choreographer of plays, 1966-1970; Director of plays, 1971-1974; Director, choreographer, and author of *Seesaw,* 1973; Co-Producer, choreographer, director, and co-author of *A Chorus Line,*1975; Director and choreographer of *Ballroom,* 1978; Choreographer of film and television programs; Member: League of New York Theatres and Producers, Society of Stage Directors and Choreographers.

Selected Works: *Seesaw: A Musical* (Adaptation), 1975. **Films:** *A Chorus Line,* PolyGram, 1985.

Other Awards: Antoinette Perry Award, Best Choreographer, 1971: *Follies.* Antoinette Perry

Award, Best Director, 1971: *Follies.* Antoinette Perry Award, Best Choreographer, 1973: *Seesaw.* Antoinette Perry Award, Best Choreographer, 1975: *A Chorus Line,* New York: Studio Duplicating Service, 1975. Antoinette Perry Award, Best Director, 1975: *A Chorus Line.* Antoinette Perry Award, Best Choreographer, 1979: *Ballroom.* Three New York Drama Critics Circle Awards: *Ballroom.* Outer Critics Circle Award. Los Angeles Drama Critics Award: *Ballroom.*

For More Information: Philp, Richard, "Michael Bennett's Ballroom—Dancing for Your Life!" *Dance Magazine,* New York. February 1979, p. 60-62; Barnes, Clive, "Michael Bennett: An Appreciation," *Dance Magazine,* New York. October 1987, p. 32; Stuart, Otis, "Michael Bennett, 1943-1987," Obituary, *Dance Magazine,* New York. October 1987, p. 33; Mandelbaum, Ken, *A Chorus Line and the Musicals of Michael Bennett,* New York: St. Martin's, 1989; Flinn, Denny Martin, *What They Did for Love: The Untold Story Behind the Making of 'A Chorus Line',* New York: Bantam Books, 1989; Kelly, Kevin, *One Singular Sensation: The Michael Bennett Story,* New York: Doubleday, 1990.

Commentary: Michael Bennett, James Kirkwood, Nicholas Dante, Marvin Hamlisch, and Edward Kleban were awarded the 1976 Pulitzer Prize in Drama for *A Chorus Line,* a story of a group of dancers who audition for a show, revealing details about themselves in the process. It premiered on July 25, 1975 at New York's Shubert Theater after a debut run at the Public Theater and became the longest running show in Broadway theatre history.

Bennett was born Michael Bennett Di Figlia in Buffalo, New York. He made his Broadway debut as a dancer in 1961 in *Subways Are for Sleeping,* and starred as a dancer in the 1960s television show *Hullabaloo.* He then moved from dancing to choreography. In addition to conceiving, directing, choreographing, and coproducing *A Chorus Line,* his other Broadway productions were *Promises, Promises* and *Dreamgirls.* He died of complications from AIDS in 1987. Bennett won eight Tony Awards.

Nicholas Dante   216
Birth: November 22, 1941; New York, NY. **Death:** May 21, 1991. **Parents:** Conrado and Maria Guadalupe (Betancourt) Morales.

Prize: *Drama,* 1976: *A Chorus Line,* New York: Studio Duplicating Service, 1975.

Career: Dancer and playwright.

Films: *A Chorus Line,* PolyGram, 1985.

Other Awards: New York Drama Critic's Circle Award, Best New Musical, 1975. Antoinette Perry Award, Best Book of Broadway Musical: *A Chorus Line.* Drama Desk Award, Outstanding Musical / Book, 1975: *A Chorus Line.*

For More Information: Weatherby, W.J., "Nicholas Dante: Stepping Out of Poverty," *Guardian,* May 24, 1991; "Nicholas Dante," *Variety,* May 27, 1991; *Contemporary Theatre, Film and Television, Volume II,* Detroit: Gale, 1994.

Commentary: Nicholas Dante, Michael Bennett, James Kirkwood, Marvin Hamlisch, and Edward Kleban were awarded the 1976 Pulitzer Prize in drama for *A Chorus Line,* a story of a group of dancers who audition for a show, revealing details about themselves in the process. It premiered on July 25, 1975 at New York's Shubert Theater after a debut run at the Public Theater and became the longest running show in Broadway theatre history.

Dante was born "Conrado Morales" in New York City. He became a dancer in Broadway shows and co-authored *A Chorus Line* with James Kirkwood. He died of complications from AIDS at the age of 49.

Marvin Hamlisch 217

Birth: June 2, 1944; New York, NY. **Parents:** Max and Lily (Schachter) Hamlisch. **Education:** Queens College, NY: BA. Juilliard School of Music, NY. **Spouse:** Terri Blair (m. 1989).

Prize: *Drama,* 1976: *A Chorus Line,* New York: Studio Duplicating Service, 1975.

Career: Composer and pianist.

Selected Works: *The Longest Line: Broadway's Most Singular Sensation, A Chorus Line* (Stevens, Gary and Alan George), 1995. **Films:** *A Chorus Line,* PolyGram, 1985.

Other Awards: Four Grammys. Golden Globe Award, Best Original Song, 1972: *Kotch.* Golden Globe Award, Best Original Song, 1974: *The Way We Were.* Academy Award, Best Music, Original Dramatic Score, 1974: *The Way We Were.* Academy Award, Best Music, Scoring Original Song Score and/or Adaptation, 1974: *The Sting.* Academy Award, Best Music, Song, 1974: *The Way We Were.* Emmy Award, Outstanding Individual Achievement in Music Direction, 1995: *Barbra Streisand: The Concert.* Emmy Award, Outstanding Individual Achievement in Music and Lyrics, 1995: *Barbra Streisand: The Concert.* ASCAP Award, Most Performed Songs for Motion Pictures, 1998: *The Mirror Has Two Faces.*

For More Information: Flinn, Denny Martin, *What They Did for Love: The Untold Story behind the Making of 'A Chorus Line',* New York: Bantam, 1989.

Commentary: Marvin Hamlisch, Michael Bennett, James Kirkwood, Nicholas Dante, and Edward Kleban were awarded the 1976 Pulitzer Prize in Drama for *A Chorus Line,* a story of a group of dancers who audition for a show, revealing details about themselves in the process. It premiered on July 25, 1975 at New York's Shubert Theater after a debut run at the Public Theater and became the longest running show in Broadway theatre history.

Hamlisch was born in New York City. His father was an accordionist and steered Marvin in the direction of music. He has composed music for the stage, film, and concerts, and has performed at the piano for audiences around the world. He has composed music for such Broadway shows as *They're Playing Our Song* and *The Goodbye Girl,* and his film credits include *The Sting, The Way We Were* and, most recently, *The Mirror Has Two Faces.* Marvin Hamlisch currently is the Principal Pops Conductor with the Pittsburgh Symphony and Baltimore Symphony orchestras.

James Kirkwood 218

Birth: August 22, 1930; Los Angeles, CA. **Death:** April 21, 1989. **Parents:** James, Sr. and Lila (Lee) Kirkwood. **Religion:** Roman Catholic. **Education:** Sanford Meisner Professional Classes, NY. New York University. University of California, Los Angeles.

Prize: *Drama,* 1976: *A Chorus Line,* New York: Studio Duplicating Service, 1975.

Career: Actor, novelist, and playwright; Served in U.S. Coast Guard Reserve; Actor, touring companies, Broadway shows, television and film; Week-day radio program, *Kirkwood-Goodman Show,* WOR radio, NY; Twenty-six week series, *Teenager Unlimited,* Mutual Network; Member: Actors Equity Association, American Federation of Television and Radio Artists, American Guild of Variety Artists, Authors League, Dramatists Guild, PEN, Screen Actors Guild.

Selected Works: *UTBU: Unhealthy to Be Unpleasant,* 1966. *American Grotesque: An Account of the Clay Shaw-Jim Garrison Affair in the City of New Orleans,* 1970. *P.S. Your Cat Is Dead! A Novel,* 1972. *Some Kind of Hero: A Novel,* 1975. *Hit Me with a Rainbow: A Novel,* 1980. *Good Times/Bad Times: A Novel,* 1983. *Diary of a Mad Playwright,* 1989. **Films:** *A Chorus Line,* PolyGram, 1985.

Other Awards: Antoinette Perry Award, Best Play, 1976: *A Chorus Line,* New York: Studio Duplicating Service, 1975. Drama Critics Circle Award, 1976: *A Chorus Line.* Drama Desk Award, 1976: *A Chorus Line.* Theatre World Award, 1976: *A Chorus Line.*

For More Information: Flinn, Denny Martin, *What They Did for Love: The Untold Story Behind the Making of 'A Chorus Line',* New York: Bantam Books, 1989.

Commentary: James Kirkwood, Michael Bennett, Nicholas Dante, Marvin Hamlisch, and Edward Kleban were awarded the 1976 Pulitzer Prize in Drama for *A Chorus Line,* a story of a group of dancers who audition for a show, revealing details about themselves in the process. It premiered on July 25, 1975 at New York's Shubert Theater after a debut run at the

Public Theater and became the longest running show in Broadway theatre history.

Kirkwood was born in Los Angeles. He was the child of silent film stars Lila Lee and James Kirkwood. As an actor he appeared in the film, *Oh God, II.* In addition to writing the lyrics for *A Chorus Line,* his works include the novel *P.S. Your Cat Is Dead!*

Edward Kleban   219

Birth: April 30, 1939; New York, NY. **Death:** 1987. **Parents:** Julian Milton and Sylvia Kleban. **Education:** Columbia University, NY: BA.

Prize: *Drama,* 1976: *A Chorus Line,* New York: Studio Duplicating Service, 1975.

Career: Composer and lyricist.

Films: *A Chorus Line,* PolyGram, 1985.

Other Awards: New York Drama Critics Award, 1975: *A Chorus Line,* New York: Studio Duplicating Service, 1975. Antoinette Perry Award, 1976: *A Chorus Line.* Drama Desk Award, 1976. Obie Award, 1975-1976: *A Chorus Line.* Los Angeles Drama Critics Award, 1977: *A Chorus Line.*

For More Information: Corman, Avery, "The Invisible Man in 'A Chorus Line'," *New York Times,* Current Events Edition, 7 April 1990.

Commentary: Edward Kleban, Michael Bennett, James Kirkwood, Nicholas Dante, and Marvin Hamlisch were awarded the 1976 Pulitzer Prize in Drama for *A Chorus Line,* a story of a group of dancers who audition for a show, revealing details about themselves in the process. It premiered on July 25, 1975 at New York's Shubert Theater after a debut run at the Public Theater and became the longest running show in Broadway theatre history.

Kleban was born in New York City. He has written lyrics for and produced Broadway shows. He and Marvin Hamlisch worked together on the lyrics and music for *A Chorus Line.*

1977

Michael Cristofer   220

Birth: January 22, 1945; Trenton, NJ. **Parents:** Joseph Peter and Mary (Muccioli) Procaccino. **Education:** Catholic University of America, Washington, DC. American University, Beirut, Lebanon.

Prize: *Drama,* 1977: *The Shadow Box,* New York: Drama Book Specialists, 1977.

Career: Screenwriter, *Witches of Eastwick (Screenplay),* 1987, *Bonfire of the Vanities (Screenplay),* 1990, *The Great American Belly Dance (Adaptation).*

Selected Works: *The Lady and the Clarinet,* 1985. **Films:** *The Witches of Eastwick,* Warner Bros., 1987; *The Bonfire of the Vanities,* Warner Bros., 1990.

Other Awards: Los Angeles Drama Critics Award, Acting, 1973. Theatre World Award for Performance, 1977: *The Shadow Box,* New York: Drama Book Specialists, 1977. Antoinette Perry Award, 1977: *The Shadow Box.*

For More Information: *Contemporary American Dramatists,* London, England: St. James, 1994.

Commentary: *The Shadow Box,* a story about terminal illness that is set in a hospice, won the 1977 Pulitzer Prize in Drama for Michael Cristofer. It premiered March 31, 1979, at New York's Morosco Theater and debuted the actor Mandy Patinkin.

Cristofer attended Catholic University in Washington, DC and American University in Lebanon. He has written a dramatization of *The Great American Belly Dance* and screenplays for *Witches of Eastwick* and *Bonfire of the Vanities.* He has also written *The Blues Are Running,* a comedy set at a park bench.

1978

Donald L. Coburn   221

Birth: August 4, 1958; Baltimore, MD. **Parents:** Guy Dabney and Ruth Margaret (Somes) Coburn. **Spouse:** Nazlee Joyce French (m. 1964; div. 1971); Marsha Woodruff Maher (m. 1975). **Children:** Donn Christopher, Kimberly (NJF).

Prize: *Drama,* 1978: *The Gin Game,* New York: Drama Book Specialists, 1978.

Career: Playwright; Served in U.S. Navy, 1958-1960; Owner and Director, Coburn and Associates Advertising Agency, Baltimore, MD, 1965-1968; Writer, Stanford Advertising Agency, Dallas, TX, 1968-1971; Creative and Marketing Consultant, Donald L. Colburn, Dallas, 1973-1976; Playwright, beginning, 1976; Member, Soaring Society of America.

Films: *The Gin Game* (TV), 1981.

For More Information: *Contemporary Authors,* Detroit: Gale, 1997.

Commentary: Donald L. Coburn was awarded the 1978 Pulitzer Prize in Drama for *The Gin Game,* a play about two nursing home residents. The play takes place over a game of gin rummy. It premiered on October 6, 1977, at New York's John Golden Theater.

Coburn was born in Baltimore, Maryland. He worked in advertising sales before becoming successful in the theatre. His other works include *Bluewater Cottage* and the screenplay for *Flights of Angels.*

1979

Sam Shepard   222

Birth: November 5, 1943; Fort Sheridan, IL. **Parents:** Samuel Shepard and Elaine (Schook) Rogers.

Education: Mount San Antonio Junior College, CA. **Spouse:** O-Lan Johnson (m. 1969; div); Jessica Lange. **Children:** Jesse Mojo (OJ); Hannah Jane, Samuel Walker (JL).

Prize: *Drama,* 1979: *Buried Child,* New York: Urizen Books, 1979.

Career: Writer, actor and director; Stable hand, Conley Arabian Horse Ranch, Chino, CA, 1958-1960; Actor, Bishop's Company Repertory Players, 1962-1963; Busboy, Village Gate, New York City, 1963-1964; Drummmer and Guitarist, Holy Modal Rounders, 1968-1971; Playwright-in-Residence, Magic Theatre, San Francisco, CA, 1974-1984; Film actor, 1978-1994; Member, American Academy and Institute of Arts and Letters.

Selected Works: *La Turista,* 1968. *Operation Sidewinder,* 1970. *The Unseen Hand and Other Plays,* 1972. *Sam Shepard: Mad Dog Blues & Other Plays,* 1972. *Hawk Moon: A Book of Short Stories, Poems, and Monologues,* 1973. *The Tooth of Crime: Geography of a Horse Dreamer: Two Plays,* 1974. *Angel City & Other Plays,* 1976. *Rolling Thunder Logbook,* 1977. *Sam Shepard Seven Plays,* 1981. *True West,* 1981. *Motel Chronicles,* 1982. *Fool for Love and Other Plays,* 1984. *Paris, Texas* (with Wim Wenders), 1984. *A Lie of the Mind: A Play in Three Acts; The War in Heaven: Angel's Monologue* (with Joseph Chaiken), 1987. *States of Shock; Far North; Silent Tongue,* 1993. *Cruising Paradise: Tales,* 1996. **Films:** *Fool for Love,* Cannon Group, 1985.

Other Awards: Obie Awards, Best Plays, *Village Voice,* 1966: *Chicago, Icarus's Mother,* and *Red Cross.* Obie Awards, Best Play, 1967: *La Turista,* Indianapolis, IN: Bobbs-Merrill, 1968. Obie Awards, Best Plays of the Off-Broadway Season, 1968: *Forensic and the Navigators* and *Melodrama Play.* Obie Award, Best Play, 1973: *The Tooth of Crime,* New York: Grove, 1974. Obie Award, Best Play, 1975: *Action.* Obie Award, Best Play, 1977: *Curse of the Starving Class.* Obie Award, Best Play, 1979: *Buried Child,* New York: Urizen Books, 1979. Obie Award, Best Play, 1984: *Fool for Love,* New York: Bantam, 1984. University of Minnesota Grant, 1966. Rockefeller Foundation Grant, 1967. Yale University Fellowship, 1967. Guggenheim Foundation Memorial Fellowships, 1968, 1971. Award for Literature, National Institute and American Academy, 1974. Brandeis University Creative Arts Award. Golden Palm Award, Cannes Film Festival, 1984: *Paris, Texas.* New York Drama Critics' Circle Award, 1986: *A Lie of the Mind.* Theater Hall of Fame, 1994.

For More Information: Mottram, Ron, *Inner Landscapes: The Theater of Sam Shepard,* Columbia: University of Missouri, 1984; Oumano, Ellen, *Sam Shepard: The Life and Work of an American Dreamer,* New York: St. Martin's, 1986; Daniels, Barry, ed., *Joseph Chaikin & Sam Shepard: Letters and Texts,*

1972-1984, New York: New American Library, 1989; Perry, Frederick J., *A Reconstruction-Analysis of Buried Child by Playwright Sam Shepard,* San Francisco: Mellen Research University Press, 1992; Tucker, Martin, *Sam Shepard,* New York: Continuum, 1992; Wade, Leslie A., *Sam Shepard and the American Theatre,* Westport, CT: Greenwood, 1997.

Commentary: *Buried Child,* a play about a homecoming to a dysfunctional family, won the 1979 Pulitzer Prize in Drama for Sam Shepard. It premiered on December 5, 1978 at New York's Theatre de Lys.

Shepard was born Samuel Shepard Rogers Jr. in Fort Sheridan, Illinois. He grew up on or near military bases where his father, a career army officer, was stationed. He attended Mount San Antonio Junior College in California and shortly thereafter began touring with an acting company. He has been an actor, a musician and a playwright. He made a reputation in experimental theatres like New York's La Mama and San Francisco's Magic Theatre. His acting roles, which include *The Right Stuff* and *Country,* have brought him into the mainstream. His other works include *Fool For Love, True West,* and *Tooth of the Crime.*

1980

Lanford Wilson   223

Birth: April 13, 1937; Lebanon, MO. **Parents:** Ralph Eugene and Violetta (Tate) Wilson. **Education:** Southwest Missouri State. San Diego State, CA. University of Chicago, IL. University of Missouri: PhD. Grinnell College, IA.

Prize: *Drama,* 1980: *Talley's Folly,* New York: Hill & Wang, 1979.

Career: Playwright.

Selected Works: *Balm in Gilead, and Other Plays,* 1965. *The Rimers of Eldritch: A Play in Two Acts,* 1967. *The Gingham Dog,* 1969. *The Sand Castle, and Three Other Plays,* 1970. *Lemon Sky,* 1970. *The Hot l Baltimore,* 1973. *Serenading Louie,* 1976. *The Mound Builders,* 1976. *5th of July,* 1978. *Angels Fall,* 1983. *Serenading Louie,* 1984. *Talley & Son: A Play in Two Acts,* 1986. *Redwood Curtain,* 1993. *Four Short Plays: Days Ahead; The Madness of Lady Bright; This Is the Rill Speaking; Say de Kooning,* 1994.

For More Information: Williams, Philip Middleton, *A Comfortable House: Lanford Wilson, Marshall W. Mason, and the Circle Repertory Theatre,* Jefferson, NC: McFarland, 1993; Bryer, Jackson R., *Lanford Wilson: A Casebook,* New York: Garland, 1994; Dean, Anne M., *Discovery and Invention: The Urban Plays of Lanford Wilson,* Rutherford, NJ: Fairleigh Dickinson University, 1994.

Commentary: Lanford Wilson was awarded the 1980 Pulitzer Prize in Drama for *Talley's Folly,* the second part of a trilogy about a disabled Vietnam veteran. It premiered on May 3, 1979 at New York's Circle Repertory and moved to Broadway.

Lanford Wilson was born in Lebanon, Missouri. He began his career at Caffe Cino in New York's Greenwich Village, writing one-act plays. The trilogy about the Talley family began with *Fifth of July* and ended with *A Tale Told.* His other works include *Lemon Sky* and *The Hot l Baltimore.*

1981

Beth Henley   224

Birth: May 8, 1952; Jackson, MS. **Parents:** Charles Boyce and Elizabeth Josephine (Becker) Henley. **Education:** Southern Methodist University, TX: BFA. University of Illinois.

Prize: *Drama,* 1981: *Crimes of the Heart,* New York: Viking, 1982.

Career: Actress, Theatre Three, Dallas, Texas, 1972-1973; Member, Acting Ensemble, Directors Colloquium, Southern Methodist University, Dallas, TX, 1973; Teacher, Creative Dramatics, Dallas Minority Repertory Theatre, 1974-1975; Teacher, Beginning acting, Lessac voice technique, University of Illinois, Urbana, 1975-1976; Actress, *Great American People Show,* summer, 1976.

Selected Works: *The Miss Firecracker Contest: A Play in Two Acts,* 1979. *Am I Blue: A Play,* 1982. *The Wake of Jamey Foster,* 1983. *The Lucky Spot: A Play,* 1987. *Abundance,* 1991. *The Debutante Ball,* 1991. **Films:** *True Stories,* Warner Bros., 1986; *Crimes of the Heart,* De Laurentis, 1986; *Miss Firecracker,* USA, 1989.

Other Awards: Co-winner, Great American Playwriting Contest, Actor's Theatre of Louisville, 1978: *Crimes of the Heart,* New York: Viking, 1982. New York Drama Critics Circle Award, Best New American Play, 1981: *Crimes of the Heart.* Guggenheim Award, *Newsday,* 1981.

For More Information: Walker, Beverly, "Beth Henley," *American Film,* December 1986; Isenberg, Barbara, "She'd Rather Do It Herself," *Los Angeles Times,* July 11, 1993.

Commentary: *Crimes of the Heart,* a play about three eccentric sisters set in a small Mississippi town, won the 1981 Pulitzer Prize in Drama for Beth Henley. After initial staging at the Actor's Theatre in Louisville, Kentucky, the play had its New York premier on December 21, 1980 at the Manhattan Theatre Club.

Henley was born in Jackson, Mississippi and attended Southern Methodist University and the University of Illinois. Hers is a regional voice in American theatre. She submitted her play to the Great American

Play Contest at the Actor's Theatre in Louisville, Kentucky and *Crimes of the Heart* was chosen. This set Henley on a course for Broadway. Her other works include *The Miss Firecracker Contest.* Her most recent plays are *Control Freaks* and *L-Play.*

1982

Charles Fuller   225

Birth: March 5, 1939; Philadelphia, PA. **Parents:** Charles H. and Lillian (Anderson) Fuller. **Education:** Villanova University, PA. La Salle College, PA. **Spouse:** Married. **Children:** Two sons.

Prize: *Drama,* 1982: *A Soldier's Play,* New York: Hill and Wang, 1981.

Career: Playwright; Co-Founder and Co-Director, Afro-American Arts Theatre, Philadelphia, PA, 1967-1971; Writer and Director, *The Black Experience,* WIP-Radio, Philadelphia, PA, 1970-1971; Professor, African-American Studies, Temple University, Philadelphia, PA, 1993; Member: Dramatists Guild, PEN, Writers Guild East.

Selected Works: *Zooman and the Sign,* 1982. **Films:** *A Soldier's Story,* Columbia, 1984.

Other Awards: Creative Artist Public Service Award, 1974. Rockefeller Foundation Fellow, 1975. National Endowment for the Arts Fellow, 1976. Guggenheim Fellow, 1977-1978. Obie Award, 1981: *Zooman and the Sign,* New York: S. French, 1982. Audelco Award, Best Writing, 1981: *Zooman and the Sign.* New York Drama Critics Award, Best American Play, 1982: *A Soldier's Play,* New York: Hill and Wang, 1981. Audelco Award, Best Play, 1982: *A Soldier's Play.* Theatre Club Award, Best Play, 1982: *A Soldier's Play.* Outer Circle Critics Award, Best Off-Broadway Play, 1982: *A Soldier's Play.* Hazelitt Award, Pennsylvania State Council on the Arts, 1984. Honorary DFAs: La Salle College, PA, 1982; Villanova University, PA, 1983; Chestnut Hill College, PA, 1985.

For More Information: Anadolu-Okur, Nilgun, *Contemporary African American Theater: Afrocentricity in the Works of Larry Neal, Amiri Baraka, and Charles Fuller,* New York: Garland, 1997.

Commentary: Charles H. Fuller Jr. was awarded the 1982 Pulitzer Prize in Drama for *A Soldier's Play,* the story of a black soldier's murder at a Louisiana training camp during World War II and the subsequent investigation. It premiered on November 20 at New York's Negro Theatre Ensemble Company and starred Denzel Washington.

Fuller was born in Philadelphia, Pennsylvania. He attended Villanova University and La Salle College. He worked for a time as a housing inspector. His first play, *In the Deepest Part of Sleep,* was performed by the Negro Theatre Ensemble in 1974. His other works include *The Brownsville Raid* and numerous screenplays.

1983

Marsha Norman   226
Birth: September 21, 1947; Louisville, KY. **Parents:** Billie Lee and Berta Mae (Conley) Williams. **Education:** Agnes Scott College, GA: BA. University of Louisville, KY. **Spouse:** Michael Norman (div. 1974); Dann C. Byck (m. 1978; div.); Timothy Dykman. **Children:** Angus, Katherine (TD).

Prize: *Drama,* 1983: *'Night, Mother,* New York: Hill and Wang, 1983.

Career: Playwright and producer; Teacher, Kentucky Department of Health, 1969-1970; Teacher, Jefferson County Public Schools, 1970-1972; Teacher, Kentucky Arts Commission, 1972-1976; Book Reviewer and Editor, *Louisville Times,* Louisville, KY, 1974-1979; Worked with disturbed children, Kentucky Central State Hospital; Director, Actors Theatre of Louisville, 1980-1981; Member: Dramatists Guild, International PEN, Writers Guild.

Selected Works: *Getting Out: Play in Two Acts,* 1979. *The Fortune Teller,* 1987. *Four Plays,* 1988. *The Secret Garden* (Adaptation) (with Lucy Simon), 1992. **Films:** *'Night Mother,* Blackbird Productions, 1986.

Other Awards: American Theater Critics Association, Best Play Produced in Regional Theatre, 1977-1978: *Getting Out,* New York: Dramatists Play Service, 1979. National Endowment for the Arts Grant, 1978-1979. Actors Theatre of Louisville. John Gassner New Playwrights Medallion. George Oppenheimer-Newsday Award, 1979: *Getting Out.* Outer Critics Circle Award, 1979: *Getting Out.* Rockefeller Playwright-in-Residence Grant, Mark Taper Forum, 1979-1980. Susan Smith Blackburn Prize. Elizabeth Hull-Kate Warriner Award, Dramatists Guild, 1983: *'Night, Mother,* New York: Hill and Wang, 1983. Literary Lion Award, New York Public Library, 1986. Antoinette Perry Award, Best Book of a Musical, 1991: *The Secret Garden,* New York: Theatre Communications Group, 1992. Drama Desk Award, Best Book of a Musical, 1991: *The Secret Garden.* American Academy and Institute for Arts and Letters Grant.

For More Information: Kintz, Linda, *The Subject's Tragedy: Political Poetics, Feminist Theory, and Drama,* Ann Arbor, NY: University of Michigan, 1992.

Commentary: *'Night, Mother,* a play about a lonely daughter's announcement of her plans to commit suicide, won the 1983 Pulitzer Prize in Drama for Marsha Norman. It premiered on March 31, 1983 at New York's John Golden Theater with Kathy Bates in the lead role.

Norman was born Marsha Williams in Louisville, Kentucky. Norman had worked with emotionally disturbed children and later taught at a middle school for gifted children in Louisville. She began to submit writing pieces to newspapers and eventually wrote *Getting Out,* a play about a rehabilitated parolee who struggles to keep her best self, which met with critical acclaim and eventually opened in New York's off-Broadway district. Her other works include *The Shakers* and *Traveler in the Dark.*

1984

David Mamet   227
Birth: November 30, 1947; Chicago, IL. **Parents:** Bernard Morris and Lenore June (Silver) Mamet. **Education:** Neighborhood Playhouse School of the Theater. Goddard College, VT: BA. **Spouse:** Lindsay Crouse (m. 1977; div); Rebecca Pidgeon (m. 1991). **Children:** Willa (RP).

Prize: *Drama,* 1984: *Glengarry Glen Ross,* New York: Grove, 1983.

Career: Playwright, screenwriter, and director; Special Lecturer in Drama, Marlboro College, 1970; Artist-in-Residence in Drama, Goddard College, 1971-1973; Founder, St. Nicholas Theater Company, Chicago, IL, 1973; Artistic director, St. Nicholas Theater Company, Chicago, IL, 1973-1976; Member, Board of Directors, St. Nicholas Theater Company, Chicago, IL, 1973; Faculty member, Illinois Arts Council, 1974; Visiting Lecturer in Drama, University of Chicago, 1975-76 and 1979; Teaching Fellow, School of Drama, Yale University, 1976-1977; Associate Artistic Director, Goodman Theater, Chicago, 1978-1979; Guest Lecturer, New York University, 1981; Associate Professor of Film, Columbia University, 1988; Chairman of the Board, Atlantic Theater Company; Member: Actors Equity Association, Dramatists Guild, PEN, Randolph A. Hollister Association, United Steelworkers of America, Writers Guild of America.

Selected Works: *Life in the Theatre* (Typescript), 1975. *American Buffalo* (Typescript), 1975. *The Water Engine: An American Fable,* 1977. *A Life in the Theatre,* 1977. *A Sermon* (Typescript), 1978. *Lone Canoe; or, the Explorer* (Typescript), 1978. *The Water Engine: An American Fable; and Mr. Happiness: Two Plays,* 1978. *Sexual Perversity in Chicago and The Duck Variations: Two Plays,* 1978. *The Postman Always Rings Twice* (Typescript), 1979. *Reunion; Dark Pony: Two Plays* (Adaptation), 1979. *The Woods: A Play,* 1979. *Edmond: A Play,* 1983. *Warm and Cold,* 1985. *The Shawl; and, Prairie du Chien: Two Plays,* 1985. *Goldberg Street: Short Plays and Monologues,* 1985. *Writing in Restaurants,* 1986. *House of Games,* 1987. *Speed-the-Plow: A Play,*

1987. *Things Change: A Screenplay* (with Shel Silverstein), 1988. *Uncle Vanya* (Adaptation), 1988. *Some Freaks,* 1989. *The Three Sisters* (Adaptation), 1990. *Five Television Plays,* 1990. *We're No Angels: A Screenplay,* 1990. *On Directing Film,* 1991. *The Cabin: Reminiscence and Diversions,* 1992. *Homicide,* 1992. *Oleanna,* 1992. *The Cryptogram,* 1995. *Passover,* 1995. *Make-Believe Town: Essays and Remembrances,* 1996. *True and False: Heresy and Common Sense for the Actor,* 1997. *The Old Religion,* 1997. **Films:** *The Verdict,* 20th Century Fox, 1982; *House of Games,* Filmhaus, 1987; *The Untouchables,* Paramount, 1987; *Homicide,* Cinehaus, 1991; *Glengarry Glen Ross,* New Line Cinema, 1992.

Other Awards: Joseph Jefferson Award, 1975: *Sexual Perversity in Chicago.* Joseph Jefferson Award, 1976: *American Buffalo.* Obie Award, *Village Voice,* Best New Playwright, 1976: *Sexual Perversity in Chicago.* Obie Award, *Village Voice,* Best New Playwright, 1976: *American Buffalo.* Obie Award, *Village Voice,* Best American Play, 1983: *Edmond,* New York: Grove, 1983. Children's Theater Grant, New York State Council on the Arts, 1976. Rockefeller Grant, 1976. Columbia Broadcasting System Fellowship, Creative Writing, 1976. New York Drama Critics Circle Award, Best American Play, 1977: *American Buffalo.* New York Drama Critics Circle Award, Best American Play, 1984: *Glengarry Glen Ross,* New York: Grove, 1983. Outer Critics Circle Award, Contributions to the American Theater, 1978. Joseph Dintenfass Award, 1984: *Glengarry Glen Ross.* Hull-Warriner Award, Dramatists Guild, 1984. American Academy and Institute of Arts and Letters, Award for Literature, 1986.

For More Information: Bigsby, C. W. E., *David Mamet,* London; New York: Methuen, 1985; Kane, Leslie, ed., *David Mamet: A Casebook,* New York: Garland, 1992; Brewer, Gay, *David Mamet and Film: Illusion/Disillusion in a Wounded Land,* Jefferson, NC: McFarland, 1993; McDonough, Carla J., *Staging Masculinity: Male Identity in Contemporary American Drama,* Jefferson, NC: McFarland, 1997.

Commentary: David Mamet was awarded the 1984 Pulitzer Prize in Drama for *Glengarry Glen Ross,* a play about five middle-aged real estate scammers competing for buyers of worthless property. It was staged initially in London and had its New York premier on March 25, 1984 at the John Golden Theater.

Mamet was born in Chicago and has become one of the preeminent writers of plays and screen stories in America today. He began as an actor at the Neighborhood Playhouse while still in college. He founded the Saint Nicholas Company as a staging ground for his plays. His *American Buffalo* premiered on Broadway in 1977 and his career took off from there. Critics compared *Glengarry* to Arthur Miller's *Death of a*

Salesman. His film credits include the scripts for *The Untouchables* and *House of Games.*

1985

James Lapine 228

Birth: January 10, 1949; Mansfield, OH. **Parents:** David Sanford and Lillian (Feld) Lapine. **Education:** Franklin and Marshall College, PA: BA. California Institute of Arts, CA: MFA. **Spouse:** Sarah Marshall Kernachan (m. 1985). **Children:** Phoebe.

Prize: *Drama,* 1985: *Sunday in the Park With George,* New York: Studio Duplicating Service, 1983.

Career: Graphic designer, photographer; Stage director and writer; Architectural Preservationist, Architectural League of NY, 1973-1975; Resident Graphic Designer and Teacher, Drama School, Yale University, CT, beginning in 1976; Teacher, Fashion Institute of Technology; Director of stage productions, 1981-1994; Director of films, 1988-1993.

Selected Works: *Twelve Dreams* (with Steven Sondheim), 1982. *Table Settings,* 1980. *Into the Woods* (with Steven Sondheim), 1989. *Falsettoland* (with William Finn), 1991. *Passion: A Musical* (with Steven Sondheim), 1994.

Other Awards: Obie Award, *Village Voice: Photograph.* George Oppenheimer/Newsday Award: *Table Settings.* New York Drama Critics Circle Award, Best Musical Book, 1984. Olivier Award: *Sunday in the Park with George.* Antoinette Perry Award, Best Musical Book, 1988: *Into the Woods.* Drama Desk Award, 1988: *Into the Woods.* New York Drama Critics Circle, Best Book from a Musical, 1988: *Into the Woods.* Evening Standard Award and London Critics Award, 1991: *Into the Woods.* Co-winner, Outer Critics Circle Award, Best Musical, 1990: *Falsettoland.* Antoinette Perry Award, Best Musical Book, 1992: *Falsettoland.* Co-winner, Antoinette Perry Award, Best Musical, 1994: *Passion.* Antoinette Perry Award Best Book of a Musical, 1994: *Passion.* Drama Desk Award, Best Book of a Musical, 1994: *Passion.* Honorary Degree, Franklin and Marshall College, 1994.

For More Information: Rosen, Carol, "Lucky Lapine," *Village Voice,* April 11, 1995; Hogrefe, Jeffrey, "On the Park with James Lapine," *Architectural Digest,* November 1995.

Commentary: Stephen Sondheim and James Lapine were awarded the 1985 Pulitzer Prize in Drama for *Sunday in the Park With George,* the musical dramatization of George Seurat's painting *A Sunday Afternoon on the Island of La Grande Jette* come to life. It premiered at New York's Booth Theater on May 2, 1984.

Lapine was born in Mansfield, Ohio. He attended

Franklin & Marshall College and the California Institute of Arts. His directing credits include *March of the Falsettos, A Midsummer Night's Dream,* and *Into the Woods.*

Stephen Sondheim 229

Birth: March 22, 1930; New York, NY. **Parents:** Herbert and Janet Leshkin (Fox) Sondheim. **Education:** Williams College, MA: BA, magna cum laude.

Prize: *Drama,* 1985: *Sunday in the Park With George,* New York: Studio Duplicating Service, 1983.

Career: Composer and lyricist; President, Dramatists Guild, 1973-1981; Visiting Professor of Drama and Musical Theater and Fellow, St. Catherine's College, Oxford University, England, 1990; Professor, Juilliard School of Music, Lincoln Center of the Performing Arts; Member: American Academy and Institute of Arts and Letters, American Society of Composers, Authors, and Publishers (ASCAP), Authors League of America, Writers Guild of America.

Selected Works: *West Side Story* (with Arthur Laurents and Jerome Robbins), 1958. *Gypsy* (with Arthur Laurents), 1960. *A Funny Thing Happened on the Way to the Forum* (with Burt Shevelove and Larry Gelbart), 1963. *Anyone Can Whistle* (with Arthur Laurents), 1965. *Do I Hear a Waltz?* (with Arthur Laurents), 1966. *Company* (with George Furth), 1970. *Follies* (with James Goldman), 1971. *A Little Night Music* (with Hugh Wheeler), 1974. *Pacific Overtures* (with John Weidman and Hugh Wheeler), 1977. *Sweeney Todd: The Demon Barber of Fleet Street* (with Hugh Wheeler), 1979. *Into the Woods* (with James Lapine), 1989. *Assassins,* 1991. *Passion* (with James Lapine), 1994. *Getting Away with Murder* (with George Furth), 1997. **Films:** *West Side Story,* United Artists, 1961.

Other Awards: Hutchinson Prize, Williams College, 1950. *Evening Standard* Drama Award, Best Musical, 1959: *Gypsy.* Antoinette Perry Award, 1963: *A Funny Thing Happened on the Way to the Forum.* Best Composer, New York Drama Critics' Poll, *Variety,* 1969-70: *Company.* Drama Desk Award, Music and Lyrics, 1969-70: *Company.* Grammy Award, Best Musical Cast Album, National Academy of Recording Arts and Sciences, 1970: *Company.* New York Drama Critics' Circle Award, Best New Musical, 1970: *Company.* Best Composer and Lyricist, New York Drama Critics' Poll, *Variety,* 1970-71: *Follies.* Drama Desk Award, Music and Lyrics, 1970-71: *Follies.* Antoinette Perry Award, Best Music, 1971: *Company.* Antoinette Perry Award, Best Lyrics, 1971: *Company.* New York Drama Critics' Circle Award, Best New Musical, 1971: *Follies.* Drama Desk Award, Music and Lyrics, 1972-73: *A Little Night Music.* Co-Winner, Edgar Allan Poe Award,

Best Motion Picture Screenplay, Mystery Writers of America, 1973: *The Last of Sheila. Evening Standard* Drama Award, Best Musical, 1973: *A Little Night Music.* Grammy Award, Best Musical Cast Album, 1973: *A Little Night Music.* Musical Salute from the American Musical and Dramatic Academy and the National Hemophilia Foundation at Shubert Theatre, 1973. New York Drama Critics' Circle Award, Best New Musical, 1973: *A Little Night Music.* Los Angeles Drama Critics' Circle Award, Music and Lyrics, 1974-75: *A Little Night Music.* Grammy Award, Song of the Year, 1975: "Send in the Clowns," from *A Little Night Music.* New York Drama Critics' Circle Award, Best New Musical, 1976: *Pacific Overtures.* Drama Desk Award, Music and Lyrics, 1978-79: *Sweeney Todd.* Antoinette Perry Award, Best Score, 1979: *A Little Night Music.* Antoinette Perry Award, Best Score, 1979: *Sweeney Todd.* Elizabeth Hull-Kate Warriner Award, Dramatists Guild, 1979: *Sweeney Todd.* Grammy Award, Best Musical Cast Album, 1979: *Sweeney Todd.* New York Drama Critics' Circle Award, Best New Musical, 1979: *Sweeney Todd.* Drama Desk Award, Music and Lyrics, 1981-82: *Merrily We Roll Along.* Brandeis University Creative Arts Award, Theater Arts, 1982. Unique Contribution Award, Drama League of New York, 1983. Drama Desk Award, Lyrics, 1983-84: *Sunday in the Park with George.* New York Drama Critics' Circle Award, Best New Musical, 1984: *Sunday in the Park with George.* Grammy Award, Best Musical Cast Album, 1984: *Sunday in the Park with George.* Common Wealth Award of Distinguished Service, Dramatic Arts, Bank of Delaware, 1984. Grammy Award, Best Musical Cast Album, 1986: *Follies in Concert.* Drama Desk Award, Lyrics and Outstanding Musical, 1987-88: *Into the Woods.* Evening Standard Drama Award, Best Musical, 1987: *Follies.* Antoinette Perry Award, Best Score, 1988: *Into the Woods.* Grammy Award, Best Musical Cast Album, 1988: *Into the Woods.* Laurence Olivier Award, Musical of the Year, Society of West End Theatre, England, 1988: *Follies.* New York Drama Critics' Circle Award, Best New Musical, 1988: *Into the Woods. Evening Standard* Drama Award, Best Musical, 1989: *Into the Woods.* Lion of the Performing Arts, New York Public Library, 1989. Los Angeles Drama Critics' Circle Award, Original Musical Score, 1989: *Into the Woods.* Academy Award, Best Original Song, 1990: "Sooner or Later (I Always Get My Man)" from *Dick Tracy.* Laurence Olivier Award, Musical of the Year, Society of West End Theatre, England, 1991: *Sunday in the Park with George.* National Medal of Arts Award, National Endowment for the Arts, 1992. Honor for Lifetime Achievement, Kennedy Center, 1993. Honorary Doctorate, Williams College, 1971.

For More Information: Zadan, Craig, *Sondheim & Co,* New York: Macmillan, 1974; Gordon, Joanne

L., *Art Isn't Easy: The Achievement of Stephen Sondheim,* Carbondale: Southern Illinois University Press, 1990; Banfield, Stephen, *Sondheim's Broadway Musicals,* Ann Arbor: University of Michigan Press, 1993; Gottfried, Martin, *Sondheim,* New York: H.N. Abrams, 1993.

Commentary: Stephen Sondheim and James Lapine were awarded the 1985 Pulitzer Prize in Drama for *Sunday in the Park With George,* the musical dramatization of George Seurat's painting *A Sunday Afternoon on the Island of La Grande Jette* come to life. It premiered at New York's Booth Theater on May 2, 1984.

Sondheim was born in New York City. As a composer and lyricist, Sondheim has produced over 40 works for the theatre, as well as film and television pieces. After attending Williams College, he studied with the composer Milton Babbitt and Oscar Hammerstein II. He has worked with Leonard Bernstein and Jules Styne, among others. He is well known for such works as *West Side Story, A Funny Thing Happened on the Way to the Forum,* and *Sweeney Todd: The Demon Barber of Fleet Street.* He teaches at the Juilliard School at Lincoln Center for the Performing Arts. He has won numerous Tony Awards.

1986
No award

1987

August Wilson   230

Birth: April 27, 1945; Pittsburgh, PA. **Parents:** Frederick August and Daisy Wilson. **Spouse:** Second marriage, Judy Oliver (m. 1981; div.); Constanza Romero. **Children:** Sakena Ansari.

Prize: *Drama,* 1987: *Fences,* New York: New American Library, 1986. *Drama,* 1990: *The Piano Lesson,* New York: Dutton, 1990.

Career: Writer; Co-Founder, Scriptwriter, and Director, Black Horizons on the Hill Theatre Company, Pittsburgh, PA, 1968-1978; Scriptwriter, Science Museum of Minnesota, St. Paul, 1979.

Selected Works: *Ma Rainey's Black Bottom,* 1985. *Joe Turner's Come and Gone,* 1988. *Two Trains Running,* 1992. *Seven Guitars,* 1996. **Films:** *The Piano Lesson* (TV), 1995.

Other Awards: New York Drama Critics Circle Award, Best Play of 1984-85, 1985: *Ma Rainey's Black Bottom,* New York: French, 1985. Whiting Writers' Award, Whiting Foundation, 1986: *Ma Rainey's Black Bottom.* Outstanding Play Award from American Theatre Critics, 1986: *Fences,* New York: New American Library, 1986. Drama Desk Outstanding New Play Award, 1986: *Fences.* New York Drama

Critics Circle Best Play Award, 1986: *Fences.* Antoinette Perry Award, Best Play, 1987: *Fences.* Outer Critics Circle Award, Best Broadway Play, 1987: *Fences.* John Gassner Award for Best American Playwright, Outer Critics Circle, 1987. Artist of the Year, *Chicago Tribune,* 1987. Literary Lion Award, New York Public Library, 1988. New York Drama Critics Circle Best Play Award, 1988: *Joe Turner's Come and Gone,* New York: New American Library, 1988. Drama Desk Outstanding New Play Award, 1990: *The Piano Lesson,* New York: Dutton, 1990. New York Drama Critics Circle Best Play Award, 1990: *The Piano Lesson.* Antoinette Perry Award, Best Play, 1990: *The Piano Lesson.* American Theatre Critics Outstanding Play Award, 1990: *The Piano Lesson.* Black Filmmakers Hall of Fame Award, 1991. American Theatre Critics' Association Award, 1992: *Two Trains Running,* New York: Plume, 1992. Clarence Muse Award, Guggenheim Foundation Fellowship.

For More Information: Pereira, Kim, *August Wilson and the African-American Odyssey,* Urbana: University of Illinois, 1995; Shannon, Sandra G., *The Dramatic Vision of August Wilson,* Washington, DC: Howard University, 1995; McDonough, Carla J., *Staging Masculinity: Male Identity in Contemporary American Drama,* Jefferson, NC: McFarland, 1997.

Commentary: August Wilson has won two Pulitzer Prizes, both in Drama. He won his first prize in 1987 for *Fences,* a play about a father and son and their disagreements. It premiered on May 26, 1987 at New York's 46th Street Theatre. His second prize was awarded in 1990 for *The Piano Lesson,* set in the 1930s and concerning a family heirloom. It premiered at New York's Manhattan Theatre Club. After winning the Pulitzer Prize, the play was moved to the Walter Kerr Theatre on April 16, 1990.

Wilson was born in Pittsburgh, Pennsylvania. He was self-educated. Wilson was a co-founder in 1968 of Black Horizons Theatre in Pittsburgh. He published poetry before turning to playwriting. His plays follow a pattern in that each is set in a different decade of the 20th century. He had his first big success with *Ma Rainey's Black Bottom* in 1985. His other works include *Joe Turner's Come and Gone* and *Seven Guitars.*

1988

Alfred Uhry   231

Birth: December 3, 1936; Atlanta, GA. **Parents:** Ralph K. and Alene Uhry. **Education:** Brown University, RI: BA. **Spouse:** Joanna Kellogg. **Children:** Emily Uhry Rhea, Elizabeth Uhry MacCurrach, Katherine, Nell.

Prize: *Drama,* 1988: *Driving Miss Daisy,* New York: Theatre Communications Group, 1988.

Career: Playwright and lyricist, worked with composer Frank Loesser, 1960-1963; Instructor, English and Drama, Calhoun High School, New York City; Affiliated, Goodspeed Opera House, 1980-1984; Instructor of Lyric Writing, New York University, New York City, 1985-1988; Comedy writer, scripts for television; Member: Academy of Motion Picture Arts and Sciences, Dramatists Guild.

Selected Works: *The Robber Bridegroom,* 1976. *The Last Night of Ballyhoo,* 1997. **Films:** *Mystic Pizza,* Samuel Goldwyn, 1988; *Driving Miss Daisy,* Warner Brothers, 1989.

Other Awards: Academy Award, Best Screenplay Adaptation, Academy of Motion Picture Arts and Sciences, 1990: *Driving Miss Daisy.*

For More Information: Graham, Keith, "Alfred Uhry Driven by His Craft," *Atlanta Constitution,* April 25, 1990; Witchel, Alex, "Remembering Prejudice, of a Different Sort," *New York Times,* February 23, 1997.

Commentary: Alfred Fox Uhry was awarded the 1988 Pulitzer Prize in Drama for *Driving Miss Daisy,* a Southern tale of the long and close relationship of a black chauffeur and his white Jewish employer. It premiered on April 15, 1987 at New York's Playwright's Horizons.

Uhry was born in Atlanta, Georgia. He attended Brown University. He has written masterfully, from experience, about Jews and blacks living closely in the South. His other works include *The Robber Bridegroom.*

1989

Wendy Wasserstein   232

Birth: October 17, 1950; New York, NY. **Parents:** Morris W. and Lola (Schleifer) Wasserstein. **Education:** Mount Holyoke College, MA: BA. City College, NY: MA. Yale University Drama School, CT: MFA.

Prize: *Drama,* 1989: *The Heidi Chronicles and Other Plays,* San Diego, CA: Harcourt Brace Jovanovich, 1990.

Career: Dramatist, screenwriter and actress; Teacher, Columbia University, NY; Teacher, New York University, NY; Board Member, British American Arts Association; Board Member, McDowell Colony; Board Member,WNET; Member of Artistic Board, Playwrights Horizons; Member, Dramatists Guild for Young Playwrights; Member of Steering and Women's Committees, Dramatists Guild.

Selected Works: *Uncommon Women and Others,* 1978. *Isn't It Romantic,* 1985. *Bachelor Girls,* 1990. *The Sisters Rosensweig,* 1993. **Films:** *The Heidi Chronicles* (TV), 1995.

Other Awards: Joseph Jefferson Award: *Uncommon Women and Others,* New York: Dramatists

Play Service, 1978. Dramalogue Award: *Uncommon Women and Others.* Inner Boston Critics Award: *Uncommon Women and Others.* Hale Mathews Foundation Award. Guggenheim Fellowship, 1983. Grant for Writing and Studying Theater in England, British-American Arts Association. Grant for Playwriting, American Playwrights Project, 1988. Antoinette Perry Award, Best Play, 1989: *The Heidi Chronicles,* San Diego, CA: Harcourt Brace Jovanovich, 1990. Drama Desk Award, 1989: *The Heidi Chronicles.* Outer Critics Circle Award, 1989: *The Heidi Chronicles.* Susan Smith Blackburn Prize Award for Best New Play, 1989: *The Heidi Chronicles.* New York Drama Critics' Circle Award, 1989: *The Heidi Chronicles.* Outer Critics Circle Award, 1993: *The Sisters Rosensweig,* New York: Harcourt Brace Jovanovich, 1993.

For More Information: Miller, Judith, "The Secret Wendy Wasserstein," *New York Times,* October 18, 1992; "The Family Wasserstein, *New York,* January 4, 1993; Green, Blake, "A Witty Playwright's Reflections on Herself," *San Francisco Chronicle,* February 8, 1993.

Commentary: *The Heidi Chronicles,* a play about a woman who questions her choices in life but manages to find happiness in the end, won the 1990 Pulitzer Prize in Drama for Wendy Wasserstein. It premiered at New York's Playwright's Horizons and moved to the Plymouth Theatre on March 9, 1989.

Wasserstein was born in New York City. She attended Mount Holyoke College and the Yale School of Drama. Her first major work, *Uncommon Women and Others,* was produced at Playwright's Horizons. *The Heidi Chronicles* was somewhat autobiographical. Her other works include *The Sisters Rosensweig* and *Pamela's First Musical.*

1990

August Wilson

Full entry appears as #**230** under "Drama," 1987.

1991

Neil Simon   233

Birth: July 4, 1927; Bronx, NY. **Parents:** Irving and Mamie Simon. **Education:** New York University. University of Denver, CO. **Spouse:** Joan Baim (m. 1953; died 1973); Marsha Mason (m. 1973; sep. 1983; div); Diana Lander (m. 1987; div. 1989; rem. 1990). **Children:** Ellen, Nancy (JB).

Prize: *Drama,* 1991: *Lost in Yonkers,* New York: Iron Mountain Productions, 1991.

Career: Playwright and producer; Served in U.S. Army Air Force Reserve; Sports Editor of *Rev-Meter,*

U.S. Army, Lowry Field Base newspaper, CO, 1946; Mail Room Clerk, Warner Brothers, NY, 1946; Comedy Writer, Goodman Ace, CBS Radio, New York City, late 1940s; Comedy Writer, Robert Q. Lewis's *The Little Show,* radio, late 1940s; Comedy Writer, *The Phil Silvers Arrow Show,* NBC TV, 1948, *The Tallulah Bankhead Show,* NBC TV, 1951, Sid Caesar's *Your Show of Shows,* NBC TV, 1956-1957, *The Phil Silvers Show,* CBS TV, 1958-1959, *The Garry Moore Show,* CBS TV, 1959-1960, for *The Jackie Gleason Show* and *The Red Buttons Show,* CBS TV; Member: Dramatists Guild, Writers Guild of America.

Selected Works: *Come Blow Your Horn: A Comedy in Three Acts,* 1961. *Barefoot in the Park,* 1964. *The Odd Couple,* 1966. *The Star-Spangled Girl,* 1967. *Plaza Suite,* 1969. *Promises, Promises* (Adaptation), 1969. *The Comedy of Neil Simon,* 1971. *The Gingerbread Lady,* 1971. *The Prisoner of Second Avenue,* 1972. *The Sunshine Boys,* 1973. *The Good Doctor* (Adaptation), 1974. *God's Favorite,* 1975. *California Suite,* 1977. *The Collected Plays of Neil Simon, Volume II,* 1979. *Chapter Two,* 1979. *They're Playing Our Song,* 1980. *I Ought to Be in Pictures,* 1981. *Fools: A Comic Fable,* 1981. *Brighton Beach Memoirs,* 1984. *Biloxi Blues,* 1986. *Broadway Bound,* 1987. *Rumors: A Farce,* 1990. *Jake's Women,* 1994. *Laughter on the 23rd Floor,* 1995. *Rewrites: A Memoir,* 1996. **Films:** *The Odd Couple,* Paramount, 1968; *The Goodbye Girl,* Warner Bros., 1977; *Lost in Yonkers,* Columbia, 1993.

Other Awards: Emmy Award, Academy of Television Arts and Sciences Award, 1957: *Your Show of Shows.* Emmy Award, Academy of Television Arts and Sciences Award, 1959: *The Phil Silvers Show.* Antoinette Perry Award Award, Best Playwright, 1965: *The Odd Couple,* Evening Standard Drama Award, London, 1967: *Sweet Charity.* Sam S. Shubert Foundation Award, 1968. Writers Guild Award, 1969: *The Odd Couple,* 1970: *Last of the Red Hot Lovers.* Writers Guild Award, 1971: *The Out-of-Towners.* Entertainer of the Year, *Cue,* 1972. Writers Guild Award, 1972: *The Trouble with People.* New York Drama Critics Circle Award, 1983: *Brighton Beach Memoirs.* Theater Hall of Fame, Uris Theater, 1983. Antoinette Perry Award Award, Best Drama, 1985: *Biloxi Blues.* Antoinette Perry Award Award, Best Drama, 1991: *Lost in Yonkers.* Neil Simon Tribute Show, Shubert Theater, March 1, 1987. Drama Desk Award, 1991: *Lost in Yonkers.* Honorary LHD, Hofstra University, NY, 1981.

For More Information: McGovern, Edythe M., *Neil Simom: A Critical Study,* New York: Ungar, 1979; Johnson, Robert K., *Neil Simon,* Boston: Twayne, 1983; Konas, Gary, ed., *Neil Simon: A Casebook,* New York: Garland, 1997.

Commentary: Neil Simon was awarded the 1991 Pulitzer Prize in Drama for *Lost in Yonkers,* a comedy set in 1942 about two boys who are dropped off at their grandmother's house, and their assorted relatives. It premiered on February 21, 1991 at the Richard Rodgers Theatre.

Simon was born Marvin Neil Simon in the Bronx section of New York City. He attended New York University and the University of Denver. A talented comic writer, he wrote for television's Sid Caesar, Phil Silvers, Garry Moore, and Jackie Gleason. His first play, *Come Blow Your Horn,* was produced in 1960. He has had one Broadway success after another ever since, with many of his plays being made into films. His many works include *Barefoot in the Park, Star Spangled Girl, The Odd Couple,* and the autobiographical trilogy *Brighton Beach Memoirs, Biloxi Blues,* and *Broadway Bound.*

1992

Robert Schenkkan   234

Birth: March 19, 1953; Chapel Hill, NC. **Parents:** Robert Frederic Sr. and Jean (McKenzie) Schenkkan. **Education:** University of Texas: BA. Cornell University, NY: MFA. **Spouse:** Mary Ann Dorward (m. 1984). **Children:** Sarah Victoria, Joshua McHenry.

Prize: *Drama,* 1992: *The Kentucky Cycle,* New York: Plume, 1993.

Career: Playwright; Actor in theater, film, and television; Member: Actors' Equity Association, American Federation of Television and Radio Artists, Dramatists Guild, Ensemble Studio Theatre, New Dramatists, Screen Actors Guild.

Selected Works: *Fourteen Plays for the Church* (with Kai Jurgensen), 1948.

Other Awards: Best of the Fringe Award, Edinburgh Festival, 1984: *The Survivalist.* Creative Artists Public Service Program Grant, State of New York, 1985: *Final Passages.* Playwrights Forum Award, 1988: *Tall Tales.* Julie Harris Playwright Award from Beverly Hills Theatre Guild, 1989: *Heaven on Earth.* Arthur Foundation Grant, 1989: *The Kentucky Cycle.* Vogelstein Foundation Grant, 1989: *The Kentucky Cycle.*

For More Information: Shirley, Don, "Drama Pulitzer Breaks N.Y. Monopoly," *Los Angeles Times,* April 8, 1992; Scheck, Frank, "Appalachia Stint Fuels Pulitzer-Winning Play," *Christian Science Monitor,* November 30, 1993; Shirley, Don, 'Cycle' Retains Power in its Return to L.A.," *Los Angeles Times,* April 27, 1995.

Commentary: *The Kentucky Cycle,* a story of three families and one piece of land over 200 years, or an exploration of the myth of the American frontier, won the 1992 Pulitzer Prize in Drama for Robert

Schenkkan. It premiered in Seattle and moved to the Mark Taper Forum in Los Angeles on February 2, 1992.

Schenkkan was born in Chapel Hill, North Carolina. He attended the University of Texas at Austin and Cornell University. He has worked as an actor and writer on Broadway, off-Broadway, and at regional theatres across the country. *The Kentucky Cycle,* favored on the West Coast, was not a critical success in New York. His other works include *Heaven on Earth, Final Passages,* and *Conversations With the Spanish Lady and Other Plays.*

1993

Tony Kushner   235

Birth: July 16, 1956; New York, NY. **Parents:** Bill and Sylvia Kushner. **Education:** Columbia University, NY: BA. New York University: MFA.

Prize: *Drama,* 1993: *Angels in America: A Gay Fantasia on National Themes. Part One, Millennium Approaches,* London, England: Royal National Theatre/Nick Hern, 1992.

Career: Switchboard Operator, United Nations Plaza Hotel, 1979-1985; Assistant Director, St. Louis Repertory Theatre, 1985-1986; Artistic Director, New York Theatre Workshop, 1987-1988; Director of Literary Services, Theatre Communication Group, New York City, 1990-1991; Playwright-in-Residence, Juilliard School of Drama, New York City, 1990-1992; Guest Artist, New York University Graduate Theatre Program; Guest Artist, Yale University; Guest Artist, Princeton University; Member, AIDS Coalition to Unleash Power (ACT UP).

Selected Works: *7 Different Plays,* 1988. *A Bright Room Called Day,* 1994. *The Holocaust and the Liberal Imagination: A Social and Cultural History,* 1994. *Thinking about the Longstanding Problems of Virtue and Happiness: Essays, a Play, Two Poems, and a Prayer,* 1995.

Other Awards: Directing Fellowship, National Endowment for the Arts, 1985, 1987, 1993. Princess Grace Award, 1986. Playwriting Fellowship, New York State Council for the Arts, 1987. John Whiting Award, Arts Council of Great Britain, 1990. Kennedy Center / American Express Fund for New American Plays Awards, 1990, 1992. Kesserling Award, National Arts Club, 1992. Will Glickman Playwriting Prize, 1992. *London Evening Standard* Award, 1992. Antoinette Perry Award, Best Play, 1993: *Millennium Approaches, Part One of Angels in America.* New York Drama Critics Circle Award, Best New Play, 1993: *Millennium Approaches, Part One of Angels in America.* American Academy of Arts and Letters Award, 1994: *Perestroika, Part Two of Angels in*

America. Antoinette Perry Award, Best Play, 1994: *Perestroika, Part Two of Angels in America.*

For More Information: Brask, Per, ed., *Essays on Kushner's Angels,* Winnipeg, Canada: Blizzard, 1995; Vorlicky, Robert, ed., *Tony Kushner in Conversation,* Ann Arbor: University of Michigan, 1998.

Commentary: Tony Kushner was awarded the 1993 Pulitzer Prize in Drama for *Angels in America: Millennium Approaches,* an unconventional play about homosexuality, AIDS, and the Reagan era. It premiered on May 4, 1992 at the Walter Kerr Theatre.

Kushner was born in New York City. He grew up mostly in Louisiana where his family owned a lumber business. He attended Columbia and New York universities. His first play, *A Bright Room Called Day,* was produced in San Francisco and Chicago. He received unanimous critical acclaim for *Angels* and its second part, *Perestroika.*

1994

Edward Franklin Albee

Full entry appears as #**210** under "Drama," 1967.

1995

Horton Foote   236

Birth: March 14, 1916; Wharton, TX. **Parents:** Albert and Hallie (Brooks) Foote. **Education:** Pasadena Playhouse School of Theatre. Tamara Darkarhovna School of Theatre. **Spouse:** Lillian Vallish (m. 1945). **Children:** Barbara Hallie, Albert Horton, Walter Vallish, Daisy Brooks.

Prize: *Drama,* 1995: *The Young Man from Atlanta,* New York: Dutton, 1995.

Career: Writer for stage, screen, and television; Actor in Broadway plays, 1932-1942; Manager and Instructor, Playwriting and Acting for Productions, Inc., Washington, DC, 1945-1949; Teleplay Writer, ABC, BBC, CBS, NBC; Member: Writers Guild of America, Authors Guild, Dramatists Guild, Fellowship of Southern Writers, Texas Institute of Letters.

Selected Works: *The Chase* (play), 1952. *The Trip to Bountiful,* 1954. *A Young Lady of Property: Six Short Plays,* 1955. *The Traveling Lady,* 1955. *The Chase,* 1956. *Harrison, Texas: Eight Television Plays,* 1956. *The Midnight Caller: A Play in One Act,* 1959. *Three Plays: Old Man, Tomorrow Adapted from Stories,* 1962. *To Kill a Mockingbird* (screenplay), 1964. *Courtship,* 1984. *Tomorrow and Tomorrow,* 1985. *Courtship, Valentine's Day, 1918: Three Plays from "The Orphans' Home Cycle,"* 1987. *Roots in a Parched Ground; Convicts; Lily Dale; The Widow Claire: The First Four Plays of "The Orphans' Home Cycle,"* 1988. *Cousins; and,*

The Death of Papa: The Final Two Plays of "The Orphans' Home Cycle," 1989. *To Kill a Mockingbird; Tender Mercies; and, The Trip to Bountiful: Three Screenplays,* 1989. *Horton Foote's Three Trips to Bountiful,* 1993. **Films:** *To Kill a Mockingbird,* Universal, 1962; *Tender Mercies,* EMI, 1983; *The Trip to Bountiful,* USA, 1985.

Other Awards: Academy Award, Best Screenplay, Academy of Motion Picture Arts and Sciences, 1962: *To Kill a Mockingbird.* Writers Guild of America Screen Award, 1962: *To Kill a Mockingbird.* Academy Award, Best Screenplay, Academy of Motion Picture Arts and Sciences, 1983: *Tender Mercies.* Evelyn Burkey Award, Writers Guild, 1989. Honorary Degrees: American Film Institute; Austin College, TX; Drew University, NJ.

For More Information: Wood, Gordon C., ed., *Horton Foote: A Casebook,* New York: Garland, 1998.

Commentary: Horton Foote was awarded the 1995 Pulitzer Prize in Drama for *The Young Man From Atlanta,* which premiered in Atlanta at the Signature Theatre Company and, two years later on March 27, 1997, opened at New York's Longacre Theatre.

Foote was born in Wharton, Texas. He attended professional theatre schools. He worked on Broadway in the 1930s and managed a theatre company in Washington, DC in the late 1940s. He has had a long and successful career in the theatre, film, and television. He wrote many screenplays, including the adaptation of Harper Lee's Pulitzer Prize-winning novel *To Kill a Mockingbird.* His other works include *The Trip to Bountiful, The Death of Papa, Cousins,* and *Tender Mercies.*

1996

Jonathan Larson 237

Birth: February 4, 1960; White Plains, NY. **Death:** January 25, 1996. **Parents:** Allan and Nanette Larson. **Education:** Adelphi University, NY.

Prize: *Drama,* 1996: *Rent,* New York: Rob Weisbach, 1997.

Career: Playwright, composer, and lyricist; Songwriter, *Sesame Street,* PBS; Waiter, Moondance Diner, New York City.

Selected Works: *Superbia. Tick, Tick...Boom!. J.P. Morgan Saves the Nation* (with Jeffrey M. Jones), 1995.

Other Awards: Richard Rodgers Development Grant: *Superbia.* Stephen Sondheim Award: *Superbia.* Richard Rodgers Studio Production Award, 1994: *Rent.* (Workshop version). Membership, American Academy of Arts and Letters, 1994: *Rent,* (Workshop version). Antoinette Perry Award, Best

Musical, 1996: *Rent.* New York: Rob Weisbach, 1997. Antoinette Perry Award, Best Original Score, 1996: *Rent.* Antoinette Perry Award, Best Musical, 1996: *Rent.*

For More Information: Feingold, Michael, "Jonathan Larson, 1961-1996," *Village Voice,* February 6, 1996; Lahr, John, "Hello and Goodbye," *New Yorker,* February 19, 1996; Kroll, Jack, "A Downtown 'La Boheme'," *Newsweek,* February 26, 1996; Wolf, Matt, "The Posthumous Hero," *Guardian,* April 10, 1996.

Commentary: *Rent,* a musical drama based on Puccini's *La Boheme* about artists living on New York's Lower East Side, won the 1996 Pulitzer Prize in Drama for Jonathan Larson. It was a posthumous award; Larson died of an aortic aneurysm on January 25, 1996, the night before the show's premiere. *Rent* premiered off-Broadway and moved to New York's Nederlander Theater on April 29, 1996.

Larson lived on the Lower East Side and worked as a waiter while writing and producing musicals including the rock monologue *Tick, Tick . . . Boom!,* which was produced off-Broadway at the New York Theater Workshop.

1997
No award

1998

Paula Vogel 238

Birth: November 16, 1951; Washington, DC. **Parents:** Donald Stephen and Phyllis (Bremerman) Vogel. **Religion:** Unitarian Universalist. **Education:** Bryn Mawr College, PA. Catholic University of America, Washington, DC: BA. Cornell University, NY: ABD.

Prize: *Drama,* 1998: *How I Learned to Drive,* New York: Dramatists Play Service, 1997.

Career: Lecturer, Theatre and Women's Studies, Cornell University, NY, 1977-1980; Production Supervisor, Theatre on Film & Tape, 1982-1984; Professor, Creative Writing and English, Brown University, RI, 1984-; Playwright-in-Residence, Arena Theatre, Washington, DC, 1998-2001.

Selected Works: *The Baltimore Waltz* (Play), 1992. *And Baby Makes Seven* (Play), 1993. *Desdemona: A Play about a Handkerchief* (Play), 1994. *Hot 'n' Throbbing* (Play), 1994. *The Mineola Twins* (Play), 1995. *The Baltimore Waltz, and Other Plays* (Play), 1996. *The Mammary Plays* (Play), 1998.

Other Awards: Obie Award, Village Voice, 1992: *The Baltimore Waltz,* Circle Repertory Theatre, NY. AT&T New Play Award, 1992: *The Baltimore Waltz.* National Endowment for the Arts Fellowship,

1980, 1991. Guggenheim Fellow, Guggenheim Foundation, 1996. Pew Charitable Trust Residency, 1995-1997: *Perseverance,* Juneau Theatre, Alaska. New York Critics Circle Award, 1997: *How I Learned to Drive,* New York: Dramatists Play Service, 1997. New York Drama Desk Award, 1997: *How I Learned to Drive.* Obie Award, 1997: *How I Learned to Drive.* Outer Critic Circle Award, 1997: *How I Learned to Drive.* Lucille Lortel Award, 1997: *How I Learned to Drive.*

For More Information: Savran, David, "Paula Vogel's Acts of Retaliation," *American Theatre,* April 1996; Sam Whiting, "How Paula Vogel Found Her Drive," *San Francisco Chronicle,* January 4, 1998; Dolan, Jill, "How I Learned to Drive," *Theatre Journal,* March 1998; Brodesser, Claude, "Vogel's 'Drive' Nabs Pulitzer," *Variety,* April 20-26, 1998; Day, Nicholas, "Perseverance Pays: Pulitzer Winner Vogel to Work at Arena," *Washington Post,* June 13, 1998.

Commentary: The 1998 Pulitzer Prize in Drama was awarded to *How I Learned to Drive,* written by Paula Vogel. It is both a humorous and gripping dramatization of a young woman's experience with child abuse. It premiered at the the Vineyard Theatre in New York City on March 12, 1997.

Paula Vogel was born in Washington, DC. She has been a professor of creative writing and English at Brown University since 1984. Vogel's theatre productions have been performed in the United States, Canada, England, Brazil, and Spain. *The Baltimore Waltz* was inspired by her brother Carl's death from AIDS. Her other dramas include *Hot 'n Throbbing* and *The Mineola Twins.*

Editorial Cartooning

1922

Rollin Kirby 239
Birth: September 4, 1874; Galva, IL. **Death:** May 9, 1952. **Parents:** George Washington Kirby and Elizabeth (Maddox). **Education:** Art Students' League, NY. **Spouse:** Estelle Carter (m. 1903, died 1943). **Children:** Janet.

Prize: *Editorial Cartooning,* 1922: *New York World,* "On the Road to Moscow," August 5, New York: New York World, 1921. *Editorial Cartooning,* 1925: *New York World,* "News from the Outside World," October 5, New York: New York World, 1924. *Editorial Cartooning,* 1929: *New York World,* "Tammany," September 24, New York: New York World, 1928.

Career: Magazine illustrator, 1901-10; Cartoonist, *New York Evening Mail,* 1911; Cartoonist, *New York Sun,* 1912; Cartoonist, *New York World,* 1913; Political Cartoonist, *New York World,* 1914-31; Political Cartoonist, *New York World-Telegram,* 1931-39; Political Cartoonist, *New York Post,* 1939-42; Political Cartoonist, *New York Post,* 1942-; Writer.

Selected Works: *Highlights: A Cartoon History of the Nineteen Twenties,* 1931.

Other Awards: Universal Peace League, 1935.

For More Information: *New York World,* April 27, 1925; *New York Times,* May 3, 1925: 11; *Current History,* August, 1939: 31+; *Quill,* 27:4 (April 1939): 6-7+; *New York Times,* May 10, 1952: 21; Lent, John A., *Animation, Caricature, and Gag and Political Cartoons in the United States and Canada: An International Bibliography, Bibliographies and Indexes in Popular Culture, Number 3,* Westport, CT: Greenwood Press, 1994.

Commentary: Rollin Kirby was the first three-time winner of a Pulitzer Prize. His winning cartoons dealt with international affairs and the local political agenda. His editorial cartoons ranged from commentary on the presidents and prohibition to facism and other radical issues. He also wrote poetry, articles, and book reviews. He authored the article on cartooning in the 14th edition of the *Encyclopaedia Britannica.*

1923
No award

1924

Jay Norwood Darling 240
Birth: October 21, 1876; Norwood, MI. **Death:** February 12, 1962. **Parents:** Marcellus Warner Darling and Clara R. (Woolson). **Religion:** Congregationalist. **Education:** Yankton College, SD. Beloit College, WI: PhB. **Spouse:** Genevieve Pendleton (m. 1906, died 1968). **Children:** John, Mary.

Prize: *Editorial Cartooning,* 1924: *Des Moines Register and Tribune,* "In Good Old USA," May 6, Des Moines, IA: Des Moines Register and Tribune, 1923. *Editorial Cartooning,* 1943: *Des Moines Register and Tribune,* "What a Place for a Waste Paper Salvage Campaign," September 13, Des Moines, IA: Des Moines Register and Tribune, 1942.

Career: Cub Reporter, *Sioux City (IA) Tribune,* 1899; Reporter/Cartoonist, *Sioux City (IA) Journal,* 1900; Cartoonist, *Sioux City (IA) Journal,* 1901-06; Cartoonist, *Des Moines (IA) Register and Leader,* 1906-11; Cartoonist, *New York Globe,* 1911-13; Cartoonist, *Des Moines (IA) Register,* 1913-49; Cartoonist, *New York Herald-Tribune,* 1917-49; Chief, Bureau of Biological Survey, 1934-35.

Selected Works: *Cartoons from the Files of the Register and Leader,* 1908. *Cartoons from the Pen of Jay N. Darling "Ding," 1908,* 1908. *The Education of Alonzo Applegate and Other Cartoons,* 1910. *Cartoon Book No. III: Cartoons by Jay N. Darling from 1910 and 1911 Files of the Des Moines Ledger and Leader,* 1911. *Condensed Ink, an Iowa Breakfast Food: Being Cartoons from the Register and Leader, of Des Moines, by "Ding,"* 1914. *In Peace and War: Cartoons from the Des Moines Register,* 1914. *Our Sons at Camp Dodge: A Book of Pictures,* 1917. *Aces and Kings: Cartoons from the Des Moines Register,* 1918. *Aces and Kings: Cartoons from the Nebraska State Journal,* 1918. *The Jazz Era, Cartoon Book 7,* 1920. *Our Own Outlines of History for 1921 and 1922: Cartoons by J.N. Darling, Book 8,* 1922. *The 1928 Election. Ding Goes to Russia,* 1932. *Game Management on the Farm, Farmers' Bulletin (United States Department of Agriculture), Number 1759* (with H.P. Sheldon and Ira Noel Gabrielson), 1936. *The Cruise of the Bouncing Betsy: A Trailer Travelogue,* 1937. *Poverty or Conservation: Your National Problem,* 1945. *Our Great Out-of-Doors, a Portfolio of Cartoons* (with John M. Henry), 1947. *As Ding Saw Hoover,* 1954. *It Seems Like Only Yesterday,* 1960. *Ding's Half Century,* 1962. *In Peace and War: Cartoons from the Des Moines Register,* 1976. *J.N.*

"Ding" Darling's Conservation and Wildlife Cartoons, 1991. *As Ding Saw Herbert Hoover: Iowa Heritage Collection* (with John M. Henry), 1996.

Other Awards: National Audubon Society's Medal, 1960. Florence K. Hutchinson Award, Garden Club of America. Hall of Fame, Izaak Walton League of America. Honorary Degrees: Beloit College, WI, 1925; Drake University, IA, 1926.

For More Information: *People's Popular Monthly,* October (1923): 7, 39, 45; *Quill,* January (1943): 12-15; *The World of Comic Art,* 1:1 (June 1966): 18-25; Lendt, David, *Ding—The Life of Jay Norwood Darling,* Ames: Iowa State University Press, 1979; *Los Angeles Times,* April 8, 1990: part E; Lent, John A., *Animation, Caricature, and Gag and Political Cartoons in the United States and Canada: An International Bibliography, Bibliographies and Indexes in Popular Culture, Number 3,* Westport, CT: Greenwood Press, 1994.

Commentary: By the time Jay N. "Ding" Darling retired, he had drawn more than 15,000 daily cartoons, which appeared in 130 leading newspapers. When Ding was 38, a partial paralysis of his drawing arm threatened to end his career.

He was appointed by FDR to head the Bureau of Biological Survey, which was the predecessor of the United States Fish and Wildlife Service. He was a founder and the first president of the National Wildlife Foundation. He created the first duck hunting stamp in 1934, and duck hunters still must have a current stamp in their possession.

1925

Rollin Kirby

Full entry appears as **#239** under "Editorial Cartooning," 1922.

1926

Daniel Robert Fitzpatrick   241

Birth: March 5, 1891; Superior, WI. **Death:** May 18, 1969. **Parents:** Patrick Fitzpatrick and Delia Ann (Clark). **Education:** Art Institute of Chicago, IL. **Spouse:** Lee Dressen (m. 1913, died 1965).

Prize: *Editorial Cartooning,* 1926: *St. Louis Post-Dispatch,* "The Laws of Moses and the Laws of Today," April 12, St. Louis: St. Louis Post-Dispatch, 1925. *Editorial Cartooning,* 1955: *St. Louis Post-Dispatch,* "How Would Another Mistake Help?" June 8, St. Louis: St. Louis Post-Dispatch, 1954.

Career: Staff Artist, *Chicago Daily News,* 1911; Cartoonist, *Chicago Daily News,* 1912; Cartoonist, *St. Louis (MO) Post-Dispatch,* 1913-58; Staff Cartoonist, *Collier's Weekly.*

Selected Works: *Cartoons,* 1947. *As I Saw It: A Revue of Our Times with 311 Cartoons and Notes,* 1953. *Editorial Cartoons 1913-1965 from the Editorial Page of the St. Louis Post-Dispatch* (with others), 1965.

Other Awards: John Frederick Lewis Prize for Caricature, 1924. Special Award, Sidney Hillman Foundation, 1955. Distinguished Service to Journalism Medal, University of Missouri, 1958. Honorary Degree, Washington University, MO, 1949.

For More Information: *Time,* May 5, 1941: 48; *Cartoonist PROfiles,* 54 (June 1982): 37-41; Lent, John A., *Animation, Caricature, and Gag and Political Cartoons in the United States and Canada: An International Bibliography, Bibliographies and Indexes in Popular Culture, Number 3,* Westport, CT: Greenwood Press, 1994.

Commentary: D.R. Fitzpatrick knew from the age of 10 that he wanted to be a cartoonist. He left high school to enroll at the Art Institute in Chicago and after three years, he went to work for the *Chicago Daily News.* Two years later, he joined the staff of the *St. Louis Post-Dispatch,* where he would stay for 45 years.

He won the Pulitzer Prize twice. The first was for a cartoon that depicted the two tablets of laws of Moses dwarfed by mountains of paper labeled the "laws of today." His second was a commentary, prior to the beginning of the Vietnam War, which had Uncle Sam poised, about to walk into a swamp titled "French Mistakes in Indo-China."

1927

Nelson Harding   242
Birth: October 31, 1879; Brooklyn, NY. **Death:** December 30, 1944. **Parents:** Charles Nelson Harding and Flora (McGregor). **Religion:** Episcopalian. **Education:** Art Students' League, NY. New York School of Art. **Spouse:** Anna Seamon (m. 1911, died 1936). **Children:** Peggy, Jean.

Prize: *Editorial Cartooning,* 1927: *Brooklyn Daily Eagle,* "Toppling the Idol," September 19, Brooklyn, NY: Brooklyn Daily Eagle, 1926. *Editorial Cartooning,* 1928: *Brooklyn Daily Eagle,* "May His Shadow Never Grow Less," December 15, Brooklyn, NY: Brooklyn Daily Eagle, 1927.

Career: U.S. Volunteers, Spanish-American War; Lithographer, 1899-1907; Freelance cartoonist, 1907-08; Cartoonist, *Brooklyn (NY) Eagle,* 1908-29; Cartoonist, *New York Journal,* 1929-42.

Selected Works: *The Political Campaign of 1912 in Cartoons: The Eagle Library, No. 170,* 1912. *Ruthless Rhymes of Martial Militants: The Eagle Library, No. 185,* 1914.

For More Information: *New York Times,* May 3, 1927: 7; *New York Times,* May 8, 1928: 4; *New York Times,* January 2, 1945: 19.

Commentary: Nelson Harding was the second cartoonist to win the Pulitzer Prize twice. He was the first winner to be awarded back-to-back awards. Harding was a member of the New York National Guard for 10 years. He also participated in the Battle of San Juan Hill and was a First Lieutenant during World War I.

1928

Nelson Harding
Full entry appears as #**242** under "Editorial Cartooning," 1927.

1929

Rollin Kirby
Full entry appears as #**239** under "Editorial Cartooning," 1922.

1930

Charles Raymond Macauley   243
Birth: March 19, 1871; Canton, OH. **Death:** November 24, 1934. **Parents:** John K. Macauley and Abbie (Burry). **Spouse:** Clara Hatter (m. 1893, d.); Emma Worms (m. 1897, d.); Edythe Belmont Lott (m. 1914). **Children:** Clara (CH).

Prize: *Editorial Cartooning,* 1930: *Brooklyn Daily Eagle,* "Paying for a Dead Horse," Brooklyn, NY: Brooklyn Daily Eagle, 1929.

Career: Cartoonist, *Cleveland (OH) World,* 1891, *Cleveland (OH) Plain Dealer, Cleveland (OH) Leader;* Cartoonist, *Philadelphia (PA) Inquirer,* 1899-1901; Freelance cartoonist; Cartoonist, *New York Morning World,* 1904-14; Editorial Cartoonist, *Brooklyn (NY) Daily Eagle,* 1929-30; Staff Cartoonist, *New York Daily Mirror,* 1931-34.

Selected Works: *Emblemland* (with John Kendrick Bangs), 1902. *Fantasma Land,* 1904. *Red Tavern,* 1914.

For More Information: *New York Times,* 25 November (1934): 30; *Target: The Political Cartoon Quarterly,* Winter (1984): 14-19.

Commentary: Charles Raymond Macauley chose his career when he won the $50 first prize in a contest sponsored by the *Cleveland World.* He joined the staff of that paper two weeks later. He worked for several Ohio papers before heading East. His cartoons were published in newspapers and magazines in New York and Philadelphia for 40 years. He had an innate sense of justice and supported social causes.

1931

Edmund Duffy   244
Birth: March 1, 1899; Jersey City, NJ. **Death:** September 13, 1962. **Parents:** John J. Duffy and Anna (Hughes). **Education:** Art Students' League, NY. **Spouse:** Anne Rector (m. 1924, died 1970). **Children:** Sara.

Prize: *Editorial Cartooning,* 1931: *Baltimore Sun,* "An Old Struggle Still Going On," Baltimore, MD: Baltimore Sun, 1930. *Editorial Cartooning,* 1934: *Baltimore Sun,* "California Points with Pride!!" November 28, Baltimore, MD: Baltimore Sun, 1933. *Editorial Cartooning,* 1940: *Baltimore Sun,* "The

Outstretched Hand," October 7, Baltimore, MD: Baltimore Sun, 1939.

Career: Magazine contributor, illustrations and sketches, 1918-23; Staff member, *Brooklyn (NY) Daily Eagle,* 1923; Political Cartoonist, *New York Leader,* 1923; Political Cartoonist, *Baltimore (MD) Sun,* 1924-48; Editorial Page Cartoonist, *Saturday Evening Post,* 1949-57; Contributor, cartoon illustrations, newspapers, magazines.

For More Information: *New York Times,* May 7, 1940: 20; *Editor and Publisher,* 81:25 June 19, 1948: 11; *Saturday Evening Post,* 221:29 January 15, 1949: 136; *New York Times,* September 13, 1962: 37.

Commentary: Edmund Duffy estimated that by the time he retired from the *Baltimore Sun,* he had drawn about 8,000 cartoons. His colleagues at the *Sun* considered him a "mild-mannered fellow" while others thought of him as an authority of "devastating satire and raucous caricature."

He is one of five cartoonists to win the Pulitzer Prize three times. His drawing was known for its strength and simplicity.

1932

John Tinney McCutcheon   245
Birth: May 6, 1870; near South Raub, IN. **Death:** June 10, 1949. **Parents:** John Barr McCutchen and Clarissa (Glick). **Education:** Purdue University, IN: BS. **Spouse:** Evelyn Shaw (m. 1917). **Children:** John, Evelyn, Shaw, Barr.

Prize: *Editorial Cartooning,* 1932: *Chicago Daily Tribune,* "A Wise Economist Asks a Question," August 19, Chicago: Chicago Tribune, 1931.

Career: Staff member, *Chicago Record,* 1889-1901; Staff member, *Chicago Record-Herald,* 1901-03; Cartoonist, *Chicago Tribune,* 1903-44; Contributor, articles and cartoons, Sunday *Chicago Tribune* 1944-; Cartoonist; Writer; Lecturer; War Correspondent.

Selected Works: *Chicago Record's Stories of Filipino Warfare,* 1900. *The Cartoons That Made Prince Henry Famous,* 1902. *Bird Center Cartoons,* 1904. *Cartoons by McCutcheon,* 1904. *The Mysterious Stranger and Other Cartoons,* 1905. *Congressman Pumphrey, the People's Friend,* 1907. *In Africa: Hunting Adventures in the Big Game Country,* 1910. *T.R. in Cartoons,* 1910. *History of Indiana,* 1911. *Dawson '11, Fortune Hunter,* 1912. *The Restless Age,* 1921. *Doing the Grand Canyon,* 1922. *An Heir at Large,* 1923. *War Cartoons Reproduced from the Chicago Tribune (December 8, 1941-September 28, 1942),* 1942. *History of World War II in Cartoons,* 1942. *John McCutcheon's Book,* 1948. *Drawn from Memory,* 1950.

Other Awards: Honorary Degrees: Purdue University, IN, 1926; Notre Dame University, IN, 1931; Northwestern University, IL, 1943.

For More Information: *World To-Day,* October (1908): 1021-1028; *New York Times,* May 3, 1932: 1, 16; *Quill,* 27:5 (June 1939): 10-12; *New York Times,* June 11, 1949: 17; Lent, John A., *Animation, Caricature, and Gag and Political Cartoons in the United States and Canada: An International Bibliography, Bibliographies and Indexes in Popular Culture, Number 3,* Westport, CT: Greenwood Press, 1994.

Commentary: John T. McCutcheon's winning cartoon has a squirrel asking a downtrodden man, "But why didn't you save some money for the future when times were good?" The man replies, "I did." The cartoon captured the essence of the Great Depression. McCutcheon traveled frequently. While he was on a round-the-world trip in 1898, he found himself at the Battle of Manila Bay. Since that time, he has traveled to India, Burma, Siam, China, Korea, Japan, Persia, Turkestan, Africa, Mexico, Europe, over the Andes, and down the Amazon.

1933

Harold M. Talburt   246
Birth: February 19, 1895; Toledo, OH. **Death:** October 22, 1966. **Spouse:** Marguerite Haynes Coombs (m., died 1944); Frances Karn Long (m. 1947). **Children:** Thomas M., Susan (MC).

Prize: *Editorial Cartooning,* 1933: *Washington Daily News,* "The Light of Asia," January 27, Washington, DC: Washington Daily News, 1932.

Career: High School Correspondent, *Toledo (OH) Times;* Reporter, *Toledo (OH) News-Bee,* 1916; Cartoonist, Washington (DC) Bureau, Scripps-Howard Syndicate, 1921-; Chief Washington Cartoonist, Scripps-Howard Syndicate and *Washington (DC) Daily News,* ?-1963.

Selected Works: *Talburt,* 1943. *Cartoons: Largely Political,* 1943.

For More Information: *New York Times,* May 2, 1933: 15; *New York Times,* October 23, 1966: 88; *Washington Post-Times Herald,* October 23, 1966: B4.

Commentary: Harold M. Talburt's winning cartoon depicts the treaty forming the League of Nations being used as a burning torch in a hand labeled Japan. Talburt began his career as a reporter, but his true desire was to be a cartoonist. He had the ability to draw editorial ideas effectively. He covered seven United States presidents, from Harding to Kennedy. His favorite president was Herbert Hoover.

1934

Edmund Duffy

Full entry appears as **#244** under "Editorial Cartooning," 1931.

1935

Ross Aubrey Lewis   247

Birth: November 9, 1902; Metamora, MI. **Death:** August 6, 1977. **Parents:** Nelson William Lewis and Sophia (Ross). **Education:** Milwaukee State Teachers College, WI. Layton School of Arts, WI. Art Students' League, NY. **Spouse:** Florence Olsoen Dieneck (m. 1943).

Prize: *Editorial Cartooning,* 1935: *Milwaukee Journal,* "Sure, I'll Work for Both Sides," September 1, Milwaukee, WI: Milwaukee Journal, 1934.

Career: Commercial Artist, Gugler Lithograph Company; Commercial Designer, Advertising Layouts, *Milwaukee (WI) Journal,* 1925-28; Staff Artist, *Milwaukee (WI) Journal,* 1929-32; Editorial Cartoonist, *Milwaukee (WI) Journal,* 1932-67; U.S. Coast Guard Reserve member, 1942-46.

Other Awards: Schuman Trophy Award, Association of Newspaper Advertising Executives, 1927.

For More Information: *New York Times,* May 7, 1935: 20; Lockwood, George, *The Cartoons of R.A. Lewis, Milwaukee Journal,* Milwaukee, WI: Journal, 1968; *New York Times,* August 9, 1977: 36.

Commentary: Ross A. Lewis's winning cartoon depicts a man named Violence straddling a fence between industry and striking workers.

Lewis began his career as a commercial artist and did the layouts for a prize-winning civic promotion campaign for his newspaper before moving into editorial cartooning.

1936
No award

1937

Clarence Daniel Batchelor   248

Birth: April 1, 1888; Osage City, KS. **Death:** September 5, 1977. **Parents:** Daniel L. Batchelor and Lillian E. (James). **Education:** Chicago Art Institute, IL. Art Students' League, NY. **Spouse:** Hazel Deyo (m. 1918, died); Julie Forsyth (m. 1948, died); Allegra Taylor (m. 1959).

Prize: *Editorial Cartooning,* 1937: *New York Daily News,* "Come on In, I'll Treat You Right. I Used

to Know Your Daddy," April 6, New York: New York Daily News, 1936.

Career: Staff Artist, *Kansas City (MO) Star,* 1911; Freelance magazine artist, 1914-18; Cartoonist, *New York Evening Journal, New York Mail, New York Tribune;* Cartoonist, Ledger Syndicate, *New York Post,* 1923-31; Editorial Cartoonist, *New York Daily News,* 1930-69.

Selected Works: *Truman Scrapbook: The Washington Story in Cartoons and Text,* 1951.

Other Awards: Award, Public Health Cartoons, American Medical Association, 1912. Silver Plaque, National Headliners Club, 1938. Page One Award, Newspaper Guild of New York, 1965.

For More Information: *Quill,* 27:12 (1939): 6-7+; *Cartoonist PROfiles,* Fall (1969): 55-57; *New York Times,* September 6, 1977: 42; Taft, William H., *Encyclopedia of Twentieth-Century Journalists,* New York: Garland Publishing Company, 1986.

Commentary: C.D. Batchelor's winning cartoon depicts a ghoul labeled "War" dressed enticingly, chatting with a European youth. It conveys the dismay that was felt by the world heading toward another world war and the death that will be its outcome. Batchelor worked for the *New York Daily News* for nearly 20 years and drew literally thousands of cartoons. He did over 1,000 for his automobile safety series, "Inviting the Undertaker."

1938

Vaughn Richard Shoemaker   249

Birth: August 11, 1902; Chicago, IL. **Death:** August 18, 1991. **Parents:** William H. Shoemaker. **Religion:** Seventh Day Adventist. **Education:** Chicago Academy of Fine Arts, IL. **Spouse:** Evelyn Arnold (m. 1926). **Children:** Vaughn Richard Jr.

Prize: *Editorial Cartooning,* 1938: *Chicago Daily News,* "The Road Back," November 11, Chicago: Chicago Daily News, 1937. *Editorial Cartooning,* 1947: *Chicago Daily News,* "Still Racing His Shadow," Chicago: Chicago Daily News, 1946.

Career: Art Staff member, *Chicago Daily News,* 1922-25; Chief Cartoonist, *Chicago Daily News,* 1925-52; Chief Editorial Cartoonist, *New York Herald-Tribune;* Cartoonist, *Chicago American;* Instructor, Chicago Academy of Fine Arts.

Selected Works: *1938 A.D.,* 1939. *1939 A.D.,* 1940. *1940 A.D.,* 1941. *'41 and '42 A.D.,* 1943. *'43 and '44 A.D.,* 1945. *'45 and '46 A.D.,* 1947. *Shoemaker,* 1966.

Other Awards: National Headliners Club Award, 1943.

For More Information: *Editor & Publisher,* August 6, 1938; *New York Times,* August 22, 1938: 16;

Quill, September 1938; *Los Angeles Times,* August 22, 1991: 36.

Commentary: Vaughn Shoemaker drew over 14,000 cartoons during his career. He was responsible for "John Q. Public," who appeared in his cartoons as a victim of taxes and bureaucracy and came to symbolize the average citizen.

1939

Charles George Werner   250

Birth: March 23, 1909; Marshfield, WI. **Death:** July 1, 1997. **Parents:** George J. Werner and Marie (Tippelt). **Religion:** Episcopalian. **Education:** Oklahoma City University. **Spouse:** Eloise Robertson (m. 1938, died 1993). **Children:** David, Steve, Jean.

Prize: *Editorial Cartooning,* 1939: *Daily Oklahoman,* "Nomination for 1938," October 6, Oklahoma City, OK: Daily Oklahoman, 1938.

Career: Staff Artist and Photographer, *Springfield (MO) Leader and Press,* 1930-35; Staff, Art Department, *Oklahoma City (OK) Daily Oklahoman,* 1935-37; Editorial Cartoonist, *Oklahoma City (OK) Daily Oklahoman,* 1937-41; Chief Editorial Cartoonist, *Chicago Sun,* 1941-47; Editorial Cartoonist, *Indianapolis (IN) Star,* 1947-94.

Other Awards: Sigma Delta Chi Award, 1944. National Headliners Club Award, 1951. David Roberts Award.

For More Information: *Quill,* 32:5 (1944): 12-13; *Cartoonist PROfiles,* December (1979): 56-63; *Indianapolis Star,* July 2, 1997: B1; *Indianapolis Star,* July 2, 1997: B4.

Commentary: When Charles Werner won the Pulitzer Prize in 1939, he was the youngest person to win the editorial cartooning award to that date. His winning cartoon had a tombstone marked "Grave of Czecho-Slovakis, 1919-1938," and upon the grave was a scroll marked "Nobel Peace Prize."

Werner did not have any formal training as an artist. He developed his own style and technique.

1940

Edmund Duffy

Full entry appears as **#244** under "Editorial Cartooning," 1931.

1941

Jacob Burck   251

Birth: January 10, 1904; Poland. **Death:** May 11, 1982. **Parents:** Abraham Burck and Rebecca (Lev). **Religion:** Jewish. **Education:** Cleveland School of Art, OH. Art Students' League, NY. **Spouse:** Esther Kriger (m. 1933, died 1975). **Children:** Joseph, Conrad.

Prize: *Editorial Cartooning,* 1941: *Chicago Times,* "If I Should Die before I Wake," Chicago: Chicago Times, 1940.

Career: Freelance Cartoonist, *Daily Worker;* Illustrator, *St. Louis (MO) Post-Dispatch,* 1937-38; Editorial Cartoonist, *Chicago Times,* 1938-; Editorial Cartoonist, *Chicago Sun-Times,* ?-1982.

Selected Works: *1929 Red Cartoons Reprinted from the Daily Worker* (with Fred Ellis), 1929. *Hunger and Revolt,* 1935. *Our 34th President,* 1953.

Other Awards: Sigma Delta Chi Award, 1942. Birmingham Museum of Art Award, AL, 1958. National Headliners Club Award, 1972. Marshall Field Award, 1975.

For More Information: *Chicago Sun-Times,* 12 May (1982): part 1, 4; part 1, 74; *New York Times,* 13 May (1982): D27.

Commentary: Jacob Burck's winning cartoon shows a small child kneeling in prayer in a house destroyed by bombs. The caption reads, "If I should die before I wake." It captured the fear of the destruction that world war would cause. Burck worked for the *Chicago Sun-Times* for over 44 years and drew over 10,000 cartoons.

He came to the United States with his parents when he was seven. He was always interested in drawing. He believes his family helped turn him into a cartoonist, due to the contrast between his mother's "Jewish ghetto humor" and his father's conservative nature.

1942

Herbert Lawrence Block   252

Birth: October 13, 1909; Chicago, IL. **Parents:** David Julian Block and Theresa (Lupe). **Education:** Lake Forest College, IL. Chicago Art Institute, IL.

   Prize: *Editorial Cartooning,* 1942: *NEA Service,* "British Plane," March 7, 1941. *Editorial Cartooning,* 1954: *Washington Post and Times-Herald,* "You Were Always a Great Friend of Mine, Joseph," Washington, DC: Washington Post and Times-Herald, 1953. *Editorial Cartooning,* 1979: *Washington Post,* Washington, DC: Washington Post, 1978.

   Career: Reporter, Chicago City News Bureau, 1925; Editorial Page Cartoonist, *Chicago Daily News,* 1929-33; Editorial Cartoonist, *NEA Service,* 1933-43; Served in U.S. Army, 1943-45; Editorial Cartoonist, *Washington (DC) Post,* 1946-.

   Selected Works: *Herblock Looks at Communism,* 1950. *The Herblock Book,* 1952. *Herblock's Here and Now,* 1955. *Herblock's Special for Today,* 1958. *Straight Herblock,* 1964. *The Herblock Gallery,* 1968. *Herblock's State of the Union,* 1972. *Herblock's Special Report,* 1974. *Herblock on All Fronts,* 1980. *Herblock through the Looking Glass,* 1984. *Herblock at Large,* 1987. *Herblock: A Cartoonist's Life,* 1993. *Bella and Me: Life in the Service of a Cat,* 1995.

   Other Awards: National Headliners Club Award, 1940, 1976. American Newspaper Guild Award, 1948. Heywood Brown Award, 1948. Sigma Delta Chi Award, 1948-49, 1951, 1956. Reuben Award, National Cartoonists Society, 1957. Distinguished Service to Journalism Award, University of Missouri, 1961. Fellow, Sigma Delta Chi, 1970. Fourth Estate Award, National Press Club, 1977. Presidential Medal of Freedom, 1994. Cartoon Hall of

Fame, International Museum of Cartoon Art, 1997. Honorary Degrees: Lake Forest College, IL, 1957; Rutgers, NJ, 1963; Williams College, MA, 1969; Haverford College, PA, 1977; University of Maryland, 1977; Colby College, ME, 1986.

   For More Information: *Target: The Political Cartoon Quarterly,* 4:14 (Winter 1984); Taft, William H., *Encyclopedia of Twentieth-Century Journalists,* New York: Garland Publishing Incorporated, 1986; *Cartoonist PROfiles,* December (1991): 40-47; Lent, John, *Animation, Caricature, and Gag and Political Cartoons in the United States and Canada: An International Bibliography, Bibliographies and Indexes in Popular Culture, Number 3,* Westport, CT: Greenwood Press, 1994; *Editor & Publisher,* 8 March (1997): 52.

   Commentary: Herbert "Herblock" Block's editorial cartoons have been a fixture in the nation's newspapers for over 50 years. He has won the Pulitzer Prize three times, the last for the body of his work in the preceding year. This work was exemplified by his cartoon of August 31, 1978, which showed a Roman judge handing a soldier a license to fish through the belongings of the press and saying "Bring me their heads so I can see what goes on in them." He also designed the United States postage stamp for the 175th anniversary of the Bill of Rights.

1943

Jay Norwood Darling

Full entry appears as **#240** under "Editorial Cartooning," 1924.

1944

Clifford Kennedy Berryman   253

Birth: April 2, 1869; near Versailles, Kentucky. **Death:** December 11, 1949. **Parents:** James T. Berryman and Sallie (Church). **Religion:** Presbyterian. **Spouse:** Kate Durfee (m. 1893). **Children:** Mary, Florence, James.

   Prize: *Editorial Cartooning,* 1944: *Evening Star,* "Where Is the Boat Going?" August 28, Washington, DC: Evening Star, 1943.

   Career: Draftsman, U.S. Patent Office, 1886-91; General illustrator, 1891-96; Cartoonist, *Washington (DC) Post,* 1896-1907; Cartoonist, *Washington (DC) Evening Star,* 1907-.

   Selected Works: *Berryman Cartoons,* 1900. *Pictorial History of the Schley Court of Inquiry* (with Henry Litchfield West), 1901. *Berryman's Cartoons of the 58th House,* 1903. *The Bunk Book,* 1925. *Development of the Cartoon, University of Missouri Journalism Series, No. 41,* 1926. *Cartoons and Cari-*

catures. The Campaign of '48 in Star Cartoons (with others), 1948.

Other Awards: Honorary Degree, George Washington University, Washington, DC, 1921. Distinguished Service Award, Cosmopolitan Club, 1948.

For More Information: *Quill,* 27:10 (October 1939): 10-13; *New York Times,* December 12, 1949: 33; *National Cyclopaedia of American Biography, Volume 39,* New York: James T. White & Company, 1954: 419; Mullins, Linda, *The Teddy Bear Men: Theodore Roosevelt and Clifford Berryman,* Cumberland, MO: Hobby House Press, 1987.

Commentary: Clifford K. Berryman is well known for creating the teddy bear. It came from a cartoon of Theodore Roosevelt and a bear that Roosevelt just could not shoot. A small bear in the corner of his drawings became Berryman's trademark. Berryman's son James also won a Pulitzer Prize, making them one of two pairs of parent/child winners of a Pulitzer Prize. (Malcolm and Haynes Johnson also won Pulitzer Prizes.)

1945

William Henry Mauldin   254

Birth: October 29, 1921; Mountain Park, NM. **Parents:** Sidney Albert Mauldin and Edith Katrina (Bemis). **Education:** Chicago Academy of Fine Arts, IL. **Spouse:** Norma Jean Humphries (m. 1942, div. 1946); Natalie Sarah Evans (m. 1947, died 1971); Christine Ruth Lund (m. 1972). **Children:** Bruce Patrick, Timothy (NH); Andrew, David, John, Nathaniel (NE); Kaja Lisa, Samuel Lund (CL).

Prize: *Editorial Cartooning,* 1945: United Features Syndicate, Inc., "Up Front with Mauldin," 1944. *Editorial Cartooning,* 1959: *St. Louis Post-Dispatch,* "I Won the Nobel Prize for Literature. What Was Your Crime?" St. Louis: St. Louis Post-Dispatch, 1958.

Career: Served in U.S. Army, 1940-45; Actor; Technical Advisor; Editorial Cartoonist, *St. Louis (MO) Post-Dispatch,* 1958-62; Editorial Cartoonist, *Chicago Sun-Times,* 1962-91.

Selected Works: *Star Spangled Banter,* 1941. *Sicily Sketchbook,* 1943. *Muds, Mules, and Mountains,* 1944. *News of the 45th* (with Don Robinson), 1944. *Up Front,* 1944. *This Damn Tree Leaks,* 1945. *Back Home,* 1947. *A Sort of a Saga,* 1949. *Bill Mauldin's Army,* 1951. *Bill Mauldin in Korea,* 1952. *Up High with Bill Mauldin,* 1956. *What's Got Your Back Up?,* 1961. *I've Decided I Want My Seat Back,* 1965. *Editorial Cartoons 1913-1965 from the Editorial Page of the St. Louis Post-Dispatch* (with others), 1965. *Bill of Rights Day Celebration,* 1969. *The Brass Ring,* 1972. *Name Your Poison,* 1975. *Mud and Guts,* 1978. *Let's Declare Ourselves Winners and Get the Hell Out,* 1985.

Other Awards: Purple Heart. Legion of Merit. Award, Editorial Cartoons, National Cartoonists Society, 1960. Reuben Award, National Cartoonists Society, 1962. Sigma Delta Chi Award, 1963, 1969, 1972. Walter Cronkite Award, Sigma Delta Chi, 1985. Harry S Truman Good Neighbor Award, 1996. Honorary Degree, Connecticut Wesleyan University, 1946. Honorary Degrees: Albion College, MI, 1970; Lincoln College, IL, 1970; New Mexico State University, 1972; Washington University, MO, 1984; College of Santa Fe, NM, 1986.

For More Information: Robbins, Albert and Randall Rothenberg, *Getting Angry Six Times A Week: A Portfolio of Political Cartoons,* Boston: Beacon Press, 1979; *People,* November 22, 1982: 81; *Cartoonist PROfiles,* June (1982): 12-21; Lent, John A., *Animation, Caricature, and Gag and Political Cartoons in the United States and Canada: An International Bibliography, Bibliographies and Indexes in Popular Culture, Number 3,* Westport, CT: Greenwood Press, 1994.

Commentary: Bill Mauldin is the only editorial cartoonist to win the Pulitzer Prize for work he did on a military paper. During World War II, Mauldin worked on the *Stars and Stripes* and his two GI characters, Willie and Joe, were well recognized because of the national syndication of "Up Front With Mauldin" in the United States. After the war, he acted in two movies, one of which was *The Red Badge of Courage.* He won the Pulitzer Prize a second time when he was a civilian and working at the *St. Louis Post-Dispatch.* for "I Won the Nobel Prize for Literature. What Was Your Crime?"

1946

Bruce Alexander Russell   255

Birth: August 4, 1903; Los Angeles, CA. **Death:** December 18, 1963. **Parents:** Alexander Russell and Flora Estelle (Saunders). **Education:** University of California, Los Angeles. **Spouse:** Mary Anne Morrissey (m. 1931). **Children:** Anne, Mary, Bruce Jr.

Prize: *Editorial Cartooning,* 1946: *Los Angeles Times,* "Time to Bridge That Gulch," Los Angeles, CA: Los Angeles Times, 1945.

Career: Cartoonist, *Los Angeles Evening Herald,* 1925-26; Sports and Theater Cartoonist, *Los Angeles Times,* 1927-34; Political Cartoonist, *Los Angeles Times,* 1934-63.

Other Awards: Distinguished Service Award, Sigma Delta Chi, 1948, 1950-51. National Headliners Club Award, 1949. Award, Freedoms Foundation, 1949-62. Edward A. Dickson Alumnus of the Year Award, University of California, Los Angeles, 1951. Christopher Award, 1953. United States Treasury Award, 1958.

For More Information: *Los Angeles Times,* 19 December (1963): part 2, 1+.

Commentary: Bruce Russell spent all but one year of his career at the *Los Angeles Times.* His cartoons were syndicated nationally from 1960-63. His winning cartoon has an American Bald Eagle and a Russian Bear facing off over a gulch littered with "irresponsible statements" and "deepening suspicions."

Russell was also the creator of "Rollo Rollingstone" for the *Associated Press.* The comic strip ran from 1930-33.

1947

Vaughn Richard Shoemaker

Full entry appears as **#249** under "Editorial Cartooning," 1938.

1948

Reuben Lucius Goldberg   256

Birth: July 4, 1883; San Francisco, CA. **Death:** December 7, 1970. **Parents:** Max Goldberg and Hannah (Cohen). **Education:** University of California, Berkeley: BS. **Spouse:** Irma Seeman (m. 1916). **Children:** Thomas, George.

Prize: *Editorial Cartooning,* 1948: *New York Sun,* "Peace Today," New York: New York Sun, 1947.

Career: Sports Cartoonist, *San Francisco Chronicle,* 1904-05; Sports Cartoonist, *San Francisco Bulletin,* 1905-07; Sports Cartoonist, Writer, *New York Evening Mail,* 1907-21; Syndicated Cartoonist, 1921-64; Sculptor, 1964-70; Director, Cartoon Course, "Famous Artists."

Selected Works: *Foolish Questions, with Due Thanks to the New York Evening Mail,* 1909. *Chasing the Blues,* 1912. *Seeing History at Close Range,* 1914. *Is There a Doctor in the House?,* 1929. *The Rube Goldberg Plan for the Post-War Period,* 1944. *Music in the Zoo,* 1946. *Guide to Europe,* 1954. *How to Remove the Cotton from a Bottle of Aspirin,* 1959. *I Made My Bed,* 1960. *Bobo Baxter: The Hyperion Library of Classic American Comic Strips,* 1977. *Rube Goldberg,* 1981. *Rube Goldberg: A Retrospective,* 1983.

Other Awards: Banshee's Silver Lady Award, 1959. Reuben Award, National Cartoonists Society, 1968. Cartoon Hall of Fame, International Museum of Cartoon Art.

For More Information: Kinnaird, Clark, *Rube Goldberg Vs. the Machine Age,* New York: Hastings House, 1968; Marzio, Peter C., *Rube Goldberg: His Life and Work,* New York: Harper and Row, 1973;

Cartoonist PROfiles, March (1983): 60-65; *Cartoonist PROfiles,* March (1989): 60-63; Lent, John A., *Comic Books and Comic Strips in the United States: An International Bibliography, Bibliographies and Indexes in Popular Culture, Number 4,* Westport, CT: Greenwood Press, 1994.

Commentary: Reuben "Rube" Goldberg cartoons are famous for the intricate gadgetry that he created to do a simple task. He also drew the comic strip "The Look-A-Like Boys" during the early part of the 20th century and later the strip "Boob McNutt." In 72 years of drawing, he drew nearly 50,000 cartoons.

The National Cartoonists Society, which he helped form, named its award for the Best Cartoonist of the Year after him.

1949

Lucius Curtis Pease   257

Birth: March 27, 1869; Winnemucca, NV. **Death:** August 16, 1963. **Parents:** Lucius Curtis Pease and Mary Isabel (Hutton). **Education:** Malone Academy, NY. **Spouse:** Nell Christmas McMullin (m. 1905).

Prize: *Editorial Cartooning,* 1949: *Newark Evening News,* "Who Me?" November 6, Newark, NJ: Newark Evening News, 1948.

Career: Rancher, Santa Barbara County, CA, 1887; Prospector, gold miner, Alaska; Occasional Correspondent, Yukon-Nome (AK), *Seattle (WA) Post-Intelligencer,* 1897-1901; U.S. Commissioner, Kotzebue Sound-Point Hope District, 1901-02; Political Cartoonist and Reporter, *Portland (OR) Oregonian,* 1902-05; Editor-in-Chief, *Pacific Monthly,* 1906-13; Political Cartoonist, *Newark (NJ) Evening News,* 1914-54; Portrait and landscape painter; Writer.

For More Information: *Current Biography Yearbook, 1949,* New York: H.W. Wilson Company, 1949; *Editor & Publisher,* February 19, 1949: 10; *New York Times,* August 17, 1963: 19.

Commentary: Lute Pease's artistic talent was recognized when he was six years old. He drew animals as well as sketches of his teachers for his classmates. In the earlier part of his career, journalism was his secondary profession. He was a miner in the Klondike Gold Rush of 1897-98 and in the Yukon. He also worked on a ranch, as a lumberman, and as a canvasser. As a cub reporter, he did a five-minute interview with Mark Twain, and Twain called it "the most accurate and best written of me."

1950

James T. Berryman 258

Birth: June 8, 1902; Washington, DC. **Death:** August 12, 1971. **Parents:** Clifford K. Berryman and Kate G. (Durfee). **Religion:** Presbyterian. **Education:** George Washington University, Washington, DC. Corcoran School of Art, Washington, DC. **Spouse:** Louise Rhys (m. 1926). **Children:** Rhys.

Prize: *Editorial Cartooning,* 1950: *Evening Star,* "All Set for a Super-Secret Session in Washington," Washington, DC: Evening Star, 1949.

Career: Reporter, *Albuquerque (NM) State Tribune,* 1923-24; Staff Artist, *Washington (DC) Star,* 1924-30; Editorial Illustrator, 1930-33; Sports Cartoonist, *Evening Star* and *Sporting News,* 1934-41; Magazine illustrator, 1936-66; Political Cartoonist, *Washington Star,* 1941-64; Political Cartoonist, *King Features Syndicate,* 1944-66; Graphic Arts Instructor, Southeastern University, 1937-38; Cartoonist, Association of American Railroads, 1948.

Selected Works: *The Campaign of '48 in Star Cartoons* (with others), 1948. *The Campaign of '52 in Star Cartoons* (with others), 1952.

Other Awards: Award, New York World's Fair. Award, Infantile Paralysis Foundation. Award, United States Treasury, War Bond Committee. Award, Freedoms Foundation, 1949-51, 1962. National Headliners Club Award, 1953.

For More Information: *New York Times,* 2 May (1950): 22; *New York Times,* 13 August (1971): 32; Taft, William H., *Encyclopedia of Twentieth-Century Journalists,* New York: Garland Publishing Incorporated, 1986.

Commentary: James Thomas Berryman followed in his father's footsteps and became an editorial cartoonist. Berryman and his father are one of a pair of parent/child winners of the award. They are the only pair to win in the same category. (Malcolm Johnson and his son Haynes Johnson also won Pulitzer Prizes, Malcolm in the Local Reporting category and Haynes in the National Reporting category.)

1951

Reginald West Manning 259

Birth: April 8, 1905; Kansas City, MO. **Death:** March 10, 1986. **Parents:** Charles A. Manning and Mildred A. (Joslin). **Spouse:** Ruth Littlefield (m. 1926). **Children:** David.

Prize: *Editorial Cartooning,* 1951: *Arizona Republic,* "Hats," Phoenix, AZ: Arizona Republic, 1950.

Career: Freelance cartoonist, 1924-26; Cartoonist, *Arizona Republic,* Phoenix, 1926-81; Editorial Cartoonist, McNaught Syndicate, Incorporated, New York City, 1948-71; Owner, *Reganson Cartoon Books;* Lecturer, illustrator.

Selected Works: *Reg Manning's Cartoon Guide to Arizona,* 1938. *Reg Manning's Cartoon Guide to California,* 1939. *What Kinda Cactus Izzat? A Who's Who of Strange Plants of the Southwest American Desert,* 1941. *Little Itchy Itchy, and Other Cartoons,* 1944. *From Tee to Cup,* 1954. *What Is Arizona Really Like,* 1968. *Reg Manning's Desert in Crystal,* 1973.

Other Awards: Award, Freedoms Foundation, 1950-52, 1955, 1959, 1961, 1963, 1967-69, 1973-75. National Safety Council Award, 1957. Abraham Lincoln Award, 1971-72.

For More Information: *Editor and Publisher,* 84:41, 6 October (1951): 34; Smith, Dean, *The Best of Reg,* Phoenix: Arizona Republic, 1980; *Los Angeles Times,* 16 March (1986): part 3, 19.

Commentary: Reg Manning joined the *Arizona Republican,* the precursor of the *Arizona Republic,* three days after finishing high school. He stayed with the paper for the next 50 years. He drew over 15,000 cartoons during his career. His Pulitzer Prize-winning cartoon contained top hats of United Nations diplomats and then a bullet-pierced helmet on top of a soldier's grave.

His trademark, which always accompanied his signature, was a laughing cactus. He wrote a book titled *What Kind of Cactus Izzat?,* which sold over 300,000 copies.

1952

Fred Little Packer 260

Birth: January 4, 1886; Hollywood, CA. **Death:** December 8, 1956. **Parents:** Jacob W. Packer and Elizabeth (Little). **Religion:** Presbyterian. **Education:** Los Angeles School of Art and Design, CA. Chicago Art Institute, IL. **Spouse:** Lillian Pabst Wilson (m. 1941). **Children:** Stepchild: Marjorie.

Prize: *Editorial Cartooning,* 1952: *New York Mirror,* "Your Editors Ought to Have More Sense Than to Print What I Say," October 6, New York: New York Mirror, 1951.

Career: Staff Artist, *Los Angeles Examiner,* 1906-07, *San Francisco Morning Call,* 1907-13; Art Director, *San Francisco (CA) Call Post,* 1913-18; Artist for national advertisers, 1919-32; Cartoonist, *New York Journal* and *New York American,* 1932-33; Editorial Cartoonist, *New York Daily Mirror,* 1933; Book, magazine illustrator; Vice President, Victory Builders Incorporated, 1941-45.

Other Awards: Citation, United States Treasury Department. Citation, War Production Board. Citation, American Cancer Society. Page One Award, New York Newspaper Guild, 1954, 1956-57. Art Award, Watercolor, Newspaper Guild, 1957. George

Washington Honor Medal, Freedoms Foundation, 1957.

For More Information: *Current Biography Yearbook, 1952,* New York: H.W. Wilson Company, 1952.

Commentary: Fred L. Packer's winning cartoon depicts President Truman addressing a White House press conference with the statement, "Your editors ought to have more sense than to print what I say!" Two days before the cartoon appeared, President Truman talked to press correspondents on how they should handle information of possible value.

1953

Edward D. Kuekes   261
Birth: February 2, 1901; Pittsburgh, PA. **Death:** January 13, 1987. **Parents:** Otto Kuekes and Elizabeth (Lapp). **Religion:** Methodist. **Education:** Baldwin-Wallace College, OH. Cleveland Institute of Art, OH. Chicago Academy of Fine Arts, IL. **Spouse:** Clara Gray (m. 1922). **Children:** Edward, George.

Prize: *Editorial Cartooning,* 1953: *Cleveland Plain Dealer,* "Aftermath," November 9, Cleveland, OH: Cleveland Plain Dealer, 1952.

Career: Artist, Cartoonist, *Cleveland (OH) Plain Dealer,* 1922-49; Chief Editorial Cartoonist, *Cleveland (OH) Plain Dealer,* 1949-66; Cartoonist Emeritus, *Cleveland (OH) Plain Dealer,* 1966-87; Cartoonist, Metro Newspapers, Inc., 1968-87.

Selected Works: *Funny Fables: Modern Interpretations of Famous Fabulists,* 1938. *It Happened on the Other Turn,* 1961.

Other Awards: Newspaper Guild Award, 1947. Certificate of Honor, National Safety Council, 1949. C.I.T. Foundation Award, 1949. Award, Freedoms Foundation, 1949, 1958. Distinguished Service Award, 1951, 1959-61, 1963, 1966-67. Distinguished Service Scrolls, 1952-57. Alumni Merit Award, Baldwin-Wallace College, OH, 1953. Silver T-Square Award, National Cartoonists Society, 1953. Governor's Award, 1953. Presdential Prayer Citation, United States Treasury Department, 1954. Christopher Award, 1955. Award, President Eisenhower's People to People Program, 1956. Citation, George M. Humphrey United States Treasury, 1957. First Prize Guild Award, 1958. Political Cartoon Award, Wayne State University, IN, 1960. United States Treasury Award, 1962, 1964. Award, Freedoms Foundation, 1963-69. Ohio State Senior Citizens Hall of Fame. Honorary Degree, Baldwin-Wallace College, OH, 1957.

For More Information: *New York Times,* May 5, 1953: 24; *Current Biography Yearbook, 1954,* New York: H.W. Wilson, 1954; *New York Times,* January 17, 1987: section 1, 15.

Commentary: Edward D. Kuekes proposed a standard for cartoonists to follow when he was made chief editorial cartoonist at his paper. It was, "A good drawing should be like a good golfer, the fewer the strokes the better."

Kuekes's winning cartoon depicts two soldiers carrying a third off the field of battle. One wonders if his fallen comrade had had the chance to vote. His colleague replies, "No. He wasn't old enough."

1954

Herbert Lawrence Block
Full entry appears as #252 under "Editorial Cartooning," 1942.

1955

Daniel Robert Fitzpatrick
Full entry appears as #241 under "Editorial Cartooning," 1926.

1956

Robert York   262
Birth: August 23, 1909; Minneapolis, MN. **Death:** May 21, 1975. **Parents:** Raymond York and Nelle (Johnston). **Education:** Drake University, IA. Cummings School of Art. Chicago Academy of Fine Arts, IL. **Spouse:** Lillian Lossin (m. 1936). **Children:** Robin.

Prize: *Editorial Cartooning,* 1956: *Louisville Times,* "Achilles," September 16, Louisville, KY: Louisville Times, 1955.

Career: Assistant Comic Strip Artist, *Chicago Tribune,* 1930-35; Political Cartoonist, *Nashville (TN) Banner,* 1936-37; Political Cartoonist, *Louisville (KY) Times,* 1937-43; Artist, U.S. Army Air Forces, 1943-45; Political Cartoonist, *Louisville (KY) Times,* 1945-74.

Other Awards: William Allen White Award, William Allen White Foundation, University of Kansas.

For More Information: *Louisville Courier-Journal,* May 22, 1975: D12.

Commentary: Robert York's winning cartoon depicts a robust prosperity whose tattered shoes are labelled "farm prices." As a youth, York was influenced by "Ding" Darling, who he met while he was growing up in Iowa. He once said the most difficult part of his day was selecting a subject; after that, "it was a matter of 45 minutes or so to get it down on paper."

1957

Tom Little   263

Birth: September 27, 1898; Franklin, TN. **Death:** June 20, 1972. **Parents:** John Wallace Little and Florence (Johnson). **Education:** Watkins Institute of Art, TN. Montgomery Bell Academy, TN. **Spouse:** Helen Dahnke (m. 1926, died 1938); Lillian Hannah (m. 1945).

Prize: *Editorial Cartooning,* 1957: *Nashville Tennessean,* "Wonder Why My Parents Didn't Give Me Salk Shots?" January 12, Nashville, TN: Nashville Tennessean, 1956.

Career: Reporter, *Montgomery (AL) Advertiser;* City Editor, *Nashville (TN) Tennessean,* 1916-23; Served in U.S. Army; Staff member, *New York Herald-Tribune* Syndicate, 1923-24; General Assignment Reporter, *Nashville (TN) Tennessean,* 1924-31; City Editor, *Nashville (TN) Tennessean,* 1931-37; Editorial Cartoonist, *Nashville (TN) Tennessean,* 1937; Cartoon Illustrator, *New York Times Magazine,* 1952.

Other Awards: National Headliners Club Award, 1948. Christopher Award, 1953. Freedoms Foundation Medal, 1955-56.

For More Information: *Cartoonist PROfiles,* 6 (1970): 65-70; *The World of Comic Art: The Historical Journal of Comic Art and Caricature,* 3:1 (1971).

Commentary: Tom Little started his career as a reporter, then moved into cartooning. He studied under Carey Orr, while Orr was at the *Nashville Tennessean.* Little had a great sense of humor, which was often reflected in his work.

His winning cartoon, however, was on a serious subject. It depicted a small child with leg braces watching others play. The caption said it all—"Wonder Why My Parents Didn't Give Me Salk Shots?"

1958

Bruce McKinley Shanks   264

Birth: January 29, 1908; Buffalo, NY. **Death:** April 12, 1980. **Parents:** George H. Shanks Jr. and Ellen Rose (Lattin). **Education:** Normal School of Practice. **Spouse:** Mary Louise Van Vleck (m. 1942; died 1995).

Prize: *Editorial Cartooning,* 1958: *Buffalo Evening News,* "The Thinker," August 20, Buffalo, NY: Buffalo Evening News, 1957.

Career: Copyboy, *Buffalo (NY) Express,* 1926-30; Cartoonist / Artist, *Buffalo (NY) Times,* 1933-; Cartoonist/Artist, *Buffalo (NY) Evening News,* 1933-42; Member of Intelligence, U.S. Air Force, 1942-45; Cartoonist/Artist, *Buffalo (NY) News,* 1945-51; Editorial Cartoonist, *Buffalo (NY) News,* 1951-74.

Selected Works: *1964 Cartoon Review,* 1964. *Shanks for the Memories,* 1968. *Cartoon Review of '72,* 1972.

Other Awards: Award, Freedoms Foundation, 1952-55, 1957. Page One Award, Buffalo Newspaper Guild, NY, 1956, 1959-64, 1966-71. National Award, The Christophers, 1957. Grand Award, National Safety Council, 1961.

For More Information: *Buffalo (NY) Evening News,* May 6, 1958: 3.

Commentary: Bruce M. Shanks never let being colorblind hinder his career in any way. He even enjoyed painting with water colors. His one bit of whimsy was that he always wore a yellow tie. His winning cartoon is of a union member posed in Rodin's "Thinker" position and pondering the meaning of so many highly placed union officials taking the Fifth Amendment.

Some of Shanks's cartoons on baseball are at the Baseball Hall of Fame, while others about the Federal Bureau of Investigation are hanging at the United States Department of Justice.

1959

William Henry Mauldin

Full entry appears as **#254** under "Editorial Cartooning," 1945.

1960
No award

1961

Carey Orr   265

Birth: January 17, 1890; Ada, OH. **Death:** May 16, 1967. **Parents:** Cassius Perry Orr and Martha (Rhinehart). **Education:** Chicago Academy of Fine Arts, IL. **Spouse:** Cherry Kindel (m. 1914, died). **Children:** Dorothy Jane, Cherry Sue.

Prize: *Editorial Cartooning,* 1961: *Chicago Tribune,* "The Kindly Tiger," October 8, Chicago: Chicago Tribune, 1960.

Career: Cartoonist, *Chicago Examiner,* 1912; Cartoonist, *Nashville (TN) Tennessean and American,* 1912-17; Political Cartoonist, *Chicago Tribune,* 1917-62; Instructor, Chicago Academy of Fine Arts.

Selected Works: *Nashville Business Men in Cartoon,* 1920. *Jungle Stories,* 1938. *War Cartoons. 1952 Cartoons by Orr, Parish, Holland,* 1952.

Other Awards: United States Government Gold Medal, 1918. Award, Freedoms Foundation, 1950, 1952-53.

For More Information: Campbell, Gordon, *Cartoonist PROfiles,* 47 (September 1980): 28-39.

Commentary: Carey Orr joined the staff of the *Chicago Tribune* while fellow cartoonist John T. McCutcheon was away. When McCutcheon returned, the editor asked Orr to create a comic strip. Orr came up with "Tiny Tribune." A four-pane, single strip that mimicked the paper, it included four panels—a page one, an editorial page, a sports page, and a comic page. In this way, he could continue to draw a political cartoon each day. He took over the main cartoonist position for two months each year while McCutcheon was away on vacation and, later, after McCutcheon's death.

Orr won the Pulitzer Prize for his long and dis-

tinguished career, which is exemplified by the cartoon, "The Kindly Tiger."

1962

Edmund Siegfried Valtman   266

Birth: May 31, 1914; Tallinn, Estonia. **Parents:** Johannes Valtman and Pauline Elisabet (Kukk). **Education:** Tallinn Art and Applied School, Estonia. Hartford Art School, CT. University of Hartford, CT. **Spouse:** Helmi Grunberg (m. 1943).

Prize: *Editorial Cartooning,* 1962: *Hartford Times,* "What You Need, Man, Is a Revolution Like Mine," August 31, Hartford, CT: Hartford Times, 1961.

Career: Editorial Cartoonist, *Tallinn (Estonia) Eesti Sona* and *Tallinn (Estonia) Maa Sona,* 1942-44; Editorial Cartoonist, *Geislingen (Germany) Eesti Post,* 1945-49; Editorial Cartoonist, *Hartford (CT) Times,* 1951-75; Freelance cartoonist, 1975-.

Selected Works: *Valtman: The Editorial Cartoons of Edmund S. Valtman,* 1994.

Other Awards: Leadership Medal, Greater Hartford Chamber of Commerce, CT, 1962. Frank Tripp Award, Gannett Newspapers, 1963.

For More Information: *Cartoonist PROfiles,* 15 (1972):12-19; *Hartford Courant,* March 9, 1992: C1.

Commentary: Edmund Valtman came to the United States in 1949 after four years in a displaced persons camp in Germany. He became a naturalized citizen in 1959. He made various people recognizable within his cartoons by drawing them as caricatures.

He was awarded a Pulitzer Prize for the body of his work during 1961, which was exemplified by the cartoon, "What you need, man, is a revolution like mine." In the cartoon, Fidel Castro has a chained "Cuba" and is speaking to a man, "Brazil."

1963

Frank Miller   267

Birth: 1925; Kansas City, MO. **Death:** February 17, 1983. **Education:** University of Kansas. Kansas City Art Institute, MO.

Prize: *Editorial Cartooning,* 1963: *Des Moines Register,* "I Said, We Sure Settled That Dispute, Didn't We?" Des Moines, IA: Des Moines Register, 1962.

Career: Staff Artist, *Kansas City (MO) Star;* Editorial Cartoonist, *Des Moines (IA) Register,* 1953-83.

Selected Works: *Cartoons as Commentary,* 1983. *Wolverine* (with others), 1987.

Other Awards: Award, Freedoms Foundation, 1955, 1957-58, 1960-61, 1964. National Headliners

Club Award, 1957. Courage in Journalism Award, Sigma Delta Chi, Des Moines Chapter, IA, 1961.

For More Information: *Des Moines Register,* 18 February (1983): 1, 8; *Target: The Political Cartoon Quarterly,* Spring (1983): 20-21.

Commentary: Although Frank Miller won the Pulitzer in 1963, he was not syndicated until 1981, thus many people outside of Iowa did not get to see his work.

He served in both World War II and the Korean conflict and contributed to the *Pacific Stars and Stripes.*

1964

Paul Francis Conrad 268

Birth: June 27, 1924; Cedar Rapids, IA. **Parents:** Robert H. Conrad and Florence G. (Lawler). **Religion:** Roman Catholic. **Education:** University of Iowa: BA. **Spouse:** Barbara Kay King (m. 1953). **Children:** David, James, Carol, Elizabeth.

Prize: Editorial Cartooning, 1964: *Denver Post,* Denver, CO: Denver Post, 1963. *Editorial Cartooning,* 1971: *Los Angeles Times,* Los Angeles, CA: Los Angeles Times, 1970. *Editorial Cartooning,* 1984: *Los Angeles Times,* Los Angeles, CA: Los Angeles Times, 1983.

Career: Served in U.S. Army Corps of Engineers, 1942-45; Cartoonist, college paper, *Daily Iowan;* Editorial Cartoonist, *Denver (CO) Post,* 1950-63; Chief Editorial Cartoonist, *Los Angeles Times,* 1964-93; Richard M. Nixon Lecture Chair, Whittier College (CA), 1977-78.

Selected Works: *When in the Course of Human Events* (with Malcolm Boyd), 1973. *The King and Us, Editorial Cartoons by Conrad,* 1974. *Pro and Conrad,* 1979. *Drawn and Quartered,* 1985. *Conartist: 30 Years with the Los Angeles Times* (with Norman Lewis Crown), 1993.

Other Awards: Overseas Press Club Award, 1970, 1981. Sigma Delta Chi Award, 1963, 1969, 1971, 1981-82, 1988, 1996. Southern California Journalism Award, 1972. Robert F. Kennedy Journalism Award, 1985, 1990, 1992-93. Hugh M. Hefner First Amendment Award for Print Journalism, 1990. Print Journalist of the Year, Society of Professional Journalists, Los Angeles Chapter, CA, 1992.

For More Information: *New York Times,* 5 May (1964): 39; Robbins, Albert and Randall Rothenberg, *Getting Angry Six Times a Week: A Portfolio of Political Cartoons,* Boston: Beacon Press, 1979: 105-113; *Los Angeles Times,* 25 January (1993): part A; Lent, John, *Animation, Caricature, and Gag and Political Cartoons in the United States and Canada: An International Bibliography, Bibliographies and In-*dexes in Popular Culture, Number 3, Westport, CT: Greenwood Press, 1994.

Commentary: Paul Conrad accepted a buyout in 1993 from his newspaper, the *Los Angeles Times.* He is syndicated nationally five days a week through the Los Angeles Times Syndication. He is one of five cartoonists who have won three Pulitzer Prizes. In an address to the Association of Editorial Cartoonists in 1994, he urged his colleagues to give opinions in their cartoons and not just illustrate the news. He is also a sculptor of political figures. He was a finalist for a Pulitzer Prize in 1998.

1965
No award

1966

Donald Conway Wright 269

Birth: January 23, 1934; Los Angeles, CA. **Parents:** Charles Wright and Sally (Olberg). **Spouse:** Rita Rose Blondin (m. 1960, died 1968); Carolyn Ann Jay (m. 1969).

Prize: Editorial Cartooning, 1966: *Miami News,* "You Mean You Were Bluffing?" Miami, FL: Miami News, 1965. *Editorial Cartooning,* 1980: *Miami News,* Miami, FL: Miami News, 1979.

Career: Copyboy, *Miami (FL) News;* Staff Photographer, *Miami (FL) News,* 1952-56; Signal Corps, Photographer, U.S. Army, 1955-57; Graphics Editor, *Miami (FL) News,* 1958-60; Political Cartoonist, *Miami (FL) News,* 1960-63; Editorial Cartoonist, *Miami (FL) News,* 1960-63; Syndicated Editorial Cartoonist, *Washington (DC) Star* Syndicates, 1970-76; Syndicated Editorial Cartoonist, *New York Times* Syndicate, 1976-82; Syndicated Editorial Cartoonist, Tribune Media Services, 1982-.

Selected Works: *Wright On! A Collection of Political Cartoons,* 1971. *Wright Side Up,* 1981.

Other Awards: School Bell Award, Florida Education Association, 1968. Grenville Clark Editorial Page Cartoon Award, 1969. National Headliners Club Award, 1969, 1972, 1980, 1982. Distinguished Service Award, Sigma Delta Chi, 1977. Tom Wallace Award, InterAmerican Press Association, 1982, 1986. Robert F. Kennedy Award, 1983. Overseas Press Club Award, 1985. Award, Editorial Cartoons, National Cartoonists Society, 1985.

For More Information: *Cartoonist PROfiles,* 23 (Autumn 1974): 35-39; Robbins, Albert and Randall Rothenberg, *Getting Angry Six Times A Week: A Portfolio of Political Cartoons,* Boston: Beacon Press, 1979; *Target: The Political Cartoon Quarterly,* Autumn (1981): 4-11.

Commentary: Don Wright was first a reporter, then a photographer, then a cartoonist. He learned "how you can manipulate feelings with pictures." When he was a photographer, his sketching ability was handy when photographers were not allowed in courtrooms. He would cover the story and sketch the events. Besides winning the Prize in 1966 and 1980, he was a finalist for the award in 1984, 1988, and 1993.

1967

Patrick Bruce Oliphant   270

Birth: July 24, 1935; Adelaide, Australia. **Parents:** Donald Knox Oliphant and Grace Lillian (Price). **Spouse:** Hendrika DeVries (m. 1958, div.). **Children:** Laura, Grant, Susan.

Prize: *Editorial Cartooning*, 1967: *Denver Post*, "They Won't Get Us to the Conference Table, Will They?" February 1, Denver, CO: Denver Post, 1966.

Career: Copyboy, Press Artist, *Adelaide (Australia) Advertiser*, 1953-55; Editorial Cartoonist, *Adelaide (Australia) Advertiser*, 1955-64; Political Cartoonist, *Denver (CO) Post*, 1964-1975; Political Cartoonist, *Washington (DC) Star*, 1975-81; Syndicated cartoonist.

Selected Works: *The Oliphant Book: A Cartoon History of Our Times*, 1969. *Four More Years*, 1973. *Oliphant*, 1973. *Oliphant: An Informal Gathering*, 1978. *Oliphant!*, 1980. *The Jellybean Society*, 1981. *Ban This Book!*, 1982. *But Seriously, Folks*, 1983. *The Year of Living Perilously*, 1984. *Make My Day!*, 1985. *Between a Rock and a Hard Place*, 1986. *Up to There in Alligators*, 1987. *Nothing Basically Wrong*, 1988. *What Those People Need Is a Puppy!*, 1989. *Oliphant's Presidents: Twenty-Five Years of Carica-*

ture, 1990. *Fashions for the New World Order: More Cartoons*, 1991. *Just Say No!*, 1992. *Why Do I Feel Uneasy?*, 1993. *Waiting for the Other Shoe to Drop —More Cartoons*, 1994. *Off to the Revolution*, 1995. *Reaffirm the Status Quo!*, 1996. *101 Things to Do with a Conservative* (with Dain Dunston), 1996. *So That's Where They Came from*, 1997.

Other Awards: Sigma Delta Chi Award, 1966. Reuben Award, National Cartoonists Society, 1968, 1972. National Headliners Club Award, 1979. Award, Editorial Cartoons, National Cartoonists Society, 1985, 1991. International Editorial Design Conference Award. American Illustrators Association Award.

For More Information: *American Civil Liberties Review*, September / October (1977); Robbins, Albert and Randall Rothenberg, *Getting Angry Six Times a Week: A Portfolio of Political Cartoons*, Boston: Beacon Press, 1979; *Contemporary Authors, Volume 101*, Detroit: Gale Research Company, 1981; *Cartoonist PROfiles*, June (1982): 12-21; Lent, John A., *Animation, Caricature, and Gag and Political Cartoons in the United States and Canada: An International Bibliography, Bibliographies and Indexes in Popular Culture, Number 3*, Westport, CT: Greenwood Press, 1994.

Commentary: Patrick B. Oliphant's trademark is a small penguin named Punk who adds his two cents of commentary on the cartoon. After the *Washington Star* folded in 1981, Oliphant did not join the staff of another paper. Instead he is published by syndication.

His winning cartoon has North Vietnam's President Ho Chi Minh carrying a war victim who is saying "They won't get us to the conference table, will they?"

1968

Eugene Gray Payne   271

Birth: January 2, 1919; Charlotte, NC. **Education:** Syracuse University, NY. **Spouse:** June P. **Children:** 3 children.

Prize: *Editorial Cartooning*, 1968: *Charlotte Observer*, Charlotte, NC: Charlotte Observer, 1967.

Career: Pilot, U.S. Army Air Forces, WWII; Commercial artist; Milk wagon driver; Staff, *Charlotte (NC) Observer*, 1958-; Editorial Cartoonist, *Charlotte (NC) Observer*, 1959-.

Other Awards: Sigma Delta Chi Award, 1967.

For More Information: *New York Times*, 7 May (1968): 34.

Commentary: Eugene G. Payne was born three blocks from the *Charlotte Observer*, where he would eventually spend over 40 years of his professional life. His award in 1968 was for the body of his work for the previous year.

1969

John R. Fischetti   272

Birth: September 27, 1916; Brooklyn, NY. **Death:** November 18, 1980. **Parents:** Pietro Fischetti and Emanuela (Navarra). **Education:** Pratt Institute, NY. **Spouse:** Karen Mortenson (m. 1948). **Children:** Peter, Michael.

Prize: *Editorial Cartooning,* 1969: *Chicago Daily News,* Chicago: Chicago Daily News, 1968.

Career: Cabin Boy, Western World Steamship; Freelance artist; Professional Artist, Walt Disney Company; Freelance Artist, *Los Angeles Times Magazine, Coronet Magazine,* and *Esquire Magazine;* Associate Political Cartoonist, *Chicago Sun,* 1941; Radio Operator, U.S. Army, 1942-45; Staff, U.S. Army, *Stars and Stripes,* 1945-46; Editorial Cartoonist, *New York Herald,* 2 Years; Syndicated Editorial Cartoonist, NEA Service Inc., 1951-55; Staff Cartoonist, *New York Herald-Tribune,* 1955; Cartoonist, *Publisher's Newspaper Syndicate,* 1962-67; Chief Political Cartoonist, *Chicago Daily News,* 1967-78; Editorial Cartoonist, *Chicago (IL) Sun-Times,* 1978-80.

Selected Works: *Zinga, Zinga, Za!,* 1973.

Other Awards: Sigma Delta Chi Award, 1956, 1958. Grand Award, National Safety Council. National Headliners Club Award, 1951. Page One Award, New York Newspaper Guild, 1964. Award, Editorial Cartoons, National Cartoonists Society, 1963-64. Award, American Civil Liberties Union. Honorary Degree, Colby College, ME.

For More Information: *Cartoonist PROfiles,* 10 (1971): 30-39; *Quill,* October (1973): 21-25; *New York Times,* 20 November (1980): D19; Taft, William H., *Encyclopedia of Twentieth-Century Journalists,* New York: Garland Publishing, Inc., 1986; *Dictionary of American Biography, Supplement Ten, 1976-1980,* New York: Charles Scribner's Sons, 1995.

Commentary: John Fischetti won a Pulitzer Prize for the body of his work. His favorite drawing among his 1968 cartoons is titled, "Why Don't They Lift Themselves Up By Their Bootstraps Like We Did?" It portrays a black man chained to a wall with hand irons labeled White and Racism.

Fischetti ran away from home at the age of 16. He went back to school at age 19 to study commercial art. His first professional experience was with the Walt Disney Company. He soon left that work behind to become an editorial cartoonist.

1970

Thomas Francis Darcy   273

Birth: December 19, 1932; Brooklyn, NY. **Parents:** Clinton F. Darcy and Iva (Cress). **Education:** Terry Arts Institute of Florida. School of Visual Arts, NY. **Spouse:** Audrey K. Stolzenberger (m. 1957). **Children:** Kelly Lynn, Regan Thomas, Thomas Jason, Bradley William.

Prize: *Editorial Cartooning,* 1970: *Newsday,* New York: Newsday, 1969.

Career: Served in U.S. Navy, 1951-53; Editorial Cartoonist, *Newsday (NY),* 1956-59; Cartoonist, *Phoenix (AZ) Gazette,* 1959-60; Art Director, Lenhart and Altschuler Agency, Long Island (NY), 1960-; Cartoonist, *Houston (TX) Post,* 1965-66; Editorial Cartoonist, *Philadelphia (PA) Bulletin,* 1966-68; Editorial Page Cartoonist, *Newsday (NY),* 1968-97.

Selected Works: *The Good Life,* 1970.

Other Awards: Overseas Press Club Award, 1971. United Nations Award. National Headliners Club Award, 1974. Society of Silurians Award, 1974. Page One Award, Newspaper Guild of New York, 1975.

For More Information: *New York Times,* 5 May (1970): 48; *Newsday,* 29 Janurary (1997): A31.

Commentary: Thomas Darcy won the Pulitzer Prize for the body of his work in 1969. Two major themes of his entry were the Vietnam War and inner city ghetto problems. Darcy began his career at *Newsday,* left to pursue other avenues, then returned in 1965. He remained until his retirement in 1997.

1971

Paul Francis Conrad

Full entry appears as **#268** under "Editorial Cartooning," 1964.

1972

Jeffrey Kenneth MacNelly   274

Birth: September 17, 1947; New York, NY. **Parents:** Clarence Lamont MacNelly and Ruth Ellen (Fox). **Religion:** Episcopalian. **Education:** University of North Carolina. **Spouse:** Marguerite Dewey Daniels (m. 1969, d.); Susan M. **Children:** Jeffrey Jr., Danny, Matt (MD).

Prize: *Editorial Cartooning,* 1972: *Richmond News-Leader,* Richmond, VA: Richmond News-Leader, 1971. *Editorial Cartooning,* 1978: *Richmond News-Leader,* Richmond, VA: Richmond News-Leader, 1977. *Editorial Cartooning,* 1985: *Chicago Tribune,* Chicago: Chicago Tribune, 1984.

Career: Editorial Cartoonist, college paper, *Daily Tar Heel;* Editorial Cartoonist, *Chapel Hill (NC) Weekly;* Editorial Cartoonist, *Richmond (VA) News Leader,* 1970-81; Editorial Cartoonist, *Chicago Tribune,* 1982-; Illustrator of weekly column for Dave Barry.

Selected Works: *The Election That Was—MacNelly at His Best,* 1977. *The Very First Shoe Book,* 1978. *The Other Shoe,* 1980. *The New Shoe,* 1981. *On with the Shoe,* 1982. *A Shoe for All Seasons,* 1983. *Directions,* 1984. *The Deorctionary: An Illustrated Guide to the Terms of the Primitive Texan.... The Shoe Must Go on,* 1984. *The Greatest Shoe on Earth,* 1985. *One Shoe Fits All,* 1986. *Too Old for Summer Camp and Too Young to Retire: A New Shoe Book,* 1988. *Shoe Goes to Wrigley Field,* 1988. *A Cigar Means Never Having to Say You're Sorry,* 1989. *Shake the Hand, Bite the Taco,* 1990. *Apply a Little Hardware to the Software,* 1991. *The Athletic Shoe,* 1991. *Out to Lunch: A Brand New Shoe,* 1993. *New Shoes,* 1994. *Pluggers: Calm in the Face of Disaster,* 1995. *A Golf Handbook: All I Ever Learned I Forgot by the Third Fairway,* 1996.

Other Awards: National Newspaper Association Award, 1969. George Polk Memorial Award, Long Island University, NY, 1978. Reuben Award, National Cartoonists Society, 1979-80. Sigma Delta Chi Award, 1991. Virginian of the Year, Virginia Press Association, 1996.

For More Information: *Richmond News-Leader,* 2 May (1972): 1+; *MacNelly, the Pulitzer Prize Winning Cartoonist,* Richmond, VA: Westover Publishing Company, 1972; *Cartoonist PROfiles,* 20 (1973): 54-57; *Clockwatch Review,* Spring (1985): 47-57; Lent, John A. *Animation, Caricature, and Gag and Political Cartoons in the United States and Canada: An International Bibliography, Bibliographies and Indexes in Popular Culture, Number 3,* Westport, CT: Greenwood Press, 1994; Lent, John A., *Comic Books and Comic Strips in the United States: An International Bibliography, Bibliographies and Indexes in Popular Culture, Number 4,* Westport, CT: Greenwood Press, 1994.

Commentary: Jeff MacNelly has won the Pulitzer Prize three times. Each time it was for his entire work of the previous year. He also draws the highly successful comic strip, "Shoe," which makes editorial comments in its own way. MacNelly retired from editorial cartooning in 1981 to concentrate on "Shoe" but soon joined the *Chicago Tribune* because he missed the work. He was a finalist for a Pulitzer Prize in 1998.

1973
No award

1974

Paul Michael Szep   275

Birth: July 29, 1941; Hamilton, Ontario, Canada.
Parents: Paul J. Szep and Helen (Langhorn). **Education:** Ontario College of Art, Canada. **Spouse:** Angela Garton (m. 1965, div. 1976). **Children:** Amy, Jason.

Prize: *Editorial Cartooning,* 1974: *Boston Globe,* Boston: Boston Globe, 1973. *Editorial Cartooning,* 1977: *Boston Globe,* Boston: Boston Globe, 1976.

Career: Served in Royal Canadian Army, 1957-58; Sports Cartoonist, *Hamilton (Ontario) Spectator,* 1958-61; Book illustrator; Graphics Designer; Part-time steel mills worker; Editorial Cartoonist, *Financial Post, Toronto (Canada),* 1965-66; Editorial Cartoonist, *Boston Globe,* 1966-; Contributor to *Golf Digest;* Guest Lecturer, Harvard University (MA), 1985.

Selected Works: *In Search of Sacred Cows. Keep Your Left Hand High,* 1969. *At This Point in Time,* 1973. *The Harder They Fall: Selected Editorial Cartoons,* 1975. *"Them Damned Pictures": Editorial Cartoons,* 1977. *Warts and All: A Cartoon Collection,* 1980. *To a Different Drummer,* 1983. *The Next Szep Book,* 1985. *Often in Error, Never in Doubt: Cartoons by Paul Szep,* 1987. *Not Just Another Szep Book,* 1997.

Other Awards: Sigma Delta Chi Award, 1974, 1977. Honorary Fellow, Ontario College of Art, Canada, 1975. Boston Toyl Award, Boston Jaycees, MA, 1976. National Headliners Club Award, 1977. Award, Editorial Cartoons, National Cartoonists Society, 1979. Fellow, Institute of Politics, Harvard University, MA, 1981-82. Thomas Nast Award, 1983. Award, Sports Cartoons, National Cartoonists Society, 1988. Honorary Degrees: Framingham College, MA, 1975; Worcester State College, MA, 1980; William Penn College, IA, 1981.

For More Information: *American Civil Liberties Review,* November-December (1977); Robbins, Albert and Randall Rothenberg, *Getting Angry Six Times a Week: A Portfolio of Political Cartoons,* Boston: Beacon Press, 1979: 49-59; *Contemporary Authors, Volume 128,* Detroit: Gale Research Company, 1989; Lent, John A., *Animation, Caricature, and Gag and Political Cartoons in the United States and Canada: An International Bibliography, Bibliographies and Indexes in Popular Culture, Number 3,* Westport, CT: Greenwood Press, 1994.

Commentary: Paul Szep won both of his Pulitzer Prizes for the body of his work in the preceding year. His cartoons in 1973 covered such topics as Watergate, the oil crisis, and local issues such as the lowering of the drinking age. His cartoons in 1977 did not necessarily have a theme running throughout the year, but he did once again touch on the topic of presidential corruption. He was a finalist for a Pulitzer Prize in 1981. A native of Canada, he worked in a steel mill and was a semi-pro hockey player before becoming a cartoonist.

1975

Garretson Beekman Trudeau   276

Birth: July 21, 1948; New York, NY. **Parents:** Robert Trudeau and Jean (Amory). **Education:** Yale University, CT: BA. Yale University, CT: MFA. **Spouse:** Jane Pauley (m. 1980). **Children:** Ross, Rachel, Thomas.

Prize: *Editorial Cartooning,* 1975: Universal Press Syndicate, 1974.

Career: Creator, "Bulls Tales" Comic Strip, college paper, *Yale Daily News,* 1969-70; Editor, *Trilingual Magazine,* Diplomatic Corps, Washington, DC; Designer and Constructor of light murals, Mayor Lindsay, New York City; Photographic Researcher, *Time-Life;* Assistant to Original Producer of Off-Broadway Hit, *Futz;* Manager of graphics studio, New Haven (CT), "Calligraph," 1970; Launched *Doonesbury,* 1970; Cartoonist, series of columns on 1972 conventions, *Miami (FL) Herald.*

Selected Works: *Doonesbury,* 1971. *Still a Few Bugs in the System,* 1972. *Just a French Major from the Bronx,* 1972. *Bravo for Life's Little Ironies,* 1973. *But This War Had Such Promise,* 1973. *The President Is a Lot Smarter Than You Think,* 1973. *The Fireside Watergate* (with Nicholas Von Hoffman), 1973. *Call Me When You Find America,* 1973. *Guilty, Guilty, Guilty!,* 1973. *Joanie: Cartoons for New Children,* 1974. *Dare to Be Great, Ms. Caucus,* 1975. *What Do We Have for the Witness, Johnnie?,* 1975. *Wouldn't a Gremlin Have Been More Sensible?,* 1975. *We'll Take It from Here, Sarge,* 1975. *The Doonesbury Chronicles,* 1975. *Speaking of Inalienable Rights, Amy,* 1976. *You're Never Too Old for Nuts and Berries,* 1976. *Tales from the Margaret Mead Taproom* (with Nicholas Von Hoffman), 1976. *The Original Yale Cartoons,* 1976. *An Especially Tricky People,* 1977. *As the Kid Goes for Broke,* 1977. *Doonesbury Special: A Director's Notebook,* 1977. *Stalking the Perfect Tan,* 1978. *Doonesbury's Greatest Hits,* 1978. *Any Grooming Hints for Your Fans, Rollie?,* 1978. *Doonesbury Classics: 4 Volumes,* 1980. *Doonesbury Dossier: The Reagan Years,* 1980-1984. *A Tad Overweight, but Violet Eyes to Die for,* 1980. *In Search of Reagan's Brain,* 1981. *The People's Doonesbury,* 1981. *Ask for May, Settle for June,* 1982. *The Week of the "Rusty Nail,"* 1983. *Doonesbury: A Musical Comedy* (Play), 1983. *Rap Master Ronnie* (Play), 1984. *Doonesbury Deluxe: Selected Glances Askance,* 1987. *Downtown Doonesbury,* 1987. *Calling Dr. Whoopee! A Doonesbury Book,* 1987. *Doonesbury's Greatest Hits,* 1988. *Talkin' about My G-G-Generation,* 1988. *We're Eating More Beets!,* 1988. *Read My Lips, Make My Day, Eat Quiche and Die!,* 1989. *Give Those Nymphs Some Hooters!,* 1989. *Recycled Doonesbury: Second Thoughts on a Gilded Age,* 1990. *You're Smokin' Now, Mr. Butts!,* 1990. *I'd Go with the Helmet, Ray,* 1991. *Welcome to Club Scud: A Doonesbury Book,* 1991. *What Is It, Tink, Is Pan in Trouble?,* 1992. *Action Figure!,* 1992. *Quality Time on Highway 1,* 1993. *The Portable Doonesbury,* 1993. *Washed out Bridges and Other Disasters,* 1994. *In Search of Cigarette Holder Man,* 1994. *Doonesbury Nation: A Doonesbury Book,* 1995. *Flashbacks: Twenty-Five Years of Doonesbury,* 1995. *Virtual Doonesbury,,* 1996. *Planet Doonesbury: A Doonesbury Book,* 1997. **Films:** *A Doonesbury Special,* 1977; *Tanner* T.V. Series, 1988.

Other Awards: Academy Award Nomination, Animated Film, 1977: *A Doonesbury Special.* Special Jury Prize, Cannes Film Festival, France. Spirit of Liberty Award, People for the American Way, 1995. Reuben Award, National Cartoonists Society, 1996. Honorary Degrees: Colby College, ME, 1981; University of Vermont, 1981; DePauw University, IN, 1983; Fairleigh Dickinson University, Rutherford, NJ, 1983; Duke University, NC, 1988; Johns Hopkins University, MD, 1990; Colgate University, NY; Smith College, MA; Williams College, MA; Yale University, CT; Colorado College, 1997.

For More Information: *Current Biography Yearbook,* 1975, New York: H.W. Wilson, 1975; *Target: The Political Cartoon Quarterly,* 23 (Spring 1987): 13-21; *Contemporary Authors, New Revision Series, Volume 31,* Detroit: Gale Research Company, 1990; Lent, John A., *Comic Books and Comic Strips in the United States: An International Bibliography,*

Bibliographies and Indexes in Popular Culture, Number 4, Westport, CT: Greenwood Press, 1994.

Commentary: Garry Trudeau was awarded the Pulitzer Prize for his comic strip, *Doonesbury.* It was the first time that a cartoonist who drew a comic strip won the award. Trudeau started the strip as *Bull Tales* while he was an undergraduate at Yale University. His use of recognizable personalities along with his particular sense of humor has caused several controversies over the 25 years that the strip has been syndicated. Newspapers have disagreed with the strips to such an extent that some have dropped it from their publications. Currently he is syndicated in approximately 1,400 papers. He was a finalist for a Pulitzer Prize in 1990.

1976

William Anthony Auth Jr. 277
Birth: May 7, 1942; Akron, OH. **Parents:** William Anthony Auth and Julia Kathleen (Donnally). **Education:** University of California, Los Angeles: BA. **Spouse:** Eliza Drake (m. 1982). **Children:** Katie, Emily.

Prize: *Editorial Cartooning,* 1976: *Philadelphia Inquirer,* "O Beautiful for Spacious Skies, For Amber Waves of Grain," Philadelphia, PA: Philadelphia Inquirer, 1975.

Career: Chief Medical Illustrator, Rancho Los Amigos Hospital, 1964-71; Freelance cartoonist, *Open City (CA);* Freelance cartoonist, University of California, Los Angeles, college paper, *Daily Bruin;* Staff Editorial cartoonist, *Philadelphia (PA) Inquirer,* 1971-; Editorial Board Member.

Selected Works: *Behind the Lines,* 1977. *The Gang of Eight,* 1985. *Lost in Space: The Reagan Years,* 1988. *Sleeping Babies: A Big Golden Book,* 1989. *The Sky of Now,* 1995.

Other Awards: Distinguished Service in Journalism Award, Sigma Delta Chi, 1976. Overseas Press Club Award, 1976, 1984, 1986.

For More Information: *Cartoonist PROfiles,* 17 (1973): 14-23; *Philadelphia Inquirer,* May 4, 1976: 1; *American Civil Liberties Review,* July / August (1977); Robbins, Albert and Randall Rothenberg, *Getting Angry Six Times a Week: A Portfolio of Political Cartoons,* Boston: Beacon Press, 1979; *Contemporary Authors, Volume 108,* Detroit: Gale Research Company, 1983; *Comics Journal,* December (1987): 106-116.

Commentary: Tony Auth used his degree in biological illustration to start his career as a medical illustrator, but at the same time published political cartoons in the University of California, Los Angeles campus paper for free as his avocation. Eventually that

led to full-time employment as an editorial cartoonist. Auth was also a finalist for a Pulitzer Prize in 1983.

1977

Paul Michael Szep
Full entry appears as **#275** under "Editorial Cartooning," 1974.

1978

Jeffrey Kenneth MacNelly
Full entry appears as **#274** under "Editorial Cartooning," 1972.

1979

Herbert Lawrence Block
Full entry appears as **#252** under "Editorial Cartooning," 1942.

1980

Donald Conway Wright
Full entry appears as **#269** under "Editorial Cartooning," 1966.

1981

Michael Bartley Peters 278
Birth: October 9, 1943; St. Louis, MO. **Parents:** William Ernst Peters and Charlotte Burt (Wiedeman). **Education:** Washington University, MO: BFA. **Spouse:** Marian Connole (m. 1965). **Children:** Michelle, Patricia, Martha.

Prize: *Editorial Cartooning,* 1981: *Dayton Daily News,* Dayton, OH: Dayton Daily News, 1980.

Career: Art Staff member, *Chicago Daily News,* 1965-66; Artist, Seventh Psychological Operations Group, U.S. Army, Okinawa (Japan), 1966-68; Editorial Cartoonist, *Chicago Daily News,* 1968; Editorial Cartoonist, *Dayton Daily News,* 1969-; Syndicated cartoonist.

Selected Works: *The Nixon Chronicles,* 1976. *Clones, You Idiot...I Said Clones,* 1978. *Win One for the Geezer,* 1982. *The World of Cartooning with Mike Peters: How Caricatures Develop,* 1985. *On the Brink,* 1986. *Mother Goose and Grimm,* 1986. *Grimm's Furry Tales,* 1987. *The Portable Mother Goose and Grimm,* 1987. *Oh God! It's Grimm,* 1988. *Steel-Belted Grimm,* 1988. *Four-Wheel Grimmy,*

1989. *Grimmy, So Many Trees, So Little Time,* 1989. *Grimmy, Best in Show,* 1989. *Grimmy Come Home,* 1990. *It's Grimmy,* 1990. *Grimmy, Pick of the Litter,* 1990. *Mother Goose and Grimm's Night of the Living Vacuum,* 1991. *Grimmy, Top Dog,* 1991. *Happy Days Are Here Again!,* 1992. *Grimmy, Bone in the U.S.A.,* 1992. *Grimmy, and the Temple of the Groom,* 1992. *Grimmy: On the Move,* 1992. *On the Edge: 25 Years of Cartooning at the Dayton Daily News,* 1994. *Grimmy: What a Wag,* 1994. *Grimmy: Friends Don't Let Friends Own Cats,* 1996. *Grimmy: The Postman Always Screams Twice,* 1996. *Grimmy: King of the Heap,* 1997.

Other Awards: Distinguished Service Award, Sigma Delta Chi, 1976. Ohio Man of the Year, American Civil Liberties Union, 1981. Distinguished Alumni Award, Washington University, MO, 1982. National Headliners Club Award, 1982, 1987, 1994. Reuben Award, National Cartoonists Society, 1992.

For More Information: *Cartoonist PROfiles,* 22 (1974): 6-10; *American Civil Liberties Review,* March-April (1978); Robbins, Albert and Randall Rothenberg, *Getting Angry Six Times A Week: A Portfolio of Political Cartoons,* Boston: Beacon Press, 1979; *Ohio Magazine,* June (1981): 22-28; *Contemporary Authors, Volume 108,* Detroit: Gale Research Company, 1983; Lent, John A., *Animation, Caricature, and Gag and Political Cartoons in the United States and Canada: An International Bibliography, Bibliographies and Indexes in Popular Culture, Number 3,* Westport, CT: Greenwood Press, 1994; *Quill,* 83 (January/February 1995): 27-29.

Commentary: Mike Peters's newspaper has been picketed by readers irate about his cartoons. Both D.R. Fitzpatrick and Bill Mauldin were acquaintances and influences of his when he was growing up. Mauldin even called the editor of the *Dayton Daily News* for Peters when he knew there was a job open. Peters is also known for the comic strip he draws, *Mother Goose and Grimm.* He was a finalist for a Pulitzer Prize in 1986.

1982

Ben Sargent   279

Birth: December 26, 1948; Amarillo, TX. **Parents:** Joseph N. Sargent and Dorothy (Brown). **Religion:** Roman Catholic. **Education:** Amarillo College, TX: AA. University of Texas: BA. **Spouse:** Kathryn Abbott (m. 1969, div. 1983); Diane Holloway (m. 1984). **Children:** Elizabeth (KA); Sam (DH).

Prize: *Editorial Cartooning,* 1982: *Austin American-Statesman,* Austin, TX: Austin American-Statesman, 1981.

Career: Proof Runner; Reporter, *Corpus Christi (TX) Caller-Times,* 1969; Reporter, Long News Serv-

ice, 1969-71; Reporter, *Austin (TX) American-Statesman,* 1971-72; Reporter, Long News Service, 1972-74; Reporter, United Press International, 1972; Editorial Cartoonist, *Austin (TX) American-Statesman,* 1974-.

Selected Works: *Texas Statehouse Blues,* 1980. *Big Brother Blues,* 1984.

Other Awards: "Outstanding Communicator" Award, Women in Communication Incorporated, 1981. Media Award, Texas Women's Political Caucus, 1982. H.L. Mencken Award, 1988. Outstanding Young Texas Eyes Award, University of Texas, 1989. Public Service Award, Common Cause of Texas, 1990.

For More Information: *American Civil Liberties Review,* May/June (1978); Robbins, Albert and Randall Rothenberg, *Getting Angry Six Times A Week: A Portfolio of Political Cartoons,* Boston: Beacon Press, 1979; *Target: The Political Cartoon Quarterly,* Summer (1983): 4-10; *Contemporary Authors, Volume 113,* Detroit: Gale Research Company, 1985.

Commentary: Ben Sargent worked as a reporter for five years before becoming an editorial cartoonist. He is the first full-time cartoonist that the *Austin American-Statesman* has employed. His cartoons typically make a strong statement on state politics, but he also turns his commentary pen toward national and international issues.

He grew up in a newspaper family, with both his parents working for the *Amarillo News and Globe Times.* He was also the president of the Association of American Editorial Cartoonists from 1988-89.

1983

Richard Earl Locher   280

Birth: June 4, 1929; Dubuque, IA. **Parents:** Joseph John Locher and Lucille (Jungk). **Education:** Loras College, IA. University of Iowa. Chicago Academy of Fine Arts, Art Center of Los Angeles. **Spouse:** Mary Therese Cosgrove (m. 1957). **Children:** Steve, John, Jana.

Prize: *Editorial Cartooning,* 1983: *Chicago Tribune,* Chicago: Chicago Tribune, 1982.

Career: U.S. Air Force Test Pilot, 1951-71; Assistant, Rick Yager, 1955; Assistant, Chester Gould (Creator of Dick Tracy), 1958-61; President of Firm, Novamark Corporation Art Studio, 1962-72; Staff Cartoonist, *Chicago Tribune,* 1973-; Illustrator, *Dick Tracy,* 1983-; Illustrator, *Clout Street,* 1983-; Painter, Sculptor, Aircraft Designer, Inventor.

Selected Works: *Dick Locher Draws Fire: Chicago Tribune Editorial Cartoons,* 1980. *Send in the Clowns: Chicago Tribune Editorial Cartoons by Locher,* 1982. *Flying Can Be Fun* (with Michael Kilian), 1985. *Dick Tracy: Tracy's Wartime Memories* (with

Max Collins), 1986. *Vote for Me, and It Serves You Right (and Left)*, 1988. *The Dick Tracy Casebook: Favorite Adventures, 1931-1990* (with Max Collins), 1990. *Dick Tracy's Fiendish Foes: A 60th Anniversary Celebration* (with Max Collins), 1991. *Dick Tracy and the Nightmare Machine* (with Max Collins), 1991. *Which One Is the None of the Above Button?*, 1992. *The Daze of Whine and Neurosis*, 1995.

Other Awards: Dragonslayer Award, National Educational Society, 1976-78, 1983. Special Citation, Scripps-Howard Foundation, 1978. Distinguished Health Journalism Award, American Chiropractic Association, 1983. Distinguished Service in Journalism Award, Sigma Delta Chi, 1983. Overseas Press Club Award, 1983-84. John Fischetti Award, 1987.

For More Information: *Cartoonist PROfiles,* 40 (December 1978): 14-23; *Chicago Tribune,* April 10, 1983: 1, 4; *Cartoonist PROfiles,* 64 (December 1984): 70-74; *Cartoonist PROfiles,* June (1989): 28-33.

Commentary: Dick Lochner entered the editorial cartooning business later in life than most of his contemporaries. He first was a test pilot for the Air Force; he assisted Chester Gould, the creator of Dick Tracy; and he started his own art studio which he ran for 10 years.

1984

Paul Francis Conrad

Full entry appears as **#268** under "Editorial Cartooning," 1964.

1985

Jeffrey Kenneth MacNelly

Full entry appears as **#274** under "Editorial Cartooning," 1972.

1986

Jules Ralph Feiffer   281

Birth: January 26, 1929; Bronx, NY. **Parents:** David Feiffer and Rhoda (Davis). **Religion:** Jewish. **Education:** Art Students' League, NY. Pratt Institute, NY. **Spouse:** Judith Sheftel (m. 1961, div. 1983); Jennifer Allen (m. 1983). **Children:** Kate (JS); Hallie, Julie (JA).

Prize: *Editorial Cartooning,* 1986: *Village Voice,* New York: Village Voice, 1985.

Career: Assistant, Will Eisner (Drew "The Spirit"), 1946-51; Syndicated Cartoonist, *Clifford,* 1949-51; Served in U.S. Army, 1951-53; Writer, CBS TV, *Terry Toon;* Cartoonist, *Village Voice (NY),* 1956-96; Cartoonist, *Playboy;* Writer-in-Residence, Northwestern University, 1996-97; Writer-in-Residence, Columbia University Graduate School of Journalism, 1997-.

Selected Works: *Sick, Sick, Sick,* 1958. *Passionella and Other Stories,* 1958. *The Explainers,* 1960. *Boy, Girl, Boy, Girl,* 1961. *The Feiffer Album,* 1962. *Hold Me!,* 1962. *Harry: The Rat with Women, a Novel,* 1963. *Feiffer's Album,* 1963. *The Unexpurgated Memoirs of Bernard Mergendeiler,* 1964. *Feiffer on Civil Rights,* 1966. *The Penguin Feiffer,* 1966. *Feiffer's Marriage Manual,* 1967. *Pictures at a Prosecution,* 1971. *Feiffer on Nixon, the Cartoon Presidency,* 1974. *Tantrum,* 1979. *Jules Feiffer's America: From Eisenhower to Reagan,* 1982. *Marriage Is an Invasion of Privacy and Other Dangerous Views,* 1984. *Feiffer's Children,* 1986. *Ronald Reagan in Movie America,* 1988. *The Man in the Ceiling,* 1993. *A Barrel of Laughs, a Vale of Tears,* 1995. *Meanwhile—,* 1997. *I Lost My Bear,* 1998.

Other Awards: Page One Award, Newspaper Guild of New York. Capital Press Club Award. Academy Award, Short Subject, 1961: *Munro.* Special George Polk Memorial Award, Long Island University, NY, 1962. Obie Award, 1969. Outer Circle Drama Critics Award, 1969-70.

For More Information: *Contemporary Authors, First Revision, Volumes 17-20,* Detroit: Gale Research Company, 1976: 117-118; Robbins, Albert and Randall Rosenberg, *Getting Angry Six Times a Week: A Portfolio of Political Cartoons,* Boston: Beacon Press, 1979: 12-27; *New York Times,* 15 December (1981): C9; *Los Angeles Times,* 30 September (1993): part E; Lent, John A., *Animation, Caricature, and Gag and Political Cartoons in the United States and Canada: An International Bibliography, Bibliographies and Indexes in Popular Culture, Number 3,* Westport, CT: Greenwood Press, 1994; Lent, John A., *Comic Books and Comic Strips in the United States: An International Bibliography, Bibliographies and Indexes in Popular Culture, Number 4,* Westport, CT: Greenwood Press, 1994.

Commentary: Jules Feiffer is very versatile. Besides his cartooning, he has also written plays, screenplays, fiction, and children's books. He currently teaches. He left his long time employer, the *Village Voice,* after a dispute in 1996. His cartoon strip is currently syndicated nationally weekly and is "characterized by sharp social commentary." He was a finalist for a Pulitzer Prize in 1981.

1987

Guy Berkeley Breathed   282

Birth: June 21, 1957; Encino, CA. **Parents:** John W. Breathed and Martha Jane (Martin). **Education:** University of Texas: BA. **Spouse:** Jody Boyman (m. 1986).

Prize: *Editorial Cartooning,* 1987: *Washington Post,* Washington, DC: Washington Post, 1986.

Career: Photographer/Columnist, college paper, *Daily Texan,* 1976-78; Cartoonist, 1978-.

Selected Works: *The Academia Waltz,* 1979. *Bloom County: Loose Tails,* 1983. *'Toons for Our Times,* 1984. *Penguin Dreams and Stranger Things,* 1985. *Bloom County Babylon,* 1986. *Billy and the Boingers Bootleg,* 1987. *Tales Too Ticklish to Tell,* 1988. *The Night of the Mary Kay Commandos,* 1989. *Happy Trails,* 1990. *Classics of Western Literature: Bloom County, 1986-1989,* 1990. *A Wish for Things That Work: An Opus Christmas Story,* 1991. *Politically, Fashionably, and Aerodynamically Incorrect: The First Outland Collection,* 1992. *The Last Basselope: One Ferocious Story,* 1992. *Goodnight Opus,* 1993. *His Kisses Are Dreamy — But Those Hairballs Down My Cleavage —! Another Tender Outland Collection,* 1994. *Red Ranger Came Calling: A Guaranteed True Christmas Story,* 1994. *One Last Little Peek, 1980-1995: The Final Strips, the Special Hits, the Inside Tips,* 1995. *Little Murders* (Play). *Carnal Knowledge* (Play).

Other Awards: Harry A. Schweikert Jr. Disability Awareness Award, Paralyzed Vets of America, 1982.

For More Information: *Comics Collector,* Winter (1984): 48-49+; *Cartoonist PROfiles,* December (1987): 12-18; Wills, Kendall J., *The Pulitzer Prizes, Volume 1, 1987,* New York: Touchstone Book, 1987; *Comics Journal,* 125 (October 1988): 74-106; Lent, John, *Comic Books and Comic Strips in the United States: An International Bibliography, Bibliographies and Indexes in Popular Culture, Number 4,* Westport, CT: Greenwood Press, 1994.

Commentary: Berke Breathed's editorial cartooning Pulitzer Prize was the second to be awarded for a comic strip (the first was to Garry Trudeau). He has since ceased creating the strip, Bloom County, that had such unforgettable characters as Opus, a penguin, and Bill the Cat, as well as some humans to add to the mix. The strip ran in syndication from December 1980 to 1989.

1988

Douglas Nigel Marlette   283

Birth: December 6, 1949; Greensboro, NC. **Religion:** Baptist. **Education:** Seminole Community College, FL. Florida State University: BA. **Spouse:** Melinda Hartley. **Children:** Jackson.

Prize: *Editorial Cartooning,* 1988: *Atlanta Constitution,* Atlanta, GA, 1987, and *Charlotte Observer,* Charlotte, NC, 1987.

Career: College Press Service cartoonist; Editorial Cartoonist, *Charlotte (NC) Observer,* 1972-87; Creator, *Kudzu,* 1980-; Editorial Cartoonist, *Atlanta (GA) Constitution,* 1987-89; Editorial Cartoonist, *Newsday (NY),* 1989-.

Selected Works: *The Emperor Has No Clothes: Editorial Cartoons,* 1976. *If You Can't Say Something Nice: Political Cartoons,* 1978. *Drawing Blood: Political Cartoons,* 1980. *Kudzu,* 1982. *Preacher: The Wit and Wisdom of Reverend Will B. Dunn,* 1984. *It's a Dirty Job—But Somebody Has to Do It! Cartoons,* 1984. *Just a Simple Country Preacher: More Wit and Wisdom of Reverend Will B. Dunn,* 1985. *There's No Business Like Soul Business,* 1987. *Chocolate Is My Life: Featuring Doris the Parakeet,* 1987. *Shred This Book,* 1988. *St*rs and Swipes: The Fine Art of Political Satire* (with others), 1988. *I Am Not a Televangelist! The Continuing Saga of Reverend Will B. Dunn,* 1988. *'Til Stress Do Us Part: A Guide to Modern Love by Reverend Will B. Dunn,* 1989. *A Doublewide with a View: The Kudzu Chronicles,* 1989. *In Your Face: A Cartoonist at Work,* 1991. *The Before and After Book,* 1992. *Even White Boys Get the Blues: Kudzu's First Ten Years,* 1992. *Faux Bubba,* 1993. *Gone with the Kudzu,* 1995. *I Feel Your Pain,* 1996.

Other Awards: Nieman Fellow, Harvard University, MA, 1980-81. National Headliners Club Award, 1983, 1988. Robert F. Kennedy Journalism Award, 1984. Distinguished Service Award, Sigma Delta Chi, 1986. First Amendment Award, 1986. John Fischetti Award, 1986, 1992. Golden Plate Academy of Achievement, 1991.

For More Information: *Cartoonist PROfiles,* September (1978): 54-61; Robbins, Albert and Randall Rothenberg, *Getting Angry Six Times A Week: A Portfolio of Political Cartoons,* Boston: Beacon Press, 1979: 73; *Cartoonist PROfiles,* September (1988): 16-23; *WittyWorld,* Winter / Spring (1990): 50-55; Lent, John A., *Animation, Caricature, and Gag and Political Cartoons in the United States and Canada: An International Bibliography, Bibliographies and Indexes in Popular Culture, Number 3,* Westport, CT: Greenwood Press, 1994; *Target: The Political Cartoon Quarterly,* 17: 4-11.

Commentary: Doug Marlette changed his college major from art to philosophy. As a cartoonist, he uses his medium to make a point. He was the first cartoonist to win a Nieman Fellowship at Harvard University. He was awarded a Pulitzer Prize for his work done in 1987. Typical themes covered were the Reagan Administration and television evangelists. He was a finalist for the award in 1975.

Marlette grew up during the 1950s and 1960s. He applied for and was granted conscientious objector status during the Vietnam conflict.

1989

Jack Higgins   284

Birth: August 19, 1954; Chicago, IL. **Parents:** Maurice James Higgins and Helen Marie (Egan). **Religion:** Roman Catholic. **Education:** College of the Holy Cross, MA: AB. **Spouse:** Mary Elizabeth Irving (m. 1997).

Prize: *Editorial Cartooning,* 1989: *Chicago Sun-Times,* Chicago: Chicago Sun-Times, 1988.

Career: Member of Jesuit Volunteer Corporation, 1 year; Cartoonist, Northwestern University (IL) College paper, 1978-80; Editorial Cartoonist, *Chicago Sun-Times,* 1981-.

Other Awards: Peter Lisagor Award, Society of Professional Journalists, Chicago Chapter, IL, 1985, 1987, 1993-94, 1997. First Prize, International Salon of Cartoons Competition, 1988. Distinguished Service Award, Society of Professional Journalists, 1988. Alumni Medal, St. Ignatius College Prep, 1991. Herman Kogan Award, Chicago Bar Association, 1993, 1995. Illinois Journalist of the Year, 1996.

For More Information: *Cartoonist PROfiles,* 72 (December 1986): 40-47; *Bull's Eye,* 5 (1989): 8-13; *Chicago Sun-Times,* 15 September (1996): 14.

Commentary: Two years after graduating from college, Jack Higgins was drawing cartoons for the Northwestern University student newspaper before freelancing cartoons to the *Chicago Sun-Times.* In 1981 he began working for the newspaper fulltime.

Higgins wakes early, which gives him the feeling that he has "a jump on the world," and he reads, thinks, and jots down ideas before heading in to his office. He was a finalist for a Pulitzer Prize in 1986.

1990

Thomas G. Toles   285

Birth: October 22, 1951; Buffalo, NY. **Parents:** George E. Toles and Rose (Riehle). **Education:** State University of New York, Buffalo: BA, magna cum laude. **Spouse:** Gretchen Saarnijoki (m. 1973). **Children:** Amanda, Seth.

Prize: *Editorial Cartooning,* 1990: *The Buffalo News,* "First Amendment," Buffalo, NY: Buffalo News, 1989.

Career: Graphics Art Editor, college paper, *The Spectrum,* 1969-73; Staff Artist, *Buffalo (NY) Courier-Express,* 1973-80; Graphics Designer, *Buffalo (NY) Courier-Express,* 1979; Editorial Cartoonist, *Buffalo (NY) Courier-Express,* 1980-82; Editorial Cartoonist, *Buffalo (NY) News* 1982-; Cartoonist, *New Republic* magazine, 1992-94; Cartoonist, *U.S. News and World Report Magazine,* 1994-.

Selected Works: *The Taxpayer's New Clothes,* 1985. *Mr. Gazoo: A Cartoon History of the Reagan Era,* 1987. *At Least Our Bombs Are Getting Smarter,* 1991. *My Elected Representatives Went to Washington: Cartoons,* 1993. *Curious Avenue,* 1993. *Duh— and Other Observations,* 1996. *My School Is Worse Than Yours,* 1997.

Other Awards: George W. Thorn Award, University of Buffalo Alumni Association, NY, 1983. Golden Apple Award, Excellence in Educational Journalism, New York State United Teachers, 1984. John Fischetti Award, 1984. New York State Historic Preservation Award, 1985.

For More Information: *Target, The Political Cartoon Quarterly,* Autumn (1981): 22-24; *Bull's Eye,* June (1988): 4-6+; *Cartoonist PROfiles,* December (1991): 58-62; *Comics Journal,* 195 (April 1997): 68-107.

Commentary: Tom Toles has a distinctive drawing style. His editorial cartoons more often than not are made up of several panels, and usually small characters are commenting on the story line. He was a finalist for a Pulitzer Prize in 1985 and 1996.

1991

James Mark Borgman   286

Birth: February 24, 1954; Cincinnati, OH. **Parents:** James Borgman and Marian (Maly). **Education:** Kenyon College, OH: BA, summa cum laude, Phi Beta Kappa. **Spouse:** Lynn Goodwin (m. 1977). **Children:** Dylan, Chelsea.

Prize: *Editorial Cartooning,* 1991: *Cincinnati Enquirer,* Cincinnati, OH: Cincinnati Enquirer, 1989.

Career: Cartoonist, college paper, *Kenyon Collegian,* 1975; Editorial Cartoonist, *Cincinnati (OH) Enquirer,* 1976-.

Selected Works: *Smorgasborgman* (with Lynn Goodwin Borgman), 1982. *The Great Communicator,* 1985. *The Mood of America* (with others), 1986. *Jim Borgman's Cincinnati,* 1992. *Disturbing the Peace* (with Bill Watterson), 1995.

Other Awards: Anderson Cup, Kenyon College, OH, 1976. Sigma Delta Chi Award, 1978, 1995. Thomas Nast Prize, 1980. Post Corbett Award, 1981. Award, Editorial Cartoons, National Cartoonists Society, 1987-89, 1995. Ohio Governor's Award, 1989. National Headliners Club Award, 1991. The Golden Plate, 1992. Reuben Award, National Cartoonists Society, 1994.

For More Information: *Cartoonist PROfiles,* 41 (March 1979): 34-41; *Tropics,* June 16, 1985: 14-17; West, Richard S., *Target: The Political Cartoon Quarterly,* 4:19 (Spring 1986): 4-15.

Commentary: Jim Borgman began working for the *Cincinnati Enquirer* one week after graduating from college. The paper hired him after seeing 15 cartoons he had drawn for his college paper. He draws six cartoons weekly on local and national topics. Borgman was a finalist for a Pulitzer Prize in 1985, 1995, and 1996.

1992

Signe Wilkinson   287

Birth: July 25, 1959; Wichita Falls, TX. **Education:** University of Denver, CO: BA. Pennsylvania Academy of Fine Arts. University of Strasbourg, France. **Spouse:** Jon Landau. **Children:** Claire, Nikki.

Prize: *Editorial Cartooning,* 1992: *Philadelphia Daily News,* Philadelphia, PA: Philadelphia Daily News, 1991.

Career: Reporter, art director, peace activist; Housing project director, Cyprus; Stringer, *West Chester (PA) Daily Local News;* Editorial Cartoonist, *San Jose (CA) Mercury News,* 1982-85; Editorial Cartoonist, *Philadelphia (PA) Daily News,* 1985-.

Selected Works: *Abortion Cartoons on Demand,* 1992.

Other Awards: Berryman Award, National Press Foundation, 1991.

For More Information: *Target, The Political Cartoon Quarterly,* Autumn (1983): 25-26; *Editor & Publisher,* 125:37 (1992): 46-48; *WittyWorld,* Winter (1993):15-16+.

Commentary: Signe Wilkinson is the only woman to have won an editorial cartooning Pulitzer Prize. Her favorite topics are social issues, concerning mainly women and children, but her cartoons comment on all aspects of American life. In 1994-95, she was president of the Association of American Editorial Cartoonists. She was a finalist for a Pulitzer Prize in 1991.

1993

Stephen Reed Benson   288

Birth: January 2, 1954; Sacramento, CA. **Parents:** Mark A. Benson. **Religion:** Christian. **Education:** Minneapolis Art Instruction Schools, MN. Brigham Young University, UT: BS, cum laude. **Spouse:** Mary Ann Christensen. **Children:** Rebecca, Eric, Brent, Audrey.

Prize: *Editorial Cartooning,* 1993: *Arizona Republic,* Phoenix, AZ: Arizona Republic, 1992.

Career: Missionary, Japan; Editorial Cartoonist, *Arizona Republic,* Phoenix, 1980-89; Editorial Cartoonist, *Tacoma (WA) Morning News Tribune,* 1990-91; Editorial Cartoonist, *Arizona Republic,* 1991-.

Selected Works: *Fencin' with Benson,* 1984. *Evanly Days,* 1988. *Back at the Barb-B-Que: An Expanded Cartoon Collection,* 1991. *Where Do You Draw the Line? Cartoons,* 1992.

Other Awards: Arizona Press Club Award, 1980-81, 1984-85. Parched Cow Award, Arizona Department of Tourism, 1985. National Headliners Club Award, 1984. Best of the West Award, 1991-93.

For More Information: *New York Times,* 19 March (1988): section 1, 6; *Arizona Republic,* 14 April (1993): A1; *WittyWorld,* Summer (1993): 4-5.

Commentary: Steve Benson joined the *Arizona Republic* in 1980 and, except for a two-year stint in Washington state, has been there ever since. Some of the cartoons he drew in 1992 dealt with the topics of terrorism, child-molesting priests, famine, and such personalities as George Bush, Ross Perot, and Bill Clinton. Benson was a finalist for The Pulitzer Prize in 1984, 1989, 1992, and 1994.

Benson is the grandson of Ezra Taft Benson, who was the United States Secretary of Agriculture during the Eisenhower administration and the head of the Mormon Church from 1985-1994.

1994

Michael Patrick Ramirez   289

Birth: May 11, 1961; Tokyo, Japan. **Parents:** Ireneo Edward Ramirez and Fumiko Maria. **Education:** University of California, Irvine: BFA.

Prize: *Editorial Cartooning,* 1994: *Memphis Commercial Appeal,* Memphis, TN: Commercial Appeal, 1993.

Career: Staff of college paper, *New University,* 1979; Staff of *Sutton News Group,* 1979; Editorial Cartoonist, *Baker Communications, Palos Verdes (CA) Peninsula News,* 1982-89; Editorial Cartoonist, *The San Clemente (CA) Daily Sun Post,* 1989-90; Editorial Cartoonist, *Memphis (TN) Commercial Appeal,* 1990-97; Editorial Cartoonist, *Los Angeles Times,* 1997-.

Other Awards: H.L. Mencken Award, 1996. National Society of Professional Journalists Award, 1996.

For More Information: *WittyWorld,* Winter / Spring (1991): 6-11; *Los Angeles Times,* April 30, 1994: B2; *Editor & Publisher,* 130:30 (July 26, 1997): 30, *Los Angeles Times,* September 24, 1997: A3.

Commentary: Michael Ramirez's cartoons draw strong reactions from his readers. He interjects his observations with a wry humor. Typical of his work in 1993 was a cartoon with President Clinton and a sumo wrestler representing the Japanese attitude toward America. As they bow to each other, Clinton, staring at the sumo wrestler's backside, asks "Shouldn't he be facing the other way?"

Ramirez is syndicated by Copley News Service to over 950 newspapers.

1995

Mike Luckovich   290

Birth: 1960; Seattle, WA. **Education:** University of Washington: BS. **Spouse:** Margo L. **Children:** John, Mickey, Micaela.

Prize: *Editorial Cartooning,* 1995: *Atlanta Constitution,* Atlanta, GA: Atlanta Constitution, 1994.

Career: Editorial Cartoonist, college paper, *University of Washington Daily;* Life insurance agent; Cartoonist, *Bellevue (WA) Journal American;* Cartoonist, *Seattle (WA) Post Intelligencer;* Cartoonist, *Everett (WA) Herald,* 1981-84; Cartoonist, *Greenville (SC) News,* 1984-85; Editorial Cartoonist, *New Orleans (LA) Times-Picayune,* 1985-89; Editorial Cartoonist, *Atlanta (GA) Constitution,* 1989-.

Selected Works: *Lots of Luckovich,* 1996.

Other Awards: Overseas Press Club Award, 1990, 1994. National Headliners Club Award, 1992. Robert F. Kennedy Journalism Award, 1994.

For More Information: *Target: The Political Cartoon Quarterly,* Winter (1985): 28-29; *Editor & Publisher,* 119:40 (October 4, 1986): 82-83; *Cartoonist PROfiles,* March (1989): 30-35; *Atlanta Journal and Constitution,* April 19, 1995: 1C.

Commentary: Mike Luckovich has been drawing cartoons since his childhood and was the editorial cartoonist on his college paper. He settled for a job as a life insurance agent for two years, but kept a copy of the job advertisements from *Editor & Publisher,* the newspaper trade journal, with him in his car. He accepted a job in the South and has been a cartoonist ever since. He was a finalist for the Pulitzer Prize in 1986. One of his cartoons graced the cover of the January 4, 1998 issue of *Newsweek.*

1996

James Morin   291

Birth: January 30, 1953; Washington, DC. **Parents:** Charles H. Morin and Elizabeth D. **Education:** Syracuse University, NY: BFA. **Spouse:** Danielle Flood. **Children:** Elizabeth, Spencer.

Prize: *Editorial Cartooning,* 1996: *Miami Herald,* Miami, FL: Miami Herald, 1995.

Career: Editorial Cartoonist, *Beaumont (TX) Enterprise and Journal,* 1976-77; Editorial Cartoonist, *Richmond (VA) Times-Dispatch,* 1977-78; Editorial Cartoonist, *Miami (FL) Herald,* 1978-.

Selected Works: *Famous Cats,* 1982. *Jim Morin's Field Guide to Birds,* 1985. *Line of Fire,* 1991.

Other Awards: Overseas Press Club Award, 1979, 1990. H.L. Mencken Award, 1990. Award, Editorial Cartoons, National Cartoonists Society, 1993. Berryman Award, National Press Foundation, 1996.

For More Information: *Cartoonist PROfiles,* September (1979): 56-61; *Cartoonist PROfiles,* September (1989): 46-53; *Editor & Publisher,* 129 (September 28, 1996): 32-33.

Commentary: Jim Morin became interested in cartooning while he was in college. He majored in illustration and minored in painting. He was a finalist for a Pulitzer Prize in 1977 and 1990. (In both years, the Pulitzer board awarded the Prize to a non-finalist.) In 1996, he was awarded a Pulitzer Prize even though he was not a finalist that year.

According to Jim Morin, "The most important element in an editorial cartoon is not humor, but, as with written editorials and columns, the passion and thoughtfulness of the commentary, coupled with evocative draftsmanship to effectively slam the point home."

1997

Walt Handelsman 292

Birth: December 3, 1956; Baltimore, MD. **Parents:** Dr. Jacob C. Handelsman and Shirley (Silverberg). **Religion:** Jewish. **Education:** Dean Junior College, MA: AA. University of Cincinnati, OH: BA. **Spouse:** Jodie Blankman (m. 1982). **Children:** James, William.

Prize: *Editorial Cartooning,* 1997: *New Orleans Times-Picayune,* New Orleans: New Orleans Times-Picayune, 1996.

Career: Editorial Cartoonist, Patuxent Publishing Company, 1982-85; Editorial Cartoonist, *Scranton (PA) Times,* 1985-89; Editorial Cartoonist, *New Orleans (LA) Times-Picayune,* 1989-.

Selected Works: *Political Gumbo: A Collection of Editorial Cartoons,* 1994. *Draw Me Sumpthin', Mister!,* 1997.

Other Awards: National Headliners Club Award, 1989, 1993. Sigma Delta Chi Award, 1992. Robert F. Kennedy Journalism Award, 1996.

For More Information: *Cartoonist PROfiles,* December (1989): 62-68; *Baltimore Sun,* 29 May (1997): E1; *Southern Living,* 32:4 (April 1997): 150-154; *New Orleans Times-Picayune,* 5 November (1997): E1.

Commentary: Walt Handelsman joined the *New Orleans Times-Picayune* in 1989 after his friend Mike Luckovich moved to the *Atlanta Journal-Constitution.* Handelsman is a syndicated cartoonist who appears in more than 100 newspapers nationwide. His entry included 20 cartoons that he drew throughout 1996, many of them on the presidential election.

1998

Stephen P. Breen 293

Birth: April 26, 1970; Los Angeles, CA. **Parents:** Paul Howard Breen and Joanne Francis (Sundstedt). **Religion:** Roman Catholic. **Education:** University of California, Riverside: BA. **Spouse:** Catherine Macfarlane (m. 1998).

Prize: *Editorial Cartooning,* 1998: *Asbury Park Press,* Neptune, NJ: *Asbury Park Press,* 1997.

Career: Contributor, college paper, *Highlander;* Paginator, *Neptune (NJ) Asbury Park Press,* 1994-95; Art Department, *Neptune (NJ) Asbury Park Press,* 1995-96; Editorial Cartoonist, *Neptune (NJ) Asbury Park Press,* 1996-; Editorial Cartoonist, *Home News Tribune.*

Other Awards: Charles M. Schulz Award for College Cartooning, Scripps-Howard, 1991. John Locher Memorial Award for College Cartooning, Association of American Editorial Cartoonists, 1991. Outstanding College Cartoonist, National Journalism Awards, Scripps-Howard Foundation, 1991.

For More Information: *Asbury Park Press,* 15 April (1998): A1; *Asbury Park Press,* 16 April (1998): A1; *New York Times,* 19 April (1998): Section 14, 9; *Editor & Publisher,* 131:17 (25 April 1998): 44.

Commentary: Stephen P. Breen was awarded a Pulitzer Prize in Editorial Cartooning for his portfolio of cartoons in 1997. Some of the topics portrayed in his winning cartoons included political fundraising, cigarette advertising, the paparazzi, cloning, child labor, the death penalty, and China-United States foreign relations. Breen was not a finalist in the Editorial Cartooning category; the Pulitzer Prize Board asked the cartooning jury for additional finalists and then chose Breen for the award.

Breen regularly contributed "gag" cartoons to his college paper. In 1994, he began working at the *Asbury Park Press* and was allowed to draw one editorial cartoon a week. He then worked in the illustration department and the editorial department before becoming a fulltime cartoonist in 1996. His work is syndicated nationally through Copley News Service.

Editorial Writing

1917

New York Tribune   294
Founded: April 10, 1841; New York, NY. **Founder(s):** Horace Greeley.

Prize: *Editorial Writing,* 1917: *New York Tribune,* "Lusitania Anniversary," May 7, New York, NY: New York Tribune, 1916.

For More Information: Parton, James. *The Life of Horace Greeley, Editor of the New York Tribune,* New York, NY: Mason Brothers, 1855; Greeley, Horace. *Recollections of a Busy Life,* New York, NY: J.B. Ford, 1868; *The New York Tribune: A Sketch of Its History, Illustrated,* New York, NY: 1883; Baehr, Harry William. *The New York Tribune Since the Civil War,* New York, NY: Dodd, Mead & Company, 1936; *American Heritage,* 18: 6 (October 1967): 97-112; Schulze, Suzanne. *Horace Greeley: A Bio-Bibliography, Bibliographies and Indexes in American History, Number 22,* New York, NY: Greenwood Press, 1992.

Commentary: The *New York Tribune* was awarded the first Pulitzer Prize presented in the editorial writing category in 1917. Frank Herbert Simonds wrote the winning editorial on the anniversary of the sinking of the passenger oceanliner, the Lusitania, in 1915. In the editorial, he characterizes the war in Europe as "one between civilization and barbarism."

Simonds was born in Concord, Massachusetts on April 5, 1878. He was associate editor of the *New York Tribune* when his paper was awarded the Pulitzer Prize. In 1918, he became a syndicated columnist. He wrote several books about America and World War I (the Great War). He died January 23, 1936 (*New York Times,* 24 January (1936): 19).

The *New York Tribune* was founded by Horace Greeley on April 10, 1841. It was a Republican paper and expressed the opinions of its founder. In 1862, Greeley wrote an editorial in the *Tribune* titled "Prayer for Twenty Million," which encouraged President Lincoln to end slavery in America. Lincoln's reply, which was to save the Union regardless of the issue of slavery, has been cited as his real position on the issue. One of the innovations of the *Tribune* was to have correspondents write for the paper. People who wrote for the newspaper included Karl Marx, H. W. Longfellow, Edgar Allan Poe, Mark Twain, Walt Whitman, Harriet Beecher Stowe, Heywood Broun, Grantland Rice, Alva Johnston, Homer Bigart, Red Smith, and Art Buchwald. In 1944, the paper began an international edition that still exists today, the *International Herald Tribune.*

In 1924, the paper became the *New York Herald-Tribune.* It ceased publication on April 23, 1966 because of labor disputes. For a brief time, the paper became part of the *New York World Journal Tribune;* however, that paper had labor problems as well and had a short life span.

1918

Louisville Courier-Journal   295
Founded: 1868; Louisville, KY. **Founder(s):** Henry Watterson.

Prize: *Meritorious Public Service,* 1967. *Editorial Writing,* 1918. *Feature Photography,* 1976. *General News Reporting,* 1989.

Selected Works: *George Rogers Clark Centennial Edition, the Courier Journal and the Louisville Times, Commemorating the First Definite Steps to Make a Great City at the Falls of the Ohio and the Realization of That Aim and of the Nine Foot Stage, 1818-1918,* 1918. *The Story of the National Spelling Bee, Founded 1925, by the Courier-Journal, Louisville, Kentucky,* 1929. *The Civil War in Kentucky, Centennial 1861-1961,* 1960. *They're Off: A Century of Kentucky Derby Coverage by the Courier-Journal and the Louisville Times,* 1975.

Other Awards: The *Louisville Courier-Journal's* staff, editors, and reporters have won eight Pulitzer Prizes, in addition to other journalism and public service awards.

For More Information: Miller, Char, *Fathers and Sons, the Bingham Family and the American Mission,* Philadelphia, PA: Temple University, 1982; Brenner, Marie, *House of Dreams: The Bingham Family of Louisville,* New York: Random House, 1988.

Commentary: The *Louisville Courier-Journal* won the Meritorious Public Service prize in 1967 for its successful campaign to control the Kentucky strip mining industry, a notable advance in the national effort for the conservation of natural resources. The *Courier-Journal* won the Editorial Writing prize in 1918 for the two editorials written by its long-time editor, Henry Watterson, entitled "Vae Victis!" and "War Has Its Compensation." Its staff won the Feature Photography prize in 1976 for a comprehensive pictorial report on busing in Louisville's schools. The General News Reporting prize was awarded to the *Courier-Journal* in 1989 for its exemplary initial coverage of a bus crash that claimed 27 lives and its subsequent thorough and effective examination of the causes and implications of the tragedy.

The merger in 1868 of the *Louisville Courier* and the *Louisville Journal* by editor and part-owner (with the Haldeman family) Henry Watterson created the *Courier-Journal*. Watterson admired Abraham Lincoln and favored political participation by African Americans. This set the future tone for the newspaper, later to be called the voice of the New South. Robert Worth Bingham bought the paper in 1918 from the Haldeman family. The Bingham reign continued Watterson's legacy. The *Courier-Journal* was bought by the Gannett Company in 1986, and the paper still continues to operate editorially as it has in the past.

1919
No award

1920

Harvey Ellsworth Newbranch   296
Birth: April 11, 1875; Henry County, IA. **Death:** January 27, 1959. **Parents:** Oliver Peter Newbranch and Louisa A. (Rapp). **Education:** University of Nebraska: AB. **Spouse:** Evalena Rolofson (m. 1896). **Children:** Katharine Louise, Margaret Evelyn, Eleanor Isobel.

Prize: *Editorial Writing,* 1920: *Omaha Evening World Herald,* "Law and the Jungle," September 30, Omaha, NE: Omaha Evening World Herald, 1919.

Career: Campaign manager; Insurance salesman; Reporter, Editorial Writer, *Omaha (NE) World-Herald,* 1898-1905; Associate Editor, *Omaha (NE) World-Herald,* 1905-10; Editor, *Omaha (NE) World-Herald,* 1910-44; Director, World Publishing Company, 1913-53; Secretary, World Publishing Company, 1924-34; Editor-in-Chief, *Omaha (NE) World-Herald,* 1944-1949.

Selected Works: *William Jennings Bryan: A Concise but Complete Story of His Life and Services,* 1900.

Other Awards: Oberlaender Trust Fellowship for Study of Conditions in Germany and Austria, 1933. Gold Medal, Freedom's Foundation, 1949. Honorary Degree, Creighton University, NE, 1929.

For More Information: *New York Times,* 28 January (1959): 31; *National Cyclopaedia of American Biography, Volume 44,* New York: James T. White & Company, 1962: 288-289.

Commentary: Harvey E. Newbranch's winning editorial dealt with the topics of justice and race. It was written after an African-American man was arrested for the rape of a white woman and then lynched by a mob.

1921
No award

1922

Frank Michael O'Brien   297
Birth: March 31, 1875; Dunkirk, NY. **Death:** September 22, 1943. **Parents:** Michael O'Brien and Ann (Cryan). **Religion:** Catholic. **Education:** St. Joseph's College, NY. **Spouse:** Marion Mously (m. 1910). **Children:** Frank Michael.

Prize: *Editorial Writing,* 1922: *New York Herald,* "The Unknown Soldier," November 11, New York: New York Herald, 1921.

Career: Reporter, *Buffalo Courier,* 1893-94; Reporter, *Buffalo Express,* 1895-96; City Editor, *Buffalo Express,* 1896-1904; Reporter, *New York Sun,* 1904-05; Secretary to Mayor McClellan, New York City, 1906-10; Special Writer, *New York Press,* 1912-15; Editorial Writer, *New York Sun,* 1916-18; Editorial Writer, *New York Herald,* 1918-24; Chief Editorial Writer, *New York Sun,* 1924-26; Editor, *New York Evening Sun,* 1926-.

Selected Works: *With Accrued Interest,* 1914. *The Story of the Sun, New York: 1833-1928,* 1928. *Murder Mysteries of New York,* 1932.

Other Awards: Honorary Degree, Manhattan College, NY, 1938.

For More Information: *New York World,* May 28, 1922; *National Cyclopaedia of American Biography, Volume 32,* New York: James T. White & Company, 1945: 310.

Commentary: Frank O'Brien won the Editorial Writing Pulitzer Prize in 1922 for his writing about "The Unknown Soldier." The other journalist winning that year was Kirke L. Simpson, who won for his writing on the same topic.

1923

William Allen White
Full entry appears as **#41** under "Biography or Autobiography," 1947.

1924

Boston Herald   298
Founded: August 31, 1846; Boston, MA. **Founder(s):** Albert Baker, John A. French, George W. Harmon, George H. Campbell, Amos C. Clapp, J.W. Monroe, Justin Andrews, Augustus A. Wallace, James D. Stowers.

Prize: *Editorial Writing,* 1924: *Boston Herald,* "Who Made Coolidge," September 14, Boston, MA: Boston Herald, 1923.

Other Awards: Bullard, Crider, and Murray, three staff members of the *Boston Herald,* have won individual Pulitzer Prizes in Editorial Writing.

For More Information: *The Boston Herald and Its History,* Boston, MA: 1878; Boston. Tercentenary Committee. Subcommittee on Memorial History. *Fifty Years of Boston: A Memorial Volume Issued in Commemoration of the Tercentenary of 1930,* Boston, MA: 1932.

Commentary: The *Boston Herald* was awarded the Pulitzer Prize for an editorial written by Frank Buxton. Frank Buxton was not named as the winner of the Prize. As managing editor, he contributed daily to the editorial page. In 1923, shortly after Calvin Coolidge became president after the death of Warren Harding, Buxton wrote "Who Made Coolidge?" When that editorial was awarded a Pulitzer Prize, there were criticisms of its worthiness as it posed the question "Who made Calvin Coolidge?" several times throughout the editorial and then gave multiple answers to express Buxton's opinion. Buxton was a native of Woonsocket, Rhode Island. He was born in 1877 and was a graduate of Harvard University. He died in 1974. (*New York Times,* 8 September (1974): 57)

The *Boston Herald* was first published as the *Evening Herald* on August 31, 1846 and was edited by William O. Eaton. In its early incarnation the first page was mainly stories and poems. In 1847, a morning edition edited by George W. Tyler was added and the editorial staff increased. On February 10, 1847, Eaton left the paper and a notice appeared in the paper that it would now be published as it originally had been intended as an Independent paper attached to no particular political party. Also after the departure, the publishers, John A. French & Co., for the first time were mentioned in the paper. French had bought out the original publishers one at a time except for one share (which was the & Co.) By 1881, after several management changes, the publishers were R.M. Pulsifer and Company. E.B. Haskell was the editor-in-chief while Charles H. Andrews was the news manager. Its daily circulation was 183,000. In 1888, the Boston Herald Company was formed with shareholders being Pulsifer, Haskell, Andrews, John H. Holmes, E.H. Woods, and Fred E. Whiting. That company went into receivership in 1910. In the fall of the following year, a new company of the same name was formed. That company became the Boston Publishing Compan y in 1915 and was a publicly traded firm. On September 23, 1929, the company changed its name to the Boston Herald-Traveler Corp. From 1917 until the end of 1918, the paper was published as the *Boston Herald and Boston Journal.* It once

again took the name *Boston Herald* and continued under that name until 1967 when for 5 years it became the *Boston Herald Traveler.* For less than six months the paper was named the *Boston Herald Traveler and Boston Record American.* On January 1, 1973, the paper became part of the *Boston Herald American,* and in 1982, the name *Boston Herald* once again appeared on the masthead of a paper. The paper is currently owned by Patrick J. Purcell.

Frank Irving Cobb   299

Birth: August 6, 1869; Shannon County, KS. **Death:** December 21, 1923. **Parents:** Minor H. Cobb and Mathilda. **Education:** Michigan State Normal School. **Spouse:** Delia S. Bailey (m. 1897, d.); Margaret Hubbard Ayer (m. 1913, died 1965). **Children:** Jane, Hubbard.

Prize: *Editorial Writing,* 1924: *New York World,* New York: New York World, 1923.

Career: High school superintendent, Martin, MI, 1890-91; Reporter, *Grand Rapids (MI) Herald,* 1891-1893; Political Correspondent, City Editor, *Grand Rapids (MI) Eagle,* 1893-94; Political Correspondent, Editorial Writer, *Detroit Evening News,* 1894-1900; Chief Editorial Writer, *Detroit Free Press,* 1900-04; Editorial Writer, Chief Editorial Writer, Editor, *New York World,* 1904-23.

Selected Works: *Woodrow Wilson: An Interpretation,* 1921.

Other Awards: Chevalier, Legion d'Honneur, France. Chevalier, Belgian Order of Leopold.

For More Information: Heaton, John L., *Cobb of the World: A Leader in Liberalism,* New York: Dutton, 1924; *National Cyclopaedia of American Biography, Volume 22,* New York: James T. White & Company, 1932: 128-129; *Quill,* 32:1 (1944): 6-8+; *Dictionary of Literary Biography, Volume 25,* Detroit: Gale Research Company, 1984: 43-47.

Commentary: The widow of Frank I. Cobb was given a special prize in recognition of Cobb's contribution to the journalism profession and the distinction of his editorial writing. Frank Cobb was the editor of the *New York World* after Joseph Pulitzer died.

1925

Robert Lathan   300

Birth: May 5, 1881; York, SC. **Death:** September 26, 1937. **Parents:** Rev. Robert Lathan and Fannie (Barron). **Religion:** Episcopalian. **Spouse:** Bessie Agnes Early (m. 1904).

Prize: *Editorial Writing,* 1925: *Charleston News and Courier,* "The Plight of the South," November 5, Charleston, SC: Charleston News and Courier, 1924.

Career: Teacher, 1898-99; Editorial Staff member, *Columbia (SC) State,* 1900-03; Official court reporter, law student, 1903-06; State News Editor and City Editor, *Charleston (SC) News and Courier,* 1906-10; Editor, *The Charleston (SC) News and Courier,* 1910-27; Editor, *Asheville (NC) Citizen,* 1927-37.

For More Information: *New York Times,* September 27, 1937: 21.

Commentary: Robert Lathan was not named as the writer by the Pulitzer board for the 1925 award. The citation read, "No Author Named, ... For the editorial entitled 'Plight of the South.'" Lathan was the writer of the editorial. It was written on election day 1924 and printed the following day. It discusses the lack of Southern interest and leadership at the national level.

1926

Edward Martin Kingsbury   301

Birth: July 16, 1854; Grafton, MA. **Death:** January 23, 1946. **Parents:** Benjamin Kingsbury. **Religion:** Episcopalian. **Education:** Harvard University, MA. **Spouse:** Grace M. Heymer (m. 1895). **Children:** Ralph.

Prize: *Editorial Writing,* 1926: *New York Times,* "The House of a Hundred Sorrows," December 14, New York: New York Times, 1925.

Career: Staff member, encyclopedia publisher; Editorial Writer, *New York Sun,* 1881-1915; Editorial Writer, *New York Times,* 1915-44.

For More Information: *New York Times,* January 24, 1946: 20, 21.

Commentary: Edward M. Kingsbury was a very private individual. All of his editorials for more than 60 years of writing and all but a few reviews were written anonymously. His winning editorial was written for the annual Hundred Neediest Cases appeal of the *New York Times.*

Kingsbury grew up in Massachusetts, one of 10 children. He studied and passed the bar examination but never practiced law. His father had been a station master on the Underground Railroad.

1927

Frederic Lauriston Bullard   302

Birth: May 13, 1866; Wauseon, OH. **Death:** August 3, 1952. **Parents:** Frederic Lauriston Bullard and Helen Maria (Ballard). **Education:** Wooster College, OH: BA, MA, Phi Beta Kappa. Yale University, CT: BD, magna cum laude. **Spouse:** Clara Elizabeth Keil. **Children:** Edward Lauriston, Frederic Keil, Helen Dorothea, Robert Paul, Clara Elizabeth.

Prize: *Editorial Writing,* 1927: *Boston Herald,* "We Submit," October 26, Boston: Boston Herald, 1926.

Career: Minister, Presbyterian and Congregational churches for ten years; Newspaper Staff member, 1907, mostly with *Boston Herald;* Sunday Editor, *Boston Herald,* 1915-19, Chief Editorial Writer, *Boston Herald,* 1919-43.

Selected Works: *Historic Summer Haunts from Newport to Portland,* 1912. *Famous War Correspondents,* 1914. *The Public Refuses to Pay: Editorials from the Boston Herald on the Railroad and Building Situation,* 1921. *Tad and His Father,* 1915. *The Other Lincoln,* 1941. *"A Few Appropriate Remarks": Lincoln's Gettysburg Address,* 1944. *Abraham Lincoln & the Widow Bixby,* 1946. *Abe Goes Down the River,* 1948. *Lincoln in Marble and Bronze,* 1952.

Other Awards: Diploma of Honor for Distinguished Contributions to the Study of Abraham Lincoln, Lincoln Memorial University, 1941. Honorary Degrees: Rhode Island State College, 1929; Wooster College, OH, 1930; Northeastern University, MA, 1934.

For More Information: Bodge, J. Everett, *Service for F. Lauriston Bullard, Melrose, Massachusetts, August 5, 1952 ... Hillcrest Church (Congregational),* Boston: Lincoln Group of Boston, 1952; *New York Times,* August 4, 1952: 15; Lincoln Group of Boston, *Lincoln Group of Boston: Fiftieth Anniversary Publication,* Boston: Lincoln Group of Boston, 1988.

Commentary: F. Lauriston Bullard was in charge of the editorial page of the *Boston Herald* for 24 years. He was also an editorial correspondent for the *New York Times* for a quarter of a century. His prize-winning editorial was written to the Massachusetts Supreme Court, urging a new trial for the defendants in the Sacco-Vanzetti case. He was also an authority on Abraham Lincoln, writing a half-dozen books on the subject.

1928

Grover Cleveland Hall   303

Birth: January 11, 1888; Haleburg, AL. **Death:** January 9, 1941. **Parents:** William Rabun Hall and Permelia Ann (Davis). **Spouse:** Claudia McCurdy English (m. 1912). **Children:** Grover Cleveland.

Prize: *Editorial Writing,* 1928: *Montgomery Advertiser,* Montgomery, AL: Montgomery Advertiser, 1927.

Career: Printer's Devil, 1895; Staff member, *Montgomery (AL) Advertiser,* 1910; Associate Editor, *Montgomery (AL) Advertiser,* 1919-26; Editor, *Montgomery (AL) Advertiser,* 1926; Probate Judge, Montgomery County (AL), 1933.

For More Information: *New York Times,* January 10, 1941: 19.

Commentary: Grover Cleveland Hall was the first winner for a series of editorials with no one editorial singled out above any other. Hall wrote against racial and religious intolerance, floggings, and gangism, specifically the Ku Klux Klan. Two editorials that reflect his writings include "We Predict a Freeze," published August 14, 1927, and "The Glove of the Beast—Will the State Pick It Up," published on July 3, 1927.

1929

Louis Isaac Jaffe   304

Birth: February 22, 1888; Detroit, MI. **Death:** March 12, 1950. **Parents:** Phillip Jaffe and Lotta (Kahn). **Religion:** Episcopalian. **Education:** Trinity College (now Duke University), NC: AB, Phi Beta Kappa. **Spouse:** Margaret Stewart Davis (m. 1920, d.); Alice Cohn Rice (m. 1942). **Children:** Louis Christopher (MD); Louis Isaac, Jr. (AR).

Prize: *Editorial Writing,* 1929: *Norfolk Virginian-Pilot,* "Unspeakable Act of Savagery," June 22, Norfolk, VA: Norfolk Virginian-Pilot, 1928.

Career: Staff member, *Durham (NC) Sun,* 1911; Reporter and Assistant City Editor, *Richmond (VA) Times-Dispatch,* 1911-16; Served in Army Expeditionary Forces, U.S. Army, 1918-19; Director, Paris, American Red Cross News Service, 1919; Editor, *Virginian-Pilot,* 1919.

For More Information: *New York Times,* 18 May (1929): 14; *National Cyclopaedia of American Biography, Volume 38,* New York: James T. White & Company, 1953; Dvorak, James Patrick, "Louis I. Jaffe: A Southern Liberal's Critique of Lynching" (thesis), Charlottesville: University of Virginia, 1991.

Commentary: Louis Isaac Jaffe was a key force behind the Virginia anti-lynching legislation. It was his editorial in 1928, following a lynching prior to the Democratic National Convention in Texas, that brought national attention to the issue.

1930
No award

1931

Charles Silcott Ryckman   305

Birth: July 11, 1898; Fort Collins, CO. **Death:** May 9, 1966. **Parents:** John Power Ryckman and Ada (Silcott). **Religion:** Methodist. **Education:** Harvard University, MA. **Spouse:** Mary Elizabeth Redmond (m. 1922).

Prize: *Editorial Writing,* 1931: *Fremont Tribune,* "The Gentleman from Nebraska," November 7, Fremont, NE: Fremont Tribune, 1930.

Career: Served in U.S. Navy, 1917-1919, Reporter, *Fort Collins Courier,* 1920; Editor, *Fremont Tribune,* 1920-36; Editorial Writer, *Chicago Herald and Examiner,* 1936; Editorial Writer, *New York American* and *New York Journal-American,* 1936-39; Editorial Writer, *San Francisco Examiner,* 1939-66.

For More Information: *New York Times,* May 5, 1931: 16; *San Francisco Examiner,* May 10, 1966.

Commentary: Charles S. Ryckman used satire to express his displeasure with Nebraska Senator George W. Norris. In his editorial, he tried to explain why the state's voters kept sending Norris back to Congress when Norris did not necessarily do much good for his state, except to "make himself objectionable to federal officials."

1932
No award

1933

Kansas City Star   306

Founded: September 18, 1880; Kansas City, MO. **Founder(s):** William Rockhill Nelson, Samuel Morss.

Prize: *Editorial Writing,* 1933: *Kansas City Star,* Kansas City, MO, 1932. **Special Awards and Citations: Journalism,** 1952: *Kansas City Star,* Kansas City, MO, 1951. **Local General Spot News Reporting,** 1982: *Kansas City Star,* Kansas City, MO, 1981.

Other Awards: Jeff Taylor and Mike McGraw of the *Kansas City Star* won a national reporting Pulitzer Prize in 1992.

For More Information: Johnson, Icie Florence, The Life and Career of William Rockhill Nelson, Editor of the Kansas City Star, and His Contributions to the Journalism of His Times (thesis), Northwestern University, 1934; *The Story of the Kansas City Star: Including Its Paper Mill, Its Radio Station,* Kansas City, MO: Kansas City Star Co., 1948; *Kansas City Star and Times, July 12-20, 1951, Covering the Flood in Greater Kansas City,* Kansas City, MO, 1951; *Quill,* 53:9 (September 1965): 28+; *The First 100 Years: A Man, a Newspaper, and a City; Centennial Sections, Sunday, September 14, 1980,* Kansas City, MO: *Kansas City Star,* 1980.

Commentary: William Rockhill Nelson and Samuel Morss founded the *Kansas City Star* in September 1880. Nelson was 39 years old when he founded the paper. Morss left the paper within a year of its founding. The first Sunday paper was published on April 24, 1894. (Ernest Hemingway was a reporter for the *Star* for a time in 1917.) On October 19, 1901, Nelson purchased the *Kansas City Times.* Nelson died in 1915, and his will stipulated that the papers must be sold after his widow and daughter died. In 1926, the employees of the papers bought the newspapers. In 1990, the two separate papers were merged into one morning paper, the *Star.*

In 1933, the *Kansas City Star* was awarded the Editorial Writing prize for the work of its editor, Henry J. Haskell. He wrote the 19 editorials that were included in the entry for the prize. They were broken down into three series: the economic and political conditions in Europe, economic conditions in America, and government growth. Haskell was individually awarded a Pulitzer Prize in Editorial Writing in 1944.

In 1952, the *Kansas City Star* was given a special citation for its coverage of the regional flood of July 1951 that covered a great portion of land in Kansas and northwestern Missouri. Its coverage gave the information needed to achieve "the maximum of public protection." In 1982, the staffs of the two Kansas City papers, *the Kansas City Star* and the *Kansas City Times,* produced 50 pages of coverage on the collapse of two skywalks at the Hyatt Regency Hotel in Kansas City. 114 people were killed and 200 were injured in the tragedy. By the end of 1981, the papers had published more than 340 articles and hundreds of photographs.

1934

Edwin Percy Chase 307

Birth: November 2, 1879; Anita, IA. **Death:** July 10, 1949. **Parents:** Charles F. Chase. **Spouse:** Jane Colton (m. 1924).

Prize: *Editorial Writing,* 1934: *Atlantic News-Telegraph,* "Where Is Our Money," December 2, Atlantic, IA: Atlantic News-Telegraph, 1933.

Career: Staff, Iowa State University college paper; Staff member, *Chicago Tribune;* Reporter, Denver (CO) and Boise (ID) papers; Editor, Publisher, *Atlantic (IA) News-Telegraph,* 1903-37.

For More Information: *New York Times,* May 8, 1934: 20; *New York Times,* July 12, 1949: 27.

Commentary: Edwin P. Chase's prize-winning editorial dealt with the issue of economics and the causes of the Great Depression. He called for thrift on the part of the American people to end the depression, rather than government programs.

1935
No award

1936

Felix Muskett Morley 308

Birth: January 6, 1894; Haverford, PA. **Death:** March 13, 1982. **Parents:** Dr. Frank Morley and Lilian Janet (Bird). **Religion:** Episcopalian. **Education:** Haverford College, PA: AB, Phi Beta Kappa. New College, Oxford University, England: AB. London School of Economics and Politic Science, England. Brookings Institution, Washington, DC: PhD. **Spouse:** Isabel Middleton (m. 1917). **Children:** Lorna, Christina, Anthony, Felix W.

Prize: *Editorial Writing,* 1936: *Washington Post,* Washington, DC: Washington Post, 1935.

Career: Reporter, *Philadelphia (PA) Public Ledger,* 1916-17; Staff member, Washington (DC) Bureau, United Press International, 1917; Special Service member, U.S. Department of Labor, 1917-18; Staff member, *Philadelphia (PA) National American,* 1919; Editorial Staff member, *Baltimore (MD) Sun,* 1922-29, Far East Correspondent, *Baltimore (MD) Sun,* 1925-26; Lecturer, Current Political Problems, St. John's College (MD), 1924-25; Correspondent, Geneva, Switzerland, *Baltimore (MD) Sun,* 1928-29; Director, Geneva (Switzerland) Office, League of Nations Association U.S., 1929-31; Staff member, Brookings Institution, 1931-33; Editor, *Washington (DC) Post,* 1933-40; President, Haverford College (PA), 1940-45; President, Editor, Human Events, Inc., 1945-50; Washington, DC Correspondent, *Barron's Weekly,* 1950-54; Consultant, War Manpower Community, 1942-45.

Selected Works: *Unemployment Relief in Great Britain: A Study in State Socialism; Hart, Schaffner & Marx Prize Essays, XXXVIII,* 1924. *Unemployment Relief in Great Britain; Studies in Economics and Political Science, no. 77,* 1924. *Our Far Eastern Assignment,* 1926. *Aspects of the Depression,* 1932. *The Society of Nations, Its Organization and Constitutional Development,* 1932. *The Economic World Today,* 1933. *Trade Barriers and the World Economic Conference; Economics Series Presentation, no. 26* (with Henry Chalmers), 1933. *Humanity Tries Again: An Analysis of the United Nations Charter; The Human Events Pamphlets; no. 3,* 1946. *The Power in the People,* 1949. *The Foreign Policy of the United States,* 1951. *Treaty Law and the Constitution: A Study of the Bricker Amendment,* 1953. *Gumpton Island, a Fantasy of Coexistence,* 1956. *Essays on Individuality,* 1958. *Freedom and Federalism* (with Lorna Morley), 1959. *The Patchwork History of Foreign Aid,* Washington, DC: American Enterprise Association, 1961 (with Lorna Morley), 1961. *State and Society: Studies in Social Theory, no. 7,* 1978. *For the Record,* 1979.

Other Awards: Rhodes Scholar, New College, Oxford University, England, 1921. Hutchinson Research Fellow, London School of Economics and Politic Science, 1921-22. Guggenheim Fellow, Political Science, 1928-30. William Valker Distinguished Service Award, 1961. Outstanding Alumnus Award, Friends School, MD, 1977. Lifetime Achievement Award, International Women's Media Foundation, 1997. Honorary Degrees: George Washington University, Washington, DC, 1940; Hamilton College, NY, 1941; University of Pennsylvania, 1941; Bethany College, CA, 1951; Lebanon Valley College, PA, 1952; Western Maryland College, 1964; Towson State University, MD, 1979.

For More Information: *New York Times,* March 16, 1982: D22; *Washington Post,* March 16, 1982: B4; *Washington Post,* March 21, 1982: D7.

Commentary: Both Felix Morley and George B. Parker won Pulitzer Prizes in 1936 for Editorial Writing. Morley won for the body of his work: 34 of his editorials were submitted for consideration. He wrote on topics ranging from Christmas to taxes, from the kidnapping of the Lindbergh baby to the League of Nations.

George B. Parker   309

Birth: September 10, 1886; Ithaca, MI. **Death:** October 10, 1949. **Parents:** Dean S. Parker and Harriet (Johnson). **Education:** University of Oklahoma: AB, Phi Beta Kappa. **Spouse:** Adelaide Loomis (m. 1912). **Children:** George B., Mary.

Prize: *Editorial Writing,* 1936: Scripps-Howard Newspapers, 1935.

Career: Reporter, Copy Reader, City Editor, Managing Editor, Editor, *Oklahoma City (OK) News,* 1909-20; Editor, *Cleveland (OH) Press,* 1920-22; Editor-in-Chief, Southwestern Group, Scripps-Howard Newspapers, 1922-24; General Editorial Manager, Scripps-Howard Newspapers, 1925-27; Editor-in-Chief, Scripps-Howard Newspapers, 1927-.

For More Information: *New York Times,* 5 May (1936): 18; *New York Times,* 11 October (1949): 31; *National Cyclopaedia of American Biography, Volume 39,* New York: James T. White & Company, 1954.

Commentary: 1936 was the first year that there were multiple winners in the Editorial Writing category. Both George B. Parker, editor-in-chief of Scripps-Howard Newspapers, and Felix Morley, editor of the *Washington Post,* were cited. Parker wrote on a variety of topics including freedom of the press.

1937

John Whitefield Owens   310

Birth: November 2, 1884; Anne Arundel County, MD. **Death:** April 24, 1968. **Parents:** Cyrus White-

field Owens and Eliza Providence (Brashears). **Education:** Johns Hopkins University, MD. **Spouse:** Virginia Dashiell (m. 1918, died 1926). **Children:** Elizabeth, John.

Prize: *Editorial Writing,* 1937: *Baltimore Sun,* Baltimore, MD: Baltimore Sun, 1936.

Career: Staff member, *Baltimore (MD) Evening Sun,* 1911; Political Reporter, *Baltimore (MD) Sun,* 1913-20; Staff member, Washington (DC) Bureau, *Baltimore (MD) Sun,* 1920-24; London (England) Bureau Chief, *Baltimore (MD) Sun,* 1924-26; Editorial Writer, *Baltimore (MD) Sun,* 1926-27; Editor, *Baltimore (MD) Sun,* 1927-38; Editor-in-Chief, *Baltimore (MD) Sun* and *Baltimore (MD) Evening Sun,* 1938-43; Contributing Editor, *Baltimore (MD) Sun,* 1943.

For More Information: *New York Times,* 4 May (1937): 20; *New York Times,* 25 April (1968): 47.

Commentary: John W. Owens, editor of the *Baltimore Sun,* won a Pulitzer Prize for the body of his work during 1936. His editorial "The Opposition" was mentioned as carrying the most weight in the awarding of the prize. That editorial was published November 6, 1936, the day after that year's election.

1938

William Wesley Waymack   311

Birth: October 18, 1888; Savanna, IL. **Death:** November 5, 1960. **Parents:** William Edward Waymack and Emma Julia (Oberheim). **Education:** Morningside College, IA: AB. **Spouse:** Elsie Jeannette Lord (m. 1911). **Children:** Edward Randolph.

Prize: *Editorial Writing,* 1938: *Des Moines Register and Tribune,* Des Moines, IA: Des Moines Register and Tribune, 1937.

Career: Reporter, *Sioux City (IA) Journal,* 1911-14; City Editor, Chief Editorial Writer, *Sioux City Journal,* 1914-18; Editorial Writer, *Des Moines (IA) Register and Tribune,* 1918-21; Managing Editor, *Des Moines Register and Tribune,* 1921-29; Editorial Page Editor, *Des Moines Register and Tribune,* 1931-46; Vice President, Register and Tribune Company, 1939-46; Staff member, Federal Reserve Bank of Chicago (IL), 1941-46; Editor, *Des Moines Register and Tribune,* 1942-46; Special Adviser, U.S. Department of State, 1942; Original Member, U.S. Atomic Energy Commission, 1946-48.

Selected Works: *Challenge to America: National Policy Papers, Number 1,* 1940. *Looking at it from the Russian Side. On Winning the Peace: International Conciliation, Number 391,* 1943.

Other Awards: Sigma Delta Chi Award, 1938. Distinguished Service Award, Sigma Delta Chi, 1940. Award for Service to Agriculture, American Farm Bureau Federation, 1944. Award, National Confederation of Christians and Jews, 1960. Decorated Honorary Officer, Order of the British Empire. Honorary Degrees: Drake University, IA, 1937; Morningside College, IA, 1939; Parsons College, IA, 1940; Grinnell College, IA, 1941; Iowa State College, 1949.

For More Information: *New York Times,* 3 May (1938): 16; *New York Times,* 6 November (1960): 88.

Commentary: William W. Waymack won a Pulitzer Prize for his work throughout the year and no single editorial was singled out for specific attention. He was cited in 1937 for an honorable mention in the Editorial Writing category for his editorials on farm tenancy.

Waymack served on many national committees and organizations including the President's Committee on Farm Tenancy in 1936-37, National Air Law Conference in 1937, Committee to Study the Organization of Peace in 1939, and American Council for NATO in 1954.

1939

Ronald Glenn Callvert   312

Birth: September 24, 1873; Adel, IA. **Death:** February 14, 1955. **Parents:** Stephen Alexander Callvert and Rachel Barns (Berger). **Religion:** Protestant. **Spouse:** Kathryn Shotwell Andrews (m. 1909). **Children:** Ronald.

Prize: *Editorial Writing,* 1939: *Oregonian,* "My Country 'Tis of Thee," October 2, Portland, OR: Oregonian, 1938.

Career: Printer, Reporter, Editor, *Bellingham (WA) Reveille,* 1900-01; Secretary, Board of State Land Commissioner, Olympia (WA), 1901-05; Reporter, City Editor, *Los Angeles Record,* 1906-07; Correspondent, Olympia (WA), *Los Angeles Record,* 1907-09; Staff member, *Portland (OR) Oregonian,* 1909-10; Assistant Managing Editor, *Portland (OR) Oregonian,* 1910-28; Managing Editor, *Portland (OR) Oregonian,* 1928-31; Associate Editor, *Portland (OR) Oregonian* 1931-51.

For More Information: *New York Times,* May 2, 1939: 20; *New York Times,* May 15, 1955: 27.

Commentary: Ronald G. Callvert won a Pulitzer Prize for the body of his work in 1938, which was exemplified in his "My Country 'Tis of Thee" editorial. His paper distributed over 14,000 copies of the editorial in response to requests for reprints. Callvert wrote it himself rather than assigning it to a colleague so the colleague could leave for vacation. His intention was to starkly contrast the liberties in America with the increasing totalitarian military concept that was building in Europe.

1940

Bart S. Howard   313

Birth: May 13, 1871; North Brookfield, MA. **Death:** February 12, 1941. **Education:** Williams College, MA. **Spouse:** Ann Picher. **Children:** Virginia.

Prize: *Editorial Writing,* 1940: *St. Louis Post-Dispatch,* "The Kingdom of Democracy," March 7; "Europe's Emperor," March 17; "The Golden Age," April 23; "After the Battle," June 13, St. Louis: St. Louis Post-Dispatch, 1939.

Career: Professional baseball player; Cub Reporter, *Schenectady (NY) Gazette;* Editor, *Joplin (MO) News-Herald and Joplin (MO) Globe;* Managing Editor, *Columbia (OH) Sun;* Feature Writer, Columnist, *St. Louis (MO) Republic;* Reporter, *St. Louis (MO) Post-Dispatch,* 1910; Editorial Writer, *Oklahoma City (OK) Daily Oklahoma; St. Louis (MO) Post-Dispatch,* 1919.

Other Awards: Honorary Degree, Williams College, MA, 1940.

For More Information: *St. Louis Post Dispatch,* February 12, 1941: 1, 3; *New York Times,* February 13, 1941: 19.

Commentary: Bart Howard, a left-handed second baseman, left college to become a professional baseball player. He later turned to journalism as a career. He believed that there were three documents that everyone should know: the Sermon on the Mount, the Magna Carta, and the Bill of Rights. Those three had "all the religion, all the politics, and all the rules for good living that anyone needs."

Howard was capable of describing a situation with a phrase. One technique he used was alliteration. The editorials included in his prize entry covered many different areas including support for the League of Nations, opposition of government corruption, and analysis of Hitler's conquests. His winning editorials were reprinted in the *St. Louis Post-Dispatch* on May 7, 1940, page C2.

1941

Reuben Maury   314

Birth: September 2, 1899; Butte, MT. **Death:** April 23, 1981. **Parents:** Henry Lowndes Maury and Anne Henderson (Perkins). **Education:** University of Virginia: LLB. **Spouse:** Thomasine Lafayette Rose (m. 1928).

Prize: *Editorial Writing,* 1941: *New York Daily News,* "Chemistry—The New Frontier," January 3; Untitled, January 27; "Toward Totalitarianism," February 11; "Satellite Nations," March 24; "Moses' Crosstown Highway Plan," May 26; "Anti-Semitism in This Country," September 24, New York: New York Daily News, 1940.

Career: Member of Montana Bar Association since 1923; Law firm member, Maury & Maury, 1923-26; Reporter, *New York Daily News,* 1926; Movie Critic, 1926; Chief Editorial Writer, 1926-72; Author and editorial consultant, 1973-81.

Selected Works: *The Wars of the Godly: The Story of Religious Conflict in America,* 1928. *The Nature of the Enemy: A Clear, Factual Account of Red Aims, Practices and Performance, Past, Present and Future,* 1959. *Effective Editorial Writing,* 1960. *The Enemy's New Tactics: How the Communists Operate in America Today Based on Editorials in "The News"...,* 1965.

Other Awards: Christopher Editorial Award, 1954. Award, Assembly Captive European Nations, 1965. George Sokolsky Award, American League Against Communism, 1965. Decorated, Order Brilliant Star, Taiwan, China Freedoms Foundation at Valley Forge Editorial Honor Certificate, 1973. Honorary Degree, University of Virginia, 1970.

For More Information: *National Cyclopaedia of American Biography, Volume F,* New York: James T. White & Company, 1942; *New York Times,* 24 April (1981): B6; Taft, William H., *Encyclopedia of Twentieth-Century Journalists,* New York: Garland Publishing, 1986.

Commentary: Reuben Maury's editorials in 1940 covered many different topics including technology, the Metropolitan Opera, international affairs, elevated highways around Manhattan, and anti-Semitism.

Maury was a lawyer who was challenged to write after reading an interview of H.L. Mencken, then editor of the *American Mercury,* that stated, "the state of Montana had never produced a piece of presentable copy." Maury, writing under a pseudonym, sent an article to the *American Mercury.* It was published, and the founder of the *New York Daily News* sent a letter asking if he would like a job in New York. His writing was simple in manner and written to appeal to the masses.

1942

Geoffrey Parsons   315
Birth: September 5, 1879; Douglaston, NY. **Death:** December 8, 1956. **Parents:** Charles Chauncy Parsons and Julia Warth (Michael). **Religion:** Church of the Ascension. **Education:** Columbia University, NY: AB, LLB. **Spouse:** Carle Taylor (m. 1907, died 1963). **Children:** Geoffrey, David Taylor, Mary Catherine, Carl Taylor.

Prize: *Editorial Writing,* 1942: *New York Herald-Tribune,* "Plea for Unity," New York: New York Herald-Tribune, 1941.

Career: Staff member, *New York Evening Sun,* 1906-13; Staff member, *New York Tribune,* 1913-24; Chief Editorial Writer, *New York Herald-Tribune,* 1924-52; Chief Editorial Adviser, *New York Herald-Tribune,* 1952-56.

Selected Works: *The Land of Fair Play: A Textbook of American Civics for Grammar Schools ...,* 1919. *The Stream of History,* 1928. *Black Chattels: The Story of the Australian Aborigines,* 1946.

Other Awards: Medal of Excellence, Columbia University, NY, 1933. Medal, American Scenic and Historic Preservation Society, 1949. Citation of Merit, Poetry Society of America, 1950. Officer, French Legion of Honor. Honorary Degrees: Columbia University, NY, 1941; Franklin and Marshall College, PA, 1945; Louisville University, KY, 1947.

For More Information: *New York Times,* 5 May (1942): 14; *New York Times,* 9 December (1956): 88; *National Cyclopaedia of American Biography, Volume 46,* New York: James T. White & Company, 1963: 296.

Commentary: Geoffrey Parsons wrote for a Republican newspaper, but his winning series of 17 editorials, collectively called "Plea for Unity," urged bipartisan support for all to put aside their differences and work together for the common good of the country. The series of editorials began on January 15, 1941.

Parsons wrote about seven presidential elections. His paper had taken clear-cut candidate positions and he definitely played an important role in determining those positions.

1943

Forrest W. Seymour   316
Birth: July 10, 1905; Arlington, SD. **Death:** October 3, 1983. **Parents:** Arthur Hallock Seymour and Floral Margaret (Wilson). **Education:** Drake University, IA: AB, Phi Beta Kappa. **Spouse:** Pearl Bernice Yeager (m. 1927). **Children:** Arthur, Peter, Susanna, Constance.

Prize: *Editorial Writing,* 1943: *Des Moines Register and Tribune,* Des Moines, IA: Des Moines Register and Tribune, 1942.

Career: Reporter, *Des Moines (IA) Tribune,* 1923; Copyreader, Telegraph Editor, Assistant City Editor, *Des Moines (IA) Register,* 1924-27; State Editor, *Des Moines (IA) Register & Tribune,* 1927-29; Editorial Writer, *Des Moines (IA) Register & Tribune,* 1929-43; Associate Editor, *Des Moines (IA) Register & Tribune,* 1943-46; Editorial Pages Editor, *Des Moines (IA) Register & Tribune,* 1946-53; Associate Editor, *Worcester (MA) Telegram & Gazette,* 1953-

55; Editor, *Worcester (MA) Telegram & Gazette,* 1955-70; Member, Board of Managers, American Variable Annuity Life Assurance Company, Worcester, MA; President of the Cape Cod (MA) Symphony Orchestra Association, 1974-76.

Selected Works: *Sitanka: The Full Story of Wounded Knee,* 1981.

Other Awards: Stephan A. Chadwick Editorial Appreciation Award, American Legion, 1943. Honorary Degrees: Drake University, IA, 1952; Parsons College, IA, 1947; Grinnell College, IA, 1949.

For More Information: *Washington Post,* 5 October (1983): B8; *Contemporary Authors, Volume 111,* Detroit: Gale Research Company, 1984.

Commentary: Forrest W. Seymour won a Pulitzer Prize for his Editorial Writing throughout the year. His entry for the prize included 23 editorials broken down into three categories: Making Democracy Work, An Intelligent Peace, and Common Sense and Courage on the Home Front. They were dated from March 8th to December 15th, 1942.

1944

Henry Joseph Haskell   317
Birth: March 8, 1874; Huntington, OH. **Death:** August 20, 1952. **Parents:** Rev. Henry C. Haskell and Margaret (Bell). **Religion:** Unitarian. **Education:** Oberlin College, OH: BA, Phi Beta Kappa. **Spouse:** Isabel Cummings (m. 1901, died 1923); Katharine Wright (m., died 1929); Agnes Lee Hadley (m., died 1946). **Children:** Henry Cummings (IC).

Prize: *Editorial Writing,* 1944: *Kansas City Star,* Kansas City, MO: Kansas City Star, 1943.

Career: Staff member, *Kansas City (MO) World,* 1898; *Kansas City (MO) Star,* 1898; Editorial Writer, *Kansas City (MO) Star,* 1900; Chief Editorial Writer, *Kansas City (MO) Star,* 1911-28; Editor, *Kansas City (MO) Star,* 1928-52; Director, Vice President, Kansas City Star Company.

Selected Works: *The New Deal in Old Rome: How Government in the Ancient World Tried to Deal with Modern Problems,* 1939. *This Was Cicero: Modern Politics in a Roman Toga,* 1942.

Other Awards: Citation, American Classical League, 1943. Honorary Degrees: Oberlin College, OH, 1917; Marietta College, OH; University of Missouri.

For More Information: *New York Times,* 2 May (1944): 16; *New York Times,* 21 August (1952): 19; *New York Times,* 23 August (1952): 13.

Commentary: Henry J. Haskell was not named as the writer for the 1933 Pulitzer Prize. However, as editor of the *Kansas City Star,* he wrote the 19 editorials that were included in the entry for the prize. The editorials were broken down into three series: the

economic and political conditions in Europe; economic conditions in America; and government growth. In 1944, he was individually awarded a Pulitzer Prize in Editorial Writing for the body of his work throughout the year. His entry included many topics such as education, Social Security, and World War II.

Haskell's parents were missionaries in Bulgaria, and he lived there for a time in his youth. His son was foreign editor of the *Kansas City Star* in 1952.

1945

George W. Potter   318
Birth: September 20, 1899; Fall River, MA. **Death:** August 10, 1959. **Parents:** Joseph H. Potter Jr. and Ellen (McKenny). **Education:** Brown University, RI: PhD, Phi Beta Kappa. **Spouse:** Erna C. Dingwell (m. 1927).

Prize: *Editorial Writing,* 1945: *Providence Journal-Bulletin,* Providence, RI: Providence Journal-Bulletin, 1944.

Career: Reporter, *Red River (MA) Herald,* summers, 1914-16; Reporter, *New Bedford (MA) Times,* summer, 1919; Assistant in English, Brown University (RI), 1921-23; Assistant Editor, *Providence (RI) Tribune,* 1922-23; Editor, *Providence (RI) Tribune,* 1923-29; Editorial Writer, *Providence (RI) Journal,* 1929-39; Chief Editorial Writer, *Providence (RI) Journal Bulletin,* 1939-46; Journalism Instructor, Brown University Extension Department (RI), 1927-39.

Selected Works: *An Irish Pilgrimage,* 1950. *To the Golden Door: The Story of the Irish in Ireland and America,* 1960.

Other Awards: Guggenheim Fellow, 1956-57. Honorary Degrees: Brown University, RI, 1946; Bradford Durfee Technical Institute, MA, 1955.

Commentary: George W. Potter won a Pulitzer Prize for the body of his work during 1944, and a special note was drawn to those editorials dealing with freedom of the press. His entry included five editorials dated November 30, December 4, 20, 24, and 29, 1944.

1946

William Hodding Carter Jr.   319

Birth: February 3, 1907; Hammond, LA. **Death:** April 4, 1972. **Parents:** William Hodding Carter and Irma (Dutart). **Religion:** Episcopalian. **Education:** Bowdoin College, ME: BA. Columbia University, NY. Tulane University, LA. Louisiana State University. **Spouse:** Betty Werlein (m. 1931). **Children:** William Hodding III, Philip Dutartre, Thomas Hennen.

Prize: *Editorial Writing,* 1946: *Delta Democrat-Times,* "Go For Broke," August 27, Greenville, MS: Delta Democrat-Times, 1945.

Career: Teaching Fellow, Tulane University (LA), 1928-29; Reporter, *New Orleans (LA) Item-Tribune,* 1929; Night Bureau Manager, *New Orleans (LA) Item-Tribune,*1930; Manager, Jackson MS Bureau, Associated Press, 1931-32; Founder, Editor, Publisher, *Hammond (LA) Daily Courier,* 1932-36; Founder, Editor, Publisher, *Greenville (MS) Delta Star,* 1936-38; Editor and Publisher, *Greenville (MS) Delta Democrat-Times,* 1939; Editor, *PM,* 1939; Served in Mississippi National Guard, Middle East, WWII; Civilian Aide to Secretary of the Army, 1954-60; Writer-in-Residence, Tulane University (LA), 1962-68.

Selected Works: *Civilian Defense of the United States* (with Colonel R. Ernest Dupuy), 1942. *Lower Mississippi: The Rivers of America,* 1942. *The Winds of Fear,* 1944. *Flood Crest,* 1947. *Southern Legacy,* 1950. *Gulf Coast Country* (with Anthony Ragusin), 1951. *John Law Wasn't So Wrong: The Story of Louisiana's Horn of Plenty,* 1952. *Where Main Street Meets the River,* 1953. *Robert E. Lee and the Road of Honor,* 1955. *So Great a Good: A History of the Episcopal Church in Louisiana and Christ Church*

Cathedral (with Betty Carter), 1955. *The Marquis De Lafayette: Bright Sword for Freedom; World Landmark Book (W-34),* 1958. *The Angry Scar: The Story of Reconstruction: Mainstream of America Series,* 1959. *Doomed Road of Empire: The Spanish Trail of Conquest; American Trails Series,* 1963. *First Person Rural,* 1963. *The Ballad of Catfood Grimes and Other Verses,* 1964. *So the Heffners Left McComb,* 1965. *The Commandos of World War II; World Landmark Books (W-61),* 1966. *The Past as Prelude: New Orleans, 1718-1968,* 1968. *Their Words Were Bullets: The Southern Press in War, Reconstruction, and Peace; Mercer University Lamar Memorial Lectures, Number 12,* 1969. *Man and the River: The Mississippi,* 1970.

Other Awards: Nieman Fellow, Harvard University, MA, 1939-40. Guggenheim Fellowship, 1945. Southern Literary Award, 1945. War Department Citation, 1946. Elijah Parish Lovejoy Award, Colby College, ME, 1952. Fellowship, Sigma Delta Chi, 1954. National Citation of Journalistic Merit, William A. White Foundation, 1961. Bowdoin Prize, Bowdoin College, ME, 1963. Honored by the Protestant Episcopal Theological Seminary, VA, 1965. First Federation Award, 1968. Journalism Alumni Award, Columbia University, NY, 1971. Honorary Degrees: Bowdoin College, ME, 1947; Washington University, MO, 1954; Coe College, IA, 1958; Allegheny College, PA, 1960.

For More Information: *New York Times,* April 5, 1972: 48; Taft, William H., *Encyclopedia of Twentieth-Century Journalists,* New York: Garland Publishing, Inc., 1986; *Dictionary of Literary Biography, Volume 127,* Detroit: Gale Research Company, 1993; Waldron, Ann, *Hodding Carter,* Chapel Hill, NC: Algonquin Books of Chapel Hill, 1993; *Dictionary of American Biography, Supplement 9,* New York: Charles Scribner's Sons, 1994.

Commentary: Hodding Carter returned from serving in the Army in June 1945. He then concentrated on the topics of "racial, religious, and economic biases" in his editorials. "Go For Broke" deals with the topic of Japanese-Americans, but easily conveys the need for racial harmony among all.

1947

William Henry Grimes   320

Birth: March 7, 1892; Bellevue, OH. **Death:** January 14, 1972. **Parents:** Samuel L. Grimes and Lucy (Bush). **Education:** Western Reserve University, OH. **Spouse:** Iva Mae McCormick (m. 1915, died 1967). **Children:** Jane, William Henry, John Alan.

Prize: *Editorial Writing,* 1947: *Wall Street Journal,* New York: Dow Jones, 1946.

Career: Proofreader, *Sandusky (OH) Register,* 1913; Reporter, Ohio Newspapers, United Press International, 1913-20; Manager, Washington (DC) Bureau, United Press International, 1920; Manager, New York (NY) Office, United Press International, 1921; Manager, Washington (DC) Bureau, *Wall Street Journal,* 1926-34; Managing Editor, *Wall Street Journal,* 1934-41; Editor, *Wall Street Journal,* 1941-58; Vice-President, Dow Jones and Company, ?-1961.

Other Awards: Honorary Degrees: Bowdoin College, ME, 1952; New York University, 1957; Western Reserve University, OH, 1961.

For More Information: *Wall Street Journal,* 17 January (1972): 11; Taft, William H., *Encyclopedia of Twentieth-Century Journalists,* New York: Garland Publishing, Inc., 1986.

Commentary: William H. Grimes played a major role in the evolution and growth of the *Wall Street Journal.* He was at its helm from the New Deal until he retired in 1958. He once wrote in a column, "On our editorial page, we make no pretense of walking down the middle road." He would chide both the government and industry in his editorials. He won a Pulitzer Prize for his editorial commentary in 1946. Many of his editorials for that year dealt on the topics of business, labor, and economics.

1948

Virginius Dabney   321

Birth: February 8, 1901; VA. **Death:** December 28, 1995. **Parents:** Richard Heath Dabney and Lily Heth (Davis). **Religion:** Episcopalian. **Education:** University of Virginia: BA: MA. **Spouse:** Douglas Harrison Chelf (m. 1923, died 1994). **Children:** Douglas Gibson, Lucy Davis, Richard Heath II.

Prize: *Editorial Writing,* 1948: *Richmond Times-Dispatch,* Richmond, VA: Richmond Times-Dispatch, 1947.

Career: Algebra and English Teacher, Episcopal High School, Alexandria (VA), 1921-22; Reporter, *Richmond (VA) News-Leader,* 1922-28; Editorial Staff member, *Richmond (VA) Times-Dispatch,* 1928-34; Chief Editorial Writer, *Richmond (VA) Times-Dispatch,* 1934-36; Editor, *Richmond (VA) Times-Dispatch,* 1936-69; Visiting Lecturer, Princeton University (NJ), 1939-40; Visiting Lecturer, Cambridge University (England), 1954.

Selected Works: *Liberalism in the South,* 1932. *Below the Potomac,* 1942. *Dry Messiah: The Life of Bishop Cannon,* 1949. *Virginia: The New Dominion,* 1971. *Richard Heath Dabney: A Memoir,* 1973. *The Patriots: The American Revolution Generation of Genius,* 1975. *Richmond: The Story of a City,* 1976. *Across the Years: Memories of a Virginian,* 1978. *Mr. Jefferson's University,* 1981. *The Jefferson Scandals,*

1981. *Architecture of Downtown Richmond* (with others), 1982. *Bicentennial History and Roster of the Society of Cincinnati in the State of Virginia, 1783-1983,* 1983. *The Last Review: The Confederate Reunion, Richmond, 1932,* 1984. *Virginius Dabney's Virginia: Writings about the Old Dominion,* 1986. *Virginia Commonwealth University: A Sesquicentennial History,* 1987. *Pistols and Pointed Press: The Dueling Editors of Old Virginia,* 1987.

Other Awards: Oberlaender Trust Grant, 1934. Lee Editorial Award, Virginia Press Association, 1937. Sigma Delta Chi Award, 1948, 1952. Medallion of Honor, Virginians of Maryland Society, 1961. B'nai B'rith Man of the Year Award, 1966. Guggenheim Fellow, 1968. George Mason Award, Sigma Delta Chi, 1969. Grant, National Endowment for the Humanities, 1970. Raven Society Award, 1972. Thomas Jefferson Award for Public Service, 1972. Jackson Davis Award, 1975. Liberty Bell Award, Richmond Bar Association, 1976. Honorary Degree, Virginia Commonwealth University, 1976. Douglas Southall Freeman Literary Award, 1985: *The Last Review: The Confederate Reunion, Richmond, 1932,* Chapel Hill, NC: Algonquin Books, 1984. Virginia Communications Hall of Fame, Virginia Commonwealth University, 1986. Honorary Degrees: University of Richmond, VA, 1940; Lynchburg College, VA, 1944; College of William and Mary, VA, 1944.

For More Information: *Current Biography Yearbook, 1948,* New York: H.W. Wilson, 1948; Sosna, Morton, *In Search of the Silent South: Southern Liberals and the Race Issue,* Contemporary American History Series, New York: Columbia University Press, 1977; Taft, William H., *Encyclopedia of Twentieth-Century Journalists,* New York: Garland Publishing, Inc., 1986; *New York Times,* 29 December (1995): A31; *Richmond Times-Dispatch,* 29 December (1995): A1; *Washington Post,* 30 December (1995): D6.

Commentary: Virginius Dabney, a direct descendent of Thomas Jefferson through his mother, was an independent writer and scholar. He published seven books after retirement from the newspaper business. He won a Pulitzer Prize for editorials assailing segregation on buses and streetcars and attacking the poll tax in Virginia.

1949

John Henshaw Crider   322

Birth: February 26, 1906; Mount Vernon, NY. **Death:** July 8, 1966. **Parents:** James Leland Crider and Annabelle (Snodgrass). **Religion:** Presbyterian. **Education:** Virginia Military Institution. Columbia University, NY: BLitt. **Spouse:** Maxine Roemer (m. 1932). **Children:** John, Peter, Cynthia.

Prize: *Editorial Writing,* 1949: *Boston Herald,* Boston: Boston Herald, 1948.

Career: College Correspondent, *New York Times,* 1928; Police Reporter, Rewriteman, *New York Times,* 1928-29; Correspondent, Westchester County (NY), *New York Times,* 1929-37; Correspondent, Washington (DC), *New York Times,* 1937-42; Economic Correspondent, Washington (DC), *Time* magazine, 1942; Associate Editor, Whaley-Eaton Service, 1942-43; Correspondent, Washington (DC), *New York Times,* 1943-46; Editor-in-Chief, *Boston Herald,* 1946-51; News Analyst, Boston (MA), CBS TV, 1952; Assistant Editorial Page Editor, *Life* magazine, 1953; Correspondent, Washington (DC), *Barron's Weekly,* 1954-55; Diplomatic Correspondent, London, International News Service, 1956-57; Assistant Information Director, Commission for Economic Development, New York City, 1957; Staff member of Morgan Guaranty Trust Company, 1964-1966.

Selected Works: *The Bureaucrat,* 1944.

Other Awards: Nieman Fellow, Harvard University, MA, 1940-41. Award, United States Council of the International Chamber of Commerce. Sigma Delta Chi Award.

For More Information: *Current Biography Yearbook, 1949,* New York: H.W. Wilson, 1949; *New York Times,* 3 May (1949): 22; *New York Times,* 9 July (1966): 27.

Commentary: John H. Crider's editorial writing for the *Boston Herald* won him a Pulitzer Prize in 1949. Differing from most editorial writers, the ones submitted for the prize were only those written while he was out of town. Thus, the editorials "impress the reader with the editor's proximity to the news,"—from the nominating letter of Robert B. Choate

Herbert Berridge Elliston   323

Birth: November 15, 1895; Wakefield, Yorkshire, England. **Death:** January 22, 1957. **Parents:** Frederick Thomas Elliston and Elizabeth (Berridge). **Religion:** Unitarian. **Spouse:** Mildred Foster (m. 1932, div. 1941); Joanne Shaw Parker (m. 1941). **Children:** Stephen Foster (MF); Peter Berridge, Michael Shaw (JP).

Prize: *Editorial Writing,* 1949: *Washington Post,* "The Ambassador and the Law," August 16, p. 6; "Church Unity," August 29, p. 4B; "Capital Dilemma," December 13, p. 6, Washington, DC: Washington Post, 1948.

Career: Royal Horse Artillery, British Army, 1915-18; Reporter, *Coventry (England) Midland Daily Telegraph*; Reporter, *Portsmouth (England) Evening News*; Foreign Correspondent, *Manchester (England) Guardian,* 1919; Foreign Correspondent, *Shanghai (China) Times*; Foreign Correspondent, *New York (NY) Herald,* ?-1921; Assistant Cable Editor, *New York Sun;* Editorial Writer, *New York Herald,* 1922-23; Financial Advisor, Chinese Government, 1923-27; Assistant Director of Research, Council on Foreign Relations, 1927-30; Financial Editor and Columnist, *Christian Science Monitor,* 1930-40; Associate Editor, Editorial Page Editor, *Washington (DC) Post,* 1940-53; Sunday Columnist, *Washington (DC) Post,* 1953-57.

Selected Works: *Finland Fights,* 1940.

Other Awards: Order of the White Rose, Finland, 1956.

For More Information: *Current Biography Yearbook, 1949,* New York: H.W. Wilson Co., 1949; *New York Times,* January 23, 1957: 29; *National Cyclopaedia of American Biography, Volume 45,* New York: James T. White & Company, 1962: 504-505.

Commentary: Herbert Elliston wrote editorials on a variety of issues. Those submitted for the Pulitzer Prize included the topics of local racial issues, church unity, and the expulsion of General Consul Lomakin. He wrote at least one editorial daily, and many had great impact on his community.

1950

Carl Maxon Saunders   324

Birth: October 26, 1890; Grand Rapids, MI. **Death:** October 2, 1974. **Parents:** Fred Saunders and Fanny Francisci (Sommer). **Religion:** Episcopalian. **Spouse:** Grace Strong (m. 1914, died 1952); Katherine Long Taylor (m. 1955). **Children:** Dorothy, Lelia.

Prize: *Editorial Writing,* 1950: *Jackson Citizen Patriot,* Jackson, MI: Jackson Citizen Patriot, 1949.

Career: Reporter, *Grand Rapids (MI) News,* 1909; Reporter, *Kalamazoo (MI) Telegraph-Press,* 1911; Managing Editor, *Kalamazoo (MI) Telegraph-*

Press, 1912; Copy Editor, *Detroit Free Press,* 1913-14; Editorial Writer, *Grand Rapids (MI) Herald,* 1915-28; Associate Editor, *Grand Rapids (MI) Herald,* 1928-32; Editor, *Grand Rapids (MI) Herald,* 1932-33; Editor, *Jackson (MI) Citizen Patriot,* 1934-60.

Other Awards: Distinguished Service in Journalism Award, University of Minnesota, 1955. National Headliners Club Award, 1958. Citation, Michigan Medical Society. Associated Press Managing Editors Award. Honorary Degree, Albion College, MI, 1951.

For More Information: *Current Biography Yearbook, 1950,* New York: H.W. Wilson Company, 1950; *New York Times,* 4 October (1974): 42; *Contemporary Authors, Volumes 89-92,* Detroit: Gale Research Company, 1980.

Commentary: Carl M. Saunders won a Pulitzer Prize for his work throughout the year. An example is an editorial that calls for people to pray for peace. He first proposed prayer for Memorial Day in 1948 and repeated his request the following year. His editorial "First Things First" on February 20, 1949 calls for using the day for peace. A resolution was introduced in the United States Congress to have Memorial Day be one of prayer, and President Harry Truman proclaimed that for the day.

1951

William Henry Walter Fitzpatrick 325

Birth: May 23, 1908; New Orleans, LA. **Parents:** William Henry Fitzpatrick and Clara Mary (Bertel). **Religion:** Roman Catholic. **Education:** Tulane University, LA. **Spouse:** Francis Westfeldt (m. 1940). **Children:** William, Peter, Victor, Francis.

Prize: *Editorial Writing,* 1951: *New Orleans States,* "Government by Treaty," December 11-18, New Orleans, LA: New Orleans States, 1950.

Career: Reporter, *New Orleans (LA) Item,* 1933-35; Reporter, *New Orleans (LA) Times-Picayune,* 1935-40; City Editor, *New Orleans (LA) States,* 1940-41; Managing Editor, *New Orleans (LA) States,* 1941-45; Served in U.S. Naval Reserve, 1942-45; Editor, *New Orleans (LA) States,* 1945-52; Vice-President, Director, Times-Picayune Publishing Company, 1948-52; Associate Editor, *Wall Street Journal,* 1952-60; Editor, *Norfolk-Portsmouth (VA) Ledger-Star,* 1960-71; Executive Editor, Landmark Communications, Incorporated, 1971-75.

Other Awards: Freedoms Foundation Medal, 1952.

Commentary: William H. Fitzpatrick won a Pulitzer Prize for his two series of editorials, "The Cove-nant on Human Rights," and "Government By Treaty." He examined the constitutional implications for the United States if it were to ratify the United Nations Covenant on Human Rights. His second series discussed how adoption of such a treaty would supersede our constitutional law. After his editorial appeal, popular sentiment shifted against the Covenant to such an extent that the Eisenhower administration did not even submit it to the Senate for ratification.

1952

Louis La Coss 326

Birth: January 8, 1890; Erie, PA. **Death:** February 17, 1966. **Parents:** William Matthew La Coss and Caroline (Schimpff). **Religion:** Catholic. **Education:** University of Kansas: AB. **Spouse:** Edith Gregory (m. 1923, died 1935); Edith Penn (m. 1938). **Children:** Gregory Matthew (EG).

Prize: *Editorial Writing,* 1952: *St. Louis Globe-Democrat,* "The Low Estate of Public Morals," February 17, St. Louis: St. Louis Globe-Democrat, 1951.

Career: Editor, college paper, *Daily Kansan;* Newspaper Reporter, *San Diego (CA) Sun,* 1912; Reporter, *Kansas City (MO) Star,* 1913; Reporter, *Parsons (KS) Sun,* 1914; Reporter, Associated Press, 1915-23; Correspondent, Mexico City, Mexico, Associated Press, 1920-23; Reporter, Feature Writer, *St. Louis (MO) Globe-Democrat,* 1923; Assistant Editorial Writer, *St. Louis (MO) Globe-Democrat,* 1935; Editorial Page Editor, *St. Louis (MO) Globe-Democrat,* 1941-59; Sunday Columnist, Book Reviewer, *St. Louis (MO) Globe-Democrat,* 1959.

Other Awards: Distinguished Service Citation, University of Kansas.

For More Information: *New York Times,* February 19, 1966: 27.

Commentary: Louis La Coss wrote his editorial "The Low Estate of Public Morals" in response to his growing concern about the moral fiber of the country. He felt that events such as the cheating at the United States Military Academy at West Point, government corruption, and the Kefauver crime hearings indicated the direction the country was headed. His newspaper received more than 47,000 requests for reprints.

1953

Vermont Connecticut Royster

Full entry appears as **#105** under "Commentary," 1984.

1954

Donald Morison Murray   327

Birth: September 16, 1924; Boston, MA. **Parents:** John W. Murray and Jean Edith Thomas (Smith). **Education:** University of New Hampshire: BA, cum laude. Boston University, MA: Postgraduate. **Spouse:** Ellen Pinkham (m. 1946, div. 1948); Minnie Mae Emmerich (m. 1951). **Children:** Anne, Lee, Hannah (ME).

Prize: *Editorial Writing,* 1954: *Boston Herald,* Boston: Boston Herald, 1953.

Career: Paratrooper, U.S. Army, 1943-46; Copyboy, *Boston Herald,* 1948-49; Staff Reporter, *Boston Herald,* 1949-51; Editorial Writer, *Boston Herald,* 1951-54; Journalism Instructor, Boston University (MA), 1953-54; Editorial Staff member, *Time* magazine, 1954-56; Free-lance writer, 1956-63; English Professor, University of New Hampshire, Durham, 1963-; Writing Coach, *Boston Globe,* 1978.

Selected Works: *The World of Sound Recordings,* 1965. *A Writer Teaches Writing: A Practical Method of Teaching Composition,* 1968. *Write to Communicate: The Language Arts in Process* (with Burton Albert), 1973. *Learning by Teaching: Selected Articles in Writing and Teaching,* 1982. *Writing for Readers: Notes on the Writer's Craft from the Boston Globe,* 1983. *Write to Learn,* 1984. *Expect the Unexpected: Teaching Myself—and Others—to Read and Write,* 1989. *Shoptalk: Learning to Write with Writers,* 1990. *The Craft of Revision,* 1991. *A Writer in the Newsroom: A Moving Narrative of a Life as a Reporter, Writer, Teacher and Above All, Student of the World; Poynter Papers, No. 7,* 1995. *Crafting a Life in Essay, Story, Poem,* 1996.

Other Awards: Yankee Quill Award, 1981. Honorary Degree, University of New Hampshire, 1997.

For More Information: *New York Times,* 4 May (1954): 26.

Commentary: Don Murray entered more than 100 of his editorials from 1953 for a Pulitzer Prize. They all contained the theme of the "new look" in national defense about the changes in the United States military policy.

1955

Detroit Free Press   328

Founded: 1831; Detroit, MI. **Founder(s):** Sheldon McKnight.

Prize: *Meritorious Public Service,* 1945. *Editorial Writing,* 1955. *Local General Spot News Reporting,* 1968.

Selected Works: *The Ship of Silver, and Other Verses: An Anthology Selected from Contributions to the Young Verse-Writers' Corner of the Detroit Free Press* (Dorian, Sylvestre, ed.), 1925. *The People beyond 12th Street: A Survey of Attitudes of Detroit Negroes after the Riot of 1967,* the Detroit Urban League (with the Detroit Urban League and the Detroit Free Press), 1967. *Reporting the Detroit Riot, by the Staff Editors of the Detroit Free Press,* 1968.

Other Awards: The *Detroit Free Press*'s staff, editors, and reporters have won eight Pulitzer Prizes, in addition to other journalism and public service awards.

For More Information: Morton, John, "Business of Journalism: Cliffhanger in Detroit (The News and the Free Press)," *Washington Journalism Review,* Volume 8, No. 11, November 1986; Gruley, Bryan, *Paper Losses: A Modern Epic of Greed and Betrayal at America's Two Largest Newspaper Companies,* New York: Grove Press, 1993; Cleghorn, Reese, "How Free, for Whom, for What? And Then? Considering New Challenges to Free Speech and a Free Press," *American Journalism Review,* Volume 16, No. 2, Page 4, March 1994.

Commentary: The *Detroit Free Press* was awarded the Meritorious Public Service prize in 1945 for its investigation of legislative graft and corruption in Lansing, Michigan. It won the Editorial Writing prize in 1955 for an editorial by Royce Howes on "The Cause of a Strike," published on July 26, 1954, impartially and clearly analyzing the responsibility of both labor and management for a local union's unauthorized strike in July 1954, rendering the Chrysler Corporation workers idle and unpaid. By pointing out how and why the parent United Automobile Workers' Union ordered the local strike called off and stating that management let dissatisfaction get out-of-hand, the editorial made a notable contribution to public understanding of the whole program of the respective responsibilities and relationships of labor and management in this field. The *Free Press* won the Local General Spot News Reporting prize in 1968 for its coverage of the Detroit riots of 1967, recognizing both the brilliance of its detailed spot news staff work and its swift and accurate investigation into the underlying causes of the tragedy.

The *Democratic Free Press and Michigan Intelligencer* in 1831 was the first newspaper published in Michigan. (Detroit was a small frontier town at that time.) In 1853, the paper was one of the first to publish a Sunday edition. It became part of Knight Newspapers, owned by John S. Knight, in 1940. In 1974, Knight merged with Ridder and became Knight-Ridder newspapers. The *Free Press* was noted for its Civil War coverage.

1956

Lauren Kephart Soth   329

Birth: October 2, 1910; Sibley, IA. **Death:** February 9, 1998. **Parents:** Michael Ray Soth and Virginia Mabel (Kephart). **Religion:** Episcopalian. **Education:** Iowa State University: MS. Iowa State University: MS. **Spouse:** Marcella Shaw Van (m. 1934). **Children:** Michael, Sara Kathryn, Melinda.

   Prize: *Editorial Writing,* 1956: *Des Moines Register and Tribune,* "If the Russians Want More Meat...," February 10, Des Moines, IA: Des Moines Register and Tribune, 1955.

   Career: Instructor, Associate Professor of Economic Information, Iowa State University of Science and Technology, 1933-47; Principal Agricultural Economist, Office of Price Administration, Washington, DC, 1942; Served in U.S. Army, 1942-46; Editorial Writer, *Des Moines (IA) Register and Tribune,* 1947-50; Assistant Editor of Editorial Pages, *Des Moines (IA) Register and Tribune,* 1950-54; Editorial Page Editor, *Des Moines (IA) Register and Tribune,* 1954-75; Columnist, *Des Moines (IA) Register,* 1976-94.

   Selected Works: , "Presentation and Dissemination of Agricultural Economic Information for Iowa," (thesis), 1938. *Agricultural Economic Facts Basebook of Iowa; Special Report (Iowa State College, Agricultural Experiment Station), Number 1,* 1936. *Farm Trouble,* 1957. *An Embarrassment of Plenty,* 1965. *Agriculture in an Industrial Society; American Problem Series,* 1966. *The Farm Policy Game Play by Play: The Henry A. Wallace Series on Agricultural History and Rural Studies,* 1989.

   Other Awards: National Headliners Club Award, 1956. Reuben Brigham Award, Agricultural College Editors Association, 1966. Honorary Degree, Grinnell College, IA, 1990.

   For More Information: *Des Moines Register,* February 10, 1998: 3.

   Commentary: Lauren K. Soth's editorial inviting the Russians and Khrushchev to visit Iowa during the height of the Cold War won him a Pulitzer Prize. He was part of the United States delegation that returned the visit in 1955. He retired from the *Des Moines Register and Tribune* in 1975 after running the editorial page for 21 years.

1957

James Buford Boone Sr.   330

Birth: January 8, 1909; west of Newnan, GA. **Death:** February 7, 1983. **Parents:** James Edwin Boone and Maude (McKoy). **Religion:** Baptist. **Education:** Mercer University, GA: AB. **Spouse:** Frances Herin (m. 1929). **Children:** Janette Younkin, James B. Jr.

   Prize: *Editorial Writing,* 1957: *Tuscaloosa News,* "What a Price For Peace," February 7, Tuscaloosa, AL: Tuscaloosa News, 1956.

   Career: Reporter, Copydesk, City Editor, Managing Editor, *Macon (GA) Telegraph, Macon (GA) News,* 1929-42; Special Agent, Federal Bureau of Investigation, 1942-46; Editor, *Macon (GA) Telegraph,* 1946; Publisher, *Tuscaloosa (AL) News,* 1947-68; President and Publisher, Tuscaloosa Newspapers Incorporated, 1954-68; Chairman of the Board, Tuscaloosa Newspapers, Incorporated, 1968-74.

   Other Awards: Certificate of Commendation for Services, Director John Edgar Hoover, Federal Bureau of Investigation. George Washington Medal, Freedoms Foundation, 1957. Elijah Parish Lovejoy Award, Colby College, ME, 1957. Algernon Sydney Sullivan Award, University of Alabama, 1968. Alumnus Award, Mercer University, GA.

   For More Information: *New York Times,* February 9, 1983: B12; Taft, William H., *Encyclopedia of Twentieth-Century Journalists,* New York: Garland Publishing, Inc., 1986; *Buford Boone: A Voice of Justice and Reason (VHS),* Princeton, NJ: Films for the Humanities & Sciences, 1995.

   Commentary: Buford Boone's winning editorial was written in response to community unrest after Autherine Lucy enrolled at the University of Alabama. Boone, who was a descendant of Confederate Civil War veterans, was a voice of reason during the turbulent civil rights movement in the South. He won a Pulitzer Prize for his "courage and independence."

1958

Harry Scott Ashmore 331

Birth: July 28, 1916; Greenville, SC. **Death:** January 20, 1998. **Parents:** William Green Ashmore and Elizabeth (Scott). **Education:** Clemson College, SC: BS. **Spouse:** Barbara Edith Laier (m. 1940). **Children:** Anne Rogers.

Prize: *Editorial Writing,* 1958: *Arkansas Gazette,* Little Rock, AR: Arkansas Gazette, 1957.

Career: Reporter, *Greenville (SC) Piedmont;* Political Writer and State Capital Correspondent, *Greenville News;* Political Writer, *Charlotte (NC) News,* 1940-41; Lieutenant Colonel, U.S. Army, 1942-45; Associate Editor, *Charlotte News,* 1945-47; Editor, *Charlotte News,* 1947; Editorial Page Editor, *Arkansas Gazette,* 1947; Executive Editor, *Arkansas Gazette,* 1948-59; Assistant, Adlai Stevenson Presidential Campaign, 1955-56; Correspondent, *New York Herald-Tribune,* 1959; Executive Vice President, President, Center for the Study of Democratic Institutions (Santa Barbara, CA), 1959-68; Editor-in-Chief, *Encyclopaedia Britannica,* 1960-63; Senior Fellow, Duke University (NC), 1973-74; Visiting Professor, University of Michigan; Consultant, U.S. Secretary of Education; Columnist, *Los Angeles Times* Syndicate; Writer.

Selected Works: *The Negro and the Schools,* 1954. *An Epitaph for Dixie,* 1958. *The Other Side of Jordan,* 1960. *The Man in the Middle; Paul Anthony Brick Lectures, 5th series,* 1966. *Mission to Hanoi: A Chronicle of Double Dealing in High Places: A Berkeley Medallion Book* (with William C. Baggs), 1968. *Fear in the Air,* 1973. *The William O. Douglas Inquiry into the State of Individual Freedom* (with others), 1979. *Hearts and Minds: The Anatomy of Racism from Roosevelt to Reagan,* 1982. *Arkansas, a History: States and the Nation,* 1984. *Hearts and Minds: A Personal Chronicle of Race in America,* 1988. *Unreasonable Truths: The Life of Robert Maynard Hutchins,* 1989. *Civil Rights and Wrongs: A Memoir of Race and Politics 1944-1994,* 1994.

Other Awards: Nieman Fellow, Harvard University, MA, 1940-41. Sidney Hillman Foundation Award, 1958. Freedom House Award. Bronze Star and Two Oak Leaf Clusters. Robert F. Kennedy Memorial Lifetime Achievement Award, 1996. Honorary Degrees: Clemson University, SC; Oberlin College, OH, 1958; Grinnell College, IA, 1961; University of Arkansas, 1972.

For More Information: Taft, William H., *Encyclopedia of Twentieth-Century Journalists,* New York: Garland Publishing, Inc., 1986; *New York*

Times, 22 January (1998): B14; *Washington Post,* 22 January (1998): D6.

Commentary: As the executive editor of the *Arkansas Gazette,* Harry Ashmore was the voice of reason during the integration of Little Rock schools. The Pulitzer board cited his editorials "for clearness of style, moral purpose, sound reasoning, and power to influence public opinion." In a rare occurrence, the board also awarded his paper, the *Arkansas Gazette,* a Pulitzer Prize for Meritorious Public Service. Ashmore was a Southern journalist who wrote about the South and its history and about civil rights.

1959

Ralph Emerson McGill 332

Birth: February 5, 1898; Soddy, TN. **Death:** February 3, 1969. **Parents:** Benjamin Franklin McGill and Lou (Skillern). **Religion:** Episcopalian. **Education:** Vanderbilt University, TN. **Spouse:** Mary Elizabeth Leonard (m. 1929, died 1962); Mary Lynn Morgan (m. 1967). **Children:** Elizabeth, Virginia, Ralph Emerson Jr. (ML).

Prize: *Editorial Writing,* 1959: *Atlanta Constitution,* "A Church, A School. . . ," October 15, Atlanta, GA: Atlanta Constitution, 1958.

Career: Served in U.S. Marine Corps, WWI; Reporter, Sports Editor, *Nashville (TN) Banner,* 1922-28; Assistant Sports Editor, *Atlanta (GA) Constitution,* 1929-31; Sports Editor, *Atlanta (GA) Constitution,* 1931-39; Editor-in-Chief, *Atlanta (GA) Constitution,* 1942-60; Publisher, *Atlanta (GA) Constitution,* 1960-69.

Selected Works: *Two Georgians Explore Scandinavia: A Comparison of Education for Democracy in Northern Europe and Georgia* (with Thomas Cleveland David), 1938. *Israel Revisited,* 1950. *The Fleas Come with the Dog,* 1954. *A Church, a School,* 1959. *The South and the Southerner,* 1963. *Quotations,* 1970. *Ralph Emerson McGill: February 5, 1898-February 3, 1969,* 1970. *The Best of Ralph McGill: Selected Columns* (with Thomas Cleveland David), 1980. *Southern Encounter: Southerners of Note in Ralph McGill's South* (with Cal M. Logue), 1983. *No Place to Hide: The South and Human Rights* (with Call M. Logue), 1984.

Other Awards: Rosewald Fellowship, 1937-38. Medal, University of Missouri School of Journalism, 1957. Otis Brumby Award, Georgia Press Association, 1959-60. Lauterbach Award, Distinguished Service in Civil Liberties, 1960. Elijah Parish Lovejoy Award, Southern Illinois University, 1960. Chubb Fellow from Yale University, CT, 1961. Achievement Award, University of Southern California, School of Journalism, 1961. Medallion of Valor, Government of Israel, 1961. Atlantic Nonfiction Prize, 1963: *The*

South and the Southerner, Boston: Little, Brown, 1963. Presidential Medal of Freedom, 1964. National Award, Phi Epsilon Pi. Honorary Degrees: University of Miami, 1959; Colby College, ME, 1960; Mercer University, GA, 1961; Harvard University, MA, 1961; Morehouse College, GA, 1962; St. Bernard College, AL, 1963; Wayne State University, MI, 1963; Brandeis University, MA, 1963; Tufts University, MA, 1963; Oberlin College, OH, 1963; Columbia University, NY, 1963; Emory University, GA, 1963; Brown University, RI, 1964; Kenyon College, OH, 1964; Atlanta University, GA, 1965; DePaul University, IL, 1965; Temple University, PA, 1967.

For More Information: *Saturday Evening Post,* 27 December (1958); *Newsweek,* April 13, 1959: 102-03; Logue, Cal M., *Ralph McGill: Editor and Publisher,* Durham, NC: Moor Publishing Company, 1969; Martin, Harold H., *Ralph McGill, Reporter,* Boston: Little, Brown, 1973; *Dictionary of Literary Biography, Volume 29,* Detroit: Gale Research Company, 1984.

Commentary: Ralph McGill had written his daily column for 28 years when he was awarded a Pulitzer Prize in 1959. During that year, he wrote about tolerance and school integration. He won for the body of his work, but his editorial "A Church, A School ..." exemplified his writing. It was written after Atlanta's largest Jewish synagogue was bombed. He conveyed his point through lucid argument with interjections of humor and compassion.

1960

Lenoir Chambers   333

Birth: December 26, 1891; Charlotte, NC. **Death:** January 10, 1970. **Parents:** Joseph Lenoir Chambers and Grace Singleton (Dewey). **Education:** University of North Carolina: AB, Phi Beta Kappa. Columbia University, NY. **Spouse:** Roberta Burwell Strudwick (m. 1928). **Children:** Stepchild: Robert Strudwick Glenn; Elisabeth Lacy.

Prize: *Editorial Writing,* 1960: *Norfolk Virginian-Pilot,* "The Year the Schools Closed," January 1; "The Year the Schools Opened," December 31, Norfolk, VA: Norfolk Virginian-Pilot, 1959.

Career: English Teacher, Woodberry Forest School (VA), 1914-16; Staff member, Washington, DC, *New Republic News Service,* 1917; Served in Army Expeditionary Forces, U.S. Army, 1917-19; Director, University of North Carolina News Bureau, 1919-21; Reporter, City Editor, Associate Editor, *Greensboro (NC) Daily News,* 1921-29; Editor, *Norfolk Virginian-Pilot,* 1929-44; President, Director, Norfolk Forum Incorporated, 1943-46; Editor, *Norfolk (VA) Ledger-Dispatch,* 1944-50; Editor, *Norfolk Virginian-Pilot,* 1950-61.

Selected Works: *Stonewall Jackson,* 1959. *Salt Water & Printer's Ink: Norfolk and Its Newspapers, 1865-1965* (with Joseph E. Shank), 1967.

Other Awards: Honorary Degree, University of North Carolina, 1960.

For More Information: *New York Times,* January 11, 1970: 76; Powell, William S., *Dictionary of North Carolina Biography, Volume 1, A-C.* Chapel Hill, NC: University of North Carolina Press, 1979; *Contemporary Authors, Volume 111,* Detroit: Gale Research, 1984; Leidholdt, Alexander, *Standing Before the Shouting Mob: Lenoir Chambers and Virginia's Massive Resistance to Public School Integration,* Tuscaloosa: University of Alabama Press, 1997.

Commentary: Lenoir Chambers's winning editorials in 1959 dealt with the topic of desegregation in Virginia schools. He was opposed to the policy of closing schools to avoid desegregation. His first editorial of the year said that Virginians must ask themselves "what they can and will do in 1959" to avoid the tragedy of 1958. His last editorial, written 365 days later, challenged the people of Virginia to step up, to initiate, and to lead so that the coming year would be one of hope.

1961

William Joseph Dorvillier   334

Birth: April 24, 1908; North Adams, MA. **Death:** May 5, 1993. **Parents:** Joseph Dorvillier and Aurise (Champagne). **Religion:** Roman Catholic. **Education:** New York University. **Spouse:** Mary Elizabeth Johnson (m. 1938, died 1979). **Children:** William Clay.

Prize: *Editorial Writing,* 1961: *San Juan Star,* San Juan, Puerto Rico: San Juan Star, 1960.

Career: South American Desk Reporter, New York (NY), Associated Press; Caribbean Correspondent, Associated Press; War Correspondent, WWII; Editor, *Puerto Rico World Journal,* 1940-45; White House Correspondent, Washington (DC), *San Juan (Puerto Rico) El Mundo,* 1945-53; Founder, Chairman of the Board, *Puerto Rico-Dorvillier News Agency,* 1953-79; Founder, Editor, Publisher, *San Juan (Puerto Rico) Star,* 1959-67; President, Star Publishing Company, 1959-62; News Director, WAPA-TV, 1969-73.

Selected Works: *Workshop U.S.A.: The Challenge of Puerto Rico,* 1962.

For More Information: *New York Times,* 6 May (1993): D22.

Commentary: William J. Dorvillier won a Pulitzer Prize for his series of 20 editorials criticizing the Roman Catholic bishops of Puerto Rico for playing politics in the 1960 election for governor. The bishops had threatened excommunication for those who opposed them. Dorvillier resisted the pressure and continued writing the editorials. The voters also resisted the pressure and voted for the opposition.

1962

Thomas More Storke   335

Birth: November 23, 1876; Santa Barbara, CA. **Death:** October 12, 1971. **Parents:** Charles Albert Storke and Martha (More). **Education:** Stanford University, CA: AB. **Spouse:** Elsie Smith (m. 1904, died); Marion Day (m. 1920). **Children:** Jean Isabel, Elsie Margaret, Charles Albert, (ES); Thomas More (MD).

Prize: *Editorial Writing*, 1962: *Santa Barbara News-Press,* Santa Barbara, CA: Santa Barbara News-Press, 1961.

Career: Editor, Publisher, Owner, *Santa Barbara (CA) News-Press,* 1901-64; Postmaster, Santa Barbara, CA, 1914-21; Member, U.S. Senate, 1938-39; Member, California Crime Commission, 1951-52; Editor Emeritus, *Santa Barbara (CA) News-Press,* 1964-71.

Selected Works: *California Editor,* 1958. *I Write for Freedom,* 1962.

Other Awards: Lauterbach Award, 1961. Elijah Parish Lovejoy Award, Colby College, ME, 1962. Honorary Degrees: University of California, 1960; Colby College, ME, 1963.

For More Information: *Current Biography Yearbook, 1963,* New York: H.W. Wilson Company, 1963; *New York Times,* 13 October (1971): 48; *Contemporary Authors, Volumes 89-92,* Detroit: Gale Research Company, 1980; Taft, William H., *Encyclopedia of Twentieth-Century Journalists,* New York: Garland Publishing, 1986.

Commentary: Thomas More Storke, who was editor and publisher of the *Santa Barbara News-Press,* started his paper on the first day of the 20th century. He won a Pulitzer Prize for his editorials that called attention to the semi-secret John Birch Society. He was one of the first to expose the group and its beliefs. His articles on the John Birch Society were reprinted in the *New York Times Magazine* and the *Congressional Record.*

1963

Ira Brown Harkey Jr.   336

Birth: January 15, 1918; New Orleans, LA. **Parents:** Ira Brown Harkey and Flora B. (Lewis). **Education:** Tulane University, LA: BA, Phi Beta Kappa. University of Florida. Ohio State University: MA. **Spouse:** Marie E. Gore (m. 1939, div. 1963); Marion Marks Drake (m. 1963, div. 1976); Virga Quin Mioten (m.

1977). **Children:** Marie Ella, Ira III, Meg, Erik, Lewis M., Amelie, William M. (MG); Katherine B. (MD).

Prize: *Editorial Writing,* 1963: *Pascagoula Chronicle,* Pascagoula, MS: Pascagoula Chronicle, 1962.

Career: Cub Reporter, City Room, *New Orleans (LA) Times-Picayune,* 1940-42; Served in U.S. Navy, 1942-46; Cub Reporter, City Room, *New Orleans (LA) Times-Picayune,* 1946-49; Owner, *Pascagoula (MS) Chronicle,* 1949; Editor and Publisher, *Pascagoula (MS) Chronicle,* 1949-62; Journalism Faculty member, Ohio State University, 1965-66; Vice-President, Director, Coca-Cola Bottling Company, Inc., Oklahoma City, OK, 1965-80; Carnegie Visiting Professor, University of Alaska, 1968-69; Dean Stone Lecturer, University of Montana, 1970; Eric Allen Lecturer, University of Oregon, 1972; Vice-President, Director, Great Plains Industries, 1979-80; President, Indian Creek Company, 1980-93.

Selected Works: *Dedicated to the Proposition: Editorials from The Chronicle, Pascagoula, Mississippi,* 1963. *The Smell of Burning Crosses: An Autobiography of a Mississippi Newspaperman,* 1967. *Pioneer Bush Pilot: The Story of Noel Wien,* 1974. *Alton Ochsner, Surgeon of the South* (with John Wilds), 1990.

Other Awards: National Conference of Christians and Jews Award, 1963. Sidney Hillman Foundation Award, 1963. Sigma Delta Chi Award, 1963. Civil Libertarian of the Year, Mississippi Chapter of Civil Liberties Union, 1992. Hall of Fame, Mississippi Press Association, 1993.

For More Information: *Contemporary Authors, Volumes 57-60,* Detroit: Gale Research Company, 1976.

Commentary: Ira B. Harkey Jr. received a Pulitzer Prize for his editorials on integration in Mississippi. His was a voice of reason and for observance of the law when riots broke out after James Meredith was admitted as a student at the University of Mississippi.

Harkey won many awards for his writings in 1962. But many Southerners felt it was a show of Yankee approval, and Harkey was ostracized. He sold his paper in 1963.

1964

Hazel Brannon Smith   337

Birth: February 5, 1914; Gadsden, AL. **Death:** May 14, 1994. **Parents:** Dock Boad Brannon and Georgia (Freeman). **Education:** University of Alabama: BA. **Spouse:** Walter Dyer Smith (m. 1950, died 1983).

Prize: *Editorial Writing,* 1964: *Lexington Advertiser,* Lexington, MS: Lexington Advertiser, 1963.

Career: Staff member, *Gadsden (AL) Etowah Observer,* 1931-33; Managing Editor, college paper;

Owner, *Durant (MS) News,* 1936-43; Editor, Publisher, *Lexington (MS) Advertiser* and three other weekly newspapers, 1943; Publisher, *Banner (MS) County Outlook,* 1955; Publisher, *Jackson (MS) Northside Reporter,* 1956.

Other Awards: Highest Editorial Award, National Federation of Press Women, 1948, 1955-56. Elijah Parish Lovejoy Award, Southern Illinois University, 1960. Golden Quill, International Conference of Weekly Newspaper Editors, 1963. Herrick Award, National Editorial Association. Mississippi Woman of the Year, 1964.

For More Information: *St. Louis Post-Dispatch,* 26 November (1961): Everyday Magazine; *Washington Post,* 14 December (1963) *Congressional Record,* 109: 204 (12 December 1963); *Congressional Record,* 13 December (1963): 23389; *Columbia Journalism Review,* Fall (1963); *Current Biography Yearbook, 1973,* New York: H.W. Wilson Company, 1973: 384-386; *Dictionary of Literary Biography, Volume 127,* Detroit: Gale Research Company, 1993; *New York Times,* 16 May (1994): B8; Riley, Sam G., *Biographical Dictionary of American Newspaper Columnists,* Westport, CT: Greenwood Press, 1995.

Commentary: Hazel Brannon Smith owned four Mississippi weekly papers by the late 1950s. She wrote a column "Through Hazel Eyes." (Hers were actually blue.) She encouraged social reform. Her promotion of civil rights had an adverse effect on her advertising revenue, and she had to accept speaking engagements to remain solvent. The Pulitzer Prize was in recognition of her editorial stand against injustice and corruption in the face of strong opposition among community members. She was the first woman to win a Pulitzer Prize for Editorial Writing.

1965

John Raymond Harrison 338

Birth: June 8, 1933; Des Moines, IA. **Parents:** Raymond Harrison and Dorothy (Stout). **Education:** Harvard University, MA: AB. **Spouse:** Lois Cowles (m. 1955, div. 1981); Mary Gee MacQueen (m. 1981). **Children:** Gardner Mark, Kent Alfred, John Patrick, Lois Eleanor (LC).

Prize: *Editorial Writing,* 1965: *Gainesville Sun,* Gainesville, FL: Gainesville Sun, 1964.

Career: Printer, *Ft. Pierce (FL) News-Tribune;* Vice-President and President, *New York Times* Affiliated Newspaper Group; Director, *International Herald-Tribune;* Publisher, *Gainesville Sun,* 1962; Vice President, *New York Times* Company; President, *New York Times* Regional Newspaper Group, ?-1993; Harrison Charitable Foundation Staff member.

Other Awards: Bronze Medallion, Sigma Delta Chi, 1970, 1973. National Headliners Club Award,

1972. Walker Stone Award, Scripps-Howard Foundation, 1974.

For More Information: *Atlanta Journal and Constitution,* 10 June (1993): F1.

Commentary: John R. "Jack" Harrison led the campaign for minimum housing codes for the city of Gainesville, Florida. The campaign lasted approximately one month, fighting the leaders of the town who for a decade had been resisting the idea of housing codes. Harrison's writing helped win municipal approval and improve housing conditions in his community.

1966

Robert N. Lasch 339

Birth: March 26, 1907; Lincoln, NE. **Death:** April 6, 1998. **Parents:** Theodore Walter Lasch and Myrtle (Nelson). **Religion:** Unitarian Universalist. **Education:** University of Nebraska: AB. **Spouse:** Zora Schaupp (m. 1931, died 1982); Iris C. Anderson (m. 1986). **Children:** Robert Christopher, Catherine (ZS).

Prize: *Editorial Writing,* 1966: *St. Louis Post-Dispatch,* St. Louis: St. Louis Post-Dispatch, 1965.

Career: Police Reporter, *Lincoln (NE) Star;* Reporter, Editorial Writer, *Omaha (NE) World Herald,* 1931-41; Chief Editorial Writer, *Chicago Sun,* 1942-50; Editorial Writer, *St. Louis (MO) Dispatch,* 1950-57; Editorial Page Editor, *St. Louis (MO) Dispatch,* 1957-71.

Selected Works: *The Sun Looks Ahead to Postwar Chicago* (with others), 1943. *Freedom of the Press: Reprinted from the Atlantic Monthly,* 1944. *Breaking the Building Blockade,* 1946. *The Golden Dozen, 1968: Finalists, Golden Quill Award for Editorial Writing,* 1968.

Other Awards: Rhodes Scholar, Oxford University, England, 1928-30. Nieman Fellow, Harvard University, MA, 1941-42. St. Louis Civil Liberties Award, 1966.

For More Information: *St. Louis Post-Dispatch,* 16 February (1994): B4; *St. Louis Post-Dispatch,* 8 April (1998): A14.

Commentary: Robert Lasch has been connected to newspapers in some form or fashion since he was 13 years old. He was a printer's devil while he was in high school and a police reporter while attending the University of Nebraska. Many of his editorials during 1965 carried the theme of disenchantment with the United States foreign policy regarding Vietnam. One that the Pulitzer Prize board cited as representative was "The Containment of Ideas," which had been published on January 17, 1965.

1967

Eugene Corbett Patterson   340

Birth: October 15, 1923; Valdosta, GA. **Parents:** William C. Patterson and Annabel (Corbett). **Education:** North Georgia College, Dahlonega. University of Georgia: AB. **Spouse:** Mary Sue Carter (m. 1950). **Children:** Mary.

    Prize: *Editorial Writing,* 1967: *Atlanta Constitution,* Atlanta, GA: Atlanta Constitution, 1966.

    Career: Served in U.S. Army, WWII; Reporter, *Temple (TX) Daily Telegram,* and Reporter, *Macon (GA) Telegraph,* 1947-48; Reporter, Atlanta (GA) Bureau, United Press International; South Carolina Manager, United Press International; Night Manager, New York (NY) Bureau, United Press International, 1949-53; Chief Correspondent, United Kingdom, and London (England) Bureau Chief, United Press International, 1953-56; Executive Editor, *Atlanta (GA) Journal and Constitution,* 1956-60; Editor, *Atlanta (GA) Journal and Constitution,* 1960-68; Managing Editor, *Washington (DC) Post,* 1968-71; Journalism Instructor, Duke University, NC, 1971-72; Editor, *St. Petersburg (FL) Times,* 1972-88; Chairman, Chief Executive Officer, *St. Petersburg (FL) Times,* 1978-88.

    Selected Works: *Ralph McGill: Rock in a Weary Land; Ralph McGill Lectures, 1979,* 1979. *The Bridge Behind: A Family History,* 1993.

    Other Awards: William Allen White Award, William Allen White Foundation, University of Kansas, 1980. Ralph McGill Lifetime Achievement in Journalism Award, Society of Professional Journalists, Atlanta Chapter, GA, 1991. Elijah Parish Lovejoy Award, Southern Illinois University, 1994. Florida Newspaper Hall of Fame, Florida Press Association, 1997. Honorary Degrees: Tusculum College, TN;

Emory University, GA; Tuskegee Institute, AL; Oglethorpe College, GA.

    For More Information: U.S. Congress/Senate Committee on the Judiciary, Subcommittee on Constitutional Rights, *Nominations of Mrs. Frankie Muse Freeman and Mr. Eugene C. Patterson,* Washington, D.C.: U.S. G.P.O., 1964; *Washington Post,* 29 October (1994): A8; *St. Petersburg Times* 21 July (1997): B1.

    Commentary: Eugene C. Patterson grew up during the Depression, joined the Army and was a tank commander in World War II, then turned to a career in journalism. He worked as editor for three large daily newspapers, the *Atlanta Journal and Constitution,* the *Washington Post,* and the *St. Petersburg Times.* His editorials against racism won him a Pulitzer Prize.

1968

John Shively Knight   341

Birth: October 26, 1894; Bluefields, WV. **Death:** June 16, 1981. **Parents:** Charles Landon Knight and Clara Irene (Scheifley). **Religion:** Episcopalian. **Education:** Cornell University, NY. **Spouse:** Katherine McLain (m. 1921, died 1929); Beryl Zoller Comstock (m. 1932, died 1974); Elizabeth Good Augustus (m. 1976, died 1981). **Children:** John Shively Jr, Charles Landon, Frank McLain (KM); adopted: Rita (BC).

    Prize: *Editorial Writing,* 1968: Knight Newspapers, 1967.

    Career: Served in Army Air Corps and Army Expeditionary Forces, U.S. Army, 1917-19; Newspaper Reporter and Executive, 1920-25; Managing Editor, *Akron (OH) Beacon Journal,* 1925-33; Editor, *Akron (OH) Beacon Journal,* 1933-71; Editorial Chairman, *Akron (OH) Beacon Journal,* 1971-76; Editor Emeritus, *Akron (OH) Beacon Journal,* 1976-81; Editorial Director, *Springfield (OH) Sun,* 1925-27; Editorial Director, *Massilion (OH) Independent,* 1927-33; President, *Massilion (OH) Independent,* 1933-37; Chairman of the Board, *Miami (FL) Herald,* 1937-67; Owner of discontinued *Miami (FL) Tribune,* 1937; Owner, Publisher, *Detroit (MI) Free Press,* 1940; President, Editor, *Detroit (MI) Free Press,* 1940-67; Editorial Chairman, *Detroit (MI) Free Press,* 1940-76; Former Owner, Editor, Publisher, *Chicago Daily News,* 1944-59; Vice President, *Charlotte (NC) Observer,* 1954; Staff member, *Charlotte (NC) News,* 1959; Editorial Chairman, *Miami (FL) Herald,* 1967-76; Editor Emeritus, *Miami (FL) Herald,* 1976-81; President, Beacon Journal Publishing Company, Knight Newspapers, Incorporated, ?-1966; Editorial Chairman, Beacon Journal Publishing Company, Knight Newspapers, Incorporated, 1966-76; Editor Emeritus, Beacon Journal Publishing Company, Knight Newspapers, Incorporated, 1976-81;

Editor Emeritus, *Detroit Free Press,* 1976-81; Staff member, *Tallahassee (FL) Democrat.*

Selected Works: *To Speak One's Mind: An Address; The John Peter Zenger Award for Freedom of the Press and People's Right to Know,* 1967. *The Twilight of the Tyrants; Alberdi-Sarmiento Award Lectures* (with German Arciniegas), 1973.

Other Awards: Brotherhood of Children Award, 1946. Medal for Distinctive Achievement in Newspaper Publishing, Syracuse University School of Journalism, NY, 1946. Citation of Merit, Poor Richard Club, Philadelphia, PA, 1947. Howard Hawks Memorial Trophy for Service to Aviation, 1947. Distinguished Service to Journalism Award, University of Missouri, 1949. Outstanding Chicagoan in Inter-American Relations, U.S.-Uruguay Alliance, 1952. First Annual La Prensa Award, Rio de Janeiro, Brazil, 1954. America's Foundation Award, 1959. Maria Moors Cabot Gold Medal, Columbia University, NY, 1962. Governor's Award Winner, 1964. Presidential Councillor, Cornell University, NY, 1966. John Peter Zenger Award, University of Arizona, 1967. Carr Van Anda Award, Ohio University, 1970. William Allen White Award of Journalistic Merit, William Allen White Foundation, University of Kansas, 1972. Gold Medal of Achievement, 1972. Fourth Estate Award, National Press Club, 1976. Honorary Degrees: University of Akron, OH, 1945; Northwestern University, IL, 1947; Kent State University, OH, 1958; Ohio State University, 1961; University of Michigan, 1969; Oberlin College, OH, 1969; Colby College, ME, 1969; University of Kentucky, 1980.

For More Information: *Contemporary Authors, Volumes 93-96,* Detroit: Gale Research Company, 1980; *John Shively Knight, 1894-1981: A Tribute to an American Editor,* Akron, OH: Akron Beacon Journal, 1981; Whited, Charles, *Knight: A Publisher in a Tumultuous Century,* New York: Dutton, 1988.

Commentary: John S. Knight, head of the Knight chain of newspapers, won a Pulitzer Prize for his weekly column, "The Editor's Notebook," which he began writing in the 1930s. Depending on his mood, the column was serious or whimsical. His entry included 10 of his columns on his opposition to the United States' involvement in Vietnam.

1969

## Paul Greenberg				342
Birth: January 21, 1937; Shreveport, LA. **Parents:** Ben Greenberg and Sarah (Ackerman). **Religion:** Jewish. **Education:** Centenary College, LA. University of Missouri: BA. University of Missouri: MA. Columbia University, NY: Postgrad. **Spouse:** Carolyn Levy (m. 1964). **Children:** Daniel, Ruth Elizabeth.

Prize: *Editorial Writing,* 1969: *Pine Bluff Commercial,* Pine Bluff, AR: Pine Bluff Commercial, 1968.

Career: History Lecturer, Hunter College (NY), 1960-62; Editorial Page Editor, *Pine Bluff (AR) Commercial,* 1962-66; History Editor, Crowell Collier Publishing Company, NY; Editorial Writer, *Chicago Daily News,* 1966-67; Lecturer, University of Arkansas, 1967-; Editorial Page Editor, *Pine Bluff (AR) Commercial,* 1967-69; Columnist, *Pine Bluff (AR) Commercial,* 1970-; Columnist, *Los Angeles (CA) Times* Syndicate.

Selected Works: *Resonant Lives: 50 Figures of Consequence,* 1991. *Entirely Personal,* 1992. *Resonant Lives: 60 Figures of Consequence,* 1993. *No Surprises: Two Decades of Clinton-Watching,* 1996.

Other Awards: First Place, Grenville Clark Competition for Best Editorial on the Subject of World Peace Through World Law, 1964. First Place, Best Editorial Competition, National Newspaper Association, 1967. University of Missouri Journalism Medal. Distinguished Writing Award, American Society of Newspaper Editors, 1981. H.L. Mencken Award, 1987. William Allen White Award, William Allen White Foundation, University of Kansas, 1988.

For More Information: *New York Times,* 6 May (1969): 34; *Contemporary Authors, Volumes 69-72,* Detroit: Gale Research Company, 1978: 288; Taft, William H., *Encyclopedia of Twentieth-Century Journalists,* New York: Garland Publishing, Inc., 1986; Riley, Sam G., *Biographical Dictionary of American Newspaper Columnists,* Westport, CT: Greenwood Press, 1995.

Commentary: Paul Greenberg won a Pulitzer Prize for several of his editorials that ran throughout 1968. He touched on such topics as George Wallace's candidacy for President and school desegregation. He was a finalist for a Pulitzer Prize in 1978 and 1986.

1970

## Philip Laussat Geyelin			343
Birth: February 27, 1923; Devon, PA. **Parents:** Emile Camille Geyelin and Cecily (Barnes). **Education:** Yale University, CT: BA. **Spouse:** Cecilia Sherman Parker (m 1950). **Children:** Mary, Emile, Philip, Cecily.

Prize: *Editorial Writing,* 1970: *Washington Post,* Washington, DC: Washington Post, 1969.

Career: Served in U.S. Marine Corps Reserves, 1943-46; Washington (DC) Bureau, Associated Press, 1946-47; Staff member, *Wall Street Journal,* 1947-66; Diplomatic Correspondent, *Wall Street Journal,* 1960-67; Editorial Staff, *Washington (DC) Post,* 1967-79; Editorial Page Editor, *Washington (DC) Post,* 1968-79; Syndicated columnist; Editor-in-

Residence, School of Advanced International Studies, Johns Hopkins University (MD).

Selected Works: *Lyndon B. Johnson and the World,* 1966. *American Media: Adequate or Not? Rational Debate Seminars,* 1970.

Other Awards: Overseas Press Club Award, 1966. Fellow, Institute of Politics, John F. Kennedy School of Government, Harvard University, MA, 1967.

For More Information: *Washington Post,* 24 March (1979): A3; Riley, Sam G., *Biographical Dictionary of American Newspaper Columnists,* Westport, CT: Greenwood Press, 1995.

Commentary: Philip L. Geyelin wrote on a variety of topics in 1969, for which he was awarded a Pulitzer Prize. His entry of 10 editorials covered such topics as the Johnson administration's Vietnam policy, the rejection by the University of Georgia of former Secretary of State Dean Rusk for a teaching position, and President Johnson's television reminiscences.

Geyelin worked at the *Wall Street Journal* for 20 years before moving to the *Washington Post* in 1967.

1971

Horance Gibbs Davis Jr. 344

Birth: July 14, 1924; Manchester, GA. **Parents:** Horance Gibbs Davis and Florance Gray (Beavers). **Religion:** Episcopalian. **Education:** University of Florida: BA: MA, High Honors. **Spouse:** Marjorie Lucile Davis (m. 1948). **Children:** Gregory Rawson, Jennifer Diane.

Prize: *Editorial Writing,* 1971: *Gainesville Sun,* Gainesville, FL: Gainesville Sun, 1970.

Career: Served in U.S. Army Air Corps, 1943-46; Editing Staff member, *Bradford County (FL) Telegraph,* 1948; Correspondent, Gainesville (FL), *Jacksonville Florida Times Union,* 1949-50; Capital Correspondent, Tallahassee (FL), *Jacksonville Florida Times-Union,* 1950-54; Journalism Instructor, University of Florida, Gainesville, 1954-57; Editing Staff member, *Bradford County (FL) Telegraph,* 1955, 1956; Assistant Professor of Journalism, University of Florida, Gainesville, 1957-60; Reporter, *Atlanta (GA) Constitution,* 1959, 1960; Associate Professor of Journalism, University of Florida, Gainesville, 1960-77; Reporter, *Miami (FL) Herald,* 1961, 1966; Editorial Writer, *Gainesville (FL) Sun,* 1962-89; Distinguished Service Professor of Journalism, University of Florida, Gainesville, 1977-85; Weekly Columnist, *Atlanta (GA) Journal-Constitution,* 1977-79; Columnist, *New York Times* Regional Newspaper Group, 1983-89; Columnist, *Gainesville (FL) F.A.C.T.,* 1995-.

Selected Works: , "Florida Journalism during the Civil War...," (thesis), 1952. *Gainesville Sun Editorials,* 1971.

Other Awards: Sidney Hillman Award, 1964. Distinguished Service Award, Sigma Delta Chi, 1964. Distinguished Alumnus Award, University of Florida, 1971. Wells Memorial Key, Sigma Delta Chi, 1977. Ernest R. Currie Memorial Media Award, Florida Medical Association, 1985.

For More Information: Beasley, Maurine Hoffman and Richard R. Harlow, *Voices of Change: Southern Pulitzer Winners,* Baltimore, MD: University Press of America, 1979; Mikell, Ann Wayne, "In Righteous Dissent: A Profile of Southern Reformer H.G. Buddy Davis" (thesis), University of Florida, 1990; *Miami Herald,* 5 March (1995): B6.

Commentary: Horance G. "Buddy" Davis Jr. wrote more than 30 editorials supporting tolerance during the period of school desegregation in Florida in 1970. He argued that desegregation could happen without violence. The winning editorials were published between January 18 and May 15, 1969. He spent 31 years at the University of Florida teaching journalism to would-be reporters.

1972

John Strohmeyer 345

Birth: June 26, 1924; Cascade, WI. **Parents:** Louis A. Strohmeyer and Anna Rose (Saladunas). **Education:** Moravian College, PA. Muhlenberg College, PA: AB. Columbia University, NY: MS. **Spouse:** Nancy Jordan (m. 1949). **Children:** Mark, John, Sarah.

Prize: *Editorial Writing,* 1972: *Bethlehem Globe-Times,* Bethlehem, PA: Bethlehem Globe-Times, 1971.

Career: Reporter, *Nazareth (PA) Item,* 1940-41; Night Reporter, *Bethlehem (PA) Globe-Times,* 1941-43; Served in U.S. Navy, 1943-46; Investigative Reporter, *Providence (RI) Journal,* 1946-47; Editor, *Bethlehem (PA) Globe-Times,* 1956-84; Vice-President, *Bethlehem (PA) Globe-Times,* 1961-84; Director, *Bethlehem (PA) Globe-Times,* 1963-84; McFadden Professor, Lehigh University (PA), 1986-87; Atwood Professor of Journalism, University of Alaska, Anchorage, 1987-89; Writer-in-Residence, University of Alaska, Anchorage, 1989-.

Selected Works: *Crisis in Bethlehem: Big Steel's Struggle to Survive,* 1986. *Extreme Conditions: Big Oil and the Transformation of Alaska,* 1993.

Other Awards: Pulitzer Traveling Fellowship, 1948. Nieman Fellow, Harvard University, MA, 1952-53. Bronze Medallion, 50th Anniversary Honors List, Columbia University Graduate School of Journalism, NY. Comenius Award, Moravian College, PA, 1971. Fellow, Alicia Patterson Foundation, 1984-85. Honorary Degree, Lehigh University, PA, 1983.

For More Information: *New York Times,* 2 May (1972): 36; *Contemporary Authors, Volume 128,* Detroit: Gale Research Company, 1990.

Commentary: John Strohmeyer's strong editorial stand against community violence toward newly arrived Puerto Rican workers helped reduce racial tensions. For his leadership in a difficult situation, he won a Pulitzer Prize in 1972.

1973

Roger Bourne Linscott   346

Birth: January 22, 1920; Winchester, MA. **Parents:** Robert Newton Linscott and Helen Rockwell (Lathrop). **Education:** Harvard University, MA: BA. **Spouse:** Lucy Ann Richardson Goodlatte (m. 1943). **Children:** Wendy, Judith, Victoria, Rebecca.

Prize: *Editorial Writing,* 1973: *Berkshire Eagle,* Pittsfield, MA: Berkshire Eagle, 1972.

Career: Lieutenant, U.S. Navy, 1942-45; Staff member, *Cape Cod (MA) Times,* summers during college; Member of Buchanan Advertising Agency; Copywriter, Franklin Spier Agency, 1946-47; "On the Books" Weekly Columnist, *New York Herald-Tribune,* 1947-48; Reporter, *Pittsfield (MA) Berkshire Eagle,* 1948-; Editorial Page Editor, *Pittsfield (MA) Berkshire Eagle,* 1956-72; Associate Editor, *Pittsfield (MA) Berkshire Eagle,* 1973-; Visiting Professor, University of Massachusetts, 1974-75.

Other Awards: Honorary Degree, Adams State College, CO, 1974.

For More Information: *New York Times,* 8 May (1973): 32.

Commentary: Roger B. Linscott was a columnist in New York when he decided he wanted a career change. He went to an out-of-town newspaper stand and chose his next employer by evaluating the quality of other newspapers. His editorials in 1972 covered a variety of local and national issues. One of his editorials endorsed McGovern for President due to "the crooked Nixon Administration." Some local issues he tackled were the local bus service and local hospitals and a family planning project.

1974

Frederick Gilman Spencer   347

Birth: December 8, 1925; Philadelphia, PA. **Parents:** F. Gilman Spencer and Elizabeth (Hetherington). **Spouse:** Isabel Brannon (m. 1965). **Children:** Amy, Elizabeth, F. Gilman, Jonathan, Isabel Caroline.

Prize: *Editorial Writing,* 1974: *Trentonian,* Trenton, NJ: Trentonian, 1973.

Career: Served in U.S. Navy, 1943-46; Copyboy, *Philadelphia (PA) Inquirer,* 1947-49; Photographer and Cub Sports Writer, *Chester Times,* 1949; Photographer and Sports Writer, *Mount Holly Herald,* 1949-52; News and General Assignments Writer, *Chester Times,* 1952-59; Editor, *Ardmore (PA) Main Line Times,* 1959-63; Deskman, *Philadelphia (PA) Evening Bulletin,* 1963-64; Writer and Television Editorialist, WCAU-TV, CBS affiliated station, Philadelphia, PA, 1964-67; Editor, *The Trenton (NJ) Trentorian,* 1967-75; Editor, *Philadelphia (PA) Daily News,* 1975-84; Editor, *New York Daily News,* 1984-89; Editor-in-Chief, *Denver (CO) Post,* 1989-93; Syndicated Columnist, Universal Press Syndicate, 1993-96.

Other Awards: Honorary Degree, University of Colorado, 1994.

For More Information: *New York Times,* 7 May (1974): 40; *New York Times,* 15 September (1989): B3.

Commentary: F. Gilman "Gil" Spencer spent over 50 years in the news business. He began as a copy boy and worked up to editor-in-chief. His award was for his editorial campaign to focus public attention on the scandals in New Jersey state government. He persevered despite the counterattacks of the state officials that were involved in the scandal. His writings led to federal prosecution of some officials for corruption.

1975

John Daniell Maurice   348

Birth: October 23, 1913; Vivian, WV. **Parents:** John F. Maurice and Margaret May (Daniell). **Education:** Marshall University, WV: AB, magna cum laude. **Spouse:** Louise Hart (m. 1939). **Children:** Johanna Louisa, Eva.

Prize: *Editorial Writing,* 1975: *Charleston Daily Mail,* Charleston, WV: Charleston Daily Mail, 1974.

Career: Reporter, *Huntington (WV) Herald-Dispatch,* 1935-38; Reporter, *Charleston (WV) Daily Mail,* 1938-43; Served in U.S. Naval Reserve, 1943-46; Chief Editorial Writer, *Charleston (WV) Daily Mail,* 1946-53; Editor, *Charleston (WV) Daily Mail,* 1954-78.

Other Awards: Sigma Delta Chi Award, 1958. Honorary Degree, Marshall University, WV, 1964.

Commentary: John Daniell Maurice, editor of the Charleston, West Virginia *Daily Mail* wrote almost 50 editorials expressing opinion and commentary on the textbook selection process in the local public schools. He continued his campaign despite threats of violence and community unrest. Maurice retired from his post in 1978.

1976

Philip Pearce Kerby   349

Birth: December 24, 1911; Pueblo, CO. **Death:** April 28, 1993. **Parents:** William Bunyan Kerby and Olive Burdette (Hinton). **Spouse:** Elizabeth Josephine Poe (m. 1953). **Children:** David.

Prize: *Editorial Writing,* 1976: *Los Angeles Times,* Los Angeles, CA: Los Angeles Times, 1975.

Career: Reporter, Editorial Writer, *Pueblo (CO) Star-Journal-Chieftain,* 1931-42; Reporter, *Denver (CO) Post,* 1942-45; News Editor, Radio Station KGHF, 1946-47; Editor, *Rocky Mountain Life,* 1948; Editor, *Frontier Magazine,* 1949-67; Associate Editor, *The Nation,* 1967-71; Senior Editorial Writer, *Los Angeles Times,* 1971-76; Contributor, *Los Angeles Times,* 1976-85.

Other Awards: Outstanding Radio Journalist Award, Denver Press Club, 1947. Ford Fund for Adult Education Fellowship, Harvard University, MA, 1957-58. Public Service Award, State Bar of California, 1983.

For More Information: *New York Times,* 4 May (1976): 48; *Los Angeles Times,* 30 April (1993): A24.

Commentary: Philip P. Kerby, who retired in 1976 after nearly 45 years in the news business, won a Pulitzer Prize for his editorials on the increasing secrecy of the government and the attempts of judicial rulings to censor the availability of trial proceedings.

1977

Norman Francis Cardoza   350

Birth: September 3, 1930; Yreka, CA. **Parents:** John Clyde Cardoza and Emily Lourdes (Simas). **Religion:** Roman Catholic. **Education:** Shasta College, CA: AA. University of California, Berkeley. **Spouse:** Married (1975).

Prize: *Editorial Writing,* 1977: *Reno Evening Gazette* and *Nevada State Journal,* Reno, NV: 1976.

Career: Reporter, *Redding Record-Searchlight,* 1958; Reporter, *Klamath (OR) Herald and News,* 1959-61; Reporter, Reno (NV) papers, 1961; State Capital Correspondent; Editorial Page Editor, *Reno (NV) Evening Gazette,*.

For More Information: *New York Times,* 22 April (1977): C28.

Commentary: Norman Cardoza, Warren Lerude, and Foster Church were awarded a Pulitzer Prize for their editorials that publicized how Joe Conforte, a local brothel owner, had become a clandestine political force with his political contributions.

Foster Church   351

Birth: April 10, 1942; McGill, NV. **Parents:** Ben Mitchell Church and Lucille (Baker). **Education:** University of San Francisco, CA: BA. University of California, Berkeley: Postgraduate.

Prize: *Editorial Writing,* 1977: *Reno Evening Gazette* and *Nevada State Journal,* Reno, NV: 1976.

Career: Served in U.S. Army, 1967-69; County Government Reporter, *Nevada State Journal,* 1970-71; Courthouse Reporter; Entertainment Editor, *Nevada State Journal* and *Reno (NV) Evening Gazette,* 1971-74; Editorial Page Editor, *Nevada State Journal* and *Reno (NV) Evening Gazette,* 1974-79; Writer, *Portland (OR) Oregonian,* 1979-.

Commentary: Foster Church, along with his colleagues Norman F. Cardoza and Warren L. Lerude, exposed the widespread political influence that a local brothel owner, Joe Conforte, had acquired. They followed the money and showed how it was spread among a large number of officeholders.

Warren Leslie Lerude   352

Birth: October 29, 1937; Reno, NV. **Parents:** Leslie R. Lerude and Ione (Lundy). **Education:** University of Nevada: BA. **Spouse:** Jane Lagomarsino (m. 1961). **Children:** Eric Warren, Christopher Mario, Leslie Ann.

Prize: *Editorial Writing,* 1977: *Reno Evening Gazette* and *Nevada State Journal,* Reno, NV: 1976.

Career: Served in U.S. Naval Reserve, 1957-59; Managing Editor, *Fallon (NV) Eagle-Standard,* 1959; Reporter, Editor, Nevada and California, Associated Press, 1960-63; Reporter, *Nevada State Journal* and

Reno (NV) Evening Gazette, 1963-65; News Editor, *Nevada State Journal* and *Reno (NV) Evening Gazette,* 1965-68; Managing Editor, *Nevada State Journal* and *Reno (NV) Evening Gazette,* 1968-72; Executive Editor, *Nevada State Journal* and *Reno (NV) Evening Gazette,* 1972-77; Publisher, *Nevada State Journal* and *Reno (NV) Evening Gazette,* 1977-81; Journalism Professor, University of Nevada, Reno, 1981-.

Selected Works: *American Commander in Spain: Robert Hale Merriman and the Lincoln Brigade; Nevada Studies in History and Political Science Series* (with Marion Merriman), 1986. *Above Tahoe and Reno: A New Collection of Historical and Original Aerial Photographs* (with Robert Cameron), 1995.

For More Information: *New York Times,* 22 April (1977): C28.

Commentary: Warren Lerude, Foster Church, and Norman F. Cardoza shared a Pulitzer Prize for their editorials that publicized the political power a local brothel keeper had acquired through his political contributions. Lerude rose from reporter to publisher during his career in the news business. He now teaches media management, first amendment issues, and media ethics at the University of Nevada, Reno.

1978

Meg Greenfield   353

Birth: December 27, 1930; Seattle, WA. **Parents:** Lewis James Greenfield and Lorraine (Nathan). **Religion:** Jewish. **Education:** Smith College, MA: BA, summa cum laude, Phi Beta Kappa.

Prize: *Editorial Writing,* 1978: *Washington Post,* Washington, DC: Washington Post, 1977.

Career: Researcher, *Reporter Magazine,* 1957-61; Correspondent, *Reporter Magazine,* 1961-65; Editor, Washington (DC), *Reporter Magazine,* 1965; Washington, DC Bureau Chief, *Reporter Magazine,* 1966-68; Editorial Staff member, *Washington (DC) Post,* 1968-69; Deputy Editorial Page Editor, *Washington (DC) Post,* 1969-79; Columnist, *Newsweek* magazine, 1974-; Editorial Page Editor, *Washington (DC) Post,* 1979-.

Other Awards: Fulbright Scholar, Cambridge University, England, 1952-53. Lifetime Achievement Award, International Women's Media Foundation, 1997. Honorary Degrees: Smith College, MA, 1978; Georgetown University, Washington, DC, 1979; Wesleyan University, CT, 1982; Williams College, MA, 1987.

For More Information: *Washington Post,* 18 April (1978): A1; *Washington Post,* 24 March (1979): A3; Taft, William H., *Encyclopedia of Twentieth-Century Journalists,* New York: Garland Publishing, 1986.

Commentary: Meg Greenfield won a Pulitzer Prize for selected samples of her work which included editorials on a court ruling in a libel case in favor of the press as well as an editorial on redressing generations of racial inequities. Greenfield took over the helm of the editorial page after working for the *Washington Post* for 10 years.

There was some controversy in 1978 in the Editorial Writing category because the Pulitzer board overruled the jury's selection and awarded the prize to Greenfield.

1979

Edwin Milton Yoder Jr.   354

Birth: July 18, 1934; Greensboro, NC. **Parents:** Edwin M. Yoder and Mytrice M. (Logue). **Religion:** Episcopalian. **Education:** University of North Carolina: AB. Oxford University, England: MA. **Spouse:** Mary Jane Warwick (m. 1958). **Children:** Anne Daphne, Edwin Warwick.

Prize: *Editorial Writing,* 1979: *Washington Star,* Washington, DC: Washington Star, 1978.

Career: Editor, college paper, *Daily Tar Heel;* Editorial Writer, *Charlotte (NC) News,* 1958-61; Editorial Writer, *Greensboro (NC) Daily News,* 1961-64; Assistant Professor of History, University of North Carolina, Greensboro, 1964-65; Associate Editor, *Greensboro (NC) Daily News,* 1965-75; Associate Editor and Editorial Page Editor, *The Washington (DC) Star,* 1975-81; Syndicated Columnist, *The Washington (DC) Post* Writers Group, 1981-97; Professor, Journalism and Humanities, Washington and Lee University, 1992-.

Selected Works: *Night of the Old South Ball,* 1984. *The Unmaking of a Whig and Other Essays on Self-Definition,* 1990. *Joe Alsop's Cold War: A Study of Journalistic Influence and Intrigue,* 1995. *The Historical Present: Uses and Abuses of the Past,* 1997.

Other Awards: Rhodes Scholar, Oxford University, England, 1958. Walker Stone Award, Scripps-Howard Foundation, 1978. Distinguished Alumnus Award, University of North Carolina, Chapel Hill, 1980. Honorary Degrees: Grinnell College, IA, 1980; Elon College, NC, 1986; University of North Carolina, 1993; Richmond College, England.

For More Information: *Washington Post,* January 6, 1985: 9; Riley, Sam G., *Biographical Dictionary of American Newspaper Columnists,* Westport, CT: Greenwood Press, 1995; *Greensboro News And Record,* December 13, 1996: A17.

Commentary: Ed Yoder never wrote condescendingly to his readers. A scholar turned journalist, he returned to academia in 1992. Yoder wrote thoughtful and thought-provoking columns on many different subjects. His Pulitzer Prize was awarded for his editorials that covered a range of topics, including international affairs and domestic policy.

1980

Robert LeRoy Bartley   355

Birth: October 12, 1937; Marshall, MN. **Parents:** Theodore French Bartley and Iva Mae (Radach). **Education:** Iowa State University: BS. University of Wisconsin: MS. **Spouse:** Edith Jean Lillie (m. 1960). **Children:** Edith Elizabeth, Susan Lillie, Katharine French.

Prize: *Editorial Writing,* 1980: *Wall Street Journal,* New York: Dow Jones, 1979.

Career: Editor-in-Chief, college paper, *Iowa State Daily;* Reporter, *Grinnell (IA) Herald-Reporter,* 1959-60; Served in U.S. Army Reserve, 1960; Reporter, Chicago, *Wall Street Journal,* 1962-63; Reporter, Philadelphia (PA) *Wall Street Journal,* 1963-64; Editorial Page Staff member, New York, *Wall Street Journal,* 1964-72; Associate Editor and Editorial Page Editor, *Wall Street Journal,* 1972-79; Editor, *Wall Street Journal,* 1979-; Vice-President, *Wall Street Journal,* 1983-.

Selected Works: *Press, Politics and Popular Government: Domestic Affairs Studies, 3* (Will, George F., ed.), 1972. *A Pathology of Perception; Poynter Pamphlet, Number 1,* 1973. *The New Class?* (with B. Bruce-Briggs), 1981. *The Seven Fat Years, and How to Do It Again,* 1992. *Democracy & Capitalism: Asian and American Perspectives,* 1993. *Whitewater: From the Editorial Pages of the Wall Street Journal: A Journal Briefing* (with Micah Morrison), 1994. *Whitewater, Volume II: From the Edito-*

rial Pages of the Wall Street Journal: A Journal Briefing, 1996.

Other Awards: Cardinal Key, Undergraduate Award, Phi Kappa Phi. Overseas Press Club Award, 1977. Gerald Loeb Award, Anderson Graduate School of Management, University of California, Los Angeles, 1979. Honorary Degrees: Macalester College, MN, 1982; Babson College, MA, 1987; Adelphi University, NY, 1992.

For More Information: *Wall Street Journal,* 15 April (1980): A8; *Contemporary Authors, Volumes 97-100,* Detroit: Gale Research Company, 1981; *Washington Post Magazine,* 11 January (1982): 12; Taft, William H., *Encyclopedia of Twentieth-Century Journalists,* New York: Garland Publishing, Inc., 1986; *Boston Globe Magazine,* 23 January (1994): 10.

Commentary: Robert Bartley has been an editor at the *Wall Street Journal* longer than anyone in its history. He was awarded a Pulitzer Prize for the body of his work covering a wide range of issues, including economic policy, Ronald Reagan, the Strategic Arms Limitation Treaty, federal aid to large corporations, and political leadership. He is the third consecutive *Wall Street Journal* editor to win a Pulitzer Prize. His predecessors won in 1947 and 1953.

1981
No award

1982

Jacob Rosenthal   356

Birth: June 30, 1935; Tel Aviv, Palestine. **Parents:** Manfred Rosenthal and Rachel (Kaplan). **Religion:** Jewish. **Education:** Harvard University, MA: AB. **Spouse:** Marilyn Wayne Silver (m. 1963, div.); Holly Russell (m. 1985). **Children:** John, Ann (MS); Stepchildren: Christopher, Andrew (HR).

Prize: *Editorial Writing,* 1982: *New York Times,* New York: New York Times, 1981.

Career: Executive Editor, college paper, *The Crimson;* Reporter and Editor, *Portland (OR) Oregonian,* 1950-59; Served in U.S. Army, 1958; Reporter, *Portland (OR) Reporter,* 1959-61; Special Assistant to Attorney General, Robert F. Kennedy and Nicholas de Katzenbach, 1961-66; Urban Affairs Correspondent, *Life* magazine, 1968-69; National Urban Affairs Correspondent, *New York Times,* 1969-73; Assistant Sunday Editor, *New York Times,* 1973-75; Editor, *New York Times Magazine,* 1975-77; Deputy Editorial Page Editor, *New York Times,* 1977-86; Editorial Page Editor, *New York Times,* 1986-93; Assistant Managing Editor, *New York Times,* 1993-; Editor, *New York Times Magazine,* 1993-98; Editor-in-Chief, *New York Times Magazine,* 1998-.

Other Awards: Silver Gavel, American Bar Association. Outstanding Press Officer in the Government, Washington Press Corps, 1966. Fellow, Institute of Politics, Harvard University, MA, 1967-68. Gerald Loeb Award, Anderson Graduate School of Management, University of California, Los Angeles, 1973.

For More Information: *New York Times,* 22 December (1985): 58; *New York Times,* 12 October (1986): 1; *New York Times,* 12 September (1992): section 1, 9; *New York Times,* 14 January (1998): A15.

Commentary: Jacob Rosenthal won a Pulitzer Prize for the breadth of his editorials from the previous year. He covered diverse topics, ranging from the impact of President Ronald Reagan's policies to the intolerance and prejudice against fat people.

1983

Miami Herald 357

Founded: 1910; Miami, FL.

Prize: *Meritorious Public Service,* 1951. *Editorial Writing,* 1983. *National Reporting,* 1987. *Spot News Reporting,* 1991. *Meritorious Public Service,* 1993.

Selected Works: *Knights of the Fourth Estate: The Story of the Miami Herald* (with Nixon Smiley), 1974.

Other Awards: The *Miami Herald*'s staff, editors, and reporters have won 15 Pulitzer Prizes, in addition to other journalism and public service awards.

For More Information: Lawrance, David Jr., "Being There (Miami Herald, Hurricane Andrew)," *Presstime,* Volume 15, No. 1, Page 32-33, January 1993; Morris, Chase, "Herald Finds, 'In Miami, Every Story Requires Diverse Voices'," *ASNE Bulletin,* No. 750, Page 15-16, May/June, 1993; Stein, M.L., "Miami Herald Now Quadrilingual: Prints in Spanish, Creole, and Portuguese in Addition to English," *Editor & Publisher,* Volume 127, No. 15, Page 18, April 9, 1994; Contact the Florida Newspaper Project, University of Florida, Gainesville, telephone: (352) 392-0351.

Commentary: The *Miami Herald* has won two Meritorious Public Service awards. The first came in 1951 for its crime reporting during the year. The *Herald*'s Editorial Board won the Editorial Writing prize in 1983 for its campaign against the detention of illegal immigrants by federal officials. In 1987, the *Herald* was a co-winner of the National Reporting prize for its exclusive reporting and persistent coverage of the U.S. Iran-Contra connection. It was awarded the Spot News Reporting prize in 1991 for stories profiling a local cult leader, his followers, and their links to several area murders. The *Herald* won

its second Meritorious Public Service prize in 1993 for coverage that not only helped readers cope with Hurricane Andrew's devastation, but also showed how lax zoning, inspection, and building codes had contributed to the destruction.

The *Herald* was established in 1910. It has become respected as the voice of Spanish-speaking Miami and today has bureaus in Latin America. The *Herald* was purchased by John S. Knight in 1937, and it later became part of the Knight-Ridder group. Knight started an English-language international edition with circulation in more than 20 Latin American countries in 1946.

1984

Albert James Scardino 358

Birth: September 22, 1948; Baltimore, MD. **Parents:** Peter Lester Scardino and Mary Katherine (Mangelsdorf). **Education:** Columbia University, NY: BA. University of California, Berkeley: MA. **Spouse:** Marjorie Beth Morris (m. 1974). **Children:** Adelaide Katherine, William Brown, Albert Henry Hugh.

Prize: *Editorial Writing,* 1984: *Georgia Gazette,* Savannah, GA: Georgia Gazette, 1983.

Career: Intern, *Baltimore (MD) Sun;* Intern, *Atlanta (GA) Company;* Reporter, *Atlanta (GA) Weekly Star,* 1966; Reporter, *Savannah (GA) Morning News,* 1967; Editor, Reporter, college paper, *Daily Spectator,* 1967-68; Reporter, *Baltimore (MD) Evening Sun,* 1968; Reporter, *Atlanta (GA) Constitution,* 1969; Reporter, West Virginia, Associated Press, 1971; Researcher, CBS-TV, *60 Minutes,* 1975; Documentary filmmaker, 1976-78; Writer, Editor, Co-Producer, "Guale," documentary film, 1977; Co-Founder, Editor, *Savannah Georgia Gazette,* 1978-85; Founder, *Island's Gazette,* 1982; Editor, Correspondent, *New York Times,* 1985-; Adjunct Journalism Professor, Columbia University (NY), 1986-88; Press Secretary, New York City Mayor David Dinkins, 1989-91.

Selected Works: *A Lever Long Enough: The Story of the Georgia Gazette, 1978-85,* 1990.

Other Awards: Dale L. Morgan Prize in History of the American West, University of California, Berkeley, 1976. Blue Ribbon, American Film Festival, 1977: *Guale.* Paramount Award, National Education Film Festival, 1977: *Guale.* CINE Golden Eagle, Council on International Nontheatrical Events, 1977: *Guale.* Bronze Hugo, Chicago International Film Festival, 1977: *Guale.* Francis Scott Key Award, Baltimore International Film Festival, 1977: *Guale.* Golden Quill Award, American Society of Newspaper Editors, 1982. Grant, Fund for Investigative Journalism, 1983. Silver Gavel, Georgia Bar Association, 1983. Certificate of Merit, Society of Professional Journalists, Atlanta Chapter, GA, 1983.

For More Information: *Columbia Journalism Review,* July/August (1983): 14-15; *People,* August 27, 1984: 40; Rothmeyer, Karen, *Winning Pulitzers: The Stories Behind Some of the Best News Coverage of Our Times,* New York: Columbia University Press, 1991: 167-178.

Commentary: Albert Scardino won a Pulitzer Prize for his forthright writing. The *Georgia Gazette,* of which he was the editor and his wife was the publisher, went head-to-head with its larger competitor. The paper ceased publication in 1985.

1985

Richard Lloyd Aregood   359

Birth: December 31, 1942; Camden, NJ. **Parents:** Lloyd Samuel and Ruby Odell (Trousdale). **Religion:** Episcopalian. **Education:** Rutgers University, NJ: BA. **Spouse:** Barbara Sue Wittenberger (m. 1962, div. 1978); Joan Sampieri (m. 1979, div. 1992); Kathleen Shea (m. 1993). **Children:** Laurie, Christopher (BW); Deborah, David, Jennifer, William Sampiere (JS); James (KS).

Prize: *Editorial Writing,* 1985: *Philadelphia Daily News,* Philadelphia, PA: Philadelphia Daily News, 1984.

Career: Reporter, *Mount Holly (NJ) Herald,* 1964-65; Reporter, *Burlington County (NJ) Times,* 1965-66; Reporter, *Philadelphia (PA) Daily News,* 1966-71; Police Reporter, City Editor, Features Editor, Deputy Sports Editor, News Editor, Day City Editor, *Philadelphia (PA) Daily News,* 1971-; Editorial Writer, *Philadelphia Daily News,* 1973-78; Editorial Page Editor *Philadelphia Daily News,* 1978-95; Head Editorial Board, *Newark (NJ) Star-Ledger,* 1995-; Writing Instructor, Rutgers University (NJ).

Other Awards: Distinguished Writing Award, American Society of Newspaper Editors, 1985, 1991, 1993. Hall of Distinguished Alumni, Rutgers University, NJ, 1993.

For More Information: *Editor & Publisher,* 128:8 (February 8, 1995): 21; *American Journalism Review,* 17 (April 1995): 12-13.

Commentary: Richard Aregood won a Pulitzer Prize for his editorials written on a variety of subjects. He left the *Philadelphia Daily News* in 1995 as a result of pressure from management to cut editorial resources.

1986

Jack William Fuller   360

Birth: October 12, 1946; Chicago, IL. **Parents:** Ernest Brady Fuller and Dorothy Voss (Tegge). **Religion:** Protestant. **Education:** Northwestern University, IL: BS. Yale University, CT: JD. **Spouse:** Alyce Sue Tuttle (m. 1973). **Children:** Timothy, Katherine.

Prize: *Editorial Writing,* 1986: *Chicago Tribune,* Chicago: Chicago Tribune, 1985.

Career: Served in U.S. Army, 1969-70; Reporter, *City News Bureau of Chicago;* Reporter, *Chicago Daily News;* Reporter, *Washington (DC) Post;* City Desk Reporter, *Chicago Tribune,* 1973-74; Special Assistant, U.S. Attorney General, 1975-76; Correspondent, Washington (DC), *Chicago Tribune,* 1977-78; Editorial Page Writer, *Chicago Tribune,* 1978-79; Deputy Editorial Page Editor, *Chicago Tribune,* 1979-82; Editorial Page Editor, *Chicago Tribune,* 1982-87; Executive Editor, *Chicago Tribune,* 1987-89; Vice President and Editor, *Chicago Tribune,* 1989-93; President and Chief Executive Officer, *Chicago Tribune,* 1993-97; Publisher, *Chicago Tribune,* 1994-97; Executive Vice-President, Tribune Publishing Company, 1997-.

Selected Works: *Convergence,* 1982. *Fragments,* 1984. *Mass,* 1985. *Our Fathers' Shadow,* 1987. *Legends' End,* 1991. *News Values: Ideas for an Information Age,* 1996.

Other Awards: Gavel Award, American Bar Association, 1979. Cliff Dwellers Award, 1983: *Convergence,* Garden City, NY: Doubleday, 1982. Friends of American Writers Award, 1985: *Fragments,* New York: Morrow, 1984. Fellow, American Academy of Arts and Sciences.

For More Information: *Contemporary Authors, Volume 130,* Detroit: Gale Research Company, 1990; *Chicago Tribune,* 1 June (1994): Business, 1.

Commentary: Jack Fuller won a Pulitzer Prize for his writings on constitutional issues. He has worked in all aspects of journalism, starting as a reporter, taking a brief time out to practice law, returning to the *Chicago Tribune,* and eventually becoming an executive of the Tribune Publishing Company.

1987

Jonathan Freedman   361

Birth: April 11, 1950; Rochester, MN. **Parents:** Marshall Arthur Freedman and Betty (Borwick). **Religion:** Jewish. **Education:** Columbia University, NY: AB, cum laude, Phi Beta Kappa. **Spouse:** Maggie Locke (m. 1979). **Children:** Madigan, Nicholas.

Prize: *Editorial Writing,* 1987: *San Diego Tribune,* San Diego, CA: San Diego Tribune, 1986.

Career: Correspondent, San Paulo and Rio de Janeiro (Brazil), Associated Press, 1974-75; Freelance writer, 1976-81; Novelist, writing in Spain and Portugal, 1979-80; Editorial Writer, *The San Diego (CA) Tribune,* 1981-90; Syndicated columnist, 1987-89; Freelance Editorial Writer, *New York Times,*

1990-91; Freelance Columnist, *Los Angeles Times,* 1990-; Distinguished Visiting Lecturer and Adjunct Faculty member, San Diego State University, CA, 1990-; Writer.

Selected Works: *The Man Who'd Bounce the World,* 1979. *From Cradle to Grave: The Human Face of Poverty in America,* 1993.

Other Awards: Cornell Woolrich Writing Fellowship. Eugene C. Pulliam Editorial Writing Fellowship, Sigma Delta Chi Foundation. Award, Sigma Delta Chi, San Diego Chapter, 1983. Copley Ring of Truth Award, 1983. San Diego Press Club Award, 1984. Special Citation, Columbia University, Graduate School of Journalism, NY, 1985. Distinguished Service Award, Society of Professional Journalists, 1985. Distinguished Writing Award, American Society of Newspaper Editors, 1986.

For More Information: Wills, Kendall J., *The Pulitzer Prizes, Volume 1, 1987,* New York: Simon & Schuster, 1987; *San Diego Union-Tribune,* 16 April (1987): A1.

Commentary: Jonathan Freedman's award-winning entry contained nine editorials that were written between April 3rd and November 6th. The editorials were the culmination of a five-year campaign for immigration reform. He took a national issue and explored the local impact of national policies.

Freedman was a finalist for an Editorial Writing Pulitzer Prize in 1983 and 1984.

1988

Jane Elizabeth Healy   362

Birth: May 9, 1949; Washington, DC. **Parents:** Paul Francis Healy and Connie (Maas). **Education:** University of Maryland: BS. **Spouse:** James Covington Clark (m. 1977). **Children:** Randall, Kevin.

Prize: *Editorial Writing,* 1988: *Orlando Sentinel,* "Florida's Shame," Orlando, FL: Orlando Sentinel, 1987.

Career: Copygirl, Reporter, Washington (DC) *New York Daily News,* 1971-73; Metro Reporter, *Orlando (FL) Sentinel,* 1973-80; Regional Coordinator, *Orlando (FL) Sentinel,* 1980-81; Editorial Writer, *Orlando (FL) Sentinel,* 1981-85; Chief Editorial Writer, *Orlando (FL) Sentinel,* 1983-85; Associate Editor in Charge of Editorial Page, Op-Ed Page, and Sunday Insight Section, *Orlando (FL) Sentinel,* 1985-92; Managing Editor, *Orlando (FL) Sentinel,* 1993-.

Other Awards: First Place Editorial Writing, Greater Orlando Press Club, 1983. First Place Editorial Writing, Florida Press Club, 1984. First Place Editorial Writing, Sigma Delta Chi, Southeast, 1985-86. First Place Editorial Writing, Florida Society of Newspaper Editors, 1986, 1990. Paul Hansen Award, 1988. Distinguished Service Award, 1988.

For More Information: *New York Times,* 1 April (1988): B4; *Orlando Sentinel Tribune,* 17 December (1992): A3.

Commentary: Jane Healy won the first Pulitzer for her paper, the *Orlando Sentinel.* She wrote a series of editorials titled "Florida's Shame." Her writing focused on the overdevelopment of Orange County and its impact on the environment and life. She was a finalist for a Pulitzer Prize in 1985.

1989

Lois Jean Wille   363

Birth: September 19, 1931; Chicago, IL. **Parents:** Walter Kroeber and Adele S. (Taege). **Education:** Northwestern University, IL: BS. Northwestern University, IL: MS. **Spouse:** Wayne M. Wille (m. 1954).

Prize: *Editorial Writing,* 1989: *Chicago Tribune,* Chicago: Chicago Tribune, 1988.

Career: Reporter, *Chicago Daily News,* 1956-74; National Correspondent, *Chicago Daily News,* 1975-76; Associate Editor and Editorial Page Editor, *Chicago Daily News,* 1977-78; Associate Editor and Editorial Page Editor, *Chicago Sun-Times,* 1978-83; Associate Editorial Page Editor, *Chicago Tribune,* 1984-87; Editorial Page Editor, *Chicago Tribune,* 1987-91.

Selected Works: *The Anxious Majority, Chicago's Working Class,* 1970. *Forever Open, Clear, and Free: The Historic Struggle for Chicago's Lakefront,* 1972. *Interviews with Lois Wille: Oral History Transcript,* 1992. *At Home in the Loop: How Clout and Community Built Chicago's Dearborn Park,* 1997.

Other Awards: Excellence in Editorial Writing Award, William Allen White Foundation, University of Kansas, 1978. Peter Lisagor Award, Chicago Headliners Club. Chicago Journalism Hall of Fame, 1983. Honorary Degrees: Columbia College, IL, 1980; Northwestern University, IL, 1990; Rosary College, IL, 1990.

For More Information: *Chicago Tribune,* April 28, 1991: 3.

Commentary: Lois Wille, who retired from the *Chicago Tribune* in 1991, won two Pulitzer Prizes. Her first was in 1963 as a part of the *Chicago Daily News* team that won for Meritorious Public Service. The second was for a group of 10 editorials on a variety of local Chicago issues. She was a finalist for an Editorial Writing Pulitzer Prize in 1984.

1990

Thomas James Hylton   364

Birth: December 20, 1948; Reading, PA. **Parents:** William Harold Hylton and Mary Harriet (Kitzmiller). **Education:** Kutztown University, PA: BA. **Spouse:** Frances Wismer (m. 1970).

Prize: *Editorial Writing,* 1990: *Pottstown Mercury,* Pottstown, PA: Pottstown Mercury, 1989.

Career: Reporter, *Pottstown (PA) Mercury,* 1971-86; Editorial Writer, *Pottstown (PA) Mercury,* 1986-94.

Selected Works: *Save Our Lands, Save Our Towns: A Plan for Pennsylvania* (with Blair Seitz), 1995.

Other Awards: American Planning.

For More Information: *New York Times,* 13 April (1990): A17; *The Pulitzer Prizes 1990,* New York: Simon & Schuster, 1990: 289-318.

Commentary: Thomas J. Hylton believes in writing about issues that have an impact for his local readers. His Pulitzer Prize-winning editorials expounded on the need to preserve local farm land and to prevent its loss to development.

1991

Ronald Bruce Casey   365

Birth: August 21, 1951; Birmingham, AL. **Parents:** J.B. Casey and Ruby Lois (Sizemore). **Education:** University of Alabama, Tuscaloosa: BA. **Spouse:** Margaret Griffin Brooke (m. 1979). **Children:** Jefferson, Anna.

Prize: *Editorial Writing,* 1991: *Birmingham News,* Birmingham, AL: Birmingham News, 1990.

Career: Editor, college paper; Staff Writer, Police Reporter, Suburban Reporter, City Hall Reporter, Courthouse Reporter, County Legislative Delegation, Assistant City Editor, Features Editor, *Birmingham (AL) News,* 1973-83; Editorial Writer, *Birmingham (AL) News,* 1983-1990; Editorial Page Editor, *Birmingham (AL) News,* 1990-.

Other Awards: National Headliners Club Award, 1991. Journalist of the Year Award, Troy State University, AL, 1993. Award, National Education Writers Association, 1995.

For More Information: *New York Times,* 10 April (1991): A20.

Commentary: Ron Casey was born in a company house in a steel-producing area outside of Birmingham, Alabama. He has worked for the *Birmingham News* since he graduated from college in 1973.

Casey, along with Harold Jackson and Joey Kennedy, wrote a series of editorials on the inequities in the state tax laws of Alabama. The three were awarded a Pulitzer Prize in 1991 for their efforts.

Harold Jackson   366

Birth: August 14, 1953; Birmingham, AL. **Parents:** Lewis Jackson and Janye (Wilson). **Religion:** Presbyterian. **Education:** Baker University, KS: BS. **Spouse:** Denice Estell Pledger (m. 1977). **Children:** Annette Michelle, Dennis Jerome.

Prize: *Editorial Writing,* 1991: *Birmingham News,* Birmingham, AL: Birmingham News, 1990.

Career: Reporter, *The Birmingham (AL) Post-Herald,* 1975-80; Correspondent, United Press International, 1980-83; Alabama News Editor, United Press International, 1983-85; Assistant National Editor, *Philadelphia Inquirer,* 1985-86; Assistant City Editor, *Birmingham (AL) News,* 1986; Editorial Board, Editorial Writer and Columnist, *Birmingham (AL) News,* 1987-.

Other Awards: Green Eyeshade Award, 1989. Journalist of the Year, National Association of Black Journalists, 1991.

Commentary: Harold Jackson grew up in a Birmingham, Alabama housing project. He and his four brothers all went to college. After receiving his degree he returned to his hometown to work on a local paper.

He and his colleagues, Ron Casey and Joey Kennedy, won a Pulitzer Prize for a nine-part series about the Alabama state tax structure and its inequities.

Joey David Kennedy Jr.   367

Birth: March 28, 1956; Dayton, TX. **Parents:** Joe David Kennedy and Patricia Ann (Harper). **Religion:** Christian. **Education:** Nicholls State University, LA. Jacksonville State University, AL. University of Alabama, Birmingham: BA. **Spouse:** Veronica Elaine Pike (m. 1980).

Prize: *Editorial Writing,* 1991: *Birmingham News,* Birmingham, AL: Birmingham News, 1990.

Career: General Assignments Reporter, *Houma (LA) Daily Courier,* 1974-76; News Director and Sports Director, two radio stations, Louisiana, 1976-77; General Assignment Reporter, *Cullman (AL) Times,* 1977; News Editor, *Pell City (AL) St. Clair News Aegis,* 1978; Press Secretary, Louisiana Governor Guy Hunt, 1978; Sports Reporter, *Anniston (AL) Star,* 1978-80; Assistant Sports Editor, *Anniston (AL) Star,* 1980-81; Sports Copy Editor, *Birmingham (AL) News,* 1981-84; Assistant Life/Style Editor, *Birmingham (AL) News,* 1984-85; Photo Editor, *Birmingham (AL) News,* 1985-86; Sunday Editor, *Birmingham (AL) News,* 1986-89; Book Review Editor, *Birmingham (AL) News,* 1988-; Editorial Board, Editorial Writer, Columnist, Editor Op-Ed Page, *Birmingham (AL) News,* 1989-.

Selected Works: *What They Won't Tell You about Your Taxes,* 1990.

Other Awards: Alumnus of the Year, University of Alabama, 1991. Hector Award, Troy State University, AL, 1991.

Commentary: Joey Kennedy grew up in southeast Texas and southern Louisiana. He has lived in Alabama since 1977 when he joined the *Cullman Times.* He has worked in a variety of positions in Alabama newspapers.

Kennedy, along with Ron Casey and Harold Jackson, shared a Pulitzer Prize for their series on the state tax laws in Alabama.

1992

Glenda Maria Henson   368

Birth: June 17, 1960; Marion, NC. **Parents:** Douglas Bradley Henson and Glenda June (Crouch). **Education:** Wake Forest University, NC: BA, cum laude.

Prize: *Editorial Writing,* 1992: *Lexington Herald-Leader,* Lexington, KY: Lexington Herald-Leader, 1991.

Career: Reporter, *Little Rock (AR) Arkansas Democrat,* 1982-84; Reporter, *Tampa (FL) Tribune,* 1984; Statehouse Reporter, *Little Rock (AR) Arkansas Gazette,* 1984-87; Washington (DC) Bureau Chief, *Little Rock (AR) Arkansas Gazette,* 1987-89; Editorial Writer, *Lexington (KY) Herald-Leader,* 1989-1994; Editorial Writer and Columnist, *Charlotte (NC) Observer,* 1994-96; Associate Editor, *Charlotte (NC) Observer,* 1996-.

Other Awards: Woman of the Year, Wake Forest University, NC, 1992. Kentucky Press Association Award, 1992. Walker Stone Award, Scripps-Howard Foundation, 1992. Nieman Fellow, Harvard University, MA, 1993-94. Leadership Award, Duke University, NC, 1995. North Carolina Press Association Award, 1995-96. National Headliners Club Award, 1996.

For More Information: *Louisville Courier-Journal,* 8 April (1992): A1; *Charlotte Observer,* 5 November (1994): 18A; *Charlotte Observer,* 7 July (1996): 2C.

Commentary: Maria Henson's 16-month investigation and approximately 30 editorials on spouse abuse won her a 1992 Pulitzer Prize. Her editorials examined how the law does not always protect spouse abuse victims.

1993
No award

1994

Robert Bruce Dold   369

Birth: March 9, 1955; Newark, NJ. **Parents:** Robert Bruce Dold and Margaret (Noll). **Religion:** Roman Catholic. **Education:** Northwestern University, IL: BS, MS. **Spouse:** Eileen Claire Norris (m. 1982). **Children:** Megan, Kristen.

Prize: *Editorial Writing,* 1994: *Chicago Tribune,* "Killing Our Children," Chicago: Chicago Tribune, 1993.

Career: Suburban Reporter, *Chicago Tribune,* 1978-83; Critic, *Downbeat Magazine,* 1980-84; Reporter, *Chicago Tribune,* 1983-87; Political Writer, *Chicago Tribune,* 1987-90; Editorial Board, *Chicago Tribune,* 1990-95; Columnist, *Chicago Enterprise,* 1991-95; Deputy Editorial Page Editor, *Chicago Tribune,* 1995-; Reporter; Television/radio commentator; Jazz Critic.

Other Awards: Peter Lisagor Award, Sigma Delta Chi, Chicago Chapter, IL, 1988.

For More Information: *Chicago Tribune,* 13 April (1994): 7.

Commentary: R. Bruce Dold specializes in writing about government and politics. He won a Pulitzer Prize for his 10-part series, "Killing Our Children." His series discussed the failure of the Illinois Department of Children and Family Services to keep Joseph Wallace, a three-year-old child, from being murdered by his mother. The series helped push the state legislature into action, so that "the best interests of the child" would be taken into account in child custody cases. Dold worked for a year on this series. It was also a finalist in the Meritorious Public Service category.

1995

Jeffrey Good   370

Birth: January 19, 1959; St. Louis, MO. **Education:** St. Michael's College, VT. **Spouse:** Laura G. **Children:** One daughter.

Prize: *Editorial Writing,* 1995: *St. Petersburg Times,* "Final Indignities," August 28; "Broken Trusts," September 4; "Forgotten Victims," September 11; "The Road to Reform," September 18, St. Petersburg, FL: St. Petersburg Times, 1994.

Career: Intern, *Burlington (VT) Free Press;* Associate Editor, *Burlington (VT) Vermont Vanguard Press;* Editor, *Public Citizen Magazine;* Writer, *St. Petersburg (FL) Times,* 1983-; Editorial Board, *St. Petersburg (FL) Times,* 1993-; Capital Bureau Chief, *Burlington (VT) Free Press;* Freelance writer, editor.

Selected Works: *Poison Mind* (with Susan Goreck), 1995.

For More Information: *St. Petersburg Times,* April 19, 1995: A1.

Commentary: Jeffrey Good's series "Final Indignities" explored the problems and suggested solutions for the treatment of personal estates in Florida. The series was published on four consecutive Sundays and began on August 28. He wrote about heirs who never receive any of the money from loved ones' estates because of the way probate lawyers and executors are able to handle the proceedings. His research took seven months and involved analysis of court records, Florida Bar Association proceedings, and dozens of interviews of those whose lives had been affected.

1996

Robert Baylor Semple Jr.   371

Birth: August 12, 1936; St. Louis, MO. **Parents:** Robert B. Semple and Isabelle Ashby (Neer). **Religion:** Episcopalian. **Education:** Yale University, CT: BA. University of California, Berkeley: MA. **Spouse:** Susan Riker Kirk (m. 1961, div. 1980); Lisa Pulling (m. 1981). **Children:** Robert Baylor III, Elizabeth, William, Mary (SK).

Prize: *Editorial Writing,* 1996: *New York Times,* New York: New York Times, 1995.

Career: Reporter, *National Observer,* 1961-63; General Assignment Reporter, *New York Times,* 1963-68; Political Reporter, White House Correspondent, *New York Times,* 1968-72; Deputy National Editor, *New York Times,* 1973-75; London Bureau Chief, *New York Times,* 1975-77; Foreign Editor, *New York Times,* 1977-82; Op-Ed Page Editor, *New York Times,* 1982-88; Associate Editorial Page Editor, *New York Times,* 1988-.

Other Awards: Carnegie Fellow, 1959-60. Woodrow Wilson Fellow, 1960-61.

For More Information: *New York Times,* 15 April (1982): C28; *New York Times,* 15 March (1988): A17.

Commentary: Robert Semple has spent all but two years of his career at the *New York Times.* His editorials on environmental issues won him a Pulitzer Prize in 1996.

1997

Michael Gay Gartner   372

Birth: October 25, 1938; Des Moines, IA. **Parents:** Carl D. Gartner and Mary M. (Gay). **Education:** Carleton College, MN: BA. New York University: JD. **Spouse:** Barbara Jeanne McCoy (m. 1968). **Children:** Melissa, Christopher, Mike.

Prize: *Editorial Writing,* 1997: *Daily Tribune,* Ames, IA: Daily Tribune, 1996.

Career: Sports Department Staff member, *Des Moines (IA) Register;* Staff member, *Wall Street Journal,* 1960-74; Page One Editor, *Wall Street Journal,* 1970-1974; Editor and President, *Des Moines (IA) Register;* Editor, *Louisville (KY) Courier-Journal,* 1986-87; General News Executive, Gannett Company, 1987-88; President, NBC News, 1988-1993; Editor, *Ames (IA) Daily Tribune.*

Selected Works: *The Jilted Aardvark, and Other Improbable Tales from the Wall Street Journal,* 1970. *Ted Williams, Sam the Genius, and Other Sports Stories from the Wall Street Journal,* 1971. *Crime and Business: What You Should Know about the Infiltration of Crime into Business — and of Business into Crime,* 1971. *Riding the Pennsy to Ruin: A Wall Street Journal Chronicle of the Penn Central Debacle,* 1971. *The Road to the Top,* 1972. *Animal Tales from the Wall Street Journal,* 1973. *Advertising and the First Amendment,* 1989.

Other Awards: Fellow, Institute of Politics, John F. Kennedy School of Government, Harvard University, MA. Award, American Society of Newspaper Editors. Inland Press Association Award. Honorary Degrees: Simpson College, IA, 1984; James Madison University, VA, 1989; Grand View College, IA, 1990; Iowa Wesleyan College, 1997.

For More Information: *New York Times,* 28 March (1994): D1.

Commentary: Michael G. Gartner caused controversy in the journalism world when there were some lapses in impartiality and judgment while he was head of NBC News. He left that position in 1993. He joined with two partners and became editor of the Ames *Daily Tribune,* which has a circulation of 10,000.

Gartner is a third generation newspaperman. He is a lawyer as well as a journalist and writes on First Amendment issues. His winning editorials were on local issues of concern to his community and included topics such as street sign disputes and lap dancing.

1998

Bernard L. Stein   373

Birth: July 18, 1941; Cleveland, OH. **Parents:** David A. Stein and Celia (Leikind). **Religion:** Jewish. **Education:** Columbia University, NY: BA. University of California, Berkeley: Postgrad. **Spouse:** Susan Cole (m. 1963, div. 1965); Marguerite Adams (m. 1973). **Children:** Anna (MA).

Prize: *Editorial Writing,* 1998: *Riverdale Press,* Bronx, NY: *Riverdale Press,* 1997.

Career: Editor, Senior Editor, Principal Editor, *Mark Twain Papers,* University of California,

Berkeley, 1966-78; Editor, *Riverdale Press,* 1978-; Co-Publisher, *Riverdale Press,* 1980-.

Other Awards: Writer of the Year, New York Press Association, 1985. First Amendment Award, Society of Professional Journalists, 1989. Herrick Editorial Award, National Newspaper Association, 1989, 1994. Education Reporting Award, Education Writers Association, 1996.

For More Information: *Quill,* July / August (1989): 14; *New York Times,* March 14, 1989: B1; *New York Times,* April 16, 1998: B2; *American Journalism Review* 20:5 (June 1998): 12.

Commentary: Bernard L. Stein was awarded a Pulitzer Prize for his "gracefully written editorials on politics and other issues affecting New York City residents." His winning entry included editorials on economic development and its impact on neighborhood environment, racism, New York City management and its attitude toward "dispossessed New Yorkers," and freedom of speech and Salman Rushdie. Stein was a Pulitzer Prize finalist in 1987 and 1988.

Stein became editor of the *Riverdale Press* in 1978, succeeding his father who founded the paper in 1950. In 1980, after his father's retirement, Stein and his brother became co-publishers.

Explanatory Journalism

1985

Jon Daniel Franklin   374

Birth: January 13, 1942; Enid, OK. **Parents:** Benjamin Max Franklin and Wilma (Winborn). **Education:** University of Maryland: BS, High Honors. **Spouse:** Nancy Sue Creevan (m. 1959, div. 1976); Lynn Irene Scheidhauer (m. 1988). **Children:** Teresa June, Catherine Cay (NC).

Prize: *Feature Writing,* 1979: *Baltimore Evening Sun,* "Mrs. Kelly's Monster," December, Baltimore, MD: Baltimore Evening Sun, 1978. *Explanatory Journalism,* 1985: *Baltimore Evening Sun,* Baltimore, MD: Baltimore Evening News, 1984.

Career: Journalist, U.S. Navy, 1959-67; Editor and Reporter, *Hyattsville (MD) Prince Georges Post,* 1967-70; Rewriteman, *Baltimore (MD) Evening Sun,* 1970-72; Science Writer, *Baltimore (MD) Evening Sun,* 1972-76; Part-Time Instructor, Towson State University; Associate Professor, University of Maryland, College Park, 1986-89; Head, Science Journalism Department, Oregon State University, 1989-91; Creative Writing Professor, University of Oregon, Eugene, 1991-; Hearst Visiting Professional, University of Maryland, College Park, 1996.

Selected Works: *The Chesapeake: Still at Bay?* (with Bill Burton), 1977. *Shocktrauma* (with Alan Doelp), 1980. *Not Quite a Miracle: Brain Surgeons and Their Patients on the Frontier of Medicine* (with Alan Doelp), 1983. *Guinea Pig Doctors: The Drama of Medical Research through Self-Experimentation* (with John Sutherland), 1984. *The Mind Fixers,* 1984. *Writing for Story: Craft Secrets of Dramatic Nonfiction by a Two-Time Pulitzer Prize Winner,* 1986. *Molecules of the Mind,* 1987.

Other Awards: James T. Grady Medal, American Chemical Society, 1975. Honorary Degrees: University of Maryland, Baltimore, 1981; College of Notre Dame, MD, 1982.

For More Information: *Baltimore Sun,* 17 April (1979): 1; *Contemporary Authors, Volume 104,* Detroit: Gale Research Company, 1982.

Commentary: Jon Franklin won the first Pulitzer Prize given in Feature Writing as well as the first Pulitzer Prize in Explanatory Journalism. He now teaches writing and in 1997 started a literary journalism site on the Internet called "Bylines."

1986

New York Times   375

Founded: September 18, 1851; New York, NY. **Founder(s):** Henry J. Redmond, George Jones and Edward Wesley.

Prize: *Meritorious Public Service,* 1918. *Special Awards and Citations: Journalism,* 1941. *Meritorious Public Service,* 1944. *International Reporting,* 1958. *Meritorious Public Service,* 1972. *Explanatory Journalism,* 1986. *National Reporting,* 1987. *Spot News Reporting,* 1994. *International Reporting,* 1998.

Selected Works: *Words in Action* (with Robert Greenman), 1983. *The Paper's Papers: A Reporter's Journey through the Archives of The New York Times* (with Richard F. Shepard), 1996.

Other Awards: The *New York Times* and its reporters and editors have won 70 Pulitzer Prizes, more than any other publication.

For More Information: Berger, Meyer, *The Story of the New York Times, 1851-1951,* New York: Simon & Schuster, 1951; Davis, Elmer Holmes, *History of the New York Times, 1891-1921,* New York: Greenwood Press, 1969; Talese, Gay, *The Kingdom and the Power,* New York: World Publishing, 1969; Adler, Ruth, *A Day in the Life of the New York Times,* Philadelphia, PA: Lippincott, 1971; Salisbury, Harrison Evans, *Without Fear or Favor: The New York Times and Its Times,* New York: Times, 1980; Goulden, Joseph C., *Fit to Print: A.M. Rosenthal and His Times,* Secaucus, NJ: L. Stuart, 1988; Reston, James, *Deadline: A Memoir,* New York: Random House, 1991; Diamond, Edwin, *Behind the Times: Inside the New New York Times,* New York: Villard, 1993; Rudenstine, David, *The Day the Presses Stopped: A History of the Pentagon Papers Case,* Berkeley: University of California, 1996.

Commentary: The first Meritorious Public Service award was given to the *New York Times* in 1918 for publishing in full so many official reports, documents, and speeches by European statesmen relating to the progress and conduct of World War I. A special award and citation was awarded the *Times* in 1941 for the public educational value of its foreign news report, exemplified by its scope, excellence of writing and presentation, and supplementary background information, illustration, and interpretation. The Meritorious Public Service Award of 1944 was won by the *Times* for its survey of the teaching of American history. The *Times* was awarded the International

Reporting award in 1958 for its distinguished coverage of foreign news, which was characterized by admirable initiative, continuity, and high quality during the year.

The Meritorious Public Service award went to the *Times* in 1972 for the publication of the Pentagon Papers. The Nixon adminstration challenged the paper's right to publish and a 6-3 ruling from the Supreme Court decided in favor of the *Times*. Staff were awarded the prize for Explanatory Journalism in 1986 for a six-part comprehensive series on the Strategic Defense Initative, which explored the scientific, political and foreign policy issues involved in the "Star Wars" defense system. The 1987 National Reporting award went to the staff for coverage of the aftermath of the *Challenger* explosion. The coverage included stories that identified serious flaws in the shuttle's design and in the administration of America's space program. The staff was awarded the prize for Spot News Reporting in 1994 for its comprehensive coverage of the bombing of Manhattan's World Trade Center. The 1998 prize for International Reporting went to the staff for its revealing series profiling the corrosive effects of drug corruption in Mexico.

The *New York Times* was founded in 1851 by Henry J. Redmond and George Jones. Adolph Simon Ochs purchased it in 1896. His plan was to turn the *Times* into a serious news publication. He adopted the famous slogan, "All the News That's Fit to Print," used for the first time on Oct. 25, 1896. He developed the *Times* into the national "newspaper of record" and an internationally known paper with outstanding comprehensive international news coverage. The *New York Times Index* began in 1913. Arthur Ochs Sulzberger is the present publisher.

1987

Peter Gorner   376

Birth: 1942. **Education:** Northwestern University, IL. University of South Carolina.

Prize: *Explanatory Journalism,* 1987: *Chicago Tribune,* "Altered Fates, The Promise of Gene Therapy," Chicago: Chicago Tribune, 1986.

Career: Staff member, *Chicago Tribune.*

Selected Works: *Divorce, Chicago Style* (with others), 1983. *Altered Fates* (with Jeff Lyon), 1986. *Aging on Hold: Secrets of Living Younger Longer* (with Ronald Kotulak), 1992. *Altered Fates: The Story of Gene Therapy* (with Jeff Lyon), 1994.

For More Information: Wills, Kendall, *The Pulitzer Prizes, Volume 1, 1987,* New York: Simon & Schuster, 1987.

Commentary: Peter Gorner and Jeff Lyon explored the evolving medical technology and the possibility of gene therapy. Their 50,000-word series ran

for seven days in March and April 1986. They had spent months interviewing scientists; visiting the Office of Recombinant DNA Activities, the federal agency that will regulate gene therapy at the National Institutes of Health; and reading the literature of the science. Gorner was a finalist for a Pulitzer Prize in 1991 for a series of stories on genetic research.

Jeffrey R. Lyon   377

Birth: November 28, 1943; Chicago, IL. **Parents:** Herbert T. Lyon and Lyle (Hoffenberg). **Education:** Northwestern University, IL: BSJ. **Spouse:** Bonita Brodt (m. 1981). **Children:** Lindsay, Derek.

Prize: *Explanatory Journalism,* 1987: *Chicago Tribune,* "Altered Fates, The Promise of Gene Therapy," Chicago: Chicago Tribune, 1986.

Career: Reporter, *Miami (FL) Herald,* 1964-66; Reporter, *Chicago Today,* 1966-76; Columnist, *Chicago Tribune,* 1976-81; Feature Writer, *Chicago Tribune,* 1981-; Creative Writing Teacher, Columbia College, 1987; Director of Science Communication Program, Columbia College, 1988-; Staff member, *Chicago Tribune.*

Selected Works: *Playing God in the Nursery,* 1985. *Altered Fates* (with Peter Gorner), 1986. *Altered Fates: The Story of Gene Therapy* (with Peter Gorner), 1994.

Other Awards: National Headliners Club Award, 1984. Peter Lisagor Award, *Chicago Tribune,* 1990.

For More Information: Wills, Kendall, *The Pulitzer Prizes, Volume 1, 1987,* New York: Simon & Schuster, 1987; *Contemporary Authors, Volume 130,* Detroit: Gale Research Company, 1990.

Commentary: Jeff Lyon and Peter Gorner's research into the medical advances of gene therapy won them a Pulitzer Prize. Their eight-part series, "Altered Fates, The Promise of Gene Therapy," was published for seven days in March and April 1986. They spent months on research, learning the jargon, culling relevant articles, and interviewing more than 60 scientists.

1988

Daniel Hertzberg   378

Birth: February 3, 1946; New York, NY. **Parents:** Abraham Hertzberg and Joan (Naumburg). **Education:** University of Chicago, IL: AB. **Spouse:** Barbara Kantrowitz (m. 1976). **Children:** Michael, Benjamin.

Prize: *Explanatory Journalism,* 1988: *Wall Street Journal,* New York: Dow Jones, 1987.

Career: Reporter, *Buffalo (NY) Evening News,* 1968-71; Reporter, *Garden City (NY) Newsday,* 1971-77; Reporter, New York (NY), *Wall Street Journal,* 1977-87; Deputy News Editor, *Wall Street Journal,*

1987-88; Deputy Managing Editor, *Wall Street Journal,* 1995-.

Other Awards: Gerald Loeb Award, Anderson Graduate School of Management, University of California, Los Angeles, 1987. George Polk Memorial Award, Long Island University, NY, 1988. Gerald Loeb Award, 1987, 1988.

For More Information: *Wall Street Journal,* 1 April (1988): 2.

Commentary: Daniel Hertzberg and James B. Stewart reported on the United States financial markets. Their winning stories included one on the New York Stock Exchange, which came within minutes of shutting down, and another chronicled the expansion of insider trading from outsiders, such as Ivan Boesky, and from trusted establishments on Wall Street. Hertzberg was 42 when he was awarded a Pulitzer Prize.

James B. Stewart   379

Birth Place: Quincy, IL. **Education:** DePauw University, IN: BA. Harvard University, MA: JD.

Prize: *Explanatory Journalism,* 1988: *Wall Street Journal,* New York: Dow Jones, 1987.

Career: Attorney, Cravath, Swaine, & Moore, 1976-; Executive Editor, *American Lawyer* magazine, 1979; Senior Writer and Front Page Editor, *Wall Street Journal,* 1983-92; Reporter-at-Large, *New Yorker* magazine, 1993-; Writer.

Selected Works: *The Partners: Inside America's Most Powerful Law Firms,* 1983. *The Prosecutors: Inside the Offices of the Government's Most Powerful Lawyers,* 1987. *Den of Thieves,* 1991. *Blood Sport: The President and His Adversaries,* 1996.

Other Awards: George Polk Memorial Award, Long Island University, NY, 1987. Gerald Loeb Award, Anderson Graduate School of Management, University of California, Los Angeles, 1988.

For More Information: *Wall Street Journal,* 1 April (1988): A2; *Contemporary Authors, Volume 146,* Detroit: Gale Research Company, 1995.

Commentary: James B. Stewart and Daniel Hertzberg spent four weeks investigating "the scope and severity of the stock market crash" of October 1987. Their story told how the New York Stock Market came within minutes of closing. They chronicled the stock exchange events of October 19 and 20. Another story examined the spread of insider trading from outsiders, such as Ivan Boesky, to those in the most established Wall Street firms. Stewart was 36 years old when he won the award in 1988.

1989

Karen Alyce Blessen   380

Birth: December 19, 1951; Columbus, NE. **Education:** University of Nebraska: BFA.

Prize: *Explanatory Journalism,* 1989: *Dallas Morning News,* Dallas: Dallas Morning News, 1988.

Career: Freelance illustrator, 1973-86; Designer, *Dallas (TX) Morning News,* 1986-89; Freelance Illustrator, *Dallas (TX) Morning News,* 1989; Owner, Karen Blessen Illustration, 1989-.

Selected Works: *The Soozabadootch* (with Doris E. Foster), 1979. *Be an Angel* (with Dana Reynolds), 1994. *Doing Time: Notes from the Undergrad* (with Rob Thomas), 1997.

Commentary: Karen Blessen, along with her colleagues David Hanners and William Snyder, followed the 22-month investigation of the National Transportation Safety Board through the steps of examining an aviation disaster. Their four-part series was published in a special 12-page section in the *Dallas Morning News* in February 1988. Blessen worked on the project for four months, coordinating graphics. She is the first graphic artist to win a Pulitzer Prize. She now owns her own business.

David Hanners   381

Birth: June 23, 1955; Casey, IL. **Education:** Indiana State University: BS. **Spouse:** Casey Selix. **Children:** Ian.

Prize: *Explanatory Journalism,* 1989: *Dallas Morning News,* Dallas: Dallas Morning News, 1988.

Career: Night Police Beat Reporter, *Amarillo (TX) Globe-News,* 1977-; Randall County Bureau Chief, *Amarillo (TX) Globe-News,* ?-80; Federal Courts Reporter, *Brownsville (TX) Herald,* 1980-82; General Assignment Reporter, State Desk, *Dallas (TX) Morning News,* 1982-; Staff member, *St. Paul (MN) Pioneer Press,*.

Other Awards: Katie Award, Dallas Press Club, 1983-84, 1987. Individual Achievement Award, Headliners Club, 1984, 1989. H.M. Baggerly Award, Texas Farmers Union, 1986. Gavel Award, State Bar of Texas, 1988. Earl D. Osborn Premier Award, Aviation/Space Writers Association, 1989. George Polk Memorial Award, Long Island University, NY, 1990. Journalism Fellow, University of Michigan, 1992-93.

Commentary: David Hanners, William Snyder, and Karen Blessen won a Pulitzer Prize for their series of articles, "Anatomy of an Air Disaster: The Final Flight of 50 Sierra Kilo." Hanners, a reporter, and Snyder, a photographer, followed the 22-month investigation by the National Transportation Safety Board into a business jet crash in East Texas that killed seven people. Their series was published in February 1988.

William D. Snyder   382

Birth: July 1, 1959; Henderson, KY. **Parents:** Charles Gordon Snyder and Mary Odette (Galloway). **Religion:** Episcopalian. **Education:** Boston University, MA. Rochester Institute of Technology, NY: BS, Highest Honors. **Spouse:** Amy Barbara Lewy (m. 1985). **Children:** Cameron, Scott.

Prize: *Explanatory Journalism,* 1989: *Dallas Morning News,* Dallas: Dallas Morning News, 1988. *Feature Photography,* 1991: *Dallas Morning News,* Dallas: Dallas Morning News, 1990. *Spot News Photography,* 1993: *Dallas Morning News,* Dallas: Dallas Morning News, 1992.

Career: Photographer / Intern, *Henderson (KY) Gleaner,* 1974-76; Photographer, *Evansville (IN) Press,* 1977-79; Photographer Intern, *Arizona Republic,* Phoenix, AZ, 1980; Photographer, *Miami (FL) News,* 1981-83; General Assignment Photographer, *Dallas (TX) Morning News,* 1983-.

Other Awards: Region 6 Photographer of the Year, National Press Photographers Association, 1983. Pro-Football Photographer of the Year, Pro-Football Hall of Fame, 1986. National Press Photographers Assocation, 1986. Robert F. Kennedy Journalism Award, 1991. Olympic Media Award, 1997. Associated Press Managing Editors Award.

Commentary: William Snyder is the only photographer to win a Pulitzer Prize three times as well as the only person to win in three different categories. In 1989, he, along with two colleagues, examined and explained the procedure followed by the National Transportation Safety Board when it investigates a plane crash. In 1990, his photographic essay showed the condition in Romania for sick and orphaned children. In 1993, he and Ken Geiger won for their coverage of the Barcelona Olympic Games. They worked around-the-clock for three weeks. Other assignments have included a variety of sporting events, national party conventions, the first free elections in Haiti, and Germany's reunification.

1990

Stephen Wilson Coll   383

Birth: October 8, 1958; Washington, DC. **Parents:** Robert Wilson Coll and Shirley Lee (Baldwin). **Education:** Occidental College, CA: BA, cum laude, Phi Beta Kappa. Sussex University, England. **Spouse:** Susan Keselenko (m. 1984). **Children:** Alexandra, Emma, Maxwell.

Prize: *Explanatory Journalism,* 1990: *Washington Post,* Washington, DC: Washington Post, 1989.

Career: Staff Reporter, KCET-TV, Los Angeles, CA, 1982-83; Contributing Editor, *California Magazine,* 1983-84; Contributing Editor, *Inc. Magazine,*

1984-85; Staff Writer, *Washington (DC) Post,* 1985-86; Financial Correspondent, *Washington (DC) Post,* 1987-89; Correspondent, South Asia, *Washington (DC) Post,* 1989-92; Correspondent, London (England), *Washington (DC) Post,* 1992-95; Editor, *Washington (DC) Post Magazine,* 1995-98; Managing Editor, *Washington (DC) Post,* 1998-.

Selected Works: *The Deal of the Century: The Breakup of AT&T,* 1986. *The Taking of Getty Oil,* 1987. *Eagle on the Street: Based on the Pulitzer Prize-Winning Account of the SEC's Battle with Wall Street* (with David A. Vise), 1991. *On the Grand Trunk Road: A Journey into South Asia,* 1994.

Other Awards: Gerald Loeb Award, Anderson Graduate School of Management, University of California, Los Angeles, 1990. Livingston Award, University of Michigan, 1992. *Sunday* Magazine Editors' Award, 1994. Certificate of Recognition for Excellence in International Journalism, School of Advanced International Studies, Johns Hopkins University, 1996.

For More Information: Wills, Kendall, *The Pulitzer Prizes 1990,* New York: Simon & Schuster, 1990; *Contemporary Authors, Volume 137,* Detroit: Gale Research Company, 1992; *Washington Post,* 7 March (1998): A4.

Commentary: Steve Coll and David A. Vise were awarded a Pulitzer Prize for their exploration of the organization and work of the Securities and Exchange Commission. They interviewed more than 200 people about the agency and the impact of its former chairman, John Shad. In March 1998, Coll was named managing editor of the *Washington Post.*

David Allan Vise   384

Birth: June 16, 1960; Nashville, TN. **Parents:** Harry Vise and Doris Bertha (Oppenheim). **Religion:** Jewish. **Education:** University of Pennsylvania: BS, magna cum laude. London School of Economics, England. University of Pennsylvania: MBA. **Spouse:** Lori Silverman (m. 1984). **Children:** Lisa, Allison.

Prize: *Explanatory Journalism,* 1990: *Washington Post,* Washington, DC: Washington Post, 1989.

Career: Summer Intern, *Nashville (TN) Tennessean;* Intern, *Washington (DC) Post,* 1982; Investment Banker, Goldman, Sachs & Company, 1983-84; Business Reporter, *Washington (DC) Post,* 1984-90; Local Business Editor, *Washington (DC) Post,* 1990-91; Deputy Business Editor, *Washington (DC) Post,* 1991-92; Staff member, *Washington (DC) Post,* 1993-.

Selected Works: *Eagle on the Street: Based on a Pulitzer Prize-Winning Account of the SEC's Battle with Wall Street,* 1991.

Other Awards: Gerald Loeb Award, Anderson Graduate School of Management, University of California, Los Angeles, 1990.

For More Information: *Washington Post,* 13 April (1990): A4; Wills, Kendall, *The Pulitzer Prizes 1990,* New York: Simon & Schuster, 1990.

Commentary: David A. Vise and Steve Coll's investigation into the activities of the Security and Exchange Commission was the basis for their February 1989 series of stories on the agency and its former director, John Shad. They spent countless hours interviewing people and going through thousands of documents to understand the workings of the commission. The Securities and Exchange Commission, although a public agency, does most of its work behind closed doors.

1991

Susan C. Faludi   385

Birth: April 18, 1959; New York, NY. **Parents:** Steven Faludi and Marilyn (Lanning). **Education:** Harvard University, MA: BA, summa cum laude.

Prize: *Explanatory Journalism,* 1991: *Wall Street Journal,* "The Reckoning," New York: Dow Jones, 1990.

Career: Editor, Yorktown (NY) high school paper; Managing Editor, college paper, *Crimson;* Summer Intern, *Staten Island (NY) Advance,* 1980; Stringer, *Boston Globe,* 1981; News and Copy Clerk, *New York Times,* 1981-82; Reporter, Suburban Bureau, *Miami (FL) Herald,* 1983; Reporter, *Atlanta (GA) Journal-Constitution,* 1984-85; Staff Writer, Sunday Magazine, *San Jose (CA) Mercury News,* 1985-89; Affiliated Scholar, Stanford University (CA), Institute for Research on Women and Gender, 1989-91; Staff Writer, San Francisco (CA) Bureau, *Wall Street Journal,* 1990-92; Writer.

Selected Works: *Backlash: The Undeclared War against American Women,* 1991.

Other Awards: Oliver Dabney History Award for Senior Thesis, 1981. News Reporting and Feature Reporting Awards, Georgia Press Association, 1985. John Hancock Award for Excellence in Business and Financial Journalism, 1991. National Book Critics' Circle Award, 1991: *Backlash: The Undeclared War against American Women,* New York: Crown, 1991. Robert F. Kennedy Journalism Award.

For More Information: *Working Woman,* April 1992; *Contemporary Authors, Volume 138,* Detroit: Gale Research Company, 1993; *Current Biography Yearbook, 1993,* New York: H.W. Wilson, 1993: 187-190.

Commentary: Susan Faludi was able to take a business story and put a human face on it. She wrote about the leveraged buyout of Safeway Stores, Inc., and its impact on the employees, despite management assurances that "no one would be hurt." Eventually 63,000 people were laid off from the world's largest supermarket chain. In her Pulitzer citation, it was noted that Faludi "revealed the human cost of high finance."

1992

Robert S. Capers   386

Birth: July 15, 1949; Boston, MA. **Education:** Colby College, ME. University of Connecticut. **Spouse:** Married. **Children:** Children.

Prize: *Explanatory Journalism,* 1992: *Hartford Courant,* "The Looking Glass: How a Flaw Reflects Cracks in Space Science," Hartford, CT: Hartford Courant, 1991.

Career: Staff member, *Meriden Morning Record;* Reporter, 1978-; Writer, Editor, *Hartford (CT) Courant,* ?-1995.

For More Information: *University of Connecticut Advance,* 19 September (1997).

Commentary: Robert S. Capers and Eric Lipton investigated the debacle of the Hubble Space Telescope, which cost $1.5 billion and did not work because of a flawed mirror. They spent five months researching their four-part series. They wrote about the pressures of deadlines and cost cutting at NASA, the personalities of the top scientists, and the intricacies of optical physics.

Capers left the *Hartford Courant* in a voluntary buyout program in 1995.

Eric S. Lipton   387

Birth: August 13, 1965; Philadelphia, PA. **Parents:** Herbert Lipton and Helene (Slepin). **Religion:** Jewish. **Education:** University of Vermont.

Prize: *Explanatory Journalism,* 1992: *Hartford Courant,* "The Looking Glass: How a Flaw Reflects Cracks in Space Science," Hartford, CT: Hartford Courtant, 1991.

Career: Staff Writer, *Lebanon (NH) Valley News,* 1987-89; Staff Writer, *Hartford (CT) Courant,* 1989-94; Metro Reporter, *Washington (DC) Post,* 1994-.

Other Awards: Aviation and Space Writers' Award, 1991.

For More Information: *Hartford Courant,* 8 April (1992): A1; *The News Science Journalists,* New York: Ballantine Books, 1995.

Commentary: Eric Lipton and Robert S. Capers won the first Pulitzer Prize for the *Hartford Courant.* The series on the Hubble Space Telescope ran for four days in March and April 1991. It delved into the complexities of optical physics, the personalities of top scientists, and the pressures of deadlines and decision making at NASA.

1993

Michael F. Toner   388
Birth: March 17, 1944; Le Mars, IA. **Parents:** Francis F. Toner and Mary Ann (Delaney). **Education:** University of Iowa: BA. Northwestern University, IL: MS, cum laude. University of Oklahoma: Postgraduate. **Spouse:** Patricia L. Asleson (m. 1966). **Children:** Susan, Sharon.

Prize: *Explanatory Journalism,* 1993: *Atlanta Journal and Constitution,* "When Bugs Fight Back," August 23, 28; September 6, 9, 26; October 3, 16, Atlanta, GA: Atlanta Journal and Constitution, 1992.

Career: Chief Photographer, college paper, *Daily Iowan (IA),* 1964-66; Reporter and Photographer, Chicago, United Press International, 1966-67; Key West (FL) Bureau Chief, *Miami (FL) Herald,* 1967-68; Copy Editor, *Miami (FL) Herald,* 1968-69; Assistant City Editor, *Miami (FL) Herald,* 1969-70; Environmental Writer, *Miami (FL) Herald,* 1970-79; Science Writer, *Miami (FL) Herald,* 1979-84; Science Editor, *Atlanta (GA) Journal and Constitution,* 1984-91; Science Writer, *Atlanta (GA) Journal and Constitution,* 1991-; Professional-in-Residence, University of Iowa, 1993.

Selected Works: *This Land of Ours: A Profile of Florida Natural Resources,* 1976. *Florida by Paddle and Pack,* 1979. *Field Guide for Science Writers* (with others), 1997.

Other Awards: Professional Journalism Fellow, Stanford University, CA, 1974.

For More Information: *New Science Journalists,* New York: Ballantine Books, 1995; *Masterpieces of Reporting, Volume 1,* Northport, AL: Vision Press, 1997.

Commentary: Mike Toner, a 20-year veteran science writer, delved into the world of bacteria, viruses, and insects. His winning series, "When Bugs Fight Back," explores the growing level of resistance to antibiotics and pesticides. The occasional series was published in the *Atlanta Journal and Constitution* between August 23 and October 16, 1992. Excerpts were reprinted in the April 14, 1993 paper with the announcement of his award. He took a complicated subject "and made it as simple as a rock falling into a pond."

1994

Ronald Kotulak   389
Birth: July 31, 1935; Detroit, MI. **Parents:** John Kotulak and Mary (Roman). **Education:** Wayne State University, MI. University of Michigan: BA. **Spouse:** Jean Bond (m. 1961, died 1974); Donna Colucci (m. 1980). **Children:** Jeffrey, Kerry, Christopher (JB); Stepchildren: Paul Colucci, Lisa Colucci (DC).

Prize: *Explanatory Journalism,* 1994: *Chicago Tribune,* "Unlocking the Mind," April 11-15; "Unlocking the Mind: Roots of Violence," December 12-15, Chicago: Chicago Tribune, 1993.

Career: Neighborhood News Reporter, *Chicago Tribune,* 1959; Science Writer, *Chicago Tribune,* 1963-.

Selected Works: *Inside the Brain: Revolutionary Discoveries of How the Mind Works,* 1996.

Other Awards: Edward Scott Beck Award, *Chicago Tribune,* 1965, 1976, 1991, 1993. American Heart Association, 1968. American Chemical Society, 1974. Robert T. Morse Writers Award, American Psychiatric Association, 1982, 1989. American Diabetes Association, 1995.

For More Information: Taft, William H., *Encyclopedia of Twentieth Century Journalists,* New York: Garland Publishing, 1986.

Commentary: Ronald Kotulak has covered science for the *Chicago Tribune* for 30 years. He won a Pulitzer Prize for two series of stories dealing with the brain. One series dealt with new understandings on the workings of the brain and the combination of nature and nurture that determine the adults that children become. His second series reported on the biology of violence. His first series was cited by Hillary Clinton in her book *It Takes a Village* to explain the importance of early experience to brain development. He was a finalist for a Pulitzer Prize in 1991 for a series of stories on genetic research.

1995

Leon DeCosta Dash Jr.   390

Birth: March 16, 1944; New Bedford, MA. **Parents:** Leon DeCosta Dash Sr. and Ruth E. (Kydd). **Religion:** Unitarian Universalist. **Education:** Lincoln University, PA. Howard University, Washington, DC: BA. **Spouse:** Dyann Anita Waugh (m. 1968, div. 1976); Alice Carol Bonner (m. 1978, div.). **Children:** Darla, Destiny (DW).

Prize: *Explanatory Journalism,* 1995: *Washington Post,* "Rosa Lee's Story," September 18-25, Washington, DC: Washington Post, 1994.

Career: Copy Aide, *Washington (DC) Post,* 1965-66; Reporter, *Washington (DC) Post,* 1966-76; Served in Peace Corps, (Kenya), 1969-70; Reporter, *Washington (DC) Post,* 1971-78; Foreign Correspondent, *Washington (DC) Post,* 1976-84; Visiting Professor of Political Science, University of California, San Diego, 1978; West Africa Bureau Chief, *Washington (DC) Post,* 1979-84; Investigative Reporter, *Washington (DC) Post,* 1984-98; Professor, University of Illinois, Urbana-Champaign Department of Journalism and Afro-American Studies and Research Program, 1998-.

Selected Works: *The Shame of the Prisons* (with Ben H. Bagdikian), 1972. *Savimbi's 1977 Campaign against the Cubans and the MPLA: Munger Africana Library Notes, Number 40-41, 1977. When Children Want Children: The Urban Crisis of Teenage Childbearing, 1989. Rosa Lee: A Mother and Her Family in Urban America,* 1996.

Other Awards: George Polk Memorial Award, Long Island University, NY, 1974. Reporting Prize, Washington, DC-Baltimore, MD Newspaper Guild, 1974. International Reporting Awards from Africare, 1984. International Reporting Award, Capitol Press Club, 1984. General News Award, National Association of Black Journalists, 1986. Distinguished Service Award, Social Services Administration of Maryland, 1986. Public Service Award, Washington, DC-Baltimore, MD, 1987. Investigative Reporters and Editors Award, 1987. President's Award, Washington Independent Writers, 1989. PEN/Martha Albrand Special Citation, 1990: *When Children Want Children: The Urban Crisis of Teenage Childbearing,* New York: William Morrow, 1989. Robert F. Kennedy Journalism Award, 1995. Media Fellow, Henry J. Kaiser Family Foundation, 1995-96. Harry Chapin Media Award, 1997: *Rosa Lee: A Mother and Her Family in Urban America,* New York: Basic Books, 1996. Emmy from National Academy of Television Arts in Public Affairs and Services, Washington, DC Chapter. Honorary Degree, Lincoln University, PA, 1996.

For More Information: Dawkins, Wayne, *Black Journalists: The NABJ Story,* Sicklerville, NJ: August Press, 1993.

Commentary: Leon Dash and Lucian Perkins won a Pulitzer Prize for their series about three generations of poverty in one Washington, DC family. He said "he felt compelled to write about Rosa Lee Cunningham and her family because the underclass is a huge and growing problem in American Society." Dash followed Rosa Lee for four years. Dash was a finalist for a Pulitzer Prize in 1987 for a series of articles on teenage pregnancy.

Lucian Perkins   391

Birth: February 21, 1952; Fort Worth, TX. **Education:** University of Texas: BA.

Prize: *Explanatory Journalism,* 1995: *Washington Post,* "Rosa Lee's Story," Washington, DC: Washington Post, 1994.

Career: Staff member, college paper, *Daily Texan;* Intern, *Washington (DC) Post,* 1979; Photographer, *Washington (DC) Post,* 1979-; Founder, Inter-Foto Foundation.

Selected Works: *Russia: Chronicles of Change* (with others), 1996.

Other Awards: National Headliners Club Award, 1980. Newspaper Photographer of the Year, National Press Photographers Association/University of Missouri School of Journalism, 1994. Photo of the Year, World Press Association, 1996. White House News Photographers Association.

Commentary: Lucian Perkins, a photographer, and Leon Dash, an investigative reporter, chronicled the life of Rosa Lee Cunningham and her family in Washington, DC. They told the story of three generations of poverty and the life that Rosa Lee led to survive. Perkins is an award-winning photographer who has covered Chechnya, the war-torn region in Russia, and other areas of the former Soviet Union, and has had many assignments in the United States.

1996

Laurie Garrett   392

Birth: September 8, 1951; Los Angeles, CA. **Parents:** Banning Garrett and LouAnn (Pierose). **Education:** University of California, Santa Cruz, Honors. University of California, Berkeley: Doctoral Candidate.

Prize: *Explanatory Journalism,* 1996: *Newsday,* Garden City, NY: Newsday, 1995.

Career: California radio station, KPFA, 1979; Freelance Reporter for American Broadcasting Company (ABC), British Broadcasting Company (BBC); Reporter, Canadian Broadcasting Company (CBC); Science Correspondent, National Public Radio, 1980-

88; Staff member, *Newsday,* 1988-; Part Owner, Havens, Winery, Napa Valley, CA.

Selected Works: *The Coming Plague: Newly Emerging Diseases in a World out of Balance,* 1994. *Microbes versus Mankind: The Coming Plague; Headline Series, Number 309,* 1996.

Other Awards: George Foster Peabody Broadcasting Award for Science Story, 1977. Edwin Howard Armstrong Broadcast Award, 1978. National Press Club Award, 1982. Meritorious Achievement Award, Media Alliance, 1983. World Hunger Media Award, 1987. J.C. Penney, Missouri Journalism Certificate of Merit, 1990. Best Beat Reporter, Deadline Club of New York, 1993. New York State Associated Press Writing Award, 1994. Award, Press Club of Long Island, NY, 1994. Society of Silurians Award, 1994. Newsday Publisher's Award for Best Beat Reporter, 1990, 1995. Bob Considine Award, Overseas Press Club Award, 1995.

For More Information: *Contemporary Authors, Volume 148,* Detroit: Gale Research Company, 1996; *Newsday,* 10 April (1996): A31.

Commentary: Laurie Garrett spent a week in Zaire covering the outbreak of the Ebola virus. She filed her stories by cellular phone. She has covered the emergence of diseases elsewhere as well, such as AIDS in East Africa. She was president of the National Association of Science Writers in 1996. Garrett had been a finalist in the International Reporting category but was shifted to the Explanatory Journalism category by the Pulitzer board.

1997

Ron Cortes   393

Birth: March 29, 1945; San Antonio, TX. **Education:** University of Texas. University of Texas: MA. **Spouse:** Married. **Children:** One son.

Prize: *Explanatory Journalism,* 1997: *Philadelphia Inquirer,* "Final Choices: Seeking the Good Death," November 17-21, Philadelphia, PA: Philadelphia Inquirer, 1996.

Career: Teacher, Texas, California, and Tehran (Iran), 1966-76; Staff Photographer, *Wilmington (DE) News-Journal,* 1981-87; Photographer, *Philadelphia (PA) Inquirer,* 1987-.

Other Awards: Portrait/Personality, Picture of the Year, University of Missouri School of Journalism /National Press Photographers Association, 1997.

Commentary: Ron Cortes and his colleagues Michael Vitez and April Saul won a Pulitzer Prize for Explanatory Journalism in 1997. They explored the issues that critically ill individuals face and their struggle to die with dignity. Cortes has worked on projects in Cuba, Bosnia, Ethiopia, and Haiti. He was a finalist

for a Pulitzer Prize in 1991 for his photographs of a senior citizen returning to high school.

April Saul   394

Birth: May 27, 1955; New York, NY. **Education:** Tufts University, MA: BA. Ohio University: MA. **Spouse:** Steven Zerby (m., div.). **Children:** Three children.

Prize: *Explanatory Journalism,* 1997: *Philadelphia Inquirer,* "Final Choices: Seeking the Good Death," November 17-21, Philadelphia, PA: Philadelphia Inquirer, 1996.

Career: Staff Photographer, *Baltimore (MD) Sun,* 1980-81; Photographer, *Philadelphia (PA) Inquirer,* 1981-.

Other Awards: Photographer of the Year Award, Pennsylvania Press Photographers Association, 1983-84, 1996. Robert F. Kennedy Journalism Award, 1983. Nikon/National Press Photographers Documentary Sabbatical Grant, 1986. Budapest Award, World Press Photo Competition, 1991. National Headliners Club Award. Feature Picture Story Awards for Pictures of the Year Contest.

Commentary: April Saul and Ron Cortes, photographers, and Michael Vitez, a reporter, won a Pulitzer Prize for their coverage of five critically ill individuals and their fight "to die with dignity." Saul was the first recipient of the Nikon/National Press Photographers Documentary Sabbatical Grant. She used the time and funds to photograph the plight of Hmong refugees in America. She has been a Pulitzer finalist twice, in 1987 and in 1994.

Michael Vitez   395

Birth: April 11, 1957; Washington, DC. **Education:** University of Virginia. **Spouse:** Maureen Fitzgerald. **Children:** Timmy, Sally, Jonathan.

Prize: *Explanatory Journalism,* 1997: *Philadelphia Inquirer,* "Final Choices: Seeking the Good Death," November 17-21, Philadelphia, PA: Philadelphia Inquirer, 1996.

Career: Editor-in-Chief, college paper, *Cavalier Daily,* 1978-79; Staff member, *Virginian-Pilot / Ledger-Star,* 1979-80; Staff member, *Washington (DC) Star,* 1980-81; Staff member, *Hartford (CT) Courant,* 1981-85; General Assignment and Feature Writer, *Philadelphia (PA) Inquirer,* 1985-.

Selected Works: *Final Choices: Seeking the Good Death,* 1997.

Other Awards: Michigan Journalism Fellow, University of Michigan, 1994-95. Excellence in Media Award, American Association of Homes and Services for the Aging, 1997.

For More Information: *Philadelphia Inquirer,* (1997): 10.

Commentary: Michael Vitez, along with two staff photographers, April Saul and Ron Cortes, looked into the lives of five critically ill people who fought to die with dignity. For seven months he followed the five individuals who were featured in his series of articles. Vitez has covered the topic of aging since his return to the *Philadelphia Inquirer* from a fellowship at the University of Michigan in 1995.

1998

Paul F. Salopek   396
Birth: February 9, 1962; Barstow, CA. **Parents:** Paul Salopek and Ruth (Richard). **Education:** University of California, Santa Barbara: BA, Honors. **Spouse:** Linda Lynch (m. 1996).

Prize: *Explanatory Journalism,* 1998: *Chicago Tribune,* "Unlocking the Rainbow," April 27; "Genes Offer Sampling of Hope and Fear," April 28, Chicago, IL: *Chicago Tribune,* 1997.

Career: Commercial Fisherman; Police Reporter, *Roswell (NM) Daily Record,* 1984-85; Freelance Writer/Journalist, 1985-89; Reporter, *El Paso (TX) Times,* 1989-92; Writer, *National Geographic Magazine,* 1992-95; Metropolitan Staff, *Chicago Tribune,* 1996-.

Other Awards: James Aaronson Award, 1993.

For More Information: *Chicago Tribune,* April 15, 1998.

Commentary: Paul F. Salopek won a Pulitzer Prize for his "enlightening profile of the Human Genome Diversity Project, which seeks to chart the genetic relationship among all people." His two-part series described the project in writing that was engaging for a layperson to read. Salopek began his career in journalism after his motorcycle broke down in New Mexico and he joined the staff of a local paper to earn the repair money. He joined the staff of the *Chicago Tribune* after working for *National Geographic* magazine.

Feature Photography

1968

Toshio Sakai   397

Birth: March 31, 1940; Tokyo, Japan. **Education:** Meiji University, Japan: BA.

Prize: *Feature Photography,* 1968: United Press International, "Dreams of Better Times," 1967.

Career: Darkroom Technician, United Press International, 1964; Staff Photographer, United Press International, 1965-75; News Picture Editor, Southeast Asia, United Press International, 1973-75; Photo Manager, Soeul (Korea) United Press International, 1975-77; Freelance photographer, 1977-.

Selected Works: *The Photo Book on the Vietnam War* (with Eva Press), 1979. *Nanmin: Kokkyo No Ai To Shi: Foto Apiru,* 1980.

For More Information: Leekley, Sheryle and John Leekley, *Moments: The Pulitzer Prize Photographs, Updated Version: 1942-1982,* New York: Crown Publishers, Inc., 1982: 66-67; Browne, Turner, and Elaine Partnow, *Macmillan Biographical Encyclopedia of Photographic Artists & Innovators,* New York: Macmillan Publishing Company, 1983: 529.

Commentary: Toshio Sakai's winning photograph is of an American Soldier sleeping while another stands guard. Nothing disturbs his sleep—not even a pounding rain storm.

1969

Moneta J. Sleet Jr.   398

Birth: February 14, 1926; Owensboro, KY. **Death:** September 30, 1996. **Parents:** Moneta J. Sleet and Ozetta L. **Education:** Kentucky State University: BA. New York University: MA. **Spouse:** Juanita Harris. **Children:** Gregory, Lisa, Michael.

Prize: *Feature Photography,* 1969: *Ebony,* 1968.

Career: Served in U.S. Army, 1944-46; Photography Instructor, Maryland State College, 1948-49; Sportswriter, *Amsterdam (NY) News,* 1950; Photographer, *Our World* Magazine, 1950-55; Photographer, Johnson Publishing Company (NY), 1955-.

Selected Works: *Moneta Sleet, Jr.: Pulitzer Prize Photojournalist,* 1986.

Other Awards: Overseas Press Club Award, 1957. National Urban League. Photo-Journalism Award, National Association of Black Journalists, 1978. Kentucky Journalism Hall of Fame, University of Kentucky, 1989.

For More Information: McKenty, Beth, *Moneta Sleet, Faces of America,* Milwaukee, WI: Community Relations-Social Development Commission, 1978; Leekley, Sheryle and John Leekley, *Moments: The Pulitzer Prize Photographs, Updated Version: 1942-1982,* New York: Crown Publishers, Inc., 1982: 70-71; *New York Times,* 2 October (1996): D23; *Jet,* 90:22 (14 October 1996): 4-7.

Commentary: Moneta J. Sleet Jr. was the first African American to win a Pulitzer Prize in photography. His photograph of the grieving Coretta Scott King holding her daughter Bernice during her husband's funeral was distributed by the Associated Press and published throughout the country.

Sleet's interest in photography began as a hobby when he was given a box camera as a child. His first civil rights assignment was covering the Montgomery, Alabama bus boycott which was organized by Martin Luther King Jr. He also photographed King receiving his Nobel Peace Prize in Sweden in 1964.

Sleet died of cancer in 1996.

1970

Dallas Kinney   399

Birth: January 13, 1937; Buckeye, IA. **Education:** University of Iowa. **Spouse:** Lucinda K. **Children:** Allison, Rebecca.

Prize: *Feature Photography,* 1970: *Palm Beach Post,* "Migration to Misery," West Palm Beach, FL: Palm Beach Post, 1969.

Career: Writer, Photographer, *Washington (IA) Evening Journal,* 1964-66; Staff Photographer, *Dubuque (IA) Telegraph Herald, Miami (FL) Herald;* Staff Photographer, *Palm Beach (FL) Post,* 1969-, *Philadelphia (PA) Inquirer, Palm Beach (FL) Post;* Staff member, Christian Broadcast Network; Communications Consultant, Mailers and Consultants.

For More Information: *New York Times,* 5 May (1970): 48; *Washington Post,* 12 September (1982): Style-G1; Leekley, Sheryle and John Leekley, *Moments: The Pulitzer Prize Photographs, Updated Version: 1942-1982,* New York: Crown Publishers, Inc., 1982: 74-75.

Commentary: Dallas Kinney's eight-part series looked into the "other" Palm Beach. He photographed the migrant workers of one of the wealthiest regions of the country, who lived, worked, and died in poverty.

1971

Jack William Dykinga 400

Birth: January 2, 1943; Chicago, IL. **Parents:** John Richard Dykinga and Gertrude (Magnuson). **Education:** St. Procopius College, IL. Elmhurst College, IL. **Spouse:** Margaret Susan Maley (m. 1965). **Children:** Camille Marie, Peter Michael.

Prize: *Feature Photography,* 1971: *Chicago Sun-Times,* Chicago: Chicago Sun-Times, 1970.

Career: Photographer, Metro News Photos Company, 1962-64; Photographer, *Chicago Tribune,* 1964-65; Editorial Photographer, *Chicago Sun-Times,* 1965-74; Photo Assignment Editor, *Chicago Sun-Times,* 1974-76; Photo Editor, *Arizona Daily Star,* 1976-81; President, Southwestern Wilderness Travel, 1981-.

Selected Works: *Frog Mountain Blues* (with Charles Bowden), 1987. *The Sonoran Desert* (with Charles Bowden), 1992. *The Secret Forest* (with Charles Bowden), 1993. *Stone Canyons of the Colorado Plateau* (with Charles Bowden), 1996.

Other Awards: Grand Sweepstakes Award, Inland Press Association, 1971. Picture of the Year Award, University of Missouri/National Press Photographers Association, five times.

For More Information: Leekley, Sheryle and John Leekley, *Moments: The Pulitzer Prize Photographs, Updated Version: 1942-1982,* New York: Crown Publishers, Inc., 1982: 80-83; Browne, Turner, and Elaine Partnow, *Macmillan Biographical Encyclopedia of Photographic Artists & Innovators,* New York: Macmillan Publishing Company, 1983: 164.

Commentary: Jack Dykinga spent the first hour-and-a-half of his visits to the state schools in Lincoln and Dixon, Illinois just observing. He photographed the institutional care given to "retarded" children and adults. His pictures graphically showed the appalling living conditions for the inhabitants. After his series appeared, the State of Illinois reinstated funding for the Department of Mental Health. The funding had been scheduled to be cut.

1972

David Hume Kennerly 401

Birth: March 9, 1947; Roseburg, OR. **Parents:** Orlie "Tunney" Kennerly and Joanne (Hume). **Education:** Portland State College, OR. American Film Institute, CA. **Spouse:** Susan Allwardt (m. 1967, div. 1969); Mel Harris (m. 1983, div. 1988); Carol Huston (m. 1989, div.); Rebecca Soladay. **Children:** Byron (MH); Nicholas (RS).

Prize: *Feature Photography,* 1972: United Press International, 1971.

Career: Photographer, *Lake Oswego (OR) Review,* 1965; Photographer, *Portland (OR) Oregon Journal,* 1966; Photographer, *Portland (OR) Oregonian,* 1967; Photographer, United Press International, Los Angeles Bureau, 1967-68, New York, 1968-69, Washington DC, 1969-70, Saigon, South Vietnam, 1971-72; Contract Photographer in Southeast Asia, *Life* magazine, 1972; Photographer, *Time* magazine, 1973-74; Official Photographer, White House, 1974-77; Photographer, *Time* magazine, 1977; Freelance photographer, 1977; Director of Photography, *Philip Morris Magazine,* 1987-; Producer, Warner Bros. Television, 1990-92; President, Red Star Productions, 1990-; Contributing Editor, *Newsweek,* 1996.

Selected Works: *Shooter,* 1979. *Passage to Vietnam, Eight Days a Week,* 1994. *Photo Op,* 1995. **Films:** *The Taking of Flight 847: The Uli Derickson Story.*

Other Awards: Special Citation, National Press Photographers Association, 1976. World Press Photo Award, 1976. Olivier Rebbot Award, Overseas Press Club, 1985. Front Page Award, New York Newspaper Guild, 1985-86.

For More Information: Leekley, Sheryle and John Leekley, *Moments: The Pulitzer Prize Photographs, Updated Version: 1942-1982,* New York: Crown Publishers, Inc., 1982: 86-87; *Austin American-Statesman,* 1 December (1995): F1; *Los Angeles Times,* 5 May (1996): Part E.

Commentary: David Kennerly won a Pulitzer Prize for his combat photographs. One photograph shows a soldier cautiously approaching a bunker amid the denuded landscape—the result of mass chemical defoliation. His career has included photographing heads of state and historical events. His autobiography, *Shooter,* was made into a movie.

1973

Brian Timothy Lanker 402

Birth: August 31, 1947; Detroit, MI. **Parents:** Merrill Ross Lanker and Gertrude Pearl (Geisen). **Education:** Phoenix College, AZ. **Spouse:** Lynda L. **Children:** Julie, Jackie, Dustin.

Prize: *Feature Photography,* 1973: *Topeka Capital-Journal,* "Moment of Life," Topeka, KS: Topeka Capital-Journal, 1972.

Career: Staff Photographer, *Phoenix (AZ) Gazette,* 1966-69; Staff Photographer, *Topeka (KS) Capital-Journal,* 1969-74; Chief Photographer and Director of Graphic Services, *Eugene (OR) Register-Guard,* 1974-82; Freelance photographer, 1982.

Selected Works: *I Dream a World: Portraits of Black Women Who Changed America* (Summers, Barbara, ed.), 1989.

Other Awards: Regional Photographer of the Year, 1968-73. Newspaper Photographer of the Year, National Press Photographers Association, 1971, 1976. Joseph A. Sprague Memorial Award, National Press Photographers Association, 1979.

For More Information: Leekley, Sheryle and John Leekley, *Moments: The Pulitzer Prize Photographs, Updated Version: 1942-1982,* New York: Crown Publishers, Inc., 1982: 90-93; *Seattle Times,* 10 November (1991): 14.

Commentary: Brian Lanker's winning photographs were of the miracle of life. He captured the birth of a child and the joy and intensity of that moment.

1974

Slava Veder   403

Birth: August 30, 1926; Berkeley, CA. **Parents:** John B. Veder and Anna K. (Isvoschikova). **Education:** Modesto Junior College, CA. College of the Pacific, CA. Diablo College, CA. Sacramento State College, CA. **Spouse:** Petronella V. (m. 1972). **Children:** Tom, Tim, Kathleen, Joni, Kathryn.

Prize: *Feature Photography,* 1974: Associated Press, 1973.

Career: Sportswriter, *Richmond (CA) Independent;* Staff member, *Alameda (CA) Times-Star,* 1949-52; Assistant Sunday Editor, *Tulsa (OK) World,* 1952-56; Photographer, Sacramento (CA), Associated Press, 1961-62; Photo Editor, San Francisco (CA), Associated Press, 1962-67; Photographer, San Francisco (CA), Associated Press, 1967-91; Photographer, Sacramento (CA), Associated Press, 1991-93.

Other Awards: World Press Photo Award. Best News Photography Award, National Press Photographers Association.

For More Information: Leekley, Sheryle and John Leekley, *Moments: The Pulitzer Prize Photographs, Updated Version: 1942-1982,* New York: Crown Publishers, Inc., 1982: 96-97.

Commentary: Slava Veder captured the joy of families who see their American soldiers return home safe and sound. His photograph is of Lieutenant Colonel Robert Stirm, a prisoner of war for more than five years, and his reunion with his wife and children.

1975

Matthew Lewis   404

Birth: March 8, 1930; McDonald, PA. **Parents:** Matthew Lewis and Alzenia (Heath). **Education:** Howard University, Washington, DC. University of Pittsburgh, PA. **Spouse:** Jeannine Wells. **Children:** Charlene, Matthew, Kevin.

Prize: *Feature Photography,* 1975: *Washington Post,* Washington, DC: Washington Post, 1974.

Career: Hospital Corpsman, U.S. Navy, 1949-52; Instructor, Morgan State College (MD), 1957-65; Photographer, *Washington (DC) Post,* 1965-; Editor, *Washington (DC) Post;* Assistant Manager, *Washington (DC) Post.*

Other Awards: Special Merit Award, New York Institute of Photography, 1957. Award, National Newspaper Publishers Association, 1964. White House News Photographers Association, 1968, 1971. Washington, DC-Baltimore, MD, Newspaper Guild, 1971-72. Bill Pryor Award, Washington, DC-Baltimore, MD, Newspaper Guild, 1971-72.

For More Information: *New York Times,* 6 May (1975): 34; Leekley, Sheryle and John Leekley, *Moments: The Pulitzer Prize Photographs, Updated Version: 1942-1982,* New York: Crown Publishers, Inc., 1982: 100-103.

Commentary: Matthew Lewis's series of winning photographs looked at the decade of the 1970s.

1976

Louisville Courier-Journal

Full entry appears as #**295** under "Editorial Writing," 1918.

1977

Robin Lee Hood   405

Birth: September 22, 1944; Chattanooga, TN. **Parents:** James Lee Hood and Betty Jean (Grandin). **Education:** University of Tennessee, Chattanooga. **Spouse:** Peggy Jean Jones (m. 1970). **Children:** Farrar Jean Jones, Nicole Irene Grandin.

Prize: *Feature Photography,* 1977: *Chattanooga News-Free Press,* Chattanooga, TN: Chattanooga News-Free Press, 1976.

Career: Served in U.S. Army, 1967-70; Information Officer, U.S. Army, 1970-71; Staff Photographer, *Chattanooga (TN) News-Free Press,* 1971-80; Freelance photographer; Director of Media Services, Governor's Office; Owner, Robin Hood Photography, 1985-; President and Co-Publisher, Parker Hood Press, 1995-.

Selected Works: *The Tennesseans: A People and Their Land* (with Barry Parker), 1997. *Friends: Japanese and Tennesseans* (with Barry Parker), 1997. *The Tennesseans: A People Revisited* (with Barry Parker), 1997.

Other Awards: Centennial Distinguished Alumnus Award, University of Tennessee, Chattanooga, 1986.

For More Information: Leekley, Sheryle and John Leekley, *Moments: The Pulitzer Prize Photographs, Updated Version: 1942-1982,* New York: Crown Publishers, Inc., 1982: 116-117; *Chattanooga Free Press,* 30 June (1996).

Commentary: Robin Hood's photograph of a disabled Vietnam veteran holding a child close to him in his wheelchair captured the feelings of those present at an Armed Forces Day Parade.

Robin Hood is the only Tennessee man to win a Pulitzer Prize in photography. He has documented Tennessee for over 20 years, and his photograph of the east elevation of the state capitol was chosen to be on the United States Postal Service Commemorative stamp on Tennessee's statehood.

1978

J. Ross Baughman   406

Birth: May 7, 1953; Dearborn, MI. **Parents:** Charles T. Baughman and Patricia Jane (Hill). **Education:** Kent State University, OH: BA, cum laude. **Spouse:** Jonalyn Sue Schuon (m. 1987, div. 1995). **Children:** Henry.

Prize: *Feature Photography,* 1978: Associated Press, 1977.

Career: Photographer and Writer, *Lorain (OH) Journal,* 1974-77; Contract Photographer, Africa, Middle East, Associated Press, 1977-78; Co-Founder, Visions International, Incorporated, 1978; President, Visions Photo Group, 1978; Instructor, New School for Social Research (NY), 1979; Instructor, New York University, 1980-82; Program Director/Co-Founder, Focus Photography Symposiums, 1981-88; Adjunct Journalism Professor, University of Missouri, 1984-86.

Selected Works: *Graven Images: A Thematic Portfolio,* 1976. *Forbidden Images: A Secret Portfolio,* 1977. *Apart from the World,* 1997.

For More Information: *Lorain Journal,* 18 April (1978); *New York Times,* 18 April (1978): 28; Leekley, Sheryle and John Leekley, *Moments: The Pulitzer Prize Photographs, Updated Version: 1942-1982,* New York: Crown Publishers, Inc., 1982: 120-123; Rigsby, Gwendolyn Gezelle, "A History of Associated Press Pulitzer Prizes" (thesis), University of South Carolina, 1993.

Commentary: J. Ross Baughman's photographs of Rhodesian soldiers sparked controversy. Questions were raised about the amount of support given to the army before Baughman was allowed to go with them and take the photos.

1979

Boston Herald American   407

Founded: June 19, 1972.

Prize: *Feature Photography,* 1979: *Boston Herald American,* Boston, 1978.

Commentary: The entire staff of the *Boston Herald American* was awarded a Pulitzer Prize for its coverage of the blizzard that hit eastern Massachusetts on February 6, 7, and 8, 1978. They recorded history with their photographs of the devastation caused by nature. The 16 staff photographers were Kevin Cole (chief photographer), Mike Andersen, Paul Benoit, Dennis Brearley, Gene Dixon, Stanley Forman, Ted Gartland, Frank Hill, Bob Howard, Angela Kaloventzos, Ray Lussier, Roland Oxton, Leo Renahan, Dick Thomson, John Thompson, and M. Leo Tierney.

The *Boston Herald American,* a Hearst Newspaper, started publishing in June 1972. It was a merger of the former *Boston Herald Traveler* and the *Boston Record American.* Those papers themselves were mergers of former Boston newspapers. In 1982, the *Boston Herald American* became the *Boston Herald.*

1980

Erwin Harrison Hagler   408

Birth: August 7, 1947; Fort Worth, TX. **Parents:** Erwin Harrison Hagler and Alice V. (Harnbeck). **Education:** University of Texas: BArch. **Spouse:** Becky Ann Weatherly (m. 1977). **Children:** Casey, Cody, Katy Beth, Clay.

Prize: *Feature Photography,* 1980: *Dallas Times Herald,* Dallas: Dallas Times Herald, 1979.

Career: Staff Photographer, *Waco (TX) News-Tribune,* 1971-72; Staff Photographer, *Fort Worth (TX) Star-Telegram,* 1972-74; Staff Photographer, *Dallas (TX) Times-Herald,* 1974-88; Freelance photographer, 1988-.

Selected Works: *Where Texas Meets the Sky: A Coastal Portrait* (with Bryan Wooley), 1985.

Other Awards: Regional Photographer of the Year, National Press Photographers Association, 1972, 1974.

For More Information: *Dallas Times Herald,* 15 April (1980); Leekley, Sheryle and John Leekley, *Moments: The Pulitzer Prize Photographs, Updated Version: 1942-1982,* New York: Crown Publishers, Inc., 1982: 134-139.

Commentary: Erwin "Skeeter" Hagler's photographs are of the folk hero of the West, the cowboy. Many of those photographed still seem to live more in the 19th century than the 20th.

1981

Taro Michael Yamasaki 409

Birth: December 19, 1945; Detroit, MI. **Parents:** Minoru Yamasaki and Teruko (Hirashiki). **Education:** University of Michigan. **Spouse:** Married. **Children:** Two children.

Prize: *Feature Photography,* 1981: *Detroit Free Press,* December 14-20, Detroit, MI: Detroit Free Press, 1980.

Career: Photographer, New York City, 1968; Fashion Photographer's Assistant; Printer; Kindergarten Teacher; Photographer for Cesar Chavez's United Farm Workers, Denver, CO; Founder, Carpentry Company; Staff Photographer, *Detroit Free Press,* 1977-.

Selected Works: *Mariotti* (with others), 1988.

For More Information: *Detroit Free Press,* 14 April (1981): 1, 4; Leekley, Sheryle and John Leekley, *Moments: The Pulitzer Prize Photographs, Updated Version: 1942-1982,* New York: Crown Publishers, Inc., 1982: 144-149.

Commentary: Taro Yamasaki's winning photographic essays explored the lives and living conditions of inmates at the State Prison of Southern Michigan in Jackson. The prison is the largest walled jail in the world. There was a referendum to increase funding for prisons, but it was defeated. Five months later, a riot erupted at Jackson.

1982

John Henry White 410

Birth: March 18, 1945; Lexington, NC. **Parents:** Reid Ross White and Ruby Mae (Leverette). **Religion:** African Methodist Episcopalian. **Education:** Central Piedmont Community College, NC: AAS. **Spouse:** Emily Lee Miller (m. 1966). **Children:** Deborah, Angela, Ruby, John Henry.

Prize: *Feature Photography,* 1982: *Chicago Sun-Times,* Chicago: Chicago Sun-Times, 1981.

Career: Photographer, U.S. Marine Corps, 1966-68; Lab Technician, Tom Walters Photography, 1968-69; Press Photographer, *Chicago Daily News,* 1969-78; Volunteer Photography Teacher, Southside Art Center, Chicago, IL, 1970; Press Photographer, *Chicago Sun-Times,* 1978-; Instructor, Columbia College (IL), 1978-.

Selected Works: *This Man Bernardin* (with Eugene Kennedy), 1996. *The Final Journey of Joseph Cardinal Bernardin,* 1997.

Other Awards: National Press Photography Award, 1970. World Press Photography Award, 1971. Illinois Press Photographers Association, 1971, 1979, 1982. Feature Story Award, Picture of the Year Competition, 1975. Marshall Field Award, Newspaper Division of Field Enterprises, Inc., 1976. Photographer of the Year, Chicago Press Photographers Association, 1972-73, 1975, 1979. United Press International Award. Chicago Newspaper Guild Award. Inland Daily Press Association. Outstanding Photojournalist Award, Chicago Association of Black Journalists, 1981.

For More Information: *Chicago Sun-Times,* 13 April (1982): 1+; *Contemporary Authors, Volume 124,* Detroit: Gale Research Company, 1988.

Commentary: John Henry White won a Pulitzer Prize for a variety of photographs taken in 1981, including an Illinois Army National Guard unit singing while marching and a Chicago police officer searching for weapons at a housing project.

White bought his first camera with 50 cents and 10 Bazooka gum wrappers. He covered the major events of the life of Cardinal Joseph Bernardin of Chicago including the Cardinal's receiving the Presidential Medal of Freedom in 1996. White was a finalist for a Pulitzer Prize in 1981 and 1983.

1983

James Bruce Dickman 411

Birth: March 25, 1949; St. Louis, MO. **Parents:** Joseph Edward Dickman and Isabel Catherine (Brown). **Education:** University of Texas, Arlington. **Spouse:** Mary Kay Thomas (m. 1968, div.); Rebecca Lauren Skelton (m. 1983). **Children:** Kristi, Gavin.

Prize: *Feature Photography,* 1983: *Dallas Times-Herald,* Dallas: Dallas Times-Herald, 1982.

Career: Photographer, McKinney Job Corps, Texas, 1969-70; Photographer, *Dallas (TX) Times Herald,* 1970-; Freelance photographer.

Other Awards: World Press Photo of the Year, 1983.

Commentary: James Dickman made three trips to El Salvador in November 1981 and March 1982. He was there during the countrywide elections and he was among the first foreign photographers to see "El Playton," a hill of black lava rock that had become the dumping ground for over 60 bodies. His photographs were printed in his paper, the *Dallas Times Herald* on January 20 and July 18, 1982.

1984

Anthony Suau 412

Birth: October 16, 1956; Peoria, IL. **Parents:** Elio Suau and Elaine (Martin). **Education:** Rochester Institute of Technology, NY.

Prize: *Feature Photography,* 1984: *Denver Post,* Denver, CO: Denver Post, 1983.

Career: Staff Photographer, *Chicago Sun-Times,* 1979-81; Staff Photographer, *Denver (CO) Post,* 1981-84; Freelance Photojournalist, *Black Star,* 1984-; Contract Photographer, *Time* magazine.

Selected Works: *On a Deux Yeux de Trop: Avec les Refugies Rwandais, Goma, Zaire, 1994; Voir et Dire,* 1995.

Other Awards: Illinois Press Photographer of the Year, 1981. World Press Photo of the Year, 1987. Magazine Photographer of the Year, National Press Photographers Association, 1987-93.

Commentary: Anthony Suau was awarded a Pulitzer Prize for his photographs of the ravages of famine in Ethiopia and a photograph of a woman visiting her husband's grave on Memorial Day.

1985

Stan Grossfeld   413

Birth: December 20, 1951; Bronx, NY. **Parents:** Purroy Grossfeld and Mildred (Hadburg). **Education:** Rochester Institute of Technology, NY: BS. Boston University, MA: MJ.

Prize: *Spot News Photography,* 1984: *Boston Globe,* Boston: Boston Globe, 1983. *Feature Photography,* 1985: *Boston Globe,* Boston: Boston Globe, 1984.

Career: Staff Photographer, *Newark (NJ) Star-Ledger,* 1973-75; Staff Photographer, *Boston Globe,* 1975-82, Chief Photographer, *Boston Globe,* 1983-85, Director of Photography, *Boston Globe,* 1985-86, Associate Editor, *Boston Globe,* 1987-.

Selected Works: *Nantucket: The Other Season,* 1982. *The Eyes of the Globe: Twenty-Five Years of Photography from the Boston Globe,* 1985. *Two on the River* (with Will Haygood), 1986. *Whisper of Stars: A Siberian Journey,* 1988. *Lost Futures: Our Forgotten Children,* 1997.

Other Awards: Photographer of the Year Award, Boston Press Photographers' Association, 1979-81, 1984, 1985. Best Photographic Reporting from Abroad Award, Overseas Press Club of America, 1984. Humanitarian Award, 1985. Canon Photo Essayist Award, University of Missouri, Columbia, 1985. Gold Medal, Society of Newspaper Designers, 1985. World Hunger Media Award, 1986. Nieman Fellow, Harvard University, MA, 1991-92. Lowell Thomas Award for Best Travel Book. UNICEF Local Hero Award, 1996.

Commentary: Stan Grossfeld is a two-time winner of a photography Pulitzer Prize. His first was for his coverage and images of the war in Lebanon. His second prize was for his coverage of the famine in Ethiopia and of illegal aliens along the Mexico-United States border. He was a finalist for a Pulitzer Prize in 1994 and 1996.

Larry C. Price   414

Birth: February 23, 1954; Corpus Christi, TX. **Education:** Sam Houston State, TX. University of Texas. **Spouse:** Debbi M.

Prize: *Spot News Photography,* 1981: *Fort Worth Star-Telegram,* Fort Worth, TX: Fort Worth Star-Telegram, 1980. *Feature Photography,* 1985: *Philadelphia Inquirer,* Philadelphia, PA: Philadelphia Inquirer, 1984.

Career: Staff Photographer, college paper, *Daily Texan;* Staff Photographer, *El Paso (TX) Times,* 1977; Staff Photographer, *Fort Worth (TX) Star Telegram,* 1979-82; Staff Photographer, *Philadelphia (PA) Inquirer,* 1983-; Director of Photography, *Philadelphia (PA) Inquirer* Sunday magazine; Associate Editor for Photography, Graphics and Design, *Fort Worth (TX) Star-Telegram.*

For More Information: Leekley, Sheryle and John Leekley, *Moments: The Pulitzer Prize Photographs, Updated Version: 1942-1982,* New York: Crown Publishers, Inc., 1982: 140-143.

Commentary: Larry C. Price won his first Pulitzer Prize for his first foreign assignment. He went to Liberia because many Southern Baptist missionaries in Liberia studied at the Southwestern Baptist Theological Seminary in Fort Worth. He was the only American photographer to witness the execution by firing squad of 13 members of the previous government.

He won his second Pulitzer Prize for his coverage of the civil wars in Angola and El Salvador. He spent most of 1984 either in Africa or Central America. His photographs revealed how the atrocities of war had become a part of life. He had been nominated in the Spot News Photography category but was shifted to the Feature Photography category by the Pulitzer board.

1986

Tom Gralish   415

Birth Place: Mount Clemens, MI.

Prize: *Feature Photography,* 1986: *Philadelphia Inquirer,* Philadelphia, PA: Philadelphia Inquirer, 1985.

Career: Photographer, United Press International; Staff Photographer, *Las Vegas (NV) Valley Times;* Staff Photographer and Picture Editor, *Philadelphia (PA) Inquirer,* 1983-.

Commentary: Tom Gralish was 29 years old when he won a Pulitzer Prize for his series of photographs of the homeless in Philadelphia.

1987

David Charles Peterson   416

Birth: October 22, 1949; Kansas City, MO. **Parents:** John Edward Peterson and Florence Athene (Hobbs). **Education:** Kansas State University: BS. University of Kansas: BS. **Spouse:** Adele Mae Johnson. **Children:** Brian, Scott, Anna.

Prize: *Feature Photography,* 1987: *Des Moines Register,* Des Moines, IA: Des Moines Register, 1986.

Career: Photographer, *Topeka (KS) Capital-Journal,* 1975-77; Staff Photographer, *Des Moines (IA) Register,* 1977-.

Other Awards: Regional Photographer of the Year, 1979-81. National Press Photographers Association/Nikon Documentary Sabbatical Grant, 1986.

For More Information: *American Photographer,* 20:1 (January 1988): 60-68.

Commentary: David Peterson used his National Press Photographers Association / Nikon Documentary Sabbatical grant to chronicle the farm crisis in middle America. He broke the sabbatical into three month-long segments, one in spring, summer, and fall, to cover the growing cycle. He captured the desperation of the times by photographing a family forced to sell their land, a boarded-up and nearly deserted town, and a wife visiting her husband's grave after he committed suicide.

1988

Michel duCille   417

Birth: January 24, 1956; Kingston, Jamaica. **Parents:** Frank Olivier duCille and Loleta (duMont). **Religion:** Presbyterian. **Education:** Indiana University: BA.

Ohio University: MS. **Spouse:** Christine Clarke (m. 1982). **Children:** Leighton; Lesley Anne.

Prize: *Spot News Photography,* 1986: *Miami Herald,* Miami, FL: Miami Herald, 1985. *Feature Photography,* 1988: *Miami Herald,* Miami, FL: Miami Herald, 1987.

Career: Photo Staff member, *Miami (FL) Herald,* 1981-; Photography Editor, *Washington (DC) Post;* Board of directors of region 4 of the National Press Photographers Association.

Other Awards: Ross Hazeltine Travel Grant, 1981. Best in Show, Atlanta Photojournalism Seminar, GA, 1987. Feature Picture Story Award, Atlanta Photojournalism Seminar, GA, 1987. Distinguished Service Award, Society of Professional Journalists. Photojournalism Award, National Association of Black Journalists, 1987. Journalist of the Year, National Association of Black Journalists, 1989.

For More Information: *Miami Herald,* 18 April (1986): A1; *Miami Herald,* 1 April (1988): A1.

Commentary: Michel duCille and Carol Guzy won a photography Pulitzer Prize for their coverage of the volcanic eruption of Nevado del Ruiz and its devastating effect in Colombia. Ducille's second Pulitzer Prize was for his chronicle of the decay and restoration of a housing project that had been overrun by users of the drug crack.

1989

Manny Crisostomo   418

Birth: November 28, 1958; Guam. **Education:** University of Guam. University of Missouri.

Prize: *Feature Photography,* 1989: *Detroit Free Press,* Detroit, MI: Detroit Free Press, 1988.

Career: Staff member, *Columbia Missourian;* Intern, *Jackson (MI) Citizen Patriot;* Intern, *Detroit Free Press;* Staff Photographer, *Detroit Free Press.*

Selected Works: *Main Street: A Portrait of Small-Town Michigan* (with Marcia Joy Prouse), 1986. *Moving Pictures: A Look at Detroit from High Atop the People Mover,* 1987. *Legacy of Guam,* 1991.

Other Awards: Michigan Photographer of the Year, Michigan Press Photographers' Association, 1987-88. Robert F. Kennedy Journalism Award. Picture of the Year Award, University of Missouri / National Press Photographers Association.

Commentary: Manny Crisostomo's 12-page article, "A Class Act, The Life and Times of Southwestern High School," examined the violence that faces young people in Detroit. He took photographs, interviewed students, and wrote the introduction to the story.

1990

David Carl Turnley   419
Birth: June 22, 1955; Fort Wayne, IN. **Parents:** William Lloyd Turnley and Elizabeth Ann (Protsman). **Education:** University of Michigan: BA. Sorbonne University, Paris, France. **Spouse:** Karin Nicolette Louw (m. 1989).

Prize: *Feature Photography,* 1990: *Detroit Free Press,* Detroit, MI: Detroit Free Press, 1989.

Career: Staff Photographer, *Northville (MI) Sliger* Home Newspapers, 1978-80; Photographer, *Detroit Free Press,* 1980-; Photographer, South Africa, *Detroit Free Press,* 1985-87; Photographic Correspondent, Paris, France, *Detroit Free Press,* 1987-.

Selected Works: *Why Are They Weeping? South Africans under Apartheid,* 1988. *Beijing Spring,* 1989. *Moments of Revolution: Eastern Europe,* 1990. *The Russian Heart: Days of Crisis and Hope in the Soviet Union,* 1992. *David and Peter Turnley: In Times of War and Peace,* 1996.

Other Awards: Overseas Press Club Award, 1982, 1984-85, 1991. Canon Essay Award, University of Missouri/National Press Photographers Association, 1985. Oscar Barnack Award, World Press Photo Foundation, 1985. Picture of the Year Award, World Press Photo Foundation, 1988, 1991. Robert Capa Gold Medal, Overseas Press Club, 1990. Nieman Fellow, Harvard University, MA, 1997-98. Honorary Degree, Keele University, England, 1991.

For More Information: *People,* 7 May (1990): 197; *The Pulitzer Prizes 1990,* New York: Simon & Schuster, 1990: 276-288.

Commentary: David C. Turnley, whose twin brother is also a photographer, documented a year of revolutions. He took photographs of the suppression of the democratic movement in China, the overthrow of the Ceausescu government in Romania, and the destruction of the Berlin Wall. He was a finalist for a Pulitzer Prize in 1992 and 1996.

1991

William D. Snyder
Full entry appears as **#382** under "Explanatory Journalism," 1989.

1992

John Kaplan   420
Birth: August 21, 1959; Wilmington, DE. **Parents:** Ralph Benjamin Kaplan and Ruth Jillya (Denkin). **Education:** Ohio University: BJ.

Prize: *Feature Photography,* 1992: *Block Newspapers,* Toledo, OH: Block Newspapers, 1991.

Career: Staff member, college paper, *The Post;* Photojournalist, *Spokane (WA) Review / Chronicle,* 1983-84; Photojournalist, *Pittsburgh (PA) Press,* 1984-90; Visiting Lecturer, Bradley University (IL), 1989; Founder and Director, Pittsburgh (PA) Media Alliance, 1990-; Photojournalist, *Pittsburgh (PA) Post-Gazette,* 1990-92; Special Correspondent, *Block Newspapers,* 1992-94; Adjunct Professor, Syracuse University (NY), London Campus, 1993; Adjunct Professor, University of Pittsburgh (PA) 1996-.

Selected Works: *Mom and Me,* 1996.

Other Awards: Regional Photographer of the Year, 1985-89. Robert F. Kennedy Journalism Award, 1989. Nikon Documentary Sabbatical Award, 1990. National Photographer of the Year, Pictures of the Year Competition, 1992. *Matrix* Magazine Award, Women in Communications, 1992. Distinguished Graduate Award, Ohio University, 1993. Hall of Fame, Ohio University College of Communications, 1993.

For More Information: *New York Times,* 8 April (1992): B6; *New York Times,* 31 May (1992): Section 9, 7.

Commentary: John Kaplan was awarded a Pulitzer Prize for his photographic essays on the diverse lifestyles of seven 21-year olds. He spent up to three weeks with each individual, capturing the photographs he wanted. A $15,000 Nikon Sabbatical grant allowed him to spend the extraordinary amount of time pursuing this project.

1993

Associated Press   421
Founded: 1848.

Prize: *Spot News Photography,* 1992: Associated Press, 1991. *Feature Photography,* 1993: Associated Press, 1992. *Feature Photography,* 1995: Associated Press, 1994.

Other Awards: Staff of the Associated Press have won 34 individual Pulitzer Prizes.

For More Information: Gramling, Oliver, *AP: The Story of News,* New York: Farrar and Rinehart, Inc., 1940; *Editor & Publisher,* 128:27 (8 July 1995): 18.

Commentary: The Associated Press began in May 1848 when ten men representing six New York newspapers met to form a cooperative news-gathering association. In 1998, 150 years after it was organized, the Associated Press has 237 bureaus, 144 in the United States and 93 bureaus in 71 other countries. 7,700 daily and weekly newspapers, radio stations, and television stations in the United States receive information from the Associated Press. It also has

8,500 international subscibers for its news and photographs.

Members of the photographic staff of the Associated Press won a Pulitzer Prize in 1992 for their pictures of the attempted coup in Russia and the collapse of the Soviet Union. The staff cited for the award included Liu Heung-Shing, Olga Shalygin, Czarek Sokolowski, Boris Yurchenko, and Alexander Zemlianichenko.

In 1993, a team of photographers from across the United States won a Feature Photography Pulitzer Prize for its coverage of the 1992 presidential campaign. The team members included Scott Applewhite, Richard Drew, Greg Gibson, David Longstreath, Doug Mills, Marcy Nighswander, Amy Sancetta, Stephen Savoia, Reed Saxon, and Lynn Sladky. It was the third time since prizes were awarded in photography that the Associated Press had won three years in a row.

In 1995, for the fourth time in five years, the Associated Press won a Pulitzer Prize in photography. The winning photographers chronicled the devastating civil war between the Hutus and the Tutsis in Rwanda. The team of photographers included Jacqueline Artz, Javier Bauluz, Jean-Marc Bouju, and Karsten Thielker.

1994

Kevin Carter   422

Birth: September 13, 1960; Johannesburg, South Africa. **Death:** July 27, 1994. **Parents:** Jimmy Carter and Roma. **Children:** Megan.

Prize: *Feature Photography,* 1994.

Career: Sports and News Photographer, *Sunday Express,* 1983-84; Photographer, Johannesburg, South Africa Star, 1984-87; Stringer, South Africa Associated Press, 1988-89; Chief Photographer, Johannesburg Bureau, *The Sunday Tribune,* 1989-90; Head of Photographic Department, *Rand South Africa Daily Mail,* 1990; Photo Editor, *Rand South Africa Weekly Mail,* 1993; Photography Editor, *Mail and Guardian;* Photography Stringer, *Reuters;* Freelance photographer.

Other Awards: Ilford Photo Press Award. News Picture of the Year, 1993.

For More Information: *Columbia Journalism Review,* 33:4 (November / December 1994): 57-60; *Los Angeles Times,* July 30, 1994: 24; *Time,* 144 (September 12, 1994): 70-73; *Johannesburg Weekly Mail and Guardian,* 10:30 (July 29-August 4, 1994): 3.

Commentary: Kevin Carter won a Pulitzer Prize for a 1993 photograph of a small Sudanese girl making her way to a feeding center. The photo captured the bleak reality of the famine in the country; a vulture watched over her as she made her way.

1995

Associated Press

Full entry appears as #421 under "Feature Photography," 1993.

1996

Stephanie Welsh   423

Birth: June 27, 1973; Quantico, VA. **Parents:** Donald Welsh and Susan (Stevens). **Education:** Syracuse University, NY.

Prize: *Feature Photography,* 1996: Newhouse News Service, 1995.

Career: Intern, Syracuse Newspapers; Photography Intern, *Nairobi Daily Nation,* 1994; Photography Intern, *Palm Beach (FL) Post,* 1996; Staff Photographer, *Palm Beach (FL) Post,* 1996-.

Other Awards: Exceptional Merit Media Award, National Women's Political Caucus, 1997.

For More Information: *Editor & Publisher,* 129 (21 September 1996): 12-13; *News Photographer,* 51:7 (July 1996): 24-27.

Commentary: Stephanie Welsh took a break from college and traveled to Africa. She was 21 years old and did not know the language, but she got a job on a local paper. Her photographic series documents the rite of female circumcision in Kenya. She was 22 years old when she won her Pulitzer Prize in 1996.

1997

Alexander Vadimovich Zemlianichenko   424

Birth: May 7, 1950; Saratov, Russia. **Parents:** Vadim Zemlianichenko and Nadezhoa (Mechkovskata). **Education:** Saratov Technical Institute. Juilliard School of Music, NY. **Spouse:** Larissa Z. (m. 1980?). **Children:** Alexander.

Prize: *Feature Photography,* 1997: Associated Press, 1996.

Career: Photographer, Moscow, *Yomsolmolskaya Pravda* Newspaper, 1980-84; Photographer, Moscow, *Soviet Union Magazine,* 1984-88; Photographer, Moscow, *Motherland Magazine,* 1988-90; Stringer, Moscow, Associated Press, 1988-90; Photographer, Associated Press, Moscow, 1990-.

Other Awards: National Headliners Club Award, 1994, 1997. Picture of the Year Award, University of Missouri National Press Photographers Association, 1994. Associated Press Managing Editors Award, 1996. World Press Photography Award, 1997.

Commentary: Alexander Zemlianichenko's winning photograph is of Russian leader Boris Yeltsin dancing at a rock concert. Zemlianichenko was also part of the Associated Press group of photographers who won a Pulitzer Prize in 1992.

1998

Clarence Williams   425

Birth: January 22, 1967; Philadelphia, PA. **Education:** Temple University, PA: BA.

Prize: *Feature Photography,* 1998: *Los Angeles Times,* Los Angeles, CA: *Los Angeles Times,* 1997.

Career: Photography Intern, *Philadelphia (PA) Tribune,* 1992-93; Summer Photography Intern, *York (PA) Daily Record,* 1993; Staff Photographer, *Reston (VA) Times Community Newspapers,* 1993-94; Staff Photographer, *METPRO,* 1994; Temporary Staff Photographer, *Los Angeles Times,* 1995-96; Staff Photographer, *Los Angeles Times,* 1996-.

Other Awards: Kay Kreighbaum Photojournalist Award, 1992. Illustration Award, National Press Photographers Association National Monthly Clip Contest, 1995. Issues Reporting Award, Pictures of the Year/National Press Photographers Association, 1996. National Headliners Club Award, 1996. Harry Chapin Media Award, 1998. Robert F. Kennedy Journalism Award, 1998.

For More Information: *Los Angeles Times,* 15 April (1998): A1, A15.

Commentary: Clarence Williams was awarded a Pulitzer Prize in Feature Photography for his "powerful images documenting the plight of young children with parents addicted to alcohol and drugs." Williams's photographs accompanied a two-part series titled "Orphans of Addiction," published in November 1997.

His photographs sparked some controversy over the idea of the non-intrusiveness of a journalist or a photographer capturing a story and the need to intervene in the lives of children at risk. Within days of publication, the children covered in the series were taken into protective services.

Feature Writing

1979

Jon Daniel Franklin

Full entry appears as **#374** under "Explanatory Journalism," 1985.

1980

Madeleine H. Blais   426

Birth: August 25, 1947; Holyoke, MA. **Parents:** Raymond Joseph Blais and Maureen (Shea). **Education:** College of New Rochelle, NY: BA. Columbia University, NY: MS. **Spouse:** John Katzenbach. **Children:** Nicholas, Justine.

Prize: *Feature Writing,* 1980: *Miami Herald,* "Zepp's Last Stand," Miami, FL: Miami Herald, 1979.

Career: Freelance Suburban Reporter, *Boston Globe,* 1970-71; Boston Bureau, *Women's Wear Daily;* Writer, *Trenton (NJ) Times,* 1974-76; Freelance Writer, *Miami (FL) Herald;* Staff Writer, *Miami (FL) Herald Tropic* Magazine, 1979-87; Columnist, *Newsday (NY),* 1989-1993; Associate Professor of Journalism, University of Massachusetts, Amherst, 1987-.

Selected Works: *They Say You Can't Have a Baby: The Dilemma of Infertility,* 1979. *The Heart Is an Instrument: Portraits in Journalism,* 1992. *In These Girls, Hope Is a Muscle,* 1995.

Other Awards: Nieman Fellow, Harvard University, MA, 1985-86. Honorary Degree, Springfield College, MA, 1996.

For More Information: *Contemporary Authors, Volume 104,* Detroit: Gale Research Company, 1982; Belford, Barbara, *Brilliant Bylines: A Biographical Anthology of Notable Newspaperwomen in America,* New York: Columbia University Press, 1986: 350-368; *Newsday,* 4 February (1989): Part 2, 2.

Commentary: Madeleine Blais's writing for the *Miami Herald* won the Feature Writing award in 1980. Her winning article was about a World War I soldier who was a conscientious objector and had been discharged with dishonor, and his fight to have his military record cleared and his discharge changed to honorable. Her articles on families and individual were frequently cover stories in the paper's Sunday magazine. She has also written a column on mothering that appeared in *New York Newsday.* She was a finalist for a Pulitzer Prize in 1981.

1981

Teresa Suzanne Carpenter   427

Birth: August 1, 1948; Independence, MO. **Parents:** Rawlin Mack Carpenter and Gloria Lee Harvey (Thompson). **Education:** Graceland College, IA: BA. University of Missouri: MA.

Prize: *Feature Writing,* 1981: *Village Voice,* "Death of a Playmate," New York City, NY: Village Voice, 1980.

Career: Senior Editor, Princeton (NJ), *New Jersey Monthly,* 1976-79; Freelance journalist, NY, 1979-81; Staff Writer, *Village Voice (NY),* 1981-.

Selected Works: *Missing Beauty: A True Story of Murder and Obsession,* 1988. *Mob Girl: A Woman's Life in the Underworld,* 1992. *Without a Doubt* (with Marcia Clark), 1997.

Other Awards: Fairchild Fellow, University of Missouri, 1975-76. Page One Award, New York Newspaper Guild, 1981. Front Page Award, New York Newspaperwomen's Club, 1981. Clarion Award, Women in Communications, 1982, 1986.

For More Information: *Chicago Tribune,* 27 June (1988): Tempo, 3.

Commentary: Teresa Carpenter was awarded a Pulitzer Prize after the *Washington Post* gave back the award that had been given to Janet Cooke because Cooke's story was found (after the prize had been awarded) to have been fictitious. Carpenter had originally been the jury's recommendation, but the Pulitzer board overruled the jury and gave the prize to Cooke.

Carpenter wrote on three murders, one of which was that of Dorothy Stratten, a Playboy Playmate of the Year. The television movie *Star 80* was based on her story.

1982

Saul Pett   428
Birth: March 18, 1918; Passaic, NJ. **Death:** June 13, 1993. **Parents:** Nathan Pett and Ida (Litsky). **Education:** University of Missouri: BA. **Spouse:** Lenore Green (m. 1941, died 1978). **Children:** Kathy, Amy, Sukey.

Prize: *Feature Writing,* 1982: Associated Press, 1981.

Career: Copyboy, *New York Daily News,* 1940; Detroit (MI), Chicago (IL), New York (NY), International News Service, 1940-46; Features Department, New York (NY), Associated Press, 1946-64; Special Correspondent, New York (NY), Associated Press, 1964-89; Special Correspondent, Washington (DC), Associated Press, 1989-91.

Selected Works: *The Instant It Happened* (with Hal Buell), 1972. *The Torch Is Passed: The Associated Press Story of the Death of a President,* 1963. *Lightning out of Israel: The Six-Day War in the Middle East* (with others), 1967. *An American Ordeal: The Deception and Descent of Richard M. Nixon,* 1975.

Other Awards: Honor Medal, University of Missouri, 1956. Distinguished Writing Award, American Society of Newspaper Editors. General Reporting Award, Sigma Delta Chi, 1963. Overseas Press Club Award, 1964. Top Performance Award, Associated Press Managing Editors, 1981.

For More Information: Rigsby, Gwendolyn Gezelle, "A History of Associated Press Pulitzer Prize" (thesis), University of South Carolina, 1993; *Los Angeles Times,* 14 June (1993): A16; *Washington Post,* 14 June (1993): B6.

Commentary: Saul Pett's first major story was of an automobile/train crash that killed seven teenagers in 1959. The story was 3,500 words long. Because of its length, it was distributed by mail by the Associated Press rather than by wire. Pett wrote intensely researched stories that were extremely readable. His winning story is an 8,571-word description of the federal bureaucracy. The story's dateline was June 14, 1981.

1983

Nan Robertson   429

Birth: July 11, 1926; Chicago, IL. **Parents:** Frank William Robertson and Eva (Morrish). **Religion:** Episcopalian. **Education:** Northwestern University, IL: BS. **Spouse:** Allyn Zelton Blum (m. 1950, div. 1961); Stan Levey (m. 1961, died 1971).

Prize: *Feature Writing,* 1983: *New York Times,* "Toxic Shock," September 19, New York: New York Times, 1982.

Career: Reporter, Copyreader, *Stars and Stripes,* 1948-49; Fashion publicist, 1950; Correspondent, Germany, *Milwaukee (WI) Journal,* 1951-53; Feature Writer and Columnist, Germany, *New York Herald-Tribune,* 1952-53; Reporter, Copyreader, London (England), *American Daily,* 1953-54; Fashion Correspondent, London (England), *New York Times,* 1954; General Assignment and Women's News Department, *New York Times,* 1955-63; Correspondent, Washington (DC), *New York Times,* 1963-72; European Correspondent, *New York Times,* 1972-75; Living/Style Staff member, *New York Times,* 1975-82; Cultural News Staff member, *New York Times,* 1983-88; Visiting Fellow, Duke University (NC), 1988; Josephine B. and Newton N. Minow Visiting Professor in Communications, Northwestern University (IL), 1992; Eugene L. Roberts Visiting Professor, University of Maryland, College Park, 1994.

Selected Works: *Getting Better: Inside Alcoholics Anonymous,* 1988. *The Girls in the Balcony: Women, Men, and the New York Times,* 1992. *Under the Influence: 11 Million Americans Are Hooked on Alcohol, 76 Million Have an Alcoholic in Their Family: Who Gets Hurt? How Can We Stop It?,* 1992.

Other Awards: Feature Writing Award, New York Newspaper Women's Club, 1962. Best Feature of 1980, Front Page Award, Newswomen's Club of New York, 1981. Fellow, MacDowell Colony, 1981, 1983. Page One Award, Newspaper Guild of New York, 1983. Woodrow Wilson National Fellow, 1983. Francis E. Willard Award, Alpha Phi, 1984. Merit Award, Northwestern Alumni Association, 1988. Alumnae Award, Alumnae of Northwestern University, IL, 1991. Lifetime Achievement Award, International Women's Media Foundation, 1993. Honorary Degree, Northwestern University, IL, 1992.

For More Information: *People,* December 13, 1982: 95; *New York Times,* April 19, 1983: B4; *Contemporary Authors, Volume 121,* Detroit: Gale Research Company, 1987.

Commentary: Nan Robertson was the third woman on the staff of the *New York Times* to win a Pulitzer Prize. Her winning story is of her own experience after an attack of Toxic Shock Syndrome that made her deathly ill. Her story attracted attention to the then little-known disease.

1984

Peter Mark Rinearson   430

Birth: August 4, 1954; Seattle, WA. **Parents:** Peter Morley Rinearson and Jeannette Irene (Love). **Education:** University of Washington. **Spouse:** Jill Chan (m. 1991).

Prize: *Feature Writing,* 1984: *Seattle Times,* "Making It Fly," Seattle, WA: Seattle Times, 1983.

Career: Editor, *Redmond (WA) Sammamish Valley News,* 1975-76; Reporter, *Seattle (WA) Times,* 1976-79; Political Reporter, *Seattle (WA) Times,* 1979-81; Aerospace Writer, *Seattle (WA) Times,* 1982-84; Asian Correspondent, *Seattle (WA) Times,* 1985-86; President, Alki Software Corporation, 1990-; President, Raster Ranch, Ltd., 1995-.

Selected Works: *Word Processing Power with Microsoft Word,* 1985. *Microsoft Word Style Sheets* (with JoAnne Woodcock), 1987. *Quick Reference Guide to Microsoft Word for the IBM PC,* 1988. *Quick Reference Guide to Microsoft Word 5.0,* 1989. *Microsoft Word Companion Disk,* 1989. *Running Microsoft Word 5.5,* 1991. *The Road Ahead* (with Bill Gates), 1995. *A Genealogy of the Reyniersen Family* (with Arthur P. Rynearson), 1997.

Other Awards: Special Paul Myhre Award, University of Missouri/J.C. Penney Newspaper Awards, 1983. Distinguished Writing Award, American Society of Newspaper Editors, 1984. Lowell Thomas Travel Writing Award, Society of American Travel Writers Foundation, 1984. John Hancock Award, 1985. U.S. Japan Leadership Program Fellow, Japan Society, 1988.

For More Information: *New York Times,* 17 April (1984): B4.

Commentary: Peter Rinearson wrote about the development of the Boeing 757. He had just started the aerospace beat at the *Seattle Times* and undertook the story to better understand the making of a plane. He described the process of the 757 from the decision to manufacture, the compromises in its development, and the complexities of the process. Rinearson later left journalism to work in the publishing industry.

1985

Alice Steinbach   431

Birth Place: Baltimore, MD. **Education:** University of London, England. **Spouse:** Irvin Steinbach (m., div.). **Children:** Andrew, Samuel.

Prize: *Feature Writing,* 1985: *Baltimore Sun,* "A Boy of Unusual Vision," Baltimore, MD: Baltimore Sun, 1984.

Career: Director, Public Information, Baltimore Museum of Art, 1976-81; Feature Writer, *Baltimore (MD) Sun,* 1981-; Columnist, *Baltimore (MD) Sun;* Freelance writer.

Selected Works: *The Miss Dennis School of Writing and Other Lessons from a Women's Life,* 1996.

Other Awards: Best Feature Story Award, Chesapeake Associated Press, 1985, 87. Quality of Writing Award, United Press International, 1987.

For More Information: *New York Times,* 25 April (1985): B10; Ricchiardi, Sherry and Virginia Young, *Women on Deadline: A Collection of America's Best,* Ames: Iowa State University Press, 1991: 53-70.

Commentary: Alice Steinbach's story about the life of Calvin Stanley, a blind 10-year-old, won her the 1985 Feature Writing Pulitzer Prize. She spent over a month researching the project and one week writing the story.

1986

John Roswell Camp   432

Birth: February 23, 1944; Cedar Rapids, IA. **Parents:** Roswell Sandford Camp and Anne (Barron). **Religion:** Roman Catholic. **Education:** University of Iowa: BA. University of Iowa: MA. **Spouse:** Susan Lee Jones. **Children:** Roswell, Emily.

Prize: *Feature Writing,* 1986: *St. Paul Pioneer Press Dispatch,* "Life on the Land: An American Farm Family," St. Paul, MN: St. Paul Pioneer Press Dispatch, 1985.

Career: Freelance Writer, college paper, *Daily Iowan;* Served in U.S. Army, 1966-68; General Assignment Reporter, *Cape Girardeau (MO) Southeast Missourian,* 1968-69; Reporter, *Miami (FL) Herald,*

1971-78; Feature Writer, *St. Paul (MN) Pioneer Press,* 1978-80; Columnist, General Reporter, *St. Paul (MN) Pioneer Press,* 1980-89; Writer.

Selected Works: *Great Dakota Conflict* (with others), 1987. *The Eye and the Heart: Watercolors of John Stuart Ingle,* 1988. *Plastic Surgery: The Kindest Cuts,* 1989. *The Fool's Run,* 1989. *Rules of Prey,* 1989. *Shadow Prey,* 1990. *Eyes of Prey,* 1991. *The Empress File,* 1991. *Silent Prey,* 1992. *Winter Prey,* 1993. *Night Prey,* 1994. *Mind Prey,* 1995. *Sudden Prey,* 1996. *The Night Crew,* 1997.

Other Awards: Distinguished Writing Award, American Society of Newspaper Editors, 1986.

For More Information: *Contemporary Authors, Volume 138,* Detroit: Gale Research Company, 1993; *Minneapolis Star-Tribune,* 8 May (1995): Books and Games, 10; *Newsday,* 11 April (1996): B3.

Commentary: John Camp won a Pulitzer Prize for his examination of the farm crisis and life on the land. He was a finalist for a Prize in 1980 for a series of articles on Native Americans. He left journalism in 1989 to pursue writing fiction fulltime. He has had several bestselling novels that he wrote under the pseudonym John Sandford.

1987

Stephen M. Twomey   433

Birth: May 30, 1951; Niles, MI. **Parents:** Michael Twomey and Mary Lou (Sigler). **Education:** Northwestern University, IL. **Spouse:** Kathleen Carroll (m. 1985). **Children:** Nicholas.

Prize: *Feature Writing,* 1987: *Philadelphia Inquirer,* Philadelphia, PA: Philadelphia Inquirer, 1986.

Career: Reporter, Education Writer, Labor Reporter, West Coast Correspondent *Philadelphia (PA) Inquirer,* 1973-83; Correspondent, Paris (France), *Philadelphia (PA) Inquirer,* 1983-1987; Reporter, *Philadelphia (PA) Inquirer,* 1987-; Staff Writer, *Washington (DC) Post,* 1989-1991; Columnist, *Washington (DC) Post,* 1991-.

Other Awards: Chesapeake Associated Press Editor Award, 1994. Maryland-Delaware-DC Press Association Award, 1993-94.

Commentary: Steve Twomey, who was 35 when he won his Pulitzer Prize, profiled life aboard *America,* a giant aircraft carrier. He wrote about daily life for the personnel and questioned the value of spending half a million dollars a day to operate the ship. Twomey is currently a columnist for the Washington Post.

1988

Jacqueline Marie Banaszynski   434

Birth: April 17, 1952; Pulaski, WI. **Parents:** Eugene Francis Banaszynski and Ethel Marie (McGillivray). **Education:** Marquette University, WI: BA, magna cum laude.

Prize: *Feature Writing,* 1988: *St. Paul Pioneer Press Dispatch,* "AIDS in the Heartland," St. Paul, MN: St. Paul Pioneer Press Dispatch, 1987.

Career: Reporter / Editor, *Pulaski (WI) News;* Reporter, college paper, *Marquette Tribune;* Intern, Boston (MA) Bureau, *Wall Street Journal,* 1973; Intern, *Indianapolis (IN) Star;* Reporter, *Janesville (WI) Gazette, Duluth (MN) News-Tribune, Eugene (OR) Register-Guard, Minneapolis (MN) Star and Tribune;* Labor, Workplace Beat Reporter, *St. Paul (MN) Pioneer Press Dispatch,* 1984-85; Special Projects Reporter and Feature Writer, *St. Paul Pioneer Press Dispatch,* 1985-; Editor, *St. Paul Pioneer Press Dispatch,* ?-1994; Senior Projects Editor, *Portland (OR) Oregonian,* 1994-.

Other Awards: Pulliam Fellowship, *Indianapolis Star,* 1974. Reporter of the Year, St. Paul Pioneer Press and Dispatch Executive Editor's Awards, 1985. Gene O'Brien Award, Minnesota Press Club, 1986. Society of Professional Journalists, 1987.

For More Information: Ricchiardi, Sherry, and Virginia Young, *Women on Deadline: A Collection of America's Best,* Ames: Iowa State University Press, 1991: 23-51.

Commentary: Jacqui Banaszynski told the story of two Minnesota men as they were dealing with life with AIDS.

She began her career in journalism during high school. Her school published her community's paper. She was a finalist for the Pulitzer Prize in 1986 for her reporting of the African famine.

1989

David Alan Zucchino   435

Birth: November 14, 1951; McPherson, KS. **Parents:** Ernest Joseph Zucchino and Maxine Loree (Jones). **Education:** University of North Carolina: BA. **Spouse:** Kacey Anne Chapp (m. 1981). **Children:** Adrien, Emily, Natalie.

Prize: *Feature Writing,* 1989: *Philadelphia Inquirer,* "Being Black in South Africa," Philadelphia, PA: Philadelphia Inquirer, 1988.

Career: Reporter, *Raleigh (NC) News and Observer,* 1973-78; Reporter, *Detroit Free Press,* 1978-80; Foreign Correspondent, *Philadelphia (PA) Inquirer,* 1980-; Middle East Correspondent, *Philadelphia (PA) Inquirer,* 1982-84; Africa Correspondent, *Philadelphia (PA) Inquirer,* 1986-1990; Staff Writer, *Philadelphia (PA) Inquirer,* 1990-1995; Foreign Editor, *Philadelphia (PA) Inquirer,*.

Selected Works: *Myth of the Welfare Queen: A Pulitzer Prize-Winning Journalist's Portrait of Women on the Line,* 1997.

Other Awards: American Society of Newspaper Editors, 1985. Overseas Press Club Award, 1989. International Print Reporting Award, National Association of Black Journalists, 1989.

For More Information: *Philadelphia Inquirer,* 31 March (1989): 1A, 4A.

Commentary: David Zucchino's series on "Being Black in South Africa" was moved from the International Reporting category to the Feature Writing category by the Pulitzer Prize board. His nine-part series studied the lives of blacks in South Africa. His reporting included the indigent as well as the rich and powerful. Zucchino did not know his paper had nominated him until he received a call from the *Inquirer*'s foreign editor to tell him he won. He was a finalist for a Pulitzer Prize in 1985 for his dispatches from Lebanon and in 1995 for a series of stories about the history and impact of violence in America.

1990

David Stephen Curtin   436

Birth: December 18, 1955; Kansas City, MO. **Parents:** Gerald Curtin and Nadine (Pemberton). **Religion:** Methodist. **Education:** University of Colorado: BS.

Prize: *Feature Writing,* 1990: *Colorado Springs Gazette Telegraph,* "Adam & Megan: A Story of One Family's Courage," January 8, Colorado Springs, CO: Colorado Springs Gazette Telegraph, 1989.

Career: Part-Time Sportswriter and City Reporter, *Littleton (CO) Independent,* 1975-77; Sportswriter and City Reporter, *Boulder (CO) Daily Camera,* 1977-78; Sportswriter and Photographer, *Greeley (CO) Tribune,* 1977-81; Police Reporter and Photographer, *Greeley (CO) Tribune,* 1981-84; General Assignment Reporter and Photographer, *Durango (CO) Herald,* 1984-87; Police and Assignment Reporter, *Colorado Springs (CO) Gazette-Telegraph,* 1987-97; Journalism Instructor, University of Colorado, Colorado Springs; Staff Writer, *Denver (CA) Post,* 1997-.

Selected Works: *Colorado Springs: Rocky Mountain Majesty* (with Rob Lynde), 1995.

Other Awards: Greeley Colorado Press Club Awards, 1979-80, 1983. Inland Daily Press Association Award, 1986. Colorado Society of Professional Journalists Award, 1990.

For More Information: *The Pulitzer Prizes 1990,* New York: Simon & Schuster, 1990: 379-404; *New York Times,* April 13, 1990: A17.

Commentary: Dave Curtain won a Pulitzer Prize in Feature Writing for his account of a family and their lives after several of them were burned in an explosion. He has worked at several Colorado papers and has taught journalism at the University of Colorado.

1991

Sheryl Teresa James   437

Birth: October 7, 1951; Detroit, MI. **Parents:** Reese Louis James and Dava Helen (Bryant). **Religion:** Roman Catholic. **Education:** Eastern Michigan University: BS. **Spouse:** Eric Torgeir Vigmostad (m. 1974). **Children:** Teresa, Kelsey.

Prize: *Feature Writing,* 1991: *St. Petersburg Times,* "A Gift Abandoned," February 18-21, St. Petersburg, FL: St. Petersburg Times, 1990.

Career: Writer, *City Magazine* in Lansing, Michigan, 1979-82; Feature Writer, *Greensboro (NC) News and Record,* 1982-86; Feature Writer, *St. Petersburg (FL) Times,* 1986-91; Staff Writer, *Detroit Free Press,* 1991-.

Other Awards: Penney-Missouri Award, University of Missouri/J.C. Penney, 1985. Feature Writing Award, Florida Society Newspaper Editors, 1991. Alumna Achievement Award, Eastern Michigan University, 1992.

For More Information: *St. Petersburg Times,* April 10, 1991: A1; *St. Petersburg Times,* July 15, 1992: B3.

Commentary: Sheryl James's winning four-part series was about abandoned babies in Florida. She followed the story for several months, from the time Judy Pemberton left her infant under an oak tree to the investigators' search for the mother and the trial of Pemberton for abandonment. James spent eight months working on the story. After she won the Pulitzer Prize, the *St. Petersburg Times* reprinted the series on April 14, 1991. James was a Pulitzer finalist in 1992 for a series of stories about organ transplants.

1992

Howell Hiram Raines   438

Birth: February 5, 1943; Birmingham, AL. **Parents:** W.S. Raines and Bertha Estelle (Walker). **Education:** Birmingham-Southern College, AL: BA. University of Alabama, Tuscaloosa: MA. **Spouse:** Laure Susan Woodley (m. 1969, div.). **Children:** Ben, Jeffrey.

Prize: *Feature Writing,* 1992: *New York Times,* "Grady's Gift," December 1, New York: New York Times, 1991.

Career: Reporter, *Birmingham (AL) Post-Herald,* 1964-65; Staff Writer, Birmingham (AL), WBRC-TV, 1965-67; Served in U.S. Army National Guard, 1965-71; Reporter, *Tuscaloosa (AL) News,* 1968-69; Reporter, *Birmingham (AL) News,* 1970-71; Political Editor, *Atlanta (GA) Constitution,* 1971-76; Political Editor, *St. Petersburg (FL) Times,* 1976-78; National Correspondent, *New York Times,* 1978-79; Atlanta (GA) Bureau Chief, *New York Times,* 1979-81; White House Correspondent, *New York Times,* 1981-84; National Political Correspondent, *New York Times,* 1984-85; Deputy Washington (DC) Editor, *New York Times,* 1985-87; London (England) Bureau Chief, *New York Times,* 1987-88; Washington (DC) Editor, *New York Times,* 1988-92; Editorial Page Editor, *New York Times,* 1993-.

Selected Works: *Campaign Money: Reform and Reality in the United States* (with others), 1976. *My Soul Is Rested: Movement Days in the Deep South Remembered,* 1977. *Whisky Man,* 1977. *Fly Fishing through the Midlife Crisis,* 1993.

For More Information: *Contemporary Authors, Volumes 73-76,* Detroit: Gale Research Company, 1978; *New York Times,* September 12, 1992: Section 1, 9; *Washington Post,* May 10, 1993: B1.

Commentary: Howell Raines, who was born in Alabama in 1943, grew up in the deep South. His composition on his youth, his relationship with Grady Hutchinson, the family's black housekeeper, and his reunion with her over 30 years later won him a Pulitzer Prize.

1993

George Lardner Jr.   439
Birth: August 10, 1934; Brooklyn, NY. **Parents:** George Edmund Lardner and Rosetta (Russo). **Religion:** Roman Catholic. **Education:** Marquette University, WI: AB, summa cum laude. Marquette University, WI: MA. **Spouse:** Rosemary Schalk (m. 1957). **Children:** Helen, Edmund, Richard, Charles, Kristin.

Prize: *Feature Writing,* 1993: *Washington Post,* "The Stalking of Kristin," November 22, Washington, DC: *Washington Post,* 1992.

Career: Reporter, *Worcester (MA) Telegram,* 1957-59; Reporter, *Miami (FL) Herald,* 1959-63; Reporter, *Washington (DC) Post,* 1963-64; Columnist, *Washington (DC) Post,* 1964-66; Reporter, *Washington (DC) Post,* 1966-.

Selected Works: *The Stalking of Kristin: A Father Investigates the Murder of His Daughter,* 1995.

Other Awards: Byline Award, Marquette University, WI, 1967. Certificate of Merit, American Bar Association, 1977. Front Page National News Award, Washington/Baltimore Newspaper Guild, 1984, 1986.

Commentary: George Lardner Jr. was awarded a Pulitzer Prize for the haunting story of his daughter's murder. He has been with the *Washington Post* since the early 1960s. According to Mr. Lardner, "The article was about the murder of my daughter Kristin in Boston in 1992. It was about her, the young man she met, and the disjointed system of justice that left him free to stalk and kill her. It was the most important story I ever wrote."

1994

Isabel Alexis Wilkerson   440
Birth: March 8, 1960; Washington, DC. **Parents:** Alexander M. Wilkerson. **Education:** Howard University, Washington, DC: BA. **Spouse:** Roderick Jeffrey Watts (m. 1989).

Prize: *Feature Writing,* 1994: *New York Times,* "Cruel Flood," August 26; "First Born, Fast Grown," April 4, New York: New York Times, 1993.

Career: Editor-in-Chief, college paper, *The Hilltop;* Editor, student magazine, *Extensions;* Intern, *St. Petersburg (FL) Times;* Intern, *Atlanta (GA) Journal;* Intern, *Washington (DC) Star;* Intern, *Washington (DC) Post;* Intern, *Los Angeles Times,* ?-1984; Metropolitan Reporter, *New York Times,* 1984-87; Correspondent, Chicago (IL), *New York Times,* 1987-91; Chicago (IL) Bureau Chief, *New York Times,* 1991-95; Senior Writer, *New York Times,* 1995-.

Other Awards: Mark of Excellence Award, Sigma Delta Chi, 1983. New York Association of Black Journalists Award, 1991, 1993. Journalist of the Year, National Association of Black Journalists, 1994. George Polk Memorial Award, Long Island University, NY, 1994. Casey Medal, University of Maryland, 1995.

Commentary: Isabel Wilkerson won a Pulitzer Prize for her stories that told the tale of the town whose cemetery was washed away during the flooding in the Midwest, and of the fourth grader who survives in a dangerous Chicago neighborhood. She spent weeks with Nicholas, the fourth grader, and his family before writing the story and refrained from using many quotes because "Why have someone say what you can show the reader?"

1995

Ronald Steven Suskind   441
Birth: November 20, 1959; Kingston, NY. **Parents:** Walter Burton Suskind and Shirley Lila (Berman). **Education:** University of Virginia: BA. Columbia University, NY: MS. **Spouse:** Cornelia Kennedy (m. 1986). **Children:** Walter, Harry Owen.

Prize: *Feature Writing,* 1995: *Wall Street Journal,* "Against All Odds," May 26; "Desperately Trying to Stay on Course," May 26, New York: Dow Jones, 1994.

Career: News Assistant and Interim Reporter, *New York Times,* 1983-85; City/State Staff Writer, *St. Petersburg (FL) Times,* 1985-87; Senior Editor, *Boston Business Magazine,* 1987-88; Editor, *Boston Business Magazine,* 1988-89; Reporter, Boston (MA) Bureau, *Wall Street Journal,* 1990; Senior National Affairs Reporter, *Wall Street Journal;* Page One Editor, *Wall Street Journal;* Journalism Instructor, Harvard University (MA).

Other Awards: Grand Prize, Benjamin Fine Awards, 1995. National Writing Award, Ball State University, IN, 1995.

For More Information: *Wall Street Journal,* April 19, 1995: A2.

Commentary: Ron Suskind chronicled the lives of the top students at Frank W. Ballou Senior High, an inner city school. He described the harsh reality of the crime in their environment and revealed their hopes for the future.

1996

Ricky Edward Bragg   442

Birth: July 26, 1959; Piedmont, AL. **Parents:** Charles Bragg and Margaret Marie (Bundrum). **Education:** Jacksonville State University, AL. **Spouse:** Lisa B. (m., div.).

Prize: *Feature Writing,* 1996: *New York Times,* New York: New York Times, 1995.

Career: Reporter, *Jacksonville (AL) News,* 1978; Reporter, *Talladega (AL) Daily Home,* 1978; Reporter, *Anniston (AL) Star,* 1979-84; Reporter *Birmingham (AL) News,* 1985-89; Miami (FL) Bureau Chief, *St. Petersburg (FL) Times,* 1989-93; Reporter, *Los Angeles Times,* 1993; Metropolitan Reporter, *New York Times,* 1994; Correspondent, Atlanta (GA) Bureau, *New York Times,* 1994-.

Selected Works: *All Over but the Shoutin',* 1997.

Other Awards: Distinguished Writing Award, American Society of Newspaper Editors, 1991, 1996. George Polk Memorial Award, Long Island University, NY. Nieman Fellow, Harvard University, MA, 1992-93. Casey Medal, University of Maryland, 1995.

For More Information: *New York Times,* 10 April (1996): B6.

Commentary: Rick Bragg's writing is influenced by his rural Southern upbringing. He was raised by his mother after his father abandoned his family. The citation by the Pulitzer board noted that his award was "for his elegantly written stories about contemporary America."

1997

Lisa K. Pollak   443

Birth: April 28, 1969; Ann Arbor, MI. **Education:** University of Michigan. Northwestern University, IL: MS.

Prize: *Feature Writing,* 1997: *Baltimore Sun,* "Umpire's Sons," December 29, Baltimore, MD: Baltimore Sun, 1996.

Career: College paper, *The Michigan Daily,* 1987-90; Intern, *Detroit Free Press,* 1992; Staff member, *Charlotte (NC) Observer, Raleigh (NC) News and Observer,* ?-1996; General Assignment Features Writer, *Baltimore (MD) Sun,* 1996-.

Other Awards: Ernie Pyle Award, 1995.

For More Information: *New York Times,* April 8, 1997: B7; *Baltimore Sun,* April 8, 1997: A1.

Commentary: Lisa Pollak's winning article tells "the story behind the story." She wrote an in-depth portrait of John Hirschbeck, a baseball umpire, and his family. (Hirschbeck was the official who was spat upon by Roberto Alomar.) Pollak's story clearly shows the courage of the Hirschbeck family, who lost one son to a rare neurological disease and have another with the same ailment.

1998

Thomas French   444

Birth: January 3, 1958; Columbus, OH. **Parents:** Hans French and Katharine (Darst). **Education:** Indiana University: BJ. **Spouse:** Linda F. **Children:** Nathaniel, Samuel.

Prize: *Feature Writing,* 1998: *St. Petersburg Times,* "Angels and Demons," October 26-November 9, St. Petersburg, FL: *St. Petersburg Times,* 1997.

Career: Editor-in-Chief, college paper, *Indiana Daily Student,* 1980; Night Police Reporter, *St. Petersburg (FL) Times,* 1981; Courts Reporter, *St. Petersburg (FL) Times,* 1982-84; General Assignment Reporter, *St. Petersburg (FL) Times,* 1984-88; Narrative Projects Reporter, *St. Petersburg (FL) Times,* 1988-.

Selected Works: *Unanswered Cries: A True Story of Friends, Neighbors, and Murder in a Small Town,* 1991. *South of Heaven: Welcome to High School at the End of the Twentieth Century,* 1993.

Other Awards: Poynter Scholarship, Indiana University. Feature Writing Award, Hearst Competition. Livingston Award for Young Journalists, Mollie Parnis Livingston Foundation, University of Michigan, 1991.

Commentary: Thomas French joined the *St. Petersburg Times* after graduating from college. His two books, *Unanswered Cries* and *South of Heaven,* were first published as long narrative series in the *St. Petersburg Times.*

"Angels & Demons, the series that won the Pulitzer, follows the case of a mother and her two daughters who came to Florida and were murdered during the first family vacation of their lives. It's a story about faith, about what keeps us going after the unthinkable happens." —T. French

Fiction

1948

James Albert Michener 445

Birth: February 3, 1907; New York, NY. **Death:** October 16, 1997. **Parents:** Mabel (Haddock) Michener. **Religion:** Quaker. **Education:** Swarthmore College, PA: AB, summa cum laude. Colorado State College of Education, CO: AM. University of Pennsylvania. University of Virginia. Ohio State University. Harvard University, MA. University of St. Andrews, Scotland. University of Siena, Italy. **Spouse:** Patti Koon (m. 1935; div. 1948); Vange Nord (m. 1948; div. 1955); Mari Yoriko Sabusawa (m. 1955; died 1994).

Prize: *Fiction*, 1948: *Tales of the South Pacific*, New York: Macmillan, 1947.

Career: Freelance writer; Actor and sports columnist; Teacher, Hill School, PA, 1932; Teacher, George School, PA, 1933-1936; Associate Professor, Colorado State College of Education (now University of Northern Colorado), Greeley, 1936-1941; Visiting Professor, Harvard University, MA, 1940-1941; Associate Editor, Macmillan, NY, 1941-1942; Lieutenant Commander, U.S. Naval Reserve, 1942-1945; Naval historian in the South Pacific; Associate Editor, Macmillan, NY, 1946-1949; Member, Advisory Committee on the Arts, U.S. State Department, 1957; Creator, *Adventures in Paradise* television series, 1959; Chairman, President Kennedy's Food for Peace Program, 1961; Congressional candidate from Pennsylvania's Eighth District, 1962; Secretary of Pennsylvania Constitutional Convention, 1967-1968; Member, Advisory Committee, U.S. Information Agency, 1970-1976; Member, Committee to Reorganize U.S.I.S., 1976; Member, Advisory Committee, U.S. Postal Service, 1978-1987; Member, Advisory Council, National Aeronautics and Space Administration, 1979-1983; Visiting Professor, University of Texas at Austin, 1983; Member, U.S International Broadcasting Board, 1983-1989; Member, Phi Beta Kappa.

Selected Works: *The Fires of Spring*, 1949. *Return to Paradise*, 1951. *The Voice of Asia*, 1951. *The Bridges at Toko-ri*, 1953. *Sayonara,* 1954. *Rascals in Paradise*, 1957. *The Bridge at Andau*, 1957. *Hawaii*, 1959. *Report of the County Chairman*, 1961. *Caravans*, 1963. *The Source*, 1965. *Iberia*, 1968. *Presidential Lottery*, 1969. *The Quality of Life*, 1970. *Kent State*, 1971. *The Drifters*, 1971. *Centennial*, 1974. *Sports in America*, 1976. *The Covenant*, 1980. *Space*, 1982. *Collectors, Forgers—and a Writer*, 1983. *Po-*land, 1983. *Texas*, 1985. *The Legacy*, 1987. *Journey*, 1988. *Alaska*, 1988. *Caribbean*, 1989. *Six Days in Havana* (Michener and Kings, John), 1989. *The Eagle and the Raven*, 1990. *Pilgrimage: A Memoir of Poland and Rome*, 1990. *The Novel*, 1991. *Mexico*, 1992. *James A. Michener's Writer's Handbook*, 1992. *The World Is My Home*, 1992. *Creatures of the Kingdom: Stories of Animals and Nature*, 1993. *Recessional*, 1994. *Miracle in Seville*, 1995. *This Noble Land: My Vision for America*, 1996.

Other Awards: National Association of Independent Schools Award, 1954, 1958. Einstein Award, 1967. Bestsellers Paperback of the Year Award, 1968: *The Source*, New York: Random House, 1965. George Washington Award, Hungarian Studies Foundation, 1970. U.S. Medal of Freedom, 1977. Franklin Award for Distinguished Service, Printing Industries of Metropolitan New York, 1980. Citation for Long-Standing Support of the Iowa Workshop Writer's Project, University of Iowa, President's Committee on the Arts and the Humanities, 1983. Lippincott Travelling Fellowship, British Museum. Distinguished Service Medal, NASA. Golden Badge of Order of Merit, 1988. Honorary DHLs: Rider College, NJ, 1950; Swarthmore College, PA, 1954. Honorary LLD, Temple University, PA, 1957. Honorary LittDs: American International College, 1957, Washington University, MO, 1967.

For More Information: Day, Arthur Grove, *James Michener*, Boston: Twayne, 1977; Becker, George Joseph, *James A. Michener*, New York: F. Ungar, 1983; Severson, Marilyn S., *James A. Michener: A Critical Companion*, Westport, CT: Greenwood, 1996.

Commentary: The 1948 Pulitzer Prize for Fiction was awarded to James Michener for his *Tales of the South Pacific*. The 18 tales are based on Michener's World War II experiences in the Navy. Each story stands on its own, but characters move from one story to the next. Richard Rodgers and Oscar Hammerstein II created an adaptation with music and lyrics and turned the *Tales* into the Broadway musical *South Pacific*. (They were rewarded with a Pulitzer Prize for Drama in 1950.)

Michener was adopted as an infant by a widow, Mabel Michener, who raised him and a number of foster children in her Doylestown, Pennsylvania home. Michener attended Swarthmore College and during the war served as a naval historian. His writing was geographically oriented. He would pick a location and write about its history, people, and issues. He methodically researched his subject and produced fact-filled mega-novels. He even traveled with a research team charged with getting the facts. The locations ranged from Hawaii to Israel to Poland to Japan to Texas. He died in 1997, having completed close to 40 novels.

readers.

Cozzens had an admiration for order. He felt that humans adapt well to structure and perform at their peak when it is in place. This is exemplified by his reliance on structure in his writing. Cozzens's most successful work was *The Last Adam.*

1949

James Gould Cozzens   446

Birth: August 19, 1903; Chicago, IL. **Death:** August 9, 1978. **Parents:** Henry William and Bertha (Wood) Cozzens. **Education:** Harvard University, MA. **Spouse:** Sylvia Bernice Baumgarten (m. 1927; died 1978).

Prize: *Fiction,* 1949: *Guard of Honor,* New York: Harcourt, Brace, 1948.

Career: Writer; Teacher, Tuinucu, Cuba, 1925-1926; Tutor, 1926-1927; Librarian, New York Athletic Club, 1927; Associate Editor, *Fortune* magazine, 1938; Major, U.S. Army Air Forces, 1942-1945; Member, National Institute of Arts and Letters.

Selected Works: *Confusion,* 1924. *Michael Scarlett: A History,* 1925. *Cock Pit,* 1928. *The Son of Perdition,* 1929. *S. S. San Pedro,* 1931. *The Last Adam,* 1933. *Men and Brethren,* 1936. *Ask Me Tomorrow,* 1940. *The Just and the Unjust,* 1942. *By Love Possessed,* 1957. *Children and Others,* 1964. *Morning, Noon, and Night,* 1968. *A Flower in Her Hair,* 1974. *A Time of War: Air Force Diaries and Pentagon Memos, 1943-1945,* 1984.

Other Awards: O. Henry Memorial Award, 1931. "A Farewell to Cuba." O. Henry Memorial Award, 1936: "Total Stranger." William Dean Howells Medal, American Academy of Arts and Letters, 1960: *For Love Possessed,* New York: Harcourt, Brace, 1957. Honorary LittD, Harvard University, MA, 1952.

For More Information: Bracher, Frederick George, *The Novels of James Gould Cozzens,* New York: Harcourt, Brace, 1959; Mooney, Harry John, *James Gould Cozzens,* Pittsburgh, PA: University of Pittsburgh, 1963; Michel, Pierre, *James Gould Cozzens,* New York: Twayne, 1974; Bruccoli, Matthew Joseph, *James Gould Cozzens: A Life Apart,* San Diego: Harcourt Brace Jovanovich, 1983.

Commentary: *Guard of Honor* won the Pulitzer Fiction prize in 1949. The story, set on an air force base during World War II, grew out of a detailed diary kept by Cozzens while he was stationed on an army base near Washington, DC. Writing training guides, manuals, and special reports, he gained a broad insight into the scope of military operations. The immensity of this organization and the seeming ease with which manpower, equipment, and operations worked together in harmony made him want to relay this to

1950

A.B. Guthrie Jr.   447

Birth: January 13, 1901; Bedford, IN. **Death:** April 26, 1991. **Parents:** Alfred Bertram and June (Thomas) Guthrie. **Education:** University of Washington. University of Montana: AB. Harvard University, MA. **Spouse:** Harriet Larson (m. 1931; div. 1963); Carol Bischman (m. 1969). **Children:** Alfred Bertram III, Helen Guthrie Atwood (HL).

Prize: *Fiction,* 1950: *The Way West,* New York: W. Sloane, 1949.

Career: Reporter, 1926-1929, City Editor and Editorial Writer, 1929-1945, Executive Editor, 1945-1947, *Lexington Leader,* Lexington, KY; Creative Writing Teacher, University of Kentucky, Lexington, 1947-1952; Writer.

Selected Works: *The Big Sky,* 1947. *These Thousand Hills,* 1956. *The Big It and Other Stories,* 1960. *The Blue Hen's Chick,* 1965. *Arfive,* 1970. *The Last Valley,* 1975. *No Second Wind,* 1980. *Fair Land, Fair Land,* 1982. *Playing Catch-Up,* 1985. *Murder in the Cotswolds,* 1989. *A Field Guide to Writing Fiction,* 1991.

Other Awards: Western Heritage Wrangler Award, 1970: *Arfive,* Boston: Houghton Mifflin, 1970. Distinguished Achievement Award, Western Literature Association, 1972. Doctor of Humane Letters, Indiana State University, 1975. Montana Governor's Award, Distinguished Achievement in the Arts. Kentucky Governor's Award. Indiana Governor's Award. Honorary LittD, University of Montana, 1949.

For More Information: Ford, Thomas W., *A. B. Guthrie, Jr.,* Austin, TX: Steck-Vaughn, 1968; Vinson, James, *Contemporary Novelists,* New York: St. Martin's, 1982; Obituary, *New York Times,* April 27, 1991; Obituary, *Washington Times,* April 29, 1991.

Commentary: A.B. Guthrie was awarded the Pulitzer Fiction prize for *The Way West* in 1950. The novel, considered one of the great tales of the American migration to the Pacific Coast, takes its reader on a trail ride west with pioneers to Oregon. It is both a love story and an adventure. The characters display the qualities necessary to endure hardships and keep going, as well as the excitement of being on the frontier.

Guthrie was a newspaper man for many years before he began writing novels. He lived in Montana most of his life and it is the subject of his novel *The Big Sky*. His great love for the West is apparent in his writing, including short stories and poems.

1951

Conrad Richter 448

Birth: October 13, 1890; Pine Grove, PA. **Death:** October 30, 1968. **Parents:** John Absalom and Charlotte Esther (Henry) Richter. **Spouse:** Harvena M. Achenbach (m. 1915). **Children:** Harvena.

Prize: *Fiction,* 1951: *The Town,* New York: A. Knopf, 1950.

Career: Journalist and Editor, Johnstown, and Pittsburgh, PA; Private Secretary, Cleveland, OH, 1910-1924; Writer, 1924-1968; Member: National Institute of Arts and Letters, Authors League, PEN.

Selected Works: *Brothers of No Kin: And Other Stories,* 1924. *Human Vibration: The Mechanics of Life and Mind,* 1925. *Early Americana and Other Stories,* 1936. *The Sea of Grass,* 1937. *The Trees,* 1940. *Tacey Cromwell,* 1942. *The Free Man,* 1943. *The Fields,* 1946. *Always Young and Fair,* 1947. *The Light in the Forest,* 1953. *The Mountain on the Desert,* 1955. *The Lady,* 1957. *The Waters of Kronos,* 1960. *A Simple Honorable Man,* 1962. *The Grandfathers,* 1964. *A Country of Strangers,* 1966. *Over the Blue Mountain,* 1967. *The Rawhide Knot and Other Stories,* 1978.

Other Awards: Gold Medal for Literature from Society of Libraries, New York University, 1942: *The Sea of Grass,* New York: Knopf: 1937; *The Trees,* New York: Knopf, 1940. Ohioana Library Medal, 1947. Literature Grant, National Institute of Arts and Letters, 1959. Maggie Award, 1959: *The Lady,* New York: Knopf, 1957. National Book Award, 1961: *The Waters of Kronos,* New York: Knopf, 1960. Honorary LittDs: Susquehanna University, PA, 1944, University of New Mexico, 1958; Lafayette College, PA, 1966; Honorary LLD, Temple University, PA, 1966. Honorary LHD, Lebanon Valley College, PA, 1966.

For More Information: Barnes, Robert J., *Conrad Richter,* Austin, TX: Steck-Vaughn, 1968; La-Hood, Marvin J., *Conrad Richter's America,* The Hague, The Netherlands: Mouton, 1975; Richter, Harvena, *Writing to Survive: The Private Notebooks of Conrad Richter,* Albuquerque: University of New Mexico, 1988; Gaston, Edwin W., *Conrad Richter,* Boston: Twayne, 1989.

Commentary: *The Town* won Conrad Richter the Pulitzer Fiction award in 1951. It is the final story of Richter's trilogy, *The Awakening;* it followed *The Trees* and *The Fields.* All three tales diagram pioneer life—cutting through forests, clearing land, and building a community. Richter was from an immigrant German family that settled in Pennsylvania.

He began his writing career by publishing short stories for more than 10 years before attempting the long story, *Human Vibrating,* published in 1926. He moved his family to New Mexico due to his wife's ill health. There he began a long creative phase, producing such works as *The Light in the Forest, Tacey Cromwell,* and *The Sea of Grass.*

1952

Herman Wouk 449

Birth: May 27, 1915; New York, NY. **Parents:** Abraham Isaac and Esther (Levine) Wouk. **Religion:** Jewish. **Education:** Columbia University, NY: BA, honors. **Spouse:** Betty Sarah Brown (m. 1945). **Children:** Abraham Isaac, Nathaniel, Joseph.

Prize: *Fiction,* 1952: *The Caine Mutiny,* Garden City, NY: Doubleday, 1951.

Career: Writer; Comedy writer, radio, NY, 1934-1935; Scriptwriter, Fred Allen Radio Show, 1936-1941; Writer and producer, promotional films, U.S. Treasury Department, 1941; Lieutenant, U.S. Navy, 1942-1946; Visiting Professor, Yeshiva University, 1953-1957; Scholar-in-Residence, Aspen Institute of Humanistic Studies, 1973-1974; Trustee, College of the Virgin Islands, 1962-1969; Member, Board of Directors, Washington National Symphony, 1969-1971; Member, Board of Directors, Kennedy Center Productions, 1974-1975; Member, Advisory Council, Center for U.S.-China Arts Exchange, 1981-1987; Lecturer, China, 1982; Member, Authors Guild; Member: Bohemian Club (San Francisco, CA), Century Club, (NY), Cosmos Club (Washington, DC), Dramatists Guild, International Platform Association, Metropolitan Club (Washington, DC), PEN, Reserve Officers Association of the U.S., Writers Guild of America East.

Selected Works: *Aurora Dawn,* 1947. *The Traitor: A Play in Two Acts* (Play), 1949. *The City Boy,* 1952. *The Caine Mutiny Court-Martial: A Play* (Play), 1954. *Marjorie Morningstar,* 1955. *Nature's Way: A Comedy in Two Acts* (Play), 1958. *Youngblood Hawke,* 1962. *Don't Stop the Carnival,* 1965. *City Boy: The Adventures of Herbie Bookbinder,* 1969. *The Winds of War,* 1971. *War and Remembrance,* 1978. *This Is My God,* 1988. *Inside, Outside,* 1985. *The Glory,* 1994. *The Hope,* 1993.

Other Awards: Richard H. Fox Prize, 1934. Four Campaign Stars, US Navy, WWII. Presidential Unit Citation, WWII. Medal of Excellence, Columbia University, NY, 1952. Alexander Hamilton Medal, Columbia College Alumni Association, NY, 1980. Ralph Waldo Emerson Award, International Platform Association, 1981. Berkeley Medal, University of California, CA, 1984. Golden Plate Award, American Academy of Achievement, 1986. Washingtonian

Book Award, 1986: *Inside, Outside,* Boston: Little, Brown, 1985. Yad Vashem Kazetnik Award, 1990. Honorary LHD, Yeshiva University, NY, 1955. Honorary LLD, Clark University, MA, 1960. Honorary LittD, American International University, 1979. Honorary PhD, Bar-Ilan University, Israel, 1990.

For More Information: Beichman, Arnold, *Herman Wouk, The Novelist as Social Historian,* New Brunswick, NJ: Transaction, 1984; Mazzeno, Laurence W., *Herman Wouk,* New York: Twayne, 1994; "Fiction's Truest Voice: Herman Wouk Lauded at the Library of Congress," *Washington Post,* May 16, 1995.

Commentary: Herman Wouk's *The Caine Mutiny* won the 1952 Pulitzer Fiction award. The story takes place aboard the *U.S.N.S. Caine* on mission in the Pacific during World War II. Captain Queeg's inability to impose orders or make a decision is seen through the eyes of young Lt. Keefer. The situation deepens until a mutiny by the officers occurs, ending in a military inquiry. The stage and movie versions of the story followed. The movie is memorable for Humphrey Bogart's portrayal of Captain Queeg and Fred MacMurray in the role of Lt. Keefer.

Wouk's *Marjorie Morningstar,* a bestseller, was also made into a motion picture starring Natalie Wood. Wouk also won acclaim for *The Winds of War* and *War and Remembrance,* which became two very popular television miniseries.

1953

Ernest Hemingway 450

Birth: July 21, 1899; Oak Park, IL. **Death:** July 2, 1961. **Parents:** Clarence Edmunds and Grace (Hall) Hemingway. **Spouse:** Hadley Richardson (m. 1921;

div. 1927); Pauline Pfeiffer (m. 1927; div. 1940); Martha Gellhorn (m. 1940; div. 1945); Mary Welsh (m. 1946). **Children:** John Hadley Nicanor (HR); Patrick, Gregory (PP).

Prize: *Fiction,* 1953: *The Old Man and the Sea,* New York: Scribners, 1952.

Career: Writer, 1917-1961; Cub Reporter, *Kansas City Star,* Kansas City, MO, 1917-1918; Ambulance driver, Red Cross Ambulance Corps, Italy, 1918-1919; Writer, Co-operative Commonwealth, Chicago, IL, 1920-1921; Correspondent, *Toronto Star,* Toronto, Ontario, Canada, 1920-1924; Correspondent, Spanish Civil War, 1937-1938; War correspondent, China, 1941; War correspondent, Europe, 1944-1945, North American Newspaper Alliance.

Selected Works: *The Sun Also Rises,* 1926. *The Torrents of Spring: A Romantic Novel in Honor of the Passing of a Great Race,* 1926. *Men without Women,* 1927. *A Farewell to Arms,* 1929. *Introduction to Kiki of Montparnasse,* 1929. *In Our Time,* 1930. *Death in the Afternoon,* 1932. *Winner Take Nothing,* 1933. *Green Hills of Africa,* 1935. *To Have and Have Not,* 1937. *The Fifth Column, and the First Forty-Nine Stories,* 1938. *The Fifth Column: A Play in Three Acts* (Play), 1940. *For Whom the Bell Tolls,* 1940. *Across the River and into the Trees,* 1950. *In Our Time: Stories,* 1953. *The Snows of Kilimanjaro, and Other Stories,* 1961. *A Moveable Feast,* 1964. *Islands in the Stream,* 1970. *Ernest Hemingway, Cub Reporter: Kansas City Star Stories,* 1970. *The Nick Adams Stories,* 1972. *A Divine Gesture,* 1974. *The Dangerous Summer,* 1985. *The Garden of Eden,* 1986.

Other Awards: Nobel Prize for Literature, 1954. Award of Merit, American Academy of Arts and Letters, 1954.

For More Information: Burgess, Anthony, *Ernest Hemingway and His World,* New York: Scribner, 1978; Meyers, Jeffrey, *Hemingway, A Biography,* New York: Harper & Row, 1985; Lynn, Kenneth Schuyler, *Hemingway,* New York: Simon & Schuster, 1987; Wagner, Linda W., ed., *Ernest Hemingway: Six Decades of Criticism,* East Lansing: Michigan State University, 1987; Oliver, Charles M., ed., *A Moving Picture Feast: The Filmgoer's Hemingway,* New York: Praeger, 1989; Mellow, James R., *Hemingway: A Life Without Consequences,* Boston: Houghton Mifflin, 1992; Henderson, William McCranor, *I Killed Hemingway,* New York: St. Martin's, 1993; Bruccoli, Matthew Joseph, *Fitzgerald and Hemingway: A Dangerous Friendship,* New York: Carroll & Graf, 1994; Josephs, Allen, *For Whom the Bell Tolls: Ernest Hemingway's Undiscovered Country,* New York: Twayne, 1994; Nagel, James, ed., *Ernest Hemingway: The Oak Park Legacy,* Tuscaloosa: University of Alabama, 1996; Burwell, Rose Marie, *Hemingway: The Postwar Years and the Posthumous Novels,* New York: Cambridge University, 1996; *The*

Cambridge Companion to Hemingway, New York: Cambridge University, 1996; Bruccoli, Matthew J., ed., *The Only Thing That Counts: The Ernest Hemingway / Maxwell Perkins Correspondence, 1925-1947,* New York: Scribner, 1996.

Commentary: *The Old Man and the Sea,* Ernest Hemingway's poignant tale of an old Cuban fisherman's long period without a catch, won the 1953 Pulitzer Fiction prize. The drama of 84 days without a bite ends on the 85th day with the wrench of a giant marlin at the end of the fisherman's line. A two-day struggle ensues between the fisherman and the great fish. When the fisherman can no longer endure, he uses a harpoon to end the fight. Before he can salvage the marlin, he watches as sharks swiftly move in and devour his great catch, leaving only a carcass. Metaphorically this is viewed as perseverance, courage, and eventual defeat.

Hemingway's life and passions sent him on a romantic path where his occupation was defined by ideas—war correspondent, the Italian front in World War I, first love, bullfighting in Spain, the Spanish Civil War, the just cause, Cuba, the end of the road. He won the 1954 Nobel Prize for Literature. He took his own life in 1961. This expatriate's life has inspired and motivated countless reporters and writers since. Much like Hemingway's personal motto, "in life, one must endure," the analysis, criticism, and dissection of his work endures.

1954
No award

1955

William Faulkner   451

Birth: September 25, 1897; Byhalia, MS. **Death:** July 6, 1962. **Parents:** Murray Cuthbert and Maud (Butler) Faulkner. **Education:** University of Mississippi. **Spouse:** Lida Estelle Oldham Franklin (m. 1929). **Children:** Alabama, Jill Dilwyn Summers; stepchildren: Victoria, Malcolm Argyle.

Prize: *Fiction,* 1955: *A Fable,* New York: Random House, 1954. *Fiction,* 1963: *The Reivers: A Reminiscence,* New York: Random House, 1962.

Career: Clerk, First National Bank, Oxford, MS, 1916; Clerk, Winchester Repeating Arms Company, New Haven, CT, 1918; Cadet Pilot and Second Lieutenant, British Royal Air Force, 1918; Clerk, Lord & Taylor, NY, 1921; Postmaster, University of Mississippi, Oxford, MS, 1921-1924; Roof Painter, Carpenter, and Paper Hanger, New Orleans, LA, 1925; Deckhand, freighter, 1925; Writer, 1925-1962; Screenwriter, Metro-Goldwyn-Mayer, 1932-1933; Screenwriter, Warner Brothers, 1942-1945, 1951, 1953, and 1954; Writer in Residence, University of Virginia, 1957-1962; Member: American Academy of Arts and Letters, Sigma Alpha Epsilon.

Selected Works: *The Marble Faun,* 1924. *Soldiers' Pay,* 1926. *Mosquitoes,* 1927. *The Sound and the Fury,* 1929. *Sartoris,* 1929. *As I Lay Dying,* 1930. *Sanctuary,* 1931. *These 13: Stories,* 1931. *Light in August,* 1932. *A Green Bough,* 1933. *Doctor Martino and Other Stories,* 1934. *Pylon,* 1935. *Absalom, Absalom!,* 1936. *The Unvanquished,* 1938. *The Wild Palms,* 1939. *The Old Man,* 1939. *The Hamlet,* 1940. *Go Down, Moses, and Other Stories,* 1942. *Intruder in the Dust,* 1948. *Knight's Gambit,* 1949. *Requiem for a Nun,* 1951. *Mirrors of Chartres Street,* 1953. *Jealousy, and Episode: Two Stories,* 1955. *Big Woods,* 1955. *Faulkner at Nagano,* 1956. *The Town,* 1957. *New Orleans Sketches* (Collins, Carvel, ed.), 1958. *The Mansion,* 1959. *The Wishing Tree,* 1964. *Essays, Speeches & Public Letters* (Meriwether, James B., ed.), 1965. *Mississippi Poems,* 1979. *To Have and Have Not: Screenplay* (with Jules Furthman), 1980. *Thinking of Home: William Faulkner's Letters to His Mother and Father, 1918-1925* (Watson, James G., ed.), 1992.

Other Awards: O. Henry Memorial Award, 1939. O. Henry Memorial Award, 1940. O. Henry Memorial Award, 1949. Nobel Prize for Literature, 1949. William Dean Howells Medal, American Academy of Arts and Letters, 1950. National Book Award, 1951: Collected Stories. Legion of Honor, France, 1951. National Book Award, 1955: *A Fable,* New York: Random House, 1954. Silver Medal, Greek Academy, 1957. Gold Medal for Fiction, National Institute of Arts and Letters, 1962.

For More Information: Oates, Stephen B., *William Faulkner: The Man and the Artist, A Biography,* New York: Harper & Row, 1987; Dowling, David, *William Faulkner,* New York: St. Martin's, 1989;

Williamson, Joel, *William Faulkner and Southern History,* New York: Oxford University, 1993; Jones, Diane Brown, *A Reader's Guide to the Short Stories of William Faulkner,* New York: G.K. Hall, 1994; Inge, M. Thomas, *William Faulkner—The Contemporary Reviews,* New York: Cambridge University, 1995; Weinstein, Philip M., *The Cambridge Companion to William Faulkner,* New York: Cambridge University, 1995; Fowler, Doreen, *Faulkner: The Return of the Repressed,* Charlottesville: University Press of Virginia, 1997; Godden, Richard, *Fictions of Labor: William Faulkner and the South's Long Revolution,* New York: Cambridge University, 1997; Millgate, Michael, *Faulkner's Place,* Athens, GA: University of Georgia, 1997; Singal, Daniel Joseph, *William Faulkner: The Making of a Modernist,* Chapel Hill: University of North Carolina, 1997.

Commentary: William Faulkner won the 1955 Pulitzer Fiction prize for his novel *A Fable.* It is the story of a young man who enlists in the French army and incites mutiny. He is exposed and sentenced to death with two others for the crime. His body is blown to bits in its grave by a bombshell. The story is an allegory for the individual who is subdued and destroyed by authority and, like Christ, becomes a martyr. Faulkner received the Nobel Prize for Literature in 1949. In his acceptance speech he stated that the writer's task "is to create out of materials of the human spirit something which did not exist before." He published three books of poetry and worked as a screenwriter on such films as *To Have and Have Not, The Big Sleep,* and *Land of the Pharoahs.*

1956

MacKinlay Kantor   452

Birth: February 4, 1904; Webster City, IA. **Death:** 1977. **Parents:** John Martin and Effie Rachel (MacKinley) Kantor. **Spouse:** Florence Irene Coyne (m. 1926). **Children:** Layne Kantor Shroden, Thomas.

Prize: *Fiction,* 1956: *Andersonville,* New York: World Publishing, 1955.

Career: Reporter, *Webster City Daily News,* Webster City, Iowa, 1921-1925; Advertiser and Claim Correspondent, Chicago, IL, 1925-1926; Reporter and Freelance Writer, *Cedar Rapids Republican,* Cedar Rapids, IA, 1927; Columnist, *Des Moines Tribune,* Des Moines, IA, 1930-1931; Screen Writer, Hollywood, CA; War Correspondent, Royal Air Force, 1943; War Correspondent, U.S. Air Force, 1945; Uniformed Civilian Division, New York City Police Department, NY, 1948-1950; War Correspondent, U.S. Air Force in Korea, 1950; Technical Consultant, U.S. Air Force, 1951-1963; Trustee, Lincoln College, 1960-1968; Honorary Consultant in American Letters, Library of Congress, 1967-1973; Honor-

ary Trustee, Lincoln College, 1968-; Fellow, Society of American Historians; Member: American Society for Psychical Research, National Association of Civil War Musicians, National Council of the Boy Scouts of America; Honorary Member: Military Order of the Loyal Legion of the U.S., Sons of Union Veterans of the Civil War.

Selected Works: *Diversey,* 1928. *El Goes South,* 1930. *Long Remember,* 1934. *The Voice of Bugle Ann,* 1935. *Turkey in the Straw: A Book of American Ballads and Primitive Verse,* 1935. *Arouse and Beware,* 1936. *The Noise of Their Wings,* 1938. *Here Lies Holly Springs,* 1938. *Valedictory,* 1939. *Cuba Libre,* 1940. *Gentle Annie: A Western Novel,* 1942. *Angleworms on Toast,* 1942. *Happy Land,* 1943. *Author's Choice: 40 Stories,* 1944. *Glory for Me,* 1945. *But Look, the Morn: The Story of a Childhood,* 1947. *Midnight Lace,* 1948. *Wicked Water: An American Primitive,* 1948. *The Good Family,* 1949. *Signal Thirty-Two: A Novel,* 1950. *Don't Touch Me,* 1951. *Warwhoop: Two Short Novels of the Frontier,* 1952. *Gettysburg,* 1952. *The Daughter of Bugle Ann,* 1953. *God and My Country,* 1954. *Lobo,* 1957. *The Work of Saint Francis,* 1958. *Spirit Lake,* 1961. *If the South Had Won the Civil War,* 1961. *Story Teller,* 1967. *The Day I Met a Lion,* 1968. *Beauty Beast: A Novel,* 1968. *Missouri Bittersweet,* 1969. *I Love You, Irene,* 1972. *The Children Sing,* 1973. *Valley Forge,* 1975.

Other Awards: O. Henry Memorial Award, 1935: "Silent Grow the Guns." National Medal of Freedom. Honorary DLitts: Grinnell College, IA, 1957; Drake University, IA, 1958; Lincoln College, 1961. Honorary LLD, Iowa Wesleyan College, IA, 1961.

For More Information: Kantor, Tim, *My Father's Voice: MacKinlay Kantor Long Remembered,* New York: McGraw-Hill, 1988.

Commentary: *Andersonville* won a Pulitzer Fiction prize for MacKinlay Kantor in 1956. It is a grim story of the horrors that take place at an infamous Confederate prison during the Civil War.

Kantor's writing career followed the reporter, columnist, and writer formula. He wrote bestsellers and produced screenplays which turned out to be successful films. His novel *Glory for Me* was made into the film *The Best Years of Our Lives* and won the Academy Award for Best Picture in 1946.

1957
No award

1958

James Agee 453

Birth: November 27, 1909; Knoxville, TN. **Death:** May 16, 1955. **Parents:** Hugh James and Laura (Tyler) Agee. **Education:** Harvard University, MA: AB. **Spouse:** Olivia Sanders (m. 1933; div. 1939); Alma Mailman (m. 1939; div. 1946); Mia Fritsch (m. 1946). **Children:** Joel (AM); Julia Teresa (MF).

Prize: *Fiction,* 1958: *A Death in the Family,* New York: McDowell, Obolensky, 1957.

Career: Writer; Editorial Staff, *Time* magazine, 1930-1948; Editorial Staff member, *Fortune* magazine, 1932-1935; Motion picture actor, films include *The Bride Comes to Yellow Sky,* 1953.

Selected Works: *Let Us Now Praise Famous Men* (with Walker Evans), 1941. *The Morning Watch,* 1950. *Letters of James Agee to Father Flye,* 1962. *The Collected Short Prose of James Agee* (Fitzgerald, Robert, ed.), 1968. *The Collected Poems of James Agee* (Fitzgerald, Robert, ed.), 1968. *Knoxville: Summer 1915,* 1986.

Other Awards: Literary Award, American Academy and Institute of Arts and Letters, 1949.

For More Information: Bergreen, Laurence, *James Agee: A Life,* New York: Dutton, 1984; Spears, Ross and Jude Cassidy, eds., *Agee: His Life Remembered,* New York: Holt, Rinehart, and Winston, 1985; Maharidge, Dale and Michael Williamson, *And Their Children After Them: The Legacy of Let Us Now Praise Famous Men, James Agee, Walker Evans, and the Rise and Fall of Cotton in the South,* New York: Pantheon, 1989; Madden, David and Jeffrey J. Folks, *Remembering James Agee,* Athens, GA: University of Georgia Press, 1997.

Commentary: The 1958 Pulitzer Prize was awarded to James Agee posthumously for *A Death in the Family.* It was a semi-autobiographical account of a father's sudden death in a car accident and the bereavement process the family must go through afterwards. Agee died of a sudden heart attack two years before the novel was finished. It was pieced together from a manuscript and several versions of the text.

Agee wrote film reviews and features for *Fortune* and *Time* magazines. He is credited with writing the screenplay for the film *The African Queen,* which is based on an E.M. Forster story. He is also remembered for *Let Us Now Praise Famous Men,* his moving tribute to the lives of Southern sharecroppers.

1959

Robert Lewis Taylor 454

Birth: September 24, 1912; Carbondale, IL. **Parents:** Roscoe Aaron and Mabel (Bowyer) Taylor. **Educa-** **tion:** Southern Illinois University. University of Illinois: AB. **Spouse:** Judith Martin (m. 1945). **Children:** Martin Lewis, Elizabeth Ann.

Prize: *Fiction,* 1959: *The Travels of Jamie McPheeters,* Garden City, NY: Doubleday, 1958.

Career: Reporter, Carbondale, IL, 1934; Sailor and Correspondent, 1935-1936, *American Boy*; Reporter, *St. Louis Post Dispatch,* St. Louis, MO, 1936-1939; Profile writer, *The New Yorker,* NY, 1939-; Lieutenant Commander, U.S. Naval Reserve, 1942-1946; Member: Club Nautico, Club Monte Carlo, Down East Yacht Club (ME), Oceans Racquet and Tennis Club (FL).

Selected Works: *Doctor, Lawyer, Merchant, Chief,* 1948. *The Running Pianist,* 1950. *Winston Churchill: An Informal Study of Greatness,* 1952. *The New Yorker,* "Profiles: Evolution of an Iron-Toed Boy," April 20, 1957, p. 41+. *A Journey to Matecumbe,* 1961. *Two Roads to Guadalupe,* 1964. *Vessel of Wrath: The Life and Times of Carry Nation,* 1966. *A Roaring in the Wind: Being a History of Alder Gulch, Montana, in Its Great and Its Shameful Days,* 1978.

For More Information: *Current Biography Yearbook,* New York: Wilson, 1959.

Commentary: Robert Lewis Taylor's *The Travels of Jamie McPheeters* won the 1959 Pulitzer Fiction prize. The story humorously follows McPheeters through numerous adventures.

Taylor was a journalist, writing for the *New Yorker* magazine. He did many profiles, some of which were published as a collection in *Doctor, Lawyer, Merchant, Chief.* He wrote several biographies, including *W.C. Fields: His Follies and Fortunes* and *Winston Churchill, An Informal Study in Greatness.*

1960

Allen Stuart Drury 455

Birth: September 2, 1918; Houston, TX. **Parents:** Alden Monteith and Flora (Allen) Drury. **Education:** Stanford University, CA: BA.

Prize: *Fiction,* 1960: *Advise and Consent,* Garden City, NY: Doubleday, 1959.

Career: Writer; Editor, *Tulare Bee,* Tulare, CA, 1940-1941; County Editor, *Bakersfield Californian,* Bakersfield, CA, 1941-1942; U.S. Army, 1942-1943; Staff member, United Press International, Washington, DC, 1943-1945; Freelance Correspondent, 1946; National Editor, *Pathfinder,* Washington, DC, 1947-1953; National Staff member, *Washington Evening Star,* Washington, DC, 1953-1954; Staff member, *New York Times,* Washington, DC, 1954-1959; Political Contributor, *Reader's Digest,* Pleasantville, NY, 1959-1962; Member: National Council on the Arts, National Press Club, Sigma Delta Chi, Alpha Kappa

Lambda, Cosmos Club, University Club (Washington, DC), Bohemian Club (San Francisco, CA).

Selected Works: *A Shade of Difference: A Novel,* 1962. *A Senate Journal, 1943-1945,* 1963. *That Summer,* 1965. *Three Kids in a Cart: A Visit to Ike, and Other Diversions,* 1965. *Capable of Honor: A Novel,* 1966. *A Very Strange Society: A Journey to the Heart of South Africa,* 1967. *Preserve and Protect,* 1968. *The Throne of Saturn: A Novel of Space and Politics,* 1971. *Courage and Hesitation: Notes and Photographs of the Nixon Administration,* 1971. *Come Nineveh, Come Tyre: The Presidency of Edward M. Jason,* 1973. *The Promise of Joy,* 1975. *A God against the Gods,* 1976. *Anna Hastings: The Story of a Washington Newspaperwoman,* 1977. *Return to Thebes,* 1977. *Mark Coffin, U.S.S.: A Novel of Capitol Hill,* 1979. *Egypt: The Eternal Smile,* 1980. *The Hill of Summer,* 1981. *Decision,* 1983. *The Roads of Earth,* 1984. *Pentagon,* 1986. *Toward What Bright Glory?,* 1990. *Into What Far Harbor?,* 1993. *A Thing of State,* 1995.

Other Awards: Sigma Delta Chi Award for Editorial Writing, 1942. Honorary LittD, Rollins College, FL, 1961.

For More Information: Kemme, Tom, *Political Fiction, The Spirit of the Age, and Allen Drury,* Bowling Green, OH: Bowling Green State University Popular Press, 1987; *Celebrity Register,* Detroit: Gale, 1990; *Legends in Their Own Time,* New York: Prentice Hall, 1994.

Commentary: *Advise and Consent,* Allen Drury's first novel about the battle for Senate confirmation of a nominee for secretary of state. The story brought the public in on the drama of the confirmation process. Drury served as a U.S. Senate staff member and worked as a reporter. His experiences resulted in *Advise and Consent* and led him to write other political novels.

Another of his novels, *A Shade of Difference,* was quite contemporary on its publication. It details the political interests and relationships among the emerging African nations, the United States policy, and the United Nations. He also wrote two novels about ancient Greece, *A God Against Gods* and *Return to Thebes.*

1961

Harper Lee   456

Birth: April 28, 1926; Monroeville, AL. **Parents:** Amasa Coleman and Frances (Finch) Lee. **Religion:** Methodist. **Education:** Huntington College, AL: University of Alabama, AL. Oxford University, England.

Prize: *Fiction,* 1961: *To Kill a Mockingbird,* Philadelphia, PA: Lippincott, 1960.

Career: Reservation Clerk, Eastern Air Lines, NY, 1950s; Reservation Clerk, British Overseas Airways, NY, 1950s; Writer; Member, National Council on the Arts, 1966-1972.

Other Awards: Alabama Library Association Award, 1961. Brotherhood Award, National Conference of Christians and Jews, 1961. Bestsellers' Paperback of the Year Award, 1962: *To Kill a Mockingbird,* Philadelphia, PA: Lippincott, 1960.

For More Information: Hail, Marshall, *Knight in the Sun, Harper B. Lee, First Yankee Matador,* Boston: Little, Brown, 1962; *Interviews and Conversations with 20th Century Authors Writing in English,* Metuchen, NJ: Scarecrow, 1982; *Legends in Their Own Time,* New York: Prentice Hall, 1994.

Commentary: Harper Lee won the 1961 Pulitzer Fiction prize for *To Kill a Mockingbird.* A woman recounts memories from her childhood in an Alabama town in the 1930s and several events that changed the way she thought about life. The story is related by Scout Finch, whose father Atticus, an attorney, has agreed to take on the defense of a black man accused of raping a white woman. It becomes a case of a white woman's word against that of a black man. Gregory Peck won a Best Actor Academy Award in 1962 for his portrayal of Atticus Finch in the movie version. Harper Lee grew up in the Alabama town of Monroeville and was a close friend of Truman Capote. They both came to New York and wanted to be writers. Friends supported Lee for a year while she worked on what was to be her only novel. She assisted Capote in the research of a brutal murder that took place in a small town. The result was Capote's best-selling book, *In Cold Blood.*

1962

Edwin Greene O'Connor   457

Birth: July 29, 1918; Providence, RI. **Death:** March 23, 1968. **Parents:** John Vincent and Mary (Greene) O'Connor. **Religion:** Roman Catholic. **Education:** University of Notre Dame, IN: AB. **Spouse:** Veniette Caswell Weil (m. 1962). **Children:** One son.

Prize: *Fiction,* 1962: *The Edge of Sadness,* Boston: Little, Brown, 1961.

Career: Writer; Radio Announcer; Information Officer, U.S. Coast Guard.

Selected Works: *The Oracle,* 1951. *The Last Hurrah,* 1956. *All in the Family,* 1966.

Other Awards: Golden Book Award, Catholic Writer's Guild, 1957: *The Last Hurrah,* Boston: Little, Brown, 1956. Atlantic Prize, 1957: *The Last Hurrah.* Catholic Press Institute Award, 1962.

For More Information: Rank, Hugh, *Edwin O'Connor,* New York: Twayne, 1974; *Dictionary of*

Contemporary Catholic Writing, 1989; *Legend in Their Own Time,* New York: Prentice Hall, 1994.

Commentary: The 1962 Pulitzer Prize in Fiction was awarded to Edwin O'Connor for *The Edge of Sadness.* The story is about the effects of "God's grace" on a pastor and his congregation of Irish Americans in a city very much like Boston.

O'Connor is most noted for his previous novel, *The Last Hurrah,* which gave readers the character of Frank Skeffington. Skeffington is an Irish American political boss who decides on his 72nd birthday to run for re-election. O'Connor grew up in Rhode Island, not far from the politics and Irish-American community of Boston. He worked as a radio announcer before writing novels.

1963

William Faulkner
Full entry appears as #451 under "Fiction," 1955.

1964
No award

1965

Shirley Ann Grau   458
Birth: July 8, 1929; New Orleans, LA. **Parents:** Adolph Eugene and Katherine (Onions) Grau. **Religion:** Unitarian Universalist. **Education:** Tulane University, LA: BA. **Spouse:** James Kern Feibleman (m. 1955). **Children:** Ian James, Nora Miranda, William Leopold, Katherine Sara.

Prize: *Fiction,* 1965: *The Keepers of the House,* New York: Knopf, 1964.

Career: Novelist, Short story writer; Board member, St. Martin's Episcopal School, New Orleans, LA; Member: Authors Guild, Authors League of America, Phi Beta Kappa.

Selected Works: *The Black Prince, and Other Stories,* 1954. *The Hard Blue Sky,* 1958. *The House on Coliseum Street,* 1961. *The Condor Passes,* 1971. *The Wind Shifting West,* 1973. *Evidence of Love,* 1977. *Nine Women: Short Stories,* 1985. *Roadwalkers,* 1994.

For More Information: *Oxford Companion to Contemporary American Literature,* New York: Oxford, 1965; Schlueter, Paul, *Shirley Ann Grau,* Boston: Twayne, 1981; *Dictionary of Contemporary Catholic Writing,* 1989; *Legends in Their Own Time,* New York: Prentice Hall, 1994.

Commentary: *The Keepers of the House* won the 1965 Pulitzer Prize in Fiction for its portrayal of three generations of an interracial marriage, a white family,

and the Ku Klux Klan. It was praised for the complex family, social, and political issues it raised.

Grau has been described as a fictional anthropologist for her in-depth portraits of people and vivid painting of the atmosphere, society, and culture of the South. Grau was born in New Orleans and wrote *The House on Coliseum Street* and *The Condor Passes,* which take place in Louisiana.

1966

Katherine Anne Porter   459

Birth: May 15, 1890; Indian Creek, TX. **Death:** September 18, 1980. **Parents:** Harrison Boone and Mary Alice (Jones) Porter. **Spouse:** Eugene Dove Pressley (m. 1933; div. 1938); Albert Russel Erskine, Jr. (m. 1938; div. 1942).

Prize: *Fiction,* 1966: *Collected Stories,* New York: Harcourt, Brace, 1965.

Selected Works: *Flowering Judas and Other Stories,* 1935. *Pale Horse, Pale Rider; Three Short Novels,* 1939. *The Leaning Tower, and Other Stories,* 1944. *The Days Before,* 1952. *Ship of Fools,* 1962. *The Never-Ending Wrong,* 1977. *Correspondence* (Bayley, Isabel, ed.), 1990. *This Strange, Old World and Other Book Reviews* (Unrue, Darlene Harbour, ed.), 1991.

Other Awards: Guggenheim Fellowships, 1931, 1938. First Annual Gold Medal, Society of the Libraries, New York University, 1940: *Pale Horse, Pale Rider,* New York: Harcourt, Brace, 1939. Library of Congress Fellow, Regional American Literature, 1944. Representative of American Literature, International Expositions of the Arts in Paris, 1952. Ford Foundation Grant, 1959-1961. O. Henry Memorial Award, 1962: "Holiday." Emerson-Thoreau Bronze

Medal for Literature, American Academy of Arts and Sciences, 1962. National Book Award, 1966: *The Collected Stories of Katherine Anne Porter,* New York: Harcourt, Brace, 1965. Gold Medal, National Institute of Arts and Letters, 1967. Creative Arts Award, Brandeis University, 1971-1972. Honorary DLitts: University of North Carolina, 1949; Smith College, MA, 1958; Wheaton College, MA, 1958. Honorary DHLs: University of Michigan, 1954; University of Maryland, 1966. Honorary DFA, LaSalle College, PA.

For More Information: Givner, Joan, *Katherine Anne Porter: A Life,* New York: Simon & Schuster, 1982; Bloom, Harold, *Katherine Anne Porter,* New York: Chelsea House, 1986; Hendrick, Willene and George, *Katherine Anne Porter,* Boston: Twayne, 1988; Tanner, James T.F., *The Texas Legacy of Katherine Anne Porter,* Denton: University of North Texas, 1990.

Commentary: Katherine Anne Porter received the 1966 Pulitzer Prize in Fiction for *Collected Stories,* a volume of short stories she had written over the years. Her work was much admired by critics. She published her first collection of short stories, *Flowering Judas,* in 1930. A second collection, *Pale Rider,* also received much praise.

She was born Callie Russel Porter in Indian Creek, Texas and endured a childhood of poverty. She was educated at convent schools and worked as a reporter and freelance writer before publishing her short stories. Porter wrote one novel, *Ship of Fools,* in 1962.

1967

Bernard Malamud   460

Birth: April 28, 1914; Brooklyn, NY. **Death:** March 18, 1986. **Parents:** Max and Bertha (Fidelman) Malamud. **Religion:** Jewish. **Education:** City College, NY: BA. Columbia University, NY: MA. **Spouse:** Ann de Chiara (m. 1945). **Children:** Paul, Janna.

Prize: *Fiction,* 1967: *The Fixer,* New York: Farrar, Straus and Giroux, 1966.

Career: Census staff member, Bureau of Census, Washington, DC, 1940; English Teacher, Erasmus Hall High School, NY, 1940; English Teacher, Harlem High School, 1948-1949; Instructor and Associate Professor of English, Oregon State University, 1949-1961; Faculty, Language and Literature Division, Bennington College, Bennington, VT, 1961-1986; Visiting Lecturer, Harvard University, 1966-1968; Honorary Consultant in American Letters, Library of Congress, 1972-1975; Member: National Institute of Arts and Letters, American Academy of Arts and Sciences, PEN American Center; President, PEN American Center, 1979.

Selected Works: *The Natural,* 1952. *The Assistant,* 1957. *The Magic Barrel,* 1958. *A New Life,* 1961. *Pictures of Fidelman: An Exhibition,* 1969. *The Tenants,* 1971. *Dubin's Lives,* 1979. *God's Grace,* 1982. *The Stories of Bernard Malamud,* 1983. *The People, and Uncollected Stories* (Giroux, Robert, ed.), 1989. *Talking Horse: Bernard Malamud on Life and Work* (Cheuse, Alan, and Delbanco, Nicholas, eds.), 1996. *The Complete Stories* (Giroux, Robert, ed.), 1997.

Other Awards: Partisan Review Fellow in Fiction, 1956-1957. Richard and Hinda Rosenthal Foundation Award, 1958: *The Assistant,* New York: Farrar, Straus and Cudahy, 1957. Daroff Memorial Award, 1958: *The Assistant.* Rockefeller Grant, 1958. National Book Award in Fiction, 1959: *The Magic Barrel,* New York: Farrar, Straus and Giroux, 1958. National Book Award in Fiction, 1967: *The Fixer,* New York: Farrar, Straus and Giroux, 1966. Ford Foundation Fellow, Humanities and Arts, 1959-1961. O. Henry Memorial Award, 1969: "Man in the Drawer." Jewish Heritage Award of the B'nai B'rith, 1976. Governor's Award for Excellence in the Arts, Vermont Council on the Arts, 1979. American Library Association Notable Book Citation, 1979: *Dubin's Lives,* New York: Farrar, Straus and Giroux, 1979. Brandeis University Creative Arts Award in Fiction, 1981. Gold Medal for Fiction, American Academy and Institute of Arts and Letters, 1983. Elmer Holmes Bobst Award for Fiction, 1983. Honorary Degree, City College, CUNY, NY.

For More Information: Helterman, Jeffrey, *Understanding Bernard Malamud,* Columbia: University of South Carolina, 1985; Salzberg, Joel, *Bernard Malamud: A Reference Guide,* Boston: G.K. Hall, 1985; Bloom, Harold, ed., *Bernard Malamud,* New York: Chelsea House, 1986; Solotaroff, Robert, *Bernard Malamud: A Study of the Short Fiction,* Boston: Twayne, 1989; Abramson, Edward A., *Bernard Malamud Revisited,* New York: Twayne, 1993.

Commentary: Bernard Malamud was awarded the 1967 Pulitzer Prize for *The Fixer,* a powerful story that takes place in Tsarist Russia and is based on the historical account of a Russian Jew who was accused of murdering a Christian child. It also won the National Book Award.

Malamud was born and raised in Brooklyn, New York, the son of Russian Jewish immigrants. Although his first novel *The Natural,* a baseball story set in the Midwest, did not have any Jewish characters, Malamud's work is quintessentially Jewish in its characters, situations, and understanding of morality. *Dubin's Lives* is about a biographer whose own life mirrors that of the persons he is writing about, and as complications arise, he manages by switching biographies. Malamud's own life is somewhat similar to the one depicted in *The Assistant.*

1968

William Styron 461

Birth: June 11, 1925; Newport News, VA. **Parents:** William Clark and Pauline (Abraham) Styron. **Education:** Davidson College, NC. Duke University, NC: AB. New School for Social Research, NY. **Spouse:** Rose Burgunder (m. 1953). **Children:** Susanna, Poola, Thomas, Alexander.

Prize: *Fiction,* 1968: *The Confessions of Nat Turner,* New York: Random House, 1967.

Career: Writer; First Lieutenant, U.S. Marine Corps, 1944-1945; Associate Editor, McGraw-Hill, NY, 1947; Fellow, Silliman College, Yale University, 1964-Present; Member Editorial Board, *American Scholar,* 1970-1976; Jury President, Cannes Film Festival, 1983; Honorary Consultant in American Letters to the Library of Congress. Advisory Editor, *Paris Review;* Honorary Member, Signet Society, Phi Beta Kappa, Harvard University, MA; Member: American Academy of Arts and Letters, American Academy of Arts and Sciences, National Institute of Arts and Letters, Society of American Historians.

Selected Works: *Lie Down in Darkness: A Novel,* 1951. *Set This House on Fire,* 1960. *As He Lay Dead: A Bitter Grief,* 1962. *In the Clap Shack,* 1973. *Sophie's Choice,* 1979. *This Quiet Dust: And Other Writings,* 1982. *Darkness Visible: A Memoir of Madness,* 1990. *A Tidewater Morning: Three Tales from Youth,* 1993. *Inheritance of Night: Early Drafts of "Lie Down in Darkness,"* 1993.

Other Awards: American Academy of Arts and Letters Prix de Rome, 1952: *Lie Down in Darkness,* Indianapolis, IN: Bobbs-Merrill, 1951. William Dean Howells Medal of the American Academy of Arts and Letters, 1970: *The Confessions of Nat Turner,* New York: Random House, 1967. American Book Award, 1980: *Sophie's Choice,* New York: Random House, 1979. Connecticut Arts Award, 1984. Cino del Duca Prize, 1985. Commandeur, Ordre des Arts et des Lettres, France, 1987. Edward MacDowell Medal, 1988. National Magazine Award, 1990. National Medal of Arts, 1993. Medal of Honor, National Arts Club, 1995. Common Wealth Award, 1995. Honorary LittDs: Duke University, NC, 1968; Davidson College, NC, 1986.

For More Information: Crane, John Kenny, *The Root of All Evil: The Thematic Unity of William Styron's Fiction,* Columbia: University of South Carolina, 1984; Coale, Samuel, *William Styron Revisited,* Boston: Twayne, 1991; Cologne-Brooks, Gavin, *The Novels of William Styron: From Harmony to History,* Baton Rouge: Louisiana State University, 1995; Ross, Daniel W., *The Critical Response to William Styron,* Westport, CT: Greenwood Press, 1995.

Commentary: *The Confessions of Nat Turner* won a Pulitzer Prize in Fiction for William Styron in 1968. Nat Turner, the leader of a slave rebellion in Virginia in 1831, narrates the events. The novel was published shortly before the assassination of Martin Luther King Jr. when the Civil Rights movement was at its peak.

Styron was born and raised in Newport News, Virginia. He is known for his novels *Lie Down in Darkness* and *Sophie's Choice.* The critically acclaimed *Sophie's Choice* is somewhat autobiographical in that the character of the narrator who lives with Sophie, a Polish immigrant imprisoned in a concentration camp in Poland during the World War II, was modeled on Styron when he first lived and worked in New York. Sophie wants to escape her demons but her lover forces her to reveal all. Styron recently recovered from a deep and long depression. He has written about the experience in *Darkness Visible: A Memoir of Madness.*

1969

N. Scott Momaday 462

Birth: February 27, 1934; Lawton, OK. **Parents:** Alfred Morris and Mayme Nataochee (Scott) Momaday. **Education:** University of New Mexico: AB. Stanford University, CA: PhD. **Spouse:** Gaye Mangold (m. 1959; div.); Regina Heitzer (m. 1978). **Children:** Cael, Jill, Brit (GM); Lori (RH).

Prize: *Fiction,* 1969: *House Made of Dawn,* New York: Harper & Row, 1968.

Career: Writer, artist, educator; Assistant Professor and Associate Professor of English, University of California, Santa Barbara, 1963-1969; Assistant Professor of English and Comparative Literature, University of California, Berkeley, 1969-1973; Professor of English, Stanford University, CA, 1973-1982; Professor of English and Comparative Literature, University of Arizona, 1982-1985; Trustee, Museum of American Indians, Heye Foundation, NY; Consultant, National Endowment for the Humanities, 1970-; Consultant, National Endowment for the Arts, 1970-; Member: American Studies Association, Gourd Dance Society of the Kiowa Tribe, Modern Language Association of America, PEN.

Selected Works: *The Way to Rainy Mountain,* 1969. *American Indian Authors,* 1971. *The Names: A Memoir,* 1976. *The Gourd Dancer: Poems,* 1976. *The Ancient Child: A Novel,* 1989. *In the Presence of the Sun: Stories and Poems,1961-1991,* 1992.

Other Awards: Academy of American Poets Prize, 1962: "The Bear." Guggenheim Fellowship, 1966-1967. National Institute of Arts and Letters Grant, 1970. Co-Winner, Western Heritage Award, 1974: *Colorado: Summer/Fall/Winter/Spring.* Premio Letterario Internazionale, Mondelo, Italy, 1979.

For More Information: Schubnell, Matthias, *N. Scott Momaday, The Cultural and Literary Background,* Norman: University of Oklahoma, 1985; Contemporary Literary Criticism, Detroit: Gale, 1995.

Commentary: M. Scott Momaday won the 1969 Pulitzer Prize in Fiction for *House Made of Dawn.* The novel portrays the conflicts of a Native American World War II veteran living in a white man's world. He finds himself a stranger in both his native and adopted environments. His psyche is damaged and he returns to his native world to heal. This was Momaday's first novel and it paved the way for other Native American writers.

Momaday is a member of the Kiowa tribe and the first American Indian to win a Pulitzer Prize. Born in Oklahoma, Momaday's father was a Kiowa artist. His mother was a teacher who was descended from pioneers. Momaday grew up on Indian reservations in the Southwest. His mother's great love of memories and literature are the gifts he received from her. His next novel, *The Way to Rainy Mountain,* told the semi-mythical account of a 300-year migration of the Kiowa tribe. The book contains illustrations done by his father.

1970

Jean Stafford   463

Birth: July 1, 1915; Covina, CA. **Death:** 1979. **Parents:** John Richard and Mary (McKillop) Stafford. **Education:** University of Colorado: BA, MA. **Spouse:** Robert Lowell (m. 1940; div. 1948); Oliver Jansen (m. 1950; div. 1953); A.J. Liebling (m. 1959; died 1963).

Prize: *Fiction,* 1970: *Collected Stories,* New York: Farrar, Straus, and Giroux, 1969.

Career: Novelist and short story writer; Instructor, Stephens College, MO, 1937-1938; Lecturer, Queens College, CUNY, NY, 1945; Adjunct Professor, Columbia University, 1967-1969; Secretary, *Southern Review,* 1940-1941; Fellow, Center for Advanced Studies, Wesleyan University, CT, 1964-1965; Member, Cosmopolitan Club, NY.

Selected Works: *Boston Adventure,* 1944. *The Mountain Lion,* 1947. *The Catherine Wheel: A Novel,* 1952. *Children Are Bored on Sunday,* 1953. *Bad Characters,* 1964. *A Mother in History,* 1966.

Other Awards: Mademoiselle's Merit Award, 1944. Literature Grant, National Institute of Arts and Letters, 1945. Guggenheim Fellowship in Fiction, 1945, 1948. National Press Club Award, 1948. O. Henry Memorial Award, 1955. Ingram-Merrill Grant, 1969.

For More Information: Walsh, Mary Ellen Williams, *Jean Stafford,* Boston: Twayne, 1985; Hulbert, Ann, *The Interior Castle: The Art and Life of Jean Stafford,* New York: Knopf, 1992; Goodman, Charlotte Margolis, *Jean Stafford: The Savage Hear,* Austin: University of Texas, 1990.

Commentary: *Collected Stories* won a Pulitzer Prize in Fiction for Jean Stafford in 1970. The volume contains a selection of Stafford's short stories written in the various places she has lived. Her writing has been admired for its subtlety and vividness, and for its strict form and structure.

Stafford was born in California and lived in Colorado, Boston, New York, and Europe. The first of her three husbands was the poet Robert Lowell. *Children Are Bored on Sunday* and *Bad Characters* are collections of her short stories. She has written novels, books for children, and a non-fiction book, *A Mother in History,* which is about Lee Harvey Oswald's (President Kennedy's assassin) mother.

1971
No award

1972

Wallace Stegner   464

Birth: February 18, 1909; Lake Mills, IA. **Death:** April 13, 1993. **Parents:** George H. and Hilda (Paulson) Stegner. **Education:** University of Utah: BA. University of California. University of Iowa: MA, PhD. **Spouse:** Mary Stuart Page (m. 1934). **Children:** Stuart Page.

Prize: *Fiction,* 1972: *Angle of Repose,* Garden City, NY: Doubleday, 1971.

Career: Instructor, Augusta College, IL, 1933-1934; Instructor, University of Utah, 1934-37; Instructor, University of Wisconsin, 1937-1939; Briggs-Copeland Instructor of Composition, Harvard University, MA, 1939-1945; Professor of English, Stanford University, Stanford, CA, 1945-1993; Director of Creative Writing Program, Stanford University, 1946-1971; Writer-in-Residence, American Academy in Rome, 1960; Assistant to the Secretary, Department of the Interior, 1961; Member, National Parks Advisory Board, 1962-1966; Chairman, National Parks Advisory Board, 1965-1966; Jackson Eli Reynolds Professor of Humanities, Stanford University, 1969-1971; Bissell Professor of Canadian-U.S. Relations, University of Toronto, Toronto, Ontario, 1975; Tanner Lecturer, University of Utah, 1980; Member: American Academy of Arts and Sciences, American Antiquarian Society, American Institute and Academy of Arts and Letters, Phi Beta Kappa.

Selected Works: *Remembering Laughter,* 1937. *Fire and Ice,* 1941. *Mormon Country,* 1942. *The Big Rock Candy Mountain,* 1943. *One Nation,* 1945. *Second Growth,* 1947. *The Women on the Wall,* 1950. *The Preacher and the Slave,* 1950. *Joe Hill: A Biographical Novel,* 1950. *Beyond the Hundredth Meridian: John Wesley Powell and the Second Opening of the West,* 1954. *A Shooting Star,* 1961. *Wolf Willow: A History, a Story, and a Memory of the Last Plains Frontier,* 1962. *A Gathering of Zion: The Story of the Mormon Trail,* 1964. *All the Little Live Things,* 1967. *The Sound of Mountain Water,* 1969. *The Uneasy Chair: A Biography of Bernard DeVoto,* 1974. *The Letters of Bernard DeVoto,* 1975. *The Spectator Bird,* 1976. *Recapitulation,* 1979. *The Gathering of Zion: The Story of the Mormon Trail,* 1981. *American Places* (Page Stegner and Eliot Porter), 1981. *One Way to Spell Man,* 1982. *Crossing to Safety,* 1987. *Collected Stories of Wallace Stegner,* 1990. *Where the Bluebird Sings to the Lemonade Springs: Living and Writing in the West,* 1992.

Other Awards: Little, Brown Prize, 1937: *Remembering Laughter,* Boston: Little, Brown, 1937. O. Henry Memorial Award, 1942. O. Henry Memorial Award, 1950. O. Henry Memorial Award, 1954. Houghton-Mifflin Life-in-America Award, 1945: *One Nation,* Boston: Houghton Mifflin, 1945. Anisfield-Wolf Award, 1945: *One Nation.* Guggenheim Fellow, 1950, 1959. Rockefeller Fellow, 1950-1951. Wenner-Gren Foundation Grant, 1953. Fellow, Center for Advanced Studies in the Behavioral Sciences, 1955-1956. Blackhawk Award, 1963: *Wolf Willow,* New York: Viking, 1962. Commonwealth Club Gold Medal, 1968: *All the Little Live Things,* New York: Viking, 1967. Senior Fellow, National Endowment for the Humanities, 1972. National Book Award for Fiction, 1977: *The Spectator Bird,* Garden City, NY: Doubleday, 1976. Robert Kirsch Award, *Los Angeles*

Times, 1980. Montgomery Fellow, Dartmouth College, 1980. Honorary DLitts: University of Utah, 1968; University of Wisconsin, 1986; Montana State University, 1987. Honorary DFAs: University of California, 1969; Utah State University, 1972. Honorary DL, University of Saskatchewan, Canada, 1973. Honorary DHL, University of Santa Clara, CA, 1979.

For More Information: Robinson, Forrest Glen and Margaret G., *Wallace Stegner,* Boston: Twayne Publishers, 1977; Obituary, *New York Times,* April 15, 1993; *Wallace Stegner: Man and Writer,* Albuquerque: University of New Mexico, 1996; Benson, Jackson J., *Wallace Stegner: His Life and Work,* New York: Viking, 1996; Stegner, Page and Mary, *The Geography of Hope: A Tribute to Wallace Stegner,* San Francisco: Sierra Club, 1996.

Commentary: Wallace Stegner was awarded the 1972 Pulitzer Prize in Fiction for *Angle of Repose.* It is a fictionalization of the life of Mary Hallock Foote (1847-1938), a novelist who wrote realistic stories about the West in the 1890s and the early part of the 20th century.

Stegner was born in Iowa and educated in Utah. He taught creative writing at Stanford University. He was past 50 when he won the Pulitzer Prize and had already penned an impressive, if not well-known, collection of short stories, essays, and biographies. Most of his novels had rural settings and have been appreciated by environmentalists. He edited the historian and Pulitzer Prize-winner Bernard DeVoto's letters. His *Collected Stories* were published in 1990 and renewed an interest in his work. He died as a result of an automobile accident in 1993.

1973

Eudora Welty   465

Birth: April 13, 1909; Jackson, MS. **Parents:** Christian Webb and Chestina (Andrews) Welty. **Education:** Mississippi State College for Women. University of Wisconsin: BA. Columbia University Graduate School of Business, NY.

Prize: *Fiction,* 1973: *The Optimist's Daughter,* New York: Random House, 1972.

Career: Journalists for newspapers, radio stations, MS, 1930s; Publicity Agent, Mississippi Works Progress Administration (WPA); Staff member, *New York Times Book Review,* NY; Honorary Consultant in American letters, Library of Congress, 1958-; Member, American Academy and Institute of Arts and Letters.

Selected Works: *A Curtain of Green,* 1941. *The Robber Bridegroom,* 1942. *The Wide Net: And Other Stories,* 1943. *The Golden Apples,* 1949. *Short Stories,* 1949. *The Ponder Heart* (Play), 1954. *The Bride of the Innisfallen, and Other Stories,* 1955. *Three*

Papers on Fiction, 1962. *Losing Battles,* 1970. *The Shoe Bird,* 1964. *One Time, One Place: Mississippi in the Depression: A Snapshot Album,* 1971. *A Pageant of Birds,* 1974. *Fairy Tale of the Natchez Trace,* 1975. *The Eye of the Story: Selected Essays and Reviews,* 1978. *Women!! Make Turban in Own Home!,* 1979. *The Collected Stories of Eudora Welty,* 1980. *Twenty Photographs,* 1980. *White Fruitcake,* 1980. *One Writer's Beginnings,* 1984. *Eudora Welty: Photographs,* 1989. *The Norton Book of Friendship,* 1991. *A Curtain of Green and Other Stories,* 1991. *A Writer's Eye: Collected Book Reviews,* 1994.

Other Awards: Guggenheim Fellowship, 1942. O. Henry Memorial Award, 1942. O. Henry Memorial Award, 1943. O. Henry Memorial Award, 1968. Literature Grant, National Institute of Arts and Letters, 1944. William Dean Howells Medal, American Academy of Arts and Letters, 1955: *The Ponder Heart,* New York: Random House, 1954. Creative Arts Medal for Fiction, Brandeis University, 1966. Edward McDowell Medal, 1970. Christopher Book Award, 1972: *One Time, One Place: Mississippi in the Depression: A Snapshot Album,* New York: Random House, 1971. Gold Medal for Fiction Writing, National Institute of Arts and Letters, 1972. National Institute of Arts and Letters Gold Medal, 1972: *One Time, One Place: Mississippi in the Depression: A Snapshot Album,* National Medal for Literature, 1980. American Library Association Notable Book Award, 1980: *The Collected Stories of Eudora Welty,* New York: Harcourt Brace Jovanovich, 1980. Presidential Medal of Freedom, 1980. American Book Award, 1981: *The Collected Stories of Eudora Welty,* American Book Award, 1984: *One Writer's Beginnings,* Cambridge, MA: Harvard University, 1984. Common Wealth Award for Distinguished Service in Literature, Modern Language Association of America, 1984. Reader of the Year Award, Mystery Writers of America, 1985. National Medal of Arts, 1987. Chevalier de l'order des Arts et Lettres, 1987.

For More Information: Bloom, Harold, ed., *Eudora Welty,* New York: Chelsea House, 1986; Schmidt, Peter, *The Heart of the Story: Eudora Welty's Short Fiction,* Jackson: University Press of Mississippi, 1991; Binding, Paul, *The Still Moment: Eudora Welty: Portrait of a Writer,* London, UK: Virago, 1994; Gretlund, Jan Nordby, *Eudora Welty's Aesthetics of Place,* Newark, NJ: University of Delaware, 1994; Mortimer, Gail L., *Daughter of the Swan: Love and Knowledge in Eudora Welty's Fiction,* Athens, GA: University of Georgia, 1994; Pingatore, Diana R., *A Reader's Guide to the Short Stories of Eudora Welty,* New York: G.K. Hall, 1996; Johnston, Carol Ann, *Eudora Welty: A Study of the Short Fiction,* New York: Twayne, 1997.

Commentary: *The Optimist's Daughter* won Eudora Welty the 1973 Pulitzer Prize in Fiction. This is the story of a young working woman remembering her parents' marriage and reinterpreting her view.

Eudora Welty is a Southern writer. She grew up in Mississippi and worked as a journalist and a copywriter before she began writing short stories. Her first published collections were *A Curtain of Green* and *The Wide Net: and Other Stories.* She penned an autobiography, *One Writer's Beginnings,* which was composed of lectures she had given at Harvard University. She is noted for *The Robber Bridegroom, The Ponder Heart,* and *Losing Battles.*

1974
No award

1975

Michael Shaara   466
Birth: June 23, 1929; Jersey City, NJ. **Death:** May 5, 1988. **Parents:** Michael Joseph, Sr. and Allene (Maxwell) Shaara. **Education:** Rutgers University, NJ: BA. Columbia University, NY. University of Vermont, VT. **Spouse:** Helen Krumweide (m. 1950; div. 1980). **Children:** Jeffrey, Lila, Elise.

Prize: *Fiction,* 1975: *The Killer Angels,* New York: McKay, 1974.

Career: Paratrooper and Sergeant, U.S. Army, 1946-1949; Writer; Merchant Seaman, 1948-1949; Served in U.S. Army Reserve, 1949-1953; Police Officer, St. Petersburg Police Department, FL, 1954-55; Short Story Writer, 1955-1961; Associate Professor of English, Florida State University, Tallahassee, FL, 1961-1973; Member: Authors Guild, Delta Kappa, Gold Key, International Platform Association, Omicron.

Selected Works: *The Broken Place,* 1968. *For Love of the Game,* 1991.

Other Awards: American Medical Association Award, 1966: "In the Midst of Life." Various Short Story Awards.

For More Information: *Dictionary of Literary Biography,* Detroit: Gale, 1983; *Contemporary Authors,* Detroit: Gale, 1992; Ringle, Ken, "A Tale of Blood: Jeff Shaara's Civil War Novel Ends Where His Father's Acclaimed Book Began," *Washington Post,* July 10, 1996; Donahue, Deirdre, "Father and Son Linked by War," *USA TODAY,* July 11, 1996.

Commentary: Michael Shaara was awarded the 1975 Pulitzer Prize in Fiction for *The Killer Angels.* The novel is about the great battle at Gettysburg during the Civil War.

Shaara's son, Jeff, also a writer, has written a prequel to *The Killer Angels.* It is entitled *Gods and Generals.* Jeff Shaara also plans to write a sequel to his father's prize-winning novel.

1976

Saul Bellow 467

Birth: June 10, 1915; Lachine, Quebec, Canada. **Parents:** Abraham and Liza (Gordon) Bellow. **Education:** University of Chicago, IL. Northwestern University, IL: BS: honors. University of Wisconsin. **Spouse:** Anita Goshkin (m. 1937; div.); Alexandra Tschacbasov (m. 1956; div.); Susan Glassman (m. 1961); Alexandra Ionesco Tuleca (m. 1974; div); Janis Freedman (m. 1989). **Children:** Gregory (AG); Adam (AT); Daniel (SG).

Prize: *Fiction,* 1976: *Humboldt's Gift,* New York: Viking Press, 1975.

Career: Writer, WPA Writers Project; Instructor, Pestalozzi-Froebel Teachers College, IL, 1938-1942; Editor, "Great Books" Project, Encyclopaedia Britannica, Chicago, IL, 1943-1946; Merchant Marine, 1944-1945; Faculty, English Department, University of Minnesota, 1946; Assistant Professor, University of Minnesota, 1948-1949; Visiting Lecturer, New York University, NY, 1950-1952; Creative Writing Fellow, Princeton University, NJ, 1952-1953; Faculty member, Bard College, NY, 1953-1954; Associate Professor, English, University of Minnesota, 1954-1959; Visiting Professor of English, University of Puerto Rico, Rio Piedras, 1961; Celebrity in Residence, University of Chicago, 1962; Grunier Distinguished Services Professor, University of Chicago; Member, Committee on Social Thought, 1962-1993; Fellow, Academy for Policy Study, 1966; Chair, Committee on Social Thought, 1970-1976; Jefferson Lecturer, National Endowment for the Humanities, 1977; Professor, English, Boston University, Boston, MA, 1993-; Tanner Lecturer, Oxford University, England; Fellow, Brandford College, Yale University, CT; Member: Authors League, American Academy of Arts and Letters, PEN, Yaddo Corporation.

Selected Works: *The Victim,* 1947. *The Adventures of Augie March: A Novel,* 1953. *Seize the Day, with Three Short Stories and a One-Act Play,* 1956. *Henderson, the Rain King,* 1959. *Herzog,* 1964. *The Last Analysis: A Play* (Play), 1965. *Mosby's Memoirs and Other Stories,* 1968. *Mr. Sammler's Planet,* 1970. *Dangling Man,* 1971. *The Portable Saul Bellow,* 1974. *To Jerusalem and Back: A Personal Account,* 1976. *A Silver Dish,* 1978. *The Dean's December,* 1982. *Him with His Foot in His Mouth and Other Stories,* 1984. *A Theft,* 1989. *The Bellarosa Connection,* 1989. *Something to Remember Me By: Three Tales,* 1991. *It All Adds Up: From the Dim Past to the Uncertain Future; a Nonfiction Collection,* 1994. *Seize the Day,* 1996. *The Actual,* 1997.

Other Awards: Best American Short Stories, 1944: "Notes of a Dangling Man." Best American Short Stories, 1950: "Sermon by Doctor Pep." Guggenheim Fellowship, 1948. Grant, National Institute of Arts and Letters, 1952. National Book Award, 1954: *The Adventures of Augie March,* New York: Viking, 1953. Friends of Literature Fiction Award, 1960. O. Henry Memorial Award, 1956: "The Gonzaga Manuscripts." National Book Award, 1965: *Herzog,* New York: Viking, 1964. James L. Dow Award, 1964. Prix International de Litterature, France, 1965: *Herzog.* Jewish Heritage Award, B'nai B'rith, 1968. Croix de Chevalier, France, 1968. Formentor Prize, 1970. National Book Award, 1971: *Mr. Sammler's Planet,* New York: Viking, 1970. Nobel Prize for Literature, 1976. Gold Medal, American Academy of Arts and Letters, 1977. Emerson-Thoreau Medal, American Academy of Arts and Sciences, 1977. Neil Gunn International Fellowship, 1977. Brandeis University Creative Arts Award, 1978. O. Henry Memorial Award, 1980: "A Silver Dish." Commander, Legion of Honour, France, 1983. Malaparte Prize for Literature, Italy, 1984. Commander, Order of Arts and Letters, France, 1985. National Medal of Arts, 1988. Lifetime Achievement Award, National Book Award, 1990. Honorary LittDs: Northwestern University, IL, 1962; Bard College, NY, 1963; New York University, 1970; Harvard University, MA, 1972; Yale University, CT, 1972; McGill University, Canada, 1973; Brandeis University, MA, 1974; Hebrew Union College, OH, 1976; Trinity College, Ireland, 1976.

For More Information: Miller, Ruth, *Saul Bellow: A Biography of the Imagination,* New York: St. Martin's, 1991; Bach, Gerhard, ed., *The Critical Response to Saul Bellow:* Westport, CT: Greenwood, 1995; Friedrich, Marianne M., *Character and Narration in the Short Fiction of Saul Bellow,* New York: Peter Lang, 1995; Wasserman, Harriet, *Handsome Is: Adventures With Saul Bellow: A Memoir,* New York: Fromm International, 1997.

Commentary: Saul Bellow was awarded the 1976 Pulitzer Prize in Fiction for *Humboldt's Gift,* the story of Charles Citrine, a successful dramatist who is struggling with the death of his ex-friend, the poet and madman, Von Humboldt Fleischer. The larger theme is the idea that American materialism has killed the poet's creativity. Fleischer's character is based on the writer Delmore Schwartz, Bellow's own friend.

Bellow was born in Canada, but raised and educated in Chicago. His parents were Russian Jewish immigrants. He studied anthropology at the University of Wisconsin, but dropped it in favor of literature. He is perhaps best known for *The Adventures of Augie March* and *Herzog,* both of which have comic heroes faced with modern day intellectual dilemmas. He is at the critical forefront of American fiction. He was awarded the Nobel Prize (1976) for Literature.

1977
No award

1978

James Alan McPherson   468

Birth: September 16, 1943; Savannah, GA. **Parents:** James A., Sr. and Mable (Smalls) McPherson. **Education:** Morris Brown College, GA: Morgan State College, GA. Harvard Law School, MA: LLB. University of Iowa: MFA. Yale Law School, CT. **Children:** Rachel.

Prize: *Fiction,* 1978: *Elbow Room,* Boston: Little, Brown, 1977.

Career: Writer, educator; Writing Instructor, University of Iowa Law School, Iowa City, 1968-1969; Instructor of Afro-American Literature, University of Iowa, Iowa City, 1969; Faculty, University of California, Santa Cruz, 1969-1970; Faculty, Morgan State University, MD, 1975-1976; Faculty, University of Virginia, Charlottesville, 1976-1981; Professor, Writers Workshop, University of Iowa, 1981-; Editor, *Double Take,* 1995-; Member: American Academy of Arts and Sciences, ACLU, Authors League of America, NAACP, PEN.

Selected Works: *Hue and Cry: Short Stories,* 1969. *Crabcakes,* 1998.

Other Awards: First Prize, *Atlantic* Short Story Contest, 1965: "Gold Coast." National Institute of Arts and Letters Award in Literature, 1970. Guggenheim Fellow, 1972-1973. MacArthur Fellowship, 1981. Excellence in Technology Award, University of Iowa, IA, 1991. Best American Essays, 1990, 1993, 1994.

For More Information: Wallace, Jon, *The Politics of Style: Language as Theme in the Fiction of Berger, McGuane, and McPherson,* Durango, CO: Hollowbrook, 1992; Beavers, Herman, *Wrestling Angels Into Song: The Fictions of Ernest J. Gaines and James Alan McPherson,* Philadelphia: University of Pennsylvania, 1995.

Commentary: James Alan McPherson was awarded the 1978 Pulitzer Prize in Fiction for *Elbow Room,* a collection of his short stories detailing the tensions between rural and urban sensibilities among African Americans.

McPherson was born in Georgia and educated at Harvard University and the University of Iowa's Writer's Workshop. He is an instructor at the Workshop and he frequently does readings. He recently published his third work, *Crabcakes,* a memoir.

1979

John Cheever   469

Birth: May 27, 1912; Quincy, MA. **Death:** June 18, 1982. **Parents:** Frederick and Mary (Liley) Cheever. **Religion:** Episcopalian. **Spouse:** Mary W. Winternitz (m. 1941). **Children:** Susan, Benjamin Hale, Frederico.

Prize: *Fiction,* 1979: *The Stories of John Cheever,* New York: Knopf, 1978.

Career: Novelist and short story writer; Sergeant, U.S. Army Signal Corps, 1943-1945; Instructor, Barnard College, NY, 1956-1957; Member, Cultural Exchange Program to the USSR, 1964; Instructor, Ossining Correctional Facility, NY, 1971-1972; Instructor, Writers Workshop, University of Iowa, 1973; Visiting Professor of Creative Writing, Boston University, 1974-1975; Member, National Institute of Arts and Letters, Century Club, NY.

Selected Works: *The Way Some People Live,* 1943. *The Enormous Radio, and Other Stories,* 1953. *The Wapshot Chronicle,* 1957. *The Housebreaker of Shady Hill, and Other Stories,* 1958. *The Brigadier and the Golf Widow,* 1964. *Bullet Park,* 1969. *The Wapshot Scandal,* 1964. *The World of Apples,* 1973. *Falconer,* 1977. *Oh What a Paradise It Seems,* 1982. *Conversations with John Cheever,* 1987. *The Letters of John Cheever,* 1988. *The Journals of John Cheever,* 1991. *Thirteen Uncollected Stories,* 1994.

Other Awards: Guggenheim Fellowship, 1951. Benjamin Franklin Award, 1955: "The Five Forty-Eight." American Academy of Arts and Letters Award in Literature, 1956. O. Henry Memorial Award, 1956: "The Country Husband." O. Henry Memorial Award, 1964: "The Embarkment for Cythera." National Book Award in Fiction, 1958: *The Wapshot Chronicle,* New York: Harper, 1957. William Dean Howells Medal, American Academy of Arts and Letters, 1965: *The Wapshot Scandal.* Editorial Award, *Playboy,* 1969: "The Yellow Room." Honorary PhD, Harvard University, MA, 1978. Edward MacDowell Medal, MacDowell Colony, 1979: *The Stories of John Cheever,* New York: Knopf, 1978. National Book Critics Circle Award in Fiction, 1979: *The Stories of John Cheever.* American Book Award in Fiction, 1981: *The Stories of John Cheever.* National Medal for Literature, 1982.

For More Information: Bosha, Francis J., *John Cheever: A Reference Guide,* Boston: G. K. Hall, 1981; O'Hara, James Eugene, *John Cheever: A Study of the Short Fiction,* Boston: Twayne, 1989; Weaver, John, ed., *Glad Tidings: A Friendship in Letters: The Correspondence of John Cheever and John D. Weaver, 1945-1982,* New York: HarperCollins, 1993; Bosha, Francis J., *The Critical Response to John Cheever,* Westport, CT: Greenwood, 1994; Meanor,

Patrick, *John Cheever Revisited,* New York: Twayne, 1995.

Commentary: *The Stories of John Cheever* is a collection of 61 of Cheever's short stories. It also won the National Book Critics Circle Award. Cheever supported himself in his first years as a writer by selling stories to publications such as the *Atlantic Monthly,* the *New Yorker,* and *Collier's.*

Cheever was born in Quincy, Massachusetts. One of Cheever's novels, *The Wapshot Chronicle,* a National Book Award winner, was 20 years in the making. It follows the rise and fall of the New England Wapshots, who see their relationships to one another change. The story is particularly poignant as it captured the increasingly transitory existence of life in America.

1980

Norman Mailer 470

Birth: January 31, 1923; Long Branch, NJ. **Parents:** Isaac Barnett Mailer and Fanny (Schneider). **Education:** Harvard University, MA: SB, cum laude. Sorbonne University, France. **Spouse:** Beatrice Silverman (m. 1944; div. 1952); Adele Morales (m. 1954; div. 1962); Lady Jeanne Campbell (m. 1962; div. 1963); Beverly Rentz Bentley (m. 1963; div. 1980); Carol Stevens (m. 1980; div. 1980); Norris Church (m. 1980). **Children:** Susan (BS); Daniell, Elizabeth Anne (AM); Kate (JC); Michael Burks, Stephen McLeod (BRB); Maggie Alexandra (CS); John Buffalo (NC).

Prize: *General Non-Fiction,* 1969: *The Armies of the Night,* New York: New American Library, 1968. *Fiction,* 1980: *The Executioner's Song,* Boston: Little, Brown, 1979.

Career: Writer; Field Artillery Observer and Infantry Rifleman, Philippines and Japan, U.S. Army, 1944-1946; Lecturer, 1950-89; Candidate, Democratic nomination in mayoral race, NY, 1960 and 1969; Co-Founding Editor, *Village Voice;* University of Pennsylvania Pappas Fellow, 1983; Founder, *Fifth Estate,* 1973; President, PEN American Center, 1984-1986; Member, American Academy and Institute of Arts and Letters, National Institute of Arts and Letters.

Selected Works: *The Naked and the Dead,* 1948. *Barbary Shore,* 1951. *The Deer Park,* 1955. *The White Negro,* 1957. *Advertisements for Myself,* 1959. *Deaths for the Ladies, and Other Disasters,* 1962. *The Presidential Papers,* 1963. *An American Dream,* 1965. *Cannibals and Christians,* 1966. *The Bullfight,* 1967. *Miami and the Siege of Chicago: An Informal History of the Republican and Democratic Conventions of 1968,* 1968. *The Long Patrol: 25 Years of Writing from the Work of Norman Mailer* (Lucod, Robert F., ed.), 1971. *The Prisoner of Sex,* 1971.

Existential Errands, 1972. *The Fight,* 1975. *Genius and Lust: A Journey through the Major Writings of Henry Miller,* 1976. *A Transit to Narcissus: A Facsimile of the Original Typescript,* 1978. *Pieces and Pontifications,* 1982. *Ancient Evenings,* 1983. *Huckleberry Finn, Alive at 100,* 1984. *Tough Guys Don't Dance,* 1984. *Conversations with Norman Mailer,* 1988. *Harlot's Ghost,* 1991. *Portrait of Picasso as a Young Man: An Interpretive Biography,* 1995. *Oswald's Tale: An American Mystery,* 1995. *The Gospel According to the Son,* 1997.

Other Awards: *Story* magazine, College Fiction Prize, 1941: "The Greatest Thing in the World." National Institute and American Academy Grant in Literature, 1960. National Book Award, Nonfiction, 1968: *Miami and the Siege of Chicago,* New York: World, 1968. National Book Award, Nonfiction, 1969: *Armies of the Night,* New York: New American Library, 1968. Pulitzer Prize in Letters-General Nonfiction, 1969: *Armies of the Night.* George Polk Award, Nonfiction, 1969: *Armies of the Night.* Edward MacDowell Medal, MacDowell Colony, 1973. National Arts Club Gold Medal, 1976. Notable Book Citation, American Library Association, 1979: *The Executioner's Song.* Pappas Fellow, University of Pennsylvania. Rose Award, Lord & Taylor, 1985. Emerson-Thoreau Medal, Lifetime Literary Achievement, American Academy of Arts and Sciences, 1989.

For More Information: Mills, Hilary, *Mailer: A Biography,* New York: Empire, 1982; *Mailer, His Life and Times,* New York: Simon & Schuster, 1984; Rollyson, Carl E., *The Lives of Norman Mailer,* New York: Paragon, 1991; Merrill, Robert, *Norman Mailer Revisited,* New York: Twayne, 1992; Glenday, Michael K., *Norman Mailer,* Houndmills, England: Macmillan, 1995.

Commentary: Norman Mailer has won two Pulitzer Prizes. He was co-winner of the 1969 Pulitzer Prize in General Non-Fiction for *The Armies of the Night,* the story of Mailer's reaction to the peace march on the Pentagon in Washington, DC in 1967. Subtitled *History as Novel, and Novel as History,* it also includes commentary by other notable personages on this event. Mailer also won the 1980 Pulitzer Prize in Fiction for *The Executioner's Song,* a fictionalization of the life of death row inmate Gary Gilmore, the first person executed in the United States after restoration of the death penalty in 1976.

Mailer was born in Long Branch, New Jersey. He was educated at Harvard University and at the Sorbonne in Paris. He is a novelist, playwright, and commentator. Mailer's colorful life is itself worthy of a novel, full of plot twists and tangles. Married many times, he was a co-founder of the *Village Voice,* candidate for mayor of New York City, and has been involved in some very public quarrels. His other works include *The Naked and the Dead, Miami and the Siege of Chicago,* and *Tough Guys Don't Dance.*

1981

John Kennedy Toole   471

Birth: 1937; New Orleans, LA. **Death:** March 26, 1969. **Parents:** John and Thelma (Ducoing) Toole. **Education:** Tulane University, LA: BA. Columbia University, NY: MA.

Prize: *Fiction,* 1981: *A Confederacy of Dunces,* Baton Rouge, LA: Louisiana State University, 1980.

Career: Instructor, University of Southwestern Louisiana and St. Mary's Dominican College, LA and others, 1959-1968; Served in U.S. Army, 1962-1963.

Selected Works: *The Neon Bible,* 1989.

For More Information: *World Authors,* New York: Wilson, 1985; *Contemporary Literary Criticism,* Detroit: Gale, 1991.

Commentary: John Kennedy Toole was awarded the Pulitzer Prize in Fiction posthumously in 1981 for *A Confederacy of Dunces.* Set in New Orleans, the humorous novel's main character is Ignatius Reilly, an overweight, jobless philosopher living with his mother, who eventually tries to have him committed to a sanatorium.

Toole wrote the novel in 1963 while teaching writing at several Southern universities. He had received encouragement and advice on the manuscript from an editor at a major publishing house. He then spent three years rewriting, only to meet with a rejection. Toole committed suicide in 1969. In 1974, his mother, Thelma Toole, decided to pursue the novel's publication with no better success. Finally she approached the Southern novelist Walker Percy, who after reading it managed to have it published by Louisiana University Press.

1982

John Hoyer Updike   472

Birth: March 18, 1932; Shillington, PA. **Parents:** Wesley Russell and Linda Grace (Hoyer) Updike. **Religion:** Lutheran. **Education:** Harvard College, MA: AB. Ruskin School of Drawing and Fine Art, Oxford, England. **Spouse:** Mary Pennington (m. 1952; div. 1976); Martha Bernhard (m. 1977). **Children:** Elizabeth, David, Michael, Miranda (MP).

Prize: *Fiction,* 1982: *Rabbit Is Rich,* New York: Knopf, 1981. *Fiction,* 1991: *Rabbit at Rest,* New York: Knopf, 1990.

Career: Novelist, short story writer, poet and critic; Reporter, "Talk of the Town" column, *The New Yorker,* 1955-1957; Visited USSR, Cultural Exchange Program, U.S. Department of State, 1964;

Chancellor, American Academy and Institute of Arts and Letters.

Selected Works: *The Carpentered Hen,* 1958. *Hoping for a Hoopoe,* 1958. *The Poorhouse Fair,* 1958. *The Same Door,* 1959. *Rabbit, Run,* 1960. *Hub Fans Bid Kid Adieu,* 1960. *Pigeon Feathers, and Other Stories,* 1962. *The Same Door,* 1963. *The Centaur,* 1963. *Telephone Poles, and Other Poems,* 1963. *A Child's Calendar,* 1965. *Assorted Prose,* 1965. *Of the Farm,* 1965. *The Music School: Short Stories,* 1966. *Couples,* 1968. *Midpoint, and Other Poems,* 1969. *Bech,* 1970. *Rabbit Redux,* 1971. *Seventy Poems,* 1972. *Museums and Women, and Other Stories,* 1972. *Six Poems,* 1973. *Warm Wine,* 1973. *Query,* 1974. *Buchanan Dying* (Play), 1974. *Picked-Up Pieces,* 1975. *Couples: A Short Story,* 1976. *From the Journal of a Leper,* 1976. *Marry Me: A Romance,* 1976. *The Coup,* 1978. *Problems, and Other Stories,* 1979. *Sixteen Sonnets,* 1979. *Talk from the Fifties,* 1979. *Too Far to Go: The Maples Stories,* 1979. *People One Knows: Interviews with Insufficiently Famous Americans,* 1980. *The Chaste Planet,* 1980. *Five Poems,* 1980. *Ego and Art in Walt Whitman,* 1980. *Hawthorne's Creed,* 1981. *Invasion of the Book Envelopes,* 1981. *Bech Is Back,* 1982. *The Carpentered Hen and Other Tame Creatures,* 1982. *Hugging the Shore: Essays and Criticism,* 1983. *Confessions of a Wild Bore,* 1984. *Emersonianism,* 1984. *The Witches of Eastwick,* 1984. *Facing Nature: Poems,* 1985. *Roger's Version,* 1986. *The Afterlife,* 1987. *Trust Me: Short Stories,* 1987. *S.,* 1988. *Just Looking: Essays on Art,* 1989. *Self-Consciousness: Memoirs,* 1989. *Odd Jobs: Essays and Criticism,* 1991. *Memories of the Ford Administration,* 1992. *Collected Poems, 1953-1993,* 1993. *The Afterlife, and Other Stories,* 1994. *A Helpful Alphabet of Friendly Objects,* 1995. *Golf Dreams: Writings on Golf,* 1996. *Toward the End of Time,* 1997.

Other Awards: Guggenheim Fellowship in Poetry, 1959. American Academy and National Institute of Arts and Letters Richard and Hinda Rosenthal Foundation Award, 1960: *The Poorhouse Fair,* New York: Knopf, 1958. National Book Award in Fiction, 1963: *The Centaur,* New York: Knopf, 1963. Prix Medicis Etranger, 1966: *The Centaur.* O. Henry Award for Fiction, 1966: "The Bulgarian Poetess." Fulbright Fellow, Africa, 1972. Edward MacDowell Medal for Literature, MacDowell Colony, 1981. American Book Award, 1982: *Rabbit Is Rich,* New York: Knopf, 1981. National Book Critics Circle Award for Fiction, 1982: *Rabbit Is Rich,* National Book Critics Circle Award for Criticism, 1984: *Hugging the Shore: Essays in Criticism,* New York: Knopf, 1983. Medal of Honor for Literature, National Arts Club, NYC, 1984. PEN / Malamud Memorial Prize for Excellence in Short Story Writing, PEN / Faulkner Award Foundation, 1988. National Book

Critics Circle Award, 1991: *Rabbit at Rest,* New York: Knopf, 1990.

For More Information: Detweiler, Robert, *John Updike,* New York: Twayne, 1972; Greiner, Donald J., *John Updike's Novels,* Athens, OH: Ohio University, 1984; Luscher, Robert M., *John Updike: A Study of the Short Fiction,* New York: Twayne, 1993; O'Connell, Mary, *Updike and the Patriarchal Dilemma,* Carbondale: Southern Illinois University, 1996.

Commentary: John Updike has won two Pulitzer Prizes in Fiction for his series of Rabbit novels. The first prize was awarded in 1982 for *Rabbit Is Rich,* which was the follow-up to *Rabbit Run,* his 1961 novel that introduced readers to the protagonist Harry "Rabbit" Angstrom. He won his second Pulitzer Prize for *Rabbit at Rest* in 1991. The Rabbit novels mirror the ups and downs of life in the United States over the previous 40 years.

Updike is one the America's most popular novelists. He was born and raised in Shillington, Pennsylvania. Updike began and is still writing short stories for the *New Yorker.* He also wrote the "Talk of the Town" column for the magazine. He is said to have been greatly influenced by the writer Henry Green. His collection of short stories, *The Afterlife and Other Stories,* was critically acclaimed.

1983

Alice Walker   473
Birth: February 9, 1944; Eatonton, GA. **Parents:** Willie Lee and Minnie Tallulah (Grant) Walker. **Education:** Spelman College, GA. Sarah Lawrence College, NY: BA. **Spouse:** Melvyn Leventhal (m. 1917; div. 1976). **Children:** Rebecca.

Prize: *Fiction,* 1983: *The Color Purple,* New York: Harcourt Brace Jovanovich, 1982.

Career: Writer; Voter registration worker, GA; Worker, Head Start Program, MS; Staff member, New York City Welfare Department; Consultant on Black History, Friends of the Children of Mississippi, 1967; Writer-in-Residence and Instructor, Black Studies, Jackson State College, 1968-1969; Writer-in-Residence and Instructor, Black Studies, Tougaloo College, 1970-1971; Lecturer in Literature, Wellesley College and University of Massachusetts, Boston, 1972-1973; Distinguished Writer, Afro-American Studies Department, University of California, Berkeley, spring, 1982; Fannie Hurst Professor of Literature, Brandeis University, MA, fall, 1982; Co-Founder and Publisher, Wild Trees Press, Navarro, CA, 1984-1988; Member, Board of Trustees, Sarah Lawrence College, NY; Co-Writer and Co-Producer, *Warrior Marks,* documentary film, 1993.

Selected Works: *Once,* 1968. *The Third Life of Grange Copeland,* 1970. *In Love & Trouble: Stories of Black Women,* 1973. *Revolutionary Petunias & Other Poems,* 1973. *Meridian,* 1976. *Good Night, Willie Lee, I'll See You in the Morning: Poems,* 1979. *You Can't Keep a Good Woman Down: Stories,* 1981. *In Search of Our Mothers' Gardens: Womanist Prose,* 1983. *Horses Make a Landscape Look More Beautiful,* 1984. *To Hell with Dying,* 1987. *Living by the Word: Selected Writings, 1973-1987,* 1988. *The Temple of My Familiar,* 1989. *Finding the Green Stone,* 1991. *Her Blue Body: Everything We Know,* 1991. *Possessing the Secret of Joy,* 1992. *Warrior Marks: Female Genital Mutilation and the Sexual Blinding of Women* (with Pratibha Parmar), 1993. *Alice Walker Banned,* 1996. *The Same River Twice,* 1996. *Anything We Love Can Be Saved,* 1997.

Other Awards: Bread Loaf Writer's Conference Scholar, 1966. First Prize, American Scholar Essay Contest, 1967. Merrill Writing Fellowship, 1967. McDowell Colony Fellowship, 1967, 1977-1978. National Endowment for the Arts Grant, 1969, 1977. Radcliffe Institute Fellowship, 1971-1973. Lillian Smith Award, Southern Regional Council, 1973: *Revolutionary Petunias and Other Poems,* New York: Harcourt Brace Jovanovich, 1973. Richard and Hinda Rosenthal Foundation Award, American Academy and Institute of Arts and Letters, 1974: *In Love and Trouble: Stories of Black Women,* New York: Harcourt Brace Jovanovich, 1973. Guggenheim Fellowship, 1977-78. American Book Award, 1983: *The Color Purple,* New York: Harcourt Brace Jovanovich, 1982. Best Books for Young Adults Citation, American Library Association, 1984: *In Search of Our Mother's Gardens: Womanist Prose,* San Diego, CA: Harcourt Brace Jovanovich, 1983. O. Henry Memorial Award, 1986: "Kindred Spirits." Langston Hughes Award, New York City College, 1989. Nora Astorga Leadership Award, 1989. Fred Cody Award for Lifetime Achievement, Bay Area Book Reviewers Association, 1990. Freedom to Write Award, PEN West, 1990. California Governor's Arts Award, 1994. Honorary PhD, Russell Sage College,1972. Honorary DHL, University of Massachusetts, 1983.

For More Information: Winchell, Donna Haisty, *Alice Walker,* New York: Twayne, 1992; *Bloomsbury Guide to Women's Literature,* New York: Prentice Hall, 1992; Gates, Henry Louis, *Alice Walker: Critical Perspectives Past and Present,* New York: Amistad, 1993.

Commentary: *The Color Purple* won a Pulitzer Prize in Fiction for Alice Walker in 1983. It consists of letters addressed to God by Celie, a Southern black woman, who has been beaten by her stepfather and her husband. The story takes place in the first half of the 20th century and explores the violence in the relationships between some black women and men.

Alice Walker was born in Eatonton, Georgia, the youngest of eight children. She attended Spelman College on a scholarship and later Sarah Lawrence College, also on scholarship. Her first published work was a collection of poems, *Once. Meridian,* her second novel, is about a black female civil rights activist and her relationship with one of three civil rights activists who were killed by the Ku Klux Klan in Mississippi.

1984

William Kennedy   474
Birth: January 16, 1928; Albany, NY. **Parents:** William J. and Mary Elizabeth (MacDonald) Kennedy. **Education:** Siena College, NY: BA. **Spouse:** Ana Daisy Sosa (m. 1957). **Children:** Dana Elizabeth, Katherine Anne, Brendan Christopher.

   Prize: *Fiction,* 1984: *Ironweed,* New York: Viking, 1983.

   Career: Writer, educator; Assistant Sports Editor and Columnist, *Post Star,* Glen Falls, NY, 1949-1950; Sergeant, Sports Editor and Columnist, U.S. Army, 1950-1952; Reporter, *Times-Union,* Albany, NY, 1952-1956; Assistant Managing Editor and Columnist, Puerto Rico *World Journal,* San Juan, 1956; Reporter, *Miami Herald,* Miami, FL, 1957; Correspondent, Time-Life Publications, Puerto Rico, 1957-1959; Reporter, *Dorvillier,* newsletter, 1957-59; Reporter, Knight Newspapers, 1957-1959; Founding Managing Editor, *Star,* San Juan, Puerto Rico, 1959-1961; Full-time fiction writer, 1961-1963; Special writer, *Times-Union,* Albany, 1963-1970; Film critic, *Times-Union,* 1968-1970; Co-Founder, Cinema 750 Film Society, Rensselaer, NY, 1968-1970; Book Editor, *Look* Magazine, 1971; Lecturer, State University of New York (SUNY) at Albany, 1974-1982; Panelist, New York State Council on the Arts, 1980-1983; Visiting Professor of English, Cornell University, NY, 1982-1983; Founder, New York State Writers Institute, SUNY, Albany, 1983; Professor of English, SUNY, Albany, 1983-; Director, Writers Institute at Albany, 1984-; Member: American Academy of Arts and Letters, 1993-, PEN, Writers' Guild of America.

   Selected Works: *The Ink Truck,* 1969. *Billy Phelan's Greatest Game,* 1978. *Legs,* 1983. *O Albany!,* 1983. *Quinn's Book,* 1988. *Very Old Bones,* 1992. *Riding the Yellow Trolley Car,* 1993. *The Flaming Corsage,* 1996. **Films:** Kennedy, William, Coppola, Francis and Puzo, Mario: *The Cotton Club: Screenplay,* New York: St. Martin's, 1986; *Ironweed: A Screenplay Adapted from His Novel,* Los Angeles, CA: Taft and Barish Productions, 1987.

   Other Awards: Award for Reporting, Puerto Rican Civic Association, Miami, FL, 1957. Page One Award for Reporting, Newspaper Guild, 1965. New York State Publishers Award for Community Service, 1965: *Times-Union.* (The *Times-Union* won award on the basis of Kennedy's articles on Albany's slums.) NAACP Award for Reporting, 1965. Writer of the Year Award, Friends of the Albany Public Library, 1975. National Endowment for the Arts Fellowship, 1981. MacArthur Foundation Fellowship, 1983. National Book Critics Circle Award, 1983: *Ironweed,* New York: Viking, 1983. New York State Governor's Arts Award, 1984. "William Kennedy's Albany" Celebration, by the citizens of Albany and the State University of New York at Albany, September 6-9, 1984. Before Columbus Foundation American Book Award, 1985: *O Albany!,* New York: Viking, 1983. Brandeis University Creative Arts Award, 1986. Commander, Order of Arts and Letters, France, 1993. Honorary LHDs: Russell Sage College, NY, 1980; Rensselaer Polytechnic Institute, NY, 1987; Fordham University, 1992; Trinity College, 1992. Honorary LittDs: Siena College, NY, 1984; College of St. Rose, NY, 1985.

   For More Information: Reilly, Edward C., *William Kennedy,* Boston: Twayne, 1991; Van Dover, J. Kenneth, *Understanding William Kennedy,* Columbia: University of South Carolina, 1991; Giamo, Benedict, *The Homeless of Ironweed: Blossoms on the Crag,* Iowa City: University of Iowa, 1996.

   Commentary: William Kennedy received the 1984 Pulitzer Prize in Fiction for *Ironweed.* Set in Albany, New York, during the Depression, it is the third of Kennedy's Albany stories. Ironweed refers to a tough-stemmed member of the sunflower family and suits the character of Francis Phelan, former baseball player and now skid row bum. Phelan has been running from his ghosts and finally returns to face them.

   Kennedy was a reporter for the Albany *Times Union* and during the 1960s he wrote a series of articles on Albany's neighborhoods. They were later published as essays in *Oh, Albany!* Kennedy has put Albany on the literary map. His other Albany novels are *Legs* and *Billy Phelan's Greatest Game.*

1985

Alison Lurie   475
Birth: September 3, 1926; Chicago, IL. **Parents:** Harry and Bernice (Stewart) Lurie. **Education:** Radcliffe College, MA: AB, magna cum laude. **Spouse:** Jonathan Bishop (m. 1948; div. 1985); Edward Hower (m. 1996). **Children:** John, Jeremy, Joshua (JB).

   Prize: *Fiction,* 1985: *Foreign Affairs,* New York: Random House, 1984.

   Career: Writer, educator; Ghost writer; Librarian; Lecturer, Cornell University, NY, 1969-1973; Associate Professor, Cornell University, NY, 1973-1976; Professor of English, Cornell University, NY,

1976-; Frederic J. Whiton Professor of American Literature, Cornell University, NY, 1989-Present.

Selected Works: *V.R. Lang: A Memoir,* 1959. *Love and Friendship,* 1962. *The Nowhere City,* 1965. *Imaginary Friends,* 1967. *Real People,* 1969. *The War between the Tates,* 1974. *Poems & Plays,* 1975. *Only Children,* 1979. *Clever Gretchen and Other Forgotten Folktales,* 1980. *The Language of Clothes,* 1981. *The Truth about Lorin Jones: A Novel,* 1988. *Don't Tell the Grown-ups: Subversive Children's Literature,* 1990. *The Oxford Book of Modern Fairy Tales,* 1993. *Women and Ghosts,* 1994.

Other Awards: Yaddo Foundation Fellow, 1963, 1964, 1966. Guggenheim Grant, 1965-1966. Rockefeller Foundation Grant, 1967-1968. New York State Cultural Council Foundation Grant, 1972-1973. American Academy of Arts and Letters Award in Literature, 1978. Radcliffe College Alumnae Recognition Award, 1987. Prix Femina Etranger, 1989.

For More Information: *McGill's Survey of American Literature,* New York: Cavendish, 1991; Costa, Richard Hauer, *Alison Lurie,* New York: Twayne, 1992.

Commentary: Alison Lurie was awarded the 1985 Pulitzer Prize in Fiction for *Foreign Affairs,* a novel about a older female college English Lit professor who is an Anglophile. She studies in England for a brief time and becomes friends with a younger man. Throughout she is trailed by an imaginary mutt, Fido. The story explores issues of age and the different cultures.

Alison Lurie was born in Chicago to Latvian Jewish parents. The family moved to New York when Alison was four. She was educated at Radcliffe College. After college, she married and wrote short stories while raising a family. She published her first novel *Love and Friendship* in 1962.

1986

Larry McMurtry 476

Birth: June 3, 1936; Wichita Falls, TX. **Parents:** William Jefferson and Hazel Ruth (McIver) McMurtry. **Education:** Rice University, TX: BA, MA. North Texas State University. **Spouse:** Josephine Ballard (m. 1959; div. 1966). **Children:** James Lawrence McMurtry.

Prize: *Fiction,* 1986: *Lonesome Dove,* New York: Simon and Schuster, 1985.

Career: Writer, educator, rare book finder; Instructor, Texas Christian University, Fort Worth, 1961-1962; Lecturer of English and Creative Writing, Rice University, TX, 1963-1969; Co-owner, Booked Up Book Store, Washington, DC, 1970-; Visiting Professor, George Mason College, 1970; Visiting Professor, American University, 1970-1971; Presi-

dent, PEN American Center, 1989; Member, Texas Institute of Letters.

Selected Works: *Horseman, Pass By,* 1961. *Leaving Cheyenne,* 1963. *In a Narrow Grave,* 1968. *Moving On,* 1970. *All My Friends Are Going to Be Strangers,* 1972. *It's Always We Rambled,* 1974. *Terms of Endearment,* 1975. *Leaving Cheyenne,* 1979. *Cadillac Jack,* 1982. *The Desert Rose,* 1983. *Film Flam: Essays on Hollywood,* 1987. *Texasville,* 1987. *Anything for Billy,* 1988. *Some Can Whistle,* 1989. *Buffalo Girls,* 1990. *The Evening Star,* 1992. *Streets of Laredo,* 1993. *Pretty Boy Floyd* (with Diana Ossana), 1994. *Dead Man's Walk,* 1995. *The Late Child,* 1995. *Comanche Moon,* 1997. *Zeke and Ned,* 1997. **Films:** *The Last Picture Show,* Columbia, 1971.

Other Awards: Wallace Stegner Fellowship, 1960. Jesse H. Jones Award from Texas Institute of Letters, 1962: *Horseman, Pass By,* New York: Harper, 1961. Guggenheim Fellowship, 1964. Best Screenplay Based on Material Adapted from Another Medium, Academy of Motion Picture Arts and Sciences Award (Oscar), 1972: *The Last Picture Show,* Columbia Pictures, 1971. Barbara McCombs / Lon Tinkle Award for Continuing Excellence in Texas Letters from Texas Institute of Letters, 1986. Spur Award from Western Writers of America, Texas, 1986. Literary Award from Southwestern Booksellers Association, 1986: *Lonesome Dove,* New York: Simon and Schuster, 1985.

For More Information: Lich, Lera Patrick Tyler, *Larry McMurtry's Texas: Evolution of the Myth,* Austin, TX: Eakin, 1987; Reynolds, Clay, ed., *Larry McMurtry Casebook,* Dallas, TX: Southern Methodist University, 1989; Jones, Roger Walton, *Larry McMurtry and the Victorian Novel,* College Station: Texas A&M University, 1994; Busby, Mark, *Larry McMurtry and the West: An Ambivalent Relationship,* Denton: University of North Texas, 1995.

Commentary: *Lonesome Dove* won a Pulitzer Prize in Fiction for Larry McMurtry in 1986. A best-selling western genre novel set in the 1870s, it is an accurate depiction of a trail drive from Texas to Montana of stolen horses and cattle.

McMurtry was born in Wichita Falls, Texas. He experienced the clash of the myth of frontier life and the modern urbanization of the place where he grew up. Texas is usually the setting for his writing, such as *Texasville* and *The Last Picture Show.* His novel *Terms of Endearment* was made into an Academy Award-winning movie.

1987

Peter Hillsman Taylor 477

Birth: June 8, 1917; Trenton, TN. **Parents:** Matthew Hillsman and Katherine (Taylor) Taylor. **Education:**

Vanderbilt University, TN. Southwestern College, TN: AB. Kenyon College, OH. **Spouse:** Eleanor Lilly Ross (m. 1943). **Children:** Katherine Baird, Peter Ross.

Prize: *Fiction,* 1987: *A Summons to Memphis,* New York: Knopf, 1986.

Selected Works: *A Long Fourth, and Other Stories,* 1948. *A Woman of Means,* 1950. *The Windows of Thornton,* 1954. *Tennessee Day in St. Louis, a Comedy,* 1957. *Happy Families Are All Alike: A Collection of Stories,* 1959. *Miss Leonora When Last Seen, and Fifteen Other Stories,* 1963. *The Collected Stories of Peter Taylor,* 1968. *Presences: Seven Dramatic Pieces,* 1973. *In the Miro District and Other Stories,* 1977. *The Old Forest and Other Stories,* 1985. *The Oracle at Stoneleigh Court: Stories,* 1993. *In the Tennessee Country,* 1994.

Other Awards: Guggenheim Fellowship, 1950. National Institute of Arts and Letters Grant, 1952. Fulbright Fellowship, France, 1955. O. Henry Memorial Award, 1959: "Venus, Cupid, Folly and Time." Ohioana Book Award, 1960: *Happy Families Are All Alike,* New York: McDowell, Obolensky, 1959. Ford Foundation Fellowship, England, 1961. Rockefeller Foundation Grant, 1964. National Academy and Institute of Arts and Letters Gold Medal for Literature, 1979. Fellowship, National Endowment for the Arts, 1984. PEN/Faulkner Award for Fiction, 1986: *The Old Forest and Other Stories,* Garden City, NY: Dial, 1985. Ritz-Hemingway Prize, 1987: *Summons to Memphis,* New York: Knopf, 1986.

For More Information: Robison, James Curry, *Peter Taylor: A Study of the Short Fiction,* Boston: Twayne, 1988; Griffith, Albert J., *Peter Taylor,* Boston: Twayne, 1990; McAlexander, Hubert H., *Critical Essays on Peter Taylor,* New York: G.K. Hall, 1993; Stephens, C. Ralph, and Salamon, Lynda B., *The Craft of Peter Taylor,* Tuscaloosa: University of Alabama, 1995.

Commentary: Peter Taylor was awarded the 1987 Pulitzer Prize in Fiction for *A Summons to Memphis.* The story tells of a Southern family whose father's professional situation has changed, requiring them to relocate from Nashville to Memphis. The father has an iron will and tries to control his family. Taylor is skilled at relating the nuances of tradition and duty against which his characters must struggle for independence.

Taylor was born in Trenton, Tennessee. He was influenced by Robert Penn Warren, among others, and had roomed at Kenyon College with the poet Robert Lowell. He taught at universities for many years. Many of his short stories were published in the *New Yorker.* He is also noted for the novel *A Woman of Means.*

1988

Toni Morrison   478

Birth: February 18, 1931; Lorain, OH. **Parents:** George and Ramah (Willis) Wofford. **Education:** Howard University, Washington, DC: 1953. Cornell University, NY: MA. **Spouse:** Harold Morrison (m. 1958; div. 1964). **Children:** Harold Ford, Slade Kevin.

Prize: *Fiction,* 1988: *Beloved,* New York: Knopf, 1987.

Career: Instructor of English, Texas Southern University, Houston, 1955-1957; Instructor of English, Howard University, Washington, DC, 1957-1964; Senior Editor, Random House, NY, 1965-; Associate Professor of English, State University of New York at Purchase, 1971-1972; Visiting Lecturer, Yale University, 1976-1977; Schweitzer Professor of the Humanities, SUNY Albany, 1984-89; Visiting Lecturer, Bard College, 1986-88; Robert F. Goheen Professor of the Humanities, Princeton University, NJ, 1989-; Council Member, Authors Guild; Member: American Academy and Institute of Arts and Letters, Authors League of America, National Council on the Arts.

Selected Works: *The Bluest Eye: A Novel,* 1970. *Sula,* 1974. *Song of Solomon,* 1977. *Tar Baby,* 1981. *Jazz,* 1992. *Playing in the Dark: Whiteness and the Literary Imagination,* 1992. *Lecture and Speech of Acceptance, Upon the Award of the Nobel Prize for Literature,* 1994. *The Dancing Mind,* 1996. *Paradise: A Novel,* 1998.

Other Awards: Ohioana Book Award, 1975: *Sula,* New York: Knopf, 1974. National Book Critics Circle Award, 1977: *Song of Solomon,* New York: Knopf, 1977. American Academy and Institute of Arts and Letters Award, 1977: *Song of Solomon.* New York State Governor's Art Award, 1986. Robert F. Kennedy Award, 1988: *Beloved,* New York: Knopf, 1987. Nobel Prize in Literature, 1993. National Book Foundation Medal for Distinguished Contribution to American Letters, 1996. Elizabeth Cady Stanton Award, National Organization of Women.

For More Information: Rigney, Barbara Hill, *The Voices of Toni Morrison,* Columbus, OH: Ohio State, 1991; Peach, Linden, *Toni Morrison,* New York: St. Martin's, 1995; Furman, Jan, *Toni Morrison's Fiction,* Columbia: University of South Carolina, 1996; Kramer, Barbara, *Toni Morrison, Nobel Prize-Winning Author,* Springfield, NJ: Enslow, 1996; Rice, Herbert William, *Toni Morrison and the American Tradition: A Rhetorical Reading,* New York: P. Lang, 1996; Middleton, Daniel L., *Toni Morrison's Fiction: Contemporary Criticism,* New York: Garland, 1997.

Commentary: *Beloved* won the 1988 Pulitzer Prize in Fiction for Toni Morrison. It is a Reconstruction-era story which takes place in the vicinity of Cincinnati, Ohio. The angry ghost of a two-year-old girl named Beloved, who was murdered by her mother to prevent her from being enslaved, inhabits the farmhouse where Sethe lives. Sethe faces the dire poverty that existed for many freed slaves after the Civil War.

Toni Morrison was born Chloe Anthony Wofford in Lorain, Ohio. She attended Howard University and later taught English there. She married, had two children, and published her first novel *The Bluest Eye.* When her marriage broke up, she left teaching and sought a career in publishing, all the while writing while working and raising a family. She has been hailed as one of the greatest American writers of the last half of the century. *Sula,* a novel published in 1974, won the National Book Award.

1989

Anne Tyler   479

Birth: October 25, 1941; Minneapolis, MN. **Parents:** Lloyd and Phyllis (Mahon) Tyler. **Religion:** Quaker. **Education:** Duke University, NC: BA. **Spouse:** Taghi Madaressi (m. 1963). **Children:** Tezh, Mitra.

Prize: *Fiction,* 1989: *Breathing Lessons,* New York: Knopf, 1988.

Career: Writer; Russian Bibliographer, Duke University Library, NC, 1962-1963; Assistant to the Librarian, McGill University Law Library, Canada, 1964-1965; Member: American Academy and Institute of Arts and Letters, Authors Guild, PEN, Phi Beta Kappa.

Selected Works: *If Morning Ever Comes,* 1964. *The Tin Can Tree,* 1965. *A Slipping-Down Life,* 1970. *The Clock Winder,* 1972. *Searching for Caleb,* 1975. *Celestial Navigation,* 1975. *Earthly Possessions,* 1977. *Morgan's Passing,* 1980. *Dinner at the Homesick Restaurant,* 1982. *The Accidental Tourist,* 1985. *Saint Maybe,* 1991. *Tumble Tower,* 1993. *Ladder of Years,* 1995.

Other Awards: Mademoiselle Award for Writing, 1966. Award for Literature, American Academy and Institute of Arts and Letters, 1977. National Book Critics Circle Fiction Award Nomination, 1980. Janet Heidinger Kafka Prize, 1981: *Morgan's Passing,* New York: Knopf, 1980. PEN/Faulkner Award for Fiction, 1983: *Dinner at the Homesick Restaurant,* New York: Knopf, 1982. National Book Critics Circle Fiction Award, 1985: *The Accidental Tourist,* New York: Knopf, 1985.

For More Information: Petry, Alice Hall, *Critical Essays on Anne Tyler,* New York: G.K. Hall, 1992; Evans, Elizabeth, *Anne Tyler,* New York: Twayne, 1993; Salwak, Dale, *Anne Tyler As Novelist,* Iowa City: University of Iowa, 1994; Kissel, Susan S., *Moving On: The Heroines of Shirley Ann Grau, Anne Tyler, and Gail Godwin,* Bowling Green, OH: Bowling Green State, 1996.

Commentary: Anne Tyler was awarded the 1989 Pulitzer Prize in Fiction for *Breathing Lessons.* A Baltimore couple takes a car trip over a period of several days to the funeral of a friend's husband and their lives come into focus as they have some time to think about how they have changed and what they have become.

Tyler was born into a Quaker family living in Minneapolis, Minnesota. She attended Duke University, studying Russian. (She later was the Russian bibliographer at Duke's library.) She gave up working to write full-time in 1967. She lives with her husband and two children in Baltimore and has come to be associated with Baltimore, which is the setting for most of her novels. She writes with humor and compassion about family relationships.

1990

Oscar Hijuelos   480

Birth: August 24, 1951; New York, NY. **Parents:** Pascual and Magdalena (Torrens) Hijuelos. **Education:** City College, NY: BA, MA.

Prize: *Fiction,* 1990: *The Mambo Kings Play Songs of Love,* New York: Farrar, Straus, Giroux, 1989.

Career: Writer, educator; Advertising Media Traffic Manager, Transportation Display, Winston Network, NY, 1977-1984; Writer, 1984-; Professor of English, Hofstra University, Hempstead, NY, 1989-; Member, International PEN.

Selected Works: *Our House in the Last World: A Novel,* 1983. *The Fourteen Sisters of Emilio Montez O'Brien: A Novel,* 1993. *Mr. Ives' Christmas,* 1995.

Other Awards: Outstanding Writer Citation, Pushcart Press, 1978: "Columbus Discovering America." Oscar Cintas Fiction Writing Grant, 1978-1979. Bread Loaf Writers Conference Scholarship, 1980. Fiction Writing Grant, Creative Artists Programs Service, 1982. Fellowship for Creative Writers Award, National Endowment for the Arts, 1985: *Our House in the Last World,* New York: Persea, 1983. American Academy in Rome Fellowship in Literature, American Academy and Institute of Arts and Letters, 1985: *Our House in the Last World.*

For More Information: *Hispanic Literature Criticism,* Detroit: Gale, 1994; Shirley, Paula W., "Reading Desi Arnaz in *The Mambo Kings Play Songs of Love,*" *MELUS,* Fall 1995; McCormick, Patrick, "Forgiveness: The Gift That Brings You Back to Life," *U.S. Catholic,* May, 1996.

Commentary: Oscar Hijuelos won the Pulitzer Prize for Fiction in 1990 with *The Mambo Kings Play Songs of Love.* The Kings are transplanted Cubans who meet the pressures of their new life in America with the lure of Mambo music in 1950s New York City dance halls.

Hijuelos was born in New York City in 1951 and he attended City College. He has won grants and fellowships which have allowed him to develop his writing.

1991

John Hoyer Updike
Full entry appears as **#472** under "Fiction," 1982.

1992

Jane Graves Smiley   481
Birth: September 26, 1949; Los Angeles, CA. **Parents:** James Laverne Smiley and Frances (Graves) Smiley Nuelle. **Religion:** Agnostic. **Education:** Vassar College, NY: BA. University of Iowa: MA, MFA, PhD. **Spouse:** John Whiston (m. 1970; div. 1975); William Silag (m. 1978; div. 1985); Stephen Mortensen (m. 1987). **Children:** Phoebe, Lucy (WS); Axel James (SM).

Prize: *Fiction,* 1992: *A Thousand Acres,* New York: Knopf, 1991.

Career: Professor and Distinguished Professor, Iowa State University, IA, 1981-; Visiting Assistant Professor, University of Iowa, 1981, 1987; Member: Authors Guild, Authors League of America, Screenwriters Guild.

Selected Works: *Barn Blind,* 1980. *At Paradise Gate: A Novel,* 1981. *Duplicate Keys,* 1984. *The Age of Grief: A Novella and Stories,* 1987. *The Greenlanders,* 1988. *Catskill Crafts: Artisans of the Catskill Mountains,* 1988. *Ordinary Love, and Good Will: Two Novellas,* 1989. *The Life of the Body: A Story,* 1990. *Moo,* 1995. *The All-True Travels of Lidie Newton,* 1998.

Other Awards: Fulbright Fellowship, 1976-1977. National Endowment for the Arts Grant, 1978, 1987. Friends of American Writers Prize, 1981: *At Paradise Gate,* New York: Simon and Schuster, 1981. O. Henry Memorial Award, 1982, 1985, 1988. National Book Critics Circle Award, 1991: *A Thousand Acres.* Heartland Award, 1991: *A Thousand Acres.* Midland Authors Award, 1992.

For More Information: *Contemporary Literary Criticism,* Detroit: Gale, 1989; *Oxford Companion to Women's Writing in the United States,* New York: Oxford University Press, 1995; Adams, Lorraine, "The Moo the Merrier: Jane Smiley, Growing a Comic Novel from Her Fertile Midwestern Imagination," *Washington Post,* May 4, 1995.

Commentary: *A Thousand Acres* won the 1992 Pulitzer Prize in Fiction for Jane Smiley. The story has been called a Midwestern King Lear. An aging father wills his farm in Iowa to two of his three daughters. The father is very difficult and only willing to see his own narrow view of things. As his health deteriorates, a bitter family battle develops.

Jane Smiley was born in Los Angeles and grew up in St. Louis. She attended Vassar College and went on to the University of Iowa, where she received her PhD. She published her first novel, *Barn Blind,* in 1980. A volume of her short stories, published as *The Age of Grief,* was nominated for a National Book Critics Circle Award.

1993

Robert Olen Butler   482
Birth: January 20, 1945; Granite City, IL. **Parents:** Robert Olen and Lucille Frances (Hall) Butler. **Religion:** Roman Catholic. **Education:** Northwestern University, IL: BS. University of Iowa: MA. New School for Social Research, NY. **Spouse:** Carol Supplee (m. 1968; div.); Marilyn Geller (m. 1972; div. 1987); Maureen Donlan (m. 1987; div. 1995); Elizabeth Dewberry (m. 1995). **Children:** Joshua Robert (MD).

Prize: *Fiction,* 1993: *A Good Scent From a Strange Mountain: Stories,* New York: H. Holt, 1992.

Career: Writer, educator; Sergeant, Military Intelligence, Vietnam, U.S. Army, 1969-1972; Editor and Reporter, *Electronic News,* NY, 1972-1973; Teacher, Granite City, IL, 1973-1974; Reporter, Chicago, IL, 1974-1975; Editor-in-Chief, *Energy User News,* NY, 1975-1985; Assistant Professor and Professor, McNeese State University, LA, 1985-; Member, PEN.

Selected Works: *The Alleys of Eden,* 1981. *Sun Dogs,* 1982. *Countrymen of Bones,* 1983. *On Distant Ground,* 1985. *The Deuce,* 1989. *They Whisper,* 1994. *Tabloid Dreams: Stories,* 1997. *The Deep Green Sea: A Novel,* 1998.

Other Awards: TuDo Chinh Kien Award for Outstanding Contributions to American Culture by a Vietnam Vet, Vietnam Veterans of America, 1987. Emily Clark Balch Award for Best Work of Fiction, 1990. Virginia Quarterly Review, 1991. Richard and Hilda Rosenthal Foundation Award, American Academy of Arts and Letters, 1993: *A Good Scent from a Strange Mountain: Stories,* New York: H. Holt, 1992. Notable Book Award, American Library Association, 1993: *A Good Scent From a Strange Mountain: Stories.* Guggenheim Fellow, 1993. National Endowment for the Arts Fellow, 1994. Honorary LHD, McNeese State University, LA, 1994.

For More Information: *Biographical Dictionary of Contemporary Catholic American Writing,* New York: Greenwood, 1989; Asim, Jabari, "Robert Olen Butler: Steered by the Senses," *St. Louis Post-Dispatch,* August 22, 1993; *Contemporary Literary Criticism,* Detroit: Gale, 1994.

Commentary: Robert Olen Butler was awarded the Pulitzer Prize in Fiction in 1993 for *A Good Scent from a Strange Mountain.* It is a collection of 15 stories about different Vietnamese living in America and what they face in trying to become what they think is "American."

Butler teaches creative writing at McNeese State University in Lake Charles, Louisiana. He has published his short stories in *The Hudson Review, The Sewanee Review,* and *The Virginia Quarterly.*

1994

E. Annie Proulx 483

Birth: August 22, 1935; Norwich, CT. **Education:** Colby College, ME. University of Vermont: MA. **Spouse:** Three marriages. **Children:** Jon, Gillis, Morgan, Lang.

Prize: *Fiction,* 1994: *The Shipping News,* New York: Scribners, 1993.

Career: Writer; Founder and Editor, *Behind the Times,* VT, 1984-1986; Member: PEN, Phi Alpha Theta, Phi Beta Kappa.

Selected Works: *Sweet & Hard Cider: Making It, Using It, & Enjoying It* (with Lew Nichols), 1980. *Heart Songs and Other Stories,* 1988. *Postcards,* 1992. *Accordion Crimes,* 1996.

Other Awards: Distinguished Short Story, Best American Short Stories, 1983, 1987. Gardens Writers of America Award, 1986. Fellowship, Vermont Council on the Arts, 1989. National Endowment for the Arts Grant, 1991. Guggenheim Fellow, 1992. PEN /Faulkner Award for Fiction, 1993: *Postcards,* New York: Scribners, 1992. National Book Award for Fiction, 1993: *The Shipping News,* New York: Scribners, 1993. Chicago Tribune's Heartland Prize for Fiction, 1993: *The Shipping News.* Irish Times International Fiction Prize, 1993: *The Shipping News.* Honorary Doctor of Humane Letters, University of Maine, 1994.

For More Information: *Contemporary Literary Criticism,* Detroit: Gale, 1994; Lannon, Linnea, "The Good News on E. Annie Proulx," *Detroit Free Press,* June 9, 1996; Greenbaum, Vicky, "Beyond the Bookroom: Modern Literature, Modern Literacy, and the Teaching of E. Annie Proulx's The Shipping News," *English Journal,* December 1997.

Commentary: Edna Annie Proulx won the 1994 Pulitzer Prize in Fiction for *The Shipping News.* It is a tragi-comic tale about a hapless reporter living in Newfoundland. The book received much critical acclaim, including the National Book Award and the Irish Times International Award.

Proulx was born in Norwich, Connecticut. She had planned a career as an academic but abandoned that idea, fearing that she would not be able to find a teaching job. This led her into journalism, which is what she did for almost 20 years before she began writing short fiction. Her first book, *Heart Songs and Other Stories,* was published in 1988. She received a PEN / Faulkner Award in 1993 for her first novel, *Postcards.* Her advice to aspiring writers has been to "write about what you don't know," because she has felt the reverse advice has resulted in too much introspection and just plain boring writing.

1995

Carol Shields 484

Birth: June 2, 1935; Oak Park, IL. **Parents:** Robert and Inez Sellgren. **Education:** Hanover College, IN: BA. University of Ottawa, Canada: MA. **Spouse:** Donald Shields. **Children:** John, Anne, Catherine, Margaret, Sara.

Prize: *Fiction,* 1995: *The Stone Diaries,* New York: Viking, 1994.

Career: Editorial Assistant, *Canadian Slavonic Papers,* Ottawa, Ontario, 1972-1974; Freelance writer; Professor, University of Manitoba, 1980-; Writers Guild of Manitoba; Member: Writers' Union of Canada, PEN.

Selected Works: *Intersect: Poems,* 1974. *Small Ceremonies,* 1976. *The Box Garden,* 1977. *Susanna Moodie: Voice and Vision,* 1977. *A Fairly Conventional Woman,* 1982. *Various Miracles,* 1985. *Swann: A Mystery,* 1987. *Departures & Arrivals,* 1988. *A*

Celibate Season, 1991. *The Republic of Love,* 1992. *Thirteen Hands: A Play in Two Acts,* 1993. *Happenstance: Two Novels in One about a Marriage in Transition,* 1994. *Coming to Canada,* 1995. *Fashion, Power, Guilt and the Charity of Families,* 1995. *Larry's Party,* 1997.

Other Awards: Winner, Young Writers' Contest, Canadian Broadcasting Corporation, 1965. Canada Council Grant, 1972, 1974, 1976. Fiction Prize, Canadian Authors Association, 1976: *Small Ceremonies,* New York: McGraw-Hill Ryerson, 1976. Prize for Drama, Canadian Broadcasting Corporation, 1983. National Magazine Award, 1984, 1985. Arthur Ellis Award, 1988. Marian Engel Award, 1990. Governor General's Award for English-Language Fiction, 1994: *The Stone Diaries,* New York: Viking, 1994. National Book Critics Circle Award for Fiction, 1994: *The Stone Diaries.* Honorary PhD, University of Ottawa, Canada, 1995.

For More Information: *Feminist Companion to Literature in English,* New Haven, CT: Yale, 1990; *Bloomsbury Guide to Women's Literature,* New York: Prentice Hall, 1992.

Commentary: *The Stone Diaries* won Carol Shields the 1995 Pulitzer Prize for Fiction. It is the rather unusual biography of a fictional woman who has lived through most of the 20th century. The story is chronicled by others.

Shields is an American-born Canadian. She grew up in Oak Park, Illinois. She is the mother of five children and lives in Manitoba, Canada. Her writing career began with the winning of a contest for poems she submitted to the Canadian Broadcasting Corporation when she was 29. Her first novel, *Small Ceremonies,* was published the week that she turned 40. She also received critical acclaim for *The Republic of Love.*

1996

Richard Ford   485

Birth: February 16, 1944; Jackson, MS. **Parents:** Parker Carrol and Edna (Akin) Ford. **Education:** Michigan State University: BA. University of California, Irvine: MFA. **Spouse:** Kristina Hensly (m. 1968).

Prize: *Fiction,* 1996: *Independence Day,* New York: Knopf, 1995.

Career: Writer; Lecturer, University of Michigan, Ann Arbor, 1974-1976; Assistant Professor of English, Williams College, MA, 1978-1979; Lecturer, Princeton University, NJ, 1979-1980; Member: PEN, Writers Guild.

Selected Works: *A Piece of My Heart,* 1976. *The Ultimate Good Luck,* 1981. *The Sportswriter,* 1986. *Communist,* 1987. *Rock Springs: Stories,* 1987. *Wild-*

life, 1990. *The Granta Book of the American Short Story,* 1992. *Women with Men: Three Stories,* 1997.

Other Awards: University of Michigan Society of Fellows, 1971-1974. Guggenheim Fellow, 1977-1978. Fellow, National Endowment for the Arts, 1979-1980, 1985-1986. One of the Five Best Books, *Time* magazine, 1986: *The Sportswriter.* Literature Award, Mississippi Academy of Arts and Letters, 1987. PEN/Faulkner Citation for Fiction, 1987: *The Sportswriter,* New York: Vintage, 1986. Literary Lion Award, New York Public Library, 1989. Literature Award, American Academy and Institute of Arts and Letters, 1989. Echoing Green Foundation Award, 1991.

For More Information: *Contemporary Literary Criticism,* Detroit: Gale, 1988; *Contemporary Novelists,* Chicago: St. James, 1991; *World Authors,* New York: Wilson, 1991.

Commentary: Richard Ford was awarded the 1996 Pulitzer Prize in Fiction for *Independence Day.* Its main character, Frank Bascombe, returns from an earlier Ford story, *The Sportswriter.* This time around, as a divorced father, he is trying to forge a closer relationship with his shoplifting son by taking him on a trip over Independence Day weekend to the Basketball and Baseball Halls of Fame.

Ford was born in Jackson, Mississippi. His father was a traveling salesman. He worked briefly for the CIA and he also studied law before turning to fiction writing. His wife supported his writing through her job. Ford writes with great familiarity about entrances and exits, overpasses and underpasses on American highways. This he views as the fabric of American society today.

1997

Steven Millhauser   486

Birth: August 3, 1943; New York, NY. **Education:** Columbia University, NY: BA. Brown University, RI. **Spouse:** Married. **Children:** Two children.

Prize: *Fiction,* 1997: *Martin Dressler: The Tale of an American Dreamer,* New York: Crown, 1996.

Career: Novelist and short story writer, *The New Yorker, Canto, Grand Street,* and *Antaeus.*

Selected Works: *Edwin Mullhouse: The Life and Death of an American Writer, 1943-1954, by Jeffrey Cartwright: A Novel,* 1972. *Portrait of a Romantic,* 1977. *From the Realm of Morpheus,* 1986. *In the Penny Arcade: Stories,* 1986. *The Barnum Museum: Stories,* 1990. *Little Kingdoms: Three Novellas,* 1993.

Other Awards: Prix Medicis Etranger, France, 1975: *Edwin Mullhouse: The Life and Death of an American Writer, 1943-1954, by Jeffrey Cartwright,* New York: Knopf, 1972.

For More Information: *Oxford Companion to American Literature,* New York: Oxford, 1983; *Contemporary Literary Criticism,* Detroit: Gale, 1989.

Commentary: Steven Millhauser won the 1997 Pulitzer Prize in Fiction for *Martin Dressler: The Tale of an American Dreamer.* The story is set in 19th-century New York and follows Martin's journey from working as a clerk in his father's cigar store to attaining the American dream until he realizes that he had "dreamed the wrong dream."

Millhauser was born in New York City and attended Columbia University and Brown University. He currently teaches at Skidmore College and lives in Saratoga Springs, New York with his wife and two children. He is the author of *Edwin Mullhouse, The Barnum Museum,* and *Little Kingdoms.*

1998

Philip Roth   487

Birth: March 19, 1933; Newark, NJ. **Parents:** Herman and Bess (Finkel) Roth. **Religion:** Jewish. **Education:** Rutgers, The State University, NJ. Bucknell University, PA. University of Chicago, IL. **Spouse:** Margaret Martinson (m. 1959; div.); Claire Bloom (m. 1990; div. 1994).

Prize: *Fiction,* 1998: *American Pastoral,* Boston: Houghton Mifflin, 1997.

Career: Novelist and short story writer.

Selected Works: *Goodbye, Columbus and Five Short Stories,* 1959. *Letting Go,* 1962. *When She Was Good,* 1967. *Portnoy's Complaint,* 1969. *Our Gang (Starring Tricky and His Friends),* 1971. *The Breast,* 1972. *My Life as a Man,* 1974. *Reading Myself and Others,* 1975. *The Professor of Desire,* 1977. *The Ghost Writer,* 1979. *Zuckerman Unbound,* 1981. *The Anatomy Lesson,* 1983. *The Counterlife,* 1986. *The Facts: A Novelist's Autobiography,* 1988. *Deception: A Novel,* 1990. *Patrimony: A True Story,* 1991. *Operation Shylock: A Confession,* 1993. *Sabbath's Theater,* 1995. **Films:** *Goodbye, Columbus,* Paramount, 1969; *Portnoy's Complaint,* Warner, 1972.

Other Awards: National Book Award, 1959: *Goodbye, Columbus and Five Short Stories,* Boston: Houghton Mifflin, 1959. Member, National Institute of Arts and Letters. Pen / Faulkner Award, 1993: *Operation Shylock,* New York: Simon & Schuster, 1993. National Book Award, 1995: *Sabbath's Theater,* Boston: Houghton Mifflin, 1995. Honorary DL, Bucknell University, PA, 1979.

For More Information: Pinsker, Sanford, *The Comedy That "Hoits": An Essay on the Fiction of Philip Roth,* Columbia: University of Missouri, 1975; Pinsker, Sanford, ed., *Critical Essays on Philip Roth,* Boston: G.K. Hall, 1982; Lee, Hermione, *Philip Roth,* New York: Methuen, 1982; Milbauer, Asher Z. and Donald G. Watson., eds., *Reading Philip Roth,* New York: St. Martin's, 1988; Searles, George J., *Conversations With Philip Roth,* Jackson: University Press of Mississippi, 1992; Appelfeld, Sharon, *Beyond Despair: Three Lectures and a Conversation with Philip Roth,* New York: Fromm International, 1994; Wade, Stephen, *The Imagination in Transit: The Fiction of Philip Roth,* Sheffield, England: Sheffield Academic, 1996; Cooper, Alan, *Philip Roth and the Jews,* Albany, NY: State University of New York, 1996.

Commentary: The 1998 Pulitzer Prize for Fiction was awarded to Philip Roth for *American Pastoral.* It is the story of Seymour Levov, also known as Swede, who finds himself pitted between the extremes of American self-reliance and individualism, straddling life's promise and its stark reality.

Philip Roth was born in Newark, New Jersey. His style has been compared at times to Saul Bellow and by turns has been autobiographical. His first book, *Goodbye, Columbus and Five Short Stories,* won the National Book Award in 1959 and was made into a motion picture 10 years later. He is known for *Portnoy's Complaint,* the comic tale of a Jewish man's relationship with his mother as told to his psychiatrist. His other works include the Zuckerman trilogy, *The Ghost Writer, Zuckerman Unbound,* and *The Anatomy Lesson.* His account of his father's death is related in *Patrimony: A True Story,* published in 1991.

General News Reporting

1985

Thomas Anthony Turcol   488

Birth: September 18, 1953; Wilmington, DE. **Parents:** Battista A. Turcol and Rose Marie (Cekine). **Education:** University of Delaware: BA.

Prize: *General News Reporting,* 1985: *Virginian-Pilot and Ledger-Star,* Norfolk, VA: Virginian-Pilot and Ledger-Star, 1984.

Career: Reporter, *Newark (DE) Weekly Post,* 1976; Reporter, *Atlantic City (NJ) Press and Sunday Press,* 1977-83; Reporter, *Norfolk (VA) Virginian-Pilot and Ledger-Star,* 1983-85; *Washington (DC) Post,* 1985-87; Staff Writer, *Philadelphia (PA) Inquirer,* 1987-.

For More Information: *New York Times,* 25 April (1985): B10.

Commentary: Thomas Turcol's investigation of a local economic development official exposed corruption and questionable financial practices. Turcol covered the City Hall beat. He disclosed allegedly false expense account claims by an official in the town of Chesapeake, Virginia.

1986

Edna Buchanan   489

Birth: 1939; Paterson, NJ. **Religion:** United Church of Christ. **Education:** Montclair State Teachers College, NJ. **Spouse:** Jim Buchanan (div. 1965); Emmett Miller (div.).

Prize: *General News Reporting,* 1986: *Miami Herald,* Miami, FL: Miami Herald, 1985.

Career: Employee of Western Electric Company (NJ); Society Reporter, *Miami Beach (FL) Sun,* 1965; General Assignment Reporter, *Miami Beach (FL) Sun;* News and Court Reporter, *Miami (FL) Herald,* 1970-73; Police Reporter, *Miami (FL) Herald,* 1973-88; Writer; Instructor, Florida International University, 1990.

Selected Works: *Carr: Five Years of Rape and Murder: From the Personal Account of Robert Frederick Carr III* (with Robert Frederick Carr), 1979. *The Corpse Had a Familiar Face: Covering Miami, America's Hottest Beat,* 1987. *Nobody Lives Forever,* 1990. *Never Let Them See You Cry: More from Miami, America's Hottest Beat,* 1992. *Contents under Pressure,* 1992. *Miami, It's Murder,* 1994. *Suitable for Framing,* 1995. *Act of Betrayal,* 1996. *Margin of Error,* 1997. *In the Silent Night,* 1998.

Other Awards: Paul Hansell Award for Distinguished Journalism, Florida Society of Newspaper Editors, 1979-80.

For More Information: *Miami Herald,* 18 April (1986): A1; *New Yorker,* 17 February (1986); *Contemporary Authors, Volume 132,* Detroit: Gale Research Company, 1991; Rothmeyer, Karen, *Winning Pulitzers: The Stories Behind Some of the Best News Coverage of Our Time,* New York: Columbia University Press, 1991: 179-190; *Publishers Weekly,* 239:42 September (1992): 54; *Current Biography,* New York: H.W. Wilson, September (1997):6-8.

Commentary: Edna Buchanan is a successful mystery novelist. Her protagonist, Britt Montero, is a journalist who covers the police beat for her paper.

Buchanan's writing while on the police beat in Miami made that one of the hottest beats on the paper. Her thorough reporting brought closure to many stories.

1987

Akron Beacon Journal   490

Founded: June 7, 1897; Akron, OH. **Founder(s):** C.L. Knight.

Prize: *Local General Spot News Reporting,* 1971. *General News Reporting,* 1987. *Meritorious Public Service,* 1994.

Other Awards: The *Akron Beacon Journal*'s staff, editors, and reporters won three Pulitzer Prizes, in addition to other journalism and public service awards.

Commentary: The *Akron Beacon Journal* was awarded the Meritorious Public Service prize in 1994 for its broad examination of local racial attitudes and its subsequent effort to promote improved communication in the community, in the newspaper's project "A Question of Color." *Journal* staff were awarded the Local General Spot News Reporting prize in 1971 for coverage of the Kent State University tragedy on May 4, 1970. The *Journal* was awarded the General News Reporting prize in 1987 for coverage, under deadline pressure, of the attempted takeover of Goodyear Time and Rubber Company by a European financier.

The *Summit Beacon* was founded on April 15, 1839. It went from a weekly to daily publication on December 6, 1869. The *Beacon* merged with the *Akron Journal* in 1897 to form the *Akron Beacon Journal*, and its first edition was printed on June 7, 1897. The Knight group of newspapers began in 1903 with Charles Landon Knight's purchase of the *Akron Beacon Journal*.

1988

Alabama Journal   491
Founded: 1889.

Prize: *General News Reporting,* 1988: *Alabama Journal,* "A Death in the Family," Montgomery, AL, 1987.

For More Information: *Washington Journalism Review,* 10:7 (September 1988): 34-37.

Commentary: The *Alabama Journal,* a 100-year-old newspaper with a circulation of 20,000, used half of its city staff — Frank Bass, Emily Bentley, Susan Eggerling, and Peggy Roberts — to delve into the infant mortality rate in Alabama, which was the highest in the nation. The reporters worked for three months on the series, "A Death in the Family." The series contained more than 20 articles and was published the last week of September 1987. Jim Tharpe, the managing editor, and Ann Green, the city editor, coordinated the reporting.

The *Alabama Journal* traces its history back to the *Evening Journal* in 1889. In 1891, it became the *Montgomery Journal,* and in 1927, the *Alabama Journal and the Times.* On September 9, 1940, the name was shortened to the *Alabama Journal.*

Lawrence Eagle-Tribune   492
Founded: July 20, 1868.

Prize: *General News Reporting,* 1988: *Lawrence Eagle-Tribune,* Lawrence, MA, 1987.

Commentary: The staff of the Massachusetts paper, the *Lawrence Eagle-Tribune,* published over 175 articles on the furlough system in place in the state's prison system. The system allowed convicted felons to leave prison for short periods. After the series appeared, the Massachusetts legislature passed a statute limiting furloughs. The two lead reporters for the series were Susan Forrest and Barbie Walsh. The paper was a finalist for the Spot News Reporting Pulitzer Prize in 1996 for its coverage of a fire that destroyed the plant of the city's largest employer.

The *Lawrence Daily Eagle* was first published in 1868 and the Lawrence *Evening Tribune* was first published on April 12, 1890. In 1898, Alexander H. Rogers and a partner bought the two papers; when the partner died in 1909, Rogers bought his interest in the papers. On September 28, 1959, Rogers merged the two newspapers into the *Lawrence Eagle-Tribune.* Irving E. Rogers Sr. continued publishing the papers upon Alexander H. Rogers's death. In 1998, Irving E. Rogers Jr. was the publisher of the *Lawrence Eagle-Tribune* while his son, Irving E. Rogers III, was the general manager.

1989

Louisville Courier-Journal
Full entry appears as **#295** under "Editorial Writing," 1918.

1990

San Jose Mercury News   493
Founded: 1851, 1853.

Prize: *General News Reporting,* 1990: *San Jose Mercury News,* San Jose, CA, 1989.

Commentary: For its detailed coverage of the October 17, 1989 Bay Area earthquake, the staff of the *San Jose Mercury News* won a Pulitzer Prize in General News Reporting. The staff used emergency generators to put out a post-quake edition. The paper had kept 12 pages open to cover the baseball World Series. Instead it used the space for information regarding the earthquake, which occurred just prior to what would have been the start of the third game of the World Series, which was being played in San Francisco's Candlestick Park.

General Non-Fiction

1962

Theodore H. White   494
Birth: May 6, 1915; Boston, MA. **Death:** 1986. **Parents:** David and Mary (Winkeller) White. **Education:** Harvard University, MA: AB, summa cum laude. **Spouse:** Nancy Ariana Van Der Heyden Bean (m. 1947; div. 1971); Beatrice Kevitt Hofstadter (m. 1974). **Children:** Ariana, David Fairbank (NAVB).

Prize: *General Non-Fiction,* 1962: *The Making of the President, 1960,* New York: Atheneum Publishers, 1961.

Career: Correspondent and Bureau Chief, Far East, *Time* Magazine; President, Foreign Correspondents Club, 1944-1945; Editor, *New Republic,* 1947; Chief European Correspondent, Overseas News Agency, NY, 1948-1950; Chief Foreign Correspondent, *Reporter,* NY, 1950-1953; National Correspondent, *Collier's,* 1955-1956; Freelance Writer and Correspondent, *Collier's,* 1956-1986; Member of Board of Overseers, Harvard University, 1968-1974; Member: Century Club, Council on Foreign Relations, Foreign Correspondents Club, Harvard Club, Phi Beta Kappa.

Selected Works: *Thunder out of China* (with Annalee Jacoby), 1946. *Fire in the Ashes: Europe in Mid-Century,* 1953. *The Mountain Road,* 1958. *The View from the Fortieth Floor,* 1960. *The Making of the President, 1964,* 1965. *Caesar at the Rubicon: A Play about Politics,* 1968. *The Making of the President, 1968,* 1969. *The Making of the President, 1972,* 1973. *Breach of Faith: The Fall of Richard Nixon,* 1975. *In Search of History: A Personal Expedition,* 1978. *America in Search of Itself: The Making of the President, 1956-1980,* 1982. *Theodore H. White at Large: The Best of His Magazine Writing, 1939-1986* (Thompson, Edward T., ed.), 1992. **Films:** *China: The Roots of Madness, Documentary,* New York: Norton, 1968.

Other Awards: Sidney Hillman Foundation Award, 1954: *Fire in the Ashes,* New York: Sloane, 1953. National Association of Independent Schools Award, 1954: *Fire in the Ashes.* Benjamin Franklin Magazine Award, 1956: "Germany—Friend or Foe?" *Collier's.* Ted V. Rodgers Award, 1956. National Association of Independent Schools Award, 1962: *The Making of the President: 1960,* New York, Atheneum Publishers, 1961. Emmy Award, Best Television Film in All Categories, National Academy of Television Arts and Sciences, 1964: *The Making of the President: 1960.* Emmy Award, Best Documen-tary Television Writing, 1967: *China: The Roots of Madness.* Emmy Award, Best Documentary Television Writing, 1985: *Television and the Presidency.* Fourth Estate Award, National Press Club. Journalist of the Year Award, Columbia School of Journalism. Honorary DHL, Hebrew Union College, OH, 1985.

For More Information: American China Policy Association, *Blunder Out of China: A Commentary on the White-Jacoby Book,* New York: American China Policy Association, 1947; Hoffmann, Joyce, *Theodore H. White and Journalism As Illusion,* Columbia: University of Missouri, 1995; Griffith, Thomas, *Harry and Teddy: The Turbulent Friendship of Press Lord Henry R. Luce and His Favorite Reporter, Theodore H. White,* New York: Random House, 1995.

Commentary: *The Making of the President* won the 1962 Pulitzer Prize in General Non-Fiction for Theodore H. White. White provided an insider's view of the 1960 presidential election. He followed candidate John F. Kennedy in the years leading up to the race and through the campaign, and in a comprehensive analysis explained Kennedy's extraordinary victory over Richard M. Nixon. White wrote similar election analyses on the presidential elections through 1980, all under the series title, *The Making of the President.*

Theodore H. White was born in Boston. He was educated at Harvard University, where he studied the Chinese language and culture. He worked as a journalist for *Time* magazine, reporting from China during World War II. His experiences there are well-documented in Thomas Griffith's *Harry and Teddy: The Turbulent Friendship of Press Lord Henry R. Luce and His Favorite Reporter, Theodore H. White.* He is credited with creating the legend of the Kennedy White House as Camelot. Articles covering China, Europe, and America, written during White's journalistic career, are collected in *Theodore H. White at Large.*

1963

Barbara W. Tuchman   495
Birth: January 30, 1912; New York, NY. **Death:** February 6, 1989. **Parents:** Maurice and Alma (Morgenthau) Wertheim. **Education:** Radcliffe College, MA: BA. **Spouse:** Lester R. Tuchman (m. 1940). **Children:** Lucy, Jessica, Alma.

Prize: *General Non-Fiction,* 1963: *The Guns of August,* New York: Macmillan, 1962. *General Non-Fiction,* 1972: *Stilwell and the American Experience in China, 1911-1945,* New York: Macmillan, 1970.

Career: Research and Editorial Assistant, Institute of Pacific Relations, NY, 1933 and Tokyo, 1934-1935; Staff Writer and Foreign Correspondent, *The Nation,* NY, 1935-1937 and Madrid Correspondent, 1937-1938; Staff Writer, *The War With Spain,* London, England, 1937-1938; Correspondent, *New Statesman* and *The Nation,* London, 1939; Editor for Far Eastern Affairs, Office of War Information, New York City, 1943-1945; Trustee, Radcliffe College, 1960-1972; President, Society of American Historians, 1970-1973; President, American Academy of Arts and Letters, 1979; Jefferson Lecturer for the National Endowment for the Humanities, 1980; Trustee, New York Public Library, 1980-1989; Council Member, Authors League of America; Lecturer, Harvard University; Lecturer, University of California; Lecturer, U.S. Naval War College; Member: American Academy of Arts and Sciences, Cosmopolitan Club, Treasurer, Authors Guild.

Selected Works: *Bible and Sword: England and Palestine from the Bronze Age to Balfour,* 1956. *The Zimmermann Telegram,* 1958. *The Proud Tower: A Portrait of the World before the War, 1890-1914,* 1966. *Notes from China,* 1972. *A Distant Mirror: The Calamitous 14th Century,* 1978. *The Palestine Question in American History* (with Clark Clifford and Eugene V. Rostow), 1978. *Practicing History: Selected Essays,* 1981. *The March of Folly: From Troy to Vietnam,* 1984. *The First Salute,* 1988.

Other Awards: Gold Medal for History, American Academy of Arts and Sciences, 1978. Regent Medal of Excellence, University of the State of New York, 1984. Sarah Josepha Hale Award, 1985. Abraham Lincoln Literary Award, Union League Club, 1985. Order of Leopold from the Kingdom of Belgium. Honorary DLitts: Yale University, CT; Columbia University, NY; New York University; Williams College, MA; Smith College, MA; Mount Holyoke College, MA; Boston University, MA; Harvard University, MA; Hamilton College, NY.

For More Information: Bowman, Kathleen, *New Women in Social Sciences,* Creative Education, 1976; *American Women Writers, 1979-1982,* New York: Ungar, 1983.

Commentary: Barbara Tuchman won two Pulitzer Prizes, both in General Non-Fiction. She won her first prize in 1963 for *The Guns of August,* which traced the diplomatic and military history of the first 30 days of World War I in 1914. Tuchman won her second prize in 1972 for *Stilwell and the American Experience in China,* a history of America's relationship with China from 1911-1945 and biography of General Joseph Stilwell, commander of the China-

Burma-India theater during World War II.

Tuchman was born in New York City. The daughter of the owner of the *Nation* magazine, she was educated at Radcliffe and then pursued a career as journalist and a non-academic historian. She reported on the Spanish Civil War from Madrid for the *Nation.* Several more correspondent positions and her interest in international affairs led her into historical writing, at which she was very successful, with six bestsellers. Her other works include *The March of Folly: From Troy to Vietnam* and *The First Salute.*

1964

Richard Hofstadter   496
Birth: August 6, 1916; Buffalo, NY. **Death:** October 24, 1970. **Parents:** Emil A. and Catherine (Hill) Hofstadter. **Education:** University of Buffalo, NY: BA. Columbia University, NY: MA, PhD. **Spouse:** Felice Swados (m. 1936; div. 1945); Beatrice Kevitt (m. 1947). **Children:** Don (FS); Sarah (BK).

Prize: *History,* 1956: *The Age of Reform: From Bryan to F.D.R.,* New York: Knopf, 1955. *General Non-Fiction,* 1964: *Anti-Intellectualism in American Life,* New York: Knopf, 1963.

Career: Assistant Professor of History, University of Maryland, College Park, 1942-1946; Assistant Professor, Columbia University, NY, 1946-1950; Associate Professor, Columbia University, 1950-1952; Visiting Professor, Princeton University, 1950; Pitt Professor of American History and Institutions, Cambridge University, 1958-1959; Professor of History, Columbia University, 1959-1970; DeWitt Clinton Professor of American History, Columbia University, 1959-1970; Corresponding Member, Massachusetts Historical Society; Member: American Academy of Arts and Sciences, American Historical Association, American Philosophical Society, American Studies Association.

Selected Works: *The American Political Tradition and the Men Who Made It,* 1951. *The Development and Scope of Higher Education in the United States* (Hofstadter, Richard and Hardy, C. De Witt, eds.), 1952. *The Development of Academic Freedom in the United States* (with Walter P. Metzger), 1955. *Social Darwinism in American Thought,* 1955. *The United States: The History of a Republic* (with William Miller and Daniel Aaron), 1957. *Great Issues in American History: A Documentary Record,* 1958. *American Higher Education: A Documentary History* (Hofstadter, Richard, and Smith, Wilson, eds.), 1961. *Anti-Intellectualism in American Life,* 1963. *The Progressive Movement, 1900-1915,* 1963. *The Paranoid Style in American Politics,* 1965. *Turner and the Sociology of the Frontier* (Hofstadter, Richard, and Lipset, Seymour M., eds.), 1968. *The Progressive*

Historians: Turner, Beard, Parrington, 1968. *The Idea of a Party System: The Rise of Legitimate Opposition in the United States, 1780-1840,* 1969. *The American Republic* (with William Miller and Daniel Aaron), 1970. *American Violence: A Documentary History* (with Michael Wallace), 1970. *America at 1750: A Social Portrait,* 1971. *The American Political Tradition and the Men Who Made It,* 1973. *Great Issues in American History: From Reconstruction to the Present Day, 1864-1981* (with Beatrice K. Hofstadter), 1982. *Social Darwinism in American Thought (Revised),* 1992. *The Paranoid Style in American Politics, and Other Essays,* 1996.

Other Awards: Beveridge Award, American Historical Association, 1942: *Social Darwinism in American Thought,* Philadelphia: University of Pennsylvania Press, 1944. Fellowship in History, 1945: *The American Political Tradition,* New York: Knopf, 1951. Sidney Hillman Award, 1964.

For More Information: Cremin, Lawrence Arthur, *Richard Hofstadter (1916-1970): A Biographical Memoir,* Syracuse, NY: National Academy of Education, 1972; Elkins, Stanley and Eric McKitrick, eds., *The Hofstadter Aegis, A Memorial,* New York: Knopf, 1974; Baker, Susan Stout, *Radical Beginnings: Richard Hofstadter and the 1930s,* Westport, CT: Greenwood, 1985.

Commentary: Richard Hofstadter has won two Pulitzer Prizes. His first award was the 1956 Pulitzer Prize in History for *The Age of Reform: From Bryan to F.D.R.* Hofstadter won a second award, the 1964 Pulitzer Prize in General Non-Fiction, for *Anti-Intellectualism in American Life.*

Hofstadter was born in Buffalo, New York. He studied at the University of Buffalo and Columbia University. Most of his teaching career was spent at Columbia University, where he was DeWitt Clinton Professor of American History. He is also known for *The Paranoid Style in American Politics.*

1965

Howard Mumford Jones　　　497

Birth: April 16, 1892; Saginaw, MI. **Parents:** Frank Alexander Jones and Josephine Whitman (Miles). **Education:** University of Wisconsin: BA. University of Chicago, IL: MA. **Spouse:** Bessie Judith Zaban (m. 1927); Clara Edgar McLure (m. 1988). **Children:** Eleanor McLure (CEM).

Prize: *General Non-Fiction,* 1965: *O Strange New World,* New York: Viking, 1964.

Career: Adjunct Professor of English, University of Texas, Austin, 1916-1917; Assistant Professor of English, Montana State University, Missoula, 1917-1919; Associate Professor, Comparative Literature and Head of Department, University of Texas, 1919-

1924; Associate Professor, University of North Carolina, Chapel Hill, 1924-1927; Professor of English, University of North Carolina, Chapel Hill, 1927-1930; Professor of English, University of Michigan, Ann Arbor, 1930-1936; Lecturer, University of Bristol, 1933; Professor of English, Harvard University, MA, 1936-1960; Dean, Graduate School of Arts and Sciences, Harvard University, MA, 1943-1944; President, American Academy of Arts and Sciences, 1944-1951; Rushton Lecturer, Harvard University, MA, 1946; Messenger Lecturer, Cornell University, 1948; Lecturer, American Institute, Munich, West Germany, 1950; Head, American Council of Learned Societies, 1955-1959; Fellow, Center for Advanced Studies in the Behavioral Sciences, 1957-1958; Head, Frank L. Weil Institute for Studies in Religion and the Humanities, 1959-1961; Editor-in-Chief, *John Harvard Library,* 1959-1962; Abbott Lawrence Lowell Professor of Humanities, Harvard University, MA, 1960-1962; Lowell Professor Emeritus, Harvard University, MA, 1962-; Visiting Professor, Massachusetts Institute of Technology, 1962-1963; Lecturer, York University, 1962; Knapp Distinguished Professor, University of Wisconsin, Madison, 1963; Paley Visiting Professor, Hebrew University of Jerusalem, 1964; President, Modern Language Association of America, 1965; Weil Lecturer, Hebrew Union College, 1967; Samuel S. Stratton Lecturer, Middlebury College, 1967; Rockefeller Distinguished Lecturer, University of Arkansas, 1975; Research Associate, Henry E. Huntington Library; Member: American Antiquarian Society, American Historical Association, American Philosophical Society, Colonial Society of Massachusetts, Delta Sigma Rho, Massachusetts Historical Society, Texas Philosophical Society, Phi Beta Kappa.

Selected Works: *Gargoyles, and Other Poems,* 1918. *America and French Culture, 1750-1848,* 1927. *The Life of Moses Coit Tyler,* 1933. *They Say the Forties,* 1937. *The Harp That Once—: A Chronicle of the Life of Thomas Moore,* 1937. *Ideas in America,* 1944. *Major American Writers* (with Ernest E. Leisy), 1945. *Education and World Tragedy,* 1946. *Primer of Intellectual Freedom,* 1949. *The Bright Medusa,* 1952. *Major American Writers* (Jones, Howard M., Ernest E. Leisy, and Richard M. Ludwig, eds.), 1952. *The Pursuit of Happiness,* 1953. *American Humanism: Its Meaning for World Survival,* 1957. *Reflections on Learning,* 1958. *Guide to American Literature and Its Backgrounds Since 1890,* 1959. *One Great Society: Humane Learning in the United States,* 1959. *The Scholar as American,* 1960. *History and the Contemporary: Essays in Nineteenth-Century Literature,* 1964. *The Theory of American Literature,* 1965. *Jeffersonianism and the American Novel,* 1966. *Belief and Disbelief in American Literature,* 1967. *The Literature of Virginia in the Seventeenth Century,*

1968. *Violence and Reason: A Book of Essays,* 1969. *Guide to American Literature and Its Backgrounds Since 1890* (with Richard M. Ludwig), 1972. *Revolution & Romanticism,* 1974. *The Many Voices of Boston: A Historical Anthology, 1630-1975* (Jones, Howard M., and Bessie Zaban, eds.), 1975. *Howard Mumford Jones: An Autobiography,* 1979.

Other Awards: Jusserand Medal from American Historical Association, 1934: *America and French Culture,* Westport, CT: Greenwood, 1927. Guggenheim Fellowship, 1964-1965. Ralph Waldo Emerson Prize, Phi Beta Kappa, 1965: *O Strange New World,* New York: Viking, 1964. Hubbell Medal, Modern Language Association, 1970. Jaffe Medal, Phi Beta Kappa, 1973. Award for Distinction in Humanistic Scholarship, University of Chicago Alumni, 1974. Honorary LittDs: Harvard University, MA, 1936; University of Colorado, 1938; University of Wisconsin, Madison, 1948; Case Western Reserve University, OH, 1948; Clark University, MA, 1952. Honorary LHD, Tulane University, LA, 1938. Honorary DHLs: Ohio State University, 1960; Hebrew Union College, IL, 1960; Northwestern University, IL, 1966; Clarkson College of Technology, NY, 1968; New York University, 1969; University of Pennsylvania, 1976. Honorary LLDs: Colby College, ME, 1962; University of Utah, 1966; University of Windsor, Canada, 1969.

For More Information: Brier, Peter A., *Howard Mumford Jones and the Dynamics of Liberal Humanism,* Columbia: University of Missouri, 1994.

Commentary: Howard Mumford Jones was awarded the 1965 Pulitzer Prize in General Non-Fiction for *O Strange New World,* a study of the formative years in American culture beginning with the Columbus discovery.

Jones was born in Saginaw, Michigan and educated at the University of Wisconsin and the University of Chicago. He was an educator, a poet, and a critic. In addition to writing verse, he has written about American culture and its relationship to Europe and American literature in relation to the development of the American nation. His other works include *Gargoyles, Ideas in America,* and *Primer of Intellectual Freedom.*

1966

Edwin Way Teale   498
Birth: June 2, 1899; Joliet, IL. **Death:** October 18, 1980. **Parents:** Oliver Cromwell and Clara Louise (Way) Teale. **Education:** Earlham College, IN: AB. Columbia University, NY: AM. **Spouse:** Nellie Imogene Donovan (m. 1923). **Children:** David Allen.

Prize: *General Non-Fiction,* 1966: *Wandering Through Winter, A Naturalist's Record of a 20,000-Mile Journey Through the North American Winter,* New York: Dodd, Mead, 1965.

Career: Instructor of English and Public Speaking, and Editorial Assistant, Friends University, Wichita, KS, 1922-1927; Feature Writer, *Popular Science,* NY, 1928-1941; Freelance writer and photographer, 1941-1980; President, New York Entomological Society, 1944; President, Brooklyn Entomological Society, 1949-1953; President, Thoreau Society, 1958; Fellow, American Association for the Advancement of Science; Member, American Ornithologists' Union; Associate, Royal Photographic Society; Fellow, New York Academy of Sciences; Member, Explorers Club, NY.

Selected Works: *Dune Boy: The Early Years of a Naturalist,* 1943. *Journey into Summer: A Naturalist's Record of a 19,000-Mile Journey through the North American Summer,* 1960. *The Lost Dog,* 1961.

Other Awards: John Burroughs Medal, 1943. Christopher Medal, 1957. Indiana Authors Day Award, 1960. Eva L. Gordon Award, American Nature Study Society, 1965. Sarah Chapman Francis Medal, Garden Club of America, 1965. Sarah Josepha Hale Award, 1975. Ecology Award, Massachusetts Horticulture Society, 1975. Conservation Medal, New England Wildflower Society, 1975. Honorary LLDs: Earlham College, IN, 1957; Indiana University, 1978. Honorary ScD, University of New Haven, CT, 1978.

For More Information: Dodd, Edward, *Of Nature, Time, and Teale,* New York: Dodd, Mead, 1960.

Commentary: Edwin Way Teale won the 1966 Pulitzer Prize in General Non-Fiction for *Wandering Through Winter,* one of a series of books he wrote about nature as it moves through the seasons in North America. Other books in the series include *North With Spring, Autumn Across America,* and *Journey Into Summer.*

Teale was born in Joliet, Illinois and educated at Earlham College and at Columbia University. He was an editorial assistant at *Popular Science* and began writing books on nature, such as *Boys' Book of Insects.* He also developed new techniques of photography for close-up shots of insects and other living creatures. Teale attributed his interest in nature to his boyhood summers spent at his grandfather's Indiana farm, a story told in *Dune Boy.* His writings have helped to promote a deeper appreciation of the environment.

1967

David Brion Davis   499
Birth: February 27, 1927; Denver, CO. **Parents:** Clyde Brion and Martha (Wirt) Davis. **Education:** Dartmouth College, NH: AB, summa cum laude. Har-

vard University, MA: AM, PhD. Oxford University, England: MA. Yale University, CT: MA. **Spouse:** Toni Hahn (m. 1971). **Children:** Jeremiah, Martha, Sarah (first marriage); Adam, Noah (TH).

Prize: *General Non-Fiction, 1967: The Problem of Slavery in Western Culture,* Ithaca, NY: Cornell University, 1966.

Career: Served in U.S. Army, 1945-1946; Instructor of History and Ford Fund for the Advancement of Education Intern, Dartmouth College, NH, 1953-1954; Assistant Professor, Cornell University, NY, 1955-1958; Associate Professor, Cornell University, NY, 1958-1963; Ernest I. White Professor of History, Cornell University, NY, 1963-1969; Professor of History, Yale University, CT, 1969-1972; Farnham Professor of History, Yale University, CT, 1972-1978; Sterling Professor of History, Yale University, CT, 1978-; Fulbright Lecturer, India, 1967, Guyana and the West Indies, 1974; Commissioner, Public Library Commission, Orange, CT, 1974-1975; Associate Director, National Humanities Institute, Yale University, CT, 1975; Executive Board Member, Organization of American Historians, 1987-1992; President, Organization of American Historians, 1988-1989; Council Member, Institute of Early American History and Culture; Member of Pulitzer Prize and Beveridge Prize Committees, American Historical Association; Member: American Antiquarian Society, American Philosophical Society, American Academy of Arts and Sciences, British Academy, Phi Beta Kappa, Society for American Historians.

Selected Works: *Homicide in American Fiction, 1798-1860: A Study in Social Values,* 1957. *Ante-Bellum Reform,* 1967. *The Slave Power Conspiracy and the Paranoid Style,* 1969. *The Fear of Conspiracy: Images of Un-American Subversion from the Revolution to the Present,* 1971. *The Emancipation Moment,* 1983. *Slavery and Human Progress,* 1984. *From Homicide to Slavery: Studies in American Culture,* 1986. *Revolutions: Reflections on American Equality and Foreign Liberations,* 1990. *Antebellum American Culture: An Interpretive Anthology* (Davis, David, ed.), 1997.

Other Awards: Guggenheim Fellow, 1958-1959. Anisfield-Wolf Award, 1967. National Mass Media Award, National Conference of Christians and Jews, 1967. Center for Advanced Study in the Behavioral Sciences Fellow, 1972-1973. Albert J. Beveridge Award, American Historical Association, 1975. National Book Award for History, 1976: *The Problem of Slavery in the Age of Revolution, 1770-1823,* Ithaca, NY: Cornell University, 1966. Bancroft Prize, 1976. Henry E. Huntington Library Fellow, 1976. National Endowment for the Humanities, Research Grants, 1979-1980, 1980-1981. Fellowship for Independent Study and Research, 1983-1984. Fulbright Traveling Fellow, 1980-1981. Corresponding Fellow, Massa-

chusetts Historical Society, 1989. Presidential Medal for Outstanding Leadership and Achievement, Dartmouth College, 1991. Corresponding Fellow, British Academy, 1992. Honorary LittD, Dartmouth College, NH, 1977. Honorary LHD, University of New Haven, CT, 1986.

For More Information: *Oxford Companion to American Literature,* New York: Oxford, 1983.

Commentary: *The Problem of Slavery in Western Culture* won the 1967 Pulitzer Prize in General Non-Fiction for David Brion Davis. The work was a study of the growth of anti-slavery sentiment in the Atlantic world through the 19th century. The book also won Davis the Anisfield-Wolf Award for the promotion of race relations.

Davis was born in Denver, Colorado, and he was educated at Dartmouth College and at Harvard University. Davis taught at Cornell University and has been the Sterling Professor of History at Yale University since 1969. Davis followed his prize-winning book with *The Problem of Slavery in the Age of Revolution, 1770-1823,* which won the National Book Award for History in 1976. He is currently working on a final volume, *The Problem of Slavery in the Age of Emancipation.* He served as a consultant on Steven Spielberg's film *Amistad.*

1968

Ariel Durant   500

Birth: 1898; Proskurov, Ukraine. **Death:** 1982. **Spouse:** Will Durant (m. 1913). **Children:** Ethel Benvenuta, Louis R.

Prize: *General Non-Fiction, 1968: Rousseau and Revolution,* Vol. 10 in *The Story of Civilization,* New York: Simon and Schuster, 1935-1975.

Career: Researcher, writer.

Selected Works: *The Age of Louis XIV* (with Will Durant), 1963. *The Lessons of History* (with Will Durant), 1968. *Interpretations of Life: A Survey of Contemporary Literature* (with Will Durant), 1970. *A Dual Autobiography* (with Will Durant), 1977.

Other Awards: Cowinner (with husband Will Durant) Huntington Hartford Foundation Award for Literature, 1963: *The Age of Louis XIV,* New York: Simon and Schuster, 1963. Co-Winner (with husband Will Durant) California Literature Medal Award, 1971: *Interpretations of Life,* New York, Simon and Schuster, 1970. Co-Winner (with husband Will Durant) Medal of Freedom, 1977.

For More Information: *Annual Obituary,* New York: St. Martin's, 1982; *Legends in Their Own Time,* New York: Prentice Hall, 1994.

Commentary: Will and Ariel Durant won the 1968 Pulitzer Prize in General Non-Fiction for *Rousseau and Revolution,* the 10th volume of the 11-volume series *The Story of Civilization.* A husband-and-wife team, they worked together on the last five volumes in the series.

Ariel Durant was born Chaya Kaufman in Proskurov, Russia. Her family immigrated to the United States and she became a student at the Ferrer Modern School in New York City where Will Durant was teaching. They fell in love and were married in 1913. They enjoyed a long and close married life. They traveled around the world together in researching *The Story of Civilization.* She helped with much of the preparation, and by the seventh volume was fully half-author. They died within a year of one another.

William James Durant   501

Birth: November 5, 1885; North Adams, MA. **Death:** November 7, 1981. **Parents:** Joseph and Marie (Allors) Durant. **Religion:** Agnostic. **Education:** St. Peter's College, NJ: BA, MA. Columbia University, NY: PhD. **Spouse:** Ariel Kaufman (m. 1913). **Children:** Ethel Benvenuta, Louis R.

Prize: *General Non-Fiction,* 1968: *Rousseau and Revolution,* Vol. 10 in *The Story of Civilization,* New York: Simon and Schuster, 1935-1975.

Career: Writer; Instructor of Latin and French, Seton Hall College, NJ, 1907-1911; Reporter, *New York Evening Journal,* 1908; Teacher, Ferrer Modern School, NY, 1911-1913; Director and Lecturer, Labor Temple School, NY, 1914-1927; Instructor of Philosophy, Columbia University, New York City, 1917; Professor of Philosophy, University of California, Los Angeles, 1935; Member, National Institute of Arts and Letters.

Selected Works: *Philosophy and the Social Problem,* 1917. *The Story of Philosophy: The Lives and Opinions of the Greater Philosophers,* 1926. *Transition: A Sentimental Story of One Mind and One Era,* 1927. *The Mansions of Philosophy: A Survey of Human Life and Destiny,* 1929. *The Case for India,* 1930. *Adventures in Genius,* 1931. *A Program for America,* 1931. *On the Meaning of Life* (Durant, Will, ed.), 1932. *The Tragedy of Russia: Impressions from a Brief Visit,* 1933. *The Lesson of Russia,* 1933. *The Foundations of Civilization,* 1936. *Caesar and Christ: A History of Roman Civilization and of Christianity from Their Beginnings to A.D. 325,* 1944. *The Age of Faith: A History of Medieval Civilization—Christian, Islamic, and Judaic—from Constantine to Dante: A.D. 325-1300,* 1950. *The Age of Louis XIV* (with Ariel Durant), 1963. *The Lessons of History* (with Ariel Durant), 1968. *Interpretations of Life: A Survey of Contemporary Literature* (with Ariel Durant), 1970. *A Dual Autobiography* (with Ariel Durant), 1977.

Other Awards: Cowinner (with wife Ariel K. Durant), Huntington Hartford Foundation Award for Literature, 1963: *The Age of Louis XIV,* New York:

Simon and Schuster, 1963. Cowinner (with wife Ariel K. Durant) California Literature Medal Award, 1971: *Interpretations of Life,* New York: Simon and Schuster, 1970. Cowinner (with wife Ariel K. Durant) Medal of Freedom, 1977. Honorary LHD, Syracuse University, 1930.

For More Information: Frey, Raymond, *William James Durant: An Intellectual Biography,* Lewiston, NY: Mellen, 1991.

Commentary: Will and Ariel Durant won the 1968 Pulitzer Prize in General Non-Fiction for *Rousseau and Revolution,* the 10th volume of the 11-volume series *The Story of Civilization.* A husband-and-wife team, they worked together on the last five volumes in the series.

Will Durant was born in North Adams, Massachusetts and educated at St. Peter's College in New Jersey and at Columbia University. He taught at private schools in New York City, including the Ferrer Modern School, an experiment in libertarian education. He was a professor of philosophy at several colleges and universities, including the University of California at Berkeley. He wrote *The Story of Philosophy,* which was a commercial success, allowing him to quit teaching and concentrate on writing. He and Ariel attempted to write a series that would appeal to the general reader and popularize the subjects of history and philosophy, instead of writing just for scholars. They succeeded in making the history of ideas available to a wide audience while still gaining critical approval.

1969

Rene Jules Dubos   502

Birth: 1901; Saint Brice, France. **Death:** 1982.

Prize: *General Non-Fiction,* 1969: *So Human an Animal,* New York: Scribner, 1968.

Career: Microbiologist, researcher, author.

Selected Works: *Bacterial and Mycotic Infections of Man,* 1948. *Louis Pasteur, Free Lance of Science,* 1950. *Mirage of Health: Utopias, Progress, and Biological Change,* 1959. *The Unseen World,* 1962. *The Torch of Life: Continuity in Living Experience,* 1962. *Man Adapting,* 1965. *A God Within,* 1972. *Only One Earth: The Care and Maintenance of a Small Planet* (with Barbara Ward), 1972. *Of Human Diversity,* 1974. *Beast or Angel? Choices That Make Us Human,* 1974. *Louis Pasteur, Free Lance of Science,* 1976. *Quest: Reflections on Medicine, Science, and Humanity* (with Jean-Paul Escande), 1980. *The Wooing of Earth,* 1980. *Celebrations of Life,* 1981.

For More Information: *Asimov's Biographical Encyclopedia of Science and Technology,* Garden City, NY: Doubleday, 1972; *Current Biography,* New York: Wilson, 1982; *Oxford Companion to Medicine,* New York: Oxford, 1986.

Commentary: Rene Jules Dubos was a co-winner of the 1969 Pulitzer Prize in General Non-Fiction for *So Human An Animal, The Development of Pessimism in America.* Dubos examined the relationship of humans to their environment.

Dubos was born in Saint Brice, France. He spent most of his professional life at Rockefeller University in New York. Dubos originally studied soil bacteria but branched out to include investigations of bacterial enzymes and toxins, infectious diseases, and the relationship between microbes and other life on earth. He is credited with the discovery of the first commercially produced antibiotic effective in the destruction of certain types of bacteria that cause pneumonia. Dubos also developed a new technique for the cultivation of the tuberculosis bacillus. His other works include *Bacterial and Mycotic Infections of Man, The Cultural Roots and the Social Fruits of Science, The Dreams of Reason: Science and Utopias,* and *Beast or Angel? Choices That Make Us Human.*

Norman Mailer

Full entry appears as **#470** under "Fiction," 1980.

1970

Erik H. Erikson   503

Birth: June 15, 1902; Frankfurt-am-Main, Germany. **Death:** 1994. **Education:** Vienna Psychoanalytic Institute, Austria. Psychiatry Clinic, Harvard University, MA. **Spouse:** Joan Mowat Serson (m. 1930). **Children:** Kai T., Jon M., Sue.

Prize: *General Non-Fiction,* 1970: *Gandhi's Truth on the Origins of Militant Nonviolence,* New York: Norton, 1969.

Career: Practicing psychoanalyst, 1933-1994; Teacher and Researcher, Harvard University, School of Medicine, Department of Neuropsychiatry, MA, 1934-1935; Yale University, School of Medicine, New Haven, CT, 1936-1939; University of California, Berkeley, and San Francisco, 1939-1951; San Francisco Psychoanalytic Institute, San Francisco, CA, and Menninger Foundation, Topeka, KS, 1944-1950; Senior Staff member, Austen Riggs Center, Stockbridge, MA, 1951-1960; Visiting Professor, Western Psychiatric Institute, PA, and Visiting Professor, Massachusetts Institute of Technology, Boston, MA, and Visiting Professor, University of Pittsburgh, School of Medicine, PA, 1951-1960; Professor of Human Development and Lecturer of Psychiatry, Harvard University, MA, 1969-1970; Professor Emeritus, Harvard University, 1970-1994; Distinguished Visiting Professor, Erikson Center, Harvard University, MA, 1982-1994; Fellow: American Academy of Arts and Science, American Psychological Association; Honorary Member, Phi Beta Kappa; Member: American Psychoanalytic Association, Cambridge Scientific Club, Signet Society; Member Emeritus, National Academy of Education; Trustee, Radcliffe College, MA.

Selected Works: *Young Man Luther: A Study in Psychoanalysis and History,* 1962. *Youth: Change and Challenge,* 1963. *Childhood and Society,* 1963. *Insight and Responsibility: Lectures on the Ethical Implications of Psychoanalytic Insight,* 1964. *Identity, Youth, and Crisis,* 1968. *In Search of Common Ground: Conversations with Erik H. Erikson and Huey P. Newton,* 1973. *Dimensions of a New Identity,* 1974. *Life History and the Historical Moment,* 1975. *Toys and Reasons: Stages in the Ritualization of Experience,* 1977. *Adulthood,* 1978. *The Life Cycle Completed: A Review,* 1982. *Vital Involvement in Old Age* (with Joan M. Erikson and Helen Q. Kivnik), 1986. *A Way of Looking at Things: Selected Papers from 1930 to 1980,* 1987.

Other Awards: Harvard University, MA, MS, LLD. University of California, CA, LLD. Loyola University, CA, ScD. National Book Award, Philosophy and Religion, 1970: *Gandhi's Truth,* New York: Norton, 1969. National Association for Mental Health Research Award, 1974. Aldrich Award from American Academy of Pediatrics, 1974. Golden Bagel Award, Mt. Zion Hospital, San Francisco, CA, 1976. Honorary FilDrHC, Lund University, 1980. Honorary SocScDs: Yale University, 1971; Copenhagen University, 1987. Honorary LLD, Brown University, 1972.

For More Information: Coles, Robert, *Erik H. Erikson: The Growth of His Work,* Boston: Little, Brown, 1970; Roazen, Paul, *Erik H. Erikson: The Power and Limits of a Vision,* New York: Free Press, 1976; Wright, J. Eugene, *Erikson, Identity and Relig-*

ion, New York: Seabury, 1982; Knowles, Richard T., *Human Development and Human Possibility: Erikson in the Light of Heidegger,* Lanham, MD: University Press of America, 1986; Gross, Francis L., *Introducing Erik Erikson: An Invitation to His Thinking,* Lanham, MD: University Press of America, 1987.

Commentary: *Gandhi's Truth on the Origins of Militant Nonviolence,* won the 1970 Pulitzer Prize in General Non-Fiction for Erik H. Erikson. Erikson sought to explain Gandhi's ability to lead a nation through his recognition of the damage done to the population's psyche by an oppressor and his ability to know exactly what to do to overcome the damage.

Erikson was born in Frankfurt-am-Main, Germany. He was educated at the Vienna Psychoanalytic Institute in Austria, where he studied under Anna Freud, and at Harvard University. Erikson is known for his research in developmental psychology, which led to his theory of the eight psychosocial stages in the life cycle, from infancy through adulthood. He introduced the term "identity crisis," which has been adapted into common usage. His first book, *Childhood and Society,* was widely read. He attempted to apply his theories to subjects of popular interest with his study of Mahatma Gandhi and *Young Man Luther: A Study in Psychoanalysis and History,* which focused on Martin Luther.

1971

John Toland 504
Birth: June 29, 1912; La Crosse, WI. **Parents:** Ralph and Helen (Snow) Toland. **Education:** Williams College, MA: BA. Yale University Drama School, CT. **Spouse:** Toshiko Matsamura (m. 1960). **Children:** Diana, Marcia (first marriage); Tamiko (TM).

Prize: *General Non-Fiction,* 1971: *The Rising Sun: The Decline and Fall of the Japanese Empire, 1936-1945,* New York: Random House, 1970.

Career: Captain, U.S. Air Force; Advisor, National Archives; Honorary Vice President, Western Front Association; Member: Accademia del Mediterrano, Overseas Press Club, PEN, Writers Guild.

Selected Works: *Ships in the Sky: The Story of the Great Dirigibles,* 1957. *Battle: The Story of the Bulge,* 1959. *But Not in Shame: The Six Months After Pearl Harbor,* 1961. *The Dillinger Days,* 1963. *The Last 100 Days,* 1966. *The Great Dirigibles: Their Triumphs and Disasters,* 1972. *Adolf Hitler,* 1976. *Hitler: The Pictorial Documentary of His Life,* 1978. *No Man's Land: 1918, The Last Year of the Great War,* 1980. *Infamy: Pearl Harbor and Its Aftermath,* 1982. *Gods of War,* 1985. *Occupation,* 1987. *In Mortal Combat: Korea, 1950-1953,* 1991. *Captured by History: One Man's Vision of Our Tumultuous Century,* 1997.

Other Awards: Overseas Press Club Award, 1961: *But Not in Shame,* London, England: Gibbs, 1961. Overseas Press Club Award, 1967: *The Last 100 Days,* New York: Random House, 1966. Overseas Press Club Award, 1970: *The Rising Sun: The Decline and Fall of the Japanese Empire, 1936-1945,* New York: Random House, 1970. Van Wyck Brooks Award for Nonfiction, 1970: *The Rising Sun: The Decline and Fall of the Japanese Empire, 1936-1945.* Overseas Press Club Award, 1976: *Adolf Hitler,* Garden City, NY: Doubleday, 1976. National Society of Arts and Letters Gold Medal, 1977: *Adolf Hitler.* Accademia del Mediterrano, 1978. Honorary LHDs: Williams College, MA, 1968; University of Alaska, 1977; University of Connecticut, 1986.

For More Information: *Something About the Author,* Detroit: Gale, 1985.

Commentary: John Toland won the 1971 Pulitzer Prize in General Non-Fiction for *The Rising Sun: The Decline and Fall of the Japanese Empire, 1936-1945.* Toland chronicled the aggressions committed by the Japanese in the years before and during World War II.

Toland was born in La Crosse, Wisconsin and educated at Williams College and at the Yale Drama School. His interest in writing led him into journalism. He wrote regularly for *American Magazine* and *Coronet.* He contracted with a publisher to write a book about dirigibles and, upon completion, he signed another book contract. He wrote *The Battle of the Bulge,* a bestseller that was made into a popular motion picture. His histories have a dramatic flair that make them very readable. He tells his own story in *Captured By History.* His other works include *Infamy* and a biography, *Adolf Hitler.*

1972

Barbara W. Tuchman
Full entry appears as **#495** under "General Non-Fiction," 1963.

1973

Robert Coles 505
Birth: October 29, 1929; Boston, MA. **Parents:** Philip and Sandra (Young) Coles. **Education:** Harvard University, MA: AB. Columbia University, NY: MD. **Spouse:** Jane Hallowell. **Children:** Robert, Daniel, Michael.

Prize: *General Non-Fiction,* 1973: *Children of Crisis: A Study of Courage and Fear,* Vol II and III in *Children of Crisis,* Boston: Little, Brown, 1967.

Career: Intern, Clinics, University of Chicago, 1954-1955; Resident, Psychiatry, Massachusetts

General Hospital, 1955-1956; Teaching Fellow, Staff and Clinical Assistant, Psychiatry, Harvard Medical School, 1955-1958; Resident, McLean Hospital, MA, 1956-1957; Resident, Judge Baker Guidance Center-Children's Hospital, MA, 1957-1958; Staff, Children's Unit, Metropolitan State Hospital, MA, 1957-1958; Staff, Alcoholic Clinic, Massachusetts General Hospital; Child Psychiatrist and Fellow, Judge Baker Guidance Center, Children's Hospital, MA, 1960-1961; Research Psychiatrist, Health Services, Harvard University, MA, 1963-; Member, National Advisory Committee on Farm Labor, 1965-; Lecturer, General Education, Harvard University, MA, 1966-; Contributing Editor, *New Republic,* 1966; Editorial Board, *Integrated Education,* 1967; Board of Directors, Field Foundation, 1968-; Trustee, Robert F. Kennedy Memorial, 1968; Editorial Board, *Child Psychiatry and Human Development,* 1969; Fellow, Rockefeller Foundation, 1969; Fellow, Ford Foundation, 1969; Member, Boston Children's Service, 1970; Board of Directors, Twentieth Century Fund, 1971; Contributing Editor, *American Poetry,* 1972; Member, Americans for Children's Relief, 1972; Member, National Committee for the Education of Young Children, 1972; Member, Institute of Medicine, National Academy of Sciences, 1973-1978; Visiting Professor, Public Policy, Duke University, NC, 1973-; Contributing Editor, *Aperture,* 1974; Fellow, Davenport College, MI, 1976; Fellow, Yale University, CT, 1976; Member, National Advisory Council for Rural America, 1976; Member, Advisory Committee for National Indian Education Association, 1976; Trustee, Austin Riggs Foundation, 1976; Editorial Board, *Grants Magazine,* 1977; Board of Directors, Boys Club, Boston, MA, 1977; Professor of Psychiatry and Medical Humanities, Harvard University, MA, 1977-; Member, Children's Committee, Edna McConnell Clark Foundation, 1978; Editorial Board, *Learning Magazine,* 1978; Board of Editors, *Parents Choice* magazine, 1978; Editor, *Children and Youth Services Review,* 1978; Board of Directors, Lyndhurst Foundation, 1978; Contributing Editor, *Literature and Medicine,* 1981; Board of Directors, Center for Documentary Studies, Duke University, NC; Visiting Professor, Dartmouth College, NH, 1989; Fellow, American Academy of Arts and Sciences; Fellow, Institute for Society, Ethics and the Life Sciences; Member: American Psychiatric Association, Academy of Psychoanalysis, National Organization of Migrant Children.

Selected Works: *The Desegregation of Southern Schools: A Psychiatric Study,* 1963. *Dead End School,* 1968. *Still Hungry in America,* 1969. *Wages of Neglect* (with Maria Piers), 1969. *Uprooted Children: The Early Life of Migrant Farm Workers,* 1970. *Erik H. Erikson: The Growth of His Work,* 1970. *The South Goes North,* 1971. *The Middle Americans: Proud and Uncertain,* 1971. *Migrants, Sharecroppers, Mountaineers,* 1971. *Saving Face,* 1972. *The Old Ones of New Mexico,* 1973. *Riding Free,* 1973. *A Spectacle Unto the World: The Catholic Worker Movement,* 1973. *Children and Political Authority,* 1974. *William Carlos Williams: The Knack of Survival in America,* 1975. *Headsparks,* 1975. *The Mind's Fate: Ways of Seeing Psychiatry and Psychoanalysis,* 1975. *Eskimos, Chicanos, Indians,* 1977. *Women of Crisis: Lives of Struggle and Hope* (with Jane Hallowell), 1978. *The Last and First Eskimos,* 1978. *Walker Percy: An American Search,* 1978. *Flannery O'Connor's South,* 1980. *Sex and the American Teenager* (with Geoffrey Stokes), 1985. *Agee: His Life Remembered* (Spears, Ross, and Cassidy, Jude, eds.), 1985. *The Moral Life of Children,* 1986. *The Political Life of Children,* 1986. *Simone Weil: A Modern Pilgrimage,* 1987. *Dorothy Day: A Radical Devotion,* 1987. *Harvard Diary: Reflections on the Sacred and the Secular,* 1988. *Times of Surrender: Selected Essays,* 1988. *The Call of Stories: Teaching and the Moral Imagination,* 1989. *Rumors of Separate Worlds: Poems,* 1989. *The Spiritual Life of Children,* 1990. *Women of Crisis II: Lives of Work and Dreams* (with Jane Hallowell), 1990. *Breaking the Cycle: Survivors of Child Abuse and Neglect* (with Pamela Fong), 1991. *Anna Freud: The Dream of Psychoanalysis,* 1992. *The Call of Service: A Witness to Idealism,* 1993. *A Robert Coles Omnibus,* 1993. *The Story of Ruby Bridges,* 1995. *The Youngest Parents: Teenage Pregnancy as It Shapes Lives,* 1997. *Doing Documentary Work,* 1997.

Other Awards: Ralph Waldo Emerson Prize, Phi Beta Kappa, 1967: *Children of Crisis,* Boston: Little, Brown, 1967. Anisfield-Wolf Award in Race Relations, *Saturday Review,* 1968: *Children of Crisis.* Hofheimer Award, American Psychiatric Association, 1968: *Children of Crisis.* Sidney Hillman Prize, 1971: *Children of Crisis.* Weatherford Prize, Berea College, 1973: *Children of Crisis.* Lillian Smith Award, Southern Regional Council, 1973: *Children of Crisis.* McAlpin Medal, National Association of Mental Health, 1972: *Children of Crisis.* Distinguished Scholar Medal, Hofstra University, 1974. William A. Schoenfeld Award, American Society of Adolescent Psychiatry, 1971. MacArthur Foundation Award, 1981. Sarah Josepha Hale Award, 1986.

For More Information: Ronda, Bruce A., *Intellect and Spirit: The Life and Work of Robert Coles,* New York: Continuum, 1989; Hilligoss, Susan, *Robert Coles,* New York: Twayne, 1997.

Commentary: Robert Coles was a co-winner of the 1973 Pulitzer Prize in General Non-Fiction for *Children of Crisis,* Vols. II and III, a study in courage and fear that looked at the children of migrants, sharecroppers, and African Americans moving to Northern cities. This series, when completed, comprised five volumes and included studies of Eskimo, Indian, and

Latino children.

Coles was born in Boston, Massachusetts and educated at Harvard University and Medical School and at Columbia University. He is an educator, pediatrician, and child psychologist. He has devoted his career to the study of the psyche of children and has grown to appreciate their ability to overcome adversity. His other works include *Women of Crisis: Lives of Work and Dreams* and *The Spiritual Life of Children.*

Frances Fitzgerald   506

Birth: October 21, 1940; New York. **Parents:** Desmond Fitzgerald and Marietta Endicott (Peabody) Fitzgerald Tree. **Education:** Radcliffe College, MA: BA, magna cum laude.

Prize: *General Non-Fiction,* 1973: *Fire in the Lake: The Vietnamese and the Americans in Vietnam,* Boston: Little, Brown, 1972.

Career: Journalist, author, visiting professor.

Selected Works: *America Revised: History Schoolbooks in the Twentieth Century,* 1979. *Cities on a Hill: A Journey through Contemporary American Cultures,* 1986.

Other Awards: National Book Award, 1973: *Fire in the Lake,* Boston: Little, Brown, 1972.

For More Information: McLendon, Winzola, *Don't Quote Me: Washington Newswomen and the Power Society,* New York, Dutton, 1970; *Time,* August 28, 1972; *People,* Sepetember 15, 1980.

Commentary: Frances Fitzgerald was a co-winner of the 1973 Pulitzer Prize in General Non-Fiction for *Fire in the Lake: The Vietnamese and the Americans in Vietnam.* Fitzgerald spent five years writing this analysis of the culture of Vietnam and its political and social response to the American occupation during the long years of war.

Fitzgerald was born in in New York City and educated at Radcliffe College. Her other works include *America Revised: History Schoolbooks in the Twentieth Century,* and *Cities on a Hill.*

1974

Ernest Becker   507

Birth: 1925. **Death:** 1974. **Education:** Syracuse University, NY: PhD.

Prize: *General Non-Fiction,* 1974: *The Denial of Death,* New York: Free Press, 1973.

Career: Writer; Staff member, U.S. Embassy, Paris, France; State University of New York, Instructor, 1962-1965; University of California, Berkeley, Lecturer, beginning in 1965; Instructor, San Francisco State University; Instructor, Simon Fraser University in Burnaby, British Columbia.

Selected Works: *Zen: A Rational Critique,* 1961. *The Birth and Death of Meaning: A Perspective in Psychiatry and Anthropology,* 1962. *The Revolution in Psychiatry: The New Understanding of Man,* 1964. *Beyond Alienation: A Philosophy of Education for the Crisis of Democracy,* 1967. *Angel in Armor: A Post-Freudian Perspective on the Nature of Man,* 1969. *The Birth and Death of Meaning: An Interdisciplinary Perspective on the Problem of Man,* 1971. *The Lost Science of Man,* 1971. *Escape from Evil,* 1975.

For More Information: Sontag, Frederick, *The Return of the Gods: A Philosophical / Theological Reappraisal of the Writings of Ernest Becker,* New York: Lang, 1989; Evans, Ronald V., *The Creative Myth and the Cosmic Hero: Text and Context in Ernest Becker's, "The Denial of Death,"* New York: Lang, 1992; Liechty, Daniel, *Transference and Transcendence: Ernest Becker's Contribution to Psychotherapy,* Northvale, NJ: Aronson, 1995.

Commentary: *The Denial of Death* won the 1974 Pulitzer Prize in General Non-Fiction for Ernest Becker, awarded posthumously, as Becker had died two months earlier. Becker examined the arguments for the universality of fear of death, and believed that humans devise intricate belief systems and behavior patterns to promote their own feeling of immortality in the face of the inevitability of death.

Becker was an academic who was not accepted because of his theories. He was ousted as an instructor from Syracuse University for agreeing with another professor who dissented with the diagnosis of "mentally ill" for patients at mental institutions. He was eventually offered a position at the University of California at Berkeley where he was quite popular and was able to write. Becker saw mortality as the basis of man's repression—not sexuality, as Sigmund Freud thought. His work has become more accepted since his death. His other works include *The Birth and Death of Meaning: An Interdisciplinary Perspective on the Problem of Man, Escape from Evil,* and *Angel in Armor: A Post-Freudian Perspective on the Nature of Man.*

1975

Annie Dillard   508

Birth: April 30, 1945; Pittsburgh, PA. **Parents:** Frank and Pam (Lambert) Doak. **Religion:** Roman Catholic. **Education:** Hollins College, VA: BA, MA. **Spouse:** Richard Dillard (m. 1964; div.); Gary Clevidence (m. 1980; div.); Robert D. Richardson, Jr. (m. 1988). **Children:** Cody Rose, Carin, Shelly (GC).

Prize: *General Non-Fiction,* 1975: *Pilgrim at Tinker Creek,* New York: Harper's Magazine, 1974.

Career: Writer; Columnist, "The Living Wilderness," The Wilderness Society, 1973-1975; Editor,

Harper's magazine, 1973-1985; Scholar-in-Residence, Western Washington University, WA 1975-1979; Distinguished Visiting Professor, Wesleyan University, CT, 1979-1982; Adjunct Professor, Wesleyan University, CT, 1983-1986; Writer-in-Residence, Wesleyan University, CT, 1987-present; Member, U.S. Cultural Delegation to China, 1982; Board Member and Chairman, Wesleyan Writers' Conference, 1991-present; Jury, Pulitzer Prize, 1985, 1991; Jury, Bollingen Prize; Board Member, Authors League Fund; Board Member, Catholic Commission on Intellectual and Cultural Affairs; Board Member, Key West Literary Seminar; Board Member, Milton Centre; Board Member, National Committee for United States-China Relations; Board Member, Western States Arts Foundation; Member: Century Association, International PEN, New York Public Library National Literacy Committee, Panel on Usage, American Heritage Dictionary, Phi Beta Kappa, Poetry Society of America, Western Writers of America.

Selected Works: *Tickets for a Prayer Wheel: Poems,* 1974. *Holy the Firm,* 1977. *Teaching a Stone to Talk: Expeditions and Encounters,* 1982. *Living by Fiction,* 1982. *An American Childhood,* 1987. *The Writing Life,* 1989. *The Living,* 1992. *The Annie Dillard Reader,* 1994. *Modern American Memoirs* (Dillard, Annie E., and Conley, Cort, eds.), 1995. *Mornings Like This: Found Poems,* 1995.

Other Awards: New York Press Club Award for Excellence, 1975. Washington State Governor's Award for Literature, 1978. Grants from National Endowment for the Arts, 1980-1981. Guggenheim Foundation Award, 1985-1986. Appalachian Gold Medallion, University of Charleston, 1989. St. Botolph's Club Foundation Award, Boston, 1989. English-Speaking Union Ambassador Book Award, 1990: *The Writing Life,* New York: Harper & Row, 1989. History Maker Award, Historical Society of Western Pennsylvania, 1993. Campion Award, Christian Lit, 1994. Honorary Degrees: Boston College, 1986; Connecticut College, 1993; University of Hartford, 1993.

For More Information: Smith, Linda L., *Annie Dillard,* New York: Twayne, 1991; Johnson, Sandra Humble, *The Space Between: Literary Epiphany in the Work of Annie Dillard,* Kent, OH: Kent State University, 1992.

Commentary: Annie Dillard was awarded the 1975 Pulitzer Prize in General Non-Fiction for *Pilgrim at Tinker Creek,* a book of musings on nature and things understood and things not.

Dillard was born in Pittsburgh, Pennsylvania. She was educated at Hollins College. Her other works include *The Living, Mornings Like This,* and her autobiography, *An American Childhood.*

1976

Robert Neil Butler   509

Birth: January 21, 1927; New York, NY. **Parents:** Fred and Esther (Dikeman) Butler. **Education:** Columbia University, NY: BA, MD. **Spouse:** Diane McLaughlin (m. 1950; d. 1973); Myrna Lewis (m. 1975). **Children:** Ann Christine, Carole Melissa, Cynthia Lee (DM).

Prize: *General Non-Fiction,* 1976: *Why Survive? Being Old in America,* New York: Harper & Row, 1975.

Career: Gerontologist and psychiatric researcher; Staff, U.S. Public Health Service, 1955-; Researcher, National Institute of Mental Health, MD, 1958-1962; Senior Surgeon, U.S. Public Health Service, 1961; Member, Executive Committee, Washington School of Psychiatry, 1961-1976; Board of Directors, National Ballet Society, 1961-1975; Founding Member, National Ballet, 1962-1975; Inactive Reserve, U.S. Public Health Service, 1962-1976; Member, Subcommittee on Employment, District of Columbia Inter-Departmental Committee on Aging, 1966-1967; Board of Directors, National Council on Aging, 1969-; Chairman, District of Columbia Advisory Committee on Aging, 1969-1972; Member, District of Columbia Advisory Committee on Aging, 1969-; Member, Mental Health Technical Advisory Committee to Health Planning Advisory Committee, District of Columbia Department of Public Health, 1970-1971; Medical Director, U.S. Public Health Service, 1976-; Research Psychiatrist and Gerontologist, Washington School of Psychiatry, Washington, DC, 1962-1976; Director, National Institute on Aging, MD, 1976-; Associate Clinical Professor, Howard University, School of Medicine; Associate Clinical Professor, George Washington University School of Medicine; Faculty, Washington Board of Trustees, National Council on Aging; Board of Trustees, National Caucus on the Black Aged; Board of Trustees, Legal Research and Services for the Elderly; Board of Trustees, District of Columbia Commission on Aging; Consultant, Center for Law and Social Policy; Consultant, Langley Porter Neuropsychiatric Institute; Consultant, St. Elizabeth Hospital; Consultant, U.S. Senate Special Committee on Aging; Fellow, American Psychiatric Association; Founding Fellow, American Geriatrics Society; Founding Member, Forum for Professionals and Executives; Member: American Medical Association, Cosmos Club (Washington, DC), District of Columbia Medical Society, Gerontological Society, Group for the Advancement of Psychiatry, National Council of Senior Citizens, Washington Psychiatric Society.

Selected Works: *Aging and Mental Health: Positive Psychosocial and Biomedical Approaches* (with Myrna I. Lewis), 1982. *Love and Sex after 40: A Guide for Men and Women for Their Mid and Later Years* (with Myrna I. Lewis), 1986. *Who Is Responsible for My Old Age?* (Butler, Robert Neil, and Kiikuni, Kenzo, eds.), 1993.

Other Awards: Certificate of Appreciation, American Medical Writers Association, 1976. Community Service Award, District of Columbia Medical Society, 1976.

For More Information: *American Men and Women of Science,* New York: Bowker, 1971; "Lifeline: Robert N. Butler," *Lancet,* March 21, 1998.

Commentary: Robert N. Butler won the 1976 Pulitzer Prize in General Non-Fiction for *Why Survive? Being Old in America,* a book which examined what the aging process involves and what to expect in old age.

Butler was born in New York City. He was the founding director of the National Institute on Aging. He founded the first department of geriatrics at a medical school in the United States, at the Mount Sinai Medical Center. He was chairman of the department and a professor there until 1995. He became the director of the United States branch of the International Longevity Center (ILC), which he established in 1990. The Center conducts studies of the impact of longevity on society, on institutions, and on the lives of children. He is the co-author of *Aging and Mental Health, Love and Sex after 40,* and *Love and Sex after 60.* He is currently working on a new book, *The Longevity Revolution.*

1977

William Whitesides Warner   510

Birth: April 2, 1920; New York, NY. **Parents:** Charles Jolly and Leonora (Haberle) Warner. **Religion:** Roman Catholic. **Education:** Princeton University, NJ: AB. **Spouse:** Kathleen Berryman McMahon (m. 1951). **Children:** John B., Alleta B., Georgina B., Alexandra DeP., William A., Elizabeth S.

Prize: *General Non-Fiction,* 1977: *Beautiful Swimmers: Watermen, Crabs, and the Chesapeake Bay,* Boston: Little, Brown, 1976.

Career: Essayist; Lieutenant, U.S. Navy, 1944-1946; Public Affairs Officer in Latin America, U.S. Information Agency, Washington, DC, 1951-1962; Vice President, Audubon Naturalist Society of the Central Atlantic States, 1961-1964; Executive Secretary and Program Coordinator for Latin America, Peace Corps, Washington, DC, 1962-1963; Director of Office of International Activities, Smithsonian Institution, Washington, DC, 1964-1967; Assistant Secretary for Public Service, Smithsonian Institution, Washington, DC, 1967-1973; Consultant and Research Associate, Smithsonian Institution, 1973-

1988; Vice President, Rachel Carson Trust for the Living Environment, 1966-1973; Trustee, Chesapeake Bay Foundation; Board of Directors, PEN/Faulkner Foundation; Member: Authors Guild, Chesapeake Bay Foundation, PEN, Sigma Xi.

Selected Works: *Distant Water: The Fate of the North Atlantic Fisherman,* 1983. *At Peace with All Their Neighbors: Catholics and Catholicism in the National Capital, 1787-1860,* 1994.

Other Awards: Commendation Ribbon, United States Navy. Phi Beta Kappa Award in Science, 1977: *Beautiful Swimmers,* Boston: Little, Brown, 1976. Christopher Award, 1977: *Beautiful Swimmers.* First Place, History-Biography, Catholic Press Association Book Awards, 1994: *At Peace with All Their Neighbors: Catholics and Catholicism in the National Capital, 1787-1860,* Washington, DC: Georgetown University, 1994. Honorary DSci, Memorial University of Newfoundland, Canada, 1992.

For More Information: "Washington Talk," *New York Times,* May 13, 1983; "Accent" section, *Baltimore Sun,* April 5, 1983; *World Authors, 1975-1980,* p. 779-780, New York: Wilson, 1985; *At Peace with All Their Neighbors: Catholics and Catholicism in the National Capital, 1787-1860,* Washington, DC: Georgetown University, 1994.

Commentary: *Beautiful Swimmers: Watermen, Crabs, and the Chesapeake Bay* won the 1977 Pulitzer Prize in General Non-Fiction for William W. Warner. This book is an immersion course in the habitat of the Maryland crab. The prize came as a total surprise to Warner. Twenty-three years after its publication, it is still available in paperback.

Warner was born in New York City. He was educated at Princeton University and Memorial University of Newfoundland. He worked for the United States Department of State from 1953 to 1962, the Peace Corps in the early 1960s, and at the Smithsonian Institution as Assistant Secretary for Public Service. His other works include *Distant Water* and *At Peace With All Their Neighbors: Catholics and Catholicism in the National Capital, 1787-1860.*

1978

Carl Sagan   511

Birth: November 9, 1934; New York, NY. **Death:** December 19, 1996. **Parents:** Samuel Sagan and Rachel (Gruber). **Education:** University of Chicago, IL: AB, general and special honors: BS, MS, PhD. **Spouse:** Lynn Alexander (m. 1957); Linda Salzman (m. 1968); Ann Druyan. **Children:** Dorian Solomon, Jeremy Ethan; Nicholas; Alexandra, Rachel, Samuel Democritus.

Prize: *General Non-Fiction,* 1978: *The Dragons of Eden: Speculations on the Evolution of Human Intelligence,* New York: Random House, 1977.

Career: Astrophysicist and author; Miller Research Fellow in Astronomy, University of California, Berkeley, 1960-1962; Assistant Professor of Astronomy, Harvard University, MA, 1962-1968; Astrophysicist, Smithsonian Institution, Astrophysical Observatory, MA, 1962-1968; Visiting Assistant Professor of Genetics, Stanford University Medical School, 1962-1963; Condon Lecturer, University of Oregon and Oregon State University, 1967-1968; Associate Professor, Cornell University, NY, 1968-1970; Director, Laboratory for Planetary Studies, Cornell University, NY, 1968-1996; Lecturer in Astronaut Training Program, National Aeronautics and Space Administration (NASA) 1969-1972; Professor of Astronomy and Space Sciences, Cornell University, NY, 1970-1996; Holiday Lecturer, American Association for the Advancement of Science, 1970; Associate Director, Center for Radiophysics and Space Research, Cornell University, NY, 1972-1981; Member, Board of Directors, Council for the Advancement of Science Writing, 1972-1977; Vanuxem Lecturer, Princeton University, 1973, 1985; Smith Lecturer, Dartmouth College, 1974, 1977; Judge, National Book Awards, 1975; Wagner Lecturer, University of Pennsylvania, 1975; Philips Lecturer, Haverford College, 1975; Jacob Bronowski Lecturer, University of Toronto, 1975; Chairman, Astronomy Section, American Association for the Advancement of Science, 1975; Member of Council, Smithsonian Institution, 1975-1985; Chairman, Division of Planetary Sciences, American Astronomical Society, 1975-1976; David Duncan Professor of Astronomy and Space Sciences, Cornell University, NY, 1976-1996; Member of Council, American Astronautical Society, 1976-1981; Anson Clark Memorial Lecturer, University of Texas at Dallas, 1976; Danz Lecturer, University of Washington, 1976; Member, Usage Panel, *American Heritage Dictionary of the English Language,* 1976-1996; Member, Fellowship Panel, John S. Guggenheim Memorial Foundation, 1976-1981; Chairman, Study Group on Machine Intelligence and Robotics, NASA, 1977-1979; Stahl Lecturer, Bowdoin College, ME, 1977; Christmas Lecturer, Royal Institution, London, 1977; Fellow and Member of Council, Federation of American Scientists, 1977-1981 and 1984-1988; Menninger Memorial Lecturer, American Psychiatric Association, 1978; President, Planetary Society, 1979-1996; Member of Council, International Academy of Astronautics, International Society for the Study of the Origin of Life, 1980-1996; President, Planetology Section, American Geophysical Union, 1980-1982; Member, Board of Directors, Council for a Livable World Education Fund, 1980-1996; Carver Memorial Lecturer, Tuskegee Institute,

1981; Feinstone Lecturer, U.S. Military Academy, 1981; Class Day Lecturer, Yale University, 1981; President, Carl Sagan Productions, 1981-1996; George Pal Lecturer, Motion Picture Academy of Arts and Sciences, 1982; Phelps Dodge Lecturer, University of Arizona, 1982; H. L. Welsh Lecturer in Physics, University of Toronto, 1982; Member, Advisory Panel, Civil Space Station Study, Office of Technology Assessment, U.S. Congress, 1982-1996; Fellow, Robotics Institute, Carnegie-Mellon University, 1982-1996; Distinguished Lecturer, U.S. Air Force Academy, Colorado Springs, 1983; Member, American Committee on U.S.-Soviet Relations, 1983-1996; Adolf Meyer Lecturer, American Psychiatric Association, 1984; Lowell Lecturer, Harvard University, 1984; Jack Distinguished American Lecturer, Indiana University, PA, 1984; Distinguished Lecturer, Southern Methodist University, 1984; Keystone Lecturer, National War College, National Defense University, Washington, DC, 1984-1986; Marshall Lecturer, Natural Resources Defense Council, Washington, DC, 1985; Johnson Distinguished Lecturer, Johnson Graduate School of Management, Cornell University, 1985; Gifford Lecturer in Natural Theology, University of Glasgow, 1985; Lilenthal Lecturer, California Academy of Science, 1986; Dolan Lecturer, American Public Health Association, 1986; Distinguished Visiting Scientist, Jet Propulsion Laboratory, California Institute of Technology, 1986-1996; Distinguished Lecturer, The Japan Society, 1987; Cohen Lecturer, Moravian College, PA, 1987; Barrack Lecturer, University of Nevada, 1987; Von Braun Lecturer, University of Alabama, 1987; Commonwealth Lecturer, University of Massachusetts, Amherst, 1988; Gilbert Grosvenor Centennial Lecturer, National Geographic Society, 1988; Olin Lecturer, Cornell University, 1988; Member, Board of Advisors, Children's Health Fund, 1988-1996; Co-Chairman, Science, Global Forum of Spiritual and Parliamentary Leaders on Human Survival, 1988-1996; Murata Lecturer, Kyoto, Japan, 1989; Bart Bok Centennial Lecturer, Astronomical Society of the Pacific, University of California at Berkeley, 1989; James Forrestal Lecturer, U.S. Naval Academy, 1989; Robert W. Beggs Memorial Lecturer, Cornell University Center for Religion, Ethics, and Social Policy, 1989; National Telephone and Telegraph Company Centennial Lecturer, Tokyo, 1990; Distinguished Speaker, State University of New York at Buffalo, 1990; Member, International Board of Advisors, Asahi Shimbun, Tokyo, 1991-1996; Member, Advisory Council, National Institutes for the Environment, 1991-1996; Consultant, National Academy of Science; Fellow: American Academy of Arts and Sciences, American Federation of Television and Radio Artists, American Institute of Aeronautics and Astronautics, American Physical Society, Society for the Study of Evolution, British

Interplanetary Society; Member: Astronomical Society of the Pacific, Authors Guild, Authors League of America, Council on Foreign Relations, Explorers Club, Genetics Society of America, PEN International, Phi Beta Kappa, Sigma Xi; Member of Organizing Committee, Commission of Physical Study of Planets, International Astronomical Union; Member, Writers Guild of America Vice Chairman, Working Group on Moon and Planets, Committee on Space Research International Council of Scientific Unions.

Selected Works: *Planetary Exploration,* 1970. *UFO's: A Scientific Debate* (Sagan, Carl, and Page, Thornton, eds.), 1972. *Planets* (with Jonathan Norton), 1972. *Communication with Extraterrestrial Intelligence (CETI)* (Sagan, Carl, ed.), 1973. *The Cosmic Connection: An Extraterrestrial Perspective,* 1973. *Murmurs of Earth: The Voyager Interstellar Record,* 1978. *Broca's Brain: Reflections on the Romance of Science,* 1979. *Cosmos,* 1980. *The Cold and the Dark: The World after Nuclear War* (with Paul Erhlich), 1984. *Comet* (with Ann Druyan), 1985. *Contact,* 1985. *A Path Where No Man Thought: Nuclear Winter and the End of the Arms Race* (with Richard Turco), 1990. *Shadows of Forgotten Ancestors: A Search for Who We Are* (with Ann Druyan), 1992. *Pale Blue Dot: A Vision of the Human Future in Space,* 1994. *The Demon-Haunted World: Science as a Candle in the Dark,* 1996.

Other Awards: National Science Foundation Pre-Doctoral Fellowship, 1955-1958. Alfred P. Sloan Foundation Research Fellowship, Harvard University, 1963-1967. A. Calvert Smith Prize, Harvard University, 1964. National Aeronautics and Space Administration, Apollo Achievement Award, 1970. Medal for Exceptional Scientific Achievement, 1972. Medal for Distinguished Public Service, 1977, 1981. Prix Galabert (International Astronautics Prize), 1973. Klumpke-Roberts Prize, Astronomical Society of the Pacific, 1974. John W. Campbell Memorial Award, World Science Fiction Convention, 1974: *The Cosmic Connection,* Garden City, NY: Anchar, 1973. Golden Plate Award, American Academy of Achievement, 1975. Joseph Priestly Award, Dickinson College, 1975. Washburn Medal, Boston Museum of Science, 1978. Rittenhouse Medal, Franklin Institute /Rittenhouse Astronomical Society, 1980. 75th Anniversary Award, Explorers Club, 1980. Best Books for Young Adults, American Library Association, 1980: *Cosmos,* New York: Random House, 1980. New York Public Library's Books for the Teen Age, 1980: *Broca's Brain,* and; *Murmurs of Earth,* New York: Random House, 1978. Academy of Family Films and Family Television Award, Best Television Series, 1980. American Council for Better Broadcasts Citation for Highest Quality Television Programming, 1980-1981. Silver Plaque from Chicago Film Festival. President's Special Award from Western Educa-

tional Society for Telecommunication, 1981. George Foster Peabody Award for Excellence in Television Programming, University of Georgia, 1981. Ohio State University Annual Award for Television Excellence, 1982: *Cosmos.* Humanist of the Year Award, American Humanist Association, 1981. Glenn Seaborg Prize for Communicating Science from the Lecture Platform, American Platform Association, 1981. Ralph Coats Roe Medal, American Society of Mechanical Engineers, 1981. Hugo Award, World Science Fiction Convention, 1982: *Cosmos.* Co-Winner, Stony Brook Foundation Award, Distinguished Contributions to Higher Education, 1982. John F. Kennedy Astronautics Award, American Astronautical Society, 1983. Locus Award, 1986: *Contact.* Honda Prize, Honda Foundation, 1985. Arthur C. Clarke Award for Exploration and Development of Space, 1984. Peter Lavan Award for Humanitarian Service, Bard College, 1984. New Priorities Award, Fund for New Priorities in America, 1984. Sidney Hillman Foundation Prize Award, 1984. SANE National Peace Award, 1984. Regents Medal for Excellence, Board of Regents, University of the State of New York, 1984. Olive Branch Award, New York University, 1984, 1986, 1989. Physicians for Social Responsibility Annual Award for Public Service, 1985. Co-Winner, Leo Szilard Award for Physics in the Public Interest, American Physical Society, 1985. Distinguished Service Award, World Peace Film Festival, Marlboro College, 1985. Nahum Goldmann Medal, World Jewish Congress, 1986. Brit Ha Dorot Award, Shalom Center, 1986. Annual Award of Merit, American Consulting Engineers Council, 1986. Maurice Eisendrath Award for Social Justice, Central Conference of American Rabbis and the Union of American Hebrew Congregations, 1987. In Praise of Reason Award, Committee for the Scientific Investigation of Claims of the Paranormal, 1987. Konstantin Tsiolkovsky Medal, Soviet Cosmonautics Federation, 1987. George F. Kennan Peace Award, SANE/Freeze, 1988. Helen Caldicott Peace Leadership Award, with Ann Druyan, Women's Action for Nuclear Disarmament, 1988. Distinguished Service Award for Innovation in Higher Education, University without Walls International Council, 1988. Roger Baldwin Award, Massachusetts Civil Liberties Union, 1989. Oersted Medal, American Association of Physics Teachers, 1990. Annual Award for Outstanding Television Script, Writers Guild of America, 1991. Presidential Award, National Science Supervisors Association, 1991. UCLA Medal, University of California at Los Angeles, 1991. Distinguished Leadership Award, Nuclear Age Peace Foundation, 1993. First Carl Sagan Understanding of Science Award, 1994. Public Welfare Medal, NAS, 1994. Award for Public Understanding of Science and Technology, AAAS, 1995. Honorary DScL, University of Illinois,

1990. Honorary DHum, University of Hartford, 1991. Honorary DScs: Rensselaer Polytechnic University, NY, 1975; Denison University, OH, 1976; Clarkson College, NY, 1977; Whittier College, CA, 1978; Clark University, MA, 1978; American University, Washington, DC, 1980; University of South Carolina, 1984; Hofstra University, NY, 1985; Long Island University, 1987; Tuskegee University, AL, 1988; Lehigh University, AL, 1990. Honorary LLDs: University of Wyoming, 1978; Drexel University, PH, 1986. Honorary DHLs: Skidmore College, NY 1976; Lewis and Clark College, OR, 1980; Brooklyn College, NY, 1982.

For More Information: Ginenthal, Charles, *Carl Sagan & Immanuel Velikovsky,* Tempe, AZ: New Falcon, 1995; Jones, Tony, "A Fond Farewell from Carl Sagan," *New Scientist,* September 27, 1997; Joson, Imelda B, "Sagan's Sagacious Legacy," *Sky and Telescope,* February 1998; Plait, Philip, "Sagan's Legacy: Astronomy Shines in Contact," *Astronomy,* April 1998.

Commentary: Carl Sagan won the 1978 Pulitzer Prize in General Non-Fiction for *The Dragons of Eden: Speculations on the Evolution of Human Intelligence,* a study of genetics, evolution, and the human brain.

Carl Sagan was deeply interested in the possibility of life on other planets. He made significant contributions to understanding the planets Mars and Venus. He participated in and developed experiments for the Mariner and Viking missions to Mars, and also the Pioneer and Voyager missions. Sagan's search for intelligent life in the universe found a wide public audience through his numerous television appearances as a guest on the *Tonight Show,* his 1980 series for PBS, *Cosmos,* and the bestselling book by the same title. He wrote numerous books and articles on the possibility of life elsewhere in the universe.

1979

Edward Osbourne Wilson   512

Birth: June 10, 1929; Birmingham, AL. **Parents:** Edward O., Sr., and Inez (Crumley) Wilson. **Education:** University of Alabama: BS, MS. Harvard University, MA: PhD. **Spouse:** Irene Kelley (m. 1955). **Children:** Catherine Irene.

Prize: *General Non-Fiction,* 1979: *On Human Nature,* Cambridge, MA: Harvard University, 1978. *General Non-Fiction,* 1991: *The Ants,* Cambridge, MA: Belknap, 1990.

Career: Writer; Assistant Professor of Biology, Harvard University, MA, 1956-1958; Associate Professor of Zoology, Harvard University, MA, 1958-1964; Professor of Zoology, Harvard University, MA, 1964-1976; Curator of Entomology at Museum of Comparative Zoology, Harvard University, MA, 1972-present; Frank B. Baird, Jr. Professor of Science, Harvard University, MA, 1976-1994; Member, Selection Committee, J. S. Guggenheim Foundation, 1982-1989; Board of Directors, World Wildlife Fund, 1983-1994; Pellegrino University Professor, Harvard University, 1994-1997; Pellegrino University Professor Emeritus, 1997-; Fellow: American Philosophical Society, American Academy of Arts and Sciences, Deutsche Akademie Naturforscher, German Academy of Sciences, Society for the Study of Evolution; Honorary Life Member: American Genetics Association, American Humanist Society, British Ecological Society, Entomological Society of America, Zoological Society of London; Member: American Academy of Liberal Education, National Academy of Sciences, Royal Society London; Trustee, Marine Biological Laboratory, Woods Hole, MA.

Selected Works: *The Theory of Island Biogeography* (with Robert H. MacArthur), 1967. *The Insect Societies,* 1971. *Sociobiology: The New Synthesis,* 1975. *Genes, Mind, and Culture: The Coevolutionary Process* (with Charles J. Lumsden), 1981. *Promethean Fire: Reflections on the Origin of Mind* (with Charles J. Lumsden), 1983. *Biophilia,* 1984. *The Diversity of Life,* 1992. *Naturalist,* 1994. *Journey to the Ants: A Story of Scientific Exploration* (with Bert Holldobler), 1994. *In Search of Nature,* 1996.

Other Awards: Award from American Association for the Advancement of Science, 1969. Mercer Award, Ecological Society of America, 1971. Founders Memorial Award, Entomological Society of America, 1972. Distinguished Service Award, American Institute of Biological Sciences, 1976. National Medal of Science, 1977. Leidy Medal, Academy of Natural Sciences, 1979. Sesquicentennial Medal, University of Alabama, 1981. Distinguished Humanist Award, American Humanist Association, 1982. Richard M. Weaver Award for Scholarly Letters, Ingersoll Foundation, 1989. Crafoord Prize, Royal Swedish Academy of Sciences, 1990. Prix d'Institute de la Vie, Paris, 1990. Achievement Award, National Wildlife Federation, 1992. Shaw Medal, Missouri Botanical Garden, 1993. International Prize for Biology, Government of Japan, 1993. Wildlife Society Book Award, 1993: *The Diversity of Life,* Cambridge, MA: Belknap, 1992. Eminent Ecologist Award, Ecological Society of America, 1994. Distinguished Achievement Award, Educational Press Association of America, 1994. Sir Peter Kent Conservation Book Prize, Book Trust, United Kingdom, 1994: *The Diversity of Life.* Audubon Medal, Audubon Society, 1995. John Hay Award, Orion Society, 1995. *Los Angeles Times,* Book Review Award for Science and Technology, 1995. Phi Beta Kappa Award, Science, 1995: *Journey to the Ants,* Cambridge, MA: Belknap, 1990. Benjamin Franklin Award, Publishers Marketing Association, 1995: *Naturalist,* Washington, DC: Island Press / Shearwater, 1994. William Procter Prize for Scientific Achievement, Sigma Xi, 1997.

For More Information: Hoyt, Erich, *The Earth Dwellers: Adventures in the Land of Ants,* New York: Simon & Schuster, 1996; "E.O. Wilson Receives Procter Prize," *American Scientist,* November / December 1996; "E.O. Wilson's Last Class," *Nieman Reports,* Spring 1997; Pratter, Frank, "How Billions of Humans Can Evolve In Harmony on Planet Earth," *Christian Science Monitor,* April 9, 1998.

Commentary: Edward O. Wilson won two Pulitzer Prizes, both in General Non-Fiction. He won his first prize in 1979 for *On Human Nature,* an elucidation of his key ideas on the implications of sociobiology for the understanding of human nature. He and co-author, Bert Holldobler, won the prize in 1991 for *The Ants,* a comprehensive study of the evolution, taxonomy, physiology, ecology, and social behavior of ants.

Wilson was born in Birmingham, Alabama. He was educated at the University of Alabama and at Harvard University. A Harvard University entomologist and Frank B. Baird Jr. Professor of Science, Wilson is a leader in documenting the destruction of the earth's biodiversity and in promoting a strong conservation ethic. His other works include *The Insect Societies, Sociobiology: The New Synthesis, Biophilia,* and *Consilience: The Unity of Knowledge.*

1980

Douglas R. Hofstadter 513

Birth: February 15, 1945; New York, NY. **Parents:** Robert and Nancy (Givan) Hofstadter. **Education:** Stanford University, CA: BS, with distinction. University of Oregon: MS, PhD. **Spouse:** Carol Ann Brush (m. 1948; died 1993). **Children:** Daniel Frederic, Monica Marie.

Prize: *General Non-Fiction,* 1980: *Godel, Escher, Bach: An Eternal Golden Braid,* New York: Vintage, 1979.

Career: Assistant Professor, Indiana University, Bloomington, 1977-1980; Associate Professor of Computer Science, Indiana University, Bloomington, 1980-1984; Walgreen Professor of Cognitive Science, University of Michigan, Ann Arbor, 1984-1988; Professor of Cognitive Science and Computer Science, Indiana University, Bloomington, 1988-present; Director, Center for Research on Concepts and Cognition, Indiana University; Member: American Association for Artificial Intelligence, Association for Computing Machinery, Association of Computational Linguistics, Cognitive Science Society.

Selected Works: *The Mind's I: Fantasies and Reflections on Self and Soul* (with Daniel C. Dennett),

1981. *Metamagical Themas: Questing for the Essence of Mind and Pattern,* 1985. *Fluid Concepts and Creative Analogies: Computer Models of the Fundamental Mechanisms of Thought* (with Fluid Analogies Research Group), 1995. *Rhapsody on a Theme of Clement Merot* (Grace A. Tanner Lecture in Human Values), 1996. *Le Ton beau de Marot: In Praise of the Music of Language,* 1997.

Other Awards: American Book Award, 1980: *Godel, Escher, Bach: An Eternal Golden Braid,* New York: Vintage, 1979. Sigma Xi Distinguished Lecturer Award, 1980. Guggenheim Fellowship, 1980-1981. Leather Medal Award, Indiana University Chapter of Sigma Delta Chi, Society of Professional Journalists, 1982. Young Alumnus of the Year, University of Oregon, 1983. Polya Prize, Best Article Written for Two-Year College Mathematics Journal. Golden Plate Recipient, American Academy of Achievement, 1984. Senior Fellow, Michigan Society of Fellows, 1985.

For More Information: Kelly, Kevin, "By Analogy," *Wired,* November 1995; Boden, Margaret A, "Artificial Genius," *Discover,* October 1996; Griffiths, Paul, "Translating a 'Universal Language,'" *New York Times,* September 21, 1997.

Commentary: *Godel, Escher, Bach: An Eternal Golden Braid* won the 1980 Pulitzer Prize in general nonfiction for Douglas R. Hofstadter. This book is an observation about the products of the workings of the human mind, wherein Hofstadter ties together the work of mathematician Godel, graphic artist Escher, and composer Bach.

Hofstadter was born in New York City and educated at Stanford University and the University of Oregon. Hofstadter is a professor of cognitive science and computer science at Indiana University. He has written about human and artificial intelligence. His other works include *Metamagical Themas: Questing for the Essence of Mind and Pattern, Fluid Concepts and Creative Analogies: Computer Models of the Fundamental Mechanisms of Thought,* and *The Mind's I.*

1981

Carl E. Schorske 514

Birth: March 15, 1915; New York, NY. **Parents:** Theodore A. and Gertrude (Goldschmidt) Schorske. **Education:** Columbia University, NY: AB. Harvard University, MA: MA, PhD. **Spouse:** Elizabeth Rorke (m. 1941). **Children:** Theodore, Anne Schorske Edwards, Stephen, John, Richard.

Prize: *General Non-Fiction,* 1981: *Fin-de-Siecle Vienna: Politics and Culture,* New York: Knopf, 1979.

Career: Political Analyst for Office of Strategic Services, 1941-1946; Lieutenant, U.S. Naval Reserve, 1943-1946; Assistant Professor, Wesleyan University, CT, 1946-1950; Member, Council on Foreign Relations, 1946-1950; Associate Professor, Wesleyan University, CT, 1950-1955; Visiting Lecturer, Harvard University, 1951-1952, Visiting Lecturer, Yale University, 1952-1953; Professor of History, Wesleyan University, CT, 1955-1960; Fellow, Center on Advanced Studies in Behavioral Sciences, 1959-1960; Professor of History, University of California, Berkeley, 1960-1969; Member of Council, American Historical Association, 1964-1968; Fellow, Institute of Advanced Studies, Princeton University, NJ, 1967-1968 and 1969-1972; Dayton-Stockton Professor of History, Princeton University, NJ, 1969-present; Director of European Cultural Studies, Princeton University, NJ, 1973-present; Member: American Academy of Arts and Sciences, American Historical Association, Board of Trustees, Institute of Architecture and Urban Studies, Board of Trustees, Institute of Humanities, Phi Beta Kappa.

Selected Works: *The Problem of Germany* (with Hoyt Price), 1947. *German Social Democracy, 1905-1917: The Development of the Great Schism,* 1955. *Gustav Mahler: Formation and Transformation,* 1992. *Budapest and New York: Studies in Metropolitan Transformation, 1870-1930* (Schorske, Carl E. and Bender, Thomas, eds.), 1994.

Other Awards: Harvard University Fellow, 1938-1941. Award from Social Sciences Research Council, 1946. Rockefeller Fellow, 1949. Toppan Prize from Harvard University, 1950. Guggenheim Fellow, 1954-1955. Honorary DLH, Wesleyan University, Middletown, CT, 1967.

For More Information: Roth, Michael S., "Performing History: Modernist Contextualism in Carl Schorske's Fin-de-Siecle Vienna," *American Historical Review,* June 1994.

Commentary: Carl E. Schorske was awarded the 1981 Pulitzer Prize in General Non-Fiction for *Fin-de-Siecle Vienna: Politics and Culture,* a look back at the city of Vienna at the end of the 19th century—the arts, the growth of the field of psychology, and other ideas which would rapidly shape the 20th century.

Schorske was born in New York City and educated at Columbia and Harvard Universities. He has been a professor of history at Wesleyan University and the University of California at Berkeley and he is currently Professor Emeritus at Princeton. His other works include *The Problem of Germany* and *German Social Democracy, 1905-1917.*

1982

John Tracy Kidder   515

Birth: November 12, 1945; New York, NY. **Parents:** Henry Maynard and Reine Maria Melanie (Tracy) Kidder. **Education:** Harvard University, MA: AB. University of Iowa: MFA. **Spouse:** Frances Toland (m. 1971). **Children:** Nathaniel T., Alice T.

Prize: *General Non-Fiction,* 1982: *The Soul of a New Machine,* Boston: Little, Brown, 1981.

Career: Writer, 1974-present; Contributing Editor, *Atlantic Monthly,* Boston, 1982-present; Visiting Lecturer, Smith College, MA, 1985, 1986; Writer-in-Residence, Northwestern University, 1995.

Selected Works: *The Road to Yuba City,* 1974. *Among Schoolchildren,* 1985. *Old Friends,* 1993.

Other Awards: Atlantic First Award, *Atlantic Monthly:* "The Death of Major Great." Sidney Hillman Foundation Prize, 1978: "Soldiers of Misfortune." American Book Award, 1982: *The Soul of a New Machine,* Boston: Little, Brown, 1981. Robert F. Kennedy Award, 1990: *Among Schoolchildren,* Boston: Houghton Mifflin, 1985. Ambassador Book Award, 1990: *Among Schoolchildren.* New England Book Award, 1994. Honorary DHLs: University of Massachusetts; Springfield College; Clarkson University, NY.

For More Information: Smith, Amanda, "Tracy Kidder," *Publishers Weekly,* September 15, 1989; Richards, Evelyn, "Data General Struggles to Regain Its Balance," *Washington Post,* August 22, 1990; Blades, John, "Elder Statesman," *Chicago Tribune,* November 10, 1993.

Commentary: Tracy Kidder won the 1982 Pulitzer Prize in General Non-Fiction for *The Soul of a New Machine,* the story of the development and building of a new super mini-computer at Data General Corporation.

Kidder was born in New York City. He was educated at Harvard University and at the University of Iowa. He has written short stories and nonfiction articles for such publications as *Atlantic,* the *New Yorker,* and *Granta.* His other works include *The Road to Yuba City* and *Among Schoolchildren.*

1983

Susan Sheehan   516

Birth: August 24, 1937; Vienna, Austria. **Parents:** Charles and Kitty C. (Hermann) Sachsel. **Education:** Wellesley College, MA: BA. **Spouse:** Neil Sheehan (m. 1963). **Children:** Maria Gregory, Catherine Fair.

Prize: *General Non-Fiction,* 1983: *Is There No Place on Earth for Me?,* Boston: Houghton Mifflin, 1982.

Career: Writer; Editorial Researcher, *Esquire*, NY, 1959-1960; Freelance writer, NY, 1960-1961; Staff Writer, *The New Yorker*, NY, 1961-present; Member, Advisory Committee on Employment and Crime, Vera Institute of Justice, 1978-1984; Member, Literature Panel, District of Columbia Commission on Arts and Humanities, 1979-1984; Consultant, 42nd St. Redevelopment Project, New York City Department of City Planning; Judge, Robert F. Kennedy Journalism Awards, 1980, 1984; Literary Panel, National Mental Health Association, 1982-1983; Chair, Pulitzer Prize Nominating Jury, General Nonfiction, 1988; Member, Pulitzer Prize Nominating Jury, General Nonfiction, 1991; Contributor to many publications including the *New York Times Sunday Magazine, Harper's, Atlantic* and *New Republic;* Member: American Society of Historians, National Mental Health Association, Phi Beta Kappa.

Selected Works: *Ten Vietnamese*, 1967. *A Welfare Mother*, 1976. *A Prison and a Prisoner*, 1978. *Kate Quinton's Days*, 1984. *A Missing Plane*, 1986. *Robert Indiana Prints: A Catalogue Raisonne, 1951-1991*, 1991. *Life for Me Ain't Been No Crystal Stair*, 1993.

Other Awards: Guggenheim Fellow, 1975-1976. Sidney Hillman Foundation Award, 1976: *A Welfare Mother*, Boston, NY: Houghton Mifflin, 1976. Gavel Award, American Bar Association, 1978: *A Prison and a Prisoner*. Fellow, Woodrow Wilson Center for International Scholars, 1981. Mental Health Media Award for Individual Reporting, National Mental Health Association, 1981: "The Patient." Distinguished Alumni Award, Wellesley College, 1984. Feature Writing Award, New York Press Club, 1984. Fellow, Ford Foundation. Distinguished Graduate Award, Hunter College High School, NY, 1995. Honorary DHL, University of Massachusetts, 1991.

For More Information: Warren, James, "The Remarkable Sheehans," *Chicago Tribune*, April 15, 1990; Warren, James, "She Needs Her Space," *Chicago Tribune*, September 26, 1993.

Commentary: *Is There No Place on Earth for Me?* won the 1983 Pulitzer Prize in General Non-Fiction for Susan Sheehan. It chronicled Sylvia Frumkin's battle with schizophrenia at Creedmoor Psychiatric Center on Long Island, New York.

Sheehan was born in Vienna, Austria and educated at Wellesley College. She is married to Neil Sheehan, who is also a Pulitzer Prize winner in General Non-Fiction (1989). Her biography of Frumkin originally appeared in parts in the *New Yorker* magazine. She has written for many magazines. Sheehan's other works include *Missing Plane* and *Life for Me Ain't Been No Crystal Stair*.

1984

Paul Starr 517

Birth: May 12, 1949; New York, NY. **Parents:** Saul Starr and Sarah Marion (Buzen). **Education:** Columbia University, NY: BA, summa cum laude. Harvard University, MA: PhD. **Spouse:** Sandra Lurie Stein (m. 1982). **Children:** Three children.

Prize: *General Non-Fiction*, 1984: *The Social Transformation of American Medicine*, New York: Basic, 1982.

Career: Assistant Professor, Harvard University, MA, 1978-1983; Associate Professor of Sociology, Harvard University, MA, 1983-1985; Professor of Sociology, Princeton University, Princeton, NJ, 1985-Present; Project Director, Center for Study of Responsive Law, 1971-1972; Member, Institute for Advanced Study, 1984-1985; Member, Phi Beta Kappa.

Selected Works: *The University Crisis Reader* (Starr, Paul, and Wallerstein, Immanuel, eds.), 1971. *The Discarded Army: Veterans after Vietnam; the Nader Report on Vietnam Veterans and the Veterans Administration*, 1973. *Privatization / Project on the Federal Social Role*, 1985. *The Politics of Numbers* (with William Alonso), 1987. *The Limits of Privatization*, 1988.

Other Awards: Guggenheim Fellow, 1981-1982. C. Wright Mills Award, Society for the Study of Social Problems, 1983. Bancroft Prize in American History and Diplomacy, Columbia University. James A. Hamilton Hospital Administrators' Book Award, American College of Healthcare Executives, 1984: *The Social Transformation of American Medicine*, New York: Basic, 1982. Honorary DHL, State University of New York, 1986.

For More Information: Alter, Jonathan, "Can Ideas Grow out of Ashes?" *Newsweek*, April 30, 1990; Pearlstein, Steven, "Clinton's Professorial Point Man on Health Care Reform," *Washington Post*, May 23, 1993; Millenson, Michael L, "From Health Care's Tom Paine, Dose of 'Common Sense,'" *Chicago Tribune*, September 5, 1993.

Commentary: Paul Starr was awarded the 1984 Pulitzer Prize in General Non-Fiction for *The Social Transformation of American Medicine*, a documentation of the rise of the medical profession, which offers superb sociology and history of American medicine.

Starr was born in New York City and educated at Columbia and Harvard Universities. He is currently a professor of sociology at Princeton University, co-editor of *The American Prospect*, and founder of *The Electronic Policy Network*. In *The Logic of Health-Care Reform*, he presented a case for a system of universal health insurance based on consumer choice among private health plans and a budget cap on spending growth. He has been an advisor to President Clinton on health care policy. *The Social Transformation of American Medicine* won the 1984 Pulitzer Prize for Nonfiction, the C. Wright Mills Award, the James Hamilton Prize of the American College of Healthcare Executives, and the Bancroft Prize in American History and Diplomacy.

1985

Studs Terkel   518

Birth: May 16, 1912; New York, NY. **Parents:** Samuel and Anna (Finkel) Terkel. **Education:** University of Chicago, IL: PhB, JD. **Spouse:** Ida Goldberg (m. 1939). **Children:** Paul.

Prize: *General Non-Fiction,* 1985: *The Good War: An Oral History of World War Two,* New York: Pantheon, 1984.

Career: Author; Civil Service Employee, Washington, DC; Stage Actor and Movie House Manager, 1930s and 1940s; Host, interview show, WFMT, Chicago, IL, 1945-Present; Moderator, *Studs' Place,* Television program, Chicago, 1950-1953; Master of Ceremonies, Ravinia Music Festival, Ravinia, IL, 1959; Master of Ceremonies, Newport Folk Festival, 1959 and 1960; Master of Ceremonies, University of Chicago Folk Festival, 1961.

Selected Works: *Division Street: America,* 1967. *Hard Times: An Oral History of the Great Depression,* 1970. *Working,* 1974. *Giants of Jazz,* 1975. *American Dreams, Lost and Found,* 1980. *Envelopes of Sound: The Art of Oral History* (with Ronald J. Grele), 1985. *Race: How Blacks and Whites Think and Feel about the American Obsession,* 1992. *Coming of Age: The Story of Our Century by Those Who've Lived It,* 1995. *Talking to Myself: A Memoir of My Times,* 1995. *My American Century,* 1997.

Other Awards: Ohio State University Award, 1959. UNESCO Prix Italia Award, 1962: *Wax Museum,* New York: Pantheon, 1980. Communicator of the Year Award, University of Chicago Alumni Association, 1969. George Foster Peabody Broadcasting Award, 1980. Society of Midland Authors Award, 1982: *American Dreams: Lost and Found,* New York: Pantheon, 1980. Best Writer, Society of Midland Authors Award, 1983. Eugene V. Debs Award for Public Service, 1983. Hugh M. Hefner First Amendment Award for Lifetime Achievement, 1990.

For More Information: Baker, James Thomas, *Studs Terkel,* New York: Twayne, 1992; Parker, Tony, *Studs Terkel: A Life in Words,* New York: Holt, 1996.

Commentary: Studs Terkel won the 1985 Pulitzer Prize in General Non-Fiction for *The Good War: An Oral History of World War Two,* the story of the war from the perspectives of those who fought on the front lines and on the home front.

Terkel was born in New York City and educated at the University of Chicago. After college, he stayed in Chicago and had a career as both a radio and a television personality. He is in touch with all walks of life in America and is the consummate interviewer, with an uncanny ability to get his subjects to talk. His other works include an oral history of the Depression, *Hard Times, Race: How Blacks and Whites Think and Feel About the American Obsession,* and *My American Century.*

1986

Joseph Lelyveld   519

Birth: April 5, 1937; Cincinnati, OH. **Parents:** Arthur Joseph and Toby (Bookholtz) Lelyveld. **Education:** Harvard University, MA: AB, summa cum laude: MA. Columbia University, NY: MS. **Spouse:** Carolyn Fox (m. 1959). **Children:** Amy, Nita.

Prize: *General Non-Fiction,* 1986: *Move Your Shadow: South Africa Black and White,* New York: Times, 1985.

Career: U.S. Army Reserves, 1961-1967; Staff member, *New York Times,* NY, 1962-present; Correspondent, Congo and South Africa, *New York Times,* 1965-1966; Correspondent, London, England, *New York Times,* 1966; Correspondent, India and Pakistan, *New York Times,* 1966-1969; Correspondent, Hong Kong, *New York Times,* 1973-1975; Deputy Foreign Editor, *New York Times,* 1978-1980; Correspondent, South Africa, *New York Times,* 1980-1983; Staff Writer, *New York Times Magazine,* NY, 1984-1985; London Bureau Chief, *New York Times,* 1985-1986; Foreign Editor, *New York Times,* 1987; Executive Editor, *New York Times,* Present.

Selected Works: *Young Americans Abroad,* 1963.

Other Awards: Fulbright Fellowship, Burma, 1960. Page One Award, New York Newspaper Guild, 1970: Article on death of twelve-year-old heroin user in Harlem. George Polk Memorial Award, 1972: Series of articles on a fourth-grade class. George Polk Memorial Award, 1984: Coverage of South Africa. Guggenheim Fellowship, 1984. *Los Angeles Times* Book Award, 1986: *Move Your Shadow: South Africa Black and White.*

For More Information: "The Talk of the Town: In His Times," *New Yorker,* July 11, 1994; Wechsler, Pat and Roger D. Friedman, "Joseph Lelyveld, Your Times Pen Pal," *New York,* January 2, 1995; "The Times Announces 2 Senior Appointments," *New York Times,* Current Events Edition, April 18, 1995; Zoglin, Richard, "The Last Great Newspaper," *Time,* September 29, 1997.

Commentary: Joseph P. Lelyveld was a co-winner of the 1986 Pulitzer Prize in General Non-Fiction for *Move Your Shadow: South Africa Black and White,* an authoritative report of the ordeals of daily black life under the apartheid regime and a discussion of what the future might bring.

Lelyveld was born in Cincinnati, Ohio and educated at Harvard University and at Columbia University. He has been with the *New York Times* since 1962 as a correspondent and he is currently the executive editor. He was based in South Africa in the 1960s and again in the 1980s. He has won numerous awards, including two George Polk Memorial Awards.

J. Anthony Lukas 520

Birth: April 25, 1933; New York, NY. **Death:** June 5, 1997. **Parents:** Edwin Jay Lukas and Elizabeth (Schamberg). **Religion:** Jewish. **Education:** Harvard University, MA: BA, magna cum laude, Phi Beta Kappa. Free University of Berlin, Germany: Postgrad. **Spouse:** Linda Healey (m. 1982).

Prize: *Local Investigative Specialized Reporting,* 1968: *New York Times,* New York: New York Times, 1967. *General Non-Fiction,* 1986: *Common Ground: A Turbulent Decade in the Lives of Three American Families,* New York: Knopf, 1985.

Career: Assistant Manager, college paper, *Harvard Crimson;* News Commentator and Writer, U.S. Army, 1956-58; City Hall Correspondent, *Baltimore (MD) Sun,* 1958-62; Reporter, Washington (DC) and United Nations Bureaus, *New York Times,* 1962; Correspondent, Congo, *New York Times,* 1962-65; Correspondent, India, *New York Times,* 1965-67; Metropolitan Staff member, *New York Times,* 1967-68; National Correspondent, *New York Times,* 1969-70; Staff member, Sunday magazine, *New York Times,* 1970-71; Founder, *More Magazine,* 1971-77; Visiting Lecturer, Yale University (CT), 1973; Adjunct Professor, School of Public Communications, Boston University, 1977-78; Visiting Lecturer, Kennedy School of Government, Harvard University (MA), 1979-80; Writer.

Selected Works: *The Barnyard Epithet and Other Obscenities: Notes on the Chicago Conspiracy Trial,* 1970. *Don't Shoot—We Are Your Children!,* 1971. *Watergate: The Story So Far,* 1973. *Nightmare: The Underside of the Nixon Years,* 1976. *Big Trouble: A Murder in a Small Western Town Sets off a Struggle for the Soul of America,* 1997.

Other Awards: Adenauer Fellow, Free University of Berlin, Germany, 1956. George Polk Memorial Award, Long Island University, NY, 1968. Mike Berger Award, Columbia University, NY, 1968. Page One Award, New York Newspaper Guild, 1968. Byline Feature Award, Newspaper Reporters Association, 1968. Nieman Fellow, Harvard University, MA, 1968-69. Fellow, Kennedy Institute of Politics, Har-

vard University, MA, 1976-77. Guggenheim Fellow, 1978-79. American Book Award, 1985: *Common Ground: A Turbulent Decade in the Lives of Three American Families,* New York: Knopf, 1985. National Book Critics Circle Award, 1985: *Common Ground: A Turbulent Decade in the Lives of Three American Families.* Robert F. Kennedy Book Award, 1985: *Common Ground: A Turbulent Decade in the Lives of Three American Families.* Honorary Degree, Northeastern University, MA.

For More Information: *Times Talk,* 20:10 (May 1968): 1; *New Yorker,* 23 February (1976); *Contemporary Authors, New Revision Series, Volume 2,* Detroit: Gale Research Company, 1981: 428-29; *Current Biography Yearbook, 1987,* New York: H.W. Wilson Company, 1987: 371-374; *New York Times,* 7 June (1997): 17; *Harvard Magazine,* September/October (1997).

Commentary: J. Anthony Lukas's first Pulitzer Prize was presented for a story contrasting the affluent upbringing and the counterculture lifestyle of a girl found beaten to death with her boyfriend in New York City's East Village. His second Pulitzer Prize was awarded for the book *Common Ground,* which was about school desegregation and bussing, and the impact on two low-income families in Boston. The research and writing of the book took him seven years.

Lukas is believed to have coined the phrase "barnyard epithet." He committed suicide in 1997.

1987

David K. Shipler 521

Birth: December 3, 1942; Orange, NJ. **Parents:** Guy Emery, Jr. and Eleanor (Karr) Shipler. **Religion:** Protestant. **Education:** Dartmouth College, NH: AB. Russian Institute, Columbia University, NY. **Spouse:** Deborah S. Isaacs (m. 1966). **Children:** Jonathan Robert, Laura Kerr, Michael Edmund.

Prize: *General Non-Fiction,* 1987: *Arab and Jew: Wounded Spirits in a Promised Land,* New York: Times, 1986.

Career: Lieutenant, U.S. Naval Reserve, 1964-1966; News Clerk, *New York Times,* NY, 1966-1968; Reporter, *New York Times,* NY, 1968-1973; Foreign correspondent in Saigon, *New York Times,* 1973-1975; Foreign correspondent in Moscow, *New York Times,* 1975-1979; Chief, Moscow Bureau, *New York Times,* 1977-1979; Chief, Jerusalem Bureau, *New York Times,* 1979-1984; Guest Scholar, Brookings Institution, Washington, DC, 1984-1985; State Department diplomatic correspondent, *New York Times,* Washington Bureau, Washington, DC, 1985- ; Member: Authors Guild, Authors League of America, New York Newspaper Guild.

Selected Works: *Russia: Broken Idols, Solemn Dreams,* 1983. *Through Different Eyes: Two Leading Americans, a Jew and an Arab, Debate U.S. Policy in the Middle East* (with Bookbinder and Abourezk), 1987. *A Country of Strangers: Blacks and Whites in America,* 1997.

Other Awards: Award for Distinguished Reporting, Society of Silurians, 1971. Award, Distinguished Public Affairs Reporting, American Political Scientists Association, 1971. Page One Award for Best Local Reporting, New York Newspaper Guild, 1973. Award, New York Chapter of Sigma Delta Chi, 1973. George Polk Award in Journalism, Long Island University, 1983. Overseas Press Club Award, 1984.

For More Information: Halkin, Hille, "Neighbors and Strangers," *New Republic,* November 10, 1986; Schrage, Steven S., "A Journalist with 'Perfect Pitch,'" *National Journal,* Dec 3, 1994; Browne, J. Zamgba, "A Pulitzer Prize-Winner Explores America's Racial Landscape," *Amsterdam News,* November 6, 1997.

Commentary: David K. Shipler won the 1987 Pulitzer Prize in General Non-Fiction for *Arab and Jew: Wounded Spirits in a Promised Land,* an examination of attitudes and their roots on the part of the Jews and the Arabs living in the Middle East.

Shipler was educated at Dartmouth College. He served as an officer on an Atlantic Fleet destroyer in the United States Navy for two years after college. He became a reporter and was a correspondent for the *New York Times,* based in Washington, Vietnam, Israel, and the Soviet Union. He is the Ferris Professor of Journalism and Public Affairs at Princeton University. His other works include *Russia: Broken Idols, Solemn Dreams* and *A Country of Strangers: Blacks and Whites in America.*

1988

Richard Rhodes   522

Birth: July 4, 1937; Kansas City, KS. **Parents:** Arthur and Georgia (Collier) Rhodes. **Education:** Yale University, CT: BA, cum laude. **Spouse:** Linda Iredell Hampton (m. 1960; div. 1974); Mary Magdalene Evans (m. 1976; div.); Ginger Untrif (m. 1993). **Children:** Timothy James, Katherine Hampton (LIH).

Prize: *General Non-Fiction,* 1988: *The Making of the Atomic Bomb,* New York: Simon and Schuster, 1986.

Career: Writer Trainee, *Newsweek,* NY, 1959; Staff Assistant, Radio Free Europe, NY, 1960; Instructor of English, Westminster College, MO, 1960-1961; Surgical Technician, U.S. Air Force Reserve, 1960-1965; Book Editing Manager, Hallmark Cards, Inc., MO, 1962-1970; Contributing Editor, *Harper's,* NY, 1970-1974; Writer in Residence, Kansas City

Regional Council for Higher Education, 1972; Contributing Editor, *Playboy,* IL, 1974-present; Fellow, John Simon Guggenheim Memorial Foundation, 1974-1975; Fellow, National Endowment for the Arts, 1978; Fellow, Ford Foundation, 1981-1983; Fellow, Alfred P. Sloan Foundation, 1985, 1988, 1991-1994; Visiting Fellow, Defense and Arms Control Studies Program, Massachusetts Institute of Technology, 1988-1989; Visiting Scholar, History of Science Department, Harvard University, MA, 1989-1990; Fellow, Program on Peace and International Cooperation, MacArthur Foundation, 1990-1991; Advisor, Alfred P. Sloan Foundation, 1990-present.

Selected Works: *The Ungodly: A Novel of the Donner Party,* 1973. *Holy Secrets,* 1978. *Looking for America: A Writer's Odyssey,* 1979. *The Last Safari,* 1980. *Farm: A Year in the Life of an American Farmer,* 1989. *A Hole in the World: An American Boyhood,* 1990. *The Inland Ground: An Evocation of the American Middle West,* 1991. *Making Love: An Erotic Odyssey,* 1992. *Nuclear Renewal: Common Sense about Energy,* 1993. *Dark Sun: The Making of the Hydrogen Bomb,* 1995. *How to Write: Advice and Reflections,* 1995. *Deadly Feasts: Tracking the Secrets of a Terrifying New Plague,* 1997.

Other Awards: Editorial Award, *Playboy,* 1972. Guggenheim Fellowship, 1974-1975. Writing Grant, National Endowment for the Arts, 1978. Ford Foundation Fellowship, 1981-1983. Alfred P. Sloan Foundation Grant, 1984. National Book Award, Nonfiction, 1987: *The Making of the Atomic Bomb.* National Book Critics Circle Award, General Nonfiction, 1987: *The Making of the Atomic Bomb.* Honorary DHL, Westminster College, MO, 1988.

For More Information: Mueller, Jane, "Lusty Rhodes," *Times-Picayune,* January 17, 1993; Giffin, Glenn, "Soviet Archives Opened Door for Rhodes," *Denver Post,* September 17, 1995.

Commentary: Richard Rhodes won the 1988 Pulitzer Prize in General Non-Fiction for *The Making of the Atomic Bomb,* a comprehensive history of the invention that forever changed the course of human history. It also received the National Book Award.

Rhodes was educated at Yale University. His other works include *Dark Sun: The Making of the Hydrogen Bomb.*

1989

Neil Sheehan   523

Birth: October 27, 1936; Holyoke, MA. **Parents:** Cornelius Joseph and Mary (O'Shea) Sheehan. **Education:** Harvard University, MA: AB, cum laude. **Spouse:** Susan Sachsel (m. 1963). **Children:** Maria Gregory, Catherine Fair.

Prize: *General Non-Fiction,* 1989: *A Bright Shining Lie: John Paul Vann and America in Vietnam,* New York: Random House, 1988.

Career: Reporter, writer.

Selected Works: *The Pentagon Papers: As Published by the New York Times* (Gold, Siegel, and Abt, eds.), 1971. *The Arnheiter Affair,* 1971. *After the War Was Over: Hanoi and Saigon,* 1992.

Other Awards: United States Army Commendation Medal, 1961. Department of the Army Award, Best Division Newspapers, 1961. Louis M. Lyons Award for Conscience and Integrity in Journalism, 1964. Silver Medal, Poor Richard Club of Philadelphia, 1964. Certificate of Appreciation for Best Article on Asia, Overseas Press Club of America, 1967. First Annual Drew Pearson Prize for Excellence in Investigative Reporting, 1971. Columbia Journalism Award, 1972. Sidney Hillman Foundation Award, 1972. Page One Award, Newspaper Guild of New York, 1972. Distinguished Service Award for Washington Correspondence and Bronze Medallion, Sigma Delta Chi, Society of Professional Journalists, 1972. Citation for Excellence, Overseas Press Club of America, 1972. Guggenheim Fellow, 1973-1974. Adlai Stevenson Fellow, 1973-1975. Lehrman Institute Fellow, 1975-1976. Rockefeller Foundation Fellow in Humanities, 1976-1977. Woodrow Wilson International Center for Scholars Fellow, 1979-1980. Memorial Society of American Historians, American Academic Achievement. National Book Award, Nonficiton, 1988: *A Bright Shining Lie: John Paul Vann and America in Vietnam,* New York: Random House, 1988. Robert F. Kennedy Book Award, 1989: *A Bright Shining Lie: John Paul Vann and America in Vietnam.* Vetty Award, Vietnam Vets Ensemble Theatre, 1989. Special Achievement Award, Vietnam Veterans of America, 1989. Outstanding Investigative Reporting Award, Investigative Reporters and Editors, 1989. Ambassador Award, English-Speaking Union, 1989. John F. Kennedy Award, Holyoke, 1989. Literary Lion Award, New York Public Library, 1992. Honorary DHL, Columbia College, IL, 1972.

For More Information: Goldman, John J., "Neil Sheehan Wins Pulitzer for History of Vietnam War," *Los Angeles Times,* March 31, 1989; Warren, James, "The Remarkable Sheehans," *Chicago Tribune,* April 15, 1990; Lehmann-Haupt, Christopher, "Sheehan Turns to Peace in Vietnam," *New York Times,* Current Events Edition, July 27, 1992; Warsh, David, "The Greatest Story of the Vietnam War: What It Was and the Reporter Who Got It," *Boston Globe,* August 29, 1993; Prochnau, William W., "The Boys of Saigon," *Vanity Fair,* November 1995; Prochnau, William W., *Once Upon a Distant War,* New York: Times, 1995.

Commentary: Neil Sheehan won the 1989 Pulitzer Prize in General Non-Fiction for *A Bright Shining Lie,* a study of American involvement in Vietnam

and Lieutenant Colonel John Paul Vann, the American military adviser who, early on, saw the fulitity of sending in more troops and firepower.

Sheehan was born in Holyoke, Massachusetts and educated at Harvard University. He has been at the center of recent American history. He acquired the Pentagon Papers from Daniel Ellsberg and they were published in the *New York Times* as a result of his investigative reporting. He spent 16 years writing *A Bright Shining Lie,* which was interrupted by the Pentagon Papers tumult and by a car accident which took a year away from Sheehan's work. He is married to Susan Sheehan, also a General Non-Fiction Pulitzer Prize winner (1983). His most recent works are *After the War Was Over: Hanoi and Saigon* and *Two Cities: Hanoi and Saigon.*

1990

Dale Dmitro Maharidge 524

Birth: October 24, 1956; Cleveland, OH. **Parents:** Steve and John (Kopfstein) Maharidge. **Education:** Cuyahoga Community College, OH. Cleveland State University, OH.

Prize: *General Non-Fiction,* 1990: *And Their Children After Them,* New York: Pantheon, 1989.

Career: Machinery worker, Cleveland, OH, 1971-1976; Freelance writer, 1977; Staff Writer, *Gazette,* Medina, OH, 1977-1978; Freelance writer, 1978-1980; Journalist, *Sacramento Bee,* CA, 1980-1991; Assistant Professor, Columbia University, NY, 1991-1992; Lecturer, Stanford University, Stanford, CA, 1992-Present; Member, Newspaper Guild.

Selected Works: *Journey to Nowhere: The Saga of the New Underclass* (with Michael Williamson), 1985. *The Last Great American Hobo* (with Michael Wiliamson), 1993. *The Coming White Minority: California's Eruptions and America's Future,* 1996.

Other Awards: First Place Award, Feature Articles, San Francisco Press Club, 1982, 1987. Award for Best Series, United Press International, California-Nevada, 1984. World Hunger Award, 1987. Lucius W. Nieman Fellowship, Harvard University, MA, 1988. Pope Foundation Award, Mid-Career Achievement, 1994. Professors' Publishing Program Grant, Freedom Forum, 1995.

For More Information: Yardley, Jonathan, "Children of Poverty," *Washington Post,* May 14, 1989; Schoenberg, Tom, "Professor's Research Inspires a Rock Star," *Chronicle of Higher Education,* January 19, 1996.

Commentary: *And Their Children After Them* won the 1990 Pulitzer Prize in General Non-Fiction for Dale Maharidge and Michael Williamson. Maharidge, a reporter, and Williamson, a photographer, found 128 survivors and offspring of the original 22 family members of the Alabama sharecroppers portrayed by James Agee and photographed by Walker Evans in *Let Us Now Praise Famous Men.*

Maharidge was born in Cleveland, Ohio and was educated at Cleveland State University. He was a reporter for the *Sacramento Bee* at the time that he won the Pulitzer Prize. He is a lecturer in communications at Stanford University and he writes articles for newspapers and magazines. His most recent work is *The Coming White Minority: California's Eruptions and the Nation's Future.*

Michael Williamson   525

Birth: 1957; Washington, DC. **Education:** Contra Costa College, CA. American Rover College, CA. **Spouse:** Michelle. **Children:** Sophia, Valerie.

Prize: *General Non-Fiction,* 1990: *And Their Children After Them,* New York: Pantheon, 1989.

Career: Staff Writer, *West County (CA) Times,* 1975-1977; Staff Photographer, *Sacramento Bee,* 1978-1991; President, California Press Photographers Association, 1980-1982; Documentary Film Field Producer, Writer, and Director, German public television (ZDF) and British Broadcasting Company (BBC), 1984-1992; Resident Photojournalist, Western Kentucky University, Bowling Green, KY, summer 1991-winter 1992; Staff Photographer, *Washington Post,* 1993-present.

Selected Works: *Journey to Nowhere: The Saga of the New Underclass* (with Dale Dmitro Maharidge), 1988. *The Last Great American Hobo* (with Dale Dmitro Maharidge), 1993.

Other Awards: Photographer of the Year, San Francisco Bay Area Photographers Association, 1989; Kodak Crystal Eagle Award for Impact in Photojournalism, 1994; Newspaper Photographer of the Year, NPPA, 1995; Northern Photographer of the Year, NPPA, 1995; Southern Photographer of the Year, 1996 and 1998

For More Information: "Messages from Michael Williamson," *News Photographer,* June 1996; Peattie, Peggy and Jim Gordon, "Making a Difference," *News Photographer,* June 1996; "A Gift of Gab That Can Put Anyone at Ease...," *News Photographer,* June 1996.

Commentary: *And Their Children After Them* won the 1990 Pulitzer Prize in General Non-Fiction for Dale Maharidge and Michael Williamson. Maharidge, a reporter, and Williamson, a photographer, found 128 survivors and offspring of the original 22 family members of the Alabama sharecroppers portrayed by James Agee and photographed by Walker Evans in *Let Us Now Praise Famous Men.*

Williamson was a photographer for the *Sacramento Bee* at the time that he won the Pulitzer Prize. He is currently a news photographer for the *Washington Post.* He has been working as a journalist since

high school and has covered wars in Nicaragua, Guatemala, Rwanda, and Bosnia.

1991

Bert Holldobler   526

Birth: June 25, 1936; Erling-Andechs, Germany. **Parents:** Karl and Maria (Russman) Holldobler. **Education:** University of Wurzburg, Germany: Doctor. University of Frankfurt, Germany: Doctor. **Spouse:** Frederike M. Probst (m. 1980). **Children:** Jacob, Stefan, Sebastian.

Prize: *General Non-Fiction,* 1991: *The Ants,* Cambridge, MA: Belknap, 1990.

Career: Scientific Assistant, Zoological Institute of the University of Frankfurt, Germany, 1966-1969; Research Associate, Biological Department, Harvard University, MA, 1969-1971; Professor of Zoology, University of Frankfurt, Germany, 1971-1972; Professor of Biology, Harvard University, MA, 1973-1990; Member, American Academy of Arts and Sciences, 1974; Member, Deusche Akademie der Naturforscher, Leopoldina, 1975; Co-Editor, Behavioral Ecology and Sociobiology, 1976-1989; Fellow, American Association for the Advancement of Sciences, 1979; Alexander Agassiz Professor of Zoology, Harvard University, MA, 1982-1990; Member, Psychobiology-Behavioral Physiology, National Science Foundation Panel, 1984-1987; Adjunct Professor, University of Arizona, 1989-; Editorial Board, Behavioral Ecology and Sociobiology, 1989-; Professor of Zoology (Ordinarius), University of Wurzburg, Germany, 1989-; Research Associate, Museum of Comparative Zoology, Harvard University, 1990-; Member, Selection Committee for Senior Scientist Prize, Alexander von Humboldt Foundation, 1990-, Member, Senate of Leopoldina, 1991-; Fellow, American Animal Behavior Society, 1992; Member, Academia Europea, 1994; Chairman, Department of Biology, University of Wurzburg, Germany, 1993-1995; Co-Editor, Die Naturwissenschaften, 1995-; Corresponding Member, Berlin-Brandenburgische Akademie der Wissenschaften, 1995; Member, German National Science Council, 1996-; Vice President, Society for the Study of Evolution (SSE), 1997; Advisory Board, Humboldt Museum of Natural History, Berlin, Germany; Member: International Union for the Study of Social Insects, Cambridge Entomological Society, Animal Behavior Society, Society for the Study of Evolution, Society of American Naturalists, International Society for Behavioral Ecology, International Society of Neuroethology.

Selected Works: *Experimental Behavioral Ecology and Sociobiology: In Memoriam Karl von Frisch, 1886-1982* (with Martin Lindauer), 1985.

Other Awards: Guggenheim Fellow, 1980-1981. United States Senior Scientist Prize, Alexander von Humboldt Foundation, 1986-1987. Liebniz Prize, German Science Foundation, 1990. Co-Winner, R.R. Hawkins Prize of the Association of American Publishers, Most Outstanding Professional Reference Work, 1990: *The Ants,* Cambridge, MA: Belknap, 1990. Co-Winner, Phi Beta Kappa Prize, 1995: *The Ants,* Karl Ritter von Frisch Medal and Science Prize of the German Zoological Society, 1996. Korber Prize for European Sciences, 1996.

For More Information: Weiner, Jonathan, "In Love with Living Things," *Los Angeles Times,* October 23, 1994; Detjen, Jim, "Entomologist Has a Way With Ants and With Stories," *Detroit Free Press,* December 4, 1994; Powers, Katherine A, "Antsy About the Plight of Endangered Species? It's Only Natural," *Boston Globe,* January 28, 1996.

Commentary: Bert Holldobler and Edward O. Wilson won the 1991 Pulitzer Prize in General Non-Fiction for *The Ants.*

Holldobler was born in Erling-Andechs, Germany. He was educated at the University of Wurzburg and the University of Frankfurt, both in Germany. He is currently professor of zoology at the University of Wurzburg. He has done field research in Argentina, Australia, Costa Rica, Germany, Finland, Kenya, India, Jamaica, Panama, and Sri Lanka.

Edward Osbourne Wilson

Full entry appears as **#512** under "General Non-Fiction," 1979.

1992

Daniel Yergin   527

Birth: February 6, 1947; Los Angeles, CA. **Parents:** Irving H. and Naomi Y. Yergin. **Education:** Yale University, CT: BA. Cambridge University, England: Marshall Scholar, MA, PhD. **Spouse:** Angela Stent (m. 1975). **Children:** Alexander George, Rebecca Isabella.

Prize: *General Non-Fiction,* 1992: *The Prize: The Epic Quest for Oil, Money and Power,* New York: Simon and Schuster, 1991.

Career: Writer; consultant; Contributing Editor, *New York* Magazine, 1968-1970; Research Fellow, Harvard University, MA, 1974-1976; Fellow, Rockefeller Foundation, 1975-1979; Lecturer, Harvard Business School, Harvard University, MA, 1976-1979; Member, Advance Board, Solar Energy Research Institute, CO, 1979-1981; Lecturer, John F. Kennedy School of Government, Harvard University, MA, 1979-1983; Fellow, German Marshall Fund, 1980-1981; President, Cambridge Energy Research Associates, 1982-; Advisory Panel, U.S.-Japan Rela-

tions, Harvard University, MA; Associate, PEN Lehrman Institute; Board of Directors, Marshall Scholars, 1988-1991; Board of Directors, U.S. Energy Associates; Board of Energy Experts, *Dallas Morning News;* Fellow, Atlantic Institute for International Affairs; Member: American History Association, Council on Foreign Relations, Harvard Club (NY), International Panel of Advisors, Asia-Pacific Petroleum Conference, National Petroleum Council, Yale Club (NY).

Selected Works: *Shattered Peace: The Origins of the Cold War and the National Security State,* 1977. *Energy Future: Report of the Energy Project at the Harvard Business School* (Yergin, Daniel, and Stobaugh, Robert, eds.), 1979. *Global Insecurity: A Strategy for Energy and Economic Renewal* (Yergin, Daniel, and Hillenbrand, Martin, eds.), 1982. *Russia 2010—and What It Means for the World: The CERA Report* (with Thane Gustafson), 1993.

For More Information: Parrish, Michael, "He Knows Oil: Daniel Yergin Built a Company and Penned a Best-Selling History," *Los Angeles Times,* January 9, 1993; Judice, Mary. "'The Key Frontier': Author Predicts Dawn of Oil Boom," *Times-Picayune,* April 30, 1996.

Commentary: Daniel Yergin was awarded the 1992 Pulitzer Prize in General Non-Fiction for *The Prize: The Epic Quest for Oil, Money, and Power,* a history of the impact of oil on world affairs since 1854. In that year, a group of New York investors commissioned a Yale chemist to analyze the properties of oil as a possible competitor of coal and the future prospects for energy needs.

Yergin was born in Los Angeles. He was educated at Cambridge University in England. He has been a contributing editor to *New York* Magazine. A historian and energy expert, Yergin is the president of Cambridge Energy Research Associates, advisors to international organizations. His other works include *Shattered Peace,* a classic history of the origins of the Cold War.

1993

Garry Wills   528

Birth: May 22, 1934; Atlanta, GA. **Parents:** John H. and Mayno (Collins) Wills. **Education:** St. Louis University, MO: AB. Xavier University, OH: MA. Yale University, CT: MA, PhD. **Spouse:** Natalie Cavallo (m. 1959). **Children:** John Christopher, Garry Laurence, Lydia Mayno.

Prize: *General Non-Fiction,* 1993: *Lincoln at Gettysburg: The Words That Remade America,* New York: Simon & Schuster, 1992.

Career: Associate Editor, *Richmond News Leader,* VA, 1961; Fellow, Center for Hellenic Studies, Washington, DC, 1961-1962; Assistant Professor, Johns Hopkins University, MD, 1962-1967; Visiting Lecturer, Classics, Johns Hopkins University, 1968-1969; Regents Lecturer, University of California, 1971; Adjunct Professor of Humanities, Johns Hopkins University, 1973-present; Henry R. Luce Professor of American Culture and Public Policy, Northwestern University.

Selected Works: *Chesterton, Man and Mask,* 1961. *Politics and Catholic Freedom,* 1964. *Roman Culture: Weapons and the Man,* 1966. *Jack Ruby* (with Ovid Demaris), 1968. *The Second Civil War: Arming for Armageddon,* 1968. *Nixon Agonistes: The Crisis of the Self-Made Man,* 1970. *Bare Ruined Choirs: Doubt, Prophecy, and Radical Religion,* 1972. *Values Americans Live By* (Wills, Gary, ed.), 1974. *Inventing America: Jefferson's Declaration of Independence,* 1978. *Confessions of a Conservative,* 1979. *Explaining America: The Federalist,* 1981. *The Kennedy Imprisonment: A Meditation on Power,* 1982. *Lead Time: A Journalist's Education,* 1983. *Cincinnatus: George Washington and the Enlightenment,* 1984. *Reagan's America,* 1988. *Certain Trumpets: The Call of Leaders,* 1994. *Witches and Jesuits: Shakespeare's Macbeth,* 1995. *John Wayne's America: The Politics of Celebrity,* 1997.

Other Awards: Merle Curti Award, Organization of American Historians, 1978. National Book Critics Circle Award, 1979: *Inventing America,* Garden City, NY: Doubleday, 1978. John D. Rockefeller III Award, 1979: *Inventing America.*

For More Information: Buell, Thomas B., "From Socrates to Perot: Garry Wills on Leadership," *Chicago Tribune,* May 8, 1994; Edelstein, Barry, "In the Cauldron of History," *Washington Post,* October 30, 1994; Donahue, Deirdre, "The Duke as a Cultural Icon in John Wayne: Historian Garry Wills Finds Manifest Destiny," *USA Today,* April 9, 1997.

Commentary: Garry Wills won the 1993 Pulitzer Prize in General Non-Fiction for *Lincoln at Gettysburg: The Words That Remade America.* The words Lincoln spoke in the Gettysburg Address are examined by a Greek scholar within the political context of the day, November 19, 1863, and compared to the funeral orations of Pericles and Gorgias in the fifth century B.C.

Wills was born in Atlanta, Georgia. He was educated at Yale University and taught Greek there. Wills has been a magazine writer, writing for *Esquire, The New York Times Magazine, The New York Review of Books,* and *New York Magazine.* He is currently the Henry R. Luce Professor of American Culture and Public Policy at Northwestern University. Wills has authored works on politics, history, and philosophy, including *Witches and Jesuits.*

1994

David Remnick   529

Birth: October 29, 1958; Hackensack, NJ. **Parents:** Edward C. and Barbara (Seigel) Remnick. **Education:** Princeton University, NJ: AB. **Spouse:** Esther B. Fein. **Children:** Alexander, Noah.

Prize: *General Non-Fiction,* 1994: *Lenin's Tomb: The Last Days of the Soviet Empire,* New York: Random House, 1993.

Career: Reporter, *Washington Post,* 1982-1991; Staff Writer, *The New Yorker,* 1992-1998; Editor, *The New Yorker,* 1998—.

Selected Works: *Black in America,* 1996. *The Devil Problem: And Other True Stories,* 1996. *Resurrection: The Struggle for a New Russia,* 1997.

Other Awards: Livingston Award, 1991. George Polk Award, 1994: *Lenin's Tomb: The Last Days of the Soviet Empire,* New York: Random House, 1993. Helen Bernstein Award, New York Public Library, 1994.

For More Information: "Talking With ... David Remnick," *People Weekly,* July 12, 1993; Marquand, Robert, "Writer's Reflections on Years in Moscow," *Christian Science Monitor,* July 29, 1993; Skube, Michael, "Remnick's Mastery of the Long Form," *Atlanta Constitution,* October 6, 1996.

Commentary: *Lenin's Tomb: The Last Days of the Soviet Empire* won the 1994 Pulitzer Prize in General Non-Fiction for David Remnick. This is Remnick's eyewitness account of the end of the Soviet Union and the beginnings of democracy in the newly formed Russia.

Remnick was born in Hackensack, New Jersey and educated at Princeton University. He spent 10 years as a reporter for the *Washington Post.* Remnick has just been appointed editor of the *New Yorker.* His other works include *The Devil Problem: And Other True Stories* and *Resurrection: The Struggle for a New Russia.*

1995

Jonathan Weiner   530

Birth: November 26, 1953; New York, NY. **Parents:** Jerome Harris and Ponnie (Mensch) Weiner. **Religion:** Jewish. **Education:** Harvard University, MA: BA, cum laude. **Spouse:** Deborah Heiligman (m. 1982). **Children:** Aaron.

Prize: *General Non-Fiction,* 1995: *The Beak of the Finch: A Story of Evolution in Our Time,* New York: Knopf, 1994.

Career: Assistant Editor, *Moment,* Boston, MA, 1978; Senior Editor, *The Sciences,* New York Academy of Sciences, NY, 1978-1984; Contributing Editor and Author, "Field Notes" Column, *The Sciences,* 1984-present; Member, National Association of Science Writers.

Selected Works: *Planet Earth,* 1986. *The New Medical Marketplace: A Physician's Guide to the Health Care Revolution* (with Anne M. Stoline), 1988. *The Next One Hundred Years: Shaping the Fate of Our Living Earth,* 1990. *The New Medical Marketplace: A Physician's Guide to the Health Care System in the 1990s* (with Anne M. Stoline), 1993.

Other Awards: Best Column, National Association of Association Publications, 1985: *The Sciences.* "Field Notes." Outstanding Contribution to Public Understanding of Geology Award, American Geological Institute, 1986: *Planet Earth,* New York: Bantam, 1986. James H. Shea Award, 1996.

For More Information: Hanson, Beth, "Bird's-Eye View of Evolution," *Los Angeles Times,* June 19, 1994; Gutin, JoAnn C. "Evolving Before Your Very Eyes," *Washington Post,* July 24, 1994; "Jonathan Weiner—1996 James H. Shea Awardee," *Journal of Geoscience Education,* January, 1997.

Commentary: Jonathan Weiner won the 1995 Pulitzer Prize in General Non-Fiction for *The Beak of the Finch: A Story of Evolution in Our Time,* the story of a team of biology researchers from Princeton University busily measuring the beaks of finches to document the existing variety and changes that have "evolved" since Darwin first set forth his theory of evolution.

Weiner was born in New York City and educated at Harvard University. His other works include *The Next One Hundred Years: Shaping the Fate of Our Living Earth* and *The New Medical Marketplace: A Physician's Guide to the Health Care System in the 1990s.*

1996

Tina Rosenberg 531

Birth: April 14, 1960; Brooklyn, NY. **Parents:** Barnett and Ritta Rosenberg. **Religion:** Jewish. **Education:** Northwestern University, IL: BS,MS.

Prize: *General Non-Fiction,* 1996: *The Haunted Land: Facing Europe's Ghosts After Communism,* New York: Random House, 1995.

Career: Reporter, writer; Resident and reporter, Latin America, 1985-1990; Resident and reporter, Former Soviet Union, 1991-1994; Contributor, *The New Yorker, Harper's, The New Republic, The Atlantic, Rolling Stone,* and other publications; Senior Fellow, World Policy Institute, New School for Social Research, NY, Present.

Selected Works: *Children of Cain: Violence and the Violent in Latin America,* 1991.

Other Awards: MacArthur Fellowship, 1987.

For More Information: Richman, Ruth, "'Genius Grant' Recipients Pause, Reflect," *Houston Chronicle,* December 9, 1993; Weil, Elizabeth, "Slipping and Sliding Into the Success Zone: Tina Rosenberg," *Los Angeles Times,* June 28, 1996.

Commentary: Tina Rosenberg won the 1996 Pulitzer Prize in General Non-Fiction for *The Haunted Land: Facing Europe's Ghosts After Communism.* Rosenberg examines the process of confronting the past that is being carried out in four neighboring societies where more than four decades of Soviet-shaped Communist rule came to an abrupt end in 1989.

Rosenberg was born in Brooklyn, New York and educated at Northwestern University. She lived in Latin America from 1985 to 1990 and reported from there for the *Atlantic* and the *New Republic.* She is also the author of *Children of Cain.*

1997

Richard Kluger 532

Birth: September 18, 1934; Paterson, NJ. **Parents:** David and Ida (Abramson) Kluger. **Education:** Princeton University, NJ: BA, cum laude. **Spouse:** Phyllis Schlain (m. 1957). **Children:** Matthew Harold, Leonard Theodore.

Prize: *General Non-Fiction,* 1997: *Ashes to Ashes: America's Hundred-Year Cigarette War, the Public Health and the Unabashed Triumph of Philip Morris,* New York: Knopf, 1996.

Career: Author, Editor, Critic; City Editor, *Wall Street Journal,* NY, 1956-1957; Editor and Publisher, *County Citizen,* New York City, NY, 1958-1960; Staff Writer, *New York Post,* NY, 1960-1961; Associate Editor, *Forbes,* NY, 1962; General Book Editor, *New York Herald-Tribune,* 1962-1963; Book Editor, *New York Herald-Tribune,* 1963-1966; Editor, *Book Week,* NY, 1963-1966; Managing Editor, Simon & Schuster, NY, 1966-1968; Executive Editor, Simon & Schuster, NY, 1968-1970; Editor-in-Chief, Atheneum Publishers, NY, 1970-1971; President and Publisher, Charterhouse Books, NY, 1972-1973; Member, Princeton Club, NY.

Selected Works: *When the Bough Breaks,* 1964. *National Anthem,* 1969. *Simple Justice: The History of Brown v. Board of Education and Black America's Struggle for Equality,* 1975. *Members of the Tribe,* 1977. *Star Witness,* 1979. *Un-American Activities,* 1982. *The Paper: The Life and Death of the New York Herald Tribune,* 1986. *The Sheriff of Nottingham,* 1992.

Other Awards: Sidney Hillman Prize, 1976: *Simple Justice: A History of Brown v. Board of Education,* New York: Knopf, 1975. George Polk Prize,

1987: *The Paper: The Life and Death of the New York Herald Tribune,* New York: Knopf, 1986.

For More Information: Lehmann-Haupt, Christopher, "A Tale of Tobacco, Pleasure, Profits and Death," *New York Times,* April 15, 1996; LaMay, Craig L., "Clearing Away the Smoke," *Chicago Tribune,* May 5, 1996; Galloway, Paul, "Tobacco's Road," *Chicago Tribune,* October 17, 1996.

Commentary: *Ashes to Ashes: America's Hundred-Year Cigarette War, the Public Health, and the Unabashed Triumph of Philip Morris* won the 1997 Pulitzer Prize in General Non-Fiction for Richard Kluger. This is a history of the American tobacco industry since the late 19th century, the industry's growth, and its methods for dealing with critics and health warnings, in particular Philip Morris, the company with the largest market share.

Kluger was born in Paterson, New Jersey. He was educated at Princeton University. His other works include *Simple Justice,* about the Supreme Court decision in *Brown v. Board of Education,* and *The Paper,* a story of the now-defunct *New York Herald Tribune.* He has also written novels such as *The Sheriff of Nottingham* and *Un-American Activities.*

1998

## Jared Mason Diamond				533

Birth: September 10, 1937; Boston, MA. **Parents:** Louis and Flora (Klein) Diamond. **Education:** Harvard University, MA: BA. Cambridge University, England: PhD. **Spouse:** Marie Cohen (m. 1982). **Children:** Max, Joshua.

Prize: *General Non-Fiction,* 1998: *Guns, Germs, and Steel: The Fates of Human Societies,* New York: Norton, 1997.

Career: Professor of Physiology, University of California, Los Angeles School of Medicine, 1966-present; Contributor, design of national park systems in Irian Jaya, Papua New Guinea, and the Solomon Islands; Founding Member, Club of the Earth; Founding Member, Society for Conservation Biology; Member, Board of Directors, World Wildlife U.S.A.;

Author of over 200 articles in *Discover, Natural History, Nature,* and *Geo* magazines.

Selected Works: *Ecology and Evolution of Communities* (Diamond, Jerod and Cody, Martin L., eds), 1975. *Birds of Karkar and Bagabag Islands, New Guinea* (with Mary Lecroy), 1979. *The Third Chimpanzee: The Evolution and Future of the Human Animal,* 1992. *Why Is Sex Fun? The Evolution of Human Sexuality,* 1997. **Films:** *Discovering Great Minds: Evolution, with Dr. Jared Diamond* (VHS), Pangea Digital Pictures, 1995.

Other Awards: Britain's Science Book Prize, 1997: *The Rise and Fall of the Third Chimpanzee.* London, England: Radius, 1991.

For More Information: Hoffman, Paul, "Diamond Vision," *Discover,* May 1989; Alfred W. Crosby, "Geography Is Fate; Guns, Germs, and Steel: The Fates of Human Societies," *Los Angeles Times,* March 9, 1997; Schreuder, Cindy, "Jared Diamond, Physiologist and Evolutionary Biologist," *Chicago Tribune,* March 23, 1997.

Commentary: The 1998 Pulitzer Prize in General Non-Fiction was awarded to *Guns, Germs, and Steel,* written by Jared M. Diamond. The book examines the biological consequences of conquerors upon their victim populations.

Jared Mason Diamond was born in Boston, Massachussetts. Diamond was a bird-watcher when he was a boy and he pursued a degree in animal physiology. During his career, he has traveled to New Guinea to study ornithology and helped in the design of the national parks system in Irian Jaya, Papua New Guinea, and the Solomon Islands. He is a natural historian, conservation biologist, ornithologist, and professor of physiology at the University of California at Los Angeles. He is a leader in the biological research forming the basis for preserving biodiversity. His research interests are regulation of nutrient transport and integrative and evolutionary physiology. He drew much attention with his book, *Why Is Sex Fun?: The Evolution of Human Sexuality,* which differentiated the sex habits of homo sapiens from those of other species.

History

1917

Jean Adrien Antoine Jules Jusserand   534

Birth: February 18, 1855; Lyons, France. **Death:** July 18, 1932. **Education:** College des Chartreaux, Lyons, France. **Spouse:** Elise Richards.

Prize: *History,* 1917: *With Americans of Past and Present Days,* New York: C. Scribner, 1916.

Career: French Minister to Denmark, 1890; French Ambassador to the U.S., 1902-1905.

Selected Works: *Les Anglais au Moyen ge: La Vie Nomade et les Routes d'Angleterre au XIV e Sicle,* 1884. *Le Roman Anglais: Origine et Formation des Grandes coles de Romanciers du XVIII e Sicle,* 1886. *A French Ambassador at the Court of Charles the Second: Le Comte de Cominges,* 1892. *Paul Scarron: A Study,* 1892. *Histoire Littraire du Peuple Anglais,* 1894. *Piers Plowman: A Contribution to the History of English Mysticism,* 1894. *English Essays from a French Pen,* 1895. *Le Roman d'un Roi d'cosse,* 1895. *The Romance of a King's Life,* 1896. *What to Expect of Shakespeare,* 1911. *English Wayfaring Life in the Middle Ages (XIVth Century),* 1912. *Ronsard,* 1913. *En Amrique Jadis & Maintenant,* 1918. *The French and American Independence,* 1918. *Brothers in Arms,* 1919. *The School for Ambassadors and Other Essays,* 1924. *The Writing of History* (with Wilbur C. Abbott, Charles W. Colby, and John S. Bassett), 1926. *Le Sentiment Americain Pendant la Guerre,* 1931. *What Me Befell: The Reminiscences of J.J. Jusserand,* 1933.

For More Information: *Jean Jules Jusserand, Ambassador of the French Republic to the United States of America 1903-1925,* New York: Jusserand Memorial Committee, 1937.

Commentary: Jean Jules Jusserand was awarded the 1917 Pulitzer Prize in History for *With Americans of Past and Present Days.* This volume contained a selection of speeches on the relationship between France and the United States at various times in each nation's history and was dedicated to Rochambeau and the French in America.

Jusserand was a historian and a diplomat with an avid interest in English literature and history. He was appointed ambassador to the United States in 1902. He is most noted for the work *Literary History of the English People.* He was the only non-American to be elected president of the American Historical Society. Franklin D. Roosevelt spoke at his memorial service.

1918

James Ford Rhodes   535

Birth: May 1, 1848; Cleveland, OH. **Death:** January 22, 1927. **Education:** New York University. University of Chicago, IL. College de France. **Spouse:** Ann Card (m. 1910). **Children:** One son.

Prize: *History,* 1918: *History of the Civil War, 1861-1865,* New York: Macmillan, 1917.

Career: Rhodes & Company, coal and iron business, 1874-1885; Historian.

Selected Works: *History of the United States from the Compromise of 1850 to the Final Restoration of Home Rule at the South in 1877,* 1892-1906. *History of the United States from the Compromise of 1850 to the McKinley-Bryan Campaign of 1896,* 1892-1919. *Historical Essays,* 1909. *The McKinley and Roosevelt Administrations, 1897-1909,* 1922.

Other Awards: Corresponding Fellow, British Academy. Loubat Prize, Berlin Academy, 1901. Gold Medal, National Institute of Arts and Letters, 1910. Honorary PhDs: Yale University, CT; Harvard University, MA; Princeton University, NJ; Oxford University, England.

For More Information: Howe, M.A. De Wolfe, *James Ford Rhodes, American Historian,* New York: D. Appleton, 1929; *The Barber and the Historian: The Correspondence of George A. Myers and James Ford Rhodes, 1910-1923,* Columbus: Ohio Historical Society, 1956; Cruden, Robert, *James Ford Rhodes: The Man, The Historian, and His Work,* Westport, CT: Greenwood Press, 1961.

Commentary: James Ford Rhodes won the Pulitzer Prize in History in 1918 for *A History of the Civil War.*

Rhodes was born in Cleveland, Ohio. He was in the coal and iron business before devoting his full attention to the role of historian. He was greatly influenced by Henry Thomas Buckle's *History of Civilization.* He retired from business to write a *History of the United States from the Compromise of 1850,* which, when completed, was a seven-volume work ending with the restoration of Southern home rule in 1877. It was well received by critics as the work of a professional historian. His other major work is *History of the U.S. from Hayes to McKinley.*

1919
No award

1920

Justin Harvey Smith   536

Birth: January 13, 1857; Boscowan, NH. **Death:** March 31, 1930. **Parents:** Rev. Ambrose and Cynthia (Egerton) Smith. **Education:** Dartmouth College, NH: BA, with honors: MA. Union Theological Seminary, NY. **Spouse:** Mary E. Barnard (m. 1892; div. 1894).

Prize: *History,* 1920: *The War with Mexico,* Gloucester, MA: P. Smith, 1919.

Career: Scribners, NY; Editorial Staff, Ginn & Company, NY; Professor, Modern History, Dartmouth College, NH, 1899-1908; Chairman, Historical Manuscripts, American Historical Society.

Selected Works: *The Troubadours at Home: Their Lives and Personalities, Their Songs and Their World,* 1899. *Arnold's March from Cambridge to Quebec: A Critical Study, Together with a Reprint from Arnold's Journal,* 1903. *Our Struggle for the Fourteenth Colony: Canada, and the American Revolution,* 1907. *The Annexation of Texas,* 1971.

Other Awards: Loubat Prize, 1923: *The War with Mexico.* Gloucester, MA: P. Smith, 1919. Honorary LittD, Dartmouth College, NH 1920.

For More Information: *Who Was Who in America, Volume 1, 1897-1942,* Chicago: Marquis, 1942; *Dictionary of American Biography,* New York: Scribners, 1964; *American Authors and Books,* New York: Crown, 1972; *American Biographies,* Detroit: Gale, 1974.

Commentary: Justin H. Smith was awarded the 1920 Pulitzer Prize in History for *The War with Mexico,* a two-volume work.

Smith was born in Boscawen, New Hampshire. He was a historian, educator, and publisher. He taught modern history at Dartmouth College. He is also known for *The Troubadors at Home* and *The Annexation of Texas.*

1921

Burton Jesse Hendrick

Full entry appears as #19 under "Biography or Autobiography," 1923.

William Sowden Sims   537

Birth: October 15, 1858; Port Hope, Ontario, Canada. **Death:** September 28, 1936. **Education:** United States Naval Academy, MD.

Prize: *History,* 1921: *The Victory at Sea,* Garden City, NY: Doubleday, Page, 1920.

Career: Rear Admiral, U.S. Navy, January 1917; Vice Admiral, U.S. Navy, May, 1917; Commander, U.S. Naval Operations, April 1917-March 1919; Admiral, U.S. Navy, December 1918; U.S. Navy, retired, 1922.

Selected Works: *The Great War,* 1915-1921.

For More Information: Kittredge, Tracy Barrett, *Naval Lessons of the Great War, A Review of the Senate Naval Investigation of the Criticisms by Admiral Sims of the Policies and Methods of Josephus Daniels,* Garden City, NY: Doubleday, Page, 1921; Morison, Elting Elmore, *Admiral Sims and the Modern American Navy,* New York: Russell & Russell, 1942.

Commentary: William Sowden Sims was awarded the 1921 Pulitzer Prize in History for *The Victory at Sea.* The work is both a history and Sims's personal narrative detailing the reasons why an allied victory in World War I could have been accomplished one year earlier, had American naval operations and procedures been more efficient and serious errors avoided. Sims collaborated with J. Burton Hendrick in writing this volume. Hendrick was also awarded the Pulitzer Prize.

Sims was born in Canada and attended the United States Naval Academy in Annapolis, Maryland. He was a career navy officer, reaching the rank of admiral and was Commander of United States Naval Operations during World War I. His experience served as the basis for the history. Sims was a proponent of the "all-big-gun" battleship. He is regarded as the father of destroyer tactics, which were in use up until the end of World War II.

1922

James Truslow Adams   538

Birth: October 18, 1878; Brooklyn, NY. **Death:** May 18, 1949. **Parents:** William Newton and Elizabeth Harper (Truslow) Adams. **Education:** Yale University, CT. Polytechnic Institute, NY: AB. **Spouse:** Kathryn M. Seeley (m. 1927).

Prize: *History,* 1922: *The Founding of New England,* Boston: Atlantic Monthly Press, 1921.

Career: Stockbroker; Served in U.S. Military Intelligence, WWI; Planner, Peace Conference, end of WWI; Essayist and Historian; Pulitzer Prize History Jurist, 1924-1932; Chairman, Pulitzer Prize History Jury, 1930-1932; General Editor, *Dictionary of American History,* 1940.

Selected Works: *Memorials of Old Brideghampton,* 1916. *History of the Town of Southampton,* 1918. *Revolutionary New England, 1691-1776,* 1923. *New England in the Republic, 1776-1850,* 1926. *Jeffersonian Principles* (Adams, James Truslow, ed.), 1928. *Our Business Civilization: Some Aspects of American Culture,* 1929. *A Searchlight on America,* 1930. *The Adams Family,* 1930. *The Epic of America,* 1931. *The Tempo of Modern Life,* 1931. *The Epic of America,*

1932. *The March of Democracy,* 1932-1933. *Jeffersonian Principles and Hamiltonian Principles,* 1932. *Henry Adams,* 1933. *America's Tragedy,* 1934. *The Record of America* (with Garrett Vannest), 1935. *The Living Jefferson,* 1936. *Building the British Empire: To the End of the First Empire,* 1938. *Constitution of the United States,* 1941. *Dictionary of American History Index* (Adams, James Truslow and Coleman, R.V., eds.), 1940. *Empire on the Seven Seas: The British Empire, 1784-1939,* 1940. *The American: The Making of a New Man,* 1943. *Atlas of American History* (Adams, James Truslow, ed.), 1943. *Album of American History* (Adams, James Truslow, ed.), 1944-1949. *America's World Backgrounds* (Freeland, George Earl and Adams, James Truslow, eds.), 1944. *Frontiers of American Culture: A Study of Adult Education in a Democracy,* 1944. *Dictionary of American History,* 1976-1978. *Atlas of American History* (Adams, James Truslow and Jackson, Kenneth J., eds.), 1978.

For More Information: Nevins, Allan, 1890-1971, *James Truslow Adams: Historian of the American Dream,* Urbana: University of Illinois, 1968; *Who's Who Among North American Authors, 1921-1939,* Detroit: Gale, 1976; *Webster's American Biographies,* Springfield, MA: Merriam, 1974.

Commentary: James Truslow Adams won the 1922 Pulitzer Prize in History for *The Founding of New England.* Adams's history of New England put forth his idea of the cardinal American values: work, morality, individualism, fiscal responsibility, and dedication to duty. These were the values he saw present in the character of the early New Englanders. "Americans love property but hate privilege" was his supporting theory.

Adams was born in Brooklyn, New York. He worked as a stockbroker and accumulated a fortune early. This allowed him to devote his time to the study and writing of history. He was the foremost authority on the New England Adamses. He began writing history after World War I and was the general editor of the *Dictionary of American History,* an undertaking of six volumes, completed in 1940. He believed strongly that big business was necessary as a function of American democracy. He was involved in the information gathering for the Paris peace conference. He attended the conference as a cartographer.

1923

Charles Warren 539

Birth: March 9, 1868; Boston, MA. **Death:** August 16, 1954. **Education:** Harvard University, MA: BA, MA. Harvard Law School, MA. **Spouse:** Annie Louise Bliss (m. 1904). **Children:** No children.

Prize: *History,* 1923: *The Supreme Court in United States History,* Boston: Little Brown, 1922.

Career: Lawyer and writer; Assistant Attorney General of the U.S., 1914-1918.

Selected Works: *The Girl and the Governor,* 1900. *A History of the American Bar,* 1911. *The Making of the Constitution,* 1928. *Jacobin and Junto: Or, Early American Politics as Viewed in the Diary of Dr. Nathaniel Ames, 1758-1822,* 1931. *The Supreme Court in United States History,* 1935. *The Making of the Constitution,* 1937. *Odd Byways in American History,* 1942. *Congress, the Constitution and the Supreme Court,* 1968.

Other Awards: Honorary LLD, Columbia University, NY, 1904.

For More Information: *Webster's American Biographies,* Springfield, MA: Merriam, 1974.

Commentary: *The Supreme Court in United States History* won the 1923 Pulitzer Prize in History for Charles Warren. Written by a former assistant attorney general of the United States, the two-volume book discussed the history of Supreme Court law in the United States.

Warren, who was born in Boston, Massachusetts, was a legal historian who served in a series of high-level government administrative positions. He served as private secretary to Governor William E. Russell of Massachusetts and later was chairman of the Massachusetts Civil Service Commission from 1905 to 1911. He served as assistant attorney general from 1914 to 1918. He lectured in law at Cornell, Princeton, Johns Hopkins, and several other universities.

1924

Charles Howard McIlwain 540

Birth: March 15, 1871; Saltsburg, PA. **Death:** 1968. **Parents:** William R. and Anne Elizabeth (Galbraith) McIlwain. **Education:** Princeton University, NJ. Harvard University, MA. Oxford University, England: MA, PhD. **Spouse:** Mary B. Irwin (m. 1899, died); Kathleen Thompson (m. 1916). **Children:** Two sons, two daughters.

Prize: *History,* 1924: *The American Revolution: A Constitutional Interpretation,* Ithaca, NY: Great Seal, 1923.

Career: Professor of History, Miami University, Oxford, OH, 1903-1905; Precept, Princeton University, NJ, 1905-1910; Thomas Brackett Reed Professor of History and Political Science, Bowdoin College, ME, 1910-1911; Assistant Professor, Harvard University, MA, 1911-1916; Professor of History and Government, Harvard University, MA, 1916-1925; Eaton Professor of the Science of Government, Harvard University, MA, 1925-1948; Visiting Professor at Yale University, 1930-1931; George Eastman Visiting Professor, Oxford University, England, 1944; Lecturer, Princeton University, 1947-1949; Emeritus Member of Board of Trustees, Princeton University, 1949-1968.

Selected Works: *The High Court of Parliament and Its Supremacy: An Historical Essay on the Boundaries between Legislation and Adjudication in England,* 1910. *The Growth of Political Thought in the West: From the Greeks to the End of the Middle Ages,* 1932. *Constitutionalism & the Changing World: Collected Papers,* 1939. *Constitutionalism, Ancient and Modern,* 1940. *Federalism as a Democratic Process: Essays by Roscoe Pound* (with Roy F. Nichols), 1942. *Constitutionalism, Ancient and Modern,* 1947.

Other Awards: Honorary LHH, LittD, LLD, and DCL from many institutions.

For More Information: Wittke, Carl, *Essays in History and Political Theory in Honor of Charles Howard McIlwain,* New York: Russell & Russell, 1964.

Commentary: Charles Howard McIlwain was awarded the 1924 Pulitzer Prize in History for *The American Revolution: A Constitutional Interpretation.* This volume covered the history and the causes of the American Revolution (1775-1783) from a constitutional perspective.

McIlwain was born in Saltsburg, Pennsylvania. He was a historian and a political scientist. He held the chair of Eaton Professor of the Science of Government at Harvard University from 1926 to 1946. He is also known for *The High Court of Parliament and Its Supremacy,* which analyzed the historical roots and development of the British Parliament as a lawmaking body starting in the year 1066. His other influential history was *Constitutionalism: Ancient and Modern.* McIlwain, as an expert in constitutional history, greatly feared the rise of totalitarianism.

1925

Frederic Logan Paxson   541

Birth: 1877; Philadelphia, PA. **Death:** October 24, 1948. **Education:** University of Pennsylvania: MA, PhD. Harvard University, MA. **Spouse:** Helen Hale (m. 1906). **Children:** Jane, Emma, Patricia.

Prize: *History,* 1925: *History of the American Frontier, 1763-1893,* Boston, MA: Houghton Mifflin, 1924.

Career: Historian.

Selected Works: *The Independence of the South-American Republics: A Study in Recognition and Foreign Policy,* 1903. *The Public Archives of the State of Colorado,* 1904. *The Boundaries of Colorado,* 1904. *The Last American Frontier,* 1910. *The American Civil War,* 1911. *Guide to the Materials in London*

Archives for the History of the United States Since 1783 (with Charles O. Paullin), 1914. *T. Turnbull's Travels from the United States across the Plains to California,* 1914. *The Independence of the South American Republics: A Study in Recognition and Foreign Policy,* 1916. *Recent History of the United States,* 1921. *The United States in Recent Times,* 1926. *When the West Is Gone,* 1930. *American Democracy and the World War,* 1936-48. *The Great Demobilization, and Other Essays,* 1941.

For More Information: *Wisconsin Writers,* Detroit: Gale, 1924.

Commentary: Frederic L. Paxson won the 1925 Pulitzer Prize in History for *History of the American Frontier.* This volume traced with depth and precision the history of the settlement of the American western frontier up to the Mississippi River Valley.

Paxson was regarded by many as the foremost historian of frontier history. He believed the role of the frontier was a reaction by the East and the West, the settled and the unsettled, to each other's outlook on what it meant to be "American." He was adept at portraying the process of the frontier experience.

1926

Edward Channing   542

Birth: June 15, 1856; Dorchester, MA. **Death:** January 7, 1931. **Parents:** William Ellery Channing and Ellen Kilshaw (Fuller) Channing. **Education:** Harvard University, MA: BA, PhD. **Spouse:** Alice Thatcher (m. 1886). **Children:** Two daughters.

Prize: *History,* 1926: *A History of the United States, The War of Independence, Volume VI,* New York: Macmillan, 1921-1932.

Career: Instructor, History, Harvard University, MA, 1883-1896; Assistant Professor, Harvard University, 1897; McLean Professor of Ancient and Modern History, Harvard University, 1913; Retired, 1929.

Selected Works: *Lectures Read to the Seniors in Harvard College,* 1856. *Town and County Government in the English Colonies of North America. The Toppan Prize Essay for 1883,* 1884. *The Genesis of the Massachusetts Town, and the Development of Town-Meeting Government* (with Charles F. Adams, Abner Goodell, and Meller Chamberlain), 1892. *English History for American Readers* (with Thomas Wentworth Higginson), 1893. *The United States of America, 1765-1865,* 1896. *Guide to the Study of American History* (with Albert Bushnell Hart), 1896. *A Student's History of the United States,* 1898. *First Lessons in United States History,* 1906. *A Students' History of the United States,* 1907. *The Story of the Great Lakes* (with Marion Florence Lansing), 1909. *Elements of United States History* (with Susan J. Ginn), 1910. *The Barrington-Bernard Correspon-*

dence and Illustrative Matter, 1760-1770 (Channing, Edward and Coolidge, Archibald Cary, eds.), 1912. *The American Nation, a History: From Original Sources by Associated Scholars,* 1904-1918. *English History for Americans,* 1912. *Guide to the Study and Reading of American History* (with Albert Bushnell Hart and Frederick Jackson Turner), 1912. *A Student's History of the United States,* 1913.

For More Information: Preston, Wheeler, *American Biographies,* New York: Harper, 1940; Joyce, Davis D., *Edward Channing and the Great Work,* The Hague, Netherlands: Martinus Nijhoff, 1974; *Harper's Encyclopedia of American History,* Detroit: Gale, 1974.

Commentary: *A History of the United States* won the 1926 Pulitzer Prize in History for Edward Channing. This was a monumental work consisting of seven volumes. It began with the New World in the period from 1000 to 1600 and ended with the period of the Civil War. The first volume appeared in 1905 and the final volume was published in 1925.

Channing was born in Dorchester, Massachusetts. He was a student of the historian Henry Adams at Harvard University and decided early on a career as a historian. Channing undertook much original research for his histories. He viewed his earlier histories as preparation for the "great work," the series on United States history. The series was the focus of his professional career. Channing died while working on the seventh volume. He has the distinction of having delivered the first paper ever presented at the first meeting of the American Historical Association in 1883. The paper, "Town and Country Government in the English Colonies," launched his career as a historian.

1927

Samuel Flagg Bemis

Full entry appears as #44 under "Biography or Autobiography," 1950.

1928

Vernon Louis Parrington   543

Birth: August 3, 1871; Aurora, IL. **Death:** June 17, 1929. **Parents:** John William and Louise (McClelland) Parrington. **Education:** Harvard University, MA: AB. College of Emporia, KS: MA.

Prize: *History,* 1928: *Main Currents in American Thought: An Interpretation of American Literature from the Beginnings to 1920,* New York: Harcourt, Brace, 1930.

Career: Instructor, College of Emporia, KS, 1893-1897; Professor of English, University of Okla-

homa, 1897-1908; Assistant Professor of English, University of Washington, WA, 1908-1912; Professor of English, University of Washington, 1912-1929.

Selected Works: *The Connecticut Wits,* 1926. *Sinclair Lewis, Our Own Diogenes,* 1927.

For More Information: Hofstadter, Richard, *The Progressive Historians: Turner, Beard, Parrington,* New York: Knopf, 1968; Hall, H. Lark, *V. L. Parrington: Through the Avenue of Art,* Kent, OH: Kent State University, 1994.

Commentary: Vernon Louis Parrington won the 1928 Pulitzer Prize in History for *Main Currents in American Thought: An Interpretation of American Literature from the Beginnings to 1920.* At the time of the award, two volumes of the three-volume history were completed. They made a reputation for Parrington because his was the first attempt ever made to survey American intellectual history.

Parrington was born in Aurora, Illinois, and grew up in Kansas. He was a teacher, historian, critic, and biographer. He attributed his exposure to populism while growing up as having shaped his future views. He both attended and taught at the College of Emporia in Kansas. Parrington's first volume of *Main Currents* was *The Colonial Mind.* In it he put forth the idea of Puritan society as a closed society. He saw the Puritans as resistant to the liberalism, which in the 18th century became accepted as "the right and duty of citizens to re-create social and political institutions to the end that they further social justice." In the time since its publication, *Main Currents* has received more criticism than acclaim. Parrington died while working on the third volume.

1929

Fred Albert Shannon   544

Birth: February 12, 1893; Sedalia, MO. **Death:** February 4, 1963. **Parents:** Louis Tecumseh and Sarah Margaret (Sparks) Shannon. **Education:** Indiana State Teachers College: BA. Indiana University: MA. University of Iowa: PhD.

Prize: *History,* 1929: *The Organization and Administration of the Union Army, 1861-1865,* Cleveland, OH: Clark, 1928.

Career: Assistant Professor of History, Iowa State Teachers College.

Selected Works: *The Farmer's Last Frontier: Agriculture, 1860-1897,* 1945. *American Farmers' Movements,* 1957. *The Centennial Years: A Political and Economic History of America from the Late 1870s to the Early 1890s,* 1967.

For More Information: *Dictionary of American Biography,* New York: Scribners, 1964; *Who Was Who Among North American Writers, 1921-1939,* Detroit: Gale, 1976.

Commentary: Fred Albert Shannon was awarded the 1929 Pulitzer Prize in History for his two-volume *The Organization and Administration of the Union Army, 1861-1865.* It covered the history of the Union Army, including recruitment and enlistment, during the period of the Civil War.

Shannon wrote history from the perspective of the common American. He had a low regard for the wealthy and well-born and felt that it was the common man's values that shaped America. He was painstaking in his analysis of census data as a source of information for this work. He worked closely with Arthur M. Schlesinger Sr. at the University of Iowa.

1930

Claude H. Van Tyne   545

Birth: October 16, 1869; Tecumseh, MI. **Death:** March 21, 1930. **Parents:** Lawrence M. and Helen (Rosecrans) Van Tyne. **Education:** University of Michigan: BA: University of Pennsylvania, PA: PhD. **Spouse:** Belle Josling (m. 1896). **Children:** Three sons, one daughter.

Prize: *History,* 1930: *The War of Independence; American Phase, Being the Second Volume of a History of the Founding of the American Republic,* Boston: Houghton Mifflin, 1929.

Career: Assistant Professor of History, University of Michigan, 1903-1906; Professor of History, University of Michigan, 1906; Head, History Department, University of Michigan, 1911-1930.

Selected Works: *The Letters of Daniel Webster,* 1902. *The Loyalists in the American Revolution,* 1902. *Guide to the Archives of the Government of the United States in Washington* (with Waldo G. Leland), 1904. *A History of the United States for Schools* (with Andrew C. McLaughlin), 1911. *The Causes of the War of Independence,* 1922. *India in Ferment,* 1923. *England & America: Rivals in the American Revolution,* 1969.

For More Information: *Dictionary of American Authors,* Boston: Houghton, Mifflin, 1905; Obituary, *New York Times,* March 22, 1930; *American History Review,* July 1930.

Commentary: *The War of Independence* won the 1930 Pulitzer Prize in History for Claude Van Tyne. It covered the history and causes of the American Revolution from 1775 to 1783.

Van Tyne was born in Tecumseh, Michigan. He studied at the University of Michigan and the University of Pennsylvania. He lectured in France and was invited to India to tour. His work was lauded as very readable.

1931

Bernadotte Everly Schmitt   546

Birth: May 19, 1886; Strasburg, VA. **Death:** 1969. **Parents:** Cooper Davis and Rose V. (Everly) Schmitt. **Education:** University of Tennessee: AB. Oxford University, England: Rhodes Scholar, BA, MA. University of Wisconsin: PhD. **Spouse:** Demaris Kathryn Ames (m. 1939).

Prize: *History,* 1931: *The Coming of the War, 1914,* New York: Scribners, 1930.

Career: Instructor and Professor of History, Western Reserve University, Cleveland, OH, 1910-1925; Second Lieutenant, U.S. Army, Field Artillery, 1918; Professor, University of Chicago, 1925-1939; Professor of Diplomatic History, Graduate Institute of International Studies, Geneva, Switzerland, 1931-32; Andrew MacLeish Distinguished Service Professor of Modern History, University of Chicago, 1939-1946; Trustee, Newbery Library, Chicago, 1941-1947; Visiting Professor at Washington and Jefferson College, 1942; U.S. Department of State, Historical Division, 1945-52; Professor Emeritus, University of Chicago, 1946; Visiting Professor at University of South Carolina, 1956; President, American Historical Association, 1960; Honorary Member, Historical Association of Great Britain; Member: American Philosophical Society, American Academy of Arts and Sciences, American Political Science Association, Cosmos Club and Literary Society (Washington, DC), Chicago Literary Club, Phi Beta Kappa, Phi Kappa Phi, Phi Gamma Delta.

Selected Works: *England and Germany, 1740-1914,* 1918. *Triple Alliance and Triple Entente,* 1934. *The Annexation of Bosnia, 1908-1909,* 1937. *Some Historians of Modern Europe: Essays in Historiography* (Schmitt, Bernadette E., ed.), 1942. *The Fashion and Future of History: Historical Studies and Addresses,* 1960. *England and Germany, 1740-1914,* 1967. *The World in the Crucible, 1914-1919* (with Harold C. Vedeler), 1984.

Other Awards: George Louis Beer Prize, American Historical Association, 1930. Honorary LLD from Western Reserve University, OH, 1941. Honorary, LittD, Pomona College, CA 1941.

For More Information: Cochran, Michael Hermond, *Germany Not Guilty in 1914,* Boston: Stratford, 1931; Halperin, Samuel William, *Some 20th-Century Historians: Essays on Eminent Europeans,* Chicago: University of Chicago, 1961.

Commentary: Bernadotte Everly Schmitt won the 1931 Pulitzer Prize in History for *The Coming of the War, 1914.* A work in two volumes, it examined the causes leading up to World War I and politics and government in Europe from 1871 to 1918.

Schmitt was born in Strasburg, Virginia. He was

a professor of modern and diplomatic history. He taught at the University of Chicago from 1910 until 1939 when he was made Distinguished Service Professor of Modern History there.

1932

John J. Pershing 547

Birth: September 13, 1860; Laclede, MO. **Death:** July 15, 1948. **Parents:** John Frederic Pershing (name originally Pforershing). **Education:** University of Nebraska: Law Degree. **Spouse:** Frances Warren (died, 1915). **Children:** Three daughters, one son.

Prize: *History,* 1932: *My Experiences in the World War,* New York: Frederick A. Stokes, 1931.

Career: U.S. Army General.

Selected Works: *Final Report of Gen. John J. Pershing,* 1919. *The Official Story of American Operations in France,* 1919. *Report of the First Army, American Expeditionary Forces,* 1923.

For More Information: Hill, Ruth, *John Joseph Pershing: A Story and a Play,* Boston: Badger, 1919; McCracken, Harold, *Pershing, The Story of a Great Soldier,* New York: Brewer & Warren, 1931; Army Times Publishing Company, *The Yanks Are Coming: The Story of General John J. Pershing,* New York: Putnam, 1960; O'Connor, Richard, *Black Jack Pershing,* Garden City, NY: Doubleday, 1961; Smythe, Donald, *Guerrilla Warrior: The Early Life of John J. Pershing,* New York: Scribner, 1973; Vandiver, Frank Everson, *Black Jack: The Life and Times of John J. Pershing,* College Station: Texas A&M University, 1977; Goldhurst, Richard, *Pipe Clay and Drill: John J. Pershing, The Classic American Soldier,* New York: Reader's Digest, 1977;

Smythe, Donald, *Pershing, General of the Armies,* Bloomington, IN: Indiana University, 1986.

Commentary: John Joseph Pershing was awarded the 1932 Pulitzer Prize in History for *My Experiences in the World War.* Written in two volumes, it is both a history of the United States Army in World War I and the autobiography of "Black Jack" Pershing, the general responsible for organizing and controlling 2 million American troops in Europe.

Pershing was born near Laclede, Missouri. Pershing grew up on a farm and taught school in his youth. He was a man who inspired confidence through his strict discipline, steadfastness, and sense of duty. Pershing had participated in the Indian Campaigns against Geronimo and at Wounded Knee. He was ordered to lead ten thousand troops to capture the infamous Pancho Villa in 1916. The experience of leading a large force and using modern equipment such as automobiles, radios, trucks, machine guns, and aircraft made him best qualified to lead when America joined the war in Europe. Pershing was made "General of the Armies" in 1919, the only so-ranked general since George Washington.

1933

Frederick J. Turner 548

Birth: November 14, 1861; Portage, WI. **Death:** March 14, 1932. **Parents:** Andrew Jackson and Mary (Hanford) Turner. **Education:** University of Wisconsin: AB, MA. Johns Hopkins University, MD: PhD. **Spouse:** Caroline Mae Sherwood (m. 1889). **Children:** Two daughters, one son.

Prize: *History,* 1933: *The Significance of Sections in American History,* New York: Holt, 1932.

Career: Reporter, Madison, WI; Assistant Professor of History, University of Wisconsin, 1892-1910; Professor of History, Harvard University, MA, 1910-1924; Professor Emeritus, Harvard University, 1924; Research Associate, Henry E. Huntington Library, 1927-1928.

Selected Works: *Outline Studies in the History of the Northwest,* 1888. *The Character and Influence of the Fur Trade in Wisconsin,* 1889. *The Old West,* 1909. *Guide to the Study and Reading of American History* (with Edward Channing and Albert Bushnell Hart), 1912. *List of References on the History of the West,* 1913. *Reuben Gold Thwaites,* 1914. *The Frontier in American History,* 1928. *The United States, 1830-1850: The Nation and Its Sections,* 1935. *The Early Writings of Frederick Jackson Turner* (Edward, Everett E., ed.), 1938. *Essays in American History: Dedicated to Frederick Jackson Turner,* 1951.

For More Information: Hart, Albert Bushnell, *The American Nation, A History: From Original Sources by Associated Scholars,* New York: Harper,

1904-1918; Billington, Ray Allen, *"Dear Lady": The Letters of Frederick Jackson Turner and Alice Forbes Perkins Hooper, 1910-1932,* San Marino, CA: Huntington Library, 1970; *Frederick Jackson Turner: Historian, Scholar, Teacher,* New York: Oxford University, 1973; Carpenter, Ronald H., *The Eloquence of Frederick Jackson Turner,* San Marino, CA: Huntington Library, 1983; Mattson, Vernon E. and William E. Merion, *Frederick Jackson Turner: A Reference Guide,* Boston: G.K. Hall, 1985; Faragher, John Mack, *Rereading Frederick Jackson Turner,* New York: Holt, 1994; Jacobs, Wilbur R., *On Turner's Trail: 100 Years of Writing Western History,* Lawrence, KS: University Press, 1994.

Commentary: Frederick Jackson Turner won the 1933 Pulitzer Prize in History for *The Significance of Sections in American History.* Published in the year that Turner died, it is a history of sectionalism in the United States. It was edited by Max Farrand and Avery Odelle Craven.

Turner was born in Portage, Wisconsin. He was educated at the University of Wisconsin and Johns Hopkins University. Upon presenting a paper, "The Significance of the Frontier in American History," at a meeting of the American Historical Association in 1893, he became indelibly linked to frontier history. In this essay, he offered what became known as the "Turner Thesis" in which the frontier, as a source of individualism, restless energy, self-reliance, and inventiveness, produced uniquely American ideals and shaped the American character. He posited that perhaps the "free environment" of the frontier produced new traits in the Europeans who left behind countries that were decidedly "not free" due to social and economic pressures. This became the main approach to the teaching of American history.

1934

Herbert Agar   549

Birth: September 29, 1897; New Rochelle, NY. **Parents:** John Giraud and Agnes Louise (McDonough) Agar. **Education:** Columbia University, NY: BA. Princeton University, NJ: MA, PhD. **Spouse:** Adelaine Scott (m. 1918; div. 1933); Eleanor Caroll Chilton (m. 1933; div. 1945); Barbara Tylas Wallace (m. 1945). **Children:** William Scott, Agnes (AS).

Prize: *History,* 1934: *The People's Choice, From Washington to Harding: A Study in Democracy,* Boston: Houghton Mifflin, 1933.

Career: U.S. Naval Reserve, 1917-1918; Correspondent, London, England, *Louisville Courier-Journal* and *Louisville Times,* KY, 1929-1934; Daily Columnist, *Louisville Courier-Journal,* 1935-1939; Editor, *Louisville Courier-Journal,* 1940-1942; Founder and First President, Freedom House, 1941;

Lieutenant Commander, U.S. Naval Reserve, 1942; Director of British Division, Office of War Information, London, England, 1943-1946; Special Assistant to American Ambassador in London, 1943-1946; Counsellor for Public Affairs at U.S. Embassy in England, 1946; Director, Rupert Hart-Davis Publishing, London, 1951-1963; Director, T.W.W. Ltd. (Independent Television South Wales and West of England), London, 1953-1965; Member: National Arts Club, Phi Beta Kappa, Century Club, Savile Club.

Selected Works: *Fire and Sleet and Candlelight* (with Eleanor Carroll Chilton and Willis Fisher), 1928. *The Garment of Praise: The Necessity for Poetry* (with Eleanor Carroll Chilton), 1929. *Pursuit of Happiness: The Story of American Democracy,* 1938. *The City of Man: A Declaration on World Democracy,* 1940. *Beyond German Victory* (with Helen Hill), 1940. *World-Wide Civil War,* 1942. *A Time for Greatness,* 1942. *The Price of Union,* 1950. *A Declaration of Faith,* 1952. *Abraham Lincoln,* 1952. *Nationality versus Nationalism,* 1954. *The Price of Power: America Since 1945,* 1957. *The Unquiet Years: U.S.A. 1945-1955,* 1957. *The Saving Remnant: An Account of Jewish Survival,* 1960. *The Americans: Ways of Life and Thought,* 1962. *The Perils of Democracy,* 1965. *Britain Alone, June 1940-June 1941,* 1972.

Other Awards: Honorary LittD, Southwestern University, TN. Honorary LLD, Boston University.

For More Information: *Current Biography Yearbook,* New York: Wilson, 1944; *Time,* November 9, 1942 and December 9, 1946.

Commentary: *The People's Choice* won the 1934 Pulitzer Prize in History for Herbert Agar. The volume was a study of presidents from Washington to Harding.

1935

Charles McLean Andrews   550

Birth: February 22, 1863; Wethersfield, CT. **Death:** September 9, 1943. **Education:** Trinity College, CT. Johns Hopkins University, MD: PhD. **Spouse:** Evangeline H. Walker (m. 1895). **Children:** One daughter, one son.

Prize: *History,* 1935: *The Colonial Period of American History,* New Haven, CT: Yale University, 1934-1938.

Career: Associate Professor of History, Bryn Mawr College, 1889-1907; Professor of History, Johns Hopkins University, MD, 1907-1910; Farnam Professor of American History, Yale University, CT, 1910-1931; Editor, History Publications, Yale University, 1912-1933; President, American Historical Association, 1925; Director, History Publications, Yale University, 1931-1933.

Selected Works: *The River Towns of Connecticut: A Study of Wethersfield, Hartford, and Windsor,* 1889. *The Old English Manor: A Study in English Economic History,* 1892. *The Historical Development of Modern Europe: From the Congress of Vienna to the Present Time, 1815-1897,* 1906. *Guide to the Manuscript Materials for the History of the United States to 1783, in the British Museum, in Minor London Archives, and in the Libraries of Oxford and Cambridge* (with Frances G. Davenport), 1908. *The Colonial Period,* 1912. *Guide to the Materials for American History, to 1783, in the Public Record Office of Great Britain,* 1912-1914. *Short History of England,* 1912. *List of Commissions, Instructions, and Additional Instructions Issued to the Royal Governors and Others in America,* 1913. *Narratives of the Insurrections: 1675-1690,* 1915. *Connecticut's Place in Colonial History,* 1924. *The Colonial Background of the American Revolution: Four Essays in American Colonial History,* 1931. *Our Earliest Colonial Settlements, Their Diversities of Origin and Later Characteristics,* 1933. *Journal of a Lady of Quality* (with Evangeline W. Andrews), 1939. *The Colonial Background of the American Revolution: Four Essays in American Colonial History,* 1958.

For More Information: *Pennsylvania Magazine of History and Biography,* July 1935; *Time,* December 28, 1936.

Commentary: Charles McLean Andrews was awarded the 1935 Pulitzer Prize in History for *The Colonial Period of American History.* A four-volume work, it told the story of England's American settlements from 1600 to 1775, and covered England's commercial and colonial policy.

Andrews was born in Wethersfield, Connecticut. He was an expert on colonial history and institutions. His prize-winning work broke ground because Andrews thought the American Revolution was, first, a political and constitutional movement and, second, a financial, commercial, or social movement. He conducted much of his research in British archives. He also wrote *Historical Development of Modern Europe, 1815-1897* and *The Boston Merchants and the Non-Importation Movement.* Andrews taught at Yale University from 1910 until his retirement.

1936

Andrew C. McLaughlin 551

Birth: February 14, 1861; Beardstown, IL. **Death:** September, 24, 1947. **Education:** University of Michigan. University of Michigan Law School, MI. **Spouse:** Lois Thompson Angell (m. 1890). **Children:** Three sons, three daughters.

Prize: *History,* 1936: *A Constitutional History of the United States,* New York: Appleton-Century, 1935.

Career: Latin Teacher, University of Michigan, 1886; Instructor of History, University of Michigan, 1887-1897; Editor, *American History Review,* 1898-1914; Managing Editor, *American History Review,* 1901-1905; Head, Bureau of Historical Research, Carnegie Institute, 1903; Head, Department of History, University of Chicago, 1906; Professor Emeritus, University of Chicago, 1929.

Selected Works: *Lewis Cass,* 1891. *A History of the American Nation,* 1899. *Report on the Diplomatic Archives of the Department of State, 1789-1840,* 1904. *A History of the United States for Schools* (with Claude H. Van Tyne), 1911. *A History of the American Nation,* 1912. *Readings in the History of the American Nation,* 1914. *A History of the United States for Schools* (with Claude H. Van Tyne), 1916. *A History of the American Nation,* 1916. *Source Problems in United States History* (with William E. Dodd, Marcus W. Jernegan, and Arthur P. Scott), 1918. *America and Britain,* 1918. *Steps in the Development of American Democracy,* 1920. *Aspects of the Social History of America* (with Dixon R. Fox, Henry S. Canby, and Theodore Sizer), 1931. *The Foundations of American Constitutionalism,* 1932. *Cyclopedia of American Government* (with Albert B. Hart), 1942.

For More Information: Obituary, *New York Times,* September 25, 1947; *American Historical Review,* January 1948; *National Encyclopedia of American Biography,* New York: White, 1950.

Commentary: Andrew Cunningham McLaughlin won the 1936 Pulitzer Prize in History for *A Constitutional History of the United States.*

McLaughlin was a historian and constitutional scholar. He was more interested in ideas and institutions than in individuals. He was considered at his best when tracing the evolution of concepts, practices, and governmental forms basic to American constitutionalism. He taught at the University of Chicago from 1906 to 1929.

1937

Van Wyck Brooks   552

Birth: February 16, 1886; Plainfield, NJ. **Death:** May 2, 1963. **Parents:** Charles Edward Brooks and Sarah Bailey (Ames). **Religion:** Episcopalian. **Education:** Harvard University, MA: AB. **Spouse:** Eleanor Keagan Stimson (m. 1911; died 1946); Gladys Rice Billings (m. 1947). **Children:** Charles, Oliver Keagan (EKS).

Prize: *History,* 1937: *The Flowering of New England, 1815-1865,* New York: Dutton, 1936.

Career: Editor, Translator, and Writer, *Standard Dictionary, Collier's Encyclopedia,* and *World's Work;* Instructor, English, Stanford University, 1911-1913; French Translator, Century Company, NY, 1914; Associate Editor, *Seven Arts,* 1917-1918; Associate Editor, *Freeman,* 1920-1924; Historian; Chancellor, American Academy of Arts and Sciences, 1957; Fellow, Royal Society of Literature; Member: American Academy of Arts and Letters, American Philosophical Society, Century Club, Phi Beta Kappa, The Players.

Selected Works: *The Wine of the Puritans: A Study of Present-Day America,* 1908. *The Malady of the Ideal: Obermann, Maurice de Gurin and Amiel,* 1913. *John Addington Symonds: A Biographical Study,* 1914. *America's Coming-of-Age,* 1915. *The World of H.G. Wells,* 1915. *The Flame That Is France,* 1918. *Letters and Leadership,* 1918. *History of a Literary Radical, and Other Essays,* 1920. *The Ordeal of Mark Twain,* 1920. *Henry Thoreau, Bachelor of Nature, by Lon Bazalgette* (Translation), 1924. *The Pilgrimage of Henry James,* 1925. *Emerson and Others,* 1927. *The Road, by Andre Chamson* (Translation), 1929. *The Crime of the Just, by Andre Chamson* (Translation), 1930. *Philine, from the Unpublished*

Journals of Henri-Frederic Amiel (Translation), 1930. *Sketches in Criticism,* 1932. *The Journal of Gamaliel Bradford, 1883-1932,* 1933. *The Letters of Gamaliel Bradford, 1918-1931,* 1934. *Three Essays on America,* 1934. *New England: Indian Summer, 1865-1915,* 1940. *On Literature Today,* 1941. *Opinions of Oliver Allston,* 1941. *The World of Washington Irving,* 1944. *The Times of Melville and Whitman,* 1947. *The Malady of the Ideal: Obermann, Maurice de Gurin and Amiel,* 1947. *A Chilmark Miscellany,* 1948. *The Confident Years: 1885-1915,* 1952. *The Writer in America,* 1953. *Scenes and Portraits: Memories of Childhood and Youth,* 1954. *Our Literary Heritage: A Pictorial History of the Writer in America* (with Otto L. Bettmann), 1956. *Helen Keller: Sketch for a Portrait,* 1956. *Days of the Phoenix: The Nineteen-Twenties I Remember,* 1957. *The Dream of Arcadia: American Writers and Artists in Italy, 1760-1915,* 1958. *From the Shadow of the Mountain: My Post-Meridian Years,* 1961. *A New England Reader,* 1962. *Fenollosa and His Circle: With Other Essays in Biography,* 1962. *An Autobiography,* 1965.

Other Awards: Dial Prize, Distinguished Critical Work, 1923. National Book Award, 1937: *The Flowering of New England,* New York: Dutton, 1936. Gold Medal of National Institute of Arts and Letters, 1946. Theodore Roosevelt Medal, 1954. Wing Dedicated, Burnham Public Library, Bridgewater, CT. Honorary LittDs: Harvard University, MA; Columbia University, NY; Boston University, MA; Bowdoin College, MA; Dartmouth College, NH; Northwestern University, MA; Union College; Northeastern University, IL; Tufts University, MA; University of Pennsylvania; Fairleigh Dickinson University, NJ. Honorary LHD, Northwestern University, IL.

For More Information: *Current Biography Yearbook,* New York: Wilson, 1955; *Oxford Companion to American Literature,* New York: Oxford, 1965; Hoopes, James, *Van Wyck Brooks: In Search of American Culture,* Amherst: University of Massachusetts, 1977; Vitelli, James R., *Van Wyck Brooks: A Reference Guide,* Boston: Hall, 1977; Wasserstrom, William, ed., *Van Wyck Brooks, The Critic and His Critics,* Port Washington, NY: Kennikat, 1979; Nelson, Raymond, *Van Wyck Brooks: A Writer's Life,* New York: Dutton, 1981.

Commentary: *The Flowering of New England, 1815-1865* won the 1937 Pulitzer Prize in History for Van Wyck Brooks. This work provided both a history and criticism of American literature in New England during the 19th century.

Brooks was born in Plainfield, New Jersey. A graduate of Harvard University, he was an editor and translator in addition to writing literary history. He contributed articles to the *Standard Dictionary* and *Collier's Encyclopedia.* Brooks penned a sequel to

Flowering; published in 1940, it was titled *New England: Indian Summer, 1865-1915.*

1938

Paul Herman Buck 553

Birth: August 25, 1899. **Death:** 1978. **Parents:** Henry John and Adele (Kreppelt) Buck. **Education:** Ohio State University: Harvard University, MA: PhD. **Spouse:** Sally Burwell Botts (m. 1927).

Prize: *History,* 1938: *The Road to Reunion, 1865-1900,* Boston: Little, Brown, 1937.

Career: History Instructor, Harvard University, MA, 1926-1927; Assistant Professor, Harvard University, 1936; Associate Dean of Faculty, Harvard University, 1938; Associate Professor, Harvard University, 1939; Board of Editors, Journal of Southern History, 1941-; Dean of Faculty, Harvard University, MA, 1942.

Selected Works: *The Role of Education in American History,* 1957. *Libraries & Universities: Addresses and Reports,* 1964.

Other Awards: Sheldon Travelling Fellowship, 1927.

For More Information: *Current Biography Yearbook,* New York: Wilson, 1955; *One Hundred Authors Who Shaped World History,* San Mateo, CA: 1996.

Commentary: Paul Herman Buck was awarded the 1938 Pulitzer Prize in History for *The Road to Reunion, 1865-1900.* It provided a history of politics and government during the Reconstruction years. He viewed the era as one in which two bitter foes were joined or harmonized, building a core for American life since.

Buck taught history at Harvard University and became dean of the faculty in 1942. Buck claimed that he wouldn't have written this history if it hadn't been for the constant encouragement of Arthur M. Schlesinger Sr.

1939

Frank Luther Mott 554

Birth: April 4, 1886; What Cheer, IA. **Death:** 1964. **Parents:** David C. and Mary E. Mott. **Education:** Simpson College, IA. University of Chicago, IL: PhB. Columbia University, NY: MA, PhD. **Spouse:** Vera Ingram (1910). **Children:** Mildred.

Prize: *History,* 1939: *A History of American Magazines, 1741-1850, Vols. II and III,* New York: Appleton, 1930.

Career: Newspaperman; Co-Editor, *Marengo Republican,* Marengo, IA, 1907-1914; Editor and Publisher, *Grand Junction Globe,* Grand Junction, IA, 1914-1917; Professor of English, Simpson College, IA, 1919-1921; Assistant Professor of English, State University of Iowa, 1921-1925; Associate Professor, State University of Iowa, 1925-1927; Professor of Journalism and Director of School of Journalism, State University of Iowa, 1927-1942; Dean of School of Journalism, University of Missouri, 1942-1951; Professor of Journalism, University of Missouri, 1942-1956; Member, Government Journalism Mission, France, 1945-1946; Adviser to General MacArthur's staff and to newspaper leaders, Japan, 1947; Dean Emeritus and Professor Emeritus, University of Missouri, 1956-1964; Board of Trustees, State Historical Society of Missouri; Fellow: Sigma Delta Chi, Society of American Historians; Former Chairman, National Council for Research in Journalism; Honorary Member, Phi Beta Kappa; Member, American Association of Schools and Departments of Journalism; President, Kappa Tau Alpha.

Selected Works: *Literature of Pioneer Life in Iowa,* 1923. *A History of American Magazines, 1741-1850,* 1930. *American Journalism: A History of Newspapers in the United States through 250 Years, 1690-1940,* 1941. *Golden Multitudes: The Story of Best Sellers in the United States,* 1947. *The News in America,* 1952. *American Journalism: A History of Newspapers in the United States through 260 Years: 1690 to 1950,* 1956. *American Journalism: A History, 1690-1960,* 1962. *The Old Printing Office,* 1962. *Time Enough: Essays in Autobiography,* 1962. *Missouri Reader,* 1964.

Other Awards: Bancroft Prize, 1957. Sigma Delta Chi Award for Research, 1939, 1958. 1957. Kappa Tau Alpha National Research Award, 1958. Honorary LittDs: Simpson College, IA; Temple University, PA. Honorary LHD, Boston University. Honorary LLD, Marquette University, WI.

For More Information: *Current Biography Yearbook,* New York: Wilson, 1964; *Encyclopedia of American Biography,* New York: Harper Collins, 1967; *Encyclopedia of Journalism,* New York: Facts on File, 1983.

Commentary: Frank Luther Mott won the 1939 Pulitzer Prize in History for *A History of American Magazines.* It provided a complete reference work on American magazines in five volumes.

Mott was born in What Cheer, Iowa. He was educated at the University of Chicago and Columbia University. He was a newspaper editor and publisher before taking on an academic career teaching English and journalism. He also published *American Journalism: A History of Newspapers in the United States Through the Years, 1690-1940,* which he later updated through 1950.

1940

Carl Sandburg   555

Birth: January 6, 1878; Galesburg, IL. **Death:** July 22, 1967. **Parents:** August and Clara (Anderson) Sandburg. **Education:** Lombard College, IL. **Spouse:** Lillian ("Paula") Steichen (m. 1908). **Children:** Margaret, Janet, Helga.

Prize: *Poetry,* 1919: *Cornhuskers,* New York: Holt and Company, 1918. *History,* 1940: *Abraham Lincoln: The War Years,* New York: Harcourt, Brace, 1939. *Poetry,* 1951: *Complete Poems,* New York: Harcourt, Brace, 1950.

Career: Poet, historian and folk singer; Sixth Illinois Volunteers, 1898; Served in Puerto Rico, Spanish-American War; Organizer, Wisconsin Socialist Democratic Party; Reporter, *Milwaukee Sentinel* and *Milwaukee Daily News;* City Hall Reporter, *Milwaukee Journal;* Secretary, Mayor Emil Seidel, Milwaukee, WI, 1910-1912; Reporter, *Milwaukee Leader* and *Chicago World,* 1912; Reporter, *Day Book,* Chicago, IL, 1912-1917; Associate Editor, *System: The Magazine of Business,* Chicago, 1913; Reporter, *Chicago Evening American,* 1917; Reporter, Editor, Columnist, *Chicago Daily News,* 1917-1932; Stockholm Correspondent, Newspaper Enterprise Association, 1918; Chicago Office, Newspaper Enterprise Association, 1919; Weekly Syndicated Presidential Medal of Freedom Lecturer, University of Hawaii, 1934; Walgreen Foundation Lecturer, University of Chicago, 1940; Columnist, *Chicago Daily Times,* beginning in 1941; Contributing Columnist, Chicago Times Syndicate; Member: American Academy of Arts and Letters, National Institute of Arts and Letters; Honorary Member: Phi Beta Kappa, Tavern Club (Chicago), Swedish Club (Chicago).

Selected Works: *Chicago Poems,* 1916. *The Chicago Race Riots, July 1919,* 1919. *Smoke and Steel,* 1920. *Rootabaga Stories,* 1922. *Slabs of the Sunburnt West,* 1922. *Rootabaga Pigeons,* 1923. *Abraham Lincoln: The Prairie Years,* 1925. *Selected Poems of Carl Sandburg* (West, Rebecca [pseudonym], ed.), 1926. *The American Songbag,* 1927. *Parrot Pie, Parodies and Imitations of Contemporaries,* 1927. *Abe Lincoln Grows Up,* 1928. *Good Morning, America,* 1928. *Rootabaga Country, Selections from Rootabaga Stories and Rootabaga Pigeons,* 1929. *Early Moon,* 1930. *The People, Yes,* 1936. *Smoke and Steel; Slabs of the Sunburnt West; Good Morning America,* 1942. *Home Front Memo,* 1943. *Poems of the Midwest,* 1946. *Remembrance Rock,* 1948. *Always the Young Strangers,* 1953. *Potato Face,* 1953. *Abraham Lincoln: The Prairie Years and the War Years,* 1954. *Harvest Poems, 1910-1960,* 1960. *The World of Carl Sandburg,* 1961. *Honey and Salt,* 1963. *The Wedding Procession of the Rag Doll and the Broom Handle and Who Was in It,* 1967.

Other Awards: Levinson Prize, 1914. Poetry Society of America Prize, 1919, 1921. Friend of American Writers Award. Phi Beta Kappa Poet, Harvard University, 1928. Phi Beta Kappa Poet, William & Mary College, 1943. Friends of Literature Award, 1934: *Lincoln: The Prairie Years.* Theodore Roosevelt Distinguished Service Medal, 1939. American Academy of Arts and Letters, Gold Medal for History, 1952, 1953. Poetry Society of America, Gold Medal for Poetry, 1953. Taminent Institution Award, 1953: *Always the Young Strangers,* New York: Harcourt, Brace, 1953. Seventy-Fifth Birthday Honor, Sweden's Commander, Order of the North Star, January 6, 1953. New York Civil War Round Table Silver Medal, 1954. University of Louisville Award of Merit, 1955. Albert Einstein Award, Yeshiva College, 1956. Roanoke-Chowan Poetry Cup, 1960: *Harvest Poems, 1910-1960,* New York: Harcourt, Brace, 1960. Roanoke-Chowan Poetry Cup, 1961: *Wind Song.* International Poet's Award, 1963. National Association for the Advancement of Colored People Award, 1965. Carl Sandburg acclaimed as "a major prophet of civil rights in our time." Honorary LittDs: Lombard College, 1928; Knox College, IL, 1929; Northwestern University, IL, 1931; Harvard University, MA, 1940; Yale University, CT, 1940; New York University, 1940; Wesleyan University, MA, 1940; Lafayette College, PA, 1940; Syracuse University, NY, 1941; Dartmouth College, NH, 1941; University of North Carolina, 1955. Honorary LLDs: Rollins College, FL, 1941; Augustana College, GA, 1948; University of Illinois, 1953. Honorary PhD, Upsala College, NJ, 1948.

For More Information: Salwak, Dale, *Carl Sandburg: A Reference Guide,* Boston: Hall, 1988; Niven, Penelope, *Carl Sandburg: A Biography,* New York: Scribners, 1991; Yannella, Philip, *The Other Carl Sandburg,* Jackson, MS: University Press of Mississippi, 1996.

Commentary: Carl Sandburg won three Pulitzer Prizes, two in Poetry and one in Biography. He was the co-winner of the 1919 Poetry prize for *Cornhuskers.* Sandburg won his second Pulitzer Prize for part of his four-volume biography of Abraham Lincoln. A third Pulitzer Prize was awarded to Sandburg in 1951 for his *Complete Poems.*

Sandburg was born in Galesburg, Illinois, the son of Swedish immigrant parents. He worked at various odd jobs before attending Lombard College, and later becoming a reporter. Sandburg's great love for America and for democracy was evident in much of his work. His poetry was first published in *Poetry* magazine and he followed with several volumes, including *Chicago Poems, Cornhuskers,* and *Smoke and Steel.* His hero was Abraham Lincoln and his masterful biography was actually two sets. The first two-volume set, *Abraham Lincoln: The Prairie Years,* was published in 1926. He wrote, collected, and performed American folk songs that were published in *The American Songbag.* He also wrote under the pseudonyms Charles August Sandburg, Militant, and Jack Phillips.

1941

Marcus Lee Hansen   556

Birth: December 8, 1892; Neenah, WI. **Death:** May 11, 1938. **Education:** Central College, IA: BA. University of Iowa: MA. Harvard University, MA: PhD.

Prize: *History,* 1941: *The Atlantic Migration, 1607-1860: A History of the Continuing Settlement of the United States,* Cambridge, MA: Harvard University, 1940.

Career: U.S Army, WWI; Associate Professor of History, University of Illinois, 1928-1930; Professor, University of Illinois, 1930-1938.

Selected Works: *Old Fort Snelling, 1819-1858,* 1918. *Welfare Campaigns in Iowa,* 1920. *Welfare Work in Iowa,* 1921. *The Immigrant in American History,* 1940. *The Mingling of the Canadian and American Peoples* (with John B. Brebner), 1940.

Other Awards: Social Science Research Council Stipend, 1924-1928. Study of Immigration.

For More Information: Obituary, *New York Times,* May 12, 1938; *American Historical Review,* July 1938; *Oxford Companion to American History,* New York: 1966; *Lincoln Library of Language Arts,* Columbus, OH: Frontier, 1978; Kivisto, Peter and Dag Blanck, eds., *American Immigrants and Their Generations: Studies and Commentaries on the Hansen Thesis After Fifty Years,* Urbana: University of Illinois, 1990.

Commentary: *The Atlantic Migration, 1607-1860* won the 1941 Pulitzer Prize in History for Marcus Lee Hansen. This was an ambitious history of the continuing settlement of the United States by Europeans. It included coverage of the social conditions in Europe during this long migration.

Hansen was born in Neenah, Wisconsin. He studied at the University of Iowa and Harvard University, under the tutelage of Frederick Jackson Turner. He decided to focus on the history of immigration and received a two-year grant enabling him to travel to European countries where he spent several years studying migration records. He realized that much more research would be necessary to adequately conduct a survey for *The Atlantic Migration.* His other works are *The Mingling of the Canadian and American Peoples* and *The Immigrant in American History.* Arthur M. Schlesinger Sr. was the editor of two of Hansen's books. Hansen died in Redlands, California, at the age of 46.

1942

Margaret Leech   557

Birth: November 7, 1893; Newburgh, NY. **Death:** February 24, 1974. **Parents:** William and Rebecca (Taggart) Leech. **Education:** Vassar College, NY: BA. **Spouse:** Ralph Pulitzer (m. 1938; died 1939). **Children:** Susan, Marietta.

Prize: *History,* 1942: *Reveille in Washington, 1860-1865,* New York: Harper, 1941. *History,* 1960: *In the Days of McKinley,* New York: Harper, 1959.

Career: Novelist, biographer, and historian; Publicity Agent for numerous fund-raising organizations, WWI; Staff member, publishing and advertising agencies, NY.

Selected Works: *The Back of the Book,* 1924. *Tin Wedding,* 1926. *The Feathered Nest,* 1928. *Anthony Comstock, Roundsman of the Lord* (with Heywood Broun), 1927. *The Garfield Orbit* (with Harry J. Brown), 1978.

Other Awards: Bancroft Prize, Columbia University, NY, 1960: *In the Days of McKinley.* New York: Harper, 1959.

For More Information: *Current Biography Yearbook,* New York: Wilson, 1974; *Oxford Companion to American Literature,* New York: Oxford, 1983.

Commentary: Margaret Leech won two Pulitzer Prizes, both in History. The first was awarded in 1942 for *Reveille in Washington, 1860-1865,* an examination of the Civil War. She won a second prize in 1960 for *In the Days of McKinley,* a history of the presidency of William McKinley (1897-1901).

Leech was born in Newburgh, New York and educated at Vassar College. Leech worked as a publicity agent and in the advertising and publishing fields before writing history and biography. Her other works include *Anthony Comstock, Roundsman of the Lord* and *The Garfield Orbit.*

1943

Esther Forbes   558

Birth: June 28, 1891; Westborough, MA. **Death:** 1967. **Parents:** William Trowbridge and Harriet (Marrifield) Forbes. **Education:** Bradford Junior College, WI. University of Wisconsin.

Prize: *History,* 1943: *Paul Revere and the World He Lived In,* Boston: Houghton Mifflin, 1942.

Career: Author; Editor, Houghton Mifflin, MA, 1920-1926, 1942-1946; Member: American Academy of Arts and Sciences, American Antiquarian Society, Society of American Historians.

Selected Works: *O Genteel Lady!,* 1926. *A Mirror for Witches in Which Is Reflected the Life, Machinations, and Death of Famous Doll Bilby, Who, With a More Than Feminine Perversity, Preferred a Demon to a Mortal Lover,* 1928. *Miss Marvel,* 1935. *Paradise,* 1937. *The General's Lady,* 1938. *Johnny Tremain,* 1943. *America's Paul Revere,* 1946. *The Boston Book,* 1947. *The Running of the Tide,* 1948. *Rainbow on the Road,* 1954.

Other Awards: John Newbery Medal, Most Distinguished Contribution of Year to Children's Literature, 1944: *Johnny Tremain: A Novel for Young and Old,* Boston: Houghton Mifflin, 1943. Metro-Goldwyn-Mayer Novel Award, 1948. Honorary LittDs: Clark University, MA, 1943; University of Maine; University of Wisconsin; Northeastern University, MA; Wellesley College, MA. Honorary LLD, Tufts University, MA.

For More Information: *Oxford Companion to American History,* New York: Oxford, 1966; *Oxford Companion to American Literature,* New York: 1966; *Dictionary of Literary Biography,* Detroit: Gale, 1983.

Commentary: Esther Forbes was awarded the 1943 Pulitzer Prize in History for *Paul Revere and the World He Lived In.*

Forbes was born in Westborough, Massachusetts, and she was educated at the University of Wisconsin. She was an editor at Houghton Mifflin Publishing Company during two periods of her life. She has primarily been an author of children's literature, history, and biography. Her other works include *Johnny Tremain: A Novel for Young and Old, The Running of the Tide,* and *Rainbow on the Road.*

1944

Merle Curti   559

Birth: September 15, 1897; Papillon, NE. **Death:** March 9, 1996. **Parents:** John Eugene and Alice (Hunt) Curti. **Education:** Harvard University, MA: AB, summa cum laude: AM, PhD. Sorbonne University, France. **Spouse:** Margaret Wooster (m. 1925; died); Frances Howard Becker (m. 1968; died 1978). **Children:** Nancy Alice Curti Holub, Felicitas (MW).

Prize: *History,* 1944: *The Growth of American Thought,* New York: Harper & Brothers, 1943.

Career: Instructor, Beloit College, WI, Simmons College, MA; Assistant Professor, Smith College, MA, 1925; Dwight Morrow Professor of History, Smith College, MA, 1936-1937; Professor of History, Columbia University, NY, 1937-1942; Professor, University of Wisconsin, Madison, 1942-1947; Visiting Professor at universities in India, Watmull Foundation, 1946-1947; Frederick Jackson Turner Professor of History, University of Wisconsin, Madison, 1947-1968; President, Organization of American Historians, 1951-1952; Fulbright Visiting Lecturer, Cambridge University, 1953; President, American Historical Association, 1954; Vice-President, American Studies Association; Vice-Chairman and Member of Board of Directors, American Council of Learned Societies, 1958-1959; Visiting Professor, University of Tokyo, 1959-1960; Member: Social Science Research Council, American Academy of Arts and Sciences, American Philosophical Society, Madison Club, University Club (Madison, WI); Senator, Phi Beta Kappa, 1947-1952.

Selected Works: *The American Peace Crusade,* 1929. *The Social Ideas of American Educators,* 1935. *Peace or War: The American Struggle, 1636-1936,* 1936. *The Learned Blacksmith: The Letters and Journals of Elihu Burritt,* 1937. *The Roots of American Loyalty,* 1946. *Prelude to Point Four: American Technical Missions Overseas, 1838-1938* (with Kendall Birr), 1954. *The University of Wisconsin: A History* (with Vernon Carstensen), 1949. *Probing Our Past,* 1955. *American Paradox: The Conflict of Thought and Action,* 1956. *The Making of an American Community: A Case Study of Democracy in a Frontier County,* 1959. *The Social Ideas of American Educators,* 1959. *American Philanthropy Abroad: A History,* 1963. *Rise of the American Nation* (with Lewis Paul Todd), 1964. *Philanthropy in the Shaping of American Higher Education,* 1965. *The 1920s in Historical Perspective,* 1966. *Human Nature in American Thought: A History,* 1980.

Other Awards: Fellow, Center for Advanced Study in the Behavioral Sciences, 1956. Award for Distinguished Scholarship in Humanities, American Council of Learned Societies, 1960. Order of the Northern Star, Swedish Government, 1965. Honorary LHDs: Northwestern University, IL; University of Pennsylvania; Western Reserve University, OH; Adelphi University, NY; University of Michigan; Beloit College, WI.

For More Information: Saxon, Wolfgang, "Merle Eugene Curti, 98, Scholar Who Won Pulitzer for History," *New York Times,* March 17, 1996; Lillibridge, G. D, "So Long, Maestro: A Portrait of Merle Curti," *American Scholar,* Spring 1997.

Commentary: *The Growth of American Thought* won the 1944 Pulitzer Prize in History for Merle Curti. This was a story of intellectual life in the United States.

Curti was born in Papillon, Nebraska and educated at Harvard University and the Sorbonne in Paris. He taught history at Columbia University and the University of Wisconsin, where he was the Frederick Jackson Turner Professor of History from 1947 to 1968. His other works include *American Paradox: The Conflict of Thought and Action* and *The Social Ideas of American Educators.* He died at the age of 98.

1945

Stephen Bonsal   560

Birth: March 29, 1865. **Death:** June 8, 1951. **Parents:** Stephen and Frances (Leigh) Bonsal. **Education:** University of Heidelberg, Germany. University of Bonn, Germany. University of Vienna, Germany. **Spouse:** Henrietta Fairfax Morgan (m. 1900). **Children:** Four sons.

Prize: *History,* 1945: *Unfinished Business,* Garden City, NY: Doubleday, Doran, 1944.

Career: Reporter and Correspondent, *New York Herald,* 1887-.

Selected Works: *The American Mediterranean,* 1912. *Heyday in a Vanished World,* 1937. *When the French Were Here,* 1945. *Suitors and Suppliants: The Little Nations at Versailles,* 1946.

For More Information: *Current Biography Yearbook,* New York: Wilson, 1945; *Saturday Review of Literature,* June 1, 1946.

Commentary: Stephen Bonsal won the 1945 Pulitzer Prize in History for *Unfinished Business.* The work provided a detailed history of the League of Nations, the Peace Conference, and the resulting Treaty of Versailles from 1919 to 1920. Bonsal was in a unique position; acting as confidential interpreter for Woodrow Wilson at the Peace Conference, he had an eyewitness perspective on the events and discussions at Versailles. Bonsal saw "history repeating itself" with World War II and felt it important to publish what he knew about the events at Versailles.

Bonsal was educated in Europe at the Universities of Heidelberg and Bonn in Germany and the University of Vienna in Austria. As a reporter for the *New York Herald,* he covered every major international conflict from the Bulgarian-Serbian War of 1888 to World War I. He was known as one of the "Three Musketeers of Journalism," along with Richard Harding Davis and Arthur Brisbane. He also briefly served in the United States Foreign Service.

He penned a sequel to the prize-winning history entitled *Suitors and Suppliants: The Little Nations at Versailles.*

1946

Arthur Meier Schlesinger Jr.

Full entry appears as **#59** under "Biography or Autobiography," 1966.

1947

James Phinney Baxter III   561

Birth: February 15, 1893; Portland, ME. **Death:** 1975. **Parents:** James Phinney Baxter and Nellie Furbish (Carpenter). **Religion:** Episcopalian. **Education:** Williams College, MA: AB, summa cum laude: AM. Harvard University, MA: AM, PhD. **Spouse:** Anne Holden Strong (m. 1919; died 1962). **Children:** James Phinney, Arthur Brown, Steven Barton.

Prize: *History,* 1947: *Scientists Against Time,* Boston: Little, Brown, 1946.

Career: Member of Staff, Industrial Finance Corporation, NY, 1914-1915; Instructor of History, Colorado College, 1921-1922; Instructor, Harvard University, MA, 1925-1927; Assistant Professor, Harvard University, 1927-1931; Associate Professor, Harvard University, 1931-1936; Master of Adams House, Harvard University, 1931-1937; Lecturer, Lowell Institute, 1931; Lecturer, Naval War College, 1932; Trustee of Williams College, 1934-1937; Professor of History, Harvard University, 1936-1937; Lecturer, Cambridge University, 1936; President, Williams College, MA, 1937-1961; Member of Executive Committee, American Historical Association,

1937-1938; Educational Adviser, U.S. Military Academy; Director, Research and Analysis, Office of the Coordinator of Information, 1941-1942; Deputy Director, Office of Strategic Services, 1942-1943; Historian, Office of Scientific Research and Development, 1943-1946; President, Association of American Colleges, 1945; President, Society of American Historians, 1945-1946; Lecturer, Army War College, 1946; Member, Gaither Commission, 1950s; Trustee, Teachers Insurance and Annuity Association, 1955-1959; Term Trustee, Massachusetts Institute of Technology, 1956-1961; President Emeritus, Williams College, MA, 1961-1975; Senior Fellow, Council on Foreign Relations, 1961-1965; Trustee: World Peace Foundation, Phillips Andover Academy, Radcliffe College, American Military Institute; Member, Board of Overseers, Harvard University; Board of Directors, State Mutual Life Insurance Company, MA; Fellow: American Academy of Arts and Sciences, American Association for the Advancement of Science; Member: American Antiquarian Society, American Council on Education, American Political Science Association, American Society of International Law, Century Club, Colonial Society of Massachusetts, Gargoyle Society, Harvard Club, Kappa Alpha, Maine Historical Society, Massachusetts Historical Society, Naval Historical Society, Phi Beta Kappa Tavern Club (MA), Williams Club (NY).

Selected Works: *The Introduction of the Ironclad Warship,* 1933.

Other Awards: Presidential Certificate of Merit. Honorary LLDs: Harvard University, MA; Amherst College, MA, 1938; University of Maine, 1939; Wesleyan University, CT, 1939; Hobart College, NY, 1942; Bowdoin College, ME, 1944; Williams College, MA, 1947. Columbia University, NY, 1954; Brown University, RI, 1956; University of Rochester, 1960. Honorary LHDs: Case Institute of Technology, 1948; American International College, 1954. Honorary DScs: Union College, 1949; Kenyon College, OH, 1949. Honorary LittD, Syracuse University, 1954.

For More Information: *Current Biography Yearbook,* New York: Wilson, 1947; *Oxford Companion to American Literature,* New York: Oxford, 1965; Kinnell, Susan, *People in History,* Santa Barbara, CA: ABC-CLIO, 1988.

Commentary: *Scientists Against Time* won the 1947 Pulitzer Prize in History for James Phinney Baxter III. It was the first of a ten-volume series, *Science in World War II, Office of Scientific Research and Development,* which documented the activities of the United States Office of Scientific Research and Development.

Baxter was born in Portland, Maine, and educated at Williams College and Harvard University. He was the director of research in what became known as the Office of Strategic Services (OSS) during the first half of World War II. He then became the historian of the Office of Scientific Research and Development from 1943 to 1946. He also wrote *The History of the Ironclad Warship.*

1948

Bernard De Voto   562

Birth: January 11, 1897; Ogden, UT. **Death:** 1955.
Parents: Florian and Rhoda (Pye) De Voto. **Education:** University of Utah. Harvard University, MA, Phi Beta Kappa. **Spouse:** Helen Avis MacVicar (m. 1923). **Children:** One son.

Prize: *History,* 1948: *Across the Wide Missouri,* Boston: Houghton Mifflin, 1947.

Career: Assistant Professor of English, Northwestern University, IL, 1922-1927; Instructor, Harvard University, MA, 1929-; Columnist, "Easy Chair," *Harper's* Magazine, 1935; Editor, *Saturday Evening Review of Literature,* 1936.

Selected Works: *The Crooked Mile,* 1924. *The Chariot of Fire: An American Novel,* 1926. *The Writer's Handbook: A Manual of English Composition* (with W. F. Bryan and Arthur H. Nethercot), 1927. *The House of Sun-Goes-Down,* 1928. *The Life and Adventures of James P. Beckwourth* (De Voto, Bernard, ed.), 1931. *Mark Twain's America,* 1932. *We Accept with Pleasure,* 1934. *Forays and Rebuttals,* 1936. *Minority Report,* 1940. *Mark Twain at Work,* 1942. *The Year of Decision, 1846,* 1943. *The Literary Fallacy,* 1944. *The Portable Mark Twain,* 1946. *Mountain Time,* 1947. *The World of Fiction,* 1950. *The Hour,* 1951. *The Course of Empire,* 1952. *The Journals of Lewis and Clark,* 1953. *The Louisiana Purchase,* 1953. *The Easy Chair,* 1955. *Spectator*

Sampler: Essays, 1955. *Women and Children First,* 1955. *Mark Twain's America, and Mark Twain at Work,* 1967. *The Letters of Bernard De Voto* (Stegner, Wallace, ed.), 1975. *The Portable Mark Twain* (De Voto, Bernard, ed.), 1977. *The Year of Decision, 1846,* 1989.

For More Information: *Saturday Revue of Literature,* June 16, 1934; *New Republic,* February 3, 1937; *Time,* August 26, 1940; Sawey, Orlan, *Bernard De Voto,* New York: Twayne, 1969; Stegner, Wallace E., *Robert Frost & Bernard De Voto,* Stanford, CA: Associates of the Stanford University Libraries, 1974; Stegner, Wallace E., *The Uneasy Chair: A Biography of Bernard De Voto,* Garden City, NY: Doubleday, 1974.

Commentary: Bernard De Voto was awarded the 1948 Pulitzer Prize in History for *Across the Wide Missouri.* It told the story of the Western fur trade up to the year 1848. A movie version with the same title was made by MGM Studios in 1951 and starred Clark Gable and Adolphe Menjou.

De Voto was born in Ogden, Utah. He was educated at Harvard University, where he also taught history. He wrote a column called the "Easy Chair" for *Harper's* in 1935 and was editor of the *Saturday Evening Review* in 1936. He sometimes wrote under the pseudonym John August. He also wrote *The Louisiana Purchase* and was the editor of *The Portable Mark Twain.*

1949

Roy Franklin Nichols   563

Birth: March 3, 1896; Newark, NJ. **Parents:** Franklin C. and Anna (Cairns) Nichols. **Religion:** Baptist. **Education:** Rutgers, The State University, NJ: AB, AM. Columbia University, NY: PhD. **Spouse:** Jeanette Paddoch.

Prize: *History,* 1949: *The Disruption of American Democracy,* New York: Macmillan, 1948.

Career: Instructor, History, Columbia University, NY, 1921-1925; Assistant Professor, University of Pennsylvania, 1925-1930; Professor of History, University of Pennsylvania, 1930-1966; President, Middle States Association of History Teachers, 1932-1933; President, Pennsylvania Federation of Historical Societies, 1940-1942; Member, Pennsylvania Historical Commission, 1940-1943; Member of Council, American Historical Association 1943-1947; Visiting Professor, Columbia University, 1944-1945; Executive Committee, American Historical Association 1945-1947; Visiting Professor, Cambridge University, 1948-1949; Chairman, Social Science Research Council, 1949-1953; Trustee, Rutgers State University, 1950-1973; Visiting Professor, Stanford University, 1952; Dean, Graduate School of

Arts and Sciences, University of Pennsylvania, 1952-1966; Vice Provost, University of Pennsylvania, 1953-1966; Board of Governors, 1956-1973; Fulbright Lecturer, India and Japan, 1962; President, Association of Graduate Schools of the American Association of Universities, 1963-1964; Vice President, American Historical Association 1964-1965; President, American Historical Association 1965-1966; Chairman, Council of Graduate Schools in the U.S., 1965; Professor Emeritus, University of Pennsylvania, 1966-1973; Senator, United Chapters, Historical Society of Pennsylvania; Member: American Philosophical Society, Authors Club (London, England), Century Club (NY), Cosmos Club (Washington, DC), Phi Alpha Theta, Phi Beta Kappa, Philadelphia Historical Commission, Pi Gamma Mu, Rittenhouse Club (Philadelphia, PA).

Selected Works: *The Democratic Machine, 1850-1854,* 1923. *A Syllabus for the General Course in American History* (with John A. Krout), 1923. *Syllabus for the History of Civilization* (with Witt Bowden), 1927. *The Growth of American Democracy: Social, Economic, Political* (with Jeanette P. Nichols), 1939. *Advance Agents of American Destiny,* 1956. *The Stakes of Power, 1845-1877,* 1961. *Blueprints for Leviathan: American Style,* 1963. *The Invention of the American Political Parties,* 1967. *The Pennsylvania Historical and Museum Commission: A History,* 1967. *A Historian's Progress,* 1968. *The Stakes of Power, 1845-1877* (with Eugene H. Berwanger), 1982.

Other Awards: Silver Medal of Philadelphia Club of Advertising Women. Haney Medal for Literary Excellence, 1961. Athenaeum Award, 1962. Honorary LittDs: Franklin and Marshall College, PA, 1937; Muhlenberg University, 1956; University of Chattanooga, 1966. Honorary MA, Cambridge University, England, 1940. Honorary LHD, Rutgers, NJ, 1941. Honorary LLDs: Moravian College, PA, 1953. Lincoln University, 1959; Knox College, 1960. Honorary SScD, Lebanon Valley College, PA, 1961. Honorary DPed, Susquehanna University, PA, 1964.

For More Information: *Current Biography Yearbook,* New York: Gale, 1949; *Fifty Western Writers,* Westport, CT: Greenwood, 1982.

Commentary: Roy Franklin Nichols won the 1949 Pulitzer Prize in History for *The Disruption of American Democracy.* This book relates the history of the Democratic Party from 1857 to 1861.

Nichols was born in Newark, New Jersey, and educated at Rutgers and Columbia Universities. He was professor of history at the University of Pennsylvania from 1930 to 1966. His other works include *Advance Agents of American Destiny* and *The Invention of American Political Parties.*

1950

Oliver W. Larkin   564

Birth: August 17, 1896; Medford, MA. **Death:** 1973. **Parents:** Charles Ernest and Kate Mary (Waterman) Larkin. **Education:** Harvard University, MA: AB, AM. **Spouse:** Ruth Lilye McIntire (m. 1925). **Children:** Peter Sidney.

Prize: *History,* 1950: *Art and Life in America,* New York: Rinehart, 1949.

Career: Soldier, 73rd Regiment, U.S. Army, 1918-1919; Assistant, Harvard University, Cambridge, MA, 1921-1924; Faculty member, Smith College, Northampton, MA, 1924-1964; Jessie Wells Post Professor of Art, Smith College, MA; Retired, 1964; Member: College Art Association of America, American Association of University Professors, Phi Beta Kappa; President, Northampton Historical Society.

Selected Works: *Samuel F.B. Morse and American Democratic Art,* 1954. *Daumier in His Time and Ours,* 1962. *Daumier, Man of His Time,* 1966.

For More Information: *New York Times,* May 2, 1950; *New York Herald Tribune,* May 2, 1950.

Commentary: *Art and Life in America* won the 1950 Pulitzer Prize in History for Oliver Waterman Larkin. This work was a comprehensive history of art and artists in the United States.

Larkin was born in Medford, Massachusetts. He was educated at Harvard University. After serving in World War I, he was professor of art at Smith College from 1924 to 1964. He also wrote *Samuel F.B. Morse and American Democratic Art* and *In His Time and Ours.*

1951

R. Carlyle Buley   565

Birth: July 8, 1893; Floyd County, IN. **Parents:** David Marion and Nora (Keithly) Buley. **Education:** Indiana University: AB, AM. University of Wisconsin: PhD. **Spouse:** Ester Giles (m. 1919; died 1921); Evelyn Bennet (m. 1926).

Prize: *History,* 1951: *The Old Northwest: Pioneer Period, 1815-1840,* Indianapolis, IN: Indiana Historical Society, 1950.

Career: High school teacher, Delphi and Muncie, IN, 1914-1918; Sergeant, U.S. Army, 1918-1919; Head, History Department and Assistant Principal, high school, Springfield, IL, 1919-1923; Assistant Instructor, University of Wisconsin, 1923-1925; Instructor and Professor of History, Indiana University, Bloomington, 1925-1964; Professor Emeritus, Indiana University, 1964-1968; Member: American Historical Association, Indiana Historical Society, Ohio

Historical Society, Organization of American Historians.

Selected Works: *The American Life Convention, 1906-1952: A Study in the History of Life Insurance,* 1953. *The Equitable Life Assurance Society of the United States: One Hundredth Anniversary History, 1859/1959,* 1959. *The Equitable Life Assurance Society of the United States, 1859-1964,* 1967.

Other Awards: Elizur Wright Award, 1954: *The American Life Convention, 1906-1952.* Honorary LittD, Muhlenberg University, 1956. Honorary DLitt, Coe College, IA, 1958.

For More Information: *Current Biography Yearbook,* New York: 1951; Obituary, *New York Times,* May 8, 1951.

Commentary: R. Carlyle Buley won the 1951 Pulitzer Prize in History for *The Old Northwest, Pioneer Period 1815-1840.*

Buley was born in Floyd County, Indiana. He was educated at Indiana University and the University of Wisconsin. After serving in World War I, he taught high school history. He also taught history at Indiana University in Bloomington from 1924 to 1963 and was appointed Professor Emeritus there in 1964. He also wrote a history of insurance in *The American Life Convention, 1906-1952: A Study of the History of Life Insurance.*

1952

Oscar Handlin   566

Birth: September, 29, 1915; New York, NY. **Parents:** Joseph and Ida (Yanowitz) Handlin. **Religion:** Jewish. **Education:** Brooklyn College, NY: BA. Harvard University, MA: PhD. **Spouse:** Mary Flug (m. 1937; div. 1976); Lilian Bonbach (m. 1977). **Children:** Joanna, David, Ruth (MF).

Prize: *History,* 1952: *The Uprooted: The Epic Story of the Great Migrations That Made the American People,* New York: Grosset & Dunlap, 1957.

Career: Instructor, History, Brooklyn College, NY, 1936-1938; Instructor, Harvard University, 1939-1944; Assistant Professor of History, Harvard University, 1944-1947; Assistant Professor of Social Science, Harvard University, 1947-1948; Associate Professor, Harvard University, 1948-1954; Professor of History, Harvard University, 1954-1962; Director, Center for Study of Liberty in America, Harvard University, 1958-1966; Winthrop Professor of History, Harvard University, 1962-1965; Vice Chairman, U.S. Board of Foreign Scholarships, 1962-1965; Director, Charles Warren Center for Studies in American History, Harvard University, MA, 1965-1972; Chairman, U.S. Board of Foreign Scholarships, 1965-1968; Fellow, Brandeis University, 1965-; Charles H. Pforzheimer University Professor, Harvard University, MA, 1970-; Harmsworth Professor, Oxford University, England, 1972-1973; Vice President, American Jewish Historical Society, 1973-; Trustee, New York Public Library, 1973-1980; Director, Harvard University Library, 1979-1985; Associate, National Academy of Education; Member: American Historical Association, American Academy of Arts and Sciences, American Antiquarian Society, Colonial Society of Massachusetts, Massachusetts Historical Society, National Education Association, St. Botolph's Club.

Selected Works: *This Was America: True Accounts of People and Places, Manners and Customs, as Recorded by European Travelers to the Western Shore in the Eighteenth, Nineteenth and Twentieth Centuries,* 1949. *John Dewey's Challenge to Education: Historical Perspectives on the Cultural Context,* 1950. *The American People in the Twentieth Century,* 1954. *Chance or Destiny: Turning Points in American History,* 1955. *Harvard Guide to American History,* 1955. *Race and Nationality in American Life,* 1957. *Readings in American History,* 1957. *Al Smith and His America,* 1958. *Boston's Immigrants 1790-1880: A Study in Acculturation,* 1959. *Immigration as a Factor in American History,* 1959. *The Newcomers: Negroes and Puerto Ricans in a Changing Metropolis,* 1959. *The Dimensions of Liberty* (with Mary Handlin), 1961. *The Americans: A New History of the People of the United States,* 1963. *The Historian and the City* (Handlin, Oscar and Burchard, John, eds.), 1963. *Fire-Bell in the Night: The Crisis in Civil Rights,* 1964. *Jews in the Culture of Middle Europe,* 1964. *Children of the Uprooted,* 1966. *The Popular Sources of Political Authority: Documents on the Massachusetts Constitution of 1780* (Handlin, Oscar and Handlin, Mary F., eds.), 1966. *America: A History,* 1968. *Commonwealth: A Study of the Role of Government in the American Economy; Massachusetts, 1774-1861* (with Mary F. Handlin), 1969. *The American College and American Culture* (with Mary F. Handlin), 1970. *Facing Life: Youth and the Family in American History* (with Mary F. Handlin), 1971. *Statue of Liberty,* 1971. *A Pictorial History of Immigration,* 1972. *One World: The Origins of an American Concept,* 1974. *The Wealth of the American People: A History of American Affluence* (with Mary F. Handlin), 1975. *Abraham Lincoln and the Union,* 1980. *The Distortion of America,* 1981. *A Restless People: Americans in Rebellion, 1770-1787* (with Lilian Handlin), 1982. *The Road to Gettysburg,* 1987. *Boston's Immigrants, 1790-1880: A Study in Acculturation,* 1991. *Liberty in America, 1600 to the Present* (with Lilian Handlin), 1986-1994. *From the Outer World* (Handlin, Oscar and Handlin, Lilian, eds.), 1997.

Other Awards: Union League Club Award for History, 1934. J. H. Dunning Prize, American Histori-

cal Association, 1941: *Boston's Immigrants, 1790-1865: A Study in Acculturation.* Award of Honor, Brooklyn College, 1945. Guggenheim Fellowship, 1954-1955. Christopher Award, 1958: *Al Smith and His America.* Robert H. Lord Award, 1972. Fulbright Distinguished American Fellow, 1986. Honorary LLD, Colby College, 1962. Honorary LittDs: Hebrew Union College, OH, 1967; Northern Michigan University, 1969; Lowell University, MA, 1980. Honorary HHD, Oakland University, MI, 1968. Honorary DHLs: Seton Hall University, NJ, 1972; Boston College, MA, 1975. Honorary DLetters, Brooklyn College of the City University of New York, 1972. Honorary LHD, University of Cincinnati, OH, 1981.

For More Information: Jaher, Frederic C., *Oscar Handlin's The Uprooted: A Critical Commentary,* New York: American R.D.M., 1966; Bushman, Richard L., *Uprooted Americans: Essays to Honor Oscar Handlin,* Boston: Little, Brown, 1979.

Commentary: Oscar Handlin was awarded the 1952 Pulitzer Prize in History for *The Uprooted.* It is the epic story of the great migrations that made the American people. Handlin has said, "Once I thought to write a history of the immigrants in America. Then I discovered that the immigrants were American history."

Handlin was born in New York City and educated at Brooklyn College and Harvard University. He was professor of history at Harvard and he has taught and lectured at other institutions as well. He has written many books and continues to write. His most recent publication is *From the Outer World.*

1953

George Dangerfield 567

Birth: October 28, 1904; Newbury, Berkshire, England. **Death:** 1986. **Parents:** George and Ethel (Tyrer) Dangerfield. **Religion:** Church of England. **Education:** Oxford University, England: BA, MA. **Spouse:** Helen Mary Spedding (m. 1928); Mary Louise Schott (m. 1941). **Children:** Mary Jo, Hilary, Anthony (MLS).

Prize: *History*, 1953: *The Era of Good Feelings*, New York: Harcourt, Brace, 1952.

Career: Assistant Editor, Brewer, Warren & Putnam Publishers, NY, 1930-1932; Literary Editor, *Vanity Fair*, NY, 1933-1935; Served in Infantry, U.S. Army, 1942-1945; Lecturer, Anglo-American History, University of California, Santa Barbara, 1968-; Member: American Civil Liberties Union, Americans for Democratic Action, American Historical Association, Friends of Santa Barbara Public Library, National Association for the Advancement of Colored People.

Selected Works: *Bengal Mutiny: The Story of the Sepoy Rebellion*, 1933. *The Strange Death of Liberal England*, 1935. *Victoria's Heir: The Education of a Prince*, 1941. *Chancellor Robert R. Livingston of New York, 1746-1813*, 1960. *The Awakening of American Nationalism, 1815-1828*, 1965. *The Damnable Question: A Study in Anglo-Irish Relations*, 1976.

Other Awards: Bancroft Prize, Columbia University, 1953: *The Era of Good Feelings*. Benjamin D. Shreve Fellow, Princeton University, 1957-1958. California Literature Silver Medal Award, 1961: *Chancellor Robert R. Livingston of New York*. Guggenheim Fellow, 1970-1971. Marquis Biographical Award, 1961: *Chancellor Robert R. Livingston of New York*.

Commentary: George Dangerfield won the 1953 Pulitzer Prize in History for *The Era of Good Feelings*. The story concerns the years 1814 to 1829 on the Caribbean island of Barbados where the government has just saluted an American ship, a recognition of the American nation, as it arrives in the harbor.

Dangerfield was born in Newbury, Berkshire, England and educated at Oxford University. He wrote several other histories, including *The Strange Death of Liberal England* and *The Damnable Question: A Study in Anglo-Irish Relations*.

1954

Bruce Catton   568

Birth: October 9, 1899; Petoskey, MI. **Death:** August 28, 1978. **Parents:** George Robert and Adella Maude (Patten) Catton. **Religion:** Presbyterian. **Education:** Oberlin College, OH. **Spouse:** Hazel Cherry (m. 1925; died 1969). **Children:** William Bruce.

Prize: *History*, 1954: *A Stillness at Appomattox*, Garden City, NY: Doubleday, 1953.

Career: Writer; Served in Navy, WWI; Reporter, *Cleveland News*, OH, and *Boston American*, MA, 1920-1924; Reporter, *Cleveland Plain Dealer*, OH, 1925; Writer and Columnist, Scripps Howard Newspapers, 1926-1939; Associate Director of Information, U.S. War Production Board, 1942; Director of Information, U.S. War Production Board, 1942-1945; Director of Information, U.S. Department of Commerce, 1945-1947; Special Assistant, U.S. Secretary of Commerce, 1948; Associate Director of Information, U.S. Department of Interior, 1950-1952; Member: American Academy of Arts and Letters, Players Club, Century Club, and Lotos Club (all New York).

Selected Works: *Mr. Lincoln's Army*, 1951. *Glory Road: The Bloody Route from Fredericksburg to Gettysburg*, 1952. *U. S. Grant and the American Military Tradition*, 1954. *Banners at Shenandoah: A Story of Sheridan's Fighting Cavalry*, 1955. *This Hallowed Ground: The Story of the Union Side of the Civil War*, 1956. *America Goes to War*, 1958. *The American Heritage Picture History of the Civil War*, 1960. *The Centennial History of the Civil War*, 1961-1965. *Two Roads to Sumter* (with William Catton), 1963. *Grant Takes Command*, 1969. *Waiting for the Morning Train: An American Boyhood*, 1972. *Gettysburg: The Final Fury*, 1974. *Michigan: A Bicentennial History*, 1976. *The Bold and Magnificent Dream: America's Founding Years, 1492-1815* (with William Catton), 1978. *Reflections on the Civil War*, 1981. *The American Heritage New History of the Civil War*, 1996.

Other Awards: Ohioana Book Award, Ohioana Library Association, 1952: *Mr. Lincoln's Army*, Garden City, NY: Doubleday, 1951. Ohioana Book Award, 1962: *The Coming Fury*, Garden City, NY: Doubleday, 1961. National Book Award, 1954: *A Stillness at Appomattox*, Garden City, NY: Doubleday, 1953. Fletcher Pratt Award, The Civil War Round Table of New York, 1957: *This Hallowed Ground*, Garden City, NY: 1956. Fletcher Pratt Award, 1970: *Grant Takes Command*, Boston: Little Brown, 1969. Meritorious Service in the Field of Civil War History Award, 1959. Christopher Book Award, The Christophers, 1961: *The Coming Fury*. Bruce Catton Day, Petoskey, MI, 1965. Bruce Catton Day, Benzie County, MI, 1972. Presidential Medal of Freedom, 1976. Honorary LittDs: University of Maryland, 1955; Wesleyan University, CT, 1955; Dickinson College, PA, 1955; Oberlin College, OH, 1956; Lincoln College, IL, 1956; Harvard University, MA, 1957; Syracuse University, NY, 1957; Illinois College, 1958; Western Michigan College, 1958. Honorary DLC, Union College, 1956. Honorary LLD, Knox College, IL, 1958.

For More Information: *Current Biography Yearbook*, New York: Wilson, 1954; *New York Times*,

May 5, 1954; *Dictionary of Literary Biography,* Detroit: Gale, 1983.

Commentary: *A Stillness at Appomattox* won the 1954 Pulitzer Prize in History for Bruce Catton. It is the story of the Appomattox Campaign of 1865 and the Civil War.

Catton was born in Petoskey, Michigan, and educated at Oberlin College in Ohio. After serving in World War I, he worked as a reporter and correspondent for several news organizations. He also worked for the United States Department of Commerce during World War II. He has written, probably more than anyone, on the many battles and figures of the Civil War era. He has worked with network television on several Civil War dramatizations and was co-host with President Eisenhower in 1963 of a television special on the Battle of Gettysburg.

1955

Paul Horgan   569

Birth: August 1, 1903; Buffalo, NY. **Death:** March 8, 1995. **Parents:** Edward Daniel and Rose Marie (Rohr) Horgan. **Religion:** Roman Catholic. **Education:** New Mexico Military Institute, NM.

Prize: *History,* 1955: *Great River: The Rio Grande in North American History,* New York: Rinehart, 1954. *History,* 1976: *Lamy of Santa Fe, His Life and Times,* New York: Farrar, Straus and Giroux, 1975.

Career: Novelist, biographer; Member, Production Staff, Eastman Theatre, Rochester, NY, 1923-1926; Librarian, New Mexico Military Institute, Roswell, 1926-1942; Chief and Lieutenant Colonel, Army Information Branch, U.S. Army, 1942-1946; Visiting Lecturer, University of Iowa, 1946; Assistant

to President, New Mexico Military Institute, Roswell, 1947-1949; President, Board of Directors, Roswell Museum, 1948-1955; Board of Directors, Roswell Public Library, 1958-1962; Chairman, Board of Directors, Santa Fe Opera, NM, 1958-1971; Board of Managers, School of American Research, 1959-1995; Fellow, Center for Advanced Studies, Wesleyan University, CT, 1959, 1961; Member of Advisory Board, John Simon Guggenheim Foundation, 1961-1967; Director, Center for Advanced Studies, Wesleyan University, 1962-1967; Lay Trustee, St. Joseph's College, West Hartford, CT, 1964-1968; Hoyt Fellow, Saybrook College of Yale University, 1965; Associate Fellow, Saybrook College of Yale University, 1966-1995; Adjunct Professor of English, Wesleyan University, 1967-1971; Scholar-in-Residence, Aspen Institute for Humanistic Studies, 1968, 1971, 1973; Visiting Lecturer, Yale University, 1969; Board of Judges, Book-of-the-Month Club, 1969-1972; Professor Emeritus and Author-in-Residence, Wesleyan University, 1971-1995; Board of Directors, Witter Bynner Foundation, 1972-1979; Associate, Book-of-the-Month Club, 1972-73; Fellow, Aspen Institute for Humanistic Studies, 1973-1995; Fellow, Pierpont Morgan Library, 1974-1995; Council of Fellows, Pierpont Morgan Library, 1975-1979, 1982; Council of Fellows, Yale University Library, 1976-1979; Founding Trustee, Lincoln County Heritage Trust, NM, 1976-1995; Life Fellow, Pierpont Morgan Library, 1977-1995; Fellow, School of American Research, 1978; Trustee, Associates Member, National Advisory Board, Center for the Book, Library of Congress, 1978-1995; Fellow, Society of American Historians; American Academy of Arts and Sciences; National Institute of Arts and Letters; Fellow, Connecticut Academy of Arts and Sciences; Member: Athenaeum Club (London, England), Century Club (NY), Phi Beta Kappa, Yale Club (NY).

Selected Works: *The Fault of Angels,* 1933. *No Quarter Given,* 1935. *The Return of the Weed,* 1936. *Main Line West,* 1936. *A Lamp on the Plains,* 1937. *Far from Cibola,* 1938. *Figures in a Landscape,* 1940. *The Devil in the Desert,* 1950. *One Red Rose for Christmas,* 1952. *Humble Powers,* 1954. *Great River: The Rio Grande in North American History,* 1954. *The Saintmaker's Christmas Eve,* 1955. *Give Me Possession,* 1957. *Rome Eternal,* 1959. *A Distant Trumpet,* 1960. *Citizen of New Salem,* 1961. *Conquistadors in North American History,* 1963. *Things as They Are,* 1964. *Songs after Lincoln,* 1965. *Memories of the Future,* 1966. *Everything to Live For,* 1968. *The Heroic Triad: Essays in the Social Energies of Three Southwestern Cultures,* 1970. *Whitewater,* 1970. *Encounters with Stravinsky: A Personal Record,* 1972. *Approaches to Writing,* 1973. *The Thin Mountain Air,* 1977. *Josiah Gregg and His Vision of the Early West,* 1979. *Of America, East and West,* 1984. *The Cleri-*

hews of Paul Horgan, 1985. *A Certain Climate: Essays on History, Arts, and Letters,* 1988. *A Writer's Eye: Field Notes and Watercolors,* 1988. *Tracings: A Book of Partial Portraits,* 1993. *Henriette Wyeth: The Artifice of Blue Light,* 1994.

Other Awards: Harper Prize Novel Award, 1933: *The Fault of Angels,* New York: Harper, 1933. Legion of Merit, United States Army. Guggenheim Fellow, 1945, 1959. Carr P. Collins Award, Texas Institute of Letters, 1955: *Great River,* New York: Rinehart, 1954. Carr P. Collins Award, Texas Institute of Letters, 1976: *Lamy of Santa Fe.* Bancroft Prize, Columbia University, 1955: *Great River.* Campion Award, Eminent Service to Catholic Letters, Catholic Book Club, 1957: *The Centuries of Santa Fe.* Knight of St. Gregory, 1957. National Catholic Book Award for Fiction, Catholic Press Association, 1965: *Things as They Are,* New York: Farrar Straus, 1969. National Catholic Book Award for Fiction, Catholic Press Association, 1969: *Everything to Live For.* Jesse H. Jones Award, Texas Institute of Letters, 1971: *Whitewater.* Western Writers of America Award and Christopher Book Award, 1976: *Lamy of Santa Fe.* Laetare Medal, University of Notre Dame, 1976. Copley Medal, National Portrait Gallery, 1981. Baldwin Medal, Wesleyan University, 1982. James L. McConaughy Memorial Award, 1986. Robert Kirsch Award, *Los Angeles Times,* 1987. Paul Horgan Library, New Mexico Military Institute. Paul Horgan Art Center of Roswell Museum. Paul Horgan Gallery, Roswell Museum. Honorary LittDs: Wesleyan University, CT, 1956; Southern Methodist University, TX, 1957; University of Notre Dame, IN, 1958; Boston College, MA, 1958; New Mexico State University, 1961; College of the Holy Cross, MA, 1962; University of New Mexico, 1963; Fairfield University, CT, 1964; St. Mary's College, 1976; Yale University, CT, 1977. Honorary DHLs: Canisius College, NY, 1960; Georgetown University, Washington, DC, 1963; Lincoln College, IL, 1968; Loyola College, Baltimore, 1968; D'Youville College, NY, 1968; Pace University, NY, 1968; St. Bonaventure University, NY, 1970; La Salle University, PA, 1971; Catholic University of America, Washington, DC, 1973; University of Hartford, CT, 1987.

For More Information: Day, James M., *Paul Horgan,* Austin, TX: Steck-Vaughn, 1967; *Current Biography Yearbook,* New York: Wilson, 1971; Gish, Robert, *Nueva Granada: Paul Horgan and the Southwest,* College Station: Texas A&M University, 1995.

Commentary: Paul Horgan won two Pulitzer Prizes, both in History. The first award was in 1955 for *Great River: The Rio Grande in North American History,* a two-volume work. The first volume is about the American Indians and Spain, and the second is about Mexico and the United States. Horgan's second award was in 1976 for *Lamy of Santa Fe,* which tells

the life story of Archbishop Juan Bautista Lamy, the pioneer priest. (Lamy was also the subject of Willa Cather's *Death Comes to the Archbishop.*)

Horgan was born in Buffalo, New York. Through his writing he is most closely associated with New Mexico. He was a novelist and a historian, writing popular narratives that conveyed a vivid portrait of the people and landscape of the Southwest. He was also much admired by other writers and historians for his craftsmanship and understanding.

1956

Richard Hofstadter

Full entry appears as **#496** under "General Non-Fiction," 1964.

1957

George F. Kennan

Full entry appears as **#61** under "Biography or Autobiography," 1968.

1958

Bray Hammond   570
Birth: 1886. **Death:** 1968.

Prize: *History,* 1958: *Banks and Politics in America, from the Revolution to the Civil War,* Princeton, NJ: Princeton University, 1957.

Selected Works: *Sovereignty and an Empty Purse: Banks and Politics in the Civil War,* 1970.

For More Information: *Oxford Companion to American Literature,* New York: Oxford, 1965; Golembe, Carter H., "Memorandum Re: Of Myths and History — And Current Fears of Bank Size," *Golembe Reports,* August 15, 1985; "Notable & Quotable," *Wall Street Journal,* May 15, 1992.

Commentary: Bray Hammond was awarded the 1958 Pulitzer Prize in History for *Banks and Politics in America.* This was a history of banks and the banking industry in the United States.

1959

Jean Schneider   571

Prize: *History,* 1959: *The Republican Era: 1869-1901: A Study in Administrative History,* New York: Macmillan, 1958.

Selected Works: *The Practice of Public Administration* (with Ernst von Harnack).

Commentary: *The Republican Era: 1869-1901: A Study in Administrative History* won the 1959 Pulitzer Prize in history for Leonard Dupee White and Jean Schneider, his assistant.

Leonard Dupee White   572

Birth: 1891; Acton, MA. **Death:** 1958. **Education:** Dartmouth College, NH. University of Chicago, IL: PhD.

Prize: *History,* 1959: *The Republican Era, 1869-1901: A Study in Administrative History,* New York: Macmillan, 1958.

Career: Political Scientist; Professor, University of Chicago, 1920-56; Member, Committee on Social Trends, 1929; Commissioner, U.S. Civil Service Commission, 1934-37; Member, Committee on Civil Service Improvement, 1939-41; Chairman, Department of Political Science, University of Chicago, 1940-48; President, American Political Science Association, 1944.

Selected Works: *Introduction to the Study of Public Administration,* 1926. *The City Manager,* 1927. *Chicago: An Experiment in Social Science Research* (with T. V. Smith), 1929. *The Prestige Value of Public Employment in Chicago: An Experimental Study,* 1929. *The Civil Service in the Modern State,* 1930. *The New Social Science,* 1930. *Further Contributions to the Prestige of Public Employment,* 1932. *Trends in Public Administration,* 1933. *Whitley Councils in the British Civil Service: A Study in Conciliation and Arbitration,* 1933. *Government Career Service,* 1935. *The Frontiers of Public Administration* (with John M. Gaus and Marshall E. Dimock), 1936. *Politics and Public Service: A Discussion of the Civic Art in America* (with T. V. Smith), 1939. *The Future of Government in the United States: Essays in Honor of Charles E. Marriam* (White, Leonard Dupee, ed.), 1942. *Civil Service in Wartime,* 1945. *The Jeffersonians: A Study in Administrative History, 1801-1829,* 1951. *The Federalists: A Study in Administrative History,* 1948. *Introduction to the Study of Public Administration,* 1948. *The States and the Nation,* 1953. *The Jacksonians: A Study in Administrative History, 1829-1861,* 1954. *The State of the Social Sciences: Papers Presented at the 25th Anniversary of the Social Science Research Building, the University of Chicago, November 10-12, 1955,* 1956.

For More Information: *Biographical Dictionary of American Educators,* Westport, CT: Greenwood, 1978.

Commentary: *The Republican Era, 1869-1901: A Study in Adminstrative History* won the 1959 Pulitzer Prize in History for Leonard Dupee White and Jean Schneider, his assistant. White was born in Acton, Massachusetts. He was educated at Dartmouth College and the University of Chicago, where he taught from 1924 to 1956. He was a commissioner of

the United States Civil Service Commission from 1934 to 1937. He served on President Franklin D. Roosevelt's Committee on Civil Service Improvement. He is credited with launching the study of public administration in higher education. He wrote the standard introductory text and developed civil service examinations and training materials for university graduates. His works include a four-volume history of public administration.

1960

Margaret Leech

Full entry appears as **#557** under "History," 1942.

1961

Herbert Feis   573

Birth: June 7, 1893; New York, NY. **Death:** 1972. **Parents:** Louis J. and Louise (Waterman) Feis. **Education:** Harvard University, MA: AB, PhD. **Spouse:** Ruth Stanley-Brown (m. 1922). **Children:** Maria Felicia Feis.

Prize: *History,* 1961: *Between War and Peace; The Potsdam Conference,* Princeton, NJ: Princeton University, 1960.

Career: Lieutenant, U.S. Naval Reserve, WWI; Associate Professor of Economics, University of Kansas, Lawrence, 1922-1925; Adviser, American Industrial Relations, International Labor Office, League of Nations, 1922-1927; Head, Department of Economics, University of Cincinnati, Cincinnati, Ohio, 1926-1929; Staff, Council on Foreign Relations, New York, 1930-1931; Economic Adviser, U.S. Department of State, Washington DC, 1931-1937; Adviser to U.S.

Delegation, World Economic and Monetary Conference, London, 1933; Adviser to U.S. Delegation, Inter-American Conference for the Maintenance of Peace, Buenos Aires, 1936; Adviser on International Economic Affairs, Department of State, 1937-1943; Adviser to U.S. Delegation, Conferences of American States in Lima, 1938, and Panama, 1939; Special Consultant to Secretary of War, 1944-1946; Member, Institute for Advanced Study, Princeton, NJ, 1948-1950, 1951-1963; Member, Policy Planning Staff, Department of State, 1950-1951; Visiting Professor at Harvard University, 1957, 1965-1966; Visiting Professor at Columbia University, 1961; Consultant to National Broadcasting Company, 1964.

Selected Works: *Seen from E. A.: Three International Episodes,* 1946. *The Spanish Story: Franco and the Nations at War,* 1948. *The Diplomacy of the Dollar: First Era, 1919-1932,* 1950. *The Road to Pearl Harbor: The Coming of the War between the United States and Japan,* 1950. *The China Tangle: The American Effort in China from Pearl Harbor to the Marshall Mission,* 1953. *Churchill, Roosevelt, Stalin: The War They Waged and the Peace They Sought,* 1957. *Between War and Peace: The Potsdam Conference,* 1960. *Japan Subdued: The Atomic Bomb and the End of the War in the Pacific,* 1961. *Foreign Aid and Foreign Policy,* 1964. *1933: Characters in Crisis,* 1966.

Other Awards: Guggenheim Fellow, 1926. American Library Association Liberty and Justice Award, 1958: *Churchill-Roosevelt-Stalin,* Princeton, NJ: Princeton University, 1957. Honorary DLitt, Princeton University, NJ, 1960.

Commentary: Herbert Feis won the 1961 Pulitzer Prize in History for *Between War and Peace: The Potsdam Conference.* This was Feis's continuation of the narrative he began in *Churchill-Roosevelt-Stalin,* published in 1957.

Feis was born in New York City and educated at Harvard University. He taught economics at several universities and was an economic advisor to the presidents of the International Telephone and Telegraph Corporation and the Anaconda Copper Company at intervals during the 1920s. He also advised the United States Department of State during the 1930s. He wrote histories from the 1940s through the 1960s. His other works include *The Diplomacy of the Dollar: First Era, 1919-1932* and *Foreign Aid and Foreign Policy.*

1962

Lawrence Henry Gipson   574

Birth: December 7, 1880; Greeley, Colorado. **Death:** September 26, 1971.

Prize: *History,* 1962: *The Triumphant Empire: Thunder-Clouds Gather in the West, 1763-1766,* New York: Knopf, 1961.

Selected Works: *The British Empire before the American Revolution,* 1936-1970. *The Moravian Indian Mission on White River: Diaries and Letters, May 5, 1799, to November 12, 1806* (Gipson, Lawrence Henry, ed.), 1938. *Lewis Evans,* 1939.

For More Information: *Oxford Companion to American Literature,* New York: 1965; *Current Biography Yearbook,* New York: Wilson, 1971.

Commentary: Lawrence Gipson was awarded the 1962 Pulitzer Prize in History for *The Triumphant Empire: Thunder-Clouds Gather in the West, 1763-1766.*

Gipson was born in Greeley, Colorado. He taught history at the College of Idaho, Wabash College, and Lehigh University. He was from the "Imperial School" of historians of the colonial era, believing London to be at the center of colonial history. He is known for the 15-volume *The British Empire Before the American Revolution,* which he wrote over the period 1936 to 1970.

1963

Constance McLaughlin Green   575

Birth: August 21, 1897; Ann Arbor, MI. **Death:** 1975. **Parents:** Andrew Cunningham and Lois Thompson (Angill) McLaughlin. **Religion:** Congregationalist. **Education:** University of Chicago, IL. Smith College, MA: AB. Mount Holyoke College, MA. Yale University, CT: PhD. **Spouse:** Donald Ross Green (m. 1921; died 1946). **Children:** Lois Angill, Donald Ross, Elizabeth L.

Prize: *History,* 1963: *Washington,* Princeton, NJ: Princeton University, 1962-63.

Career: Instructor of English, University of Chicago, 1919-1920; Instructor of History, Mount Holyoke College, MA, 1925-1932; Instructor of History, Smith College, Northampton, MA, 1938-1939; Director of Research, Council of Industrial Studies, 1939-1946; Historian, U.S. Army Ordnance Department, Springfield, MA, 1942-1945; Historian, American National Red Cross, Washington, DC, 1947-1948; Chief Historian, U.S. Army Ordnance Corps, Washington, DC, 1948-1951; Historian, Office of Secretary of Defense, Research and Development Board, 1951-1954; Commonwealth Fund Lecturer in American History, University College, University of London, England, 1951; Director, Washington History Project administered by American University, Washington, DC, 1954-1960; Corresponding Secretary, Washington Literary Society, 1961-1963; Visiting Professor of History, Dartmouth College, 1971; Member: Americans for Democratic Action, American Historical Association, Capitol Hill Restoration Society, Committee on the History of Social Welfare, Economic History Association, Landmarks Committee, National Capital Planning Commission, Organization of American Historians, U.S. Capitol Historical Society.

Selected Works: *Holyoke, Massachusetts: A Case History of the Industrial Revolution in America,* 1939. *History of Naugatuck, Connecticut,* 1948. *The Ordnance Department: Planning Munitions for War,* 1955. *Eli Whitney and the Birth of American Technology,* 1956. *American Cities in the Growth of the Nation,* 1957. *The Rise of Urban America,* 1965. *The Secret City: A History of Race Relations in the Nation's Capital,* 1967. *The Church on Lafayette Square: A History of St. John's Church, Washington, D.C., 1815-1970,* 1970. *Washington: A History of the Capital, 1800-1950,* 1976.

Other Awards: Eggleston Prize in History, Yale University, CT: *Holyoke, Massachusetts: A Case History of the Industrial Revolution in America,* New Haven, CT: Yale University, 1939. Honorary LittDs: Smith College, MA, 1963; Pace College, NY.

For More Information: *Current Biography Yearbook,* New York: Wilson, 1963; *Oxford Companion to American Literature,* New York: 1965.

Commentary: *Washington, Village and Capital, 1800-1878* won the 1963 Pulitzer Prize in History for Constance McLaughlin Green. Green's two-volume history covered the development of the city of Washington, DC, as a village and capital from 1800 to 1878 and as a capital city, from 1879 to 1950.

Green was born in Ann Arbor, Michigan, and educated at the University of Chicago and at Smith and Mount Holyoke colleges. She taught history at the latter two institutions. She was director of the Washington History Project, which was administered by American University from 1954 to 1960. She focused her interests on the urbanization of the United States. Her other works include *American Cities in the Growth of the Nation* and *The Rise of Urban America.*

1964

Sumner Chilton Powell   576

Birth: October 2, 1924; Northampton, MA. **Parents:** Chilton Latham Powell and Theodora (Sumner). **Religion:** Episcopalian. **Education:** Amherst College, MA: BA. Harvard University, MA: PhD.

Prize: *History,* 1964: *Puritan Village: The Formation of a New England Town,* Middletown, CT: Wesleyan University, 1963.

Career: Served in Communications, U.S. Naval Reserve, 1943-1946; Vice-President, Ewen Knight Corporation, MA, 1953-1954; Teacher, Choate School, Wallingford, CT, 1954-1960; President,

Powell Associates, New Haven, CT, 1960-1962; History Faculty, Iona College, New Rochelle, NY, 1962-; Teacher, Barnard School for Boys, NY, 1962-1963; Member: American Historical Association, Phi Beta Kappa.

Selected Works: *From Mythical to Medieval Man,* 1957.

For More Information: *Oxford Companion to American Literature,* New York: Oxford, 1965.

Commentary: Sumner Chilton Powell won the 1964 Pulitzer Prize in History for *Puritan Village: The Formation of a New England Town.* This was a study of municipal government passed on from Great Britain to the colonies, specifically Sudbury, Massachusetts, in the period 1600 to 1775.

Powell was born in Northampton, Massachusetts, and studied at Amherst College and Harvard University. He worked in the private sector before beginning a teaching career. He also wrote *From Mythical to Medieval Man.*

1965

Irwin Unger   577

Birth: May 2, 1927; Brooklyn, NY. **Parents:** Elias C. and Mary (Roth) Unger. **Religion:** Jewish. **Education:** City College, NY: BSS. Columbia University, NY: MA, PhD. University of Washington. **Spouse:** Bernate Spaet (m. 1956; died 1970); Debi Irene Marcus (m. 1970). **Children:** Brooke David, Miles Jeremy, Paul Joshua (BS); Anthony Allen, Elizabeth Sarah (DIM).

Prize: *History,* 1965: *The Greenback Era: A Social and Political History of American Finance, 1865-1879,* Princeton, NJ: Princeton University, 1964.

Career: Served in U.S. Army, 1952-1954; Instructor of History, Columbia University, NY, 1956-1958; Assistant Professor of History, Long Beach State College (now California State University), CA, 1959-1962; Assistant Professor, University of California, Davis, 1962-1963; Associate Professor of History, University of California, Davis, 1964-65; Professor of History, New York University, NY, 1966-present; Member: American Historical Association, Economic History Association, Organization of American Historians.

Selected Works: *Essays on the Civil War and Reconstruction,* 1970. *The Slavery Experience in the United States* (Unger, Irwin and Reimers, David, eds.), 1970. *Beyond Liberalism: The New Left Views American History,* 1971. *The American Past: A Social Record, 1607-Present* (Unger, Irwin, Brody, David, and Goodman, Paul, eds.), 1971. *The Movement: A History of the American New Left, 1959-1972,* 1974. *The Vulnerable Years: The United States, 1896-1917* (with Debbie Unger), 1977. *Turning Point, 1968* (with Debbie Unger), 1988. *Twentieth Century America* (with Debbie Unger), 1990. *The Best of Intentions: The Triumphs and Failures of the Great Society under Kennedy, Johnson, and Nixon,* 1996.

Other Awards: Guggenheim Fellowship, 1972-1973. Rockefeller Humanities Fellowship, 1979-1980.

For More Information: *Oxford Companion to American Literature,* New York: Oxford, 1965; Casse, Daniel, "At War with Newt and His Revolution," *Wall Street Journal,* May 13, 1996; Davis, Bob, "Unger Offers a Thorough Study of the Great Society's Birth," *Chicago Tribune,* September 4, 1996.

Commentary: Irwin Unger was awarded the 1965 Pulitzer Prize in History for *The Greenback Era.* Unger's history covered politics and government during the period of greenbacks, the currency in place in the United States in the post-Civil War period of 1865 to 1877.

Unger was born in Brooklyn, New York. He was educated at City College and Columbia University, both in New York City. Unger served in the Korean War. He taught history most recently at New York University. His other works include *Essays on the Civil War and Reconstruction, The Movement: A History of the American New Left,* and *Turning Point, 1968.*

1966

Perry Gilbert Eddy Miller   578

Birth: February 25, 1905; Chicago, IL. **Death:** 1963. **Parents:** Perry Sturgis and Gertrude (Eddy) Miller. **Education:** University of Chicago, IL: PhB, PhD. **Spouse:** Elizabeth Williams (m. 1930).

Prize: *History,* 1966: *The Life of the Mind in America, From the Revolution to the Civil War,* New York: Harcourt, Brace & World, 1965.

Career: Instructor, American History, Harvard University, MA, 1931-1938; Associate Professor, Harvard University, 1939-1945; Captain, U.S. Army, 1942-1945; Professor, Harvard University, 1946-1963; Major, Office of Strategic Services.

Selected Works: *The Puritans* (with Thomas H. Johnson), 1938. *The New England Mind: The Seventeenth Century,* 1939. *Images or Shadows of Divine Things,* 1948. *Jonathan Edwards,* 1949. *The Transcendentalists: An Anthology,* 1950. *The New England Mind: From Colony to Province,* 1953. *Errand into the Wilderness,* 1956. *The Raven and the Whale,* 1956. *The Works of Jonathan Edwards* (Miller, Perry, ed.), 1957. *The American Transcendentalists, Their Prose and Poetry,* 1957. *Consciousness in Concord,* 1958. *The Golden Age of American Literature* (Miller, Perry, ed.), 1959. *The Legal Mind in America: From*

Independence to the Civil War, 1962. *The Life of the Mind in America, from the Revolution to the Civil War,* 1965. *Nature's Nation,* 1967. *Margaret Fuller: American Romantic,* 1970. *The Responsibility of Mind in a Civilization of Machines: Essays,* 1979. *Sources for the New England Mind: The Seventeenth Century,* 1981. *The American Puritans, Their Prose and Poetry* (Miller, Perry, ed.), 1982.

For More Information: *Oxford Companion to American Literature,* New York: Oxford, 1983; *Dictionary of Literary Biography,* Detroit: Gale, 1988.

Commentary: Perry Miller was awarded the 1966 Pulitzer Prize in History for *The Life of the Mind in America.* Miller's history charted intellectual life in the United States from the Revolution to the Civil War.

Miller was born in Chicago and educated at the University of Chicago. A literary historian and professor of literature at Harvard, he pioneered serious study of colonial literature and theology in *The New England Mind: The Seventeenth Century.* It was seen as a reinterpretation of the Puritans through an intellectual history. The Pulitzer award was posthumous; Miller died in 1963.

1967

William Henry Goetzmann   579

Birth: July 20, 1930; Washington, DC. **Parents:** Harry William and Viola M. (Nelson) Goetzmann. **Education:** Yale University, CT: BA, PhD. **Spouse:** Mewes L. Mueller (m. 1953). **Children:** William Nelson, Anne Stimson, Stephen Russell.

Prize: *History,* 1967: *Exploration and Empire: The Explorer and the Scientist in the Winning of the American West,* New York: Knopf, 1966.

Career: Instructor, Yale University, CT, 1957-1959; Assistant Professor, Yale University, 1959-63; Associate Professor of History and American Studies, Yale University, 1963-64; Associate Professor, University of Texas, Austin, 1964-1966; Professor of History and American Studies, University of Texas, 1966-1967; Stiles Professor of American Studies and History, University of Texas, 1967-present; Director of American Studies Program, University of Texas; Vice-President, Wilgo Games; Chief Historical Consultant, U.S. National Atlas Project; Member: American Studies Association, American Historical Association, Organization of American Historians, Society of American Historians, Texas Academy of Arts and Letters, Texas State History Association, Western History Association, Phi Beta Kappa.

Selected Works: *Army Exploration in the American West, 1803-1863,* 1959. *When the Eagle Screamed,* 1966. *The Colonial Horizon,* 1969. *American Civilization: A Portrait from the Twentieth Cen-*

tury, 1972. *The American Hegelians: An Intellectual Episode in the History of Western America* (Goetzmann, William Henry, ed.), 1973. *The West as Romantic Horizon* (with Joseph C. Porter and David C. Hunt), 1981. *Texas Images & Visions,* 1983. *The West of the Imagination* (with William N. Goetzmann), 1986. *New Lands, New Men: America and the Second Great Age of Discovery,* 1986. *Looking at the Land of Promise: Pioneer Images of the Pacific Northwest,* 1988. *The Atlas of North American Exploration* (with Glyndwr Williams), 1992. *Sam Chamberlain's Mexican War: The San Jacinto Museum of History Paintings,* 1993.

Other Awards: Buffalo Award of New York Posse of The Westerners, 1960: *Army Exploration in the American West,* New Haven, CT: Yale University, 1959. Francis Parkman Award, 1967: *Exploration and Empire,* New York: Knopf, 1966. Friends of the Dallas Public Library Award, 1967: *Exploration and Empire.* Golden Plate Award, American Academy of Achievement, 1968. Honorary LLD, St. Edward's University, TX, 1967.

For More Information: *Reader's Encyclopedia of the American West,* New York: Crowell, 1977.

Commentary: *Exploration and Empire: The Explorer and the Scientist in the Winning of the American West* won the 1967 Pulitzer Prize in History for William H. Goetzmann. This story recounted the events of discovery and exploration of the Western United States during the period of expansion.

Goetzmann enjoyed critical success with *The Explorer and the Scientist* for its synthesis of wide-ranging scholarship.

1968

Bernard Bailyn 580

Birth: September 10, 1922; Hartford, CT. **Parents:** Charles Manuel and Esther (Schloss) Bailyn. **Education:** Williams College, MA: AB. Harvard University, MA: MA, PhD. **Spouse:** Lotte Lazerfeld (m. 1952). **Children:** Charles David, John Frederick.

Prize: History, 1968: *The Ideological Origins of the American Revolution,* Cambridge, MA: Belknap, 1967. *History,* 1987: *Voyagers to the West: A Passage in the Peopling of America on the Eve of the Revolution,* New York: Knopf, 1986.

Career: Served in Army Signal Corps and Army Security Agency, U.S. Army, 1943-46; Instructor in Education, Harvard University, MA, 1953-54; Assistant Professor, Harvard University, 1954-1958; Associate Professor, Harvard University, 1958-1961; Professor of History, Harvard University, 1961-1966; Colver Lecturer, Brown University, 1965; Winthrop Professor of History, Harvard University, 1966-1981; Phelps Lecturer, New York University, 1969; Treve-

lyan Lecturer, Cambridge University, 1971; Becker Lecturer, Cornell University, 1975; Adams University Professor, Harvard University, 1981-present; President, American Historical Association, 1981; Director of Charles Warren Center for Studies in American History, Harvard University, 1983-1994; Walker-Ames Lecturer, University of Washington, 1983; Curti Lecturer, University of Wisconsin, 1984; Trustee, Institute of Advanced Study, Princeton, 1984-1994; Lewin Visiting Professor, Washington University, MO, 1985; Pitt Professor of American History, Cambridge University, England, 1986-1987; James Duncan Phillips Professor of Early American History, Harvard University, 1991-present; Montgomery Fellow, Dartmouth College, 1991; Thompson Lecturer, Pomona College, 1991; Fellow, British Academy, England; Fellow, Christ's College, Cambridge University, England; Member: American Academy of Arts and Sciences, American Philosophical Society, Mexican Academy of History and Geography, National Academy of Education, Royal Historical Society, Russian Academy of Sciences.

Selected Works: *Massachusetts Shipping, 1697-1714: A Statistical Study* (with Lottie Bailyn), 1959. *Pamphlets of the American Revolution, 1750-1776* (Bailyn, Bernard, ed.), 1965. *The Origins of American Politics,* 1968. *The Intellectual Migration: Europe and America, 1930-1960* (Bailyn, Bernard and Fleming, Donald, eds.), 1969. *Law in American History* (Bailyn, Bernard and Fleming, Donald, eds.), 1971. *The Ordeal of Thomas Hutchinson,* 1974. *The Great Republic: A History of the American People,* 1977. *The Press & the American Revolution* (Bailyn, Bernard and Hench, John B., eds.), 1980. *Glimpses of the Harvard Past,* 1986. *The Peopling of British North America: An Introduction,* 1986. *Faces of Revolution: Personalities and Themes in the Struggle for American Independence,* 1990. *Strangers within the Realm: Cultural Margins of the First British Empire* (with Philip D. Morgan), 1991. *On the Teaching and Writing of History: Responses to a Series of Questions,* 1994.

Other Awards: Harvard Faculty Prize, 1965: *Pamphlets of the American Revolution, Volume 1.* Cambridge, MA: Belknap, 1965. Bancroft Prize, Columbia University, 1967: *The Ideological Origins of the American Revolution,* Cambridge, MA: Belknap, 1967. First Robert H. Lord Award, Emmanuel College, MA, 1967. National Book Award in History, 1975: *The Ordeal of Thomas Hutchinson,* Cambridge, MA: Belknap, 1974. Saloutos Award, Immigration History Society, 1986: *Voyagers to the West: A Passage in the Peopling of America on the Eve of the Revolution,* New York: Knopf, 1986. Triennial Book Award, 1986: *Voyagers to the West: A Passage in the Peopling of America on the Eve of the Revolution.* Thomas Jefferson Medal of the American Philosophical Society, 1993. Henry Allen Moe Prize of the American Philosophical Society, 1994. Honorary LHDs: Lawrence University, WI, 1967; Bard College, NY, 1968; Clark University, MA, 1975; Yale University, CT, 1976; Grinnell College, IA, 1979; Manhattanville College, NY, 1991; Dartmouth College, NH, 1991; University of Chicago, 1991; William and Mary College, VA, 1994. Honorary LittDs: Williams College, MA, 1969; Rutgers University, NJ, 1976; Fordham University, NY, 1976; Washington University, MO, 1988.

For More Information: Losos, Joseph, "Battle of Learned Men and Great Ideas," *St. Louis Post-Dispatch,* September 16, 1990; Feeney, Mark, "The Art of the Historian," *Boston Globe,* July 7, 1991; Kenyon, John, "Wisdom and Charm—On the Teaching and Writing of History: Responses to a Series of Questions by Bernard Bailyn," *Times Literary Supplement,* September 1, 1995.

Commentary: Bernard Bailyn won two Pulitzer Prizes, both in History. The first award came in 1968 for *The Ideological Origins of the American Revolution.* This was an enlarged version of the general introduction to Bailyn's *Pamphlets of the American Revolution,* Volume One, published in 1965. He won a second Pulitzer in 1987 for *Voyagers to the West,* an examination of emigration and immigration from Great Britain to the United States in the 18th century.

Bailyn was born in Hartford, Connecticut and educated at Williams College and Harvard University. He was Adams University Professor and James Duncan Phillips Professor of Early American History, Emeritus, at Harvard University. His other works include *The Ordeal of Thomas Hutchinson* and *On the Teaching and Writing of History: Responses to a Series of Questions.*

1969

Leonard W. Levy   581

Birth: April 9, 1923; Toronto, Ontario, Canada. **Parents:** Albert and Rae (Williams) Levy. **Religion:** Jewish. **Education:** University of Michigan. Columbia University, NY: BS, MA, PhD. **Spouse:** Elyse Gitlow (m. 1944). **Children:** Wendy Ellen, Leslie Anne.

Prize: *History,* 1969: *Origins of the Fifth Amendment: The Right Against Self-Incrimination,* New York: Oxford University, 1968.

Career: Sergeant, U.S. Army, 1943-1946; Research Assistant, Columbia University, NY, 1950-1951; Instructor, Associate Professor, Brandeis University, 1951-1970; Earl Warren Professor of American Constitutional History, Brandeis University, 1958-1970; Dean of Graduate School of Arts and Sciences and Associate Dean of Faculty, Brandeis University, 1957-1963; Dean of Arts and Sciences

Faculty, Brandeis University, 1963-1966; Chairman, Department of History, Brandeis University, 1963-1964, 1967-1968; Board of Directors, American Society for Legal History, 1965-1970; Chairman, Graduate Program in the History of American Civilization, Brandeis University, 1966-1967, 1969-1970; Member of U.S. Commission on the American Revolution Bicentennial, 1966-1968; Consultant to DaCapo Press, 1969-1975; William W. Clary Professor of History, Claremont Graduate School, Claremont, CA, 1970-1974; Member, Executive Council, Institute for Early American History and Culture, 1970-1973; History, Claremont Graduate School, 1970-1989; Gaspar Bacon Lecturer, Boston University Law School, 1972; Sheldon Elliott Lecturer, University of Southern California Law School, 1972; Andrew W. Mellon All-Claremont Professor of Humanities, Claremont Graduate School, 1974-1990; Chairman, Graduate Faculty of Hugo L. Black Lecturer, University of Alabama, 1976; Mellon Professor Emeritus, Claremont Graduate School, 1990-present; Distinguished Scholar-in-Residence, 1991-present; Member: American Historical Association, American Studies Association, American Antiquarian Society, Organization of American Historians, National Advisory Council, American Civil Liberties Union, Society of American Historians.

Selected Works: *The Law of the Commonwealth and Chief Justice Shaw,* 1957. *Legacy of Suppression: Freedom of Speech and Press in Early American History,* 1960. *The American Political Process* (Levy, Leonard W. and Roche, John P., eds.), 1963. *Jefferson & Civil Liberties: The Darker Side,* 1963. *The Judiciary* (with John P. Roche), 1964. *Parties and Pressure Groups,* 1964. *American Constitutional Law: Historical Essays,* 1966. *Essays on the Making of the Constitution,* 1969. *Judgments: Essays on American Constitutional History,* 1972. *Against the Law: The Nixon Court and Criminal Justice,* 1974. *Emergence of a Free Press,* 1985. *Constitutional Opinions: Aspects of the Bill of Rights,* 1986. *Encyclopedia of the American Constitution* (Levy, Leonard W., ed.), 1986. *The Establishment Clause: Religion and the First Amendment,* 1986. *The Framing and Ratification of the Constitution* (Levy, Leonard W. and Mahoney, Dennis J., eds.), 1987. *Blasphemy: Verbal Offense against the Sacred, from Moses to Salman Rushdie,* 1993. *Encyclopedia of the American Presidency* (Levy, Leonard W. and Fisher, Louis, eds.), 1994. *Seasoned Judgments: The American Constitution, Rights, and History,* 1995. *A License to Steal: The Forfeiture of Property,* 1996.

Other Awards: Columbia University Fellow, 1949-1950. Guggenheim Fellowship, 1957-1958. Sigma Delta Chi Prize, 1960. Kappa Tau Alpha Award, 1960: *Legacy of Suppression,* Cambridge, MA: Belknap, 1960. Frank Luther Mott Award for

Best Research in Journalism History, 1961. Harvard University Center for the Study of Liberty in America Senior Fellow, 1961-1962. American Council of Learned Societies Grant, 1973. American Bar Foundation Legal Merit Fellow, 1973. National Endowment for the Humanities Senior Fellow, 1974. National Endowment for the Humanities Research Grant, 1979-1982. California Literature Silver Medal Award, 1974: *Against the Law: The Nixon Court and Criminal Justice,* New York: Harper & Row, 1974. Commonwealth Club Prize for Nonfiction, 1975.

For More Information: *Who's Who in World Jewry,* New York: Pittman, 1978; Stone, Christopher D., "The Peculiar Persistence of Original Intent," *Los Angeles Times,* January 8, 1989; McDowell, Gary L., "Two Views of Constitution: One Scholar, One Hothead," *Washington Times,* January 16, 1989.

Commentary: *Origins of the Fifth Amendment* won the 1969 Pulitzer Prize in History for Leonard W. Levy. Levy recounts the British and American beginnings of the amendment allowing for the right against self-incrimination.

Levy was born in Toronto, Canada, and educated at the University of Michigan and Columbia University. He is a leading constitutional historian. He was the Earl Warren Professor of American Constitutional History at Brandeis University from 1958 to 1970. He has been Mellon Professor Emeritus at the Claremont Graduate School since 1990. His other works include *Emergence of a Free Press, Original Intent and the Framers' Constitution,* and *A License to Steal: The Forfeiture of Property.*

1970

Dean Acheson   582

Birth: April 11, 1893; Middleton, CT. **Death:** 1971. **Parents:** Bishop Edward Campion and Eleanor (Gooderham) Acheson. **Religion:** Episcopalian.

Education: Yale University, CT: BA. Harvard University, MA: LLB. **Spouse:** Alice Stanky (m. 1917). **Children:** Jane, David Campion, Mary Eleanor.

Prize: *History,* 1970: *Present at the Creation: My Years in the State Department,* New York: Norton, 1969.

Career: Lawyer, Statesman; Ensign, U.S. Navy, 1917-1918; Private Secretary to Justice Louis D. Brandeis, U.S. Supreme Court, Washington, DC, 1919-1921; Associate, Covington, Burling & Rublee, 1921-1933; Undersecretary of the Treasury, May 1933 to November 1933; Partner, Covington, Burling, Rublee, Acheson & Shorb, 1934-1941; Fellow, Yale Corporation, 1936-1961; Assistant Secretary of State, 1941-1945; Undersecretary of State, 1945-1947; Partner, Covington, Burling, Acheson, O'Brian & Shorb, 1947-1949; Chairman, American Section, Canadian-U.S. Permanent Joint Defense Board, 1947-1949; Secretary of State, 1949-1953; Attorney, private law practice, Covington & Burling, beginning in 1953; Vice-Chairman, Commission on Organization of the Executive Branch of the Government (Initial Hoover Commission); Chairman, Advisory Committee on Civil Rules, U.S. Judicial Conference, beginning in 1959; Board of Directors Member, Franklin D. Roosevelt Foundation; Board of Directors Member, Harry S. Truman Library Institute; Advisor to President Kennedy; Advisor to President Johnson; Advisor to President Nixon; Member: American Bar Association, American Society of International Law, American Academy of Arts and Sciences, Century Association, Delta Kappa Epsilon, District of Columbia Bar Association, Foreign Policy Association, Metropolitan Club (Washington DC), Phi Beta Kappa.

Selected Works: *The Pattern of Responsibility* (Bundy, McGeorge, ed.), 1951. *A Democrat Looks at His Party,* 1955. *A Citizen Looks at Congress,* 1957. *Sketches from Life of Men I Have Known,* 1961. *Morning and Noon,* 1965. *Dean Acheson on the Rhodesian Question,* 1969. *Grapes from Thorns,* 1972. *This Vast External Realm,* 1973. *Reviews of the World Situation, 1949-1950,* 1974. *Official Conversations and Meetings of Dean Acheson, 1949-1953,* 1980.

Other Awards: Grand Cross of the Royal Order of Cambodi Grand Cross of the Order of Leopold, Belgium. Great Cross of the Order of Boyaca, Colombi National Order of the Southern Cross, Brazil. Order of the Aztec Eagle, Mexico. Order of the Rising Sun, Japan. Order of Vasa, Sweden. Honorary MA, Yale University, CT, 1936. Honorary LLDs: Wesleyan University, CT, 1947; Harvard University, MA, 1950; Cambridge University, England, 1958; Yale University, CT, 1962; Johns Hopkins University, MD, 1963. Honorary DHL, Brandeis University, MA, 1956. Honorary DCLs: Oxford University, England, 1952; University of Michigan, 1967.

For More Information: McLellan, David S., *Dean Acheson: The State Department Years,* New York: Dodd, Mead, 1976; McLellan, David C., *Among Friends: Personal Letters of Dean Acheson,* New York: Dodd, Mead, 1980; Brinkley, Douglas, *Dean Acheson: The Cold War Years, 1953-1971,* New Haven, CT: Yale University, 1992; Acheson, David C., *Acheson Country: A Memoir,* New York: Norton, 1993; Glothlen, Ronald L., *Controlling the Waves: Dean Acheson and U.S. Foreign Policy in Asia,* New York: Norton, 1993; Brinkley, David, ed., *Dean Acheson and the Making of U.S. Foreign Policy,* New York: St. Martin's, 1993; Harper, John Lamberton, *American Visions of Europe: Franklin D. Roosevelt, George F. Kennan, and Dean G. Acheson,* New York: Cambridge University, 1994.

Commentary: Dean Acheson won the 1970 Pulitzer Prize in History for *Present at the Creation: My Years in the State Department.* Acheson served as President Truman's Secretary of State from 1949 to 1953.

Acheson was born in Middleton, Connecticut and educated at Yale University and Harvard Law School. After law school, Acheson clerked for Supreme Court Justice Louis Brandeis. His career in the United States Department of State began in 1941 when he was appointed assistant secretary of state. Acheson was central to the formation of NATO, the Truman Doctrine, and the Marshall Plan. He was integral to the resolution of the Korean conflict. He later was advisor to Presidents Kennedy, Johnson, and Nixon. He died in 1971, the year after receiving the Pulitzer Prize.

1971

James MacGregor Burns   583
Birth: August 3, 1918; Melrose, MA. **Parents:** Robert Arthur and Mildred Curry (Bunce) Burns. **Education:** Williams College, MA: BA. National Institute of Public Affairs. Harvard University, MA: MA, PhD. London School of Economics, England. **Spouse:** Janet Thompson Dismorr (m. 1942; died 1968); Joan Simpson (m. 1968; died 1991). **Children:** David M., Stewart, Deborah H., Margaret Rebecca Antonia (JTD).

Prize: *History,* 1971: *Roosevelt: The Soldier of Freedom,* New York: Harcourt Brace Jovanovich, 1970.

Career: Combat Historian in the Pacific, U.S. Army, 1943-1945; Assistant Professor, Political Science, Williams College, MA, 1947-1950; Member of Staff, Hoover Commission, 1948; Associate Professor, Williams College, MA, 1950-1953; Massachusetts Delegate, Democratic National Convention, 1952, 1956, 1960, 1964; Professor of Political Science, Williams College, MA, 1953-1986; Faculty

member, Salzburg Seminar in American Studies, 1954, 1961; Democratic candidate for Congress, 1958; President, New England Political Science Association, 1960-1961; Woodrow Wilson Professor of Government, Williams College, MA, 1962-1986; Lecturer, Institute of History of the Soviet Academy of Sciences, Moscow and Leningrad, 1963; Member of Advisory Board, Berkshire Community College, 1963-1964; President, American Political Science Association, 1975-1976; President, International Society of Political Psychology, 1982-1983; Professor Emeritus, Williams College, MA, 1986-present; Senior Scholar, Jepson School of Leadership Studies, University of Richmond, VA, 1990-1993; Senior Scholar, Academy of Leadership, University of Maryland, 1997-present; Member: American Civil Liberties Union, American Historical Association, American Legion, American Philosophical Association, Delta Sigma Rho, Phi Beta Kappa.

Selected Works: *Congress on Trial: The Legislative Process and the Administrative State,* 1949. *Roosevelt: The Lion and the Fox,* 1956. *John Kennedy: A Political Profile,* 1960. *The Deadlock of Democracy: Four-Party Politics in America,* 1963. *Presidential Government: The Crucible of Leadership,* 1965. *Congress on Trial: The Legislative Process and the Administrative State,* 1966. *To Heal and to Build: The Programs of Lyndon B. Johnson* (Burns, James M., ed.), 1968. *Uncommon Sense,* 1972. *Edward Kennedy and the Camelot Legacy,* 1976. *Leadership,* 1978. *The Vineyard of Liberty: The American Experiment, Vol. 1,* 1981. *The Power to Lead: The Crisis of the American Presidency,* 1984. *The Workshop of Democracy: The American Experiment, Vol. 2,* 1985. *The Crosswinds of Freedom: The American Experiment, Vol 3,* 1989. *Cobblestone Leadership: Majority Rule, Minority Power,* 1990. *Government by the People* (with J. W. Peltason and Thomas E. Cronin), 1990. *A People's Charter: The Pursuit of Rights in America* (Burns, James M. and Stewart Burns), 1991. *The Democrats Must Lead: The Case for a Progressive Democratic Party* (Burns, James M., ed.), 1992. *State and Local Politics: Government by the People,* 1993.

Other Awards: Four Battle Stars, WWII. Bronze Star, WWII. Tamiment Institute Award, Best Biography, 1956: *Roosevelt: The Lion and the Fox,* New York: Harcourt, Brace, 1956. Woodrow Wilson Prize, 1956: *Roosevelt: The Lion and the Fox.* Francis Parkman Prize, Society of American Historians. National Book Award for History and Biography, 1971: *Roosevelt: The Soldier of Freedom,* New York: Harcourt Brace Jovanovich, 1970. Sarah Josepha Hale Award for General Literary Achievement, 1979. Christopher Award, 1983.

For More Information: Beschloss, Michael R. and Thomas Cronin, eds., *Essays in Honor of James*

MacGregor Burns, Englewood Cliffs, NJ: Prentice Hall, 1989; C-SPAN, James MacGregor Burns, Author: *Crosswinds of Freedom;* Book Review, C-SPAN's *Booknotes,* June 4, 1989, C-SPAN Archives at Purdue University, 1989.

Commentary: James MacGregor Burns was awarded the 1971 Pulitzer Prize in history for *Roosevelt: The Soldier of Freedom.* The history followed President Franklin Delano Roosevelt during the World War II years of 1939 to 1945. As to writing this volume, Burns stated, "Having grown up in the Roosevelt years, and having served in the U.S. Army in the Pacific, I developed a great interest in FDR's career."

Burns was born in Melrose, Massachusetts, and educated at Williams College and Harvard University. He is the Woodrow Wilson Professor of Government Emeritus at Williams College. He is currently Senior Scholar at the Academy of Leadership of the University of Maryland. He has written biographies of John F. Kennedy and Edward Kennedy. His other works include *Congress on Trial, The Deadlock of Democracy, Roosevelt: The Lion and the Fox, Leadership, The People's Charter,* and *The American Experiment,* in three volumes.

1972

Carl N. Degler   584
Birth: February 6, 1921; Orange, NJ. **Parents:** Casper and Jewell (Neumann) Degler. **Education:** Upsala College, NJ: AB. Columbia University, NY: MA, PhD. **Spouse:** Catherine Grady (m. 1948). **Children:** Paul Grady, Suzanne Catherine.

Prize: *History,* 1972: *Neither Black Nor White: Slavery and Race Relations in Brazil and the United States,* New York: Macmillan, 1971.

Career: Weather Service, U.S. Army Air Forces, 1942-1945; Instructor in History, CUNY Hunter College, NY, 1947-1948; Instructor in History, New York University, NY, 1947-1950; Instructor in History, Adelphi University, NY, 1950-1951; Instructor and Professor of History, Vassar College, NY, 1952-1968; Visiting Summer Professor of History, Ripon College, 1959; Visiting Professor of History, Columbia University, NY, 1963-1964; Visiting Professor of History, Stanford University, CA, 1964; Chairman of Department of History, Vassar College, NY, 1966-1968; Professor of History, Stanford University, CA, 1968-present; Executive Board, Organization of American Historians, 1970-present; President, Pacific Coast Branch, American Studies Association, 1971-1972; Margaret Byrne Professor of American History, Stanford University, CA, 1972-present; Member, Harmsworth Professor of American History, Oxford University, England, 1973-1974; President, Organi-

zation of American Historians, 1979-1980; Member: American Academy of Arts and Sciences, American Historical Association, American Association of University Professors, Economic History Association, Southern Historical Association.

Selected Works: *The New Deal* (Degler, Carl N., ed.), 1970. *Out of Our Past: The Forces That Shaped Modern America,* 1970. *The Other South: Southern Dissenters in the Nineteenth Century,* 1974. *Perspectives and Irony in American Slavery: Essays,* 1976. *Place over Time: The Continuity of Southern Distinctiveness,* 1977. *At Odds: Women and the Family in America from the Revolution to the Present,* 1980. *In Search of Human Nature: The Decline and Revival of Darwinism in American Social Thought,* 1991.

Other Awards: American Council of Learned Societies Fellow, 1964-1965; Bancroft Prize, Columbia University, 1972: *Neither Black nor White,* New York: Macmillan, 1971. Beveridge Prize, American Historical Association, 1972: *Neither Black nor White.* Guggenheim Fellowship, 1972-1973. National Endowment for the Humanities Senior Fellow, 1976-1977. Center for Advanced Studies in the Behavioral Sciences Fellow, 1979-1980. Honorary Degrees: Colgate University, NY; Ripon College, WI; Oxford University, England; Upsala College, NJ.

For More Information: Winkler, Karen J., "Revisiting the Nature vs. Nurture Debate, Historian Looks Anew at Influence of Biology on Behavior," *The Chronicle of Higher Education,* May 22, 1991.

Commentary: Carl N. Degler is Margaret Byrne Professor of American History at Stanford University and served as the president of the Organization of American Historians from 1979 to 1980. His other works include *The Other South: Southern Dissenters in the Nineteenth Century, At Odds: Women and the Family in America from the Revolution to the Present,* and *In Search of Human Nature: The Decline and Revival of Darwinism in American Social Thought.*

1973

Michael Kammen   585
Birth: October 25, 1936; Rochester, NY. **Parents:** Jacob Merson and Blanche (Lazerow) Kammen. **Education:** George Washington University, Washington, DC: BA, with distinction. Harvard University, MA: MA, PhD. **Spouse:** Carol Koyen (m. 1961). **Children:** Daniel Merson, Douglas Anton.

Prize: *History,* 1973: *People of Paradox: An Inquiry Concerning the Origins of American Civilization,* New York: Knopf, 1972.

Career: Instructor, Harvard University, Cambridge, MA, 1964-1965; Assistant Professor, Cornell University, NY, 1965-1967; Associate Professor, Cornell University, NY, 1967-1969; Fellow, Humanities Center, Johns Hopkins University, MD, 1968-1969; Professor of American History, Cornell University, NY, 1969-1973; Newton C. Farr Professor of American History and Culture, Cornell University, NY, 1973-present; Chairman of History Department, Cornell University, NY, 1974-1976; Host and moderator, "The States of the Union," Series, fifty one-hour radio programs broadcast by National Public Radio, 1975-1976; Director, Society for the Humanities, 1977-1980; Directeur d'Etudes Associes, Ecole des Hautes Etudes en Sciences Sociale, Paris, France, 1980-1981; Member of the Board of Directors, Social Science Research Council, 1980-1983; Trustee, New York State Historical Association, 1981-1994; Member, Executive Board, Organization of American Historians, 1989-1992; Times-Mirror Research Professor, The Huntington Library, 1993-1994; President, Organization of American Historians, 1995-1996; Member: American Academy of Arts and Sciences American Antiquarian Society, American Historical Association, American Society of Legal History, Colonial Society of Massachusetts, Institute of Early American History and Culture, International Commission for the History of Representative and Parliamentary Institutions, Massachusetts Historical Society, Phi Beta Kappa, Society of American Historians.

Selected Works: *A Rope of Sand: The Colonial Agents, British Politics, and the American Revolution,* 1968. *Empire and Interest: The American Colonies and the Politics of Mercantilism,* 1970. *The Contrapuntal Civilization: Essays toward a New Understanding of the American Experience* (Kammen, Michael, ed.), 1971. *"What Is the Good of History?" Selected Letters of Carl L. Becker, 1900-1945* (Kammen, Michael, ed.), 1973. *Colonial New York: A History,* 1975. *From Abundance to Scarcity: Implications for the American Tradition* (with Kenneth E. Boulding and Seymor M. Lipset), 1978. *A Season of Youth: The American Revolution and the Historical Imagination,* 1978. *The Past before Us: Contemporary Historical Writing in the United States* (Kammen, Michael, ed.), 1980. *A Machine That Would Go of Itself: The Constitution in American Culture,* 1986. *The Origins of the American Constitution: A Documentary History* (Kammen, Michael, ed.), 1986. *Spheres of Liberty: Changing Perceptions of Liberty in American Culture,* 1986. *Selvages & Biases: The Fabric of History in American Culture,* 1987. *Sovereignty and Liberty: Constitutional Discourse in American Culture,* 1988. *The Transformation of Early American History: Society, Authority, and Ideology* (with James A. Henretta and Stanley N. Katz), 1991. *Mystic Chords of Memory: The Transformation of Tradition in American Culture,* 1991. *Meadows of Memory: Images of Time and Tradition in American Art and Culture,* 1992. *The Lively Arts: Gilbert Seldes*

and the Transformation of Cultural Criticism in the United States, 1996.

Other Awards: National Endowment for the Humanities Fellowship, 1967, 1972-1973, 1984-1985. George Washington University Alumni Achievement Award, 1974. Center for Advanced Study in the Behavioral Sciences Fellowship, 1976-1977. Guggenheim Fellow, 1980-1981. Francis Parkman Prize, 1987: *A Machine That Would Go of Itself: The Constitution in American Culture,* New York: Knopf, 1986. Henry Adams Prize, 1987: *A Machine That Would Go of Itself: The Constitution in American Culture.* Smithsonian Institution Regents Fellow, 1990. Honorary Doctor, Humane Letters, George Washington University, 1991.

For More Information: Kelley, Mary, "The Politics of Memory in America," *Boston Globe,* November 24, 1991; David Walton, "In the Past Lane," *New York Times Book Review,* October 19, 1997.

Commentary: Michael Kammen won the 1973 Pulitzer Prize in History for *People of Paradox: An Inquiry Concerning the Origins of American Civilization.* Kammen looked at the American colonies and nation up until 1783 to extract what he saw as American national characteristics. This volume remains in print after 26 years and has been translated into 10 languages.

Kammen was born in Rochester, New York and educated at George Washington and Harvard Universities. He is Newton C. Farr Professor of American History and Culture at Cornell University. He has written extensively on constitutionalism. He hosted *The States of the Union,* a series of 51 one-hour radio programs on National Public Radio from 1975 to 1976. His other works include *A Season of Youth, A Machine That Would Go of Itself,* and *Selvages and Biases.*

1974

Daniel J. Boorstin   586

Birth: October 1, 1914; Atlanta, GA. **Parents:** Samuel Aaron and Dora (Olson) Boorstein. **Religion:** Jewish. **Education:** Harvard University, MA: AB, summa cum laude. Balliol College, Oxford University, England: Rhodes Scholar, BA, first class honors: BCL, first class honors. Yale University, CT: Sterling Fellow, JSD. **Spouse:** Ruth Carolyn Frankel (m. 1941). **Children:** Paul Terry, Jonathan, David West.

Prize: *History,* 1974: *The Americans: The Democratic Experience,* New York: Random House, 1973.

Career: Barrister-at-law, Inner Temple, London, England, 1937; Massachusetts Bar Association member, 1942; History Instructor, Harvard University, Cambridge, MA, 1939-1942; Legal History Lecturer, Harvard Law School, 1939-1942; Senior Attorney,

Office of Lend-Lease Administration, Washington, DC, 1942; Assistant Professor of History, Swarthmore College, Swarthmore, PA, 1942-1944; Assistant Professor, University of Chicago, 1944-1949; Associate Professor, University of Chicago, 1949-1956; Fulbright Visiting Lecturer, University of Rome, 1950-1951; Preston and Sterling Morton Distinguished Professor of History, University of Chicago, 1956-1969; Fulbright Visiting Lecturer, Kyoto University, 1957; International Lecturer for U.S. Department of State, 1959-1960, 1968, 1974; First Occupant of American History Chair, Sorbonne, Paris, 1961-1962; Fellow of Trinity College, and Pitt Professor of American History and Institutions, Cambridge University, 1964-1965; Shelby and Kathryn Cullom Davis Lecturer, Graduate Institute of Trustee, Colonial Williamsburg, 1967-1985; Director of National Museum of History and Technology (now National Museum of American History), Smithsonian Institution, Washington, DC, 1969-1973; President, American Studies Association, 1969-1970; Member, American Film Institute at Kennedy Center, 1972-present; Senior Historian, Smithsonian Institution, 1973-1975; International Studies, Geneva, Switzerland, 1973-1974; Member, Indo-American Subcommittee for Education and Culture, 1974-1981; Trustee, Kennedy Center, 1975-1987; Lecturer, Reith Lectures on radio for British Broadcasting Corp. (BBC), 1975; Librarian, Library of Congress, Washington, DC, 1975-1987; Member, Japan-American Commission, 1978-present; Librarian Emeritus, Library of Congress, 1987-present; Editor-at-Large, Doubleday and Company, NY, 1987-present; Member: American Academy of Arts and Sciences, American Antiquarian Society, American Historical Association, American Philosophical Society, Authors Guild, Authors League of America, Carl Albert Congressional Research and Studies Center, Colonial Society of Massachusetts, Cosmos Club (Washington, DC), Elizabethan Club (Yale University), International House of Japan, Japan-U.S. Friendship Commission, Organization of American Historians, Phi Beta Kappa, Presidential Task Force on the Arts and Humanities, Royal Historical Society (London).

Selected Works: *The Lost World of Thomas Jefferson,* 1948. *The Genius of American Politics,* 1953. *The Americans: The Colonial Experience,* 1958. *America and the Image of Europe: Reflections on American Thought,* 1960. *The Image: Or, What Happened to the American Dream,* 1961. *The Americans: The National Experience,* 1965. *An American Primer,* 1966. *The Decline of Radicalism: Reflections on America Today,* 1969. *Democracy and Its Discontents: Reflections on Everyday America,* 1974. *The Exploring Spirit: America and the World Experience,* 1976. *The Republic of Technology: Reflections on*

Our Future Community, 1978. *The Discoverers,* 1983. *Hidden History,* 1987. *The Republic of Letters: Librarian of Congress Daniel J. Boorstin on Books, Reading, and Libraries, 1975-1987,* 1989. *The Creators,* 1992. *Cleopatra's Nose: Essays on the Unexpected,* 1994.

Other Awards: Bancroft Prize, Columbia University, 1959: *The Americans: The Colonial Experience,* New York: Random House, 1958. Friends of American Literature Prize, 1959: *The Americans: The Colonial Experience.* Francis Parkman Prize, Society of American Historians, 1966: *The Americans: The National Experience,* New York: Random House, 1965. Patron Saints Award of Society of Midland Authors, 1966: *The Americans: The National Experience.* Honorary LittD, Cambridge University, 1968. Distinguished Service Professor, University of Chicago, 1968. Dexter Prize, History: 1974: *The Americans: The Democratic Experience,* New York: Random House, 1973. La Decoration d'Officer de l'Ordre de la Couronne from His Majesty the King of the Belgians, 1980. Chevalier de l'Ordre de la Legion d'Honneur, France, 1984: *The Discoverers,* New York: Random House, 1983. Grand Officer of the Order of Prince Henry the Navigator, Portugal, 1985: *The Discoverers.* Watson-Davis Prize of the History of Science Society, 1986: *The Discoverers.* First Class Order of the Sacred Treasure, Japan, 1986. Phi Beta Kappa Prize, Distinguished Service to the Humanities, 1988. Honorary Fellow, American Geographical Society. Honorary Member, Academy of Political Science.

For More Information: *Nomination of Daniel J. Boorstin of the District of Columbia to be Librarian of Congress: Hearings Before the Committee on Rules and Administration,* United States Senate, Ninety-Fourth Congress, July 30 and 31, and September 10, 1975, Washington, DC: United States Government Printing Office, 1975; *Current Biography Yearbook,* New York: Wilson, 1984.

Commentary: Daniel J. Boorstin won the 1974 Pulitzer Prize in History for *The Americans: The Democratic Experience.* It was the final volume in a trilogy on Americans that looked first at the colonial experience; second, the national experience; and finally, the economic experience.

Boorstin was born in Atlanta, Georgia. He was educated at Harvard University and attended Oxford University as a Rhodes Scholar. He taught history and served as Morton Distinguished Service Professor at the University of Chicago. He is Librarian of Congress Emeritus. His other works include *The Discoverers, The Creators,* and *Cleopatra's Nose: Essays on the Unexpected.*

1975

Dumas Malone   587

Birth: January 10, 1892; Coldwater, MS. **Death:**
1986. **Parents:** John W. and Lillian (Kemp) Malone.
Education: Emory College, GA: BA. Yale University, CT: PhD. **Spouse:** Elisabeth Gifford (m. 1925).
Children: Gifford, Pamela.

Prize: *History,* 1975: *Jefferson and His Times,
Volumes I-V,* Boston: Little, Brown, 1948-1981.

Career: Second Lieutenant, U.S. Marine Corps,
1917-1919; Instructor of History, Yale University,
New Haven, CT, 1919-1923; Associate Professor,
Professor of History, University of Virginia, Charlottesville, 1923-1929; Visiting Professor of American
History, Yale University, 1926-1927; Editor, *Dictionary of American Biography,* 1929-1931; Editor-in-Chief, *Dictionary of American Biography,* 1931-36;
Director, Harvard University Press, Cambridge, MA,
1936-1943; Professor of History, Columbia University, NY, 1945-1959; Editor, History Book Club,
1948-1986; Thomas Jefferson Foundation Professor
of History, University of Virginia, 1959-1962; Biographer-in-Residence, University of Virginia, 1962-1986; Member: American Academy of Arts and
Sciences, American Antiquarian Society, American
Historical Association, Century Club (NY), Cosmos
Club (Washington, DC), Delta Kappa, Massachusetts
Historical Society, Omicron, Phi Beta Kappa, Southern Historical Association.

Selected Works: *The Public Life of Thomas Cooper, 1783-1839,* 1926. *Correspondence between
Thomas Jefferson and Pierre Samuel du Pont de
Nemours, 1798-1817* (Malone, Dumas, ed.), 1930.
Saints in Action, 1939. *Edwin A. Alderman: A Biography,* 1940. *George Washington: A Biography,*
1948-1957. *The Story of the Declaration of Independence,* 1954. *Thomas Jefferson as Political
Leader,* 1963. *Malone & Jefferson: The Biographer
and the Sage,* 1981.

Other Awards: John Addison Porter Prize from
Yale University, 1923: *The Public Life of Thomas
Cooper,* New Haven, CT: Yale University, 1926.
Guggenheim Fellow, 1951-1952, 1958-1959.
Thomas Jefferson Award from University of Virginia,
1964. Wilbur Lucius Cross Medal from Yale University, 1972. John F. Kennedy Medal from Massachusetts Historical Society, 1972. Honorary DLitt,
College of William and Mary, VA, 1977.

For More Information: *Encyclopedia of American Agricultural History,* Westport, CT: Greenwood,
1975; *Oxford Companion to American History,* New
York: Oxford, 1983.

Commentary: *Jefferson and His Times, Volumes
I-V* won the 1975 Pulitzer Prize in History for Dumas
Malone. The volumes were as follows: One, *Jefferson*

the Virginian; two, *Jefferson and the Rights of Man;*
three, *Jefferson and the Ordeal of Liberty;* four, *Jefferson the President, First Term, 1801-1805;* and five,
Jefferson the President, Second Term, 1805-1809. A
sixth and final volume was published in 1981, *The
Sage of Monticello.*

Malone was born in Coldwater, Mississippi. He
was educated at Emory College and Yale University
and taught at Columbia University from 1945 to 1959.
He was the Thomas Jefferson Foundation Professor
of History at the University of Virginia from 1959 to
1962, when he was named biographer-in-residence.

1976

Paul Horgan

Full entry appears as **#569** under "History," 1955.

1977

Don E. Fehrenbacher   588

Birth: August 21, 1920; Sterling, IL. **Death:** December 13, 1997. **Parents:** Joseph Henry and Mary (Barton) Fehrenbacher. **Education:** Cornell College, IA:
AB. University of Chicago, IL: MA, PhD. Oxford
University, England: MA. **Spouse:** Virginia Ellen
Swaney (m. 1944). **Children:** Rush, Susan, David.

Prize: *History,* 1977: *The Impending Crisis,
1848-1861,* New York: Harper & Row, 1976. *History,*
1979: *The Dred Scott Case: Its Significance in American Law and Politics,* New York: Oxford University,
1978.

Career: First Lieutenant, U.S. Army Air Forces,
1943-1945; Assistant Professor of History, Coe College, Cedar Rapids, Iowa, 1949-1953; Assistant Professor, Stanford University, Stanford, CA,
1953-1957; Associate Professor, Stanford University,
1957-1962; Professor of History, Stanford University, 1962-1966; William R. Coe Professor of History,
Stanford University, beginning in 1966; Coe Professor of History and American Studies Emeritus, Stanford University; Harmsworth Professor of American
History, Oxford University, England, 1967-1968;
Graduate Record Exam, Member of Committee of
Examiners in History, 1972-1978; Harrison Professor
of History, College of William and Mary, 1973-1974;
Chairman, Committee of Examiners in History, 1974-1978; Walter Lynwood Fleming Lecturer of Southern
History, Louisiana State University, 1978; Commonwealth Fund Lecturer, University College, London,
1978; Member: American Academy of Arts and Sciences, American Antiquarian Society, American Historical Association, Organization of American
Historians, Southern Historical Association.

Selected Works: *Chicago Giant: A Biography of "Long John" Wentworth,* 1957. *Prelude to Greatness: Lincoln in the 1850s,* 1962. *A Basic History of California,* 1964. *California: An Illustrated History* (with Norman E. Tuturow), 1968. *The Changing Image of Lincoln in American Historiography,* 1968. *The Leadership of Abraham Lincoln,* 1970. *Tradition, Conflict, and Modernization: Perspectives on the American Revolution* (Fehrenbacher, Don E. and Brown, Richard Maxwell, eds.), 1977. *The Minor Affair: An Adventure in Forgery and Detection,* 1979. *Slavery, Law, and Politics: The Dred Scott Case in Historical Perspective,* 1981. *Constitutions and Constitutionalism in the Slaveholding South,* 1989. *South and Three Sectional Crises,* 1995. *Recollected Words of Abraham Lincoln* (Fehrenbacher, Don E. and Fehrenbacher, Virginia, eds.), 1996.

Other Awards: Awarded Distinguished Flying Cross, Air Medal with Three Clusters, WWII. Guggenheim Fellow, 1959-1960. Annual Prize, Pacific Coast Branch, American Historical Association: *Chicago Giant,* Madison, WI: American History Research Center, 1957. National Endowment for the Humanities Fellow, 1975-1976. Honorary DHL, Cornell College, IA, 1970.

For More Information: Pace, Eric, "Don E. Fehrenbacher, 77, Authority on the Civil War, Obituary," *New York Times,* December 17, 1997.

Commentary: Don E. Fehrenbacher won two Pulitzer Prizes, both in History. He won the 1977 award for completing *The Impending Crisis: 1848-1861,* a manuscript begun by David C. Potter (Potter was also given the award posthumously). He won the second award in 1979 for *The Dred Scott Case: Its Significance in American Law and Politics,* a history of the decision in 1857 which declared that under the United States Constitution blacks were so far inferior that they had no rights that the white man was bound to respect. The outrage at this decision in the free states led to the election of Abraham Lincoln and the outbreak of the Civil War.

Fehrenbacher was born in Sterling, Illinois. During World War II, he navigated 30 missions in B-24s over occupied Europe and Germany. He was a Lincoln scholar and Coe Professor of History and American Studies Emeritus at Stanford University until his death in 1997. His other works include *The Leadership of Abraham Lincoln, Constitutions and Constitutionalism in the Slaveholding South,* and *Recollected Words of Abraham Lincoln.*

David M. Potter   589

Birth: December 10, 1910; Augusta, GA. **Death:** February 18, 1971. **Parents:** David Morris and Katie (Brown) Potter. **Education:** Emory University, GA: AB. Yale University, CT: MA, PhD. Oxford University, England: MA. **Spouse:** Ethelyn E. Henry (m. 1939; div. 1945); Dilys Mary Roberts (m. 1948; died 1969). **Children:** Catherine Mary.

Prize: *History,* 1977: *The Impending Crisis, 1848-1861,* New York: Harper & Row, 1976.

Career: Instructor of History, University of Mississippi, 1936-1938; Instructor of History, Rice Institute, Houston, TX, 1938-1942; Assistant Professor, Yale University, New Haven, CT, 1942-1947; Harmsworth Professor of American History, Queen's College, Oxford, England, 1947-1948; Associate Professor, Yale University, 1947-1949; Visiting Professor, Connecticut College, 1947; Professor, Yale University, 1949-50; Coe Professor of American History, 1950-1961; Walgreen Lecturer, University of Chicago, 1950; Visiting Professor, University of Wyoming, 1952 and 1955; Visiting Professor, University of Delaware, 1954; Visiting Professor, Stanford University, 1957 and 1958; Visiting Professor, Stetson University, 1959; Coe Professor of American History, Stanford University, Stanford, CA, 1961-1971; Commonwealth Fund Lecturer, University College, London, England, 1963; Visiting Professor, State University of New York, 1966; Walter L. Fleming Lecturer, Louisiana State University, 1968; Fellow, American Academy of Arts and Sciences; Past President, American Historical Association; Past President, Organization of American Historians; Member: American Philosophical Society, Omicron Delta Kappa, Phi Beta Kappa.

Selected Works: *Lincoln and His Party in the Secession Crisis,* 1942. *People of Plenty: Economic Abundance and the American Character,* 1954. *Party Politics and Public Action, 1877-1917* (revised by Howard R. Lamar), 1960. *The South and the Sectional Conflict,* 1968. *The South and the Concurrent Majority* (Fehrenbacher, Don E. and Degler, Carl N., eds.), 1972. *Division and the Stresses of Reunion, 1845-1876,* 1973. *History and American Society: Essays of David M. Potter* (Fehrenbacher, Don E., ed.), 1973. *Freedom and Its Limitations in American Life* (Fehrenbacher, Don E., ed.), 1976. *Japan's Foreign Aid to Thailand and the Philippines,* 1996.

Other Awards: Jules F. Landry Award, Louisiana State University Press, 1968: *The South and the Sectional Conflict,* Baton Rouge, LA: Louisiana State University, 1968. Honorary LLD, University of Wyoming, 1955. Honorary LittD, Emory University, GA, 1957.

For More Information: *World Authors,* New York: Wilson, 1980.

Commentary: The 1977 Pulitzer Prize in History was awarded to David M. Potter posthumously for *The Impending Crisis: 1848-1861.* The volume was completed by Don E. Fehrenbacher after Potter's death. (Fehrenbacher also received a Pulitzer Prize.) It was part of the New American Nation series and dealt with the causes leading up to the Civil War.

Potter was born in Augusta, Georgia. He was educated at Emory, Yale, and Oxford Universities. He taught at Yale and Stanford Universities. At Stanford he was the Coe Professor of American History from 1961-1971. His works include *The South and Sectional Conflict* and *People of Plenty: Economic Abundance and the National Character.*

1978

Alfred D. Chandler Jr.   590

Birth: September 15, 1918; Guyencourt, DE. **Parents:** Alfred DuPont Chandler and Coral (Ramsey). **Education:** Harvard University, MA: AB, MA, PhD. University of North Carolina: MA. **Spouse:** Faye Martin (m. 1944). **Children:** Alpine Douglass Chandler Bird, Mary Morris Chandler Watt, Alfred DuPont III, Howard Martin.

Prize: *History,* 1978: *The Visible Hand: The Managerial Revolution in American Business,* Cambridge, MA: Belknap, 1977.

Career: Lieutenant Commander, U.S. Navy, 1941-1945; Research Associate, Massachusetts Institute of Technology, Cambridge, 1950-1951; Instructor, Massachusetts Institute of Technology, 1951-1953; Assistant Professor, Massachusetts Institute of Technology, 1953-1958; Research Fellow, Harvard University, Cambridge, MA, 1953; Consultant, U.S. Naval War College, 1954; Trustee, Park School, Brookline, MA, 1957-1963, 1965-1969; Associate Professor, Massachusetts Institute of Technology, 1958-1962; Trustee, Brookline Public Library, 1959-1963; Chairman, Park School, 1961-1963; Professor of History, Massachusetts Institute of Technology, 1962-1963; Governor, Nantucket Yacht Club, 1963-1966; Professor of History, Johns Hopkins University, Baltimore, MD, 1963-1971; Chairman, Department of History, Johns Hopkins University, 1966-1970; Trustee, Economic History Association, 1966-1970; Executive Board, Organization of American Historians, 1969-1972; Chairman, Advisory Historical Committee, Energy Reorganization Act, 1969-1977; Distinguished Visiting Professor, Harvard University, 1970-1971; Member, National Advisory Council on Education Professions Development, 1970-1971; Ford Straus Professor of Business History, Harvard University, Graduate School of Business Administration, Boston, MA, 1971-1989; President, Economic History Association, 1971-1972; Trustee, Johns Hopkins University, 1971-; Director, Landmark Communications, 1974-; Visiting Fellow, All Souls College, Oxford University, England, 1975; Executive Council, Massachusetts Historical Society, 1977-; Visiting Professor, Institute for Studies in Advanced Management, Brussels, Belgium, 1979; Straus Professor of Business History

Emeritus, Harvard University, Graduate School of Business Administration, 1989-present; Member: American Academy of Arts and Sciences, American Antiquarian Society, American Historical Association, Guana Island Club (Virgin Islands), Harvard Club (New York) St. Botolph Club (Boston).

Selected Works: *Henry Varnum Poor, Business Editor, Analyst, and Reformer,* 1956. *Strategy and Structure: Chapters in the History of the Industrial Enterprise,* 1962. *The Railroads, the Nation's First Big Business: Sources and Readings* (Chandler, Alfred D., Jr., ed.), 1965. *The Papers of Dwight David Eisenhower* (Chandler, Alfred D., Jr. and Ambrose, Stephen, eds.), 1970. *Pierre S. DuPont and the Making of the Modern Corporation* (with Stephen Salsbury), 1971. *The Coming of Managerial Capitalism: A Casebook on the History of American Economic Institutions* (with Richard S. Tedlow), 1985. *The Essential Alfred Chandler: Essays toward a Historical Theory of Big Business* (McCraw, Thomas, ed.), 1988. *Scale and Scope: The Dynamics of Industrial Capitalism,* 1990. *Big Business and the Wealth of Nations* (Chandler, Alfred D., Jr., Franco Amatori, and Takashi Hikine, eds.), 1997.

Other Awards: Commendation Ribbon, United States Navy, WWII. Guggenheim Fellow, 1958-1959. Thomas Newcomen Award, 1964: *Strategy and Structure,* Cambridge, MA: MIT, 1962. Thomas Newcomen Award, 1980: *The Visible Hand: The Managerial Revolution in American Business,* Cambridge, MA: Belknap Press, 1977. Bancroft Prize, 1978: *The Visible Hand: The Managerial Revolution in American Business.* Honorary PhDs: University of Leuven, Belgium, 1976; University of Antwerp, Belgium, 1979.

For More Information: Koselka, Rita, "Advice To Small Companies: Think Big," *Forbes,* November 13, 1989; "A Chat with the Dean of American Business History," *Financial World,* June 25, 1991; Alford, B.W.E, "Chandlerism, the New Orthodoxy of US and European Corporate Development?" *The Journal of European Economic History,* Winter, 1994.

Commentary: *The Visible Hand: The Managerial Revolution in American Business* won the 1978 Pulitzer Prize in History for Alfred D. Chandler. This volume was a history of management in United States business and industry.

Chandler was born in Guyencourt, Delaware, a member of the DuPont family. He was educated at Harvard University and the University of North Carolina. He is the Isador Straus Professor of Business History, Emeritus, at the Harvard Business School. His other works include *Strategy and Structure* and *Scale and Scope: The Dynamics of Industrial Capitalism.*

1979

Don E. Fehrenbacher

Full entry appears as **#588** under "History," 1977.

1980

Leon Frank Litwack 591

Birth: December 2, 1929; Santa Barbara, CA. **Parents:** Julius and Minnie (Nitkin) Litwack. **Education:** University of California, Berkeley: BA, MA, PhD. **Spouse:** Rhoda Lee Goldberg (m. 1952). **Children:** John, Ann.

Prize: *History,* 1980: *Been in the Storm So Long: The Aftermath of Slavery,* New York: Knopf, 1979.

Career: Served in U.S. Army, 1953-1955; Instructor, University of Wisconsin, Madison, 1958-1959; Assistant Professor, University of Wisconsin, Madison, 1959-1963, Associate Professor, University of Wisconsin, Madison, 1963-1965; Associate Professor, University of California, Berkeley, 1965-1972; Professor, University of California, Berkeley, 1972-; Member, American Historical Association; Member, Organization of American Historians.

Selected Works: *North of Slavery: The Negro in the Free States, 1790-1860,* 1961. *The American Labor Movement,* 1962. *Reconstruction: An Anthology of Revisionist Writings* (Litwack, Leon F. and Stampp, Kenneth M., eds.), 1969. *Black Leaders of the Nineteenth Century* (Litwack, Leon F. and Meier, August, eds.), 1988. *The United States* (with Winthrop D. Jordan), 1990.

Other Awards: Social Science Research Council Faculty Fellow, 1961-1962. Guggenheim Fellowship, 1967-1968. Distinguished Teaching Award, University of California, Berkeley, 1971. Humanities Research Fellow, 1976.

Commentary: Leon Litwack received the 1980 History Pulitzer Prize for *Been in the Storm So Long: The Aftermath of Slavery.* Litwack's history examined the social conditions facing African Americans during the Civil War and Reconstruction period of 1863-1877.

Litwack was born in Santa Barbara, California. He was educated at the University of California at Berkeley. He is the A.F. and May T. Morrison Professor of History at Berkeley. Litwack has been a consultant to public television on *Africans in America* and *The American Experience.* He also has worked on film projects such as *Behind the Veil: The Age of Jim Crow.* His works include *The American Labor Movement, North of Slavery: The Negro in the Free States, 1790-1860,* and *Trouble in Mind: Black Southerners in the Age of Jim Crow.*

1981

Lawrence A. Cremin 592

Birth: October 31, 1925; New York, NY. **Death:** September 3, 1990. **Parents:** Arthur T. Cremin and Theresa (Borowich). **Education:** City College, NY: BSS. Columbia University, NY: AM, PhD. **Spouse:** Charlotte Ramp (m. 1956). **Children:** Joanne Laura, David Lawrence.

Prize: *History,* 1981: *American Education, The National Experience, 1783-1876,* New York: Harper and Row, 1980.

Career: Served in U.S. Army Air Forces, 1944-1945; Instructor, Teachers College, Columbia University, NY, 1949-1951; Assistant Professor, Teachers College, Columbia University, 1951-1954; Associate Professor, Teachers College, Columbia University, 1954-1957; Visiting Associate Professor of Education, University of California, Los Angeles, 1956; Visiting Professor of Education, Seminar in American Studies, Salzburg, 1956; Visiting Associate Professor of Education, Harvard University, 1957; Professor, Teachers College, Columbia University, 1957; Director, Division of Philosophy, Social Sciences, and Education, Teachers College, Columbia University, 1958-1974; President, History of Education Society, 1959; Visiting Professor of Education, Harvard University, 1961; Frederick A. P. Barnard Professor of Education, Teachers College, Columbia University, 1961-1974; President, National Society of College Teachers of Education, 1961; Chairman, Curriculum Improvement Panel, U.S. Office of Education, 1963-1965; Fellow, Center for Advanced Study in the Behavioral Sciences, 1964-1965; Chairman, Regional Laboratories Panel, U.S. Office of Education, 1965-1966; Horace Mann Lecturer, University of Pittsburgh, 1965; Director, Institute of Philosophy and Politics of Education, Teachers College, Columbia University, 1965-1974; Vice-Chairman, White House Conference on Education, 1965; Chairman, Carnegie Commission on the Education of Educators, 1966-1970; Sir John Adams Memorial Lecturer, University of London, 1966; President, Member, National Academy of Education, 1969-1973; Cecil H. Green Visiting Professor, University of British Columbia, 1972; Visiting Professor of Education, Stanford University, 1973; President, Teachers College, Columbia University, 1974-1984; Merle Curti Lecturer, University of Wisconsin, 1976; Sir John Adams Memorial Lecturer, University of California at Los Angeles, 1976; Vera Brown Memorial Lecturer, National Institute of Education, 1978; Distinguished Visiting Lecturer, Simon Fraser University, 1982; President, Spencer Foundation, Chicago, 1985-; Trustee, Charles F. Kettering Foundation; Trustee, John and Mary Markle Foundation; Trustee, Spencer Foundation;

Visiting Instructor, University of Wisconsin; Visiting Instructor, Bank Street College of Education; Member: American Academy of Arts and Sciences, American Antiquarian Society, American Philosophical Society, Council on Foreign Relations, Phi Beta Kappa, Society of American Historians.

Selected Works: *The American Common School: An Historic Conception,* 1951. *A History of Education in American Culture* (with R. Freeman Butts), 1953. *A History of Teachers College, Columbia University* (with David T. Shannon and Mary E. Townsend), 1954. *Public Schools in Our Democracy* (with Merle L. Borrowman), 1956. *The Transformation of the School: Progressivism in American Education, 1876-1957,* 1961. *American Education: The Colonial Experience, 1607-1783,* 1970. *Richard Hofstadter (1916-1970): A Biographical Memoir,* 1972. *Public Education,* 1976. *Traditions of American Education,* 1977. *Popular Education and Its Discontents,* 1990.

Other Awards: Guggenheim Fellowship, 1957-1958. Bancroft Prize in American History, 1962: *The Transformation of the School,* New York: Knopf, 1961. American Educational Research Association Award, Distinguished Contributions to Education Research, 1969. Creative Educational Leadership Award, New York University, 1971. Butler Medal, Columbia University, 1972. Townsend Harris Medal, College of the City of New York, 1974. Medal for Distinguished Service to Public Education, New York Academy of Public Education, 1982. President's Medal, Hunter College, 1984. Carnegie Corporation of New York Medal, 1988. Honorary LittDs: Columbia University, NY, 1975; Rider College, NJ, 1979. Honorary LHDs: Ohio State University, 1975; Kalamazoo College, MI, 1976; Widener University, PA, 1983; George Washington University, Washington, DC, 1985. University of Rochester, NY, 1980; Miami University, 1983. Honorary LLD, University of Bridgeport, CT, 1975.

For More Information: *Who's Who in World Jewry,* Tel Aviv, Israel: Olive, 1978; Fowler, Glenn, "Lawrence Cremin, 64, Educator and a Prize-Winning Historian," *New York Times,* September 5, 1990; Ravitch, Diane, "Lawrence A. Cremin," *The American Scholar,* Winter 1992; Lagemann, Ellen Condliffe, "Lawrence A. Cremin: A Biographical Memoir," *Teachers College Record,* Fall 1994.

Commentary: The 1981 Pulitzer Prize in History was awarded to Lawrence A. Cremin for *American Education: The National Experience, 1783-1876,* a history of education in the United States during its first century.

Cremin was born in New York City and he was educated at City College of the City University of New York and at Columbia University, and he served in World War II. His other works include *American*

Education: The Colonial Experience, 1607-1783 and *Popular Education and Its Discontents.*

1982

Comer Vann Woodward   593

Birth: November 13, 1908; Vanndale, AK. **Parents:** Hugh Alison and Bess (Vann) Woodward. **Education:** Emory University, GA: AB. Columbia University, NY: MA. University of North Carolina: PhD. **Spouse:** Glenn Byrd MacLeod (m. 1937). **Children:** Peter V.

Prize: *History,* 1982: *Mary Chesnut's Civil War,* New Haven, CT: Yale University, 1981.

Career: Instructor of English, Georgia School of Technology (now Georgia Institute of Technology), Atlanta, 1930-1931, 1932-1933; Worked for Works Progress Administration, 1933-1934; Assistant Professor of History, University of Florida, Gainesville, 1937-1939; Visiting Assistant Professor of History, University of Virginia, 1939; Associate Professor of History, Scripps College, Claremont, CA, 1940-1943; Lieutenant, U.S. Naval Reserve, 1943-1946; Professor of History, Johns Hopkins University, Baltimore, MD, 1946-1961; President, Southern Historical Association, 1952; James W. Richard Lecturer in History, University of Virginia, 1954; Commonwealth Lecturer, University of London, University of Virginia, 1954; Harold Vyvyan Harmsworth Professor of American History, Oxford University, England, 1954-1955; Sterling Professor of History, Yale University, New Haven, CT, 1961-1977; President, Organization of American Historians, 1968-1969; President, American Historical Association, 1969; Professor Emeritus, Yale University, New Haven, CT, 1977-; Jefferson Lecturer in Humanities, 1978; Vice-President, American Academy of Arts and Sciences, 1988-1989; Member: American Academy of Arts and Letters, American Philosophical Society, Royal Historical Society, British Academy.

Selected Works: *Tom Watson, Agrarian Rebel,* 1938. *Reunion and Reaction: The Compromise of 1877 and the End of Reconstruction,* 1951. *Origins of the New South, 1877-1913,* 1951. *The Strange Career of Jim Crow,* 1955. *The Burden of Southern History,* 1960. *Cannibals All! or, Slaves without Masters* (Woodward, C. Vann, ed.), 1960. *A Southern Prophecy: The Prosperity of the South Dependent upon the Elevation of the Negro (1889)* (Woodward, C. Vann, ed.), 1964. *The Old World's New World,* 1991. *The Oxford History of the United States* (Woodward, C. Vann, ed.), 1982. *The Burden of Southern History,* 1993.

Other Awards: Bancroft Prize, One of the Year's Two Best Works in American History, 1952: *Origins of the New South: 1877-1913,* Baton Rouge, LA:

Louisiana State University, 1951. National Institute of
Arts and Letters Award in Literature, 1954. Annual
Award of American Council of Learned Societies,
1962. Brandeis University Creative Arts Award,
1982. American Historical Society Life Work Award,
1986. American Academy of Arts and Letters, Gold
Medal for History, 1990. Honorary LLDs: University
of Arkansas, 1971; University of North Carolina,
1971; University of Michigan, 1971. Honorary
LittDs: Princeton University, NJ, 1971; Cambridge
University, England, 1975. Honorary LHDs: Columbia University, NY, 1972; Northwestern University,
IL, 1977; Johns Hopkins University, MD, 1991.

For More Information: *McGraw-Hill Encyclo-
pedia of World Biographies,* New York: McGraw-
Hill, 1973; Feldman, Glenn, "C. Vann Woodward:
Liberalism, Iconoclasm, Irony, and Belles-Lettres in
Southern History," *Southern Humanities Review,*
Spring 1995; Scroggins, Deborah, "Conversations
about the South: C. Vann Woodward Legacy: Work
Stands Nearly Unchallenged," *Atlanta Journal-Con-
stitution,* January 12, 1997; Roper, John Herbert, ed.,
*C. Vann Woodward: A Southern Historian and His
Critics,* Athens: University of Georgia, 1997.

Commentary: C. Vann Woodward received the
1982 Pulitzer Prize in History for *Mary Chesnut's
Civil War.* Woodward provided a newer interpretation
of Mary Chesnut's experiences and views based upon
the fictionalization she made of the diary.

Woodward was born in Vandale, Arkansas. He
was educated at Emory and Columbia Universities
and the University of North Carolina. He is the editor
of *The Oxford History of the World.* His other works
include *The Burden of Southern History* and *The Old
World's New World.*

1983

Rhys Llywelyn Isaac   594
Birth: November 20, 1937; Cape Town, South Africa. **Parents:** William Edwyn and Frances
(Leighton) Isaac. **Education:** University of Cape
Town, South Africa: BA. Oxford University, England: BA. **Spouse:** Colleen Malherbe (m. 1962). **Children:** Meg, Lyn.

Prize: *History,* 1983: *The Transformation of Virginia, 1740-1790,* Chapel Hill, NC: University of
North Carolina, 1982.

Career: Lecturer, University of Melbourne, Melbourne, Victoria, Australia, 1963-1970; Senior Lecturer, La Trobe University, Bundoora, Victoria,
Australia, 1970-1978; Visiting Professor, Johns Hopkins University, 1975; Reader in History, La Trobe
University, 1978-; Visiting Professor, Davis Center
for History, Princeton University, 1981-1982; Member, Virginia Baptist Historical Society.

Selected Works: *Worlds of Experience: Communities in Colonial Virginia,* 1987.

Other Awards: Rhodes Scholarship, 1958.
Douglass Adair Medal, Best Article Published in the
William and Mary Quarterly, *Institute of Early Ameri-
can History,* 1980. "Evangelical Revolt: The Nature
of the Baptists' Challenge to the Traditional Order in
Virginia, 1765-1775."

Commentary: Rhys L. Isaac received the 1983
Pulitzer Prize in History for *The Transformation of
Virginia, 1740-1790.* Isaac charted the religious and
political confrontations that brought dramatic changes
to the social life and customs in Virginia at the end of
the 18th century.

Isaac was born in Cape Town, South Africa. He
was educated at the University of Cape Town and
Oxford University. He has lectured at the University
of Melbourne in Australia.

1984
No award

1985

Thomas K. McCraw   595
Birth: September 11, 1940; Corinth, MS. **Parents:**
John Carey and Olive (Kincaid) McCraw. **Religion:**
Roman Catholic. **Education:** University of Missis-
sippi: BA. University of Wisconsin: MA, PhD.
Spouse: Susan Morehead (m. 1962). **Children:**
Elizabeth, Thomas, Susan.

Prize: *History,* 1985: *Prophets of Regulation:
Charles Francis Adams, Louis D. Brandeis, James M.
Landis, Alfred E.Kahn,* Cambridge, MA: Belknap,
1984.

Career: Officer, U.S. Navy, 1962-1966; Teaching Assistant, University of Wisconsin, Madison,
1967-1969; Assistant Professor of History, University
of Texas, Austin, 1970-1974; Director of Undergraduate Advising in History, University of Texas,
1971-1973; Associate Professor of History, University of Texas, 1974-1978; Director of Undergraduate
Advising in History, University of Texas, 1974-1976;
Visiting Associate Professor of History, Harvard University Graduate School of Business Administration,
1976-1978; Professor, Harvard University, Graduate
School of Business Administration, 1978-1989; Editorial Board, *Harvard Buisness Review,* Harvard University, 1978-1983; Editorial Advisory Board,
Business History Review, Harvard University, 1978-
1994; Member, Advisory Board, Nomura School of
Advanced Management, Tokyo, Japan, 1981-; Historical Advisory Board, National Aeronautics and
Space Administration, 1983-1987; Publications Review Board, Harvard Business School, 1985-1987;

Director of Research, Harvard Business School, 1985-1987; Trustee, Business History Conference, 1986-1988; Chair, Business, Government and Competition Area, Harvard Business School, 1986-1989; Council, Massachusetts Historical Society, 1987-1992; Straus Professor of Business History, Harvard University Graduate School of Buiness Administration, 1989-; Co-Chair, Business, Government and Competition Area, Harvard Business School 1989-; President, Business History Conference, 1989-1990; Editor, Harvard Studies in Business History monograph series, 1991-; Editorial Advisory Board, *Reviews in American History,* 1992-; Associate Editor, *Encyclopedia of the U.S. in the Twentieth Century;* Advisory Board, *Oxford Companion to American History;* Editor, *Business History Review,* 1994-.

Selected Works: *Morgan versus Lilienthal: The Feud within the TVA,* 1970. *TVA and the Power Fight, 1933-1939,* 1971. *Regulation in Perspective: Historical Essays* (McCraw, Thomas K., ed.), 1981. *America versus Japan* (McCraw, Thomas K., ed.), 1986. *The Essential Alfred Chandler: Essays Toward a Historical Theory of Big Business* (with Alfred D. Chandler, Jr. and Richard S. Tedlow), 1988. *Management, Past and Present: A Casebook on the History of American Business* (with Alfred D. Chandler, Jr. and Richard S. Tedlow), 1996. *Creating Modern Capitalism,* 1997.

Other Awards: Woodrow Wilson Fellowship, 1966-1967. Ford Foundation Fellowship, 1967-1968. American Jurisprudence Award, 1969. William P. Lyons Master's Essay Award, 1969. University of Wisconsin Fellowships, 1968-1979. Harvard-Newcomen Fellowship in Business History, 1973-1974. University of Texas Research Institute Award, 1973-1974. National Endowment for the Humanities Younger Humanist Award, 1975. Eleanor Roosevelt Institute Award, 1976. Pulitzer Prize in History, 1985. Thomas Newcomen Book Award, 1986.

Commentary: *Prophets of Regulation: Charles Francis Adams, Louis D. Brandeis, James M. Landis, Alfred E.Kahn* won the 1985 Pulitzer Prize in History for Thomas K. McCraw. This volume delves into the history of trade and industry regulation in the United States, profiling those individuals who had great influence.

McCraw was born in Corinth, Mississippi. He was educated at the University of Mississippi and University of Wisconsin. A student of Alfred D. Chandler's, he is currently the Isador Straus Professor of Business History at the Harvard Business School. *Prophets of Regulation* also won the 1986 Thomas Newcomen Award for the best book on the history of business published during the preceding three years. He recently edited *Creating Modern Capitalism: How Entrepreneurs, Companies, and Countries Triumphed in Three Industrial Revolutions.*

1986

Walter Allen McDougall   596

Birth: December 3, 1946; Washington, DC. **Parents:** D. Stewart and Carol (Bruggeman) McDougall. **Religion:** Anglican. **Education:** Amherst College, MA: BA. **Spouse:** Elizabeth Swope (m. 1970; div. 1979).

Prize: *History,* 1986: *The Heavens and the Earth: A Political History of the Space Age,* New York: Basic, 1985.

Career: Served in Artillery, Vietnam, U.S. Army, 1968-1970; Assistant Professor, University of California, Berkeley, 1975-1983; Associate Professor, University of California, 1983-1987; Professor of History, University of California, 1987-; Senior Fellow, Foreign Policy Research Institute; Editor-in-Chief, *Orbis: A Journal of World Affairs;* Vestryman at St. Peter's Episcopal Church; Member: American Church Union, Delta Kappa Epsilon, Pumpkin Papers Irregulars.

Selected Works: *France's Rhineland Diplomacy, 1914-1924: The Last Bid for a Balance of Power in Europe,* 1978. *The Grenada Papers* (McDougall, Walter Allen and Seabury, Paul, eds.), 1984. *Let the Sea Make a Noise: A History of the North Pacific from Magellan to MacArthur,* 1993. *Promised Land, Crusader State: The American Encounter with the World Since 1776,* 1997.

Other Awards: Fellow, Smithsonian Institution, Woodrow Wilson, International Center for Scholars, 1981-1982. Fellow, National Air and Space Museum, 1982. Esquire Magazine, One of "Men and Women under 40 Who are Changing America," 1984. Finalist for American Book Award, Nonfiction, Association of American Publishers, 1985: *The Heavens and the Earth.* Visiting Scholar, Hoover Institution, 1986. *Insight Magazine,* One of America's Ten Best College Professors, 1987. Dexter Prize, Best Book, Society for the History of Technology, 1987.

For More Information: *International Authors,* Cambridge, England: International Biographical Centre, 1982.

Commentary: Walter A. McDougall won the 1986 Pulitzer Prize for History for *The Heavens and the Earth,* a political history of the Space Age. McDougall's work is based upon published and declassified materials, archival research, and interviews, which illustrated the race for space between the United States and the former Soviet Union.

McDougall was born in Washington, DC and educated at Amherst College. He is currently the Alloy-Ansin Professor of International Relations at the University of Pennsylvania and the editor-in-chief of *Orbis: A Journal of World Affairs.*

1987

Bernard Bailyn
Full entry appears as **#580** under "History," 1968.

1988

Robert V. Bruce   597
Birth: December 19, 1923; Malden, MA. **Parents:** Robert G. and Bernice I. (May) Bruce. **Education:** Massachusetts Institute of Technology. University of New Hampshire: BS. Boston University, MA: AM, PhD.

Prize: *History,* 1988: *The Launching of Modern American Science, 1846-1876,* New York: Knopf, 1987.

Career: Served as member of Combat Engineers, U.S. Army, 1943-1946; Instructor of History, University of Bridgeport, CT, 1947-1948; History Master, Lawrence Academy, Groton, MA, 1948-1951; Instructor, Boston University, 1955-1958; Assistant Professor, Boston University, 1958-1960; Associate Professor, Boston University, 1960-1966; Professor of History, Boston University, 1966-; President, Lincoln Group of Boston, 1969-1974; Advisory Council, Society for the History of Technology, 1974-; Fellow, Society of American Historians; Fellow, American Association for the Advancement of Science; Member: American Historical Association, Organization of American Historians.

Selected Works: *Lincoln and the Tools of War,* 1956. *1877: Year of Violence,* 1959. *Bell: Alexander Graham Bell and the Conquest of Solitude,* 1973. *Alexander Graham Bell, Teacher of the Deaf,* 1974. *Lincoln and the Riddle of Death,* 1981.

Other Awards: Guggenheim Fellowship, 1956. Henry E. Huntington Fellowship, 1966.

For More Information: "Pulitzer Prizewinners Include 5 Academics," *Chronicle of Higher Education,* April 6, 1988; Lurie, Edward, "Reviews of Books: The Launching of Modern American Science, 1846-1876," *American Historical Review,* February 1990.

Commentary: *The Launching of Modern American Science 1846-1876* won a Pulitzer Prize in History for Robert V. Bruce in 1988. Bruce demonstrated the remarkableness of America's position of dominance in the sciences by the 1930s, when the Civil War just six decades earlier had brought most American scientific studies to a standstill.

Bruce was born in Malden, Massachusetts and was educated at the University of New Hampshire and Boston University. He taught history at Boston University beginning in 1955. He signed the contract for his prize-winning book in 1962 as part of Knopf's series on the Civil War edited by Allan Nevins. He worked on it sporadically along with other books and in 1986, a volume of larger scope was completed.

1989

Taylor Branch   598
Birth: January 14, 1947; Atlanta, GA. **Parents:** Frankin T. and Jane (Worthington) Branch. **Education:** University of North Carolina: AB. Princeton University, NJ. **Spouse:** Christina Macy. **Children:** One daughter, one son.

Prize: *History,* 1989: *Parting the Waters: America in the King Years, 1954-63,* New York: Simon and Schuster, 1988.

Career: Historian; Advisor, speechwriter, President William Jefferson Clinton, 1992-.

Selected Works: *Blowing the Whistle: Dissent in the Public Interest* (with Charles Peters), 1972. *Second Wind: The Memoirs of an Opinionated Man* (with Bill Russell), 1979. *The Empire Blues: A Novel,* 1981. *Labyrinth* (with Eugene M. Popper), 1982.

For More Information: Eisenberg, Lee, "Topping the List," *Esquire,* May 1989; Holt, Patricia. "How Branch Parted History's 'Waters,'" *San Francisco Chronicle,* February 20, 1990; Feeney, Mark, "Taylor Branch's Vision: White Leaders Share Burden For Change, Historian Says," *Boston Globe,* January 20, 1998; Bumiller, Elisabeth, "No Illusions for Historian and Friend of Bill," *New York Times,* January 27, 1998.

Commentary: Taylor Branch won the 1989 Pulitzer Prize in History for *Parting the Waters; America in the King Years, 1954-1963.* This first volume of a social history of the Civil Rights movement focused on Martin Luther King Jr.

Branch was born in Atlanta, Georgia, and educated at the University of North Carolina and Princeton University. He is currently teaching the history of the Civil Rights movement at Goucher College in Maryland. Branch followed *Parting the Waters* with *Pillar of Fire: America in the King Years, 1963-65.*

James M. McPherson   599
Birth: October 11, 1936; Valley City, ND. **Parents:** James Munro and Mirium (Osborn) MacPherson. **Religion:** Presbyterian. **Education:** Gustavus Adolphus College, MN: BA. Johns Hopkins University, MD: PhD. **Spouse:** Patricia Rosche (m. 1957). **Children:** Joanna Erika.

Prize: *History,* 1989: *Battle Cry of Freedom: The Era of the Civil War,* The Oxford History of the United States, Volume 6, New York: Oxford University, 1988.

Career: Instructor, Princeton University, NJ, 1962-1965; Assistant Professor, Princeton University, 1965-1966; Associate Professor, Princeton University, 1966-1972; Professor of History, Princeton University, 1972-1982; Elder, Nassau Presbyterian Church, 1976-1979; Edwards Professor of History, Princeton University, 1982; Fellow, Behavioral Sciences Center, Stanford University, CA, 1982-1983; Consultant, Social Science Program, Education Research Council, OH; Member: American Historical Association, Assocation for the Study of Negro Life and History, Organization of American Historians, Phi Beta Kappa, Southern Historical Association.

Selected Works: *The Struggle for Equality: Abolitionists and the Negro in the Civil War and Reconstruction, 1964. The Negro's Civil War: How American Negroes Felt and Acted during the War for the Union, 1965. Marching toward Freedom: The Negro in the Civil War, 1861-1865, 1967. The Abolitionist Legacy: From Reconstruction to the NAACP, 1975. Ordeal by Fire: The Civil War and Reconstruction, 1982. Region, Race, and Reconstruction: Essays in Honor of C. Vann Woodward* (McPherson, James M. and Kousser, Morgan, eds.), *1982. How Lincoln Won the War with Metaphors, 1985. Abraham Lincoln and the Second American Revolution, 1990. The Atlas of the Civil War, 1994. What They Fought For, 1861-1865, 1994. The Abolitionist Legacy: From Reconstruction to the NAACP, 1995. "We Cannot Escape History": Lincoln and the Last Best Hope of Earth, 1995. Drawn with the Sword: Reflections on the American Civil War, 1996. For Cause and Comrades: Why Men Fought in the Civil War, 1997.*

Other Awards: Danforth Fellow, 1958-1962. Proctor & Gamble Faculty Fellowship. Anisfield-Wolf Award in Race Relations, 1965: *The Struggle for Equality: Abolitionists and the Negro in the Civil War and Reconstruction,* Princeton, NJ: Princeton University, 1964. Guggenheim Fellow, 1967-1968. National Endowment for the Humanities-Huntington Fellowship, 1977-1978. Huntington-Seaver Institute Fellow, 1987-1988.

For More Information: *Something About the Author,* Detroit: Gale, 1979; Hyman, Harold M., "Reviews of Books: Battle Cry of Freedom," *American Historical Review,* February 1990; Deitch, Joseph, "James M. McPherson," *Publishers Weekly,* January 18, 1991; Kennedy, J. Michael, "The Historian and His Friend Abe," *Los Angeles Times,* June 27, 1994.

Commentary: James M. McPherson was awarded the 1989 Pulitzer Prize in History for *Battle Cry of Freedom: the Civil War Era.* The sixth volume of the Oxford History of the United States series, it recaptured America at mid-century and examined the forces which led to the Civil War.

McPherson was born in Valley City, North Dakota. He was educated at Gustavus Adolphus College and Johns Hopkins University. McPherson is the George Henry Davis 1886 Professor of American

History at Princeton University, where he has taught since 1962. McPherson has written seven books on the Civil War era. He was most interested in the slavery issue, but also in the revolutionary nature of the war. His most recent book is *Images of the Civil War.*

1990

Stanley Karnow   600

Birth: February 4, 1925; New York, NY. **Parents:** Harry and Henriette (Koeppel) Karnow. **Education:** Harvard University, MA: AB. Sorbonne University, France. Ecole des Sciences Politiques, France. **Spouse:** Claude Sarraute (m. 1948; div. 1955); Annette Kline Andrew (m. 1959). **Children:** Curtis Edward, Catherine Anne, Michael Franklin.

Prize: *History,* 1990: *In Our Image: America's Empire in the Philippines,* New York: Random House, 1989.

Career: Served in U.S. Army Air Forces, 1943-1946; Paris Correspondent, *Time,* New York City, France, 1950-1957; Bureau Chief in North Africa, Time-Life, 1958-1959; Special Correspondent, Hong Kong, Time-Life, 1959-1962; Correspondent for *London Observer,* 1961-1965; Writer, *Time,* NY, 1962-1963; Far East Correspondent, *Saturday Evening Post,* 1963-1965; Far East Correspondent, *Washington Post,* 1965-1971; Diplomatic Correspondent, *Washington Post,* 1971-1972; Special Correspondent, NBC News, Washington, DC, 1972-1973; Associate Editor, *New Republic,* Washington, DC, 1973-1975; Syndicated Columnist, Register & Tribune Syndicate, 1974-; Syndicated Columnist, King Features, 1975-1987; Correspondent, Public Television, 1975-; President and Editor-in-Chief, International Writers Service, Washington, DC, 1975-1986; Columnist, *Le Point,* Paris, 1981-1986; Chief Correspondent, PBS-TV Series "Vietnam: A Television History," 1983; Commentator, National Public Radio, 1985-1986; Chief Correspondent, PBS-TV Series "The U.S. in the Philippines: In Our Image," 1989; Fellow, Nieman Institute, Harvard University, 1957-1958; Fellow, Institute of Politics, John F. Kennedy School of Government, 1970-1971; Fellow, East Asian Research Center, Harvard University, 1970-1971; Member: Asia Society, Authors Guild, Authors League of America, Century Association, Council on Foreign Relations, Foreign Correspondents Club, Harvard Club, PEN American Center, Shek-O Club (Hong Kong), Signet Society, Society of American Historians, White House Correspondents Association.

Selected Works: *Mao and China: From Revolution to Revolution, 1972. Mao and China: A Legacy of Turmoil, 1990. Asian Americans in Transition*

(with Nancy Yoshihara), 1992. *Paris in the Fifties,* 1997. *Vietnam: A History,* 1997.

Other Awards: Citation from Overseas Press Club, 1966. Annual Award, Best Daily Newspaper Reporting on Foreign Affairs, Overseas Press Club, 1967, 1968. Emmy Awards, 1984: *Vietnam: A Television History.* Polk Award, 1984: *Vietnam: A Television History.* Dupont Award, 1984: *Vietnam: A Television History.* Ambassador of Honor, English-Speaking Union of the United States, 1984: *In Our Image.*

For More Information: Trueheart, Charles, "Stanley Karnow: History of a Journalist," *Washington Post,* April 13, 1990; Marine, Craig, "Falling In Love with Paris: Pulitzer-Prize Winner Stanley Karnow Writes About that Certain *je ne sais quoi*," *San Francisco Examiner,* November 9, 1997.

Commentary: Stanley Karnow was awarded the 1990 Pulitzer Prize in History for *In Our Image: America's Empire in the Philippines, 1889-1946.* Karnow tells the story of America going abroad for the first time in its history at the turn of the century and becoming a colonial power.

Karnow was born in New York City and began his professional career as a correspondent for *Time* in 1950. Most of his work has focused on Asia. He spent 25 years traveling to Vietnam and the result was *Vietnam: A History,* which was made into a documentary series for public television. He has won numerous awards.

1991

Laurel Thatcher Ulrich   601
Birth: July 11, 1938; Sugar City, ID. **Religion:** Mormon. **Education:** University of Utah: BA. Simmons College, MA: MA. University of New Hampshire: PhD. **Children:** Five children.

Prize: *History,* 1991: *A Midwife's Tale: The Life of Martha Ballard, Based on Her Diary, 1785-1812,* New York: Knopf, 1990.

Career: Instructor of English, 1972-1973; Instructor of History; Assistant Professor and Associate Professor, History, University of New Hampshire, Durham, 1980-1995; Professor of History, Harvard University, 1995-present; Member: Mormon Historical Association, National Women Studies Association, Organization of American Historians.

Selected Works: *Good Wives: Image and Reality in the Lives of Women in Northern New England, 1650-1750,* 1982.

Other Awards: Bancroft Prize, Columbia University, 1991: *A Midwife's Tale: The Life of Martha Ballard, Based on Her Diary, 1785-1812.* John S. Dunning Prize, American Historical Association, 1990: *A Midwife's Tale: The Life of Martha Ballard,*

Based on Her Diary, 1785-1812. Joan Kelly Memorial Prize, American Historical Association, 1990: *A Midwife's Tale: The Life of Martha Ballard, Based on Her Diary, 1785-1812.* Society of Historians of the Early Republic, Book Prize, 1990: *A Midwife's Tale: The Life of Martha Ballard, Based on Her Diary, 1785-1812.* New England Historical Association Award, 1991: *A Midwife's Tale: The Life of Martha Ballard, Based on Her Diary, 1785-1812.* Association of Mormon Letters Biography Prize, 1991: *A Midwife's Tale: The Life of Martha Ballard, Based on Her Diary, 1785-1812.* Guggenheim Fellowship, 1991-1992. MacArthur Fellowship (Genius Award), 1992-1997. Charles Frankel Award, National Endowment for the Humanities, 1993. Sarah Josepha Hale Award, 1994.

For More Information: Trueheart, Charles, "The Arts of the Pulitzer Winners: Laurel Ulrich, Giving Birth to History," *Washington Post,* April 10, 1991; Winkler, Karen J., "A Prize-Winning Historian in Spite of Herself," *Chronicle of Higher Education,* June 26, 1991; "Dangerous History: Laurel Ulrich and Her Mormon Sisters," *Christian Century,* October 20, 1993.

Commentary: *A Midwife's Tale* won a Pulitzer Prize in History for Laurel Thatcher Ulrich in 1991. It is the tale of Martha Ballard (1735-1812), a mother and midwife, who lived in the area of Augusta, Maine. Ulrich used Ballard's diary entries as a framework. The diary contained information on her daily life, customs, patients, maladies, and the herbal remedies used at that time.

Ulrich was born in the Mormon community of Sugar City, Utah. She has also written *Good Wives: Image and Reality in the Lives of Women in Northern New England, 1650-1750.*

1992

Mark E. Neeley Jr.   602
Birth: November 10, 1944; Amarillo, TX. **Parents:** Mark Edward and Lottie (Wright) Neeley. **Education:** Yale University, CT: BA, PhD. **Spouse:** Sylvia Eakes (m. 1966).

Prize: *History,* 1992: *The Fate of Liberty: Abraham Lincoln and Civil Liberties,* New York: Oxford University, 1991.

Career: Visiting Instructor of American History, Iowa State University, Ames, 1971-1972; Director, Louis A. Warren Lincoln Library and Museum, Fort Wayne, IN, 1972-present; Member, Advisory Board, Indiana Historical Bureau, 1980-present; Member, Board of Directors, Abraham Lincoln Association, 1981-present; President, Society of Indiana Archivists, 1980-1981; President, Indiana Association of Historians, 1987-1988.

Selected Works: *The Extra Journal: Rallying the Whigs in Illinois,* 1982. *The Abraham Lincoln Encyclopedia,* 1982. *The Lincoln Image: Abraham Lincoln and the Popular Print* (with Harold Holzer and Gabor S. Borritt), 1984. *The Insanity File: The Case of Mary Todd Lincoln* (with R. Gerald McMurty), 1986. *The Confederate Image: Prints of the Lost Cause* (with Harold Holzer and Gabor S. Boritt), 1987. *The Lincoln Family Album* (with Harold Holzer), 1990. *Confederate Bastille: Jefferson Davis and Civil Liberties,* 1993. *The Last Best Hope of Earth: Abraham Lincoln and the Promise of America,* 1993. *Mine Eyes Have Seen the Glory: The Civil War in Art* (Neely, Mark Edward, Jr. and Holzer, Harold, eds.), 1993.

Other Awards: Barondess Lincoln Award of Civil War Round Table of New York, 1981. Honorary DHL, Lincoln College, IL, 1981.

For More Information: Mitgang, Robert, "Lincoln, Revolution and Civil Liberties," *New York Times Current Events Edition,* February 9, 1991; Kenney, Michael, "Lincoln Biography Goes Beyond the Myth and Anecdotes," *Boston Globe,* November 25, 1993; Sears, Stephen W., "Lincoln's Lessons," *Houston Post,* March 27, 1994.

Commentary: Mark Edward Neeley Jr. won the 1992 Pulitzer Prize in History for *The Fate of Liberty: Abraham Lincoln and Civil Liberties.* This volume looks at the suspension of the writ of habeas corpus by Lincoln during the Civil War and what it meant for the nation. Neeley estimated that a minimum of 10,000 arrests were made. He examined the 1,000 arrest records available at the National Archives in drawing his conclusions.

Neeley was born in Amarillo, Texas, and educated at Yale University. Neeley has been director of the Louis A. Warren Lincoln Library and Museum in Fort Wayne, Indiana, since 1973. His other works include *The Insanity File: The Case of Mary Todd Lincoln* and *The Confederate Image: Prints of the Lost Cause.*

1993

Gordon Stewart Wood   603

Birth: November 27, 1935; Concord, MA. **Parents:** Herbert G. and Marion (Friberg) Wood. **Education:** Tufts University, MA: AB, summa cum laude. Harvard University, MA: AM, PhD. **Spouse:** Louise Goss (m. 1956). **Children:** Christopher, Elizabeth, Amy.

Prize: *History,* 1993: *The Radicalism of the American Revolution,* New York: Knopf, 1992.

Career: First Lieutenant, U.S. Air Force, 1955-1958; Assistant Professor, College of William and Mary, VA, 1964-1966; Assistant Professor of History, Harvard University, MA, 1966-1967; Associate Professor of History, University of Michigan, Ann Arbor, 1967-1969; Associate Professor, Brown University, RI, 1969-1971; Professor of History, Brown University, RI, 1971-present; Pitt Professor, Cambridge University, England, 1982-1983; Chairman, Department of History, Brown University, 1983-1986; University Professor, Brown University, 1990-present; Member: American Historical Association, International Conferences of Americanists, Organization of American Historians, Rhode Island Historical Society, Society of American Historians.

Selected Works: *The Creation of the American Republic, 1776-1787,* 1969. *Revolution and the Political Integration of the Enslaved and Disenfranchised,* 1974. *Russian-American Dialogue on the American Revolution* (with Louise G. Wood), 1995.

Other Awards: Delancey K. Jay Prize, Harvard University, 1963-1964. Institute of Early Culture Fellowship, 1964-1966. National Endowment for the Humanities Fellowship, 1967. John H. Dunning Prize from American Historical Association, 1970: *The Creation of the American Republic,* Chapel Hill, NC: University of North Carolina, 1969. Bancroft Award, 1970: *The Creation of the American Republic.* National Endowment for the Humanities Grant, 1972-1973. Kerr Prize, Best Article in *New York History,* New York Historical Assocation, 1981. Douglass Adair Award, 1984. Frances Tavern Museum Book Award, 1992. Ralph Waldo Emerson Award of Phi Beta Kappa, 1992.

For More Information: *William and Mary Quarterly,* No. 44, 1987; Smoler, Fredric, "The Radical Revolution," *American Heritage,* December 1992; Gussow, Mel, "Rethinking America's Radical Revolution," *Boston Globe,* February 12, 1992; Thompson, Carlton, "A Voice Emerges from the Dark," *Houston Post,* June 24, 1993; *William and Mary Quarterly,* No. 44, 1994.

Commentary: Gordon S. Wood won the 1993 Pulitzer Prize in History for *The Radicalism of the American Revolution.* Wood assessed the social aspects of the American Revolution and what democratization meant for the society at that time.

Wood was born in Concord, Massachusetts. He was educated at Tufts and Harvard Universities. He is a professor of history at Brown University, where he served as chairman of the department from 1983 to 1986. His most recent publications are *Russian-American Dialogue on the American Revolution* and *Government Structures in the U.S.A. and the Sovereign States of the Former U.S.S.R.*

1994
No award

1995

Doris Kearns Goodwin   604

Birth: January 4, 1943; Rockville Centre, NY. **Parents:** Michael Aloysius and Helen (Miller) Kearns. **Religion:** Roman Catholic. **Education:** Colby College, ME: BA, magna cum laude. Harvard University, MA: PhD. **Spouse:** Richard Goodwin (m. 1975). **Children:** Richard, Michael, Joseph.

Prize: *History,* 1995: *No Ordinary Time: Franklin and Eleanor Roosevelt: The Home Front in World War II,* New York: Simon & Schuster, 1994.

Career: Intern, U.S. Department of State, 1963; Intern, U.S. House of Representatives, 1965; Research Associate, U.S. Department of Health, Education, and Welfare, 1966; Special Assistant to Willard Wirtz, U.S. Department of Labor, 1967; Special Assistant to President Lyndon Johnson, 1968; Assistant Professor, Harvard University, MA, 1969-1971; Assistant Director of Institute of Politics, Harvard University, MA, 1971-; Associate Professor of Government, Harvard University, MA, 1972-; Hostess of television show, *What's the Big Idea,* WGBH-TV, Boston, MA, 1972; Political Analyst, News Desk, WBZ-TV, Boston, 1972; Member, Democratic Party Platform Committee, 1972; Member, Steering Committee, Women's Political Caucus in Massachusetts, 1972-; Member, Harvard Board of Overseers; Member, Society of American Historians.

Selected Works: *Lyndon Johnson and the American Dream,* 1976. *The Johnson Presidential Press Conferences,* 1978. *The Fitzgeralds and the Kennedys,* 1987. *Wait Till Next Year: A Memoir,* 1997.

Other Awards: Fulbright Fellow, 1966. Woodrow Wilson Fellow, Harvard University. Outstanding Young Woman of the Year Award, Phi Beta Kappa, 1966. White House Fellow, 1967. Harold Washington Literary Award: *No Ordinary Time,* New York: Simon & Schuster, 1994. New England Bookseller Association Award: *No Ordinary Time.* Ambassador Award: *No Ordinary Time.* Washington Monthly Book Award: *No Ordinary Time.*

For More Information: Dezell, Maureen, "Goodwin's Prose Offers Some Unusual Insights," *Boston Globe,* April 19, 1995; Gussow, Mel, "Foundations of a Lifetime, Found in the Box Scores," *New York Times,* November 12, 1997.

Commentary: *No Ordinary Time, Franklin and Eleanor Roosevelt: The Home Front in World War II* won a Pulitzer Prize in History for Doris Kearns Goodwin in 1995. Goodwin recounted the Roosevelts' many accomplishments, activities, and relationships during the war effort and effectively brought them both to life. Goodwin illustrated how President Roosevelt moved America out of the Great Depression and into the role of mighty industrial nation.

Goodwin was born in Rockville Centre, Long Island, New York. She was educated at Colby College and Harvard University. She is a frequent commentator and political analyst on news programs, especially on issues related to the presidency. She has also written about President Lyndon B. Johnson.

1996

Alan Taylor   605

Birth: June 17, 1955; Portland, ME. **Parents:** Ruel Edward, Jr. and Virginia (Craig) Taylor. **Education:** Colby College, ME: BA. Brandeis University, MA: PhD.

Prize: *History,* 1996: *William Cooper's Town: Power and Persuasion on the Frontier of the Early American Republic,* New York: Knopf, 1995.

Career: Instructor, Colby College, ME, 1984-1985; Assistant Professor, Boston University, MA, 1987-1992; Associate Professor, Boston University, 1992-95; Professor of History, University of California at Davis, CA, 1995-present.

Selected Works: *Liberty Men and Great Proprietors: The Revolutionary Settlement on the Maine Frontier, 1760-1820,* 1990.

Other Awards: Fellow, Institute of American History and Culture. Huntington Fellow, 1994.

For More Information: Kenney, Michael, "The Revolution After the Revolution," *Boston Globe,* September 28, 1995; Winkler, Karen J., "Examining a Slice of Early America," *The Chronicle of Higher Education,* May 3, 1996; Barnes, Harper, "Three Bad Guys With Good Hearts," *St. Louis Post-Dispatch,* December 6, 1996.

Commentary: *William Cooper's Town: Power and Persuasion on the Frontier of the Early American Republic* won a Pulitzer Prize in History for Alan Taylor in 1996. Taylor wrote a social history through the biography and literary analysis of the lives of William Cooper, the founder of Cooperstown, New York and his son James Fenimore Cooper.

Taylor, a professor of history at the University of California at Davis, was also awarded the 1995 New York State Historical Association Manuscript Award, and the Bancroft Prize in American history from the American Historical Association for this work.

1997

Jack N. Rakove   606

Birth: June 4, 1947; Chicago, IL. **Parents:** Milton C. and Shirley (Bloom) Rakove. **Education:** University of Edinburgh, Scotland. Haverford College, PA: AB.

Harvard University, MA: PhD. **Spouse:** Helen Scharf (m. 1969). **Children:** Robert, Daniel.

Prize: *History,* 1997: *Original Meanings: Politics and Ideas in the Making of the Constitution,* New York: Knopf, 1996.

Career: Served in U.S. Army Reserve, 1968-1974; Assistant Professor of History, Colgate University, NY, 1975-1980; Assistant Professor of History, Stanford University, CA, 1980-1982; Associate Professor of History, Stanford University, 1982-1990; Coe Professor of History and American Studies, 1996-present; Member: American Association of University Professors, Organization of American Historians.

Selected Works: *The Beginnings of National Politics: An Interpretive History of the Continental Congress,* 1979. *Interpreting the Constitution: The Debate over Original Intent,* 1990. *James Madison and the Creation of the American Republic,* 1990.

Other Awards: Fellow, Brookings Institution, 1980-1981.

For More Information: Reidinger, Paul, "Politically Expedient," *ABA Journal,* October 1996; McCabe, Michael, "Stanford Professor a Winner / 'Original Meaning' and Constitution," *San Francisco Chronicle,* April 8, 1997; Rosen, Jeffrey, "The Politics of Justice," *New Republic,* May 5, 1997.

Commentary: *Original Meanings: Politics and Ideas in the Making of the Constitution* won a Pulitzer Prize in history for Jack N. Rakove in 1997. This work examines the framers of the Constitution and answers contemporary questions of original intent.

Rakove was born in Chicago. He was educated at the University of Edinburgh, Haverford College, and Harvard University. He is a constitutional scholar. Rakove hoped that the book would appeal to serious lay readers as well as to academics across the political spectrum. It takes an ongoing controversy in law and politics and attempts to do justice of its own kind to the arguments about history that this controversy makes. Rakove is the William R. Coe Professor of History and American Studies at Stanford University.

1998

Edward John Larson   607

Birth: September 21, 1953; Mansfield, OH. **Parents:** Rex and Jean (Uncapher) Larson. **Religion:** Christian. **Education:** University of Michigan. Williams College, MA: AB. Harvard Law School, MA: JD. University of Wisconsin: MA, PhD. **Spouse:** Lucy Kaiser Larson (m. 1990). **Children:** Sarah Marie, Luke Anders.

Prize: *History,* 1998: *Summer for the Gods: The Scopes Trial and America's Continuing Debate over Science and Religion,* New York: BasicBooks, 1997.

Career: Analyst, Wisconsin State Senate, Madison, WI, 1974-1976; Member, Washington State Bar Association, 1979-present; Attorney, Davis, Wright & Tremaine, Seattle, WA, 1979-1982; Counsel, Washington, State House of Representatives, Olympia, WA, 1981-1982; Associate Counsel, Committee on Education and Labor, U.S. Congress, 1983-1986; Member, History of Science Society, 1984-present; Visiting Scholar, University of Washington, 1986, 1988 and 1992; Counsel, Office of Educational Research and Labor, U.S. Department of Education, 1986-1987; Counsel, Office of Educational Research and Improvement, 1986-1996; Professor, History and Law, University of Georgia, 1987-present; Reviewer, U.S. Department of Education School Recognition Program, 1987-1989; Science Education Project Reviewer, National Diffusion Network, U.S. Department of Education, 1989; Panelist, National Institutes of Health, Ad Hoc Section for Ethical, Legal and Social Consideration of the U.S. Human Genome Project, 1990, 1995, 1997; Chair, Book Prize Committee, Forum for the History of Science in America, 1992; University of Georgia Council Member, 1992-1999; Chair, Coordinating Committee, Forum for the History of Science in America, 1993-1995; Chair, Student Affairs Committee, University of Georgia, 1993-1996; Chair, Watson-Davis Prize Committee, History of Science Society in America, 1993-1994; Member, Executive Committee, University of Georgia, 1993-1995; Panelist, Joint Dissemination Review and Program Effectiveness Panels; U.S. Visiting Professor, Institut de Droit Compare, Universite Jen Moulin, Lyon, France, 1996; Resident Scholar, Rockefeller Foundation's Bellagio Study and Conference Center, Bellagio, Italy, 1996; Admitted to practice law before the U.S. Supreme Court, Nine Circuit U.S. Court of Appeals, U.S. District Court for the Western District of Washingon and the U.S. Tax Court.

Selected Works: *Trial and Error: The American Controversy over Creation and Evolution,* 1985. *Sex, Race, and Science: Eugenics in the Deep South,* 1995.

Other Awards: Member, Phi Beta Kappa, 1974. University Fellow, University of Wisconsin, WI, 1983-1984. Sarah H. Moss Fellowship, University of Georgia, 1988. Parks-Heggoy Award for Excellence in Teaching History, University of Georgia Chapter, Phi Alpha Theta, 1989. Richard B. Russell Award for Undergraduate Teaching, University of Georgia, 1992. Templeton Prize for Outstanding Article in Science and Religion, 1997.

For More Information: Degler, Carl N., "Sex, Race, and Science (Book Review): Eugenics in the Deep South," *American Scientist,* July/August, 1996; Smolla, Rodney A., "Monkey Business (Book Review)," *New York Times,* October 5, 1997.

Commentary: The 1998 Pulitzer Prize in History was awarded to *Summer for the Gods: The Scopes Trial and America's Continuing Debate Over Science and Religion,* written by Edward John Larson. The 1925 Scopes trial, also called the "monkey trial," pitted religious fundamentalism against Darwinism, with William Jennings Bryan holding forth for creationism and Clarence Darrow carrying the banner for evolution. Larson's history reveals how Darwinism evolved to the point of challenging the Bible's explanation of creation.

Edward J. Larson was born in Mansfield, Ohio. He is a former associate counsel for the U.S. House of Representatives Committee on Education and Labor and holds a joint appointment in history and law at the University of Georgia. His Pulitzer Prize-winning book was written while Larson was on a fellowship at the Rockefeller Foundation's Bellagio Center. Larson's other works include *Sex, Race, and Science: Eugenics in the Deep South,* and *Trial and Error: The American Controversy Over Creation and Evolution.*

International Reporting

1948

Paul William Ward   608

Birth: October 9, 1905; Lorain, OH. **Death:** November 24, 1976. **Parents:** Thomas Joseph Ward and Dyma Nora (Hire). **Education:** University of Akron, OH. West Virginia University. Middlebury College, VT: AB. **Spouse:** Dorothy I. Cate (m. 1927). **Children:** Kerry, Marren.

Prize: *International Reporting,* 1948: *Baltimore Sun,* "Life in the Soviet Union," April 30-May 18, Baltimore, MD: Baltimore Sun, 1947.

Career: Staff member, Powers Photo-Engraving Company, New York, 1925-26; *New Bedford (MA) Standard,* 1926-30; Staff member, *Baltimore (MD) Sun,* 1930-32; Reporter, Washington (DC), *Baltimore (MD) Sun,* 1932-37; Correspondent, Washington (DC), *The Nation,* 1936-37; London (England) Bureau Chief, *Baltimore (MD) Sun,* 1937-40; Foreign Affairs Specialist, U.S. State Department, Washington (DC), *Baltimore (MD) Sun,* 1940-70; Correspondent, *Agence Francaise Independente,* 1943-44; Correspondent, *Paris (France) Le Pays,* 1945; Washington (DC) Bureau Chief, *Baltimore (MD) Sun,* 1970-76.

Selected Works: *Sovereignty: A Study of Contemporary Political Nations,* 1928. *Intelligence in Politics: An Approach to Social Problems,* 1931. *A Short History of Political Thinking,* 1939. *Life in the Soviet Union,* 1947. *What the Iron Curtain Hides,* 1951.

Other Awards: Chevalier, Legion of Honor, France.

For More Information: *New York Times,* November 25, 1976; *Washington (D.C.) Post,* November 25, 1976; *National Cyclopaedia of American Biography, Volume 59,* New York: James T. White & Company, 1980.

Commentary: Paul W. Ward's series of 19 articles titled "Life in the Soviet Union" won the International Reporting Pulitzer Prize in 1948. The articles were done on his own initiative beyond his specific assignment in Moscow.

Although based in Washington, DC from 1940 until his death, he undertook various international assignments for his paper. Some of these include covering the Dumbarton Oaks Conference in 1944, the San Francisco Peace Conference of 1945, and the Moscow Foreign Ministers Conference on peace terms for Germany and Austria.

1949

Price Day   609

Birth: November 4, 1907; Plainview, TX. **Death:** December 9, 1978. **Parents:** John Walter Day and Zillah (Price). **Education:** Princeton University, NJ: AB. **Spouse:** Alice Alexander (m. 1931). **Children:** Anthony, Joseph, Thomas, James.

Prize: *International Reporting,* 1949: *Baltimore Sun,* "Experiment in Freedom — India and Its First Year of Independence," November 28-December 9, Baltimore, MD: Baltimore Sun, 1948.

Career: Cartoonist, Occasional freelance writer, New York and Florida, 1929-35; Reporter, *Fort Lauderdale (FL) News,* 1930; Ticket seller, Hialeah Park, and Freelance writer, 1935-41; Contributor, magazines, 1935-41; City Editor, *Fort Lauderdale (FL) Times,* 1942; Rewriteman, *Baltimore (MD) Evening Sun,* 1942; War Correspondent, *Baltimore (MD) Sun,* 1943-45; Foreign correspondent, 1945-60; Editor-in-Chief, *Baltimore (MD) Sun,* 1960-75; Reporter, War correspondent, columnist, political commentator, editor.

Selected Works: *Well, about the Penguin,* 1939. *Crisis in South Africa: The First of a Series of Reports on the Strength and Weaknesses of the British Commonwealth and Empire,* 1948. *Experiment in Freedom: India and Its First Year of Independence; Report Number 3 in the Sun's Worldwide Study of the Strengths and Weaknesses of the British Commonwealth and Empire,* 1948. *Day in the Sun: The Columns of Price Day, Reporter, War Correspondent, Editor, the Baltimore Sun, 1942-1979* (with Anthony Day), 1993.

For More Information: *New York Times,* December 11, 1978: D12.

Commentary: Price Day's reporting on India and the country's new state of independence won him a Pulitzer Prize. Day, a former combat correspondent during World War II, had covered the Potsdam Conference and the Nuremberg trials. He was the only reporter from an individual paper present at Germany's surrender at Reims. All four of his sons became journalists.

1950

Edmund William Stevens   610

Birth: July 22, 1910; Denver, CO. **Death:** May 24, 1992. **Parents:** Edmund William Stevens and

Florence (Ballance). **Religion:** Episcopalian. **Education:** Columbia University, NY: BA. Moscow University. **Spouse:** Nina Andreyevna Bondarenko (m. 1935). **Children:** Edmund William Jr., Anastasia.

Prize: *International Reporting,* 1950: *Christian Science Monitor,* Boston: Christian Science Monitor, 1949.

Career: Translator, Moscow, publishing company, 1935-37; Correspondent, Moscow (Russia), *Manchester (England) Guardian, London (England) Daily Herald, Observer,* and *Reuters,* 1937-39; War Correspondent, *Christian Science Monitor,* 1939-44; Correspondent, Moscow (Russia), *Christian Science Monitor,* 1946-49; Head, Mediterranean News Bureau, *Christian Science Monitor,* 1950-55; Correspondent, Moscow (Russia), *Look* magazine, 1955-58; Moscow (Russia) Bureau Chief, *Time* magazine, 1963-; Special Correspondent, *Saturday Evening Post* 1971; Reporter, NBC-Radio, 1971.

Selected Works: *Russia Is No Riddle,* 1945. *This Is Russia, Uncensored,* 1950. *North African Powder Keg,* 1955.

Other Awards: Overseas Press Club Award, 1956-58. George Polk Memorial Award, Long Island University, NY, 1958.

For More Information: *Daily Telegraph,* 27 May (1992): 23; *New York Times,* 27 May (1992): D20; *Christian Science Monitor,* 5 June (1992): 19.

Commentary: Edmund Stevens first traveled to Russia in 1934 and with that trip, he began his life as a foreign correspondent. His award in 1950 was for his series, "This is Russia—Uncensored," written after returning to the United States in 1949. There were 44 articles in the series. His award was the first Pulitzer Prize for the *Christian Science Monitor.*

He was one of three American newspapermen in Oslo when Russia attacked Finland in 1939. He and his wife returned to Moscow in 1956, where he lived until his death in 1992.

1951

Keyes Beech   611

Birth: August 13, 1913; Pulaski, TN. **Death:** February 15, 1990. **Parents:** Walter William Beech and Leona (Cardin). **Spouse:** Linda Corley Mangelsdorf (m. 1951, div. 1969); Yuko Horiguchi (m. 1973). **Children:** Keyes Jr., Barnaby, Walter, (LM); Hannah (YH).

Prize: *International Reporting,* 1951: *Chicago Daily News,* Chicago: Chicago Daily News, 1950.

Career: Copyboy, *St. Petersburg (FL) Evening Independent,* 1930-36; Reporter, *St. Petersburg Evening Independent,* 1936-37; Feature Writer, *Akron (OH) Beacon Journal,* 1937-43; Combat Correspondent, U.S. Marine Corps, 1943-45; Correspondent,

Washington (DC), *Honolulu (HI) Star-Bulletin,* 1945-47; Far East Correspondent, *Chicago Daily News,* 1947-77; Correspondent, Bangkok (Thailand), *Los Angeles Times,* 1979-81; Freelance writer.

Selected Works: *Uncommon Valor: Marine Divisions in Action* (with others), 1946. *Tokyo and Points East,* 1954. *Not without the Americans: A Personal History,* 1971. *U.S. Marines on Iwo Jima: Elite Unit Series, 6* (with others), 1987.

Other Awards: Sigma Delta Chi Award, 1951. Nieman Fellow, Harvard University, MA, 1952-53.

For More Information: *New York Times,* 16 February (1990): D19; *Los Angeles Times,* 17 February (1990): A36.

Commentary: Keyes Beech was one of many foreign correspondents who were cited for their coverage of the Korean War. He covered Asia for four decades starting during World War II. He was the first correspondent to go to the top of Mount Suribachi on Iwo Jima.

Homer William Bigart   612

Birth: October 25, 1907; Hawley, PA. **Death:** April 16, 1991. **Parents:** Homer S. Bigart and Anna (Schardt). **Education:** Carnegie Institute of Technology, PA. New York University. **Spouse:** Alice Veit (m., div.); Alice Weel (m. 1963; died 1969); Else Holmelund Minarik (m. 1970). **Children:** Stepchild: Brooke Minarik (EM).

Prize: *Telegraphic Reporting (International),* 1946: *New York Herald-Tribune,* March 9-September 5, New York: New York Herald-Tribune, 1945. *International Reporting,* 1951: *New York Herald-Tribune,* July 12-December 6, New York: New York Herald-Tribune, 1950.

Career: Night Copyboy, *New York Herald-Tribune,* 1929; Copyboy, *New York Herald-Tribune,* 1929-33; General Assignment Reporter, *New York Herald-Tribune,* 1933-42; War Correspondent, *New York Herald-Tribune, 1942-45;,* Roving Correspondent, *New York Herald-Tribune,* 1945-55; Foreign Correspondent, *New York Times,* 1955-63; National Correspondent, *New York Times,* 1963-72.

Selected Works: *Hunger in America,* 1969. *Forward Positions: The War Correspondence of Homer Bigart* (with Betsy Wade), 1992.

Other Awards: Overseas Press Club Award, 1950, 1952. George Polk Memorial Award, Overseas Press Club, 1948, 1952. Meyer Berger Award. Page One Award.

For More Information: *New York Times,* April 17, 1991: A20; *Los Angeles Times,* April 18, 1991: 28; *World Journalism Review,* 13 (November 1991): 34-35; Rothmeyer, Karen, *Winning Pulitzers: The Story Behind Some of the Best News Coverage of Our Time,* New York: Columbia University Press, 1991: 61-68.

Commentary: Homer Bigart was well known for his writing and for his carefully chosen words and phrases which convey the scene and the story to the reader. He spoke with a slight stammer, which he turned into an effective interviewing mechanism by having the person being interviewed expand on the topic. His first Pulitzer Prize was for his dispatches from the Pacific during World War II and his second was for his reporting of the Korean War.

Other stories that he covered in his career included the trial of the Nazi war criminal Adolf Eichmann, the Greek Civil War, and the Civil Rights movement. He was one of the first journalists in Hiroshima after it was bombed in 1945.

Marguerite Higgins   613

Birth: September 3, 1920; Hong Kong, China. **Death:** January 3, 1966. **Parents:** Lawrence Higgins and Marguerite (Goddard). **Education:** University of California, Berkeley: AB, cum laude, Phi Beta Kappa. Columbia University, NY: MS. **Spouse:** Stanley Moore (m. 1942, div.); William E. Hall (m. 1952). **Children:** Lawrence O'Higgins, Linda Marguerite (WH).

Prize: *International Reporting,* 1951: *New York Herald-Tribune,* June 29-December 8, New York: New York Herald-Tribune, 1950.

Career: Reporter, *New York Herald-Tribune,* 1942-44; War Correspondent, *New York Herald-Tribune,* 1944-45; Berlin (Germany) Bureau Chief, *New York Herald-Tribune,* 1946-50; Tokyo (Japan) Bureau Chief, *New York Herald-Tribune,* 1950; War Correspondent in Korea, *New York Herald-Tribune,* 1950-58; Diplomatic Correspondent, Washington, DC 1958-62; Staff member, *Newsday (NY),* 1963-.

Selected Works: *War in Korea: Report of a Woman Combat Correspondent,* 1951. *News Is a Singular Thing,* 1955. *Red Plush and Black Bread,* 1955. *Jessie Benton Fremont: North Star Books, 32,* 1962. *Overtime in Heaven: Adventures in the Foreign Service* (with Peter Lisagor), 1964. *Our Vietnam Nightmare,* 1965.

Other Awards: United States Army Combat Ribbon. Best Piece of Foreign Reporting, New York Newspaper Women's Association, 1945. Overseas Press Club Award, 1951. George Polk Memorial Award, Long Island University, NY. Front Page Award, Veterans of Foreign Wars.

For More Information: *Current Biography Yearbook, 1951,* New York: H.W. Wilson Company, 1951; *New York Herald-Tribune,* January 4, 1966; *New York Times,* January 4, 1966: 27; Jakes, John, *Great War Correspondents,* New York: G.P. Putnam's Sons, 1967: 157-173; May, Antoinette, *Witness to War: A Biography of Marguerite Higgins,* New York: Beaufort Books, 1983; Belford, Barbara, *Brilliant Bylines: A Biographical Anthology of Notable Newspaperwoman in America,* New York: Columbia University Press, 1986: 284-295; Riley, Sam G., *Biographical Dictionary of American Newspaper Columnists,* Westport, CT: Greenwood Press, 1995.

Commentary: Marguerite Higgins's war correspondence from Korea won her a Pulitzer Prize. She shared the award with five other journalists including Homer Bigart, a rival from her own paper. She began her foreign correspondence work during World War II. She was at Dachau when the camp was liberated by the Allies.

Relman George Morin   614

Birth: September 11, 1907; Freeport, IL. **Death:** July 16, 1973. **Parents:** Frederick Upton Morin and Wilhelmina Louise (Relman). **Education:** Pomona College, CA: AB. Lingham University, Canton, China.

Shanghai College, China. Yenching University, Peking, China. **Spouse:** Florence Pine (m. 1936, div. 1946); Dorothy Wright Liebes (m. 1948, died 1972). **Children:** Mary Frances (FP).

Prize: *International Reporting,* 1951: Associated Press, 1950. *National Reporting,* 1958: Associated Press, 1957.

Career: Reporter, *Los Angeles Times,* 1923-29; Staff member, *Shanghai (China) Evening Post,* 1930; Movie Columnist, *Los Angeles Record,* 1931-34; Reporter, Associated Press, 1934-37; Correspondent, Tokyo (Japan), 1937-40; Roving Correspondent, Far East, Associated Press, 1940-41; Prisoner of War, 1941-42; War Correspondent, England, North Africa, Italy, India, Middle East, Associated Press, 1942-45; Paris (France) Bureau Chief, Associated Press, 1945-47; Washington (DC) Bureau Chief, Associated Press, 1947-48; Staff member, New York (NY), Associated Press, 1948-72; General Executive, Associated Press, 1949-56.

Selected Works: *Circuit of Conquest,* 1943. *Newsmen Speak: Journalists on their Craft* (with others), 1954. *Southern Schools: Progress and Problems* (with others), 1959. *East Wind Rising,* 1960. *Churchill: Portrait of Greatness,* 1965. *Assassination: The Death of President Kennedy,* 1968. *Dwight D. Eisenhower, a Gauge of Greatness: An Associated Press Biography,* 1969. *The Associated Press Story of Election 1968,* 1969.

Other Awards: George Polk Memorial Award, Long Island University, NY, 1954, 1957. Guggenheim Fellow, 1961. Honorary Degree, Pomona College, CA, 1963. Benjamin Franklin Fellow, Royal Society of Arts, Memorial Archaeology Institute.

For More Information: *Current Biography Yearbook, 1958,* New York: H.W. Wilson Company, 1958; *New York Times,* 17 July (1973): 42; *Contemporary Authors, Volumes 41-44,* Detroit: Gale Research Company, 1979; Rigsby, Gwendolyn Gezelle, A History of Associated Press Pulitzer Prizes (thesis), University of South Carolina, 1993.

Commentary: Relman Morin, along with five other correspondents, won the 1951 International Reporting Pulitzer Prize for their dispatches on the Korean War. Morin had left a general executive job in New York to go to the front.

Morin's second winning effort was his dramatic on-the-spot coverage (from a glass phone booth across the street) of mob violence that broke out in Little Rock, Arkansas on September 23, 1957, during that city's school integration crisis. He did not limit himself to that one incident, but followed up with stories that looked into the significance of the riots and reaction to the incident throughout the South.

Fred Sparks   615

Birth: May 27, 1915; New York, NY. **Death:** February 18, 1981. **Parents:** Bennett Edward Siegelstein and Fannie (Lukather). **Religion:** Jewish.

Prize: *International Reporting,* 1951: *Chicago Daily News,* Chicago: Chicago Daily News, 1950.

Career: Copyboy, Arthur Brisbane, 1932; Rewriteman and Reporter, Hearst Newspapers, 1941-43; Contributor, *Look* magazine, 1944-46; Editor, *Parade* magazine, 1945; Journalism Instructor, New York University, 1945; Reporter, *Chicago Daily News,* 1946-; Reporter, Columnist, *New York (NY) World-Telegram and Sun.*

Selected Works: *The $20,000,000 Honeymoon: Jackie and Ari's First Year,* 1970.

For More Information: *Newsweek,* 49:8 (25 February 1957): 96+; *New York Times,* 19 February (1981): D19; *Washington Post,* 17 April (1982): A2.

Commentary: Fred Sparks changed his name from Siegelstein when he began his career as a newspaperman. He won a Pulitzer Prize for his dispatches from Korea. He was one of the eight reporters accredited to the Byrd expedition to the South Pole. He covered many of the hot spots of the world for various newspapers and had a theory that "no one ever shoots at a man carrying an umbrella." Thus, he was seen carrying an umbrella even in countries where it hardly ever rained.

He died in 1981 after a two-year battle with cancer. His will was somewhat controversial; he left 10% of his approximately $300,000 estate to the Palestine Liberation Organization. Several groups challenged the bequest in court, and the funds eventually went to the International Committee of the Red Cross to aid Palestinian refugees.

Don Ford Whitehead   616

Birth: April 8, 1908; Inman, VA. **Death:** January 12, 1981. **Parents:** Harry Ford Whitehead and Elizabeth (Bond). **Education:** University of Kentucky. **Spouse:** Marie Patterson (m. 1928, died 1979). **Children:** Ruth.

Prize: *International Reporting,* 1951: Associated Press, 1950. *National Reporting,* 1953: Associated Press, "The Great Deception," 1952.

Career: Reporter, college paper, *Kentucky Kernel;* City Editor, *Harlan (KY) Daily Enterprise,* 1930-34; Reporter, *Knoxville (TN) Journal,* 1934-35; Night Editor, Memphis (TN) Bureau, Associated Press, 1935-; Knoxville (TN) Correspondent, *Associated Press;* Feature Writer, New York (NY), Associated Press, 1941-42; War Correspondent, Associated Press, 1942-45; Hawaii Bureau Chief, Associated Press, 1945-48; Special Correspondent, Political Reporter, Washington (DC), Associated Press, 1948-56; Washington (DC) Bureau Chief, *New York Herald-*

Tribune, 1956-57; Columnist, *Knoxville (TN) News-Sentinel,* 1957-78; Freelance writer.

Selected Works: *The FBI Story: A Report to the People,* 1956. *Journey into Crime,* 1960. *Border Guard: The Story of the United States Customs Service,* 1963. *The Dow Story: The History of the Dow Chemical Company,* 1968. *Attack on Terror: The FBI against the Ku Klux Klan in Mississippi,* 1970.

Other Awards: Medal of Freedom, United States Army, World War II. Honorary Degree, University of Kentucky, 1947. Sigma Delta Chi Award, 1950. George Polk Memorial Award, Long Island University, NY, 1951. Christopher Award, 1957. Freedoms Foundation Award, 1957.

For More Information: *New York Times,* 14 January (1981): B4; Broadbooks, Jon Karl, "Reporting From the Devil's Cauldron: The Wartime Associated Press Dispatches of Don Whitehead" (thesis), Knoxville: University of Tennessee at Knoxville, 1993; Rigsby, Gwendolyn Gezelle, "A History of Associated Press Pulitzer Prizes" (thesis), University of South Carolina, 1993.

Commentary: Don Whitehead, along with five other foreign correspondents, won a Pulitzer Prize for his reporting from Korea. He had also been a war correspondent during World War II and landed with the Allied forces on the Normandy beaches on D-Day. He was the first American reporter to file a story out of liberated Paris, and he covered the atomic bomb tests on Bikini Island. His second Pulitzer Prize, which he won two years after his first, was for covering the "intricate arrangements" of President-elect Eisenhower's trip from New York to Korea.

1952

John Murmann Hightower   617

Birth: September 17, 1909; Coal Creek, TN. **Death:** February 9, 1987. **Parents:** James Edward Hightower and Mary Elizabeth (Murmann). **Education:** University of Tennessee. **Spouse:** Martha Nadine Joiner (m. 1938, died 1983); Shelley H. **Children:** John Murmann, Leslie, James Edward (MJ).

Prize: *International Reporting,* 1952: Associated Press, 1951.

Career: Associate Editor, *Drug Topics Magazine,* 1929-30; Reporter, *Knoxville (TN) News-Sentinel,* 1931-87; Reporter, Editor, Nashville (TN), Associated Press, 1933-36; Washington Bureau, Associated Press, 1936-71; General Reporter, News Editor, Associated Press, 1936-40; Navy Department Correspondent, Associated Press, 1940-42; U.S. Department of State, International Affairs Coverage, Associated Press, 1943-71; Special Correspondent, Associated Press, 1964-71; Associate Professor of Journalism, University of New Mexico at Albuquer-

que, 1971-74; Columnist, *Sante Fe (NM) New Mexican,* 1971-.

Selected Works: *Story of Radar,* 1943. *Eisenhower Administration Project: Columbia University Oral History Collection, Part 5* (with John Luter), 1968.

Other Awards: Raymond Clapper Memorial Award, 1952. Sigma Delta Chi Award, 1952. Overseas Press Club Award, 1955. American Academy Achievement Award for Washington Correspondence, 1970. Commander's Cross Order Merit. Chevalier Legion d'Honneur, France. Hall of Fame, Society of Professional Journalists, Washington, DC, Chapter, 1980. Alumni Academic Hall of Fame, University of Tennessee, 1994.

For More Information: Rigsby, Gwendolyn Gezelle, "A History of Associated Press Pulitzer Prizes" (thesis), University of South Carolina, 1993; *New York Times,* 10 January (1987): B18.

Commentary: John M. Hightower was cited for the sustained quality of his reporting throughout 1951. Some of the stories he covered included the dismissal of General of the Army Douglas MacArthur, truce talks in Korea, and negotiation of the Japanese Peace Treaty. Hightower was a careful and conscientious reporter who as legend has it "checked an inside story given to him by a Secretary of State with two independent sources before sending it out."

1953

Austin Carl Wehrwein   618

Birth: January 12, 1916; Austin, TX. **Parents:** George S. Wehrwein and Anna (Ruby). **Education:** University of Wisconsin: BA. Columbia University, NY: LLB. London School of Economics, England.

Prize: *International Reporting,* 1953: *Milwaukee Journal,* "Canada's New Century," Milwaukee, WI: Milwaukee Journal, 1952.

Career: Reporter, *Milwaukee (WI) Journal,* 1937; Reporter, Washington (DC) United Press International, 1941-43; Served in U.S. Army Air Forces, 1943-45; Staff member, Shanghai Edition *Stars and Stripes,* 1945-46; Reporter, Washington (DC), United Press International, 1946-48; Information Specialist, Economic Co-operation Administration, 1948-51; Financial Writer, *Milwaukee (WI) Journal,* 1951-53; Correspondent, Chicago, *Time* magazine, 1953-55; Reporter, *Chicago Sun-Times,* 1955-56; Financial Editor, *Chicago Sun-Times,* 1956-57; Chicago Bureau Chief, *New York Times,* 1957-66; Editorial Writer, *Minneapolis (MN) Star,* 1966-; Editor, *Observer,* Journal of the Minnesota Newspaper Foundation.

Selected Works: *Canada's New Century,* 1953. *Wisconsin's Balance Sheet,* 1953.

Other Awards: Gavel Award, American Bar Association, 1961, 1971. Distinguished Journalism Award, University of Wisconsin, 1963.

For More Information: *Contemporary Authors, Volumes 77-80,* Detroit: Gale Research Company, 1979; Taft, William H., *Encyclopedia of Twentieth-Century Journalists,* New York: Garland Publishing, 1986.

Commentary: Austin C. Wehrwein's winning articles were published in the *Milwaukee Journal* over a two-month period. The series "Canada's New Century" was popular in both the United States and Canada. His paper reprinted 5,000 copies of the series to distribute to requestors.

1954

Jim Griffing Lucas 619

Birth: June 22, 1914; Checotah, OK. **Death:** July 21, 1970. **Parents:** Jim Bob Lucas Jr. and Effie Lincoln (Griffing). **Religion:** Methodist. **Education:** University of Missouri.

Prize: *International Reporting,* 1954: Scripps-Howard Newspapers, 1953.

Career: Editor, high school newspaper; Reporter, Feature Writer, *Muskogee (OK) Daily Phoenix and Times-Democrat,* 1934-38; News Broadcaster, Muskogee (OK), KBIX, 1936-38; Reporter, Feature Writer, *Tulsa (OK) Tribune,* 1938-42; Combat Correspondent, United States Marine Corps, 1942-45; Correspondent, Scripps-Howard Newspaper Alliance, Washington, DC, 1945-70; Journalism Lecturer, University of Indiana, 1953.

Selected Works: *Combat Correspondent,* 1944. *Betio Benchhead: U.S. Marine's Own Story of the Battle for Tarawa,* 1945. *U.S. Marines on Iwo Jima*

(with others), 1945. *Report from Korea,* 1959. *Dateline: Viet Nam,* 1966. *Agnew: Profile in Conflict,* 1970.

Other Awards: Bronze Star. National Headliners Club Award, 1943. George Polk Memorial Award, Long Island University, NY. 2 Ernie Pyle Awards, 1953. General Omar N. Bradley Gold Medal, Veterans of Foreign Wars, 1953. Korean National Medal. Non Sibi Sed Patriae Medal, Marine Corps Reserves Officers Association. First Annual Fourth Estate Award, American Legion, 1958. First Annual Mark Watson Award, 1969. Honorary Member, American Seventh Division.

For More Information: *New York Times,* 22 July (1970): 41; Taft, William H., *Encyclopedia of Twentieth-Century Journalists,* New York: Garland Publishing, 1986.

Commentary: Jim G. Lucas's excellent reporting from Korea and his coverage of the war won him a Pulitzer Prize. He was a veteran combat correspondent who covered World War II for the Marines. He stayed at the front of a battle to gather his information, and he believed, "It's not your war until you've been shot at." After the Korean war, he covered the "Little Switch" and "Big Switch"—the returning of American prisoners of war.

1955

Harrison Evans Salisbury 620

Birth: November 14, 1908; Minneapolis, MN. **Death:** July 5, 1993. **Parents:** Percy Pritchard Salisbury and Georgiana (Evans). **Education:** University of Minnesota: AB. **Spouse:** Mary Hollis (m. 1933, div.); Charlotte Young Rand (m. 1964). **Children:** Michael, Stephan (MH).

Prize: *International Reporting,* 1955: *New York Times,* New York: New York Times, 1954.

Career: Editor, college paper, *Minnesota Daily;* Night staff member, St. Paul (MN), United Press International; Reporter, *Minneapolis (MN) Journal,* 1928-29; Correspondent, St. Paul (MN), Chicago (IL), Washington (DC), and New York (NY), United Press International, 1930-43; London (England) Bureau Manager, United Press International, 1943; Moscow (Russia), United Press International, 1944; Foreign News Editor, United Press International, 1944-48; Correspondent, Moscow (Russia), *New York Times,* 1949-54; Reporter, New York (NY), *New York Times,* 1954-63; Assistant Managing Editor, *New York Times,* 1964-72; Associate Editor, *New York Times,* 1972-75; Op-Ed Page Editor, *New York Times,* 1970-75.

Selected Works: *Russia on the Way,* 1946. *American in Russia,* 1955. *The Shook-Up Generation,* 1958. *To Moscow and Beyond: A Reporter's Narrative,* 1960. *Moscow Journal: The End of Stalin,* 1961. *The Northern Palmyra Affair,* 1962. *A New Russia?,* 1962. *Orbit of China,* 1967. *Behind the Lines: Hanoi,* 1967. *The Soviet Union: The Fifty Years,* 1967. *The 900 Days: The Siege of Leningrad,* 1969. *The Coming War between Russia and China,* 1969. *The Many Americas Shall Be One,* 1971. *The Eloquence of Protest: Voices of the 70s,* 1972. *To Peking and Beyond: A Report on the New Asia,* 1973. *The Gates of Hell,* 1975. *Travels around America,* 1976. *Black Night, White Snow: Russia's Revolutions, 1905-1917,* 1978. *The Unknown War,* 1978. *Russia in Revolution, 1900-1930,* 1978. *Without Fear or Favor: The New York Times and Its Times,* 1980. *China: 100 Years of Revolution,* 1983. *A Journey for Our Times: A Memoir,* 1983. *Book Enchained: The Center for the Book Viewpoint Series; 10,* 1984. *The Long March: The Untold Story,* 1985. *A Time of Change: A Reporter's Tale of Our Times,* 1988. *Disturber of the Peace: Memoirs of a Foreign Correspondent,* 1989. *The Great Black Dragon Fire: A Chinese Inferno,* 1989. *Tiananmen Diary: Thirteen Days in June,* 1989. *Essential Liberty: First Amendment Battles for a Free Press* (with others), 1991. *The New Emperors: China in the Era of Mao and Deng,* 1992. *Heroes of My Time,* 1993.

Other Awards: Distinguished Achievement Medal, University of Minnesota, 1955. George Polk Memorial Award, Long Island University, NY, 1957, 1967. Sigma Delta Chi Award, 1958. Asian Award, Overseas Press Club, 1967. Sidney Hillman Foundation Award, 1967. Montgomery Scholar, Dartmouth College, 1980. Honorary Degrees: Macalester College, MN, 1967; Maryland Institute, 1967; Assumption College, MA, 1967; University of Portland, OR, 1971; Ursinus College, PA, 1971; Columbia College, IL, 1973; Carleton College, MN, 1976; Grand View

College, IA, 1980; Amherst College, MA, 1985; Tufts University, MA, 1985; Dowling College, NY, 1986; Hofstra University, NY, 1992; Occidental College, CA, 1992.

For More Information: *Current Biography Yearbook, 1955,* New York: H.W. Wilson, 1955; McKerns, Joseph P., *Biographical Dictionary of American Journalism.* New York: Greenwood Press, 1989; *Contemporary Authors, New Revision Series, Volume 30,* Detroit: Gale Research Company, 1990.

Commentary: Harrison E. Salisbury's series of 14 articles, "Russia Re-Viewed," was based on his six years as a Moscow correspondent. The series contributed to the American understanding of Russia. He also took photographs that were published with the series. Salisbury led a long and distinguished career in journalism and was a prolific writer.

1956

Frank Conniff   621

Birth: April 24, 1914; Danbury, CT. **Death:** May 25, 1971. **Parents:** Andrew Conniff and Lucy. **Religion:** Roman Catholic. **Education:** University of Virginia. **Spouse:** Mary Elizabeth Murray (m. 1951). **Children:** Anthony, Michael, Frank, Rex, Lucy.

Prize: *International Reporting,* 1956: International News Service, 1955.

Career: Copyboy, *Danbury (CT) News Times;* Sports Writer, *Danbury (CT) News Times;* War Correspondent, International News Service, WWII; Staff member, *New York Journal-American;* National Editor, Hearst Newspapers, 1958-66; Democratic Candidate, U.S. House of Representatives, 1964; Editor, *New York City World-Journal Tribune,* 1966-67; Syndicated columnist, "East Side, West Side;" General Director, Hearst Headlines Service.

Selected Works: *How Russia Is Winning the Peace—Uncensored* (with others), 1958.

Other Awards: George R. Holmes Memorial Award for Overseas Reporting, 1944, 1947. Overseas Press Club Award, 1958.

For More Information: *New York Times,* 27 May (1971): 42; Riley, Sam G., *Biograpical Dictionary of American Newspaper Columnists,* Westport, CT: Greenwood Press, 1995.

Commentary: Frank Conniff, William Randolph Hearst Jr., and J. Kingsbury-Smith's series of interviews with top Soviet leaders gave the first indication of what Soviet policy would be for the new rulers of Russia. The group interviewed Premier Nokolai A. Bulganin, Nikita S. Khrushchev, V.M. Molotov, and Marshal Georgi Zhukov.

William Randolph Hearst Jr.   622

Birth: January 27, 1908; New York, NY. **Death:** May 14, 1993. **Parents:** William Randolph Hearst and Millicent Veronica (Willson). **Religion:** Episcopalian. **Education:** University of California, Berkeley. **Spouse:** Austine McDonnell (m. 1948, died 1991). **Children:** William Randolph III, John Augustine Chilton.

Prize: *International Reporting,* 1956: International News Service, 1955.

Career: Reporter, *New York American,* 1928-36; Reporter, Assistant to City Editor, Publisher, *New York American,* 1936-37; Publisher, *New York (NY) Journal-American,* 1937-56; War correspondent, 1943-45; Editor-in-Chief, Hearst Newspapers, 1955-.

Selected Works: *Ask Me Anything: Our Adventures with Khrushchev,* 1960. *The Hearsts: Father and Son* (with Jack Casserly), 1991.

Other Awards: Hal Boyle Award, Overseas Press Club, 1957. Overseas Press Club Award, 1958. Honorary Degree, University of Alaska.

For More Information: *Contemporary Authors, Volume 139,* Detroit: Gale Research Company, 1993; *Dictionary of Literary Biography, Volume 127,* Detroit: Gale Research Company, 1993; *New York Times,* 15 May (1993): A26; *New York Times,* 16 May (1993): A40.

Commentary: William Randolph Hearst Jr., Frank Conniff, and J. Kingsbury-Smith won a Pulitzer Prize for their exclusive interviews with top Soviet officials in February 1955.

Joseph Kingsbury-Smith   623

Birth: February 20, 1908; New York, NY. **Parents:** William Barstow Kingsbury-Smith and Maria (Jordan). **Education:** University of London, England.

Spouse: Eileen King (m. 1940). **Children:** Eileen, Diane.

Prize: *International Reporting,* 1956: International News Service, 1955.

Career: Copyboy, Cub Reporter, International News Service, 1924-26; Foreign Desk Reporter, United Press International, 1926-27; Reporter, London (England), International News Service, 1927-31; Reporter, U.S. Senate, International News Service, 1931-32; Reporter, State Department, War Department, and Navy Department, International News Service, 1932-36; London (England) Bureau Manager, International News Service, 1936-; Executive Assistant, Director of Foreign Service, London (England) Bureau, International News Service, 1940; Executive Assistant, Director of State Department, International News Service, 1941-44; European General Manager, International News Service and International News Photos, 1944-55; General Manager, International News Service and International News Photos, 1955-58; Vice President, Director, Hearst Consolidated Corporation, 1955-58; Publisher, *New York Journal-American,* 1959-66; Vice President, European Director, Hearst Corporation, 1966-76; Chief Foreign Writer, Hearst Newspapers and King Features Syndicate, 1966-76; National Editor, Hearst Newspapers, 1976-; Vice President, Hearst Corporation.

Other Awards: Legion of Honor. Knight of Malta. Knight Commander, Order St. Denis of Zahte. Distinguished Service Award, Sigma Delta Chi, 1941. George R. Holmes Memorial Award, 1941-49. National Headliners Club Award, 1941, 1947, 1950. George Polk Award, Long Island University, NY, 1950. United States Government Distinguished Service Award, 1961. Hall of Fame, Society of Professional Journalists, 1992.

Commentary: J. Kingsbury-Smith, William Randolph Hearst Jr., and Frank Conniff's exclusive interviews with top Soviet officials provided "the first definite indications of what the policy of the new rulers of Russia would be on the great issues of war and peace."

1957

Russell Jones   624

Birth: January 5, 1918; Minneapolis, MN. **Death:** June 9, 1979. **Parents:** Lewis Russell Jones and Elizabeth J. (McLeod). **Spouse:** Martha Sennyey von Kissenye (m. 1955). **Children:** Stepchildren: Jozsef Karolyi von Kissenye, Erzsebet Karoli von Nagykaroly (MK).

Prize: *International Reporting,* 1957: United Press International, 1956.

Career: Reporter, *Stillwater (MN) Post Messenger;* Reporter, Radio Columnist, *St. Paul (MN) Dispatch,* 1938-41; Co-Founder, Combat Correspondent, *Stars and Stripes,* 1942-45; Reporter, *New York Daily News;* Reporter, 1947-48; Co-Owner, Editor, (Germany), *Weekend Magazine;* Reporter, Paris (France), 1948-49; Correspondent, London (England), Prague (Czechoslovakia), Vienna (Austria), Frankfurt (Germany), Chief Eastern European Correspondent, United Press International, 1949-58; Correspondent, Middle East, CBS News, 1958-; Beirut (Lebanon) Bureau Chief, Tel Aviv (Israel), Moscow (Russia), ABC News, ?-1977.

Selected Works: *This Is Germany* (with others), 1950.

Other Awards: Sigma Delta Chi Award. George Polk Memorial Award, Long Island University, NY, 1957.

For More Information: *Current Biography Yearbook, 1957,* New York: H.W. Wilson Company, 1957; *New York Times,* 11 June (1979): section 4, 8.

Commentary: Russell Jones was the only American newspaper reporter to remain in Budapest when the Russian tanks rolled in to crush the Hungarian freedom fighters in 1956. He stayed in the country to cover the revolt until he was expelled by the government.

1958

New York Times
Full entry appears as **#375** under "Explanatory Journalism," 1986.

1959

Joseph George Martin   625
Birth: May 9, 1915; New York, NY. **Death:** January 26, 1981. **Parents:** Patrick Martin and Anne (Scully). **Spouse:** Josephine DiLorenzo (m. 1953). **Children:** Alison.

Prize: *International Reporting,* 1959: *New York Daily News,* New York: New York Daily News, 1958.

Career: Copyboy, *New York (NY) Daily News,* 1933-36; Reporter, *New York Daily News,* 1936-1943; Served in U.S. Army Air Forces, 1943-46; Reporter, *New York Daily News,* 1946-80.

Other Awards: Society of Silurians Award, 1949. George Polk Memorial Award, Long Island University, NY, 1953. Page One Award, New York Newspaper Guild, 1956-57, 1959.

For More Information: *New York Times,* 27 January (1981): B19.

Commentary: Joseph Martin and Philip Santora's ten-part series focused attention on the brutality in Cuba under then-president Fulgencio Batista.

Philip Joseph Santora   626
Birth: July 29, 1911; New York, NY. **Death:** March 28, 1993. **Education:** Syracuse University, NY. New York University. Sorbonne University, Paris, France. **Spouse:** Filamena S. (m. 1940). **Children:** Collette Courtney, Elizabeth DeForge.

Prize: *International Reporting,* 1959: *New York Daily News,* New York: New York Daily News, 1958.

Career: Boxing instructor; Hospital admitting clerk; Copyboy, Reporter, *New York Daily Mirror,* 1938-54; Reporter, *New York Daily News,* 1954-73.

Selected Works: *Animals and Statues I Have Interviewed,* 1969.

Other Awards: Society of Silurians Award, 1970, 1973.

For More Information: *New York Times,* 31 March (1993): B10.

Commentary: Phil Santora and Joseph Martin won a Pulitzer Prize for their reports on Cuba under the regime of Fulgencio Batista. Phil Santora is also known for his stories based on interviews with non-speaking subjects such as animals and statues.

1960

Abraham Michael Rosenthal 627

Birth: May 2, 1922; Sault Sainte Marie, Ontario, Canada. **Parents:** Harry Rosenthal and Sarah (Dickstein). **Education:** City College, NY: BS. **Spouse:** Ann Marie Burke (m. 1949, div.); Shirley Lord Anderson (m. 1987). **Children:** Jonathan Harry, Daniel Michael, Andrew Mark (AB).

Prize: *International Reporting,* 1960: *New York Times,* New York: New York Times, 1959.

Career: College Correspondent, *New York Times,* 1943; City Staff member, *New York Times,* 1944-46; Reporter, United Nations Staff, *New York Times,* 1946-54; Correspondent, Indian Subcontinent, *New York Times,* 1954-58; Correspondent, Warsaw (Poland), *New York Times,* 1958-59; Correspondent, Geneva (Switzerland), *New York Times,* 1959-61; Correspondent, Japan, *New York Times,* 1961-63; Metropolitan Editor, *New York Times,* 1963-66; Assistant Managing Editor, *New York Times,* 1966-68; Associate Managing Editor, *New York Times,* 1968-69; Managing Editor, *New York Times,* 1969-77; Executive Editor, *New York Times,* 1977-86; Associate Editor, *New York Times,* 1986-87; Columnist, *New York Times,* 1986-.

Other Awards: Overseas Press Club Award, 1956, 1959, 1965. George Polk Memorial Award, Long Island University, NY, 1960, 1965. Page One Award, Newspaper Guild of New York, 1960. New York County Bar Association Award, 1978. National Press Foundation Award, 1987. Honorary Degrees: City College of New York, 1974; State University of New York, 1984.

For More Information: *New York Times,* 12 October (1986): 1; Goulden, Joseph C., *Fit to Print:*

A.M. Rosenthal and His Times, Secaucus, NJ: L. Stuart, 1988.

Commentary: A.M. Rosenthal became a campus correspondent for the *New York Times* while attending the City College of New York. He has been with the *New York Times* ever since, rising through the ranks to become executive editor in 1977. He became a United States citizen in 1951.

Rosenthal won a Pulitzer Prize "for his perceptive and authoritative reporting from Poland" in 1959. He was expelled from that country, not because of false reporting, but due to the depth of his reporting into Polish affairs.

1961

Lynn Louis Heinzerling 628

Birth: October 23, 1906; Birmingham, OH. **Death:** November 21, 1983. **Parents:** Louis Heinzerling and Grace (Lawrence). **Education:** Akron University, OH. Ohio Wesleyan University. **Spouse:** Agnes C. Dengate (m. 1934). **Children:** Lynn Louis, Larry.

Prize: *International Reporting,* 1961: Associated Press, 1960.

Career: Reporter, *Cleveland (OH) Plain Dealer,* 1928-33; Editor, Cleveland (OH) and New York (NY), Associated Press, 1934-38; Foreign Correspondent, Berlin (Germany), Danzig (Poland), Helsinki (Finland), Associated Press, 1938-41; Correspondent, Associated Press, New York City 1942; Correspondent, London (England) and Cairo (Egypt), Associated Press, 1943; Army Correspondent, Italy and Austria, Associated Press, 1943-45; Vienna (Austria) Bureau Chief, Associated Press, 1945-46; Correspondent, Berlin (Germany), Associated Press, 1947-48; Geneva (Switzerland) Bureau Chief, Associated

Press, 1948-57; Johannesburg (South Africa), Associated Press, 1957-61; Assistant London (England) Bureau Chief, Associated Press, 1961-63; Columbus (OH) Bureau Chief, Associated Press, 1963-64; Chief, British and U.S. Army Operations, Africa, Associated Press, 1964-72; Freelance writer and lecturer, 1972-83.

Other Awards: Overseas Press Club Award, 1961.

For More Information: *New York Times,* 3 December (1983): 12; Rigsby, Gwendolyn Gezelle, A History of Associated Press Pulitzer Prizes (thesis), University of South Carolina, 1993.

Commentary: Lynn Heinzerling's coverage of the struggle for independence in the Congo won him a Pulitzer Prize. He had been reporting from central and southern Africa for three years and was about to be transferred when fighting and heavy rioting broke out. He stayed until November 1960 to cover the story.

Heinzerling witnessed the outbreak of World War II when the Germans seized Danzig on September 1, 1939. He covered the war from England, Egypt, Italy, and Germany. He spent his career on foreign assignments except for a brief time in Columbus, Ohio.

1962

Walter Lippmann 629

Birth: September 23, 1889; New York, NY. **Death:** December 14, 1974. **Parents:** Jacob Lippmann and Daisy (Baum). **Education:** Harvard University, MA: AB, Phi Beta Kappa. **Spouse:** Faye Albertson (m. 1917, div. 1938); Helen Byrne Armstrong (m. 1938).

Prize: *Special Awards and Citations: Journalism,* 1958: *New York Herald-Tribune,* New York:

New York Herald-Tribune, 1957. **International Reporting,** 1962: *New York Herald-Tribune* Syndicate, New York: New York Herald-Tribune Syndicate, 1961.

Career: Secretary, *Everybody's Magazine,* 1910; Associate Editor, *Everybody's Magazine;* Executive Secretary, Mayor George R. Lynn, Schenectady (NY), 1912; Founder, *New Republic* magazine, 1914; Associate Editor, *New Republic* magazine, 1914-17; Assistant to U.S. Secretary of War Newton D. Baker, 1917; Secretary, Governmental Organization, 1917; Secretary, The Inquiry, 1917-18; Member of Military Intelligence, U.S. Army, 1918-19; Staff member, *New Republic* magazine, 1919; Staff member, *New York World,* 1921-29; Editor, *New York World,* 1929-31; Columnist, *New York Herald-Tribune,* 1931-62; Columnist, *Newsweek,* 1962-.

Selected Works: *A Preface to Politics,* 1913. *Drift and Mastery an Attempt to Diagnose the Current Unrest,* 1914. *The Stakes of Diplomacy,* 1915. *The Political Scene,* 1919. *Liberty and the News,* 1920. *Public Opinion,* 1922. *Men of Destiny,* 1927. *American Inquisitors: A Commentary on Dayton and Chicago,* 1928. *A Preface to Morals,* 1929. *The Phantom Public,* 1930. *The United States in World Affairs, 1931: An Account of American Foreign Relations,* 1932. *Interpretations, 1931-32,* 1932. *The Method of Freedom,* 1934. *The Supreme Court: Independent or Controlled?,* 1937. *An Inquiry into the Principles of the Good Society,* 1937. *U.S. Foreign Policy: Shield of the Republic,* 1943. *U.S. War Aims,* 1945. *What Kind of Germany Does America Want?,* 1946. *The Cold War, a Study in U.S. Foreign Policy,* 1947. *Isolation and Alliances: An American Speaks to the British,* 1952. *Essays in the Public Philosophy,* 1956. *The Communist World and Ours,* 1959. *The Coming Tests with Russia,* 1961. *Western Unity and the Common Market,* 1962. *Public Opinion,* 1965. *The Essential Lippmann: A Political Philosophy for Liberal Democracy,* 1982.

Other Awards: Decorated Commander, Legion of Honor, France, 1942. Officer, Order of Leopold, Belgium, 1947. Knight's Cross, Order of St. Olav, Norway, 1950. Commander, Order of Orange Nassau, Netherlands, 1952. Overseas Press Club Award, 1953, 1955, 1959. George Foster Peabody Award, 1962. Presidential Medal of Freedom, 1964. Gold Medal, National Institute of Arts and Letters, 1965. Bronze Medallion, City of New York, NY, 1974. Honorary Degrees; Wake Forest College, NC, 1926; University of Wisconsin, 1927; Dartmouth College, NH, 1932; Columbia University, NY, 1932; University of California, 1933; Union College, NY, 1933; Wesleyan University, CT, 1934; Oglethorpe College, GA, 1934; University of Michigan, 1934; George Washington University, Washington, DC, 1935; Amherst College, MA, 1935; University of Rochester,

NY, 1936; College of William and Mary, VA, 1937; Drake University, IA, 1937; Harvard University, MA, 1934; University of Chicago, 1955; New School for Social Research, NY, 1955.

For More Information: Weingast, David Elliott, *Walter Lippmann: A Study in Personal Journalism,* New Brunswick, NJ: Rutgers University Press, 1949; *The Reminiscences of Walter Lippmann, Columbia University Oral History Collection,* Part 2, Number 118, 1964; *Conversations with Walter Lippmann,* Boston: Little, Brown, 1965; Stockstill, Michael Arnold, *Walter Lippmann: His Rise to Fame, 1889-1945,* Starkville, MS: 1970; Steel, Ronald, *Walter Lippmann and the American Century,* London: Bodley Head, 1980; Ricclo, Barry Daniel, *Walter Lippmann: Odyssey of a Liberal,* New Brunswick, NJ: Transaction, 1994.

Commentary: Walter Lippmann, an outstanding journalist and thinker, was a two-time winner of the Pulitzer Prize. In 1958, he was presented a special citation for his internationally syndicated column. Those columns included in his entry were dated June 6, 25; July 4, 10, 23; August 27; October 1, 8, 10, 17; November 26; and December 3, 1957. His second award was for his exclusive interview with Soviet Premier Nikita S. Khrushchev.

Lippmann had a long and varied career. He was a member of the Thinkers, an early think tank. That group developed six of the ideas that became part of President Wilson's Fourteen Points.

1963

Harold Victor Hendrix 630

Birth: February 14, 1922; Kansas City, MO. **Parents:** Clarence Virgil Hendrix and Grace Frances (Lee).

Education: Rockhurst College, MO. **Spouse:** Mary Frances Sheehan (m. 1944). **Children:** Kathleen.

Prize: *International Reporting,* 1963: *Miami News,* Miami, FL: Miami News, 1962.

Career: Staff member, *Kansas City (MO) Star,* 1944-57; Assignment Editor, Latin American Correspondent, *Kansas City (MO) Star,* 1947-57; Latin American Editor, *Miami (FL) News/Cox Newspapers,* 1957-63; Latin American Correspondent, Scripps-Howard Newspaper Alliance, 1963-67; Director Corporate Relations, Latin America, ITT Corporation, 1967-73; Director of Development, Latin America, IHC/PanAm, 1973-76; Vice-President Corporate Relations, Wackenhut Corporation, 1978-85.

For More Information: *New York Times,* 7 May (1963): 35.

Commentary: Hal Hendrix's winning series of stories was on the large Russian build-up in Cuba in 1962. He reported on the growing number of MIG-21s and the installation of missile launching pads.

1964

Malcolm Wilde Browne 631

Birth: April 17, 1931; New York, NY. **Parents:** Douglas Granzow Browne and Dorothy Rutledge (Wilde). **Education:** Swarthmore College, PA. New York University. **Spouse:** Huynh thi Le Lieu (m. 1966). **Children:** Wendy, Timothy.

Prize: *International Reporting,* 1964: Associated Press, 1963.

Career: Member of New York (NY) Firm of Consulting Chemists and Engineers, 1951-56; Korean Correspondent, U.S. Army, Pacific *Stars and Stripes,* 1956-58; Reporter and Copy Desk Editor, *Middletown (NY) Daily Record,* 1958-60; Newsman, Baltimore (MD), Associated Press, 1960-61; Foreign News Desk, New York, Associated Press; Indochina Bureau Chief, Saigon (Vietnam), Associated Press, 1961-65; Correspondent, Saigon (Vietnam), ABC, 1965-66; Freelance writer, 1966-67; Correspondent, Buenos Aires (Argentina), *New York Times,* 1967-70; Correspondent, Pakistan-Iran-Afghanistan Region, *New York Times,* 1971-72; Correspondent, Indochina, *New York Times,* 1972-73; Correspondent, Belgrade (Yugoslavia), *New York Times,* 1974; Saigon (Vietnam) Bureau Chief, *New York Times,* 1975-76; Science Correspondent, *New York Times,* 1977-81; Senior Editor, *Discover* magazine, 1981-84; Science Writer, *New York Times,* 1985-; Persian Gulf Correspondent, *New York Times,* 1991; McGraw Professor of Writing, Princeton University (NJ), 1995.

Selected Works: *The New Face of War,* 1965. *Muddy Boots and Red Socks: A War Reporter's Life,* 1993.

Other Awards: World Press Photo Award, 1963. Overseas Press Club Award, 1964. Sigma Delta Chi Award, 1964. Louis M. Lyons Award, 1964. National Headliners Club Award, 1964. Associated Press Managing Editors Award, 1964. Edward R. Murrow Fellow, Council on Foreign Relations, Columbia University, NY, 1966-67. George Polk Memorial Award, Long Island University, NY. Grady-Stack Gold Medal, American Chemical Society, 1992. Science-Writing Prize, Acoustical Society of America.

For More Information: *New York Times,* 5 May (1964): 39; Taft, William H., *Encyclopedia of Twentieth-Century Journalists,* New York: Garland Publishing, Inc., 1986; Rigsby, Gwendolyn Gezelle, A History of Associated Press Pulitzer Prizes (thesis), University of South Carolina, 1993; Prochnau, William, *Once Upon a Distant War,* New York: Times Books, 1995.

Commentary: Malcolm W. Browne sent his stories out of Vietnam in old newspapers and in the hands of travelers. His daily dispatches of the war and his coverage of the overthrow of Vietnam President Ngo Dinh Diem won him and his colleague David Halberstam a Pulitzer Prize for International Reporting. Browne wrote about the Buddhist monk who immolated himself in protest of the Diem regime. The photograph he took of the event won the World Press Photo Contest in 1963.

David Halberstam   632

Birth: April 10, 1934; New York, NY. **Parents:** Charles A. Halberstam and Blanche (Levy). **Education:** Harvard College, MA: AB. **Spouse:** Elzbieta Tchizevska (m. 1965, div. 1977); Jean Sandness Butler (m. 1979). **Children:** Julia (JB).

Prize: *International Reporting,* 1964: *New York Times,* New York: New York Times, 1963.

Career: Managing Editor, college paper, *Crimson;* Reporter, *West Point (MS) Daily Times Leader,* 1955-56; Reporter, *Nashville (TN) Tennessean,* 1956-60; Washington (DC) Bureau, *New York Times,* 1960-61; Correspondent, Congo, *New York Times,* 1961-62; Correspondent, South Vietnam, *New York Times,* 1962-63; Metropolitan Staff, *New York Times,* 1964-65; Correspondent, Warsaw (Poland), *New York Times,* 1965-66; Contributing Editor, *Harper's* Magazine, 1967-71; Author, 1971-.

Selected Works: *The Noblest Roman,* 1961. *The Making of a Quagmire,* 1965. *One Very Hot Day: A Novel,* 1967. *The Unfinished Odyssey of Robert Kennedy,* 1968. *Ho,* 1971. *The Best and the Brightest,* 1972. *CBS: The Network and the News,* 1972. *How It All Began: Working Paper No. 5,* 1973. *The Powers That Be,* 1979. *The Breaks of the Game,* 1981. *The Amateurs,* 1985. *The Reckoning,* 1986. *The Summer of '49,* 1989. *The Next Century,* 1991. *The Fifties,* 1993. *October 1964,* 1994. *The Children,* 1998.

Other Awards: Page One Award, Newspaper Guild of New York, 1962. George Polk Memorial Award, Long Island University, NY, 1964. Louis M. Lyons Award, 1964. Overseas Press Club Award, 1973. Fellow of the Society Award, Sigma Delta Chi, 1983. Political Book Award, 1986: *The Reckoning,* New York: Morrow, 1986.

For More Information: *Contemporary Authors, Volumes 69-72,* Detroit: Gale Research Company, 1978: 296; Taft, William H., *Encyclopedia of Twentieth-Century Journalists,* New York: Garland Publishing, Inc., 1986; Rothmeyer, Karen, *Winning Pulitzers: The Stories Behind Some of the Best News Coverage of Our Time,* New York: Columbia University Press, 1991: 113-122; *Time,* 4 November (1995): 73; Prochnau, William W., *Once Upon a Distant Star,* New York: Times Books, 1995.

Commentary: David Halberstam and Malcolm W. Browne both won Pulitzer Prizes for their reporting from Vietnam in 1963. Halberstam managed to send regular and accurate dispatches from Southeast Asia despite official censorship and a tapped telephone.

Halberstam left the *New York Times* in 1971 to pursue a writing career full-time. He has written over a dozen books.

1965

Joseph Arnold Livingston   633

Birth: February 10, 1905; New York, NY. **Death:** December 25, 1989. **Parents:** Solomon J. Livingston and Maud. **Education:** University of Michigan: BA. **Spouse:** Rosalie Logise Frenger (m. 1927). **Children:** Patricia.

Prize: *International Reporting,* 1965: *Philadelphia Bulletin,* "The Power Pull of the Dollar," Philadelphia, PA: Philadelphia Bulletin, 1964.

Career: Staff member, New York (NY), Daily Newspapers, 1925-30; Columnist and Executive Editor, *New York Daily Investment News,* 1931-34; Public Utilities Editor, *Financial World Magazine,* 1934-35; Economist, *Business Week* Magazine, 1936-42; Staff member, *War Progress,* (Confidential Weekly Report to the War Production Board), 1942-45; Staff member, War Mobilization and Reconversion Under James F. Byrnes and General Clay; Syndicated Columnist, "Business Outlook," 1945-; Financial Editor, *Philadelphia (PA) Record,* 1946-47; Columnist, *Washington (DC) Post,* 1946-47; Economic Columnist, *Philadelphia (PA) Bulletin,* 1948-68; Instructor, Temple University (PA), 1971; Columnist, *Philadelphia (PA) Inquirer,* 1972-89.

Selected Works: *Reconversion: The Job Ahead; Public Affairs Pamphlet, No. 94,* 1944. *The American Stockholder,* 1958.

Other Awards: Reward for Excellence in Reporting, Temple University, PA. Gerald Loeb Award, Anderson Graduate School of Management, University of California, Los Angeles, Four Times. E.W. Fairchild Award, Overseas Press Club. Hancock Award, Two Times. Honorary Degree, Temple University, PA, 1966.

For More Information: *New York Times,* 27 December (1989): D18; *Washington Post,* 28 December (1989).

Commentary: Joseph A. Livingston, a longtime financial writer and editor, won a Pulitzer Prize for his series of articles that described the economic defection of Eastern Europe from Russia. The series was a result of a 10-week journey behind the Iron Curtain.

Livingston's economic and financial column was syndicated in over 50 newspapers in 1989. His twice-yearly survey of economists was one of the nation's first consensus economic forecasts. He started the survey of economists in 1946. The Philadelphia Federal Reserve digitized the information from his surveys in 1978 and continues to produce the Livingston survey.

1966

Peter Gregg Arnett 634

Birth: November 13, 1934; Riverton, New Zealand.
Parents: Eric Lionel Arnett and Jane (Gregg).
Spouse: Nina Nguyen (m. 1964, div.). **Children:** Andrew Kim, Elsa Christina.

Prize: *International Reporting,* 1966: Associated Press, 1965.

Career: Staff member, *Invercargill (New Zealand) Southland Times,* 1951-54; Served in New Zealand Army, 1952-54; Staff member, *Standard Wellington (New Zealand),* 1955-56; Reporter, *Sydney (Australia) Sun,* 1957; Associate Editor, *Bangkok (Thailand) World,* 1958-60; Editor, *Vientian (Laos) Vientiane World,* 1960; Correspondent, Jakarta (Indonesia), Associated Press, 1961-62; Correspondent, Vietnam, Associated Press, 1962-70; Correspondent, New York (NY), Associated Press, 1970-81; International Correspondent, Cable News Network, 1981-88; Moscow (Russia) Bureau Chief, Cable News Network; National/International Security Correspondent, Cable News Network, 1988-90; Jerusalem Correspondent, Cable News Network, 1990-; Correspondent, Cable News Network.

Selected Works: *Live from the Battlefield: From Vietnam to Baghdad: 35 Years in the World's War Zones,* 1994. *Requiem: By the Photographers Who Died in Vietnam and Indochina* (with others), 1997.

Other Awards: Overseas Press Club Award, 1968, 1970. George Polk Memorial Award, Long Island University, NY, 1970. Sigma Delta Chi Award,

1970, 1983. Lifetime Achievement Award, Overseas Press Club, 1991. Fellow, Society of Professional Journalists, 1991. Lifetime Achievement Award, National Press Club of New Zealand, 1996. Award for Cable Excellence, National Academy of Cable Programmers. Achievement Award, National Association of Black Journalists.

For More Information: Taft, William H., *Encyclopedia of Twentieth-Century Journalists,* New York: Garland Publishing, Inc., 1986; *Los Angeles Times,* 27 (1991): E1; *Washington Post,* 20 (1991): F1; Rigsby, Gwendolyn Gezelle, "A History of Associated Press Pulitzer Prizes" (thesis), University of South Carolina, 1993.

Commentary: Peter Arnett is best known for his coverage of the Persian Gulf War for the *Cable News Network.* He was the only Western reporter working out of Baghdad, Iraq. He joined the cable television network in 1981 after working for the Associated Press for 20 years. It was his coverage of the Vietnam War that won him a Pulitzer Prize. Some of the stories he covered included the Vietnamese farmer who had a live grenade imbedded in his back, phony battles staged for film by the United States Information Service, and the use of tear gas by Vietnamese troops.

1967

Robert John Hughes 635

Birth: April 28, 1930; Neath, South Wales. **Parents:** Evan John Hughes and Dellis May (Williams). **Education:** School of Stationers and Newspapermakers, London. **Spouse:** Vera Elizabeth Pockman (m. 1955, div. 1987); Peggy Janeane Jordan (m. 1988). **Children:** Wendy Elizabeth, Mark Evan (VP); Evan Jordan (PJ).

Prize: *International Reporting,* 1967: *Christian Science Monitor,* Boston: Christian Science Monitor, 1966.

Career: Reporter, *Durban (South Africa) Natal Mercury,* 1946-49; Reporter, *London (England) Daily Mirror,* 1950-51; Editor, *Reuters;* News Editor, London (England) News Agencies; Bureau Chief and Sub-Editor, *Durban (South Africa) Natal Mercury,* 1954; Correspondent, Africa, *Christian Science Monitor,* 1955-61; Assistant Foreign Editor, *Christian Science Monitor,* 1962-64; Far East Correspondent, *Christian Science Monitor,* 1964-70; Managing Editor, *Christian Science Monitor,* 1970; Editor, *Christian Science Monitor,* 1970-79; Manager, Publisher, *Christian Science Monitor,* 1976-79; President and Publisher, Hughes Newspaper Incorporated, 1979-81; Associate Director, U.S. Information Agency, Washington, (DC), 1981-82; Director, Washington (DC), *Voice of America,* 1982; Chief Spokesman, Department of State, Washington (DC),

1982-85; Columnist, *Christian Science Monitor,* 1985-95; Adjunct Professor of Journalism, Boston University (MA), 1986-87; Professor of Journalism, Brigham Young University (UT), 1991-96; Director International Media Studies Program, Brigham Young University (UT), 1991-96; Assistant Secretary-General / Director of Communications, United Nations, 1995; Editor, *Deseret News (UT),* 1997-.

Selected Works: *South Africa: After 50 Years,* 1959. *The New Face of Africa South of the Sahara,* 1961. *Indonesia Upheaval,* 1967. *The Junk Merchants: The International Narcotics Traffic,* 1971.

Other Awards: Nieman Fellow, Harvard University, MA, 1961-62. Overseas Press Club Award, 1967, 1970. Yankee Quill Award, Society of Professional Journalists. Service to Journalism Award, University of Utah Department of Communications, 1997. Honorary Degrees: Colby College, ME; Southern Utah University, 1994.

For More Information: *Washington Post,* 4 August (1982): A17; *Christian Science Monitor,* 25 January (1985): 4; *Editor & Publisher,* 28 December (1996): 20; *Salt Lake Tribune,* 8 February (1997): C1.

Commentary: R. John Hughes won a Pulitzer Prize for his coverage of an attempted Communist coup in Indonesia. He has worked in many different aspects of newspapers, from foreign correspondent to editor. He is currently the first non-Mormon editor of the *Deseret News* in Salt Lake City, Utah.

1968

Alfred Friendly   636

Birth: December 30, 1911; Salt Lake City, UT. **Death:** November 7, 1983. **Parents:** Edward Rosenbaum and Harriet (Friendly). **Education:** Amherst College, MA: AB, Phi Beta Kappa. **Spouse:** Jean Ulman (m. 1937). **Children:** Alfred, Jonathan, Lucinda, Nicholas, Victoria.

Prize: *International Reporting,* 1968: *Washington Post,* Washington, DC: Washington Post, 1967.

Career: Bureau of Foreign and Domestic Commerce member, 1934-35; Member, Office of the Secretary of Commerce, 1936; Reporter, *Washington (DC) Daily News,* 1936-39; Reporter, *Washington (DC) Post,* 1939-52; Served in U.S. Army Air Forces, 1942-45; Director, Overseas Information, Economic Cooperation Administration, 1948-49; Correspondent, Washington (DC), *London (England) Financial Times,* 1949-52; Assistant Managing Editor, *Washington (DC) Post,* 1952-55; Managing Editor, *Washington (DC) Post,* 1955-65; Vice President, Associated Editor, *Washington (DC) Post,* 1963-66; Foreign Correspondent, London (England), Middle East, Africa, *Washington (DC) Post,* 1966-71.

Selected Works: *Guys on the Ground,* 1944. *Crime and Publicity: The Impact of News on the Administration of Justice* (with Ronald Goldfarb), 1967. *Beaufort of the Admirality: The Life of Sir Francis Beaufort, 1774-1857,* 1977. *The Dreadful Day: The Battle of Manzikert, 1071,* 1981.

Other Awards: Sidney Hillman Foundation Award, 1971. Honorary Degree, Amherst College, MA, 1958.

For More Information: *New York Times,* 8 November (1983): B5; *Washington Post,* 8 November (1983): B5; Taft, William H., *Encyclopedia of Twentieth-Century Journalists,* New York: Garland Publishing, Inc., 1986.

Commentary: Alfred Friendly became a foreign correspondent at the age of 56 after having been his paper's managing editor. He won a Pulitzer Prize for his coverage of the Arab-Israeli War in June 1967. He had first word of an Israeli attack 36 hours prior to the battle and dispatched firsthand accounts of the war. Later, he wrote a thorough analysis of the Six-Day War.

1969

William Klaus Tuohy   637

Birth: October 1, 1926; Chicago, IL. **Parents:** John Marshall Tuohy and Lolita (Klaus). **Education:** DePauw University, IN. Montana School of Mines. Loras College, IA. Northwestern University, IL: BS. **Spouse:** Johanna Iselin (m. 1964). **Children:** Cyril.

Prize: *International Reporting,* 1969: *Los Angeles Times,* Los Angeles, CA: Los Angeles Times, 1968.

Career: Served in U.S. Navy, 1944-46; Copyboy, *San Francisco Chronicle,* 1952; Reporter, Night City Editor, *San Francisco Chronicle,* 1952-59; Reporter, Assistant National Affairs Editor, National Political Correspondent, Saigon (Vietnam) Bureau Chief, *Newsweek,* 1959-66; Correspondent, Vietnam, *Los Angeles Times,* 1966-68; Correspondent, Middle East, *Los Angeles Times,* 1969-71; Rome (Italy) Bureau Chief, *Los Angeles Times,* 1971-77; London (England) Bureau Chief, *Los Angeles Times,* 1977-.

Selected Works: *Dangerous Company: Inside the World's Hottest Trouble Spots with a Pulitzer Prize-Winning War Correspondent,* 1987.

Other Awards: National Headliners Club Award, 1965.

For More Information: *Contemporary Authors, Volume 104,* Detroit: Gale Research Company, 1982; Taft, William H., *Encyclopedia of Twentieth-Century Journalists,* New York: Garland Publishing, 1986.

Commentary: William Tuohy was the fourth correspondent to win a Pulitzer Prize for dispatches from Vietnam. He covered the war for four years prior to winning the award. He traveled the width and the length of South Vietnam from the delta to the demilitarized zone and covered essentially all major operations from the escalation of the war in February 1965.

Tuohy moved on to the Middle East from Vietnam and from there to Europe.

1970

Seymour Myron Hersh   638
Birth: April 8, 1937; Chicago, IL. **Parents:** Isadore Hersh and Dorothy (Margolis). **Education:** University of Chicago, IL: BA, postgraduate studies. **Spouse:** Elizabeth Sarah Klein (m. 1964). **Children:** Matthew, Melissa, Joshua.

Prize: International Reporting, 1970: *Dispatch News Service,* 1969.

Career: Police Reporter, City News Bureau of Chicago, 1959-60; Public Information Officer, U.S. Army; Co-founder, weekly suburban Chicago newspaper; Correspondent, Pierre (SD), United Press International, 1961-63; Correspondent, Chicago (IL), Associated Press, 1963-65; Correspondent, Washington (DC), Associated Press, 1965-66; Pentagon Correspondent, Associated Press, 1966-67; Press Secretary, Senator Eugene McCarthy, 1968; Washington (DC) Bureau, *New York Times,* 1972-75; Investigative Reporter, *New York Times,* 1975-78; Washington (DC) Bureau, *New York Times,* 1979; Writer, 1979-; National Correspondent, *Atlantic Monthly,* 1983-86; Correspondent, *New Yorker Magazine,* 1992-.

Selected Works: *Chemical and Biological Warfare: America's Hidden Arsenal,* 1968. *My Lai 4: A Report on the Massacre and Its Aftermath,* 1970. *Cover-Up: The Army's Secret Investigation of the Massacre at My Lai 4,* 1972. *The Reporter's Obligation: An Address; The John Peter Zenger Award for Freedom of the Press and the People's Right to Know, 1975,* 1976. *The Prize of Power: Kissinger in the Nixon White House,* 1983. *"The Target Is Destroyed": What Really Happened to Flight 007 and What America Knew about It,* 1986. *The Samson Option: Israel's Nuclear Arsenal and American Foreign Policy,* 1991. *The Dark Side of Camelot,* 1997.

Other Awards: Worth Bingham Prize, 1970. Distinguished Service Award, Sigma Delta Chi, 1970, 1981. George Polk Memorial Award, Long Island University, NY, 1970, 1973-74, 1981. Front Page Award, New York Newspaper Guild, 1973. Scripps-Howard News Service Award, 1973. Sidney Hillman Foundation Award, 1974. John Peter Zenger Freedom of the Press Award, 1975. *Los Angeles Times* Book Prize in Biography, 1983: *The Prize of Power: Kissinger in the Nixon White House,* New York: Summit Books, 1983. National Book Critics Circle Award in General Nonfiction, 1984: *The Prize of Power: Kissinger in the Nixon White House,* Drew Pearson Prize.

For More Information: Downie Jr., Leonard, *The New Muckrakers,* Washington, D.C.: New Republic Book Company, Inc., 1976: 50-92; Behrens, John C., *The Typewriter Guerrillas: Closeups of 20 Top Investigative Reporters,* Chicago: Nelson-Hall, 1977: 126-135; *Contemporary Authors, New Revision Series, Volume 15,* Detroit: Gale Research Company, 1985; Taft, William H., *Encyclopedia of Twentieth-Century Journalists,* New York: Garland Publishing, Inc., 1986.

Commentary: Seymour Hersh, while not affiliated with an official news agency, uncovered and broke the silence about the massacre that took place in the small Vietnamese village of My Lai. He sold the story to 35 newspapers across the country through Dispatch News Service, which was run by his friend David Obst.

1971

Jimmie Lee Hoagland
Full entry appears as #112 under "Commentary," 1991.

1972

Peter Robert Kann   639
Birth: December 13, 1942; New York, NY. **Parents:** Robert A. Kann and Marie (Breuer). **Education:** Harvard University, MA: BA. **Spouse:** Francesca Mayer (m. 1969, died 1983); Karen Elliot House (m. 1984). **Children:** Hillary Francesca (FM); Adopted: Petra Elliot, Jason Elliot, Jade Elliot (KEH).

Prize: International Reporting, 1972: *Wall Street Journal,* New York: Dow Jones, 1971.

Career: Member of Editorial Board, Political Editor, college paper, *Crimson;* Reporter, Pittsburgh (PA), *Wall Street Journal,* 1964-65; Reporter, Los Angeles (CA), *Wall Street Journal,* 1965-66; Correspondent, Vietnam, *Wall Street Journal,* 1967-68; Asia Correspondent, Hong Kong, *Wall Street Journal,* 1968-75; Publisher and Editor, *Asian Wall Street Journal,* 1976-79; Assistant to Chairman, Dow Jones & Co., 1979-; Associate Publisher, *Wall Street Journal,* 1979-88; Executive Vice President, Dow Jones & Co., 1984-89; Publisher, *Wall Street Journal,* 1989-; President and Chief Operating Officer, Dow Jones & Co., 1989-91; Chairman and Chief Executive Officer, Dow Jones & Co., 1991-.

For More Information: *Washington Post,* 2 March (1997): H1.

Commentary: Peter R. Kann's 15-day war diary with brief vignettes of his experiences at Dacca, along with his correct predictions of the coming breakup of Pakistan, won him a Pulitzer Prize in 1972. His war diary was published later in the *Wall Street Journal.*

1973

Max Frankel   640

Birth: April 3, 1930; Gera, Germany. **Parents:** Jacob A. Frankel and Mary (Katz). **Religion:** Jewish. **Education:** Columbia University, NY: BA, Phi Beta Kappa. Columbia University, NY: MA. **Spouse:** Tobia Brown (m. 1956, died 1987); Joyce Purnick (m. 1988). **Children:** David, Margot, Jonathan (TB).

Prize: *International Reporting,* 1973: *New York Times,* New York: New York Times, 1972.

Career: Editor, college paper, *Spectator;* College Correspondent, *New York Times;* Reporter, *New York Times,* 1952; Served in U.S. Army, 1953-55; Reporter, *New York Times,* 1955-56; Europe Correspondent, *New York Times,* 1956-57; Moscow Bureau, *New York Times,* 1957-60; Chief Washington (DC) Correspondent, *New York Times,* 1961; Diplomatic Correspondent, *New York Times,* 1963-66; White House Correspondent, *New York Times,* 1966-68; Washington (DC) Bureau Chief, *New York Times,* 1968-73; Sunday Editor, *New York Times,* 1973-76; Editorial Page Editor, *New York Times,* 1977-86; Executive Editor, *New York Times,* 1986-94; Communications Columnist, *New York Times,* 1994-.

Other Awards: Overseas Press Club Award, 1965. George Polk Memorial Award, Long Island University, NY, 1970.

For More Information: Taft, William H., *Encyclopedia of Twentieth-Century Journalists,* New York: Garland Publishing, Inc., 1986; McFadden, Robert D., *New York Times,* 8 (1994): A1.

Commentary: Max Frankel was eight when the Nazis deported his family from Germany to Poland. His family moved to the United States two years later. As a college student, he was a campus correspondent for the *New York Times.* He worked for that paper for his entire career, moving up the ranks to executive editor in 1986. He stepped down from that position in 1994 and began writing a column, "Word & Image," for the *New York Times Magazine.*

Frankel won a Pulitzer Prize for his solo coverage of President Richard Nixon's historic visit to China in 1972. During the eight-day trip, he wrote thousands of words daily on the official meetings with Chinese leaders as well as writing a column, "A Reporter's Notebook," which included his own observations on the country.

1974

Hedrick Laurence Smith   641

Birth: July 9, 1933; Kilmacolm, Scotland. **Parents:** Sterling L. Smith and Phebe (Hedrick). **Education:** Williams College, MA: BA, Phi Beta Kappa. **Spouse:** Ann Bickford (m. 1957; div. 1985); Susan Zox (m. 1987). **Children:** Laurel, Jennifer, Sterling, Lesley (AB).

Prize: *International Reporting,* 1974: *New York Times,* New York: New York Times, 1973.

Career: Intelligence Officer, U.S. Air Force, 1956-59; Staff member, Memphis (TN), United Press International, 1959; Staff member, Nashville (TN), United Press International; Staff member, Atlanta (GA), United Press International, 1961-62; Cape Canaveral, United Press International, 1962; Diplomatic Correspondent, Washington (DC), *New York Times,* 1962-63; Correspondent, Saigon (South Vietnam), *New York Times,* 1963-64; Correspondent, Cairo (Egypt), *New York Times,* 1964-66; Correspondent, Washington (DC), *New York Times,* 1966-71; Panelist, PBS-TV *Washington Week in Review,* 1969-; Moscow (Russia) Bureau Chief, *New York Times,* 1971-74; Deputy National Editor, *New York Times,* 1975-75; Washington (DC) Bureau Chief, *New York Times,* 1976-79; Chief Correspondent, Washington (DC), *New York Times,* 1979-85; Visiting Journalist, American Enterprise Institute, 1985-86; Correspondent, Washington (DC), *New York Times Magazine,* 1987-88; Fellow, Foreign Policy Center, School of Advanced International Studies, Johns Hopkins University (MD), 1989-.

Selected Works: *The Russians,* 1976. *Reagan: The Man, the President; Leaders of the World,* 1981. *Counterattack: The U.S. Response to Japan,* 1983. *The Power Game: How Washington Works,* 1988. *The*

New Russians, 1990. *Inside Gorbachev's U.S.S.R.: Cooper-UNL Forum on World Issues,* 1990. *The Media and the Gulf War,* 1992. *Rethinking America,* 1995.

Other Awards: Fulbright Scholarship, Balliol College, Oxford University, England. Nieman Fellow, Harvard University, MA, 1969-70. Overseas Press Club Award, 1976: *The Russians,* New York: Quadrangle / New York Times Book Company, 1976. William Allen White National Citation, University of Kansas, 1996. Honorary Degrees: Williams College, MA, 1975; Wittenburg University, OH, 1985; Amherst College, MA, 1992; University of South Carolina, 1992.

For More Information: *New York Times,* 7 May (1974): 40; Taft, William H., *Encyclopedia of Twentieth-Century Journalists,* New York: Garland Publishing, 1986; *Contemporary Authors, Volumes 65-68,* Detroit: Gale Research Company, 1977.

Commentary: Hedrick Smith won a Pulitzer Prize for his reporting from Moscow. He became an authority on Russia and its people, and his books on the subject were considered requisite reading for anyone interested in the country. He was one of the reporters who had a wiretap placed on his phone by the Nixon Administration in its attempt to stop leaks to the press.

1975

Ovie Carter 642

Birth: March 11, 1946; Indianole, MS. **Parents:** Grover Cleveland Carter and Mary (Collins). **Education:** Forest Park Community College, IL. Ray Vogue School of Photography, IL. **Spouse:** Deborah Sue Brown (m. 1969). **Children:** Donjah, David.

Prize: *International Reporting,* 1975: *Chicago Tribune,* "The Faces of Hunger," October 13-18, Chicago: Chicago Tribune, 1974.

Career: Served in U.S. Air Force, 1966-67; Photographer, *Chicago Tribune,* 1969-.

Selected Works: *The American Millstone: An Examination of the Nation's Permanent Underclass,* 1986.

Other Awards: Press Photographer of the Year, Illinois Press Photgraphers Association, 1972-73. Edward Scott Beck Award, *Chicago Tribune,* 1974. Overseas Press Club Award, 1974. World Press Photo Award, 1975. National Association of Black Journalists Award, 1989.

For More Information: *Chicago Tribune,* May 6, 1975: 1; *New York Times,* May 6, 1975: 34.

Commentary: During the summer and fall of 1974, Ovie Carter, along with William Mullen of the *Chicago Tribune,* traveled 10,000 miles across Africa and India to report on the famine in the area. Their five-part series ran October 13-18, 1974 and was reprinted in a special booklet. Carter's photographs were cited by the Pulitzer board as showing "rare

sensitivity." Carter also initiated the use of photographic editorials at the *Chicago Tribune.*

William Charles Mullen 643

Birth: October 9, 1944; La Crosse, WI. **Parents:** Melvin Harold Mullen and Margaret (Thomley). **Education:** University of Wisconsin, La Crosse. University of Wisconsin: BA.

Prize: *International Reporting,* 1975: *Chicago Tribune,* "The Faces of Hunger," October 13-18, Chicago: Chicago Tribune, 1974.

Career: Reporter, *La Crosse Tribune,* 1966; Reporter, *Wisconsin State Journal,* 1966-67; General Assignment Reporter, *Chicago Tribune,* 1967-; Undercover Employee, Chicago Board of Election Commissioners, 1972; Lecturer, Northwestern University (IL), 1975.

Other Awards: Jakob Scher Award for Investigative Reporting, Women in Communications, 1973. Edward Scott Beck Award, *Chicago Tribune,* 1972-74. Ralph O. Nafziger Award, School of Journalism and Mass Communications, University of Wisconsin, Madison, 1976.

For More Information: *Chicago Tribune,* May 6, 1975: 1; *New York Times,* May 6, 1975: 34.

Commentary: William Mullen and Ovie Carter were awarded a Pulitzer Prize for their five-part series on famine in Africa and India. The 10,000 mile journey was Mullen's first foreign assignment.

Mullen was also part of the investigative team that helped the *Chicago Tribune* win a Pulitzer Prize in the Local General Spot News Reporting category in 1973. He took a clerk position at the Chicago Election Board and helped accumulate documentation of over 1,000 cases of voter fraud.

1976

Sydney Hillel Schanberg 644

Birth: January 17, 1934; Clinton, MA. **Parents:** Louis Schanberg and Freda (Feinberg). **Education:** Harvard University, MA: BA. **Spouse:** Janice Leah Sakofsky (m. 1967, div.). **Children:** Jessica, Rebecca.

Prize: *International Reporting,* 1976: *New York Times,* New York: New York Times, 1975.

Career: Served in U.S. Army, 1956-58; Administrative Assistant, International Latex Corporation; Copyboy, *New York Times,* 1959; Clerk and News Assistant, Metropolitan, Foreign, and Picture Desks, *New York Times,* 1959-60; Metropolitan Reporter, *New York Times,* 1960-; Albany (NY) Bureau Chief, *New York Times,* 1967-69; Correspondent, New Delhi (India), *New York Times,* 1969-73; Director, Singapore Bureau, *New York Times,* 1973; Correspondent, Southeast Asia, *New York Times,* 1973-75; Metropolitan Editor, *New York Times,* 1977-80; Columnist, *New York Times,* 1981-85; Associate Editor, Columnist, *Newsday (NY),* 1986-.

Selected Works: *The Killing Fields: The Facts behind the Film* (with Dith Pran), 1984. *The Death and Life of Dith Pran,* 1985.

Other Awards: Page One Award, Newspaper Guild of New York, 1972. George Polk Memorial Award, Long Island University, NY, 1972, 1975. Overseas Press Club Award, 1972, 1974. Bob Considine Memorial Award, 1975. Sigma Delta Chi Award. 25 Year Achievement Award, Society of Silurians, 1988.

For More Information: *Contemporary Authors, Volumes 69-72,* Detroit: Gale Research Company, 1978: 513; *Washington Post,* 16 December (1987): D1.

Commentary: Sydney H. Schanberg traveled in Cambodia from April 16 to May 8, 1975 and investigated the new rule of Communism as it took over the country. His 8,000-word, page-one story in the *New York Times* on May 9, 1975, detailed the uprooting of millions. His experience in Cambodia was the basis of the film *The Killing Fields.*

1977
No award

1978

Henry Kamm   645
Birth: June 3, 1925; Breslau, Germany. **Parents:** Rudolf Kamm and Paula (Wischnewski). **Education:** New York University: BA. **Spouse:** Barbara Lifton (m. 1950). **Children:** Alison, Thomas, Nicholas.

Prize: *International Reporting,* 1978: *New York Times,* New York: New York Times, 1977.

Career: Served in U.S. Army, 1943-46; Copyboy, Editorial Index Department, Copy Editor, *New York Times,* 1949-60; Assistant News Editor, International Edition, Paris (France), *New York Times,* 1960-64; Correspondent, Paris (France), *New York Times,* 1964-66; Correspondent, Warsaw (Poland), *New York Times,* 1966-67; Moscow (Russia) Bureau Chief, *New York Times,* 1967-69; Correspondent, Bangkok (Thailand), *New York Times,* 1969-71; Correspondent, Paris (France), *New York Times,* 1971-78; Chief Asian Diplomatic Correspondent, *New York Times,* 1978-81; Chief Correspondent, Rome (Italy), *New York Times,* 1982-85; Athens (Greece) Bureau Chief, *New York Times,* 1985-87; Central European Correspondent, Budapest (Hungary), *New York Times,* 1987-89; Senior Correspondent, Geneva (Switzerland), *New York Times,* 1989.

Selected Works: *Will the Soviet Union Survive until 1984?* (with others), 1970. *Dragon Ascending: Vietnam and the Vietnamese,* 1996.

Other Awards: Distinguished Service Award, Sigma Delta Chi, 1969. George Polk Memorial Award, Long Island, University, NY, 1969.

Commentary: Henry Kamm's reporting from Southeast Asia led to several nations opening their ports to Vietnamese refugees. His writing would not let the world forget about the refugees and shamed nations into humanitarian decisions.

Kamm came to the United States in 1941 and became a naturalized citizen in 1943. He joined the *New York Times* as a copy boy in 1949 and has been with the paper since.

1979

Richard Ben Cramer   646
Birth: June 12, 1950; Rochester, NY. **Parents:** A. Robert Cramer and Blossom (Lackritz). **Education:** Johns Hopkins University, MD: BA. Columbia University, NY: MA. **Spouse:** Carolyn White. **Children:** Ruby.

Prize: *International Reporting,* 1979: *Philadelphia Inquirer,* Philadelphia, PA: Philadelphia Inquirer, 1978.

Career: Reporter, *Baltimore (MD) Sun,* 1972-76; Transportation Writer, *Philadelphia (PA) Inquirer,* 1976-77; New York (NY) Bureau, *Philadelphia (PA) Inquirer,* 1977; Middle East Correspondent, *Philadelphia (PA) Inquirer,* 1977-83; Writer.

Selected Works: *Ted Williams: The Seasons of the Kid* (with Mark Rucker), 1991. *What It Takes: The Way to the White House,* 1992. *Bob Dole,* 1995.

Other Awards: Sigma Delta Chi Award, 1980. Ernie Pyle Award, Scripps-Howard News Service, 1980. Hal Boyle Award, Overseas Press Club, 1981. American Society of Newspaper Editors Award.

For More Information: *Philadelphia Inquirer,* 17 April (1979); *Los Angeles Times,* 5 August (1992): E1.

Commentary: Richard Ben Cramer won a Pulitzer Prize for his articles on the effect of war on individuals. His dispatches from the Middle East included the stories of a young soldier at the front, a mother learning that her daughter had died, a young man who laid down his weapons to study medicine only to be killed, and a woman who was to lose her home because of the Camp David peace accord. He was a finalist for a Pulitzer Prize in 1981 for his coverage of Afghanistan.

1980

Joel Graham Brinkley 647

Birth: July 22, 1952; Washington, DC. **Parents:** David McClure Brinkley and Ann (Fischer). **Education:** University of North Carolina: BA. **Spouse:** Sabra Elizabeth Chartrand (m. 1990).

Prize: *International Reporting,* 1980: *Louisville Courier-Journal,* "Living the Cambodian Nightmare," December, Louisville, KY: Louisville Courier-Journal, 1979.

Career: Reporter, Charlotte (NC), Associated Press, 1975; State Desk Reporter, *Richmond (VA) News Leader,* 1975-78; Reporter, *Louisville (KY) Courier-Journal,* 1978-82; Editor, *Louisville (KY) Courier-Journal,* 1982-83; Correspondent, Washington (DC), *New York Times,* 1983-86; White House Correspondent, *New York Times,* 1987; Jerusalem (Israel) Bureau Chief, *New York Times,* 1988-91; Project Editor, *New York Times,* 1991-95; Political Editor, *New York Times,* 1995-.

Selected Works: *Report of the Congressional Committees Investigating the Iran Contra Affair: With the Minority Views* (with others), 1988. *The Circus Master's Mission,* 1989. *Defining Vision: The Battle for the Future of Television,* 1997.

Other Awards: National Citizen of the Year, National Association of Social Workers, 1981. Roy W. Howard Award, Scripps-Howard Foundation, 1981-82. Consumer Journalism Award, National Press Club, 1981, 1983. Investigative Reporters and Editors Award, 1982. Clarion Award, 1982. Heywood Broun Award, 1982. National Headliners Club Award, 1983. William S. Miller Enterprise Reporting Award, 1983. Consumer Affairs Reporting Award, Penney-Missouri, 1983. George Polk Memorial Award, Long Island University, NY, 1995.

For More Information: *Louisville Courier-Journal,* April 15, 1980: 1.

Commentary: Joel Brinkley is the son of the famed news commentator David Brinkley. He went to Thailand to make the horrors of a Cambodian refugee camp relevant to the Ohio River Valley. While he was there, he contracted typhoid but still managed to make the deadline for the first article in the four-part series that won him and Jay Mather, a photographer for the *Louisville Courier-Journal,* a Pulitzer Prize.

Jay B. Mather 648

Birth: April 22, 1946; Denver, CO. **Education:** University of Colorado: BA. **Spouse:** Susan Bentley Molthop (m. 1967, div. 1984); Kathy Siebenmann (m. 1985). **Children:** Jesse, Joshua (SM).

Prize: *International Reporting,* 1980: *Louisville Courier-Journal,* "Living the Cambodian Nightmare," December, Louisville, KY: Louisville Courier-Journal, 1979.

Career: Served in Peace Corps, Malaysia, 1969-71; Staff member, *Evergreen (CO) Canyon Courier,* 1972; Staff Photographer, *Denver (CO) Sentinel* Newspapers, 1972-77; Staff Photographer, *Louisville (KY) Courier-Journal* and *Louisville (KY) Times,* 1977-86; Staff Photographer, *Sacramento (CA) Bee,* 1986-.

Selected Works: *Yosemite: A Landscape of Life,* 1990.

Other Awards: Southern Photographer of the Year, 1978. Overseas Press Club Award, 1980. Robert F. Kennedy Journalism Award, 1981. World Hunger Award, 1987.

For More Information: *Louisville Courier-Journal,* April 15, 1980: 1; *New York Times,* April 15, 1980: B8; *Macmillan Biographical Encyclopedia of Photographic Artists & Innovators,* New York: Macmillan Publishing Company, 1983: 398.

Commentary: Jay Mather and Joel Brinkley spent a week in the Cambodian refugee camps in Thailand. Mayer shot 75 rolls of film on the trip. The two brought the story of the horrors of a refugee camp to the Ohio River Valley. Their four-part series told of the appalling treatment of the Cambodian people by their Vietnamese conquerers. Mather was a finalist for a Pulitzer Prize in 1991 for his photographs of the centennial of Yosemite National Park.

1981

Shirley Ann Christian 649

Birth: January 16, 1938; Kansas City, KS. **Parents:** Herbert Walsh Christian and Minnie Lucille (Acker). **Religion:** Congregational United Church of Christ. **Education:** Kansas State College: BA. Ohio State University: MA.

Prize: *International Reporting,* 1981: *Miami Herald,* Miami, FL: Miami Herald, 1980.

Career: United Nations Correspondent, Associated Press, 1970-73; Editor, Foreign and World Desks, Associated Press, 1974-77; Adjunct Professor of Journalism, Columbia University (NY), 1977; Bureau Chief, Chile and Bolivia, Associated Press, 1977-79; Staff member, *Miami (FL) Herald,* 1979; Latin American Staff member, *Miami (FL) Herald,* 1980-83; Foreign Affairs Reporter, Washington (DC), *New York Times,* 1985-86; Visiting Professor of Journalism, Baylor University (TX), 1985; Buenos Aires (Argentina) Bureau Chief, *New York Times,* 1986-93; Freelance writer, 1993-.

Selected Works: *Nicaragua: Revolution in the Family,* 1985. *Investing and Selling in Latin America* (with others), 1995.

Other Awards: Nieman Fellow, Harvard University, MA, 1973-74. George Polk Memorial Award, Long Island University, NY, 1981. Maria Moors Cabot Prize, Columbia University, NY, 1985.

For More Information: Rosenblum, Mort, *Coups and Earthquakes: Reporting the World for America,* New York: Harper and Row, 1979; *Contemporary Authors, Volume 125,* Detroit: Gale Research Company, 1987; *Kansas City Star,* 16 February (1995): F1.

Commentary: Shirley Christian won a Pulitzer Prize for her dispatches from El Salvador. Christian wrote about the human aspect of the conflict, not just the political discord. She covered such topics as the violent funeral of Archbishop Oscar Romero, the death of four American nuns, and the effect of the war on the population.

1982

John Townsend Darnton   650

Birth: November 20, 1941; New York, NY. **Parents:** Byron Darnton and Eleanor (Choate). **Education:** Alliance Francaise, France. Sorbonne University, France. University of Wisconsin: BA. **Spouse:** Nina Lieberman (m. 1966). **Children:** Kyra, Liza, James.

Prize: *International Reporting,* 1982: *New York Times,* New York: New York Times, 1981.

Career: News Clerk and News Assistant, *New York Times,* 1966-68; Reporter, *New York Times,* 1968-71; Night Rewriteman, *New York Times,* 1971; Metropolitan Reporter, *New York Times,* 1972-75; Reporter, City Hall Bureau; Foreign Correspondent, Lagos (Nigeria), *New York Times,* 1976-77; Foreign Correspondent, Kenya, *New York Times,* 1977-79; Warsaw (Poland) Bureau Chief, *New York Times,* 1979-82; Madrid (Spain) Bureau Chief, *New York Times,* 1982-84; Deputy Foreign Editor, *New York Times,* 1984-86; Metropolitan Editor, *New York Times,* 1986-91; News Editor, *New York Times,* 1991-93; London (England) Bureau Chief, *New York Times,* 1993-96; Culture Editor, *New York Times,* 1996-.

Selected Works: *Neanderthal,* 1996.

Other Awards: George Polk Memorial Award, Long Island University, NY, 1979, 1982.

For More Information: *New York Times,* 8 December (1990): 19; *New York Times,* 10 May (1996): C30.

Commentary: John Darnton's coverage of Poland won him a Pulitzer Prize. Based in Poland, he followed the rise of Solidarity and the crackdowns of martial law. His father, Byron Darnton, had been a foreign correspondent for the *New York Times,* as well, and had died while on assignment in New Guinea.

1983

Thomas Loren Friedman   651

Birth: July 20, 1953; Minneapolis, MN. **Parents:** Harold Friedman and Margaret (Phillips). **Religion:** Jewish. **Education:** Brandeis University, MA: BA, summa cum laude. Oxford University, England: MA. University of London, England. Hebrew University, Israel. American University, Cairo, Egypt. **Spouse:** Ann Louise Bucksbaum (m. 1978). **Children:** Orly, Natalie.

Prize: *International Reporting,* 1983: *New York Times,* New York: New York Times, 1982. *International Reporting,* 1988: *New York Times,* New York: New York Times, 1987.

Career: Correspondent, London (England), United Press International, 1978-79; Correspondent, Middle East, United Press International, 1979-81; Correspondent, Beirut (Lebanon), United Press International, 1979-81; General Assignment Financial Reporter, *New York Times,* 1981-82; Beirut (Lebanon) Bureau Chief, *New York Times,* 1982-84; Israel Bureau Chief, *New York Times,* 1984-88; Chief Diplomatic Correspondent, *New York Times,* 1989-92; Chief White House Correspondent, *New York Times,* 1992-93; International Economics Correspondent, *New York Times,* 1994; Foreign Affairs Columnist, *New York Times,* 1995-.

Selected Works: *War Torn* (with Susan Vermazen), 1984. *From Beirut to Jerusalem,* 1989. *Israel, a Photobiography: The First Fifty Years* (with Micha Bar-Am), 1998.

Other Awards: Overseas Press Club Award, 1980. George Polk Memorial Award, Long Island University, NY, 1982. Livingston Award for Young Journalists, 1983. Page One Award, New York Newspaper Guild, 1984. Colonel Robert D. Heinl Jr. Memorial Award in Marine Corps History, Marine Corps Historical Foundation, 1985. Guggenheim Fellow, 1988. National Book Award, 1989: *From Beirut to Jerusalem,* New York: Farrar, Straus, Giroux, 1989. Best Book on Foreign Policy, Overseas Press Club, 1989: *From Beirut to Jerusalem,* Helen B. Bernstein Award, New York Public Library, 1990. Marshall Scholarship. Honorary Degrees: Brandeis University, MA; Macalester College, MN; Haverford College, PA; Hebrew Union College, MA.

For More Information: Rhodes, Richard, *Writing in the Era of Conflict, National Book Week Lectures,* Washington D.C.: Library of Congress, 1990; *New York Times,* 4 October (1994): C18; *Quill,* 84:9 (November 1996): 6.

Commentary: Thomas L. Friedman spent the majority of the 1980s in the Middle East. While there, he won two Pulitzer Prizes. In 1983, while he was head of the Beirut Bureau, he and Loren Jenkins won for their coverage of the massacres in the Sabra and Shatila districts. In 1988, when he was head of the Jerusalem Bureau, he was honored for his "balanced and informed coverage" of Israel. He wrote on the growing tensions in the occupied territories and the psychological damage the continued turmoil had on all involved.

Loren B. Jenkins   652

Birth: October 26, 1938; New Orleans, LA. **Parents:** Stephen B. Jenkins and Lorena (Lackey) Dabney. **Education:** University of Colorado: BA. Columbia University, NY: Postgrad. **Spouse:** Nancy Harmon (m. 1964, div. 1985); Laura Thorne (m. 1986). **Children:** Sara, Nicholas (NH).

Prize: *International Reporting,* 1983: *Washington Post,* Washington, DC: Washington Post, 1982.

Career: Ski instructor, Aspen (CO) ski school, 1958-61; Served in Peace Corps, Sierra Leone, 1961-63; Reporter, *Port Chester (NY) Daily Item,* 1964-65; Correspondent, New York (NY), London (England), Madrid (Spain), United Press International, 1965-69; Reporter, *Newsweek* magazine, 1969-79; Correspondent, Foreign Desk, *Washington (DC) Post;* 1980-89;

Publisher, Editor, *Aspen (CO) Times,* 1990-95; Senior Foreign Editor, *National Public Radio,* 1995-.

Other Awards: Overseas Press Club Award, 1976. Edward R. Murrow Fellow, Council on Foreign Relations, 1988-89.

For More Information: *Washington Post,* 19 April (1993): A1; *Rocky Mountain News,* 5 November (1995): 64A.

Commentary: Loren Jenkins and Thomas Friedman both won Pulitzer Prizes in International Reporting for their coverage of the war in Lebanon. Jenkins was cited by the Pulitzer board for his reporting under deadline pressure and for his "vivid eyewitness accounts of the aftermath of the massacre in the Shatila refugee camp."

1984

Karen Elliott House   653

Birth: December 7, 1947; Matador, TX. **Parents:** Ted Elliott and Bailey (McKeehan). **Education:** University of Texas: BJ. **Spouse:** Arthur House (m. 1975, div. 1983); Peter Kann (m. 1984). **Children:** Stepchild: Hillary (PK); Adopted: Petra Elliott; Jason Elliott; Jade Elliot.

Prize: *International Reporting,* 1984: *Wall Street Journal,* New York: Dow Jones, 1983.

Career: Stringer, *Newsweek;* Managing Editor, college newspaper, *Daily Texan;* Intern, *Houston (TX) Chronicle,* 1969; Education Reporter, *Dallas (TX) Morning News,* 1970-71; Political Reporter, Washington (DC), *Dallas (TX) Morning News,* 1971-74; Reporter, Washington (DC), *Wall Street Journal,* 1974-78; Diplomatic Correspondent, *Wall Street Journal,* 1978-83; Assistant Foreign Editor, *Wall Street Journal,* 1983-84; Foreign Editor, *Wall Street Journal,* 1984-89; Vice President International Group, Dow Jones and Company, 1989-95; President, International Group, Dow Jones and Company, 1995-.

Selected Works: *Saudi Arabia in Transition: A Wall Street Journal Series,* 1981.

Other Awards: Edward Weintal Award, Georgetown University, Washington, DC, 1980-81. Edwin M. Hood Award for Excellence in Diplomatic Reporting, National Press Club, 1982. Fellow, Institute of Politics, Harvard University, MA, 1982. Distinguished Achievement Award, University of Southern California, 1984. Bob Considine Award, Overseas Press Club, 1984, 1988. Fellow, National Academy Arts and Science.

For More Information: *New York Times,* 17 April (1984): B4; *Wall Street Journal,* 17 April (1984): A4; *Contemporary Authors, Volume 125,* Detroit: Gale Research Company, 1989.

Commentary: Karen Elliott House had over 20 exclusive interviews with Jordan's King Hussein in 1983. She wrote a series of articles that forecast the failure of the American Peace Plan in the Middle East and provided a rare understanding into the political motivations of King Hussein.

1985

Dennis Philip Bell   654
Birth: August 29, 1948; Muskegon, MI. **Death:** March 14, 1995. **Parents:** Ezra Douglas Bell and Natalie (VanArsdale). **Education:** University of Michigan. Hofstra University, NY. **Spouse:** Margie Virginia Ware (m. 1969, div.); Norma J. Davenport (m. 1978, div.); Jacqueline Nanette (m. 1984). **Children:** Tracy, Wesley (MW); Cerise, Christopher (JN).
Prize: *International Reporting*, 1985: *Newsday,* Long Island, NY: Newsday, 1984.
Career: Served in U.S. Army, 1968-70; Floor sweeper, Hofstra University (NY), 1971; Porter, Clerk, Sports Department Staff member, News Reporter, *Newsday (NY),* 1972; Assistant Suffolk County (NY) Editor, *Newsday (NY),* 1972-; Reporter Trainee, *Newsday (NY),* Nassau County and Courts Reporter, *Newsday (NY);* Reporter, Washington (DC), *Newsday (NY).*
Other Awards: Jesse M. White Award, Friends World College, 1985.
For More Information: *Newsday,* 15 March (1995): A6.
Commentary: Dennis Bell started out as a porter for the paper for which he would eventually work for more than 20 years. He worked in the sports department, covered Nassau County and the courts, and took an active interest in beginning journalists. He was selected to travel to Africa and, along with his colleagues Josh Friedman and Ozier Muhammad, won a Pulitzer Prize for reports of the famine in Ethiopia.

Joshua M. Friedman   655
Birth: November 22, 1941; Roosevelt, NJ. **Parents:** Samuel Nathaniel Friedman and Charlotte (Safir). **Education:** Rutgers University, NJ: BA. Columbia University, NY: MS. University of Chicago. **Spouse:** Carol Ash (m. 1976). **Children:** Susannah.
Prize: *International Reporting*, 1985: *Newsday,* Long Island, NY: Newsday, 1984.
Career: Served in Peace Corps, Costa Rica, 1964-66; Investigative Reporter, *Philadelphia (PA) Inquirer,* 1977-79; Editor-in-Chief, *Soho (NY) News,* 1979-81; Albany (NY) Bureau Chief, *New York Post;* United Nations Bureau Chief, Domestic and Foreign Reporting Assignments, *Newsday (NY),* 1982-; Associate Professor of Journalism, Columbia University (NY), 1992-.

Other Awards: Traveling Fellowship, Inter-American Press Association, 1967-68.
For More Information: *New York Times,* 25 April (1985): B10; *Contemporary Authors, Volume 140,* Detroit: Gale Research Company, 1993.
Commentary: Josh Friedman, Dennis Bell, and Ozier Muhammad won a Pulitzer Prize for their series on famine in Ethiopia and other African countries.

Ozier Muhammad   656
Birth: October 8, 1950; Chicago, IL. **Education:** Columbia College, IL: BFA. **Spouse:** Kimberly Satterfield. **Children:** Khalil Gibran.
Prize: *International Reporting*, 1985: *Newsday,* "Africa: The Desperate Continent," Garden City, NY: Newsday, 1984.
Career: Camera salesman, 1968-70; Staff Photographer, *Muhammad Speaks* newspaper, 1970-71; Staff Photographer, Johnson Publishing Company; Instructor, Columbia College (IL), 1972; Part-time Instructor, Columbia College (IL), 1974; Freelance photographer; Staff Photographer, *Newsday (NY),* 1980-.
Other Awards: Jesse Merton White Award for International Photography. George Polk Memorial Award, Long Island University, NY. John S. Knight Journalism Fellow. Nieman Fellow, Harvard University, MA.
For More Information: *New York Times,* 25 April (1985): B10; Willis-Thomas, Deborah, *Illustrated Bio-Bibliography of Black Photographers, 1940-1988, Garland Reference Library of the Humanities, Volume 760,* New York: Garland Publishing, 1989.
Commentary: Ozier Muhammad, a photographer, and two reporters, Dennis Bell and Josh Friedman, won a Pulitzer Prize for their coverage of the famine that struck Ethiopia and other African countries. Muhammad bought his first camera when he was 16. He also photographed the first Ali-Frazer title bout.
Muhammad is a grandson of the Honorable Elijah Muhammad, the founder of the Nation of Islam.

1986

Peter Kevin Carey   657
Birth: April 2, 1940; San Francisco, CA. **Parents:** Paul Twohig Carey and Stanleigh M. (White). **Education:** University of California, Berkeley: BS. **Spouse:** Joanne Dayl Barker (m. 1978). **Children:** Brendan, Nadia.
Prize: *International Reporting*, 1986: *San Jose Mercury News,* "Hidden Billions," June 23-25, San Jose, CA: San Jose Mercury News, 1985.

Career: Reporter, *San Francisco Examiner,* 1964; Editor, *Livermore (CA) Independent,* 1965-67; Aerospace Writer, Special Assignment Writer, Investigative Reporter, *San Jose (CA) Mercury News,* 1967-.

Selected Works: *Legislature for Sale: How Big Money Rules Lawmaking in Sacramento: Stories* (with Christopher H. Schmitt), 1995.

Other Awards: Professional Journalism Fellow, National Endowment for the Humanities, Stanford University, CA, 1983-84. California-Nevada Associated Press, 1983. Penney-Missouri Award, 1985. San Francisco Press Club Award. Mark Twain Award. George Polk Memorial Award, Long Island University, NY, 1986. Investigative Reporters and Editors Award, 1986. Jessie Meriton White Service Award, Friends World College, 1986. Thomas M. Stakes Award, Washington Journalism Center, 1991. Malcolm Forbes Award, Overseas Press Club of America, 1993. Gerald Loeb Award, Anderson Graduate School of Management, University of California, Los Angeles, 1993. Best of the West Award, 1993, 1995. Public Service Award, California Newspaper Publishers Association, 1996. Fairbanks Award for Public Service, Associated Press, 1996.

Commentary: Pete Carey, Katherine Ellison, and Lewis M. Simons won an International Reporting Pulitzer Prize for their series of articles documenting the transfer of money out of the Philippines by Ferdinand Marcos and his associates.

Carey is an investigative reporter who has written articles on different aspects of high technology in Silicon Valley, American charities in Mexico, special interest money in the California legislature, and immigration dealing.

Katherine Ellison   658

Birth: August 19, 1957; Minneapolis, MN. **Parents:** Ellis Ellison and Bernice June (Bender). **Education:** Stanford University, CA: BA.

Prize: *International Reporting,* 1986: *San Jose Mercury News,* "Hidden Billions," June 23-25, San Jose, CA: San Jose Mercury News, 1985.

Career: Intern, *Foreign Policy Magazine;* Intern, Center for Investigative Reporting; Intern, *Los Angeles Times;* Intern, *Washington (DC) Post,* 1979; Staff member, *San Jose (CA) Mercury News,* 1980-; Reporter, San Francisco (CA) Bureau, *San Jose (CA) Mercury News,* 1983-; Mexico City (Mexico) Bureau Chief, *San Jose (CA) Mercury News,* 1987-92; Latin American Correspondent, Rio de Janeiro (Brazil), *Miami (FL) Herald,* 1992-.

Selected Works: *Imelda: Steel Butterfly of the Philippines,* 1988.

Other Awards: Outstanding Print Reporting, Media Alliance of San Francisco, 1985. George Polk Memorial Award, Long Island University, NY, 1986.

Investigative Reporters and Editors Award, 1986. Inter American Press Association, 1994-95. Media Award, Latin American Studies Association, 1994. Award, National Association of Hispanic Journalists, 1997.

Commentary: Katherine Ellison, Pete Carey, and Lewis M. Simons's series of stories documenting the transfer of funds out of the Philippines by Ferdinand Marcos and his top business associates won the International Reporting Pulitzer Prize in 1986.

Ellison has been based in Latin America since 1987.

Lewis Martin Simons   659

Birth: January 9, 1939; Paterson, NJ. **Parents:** Abram Simons and Goldie (Fleisher). **Education:** New York University: BS. Columbia University, NY: MS. **Spouse:** Carol Lenore Seiderman (m. 1965). **Children:** Justine, Rebecca, Adam.

Prize: *International Reporting,* 1986: *San Jose Mercury News,* "Hidden Billions," June 23-25, San Jose, CA: San Jose Mercury News, 1985.

Career: Served in U.S. Marine Corps Reserves, 1962-66; Correspondent, Vietnam, Malaysia, Singapore, Associated Press, 1964-70; Correspondent, India, *Washington (DC) Post,* 1971-75; Correspondent, Thailand, *Washington (DC) Post,* 1975-77; Reporter, *Washington (DC) Post* 1978-82; Tokyo (Japan) Bureau Chief, *San Jose (CA) Mercury News,* 1982-88; Beijing (China) Bureau Chief, *San Jose (CA) Mercury News,* 1989-; Toyko (Japan) Bureau Chief, Knight-Ridder Newspapers, ?-1995; Foreign Policy Correspondent, *Time* Magazine, 1996-97.

Selected Works: *Worth Dying For,* 1987.

Other Awards: Edward R. Murrow Fellow, Council on Foreign Relations, 1970-71. Distinguished Investigative Reporting Award, Investigative Reporters and Editors, 1979. Front Page Award, Newspaper Guild, 1979. Citation for Excellence, Overseas Press Club, 1983. Award of Excellence, World Affairs Council, 1984, 1986, 1989, 1992. Grand Prize, Investigative Reporters and Editors, 1986. Jessie Meriton White Award, Friends World College, 1986. Overseas Press Club Award, 1987, 1992. Gerald Loeb Award, Anderson Graduate School of Management, University of California, Los Angeles, 1993.

For More Information: *New York Times,* April 18, 1986: B4; *Contemporary Authors, Volume 123,* Detroit: Gale Research Company, 1988.

Commentary: Lewis M. Simons, Pete Carey, and Katherine Ellison won the International Reporting Pulitzer Prize for their series that documented the transfer of wealth out of the Philippines by Ferdinand Marcos and several of his associates. Based in Tokyo at the time, Simons's investigation into the death of Benigno Aquino led to the story of foreign property holdings of the then-president Marcos. Simons was a finalist for a Pulitzer Prize in 1995 for a series of stories about the influence of overseas Chinese on Asia.

1987

Michael Christopher Parks 660

Birth: November 17, 1943; Detroit, MI. **Parents:** Robert James Parks and Rosalind (Smith). **Education:** University of Windsor, Canada: BA. **Spouse:** Linda Katherine Durocher (m. 1964). **Children:** Danielle Anne, Christopher, Matthew.

Prize: *International Reporting,* 1987: *Los Angeles Times,* Los Angeles, CA: Los Angeles Times, 1986.

Career: Reporter, *Detroit News,* 1962-65; Reporter, Time-Life News Service, 1965-66; Assistant City Editor, *Suffolk (NY) Sun,* 1966-68; General Assignment Reporter, *Baltimore (MD) Sun,* 1968-70; Correspondent, Saigon (Vietnam), *Baltimore (MD) Sun,* 1970-72; Correspondent, Moscow (Russia), *Baltimore (MD) Sun,* 1972-75; Correspondent, Middle East, *Baltimore (MD) Sun,* 1975-78; Hong Kong Bureau Chief, *Baltimore (MD) Sun,* 1978-79; Peking (China) Bureau Chief, *Baltimore (MD) Sun,* 1979-80; Peking (China) Bureau Chief, *Los Angeles Times,* 1980-84; Johannesburg (South Africa) Bureau Chief, *Los Angeles Times,* 1984-88; Moscow (Russia) Bureau Chief, *Los Angeles Times,* 1988-93; Jerusalem (Israel) Bureau Chief, *Los Angeles Times,* 1993-95; Deputy Foreign Editor, *Los Angeles Times,* 1995-96; Managing Editor, *Los Angeles Times,* 1996-97; Editor, *Los Angeles Times,* 1997-; Senior Vice President, *Los Angeles Times,* 1997-.

Other Awards: Editorial Award, *Los Angeles Times,* 1991, 1994.

For More Information: *Los Angeles Times,* 10 October (1997): A1.

Commentary: Michael Parks's coverage of the turmoil within South Africa was cited as being "balanced and comprehensive." After he filed 265 stories in 1986, the South African government inexplicably ordered him to leave the country. The government relented after an appeal from his editors that there was not a single "inaccurate or unfair" story.

1988

Thomas Loren Friedman

Full entry appears as **#651** under "International Reporting," 1983.

1989

Glenn Frankel 661

Birth: October 2, 1949; New York, NY. **Parents:** Herbert A. Frankel and Betty (Beck). **Education:** Columbia University, NY: BA. **Spouse:** Betsyellen Yeager (m. 1983). **Children:** Abra, Margo, Paul.

Prize: *International Reporting,* 1989: *Washington Post,* Washington, DC: Washington Post, 1988.

Career: Staff Writer, *Richmond (VA) Mercury,* 1973-75; Staff Writer, *Hackensack (NJ) Record,* 1975-79; Richmond (VA) Bureau Chief, *Washington (DC) Post,* 1979-82; Southern Africa Bureau Chief, *Washington (DC) Post,* 1983-86; Jerusalem (Israel) Bureau Chief, *Washington (DC) Post,* 1986-89; London (England) Bureau Chief, *Washington (DC) Post,* 1989-92; Deputy National News Editor, *Washington (DC) Post,* 1994-95; Special Projects Writer, *Washington (DC) Post,* 1996-.

Selected Works: *Beyond the Promised Land: Jews and Arabs on the Hard Road to a New Israel,* 1994.

Other Awards: Professional Journalism Fellow, Stanford University, CA, 1982-83. National Jewish Book Award, 1995: *Beyond the Promised Land: Jews and Arabs on the Hard Road to a New Israel,* New York: Simon & Schuster, 1994.

For More Information: *Washington Post,* 31 March (1989): A1.

Commentary: Glenn Frankel's "sensitive and balanced reports from Israel and the Middle East" during the first year of the Palestinian uprising won a Pulitzer Prize in 1989.

Bill Keller 662

Birth: January 18, 1949; Palo Alto, CA. **Education:** Pomona College, CA. **Spouse:** Ann Cooper. **Children:** Son.

Prize: *International Reporting,* 1989: *New York Times,* New York: New York Times, 1988.

Career: Reporter, *Portland (OR) Oregonian,* 1970-79; Reporter, *Congressional Quarterly Weekly Report,* 1980-82; Reporter, *Dallas (TX) Times-Herald,* 1982-84; Domestic Correspondent, Washington (DC), *New York Times,* 1984-86; Correspondent, Moscow (Russia), *New York Times,* 1986-89; Moscow (Russia) Bureau Chief, *New York Times,* 1989-92; Johannesburg (South Africa) Bureau Chief, *New York Times,* 1992-95; Foreign Editor, *New York Times,* 1995-97; Deputy Managing Editor, *New York Times,* 1997; Managing Editor, *New York Times,* 1997-.

For More Information: *New York Times,* 23 May (1997): C31.

Commentary: Bill Keller's international reporting from the Soviet Union was cited as a "resourceful and detailed coverage of events." He joined the *New York Times* in 1984. After working in the nation's capital for two years, he became a foreign correspondent. He was made managing editor of his paper in 1997.

In a rare occurrence, all three nominees for International Reporting won Pulitzer Prizes in 1989. Keller and Glenn Frankel won in the category in which the jury nominated them and David Zucchino won in the Feature Writing category. The Pulitzer board had shifted Zucchino into that category from International Reporting.

1990

Nicholas D. Kristof   663

Birth: April 27, 1959; Chicago, IL. **Parents:** Ladis K.D. Kristof and Jane (McWilliams). **Education:** Harvard University, MA: BA, Phi Beta Kappa. Magdalen College, England: Law Degree, First Class Honors. American University, Cairo, Egypt. Taipei Language Institute. **Spouse:** Sheryl WuDunn (m. 1988). **Children:** Gregory, Geoffrey.

Prize: *International Reporting,* 1990: *New York Times,* New York: New York Times, 1989.

Career: Intern, *Washington (DC) Post;* Financial Reporter, Trainee, *New York Times,* 1984-85; Reporter, *New York Times,* 1985; Correspondent, Los Angeles (CA), *New York Times,* 1985-86; Correspondent, Hong Kong, *New York Times,* 1986-87; Beijing (China) Bureau Chief, *New York Times,* 1988-93; Tokyo (Japan) Bureau Chief, *New York Times,* 1995-.

Selected Works: *Freedom of the High School Press,* 1983. *China Wakes: The Struggle for the Soul of a Rising Power* (with Sheryl WuDunn), 1994.

Other Awards: Rhodes Scholar, 1981-83. Hal Boyle Award, Overseas Press Club, 1990. George Polk Memorial Award, Long Island University, NY, 1990.

For More Information: *The Pulitzer Prizes 1990,* New York: Simon & Schuster, 1990: 237-277; *New York Times,* 13 April (1990): A17; *Daily Yomiuri,* 11 May (1995): 7.

Commentary: Nicholas D. Kristof and Sheryl WuDunn, both *New York Times* reporters, are also husband and wife. They won a Pulitzer Prize for their coverage of the democracy movement in China and its forceful suppression at Tiananmen Square.

Sheryl WuDunn   664

Birth: November 16, 1959; New York, NY. **Parents:** David WuDunn and Alice (Mark). **Education:** Cornell University, NY: BA, cum laude. Harvard University, MA: MBA. Princeton University, NJ: MPA. **Spouse:** Nicholas D. Kristof (m. 1988). **Children:** Gregory, Geoffrey.

Prize: *International Reporting,* 1990: *New York Times,* New York: New York Times, 1989.

Career: Lending Officer, Banker's Trust Company (NY), 1981-84; Summer Intern, *Miami (FL) Herald,* 1985; Summer Intern, Los Angeles (CA), *Wall Street Journal,* 1986; Correspondent, *(Hong Kong) South China Morning Post;* Correspondent, Hong Kong, *Reuters;* Correspondent, Beijing (China), *New York Times,* 1989-93; Correspondent, Tokyo (Japan), *New York Times,* 1995-.

Selected Works: *China Wakes: The Struggle for the Soul of a Rising Power* (with Nicholas D. Kristof), 1994.

Other Awards: Hal Boyle Award, Overseas Press Club, 1990. George Polk Memorial Award, Long Island University, NY, 1990.

For More Information: *New York Times,* 13 April (1990): A17; *The Pulitzer Prizes 1990,* New York: Simon & Schuster, 1990: 237-277; *Daily Yomiuri,* 11 May (1995): 7.

Commentary: Sheryl WuDunn and Nicholas D. Kristof are the first husband-and-wife team to win simultaneous Pulitzer Prizes in Journalism, for their coverage of the democracy movement in China in 1989 and its ultimate suppression at Tiananmen Square.

1991

Caryle Marie Murphy 665

Birth: November 16, 1946; Hartford, CT. **Parents:** Thomas Joseph Murphy and Muriel Kathryn (McCarthy). **Religion:** Roman Catholic. **Education:** Trinity College, Washington, DC: BA, cum laude. Johns Hopkins University, MD: MA.

Prize: *International Reporting,* 1991: *Washington Post,* Washington, DC: Washington Post, 1990.

Career: Teacher, St. Cecilia Teacher Training College, Nyeri (Kenya), 1968-71; Reporter, *Brockton (MA) Enterprise,* 1972-73; Freelance correspondent, 1974-76; Reporter, Fairfax County (VA), *Washington (DC) Post,* 1976-77; Correspondent, South Africa, *Washington (DC) Post,* 1977-82; Metropolitan News Staff member, *Washington (DC) Post,* 1982-85; National News Staff member, *Washington (DC) Post,* 1985-89; Correspondent, Middle East, *Washington (DC) Post,* 1989-94; Metropolitan Staff Writer, *Washington (DC) Post,* 1995-.

Other Awards: Courage in Journalism Award, International Women's Media Foundation, 1990. George Polk Memorial Award, Long Island University, NY, 1991. Edward Weintal Journalism Award, Georgetown University, Washington, DC, 1991. Robert F. Kennedy Journalism Award, 1994. Edward R. Murrow Fellow, Council on Foreign Relations, 1994-95.

For More Information: *New York Times* 30 August (1990): A16; *Washington Post* 10 April (1991): A1.

Commentary: Caryle Murphy was the only American reporter in Kuwait when Iraq invaded on August 2, 1990. She had her dispatches hand-carried out of the country, and after 26 days in hiding, she escaped into Saudi Arabia.

As a freelance reporter in Angola, she was expelled by the government. She has also covered South Africa.

Serge Schmemann 666

Birth: April 4, 1945; Paris, France. **Parents:** Alexander Schmemann and Juliana (Ossorguine). **Education:** Harvard University, MA: BA, cum laude, Phi Beta Kappa. Columbia University, NY: 1971. **Spouse:** Mary Schidlovsky (m. 1970). **Children:** Anne, Alexander, Nathalie.

Prize: *International Reporting,* 1991: *New York Times,* New York: New York Times, 1990.

Career: Served in U.S. Army, 1968-70; Reporter, Associated Press, 1972-80; Metropolitan Reporter *New York Times,* 1980-81; Correspondent, Moscow (Russia), *New York Times,* 1981-87; Bonn (Germany) Bureau Chief, *New York Times,* 1987-91; Correspondent, Moscow (Russia), *New York Times,*

1991-95; Jerusalem (Israel) Bureau Chief, *New York Times,* 1995-.

Selected Works: *Echoes of a Native Land: Two Centuries of a Russian Village,* 1997.

Other Awards: Hal Boyle Award, Overseas Press Club, 1986. Honorary Degree, Middlebury College, VT, 1995.

For More Information: *New York Times,* 10 April (1991): A20.

Commentary: Serge Schmemann won one of the two International Reporting Pulitzer Prizes awarded in 1991. His reporting on East Germany as it broke down and on its merger with West Germany won him the award. He was the *New York Times* Bonn bureau chief at the time. He has been a foreign correspondent since 1981 in Russia, Germany, and Israel. He was a finalist for a Pulitzer Prize in 1990.

1992

Patrick Joseph Sloyan 667

Birth: January 11, 1937; Stamford, CT. **Parents:** James Joseph Sloyan and Annamae (O'Brien). **Education:** University of Maryland: BS. **Spouse:** Phyllis Hampton (m. 1960). **Children:** Nora, Amy, Patrick, John.

Prize: *International Reporting,* 1992: *Newsday,* Garden City, NY: Newsday, 1991.

Career: Served in U.S. Army, 1955; Staff member, United Press International, 1960-; Staff member, Hearst News Service; Staff member, *Albany (NY) Times-Union;* Staff member, *Baltimore (MD) News-Post;* National Political Correspondent, *Newsday (NY),* 1974-81; European-Midwest Bureau Chief, *Newsday (NY),* 1981-86; Washington (DC) Bureau Chief, *Newsday (NY),* 1986-88; Senior Correspondent, Washington (DC), *Newsday (NY),* 1988-.

Other Awards: Deadline Writing Award, American Society of Newspaper Editors, 1981. Best Newspaper Writing Award, Modern Media Institute, 1982. George Polk Memorial Award, Long Island University, NY, 1992.

For More Information: *Best Newspaper Writing 1982: Winners, the American Society of Newspaper Editors Competition,* St. Petersburg, FL: Modern Media Institute, 1982; *New York Times,* 8 April (1992): B6; *Newsday,* 8 April (1992): 7.

Commentary: Patrick J. Sloyan's reporting on the Persian Gulf War after the war had ended won him a Pulitzer Prize. He reported on battlefield tactics of the war, including U.S. troops burying Iraqis alive as they broke Iraqi battle lines, American deaths by friendly fire, and the fact that two days after the ceasefire, the largest ground battle took place. He traveled throughout the United States and internationally to talk to soldiers and units who had been in the war.

1993

John Fisher Burns 668

Birth: October 4, 1944; Nottingham, England. **Parents:** Robert John Barrow Burns and Dorothy (Fisher). **Religion:** Church of England. **Education:** McGill University, Montreal, Canada: BA, First Class Honors. Harvard University, MA: Postgraduate. Cambridge University, Cambridge, England: Postgraduate. **Spouse:** Jane Peque Gnat (m. 1972, div. 1989); Jane Scott-Long (m. 1991). **Children:** Jamie, Emily; Stepchild: Toby (JS).

Prize: *International Reporting,* 1993: *New York Times,* New York: New York Times, 1992. *International Reporting,* 1997: *New York Times,* New York: New York Times, 1996.

Career: Reporter, *Ottawa (Canada) Citizen,* 1966-67; Reporter, *Toronto (Canada) Globe and Mail,* 1967-71; Peking (China) Bureau Chief, *Toronto (Canada) Globe and Mail,* 1971-75; Johannesburg (South Africa) Bureau Chief, *New York Times,* 1976-80; Moscow (Soviet Union) Bureau Chief, *New York Times,* 1981-84; Peking (China) Bureau Chief, *New York Times,* 1984-86; Toronto (Canada), Moscow (Soviet Union), Johannesburg (South Africa), Kabul (Afghanistan), Baghdad (Iraq) Bureau Chief, *New York Times,* 1986-90; Sarajevo (Bosnia-Herzegovina) Bureau Chief, *New York Times,* 1992-94; New Delhi (India) Bureau Chief, *New York Times,* 1994-.

Other Awards: George Polk Memorial Award, Long Island University, NY, 1977, 1997.

Commentary: John F. Burns has twice won the International Reporting Pulitzer Prize for his coverage

of war-torn regions. In 1992, his dispatches were sent from Bosnia and in 1996 he covered the turmoil in Afghanistan. He was in Kabul when the Taliban rebels overthrew the government.

Roy William Gutman 669

Birth: March 5, 1944; New York, NY. **Parents:** Ira H. Gutman and Linda (Snyder). **Religion:** Jewish. **Education:** Haverford College, PA: BA. London School of Economics, England: MS. **Spouse:** Elizabeth Jane Dribben (m. 1979). **Children:** Caroline.

Prize: *International Reporting,* 1993: *Newsday,* Long Island, NY: Newsday, 1992.

Career: Reporter, West Germany, United Press International, 1968-70; Correspondent, West Germany, Reuters News Agency, 1971-72; Belgrade (Yugoslavia) Bureau Chief, Reuters News Agency, 1973-75; Correspondent, U.S. State Department, Reuters News Agency, 1976-80; Capitol Hill Bureau Chief, Reuters News Agency, 1981; National Security Reporter, *Newsday (NY),* 1982-90; European Bureau Chief, Bonn (Germany), *Newsday (NY),* 1990-94; International Security Reporter, *Newsday (NY),* 1994-.

Selected Works: *Banana Diplomacy: The Making of American Policy in Nicaragua 1981-87,* 1988. *The Bush Administration: The New Approach to Latin America? Occasional Paper Series, Dialogues #123* (Florida International University Latin American and Caribbean Center), 1989. *A Witness to Genocide: The 1993 Pulitzer Prize-Winning Dispatches on the "Ethnic Cleansing" of Bosnia,* 1993.

Other Awards: Human Rights in Media Award, International League for Human Rights, 1992. Selden Ring Award, University of Southern California School of Journalism, 1993. George Polk Memorial Award, Long Island University, NY, 1993. Heywood Broun Award, Newspaper Guild, 1993. National Headliners Club Award, 1993. Hal Boyle Award, Overseas Press Club, 1993. Exemplary Community Service Alumni Award, Haverford College, PA, 1994.

For More Information: *Newsday,* 15 April (1993): 60.

Commentary: Roy Gutman was awarded a Pulitzer Prize for his "courageous and persistent reporting that disclosed atrocities and other human rights violations in Croatia and Bosnia-Herzegovina." Various governments first denied his reports, but his continued reporting of fact upon fact led to the truth about ethnic cleansing in the war-torn countries.

1994

Dallas Morning News 670

Founded: October 1, 1885; Dallas, TX.

Prize: *International Reporting,* 1994: *Dallas Morning News,* Dallas, 1993.

Other Awards: Individual staff members of the *Dallas Morning News* have won five Pulitzer Prizes.

For More Information: Parker, Ralph Halstead, "The History of the Dallas Morning News" (thesis), University of Texas, Austin, 1930; *Personalities in the Dallas Morning News: A Close-Up of the People Who Make Texas' Leading Newspaper,* Dallas, TX: *Dallas Morning News,* 1955; *Dallas Morning News,* 13 April (1994): A1.

Commentary: A staff of 30 reporters, editors, photographers, and graphic artists examined the international attitudes of violence directed toward women. The 14-story series "Violence Against Women: A Question of Human Rights" was published between March and June 1993. International editor Jim Landers and assistant international editor Patricia E. Gaston coordinated and headed the project. Staff members who worked on the project were Mary Carter, Ricardo Chavira, Linda Crosson, John Davidson, Kerry Gunnels, Robert Hart, Don Huff, Toni Y. Joseph, Joseph Kahn, Gregory Katz, Ed Kohorst, Melanie Lewis, Victoria Loe, Pam Maples, David L. Marcus, Paula Nelson, Gayle Reaves, Anne Reifenberg, George Rodrigue, Marco A. Ruiz, Lennox Samuels, Sue F. Smith, Karen Stallwood, Beatriz Terrazas, Lisa Thatcher, Kathleen Vincent, Judy Walgren, and Cindy Yamanaka.

A. H. Belo is the company that owns and operates the *Dallas Morning News.* In 1991, the company bought and sold the assets of the newspaper's major competitor, the *Dallas Times-Herald.*

1995

Mark Fritz   671

Birth: May 5, 1956; East Chicago, IN. **Parents:** Anthony W. Fritz Jr. and Dorothy (Horvath). **Education:** Western Michigan University. Wayne State University, MI: BA. **Spouse:** Karyn Vaughn (m. 1988).

Prize: *International Reporting,* 1995: Associated Press, 1994.

Career: General Assignment Reporter, *Kalamazoo (MI) Gazette,* 1978-83; Reporter, Michigan, Associated Press, 1984-88; Editor, International Desk (NY), Associated Press, 1988-90; Correspondent, Berlin (East Germany), Associated Press, 1990-93; West Africa Correspondent, Associated Press, 1993-94; National Writer (NY), Associated Press, 1994-96; Freelance writer, 1997-; Visiting Faculty member, Poynter Institute (FL).

Other Awards: Advancement of Justice Award, State Bar of Michigan, 1982, 1986. Associated Press Managing Editors Award, 1994. National Headliners

Club Award, 1995. Bayeux International War Correspondents Prize of France, 1995. Jesse Laventhol Prize for Deadline Writing, American Society of Newspaper Editors, 1995. Outstanding Alumni, Arts Achievement Award, Wayne State University, MI, 1996.

For More Information: *Best Newspaper Writing 1995,* St. Petersburg, FL: Poynter Institute, 1995.

Commentary: Mark Fritz won a Pulitzer Prize for his dispatches from Rwanda. In his nominating letter, William E. Ahearn, executive editor of the Associated Press, wrote, "we nominated him because he described scenes of hell in such vivid detail." Besides covering the war, Fritz probed into the causes of how people could "perpetrate such slaughter." He not only described the victims, but also talked to the killers.

Fritz also covered Germany's reunification for the *Associated Press.* He currently is a freelance writer in the New York City area.

1996

David Rohde   672

Birth: 1967. **Parents:** Harvey Rohde and Carol Ruffo. **Education:** Brown University, RI: BA.

Prize: *International Reporting,* 1996: *Christian Science Monitor,* Boston: Christian Science Monitor, 1995.

Career: Press Secretary, presidential and congressional campaigns; Production Assistant, *Turning Point,* ABC News and *ABC World News Tonight;* Freelance Reporter, Baltic Republics, *New York Times* and Associated Press, 1991; Freelance Reporter, Syria, *Washington (DC) Report on Middle East Affairs,* 1991; Freelance Reporter, Cuba, *Chris-*

tian Science Monitor, 1992; Suburban Correspondent, *Philadelphia (PA) Inquirer,* 1993-94; Roving National Correspondent, *Christian Science Monitor,* 1994; Eastern Europe Correspondent, Sarajevo (Bosnia-Herzegovina) and Zagreb (Croatia), *Christian Science Monitor,* 1994-96; Metropolitan Reporter, *New York Times,* 1997-.

Selected Works: *Endgame: The Betrayal and Fall of Srebrenica, Europe's Worst Massacre since World War II,* 1997.

Other Awards: George Polk Memorial Award, Long Island University, NY, 1996. Overseas Press Club Award. Sigma Delta Chi Award. Investigative Reporters and Editors Award. Livingston Award for Young Journalists. Paul Tobenkin Award for Human Rights Reporting.

For More Information: *Boston Globe,* 9 November (1995): section National, 1; *Christian Science Monitor,* 10 April (1996): 1.

Commentary: David Rohde was the Balkan correspondent for the *Christian Science Monitor* from 1994-1996. He covered the civil war and the "ethnic cleansing" in the former Yugoslavia. He was the first reporter to discover mass graves in Srebrenica. When he returned to the area, he was arrested and held in jail for nine days.

1997

John Fisher Burns

Full entry appears as **#668** under "International Reporting," 1993.

1998

New York Times

Full entry appears as **#375** under "Explanatory Journalism," 1986.

Investigative Reporting

1985

William Kalmon Marimow 673

Birth: August 4, 1947; Philadelphia, PA. **Parents:** Jay Marimow and Helen Alma (Gitnig). **Education:** Trinity College, CT. **Spouse:** Diane K. Macomb (m. 1969). **Children:** Ann, Scott.

Prize: *Investigative Reporting,* 1985: *Philadelphia Inquirer,* Philadelphia, PA: Philadelphia Inquirer, 1984.

Career: Staff member, *Philadelphia (PA) Inquirer,* 1972-.

Other Awards: Nieman Fellow, Harvard University, MA, 1982-83.

For More Information: Patterson, Margaret Jones and Russel, Robert H., *Behind the Lines: Case Studies in Investigative Reporting,* New York: Columbia University Press, 1986: 5-50.

Commentary: William K. Marimow investigated the Philadelphia police force's K-9 unit and uncovered that the dogs had attacked more than 350 people. A formal investigation followed the publication of the story and several officers were reassigned to other duties. The series of articles was printed in April 1984.

Marimow was also part of the team that helped the *Philadelphia Inquirer* win the Meritorious Public Service award in 1972.

Lucy Morgan 674

Birth: October 11, 1940; Memphis, TN. **Parents:** Allin Keen and Lucile (Sanders). **Religion:** Presbyterian. **Education:** Pasco-Hernando Community College, FL: AA. University of South Florida. **Spouse:** Alton F. Ware (m. 1958, d. 1967); Richard A. Morgan (m. 1968). **Children:** Lynn, Kent, Andrew, Mary.

Prize: *Investigative Reporting,* 1985: *St. Petersburg Times,* St. Petersburg, FL: St. Petersburg Times, 1984.

Career: Reporter, *Oscala (FL) Star Banner,* 1965-68; Reporter, *St. Petersburg (FL) Times,* 1967-86; Associate Editor-Capital Bureau Chief, *St. Petersburg (FL) Times,* 1986-.

Other Awards: Paul Hansel Distinguished Journalism Award, Florida Society of Newspaper Editors, 1981. Public Service Award, Florida Society of Newspaper Editors, 1982. Sigma Delta Chi Award, 1985. Hall of Fame, Kappa Tau Alpha, 1992.

For More Information: Ricchiardi, Sherry and Virginia Young, *Women on Deadline: America's Best,* Cedar Rapids: Iowa State University Press, 1991.

Commentary: Lucy Morgan and Jack Reed won a Pulitzer Prize for their research and reporting on the Pasco County, Florida sheriff. "This series of stories caused voters to reject a sheriff who ran a corrupt office and served as a lesson for many other sheriffs who have used the series to learn how *not* to run a law enforcement agency." - L. Morgan

Morgan was the first woman to win a Pulitzer Prize in the Investigative Reporting category. She has written hard-hitting stories on public corruption and drug smuggling. In 1973, she was sentenced to jail for her refusal to name a source.

Jack Louis Reed 675

Birth: September 28, 1945; Akron, OH. **Parents:** Donald Albert Reed and Sarah Elizabeth (Fanning). **Education:** University of South Florida: BS. University of Central Florida: MA. **Children:** Scott.

Prize: *Investigative Reporting,* 1985: *St. Petersburg Times,* St. Petersburg, FL: St. Petersburg Times, 1984.

Career: Social Worker, State of Florida, 1971-74; English Instructor, University of Central Florida, 1975-78; Newsletter editor for a state agency; Reporter, *Tallahassee (FL) Democrat,* 1979-81; Reporter, *St. Petersburg (FL) Times,* 1982-; City Editor, *St. Petersburg (FL) Times,* 1987-; State News Director, Editor, North Pinellas Edition, *St. Petersburg (FL) Times;* State Editor, *St. Petersburg (FL) Times,* ?-1995; Editorials Editor, North Pinellas Edition, *St. Petersburg (FL) Times,* 1996-.

Other Awards: Robert F. Kennedy Journalism Award, 1980. Florida Press Club, 1980. John S. Knight Fellow, Stanford University, CA, 1995-96.

For More Information: *St. Petersburg Times,* 3 November (1996): 2.

Commentary: Jack Reed and Lucy Morgan's investigation into the Pasco County, Florida, Sheriff's Department led to the indictment of the sheriff, John Short, and his removal from office at the next election. Also indicted was millionaire John Moorman. Short allegedly profited from selling a travel agency to Moorman as well as purchasing a home from him. In exchange, Short hired Moorman as an unpaid part-time deputy.

1986

Jeffrey A. Marx 676

Birth: September 6, 1962; New York, NY. **Education:** Northwestern University, IL.

Prize: *Investigative Reporting,* 1986: *Lexington Herald-Leader,* "Playing Above the Rules," Lexington, KY: Lexington Herald-Leader, 1985.

Career: Summer Assistant, Baltimore (MD) Colts; Sports and News Intern, *Lexington (KY) Herald-Leader;* Staff member, *Lexington (KY) Herald-Leader,* 1984-; Freelance writer; Co-Founder, Director, Wendy Marx Foundation for Organ Donor Awareness, 1990-.

Selected Works: *Inside Track* (with Carl Lewis), 1990. *One More Victory Leap* (with Carl Lewis), 1996.

Other Awards: Best Reporting Award, *Sporting News,* 1986.

Commentary: Jeffrey Marx and Michael York were awarded a Pulitzer Prize for their series, "Playing Above the Rules." The two reporters reported that University of Kentucky basketball players were receiving cash payments. Marx is currently a freelance writer and is active in promoting the awareness of organ donation.

Michael M. York 677

Birth: April 10, 1953; High Point, NC. **Education:** University of Kentucky. University of North Carolina: JD. **Spouse:** Rebecca Todd. **Children:** Emily, James.

Prize: *Investigative Reporting,* 1986: *Lexington Herald-Leader,* "Playing Above the Rules," Lexington, KY: Lexington Herald-Leader, 1985.

Career: Reporter, *Durham (NC) Morning Herald,* 1975-78; Reporter, *Washington (DC) Legal Times,* 1978; Attorney, Kentucky Legislative Research Commission, 1978-79; Staff member, *Lexington (KY) Herald-Leader,* 1979-82; Correspondent, Washington (DC), *Lexington (KY) Herald-Leader,* 1982-; Reporter and Staff Writer, *Washington (DC) Post.*

Other Awards: Best Reporting Award, *Sporting News,* 1986.

For More Information: *New York Times,* 18 April (1996): B4.

Commentary: Michael York and Jeffrey Marx wrote their series, "Playing Above the Rules," exposing University of Kentucky basketball players who had received cash payoffs.

1987

Daniel R. Biddle 678

Birth: July 19, 1953; Hyannis, MA. **Education:** University of Michigan. **Spouse:** Cynthia Roberts. **Children:** Ellery.

Prize: *Investigative Reporting,* 1987: *Philadelphia Inquirer,* "Disorder in the Court," Philadelphia, PA: Philadelphia Inquirer, 1986.

Career: Reporter, *Cleveland (OH) Plain-Dealer,* 1976-79; Reporter, City Hall Bureau, *Philadelphia (PA) Inquirer,* 1979-80; Reporter, Pennsylvania Supreme Court, *Philadelphia Inquirer,* 1980-; Assistant City Editor, *Philadelphia Inquirer,* 1991-92; New Jersey Bureau Editor, *Philadelphia Inquirer,* 1992-; Deputy Metropolitan Editor, *Philadelphia Inquirer.*

Other Awards: National Headliners Club Award. Sigma Delta Chi Award. Investigative Reporters and Editors Award.

For More Information: *Philadelphia Inquirer,* 17 April (1987): 1A, 20A.

Commentary: Daniel R. Biddle, H.G. Bissinger, and Fredric N. Tulsky's series "Disorder in the Court" exposed the corruption and incompetence within the Philadelphia court system. The team spent more than two years investigating the legal system, where judges met secretly with defense lawyers and raised campaign funds from the lawyers who argued cases before them, as well as the selection of judges for political reasons.

Henry Gerald Bissinger III 679

Birth: November 1, 1954; New York, NY. **Parents:** Harry Gerald Bissinger II and Eleanor (Lebenthal). **Education:** University of Pennsylvania: BA, cum laude. **Spouse:** Debra Stone (m. 1981, div. 1986); Sarah Whiting MacDonald (m. 1989). **Children:** Harry Gerald IV, Zachary (SM).

Prize: *Investigative Reporting,* 1987: *Philadelphia Inquirer,* "Disorder in the Court," Philadelphia, PA: Philadelphia Inquirer, 1986.

Career: Reporter, *Norfolk (VA) Ledger-Star,* 1976-78; Special Projects Reporter, *St. Paul (MN) Pioneer Press,* 1978-81; Reporter, *Philadelphia (PA) Inquirer,* 1981; Editor, *Philadelphia Inquirer,* ?-1988; Investigative Reporter, *Chicago Tribune,* 1989-; Editor, *Philadelphia Inquirer;* Freelance writer.

Selected Works: *Friday Night Lights: A Town, a Team, and a Dream,* 1990. *A Prayer for the City,* 1997.

Other Awards: Livingston Award for National Reporting, 1982. Frank Premack Memorial Award, 1982. Public Service Award, Pennsylvania Press Managing Editors, 1983. Nieman Fellow, Harvard

University, MA, 1985-86. National Headliners Club Award, 1987.

For More Information: *Philadelphia Inquirer,* 17 April (1987): 1A, 20A.

Commentary: H.G. Bissinger, Daniel R. Biddle, and Fredric N. Tulsky's investigation into the Philadelphia court system led to changes and reforms. They uncovered judges who raised campaign funds from lawyers who would later argue cases before them, as well as judges who met in secret with defense lawyers. Another tactic they uncovered was one used by defense lawyers, who would win new trials for their clients by arguing that they (the lawyers) had been incompetent at the original trial.

Fredric Neal Tulsky   680

Birth: September 30, 1950; Chicago, IL. **Parents:** George Tulsky and Helen (Mailick). **Education:** University of Missouri, Eugene Sharpe Scholar. Temple University, PA: JD, cum laude. **Spouse:** Kim Rennard (m. 1971). **Children:** Eric, Elizabeth.

Prize: *Investigative Reporting,* 1987: *Philadelphia Inquirer,* "Disorder in the Court," Philadelphia, PA: Philadelphia Inquirer, 1986.

Career: Reporter, *Saginaw (MI) News,* 1973-74; Reporter, *Port Huron (MI) Times-Herald,* 1974-75; Reporter, *Jackson (MS) Clarion-Ledger,* 1975-78; Reporter, *Los Angeles Herald-Examiner,* 1978-79; Staff Writer, *Philadelphia (PA) Inquirer,* 1979-93; Adjunct Professor of Urban Studies, University of Pennsylvania, 1990-93; Managing Editor, Center for Investigative Reporting, 1993-94; Executive Director, Center for Investigative Reporting, 1994; Reporter, *Los Angeles Times,* 1995-.

Other Awards: Sigma Delta Chi Award, 1978. Heywood Broun Award, 1978. Public Service Award, Associated Press Managing Editors, 1978. Certificate of Merit, American Bar Association, 1978. Robert F. Kennedy Journalism Award, 1979. Silver Gavel Award, American Bar Association, 1979, 1987. National Headliners Club Award, 1987. Nieman Fellow, Harvard University, MA, 1989-90. Investigative Reporters and Editors Medal, 1997.

Commentary: Fredric N. Tulsky, H.G. Bissinger, and Daniel Biddle's series of stories on the Philadelphia court system led to state and federal investigations. They uncovered corruption and conflicts of interest rife throughout the system. They spent more than two years investigating and writing the series.

Tulsky's reporting in 1996 about murder investigations within Los Angeles County was a finalist in the Meritorious Public Service category in 1997.

John William Woestendiek   681

Birth: September 5, 1953; Winston-Salem, NC. **Parents:** William John Woestendiek and Mary Josephine (Pugh). **Education:** University of North Carolina: AB. **Spouse:** Jennifer Ann Swartz (m. 1979). **Children:** Joseph.

Prize: *Investigative Reporting,* 1987: *Philadelphia Inquirer,* Philadelphia, PA: Philadelphia Inquirer, 1986.

Career: Reporter, Tucson (AZ) *Arizona Daily Star,* 1975-77; General Assignment Reporter, *Lexington (KY) Leader,* 1977-78; Assistant City Editor, *Lexington (KY) Leader,* 1978; City Editor, *Lexington (KY) Leader,* 1979-81; Reporter, *Philadelphia (PA) Inquirer,* 1981-90; National Correspondent, West Coast, *Philadelphia (PA) Inquirer,* 1990-93; Reporter, *Philadelphia (PA) Inquirer,* 1994-96; Columnist, *Philadelphia (PA) Inquirer,* 1996-.

Other Awards: Best Feature Story Award, Kentucky Press Association, 1978. Best Investigative Story Award, Kentucky Press Association, 1979. National Arc of Excellence, National Association for Retarded Citizens, 1984. Paul Tobenkin Memorial Award, Columbia University, NY, 1984. Best News Reporting Award, Associated Press Managing Editors of Pennsylvania, 1985. National Headliners Club Award, 1987. John S. Knight Fellow, Stanford University, CA, 1988-89. Sigma Delta Chi Award, 1994. Ernie Pyle Award, 1994.

Commentary: John Woestendiek's winning two-part series led to a new trial for Terence McCracken and his eventual release from prison. Woestendiek interviewed jurors and expert witnesses and heard the confession of the crime from another man. In a rare occurrence, there were two Pulitzer Prizes given out for Investigative Reporting in 1987, and the other team of reporters who won were also from the *Philadelphia Inquirer.* Woestendiek was also a Pulitzer Prize finalist in 1994 and 1995.

1988

Dean Paul Baquet   682

Birth: September 21, 1956; New Orleans, LA. **Parents:** Edward Joseph Baquet and Myrtle (Romano). **Education:** Columbia University, NY. **Spouse:** Dylan Landis (m. 1986). **Children:** Ari.

Prize: *Investigative Reporting,* 1988: *Chicago Tribune,* Chicago: Chicago Tribune, 1987.

Career: Reporter, *New Orleans (LA) Times-Picayune* and *The States-Item,* 1978-84; Investigative Reporter, *Chicago Tribune,* 1984-87; Associate Metro Editor/Chief Investigative Reporter, *Chicago Tribune,* 1987-90; Investigative Reporter, *New York Times,* 1990-92; Assistant to Managing Editor, *New*

York Times; Deputy Metropolitan Editor, City News, *New York Times,* 1992-95; National Editor, *New York Times,* 1995-.

Other Awards: William H. Jones Award, 1986-87.

For More Information: *New York Times,* 1 July (1995): 17.

Commentary: Dean Baquet, William C. Gaines, and Ann M. Lipinski's series "City Council: The Spoils of Power" examined the inner workings of Chicago's City Council and how the politics are played. The seven-part series, published from October 4-11, detailed the "waste and influence peddling" of the council members and resulted in proposals to reform the city's zoning laws.

Baquet was a finalist for a Pulitzer Prize in 1994.

William Chester Gaines   683

Birth: November 1, 1933; Indianapolis, IN. **Parents:** Philip Damon Gaines and Georgia Agnes (Smith). **Education:** Butler University, IN: BS. **Spouse:** Nellie Gilyan. **Children:** Michael, Michelle, Matthew.

Prize: *Investigative Reporting,* 1988: *Chicago Tribune,* Chicago: Chicago Tribune, 1987.

Career: Newscaster, WCTW Radio Station; Served in U.S. Army; Newscaster, radio and television stations, 1958-63; Northern Indiana Correspondent, *Chicago Daily News,* 1960-63; Investigative Reporter, *Chicago Tribune,* 1963.

Selected Works: *Investigative Reporting for Print and Broadcast,* 1994.

Other Awards: William H. Jones Award, 1987. Peter Lisagor Award, Chicago Headline Club, 1986-87.

For More Information: *Chicago Tribune,* 1 April (1988): 2.

Commentary: William Gaines, Dean Baquet, and Ann Marie Lipinski's six-month investigation into the Chicago City Council won a Pulitzer Prize. Their seven-part series documented the "waste and influence peddling" of council members. They interviewed hundreds of people, including aldermen, officials, and lobbyists. They examined land transactions, expenditure vouchers, and over 600 zoning changes.

Gaines was a member of the *Chicago Tribune* staff that won the 1976 Local Investigative Specialized Reporting Pulitzer Prize for exposing the abuses of the federal housing programs and the condition of local hospitals. He was also a finalist for a Pulitzer Prize in 1996.

Ann Marie Lipinski   684

Birth: January 1, 1956; Trenton, MI. **Education:** University of Michigan. **Spouse:** Steve Kagan. **Children:** Caroline.

Prize: *Investigative Reporting,* 1988: *Chicago Tribune,* "City Council: The Spoils of Power," October 4-11, Chicago: Chicago Tribune, 1987.

Career: Summer Intern, *Miami (FL) Herald,* 1977; Co-Editor, college paper, *Michigan Daily;* Summer Intern, *Chicago Tribune,* 1978; Reporter, *Chicago Tribune,* 1978-; Investigations Team Member, Associate Managing Editor for News, *Chicago Tribune;* Managing Editor for News, *Chicago Tribune,* 1995; Managing Editor, *Chicago Tribune,* 1995.

Other Awards: Detroit Press Club Award. Illinois Associated Press Editors Association Award, 1981. William H. Jones Award, 1987. Nieman Fellow, Harvard University, MA, 1989-90. Robert F. Kennedy Journalism Award, 1994.

For More Information: *Chicago Tribune,* January 28, 1995: 2; *Chicago Tribune,* October 3, 1995: Business, 3.

Commentary: Ann M. Lipinski, along with her colleagues Dean Baquet and William Gaines, examined in detail the Chicago City Council. Their seven-part series of articles concluded that, in some cases, the city was the last thing the council was thinking about; it was busy playing politics and making deals.

In 1993, Lipinski worked on a series of articles that documented every murder of a child under the age of 15 within the six-county metropolitan area. And in 1995, Lipinski was named managing editor of the *Chicago Tribune,* the first woman to hold that title.

1989

Bill Dedman   685

Birth: October 14, 1960; Chattanooga, TN. **Parents:** Harold C. Dedman and Bobbye (Griswold) Dedman Schroeder. **Education:** Washington University, MO. **Spouse:** Pamela J. Belluck (m. 1993). **Children:** Justin.

Prize: *Investigative Reporting,* 1989: *Atlanta Journal and Constitution,* "The Color of Money," Atlanta, GA: Atlanta Journal and Constitution, 1988.

Career: Copyboy, *Chattanooga (TN) Times,* 1976; Reporter, *Warrensburg (MO) Star-Journal,* 1981; Reporter, *Blue Springs (MO) Examiner,* 1981-82; Reporter, *Chattanooga (TN) Free Press,* 1983; Reporter, *Chattanooga (TN) Free Times, 1984-86;* Reporter, *Knoxville (TN) News Sentinel,* 1986-87; Staff Writer, *Atlanta (GA) Journal-Constitution,* 1987-89; Metropolitan Reporter, *Washington (DC) Post,* 1989-91; Freelance writer, 1991-92; Visiting Professional, University of Maryland, 1993-94; Director of Computer Assisted Reporting, Associated Press, 1994-97; Reporter, Chicago (IL), *New York Times,* 1997-.

Selected Works: *The Color of Money: Home Mortgage Lending Practices Discriminate against*

Blacks, 1988. *Power Reporting: Your Complete Guide to Computer-Assisted Journalism* (with Elliot Jaspin and Richard Mullins).

Other Awards: Southern Journalism Award, 1988. General News Award, National Association of Black Journalists, 1989. Robert F. Kennedy Journalism Award, 1989. Worth Bingham Prize, 1989. Investigative Reporters and Editors Award, 1989. Freedom Forum Fellow, Media Studies Center, 1992-93.

Commentary: Bill Dedman won a Pulitzer Prize in 1989 for his series of four articles that exposed the racial discrimination of lending institutions in the Atlanta area, specifically the practices of mortgage lenders. He spent seven months researching the topic.

"Many people contributed to 'The Color of Money,' principally Bill Kovach, Wendell Rawls Jr., Hyde Post, Sharon Bailey, Calvin Bradford, Chuck Finn, Dwight Morris, and Stan Fittesman." — B. Dedman

1990

Christopher John Ison   686

Birth: August 20, 1957; Crandon, WI. **Parents:** Luther A. Ison Jr. and Penny O. (Koyn). **Education:** University of Minnesota: BA. **Spouse:** Nancy Cassutt. **Children:** Kathryn, Allison.

Prize: *Investigative Reporting,* 1990: *Minneapolis-St. Paul Star Tribune,* Minneapolis-St. Paul, MN: Minneapolis-St. Paul Star Tribune, 1989.

Career: Managing Editor and Editor-in-Chief, college paper, *Minnesota Daily;* City Hall/State Politics Reporter, *Duluth (MN) News Tribune,* 1983-86; City Government and Investigative Projects Reporter, *Minneapolis-St. Paul (MN) Star-Tribune,* 1986-93; Federal Agencies Reporter, *Minneapolis-St. Paul (MN) Star-Tribune,* 1993-95; Investigative Projects Reporter, *Minneapolis-St. Paul (MN) Star-Tribune,* 1995-.

Other Awards: Sweepstakes Award, Investigative Reporters and Editors, 1990.

For More Information: *The Pulitzer Prizes 1990,* New York: Simon & Schuster, 1990: 149-189.

Commentary: Chris Ison and Lou Kilzer won a Pulitzer Prize for reporting about arson-for-profit in St. Paul, Minnesota.

Louis Charles Kilzer   687

Birth: February 10, 1951; Cody, WY. **Parents:** Robert Louis Kilzer and Marjorie (Harkins). **Education:** Yale University, CT: BA, cum laude. **Spouse:** Elizabeth Antonia Kovacs (m. 1975). **Children:** Louis, Xanthe.

Prize: *Investigative Reporting,* 1990: *Minneapolis-St. Paul Star Tribune,* Minneapolis-St. Paul, MN: Minneapolis-St. Paul Star Tribune, 1989.

Career: Editor, *Fort Collins (CO) Triangle Review,* 1973-; Reporter, *Denver (CO) Rocky Mountain News,* 1977-83; Reporter and Swing Editor, *Denver (CO) Post,* 1983-85; Investigative Reporter, *Denver (CO) Post,* 1985-1987; Special Projects Reporter, *Minneapolis-St. Paul (MN) Star-Tribune,* 1987-.

Selected Works: *Churchill's Deception: The Dark Secret That Destroyed Nazi Germany,* 1994.

Other Awards: George Polk Memorial Award, Long Island University, NY, 1986. Sweepstakes Award, Investigative Reporters and Editors Association, 1990.

For More Information: *The Pulitzer Prizes 1990,* New York: Simon & Schuster, 1990: 149-189.

Commentary: Lou Kilzer, along with Chris Ison, won the Pulitzer Prize for reporting about arson-for-profit in St. Paul, Minnesota.

1991

Joseph Thomas Hallinan   688

Birth: September 3, 1960; Barberton, OH. **Parents:** Neil P. Hallinan and Judith Ann (Tonovitz). **Religion:** Catholic. **Education:** College of Charleston, SC. Boston University, MA: BS, magna cum laude. **Spouse:** Joy Anne Kurts (m. 1986).

Prize: *Investigative Reporting,* 1991: *Indianapolis Star,* Indianapolis, IN: Indianapolis Star, 1990.

Career: Reporter, Police and Federal Courts Reporter, General Assignment Reporter, *Indianapolis (IN) Star,* 1984-1991; National Correspondent, Regulatory Agencies Reporter, Investigative Reporter, *Newhouse News Service,* 1991-.

Other Awards: Distinguished Alumni Award, Boston University, MA, 1992. Nieman Fellow, Harvard University, MA, 1997-98.

Commentary: Joseph T. Hallinan and Susan M. Headden's investigation into medical malpractice in Indiana led to several discoveries. Their three-part series revealed that even several malpractice liabilities did not hurt doctors professionally.

Susan M. Headden   689

Birth: June 27, 1955; Mountain Lakes, NJ. **Parents:** William P. Headden and Marie M. **Education:** Ohio Wesleyan University: BA. **Spouse:** Douglas Richardson (m. 1988). **Children:** Margaret Ann.

Prize: *Investigative Reporting,* 1991: *Indianapolis Star,* Indianapolis, IN: Indianapolis Star, 1990.

Career: *Indianapolis (IN) Star,* 1979-92; Reporter, covering General Assembly, Federal Courts; Business Reporter; Writer on five-member projects team, 1991; Associate Editor, *U.S. News and World Report* magazine, 1992-; Senior Editor, *U.S. News and World Report* magazine.

Other Awards: Lester Hunt Award. United Press International Managing Editor Award. First Amendment Award, Indiana State Bar Association. Associated Press Managing Editor Award. Overseas Press Club Award. Indiana Academy of Family Physicians Award. Unity Award, Lincoln University (MO).

Commentary: Susan Margaret Headden and Joseph T. Hallinan spent one year investigating medical malpractice in Indiana. Their three-part series revealed that doctors who were found liable for malpractice had little to worry about. The doctors neither lost their hospital privileges nor their licenses and insurance. Prior to this investigation, Headden covered the general assembly, the courts, and industry. She was 35 when she won the award in 1991.

1992

Lorraine Adams   690

Birth: October 1, 1959; Coaldale, PA. **Education:** Princeton University, NJ: BA, magna cum laude. Princeton University, NJ: MA.

Prize: *Investigative Reporting,* 1992: *Dallas Morning News,* Dallas: Dallas Morning News, 1991.

Career: Staff Writer, *Concord (NH) Monitor,* 1983-84; Reporter, *Dallas (TX) Morning News,* 1984-; Projects Reporter, *Washington (DC) Post;* Metro Reporter, *Washington (DC) Post.*

Selected Works: *Abuses of Authority: When Citizens Complain about Police: The Pulitzer-Prize Winning Investigative Series* (with Dan Malone), 1991. *A Tourist Guide to Rock Art Sites in Northern Zimbabwe,* 1991.

Other Awards: Ward Mathis Award for Creative Writing, 1980. Francis Lemoyne Page Award for Creative Writing, 1981. Dateline Award, Society of Professional Journalists, Washington, DC Chapter, 1994. Genesis Award, Art Trust, Inc., 1996.

Commentary: Lorraine Adams and Dan Malone spent two years investigating civil rights violations by law enforcement officials throughout Texas. Their series, which was published throughout 1991, included their findings of "extensive misconduct and abuses of power." At one point during their investigation, they were threatened at gunpoint.

Dan F. Malone   691

Birth: January 22, 1955; Dallas, TX. **Parents:** Charles Ted Malone and Ela Grace (Darden). **Education:** University of Texas: BJ. **Spouse:** Kathryn Ann Jones (m. 1981).

Prize: *Investigative Reporting,* 1992: *Dallas Morning News,* Dallas: Dallas Morning News, 1991.

Career: Editor-in-Chief, college paper, *Daily Texan,* 1977-78; Intern, Austin (TX) Bureau, Harte Hanks, 1978-79; Staff Writer, *Corpus Christi (TX)*

Caller-Times, 1979-81; Staff Writer, *Fort Worth (TX) Star-Telegram,* 1981-85; Reporter, *Dallas (TX) Morning News,* 1985-92; Fort Worth (TX) Bureau Chief, *Dallas (TX) Morning News,* 1992-.

Selected Works: *Abuses of Authority: When Citizens Complain about Police: The Pulitzer-Prize Winning Investigative Series* (with Lorraine Adams), 1991.

Other Awards: Fox Fellow, National News Council, 1978. Freedom of Information Award, Texas Associated Press Managing Editor's Association, 1992. Institute for Southern Studies Award, 1992.

Commentary: Dan Malone and Lorraine Adams's investigation into civil rights abuses in law enforcement departments across the state of Texas led to the indictment of a prosecutor and a police officer who were subjects within their series. Their paper, the *Dallas Morning News,* filed two successful lawsuits to obtain records, and during their two-year campaign, Malone and Adams filed between 400 and 500 open record requests.

1993

Steve Berry   692

Birth: May 2, 1948; Ft. Jackson, SC. **Parents:** Charles Berry and Marjorie (Sheehan). **Education:** University of Montevallo, AL: BA. University of North Carolina, Greensboro: Masters. **Spouse:** Cheryl B. (m. 1973). **Children:** Stephen.

Prize: *Investigative Reporting,* 1993: *Orlando Sentinel,* Orlando, FL: Orlando Sentinel, 1992.

Career: Staff member, *Dothan (AL) Eagle,* 1970-71; Reporter, *Greensboro (NC) News and Record,* 1972-81; Copy Editor, *Greensboro (NC) News and Record,* 1981-84; Reporter, *Greensboro News and Record,* 1984-89; Reporter, *Orlando (FL) Sentinel,* 1989-96; Reporter, *Los Angeles Times,* 1996-.

Other Awards: Benjamin Fine Award, 1985. National Headliners Club Award, 1993. Sports Reporting Award, Society of Professional Journalists, 1994.

For More Information: *Orlando Sentinel Tribune,* 14 April (1993): A1.

Commentary: Steve Berry and Jeff Brazil's series of articles on the Volusia County sheriff's department detailed how deputies seized cash from motorists along Interstate 95. Over a three-year period, more than $8 million had been taken in, yet only one in four people stopped were ever charged with a crime. The series, "Tainted Money," was published throughout 1992.

Jeff Brazil   693

Birth: September 21, 1962; Honolulu, HI. **Education:** Santa Clara University, CA.

Prize: *Investigative Reporting,* 1993: *Orlando Sentinel,* Orlando, FL: Orlando Sentinel, 1992.

Career: *Palo Alto (CA) Peninsula Times Tribune,* 1989; General Assignment Reporter, Lake County Bureau, *Orlando (FL) Sentinel,* 1989-91; General Assignment Reporter, Daytona Beach Bureau, *Orlando (FL) Sentinel,* 1991-; General Assignment Reporter, Volusia County Bureau, *Orlando (FL) Sentinel,* ?-1993; Reporter, Orange County, *Los Angeles Times,* 1993-; Journalism Instructor, California State University, Fullerton.

Other Awards: National Headliners Club Award, 1993. Worth Bingham Prize, 1995. Watchdog Award, Orange County Press Club, 1995.

For More Information: *Orlando Sentinel Tribune,* 14 April (1993): A1.

Commentary: Jeff Brazil and Steve Berry's reporting of the activities of the Volusia County sheriff led to a governor's task force investigation. The sheriff had seized $8 million from motorists in an anti-drug enforcement effort.

1994

Providence Journal-Bulletin 694

Founded: January 3, 1820; Providence, RI. **Founder(s):** John Miller and John Hutchens.

Prize: *Local Reporting, Edition Time,* 1953: *Providence Journal-Bulletin,* Providence, RI, 1952. *Investigative Reporting,* 1994: *Providence Journal-Bulletin,* Providence, RI, 1993.

Other Awards: George W. Potter won an editorial writing Pulitzer Prize while at the *Providence Journal-Bulletin* in 1945, and Jack White won a national reporting Pulitzer Prize in 1974.

For More Information: *Half a Century With the Providence Journal: Being a Record of the Events and Associated Connected With the Past Fifty Years of Life of Henry R. Davis, Secretary of the Company,* Providence, RI: The Journal Company, 1904; *A Hundred Years of the Providence Journal,* Providence, RI: Providence Journal, 1929; Byrnes, Garrett Davis and Charles H. Spilman, *The Providence Journal, 150 Years,* Providence, RI: Providence Journal, 1980.

Commentary: In 1953, the staff of the *Providence Journal-Bulletin* was awarded a Pulitzer Prize for Local Reporting, Edition Time. It was the first time that an entire news staff won a Pulitzer Prize. The coverage of a local bank that was robbed by an escaped psychiatric patient, the police chase, the death of a police officer, and the capture of the suspect all happened under the pressure of the newspaper's deadline.

In 1994, the staff of the *Providence Journal-Bulletin*'s investigation into corruption within Rhode Island's court system led to resignations and indictments. The reporting team members were Dan Barry, Tracy Breton, Ira Chinoy, Mike Stanton, Dean Starkman, and John Sullivan. Tom Heslin, managing editor for investigations, headed the newspaper's coverage of the story.

The *Providence Journal-Bulletin* is the oldest major daily in continuous publication in America. It began as the semiweekly *Manufacturers' & Farmers' Journal, Providence & Pawtucket Advertiser* in 1820. In 1823 John Miller bought his partner John Hutchens's share of the enterprise. In 1829, the twice-weekly paper became a daily titled the *Providence Journal,* and in 1863 the *Evening Bulletin* was added. The ownership of the company had changed several times and in June 1996, the Providence Journal Company became a publicly traded company. In September 1996, the company merged into the A.H. Belo Corporation, which also publishes newspapers in Texas.

1995

Brian R. Donovan 695

Birth: March 11, 1941; Syracuse, NY. **Education:** Syracuse University, NY. **Spouse:** Dr. Ellen Kanner (m. 1973). **Children:** Gregory, Rebecca.

Prize: *Investigative Reporting,* 1995: *Newsday,* Garden City, NY: Newsday, 1994.

Career: Reporter, *Rochester (NY) Democrat and Chronicle,* 1965-67; Reporter, *Newsday (NY),* 1967-.

Other Awards: Page One Award, Newspaper Guild of New York, 1980. George Polk Memorial Award, Long Island University, NY, 1980. Gold Typewriter Award, New York Press Club, 1995. National Headliners Club Award, 1995. National Journalism Award, Scripps-Howard Foundation, 1995. Investigative Reporting Award, Society of the Silurians, 1995.

Commentary: Brian Donovan and Stephanie Saul's investigation into disabled Long Island police officers uncovered widespread abuse of the disability system. The reporters used public records, confidential sources, and medical records to reveal how Long Island had the highest number of officers on disability pensions.

Stephanie Saul 696

Birth: January 28, 1954; St. Louis, MO. **Parents:** Elmer William Saul and Nancy (Cramer). **Education:** University of Mississippi: BA. **Spouse:** Walt Bogdanich (m. 1982). **Children:** Nicholas, Peter.

Prize: *Investigative Reporting,* 1995: *Newsday,* Garden City, NY: Newsday, 1994.

Career: Reporter, *New Albany (MS) Gazette,* 1974; Reporter, *Jackson (MS) Clarion-Ledger,* 1975-80; Reporter, *Cleveland (OH) Plain Dealer,* 1980-84;

Reporter, *Newsday (NY)*, 1984; Editor, National Desk.

Other Awards: Silver Gavel Award, American Bar Association, 1980. National Press Club Award, 1990. Gold Typewriter Award, New York Press Club, 1995. National Headliners Club Award, 1995. National Journalism Award, Scripps-Howard Foundation, 1995. Investigative Reporters and Editors Award, 1995. Investigative Reporting Award, Society of Silurians, 1995.

Commentary: Stephanie Saul and Brian Donovan's seven-part series exposed fraud within the Long Island police department's disability system. They documented one officer on disability who was a lifeguard while another flew hang gliders.

Saul is married to another Pulitzer Prize winner, Walt Bogdanich.

1996

Orange County Register 697

Founded: 1905.

Prize: *Investigative Reporting,* 1996: *Orange County Register,* Santa Ana, CA, 1995.

Selected Works: *Building for Tomorrow: The Orange County Register,* 1987.

Other Awards: Edward Humes won a Pulitzer Prize in Specialized Reporting in 1989.

For More Information: *Orange County Register,* 10 April (1996): A1, A6.

Commentary: The staff of the *Orange County Register's* investigation into fertility fraud at the University of California, Irvine's Center for Reproductive Health won a Pulitzer Prize for Investigative Reporting. The first story ran on May 16, 1995 and the whole series included more than 230 stories on topics such as egg theft, intimidation, and coverups. The investigative team included Susan Kelleher, Kim Christensen, Michelle Nicolosi, David Parrish, and Ernie Sloan. John Doussard, topic editor for health, science, and government, headed the project, along with Jim Mulvaney, investigations editor, and Terry Wimmer, assistant topic editor. Ken Brusic, executive editor, and Larry Burrough, assistant managing editor for news, supervised the project. Over 120 other staff members contributed to the series.

1997

Eric Christopher Nalder 698

Birth: March 2, 1946; Coulee Dam, WA. **Parents:** Philip Richard Nalder and Mabel Dorothy (Aurdel). **Education:** University of Washington: BA. **Spouse:** Jan Christiansen (m. 1968). **Children:** Britt.

Prize: *National Reporting,* 1990: *Seattle Times,* Seattle, WA: Seattle Times, 1989. *Investigative Reporting,* 1997: *Seattle Times,* "Tribal Housing: From Deregulation to Disgrace," Seattle, WA: Seattle Times, 1996.

Career: Reporter, *Everett (WA) Herald;* Reporter, *Seattle (WA) Post-Intelligencer;* Chief Investigative Reporter, *Seattle (WA) Times,* 1983-.

Selected Works: *Tankers Full of Trouble,* 1994.

Other Awards: Hearst Community Service Award, 1978. Writer's Education Association Award, Charles Stewart Mott Foundation, 1978. Sigma Delta Chi Award, 1986. Edward J. Meeman Award, Scripps-Howard Foundation, 1986. Thomas Stokes Award, 1990. National Headliners Club Award, 1991, 1993. Goldsmith Award for Investigative Journalism, 1993. Worth Bingham Prize, 1993. Public Service Award, Associated Press Managing Editors, 1993. Associated Press Sports Editors Award, 1993. Investigative Reporters and Editors Award, 1993, 1995. Governor's Book Award, 1995. Silver Gavel Award, American Bar Association, 1995. Clarion Award, Association for Women in Communications, 1997.

For More Information: Glazer, Myron and Penina Glazer, *The Whistleblowers: Exposing Corruption in Government and Industry,* New York: Basic Books, 1989; D'Antonio, Michael, *Atomic Harvest,* New York: Crown, 1993; Farmer, Sam, *Bitter Roses,* Champaign, IL: Sagamore, 1993.

Commentary: Eric Nalder is a two-time winner of the Pulitzer Prize. In 1990, he shared the National Reporting award for a series of articles about oil tankers. In 1997, he and his colleagues, Deborah Nelson and Alex Tizon, investigated the corrupt practices within a federally sponsored Native American housing program. They spent six months researching the story.

Deborah Nelson 699

Birth: January 13, 1953; Libertyville, IL. **Parents:** Thomas Bert Nelson and Thalia (Tetro). **Religion:** Christian. **Education:** College of Lake County, IL: AA. Arizona State University. Northern Illinois University: BS. DePaul University, IL: JD. **Spouse:** Charles Michael Jonak (m. 1976, div. 1981); Thomas Frederick Brune (m. 1990). **Children:** Molly, Anna (TB).

Prize: *Investigative Reporting,* 1997: *Seattle Times,* "Tribal Housing: From Deregulation to Disgrace," Seattle, WA: Seattle Times, 1996.

Career: Reporter, *DeKalb (IL) Daily Chronicle,* 1975-76; Reporter, *DuPage (IL) Pace Magazine,* 1976; Staff Reporter, *Arlington (IL) Daily Herald,* 1977-85; Investigative Reporter, *Chicago Sun-Times,* 1985-95; Journalism Instructor, Columbia College (IL), 1994-95; Investigative Reporter, *Seattle (WA) Times,* 1995-.

Selected Works: *IRE: Teamwork on Behalf of Press Freedom: The John Zenger Award for Freedom of the Press and the People's Right to Know, 1995* (with Rosemary Armao), 1995.

Other Awards: Investigative Reporters and Editors Award, 1983. National Housing Journalism Award, 1990. National Association of Realtors Award. Public Service Award, Illinois Associated Press, 1992. John Peter and Anna Catherine Zenger Award, 1994. Best of West Award, 1997. Clarion Award, Association for Women in Communications, 1997.

For More Information: *Editor & Publisher,* 130:15 (12 April 1997): 7-11+.

Commentary: Deborah Nelson moved with her husband and children to Washington state from Chicago to find "a more productive journalism environment." The prize-winning story on corruption and fraud in a federally sponsored Native American housing program began when Nelson learned of a 5,300-square-foot house being built with money from the program. She and her colleagues Eric Nalder and Alex Tizon spent six months researching the five-part series that appeared on page one of the *Seattle Times*.

"The story began as many others: A phone call from someone outraged over an injustice. In this case, the caller was a Native American and the outrage was a 5,300-square-foot home built for the tribal official with federal low-income housing money. I hiked through the woods to find the well-hidden estate and waded through federal records to figure out how it got there. That tip led to others and over the next six months, Eric Nalder and I teamed up to document the pervasive abuse in the government's tribal housing program—while Alex Tizon reported in poetic detail the desperate need for housing on the country's reservations. We found the problems were fostered by U.S. Department of Housing and Urban Development policies that curtailed oversight and discouraged enforcement. The series led to a Senate hearing and two federal investigations that confirmed our findings. HUD subsequently reassigned the officials in charge of the tribal housing program." —D. Nelson

Alex Tizon   700

Birth: October 30, 1959; Manila, Philippines. **Parents:** Francisco Tizon and Dr. Leticia Ascuncion Cvarak. **Education:** University of Oregon: BS, Phi Beta Kappa. Stanford University, CA: MA. **Spouse:** Melissa Quiason (m., d.). **Children:** Dylan.

Prize: *Investigative Reporting,* 1997: *Seattle Times,* "Tribal Housing: From Deregulation to Disgrace," Seattle, WA: Seattle Times, 1996.

Career: Freelance journalist, 1980-; Reporter, *Seattle (WA) Times,* 1986-; Guest Lecturer, University of Washington, Seattle University (WA), North Seattle Community College, WA, Seattle Pacific University, WA, 1986; Journalism Instructor, The Urban Journalism Workshop, 1990; Fiction writer and essayist.

Selected Works: *Choosing to Emerge* (with others), 1993.

Other Awards: Dow Jones Fellowship, Stanford University, CA. Professional Achievement Award, Filipino American National Historical Society, 1993. Penney-Missouri Multicultural Journalism Award, 1996. Society of Professional Journalists Award, 1996. Clarion Award, Association for Women in Communications, 1997. Puso Ng Pinoy Award, 1997.

For More Information: *Seattle Times,* 7 April (1997): A1; *Seattle Times,* 8 April (1997): A1; *Asian Focus,* May (1997); *Filipinas Magazine,* June (1997).

Commentary: Alex Tizon has been with the *Seattle Times* since 1986. He worked with Deborah Nelson and Eric Nalder on the fraudulent uses of government funds to build lavish homes in the Pacific Northwest. The group spent six months working on the project, conducting interviews, visiting Native American reservations, and wading through thousands of documents.

1998

Gary Cohn   701

Birth: March 9, 1952; Brooklyn, NY. **Parents:** Morton J. Cohn and Claire (Chinowsky). **Religion:** Jewish. **Education:** State University of New York, Buffalo: BA, summa cum laude, Phi Beta Kappa. University of California, Berkeley: Postgraduate.

Prize: *Investigative Reporting,* 1998: *Baltimore Sun,* "The Shipbreakers," December 7-9, Baltimore, MD: Baltimore Sun, 1997.

Career: Investigator, Southern Regional Council, 1975; Staff, Columnist Jack Anderson, 1975-80; Reporter, *Lexington (KY) Herald-Leader,* 1980-84; Reporter, Miami (FL), *Wall Street Journal,* 1984-86; Reporter, *Philadelphia (PA) Inquirer,* 1986-93; Reporter, *Baltimore (MD) Sun,* 1993-.

Other Awards: Washington Monthly Journalism Award, 1982, 1995, 1997. Investigative Reporting Award, Society of Professional Journalists, Philadelphia Chapter, PA, 1990. Outstanding Human Service Award, Governor's Commission on Latino Affairs, 1992. Special Citation for Public Service, Society of Professional Journalists, Philadelphia Chapter, PA, 1992. Media Award, Maryland Press Club, 1995. Finalist, SAIS-Ciba Prize for Excellence in International Journalism, Johns Hopkins University's Nitze School of Advanced International Studies, 1995. Excellence in Journalism Award, Society of Professional Journalists, Maryland Chapter, 1996. Inter-American Press Association Award, 1996. Overseas Press Club Award, 1996, 1998. Selden Ring

Award, University of Southern California School of Journalism Annenberg School for Communication, 1996, 1998. Times Mirror Journalist of the Year, 1996. Finalist, SAIS-Novartis Prize for Excellence in International Journalism, Johns Hopkins University's Nitze School of Advanced International Studies, 1997. George Polk Memorial Award, Long Island University, NY, 1998. Investigative Reporters and Editors Award, 1998. Society of Professional Journalists Award, 1998.

For More Information: *Baltimore Sun,* 13 March (1998): 2B; *American Journalism Review,* 20:5 (June 1998): 11.

Commentary: Gary Cohn and Will Englund won a Pulitzer Prize for "their compelling series on the international shipbreaking industry that revealed the dangers posed to workers and the environment when discarded ships are dismantled." Their reporting led Naval Secretary John H. Dalton to suspend "a proposal to send Navy ships to India, Pakistan, and Bangladesh for scrapping." Cohn's reporting on a Honduran army unit that tortured and murdered political suspects in the 1980s made him a finalist for a Meritorious Public Service Pulitzer Prize in 1996.

Will Englund   702

Birth: March 30, 1953; Pleasantville, NY. **Education:** Harvard University, MA. Columbia University, NY: MS. **Spouse:** Kathy Lally. **Children:** Two daughters.

Prize: *Investigative Reporting,* 1998: *Baltimore Sun,* "The Shipbreakers," December 7-9, Baltimore, MD: Baltimore Sun, 1997.

Career: *Bergen County (NJ) Record,* 1976-77; Copy Editor, *Baltimore (MD) Sun,* 1977-; *Glasgow (Scotland) Herald,* 1988; City Hall Reporter, *Baltimore (MD) Sun;* Education Reporter, *Baltimore (MD) Sun;* Correspondent, Moscow (Russia), *Baltimore (MD) Sun,* 1991-95; Reporter, *Baltimore (MD) Sun;* Correspondent, Moscow (Russia), *Baltimore (MD) Sun,* 1997-.

Other Awards: Fulbright Fellowship, 1988. George Polk Memorial Award, Long Island University, NY, 1998. Selden Ring Award, University of Southern California Annenberg School for Communication, 1998. Society of Professional Journalists Award, 1998.

For More Information: *Baltimore Sun,* March 13, 1998: 2B; *American Journalism Review,* 20:5 (June 1998): 11.

Commentary: Will Englund, along with Gary Cohn, won a Pulitzer Prize for their in-depth reporting of the international industry that has developed to break down large ships, many of which are decommissioned naval vessels. Englund first grew interested in the story after noting the scrapping of the Navy ship the *Coral Sea* while on a tour of shipwrecks in Baltimore Harbor.

Local General Spot News Reporting

1964

Norman Charles Miller Jr.   703

Birth: October 2, 1934; Pittsburgh, PA. **Parents:** Dr. Norman C. Miller and Elizabeth (Burns). **Education:** Pennsylvania State University: BA. **Spouse:** Mary Ann Rudy (m. 1957). **Children:** Norman III, Mary Ellen, Teresa, Scott.

Prize: *Local General Spot News Reporting,* 1964: *Wall Street Journal,* New York: Dow Jones, 1963.

Career: Staff member, *Wall Street Journal,* 1956; Served in U.S. Navy, 1956-60; Reporter, San Francisco (CA) and New York, (NY), *Wall Street Journal,* 1960-64; Detroit (MI) Bureau Chief, *Wall Street Journal,* 1964-66; Congressional Correspondent and National Political Correspondent, Washington (DC), *Wall Street Journal,* 1967-73; Washington (DC) Bureau Chief, *Wall Street Journal,* 1973-83; Columnist, *Wall Street Journal,* 1978-83; National Editor, *Los Angeles Times,* 1983-97.

Selected Works: *The Great Salad Oil Swindle,* 1965.

Other Awards: George Polk Memorial Award, Long Island University, NY, 1964. Gerald M. Loeb Award, Anderson Graduate School of Management, University of California, Los Angeles, 1967. Distinguished Alumnus Award, Pennsylvania State University, 1978.

For More Information: *New York Times,* 5 May (1964): 39; *Los Angeles Times,* 30 October (1997): A3.

Commentary: Norman C. "Mike" Miller won a Pulitzer Prize for the reporting on the bankruptcy of the Allied Crude Vegetable Oil and Refining Corporation and the multimillion dollar vegetable oil scam in New Jersey. A rogue trader had swindled $150 million from Wall Street investment firms by using nonexistent vegetable oil as collateral. Miller was the first person to win a Pulitzer Prize in the category of Local General Spot News Reporting.

1965

Melvin Harvey Ruder   704

Birth: January 19, 1915; Manning, ND. **Parents:** Moris M. Ruder and Rebecca (Friedman). **Education:** University of North Dakota: BA. Northwestern University, IL: Postgraduate. University of North Dakota: MA. **Spouse:** Ruth Bergen (m. 1950). **Children:** Patricia.

Prize: *Local General Spot News Reporting,* 1965: *Hungry Horse News,* Columbia Falls, MT: Hungry Horse News, 1964.

Career: Assistant Professor of Journalism, University of North Dakota, 1940; Industrial Relations Specialist, Westinghouse Electric Company, 1940-41; Served in U.S. Navy, 1942-45; Public Relations Member, American Machine and Foundry Company, 1946; Founder, Editor, *Columbia Falls (MT) Hungry Horse News,* 1946-78; Editor Emeritus, *Columbia Falls (MT) Hungry Horse News,* 1978.

For More Information: *Quill,* 51:3 (March 1963): 16+; *New York Times,* May 4 1965.

Commentary: Melvin Ruder, founder of the *Hungry Horse News,* won a Pulitzer Prize for his coverage of the sudden and extensive flooding of the Columbia Falls, Montana area. The crisis began on June 8, 1964. Ruder gathered all the information he could and published his weekly paper on time on Friday, June 12. He published additional editions on the 13th and the 15th of June, as well as covering the disaster for the Associated Press and telephoning local radio stations and nearby daily newspapers with updates.

1966

Los Angeles Times

Full entry appears as #91 under "Breaking News Reporting," 1998.

1967

Robert Vernon Cox   705

Birth: March 28, 1927; Chambersburg, PA. **Spouse:** Martha C. **Children:** Six children.

Prize: *Local General Spot News Reporting,* 1967: *Chambersburg Public Opinion,* Chambersburg, PA: Chambersburg Public Opinion, 1966.

Career: Served in U.S. Army Air Corps, WWII; Office Manager, food processing company; Gas serviceman; Automobile salesman; Sports Writer, *Cham-*

bersburg (PA) Public Opinion, 1959-; City Editor, *Chambersburg (PA) Public Opinion.*

For More Information: *New York Times,* 2 May (1967): 40.

Commentary: Robert V. Cox covered the raids of the "Mountain Man," an outlaw sniper in Pennsylvania mountain country, until the fugitive, William Hohenbaugh, was killed on May 18, 1966. Cox followed the story for a year as the outlaw's reign of terror peaked in the abduction of Peggy Ann Bradnick, a 17-year-old, on May 11, 1966. A sharpshooter shot the fugitive, and Ms. Bradnick was released unharmed.

1968

Detroit Free Press
Full entry appears as #328 under "Editorial Writing," 1955.

1969

John Davis Fetterman 706
Birth: February 25, 1920; Danville, KY. **Death:** June 21, 1975. **Parents:** John Lawrence Fetterman and Zora (Goad). **Religion:** Methodist. **Education:** Murray State University, KY: BS. University of Kentucky: Postgraduate. **Spouse:** Evelyn A. Maner (m. 1944). **Children:** Phyllis Lee, Mindy Nelle.

Prize: *Local General Spot News Reporting,* 1969: *Louisville Times and Courier-Journal,* Louisville, KY: Louisville Times and Courier-Journal, 1968.

Career: Member of Seabees, U.S. Navy, 1942-45; Editor, *Murray (KY) Ledger and Times,* 1946-47; Teacher, Illinois Public Schools, 1948-50; *Nashville (TN) Tennessean,* 1950-57; Writer, Photographer, *Louisville (KY) Courier-Journal,* 1957-69; Editor, *Louisville (KY) Times* magazine.

Selected Works: *Stinking Creek,* 1967. *Five Score Years Ago,* 1962.

Other Awards: National Headliners Club Award, 1969. Named Outstanding Alumnus, Murray State University, KY, 1971. Honorary Degree, University of Louisville, KY, 1974.

For More Information: *Life,* 18 August (1967); *New York Times,* 23 June (1975): 30 *Contemporary Authors, Volumes 93-96,* Detroit: Gale Research Company, 1980.

Commentary: John Fetterman's moving account of the body of a dead soldier returning to his native Kentucky won him a Pulitzer Prize. He was also a member of the reporting team of the *Louisville Courier-Journal* who won the Meritorious Public Service

award in 1967 for reporting about the effect of strip mining on the land.

1970

Thomas Fitzpatrick 707
Birth: February 2, 1928; Bronx, NY. **Education:** Washington University, MO: BA. **Spouse:** Christina F. **Children:** Three children.

Prize: *Local General Spot News Reporting,* 1970: *Chicago Sun-Times,* "A Wild Night's Ride with SDS," October 9, Chicago: Chicago Sun-Times, 1969.

Career: Paratrooper, U.S. Army, WWII; *Kent (OH) Courier-Tribune; Toledo (OH) Blade; Cleveland (OH) Plain Dealer;* Reporter, Columnist, *Chicago Tribune,* 1961-66; Sports Columnist, *Chicago Daily News,* 1966-68; Reporter, Columnist, *Chicago Sun-Times,* 1968-79; Reporter, *Arizona Republic,* 1979-80; Columnist, *Arizona Republic,* 1980-87; Staff Columnist, Phoenix (AZ) *New Times,* 1987-94.

Other Awards: Beck Award, *Chicago Tribune,* 1963.

For More Information: *New York Times,* May 5, 1970: 48; *Phoenix New Times,* October 9, 1991: features, 15; *Arizona Republic,* December 28, 1994: B1.

Commentary: Tom Fitzpatrick won a Pulitzer Prize for his coverage of the anti-war rallies in Chicago in 1969. He wrote his award-winning story in 45 minutes after running five miles with the protesters, who were avoiding the police.

1971

Akron Beacon Journal
Full entry appears as #490 under "General News Reporting," 1987.

1972

Richard Lee Cooper 708
Birth: December 8, 1946; Grand Rapids, MI. **Parents:** Harold Ralph Cooper and Elizabeth (DeSchipper). **Religion:** Presbyterian. **Education:** Grand Rapids Junior College, MI. Michigan State University: BA. **Spouse:** Carol Jean Bonjernoor (m. 1968). **Children:** Jason, Jessica.

Prize: *Local General Spot News Reporting,* 1972: *Rochester Times-Union,* Rochester, NY: Rochester Times-Union, 1971.

Career: General Assignment Reporter, *Rochester (NY) Times-Union,* 1969-77; Reporter, *Philadel-*

phia (PA) Inquirer, 1977-; Neighbors Editor, *Philadelphia (PA) Inquirer,* 1983-; Assistant City Editor, *Philadelphia (PA) Inquirer,* 1988-91; Main Line Editor, *Philadelphia (PA) Inquirer,* 1991-; Editor, *Main Line and Delaware County Neighbors,* 1993-; Editor, *Main Line and Delaware County and Chester County Neighbors,* 1995-.

Other Awards: Spot News Award, New York State Associated Press, 1972, 1976. Distinguished Alumni Award, Grand Rapids Junior College, MI, 1974. Outstanding Contributions in Public Information Award, New York State Bar Association, 1977. First Prize in Investigative Reporting, Gannett News, 1977. Fellow, University of Michigan, 1977.

For More Information: *New York Times,* 2 May (1972): 36.

Commentary: Richard Cooper and John Machacek broke the story about the true cause of death of 43 hostages and inmates during an uprising at Attica Prison in September 1971. A state official had stated that several had died of slashed throats. However, the two reporters were the first to confirm that the hostages had been shot. None of the inmates had guns and the public's perception of the uprising changed dramatically after Cooper and Machacek broke the news.

John W. Machacek   709

Birth: February 18, 1940; Cedar Rapids, IA. **Parents:** Wesley J. Machacek and Agnes (McGrane). **Religion:** Roman Catholic. **Education:** Marquette University, WI: AB. State University of New York. **Spouse:** Mary Anna S. (m. 1968). **Children:** Sarah, Rachel.

Prize: *Local General Spot News Reporting, 1972: Rochester Times-Union,* Rochester, NY: Rochester Times-Union, 1971.

Career: Summer Intern, *Kenosha (WI) News,* 1961; Summer Intern, *Waukesha (WI) Daily Freeman,* 1962; Reporter, *Milwaukee (WI) Sentinel,* 1962-64; General Assignment Reporter, *Albany (NY) Knickerbocker News,* 1964-65; Education Reporter, *Albany (NY) Knickerbocker News,* 1965-67; Transportation Reporter, *Rochester (NY) Times-Union,* 1967-69; Education Reporter, *Rochester (NY) Times-Union,* 1969-72; Environment Reporter, *Rochester (NY) Times-Union,* 1972; City Hall Reporter, *Rochester (NY) Times-Union,* 1972-76; Political Reporter, *Rochester (NY) Times-Union,* 1976-83; Washington (DC) Correspondent, Gannett News Service, 1983-.

Other Awards: Professional Journalism Fellow, Stanford University, CA, 1973-74. National Education Writing Award, National Council for the Advancement of Education Writing, 1973. "Well Done" Award, Gannett Company, 1978, 1982.

Commentary: John Machacek and Richard Cooper won the 1972 Pulitzer Prize for local general spot news reporting. "Their exclusive report revealed that

prison guard hostages in the Attica, New York, state prison uprising died of gunshots fired by state troopers. Previously, state authorities had insisted that hostages' throats were slit by rioting inmates when troopers stormed the prison. The story dramatically changed public attitudes about the insurrection." —J. Machacek

1973

Chicago Tribune   710

Founded: June 10, 1847; Chicago, IL. **Founder(s):** James Kelly, John E. Wheeler, Joseph K.C. Forrest.

Prize: *Local General Spot News Reporting, 1973: Chicago Tribune,* Chicago, 1972. *Local Investigative Specialized Reporting, 1976: Chicago Tribune,* Chicago, 1975.

Selected Works: *The Chicago Tribune News Staff: The Story of the Men and Women Who Gather, Write, Edit, and Illustrate Chicago Tribune News, Features, and Editorials,* 1957.

Other Awards: The staff of the *Chicago Tribune* has won 16 individual Pulitzer Prizes.

For More Information: Kinsley, Philip, *The Chicago Tribune, Its First Hundred Years,* Chicago: Chicago Tribune, 1946; Tebbel, John William, *An American Dynasty,* Garden City, NY: Doubleday & Company, Inc., 1947; Wendt, Lloyd, *Chicago Tribune: The Rise of a Great American Newspaper,* Chicago: Rand McNally, 1979; Gies, Joseph, *The Colonel of Chicago,* New York: Dutton, 1979; Unger, Rudolph M., *Chicago Tribune News Staff, 1920s-1960s,* Chicago, IL, 1991; Squires, James D., *Read All About It! The Corporate Takeover of America's Newspapers,* New York: Times Books, 1993; Smith, Richard Norton, *The Colonel: The Life and Legend of Robert R. McCormick, 1880-1955,* Boston: Houghton Mifflin Company, 1997.

Commentary: In 1973, the *Chicago Tribune* was awarded a Pulitzer Prize for its investigation into and exposure of the "flagrant" violations of voting procedures in the primary election on March 21, 1972.

The entire staff of the *Chicago Tribune* was awarded a Pulitzer Prize for two of its investigations in 1975. The exposure of widespread abuses in federal housing programs led to the new Secretary of the United States Department of Housing and Urban Development, Carla Hills, issuing directives to tighten mortgage practices. George Bliss and Chuck Neubauer spent seven months working on the story. The investigation into the appalling conditions at Von Solbrig and Northeast Community Hospitals resulted in their closures. The reporting team of Pamela Zekman, William Gaines, William B. Crawford, and Jay Branegan worked on the stories.

The *Chicago Tribune* began in 1847 and was an

"outgrowth of a literary weekly" published by Thomas A. Stewart, James Kelly, John E. Wheeler, and Joseph K.C. Forrest. Its first issue had a circulation of 400, but by 1865 the paper had a circulation of 40,000 per day and in 1996 it had an average daily circulation of over 680,000. Joseph Medill began his tenure with the paper in 1855 when he and his partners bought the *Chicago Tribune* on June 18, and the paper became a voice against slavery. (Medill became the mayor of Chicago in 1871.) He died in 1899. On August 29, 1911, the words, "World's Greatest Newspaper" appeared on the masthead. In 1914, Colonel Robert R. McCormick, a grandson of Medill, and his cousin, Joseph Patterson, shared editorial and publishing duties of the *Chicago Tribune.* (In 1921, the Medill School of Journalism opened at Northwestern University in Illinois.) Colonel McCormick died in 1955 at age 75. (McCormick Place, a convention center named for the former publisher, opened in 1960.) Don Maxwell was editor of the paper from 1955 to 1969 and Clayton Kirkpatrick took over in 1969. In 1983, the *Chicago Tribune* became a public company, the Tribune Company.

1974

Hugh Frederick Hough   711

Birth: April 15, 1924; Sandwich, IL. **Death:** April 16, 1986. **Parents:** Forrest Everett Hough and Lila M. (Legner). **Education:** University of Illinois: BS. **Spouse:** Ellen Marie Wesemann (m. 1948). **Children:** Hollis, Heidi, Peter, Christopher.

Prize: *Local General Spot News Reporting,* 1974: *Chicago Sun-Times,* Chicago: Chicago Sun-Times, 1973.

Career: Served in U.S. Army Air Forces, 1943-45; Editor, college paper, *Daily Illini;* Sports Editor, *Dixon (IL) Evening Telegraph,* 1951-52; Reporter, Rewriteman, *Chicago Sun-Times,* 1952-86; Columnist, *Chicago Sun-Times,* 1974-86.

Other Awards: Stick-o-Type Award, Chicago Newspaper Guild, 1960, 1965-66. Award, John Howard Association, 1961. Marshall Field Award, 1969. Newswriting Award, Illinois Association Press, 1974.

For More Information: *New York Times,* 7 May (1974): 40; *Chicago Tribune,* 17 April (1986): C10.

Commentary: Hugh Hough, along with Art Petacque, wrote a series of articles about the 1966 murder of Valerie Percy, the daughter of former United States Senator Charles Percy. That series won the two men a Pulitzer Prize. He joined with Petacque to write the column "Out Front" that took a behind-the-scenes look at local topics. Later the column was known as "Petacque-Hough."

Arthur Martin Petacque   712

Birth: July 20, 1924; Chicago, IL. **Parents:** Ralph David Petacque and Fay Nora (Brauner). **Religion:** Jewish. **Education:** University of Illinois. **Spouse:** Regina Battinus (m. 1944). **Children:** Susan, William.

Prize: *Local General Spot News Reporting,* 1974: *Chicago Sun-Times,* Chicago: Chicago Sun-Times, 1973.

Career: Reporter, *Chicago Sun,* 1942-47; Reporter, *Chicago Sun-Times,* 1947-; Investigative Reporter, *Chicago Sun-Times,* 1957-; Crime Editor, *World Book Encyclopedia,* 1970-75; Columnist, *Chicago Sun-Times,* 1974-.

Other Awards: Page One Award, Chicago Newspaper Guild, 1949, 1957, 1959, 1962-63, 1965, 1968. Joseph M. Fay Memorial Award, Chicago Newspaper Reporters Association, 1960. Investigative Reporting and Spot News Reporting Awards, 1963, 1966, 1968, 1974, 1976. Professor Jacob Scher Daily Newswriting Award, Theta Sigma Phi, Chicago Chapter, IL, 1964. John Baptist Scalabrini Award, American Community of Italian Ancestry, 1966. Marshall Field Award, 1968. Prime Minister's Medal, State of Israel, 1976. Dante Award, Civic Committee of Italian Americans, 1980. Best Spot News Coverage in Illinois, United Press International, 1980. Emmy Award, Local News Spot Reporting, 1984. Illinois Academy of Criminology Award, 1985. Chicago Journalism Hall of Fame, Chicago Headline Club, 1990. Honorary Degree, Southern Illinois University, 1987.

For More Information: *New York Times,* 7 May (1974): 40; Taft, William H., *Encyclopedia of Twentieth-Century Journalists,* New York: Garland Publishing, 1986; *Contemporary Authors, Volume 136,* Detroit: Gale Research Company, 1992; Riley, Sam G., *Biographical Dictionary of American Newspaper Columnists,* Westport, CT: Greenwood Press, 1995.

Commentary: Arthur M. Petacque, along with Hugh F. Hough, won a Pulitzer Prize for their investigation of the 1966 murder of Valerie Percy, the daughter of former United States Senator Charles Percy. He later teamed with Hough to write a column on local affairs titled "Petacque-Hough." Petacque's specialty is investigation and he has won several prizes for his work.

1975

Xenia Daily Gazette   713

Founded: November 1881; Xenia, OH.

Prize: *Local General Spot News Reporting,* 1975: *Xenia Daily Gazette,* Xenia, OH, 1974.

Commentary: The staff of the Ohio paper the *Xenia Daily Gazette* was awarded a Pulitzer Prize for its coverage of the tornado that struck the town on April 3, 1974.

The *Xenia Daily Gazette* began publishing in November 1881. In 1888, the name was changed to the *Xenia Daily Gazette and Torchlight.* Over the years, the paper has been the *Xenia Gazette,* the *Evening Gazette,* and the *Daily Gazette.* In 1974, the paper was once again the *Xenia Daily Gazette.*

1976

Gene Edward Miller   714

Birth: September 16, 1928; Evansville, IN. **Parents:** Paul E. Miller and Irene (Hudson). **Education:** Indiana University: BA. **Spouse:** Electra Sonia Yphantis (m. 1952). **Children:** Janet, Theresa, Thomas, Roberta.

Prize: *Local Investigative Specialized Reporting,* 1967: *Miami Herald,* Miami, FL: Miami Herald, 1966. *Local General Spot News Reporting,* 1976: *Miami Herald,* Miami, FL: Miami Herald, 1975.

Career: Reporter, *Evansville Press;* Reporter, *Fort Wayne (IN) Journal-Gazette,* 1950-51; Served in Counter-Intelligence Corps, U.S. Army, 1951-53; Reporter, *Wall Street Journal,* 1953-54; Reporter, *Richmond (VA) News Leader,* 1954-57; Reporter, *Miami (FL) Herald,* 1957-; Associate Editor, *Miami (FL) Herald.*

Selected Works: *83 Hours Till Dawn,* 1971. *Invitation to a Lynching,* 1975.

Other Awards: Nieman Fellow, Harvard University, MA, 1967-68. Honorary Degree, Indiana University, 1977.

For More Information: *Contemporary Authors, Volumes 97-100,* Detroit: Gale Research Company, 1981; Dygert, James H., *Investigative Journalist: Folk Heroes of a New Era,* Prentice Hall, 1976.

Commentary: Gene Miller has twice won the Pulitzer Prize for similar stories: His investigation and uncovering of evidence has helped exonerate people convicted of murder. An investigation that he began in 1967, the same year that he won his first Pulitzer Prize, culminated in his receiving the honor once again, nine years later.

1977

Margo Huston   715

Birth: February 12, 1943; Waukesha, WI. **Parents:** James Bremner and Cecile (Timlin). **Education:** University of Wisconsin. Marquette University, WI: AB. **Spouse:** James Huston (m. 1967, div.). **Children:** Sean Patrick.

Prize: *Local General Spot News Reporting,* 1977: *Milwaukee Journal,* "I'll Never Leave My Home. Would You?" October 31, Milwaukee, WI: Milwaukee Journal, 1976.

Career: Reporter, *Waukesha (WI) Freeman,* 1966-67; Feature Writer, Music and Television Critic, *Milwaukee (WI) Journal,* 1967-70; Journalism Instructor, University of Wisconsin, Milwaukee; Writer, Women and Consumer Sections, *Milwaukee (WI) Journal,* 1972; Reporter, Women and Food Sections; Editorial Writer, *Spectrum,* 1979-84; Political Reporter, *Spectrum,* 1985; Assistant Picture Editor, *Spectrum,* 1985-91; Copy Editor, *Spectrum,* 1992-95; Reporter, *Milwaukee (WI) Journal-Sentinel,* 1995-.

Other Awards: Penney-Missouri Award, 1975. Clarion Award, 1977. Knight of Golden Quill Award, Milwaukee Press Club, 1977. Writing Award, Wisconsin Associated Press, 1977. Special Award, Society of Professional Journalists, Milwaukee Chapter, WI, 1977. Paul Mynie, Penney-Missouri Award, 1978. Byline Award, Marquette University College of Journalism, WI, 1980. Best Editorial Award, Wisconsin Associated Press, 1982. Award for Journalistic Achievement, Wisconsin Women's Network, 1983. Dick Goldsohn Fund Award, 1991. Literary Arts Grantee, Wisconsin Arts Board, 1992.

Commentary: Margo Huston spent several months gathering information and interviewing the elderly for her week-long series that won a Pulitzer Prize. She described the lives of older individuals, gave an overall picture of services available to the elderly, and compiled a list of agencies and retirement communities in the area. After the series ended, Wisconsin's Lieutenant Governor and Board on Aging recommended that a study be done on home health care for the elderly.

1978

Richard Ernest Whitt 716

Birth: December 15, 1944; Beauty Ridge, KY. **Parents:** Walter Charles Whitt and Irene (Hayes). **Education:** Asland Community College, KY. University of Kentucky: BA. **Spouse:** Sharon Lyon (m. 1968, d.); Terri Bellizzi (m. 1995). **Children:** Hayes, Emily (SL); Stepchild: Christen (TB).

Prize: *Local General Spot News Reporting,* 1978: *Louisville Courier-Journal,* Louisville, KY: Louisville Courier-Journal, 1977.

Career: Served in U.S. Navy, 1962-66; Reporter, *Middlesboro (KY) Daily News,* 1970-71; Reporter, *Waterloo (IA) Daily Courier,* 1971-73; City Editor, *Kingsport (TN) Times-News,* 1972-76; Frankfort (KY) Bureau Chief, *Louisville (KY) Courier-Journal,* 1977-80; Special Projects Reporter, *Louisville (KY) Courier-Journal,* 1980-89; Investigative Reporter, *Atlanta (GA) Journal and Constitution,* 1989-.

Other Awards: Outstanding Kentucky Journalist, Sigma Delta Chi, 1977. Air Combat Medal. John Hancock Award, John Hancock Financial Services, MA, 1983. Story of the Year, Georgia Associated Press, 1994. Governor James M. Cox Award, Cox Newspapers Awards, 1994. Journalism Hall of Fame, University of Kentucky, 1995.

For More Information: *Kingston Times-News,* 18 April (1978): 1; *New York Times,* 18 April (1978): 28; *Contemporary Authors, Volumes 81-84,* Detroit: Gale Research Company, 1979.

Commentary: Richard Whitt's reporting on the tragic fire in the Beverly Hills Supper Club in Southgate, Kentucky, and his research and follow-up stories, won him a Pulitzer Prize in 1978. His reporting also led to the strengthening of the fire marshall's office by the governor of the state.

1979

San Diego Evening Tribune 717

Founded: December 2, 1895; San Diego, CA.

Prize: *Local General Spot News Reporting,* 1979: *San Diego Evening Tribune,* San Diego, CA, 1978.

Other Awards: Jonathan Freedman of the *San Diego Tribune* won an editorial writing Pulitzer Prize in 1987.

Commentary: The *San Diego Evening Tribune* won a Pulitzer Prize for extensive, accurate, and timely coverage of one of the nation's worst airline accidents, the collision of a private plane and a Pacific Southwest Airlines 727 on September 25, 1978. The paper's last edition, which was at newsstands less than six hours after the crash, carried 10 stories.

Since 1901, the *San Diego Evening Tribune* was published by the same company that published the morning paper, the *San Diego Union.* The *San Diego Union* was first published on October 10, 1865. The Spreckels family published the newspapers until 1929, when they were sold to the Copley family. On February 2, 1992, the two newspapers became the *San Diego Union-Tribune,* a morning paper.

1980

Philadelphia Inquirer 718

Founded: 1847; Philadelphia, PA.

Prize: *Meritorious Public Service,* 1978. *Local General Spot News Reporting,* 1980. *Meritorious Public Service,* 1990.

Selected Works: *Chronicle of Treason: Reprint of Series of Articles Appearing in the Philadelphia Inquirer, March 3-9, 1958, Committee on Un-American Activities, House of Representatives, Eighty-fifth Congress, Second Session* (with Francis Eugene Walter), 1958. *On Wine: The First 100 Columns from the Philadelphia Inquirer* (with Michael Pakenham), 1976.

Other Awards: The *Philadelphia Inquirer*'s staff, editors, and reporters have won 18 Pulitzer Prizes, in addition to other journalism and public service awards.

For More Information: Santangelo, Orazio de Attellis, *A Lesson to Mr. Jasper Harding, Editor of "The Pennsylvania Inquirer and Daily Courier," Philadelphia, from the School-Master, O. de A. Santangelo,* New-Orleans, LA: Benjamin Levy, 1839; Wainwright, Nicholas B., *The History of the Philadelphia Inquirer,* Supplement to the *Philadelphia Inquirer,* September 16, 1962.

Commentary: The *Philadelphia Inquirer* has won two Meritorious Public Service awards. The first came in 1978 for a series of articles showing abuses of power by the police in its home city. In 1990 the *Inquirer* shared the prize with North Carolina's *Washington Daily News*. Gilbert M. Gaul's reporting disclosed how the American blood industry operates with little governmental regulation or supervision. In 1980, the *Inquirer* won a Local Spot News Reporting Prize for coverage of the nuclear accident at Three-Mile Island.

The *Inquirer* was founded in 1847 as the *Pennsylvania Inquirer*. The name was changed to the *Philadelphia Inquirer* in 1860. In 1863, the *Inquirer* became one of the first daily newspapers to use a web-fed rotary press that could print on both sides of the paper at once. Moses L. Annenberg bought it in 1936. Circulation increased steadily under his ownership. John S. Knight purchased the *Inquirer* and the *Philadelphia Daily News* in 1969 and both papers became part of the Knight-Ridder group in 1974.

1981

Longview Daily News   719
Founded: April 2, 1923; Longview, WA.

Prize: *Local General Spot News Reporting,* 1981: *Longview Daily News,* Longview, WA: *Longview Daily News,* 1980.

For More Information: McClelland Jr., John M. *R.A. Long's Planned City: The Story of Longview,* Longview, WA: Longview Publishing Company, 1976.

Commentary: Roger A. Werth along with the entire staff of the *Longview Daily News* won a Pulitzer Prize for their coverage of the eruption of Mount St. Helens on May 18, 1980 in Washington state. The paper, which had a circulation of 26,000, produced 400 articles within two weeks of the disaster. Most of the staff worked 80 hours the first week to cover the story. Werth, who was born in Portland, Oregon in 1957, was a photographer at the paper.

Longview, Washington was a planned city developed by Robert A. Long, the principal of the Long-Bell Lumber Company. Long realized that the town newspaper should be independent and not a company publication. A council was set up to run the new newspaper. The members included Tom Fisk, A.L. Gibbs, Letcher Lambuth, S.M. Morris, and Ralph Tennal. The *Longview News* was first published on January 26, 1923. On April 2, 1923, the paper's official name became the *Longview Daily News.* The paper was managed by Ralph Tennal, who was from Missouri. He left the paper after three months. John M. McClelland, the brother-in-law of S.M. Morris, the editor, was hired to replace Tennal. Included in McClelland's employment contract was the option to purchase the paper after two years. At that time,

McClelland and Long bought the stock of the Longview Publishing Company. McClelland eventually bought out his partner. McClelland's son, John, took over as editor in 1940 and as publisher in 1955. The Longview Publishing Company grew to include other Washington state newspapers, *Washington* magazine, and a commercial printing company. In 1986, the McClelland family sold the holdings of the Longview Publishing Company. Relatives of the McClelland family, headed by Ted Natt, bought the *Longview Daily News.* Natt's company's name is Westmedia Corp. Ted Natt is currently the publisher of the paper.

1982

Kansas City Star
Full entry appears as **#306** under "Editorial Writing," 1933.

Kansas City Times   720
Founded: 1867; Kansas City, MO.

Prize: *Local General Spot News Reporting,* 1982: *Kansas City Times,* Kansas City, MO, 1981.

Other Awards: Rick Atkinson of the *Kansas City Times* won a national reporting Pulitzer Prize in 1982.

For More Information: *Kansas City Star and Times,* July 12-20, 1951, "Covering the Flood in Greater Kansas City," Kansas City, MO, 1951.

Commentary: The *Kansas City Times,* founded in 1867, was purchased by William Rockhill Nelson on October 19, 1901. Nelson was also the founder and publisher of the *Kansas City Star.* Nelson died in 1915 and in accordance with his will, the newspapers were to be sold after his heirs' deaths. In 1926, the employees of the papers purchased the papers after the death of Nelson's daughter. In 1977, Capital Cities Communications, Inc. bought the company and James H. Hale was the publisher from 1977-1992. On March 1, 1990, the two papers were merged into the *Kansas City Star.*

Within a week of the collapse of two skywalks at the Hyatt Regency Hotel in Kansas City, the staffs of the two Kansas City newspapers, the *Kansas City Times* and the *Kansas City Star,* produced 50 pages of coverage on the tragedy. By the end of the year, the two papers had published over 340 articles on the incident that had killed 114 persons and injured 200.

1983

Fort Wayne News-Sentinel   721
Founded: January 1, 1918; Fort Wayne, IN.

Prize: *Local General Spot News Reporting,* 1983: *Fort Wayne News-Sentinel,* Fort Wayne, IN, 1982.

For More Information: *The News Sentinel, One of America's Great Newspapers, Since 1833,* Fort Wayne, IN: *The News-Sentinel,* 1947.

Commentary: The *Fort Wayne News-Sentinel* won a Pulitzer Prize for its coverage of the devastating flood of March 1982. The Indiana staff, including four photographers and nine reporters, ran front page stories for six days, 96 smaller stories, and 111 photographs. Included in the disaster coverage was emergency information for the newspaper's community.

The paper traces its history back to the *Fort Wayne News* founded on June 1, 1874 and the *Daily Fort Wayne Sentinel,* first published in 1833. On January 1, 1918, the two papers merged into the *Fort Wayne News and Sentinel,* and on June 2, 1918, the name was changed to the *News-Sentinel.*

1984

Newsday 722

Founded: September 3, 1940; Garden City, NY.
Founder(s): Alicia Patterson and Harry F. Guggenheim.
Prize: *Meritorious Public Service,* 1954. *Meritorious Public Service,* 1970. *Meritorious Public Service,* 1974. *Local General Spot News Reporting,* 1984. *Spot News Reporting,* 1992. *Spot News Reporting,* 1997.
Selected Works: *The Heroin Trail* (with the Newsday Staff), 1974. *Rush to Burn: Solving America's Garbage Crisis?* (with Newsday), 1989.
Other Awards: *Newsday*'s staff, editors, and reporters have won 16 Pulitzer Prizes, in addition to other journalism and public service awards.

For More Information: Keeler, Robert F., *Newsday: A Candid History of the Respectable Tabloid,* New York: Morrow, 1990.

Commentary: *Newsday* has won three Meritorious Public Service awards. The first prize was awarded in 1954 for its expose of New York state's race track scandals and labor racketeering, which led to the extortion indictment, guilty plea, and imprisonment of William C. DeKoning Sr., New York labor racketeer. *Newsday* won its second prize in 1970 for its three-year investigation and exposure of secret land deals in eastern Long Island, which led to a series of criminal convictions, discharges, and resignations among public and political officeholders. The third prize came in 1974 for *Newsday*'s definitive report on the illicit narcotic traffic in the United States and abroad, entitled, "The Heroin Trail." *Newsday*'s team of reporters won the Local General Spot News reporting prize in 1984 for their enterprising and comprehensive coverage of the baby Jane Doe case and its far-reaching social and political implications. It won the Spot News Reporting prize in 1992 for its coverage of a midnight subway derailment in Manhattan. It won the Spot News Reporting prize in 1997 for its enterprising coverage of the crash of TWA Flight 800 and its aftermath.

Newsday was founded by Alicia Patterson and Harry F. Guggenheim in in the garage of a house in Hempstead, New York in September 1940. The first issue was published on September 3, 1940. The new paper quickly outsold its competitor, the *Nassau Daily Review-Star. Newsday* was acquired by the Times-Mirror group in 1970. The newspaper is the sixth largest metropolitan daily in the country. *Newsday* serves Nassau and Suffolk counties on Long Island, New York, and the borough of Queens in New York City.

Local Investigative Specialized Reporting

1964

Albert V. Gaudiosi   723

Birth: 1923; Philadelphia, PA. **Education:** St. Joseph's College, PA. University of Pennsylvania. **Spouse:** Married. **Children:** One daughter.

    Prize: *Local Investigative Specialized Reporting,* 1964: *Philadelphia Bulletin,* Philadelphia, PA: Philadelphia Bulletin, 1963.

    Career: Copyboy, Reporter, *Philadelphia (PA) Inquirer,* 1947-63; Suburban Desk Reporter, *Philadelphia (PA) Bulletin,* 1963-71; Deputy Executive Director, Philadelphia '76 Inc., 1972-76; City Representative and Commerce Director, City of Philadelphia, 1976-77; Democratic nominee candidate for Mayor, City of Philadelphia, 1978-79; Head, government and public relations consulting firm; Vice-President and General Manager, Publishing Division, Packard Press, 1988-.

    Commentary: Albert V. Gaudiosi, James V. Magee, and Frederick Meyer won a 1964 Pulitzer Prize for their exposure of a gambling ring in Philadelphia. Their investigations exposed police participation in the ring and led to a reorganization of a police district, 15 suspensions from the force, and 9 dismissals.

    Gaudiosi left newspaper work in 1972. He worked for the city of Philadelphia, heading the agency responsible for planning Philadelphia's celebration of the nation's bicentennial. He unsuccessfully ran for the Democratic nomination for mayor of the city, headed a consulting firm, and then began working in private industry.

James V. Magee   724

Birth: 1913; Philadelphia, PA. **Death:** September 23, 1986. **Children:** James Jr.

    Prize: *Local Investigative Specialized Reporting,* 1964: *Philadelphia Bulletin,* Philadelphia, PA: Philadelphia Bulletin, 1963.

    Career: Sports Writer, *Philadelphia (PA) Bulletin;* News Reporter, *Philadelphia (PA) Bulletin,* 1941; General Assignment Reporter, *Philadelphia (PA) Evening Bulletin,* 1941-; Served in U.S. Army, WWII.

    Other Awards: Philadelphia Press Association Award, 1952.

    For More Information: *New York Times,* 5 May (1964): 39; *Philadelphia Inquirer,* 25 September (1986): 12C.

    Commentary: James V. Magee, Albert V. Gaudiosi, and Frederick Meyer won a Pulitzer Prize for their investigation into a gambling ring in Philadelphia. Their story led to suspensions and firings in the police department.

    Magee, a veteran of World War II, landed at Normandy on D-Day and earned a Purple Heart during the Battle of the Bulge. After the war, he covered the police beat and then became an investigative reporter for the *Philadelphia Evening Bulletin.*

Frederick A. Meyer   725

Birth: 1922; Philadelphia, PA. **Death:** June 17, 1993. **Education:** Villanova University, PA. **Spouse:** Loretta Poplawski. **Children:** Gregory, Geoffrey, Garry, Grace.

    Prize: *Local Investigative Specialized Reporting,* 1964: *Philadelphia Bulletin,* Philadelphia, PA: Philadelphia Bulletin, 1963.

    Career: Copyboy, *Philadelphia (PA) Bulletin,* 1940; Served in U.S. Army Air Forces, 1941-45; Staff member, *Philadelphia (PA) Bulletin,* 1946; Staff Photographer, *Philadelphia (PA) Bulletin,* 1947-82.

    For More Information: *Philadelphia Inquirer,* 18 June (1993): C11.

    Commentary: Frederick A. Meyer, along with his colleagues James V. Magee and Albert V. Gaudiosi, won a Pulitzer Prize for the investigation into a local numbers bank which was being run under the nose of local police officers. A grand jury indicted seven men for running the gambling business. Fifteen policemen were suspended and nine were fired. Meyer took photographs of the gamblers taking bets on a Philadelphia street corner.

    Meyer enlisted in the Army Air Forces, the predecessor to the Air Force in 1941, and was shot down over Hamburg, Germany in 1944. He was a photographer for the *Philadelphia Bulletin* for 35 years. His photographs had a natural quality to them, as he did not like to pose people.

1965

Eugene Francis Goltz   726

Birth: April 30, 1930; Marquette, IA. **Parents:** Lawrence Goltz and Loraine (Breitbach). **Religion:** Roman Catholic. **Education:** University of Kansas. St. Louis University, MO. University of Missouri. **Spouse:** Rosemary Antoinette James (m. 1960). **Children:** Joseph, James, John.

    Prize: *Local Investigative Specialized Reporting,* 1965: *Houston Post,* Houston, TX: Houston Post, 1964.

    Career: Editor, high school newspaper, 1947; Automobile worker; Served in U.S. Air Force, 1957-60; General Assignment Reporter, *Houston (TX) Post,* 1962-66; Investigative Reporter, *Newsday (NY),* 1966-67; Reporter, *Detroit Free Press,* 1967-72; Head, Investigative Team, *Dayton (OH) Daily News,* 1972-75; City Editor, *Covington (KY) Post,* 1975-78; Reporter, *Washington (DC) Times,* 1982-86; Editor, Writer, Newspaper Association of America, 1986-.

    Other Awards: Heywood Broun Award, Newspaper Guild, 1964. Nieman Fellow, Harvard University, MA, 1969-70. National Headliners Club Award, 1965.

    Commentary: Gene Goltz was awarded a Pulitzer Prize for his exposure of municipal corruption in Pasadena, Texas.

1966

John Anthony Frasca   727

Birth: May 25, 1916; Lynn, MA. **Death:** December 3, 1979. **Parents:** Michele Angelo Frasca and Maria (Jordan). **Education:** Holmes Junior College, MS. Mississippi College: BA. **Spouse:** Louise Cummings (m. 1948). **Children:** Charlotte, Sydney, Karen, Michele, John Anthony.

    Prize: *Local Investigative Specialized Reporting,* 1966: *Tampa Tribune,* Tampa, FL: Tampa Tribune, 1965.

    Career: Crane Operator, General Electric Company, 1936-; Reporter, *Hattiesburg (MS) American,* 1940-42; Served in U.S. Marine Corps, 1942-45; Capital Correspondent, Austin (TX), United Press International, 1945-48; Rewriteman, *Boston American,* 1948-53; Special Feature Writer, *Philadelphia (PA) Daily News,* 1953-57; Freelance public relations director; Publicity Director, Pennsylvania Democratic Party, 1957-58; Press Secretary, Pennsylvania Governor David L. Lawrence, 1958; Radio commentator, 1958-64; Editor, *Philadelphia (PA) Sons of Haly Times,* 1959-63; Publicity Director, Senate Campaign of Pennsylvania Supreme Court John Michael Musmano, 1964; Investigative Reporter and

Columnist, *Tampa (FL) Tribune,* 1964-68; Freelance writer, 1968-79; Columnist, *Tampa (FL) La Gaceta.*

    Selected Works: *The Mulberry Tree,* 1968. *Con Man or Saint?,* 1970. *The Unstoppable Glen Turner,* 1971. *GWT Changed the World for Me: The Story of Glen W. Turner—Motivational Genius,* 1972. *The Sun Rose Late* (with D.M.J. Harris), 1974.

    Other Awards: Best Feature of the Year Award, Texas Associated Press, 1954. Pennsylvania Mental Health Bell Award, 1956. Philadelphia Good Citizenship Award, 1956. Pennsylvania Optimist Club Award, 1957. Best Writing of Year Award, Philadelphia Press Association, 1956. Best Campaign Series, 1957. Best Feature Award, 1957. Heywood Broun Award, Newspaper Guild, 1966. Green Eyeshade Award, Society of Professional Journalists, Atlanta Chapter, GA.

    For More Information: *Contemporary Authors, Volumes 49-52,* Detroit: Gale Research Company, 1975; *New York Times,* 5 December (1979): D23.

    Commentary: John Frasca's reporting uncovered several flaws in the conviction of a man sentenced to 10 years in prison for armed robbery. His reporting, and another man's confession to the armed robbery, freed Robert Lamar Watson.

    While he was working as a freelance journalist in 1961, a number of Jewish newspapers hired him to cover the trial of Adolf Eichmann in Israel.

1967

Gene Edward Miller

Full entry appears as **#714** under "Local General Spot News Reporting," 1976.

1968

J. Anthony Lukas

Full entry appears as **#520** under "General Non-Fiction," 1986.

1969

Albert Lawrence Delugach   728

Birth: October 27, 1925; Memphis, TN. **Parents:** Gilbert Delugach and Edna (Short). **Education:** University of Missouri: BJ. **Spouse:** Bernice Goldstein (m. 1950). **Children:** Joy, David, Daniel, Sharon.

    Prize: *Local Investigative Specialized Reporting,* 1969: *St. Louis Globe-Democrat,* St. Louis: St. Louis Globe-Democrat, 1968.

    Career: Served in U.S. Navy, 1943-46; Labor News and Investigative Reporter, *Kansas (MO) City*

Star, 1951-60; Rewriteman, Feature Writer, Investigative Reporter, *St. Louis (MO) Globe-Democrat,* 1960-69; Investigative Reporter, *Los Angeles Times,* 1970-89.

Other Awards: Gerald Loeb Award, Anderson Graduate School of Management, University of California, Los Angeles, 1984.

For More Information: *New York Times,* 6 May (1969): 34.

Commentary: Albert L. Delugach and Denny Walsh began an investigation in 1968 into the St. Louis Steamfitters Union Local 562. Their series of articles led to the trial and conviction of union officials. It also won them the Pulitzer Prize.

Denny Jay Walsh   729

Birth: November 23, 1935; Omaha, NE. **Parents:** Gerald Jerome Walsh and Muriel (Morton). **Education:** University of Missouri: BJ. **Spouse:** Peggy Marie Moore (m. 1966). **Children:** Catherine Camille, Colleen Cecile, Sean Joseph.

Prize: *Local Investigative Specialized Reporting,* 1969: *St. Louis Globe-Democrat,* St. Louis: St. Louis Globe-Democrat, 1968.

Career: Served in U.S. Marine Corps, 1954-58; Staff Writer, *St. Louis (MO) Globe-Democrat,* 1961-68; Assistant Editor, *Life* magazine, 1968-70; Associate Editor, *Life* magazine, 1970-73; Reporter, *New York Times,* 1973-74; Reporter, *Sacramento (CA) Bee* and *Fresno (CA) Bee,* 1974-.

Other Awards: Con Lee Kelliher Award, Sigma Delta Chi, St. Louis Chapter, MO, 1962. American Political Science Association Award, 1963. Sigma Delta Chi Award, 1968. San Francisco Press Club Award, 1977.

Commentary: Denny Walsh and Albert L. Delugach began an investigation into the St. Louis Steamfitters Union Local 562 in 1965. Their series brought about a formal investigation, trial, and conviction of union officials for using union funds in a federal election campaign. The series also won them a Pulitzer Prize in 1969.

1970

Harold Eugene Martin   730

Birth: October 4, 1923; Cullman County, AL. **Parents:** Rufus John Martin and Emma (Meadows). **Religion:** Baptist. **Education:** Howard College, AL: BA, With Honors. Syracuse University, NY: MA. **Spouse:** Jean Elizabeth Wilson (m. 1945). **Children:** Three children.

Prize: *Local Investigative Specialized Reporting,* 1970: *Montgomery Advertiser* and *Alabama Journal,* Montgomery, AL, 1969.

Career: Apprentice Printer, Birmingham (AL), 1941; Printer, Reporter, Columnist, various newspapers and commercial printing plants, 1945-55; Staff member, *Birmingham (AL) Post-Herald;* Job Foreman and Reporter, *Alexander City (AL) City Outlook,* 1954-55; Executive, Newhouse Newspapers, 1957; Advertising Instructor, Samford University (AL), 1962-63; First Vice President, Southern Newspapers Inc., Montgomery (AL), 1963-; Vice President, Editor and Publisher, *Montgomery (AL) Advertiser* and *Montgomery (AL) Alabama Journal,* 1963-; Publisher and Editor, *The Montgomery (AL) Advertiser,* 1969-77; Visiting Professor of Journalism, University of Florida, 1979-80; President, Jefferson Pilot Publications, 1980-85.

Selected Works: *Alabama Presidential Elections,* 1976.

Other Awards: Alumnus of the Year, Samford University, AL, 1970. Newswriting Award, Associated Press, 1971. Canon Award, 1972. Newswriting Award, Alabama Reporters Associated Press, 1974-75. Annual Award for Outstanding Contributions to Health Care, Alabama State Nurse's Association, 1973. News Award, Alabama State Nurse's Association, 1976. Alabama Baptist Communications Award, Alabama Baptist State Convention, 1975.

Commentary: Harold Eugene Martin's exposure of the Alabama prison system's scheme of using inmates for drug experimentation won him a Pulitzer Prize in 1970. His articles, which began in January 1969, exposed the program which had been in effect since 1962. The program also included selling prisoners' blood plasma, until a hepatitis outbreak resulted in three deaths and the prison stopped the practice. Martin's articles brought a halt to the medical experimentation on inmates. The official inquiry by the State Board of Corrections cited Martin's work.

1971

William Hugh Jones   731

Birth: May 23, 1939; Marinette, WI. **Death:** November 23, 1982. **Parents:** Hugh Fred Jones and Mildred (Festge). **Education:** University of Wisconsin, Milwaukee: BS. Northwestern University, IL: MS. Harvard University, MA. **Spouse:** Virginia Marie Murphy (m. 1964). **Children:** William Hugh, Michael Joseph, Megan Kathleen.

Prize: *Local Investigative Specialized Reporting,* 1971: *Chicago Tribune,* Chicago: Chicago Tribune, 1970.

Career: Served in U.S. Marine Corps, 1958-61; Part-Time Local Government Reporter, Lerner Newspapers (Chicago); Reporter, *Chicago Tribune,* 1965-72; City Editor, *Chicago Tribune,* 1972-74; Assistant Managing Editor, *Chicago Tribune,* 1974-75; Managing Editor-News, *Chicago Tribune,* 1975-79; Managing Editor, *Chicago Tribune,* 1979-82.

Selected Works: *The Newspaper Business* (with Laird Anderson), 1977.

Other Awards: Associated Press News Award, 1967, 1970. National Headliners Club Award, 1968. Jacob Scher Award, Theta Sigma Phi, 1969. Civic Award, Civic Foundation Northbrook, 1971. Alumni Association Award of Merit, Northwestern University, IL, 1972. Distinguished Alumnus Award, University of Wisconsin, Milwaukee, 1975.

For More Information: *New York Times,* 24 November (1982): D21; Taft, William H., *Encyclopedia of Twentieth-Century Journalists,* New York: Garland Publishing, Inc., 1986.

Commentary: William Jones won a Pulitzer Prize for an eight-part series on the collusion between police officers and private ambulance companies. He went undercover as an ambulance driver to gather the information for the story. The series was published in June 1970, and by November 1970, 16 people were indicted and many pleaded guilty. Jones went on to become managing editor for the *Chicago Tribune.* He died in 1982 of leukemia. The *Chicago Tribune's* editorial department gives an annual William H. Jones award for the best investigative reporting.

1972

Ann DeSantis   732

Birth: August 27, 1946; Schenectady, NY. **Parents:** Thaddeus B. Lewkowicz and Jill (Young). **Education:** St. Lawrence University, NY: BA. Harvard University, MA. **Spouse:** William A. DeSantis (m. 1968, died 1970); Stephen A. Kurkjian (m. 1971). **Children:** Erica Young, Adam Stephen (SK).

Prize: *Local Investigative Specialized Reporting,* 1972: *Boston Globe,* Boston: Boston Globe, 1971.

Career: Staff member, *Schenectady (NY) Gazette,* 1968-70; Staff member, *Boston Globe,* 1970-72; Publicity Director, Boston (MA) Cahners Publication Company, Inc., 1972-73; Freelance writer, 1973-85; Associate Director, Washington, DC Communications Consortium, 1987-91; Public Relations Director, Boston (MA) Foundation, 1991-.

For More Information: *New York Times,* 2 May (1972): 1+.

Commentary: Ann DeSantis, Stephen Kurkjian, Gerard O'Neill, and Timothy Leland's investigation into the corruption within Somerville, Massachusetts led to 119 indictments of present and former Somerville officials. The state legislature drafted legislation to curb expenditures in Massachusetts localities.

Stephen Anoosh Kurkjian   733

Birth: August 28, 1943; Boston, MA. **Parents:** Anooshavon Kurkjian and Rosella (Gureghian). **Education:** Boston University, MA: BA. Suffolk University, MA: JD. **Spouse:** Ann Frost Lewkowicz DeSantis (m. 1971). **Children:** Erica Young, Adam Stephen.

Prize: *Local Investigative Specialized Reporting,* 1972: *Boston Globe,* Boston: Boston Globe, 1971. *Local Investigative Specialized Reporting,* 1980: *Boston Globe,* Boston: Boston Globe, 1979.

Career: Reporter, *Boston Globe,* 1968-70; Spotlight Investigative Team, *Boston Globe,* 1970-86; Washington (DC) Bureau, *Boston Globe,* 1986-91; News Project Editor, *Boston Globe,* 1991-.

Selected Works: *Boston's Crisis in Mass Transportation: The MBTA, What's Gone Wrong* (with others), 1979. *Power & Privilege: An Examination of the Massachusetts Legislature* (with Laurence Collins), 1983.

Other Awards: Publishing Service Award, Sigma Delta Chi, 1971. National Headliners Club Award, 1977. Associated Press Managing Editors Award, 1977, 1980, 1994. Investigative Reporters and Editors, 1979. Sevellon Brown Award, New England Associated Press News Executives Association, 1979-80, 1983-84. National Educational Reporting Award, Educational Writers Association, 1982. George Polk Memorial Award, Long Island University, NY, 1985, 1994.

For More Information: Dygert, James H., *The Investigative Journalist: Folk Heroes of a New Era,* Englewood Cliffs, NJ: Prentice Hall, 1976; *Boston Globe,* 15 April (1980).

Commentary: Stephen Kurkjian, Ann DeSantis, Gerard O'Neill, and Timothy Leland's exposure of the corruption in Somerville, Massachusetts led to indictment of the current and previous town officials. Kurkjian, the only person to still be on the spotlight team eight years later, won another Pulitzer Prize for an investigation into the Boston Public Transit System.

Timothy Leland   734

Birth: September 24, 1937; Boston, MA. **Parents:** Oliver Stevens Leland and Frances Chamberlain (Ayres). **Education:** Harvard University, MA, cum laude. Columbia University, NY: Master's, Honors. **Spouse:** Natasha Bourso (m. 1964, div.). **Children:** Christian Bourso, London Chamberlain.

Prize: *Local Investigative Specialized Reporting,* 1972: *Boston Globe,* Boston: Boston Globe, 1971.

Career: Medical Editor, *Boston Herald,* 1963-64; Science Editor, *Boston Globe,* 1965-66; Chief, State House Bureau, *Boston Globe,* 1966-67; Assistant City Editor, *Boston Globe,* 1968-69; Reporter, *London (England) Sunday Times,* 1969-70; Chief, Spotlight Investigative Team, *Boston Globe,* 1970-71; Assistant Managing Editor, *Boston Globe,* 1972-75; Managing Editor, Sunday Edition, *Boston Globe,* 1976-81; Managing Editor, *Boston Globe,* 1981-.

Selected Works: *Contemporary Authors, Volume 102,* 1981. *Encyclopedia of Twentieth-Century Journalists* (Taft, William H., ed.), 1986.

Other Awards: International Fellow, Columbia University, NY, 1961. American Political Science Award, 1968. Travel Grantee, United States South African Leader Exchange Program, 1969. Civic Service Award, Sigma Delta Chi, 1972. Managing Editors Award for Public Service, Associated Press, 1974. Sevellon Brown Award, New England Associated Press News Executives Association, 1974.

Commentary: Timothy Leland, Gerard O'Neill, Stephen Kurkjian, and Ann DeSantis are the four original members of the *Boston Globe's* spotlight team that investigated the corruption in nearby Somerville, Massachusetts. They examined 6,000 public records and interviewed 120 persons. In their six-part series published in February 1971, they disclosed political favoritism, conflicts of interest, and questionable financial practices. The story led to indictments as well as new state legislation.

Gerard Michael O'Neill   735

Birth: September 1, 1942; Boston, MA. **Parents:** Richard T. O'Neill and M. Claire (Sweeney). **Education:** Stonehill College, MA: BA, cum laude. George Washington University, Washington, DC. Boston University, MA: MS. **Spouse:** Janet Reardon (m. 1968). **Children:** Brian, Shane.

Prize: *Local Investigative Specialized Reporting,* 1972: *Boston Globe,* Boston: Boston Globe, 1971.

Career: Reporter, *Quincy (MA) Patriot Ledger;* Copyboy, *Boston (MA) Globe,* 1965; Intern, *Boston Globe,* 1966; Suburban Reporter, *Boston Globe,* 1967-69; State House, City Hall Reporter, *Boston Globe,* 1968-70; Spotlight Investigative Team, *Boston Globe,* 1970-72; Chief, Spotlight Investigative Team, *Boston Globe,* 1972-80; Editor, Science and Health Section, Boston (MA) Globe, 1983-86; Chief, Spotlight Investigative Team, Boston (MA) Globe, 1986-.

Selected Works: *The Underboss: The Rise and Fall of a Mafia Family* (with Dick Lehr), 1989.

Other Awards: United Press International Award, 1971. Public Service Award, Sigma Delta Chi, 1972. Consumer Reporting Award, National Press Club, 1975. Scripps-Howard Citation, 1976. Associated Press Managing Editors Award, 1977, 1998; National Headliners Club Award, 1977; Sevellan Brown Award, 1989-90, 1992, 1997; Public Serv-

ice Award, Scripps Howard, 1991; Gerald Loeb Award, Anderson Graduate School of Managment, University of California, Los Angeles, 1992; John Hancock Award, 1992

For More Information: Behrens, John C., *The Typewriter Guerrillas: Closeups of 20 Top Investigative Reporters,* Chicago: Nelson-Hall, 1977: 180-188; *Contemporary Authors, Volumes 69-72,* Detroit: Gale Research Company, 1978: 459.

Commentary: Gerard O'Neill, Timothy Leland, Ann DeSantis, and Stephen Kurkjian examined 6,000 public documents and interviewed 120 people while investigating the widespread corruption in Somerville, Massachusetts. The six-part series, published in February 1971, led to indictments of local officials as well as new state legislation aimed at controlling expenditures of Massachusetts localities.

1973

Sun Newspapers of Omaha   736

Founding Location: Omaha, NE.

Prize: *Local Investigative Specialized Reporting,* 1973: *Sun Newspapers of Omaha,* Omaha, NE, 1972.

For More Information: Boyer, William Herbert, The Rising Sun: A History of the Sun Newspapers of Omaha, Inc. (thesis), Kansas State University, 1968.

Commentary: The *Sun Newspapers of Omaha* published a special section on March 30, 1972 on the charitable organization, Boys Town. The staff uncovered in a six-month investigation that the charity had a net worth greater than $209 million. Although the paper alleged no wrongdoing, it criticized the fund-raising practices of the charity. In response, the charity pledged $70 million in idle funds for new programs and changed its fund-raising procedures. Five members of the editorial staff working under Paul N. Williams, the managing editor, conducted the investigation. Warren Edward Buffett was the publisher of the seven weekly newspapers that made up the Sun group of newspapers. The total circulation of the seven papers was 48,000.

1974

William Sherman   737

Birth: December 9, 1946; New York, NY. **Parents:** Murray George Sherman and Beatrice Hannah (Nathanson). **Education:** Bard College, NY: BA. Boston University, MA: MS.

Prize: *Local Investigative Specialized Reporting,* 1974: *New York Daily News,* New York: New York Daily News, 1973.

Career: Reporter, *Boston Globe;* Reporter, *Village Voice;* Reporter, *New York Daily News,* 1969-; General Assignment Reporter, Rewriteman, Investigative Reporter, *New York Daily News,* 1972-; Correspondent, ABC-TV News, 1978-; Adjunct Professor of Journalism, Hunter College (NY).

Selected Works: *Times Square,* 1980.

Other Awards: Outstanding Journalism Award, Society of Silurians, 1972. George Polk Award, Long Island University, NY, 1973. Page One Award, 1973-74, 1976. Deadline Club Award, Sigma Delta Chi, 1974, 1978. Women's Press Club Award, 1974. Investigative Reporting Award, Society of Silurians, 1975.

For More Information: *New York Times,* 7 May (1974): 40; Taft, Willaim H., *Encyclopedia of Twentieth-Century Journalists,* New York: Garland Publishing, 1986.

Commentary: William Sherman's series of 14 articles revealed major fraud in the health care system. He posed as a Medicaid recipient as part of his investigation. The stories he wrote led to prosecutions and the restitution of $1 million in false billings.

1975

Indianapolis Star 738

Founded: June 6, 1903; Indianapolis, IN. **Founder(s):** George McCulloch.

Prize: *Local Investigative Specialized Reporting,* 1975.

Other Awards: In 1991, Joseph T. Hallinan and Susan M. Headden were awarded a Pulitzer Prize for Investigative Reporting.

For More Information: Carrington, John Oliver, "The Foreign Policy of the Indianapolis Star, 1918-1939" (thesis), University of Kentucky, 1958; Miller, John W., "Indiana Newspaper Bibliography: Historical Accounts of All Indiana Newspapers Published from 1804 to 1980 and Location Information for All Available Copies, Both Original and Microfilm, Indianapolis," IN: Indiana Historical Society, 1982: 285-286.

Commentary: The *Indianapolis Star* won a Pulitzer Prize for its six-month investigation into police corruption in Indianapolis. Its reporting led to the resignation of the police chief, Winston L. Churchill, public safety director, William A. Leak, assistant police chief, Donald D. Schaedel, as well as the removal of many high-ranking police officers. Reporter William E. Anderson heard rumors of corruption which led Lawrence S. Connor, the city editor, to form an investigative team. The members of that team included Anderson, Richard E. Cady, and Harley R. Bierce. Staff members Myrta J. Pulliam and Gerald W. Clark, a photographer, were soon added to the team. Robert P. Early, the managing editor, and Eugene S. Pulliam, the assistant publisher, stood by their team of reporters and printed the entire story. The *Star's* first story on the corruption was published on February 24, 1974.

The *Indianapolis Morning Star* began publication on June 6, 1903 under the direction of George McCulloch. In June 1904, the paper absorbed the *Indianapolis Journal.* In October of that year, the company was sold to a stock company headed by Daniel Reid. In April 1908, Reid's company went into receivership. That fall, John C. Shaffer, who had been the paper's editor, bought the paper. The former management challenged his purchase in court, but the United States Court of Appeals ruled in favor of Shaffer. He controlled the paper until his death in 1943. In April of 1944, the paper was sold to Eugene C. Pulliam. Pulliam acquired the *Indianapolis News* in 1946, and in 1948 he consolidated the management of the two papers. After Pulliam's death in 1975, his son Eugene S. Pulliam took over the running of the papers. The *Indianapolis Star* is a morning newspaper while the *Indianapolis News* is published in the afternoon.

1976

Chicago Tribune

Full entry appears as #710 under "Local General Spot News Reporting," 1973.

1977

Acel Moore 739

Birth: October 5, 1940; Philadelphia, PA. **Parents:** Jerry Acel Moore and Hura Mae (Harrington). **Education:** Charles Morris Price School of Journalism. **Spouse:** Carolyn Weaver (m. 1964, div. 1974); Cheryl Rice (m. 1975, d.); Linda Wright Avery (m. 1988). **Children:** Acel Jr. (CW).

Prize: *Local Investigative Specialized Reporting,* 1977: *Philadelphia Inquirer,* "The Farview Findings," Philadelphia, PA: Philadelphia Inquirer, 1976.

Career: Served in U.S. Army, 1959-61; Copyboy, *Philadelphia (PA) Inquirer,* 1962-64; Editorial Clerk, *Philadelphia (PA) Inquirer,* 1964-68; Reporter, *Philadelphia (PA) Inquirer,* 1968-80; Co-Producer, *Black Perspective on the News,* 1972-78 (nationally syndicated news program, Public Broadcasting Service); Associate Editor, *Philadelphia (PA) Inquirer,* 1981-.

Selected Works: *The Farview Findings* (with Wendell Rawls), 1976.

Other Awards: Scales of Justice Award, Pennsylvania Bar Association, 1970. Public Service

Award, Sigma Delta Chi, Philadelphia Chapter, PA, 1972, 1976. Pennsylvania Associated Press Managing Editors Association Award, 1972, 1976. Heywood Broun Award, Newspaper Guild, 1976. National Headliners Club Award, 1976. Robert F. Kennedy Journalism Award, 1976. Philadelphia Party Journalism Award, 1976. Annual Paul Robeson Award, Afro-American History Museum, 1976. Upward Bound Yvonne Motly McCabe Award, Swarthmore College, PA, 1977. National Clarion Award, Women in Communications, 1977. Nieman Fellow, Harvard University, MA, 1979-80.

For More Information: Dawkins, Wayne, *Black Journalists: The NABJ Story,* Sicklerville, NJ: August Press, 1993.

Commentary: Acel Moore and Wendell Rawls Jr.'s investigation into Farview State Hospital, an institution for the criminally insane, resulted in a widespread formal investigation which involved exhumations, psychiatric evaluations for all patients, a special grand jury, and a special prosecutor. Their story told of guards staging human cockfights, lethal beatings, and murder certified as "heart attack."

Acel Moore, a native of Philadelphia, has won awards for his writings on its black community, and he is a founding member of the National Association of Black Journalists.

Wendell Lee Rawls Jr.   740

Birth: August 18, 1941; Good Lettsville, TN. **Parents:** Wendell L. Rawls and Madolyn (Murphy). **Religion:** Protestant. **Education:** Vanderbilt University, TN: BA. **Spouse:** Kathryn Stark (m. 1971). **Children:** Amanda Coston, Matthew Bradley.

Prize: *Local Investigative Specialized Reporting,* 1977: *Philadelphia Inquirer,* "The Farview Findings," Philadelphia, PA: Philadelphia Inquirer, 1976.

Career: Served in U.S. Army Reserves, 1965-71; Sports Writer, *Nashville (TN) Tennessean;* News reporter, Trenton (NJ); Bureau Chief, Pittsburgh (PA); Bureau Chief, *Philadelphia (PA) Inquirer,* 1972-77; Reporter, *New York Times,* 1977-83; Southern Bureau Chief, *New York Times,* 1982-83; Assistant Managing Editor for Local News, *Atlanta (GA) Journal-Constitution,* 1987-89.

Selected Works: *The Farview Findings* (with Acel Moore), 1976. *Cold Storage,* 1980.

Other Awards: Special Citation, Thomas L. Stokes Competition, 1975. Pennsylvania Keystone Press Award, 1975. Robert F. Kennedy Journalism Award, 1977. National Headliners Club Award, 1977. Heywood Broun Award, Newspaper Guild, 1977. Associated Press Managing Editors Award, 1977. Sigma Delta Chi Award, 1977.

For More Information: *Contemporary Authors, New Revision Series, Volume 22,* Detroit: Gale Research Company, 1988.

Commentary: Wendell Rawls Jr. and Acel Moore spent three months investigating the Farview State Hospital, an institution for the criminally insane in Pennsylvania. They tracked down witnesses and conducted interviews as far away as Denver and Los Angeles. Their series included stories such as that of a man who was in a fistfight in 1938 and who then spent the next 32 years in Farview, guards staging human cockfights, and murder being written off as a "heart attack." Their series resulted in a formal investigation by the state, reforms at the hospital, and statewide action to protect the rights of mental patients.

Wendell Rawls Jr. first became an investigative reporter after a series of articles on cruelty to Tennessee walking horses.

1978

Anthony Rossi Dolan   741

Birth: July 7, 1948; Norwalk, CT. **Parents:** Joseph William Dolan and Margaret (Kelley). **Religion:** Roman Catholic. **Education:** Yale University, CT: BA.

Prize: *Local Investigative Specialized Reporting,* 1978: *Stamford Advocate,* Stamford, CT: Stamford Advocate, 1977.

Career: Columnist and Board Member, college paper, *Yale Daily News;* Press Aide for U.S. Senate and Gubernatorial Campaigns of James L. Buckley, 1970-73; Served in U.S. Army Reserves, 1970-76; Investigative Reporter, Police and City Hall Reporter, *Stamford (CT) Advocate,* 1974-80; Chief Speech Writer, President Ronald Reagan, 1981-86; Visiting Fellow, American Enterprise Institute.

Selected Works: *A Tribute to Whittaker Chambers: The Heritage Lectures, 31,* 1984.

Other Awards: New England Press Association Citation, 1975. National Headliners Club Award, 1977. Roy Howard Citation, 1978.

For More Information: *Contemporary Authors, Volumes 73-76,* Detroit: Gale Research Company, 1978; *New York Times,* 18 April (1978): 28.

Commentary: Anthony R. Dolan's reporting on the corruption in a local municipality led to several resignations among police, fire, public works, and parks personnel. Dolan was the chief speechwriter for President Ronald Reagan and coined the term "evil empire" to describe the Soviet Union for one of Reagan's speeches. William F. Buckley helped steer him into a newspaper career.

1979

Gilbert Martin Gaul 742

Birth: May 18, 1951; Jersey City, NJ. **Parents:** Albert Joseph Gaul and Jane (Daughton). **Education:** Fairleigh Dickinson University, NJ: BA. Montclair State College, NJ: Teacher's Certificate. **Spouse:** Cathryn Lou Candy (m. 1953). **Children:** Cary.

Prize: *Local Investigative Specialized Reporting,* 1979: *Pottsville Republican,* June 12-16, Pottsville, PA: Pottsville Republican, 1978.

Career: Teacher; Reporter, *Lehighton (PA) Times-News,* 1976-78; Reporter, *Pottsville (PA) Republican,* 1978-80; Reporter, *Philadelphia (PA) Bulletin,* 1980-81; Staff member, *Philadelphia (PA) Inquirer;* Health and Medical Reporter, *Philadelphia (PA) Inquirer.*

Selected Works: *Giant Steps: A Story of One Boy's Struggle to Walk,* 1993. *Free Ride: The Tax-Exempt Economy* (with Neill A. Borowski), 1993.

Other Awards: Edward J. Meeman Award, Scripps-Howard Foundation, 1979. Silver Gavel Award, American Bar Association, 1979. Goldsmith Prize for Investigative Reporting, 1994.

Commentary: Gilbert M. Gaul and Elliot G. Jaspin's yearlong investigation into the demise of the Blue Coal Corporation led to state reforms. Their five-part series told how a group tied to organized crime deliberately destroyed the company and left the state of Pennsylvania with $20 million in bills. Gaul was a finalist for a Pulitzer Prize in 1990 and in 1994.

Elliot Gary Jaspin 743

Birth: May 27, 1946; Mineola, NY. **Parents:** Leon Jaspin and Ethel Rica (Schoenfeld). **Education:** Colby College, ME: BA. **Spouse:** Janet Gail Thomas (m. 1977). **Children:** Jessica Megan, Katy Rebecca.

Prize: *Local Investigative Specialized Reporting,* 1979: *Pottsville Republican,* June 12-16, Pottsville, PA: Pottsville Republican, 1978.

Career: Vista volunteer, Albuquerque (NM); Magazine reporter; Reporter, *Augusta (ME) Kennebec Journal,* 1971-72; Reporter, *Pottsville (PA) Republican,* 1972-74; Wire Editor, *Lehighton (PA) Times-News,* 1974-76; Investigative Reporter, *Pottsville (PA) Republican,* 1976-79; Reporter, *Philadelphia (PA) Daily News,* 1979-81; Reporter, *Providence (RI) Journal-Bulletin,* 1981-.

Other Awards: Associated Press Managing Editors Award, 1978-79. University of Missouri School of Journalism Award, 1978. Edward J. Meeman Award, Scripps-Howard Foundation, 1979. Silver Gavel Award, American Bar Association, 1979.

For More Information: Taft, William H., *Encyclopedia of Twentieth-Century Journalists,* New York: Garland Publishing, 1986.

Commentary: Elliot G. Jaspin and Gilbert M. Gaul spent a year investigating the death of the Blue Coal Corporation. The company was once one of the nation's leading producers of anthracite. They reported the company had ties to organized crime and the possibility that Jimmy Hoffa had been a secret owner. Their five-part series had the state legislature correcting problems that had led to the abuses described in the demise of the company.

1980

Nils Johan Axel Bruzelius 744

Birth: February 27, 1947; Stockholm, Sweden. **Parents:** Axel Sture Bruzelius and Constance (Brickett). **Education:** Amherst College, MA: BA. **Spouse:** Margaret Ann Kuppinger (m. 1972).

Prize: *Local Investigative Specialized Reporting,* 1980: *Boston Globe,* Boston: Boston Globe, 1979.

Career: Reporter, *Framingham (MA) South Middlesex News,* 1968-70; Boston Bureau, Associated Press, 1970-73; Medical Writer, *Boston Globe,* 1973-79; Investigative Reporter, *Boston Globe,* 1979-81; Assistant Metropolitan Editor, *Boston Globe,* 1981-86; Health and Science Editor, *Boston Globe,* 1986-.

Other Awards: Investigative Reporters and Editors Award, 1979. Distinguished Journalism Citation, Scripps-Howard Foundation, 1979. Knight Fellow, Massachusetts Institute of Technology, 1992-93.

For More Information: *Boston Globe,* 15 April (1980).

Commentary: Nils Bruzelius, along with four of his colleagues on the *Boston Globe's* Investigative Reporting Spotlight Team, won a Pulitzer Prize for their expose of the Massachusetts Bay Transportation Authority. The 10-part series, published in December 1979, delved into why the transit system was falling apart.

Alexander Boyd Hawes Jr. 745

Birth: May 5, 1947; Washington, D.C.. **Parents:** Alexander Boyd Hawes and Elizabeth (Armstrong). **Education:** University of Denver, CO. **Spouse:** Jane Ann Gepfert (m. 1969). **Children:** Alexander Boyd III, Ellen Booth.

Prize: *Local Investigative Specialized Reporting,* 1980: *Boston Globe,* Boston: Boston Globe, 1979.

Career: General Assignment Reporter, *Pittsfield (MA) Berkshire Eagle,* 1970; Reporter, *Colorado Springs (CO) Sun,* 1972-76; General Assignment Reporter, Spotlight Investigative Team, City Hall Reporter, Human Resources Director, Assistant Managing Editor, *Boston Globe,* 1976-91; Assistant

Treasurer, Boston (MA) Affiliated Publications, Inc., 1991-93; Assistant to President, *Boston Globe,* 1994-.

Other Awards: New England Community Service Award, United Press International, 1980. Sevellon Brown Award, New England Associated Press News Executives Association, 1980.

For More Information: *Boston Globe,* 15 April (1980).

Commentary: Alexander B. Hawes Jr. and four of his coworkers won a Pulitzer Prize for their investigation into the Massachusetts Bay Transportation Authority. Their ten-part series published in December 1979 examined why the system, despite record high budgets and number of employees, had reached an all-time low on service and had come close to shutting down.

Stephen Anoosh Kurkjian

Full entry appears as #733 under "Local Investigative Specialized Reporting," 1972.

Robert Milton Porterfield   746

Birth: October 11, 1945; Portland, OR. **Parents:** Edwin Milton Porterfield and Elizabeth M. (Schimmel). **Religion:** Lutheran. **Education:** University of Oregon. **Spouse:** Marcia Anne Parker (m. 1979). **Children:** Georjeena; Elizabeth; Kassandra.

Prize: *Local Investigative Specialized Reporting,* 1980: *Boston Globe,* Boston: Boston Globe, 1979.

Career: News Staff member, *Delano (CA) Record;* Reporter, Eugene (OR), KPNW Radio; Police Officer, Washington State; Private Investigator, California; Reporter, *Roseburg (OR) News-Review,* 1969-71; Reporter, *Springfield (OR) News,* 1972-74; Reporter, *Anchorage (AK) Daily News,* 1974-78; Founder-Editor, *Alaska Journal of Commerce,* 1977; Reporter, *Boston Globe,* 1978-80; Reporter, *Newsday (NY),* 1981-.

Other Awards: National Headliners Club Award, 1976. Investigative Reporters and Editors Award, 1979. Nieman Fellow, Harvard University, MA, 1978-79. Walter Bagehot Fellow, Columbia University, NY, 1981.

For More Information: *Boston Globe,* 15 April (1980).

Commentary: Robert Porterfield and four colleagues won a Pulitzer Prize for a 10-part series on why the Massachusetts Bay Transportation System was falling apart. Their investigation lasted several months and examined all of the system's operations.

Porterfield was also part of the *Anchorage Daily News* staff when that paper won the Meritorious Public Service award for the impact the Teamsters Union had on the Alaskan economy and politics.

Joan Vennochi   747

Birth: January 27, 1953; Brooklyn, NY. **Parents:** John Joseph LoBiondo and Martha Diane (Homick). **Education:** Boston University, MA: BS. Suffolk University, MA: JD. **Spouse:** Thomas Michael Vennochi (m. 1977).

Prize: *Local Investigative Specialized Reporting,* 1980: *Boston Globe,* Boston: Boston Globe, 1979.

Career: Editor, *Thomaston (CT) Express,* 1975; Reporter, *Danbury (CT) News Times,* 1975-77; Intern, *Newsday (NY);* Reporter, *Boston Globe,* 1976-77; Reporter, Spotlight Investigative Team, *Boston Globe,* 1977-83; Reporter, City Hall Bureau, *Boston Globe,* 1983-85; State House Bureau Chief, *Boston Globe,* 1985-; Columnist, *Boston Globe,* 1994-.

For More Information: *Boston Globe,* 15 April (1980).

Commentary: Joan Vennochi and four of her colleagues' investigation into the Massachusetts Bay Transportation Authority won a Pulitzer Prize in 1980. The ten-part series looked at all major aspects of the Authority's operation and found that, mile for mile, it was the "most expensive and least productive major transit system in the nation." She researched and wrote about the transit system's failure to hire minorities and women.

1981

Clark Howard Hallas   748

Birth: May 14, 1935; Washington, DC. **Death:** 1992. **Parents:** Howard Ensley Hallas and Carol May (Harsen). **Education:** Michigan State University. Wayne State University, MI. **Spouse:** Barbara Joy Griffin (m. 1977). **Children:** Michael, Kelly.

Prize: *Local Investigative Specialized Reporting,* 1981: *Arizona Daily Star,* Tucson, AZ: Arizona Daily Star, 1980.

Career: Staff member *Birmingham (AL) Eccentric;* Served in U.S. Army, 1958-60; Reporter, United Press International, 1960-63; Assistant Night City Editor, *Delaware County (PA) Daily Times,* 1963-64; Copy Editor, *Flint (MI) Journal,* 1964-68; City Hall Bureau Chief, Political Reporter, Investigative Reporter, Business and Financial Writer, *Detroit News,* 1968-78; Investigative Reporter, *Arizona Daily Star,* 1978-, *Cleveland (OH) Plain Dealer, Pittsburgh (PA) Press.*

Other Awards: Medallion for Public Service Reporting, Detroit Press Club Foundation, 1973. Investigative Reporters and Editors Award, 1980. Newsman of the Year, Arizona Press Club, 1980. Fellow, University of Michigan, 1983.

For More Information: Patterson, Margaret Jones and Robert H. Russell, *Behind the Lines: Case Studies in Investigative Reporting,* New York: Columbia University Press, 1986: 51-93; *Detroit News,* 10 December (1992): 6.

Commentary: Clark Hallas and Bob Lowe investigated the University of Arizona athletic department. Their series disclosed that four athletes and their wives were hired by the City of Tucson for work they did not do. As a result of their reports, the head football coach resigned and was indicted for fraud.

Hallas was a finalist for a Pulitzer Prize in 1984. He, along with two colleagues, investigated the problems of Hughes Aircraft Company. He died of cancer in 1992.

Robert Brian Lowe   749

Birth: August 13, 1953; Pasadena, CA. **Parents:** Albert Chester Lowe and Rose Marie (Chin). **Education:** Stanford University, CA: BA, cum laude.

Prize: *Local Investigative Specialized Reporting,* 1981: *Arizona Daily Star,* Tucson, AZ: Arizona Daily Star, 1980.

Career: Staff member, *Arizona Republic and Gazette,* 1975-76; Phoenix (AZ) Bureau Chief and Legislative Reporter, *Arizona Daily Star,* 1976-79; Investigative Reporter, Tucson (AZ) *Arizona Daily Star,* 1979-, *Miami (FL) Herald.*

Other Awards: Don Bolles Memorial Award for Investigative Reporting, Arizona Press Club, 1979. Investigative Reporters and Editors Award, 1981. Virg Hill Newsman of the Year, Arizona Press Club, 1981.

For More Information: Patterson, Margaret Jones and Robert H. Russell, *Behind the Lines: Case Studies in Investigative Reporting,* New York: Columbia University Press, 1986: 51-93.

Commentary: Bob Lowe and Clark Hallas won a Pulitzer Prize for their investigation into the athletic department at the University of Arizona. Their reporting led to the resignation of head football coach Tony Mason. Mason was indicted along with six of his former assistants and an airline employee. The stories in the *Arizona Daily Star* questioned inconsistencies in travel vouchers submitted by Mason and his assistants.

1982

Paul Henderson III   750

Birth: January 13, 1939; Washington, DC. **Parents:** Paul Henderson Jr. and Doris Olive (Gale). **Religion:** Methodist. **Education:** University of Nebraska, Omaha. Creighton University, NE. **Spouse:** JoAnn Burnham (m. 1964, div. 1979); Janet Marie Horne (m.

1982). **Children:** Leslee, Jill, Polly Ann (JB); Peter Paul, Brady Thomas (JH).

Prize: *Local Investigative Specialized Reporting,* 1982: *Seattle Times,* Seattle, WA: Seattle Times, 1981.

Career: Served in U.S. Army, 1959-62; Reporter, *Council Bluffs (IA) Daily Nonpareil,* 1962-66; Reporter, *Omaha (NE) World-Herald,* 1966-67; Crime Reporter, Feature Writer, Investigative Reporter, *Seattle (WA) Times,* 1967-85; Private Investigator, Seattle, WA, 1985-.

Other Awards: C.B. Blethan Award, 1977, 1982. Roy W. Howard Newspaper Award, Scripps-Howard Foundation, 1982. Outstanding Achiever, American Academy of Achievement, 1982.

For More Information: *Contemporary Authors, Volume 144,* Detroit: Gale Research Company, 1994.

Commentary: Paul Henderson, a specialist on crime news and investigations, helped free an innocent man convicted of rape. When officials followed up on Henderson's lead, they found a man who resembled the defendant and who eventually confessed to the crime.

1983

Loretta A. Tofani   751

Birth: February 5, 1953; New York, NY. **Parents:** Lucio Tofani and Olga (Danise). **Religion:** Roman Catholic. **Education:** Fordham University, NY: BA. University of California, Berkeley: MA. **Spouse:** Dr. John Edward White (m. 1984).

Prize: *Local Investigative Specialized Reporting,* 1983: *Washington Post,* "Terror Behind Bars," September 26; "Justice May Not Be Served," September 27; "The Strong Inmates Exploit the Weak," September 28; "Rape Is the Way Some Master the Violent Art of Jail Survival," September 28, Washington, DC: Washington Post, 1982.

Career: Editor-in-Chief, college paper, *Ram;* Reporter, *Knoxville (TN) News-Sentinel;* Reporter, *Rochester (NY) Democrat & Chronicle;* Staff member, Portland (OR), New York (NY), Los Angeles (CA), United Press International; Reporter, Police, Local Government and Courts, *Washington (DC) Post,* 1978-87; Reporter, *Philadelphia (PA) Inquirer,* 1987-92; Foreign Correspondent, *Philadelphia Inquirer,* 1992-.

Selected Works: *Rape in the County Jail: Prince George's Hidden Horror,* 1983.

Other Awards: Front Page Award, Washington-Baltimore Newspaper Guild, 1980-82. *Washington Monthly* National Journalism Award, 1982. Mark Twain Award, Associated Press, 1982-83. Henry Miller Award, 1983. Bronze Medal, Investigative Reporters and Editors, 1983. Sigma Delta Chi Award,

1983. John F. Kennedy Journalism Award, 1983. Fulbright Fellowship, 1983-84. National Headliners Club Award, 1988. William S. Miller Award, University of Florida College of Journalism.

For More Information: *Washington Post,* April 19, 1983: A1; *Contemporary Authors, Volume 113,* Detroit: Gale Research Company, 1985.

Commentary: Loretta Tofani, who covered the police and court beats for the *Washington Post,* learned about the topic of her winning series, "Rape in the County Jail: Prince George's Hidden Horror," on the job. She was at a sentencing hearing when a lawyer told the judge that his client had been "gang raped" in the county's detention center. Tofani investigated the story for nine months. She learned that rapes occurred as often as a dozen times a week. Her series included case studies of 12 rapes. The Pulitzer Prize board observed that her series led to seven indictments of male prisoners for rape, the resignation of the director of corrections, and a $20 million bond issue to build a new prison. She was a finalist in the Feature Writing category in 1989 for a story about the pregnancy of a heroin addict and the birth of an addicted baby.

1984

Kenneth Joseph Cooper   752

Birth: December 11, 1955; Denver, CO. **Parents:** George Howard Cooper Jr. and Maxine Marie (Mosby). **Education:** Washington University, MO: BA. **Spouse:** Lucilda Loretta Dassardo (m. 1985).

Prize: *Local Investigative Specialized Reporting,* 1984: *Boston Globe,* Boston: *Boston Globe,* 1983.

Career: Associate Editor, *St. Louis (MO) American,* 1977; Staff Writer, *St. Louis (MO) Post-Dispatch,* 1977-80, *Denver (CO) Rocky Mountain News;* Staff Writer, *Boston Globe,* 1980-86; Reporter, Knight-Ridder, Inc., 1986-89; National Reporter, *Washington (DC) Post,* 1989-95; South Asia Bureau Chief, *Washington (DC) Post,* 1996-; Foreign Correspondent, *Washington (DC) Post,* 1996-.

Other Awards: Public Service Award, United Press International, 1984.

Commentary: Kenneth J. Cooper and six of his colleagues at the *Boston Globe* were awarded a Pulitzer Prize for their series of articles that studied racial tensions in the Boston area. They examined the hiring, advancement, unions, and management practices of local institutions.

Joan FitzGerald   753

Education: Bennington College, VT. Fletcher School of Law and Diplomacy, MA. **Spouse:** David.

Prize: *Local Investigative Specialized Reporting,* 1984: *Boston Globe,* Boston: *Boston Globe,* 1983.

Career: Reporter and Researcher, *Forbes* Magazine; Financial Department Staff member, *Boston Globe,* 1980-83.

Commentary: Joan FitzGerald, along with six of her colleagues at the *Boston Globe,* won a Pulitzer Prize for examining race relations in the Boston area. The series of articles looked at various Boston institutions, including the *Boston Globe.* The series of six articles also statistically compared Boston with six other metropolitan areas. FitzGerald was 35 years old when she won the award in 1984.

Jonathan Kaufman   754

Birth: April 18, 1956; New York, NY. **Parents:** H. George Kaufman and Bernice (Rosenblatt). **Religion:** Jewish. **Education:** Yale University, CT: BA. Harvard University, MA: MA.

Prize: *Local Investigative Specialized Reporting,* 1984: *Boston Globe,* Boston: *Boston Globe,* 1983.

Career: Editor, college paper, *Yale Daily News;* Reporter, *(Hong Kong) South China Morning Post,* 1978-79; Reporter, Chicago, *Wall Street Journal,* 1979-80; Reporter, Berlin (Germany) Bureau Chief, *Boston Globe,* 1982-94; Feature Writer, *Wall Street Journal,* 1995-.

Selected Works: *China and the World/The World and China,* 1983. *Broken Alliance: The Turbulent Times between Blacks and Jews in America,* 1988. *A Hole in the Heart of the World: Being Jewish in Eastern Europe,* 1997.

Other Awards: Fellow, Henry Luce Foundation, 1978. Fellow, East Asian Institute, Harvard University, MA, 1980. New England United Press International Award, 1984. Fellow, Alicia Patterson Foundation, 1986. National Jewish Book Award, 1988: *Broken Alliance: The Turbulent Times between Blacks and Jews in America,* New York: Scribner, 1988. National Headliners Club Award, 1997.

Commentary: Jonathan Kaufman and six of his colleagues at the *Boston Globe* won a Pulitzer Prize for their series of articles that examined racial tensions in the Boston area. He was a finalist for a Pulitzer Prize in 1985 for a series of articles on neighborhood activism.

Kaufman was editor of his college paper and spent a year in Hong Kong on a fellowship. He joined the *Wall Street Journal* in 1995.

Norman Alton Lockman   755

Birth: July 11, 1938; West Chester, PA. **Parents:** Norman James Lockman and Olive (White). **Religion:** Unitarian Universalist. **Education:** Pennsylvania State University. Department of Defense School of Journalism. **Spouse:** Virginia Trainer. **Children:** Holly Beth, Carey Paige, Sarah Elizabeth.

Prize: *Local Investigative Specialized Reporting,* 1984: *Boston Globe,* Boston: *Boston Globe,* 1983.

Career: Served in U.S. Air Force, 1961-65; Announcer, Coatesville (PA), WCOJ, 1965-66; Columnist, Kennett News, 1965-68; Social Worker, Delaware Department of Mental Health, 1967-69; Talk show host, Wilmington (DE), WILM, 1972-73; Correspondent, Washington (DC), *Wilmington (DE) News-Journal,* 1969-75; Staff member, *Boston Globe,* 1975-80; State House Bureau Chief, *Boston Globe,* 1981-84; Associate Editorial Page Editor, *Wilmington (DE) News-Journal,* 1984-; Associate Editor, *Wilmington (DE) News-Journal,*.

Selected Works: *Black Voices in Commentary,* 1995.

Other Awards: Maryland-Delaware-DC Press Association Award, 1969. Media Award for Government Reporting, Massachusetts Legislative Caucus, 1983. Black Achievers Award, Wilmington YMCA, DE, 1990. Achievement Award, Brandywine Professional Association, 1991.

Commentary: Norman A. Lockman and six of his colleagues won a Pulitzer Prize for their investigation into race relations in the Boston metropolitan area.

Gary W. McMillan 756

Birth: August 15, 1944; Bend, OR. **Death:** October 2, 1998. **Spouse:** Lois M.(m.,d.); Nancy Gaines (m., div.); Susan J. Fiorentini. **Children:** Wednesday A. Davison, Andrew C.

Prize: *Local Investigative Specialized Reporting,* 1984: *Boston Globe,* Boston: Boston Globe, 1983.

Career: Served in U.S. Air Force; Staff member, *Hayward (CA) Daily Review;* Staff member, *Utica (NY) Observer-Dispatch;* Staff member, *Spokane (WA) Times;* Copy Editor, *Boston Globe,* 1969-73; General Assignment Reporter, *Boston Globe,* 1974-86; Editor, *Manchester (NH) Union's Leader's New Hampshire Sunday News,* 1986-88; Executive, Boston (MA) Regan Communications, 1988-89; Press Secretary, Jim Rappaport, Massachusetts Taxpayers Committee, 1989; Director of Public Relations, James Fiorentini, U.S. Senate campaign, 1994; Director, ANG Newspapers, 1995-.

Commentary: Gary W. McMillan and six of his colleagues won a Pulitzer Prize for their examination of race relations in the Boston area. He also shared in the Meritorious Public Service award that the *Boston*

Globe won in 1975. McMillan worked for over 30 years in the newspaper business.

Kirk Scharfenberg 757

Birth: January 24, 1944; Boston, MA. **Death:** July 27, 1992. **Parents:** Clarence James Scharfenberg. **Education:** Brown University, RI. **Spouse:** Virginia S. (m., div.); Marianne Hughes. **Children:** Christa, David, Stephanie (VS); Stepchildren: Brendan Hughes, Kristen Hughes, Joseph Hughes (MH).

Prize: *Local Investigative Specialized Reporting,* 1984: *Boston Globe,* Boston: *Boston Globe,* 1983.

Career: Reporter, *Baltimore (MD) Sun;* Reporter, *Washington (DC) Post,* ?-1973; Reporter, *Berkshire Eagle,* 1973-; Reporter, *Springfield Union;* Editorial Writer, *Boston Globe,* 1977-; Assistant Managing Editor for Local News, *Boston Globe,* ?-1988; Deputy Managing Editor, *Boston Globe,* 1989-91; Editorial Page Editor, *Boston Globe,* 1991-92.

For More Information: *Boston Globe,* 31 July (1992): 17; *Boston Globe,* 28 July (1992): 21.

Commentary: Kirk Scharfenberg shared a Pulitzer Prize with six other staff members of the Boston Globe for reporting about racism in Boston. He was also a finalist in 1981 for the editorial award for a series titled "A Program for Racial Peace." He wrote over 2,000 editorials and nearly 400 columns during his tenure at the *Boston Globe.*

David M. Wessel 758

Birth: February 21, 1954; New Haven, CT. **Spouse:** Naomi Karp (m. 1984).

Prize: *Local Investigative Specialized Reporting,* 1984: *Boston Globe,* Boston: *Boston Globe,* 1983.

Career: Staff member, *Middletown (CT) Press;* Staff member, *Hartford (CT) Courant;* Business Reporter, *Boston Globe,* 1981-83; Reporter, Boston, *Wall Street Journal,* 1984-.

Other Awards: Walter E. Bagehot Fellow in Business and Economic Journalism, Columbia University, NY, 1980-81.

For More Information: *Boston Globe,* 17 April (1984).

Commentary: David Wessel, along with six of his colleagues, won a Pulitzer Prize for a study of a race relations in the Boston area. They interviewed African American and Hispanic residents in the metropolitan area, used statistics for comparison purposes, and wrote a series of six articles about the difficulties minorities had in getting hired and succeeding in the marketplace.

Local Reporting

1948

George Evans Goodwin   759

Birth: June 20, 1917; Atlanta, GA. **Parents:** George Goodwin and Carrie (Clark). **Religion:** Presbyterian. **Education:** Washington and Lee University, VA: AB. **Spouse:** Lois Milstead (m. 1940). **Children:** Clark, Allen.

Prize: *Local Reporting,* 1948: *Atlanta Journal,* Atlanta, GA: Atlanta Journal, 1947.

Career: Reporter and Feature Writer, *Atlanta (GA) Georgian,* 1939; Reporter and Feature Writer, *The Charleston (SC) News and Courier,* 1940; Reporter and Feature Writer, *The Washington (DC) Times-Herald,* 1940-41; Reporter and Feature Writer, *Miami (FL) Daily News,* 1941-42; Served in U.S. Navy, WWII; Investigative Reporter and Political Writer, *Atlanta (GA) Journal,* 1945-52; Executive Director, Central Atlanta Improvement Association, 1952-54; Vice-President, First National Bank of Atlanta, 1954-64; Executive Vice-President, Bell and Stanton, Incorporated, 1965-76; President, Atlanta (GA), Manning, Selvage, and Lee, 1976-85; Senior Counselor, Atlanta (GA), Manning, Selvage, and Lee, 1985-.

Other Awards: Purple Heart. Navy Unit Commendation. Sigma Delta Chi Award, 1948. Pall Mall Big Story Award, 1949.

For More Information: *Atlanta Business Chronicle,* 8:36 (10 February 1986): 1B.

Commentary: George Goodwin is currently a public relations executive in his hometown of Atlanta. He was the primary writer and investigator of the story about voter fraud in Telfair County, Georgia and the number of write-in votes for Herman Talmadge for governor.

1949

Malcolm Malone Johnson   760

Birth: September 27, 1904; Claremont, GA. **Death:** June 18, 1976. **Parents:** William M. Johnson and Willie Estelle (Bolding). **Education:** Mercer University, GA. **Spouse:** Ludie Adams (m. 1928, died 1972). **Children:** Haynes, Sarah, Michael, Paul.

Prize: *Local Reporting,* 1949: *New York Sun,* New York: New York Sun, 1948.

Career: Editor-in-Chief, college newspaper; Reporter, *Macon Telegraph,* 1924-28; Reporter, Night Club Columnist, War Correspondent, *New York Sun,* 1928-50; Correspondent, New York (NY), Interna-

tional News Service, 1950-54; Vice-President, Hill Knowlton, Incorporated, New York, 1954-73.

Selected Works: *Crime on the Labor Front,* 1950. *Current Thoughts on Public Relations,* 1968. *Shoe Leather and Printers' Ink, 1924-1974,* 1974. *On the Water Front: An Original Screenplay,* 1954.

Other Awards: Women's Press Club of New York Award of Merit, 1949. George Polk Memorial Award, Long Island University, NY, 1950.

For More Information: *Current Biography Yearbook, 1949,* New York: H.W. Wilson Company, 1949: 300-302; *New York Times,* 19 June (1976): 24; *Contemporary Authors, Volumes 69-72,* Detroit: Gale Research Company, 1978: 344.

Commentary: Malcolm Johnson worked on his prize-winning series of 24 articles for over five months. Many of his articles were published on page one of his newspaper, from November 8 to December 10, 1948. His exposure of organized crime on the piers of New York led to an official investigation. The film *On the Waterfront* was based on his reporting. Later in his career, he wrote the obituary for his paper, *The New York Sun,* on January 3, 1950. He also covered the surrender of the Japanese aboard the *Missouri* and the atomic bomb tests in 1946.

His son, Haynes Johnson, also won a Pulitzer Prize, making them one of two pairs of father-son winners of the award.

1950

Meyer Berger   761

Birth: September 1, 1898; New York, NY. **Death:** February 8, 1959. **Parents:** Ignace Berger and Sarah (Waldman). **Religion:** Jewish. **Spouse:** Mae Gamsu (m. 1926).

Prize: *Local Reporting,* 1950: *New York Times,* New York: New York Times, 1949.

Career: Office boy, *New York Morning World,* 1911-17; Served in U.S. Army, 1917-19; Police District Reporter, *New York World,* 1919-22; District Reporter, Rewriteman, Standard News Association, 1922-27; Reporter, *New York Times,* 1928-; Staff member, *The New Yorker,* 1938; War Correspondent, Europe, Africa, Pacific, *New York Times,* 1942-45; Columnist, "About New York," *New York Times.*

Selected Works: *The Eight Million: Journal of a New York Correspondent,* 1942. *Men of Mary Knoll* (with James Keller), 1944. *Growth of an Ideal, 1850-1950: The Story of the Manhattan Savings Bank,* 1950. *Story of the New York Times,* 1951. *New York, City on Many Waters* (with Fritz Busse), 1955. *The Library,* 1956. *Meyer Berger's New York,* 1960.

Other Awards: Purple Heart. Silver Star. Conspicious Service Cross.

For More Information: *Current Biography Yearbook, 1943,* New York: H.W. Wilson, (1943): 37-38; *Time,* 55 (8 May 1950): 68-77; *New York Times,* 9 February (1959): 28, 29, *Newsweek,* 53 (16 February 1959): 16, *Newsweek,* 53 (23 February 1959): 96; *Reader's Digest,* 75 (October 1959): 77-81; Talese, Gay, *The Kingdom and the Power,* New York: World, 1969; Liebling, A.J., *Liebling Abroad,* New York: Wideview, 1981.

Commentary: Meyer Berger began working in journalism when he was eight, as a paper boy. His column in the 1940s and 1950s told small vignettes about New York and its inhabitants. His winning story accurately captured the events of the mass killing by Howard Unruh in Camden, New Jersey.

Berger also wrote the history of the *New York Times.*

1951

Edward Samuel Montgomery 762
Birth: December 30, 1910; Fort Collins, CO. **Death:** April 6, 1992. **Education:** University of Nevada: BA. **Spouse:** Helene M. **Children:** Diana, Douglas, David.

Prize: *Local Reporting,* 1951: *San Francisco Examiner,* San Francisco: San Francisco Examiner, 1950.

Career: Reporter, *Nevada State Journal,* 1934-36; Reporter, Sports Editor, Mining Editor, *Reno (NV) Evening Gazette,* 1938-42; Served in United States Marine Corps, 1942-45; Staff Writer and Investigative Reporter, *San Francisco (CA) Examiner,* 1945-75.

For More Information: *San Francisco Chronicle,* 8 April (1992): A22.

Commentary: Edward S. Montgomery's investigation of some dishonest Internal Revenue Service employees won him a Pulitzer Prize. His hearing aid allowed him to overhear the boasting of the officials.

Montgomery also wrote about Barbara Graham. He tried to save her from dying in the California gas chamber. The story was turned into a movie in 1958 called *I Want to Live.* Susan Hayward won an Academy Award for her portrayal of Graham.

1952

George De Carvalho 763
Birth: March 10, 1921; Hong Kong, China. **Death:** April 25, 1994. **Education:** Gonzaga College, Shanghai. Sorbonne University, Paris, France. **Spouse:** Tilka D.

Prize: *Local Reporting,* 1952: *San Francisco Chronicle,* San Francisco: San Francisco Chronicle, 1951.

Career: Copyboy, *San Francisco (CA) Chronicle,* 1938-39; Rewriteman, *San Francisco (CA) Chronicle,* 1939-; Served in U.S. Army, WWII, Foreign Correspondent, Western Europe *San Francisco (CA) Chronicle,* 1946-; City Reporter, *San Francisco (CA) Chronicle,* 1950-; War Correspondent, Korea, *San Francisco (CA) Chronicle,* 1951, *Time-Life.*

Other Awards: McQuade Award, 1952. Catholic Newsman Award, 1952. Heywood Broun Award, 1952.

For More Information: *San Francisco Chronicle,* 27 April (1994): A22.

Commentary: George De Carvalho exposed the blackmail of Chinese Americans by mainland China. Many Chinese-Americans were paying ransoms so that relatives in China would not be harmed. A resolution condemning the extortion was introduced in the United Nations, and several Chinese in New York City were indicted for their roles in the racket.

Local Reporting, Edition Time

1953

Providence Journal-Bulletin
Full entry appears as #694 under "Investigative Reporting," 1994.

1954

Vicksburg Post-Herald   764
Founded: May 4, 1883; Vicksburg, MS. **Founder(s):** John Gordon Cashman.

Prize: *Local Reporting, Edition Time,* 1954: *Vicksburg Post-Herald,* Vicksburg, MS, 1953.

Commentary: For the coverage of a tornado that struck December 5, 1953 in the community of Vicksburg, Mississippi, the *Vicksburg Post-Herald* was awarded a Pulitzer Prize. The staff worked with no communications or utilities. To many of the staff, the disaster contained a personal note of tragedy. Louis P. Cashman Sr. was the editor and publisher of the paper when the Pulitzer Prize was awarded in in 1954.

The *Vicksburg Herald* was first published on July 13, 1897 and ceased publication with the March 31, 1957 edition. The *Vicksburg Evening Post* was first published in May 4, 1883.

1955

Caro Brown   765

Birth: 1908; Cleveland, TX. **Education:** College of Industrial Arts, TX. **Spouse:** Jack L. Brown. **Children:** Three children.

Prize: *Local Reporting, Edition Time,* 1955: *Alice Daily Echo,* Alice, TX: Alice Daily Echo, 1954.

Career: Associate Editor, college paper; Proofreader, *Alice (TX) Daily Echo;* Columnist, *Alice (TX) Daily Echo;* Society Editor, *Alice (TX) Daily Echo,* 1954-55; Courthouse Reporter, *Alice (TX) Daily Echo.*

Other Awards: Award, Theta Sigma Phi, Austin Chapter, TX, 1955.

For More Information: *Houston Post,* 3 May (1955): 1, 4; O'Neill, Lois Decker, *Women's Book of World Records and Achievements,* Garden City, NJ: Anchor Press, 1979: 452.

Commentary: Caro Brown exposed 40 years of corruption in Duval County, Texas. Her story of January 18, 1954 of a courthouse brawl between George B. Parr and Texas Rangers attracted national attention and led to Parr's downfall.

1956

Lee Hills   766
Birth: May 28, 1906; Granville, ND. **Parents:** Lewis Amos Hills and Lulu Mae (Lewis). **Education:** Brigham Young University, UT. University of Missouri. Oklahoma City University: LLB. **Spouse:** Leona Haas (m. 1933, died); Eileen Whitman (m. 1948, died 1961); Argentina Schifano Ramos (m. 1963). **Children:** Ronald Lee (LH); Stepchild: Mrs. Carl Griffith.

Prize: *Local Reporting, Edition Time,* 1956: *Detroit Free Press,* Detroit, MI: Detroit Free Press, 1955.

Career: Reporter, *Price (UT) News-Advocate,* 1924-25; Editor, *Price (UT) News-Advocate,* 1926; Reporter, *Oklahoma City (OK) Times,* 1929-32; Political Reporter, *Oklahoma City (OK) News,* 1932-35; Reporter, Copyreader, *Cleveland (OH) Press,* 1935-36; Editorial Writer, Associate Editor, *Indianapolis (IN) Times,* 1936-37; Editor, *Oklahoma City (OK) News,* 1938-39; Associate Editor, *Memphis (TN) Press-Scimitar,* 1939-40; Editor, *Cleveland (OH) Press,* 1940-42; Managing Editor, *Miami (FL) Herald,* 1942-51; Executive Editor, *Miami (FL) Herald,* 1951-66; Executive Editor, *Detroit Free Press,* 1951-69; Publisher, *Detroit Free Press,* 1963-79; Associate Publisher, *Miami (FL) Herald,* 1966-69; Publisher, *Miami (FL) Herald,* 1970-79; Chief Executive Officer, Knight Newspapers, Incorporated, 1973-76; Chairman of the Board, Knight Newspapers, Incorporated, 1973-79; Editorial Chairman, Knight-Ridder Incorporated, 1979-; Chairman, John S. and James L.Knight Foundation, 1991-96.

Selected Works: *Facsimile* (with Timothy J. Sullivan), 1949. *A Personal Report on Russia Today: From the Pages of the Detroit Free Press,* 1962.

Other Awards: Maria Moors Cabot Gold Medal, Columbia University, NY, 1946. Hall of Honor, University of Missouri School of Journalism, 1959. Honorary Degrees: Oklahoma City University, 1934; Cleary College, MI, 1958; University of Utah, 1969; Eastern Michigan University, 1969.

For More Information: *Contemporary Authors, Volume 101,* Detroit: Gale Research Company, 1981; Taft, William H., *Encyclopedia of Twentieth-Century Journalists,* New York: Garland Publishing, 1986.

Commentary: Lee Hills won a Pulitzer Prize for his coverage of the contract negotiations between the United Automobile Workers and the Ford Motor Company and between the United Automobile Workers and the General Motors Company. He used his inside contacts on both sides to follow the story. His series, "A Peek Behind the News Blackout," ran concurrently with the spot news coverage of his paper. Hills was executive editor of the *Detroit Free Press* at the time. He eventually became chief executive officer and chairman of the board of Knight Newspapers, Inc.

1957

Salt Lake Tribune 767
Founded: April 15, 1871; Salt Lake City, UT. **Founder(s):** George W. Crouch, William S. Godbe, E.L.T. Harrison, Oscar G. Sawyer, William H. Shearman, Edward W. Tullidge.

Prize: *Local Reporting, Edition Time,* 1957: *Salt Lake Tribune,* July 1, 1956, Salt Lake City, UT, 1956.

Selected Works: *Inside the Tribune: Behind the Headlines at One of America's Great Newspapers,* 1969. *The First 100 Years: A History of the Salt Lake Tribune, 1871-1971* (Malmquist, Orvin Nebeker, ed.), 1971. *One Hundred Years Historic Pages: The Salt Lake Tribune, 1871-1971,* 1971.

Commentary: The *Salt Lake Tribune's* coverage of what was called the world's worst commercial air disaster won the paper a Pulitzer Prize. On June 30, 1956, two airplanes struck each other and 126 people were killed. The accident was in a remote area, 22 miles northeast of the Grand Canyon, Arizona. Reporters, photographers, editors, rewritemen, and technicians worked on the story.

The *Salt Lake Tribune* was started as a secular alternative newspaper to the Mormon press in Utah.

William S. Godbe was the publisher, Oscar G. Sawyer was the managing editor, George W. Crouch and Edward W. Tullidge were the associate editors, and William H. Shearman was the business manager. Sawyer resigned in 1871 because of editorial disagreements with the other founders of the newspaper. In 1873, Fred Lockley, George F. Prescott, and A.M. Hamilton, three newspapermen from Kansas, bought the *Salt Lake Tribune.* In September 1883, Patrick H. Lannan and C.C. Goodwin purchased four-fifths of the *Salt Lake Tribune.* (Colonel O.J. Hollister had bought one-fifth of the *Tribune* the previous year.) In 1901, the paper was sold to Senator Thomas Kearns and David Keith. In 1918, both Keith and Kearns died; Keith in April, with his estate wanting cash for his share of the newspaper for tax purposes, and Kearns in October. Upon Kearns's death, John F. Fitzpatrick, formerly a chief assistant of Kearns, ran the newspaper for his estate and purchased Keith's interest in the newspaper. In 1947, the *Salt Lake Tribune* sold the *Salt Lake City Telegram* to the *Deseret News.* It established a joint operating agency to produce both the *Tribune* and the *News.*

1958

Fargo Forum 768
Founded: November 17, 1891; Fargo, ND. **Founder(s):** Major A.E. Edwards and Colonel H.C. Plumley.

Prize: *Local Reporting, Edition Time,* 1958: *Fargo Forum,* Fargo, ND, 1957.

Selected Works: *North Dakota: 100 Years,* 1988.

Commentary: Within five hours after a tornado stuck on June 20, 1957, the *Fargo Forum* published a tornado edition. It carried 24 columns of tornado news. Ten people were killed and 80 injured in the storm. Norman D. Black Jr. was the publisher of the paper and John D. Paulson was the editor at the time.

The *Fargo Forum* was founded in 1891 by Major Edwards and Colonel Plumley. It has been sold several times. In 1988, the Marcil family purchased the outstanding stock from the Lewis family and consolidated the ownership of the newspaper. In 1966, the name of the newspaper was changed to *The Forum of Fargo-Moorhead.* And in 1993, the Forum Publishing Company changed its name to Forum Communications.

1959

Mary Lou Werner   769

Birth: June 21, 1926; Alexandria, VA. **Parents:** William Joseph Werner and Anne Jeanette (Wall). **Religion:** Roman Catholic. **Spouse:** James B. Forbes. **Children:** James Werner.

Prize: *Local Reporting, Edition Time,* 1959: *Washington Evening Star,* Washington, DC: Washington Evening Star, 1958.

Career: Copygirl, *Washington (DC) Star,* 1944-46; Reporter, *Washington (DC) Star,* 1946-56; Reporter, Political Affairs, *Washington (DC) Star,* 1957-59; Editor, *Washington (DC) Star,* 1959-; Associate Editor, Editorial and Comment Section, *Washington (DC) Star,* ?-1981; Executive Editor, Source Telecomputing Corporation, 1982-; Commentary Page Editor, *Washington (DC) Times,* 1984-.

Other Awards: Education Writing Excellence Award, National Association of Education Writers, 1958. National Reporting Award, Washington DC, Newspaper Guild, 1959. Hall of Fame, Society of Professional Journalists, 1992.

For More Information: Rothmeyer, Karen, *Winning Pulitzers: The Stories Behind Some of the Best News Coverage of Our Times,* New York: Columbia University Press, 1991.

Commentary: Mary Lou Werner Forbes covered the school integration crisis in Virginia for her paper. At times, she dictated her story over the phone just before the paper went to press. Her contacts from covering the area prior to the crisis allowed her to get exclusives for her paper. She also wrote background articles to explain what was happening.

1960

John Howard Nelson   770

Birth: October 11, 1929; Talladega, AL. **Parents:** Howard Alonzo Nelson and Barbara Lena (O'Donnell). **Education:** Georgia State University. **Spouse:** Virginia Dare Dickinson (m. 1951, div. 1974); Barbara Joan Matusow (m. 1974). **Children:** Karen, John, Steven (VD).

Prize: *Local Reporting, Edition Time,* 1960: *Atlanta Constitution,* Atlanta, GA: Atlanta Constitution, 1959.

Career: Reporter, *Biloxi (MS) Daily Herald,* 1947-51; Served in U.S. Army, 1951-52; Reporter, *Atlanta (GA) Constitution,* 1952-65; Special Correspondent to the South, *Los Angeles Times,* 1965-70; Investigative Reporter, Washington (DC), *Los Angeles Times,* 1970-75; Washington (DC) Bureau Chief, *Los Angeles Times,* 1975-96; Chief Washington (DC) Correspondent, *Los Angeles Times,* 1996-.

Selected Works: *The Censors and the Schools* (with Gene Roberts Jr.), 1963. *The Orangeburg Massacre* (with Jack Bass), 1970. *The FBI and the Berrigans* (with Ronald J. Ostrow), 1972. *Captive Voices: High School Journalism in America* (with the Commission of Inquiry into High School Journalism), 1974. *Terror in the Night: The Klan's Campaign against Jews,* 1993.

Other Awards: Nieman Fellow, Harvard University, MA, 1961-62. Drew Pearson Award, 1975.

For More Information: Behrens, John C., *The Typewriter Guerrillas: Closeups of 20 Top Investigative Reporters,* Chicago: Nelson-Hall, (1977): 167-179; *Contemporary Authors, First Revision, Volumes 29-32,* Detroit: Gale Research, 1978; Taft, William H., *Encyclopedia of Twentieth-Century Journalists,* New York: Garland Publishing, 1986.

Commentary: Jack Nelson exposed the horrible conditions at the Milledgeville State Hospital in Georgia. As a result of his reporting, the mental hospital was transferred from the State Welfare Department to the State Health Department, and the state of Georgia pledged additional funds to improve the treatment of mental health patients within the state.

1961

Sanche De Gramont   771

Birth: March 31, 1932; Geneva, Switzerland. **Parents:** Gabriel Armand De Gramont and Mariette (Negroponte). **Education:** Sorbonne University, Paris, France. Yale University, CT: BA, summa cum laude. Columbia University, NY: MS. **Spouse:** Margaret Kinnicutt (m. 1958, div. 1968); Nancy Ryan (M. 1968, div. 1980). **Children:** Gabriel, Amber (NR).

Prize: *Local Reporting, Edition Time,* 1961: *New York Herald-Tribune,* New York: New York Herald Tribune, 1960.

Career: *Worcester (MA) Telegram,* 1955-56; Served in French Army, 1956-57; Reporter, New York (NY), Associated Press, 1958-59; French Press Agency, 1959; Reporter and Correspondent, Paris (France) *New York Herald-Tribune,* 1959-64; Rome (Italy) Bureau Chief, *New York Herald-Tribune,* 1962-64; Freelance reporter and writer, 1964-; Writer, *Saturday Evening Post,* 1965.

Selected Works: *The Secret War: The Story of International Espionage since World War II,* 1962. *U.S.A.,* 1966. *Epitaph for Kings,* 1968. *The French: Portrait of a People,* 1969. *Lives to Give,* 1971. *The Way up: The Memoirs of Count Gramont,* 1972. *The Strong Brown God: The Story of Niger River,* 1975. *On Becoming American,* 1978. *Maugham: A Touchstone Book,* 1981. *Rowing toward Eden,* 1981. *Churchill: Young Man in a Hurry, 1874-1915,* 1982. *FDR: A Biography,* 1985. *Literary Outlaw: The Life and Times of William S. Burroughs,* 1988. *An Uncertain Hour: The French, the Germans, the Jews, the Klaus Barbie Trial, and the City of Lyon, 1940-45,* 1990. *Wilderness at Dawn: The Settling of the North American Continent,* 1993. *A Shovel of Stars: The Making of the American West, 1800 to the Present,* 1995.

For More Information: *Contemporary Authors, New Revision Series, Volume 3,* Detroit: Gale Research Company, 1981.

Commentary: Sanche De Gramont won a Pulitzer Prize for his story on the death of Leonard Warren on the stage of the New York Metropolitan Opera House on March 4, 1960. De Gramont changed his name to Ted Morgan when he became a United States citizen in 1973. He rearranged the letters in his last name to come up with his new name.

1962

Robert D. Mullins   772

Birth: December 16, 1924; Scofield, UT. **Education:** University of Utah. **Spouse:** Donna Marie Powell (m. 1957). **Children:** Gina Marie.

Prize: *Local Reporting, Edition Time,* 1962: *Deseret News,* Salt Lake City, UT: Deseret News, 1961.

Career: Served in U.S. Army, WWII; Reporter, *Salt Lake City (UT) Deseret News;* News Bureau Manager, Price (UT), *Salt Lake City (UT) Deseret News;* 1954-87.

Commentary: Robert D. Mullins drove up to 250 miles away from his city newsroom to cover the story of the murder-kidnapping at Dead Horse Point, Utah. He was investigating the shooting of Charles Boothroyd and his fiancee, Jeannette Sullivan, and the kidnapping of Sullian's 15-year-old daughter Denise

on July 4, 1961. Mullins reported page one stories for his newspaper for seven days. He did not miss a deadline, even when the story took him away from his office.

1963

Sylvan Fox   773

Birth: June 2, 1928; Brooklyn, NY. **Parents:** Louis Fox and Sophie (Shapiro). **Education:** Juilliard School of Music, NY. Brooklyn College, NY: BA. University of California, Berkeley: MA. **Spouse:** Gloria R. Endleman (m. 1948). **Children:** Erica.

Prize: *Local Reporting, Edition Time,* 1963: *New York World-Telegram and Sun,* New York: New York World-Telegram and Sun, 1962.

Career: Reporter, *Little Falls (NY) Evening Times,* 1954; Reporter, *Schenectady (NY) Union Star,* 1954-55; Reporter, *Buffalo (NY) Evening News,* 1955-59; Rewriteman, Assistant City Editor, City Editor, *New York World-Telegram,* 1959-66; Journalism Instructor, New York University, 1965; Deputy Police Commissioner for Press Relations, New York City, 1966-67; Journalism Instructor, Long Island University (NY), 1967; Rewriteman, Reporter, *New York Times,* 1967-; Assistant Metropolitan Editor, *New York Times;* Saigon (Vietnam) Bureau Chief *New York Times,* ?-1973; Nassau County (NY) Editor, *Newsday (NY),* 1973-77; National Editor, *Newsday (NY),* 1977-; Assistant Managing Editor, National and Foreign News, *Newsday (NY),* ?-1979; Editorial Page Editor, *Newsday (NY),* 1979-88; Journalism Instructor, Baylor University (TX), 1985, 1988; Assistant Professor of Journalism, New York University, 1989-90; Travel Columnist, *Newsday (NY),* 1994-95.

Selected Works: *The Unanswered Questions about President Kennedy's Assassination,* 1965.

Other Awards: Award for Best Story Written about a Fire, Newspaper Reporter's Association, 1963. Spot News Award, Uniformed Fireman's Association.

For More Information: *New York Times,* 7 May (1963): 35; *New York World-Telegram and Sun,* 5 May (1963): 3.

Commentary: Sylvan Fox, William Longgood, and Anthony Shannon were awarded a Pulitzer Prize for their coverage of the March 1, 1962 airplane crash at Idlewild Airport. Fox wrote an article on the breaking news within a half hour of the accident. He also wrote a new 3,000-word article in the following 90 minutes.

After the demise of the *New York World-Telegram and Sun,* Fox worked for the City of New York. He then went to the *New York Times* and then *Newsday,* where he stayed until he retired in 1988.

William Frank Longgood   774

Birth: September 12, 1917; St. Louis, MO. **Parents:** William F. Longgood and Grace (Turner). **Education:** University of Missouri: BJ. **Spouse:** Margaret Henning (m. 1948). **Children:** Bret.

Prize: *Local Reporting, Edition Time,* 1963: *New York World-Telegram and Sun,* New York: New York World-Telegram and Sun, 1962.

Career: Writer, Salesman, Niagara Falls (NY) radio station, 1940-42; Writer, salesman, Santa Barbara (CA) radio station, 1942-43; Served in U.S. Army Air Forces, 1943-46; Reporter, *Newark (NY) Evening News,* 1946-48; Reporter, *New York World-Telegram and Sun,* 1948-65; Text Editor, Time-Life Books, 1965-68; Teacher, New School for Social Research (NY), 1966-72; Freelance writer, 1968-; Correspondent, Cape Cod (MA), *New York Times,* 1973-; Instructor, Columbia University Graduate School of Journalism (NY), 1973.

Selected Works: *The Suez Story,* 1957. *The Pink Slip* (with Ed Wallace), 1959. *The Poisons in Your Food,* 1960. *Talking Your Way to Success,* 1962. *Ike: A Pictorial Biography,* 1969. *Write It Right,* 1970. *Write with Feeling,* 1970. *The Darkening Land,* 1972. *The Queen Must Die, and Other Affairs of Bees and Men,* 1985. *Voices from the Earth: A Year in the Life of a Garden,* 1991.

Other Awards: George Polk Memorial Award, Long Island University, NY, 1954. Cultural Award, Newspaper Reporters Association of New York City.

New York Newspaper Guild Award. National Headliners Club Award.

For More Information: *New York World-Telegram and Sun,* 13 May (1963): 3; *Contemporary Authors, First Revision, Volumes 1-4,* Detroit: Gale Research Company, 1967; *Yankee,* August (1985).

Commentary: William Longgood, Sylvan Fox, and Anthony Shannon covered the airplane crash at Idlewild Airport on March 1, 1962. Longgood wrote about the rescue work at the scene of the accident. Ninety-five people were killed in the crash.

Anthony F. Shannon   775

Birth Place: Pittsfield, MA. **Education:** University of Maine. **Spouse:** Hope Johnson. **Children:** Gregory.

Prize: *Local Reporting, Edition Time,* 1963: *New York World-Telegram and Sun,* New York: New York World-Telegram and Sun, 1962.

Career: Served in U.S. Army, Korean War; Staff member, *Bangor (ME) Daily News, Providence (RI) Journal;* Reporter, *New York (NY) World-Telegram,* 1955-.

For More Information: *New York World Telegram and Sun,* 13 May (1963): 3.

Commentary: Anthony Shannon, William Longgood, and Sylvan Fox were awarded a Pulitzer Prize for their reporting about the airplane crash at Idlewild Airport on March 1, 1962. Shannon wrote five stories on the incident, including eyewitness accounts of the tragedy.

Local Reporting, No Edition Time

1953

Edward Joseph Mowery   776

Birth: March 8, 1906; Lancaster, OH. **Death:** December 19, 1970. **Parents:** Arlow Francis Mowery and Nellie Cecilia (O'Connor). **Religion:** Roman Catholic. **Education:** Ohio State University. Notre Dame University, IN. **Spouse:** Margaret Josephine Ryan (m. 1938). **Children:** Michael, William, Margaret.

   Prize: *Local Reporting, No Edition Time,* 1953: *New York World-Telegram and Sun,* New York: New York World-Telegram and Sun, 1952.

   Career: Founder of weekly, *Columbus (OH) Eastern News,* 1932-35; Managing Editor, *Catholic Columbian (OH);* City Editor, *Lancaster (PA) Daily Eagle;* Staff Writer, *Associated Press;* Feature Writer, *Columbus (OH) Sunday Dispatch;* Editor, *Lancaster (PA) Daily Eagle* and *Eagle Gazette;* Staff Writer, King Features Syndicate, 1937-; Editorial Writer, *Brunswick (NJ) Home News;* Financial Editor, *Newark (NJ) Star-Ledger;* Staff Writer, *New York Post;* Staff member, *New York World-Telegram & Sun,* 1943-54; Staff member, *New York Herald-Tribune;* Staff member, Washington (DC), Newhouse Newspapers; Syndicated columnist, 1960s.

   Other Awards: Pall Mall Distinguished Service "Big Story" Award, 1947, 1953. American Legion Citation for Patriotism, New York and Brooklyn Chapters, 1951. Society of Silurians Award, 1951. InterFaith Gold Medal, American Legion, 1952. Outstanding Service Award, New York Criminal-Civil Courts Bar Association, 1952. George Polk Memorial Award, Long Island University, NY, 1953. Frommer Award, Columbia University, NY, 1953.

   For More Information: *Current Biography Yearbook,* New York: H.W. Wilson Company, 1953: 438-39; *New York Times,* 21 December (1970): 38; *National Cyclopaedia of American Biography, Volume 56,* New York: James T. White & Company, 1975: 163-164.

   Commentary: Edward J. Mowery was known for going out and getting the story behind the story. He worked on his winning story for seven years. It was his efforts and reporting that cleared Louis Hoffner, who was charged with a murder he did not commit. Earlier in his career, Mowery helped clear the name of a man convicted of forgery.

1954

Alvin Scott McCoy   777

Birth: July 14, 1903; Cheney, KS. **Death:** March 8, 1988. **Education:** University of Kansas: AB, Phi Beta Kappa. **Spouse:** Marion Grey Franklin (m. 1932). **Children:** Marion S., Mary.

   Prize: *Local Reporting, No Edition Time,* 1954: *Kansas City Star,* Kansas City, MO: Kansas City Star, 1953.

   Career: Parts Department member, Ford dealership, Dodge City (KS); Reporter, *Wichita (KS) Evening Eagle,* and *Wichita (KS) Morning Eagle;* General Assignment Reporter, *Kansas City (MO) Star,* 1930-45; Pacific War Correspondent, *Kansas (MO) City Star,* 1945; Kansas Correspondent, State Politics, Legislature, News, Features, Topeka (KS) Correspondent, *Kansas City (MO) Star,* 1945-1962; Education Reporter, *Kansas City (MO) Star;* Science Editor, *Kansas City (MO) Star,* ?-1968.

   For More Information: *Kansas City Star,* 9 March (1988): 1A, 2A, 9B.

   Commentary: Alvin S. McCoy's reporting led to the resignation of C. Wesley Roberts as the chairman of the Republican National Committee. He reported on the discrepancy of funds, events leading up to the legislative investigation, and the testimony of Roberts. McCoy faced a contempt citation when he refused to name his source. He only revealed the name of his source after the person had died.

   At the age of 63, McCoy went on a three-week expedition to the South Pole. He retired in 1968.

1955

Roland Kenneth Towery   778

Birth: January 25, 1923; Smithville, MS. **Parents:** Wiley Axof Towery and Lonie Bell (Cowart). **Education:** Southwest Texas Junior College: AA. Texas A & M University. **Spouse:** Louise Ida Cook (m. 1947). **Children:** Roland Kenneth Jr., Alice Towery Russo.

   Prize: *Local Reporting, No Edition Time,* 1955: *Cuero Record,* Cuero, TX: Cuero Record, 1954.

   Career: Served in U.S. Army, 1941-46; Part-Time Farm Columnist, *Cuero (TX) Record,* 1951; Reporter, *Cuero (TX) Record,* 1952-54; Managing Editor, *Cuero (TX) Record,* 1954-56; Government Affairs Reporter, *Austin (TX) Newspapers, Inc.,* 1956-63; Administrative Assistant, U.S. Senator John

Tower, 1963-69; Deputy Director, U.S. Information Agency; Head, Development Office, University of Texas Systems, 1976-77; Administrative Officer, U.S. Senator John Tower, 1977-78; Campaign Manager, Texas for Tower, 1978; President, Austin (TX) Sentinel Corporation; Partner, Blythe, Nelson, Newton, and Towery Consulting Firm; Board Member, Corporation for Public Broadcasting, 1981-; Chairman of the Board, Corporation for Public Broadcasting, 1989-90.

Selected Works: *The Latest Monthly Public Opinion Survey from Lubbock, Texas, the Pulse of America,* 1989.

Other Awards: Distinguished Service to Journalism Award, Texas Press Association, 1955. Journalistic Achievement, Texas House of Representatives, 1963.

For More Information: *Time,* 7 March (1955); *Nominations—Corporation on Public Broadcasting: Hearing Before the Committee on Commerce, Science, and Transportation, United States Senate, Ninety-Seventh Congress, First Session, on Nominations of Sonia Shames Landau and Roland Kenneth Towery, to be Members of the Board of Directors, Corporation for Public Broadcasting, October 27, 1981,* Washington, D.C.: U.S. Government Printing Office, 1981.

Commentary: R. Kenneth Towery won a Pulitzer Prize for exposing a Texas land scandal and the Veterans Land Board. His paper had a small voice (with a circulation of 2,185), but it was heard throughout the state of Texas. Promoters were having groups of veterans apply for bank loans for land the promoters owned. The promoters then sold the land at an inflated value to the Veterans Land Board. A grand jury investigation resulted in 159 fraud indictments. Towery, who was a prisoner of war in Japan for three years, was working at his first newspaper job when he reported his winning story.

1956

Arthur John Daley   779
Birth: July 31, 1904; New York, NY. **Death:** January 3, 1974. **Parents:** Daniel Michael Daley and Mary (Greene). **Religion:** Roman Catholic. **Education:** Fordham University, NY: BA. New York University. Columbia University, NY. **Spouse:** Betty Blake (m. 1928). **Children:** Robert, Kevin, Patricia, Katharine.

Prize: *Local Reporting, No Edition Time,* 1956: *New York Times,* New York: New York Times, 1955.

Career: Assistant Editor, college paper, *Ram;* Sports Columnist, college paper, *Ram;* Sports Writer, *New York Times,* 1926-74; Columnist, "Sports of the Times," *New York Times,* 1942-74.

Selected Works: *Story of the Olympic Games* (with John Kiernan), 1941. *Times at Bat,* 1950. *Daley Delight: A Sampling of Arthur Daley's Pulitzer Prize Sports Column "Sports of the Times,"* 1957. *Sports of the Times,* 1959. *Knute Rockne, Football Wizard of Notre Dame,* 1960. *Kings of the Home Run,* 1962. *Pro Football's Hall of Fame,* 1963.

Other Awards: Grantland Rice Award, 1961. Professional Football Writers' Distinguished Writing Award, 1970. Sportswriter of the Year Award, 1973.

For More Information: *Current Biography Yearbook,* New York: H.W. Wilson, 1956: 136-138; *New York Times,* 4 January (1974): 32; Taft, William H., *Encyclopedia of Twentieth-Century Journalists,* New York: Garland Publishing, Inc., 1986.

Commentary: In the first 115 years of the *New York Times,* there were only two sports columnists. Arthur Daley was the second of the two, taking over the column "Sports of the Times" from John Kieran in 1942. It was his sports reporting that won him a Pulitzer Prize in 1956. He was the second sportswriter to be honored.

When Daley covered the Olympic Games in Berlin, it was the first time the *New York Times* sent a sports reporter abroad. He covered the Olympics from those in Los Angeles in 1932 to those in Munich in 1972.

1957

William G. Lambert   780

Birth: February 2, 1920; Langford, SD. **Death:** February 8, 1998. **Parents:** William G. Lambert and Blanche (Townsend). **Spouse:** Jean Kenway Mead (m. 1945). **Children:** Cathryn, Heather.

Prize: *Local Reporting, No Edition Time,* 1957: *Portland Oregonian,* Portland, OR: Portland Oregonian, 1956.

Career: Served in U.S. Army, WWII; Reporter, *Oregon City (OR) Banner-Courier,* 1945; News Editor, *Oregon City (OR) Banner-Courier and Enterprise,* 1945-50; Reporter, *Portland (OR) Oregonian,* 1951-59; Anchor, News Director, KPTV, Portland, OR, 1961-62; Correspondent, *Time* magazine, 1962-63; Staff Writer, Associate Editor, *Life* magazine, 1963-70; Correspondent, Time-Life News Service, 1971-73; Freelance journalist, 1973; Staff Writer, *Philadelphia (PA) Inquirer,* 1974-85; Libel litigation consultant, 1985-.

Other Awards: Heywood Broun Award, 1957, 1969-70. Nieman Fellow, Harvard University, MA, 1959-60. Magazine Reporting Award, Sigma Delta Chi, 1967. Worth Bingham Prize, 1967. George Polk Memorial Award, Long Island University, NY, 1970. National Headliners Club Award, 1970. Page One Award, 1970. Sigma Delta Chi Award, 1970.

For More Information: Taft, William H., *Encyclopedia of Twentieth-Century Journalists,* New York: Garland Publishing, 1986; *Philadelphia Inquirer,* 9 February (1998): R2; *New York Times,* 16 February (1998): A13.

Commentary: William Lambert and Wallace Turner's investigation into union corruption won them a Pulitzer Prize. Later, Lambert's story about Supreme Court Justice Abe Fortas in *Life* magazine led to Fortas's resignation.

Wallace L. Turner   781

Birth: March 15, 1921; Titusville, FL. **Parents:** Clyde H. Turner and Inabelle (Wallace). **Education:** University of Missouri: BJ. **Spouse:** Pearl Burk (m. 1943). **Children:** Kathleen J., Elizabeth A.

Prize: *Local Reporting, No Edition Time,* 1957: *Portland Oregonian,* Portland, OR: Portland Oregonian, 1956.

Career: Reporter, *Springfield (MO) Daily News,* 1943; Reporter, *Portland (OR) Oregonian,* 1943-59; News Director, KPTV, Portland, OR, 1960-61; Assistant to Secretary, U.S. Department of Health, Education, and Welfare, 1961-62; Correspondent, San Francisco (CA), *New York Times,* 1962-70; San Francisco (CA) Bureau Chief, *New York Times,* 1970-85; Seattle (WA) Bureau Chief, *New York Times,* 1985-88.

Selected Works: *Gambler's Money, the New Force in American Life,* 1965. *The Mormon Establishment,* 1966.

Other Awards: Heywood Broun Award, 1952, 1957. Nieman Fellow, Harvard University, MA, 1958-59.

For More Information: *New York Times,* 7 May (1957): 28.

Commentary: Wallace Turner and William Lambert's exposure of the corruption in Portland, Oregon won them a Pulitzer Prize. They reported on the union underworld connections and the attempted takeover of the city government. They continued their coverage despite the risk of personal reprisals.

1958

George David Beveridge Jr.   782

Birth: January 5, 1922; Washington, DC. **Death:** February 14, 1987. **Parents:** George David Beveridge and Lillian Agnes (Little). **Religion:** Presbyterian. **Education:** George Washington University, Washington, DC. **Spouse:** Betty Jean Derwent (m. 1944). **Children:** Barbara J., Deborah A., David C.

Prize: *Local Reporting, No Edition Time,* 1958: *Washington Evening Star,* Washington, DC: The Washington Evening Star, 1957.

Career: Copyboy, *Washington (DC) Star,* 1940-, Reporter, *Washington Star,* 1942-63, National Affairs Reporter, *Washington Star,* 1950-52; Reporter, Washington Metropolitan Area, *Washington Star,* 1952; Editorial Writer, *Washington Star,* 1963-74; Assistant Managing Editor, *Washington Star,* 1974-75; Ombudsman, *Washington Star,* 1976-81; Associate Editor, *Washington Star,* 1980-81; Assistant to Chairman, Allbritton Communications Company, Washington (DC), 1981-84; Senior Vice President, Communications, Riggs National Bank, Washington (DC), 1984-87.

For More Information: *Washington Evening Star,* 6 May (1958): 1+; *Contemporary Authors, Volume 102,* Detroit: Gale Research Company, 1981; *Washington Post,* 16 February (1987): 1+.

Commentary: George Beveridge's winning series of eight articles chronicled the growing problems of metropolitan Washington, DC. The articles provided information that the general public as well as those in government could use to begin discussing the problems of urbanization. His articles appeared in the *Washington Evening Star* on October 8, 13, 27, 30, and December 3, 10, 17, and 24, 1957.

1959

John Harold Brislin   783

Birth: July 8, 1911; Wilkes-Barre, PA. **Education:** University of Scranton, PA. Pennsylvania State University. **Spouse:** Gene O'Boyle. **Children:** Robert.

Prize: *Local Reporting, No Edition Time,* 1959: *Scranton Tribune* and *Scrantonion,* Scranton, PA: 1958.

Career: Copyboy, Reporter, *Scranton (PA) Times;* Staff Writer, *Scranton (PA) Tribune* and *The Scrantonian (PA).*

Other Awards: Heywood Broun Award. Sigma Delta Chi.

For More Information: *New York Times,* 22 December (1973): 28.

Commentary: John Brislin's four-year investigation into a bombing in North Scranton, Pennsylvania won him a Pulitzer Prize. A nonunion plant had been dynamited by labor radicals. He continued his investigation despite personal threats. His reporting led to a Senate hearing. Six labor leaders and four union members were convicted of the crime.

1960

Miriam Ottenberg   784

Birth: October 7, 1914; Washington, DC. **Death:** November 9, 1982. **Parents:** Louis Ottenberg and Nettie (Podell). **Religion:** Jewish. **Education:** Goucher College, MD. Columbia University, NY. University of Wisconsin: BA.

Prize: *Local Reporting, No Edition Time,* 1960: *Washington Evening Star,* "Buyer Beware," Washington, DC: Washington Evening Star, 1959.

Career: Copywriter, Chicago (IL) Neisser-Meyerhoff, 1935-36; Reporter, Woman's Department, *Akron (OH) Times-Press,* 1937, Police Reporter, *Washington (DC) Evening Star,* 1937-; Investigative Reporter, *Washington (DC) Evening Star.*

Selected Works: *The Federal Investigators,* 1962. *Debtor Beware: A Series Exposing the Debt-Consolidating Firms in the Washington Area,* 1967. *The Pursuit of Hope: A Pulitzer-Prize Winner Tells the Story of How She and Many Others Fought and Conquered the Fear, Uncertainty, and Despair of Multiple Sclerosis,* 1978.

Other Awards: Distinguished Service to Journalism Award, School of Journalism and Mass Communication, University of Wisconsin, Madison, 1961. Public Service Award, National Headliners Club, 1970. Plaque, Attorney General of the United States, Congressional Leaders, Judges, Prosecutors, and the Chief of Police. Washington Newspaper Guild Award.

For More Information: *Contemporary Authors, First Revision, Volumes 5-8,* Detroit: Gale Research Company, 1969; *Foremost Women in Communications,* New York: Foremost Americans Publishing Corp., 1970; *Washington Post,* 10 November (1982): B20; McKerns, Joseph P., *Biographical Dictionary of American Journalism,* New York: Greenwood Press, 1989.

Commentary: Miriam Ottenberg won the Pulitzer Prize for her expose of unscrupulous used car

dealers in the Washington, DC area. Her follow-up articles led to legislation to help curb the practices of those dealers.

Ottenberg also covered the Senate investigation of drug traffic and her writing campaigned successfully for stricter narcotic laws. She died of cancer in 1982.

1961

Edgar May   785

Birth: June 27, 1929; Zurich, Switzerland. **Parents:** Ferdinand May and Renee (Bloch). **Education:** Columbia University, NY. Northwestern University, IL: BS, With Highest Distinction. New England Culinary Institute. Cornell University, NY. **Spouse:** Louise T. Breason (m. 1965, died).

Prize: *Local Reporting, No Edition Time,* 1961: *Buffalo Evening News,* "Our Costly Dilemma," Buffalo, NY: Buffalo Evening News, 1960.

Career: File Clerk, *New York Times,* 1948-51; Reporter, Editor, *Bellows Falls (VT) Times,* 1951-52; Reporter, *Fitchburg (MA) Sentinel,* 1953; Served in U.S. Army, 1953-55; Part-Time Reporter, *Chicago (IL) Tribune,* 1955-56; Freelance writer, Europe, 1956; Reporter, *Buffalo (NY) Evening News,* 1958-62; Director of Public Welfare Projects, State Charities Aid Association (NY), 1962-64; Assistant Director, Office of Economic Opportunity, Washington (DC), 1964; Special Advisor, U.S. Ambassador to France, Sergeant Shiver, 1968-70; Consultant, Ford Foundation, 1970-74; Member, Vermont House of Representatives, 1975-82; Member, Vermont Senate, 1983-91; Chief Operating Officer, Special Olympics International, 1993-96.

Selected Works: *The Wasted Americans: Cost of Our Welfare Dilemmas,* 1947. *The Disjointed Trio: Poverty, Politics, and Power: California Department of Social Welfare, Selective Reading Series, No. 1,* 1963.

Other Awards: Walter O. Bingham Award, Buffalo Newspaper Guild, NY, 1959. Page One Award, Buffalo Newspaper Guild, NY, 1959. Merit Award, Northwestern University Alumni Association, IL, 1962.

For More Information: *New York Times,* 2 May (1961): 40; *Contemporary Authors, First Revision, Volumes 9-12,* Detroit: Gale Research Company, 1974.

Commentary: Edgar May spent six months investigating the cost and other problems of administrating relief. He spent three months as a case worker for the Erie County Department of Social Welfare. A result of his fourteen-part series was a 34-point reform program issued by the Department's Commissioner of Social Welfare.

1962

George William Bliss 786

Birth: July 21, 1918; Denver, CO. **Death:** September 11, 1978. **Parents:** William Lane Bliss and Marie (Brenan). **Education:** Northwestern University, IL. **Spouse:** Helen Jeanne Groble (m. 1940, died 1959); Therese O'Keefe (m. 1960, died 1978). **Children:** William R., George L., Dennis M., Marianne, Carol, Helen Jeanne (HG); Terrence (TO); Stepchildren: Charles, Kathleen, Moreen (TO).

Prize: *Local Reporting, No Edition Time,* 1962: *Chicago Tribune,* Chicago: Chicago Tribune, 1961.

Career: Staff member, *Chicago Evening American,* 1937-42; Staff member, *Chicago Tribune,* 1942-68; Labor Editor, *Chicago Tribune,* 1953-68; Chief Investigator, Better Government Association, 1968-71; Investigative Task Force, *Chicago Tribune,* 1971-78.

Other Awards: Edward Scott Beck Award, *Chicago Tribune,* 1954, 1958. Spot News Reporting Award, Chicago Newspaper Guild, 1957. Spot News Reporting Award, Illinois Associated Press, 1958-1959. Jacob Scher Award, 1973. News Writing Award, Illinois Associated Press, 1972, 1974. News Writing Award, Associated Press Editors' Association, 1974. Inland Daily Press Association Award, 1974. United Press International News Award, 1974.

For More Information: *Chicago Tribune,* 12 September (1978): 1, 18; *New York Times,* 6 November (1978); *Contemporary Authors, Volumes 85-88,* Detroit: Gale Research Company, 1980; *Dictionary of American Biography, Supplement 10,* New York: Charles Scribner's Sons, 1995.

Commentary: George Bliss wrote more than 80 stories during his investigation of the Metropolitan Sanitary District of Greater Chicago, an independent local government agency with a net worth of $3 billion. Bliss reported on fraud, incompetence, and contract cheating. As a result of the series, state and federal agencies examined the District's business practices.

Bliss was put in charge of the *Chicago Tribune*'s 1972 investigation of voter fraud that won the paper a Pulitzer Prize in the Local General Spot News Reporting category.

1963

Oscar O'Neal Griffin Jr. 787

Birth: April 28, 1933; Daisetta, TX. **Parents:** Oscar O'Neal Griffin and Myrtle Ellen (Edgar). **Education:** University of Texas: BA. Harvard University, MA: MBA. **Spouse:** Patricia Lamb (m. 1955). **Children:** Gwendolyn, Amanda, Gregory, Marguerite.

Prize: *Local Reporting, No Edition Time,* 1963: *Pecos Independent and Enterprise,* Pecos, TX: Pecos Independent and Enterprise, 1962.

Career: Served in United States Army, 1953-55; Public Relations Staff member, City of Liberty, TX, 1958-59; Editor, *Canyon (TX) News,* 1959-60; Staff member, Editor, *Pecos (TX) Independent,* 1960-62; Reporter, *Houston (TX) Chronicle,* 1962-66; White House Correspondent, *Houston (TX) Chronicle,* 1966-69; Assistant Director of Public Affairs, U.S. Department of Transportation, 1969-74; President, Griffin Well Service, Inc., 1974-88; Senior Vice-President, 395 Enterprises, Inc., 1986-88; Freelance writer, 1988-; Editor and Writer, Interfaith Ministries of Houston (TX).

Other Awards: Distinguished Service in Journalism Award, Sigma Delta Chi, Fort Worth Chapter, TX, 1962. Courage in Journalism Award, Sigma Delta Chi, Des Moines Chapter, IA, 1963. Investigative Reporting Award, Southwest Journalism Forum, 1963.

For More Information: *New York Times,* 7 May (1963): 35.

Commentary: Oscar O. Griffin Jr.'s winning series of articles on Billie Sol Estes, a Texas financier, led to Estes's prosecution and conviction for a major fraud against the United States government.

Meritorious Public Service

1917
No award

1918

New York Times
Full entry appears as #375 under "Explanatory Journalism," 1986.

1919

Milwaukee Journal   788
Founded: 1882; Milwaukee, WI. **Closed:** 1995. **Founder(s):** Lucius Nieman.

    Prize: *Meritorious Public Service*, 1919. *Meritorious Public Service*, 1967.

    Selected Works: *Picking Your Job*, 1937. *Wounded Soldiers Come Home, What Then? A Series of Articles from the Milwaukee Journal Discussing the Problem of Restoring Our Sick and Maimed Servicemen to Useful Life*, 1943.

    Other Awards: The *Milwaukee Journal*'s staff, editors, and reporters won five Pulitzer Prizes, in addition to other journalism and public service awards.

    For More Information: Conrad, William Chester. *The Milwaukee Journal: The First Eighty Years,* Madison: University of Wisconsin, 1964.

    Commentary: The *Milwaukee Journal* won two Meritorious Public Service prizes. The *Journal* won its first prize for its "strong and courageous campaign for Americanism in a constituency where foreign elements made such a policy hazardous from a business point of view." The second prize was awarded in 1967 for its successful campaign to stiffen the laws against water pollution in Wisconsin, a notable advance in the national effort for the conservation of natural resources.

    The *Milwaukee Journal* was established by Congressman Peter V. Deuster in 1882. Deuster sold it one year later to Lucius Nieman. The merger of the *Milwaukee Journal* and the *Milwaukee Sentinel* created the *Milwaukee Journal-Sentinel.* It began publishing on April 2, 1995, and is the largest daily newspaper in Wisconsin.

1920
No award

1921

Boston Post   789
Founded: 1831; Boston, MA. **Closed:** September 30, 1956. **Founder(s):** Charles G. Greene.

    Prize: *Meritorious Public Service*, 1921.

    Selected Works: *Boston Post Book of Recipes and Menus, Kitchen and Household Helps* (Caswell, Muriel, ed.), 1919.

    For More Information: Dunn, Donald H., *Ponzi!: The Boston Swindler,* New York: McGraw-Hill, 1975.

    Commentary: The *Boston Post* was awarded the Meritorious Public Service prize in 1921 for its exposure of the operations of Charles Ponzi in a series of articles that finally led to his arrest.

    The *Boston Post* was founded by Charles E. Greene in 1831 and was published as the *Boston Morning Post* until 1842, when it became the *Boston Post.* It went through several other owners and name changes and was once again the *Boston Post* in 1893. It ceased publication in 1956.

1922

New York World   790
Founded: 1883; New York, NY. **Closed:** 1931. **Founder(s):** Joseph Pulitzer.

    Prize: *Meritorious Public Service*, 1922. *Meritorious Public Service*, 1924.

    Other Awards: The *New York World*'s staff, editors, and reporters won eight Pulitzer Prizes, in addition to other journalism and public service awards.

    For More Information: *The World, Its History & Its New Home: The Pulitzer Building,* New York: Burr Printing House, 1890; Heaton, John Langdon, *The Story of a Page: Thirty Years of Public Service and Public Discussion in the Editorial Columns of the New York World,* New York: Harper, 1913; Barrett, James Wyman, *The World, the Flesh and Messrs. Pulitzer,* New York: Vanguard Press, 1931; Barrett, James Wyman, *Joseph Pulitzer and His World,* New York: Vanguard Press, 1941; Juergens, George, *Joseph Pulitzer and the New York World,* Princeton, NJ: Princeton University, 1966.

Commentary: The *New York World* won two Meritorious Public Service prizes. The first prize came in 1922 for articles published during September and October 1921, exposing the operations of the Ku Klux Klan. The second prize came in 1924 for its work in connection with the exposure of Florida peonage.

The *World* weekly was published in 1860 by Manton Marble. It became the *New York World* in 1881 and was published semi-weekly. Joseph Pulitzer purchased the paper in 1883 and began daily publication. He created the *Evening World* in 1885. The *New York World-Telegram* was formed in 1931 by the union of the *Evening World,* the *World,* and the *New York Telegram.* It was published until 1950, when *New York World-Telegram and the Sun* merged with the *New York Journal American* and the *New York Herald Tribune* to form the *World Journal Tribune.*

1923

Memphis Commercial Appeal   791

Founded: 1841; Memphis, TN. **Founder(s):** Col. Henry Van Pelt.

Prize: *Meritorious Public Service,* 1923.

Selected Works: *Commercial Appeal: Centennial Edition* (Kelley, Robert, ed.), 1940.

Other Awards: The *Memphis Commercial Appeal*'s staff, editors, and reporters have won numerous other journalism and public service awards in addition to this Pulitzer Prize.

For More Information: Baker, T.H., *The Memphis Commercial Appeal: The History of a Southern Newspaper,* Baton Rouge: Louisiana State University, 1971.

Commentary: The *Memphis Commercial Appeal* was awarded the Meritorious Public Service prize in 1923 for its courageous attitude in the publication of cartoons and the handling of news in reference to the operations of the Ku Klux Klan.

The *Commercial Appeal* was founded by Colonel Henry Van Pelt, a journeyman printer in 1841, who published a single sheet weekly. By 1878, *The Appeal* had become the *Memphis Daily Appeal.* In 1890, the *Memphis Daily Appeal* purchased a rival and became the *Appeal-Avalanche.* Another merger on July 1, 1894, gave the newspaper its current name, the *Commercial Appeal.* The newspaper is now owned by the E.W. Scripps Company. A daily, it serves the greater Memphis area and 71 counties in Tennessee, Arkansas, and Mississippi.

1924

New York World

Full entry appears as **#790** under "Meritorious Public Service," 1922.

1925
No award

1926

Columbus Enquirer Sun   792

Founded: 1828; Columbus, GA.

Prize: *Meritorious Public Service,* 1926.

Selected Works: *Letter from Ellis Bean, Colonel of Cavalry of the Mexican Republic, to Lewis Cass, Secretary of War* (with Peter Ellis Bean), 1833.

For More Information: Lisby, Gregory C., "Julian Harris and the *Columbus Enquirer Sun:* Consequences of Winning the Pulitzer Prize," *Journalism Monographs,* April 1988, No. 105; Winn, Billy. "In Columbus, Georgia, a Report on the Future Led a Newspaper to Try to Shape What Would Come," *ASNE Bulletin,* September 1992, No. 743, Pages 9-10; Kilbourne, Elizabeth Evans, *Columbus, Georgia, Newspaper Clippings (Columbus Enquirer Sun),* Savannah, GA: E.E. Kilbourne, 1997; Contact the Georgia Newspaper Project, University of Georgia Libraries, Athens, telephone: (706) 542-2131.

Commentary: The *Columbus Enquirer Sun* was awarded the Meritorious Public Service prize in 1926 for the service that it rendered in its brave and energetic fight against the Ku Klux Klan, against the enactment of a law barring the teaching of evolution, against dishonest and incompetent public officials, and for justice to the Negro and against lynching.

1927

Canton Daily News   793

Founded: 1912; Canton, OH. **Closed:** 1930.

Prize: *Meritorious Public Service,* 1927.

Commentary: The *Canton Daily News* was awarded the Meritorious Public Service prize in 1927 for its brave, patriotic, and effective fight to end a vicious state of affairs caused by collusion between city authorities and the criminal element. The fight had a tragic result; the editor of the paper, Don R. Mellett, was assassinated.

The first issue of the *Ohio Repository* was published on March 30, 1815, by John Saxton. At first the newspaper was published weekly, but it has been published daily since 1878, and a Sunday edition was added in 1892. The newspaper remained under Saxton management for 77 years. In 1892 it was taken over by George B. Frease, who sold the newspaper to Brush-Moore Newspapers in 1927. They in turn bought the *Canton Daily News* in 1930. In 1967, the newspaper was purchased by Thomson Newspapers. Today, the paper is known as the *Canton Repository.*

1928

Indianapolis Times   794
Founded: July 15, 1881; Indianapolis, IN. **Closed:** 1965. **Founder(s):** W.B. Holloway.

Prize: *Meritorious Public Service,* 1928.

For More Information: Miller, John W., *Indiana Newspaper Bibliography: Historical Accounts of all Indiana Newspapers Published from 1804 to 1980 and Locational Information for All Available Copies, Both Original and Microfilm,* Indianapolis, IN: Indiana Historical Society, 1982.

Commentary: The *Indianapolis Times* was awarded the Meritorious Public Service prize in 1928 for its work in exposing political corruption in Indiana, which caused the prosecution of the guilty and brought about a more wholesome state of affairs in civil government.

The *Indianapolis Times* was published by W.B. Holloway from July 15, 1881 to August 9, 1886. In 1887 it was published as the *Indianapolis Sun.* The newspaper was purchased by Scripps-Howard in 1922 and renamed the *Indianapolis Times.* Owned by Scripps-Howard, the *Times* was published by the Indianapolis Daily Times Company from 1922 to 1965, when it ceased publication.

1929

New York Evening World   795
Founded: 1885; New York, NY. **Closed:** 1931. **Founder(s):** Joseph Pulitzer.

Prize: *Meritorious Public Service,* 1929.

Other Awards: The *New York World-Telegram*'s staff, editors, and reporters won numerous other journalism and public service awards in addition to four Pulitzer Prizes.

Commentary: The *New York Evening World* was awarded the Meritorious Public Service prize in 1929 for its effective campaign to correct evils in the administration of justice, including the fight to curb "ambulance chasers," support for the "fence" bill, and measures to simplify procedure, prevent perjury, and eliminate politics from municipal courts. This campaign was instrumental in securing remedial action.

The *New York Evening World* was created by Joseph Pulitzer in 1885. The *New York World-Tele-*

gram was formed in 1931 by the union of the *Evening World,* the *World,* and the *New York Telegram. The Evening World, The World,* and the *New York Telegram* all appeared on the masthead from February 27 to April 6, 1931. The *World-Telegram* was published until 1950, when the *New York World-Telegram* and the *Sun* merged with the *New York Journal American* and the *New York Herald Tribune* to form the *World Journal Tribune.*

1930
No award

1931

Atlanta Constitution   796
Founded: 1868; Atlanta, GA.

Prize: *Meritorious Public Service,* 1931.

Selected Works: *Georgia Rivers, Articles from the Atlanta Journal and Constitution Magazine,* 1962.

Other Awards: The *Atlanta Constitution* has won numerous other journalism and public service awards in addition to five Pulitzer Prizes.

For More Information: Shavin, Norman, *The Atlanta Century, March, 1860-May, 1865,* Atlanta, GA: Capricorn, 1981; Farrar, Frederic, "Constitution Era Newspapers: Fourteen Survive," *Media History,* Volume 7, No. 1, Spring/Summer 1987; Shaw, Russel, and Mark Rice, "Covering the Atlanta Riots: Six Photographers, Five Reporters Attacked," *Editor & Publisher,* Volume 125, No. 19, May 9, 1992; Richards, Doug, "Report from Atlanta: Making a Point With Their Fists (Reporters Assaulted During Atlanta Riot)," *Washington Journalism Review,* June 1992, Volume 14, No. 5, Pages 24-25; Shumate, Richard, "Life after Kovach: Atlanta Newspapers are Tighter and Brighter Under Ron Martin (Atlanta Journal-Constitution)," *Washington Journalism Review,* Volume 14, No. 7, Pages 28-32, September 1992; Contact the Georgia Newspaper Project, University of Georgia Libraries, Athens, telephone: (706) 542-2131.

Commentary: The *Atlanta Constitution* was awarded the Meritorious Public Service prize in 1931 for a successful municipal graft exposure and subsequent convictions.

The *Constitution* was founded in 1868 in the Reconstruction era, under the editorial leadership of Henry W. Grady. The paper's politics have been mostly liberal. The *Constitution*'s executive editor Ralph McGill wrote strong editorials against McCarthyism and antiblack bias. In 1950, the paper was purchased by James M. Cox, who already owned the evening *Atlanta Journal,* which was founded in 1883.

1932

Indianapolis News 797
Founded: 1869; Indianapolis, IN. **Closed:** 1995.
Founder(s): John H. Halliday.

Prize: *Meritorious Public Service,* 1932.

For More Information: *The Indianapolis News Panama Libel Case: Circumstances Preceding the Return of the Indictments and Proceedings for the Removal to the District of Columbia for Trial of Delavan Smith and Charles R. Williams, Publishers of the Indianapolis News: Order for Removal Denied October 13, 1909, by the United States District Court for the District of Indiana, Hon. Albert B. Anderson, Judge,* Indianapolis, IN: Fulmer-Cornelius, 1909; Brown, Hilton Ultimus, *A Book of Memories,* Indianapolis, IN: Butler University, 1951; Halcomb, Herman Barker, *How the Indianapolis News Won the Pulitzer Prize,* Indiana University, 1965; Miller, John W., *Indiana Newspaper Bibliography: Historical Accounts of all Indiana Newspapers Published from 1804 to 1980 and Locational Information for All Available Copies, Both Original and Microfilm,* Indianapolis, IN: Indiana Historical Society, 1982.

Commentary: The *Indianapolis News* was awarded the Meritorious Public Service prize in 1932 for its successful campaign to eliminate waste in city management and to reduce the tax levy.

The *Indianapolis News* was founded in 1869 by John H. Halliday. It was published in a weekly edition from 1870 to 1876. The *News,* an afternoon paper, merged with the *Indianapolis Star* in September 1995. Eugene S. Pulliam was the publisher of both newspapers.

1933

New York World-Telegram 798
Founded: 1931; New York, NY. **Closed:** 1950.

Prize: *Meritorious Public Service,* 1933.

Selected Works: *Stylebook: A Compendium of Rules for the Guidance of Reporters, Copyreaders, Editors, Compositors and Proofreaders,* 1930.

Commentary: The *New York World-Telegram* was awarded the Meritorious Public Service prize in 1933 for its series of articles on veterans' relief, the articles on real estate bond evil, the campaign urging voters in the late New York City municipal election to "write in" the name of Joseph V. McKee, and the articles exposing the lottery schemes of various fraternal organizations.

The *World* weekly was published in 1860 by Manton Marble. It became the *New York World* in 1881 and was published semi-weekly. Joseph Pulitzer purchased the paper in 1883 and soon began daily

publication. He created the *Evening World* in 1885. The *New York World-Telegram* was formed in 1931 by the union of the *Evening World,* the *World* and the *New York Telegram.* The *Evening World,* The *World,* and *The New York Telegram* all appeared on the masthead from February 27 to April 6, 1931. It was published until 1950, when *New York World-Telegram* and the *Sun* merged with the *New York Journal American* and the *New York Herald Tribune* to form the *World Journal Tribune.*

1934

Medford Mail Tribune 799
Founded: 1906; Medford, OR.

Prize: *Meritorious Public Service,* 1934.

For More Information: Turnbull, George Stanley, *History of Oregon Newspapers,* Portland, OR: Binfords & Mort, 1939; Contact the Oregon Newspaper Project, University of Oregon Library System—USNP, Eugene, telephone: (541) 346-1838.

Commentary: The *Medford Mail-Tribune* was awarded the Meritorious Public Service prize in 1934 for its campaign against unscrupulous politicians in Jackson County, Oregon.

The *Medford Mail-Tribune* is currently owned by Ottoway Newspapers, Incorporated.

1935

Sacramento Bee 800
Founded: 1857; Sacramento, CA. **Founder(s):** James McClatchy.

Prize: *Meritorious Public Service,* 1935. *Meritorious Public Service,* 1992.

Selected Works: *Sacramento County and Its Resources: Our Capital City, Past and Present, a Souvenir of the Bee,* 1894. *California State Railroad Museum,* Sacramento, 1981. *California, the Weapons Master,* 1988. *One Hundred Twenty-Five Years in the News, 1857-1982,* 1982. *The Sting of the Bee: 125 Years of Editorial Cartoons from The Sacramento Bee, 1857-1982,* 1982.

Other Awards: The *Sacramento Bee*'s staff, editors, and reporters have won three Pulitzer Prizes, in addition to other journalism and public service awards.

For More Information: Fry, Amelia R., *Bee Perspectives of the Warren Era: Interviews,* Berkeley: Bancroft Library, University of California/Berkeley, Regional Oral History Office, Earl Warren Oral History Project, 1976; Contact the Offices of the California Newspaper Project, University of California, Berkeley, telephone: (510) 643-7680.

Commentary: The *Sacramento Bee* was awarded the Meritorious Public Service prize in 1935 for its campaign against political machine influence in the appointment of two federal judges in Nevada. The *Bee* won the Meritorious Public Service prize again in 1992 for "The Sierra in Peril," reporting by Tom Knudson that examined environmental threats and damage to the Sierra Nevada mountain range in California.

James McClatchy, a young Irishman, helped found the *Sacramento Bee* in 1857. The Sacramento area was home to more than 60 newspapers and journals during the mining era that brought an influx of thousands of workers to the area. The *Sacramento Bee* is currently owned by McClatchy Newspapers.

1936

Cedar Rapids Gazette   801

Founded: January 10, 1883; Cedar Rapids, IA.

Prize: *Meritorious Public Service,* 1936.

For More Information: Debth, James, "New Journalism: Newspapers Should be Heard, Too: Audiotex Transforms Cedar Rapids Gazette into 24-Hour News Service," *Nieman Reports,* Volume 46, No. 2, Pages 19-21, Summer 1992.

Commentary: The *Cedar Rapids Gazette* was awarded the Meritorious Public Service prize in 1936 for its crusade against corruption and misgovernment in the state of Iowa.

The *Gazette* was founded in 1883 and provides Eastern Iowa with news, announcements, and advertising. The newspaper was first published on January 10, 1883. It is currently owned by the Gazette Company.

1937

St. Louis Post-Dispatch   802

Founded: December 12, 1878; St. Louis, MO. **Founder(s):** Joseph Pulitzer.

Prize: *Meritorious Public Service,* 1937. *Meritorious Public Service,* 1941. *Special Awards and Citations: Journalism,* 1947. *Meritorious Public Service,* 1948. *Meritorious Public Service,* 1950. *Meritorious Public Service,* 1952.

Selected Works: *St. Louis Post-Dispatch: The Drift of Civilization, by the Contributors to the Fiftieth Anniversary Number of the St. Louis Post-Dispatch,* 1929. *A Report to the American People, by Joseph Pulitzer, Editor of the St. Louis Post-Dispatch* (with Joseph Pulitzer), 1945. *Mark Twain in the St. Louis Post-Dispatch, 1874-1891* (with Jim McWilliams), 1997.

Other Awards: The *St. Louis Post-Dispatch's* staff, editors, and reporters have won numerous other journalism and public service awards in addition to 16 Pulitzer Prizes.

For More Information: Markham, James Walter, *Bovard of the Post-Dispatch,* Baton Rouge: Louisiana State University, 1954; Ross, Charles Griffith, *The Story of the St. Louis Post-Dispatch,* St. Louis, MO: Pulitzer, 1954; Pulitzer, Joseph, *Pulitzer Publishing Company: Newspapers and Broadcasting in the Public Interest,* New York: Newcomen Society of the United States, 1988; Pfaff, Daniel W., "The St. Louis Post-Dispatch Debate Over Communism, 1940-1955," *Mass Communication Review,* Volume 16, No. 1&2, Pages 52-62, 1989.

Commentary: The *St. Louis Post-Dispatch* has won five Meritorious Public Service awards. The first came in 1937 for its exposure of wholesale fraudulent voter registration in St. Louis. With a coordinated news, editorial, and cartoon campaign, this newspaper succeeded in invalidating more than 40,000 fraudulent ballots in November and brought about the appointment of a new election board. The newspaper won its second Meritorious Public Service prize in 1941 for its successful campaign against the city smoke nuisance. In 1947, the *Post-Dispatch* was awarded a Special Award and Citation for its unswerving adherence to the public and professional ideals of its founder and its constructive leadership in the field of American journalism. A third Meritorious Public Service prize was awarded in 1948 for the coverage of the Centralia, Illinois mine disaster and its follow-up, which resulted in impressive reforms in mine safety laws and regulations. Its fourth Meritorious Public Service prize came in 1950 and was shared with the *Chicago Daily News* for the work of George Thiem, *Post-Dispatch,* and Roy J. Harris, *Daily News,* in exposing the presence of 37 Illinois newspapermen on an Illinois state payroll. A fifth Meritorious Public Service prize was awarded in 1952 for *Post-Dispatch* investigation and disclosures of widespread corruption in the Internal Revenue Bureau and other departments of the government.

The story of the *Post-Dispatch* began in 1878 when Joseph Pulitzer, the former publisher and part owner of the German-language *Westliche Post,* purchased the bankrupt *Dispatch* for $2,500. That same year, John A. Dillon, publisher of the *Evening Post,* proposed a merger of the two papers. Pulitzer agreed and on December 12, 1878, the first issue of the *Post and Dispatch* appeared. Three months later the newspaper changed its name to the *St. Louis Post-Dispatch.*

1938

Bismarck Tribune   **803**
Founded: 1873; Bismarck, ND. **Founder(s):** Colonel
Clement A. Lounsberry.
   Prize: *Meritorious Public Service,* 1938.
   Selected Works: *Tribune Extra,* "First Account
of the Custer Massacre," July 6, 1876.
   Commentary: The *Bismarck Tribune* was
awarded the Meritorious Public Service prize in 1938
for its news reports and editorials entitled "Self Help
in the Dust Bowl."
   The *Bismarck Tribune* was founded by Colonel
Clement A. Lounsberry in 1873. The colonel left the
Minneapolis Tribune to deliver printing equipment to
Bismarck, North Dakota. (The town had been established only the year before as "Edmonton.") The
Tribune is the oldest newspaper in North Dakota and
also the oldest surviving business in the state. It was
the first to report on General Custer's last stand,
published in an Extra early edition on the morning of
July 6, 1876. The paper is currently owned by Lee
Enterprises, Incorporated. The *Tribune* serves the
twin cities of Bismarck and Mandan and the south-
central region of North Dakota.

1939

Miami Daily News   **804**
Founded: 1903; Miami, FL. **Closed:** 1988.
   Prize: *Meritorious Public Service,* 1939.
   Selected Works: *Florida Poets and Poets Visit-
ing Florida in 1941: An Anthology of Poems Publish-
ed in the Miami Daily News* (Rader, Vivian Yeiser,
ed.), 1941.
   For More Information: Morton, John, "The
Business of Journalism: The Miami News' Profitable
Death (Joint Operating Agreements)," *Washington
Journalism Review,* Volume 10, No. 10, Page 46,
December 1988; Contact the Florida Newspaper Pro-
ject, University of Florida, Gainesville, telephone:
(352) 392-0351.
   Commentary: The *Miami Daily News* was
awarded the Meritorious Public Service prize in 1939
for its campaign for the recall of the Miami City
Commission.
   The newspaper was published as the *Daily Miami
Metropolis* from 1903 until 1907. It then became the
Miami Metropolis until 1909. The *Daily Metropolis*
was born in October 1909 and ran until August 1911.
The *Miami Daily Metropolis* started up and ran until
June 1923. Another name change occurred at that
time, and the *Miami News Metropolis* was the name
of the paper until April 1924. The *Miami Daily News
and Metropolis* was published until March 1930. The

Miami Daily News, rose up and continued publication
until November 1957. Its last incarnation was as the
Miami News, which ended publication on December
18, 1988.

1940

*Waterbury Republican &
American*   **805**
Founding Location: Waterbury, CT.
   Prize: *Meritorious Public Service,* 1940.
   For More Information: Contact the Connecticut
Newspaper Project, Connecticut State Library, Hart-
ford, telephone: (860) 566-4301.
   Commentary: Connecticut's *Waterbury Repub-
lican & American* was awarded the Meritorious Public
Service prize in 1940 for its campaign exposing mu-
nicipal graft.

1941

St. Louis Post-Dispatch
Full entry appears as **#802** under "Meritorious Public Service," 1937.

1942

Los Angeles Times
Full entry appears as **#91** under "Breaking News
Reporting," 1998.

1943

Omaha World-Herald   **806**
Founded: August 24, 1885; Omaha, NE. **Foun-
der(s):** Gilbert M. Hitchcock.
   Prize: *Meritorious Public Service,* 1943.
   Other Awards: The *Omaha World-Herald*'s
staff, editors, and reporters have won two Pulitzer
Prizes, in addition to other journalism and public
service awards.
   Commentary: The *Omaha World-Herald* was
awarded the Meritorious Public Service prize in 1943
for its initiative and originality in planning a statewide
campaign for the collection of scrap metal for the war
effort. The Nebraska plan was adopted on a national
scale by the daily newspapers, resulting in a united
effort which succeeded in supplying our war industries with necessary scrap material.
   The newspaper was founded in 1885 by Gilbert
M. Hitchcock as the *Omaha Daily World.* The *Omaha
Daily World* merged with the *Omaha Herald* in 1889.

(Hitchcock later served in the United States Senate.) The newspaper stayed in the ownership of Hitchcock and his heirs until 1962, when the heirs sold the paper to Peter Kiewit Sons, Inc. Since 1969, the newspaper has been called the *Omaha World-Herald.* After Kiewit's death, ownership shifted temporarily to the Peter Kiewit Foundation. The Foundation then followed Kiewit's instructions and sold the majority of stock to *Omaha World-Herald* employees. The foundation retains something less than 20 percent of total ownership but, in accordance with Kiewit's directive, 20 percent of the voting shares.

1944

New York Times

Full entry appears as **#375** under "Explanatory Journalism," 1986.

1945

Detroit Free Press

Full entry appears as **#328** under "Editorial Writing," 1955.

1946

Scranton Times   807

Founded: 1895; Scranton, PA. **Founder(s):** E.J. Lynett.

  Prize: *Meritorious Public Service,* 1946.

  Commentary: The *Scranton Times* was awarded the Meritorious Public Service prize in 1946 for its 15-year investigation of judicial practices in the United States District Court for the middle district of Pennsylvania, resulting in removal of the District Judge and indictment of many other persons.

  In 1895, after a history of six unsuccessful owners since the paper's birth in 1870, E.J. Lynett purchased the afternoon publication. It had a circulation of 3,200 and sold for two cents a copy. It has grown to be the third largest daily in Pennsylvania. When Mr. Lynett died in 1943, the paper's management was passed on to William R., Edward J., and Elizabeth R. Lynett. A *Sunday Times,* was published beginning in 1966 and established the Times-Shamrock newspaper group, which publishes the *Scranton Times,* the *Sunday Times,* and the *Tribune,* plus nine additional Pennsylvania newspapers, as well as two publications in New York and one in Baltimore, Maryland. The newspaper group boasts a combined circulation of 450,000. The *Times* was the first newspaper in the United States

to own and operate its own radio station, which became Shamrock Communications.

1947

Baltimore Sun   808

Founded: 1837; Baltimore, MD. **Founder(s):** Arunah Shepardson Abell.

  Prize: *Meritorious Public Service,* 1947.

  Other Awards: The *Baltimore Sun*'s staff, editors, and reporters have won 14 Pulitzer Prizes, in addition to other journalism and public service awards.

  For More Information: Johnson, Gerald W., Frank R. Kent, and H.L. Mencken, *The Sunpapers of Baltimore,* New York: Knopf, 1937; Williams, Harold A., *The Baltimore Sun, 1837-1987,* Baltimore, MD: Johns Hopkins University, 1987; Gardner, R. H., *Those Years: Recollections of a Baltimore Newspaperman,* Baltimore, MD: Sunspot Books / Galileo, 1990; Kerwin, Ann Marie, "Baltimore Sun to Ban Gun Classified Ads," *Editor & Publisher,* Volume 126, No. 17, Page 74-75, April 24, 1993.

  Commentary: The *Baltimore Sun* was awarded the Meritorious Public Service prize in 1947 for its series of articles by Howard M. Norton dealing with the administration of unemployment compensation in Maryland, resulting in guilty pleas and convictions in criminal court of 93 persons.

  The *Baltimore Sun* was founded in 1837 by Arunah Shepardson Abell. The *Sun* provided nonsensational news to the working man. Abell, working with the *Times-Picayune,* established a "pony express" of relay riders between Baltimore and New Orleans to speed the transmission of news. This allowed the *Sun* to report the news of the United States Army victory at Vera Cruz, Mexico, before the federal government had even been informed. Abell presented President James K. Polk with the news in a telegram. Abell was an admirer of Samuel F.B. Morse, whom he encouraged to develop the telegraph. The *Sun* was acquired by the Times Mirror group in 1986.

1948

St. Louis Post-Dispatch

Full entry appears as **#802** under "Meritorious Public Service," 1937.

1949

Nebraska State Journal   809

Founded: 1869; Lincoln, NE.

Prize: *Meritorious Public Service,* 1949.

Selected Works: *Willa Cather's Apprenticeship: A Collection of Her Writings in the Nebraska State Journal, 1891-1895* (with Harold Norton White), 1955.

For More Information: Alvord, Wayne A., *The Nebraska State Journal, 1867-1904,* Lincoln, NE: University of Nebraska, 1934; Contact the Nebraska Newspaper Project, University of Nebraska, Lincoln, telephone: (402) 472-3939.

Commentary: The *Nebraska State Journal* was awarded the Meritorious Public Service prize in 1949 for the campaign establishing the "Nebraska All-Star Primary" presidential preference primary, which spotlighted, through a bipartisan committee, issues early in the presidential campaign.

The *Nebraska State Journal* was established in 1869. It became the *Weekly Nebraska Journal* in 1878 and was published semi-weekly in 1892 as the *Nebraska State Journal*. It went to weekly in 1902. Novelist Willa Cather worked as a reporter for the *Journal* early in her career.

1950

Chicago Daily News 810
Founded: 1875; Chicago, IL. **Closed:** March 4, 1978.
Founder(s): Melville E. Stone.

Prize: *Meritorious Public Service,* 1950. *Meritorious Public Service,* 1957. *Meritorious Public Service,* 1963.

Selected Works: *The Chicago Daily News War Book for American Soldiers, Sailors and Marines,* 1918. *The Chicago Daily News Cook Book* (Shuck, Edith, ed.), 1930. *Survey of Daily Newspaper Home Coverage in Metropolitan Chicago,* 1934. *Done in a Day: 100 Years of Great Writing from the Chicago Daily News,* 1977.

Other Awards: The *Chicago Daily News*'s editors, reporters, and staff won 12 Pulitzer Prizes, in addition to other journalism and public service awards.

For More Information: Schmidt, Royal Jae, *Chicago Daily News and Illinois Politics, 1876-1920,* Chicago: 1957; Warren, Ellen, "March 4, 1978: Extra! Extra! Daily News's Truly Final Edition Hits The Streets," from the series: 150 Years: Events that Shaped Chicago, *Chicago Tribune,* October 19, 1997.

Commentary: The *Chicago Daily News* won three Meritorious Public Service awards. It shared the 1950 prize with the *St. Louis Post-Dispatch* for the work of George Thiem (*Daily News*) and Roy J. Harris (*Post-Dispatch*) in exposing the presence of 37 Illinois newspapermen on an Illinois state payroll. It won again in 1957 for determined and courageous public service in exposing a $2,500,000 fraud centering in

the office of the State Auditor of Illinois, resulting in the indictment and conviction of the State Auditor and others. This led to the reorganization of the State's procedures to prevent a recurrence of the fraud. Its third prize was awarded in 1963 for calling public attention to the issue of providing birth control services in the public health programs in its area.

The *Chicago Daily News* was founded in 1875 by Melville E. Stone. In 1876, Victor F. Lawson, a financier, became the newspaper's business manager and ended up owning two-thirds of its stock, taking full ownership of the paper in 1888. At its peak, the newspaper was syndicated throughout the United States. The *Daily News* was known as a writer's newspaper, employing Carl Sandburg, Ben Hecht, and Mike Royko among others. (Hecht co-authored "The Front Page," a play about the *Daily News*.) The newspaper also had a strong reputation for its international reporting.

St. Louis Post-Dispatch
Full entry appears as **#802** under "Meritorious Public Service," 1937.

1951

Brooklyn Eagle 811
Founded: October 26, 1841; Brooklyn, NY. **Closed:** January 28, 1955.

Prize: *Meritorious Public Service,* 1951.

Selected Works: *The Eagle and Brooklyn: The Record of the Progress of the Brooklyn Daily Eagle, Issued in Commemoration of Its Semi-Centennial and Occupancy of Its New Building, Together with the History of the City of Brooklyn* (Howard, Henry W. B., ed.), 1893. *Pictorial History of Brooklyn, Issued by the Brooklyn Daily Eagle on Its Seventy-Fifth Anniversary, October 26, 1916* (with Martin H. Weyrauch), 1916. *Whitman as Editor of the Brooklyn Daily Eagle* (with Thomas L. Brasher), 1970.

Other Awards: The *Brooklyn Eagle*'s staff, editors, and reporters won four Pulitzer Prizes, in addition to other journalism and public service awards.

For More Information: Schroth, Raymond A., *The Eagle and Brooklyn: A Community Newspaper, 1841-1955,* Westport, CT: Greenwood, 1974; Moses, Paul, "The Eagle Was a Tough Old Bird: Brooklyn Misses Newspaper That Was Its Voice," *Newsday,* Manhattan and Brooklyn Edition, May 14, 1995.

Commentary: The *Brooklyn Eagle* won the Meritorious Public Service prize in 1951 for its crime reporting during the year. The *Eagle* exposed police corruption in a bookmaking scandal involving Harry Gross.

The *Brooklyn Eagle* was a daily founded in 1841; its first editor was Walt Whitman. It is said to have been widely read at the time of the Civil War. The *Eagle,* a big supporter of local sports teams, especially the Brooklyn Dodgers, is credited with coining the phrase "wait 'til next year," referring to the winning of the baseball league's season pennant. "Next year" arrived for the Dodgers in 1955 when they won the World Series. The *Eagle,* unfortunately, printed its last edition on January 28, 1955, too soon to report on the Dodgers' winning season. The closing of the *Eagle* and the departure of the Dodgers for Los Angeles were two events that stunned Brooklyn.

Miami Herald
Full entry appears as **#357** under "Editorial Writing," 1983.

1952

St. Louis Post-Dispatch
Full entry appears as **#802** under "Meritorious Public Service," 1937.

1953

Tabor City Tribune   812
Founded: July 5, 1946; Tabor City, NC. **Closed:** July 31, 1991.

   Prize: *Meritorious Public Service,* 1953.

   For More Information: Contact the State Library of North Carolina, Newspaper Project, Dept. of Cultural Resources, Raleigh, telephone: (919) 733-2570.

   Commentary: North Carolina's *Whiteville News Reporter* and the weekly *Tabor City Tribune* were both awarded the Meritorious Public Service prize in 1953 for their successful campaigns against the Ku Klux Klan, waged on their own doorstep at the risk of economic loss and personal danger. Their efforts culminated in the conviction of over 100 Klansmen and put an end to terrorism in their communities.

   The *Tabor City Tribune* was first published on July 31, 1946. It closed its doors on July 31, 1991.

Whiteville News Reporter   813
Founded: 1905; Whiteville, NC.

   Prize: *Meritorious Public Service,* 1953.

   For More Information: Contact the State Library of North Carolina, Newspaper Project, Dept. of Cultural Resources, Raleigh, telephone: (919) 733-2570.

   Commentary: North Carolina's *Whiteville News Reporter* and the weekly *Tabor City Tribune* were both awarded the Meritorious Public Service prize in 1953 for their successful campaigns against the Ku

Klux Klan, waged on their own doorstep at the risk of economic loss and personal danger, culminating in the conviction of over 100 Klansmen, and putting an end to terrorism in their communities.

   The *Whiteville News Reporter* published its first issue on June 16, 1905.

1954

Newsday
Full entry appears as **#722** under "Local General Spot News Reporting," 1984.

1955

Columbus Ledger and Sunday
Ledger-Enquirer   814
Founded: 1886; Columbus, GA.

   Prize: *Meritorious Public Service,* 1955.

   Selected Works: *Letter from Ellis Bean, Colonel of Cavalry of the Mexican Republic, to Lewis Cass, Secretary of War* (with Peter Ellis Bean), 1833.

   For More Information: Contact the Georgia Newspaper Project, University of Georgia Libraries, Athens, GA, Telephone: (706) 542-2131.

   Commentary: The *Columbus Ledger* and the *Sunday Ledger-Enquirer* were awarded the Meritorious Public Service prize in 1955 for the complete news coverage and fearless editorial attack on widespread corruption in neighboring Phenix City, Alabama, which effectively destroyed a corrupt and racket-ridden city government. The newspaper exhibited an early awareness of the evils of lax law enforcement before the situation in Phenix City erupted into murder. It covered the unfolding story of the final prosecution of the wrongdoers with skill, perception, force, and courage.

1956

Watsonville Register-Pajaronian   815
Founded: 1867; Watsonville, CA.

   Prize: *Meritorious Public Service,* 1956.

   Selected Works: *Watsonville, the First Hundred Years, Incorporating the Principal Historical Data as It Appeared in the Centennial Edition of the Watsonville Register-Pajaronian of July 3, 1952,* 1953.

   For More Information: Contact the Offices of the California Newspaper Project, University of California at Berkeley, telephone: (510) 643-7680.

   Commentary: The *Watsonville-Register Pajaronian* won the Meritorious Public Service prize in 1956 for courageous exposure of corruption in public office, which led to the resignation of a district attorney and the conviction of one of his associates.

The John P. Scripps newspaper group created the *Register-Pajaronian* when it acquired and merged the *Watsonville Register* and *Evening Pajaronian* newspapers in 1937. The John P. Scripps newspaper group merged with the E.W. Scripps Company in 1986. The E.W. Scripps Company sold the *Watsonville Register-Pajaronian* to Illinois-based News Media Corporation.

1957

Chicago Daily News

Full entry appears as **#810** under "Meritorious Public Service," 1950.

1958

Arkansas Gazette   **816**

Founded: 1819; Little Rock, AR. **Closed:** October 18, 1991. **Founder(s):** William E. Woodruff.

    Prize: *Meritorious Public Service,* 1958.

    Selected Works: *25 Years of Arkansas Gazette Photography, 1950-1975* (Albright, Charles W., ed.), 1976. *The Arkansas Gazette Obituaries Index, 1819-1879* (with Stephen J. Chism), 1990.

    Other Awards: The *Arkansas Gazette*'s staff, editors, and reporters won two Pulitzer Prizes, in addition to other journalism and public service awards.

    For More Information: Ross, Margaret, *Arkansas Gazette: The Early Years, 1819-1866, A History,* Little Rock, AR: Arkansas Gazette Foundation, 1969; Duffy, Joan, "172-Year-Old Arkansas Gazette, Civil Rights Champion, Closes," Scripps Howard News Service, October 10, 1991; Reaves, Lucy Marion, *Arkansas Families: Glimpses of Yesterday Columns from the Arkansas Gazette,* Conway: Arkansas Research, 1995.

    Commentary: The *Arkansas Gazette* was awarded the Meritorious Public Service prize in 1958 for demonstrating the highest qualities of civic leadership, journalistic responsibility, and moral courage in the face of great public tension during the school integration crisis of 1957. The newspaper's fearless and objective news coverage, plus its reasoned and moderate policy, did much to restore calmness and order to an overwrought community, reflecting great credit on its editors and its management.

    The *Arkansas Gazette* was established in 1819 by William E. Woodruff. At that time, Arkansas was a territory, not a state. The *Gazette* won two Pulitzers in 1957, but lost a fifth of its readers and many advertisers with its coverage supporting integration. (They

eventually won both back.) The Heiskell-Patterson family sold the *Arkansas Gazette* to Gannett on December 1, 1986. Wehco Media Incorporated, the parent company of the *Arkansas Democrat* and the largest media company in Arkansas, bought the *Gazette* from Gannett in 1991. This created the *Arkansas Democrat Gazette.*

1959

Utica Daily Press   **817**

Founded: December 1, 1882; Utica, NY. **Closed:** March 28, 1987.

    Prize: *Meritorious Public Service,* 1959.

    Selected Works: *Presentation of the Battle Flags of the Oneida County Regiments to the Oneida Historical Society, Utica, N.Y.,* 1898.

    For More Information: Contact the New York State Newspaper Project, New York State Library, Albany, telephone: (518) 474-7491.

    Commentary: The *Utica Daily Press* was a co-winner with the *Utica Observer Dispatch* of the Meritorious Public Service prize in 1959 for their successful campaign against corruption, gambling, and vice in their home city and the achievement of sweeping civic reforms in the face of political pressure and threats of violence. By their stalwart leadership of the forces of good government, these newspapers upheld the best tradition of a free press.

    The *Utica Daily Press* was first published on December 1, 1882. The *Daily Press* ceased publication when it merged with the *Utica Observer-Dispatch* in April 1987.

Utica Observer-Dispatch   **818**

Founded: May 1, 1922; Utica, NY.

    Prize: *Meritorious Public Service,* 1959.

    For More Information: Contact the New York State Newspaper Project, New York State Library, Albany, telephone: (518) 474-7491.

    Commentary: The *Utica Observer-Dispatch* was a co-winner with the *Utica Daily Press* of the Meritorious Public Service prize in 1959 for their successful campaign against corruption, gambling, and vice in their home city and the achievement of sweeping civic reforms in the face of political pressure and threats of violence. By their stalwart leadership of the forces of good government, these newspapers upheld the best tradition of a free press.

    The *Utica-Observer Dispatch* was first published on May 1, 1922. The paper was bought by Gannett in September 1969. The *Observer-Dispatch* merged with the *Utica Daily Press* in April 1987 and continued publication as the *Observer-Dispatch.*

1960

Los Angeles Times

Full entry appears as **#91** under "Breaking News Reporting," 1998.

1961

Amarillo Globe-Times   819

Founded: 1951; Amarillo, TX. **Founder(s):** Whittenburg Family.

Prize: *Meritorious Public Service,* 1961.

Commentary: The *Amarillo Globe-Times* was awarded the Meritorious Public Service prize in 1961 for exposing a breakdown in local law enforcement with resultant punitive action that swept lax officals from their posts and brought about the election of a reform slate. The newspaper thus exerted its civic leadership in the finest tradition of journalism.

The *Amarillo Globe-Times* was established in 1951 when the Whittenburg family, owners of the *Amarillo Times* acquired the *Amarillo Globe.* The two papers merged to form the *Amarillo Globe and Times,* an afternoon daily. In 1972, the Whittenburg family sold the *Amarillo Globe-Times* to Morris Communications.

1962

Panama City News-Herald   820

Founded: March 23, 1937; Panama City, FL.

Prize: *Meritorious Public Service,* 1962.

Commentary: The *Panama City News-Herald* was awarded the Meritorious Public Service prize in 1962 for its three-year campaign against entrenched power and corruption, with resultant reforms in Panama City and Bay County.

The *Panama City News-Herald* began publication on March 23, 1937.

1963

Chicago Daily News

Full entry appears as **#810** under "Meritorious Public Service," 1950.

1964

St. Petersburg Times   821

Founded: July 25, 1884; St. Petersburg, FL.

Prize: *Meritorious Public Service,* 1964.

Other Awards: The *St. Petersburg Times*'s staff, editors, and reporters have won six Pulitzer Prizes, in addition to other journalism and public service awards.

For More Information: Pierce, Robert N., *A Sacred Trust: Nelson Poynter and the St. Petersburg Times,* Gainesville: University Press of Florida, 1993.

Commentary: The *St. Petersburg Times* was awarded the Meritorious Public Service prize in 1964 for its aggressive investigation of the Florida Turnpike Authority that disclosed widespread illegal acts and resulted in a major reorganization of the state's road construction program.

The *St. Petersburg Times* began publication as a weekly in 1884 in Dunedin, Florida. That same year, it was purchased by the Rev. R. J. Morgan and moved to St. Petersburg. It was purchased by Paul Poynter in 1912 and became a seven-day-a-week publication in 1924. In 1947, Paul's son Nelson bought a controlling interest in the newspaper and he instituted changes raising the standards for excellence at the *Times.* Nelson Poynter's ideas are carried on in the Poynter Institute, which offers journalists seminars on all aspects of media education.

1965

Hutchinson News   822

Founded: 1872; Hutchinson, KS.

Prize: *Meritorious Public Service,* 1965.

Commentary: The *Hutchinson News* was awarded the Meritorious Public Service prize in 1965 for its courageous and constructive campaign, culminating in 1964, to bring about more equitable reapportionment of the Kansas legislature, despite powerful opposition in its own community.

The *Hutchinson News* publishes a weekday morning edition and a Sunday edition.

1966

Boston Globe   823

Founded: 1872; Boston, MA.

Prize: *Meritorious Public Service,* 1966. *Meritorious Public Service,* 1975. *National Reporting,* 1983.

Selected Works: *The War in Vietnam: A Brief History of How the United States Became Involved in Vietnam* (with Charles L. Whipple), 1967. *America Rebels* (with John Harris), 1976. *The Boston Globe Historic Walks in Old Boston* (with John Harris), 1982. *Writing for Your Readers: Notes on the Writer's Craft from the Boston Globe* (with Donald Morison Murray), 1983.

Other Awards: The *Boston Globe*'s editors, reporters, and staff have won 15 Pulitzer Prizes, in addition to other journalism and public service awards.

For More Information: Morgan, James, *Charles H. Taylor, Builder of the Boston Globe, On the Fiftieth Anniversary of His Editorship, 1873-1923,* Boston: 1923; Lyons, Louis Martin, *Newspaper Story: One Hundred Years of the Boston Globe,* Cambridge, MA: Belknap Press, 1971; Harrigan, Jane T., *Read All About It! A Day in the Life of a Metropolitan Newspaper,* Chester, CT: Globe Pequot Press, 1987.

Commentary: The *Boston Globe* has won two Meritorious Public Service awards. The first came in 1966 for its campaign to prevent the confirmation of Francis X. Morrissey as a Federal District Judge in Massachussetts. The *Globe* won its second prize in 1975 for its massive and balanced coverage of the Boston school desegration. The *Globe* won the National Reporting prize in 1983 for its balanced and informative special report on the nuclear arms race.

The *Globe* was founded in 1872 and purchased by Charles H. Taylor in 1877. At the time, Boston had 10 newspapers in publication. The Taylor family owned and operated the *Globe* until 1993, when the New York Times Company acquired the paper for $1.1 billion. The *Globe* is known for its investigative reporting, commentary, and coverage of sports and politics. Its coverage of the New Hampshire primary every four years is widely read by other journalists and editors.

1967

Louisville Courier-Journal
Full entry appears as **#295** under "Editorial Writing," 1918.

Milwaukee Journal
Full entry appears as **#788** under "Meritorious Public Service," 1919.

1968

Riverside Press-Enterprise   824
Founded: 1878; Riverside, CA. **Founder(s):** James H. Roe.

Prize: *Meritorious Public Service,* 1968.

Selected Works: *The Agua Caliente Indians and Their Guardians: Selections from Pulitzer Prize Winning Entry for Meritorious Service, Published in the Riverside Press-Enterprise, Riverside, California* (with George Ringwald), 1968. *Chronological List of Articles Concerning Indian Conservatorship Investigation Series Which Appeared in the Riverside Press-Enterprise from May 20, 1967 to June 10, 1970,* 1970.

For More Information: Contact the Offices of the California Newspaper Project, University of California, Berkeley, telephone: (510) 643-7680.

Commentary: The *Riverside Press-Enterprise* was awarded the Meritorious Public Service prize in 1968 for its expose of corruption in the courts in connection with the handling of the property and estates of a California tribe of Native Americans, the Agua Caliente, and its successful efforts to punish the culprits. The series also resulted in a change in federal law which allowed the Native Americans to receive a far greater share of their own wealth.

The *Press-Enterprise* began as a weekly founded by a druggist and teacher named James H. Roe. Its title was the *Press.* The *Enterprise* began publishing as a daily seven years later. In 1880, the *Press* also became a daily and was sold to Luther M. Holt. He changed the name to the *Press & Horticulturist.* The paper helped to popularize Riverside's navel orange. In 1931, Howard H. Hays Sr. puchased a share of the newspaper in 1931 and became its director. The *Press* and the *Enterprise* were joined in 1932. Hays became vice president of the company in 1933 and later, president. Leadership of the company was passed on to Marcia McQuern in 1992. Hays remained as company chairman until the paper was sold to A.H. Belo Corporation of Dallas, Texas, in 1997. McQuern became editor and publisher in 1994.

1969

Los Angeles Times
Full entry appears as **#91** under "Breaking News Reporting," 1998.

1970

Newsday
Full entry appears as **#722** under "Local General Spot News Reporting," 1984.

1971

Winston-Salem Journal and Sentinel   825
Founded: April 3, 1897; Winston-Salem, NC. **Founder(s):** Charles Landon Knight.

Prize: *Meritorious Public Service,* 1971.

For More Information: Contact the State Library of North Carolina, Newspaper Project, Dept. of

Cultural Resources, Raleigh, telephone: (919) 733-2570.

Commentary: The *Winston-Salem Journal and Sentinel* was awarded the Meritorious Public Service prize in 1971 for coverage of environmental problems, as exemplified by a successful campaign to block a strip mining operation that would have caused irreparable damage to the hill country of northwest North Carolina.

Charles Landon Knight founded the *Journal,* an afternoon daily, in 1897 with the help of James R. Justice. (Knight left Winston-Salem that same year.) The *Western Sentinel* was "the" daily newspaper in Winston-Salem. Published first in 1856, it eventually evolved into the *Twin City Sentinel.* James O. Foy bought the *Twin City Daily* and merged it with the *Western Sentinel,* calling it the *Twin-City Daily Sentinel.* Foy would sell the paper, but purchase several others. Foy's business partner, Andrew Joyner, turned the *Journal* over to Foy and his son, Lannes. The Foys, in January 1902, merged the *Sentinel* with the *Journal* to form the *Winston-Salem Journal.* Today the paper is owned by Media General.

1972

New York Times

Full entry appears as **#375** under "Explanatory Journalism," 1986.

1973

Washington Post   826

Founded: 1877; Washington, DC.

    Prize: *Meritorious Public Service,* 1973.

    Selected Works: *Editorials from the Washington Post, 1917-1920* (with Ira E. Bennett), 1921. *Of the Press, by the Press, for the Press (and Others, Too): A Critical Study of the Inside Workings of the News Business, from the News Pages, Editorials, Columns, and Internal Staff Memos of the Washington Post* (Babb, Laura Longley, ed.), 1974. *Keeping Posted: One Hundred Years of News from the Washington Post* (Babb, Laura Longley, ed.), 1977. *The Once and Future Constitution: A Special Issue,* 1987. *Ourselves and Others: The Washington Post Sociology Companion* (with the Washington Post Writers Group), 1996.

    Other Awards: The *Washington Post*'s staff, editors, and reporters have won 31 Pulitzer Prizes, in addition to other journalism and public service awards.

    For More Information: Bernstein, Carl and Woodward, Bob, *All the President's Men,* New York: Simon & Schuster, 1974; Roberts, Chalmers

McGeagh, *The Washington Post: The First 100 Years,* Boston: Houghton Mifflin, 1977; Davis, Deborah, *Katharine the Great: Katharine Graham and the Washington Post,* New York: Harcourt Brace Jovanovich, 1979; Bray, Howard, *The Pillars of the Post: The Making of a News Empire in Washington,* New York: Norton, 1980; Rudenstine, David, *The Day the Presses Stopped: A History of the Pentagon Papers Case,* Berkeley: University of California, 1996; Graham, Katharine, *Personal History,* New York: Knopf, 1997.

    Commentary: The *Washington Post* won the Meritorious Public Service prize in 1973 for its investigation of the Watergate case—the break-in at Democratic headquarters at the Watergate Apartments by Republican "plumbers" that ultimately resulted in the resignation of President Richard M. Nixon.

The *Post* was founded in 1877 as the paper of the Democratic Party. It passed into private ownership in 1889. Eugene Meyer, a financier, purchased the newspaper in 1933. Under his ownership, the paper established independent editorial policy and well-written news coverage. Meyer passed ownership to son-in-law Philip L. Graham in 1946. Graham committed suicide in 1963 and his widow and Meyer's daughter, Katharine Graham, became the owner. Mrs. Graham won the 1998 Pulitzer Prize for her autobiography, *Personal History.* (Katharine Graham's full entry appears under "Biography or Autobiography," 1998.)

1974

Newsday

Full entry appears as **#722** under "Local General Spot News Reporting," 1984.

1975

Boston Globe

Full entry appears as **#823** under "Meritorious Public Service," 1966.

1976

Anchorage Daily News   827

Founded: January 13, 1946; Anchorage, AK.

    Prize: *Meritorious Public Service,* 1976. *Meritorious Public Service,* 1989.

    Selected Works: *The Village People,* 1966.

    Other Awards: The *Anchorage Daily News*'s staff, editors, and reporters have won two Pulitzer Prizes, in addition to other journalism and public service awards.

For More Information: Contact the Alaska Newspaper Project, Alaska State Library, Juneau, telephone: (800) 440-2919 (toll-free within Alaska).

Commentary: The *Anchorage Daily News* has won two Meritorious Public Service awards. It won its first in 1976 for its disclosures of the impact and influence of the Teamsters Union on Alaska's economy and politics. The series was called "Empire—The Alaska Teamster Story." The second prize came in 1989 for reporting about the high incidence of alcoholism and suicide among native Alaskans in a series called "A People in Peril" that focused attention on their despair and resulted in various reforms.

The *Anchorage Daily News* was established on January 13, 1946, at 16 pages. Norman Brown, the original publisher, and two publishing partners formed the Northern Publishing Company. Brown, who had worked for the *Anchorage Daily Times* since 1936, started the paper with help of his wife and two children. It is now the largest newspaper in Alaska.

1977

Lufkin News   828
Founded: 1906; Lufkin, TX.

Prize: *Meritorious Public Service,* 1977.

Commentary: The *Lufkin News* was awarded the Meritorious Public Service prize in 1977 for an obituary of a local man who died in Marine training camp. The story grew into an investigation of that death and a fundamental reform in the recruiting and training practices of the United States Marine Corps.

1978

Philadelphia Inquirer
Full entry appears as #718 under "Local General Spot News Reporting," 1980.

1979

Point Reyes Light   829
Founded: March 1, 1948; Point Reyes, CA. **Founder(s):** Dave and Wilma Rogers.

Prize: *Meritorious Public Service,* 1979.

Selected Works: *West Marin Diary* (with John Grissim), 1991.

Other Awards: The *Point Reyes Light* has won 64 state awards, mostly from the California Newspaper Publishers Association (CNPA), three regional prizes, and one Pulitzer Prize.

For More Information: Mitchell, Dave and Cathy, *The Light on Synanon: How a Country Weekly*

Exposed a Corporate Cult and Won the Pulitzer Prize, New York: Seaview Books, 1980; Contact the Offices of the California Newspaper Project, University of California, Berkeley, telephone: (510) 643-7680.

Commentary: The *Point Reyes Light,* a news weekly, was awarded the Meritorious Public Service prize in 1979 for its investigation of Synanon, a drug rehabilitation group, founded in the 1950s by Charles Dederich, which evolved into a cult-like religion implicated in a murder plot. The cult was not only abusing its tax-exempt status, it had also turned to violence in an attempt to silence critics. The violence culminated in October 1978 when Synanon members tried to murder a lawyer by putting a four-and-a-half-foot-long rattlesnake in his mailbox.

The *Point Reyes Light* was founded in 1948 as the *Baywood Press.* It is located in Marin County just north of San Francisco. In 1951, it was sold to Al and Madonna Bartlett. In 1956, it was sold to George and Nancy Sherman and in 1958, it was sold to Don and Clara Mae DeWolfe. In September 1966, the DeWolfes changed the paper's name to *The Point Reyes Light.* In 1970, the DeWolfes sold the paper to Michael and Annabelle Gahagan. In August 1975, the Gahagans sold the paper to Dave and Cathy Mitchell. In 1981, the Mitchells sold it to Rosalie Laird and her short-term partner Ace Ramos. On January 1, 1984, Dave Mitchell reacquired the *Light.* In 1995, the paper's business manager, Don Schinske, became Mitchell's partner. Dave and Cathy Mitchell wrote a book, *The Light on Synanon: How a Country Weekly Exposed a Corporate Cult and Won the Pulitzer Prize,* about the Synanon story.

1980

Gannett News Service   830
Founded: 1943. **Founder(s):** Frank Gannett.

Prize: *Special Awards and Citations: Journalism,* 1964. *Meritorious Public Service,* 1980.

Other Awards: Gannett News Service has won two and its newspapers combined have won 43 Pulitzer Prizes, and thousands of other professional awards.

For More Information: Williamson, Samuel Thurston, *Frank Gannett: A Biography,* New York: Duell, Sloan & Pearce, 1940; Williamson, Samual Thurston, *Imprint of a Publisher: The Story of Frank Gannett and His Independent Newspapers,* New York: McBride, 1948; McCord, Richard, *The Chain Gang: One Newspaper Versus the Gannett Empire,* Columbia: University of Missouri, 1996.

Commentary: In 1964, Gannett Newspaper Chain was presented with a Special Pulitzer Prize Citation. The citation was for its special coverage of success stories on "The Road to Integration." The

Pulitzer Prize Board noted that it was "a distinguished example of the use of a newspaper group's resources to complement the work of its individual newspapers." The Gannett News Service was also awarded the Meritorious Public Service prize in 1980 for its series on financial contributions to the Pauline Fathers.

In 1906, Frank Gannett and some business partners bought a half-interest in the *Elmira Gazette.* Over the years, they acquired more newspapers and in 1943 the Gannett News Service was founded as the Gannett National Service. Gannett merged with Federated Publications in 1971, with Speidel Newspaper Group in 1977, and with Combined Communications in 1979. The last merger was the largest seen in media industry at that time. Today, Gannett publishes 87 daily newspapers, including *USA Today,* and it operates 20 television stations and cable television systems in five states. It is the nation's largest newspaper publisher.

1981

Charlotte Observer 831

Founded: 1869; Charlotte, NC.

Prize: *Meritorious Public Service,* 1981. *Meritorious Public Service,* 1988.

Selected Works: *Consolidation: An Account of the Activities Surrounding the Effort to Consolidate the City of Charlotte and Mecklenburg County, North Carolina, March, 1971* (with Warren Jake Wicker), 1971.

Other Awards: The *Charlotte Observer*'s staff, editors, and reporters have won four Pulitzer Prizes, in addition to other journalism and public service awards.

For More Information: Claiborne, Jack, *The Charlotte Observer: Its Time and Place, 1869-1986,* Chapel Hill: University of North Carolina, 1986; Contact the State Library of North Carolina, Newspaper Project, Dept. of Cultural Resources, Raleigh, telephone: (919) 733-2570.

Commentary: The *Charlotte Observer* has won two Meritorious Public Service awards. The first prize was awarded in 1981 for its series on "Brown Lung: A Case of Deadly Neglect." The *Observer* won its second award in 1988 for revealing misuse of funds by the PTL television ministry through persistent coverage conducted in the face of a massive campaign by PTL to discredit the newspaper.

John S. Knight bought the *Observer* in 1954.

1982

Detroit News 832

Founded: 1873; Detroit, MI.

Prize: *Meritorious Public Service,* 1982.

Selected Works: *Washington in War Times: A Series of Articles Published in the Detroit News, July 29-August 22, 1918* (with William Cameron), 1918. *The Story of Detroit: The Detroit News* (with George B. Catlin), 1926. *Death-Fighters* (with Paul De Kruif), 1936. *Can the Cities Survive? A Thorough, Constructive Series of Reports on 1967 Big City Problems* (with Jerome Aumente), 1967.

Other Awards: The *Detroit News*'s staff, editors, and reporters have won three Pulitzer Prizes, in addition to other journalism and public service awards.

For More Information: White, Lee A., *The Detroit News: Eighteen Hundred and Seventy-Three, Nineteen Hundred and Seventeen, A Record of Progress,* Detroit: Franklin Press, 1918; Lutz, William W., *The News of Detroit: How a Newspaper and a City Grew Together,* Boston: Little, Brown, 1973; Gruley, Bryan, *Paper Losses: A Modern Epic of Greed and Betrayal at America's Two Largest Newspaper Companies,* New York: Grove Press, 1993.

Commentary: The *Detroit News* was awarded the Meritorious Public Service prize in 1982 for a series by Sydney P. Freedberg and David Ashenfelter that exposed the U.S. Navy's cover-up of circumstances surrounding the deaths of seamen aboard ship and led to significant reforms in naval procedures.

The *Detroit News* began publication in 1873. It is currently owned by the Gannett newspaper chain.

1983

Jackson Clarion-Ledger 833

Founded: 1837; Jackson, MS.

Prize: *Meritorious Public Service,* 1983.

Commentary: The *Jackson Clarion-Ledger* was awarded the Meritorious Public Service prize in 1983 for its successful campaign supporting Governor Winter in his legislative battle for reform of Mississippi's public education system.

The *Clarion-Ledger* was founded in 1837. It was bought by Thomas and Robert Hederman in 1920. It became known for its racism during the 1950s and 1960s civil rights movement. The Hedermans sold the newspaper in 1982 to the Gannett Corporation for 110 million dollars.

1984

Los Angeles Times

Full entry appears as **#91** under "Breaking News Reporting," 1998.

1985

Fort Worth Star-Telegram 834

Founded: 1906; Fort Worth, TX.

Prize: *Meritorious Public Service,* 1985.

Selected Works: *Fort Worth in the Civil War, as Published in the Fort Worth Star-Telegram* (with James Farber), 1960.

Other Awards: The *Fort Worth Star-Telegram*'s staff, editors, and reporters have won two Pulitzer Prizes, in addition to other journalism and public service awards.

For More Information: Meek, Phillip J., *Fort Worth Star-Telegram: "Where the West Begins,"* New York: Newcomen Society in North America, 1981.

Commentary: The *Fort Worth Star-Telegram* was awarded the Meritorious Public Service prize in 1985 for reporting by Mark J. Thompson, who revealed that nearly 250 United States servicemen had lost their lives as a result of a design problem in helicopters built by Bell Helicopter. This revelation ultimately led the Army to ground almost 600 Huey helicopters, pending their modification.

Knight-Ridder, Inc., purchased the *Fort Worth Star-Telegram* in 1997.

1986

Denver Post 835

Founded: 1895; Denver, CO.

Prize: *Meritorious Public Service,* 1986.

Selected Works: *Rocky Mountain Empire: Revealing Glimpses of the West in Transition from Old to New, from the Pages of the Rocky Mountain Empire Magazine of the Denver Post,* 1950. *This Is Colorado: Special Centennial Magazine Section of the Denver Post—Voice of the Rocky Mountain Empire, June 21, 1959, Gold Rush Centennial,* 1959.

Other Awards: The *Denver Post*'s staff, editors, and reporters have won four Pulitzer Prizes, in addition to other journalism and public service awards.

For More Information: Fowler, Gene, *Timber Line: A Story of Bonfils and Tammen,* New York: Covici, Friede, 1933; Martin, Lawrence Crawford, *So the People May Know: The Story of the Denver Post,* Denver, CO: Denver Post, 1950; Barker, William J., *The Wayward West,* Garden City, NY: Doubleday,

1959; Hosokawa, Bill, *Thunder in the Rockies: The Incredible Denver Post,* New York: Morrow, 1976; Hornby, William H., *Voice of Empire: A Centennial Sketch of the Denver Post,* Denver: Colorado Historical Society, 1992.

Commentary: The *Denver Post* won the Meritorious Public Service prize in 1986 for its in-depth study of "missing children." The study revealed that most are involved in custody disputes or are runaways, and it helped mitigate national fears stirred by exaggerated statistics.

Harry Tammen and Frederick G. Bonfils bought the paper in 1895.

1987

Pittsburgh Press 836

Founded: 1887; Pittsburgh, PA. **Closed:** July 28, 1992.

Prize: *Meritorious Public Service,* 1987.

Other Awards: The *Pittsburgh Press*'s staff, editors, and reporters won three Pulitzer Prizes, in addition to other journalism and public service awards.

For More Information: *The Story of the Pittsburgh Press: A Scripps-Howard Newspaper,* Pittsburgh, PA: Pittsburgh Press, 1946.

Commentary: The *Pittsburgh Press* was awarded the Meritorious Public Service prize in 1987 for reporting by Andrew Schneider and Matthew Brelis which revealed the inadequacy of the FAA's medical screening of airline pilots and led to significant reforms.

The *Pittsburgh Press* was established in 1887. It ceased publication on July 28, 1992.

1988

Charlotte Observer

Full entry appears as **#831** under "Meritorious Public Service," 1981.

1989

Anchorage Daily News

Full entry appears as **#827** under "Meritorious Public Service," 1976.

1990

Philadelphia Inquirer
Full entry appears as **#718** under "Local General Spot News Reporting," 1980.

Washington (NC) Daily News   837
Founded: 1909; Washington, NC.

   Prize: *Meritorious Public Service,* 1990.

   Commentary: North Carolina's *Washington Daily News* was a co-winner, with the *Philadelphia Inquirer,* of the Meritorious Public Service prize in 1990 for revealing that the city's water supply was contaminated with carcinogens, a problem that the local government had neither disclosed nor corrected over a period of eight years.

   Bill Coughlin was executive editor at the time the Pulitzer Prize was awarded.

1991

Des Moines Register   838
Founded: 1860; Des Moines, IA.

   Prize: *Meritorious Public Service,* 1991.

   Selected Works: *Ah, You Iowans! At Home, at Work, at Play, at War* (with Chuck Offenburger), 1992. *Iowa's Lost Summer: The Flood of 1993* (with Michael Wegner), 1993.

   Other Awards: The *Des Moines Register*'s staff, editors, and reporters won 15 Pulitzer Prizes, in addition to other journalism and public service awards.

   For More Information: Mills, George, *Harvey Ingham and Gardner Cowles, Sr.: Things Don't Just Happen,* Ames: Iowa State University, 1977.

   Commentary: The *Des Moines Register* was awarded the Meritorious Public Service prize in 1991 for reporting by Jane Schorer that, with the victim's consent, named a woman who had been raped—which prompted widespread reconsideration of the traditional media practice of concealing the identity of rape victims.

   The *Des Moines Register* was founded in 1860. It absorbed the *Des Moines Leader* in a merger in 1902, becoming the *Register and Leader.* Gardner Cowles Sr. bought the paper in 1903. He purchased an evening daily, the *Des Moines Tribune,* in 1906. The morning *Register* and the evening *Tribune,* were each managed under the Des Moines Register and Tribune Company. The *Des Moines Register* is famous for its editorial cartoonist, Jay Norwood "Ding" Darling, and George Gallup. Cowles hired Gallup, a statistician, to survey reader preferences. This led to the creation of the Gallup Poll of public opinion.

1992

Sacramento Bee
Full entry appears as **#800** under "Meritorious Public Service," 1935.

1993

Miami Herald
Full entry appears as **#357** under "Editorial Writing," 1983.

1994

Akron Beacon Journal
Full entry appears as **#490** under "General News Reporting," 1987.

1995

Virgin Islands Daily News   839
Founded: August 1, 1930; Virgin Islands of the United States West Indies.

   Prize: *Meritorious Public Service,* 1995.

   For More Information: *The Virgin Islands Daily News,* St. Thomas, United States Virgin Islands: Charlotte Amalie, 1980; Melchior, Ariel, ed., *Thoughts Along the Way: An Anthology of Editorials from the Virgin Islands Daily News, 1930-1978,* St. Thomas, United States Virgin Islands: Ariel Melchior, 1981.

   Commentary: The *Virgin Islands Daily News* was awarded the Meritorious Public Service prize in 1995 for its disclosure of the links between the region's rampant crime rate and corruption in the local criminal justice system. The reporting, largely the work of Melvin Claxton, initiated political reforms.

   The *Virgin Islands Daily News* was first published on August 1, 1930. It is now owned by Communication Corporation, which purchased the newspaper from the Gannett Company.

1996

News & Observer   840
Founded: August 12, 1894; Raleigh, NC.

   Prize: *Meritorious Public Service,* 1996.

   Selected Works: *The News & Observer's Raleigh: A Living History of North Carolina's Capital* (with David Perkins), 1994.

   Other Awards: The *News & Observer*'s staff, editors, and reporters have won two Pulitzer Prizes, in addition to other journalism and public service awards.

For More Information: Contact the State Library of North Carolina, Newspaper Project, Dept. of Cultural Resources, Raleigh, telephone: (919) 733-2570.

Commentary: The *News & Observer* was awarded the Meritorious Public Service prize in 1996 for the work of Melanie Sill, Pat Stith, and Joby Warrick on the environmental and health risks of waste disposal systems used in North Carolina's growing hog industry.

1997

Times-Picayune 841

Founded: 1837; New Orleans, LA.

Prize: *Meritorious Public Service,* 1997.

Selected Works: *Who's Who in Louisiana and Mississippi: Biographical Sketches of Prominent Men and Women of Louisiana and Mississippi,* 1918. *The Times-Picayune Guide to New Orleans,* 1924.

Other Awards: The *Times-Picayune*'s staff, editors, and reporters won two Pulitzer Prizes, in addition to other journalism and public service awards.

For More Information: Dabney, Thomas Ewing, *One Hundred Great Years: The Story of the Times-Picayune from Its Founding to 1940,* Baton Rouge: Louisiana State University, 1944; Contact the Louisiana Newspaper Project, Louisiana State University Libraries, Baton Rouge, telephone: (504) 388-6559.

Commentary: The New Orleans *Times-Picayune* was awarded the Meritorious Public Service prize in 1997 for its comprehensive series analyzing the conditions that threaten the world's fish supply.

In 1962, Samuel Irving Newhouse purchased the Times-Picayune Publishing Company, which printed both of the major newspapers in New Orleans, making him owner of more papers than any other American publisher.

1998

Grand Forks Herald 842

Founded: 1879; Grand Forks, ND. **Founder(s):** George Winship.

Prize: *Meritorious Public Service,* 1998.

Other Awards: In addition to winning the 1998 Pulitzer Prize for Meritorious Public Service, the *Grand Forks Herald* has been named the best newspaper in North Dakota for 13 years since 1985. The *Herald* has also been included in a list of "best small dailies" by the American Society of Newspaper Editors.

For More Information: Houston, Frank, "Hell and High Water," *Columbia Journalism Review,* July /August 1997; Abigail McCarthy, "Trivial Pursuits," *Commonweal,* June 5, 1998.

Commentary: The 1998 Pulitzer Prize for Meritorious Public Service was awarded to the *Grand Forks Herald* for its sustained and informative coverage, vividly illustrated with photographs, that helped hold its community together in the wake of flooding, a blizzard, and fire that devastated much of the city, including the newspaper plant itself.

The *Grand Forks Herald* was founded in 1879 by George Winship and has been published ever since. Winship's philosophy of running the newspaper in the interests of the people was followed by its second owner, Jeremiah Bacon, who bought the *Herald* in 1915. The newspaper was bought by Knight newspapers in 1929, and it is currently part of the Knight-Ridder chain.

Music

1943

William Schuman 843

Birth: August 4, 1910; New York, NY. **Death:** February 15, 1992. **Parents:** Samuel and Ray (Heilbrunn) Schuman. **Religion:** Jewish. **Education:** Malkin Conservatory of Music, NY. Teachers College, Columbia University, NY: BA, MA. Juilliard School of Music, NY. Mozartium, Austria. **Spouse:** Frances Prince (m. 1936). **Children:** Anthony William and Andrea Frances.

Prize: *Music, 1943: Secular Cantata No. 2, A Free Song.* **Special Awards and Citations: Music,** 1985, *Lifetime Achievement.*

Career: Composer, educator, administrator; Director of Publications, G. Schirmer, NY; Faculty member, Sarah Lawrence College, Bronxville, NY, 1935-45; President, Juilliard School of Music, New York City, 1945-1961; Charter President, Lincoln Center for the Performing Arts, 1962-69; Founder, Chamber Music Society of Lincoln Center; Director: Metropolitan Opera Association, Composers Forum, Koussevitzky Music Foundation, Walter W. Naumburg Foundation, National Educational Television, Film Society of Lincoln Center; Member: American Academy of Arts and Sciences, Royal Academy of Music, London, England, Advisory Committee on Cultural Information, U.S. Information Agency, Music Panel, American National Theatre and Academy.

Selected Works: *Potpourri* (Orchestra), 1932. *God's World* (Vocal), 1932. *4 Canonic Choruses* (Vocal), 1932-1933. *Canon and Fugue* (Chamber), 1934. *Pioneers!* (Vocal), 1937. *Choral Etude* (Vocal), 1937. *American Festival Overture* (Orchestra), 1939. *Prologue* (Vocal), 1939. *Prelude* (Vocal), 1939. *Quartettino* (Chamber), 1939. *This Is Our Time* (Vocal), 1940. *Newsreel, in 5 Shots* (Orchestra), 1941. *Requiescat* (Vocal), 1942. *Holiday Song* (Vocal), 1942. *A Free Song* (Vocal), 1942. *3-Score Set* (Chamber), 1943. *Prayer in Time of War* (Orchestra), 1943. *Symphony for Strings* (Orchestra), 1943. *William Billings Overture* (Orchestra), 1943. *Circus Overture: Side Show* (Orchestra), 1944. *Orpheus and His Lute* (Vocal), 1944. *Te Deum* (Vocal), 1944. *Variations on a Theme by Eugene Goosens* (Orchestra), 1944. *Undertow* (Ballet), 1945. *Undertow* (Orchestra), 1945. *Truth Shall Deliver* (Vocal), 1946. *Night Journey* (Ballet), 1947. *Judith* (Ballet), 1949. *George Washington Bridge* (Orchestra), 1950. *The Mighty Casey* (Opera), 1951-1953. *Voyage for a Theater* (Ballet), 1953. *Voyage* (Chamber), 1953. *Credendum, Article of Faith* (Orchestra), 1955. *New England Triptych* (Orchestra), 1956. *The Lord Has a Child* (Vocal), 1956. *5 Rounds on Famous Words* (Vocal), 1956-1969. *Carols of Death* (Vocal), 1958. *3 Piano Moods* (Chamber), 1958. *When Jesus Wept* (Orchestra), 1958. *A Song of Orpheus* (Orchestra), 1961. *A Song of Orpheus* (Vocal), 1961. *Variations on "America"* (Orchestra), 1963. *Deo ac veritati* (Vocal), 1963. *The Orchestra Song* (Orchestra), 1963. *Amaryllis* (Chamber), 1964. *Philharmonic Fanfare* (Orchestra), 1965. *The Witch of Endor* (Ballet), 1965. *Dedication Fanfare* (Orchestra), 1968. *Le fosse ardeatine* (Orchestra), 1968. *To Thee Old Cause* (Orchestra), 1968. *Anniversary Fanfare* (Orchestra), 1969. *In Praise of Shahn* (Orchestra), 1969. *Declaration Chorale* (Vocal), 1971. *Mail Order Madrigals* (Vocal), 1971. *Voyage for Orchestra* (Orchestra), 1972. *To Thy Love* (Vocal), 1973. *Concerto on Old English Rounds* (Vocal), 1974. *Prelude for a Great Occasion* (Orchestra), 1974. *American Muse* (Orchestra), 1975. *Be Glad Then, America* (Orchestra), 1975. *The Young Dead Soldiers* (Vocal), 1975. *Casey at the Bat* (Vocal), 1976. *In Sweet Music* (Chamber), 1978. *XXV Opera Snatches* (Chamber), 1978. *Time to the Old* (Vocal), 1979. *3 Colloquies* (Orchestra), 1979. *American Hymn* (Chamber), 1980. *American Hymn* (Orchestra), 1980. *Night Journey* (Chamber), 1980. *Esses: Short Suite for Singers on Words* (Vocal), 1982. *Perceptions* (Vocal), 1982. *Dances* (Chamber), 1984. *On Freedom's Ground: An American Cantata* (Vocal),

1985. **Films:** *Steeltown* (Film Score), 1941; *The Earth is Born* (Film Score), 1959.

Other Awards: Guggenheim Fellowship, 1939, 1940, 1941. Town-Hall-League of Composers Award, 1940. Award, National Institute of Arts and Letters, 1944. New York Critics Circle Award, 1950-51: *American Festival Overture,* New York: G. Schirmer, 1941. 1st Brandeis University Creative Arts Award in Music, 1957. Fellow, National Institute of Arts and Letters. Honorary Member, Royal Academy of Music, London, England. National Medal of Arts, 1987. Honors, Kennedy Center, 1989. Honorary PhDs: Music, Columbia University, NY; Music, New York University, NY; Music, University of Wisconsin, WI; Music, Colgate University, NY.

For More Information: Rouse, Christopher, "William Schuman Resigns as President of Lincoln Center, Dec. 16," *Dance News,* p.3, January, 1969; Page, Tim, "William Schuman at 75," *The New York Times Biographical Service,* V.16, p.917-918, August 1985; "Schuman, William Howard: Obituary," *Current Biography Yearbook,* V.53, p.644, 1992; New York: Wilson. Dorris, George E., "William Schuman (1910-1992) Obituary, *The Instrumentalist,* V.46, p.74-75, April 1992; McClatchy, J.D., "William Schuman: A Reminiscence," *The Opera Quarterly,* V.10, no. 4, p.21-37, 1994.

Commentary: *A Free Song* won the first Pulitzer Prize awarded in Music in 1943. It was William Schuman's second secular contata, which set three poems from Walt Whitman's *Drum Taps* to music for chorus and orchestra and premiered on March 26, 1943 by the Boston Symphony Orchestra, the Harvard Glee Club, and the Radcliffe Choral Society conducted by Serge Koussevitsky. Schuman was given a Special Award and Citation in 1985 for more than half a century of contribution to American music as composer and educational leader.

The child of musicians, Schuman much preferred baseball in his youth. He pursued a career in music, which led to success as a composer, teacher, and administrator. He was teaching at Sarah Lawrence College when he was selected to be president of the Juilliard School of Music, and then went on to assume the role of charter president of the Lincoln Center for the Performing Arts. His best known works are the *American Festival Overture* and *New England Triptych.*

1944

Howard Hanson 844

Birth: October 28, 1896; Wahoo, Nebraska. **Death:** February 26, 1981. **Parents:** Hans and Hilma Christina (Eckstrom) Hanson. **Education:** Luther College, IA. University of Nebraska. Institute of Musical Art (now Juilliard School of Music), NY. Northwestern University, IL: BM. **Spouse:** Margaret Elizabeth Nelson (m. 1946).

Prize: *Music,* 1944: *Symphony No. 4, Opus 34.*

Career: Assistant, Music Department, Northwestern University, IL, 1915-1916; Professor of Theory and Composition, Conservatory of Fine Arts, College of the Pacific, CA; Dean, Conservatory of Fine Arts, College of the Pacific, CA; Director, Eastman School of Music, NY, 1924-1964; Adviser, Committee on the Arts, National Cultural Center, Washington, DC; Consultant on the Arts, U.S. State Department; President, Music Teachers' National Association; President, National Association of Schools of Music; President, National Music Council; Executive Committee, UNESCO's International Music Council; Fellow: American Academy of Arts and Sciences, American Philosophical Society, Newcomen Society; Member: Bohemian Club, Century Association, Concert Advisory Panel, New York State Council of the Arts, National Institute of Arts and Letters, Phi Beta Kappa, Rochester Club, Torch Club, University Club.

Selected Works: *Symphonic Prelude* (Orchestra), 1916. *Symphonic Rhapsody* (Orchestra), 1917. *California Forest Play of 1920* (Stage), 1919. *Before the Dawn* (Orchestra), 1920. *Exultation* (Orchestra), 1920. *Nordic Symphony* (Orchestra), 1922. *Prelude and Double Concert Fugue* (Piano), 1915. *Piano Quintet* (Chamber), 1916. *Concerto da Camera*

(Chamber), 1916-1917. *4 Poems* (Piano), 1917-1918. *3 Miniatures* (Piano), 1918-1919. *Scandanavian Suite* (Piano), 1919. *3 Etudes* (Piano), 1920. *2 Yule-Tide Pieces* (Piano), 1920. *March Carillon* (Band), 1920. *Lux Aeterna* (Orchestra), 1923. *North and West* (Orchestra), 1923. *String Quartet* (Chamber), 1923. *The Lament for Beowulf* (Vocal), 1923-1925. *Pan and the Priest* (Orchestra), 1925-1926. *Heroic Elegy* (Vocal), 1927. *Romantic Symphony* (Orchestra), 1928-1930. *Merry Mount* (Stage), 1933. *3 Songs from "Drum Taps"* (Vocal), 1935. *Merry Mount Suite* (Orchestra), 1937. *Hymn to the Pioneers* (Vocal), 1938. *Requiem* (Orchestra), 1943. *Serenade for Flute, Harp and Strings* (Orchestra), 1945. *The Cherubic Hymn* (Vocal), 1948-1949. *Pastorale for Oboe Harp and Strings* (Orchestra), 1949. *Centennial Ode* (Vocal), 1950. *Fantasy—Variations on a Theme of Youth* (Orchestra), 1951. *How Excellent Thy Name* (Vocal), 1952. *Chorale and Alleluia* (Band), 1953. *Sinfonica Sacra* (Orchestra), 1954. *Elegy in Memory of My Friend, Serge Koussevitsky* (Orchestra), 1956. *The Song of Democracy* (Vocal), 1956. *Summer Seascape I* (Orchestra), 1959. *Bold Island Suite* (Orchestra), 1959-1961. *Harmonic Materials of Modern Music: Resources of the Tempered Scale* (Book), 1960. *The Song of Human Rights* (Vocal), 1963. *For the 1st Time* (Orchestra), 1963. *4 Psalms* (Vocal), 1964. *Summer Seascape II* (Orchestra), 1965. *Psalm 150, A Jubliant Song* (Vocal), 1965. *Psalm 121* (Vocal), 1968. *Streams in the Desert* (Vocal), 1969. *The Mystic Trumpeter* (Vocal), 1969. *Young Composer's Guide to the 6-Tone Scale* (Orchestra), 1971-1972. *Dies Natalis II* (Band), 1972. *Centennial March* (Band), 1974. *Laude* (Band), 1974. *New Land, New Covenant* (Vocal), 1976. *Prayer for in the Middle Ages* (Vocal), 1976. *A Sea Symphony* (Orchestra), 1977. *Nymph and Satyr* (Stage), 1978. **Films:** *Alien,* 20th Century Fox, 1979.

Other Awards: Prix de Rome, American Academy in Rome, 1921: *The California Forest Play of 1920* and *Before the Dawn.* Member, Royal Academy of Music, Sweden, 1938. George Foster Peabody Award, 1946. Laurel Leaf of the American Composers Alliance, 1957. Huntington Hartford Foundation Award, 1959.

For More Information: *Musical Quarterly,* Volume 22, April 1936, p.140-153; *Newsweek,* Volume 15, May 6, 1940, p.44; Howard, J.T., *Our American Music,* New York: Crowell, 1965; "Obituary," *New York Times,* February 28, 1981, p.19; Williams, David Russell, *Conversations with Howard Hanson,* Arkadelphia, AR: Delta, 1988.

Commentary: Howard Hanson won the 1944 Pulitzer Prize for Music for his *Symphony No. 4,* subtitled *Requiem,* a work inspired by the death of Hanson's father. It was introduced by Hanson conducting the Boston Symphony Orchestra on December 3, 1943.

Hanson was the son of Swedish immigrant parents who settled in Nebraska. His interest in music developed early with the study of piano and cello. His early idols were George Frideric Handel and Edward Grieg, and he set out to become a composer and conductor. The style he developed was romantic and traditional, reflecting his Nordic heritage, and he is sometimes referred to as the American Sibelius. He was conducting the Rochester Symphony Orchestra in the performance of his first symphony, *Nordic,* and afterwards was introduced to George Eastman by Walter Damrosch. This initial meeting led to his later taking over as director of the Eastman School of Music. Under his direction the school developed into one of the leading music institutions in the country.

1945

Aaron Copland   845

Birth: November 14, 1900; Brooklyn, NY. **Death:** December 2, 1990. **Parents:** Harris Morris and Sara (Mittenthal) Copland. **Education:** American Academy at Fontainebleau, France.

Prize: *Music,* 1945: *Appalachian Spring.*

Career: Composer, pianist and educator; Student in Fontainebleau and Paris, France, 1920-1924; Composer, 1925-1970; Member, MacDowell Colony, summers, beginning in 1925; Chairman, Executive Board of Directors, League of Composers; Founder, Copland-Sessions Concerts; Director, Copland-Sessions Concerts, 1928-1931; Staff member, Cultural Exchange in Latin America, Office of Inter-American Affairs, 1941; Founder and President, American Composers Alliance; Director, American Festivals of Contemporary Music, Yaddo, Saratoga Springs, NY;

Director, Walter Naumburg Musical Foundation; Director, American Music Center; Consultant, Koussevitsky Music Foundation; Affiliate, Composers Forum and U.S. section, International Society of Contemporary Music; Head of Composition Department, Berkshire Music Center, Tanglewood, MA; Faculty Chairman, Berkshire Music Festival, 1957-1965; Guest Conductor, Boston Symphony Orchestra's Japan tour, 1960; Composition Instructor and Lecturer, Harvard University, MA, and New School for Social Research, NY; President, American Academy of Arts and Letters.

Selected Works: *After Antwerp* (Vocal), 1917. *Melancholy* (Vocal), 1917. *Moment Musical* (Piano), 1917. *Spurned Love* (Vocal), 1917. *A Summer Vacation* (Vocal), 1918. *Dance Caracteristique* (Piano), 1918. *My Heart Is in the East* (Vocal), 1918. *Night* (Vocal), 1918. *Waltz Caprice* (Piano), 1918. *Simone* (Vocal), 1919. *Moods* (Piano), 1920-1921. *Music I Heard* (Vocal), 1920. *Old Poem* (Vocal), 1920. *Scherzo Humoristique: Le Chat et la Souris* (Piano), 1920. *Pastorale* (Vocal), 1921. *As It Fell upon a Day* (Vocal), 1923. *Rondino* (Chamber), 1923. *An Immorality* (Vocal), 1925. *Music for the Theater* (Orchestra), 1925. *The House on the Hill* (Vocal), 1925. *Symphony No. 1* (Orchestra), 1925. *Sentimental Melody* (Piano), 1926. *Ukelele Serenade* (Chamber), 1926. *Poet's Song* (Vocal), 1927. *Symphonic Ode* (Orchestra), 1927-1929. *Lento Molto* (Chamber), 1928. *Vitebsk, Study on a Jewish Theme* (Chamber), 1928. *Vocalise* (Vocal), 1928. *A Dance Symphony* (Orchestra), 1930. *Short Symphony* (Orchestra), 1932-1933. *Statements* (Orchestra), 1932-1935. *El Salon Mexico* (Orchestra), 1933-1936. *Sunday Afternoon Music (The Young Pioneers)* (Piano), 1935. *Music for Radio* (Orchestra), 1937. *An Outdoor Overture* (Orchestra), 1938. *Lark* (Vocal), 1938. *What Do We Plant* (Vocal), 1938. *Quiet City* (Orchestra), 1939. *What to Listen for in Music* (Book), 1939. *Billy the Kid* (Orchestra), 1940. *John Henry* (Orchestra), 1940. *Our Town* (Orchestra), 1940. *Our New Music* (Book), 1941. *Danzon Cubano* (Orchestra), 1942. *Fanfare of the Common Man* (Orchestra), 1942. *Las Agachadas* (Vocal), 1942. *Lincoln Portrait* (Orchestra), 1942. *Music for Movies* (Orchestra), 1942. *Rodeo 4* (Orchestra), 1942. *The Younger Generation* (Vocal), 1943. *Letter from Home* (Orchestra), 1944. *Variations on a Theme by Eugene Goosens* (Orchestra), 1944. *Appalachian Spring* (Orchestra), 1945. *In the Beginning* (Vocal), 1947. *The Red Pony* (Orchestra), 1948. *12 Poems of Emily Dickinson* (Vocal), 1949. *Preamble for a Solemn Occasion* (Orchestra), 1949. *Old American Songs for Voice* (Vocal), 1950. *Music and Imagination* (Book), 1952. *Dirge in the Woods* (Vocal), 1954. *Canticle of Freedom* (Vocal), 1955. *Copland on Music* (Book), 1960. *Nonet* (Chamber), 1960. *Connotations* (Orchestra), 1962. *Down on a Country Lane* (Piano), 1962. *Rodeo*

(Piano), 1962. *Danza de Jalisco* (Piano), 1963. *Down a Country Lane* (Orchestra), 1964. *Music for a Great City* (Orchestra), 1964. *Dance Panels* (Piano), 1965. *Inscape* (Orchestra), 1967. *The New Music* (Book), 1968. *In Evening Air* (Piano), 1969. *Inaugural Fanfare* (Orchestra), 1969. *3 Latin American Sketches* (Orchestra), 1972. *Threnody I: Igor Stravinsky, in Memorium* (Chamber), 1971. *Vocalise* (Chamber), 1972. *Night Thoughts (Hommage to Ives)* (Piano), 1972. *Threnody II: Beatrice Cunningham, in Memorium* (Chamber), 1973. *Midsummer Nocturne* (Piano), 1977. *Midday Thoughts* (Piano), 1982. *Proclamation* (Orchestra), 1982. *Proclamation* (Piano), 1982. *Copland* (Book), 1984. **Films:** *The City* (Film Score), American Documentary Films for the American Institute of Planners, 1939; *Of Mice and Men* (Film Score), United Artists, 1939; *Our Town* (Film Score), United Artists, 1940; *North Star* (Film Score), Goldwyn Pictures Corporation/RKO, 1943; *The Cunningham Story* (Film Score), 1945; *The Red Pony* (Film Score), Republic Pictures, 1948; *The Heiress* (Film Score), Paramount, 1948; *Something Wild* (Film Score), Prometheus Enterprises, 1961.

Other Awards: Guggenheim Fellow, Guggenhiem Foundation, 1925-1926. New York Music Critics Circle Award, 1945, 1946. Boston Symphony Award of Merit, 1946. Member, National Institute of Arts and Letters. Gold Medal for Music. Creative Arts Medal, Brandeis University, MA. Edward MacDowell Medal, 1961. Henry Hadley Medal, 1964. Presidential Medal of Freedom presented by President Lyndon B. Johnson, 1964. Henry Howland Memorial Prize, Yale University, 1970. Commander's Cross of Merit, Federal Republic of Germany, 1970. Gold Baton, American Symphony Orchestra League, 1978. Kennedy Center Award, 1979: Lifetime of significant contribution to American culture in the arts. Honorary Member, Accademia Santa Cecilia, Rome, Italy. Honorary MusDs: Brandeis University, MA; Harvard University, MA; Princeton University, NJ; New York University; Rutgers University, NJ; Brooklyn College, NY; University of Portland, OR; Columbia University, NY; University of Rochester, NY; Tulane University, LA; York University, England; Leeds University, England.

For More Information: Berger, Arthur Victor, *Aaron Copland,* New York: Oxford University, 1953; Butterworth, Neil, *The Music of Aaron Copland,* London, England: Toccata, 1985; Copland, Aaron and Viviana Perlis, *Copland: Since 1943,* New York: St. Martin's, 1989.

Commentary: Aaron Copland was awarded the 1945 Pulitzer Prize in Music for *Appalachian Spring,* a ballet commissioned by the Elizabeth Sprague Coolidge Foundation for Martha Graham. It premiered on October 30, 1944 in Washington, DC.

Aaron Copland was a composer of orchestral,

choral, ballet, and movie music. He is considered by many to be the most outstanding American composer of the 20th century. He bypassed formal schooling at American music schools for special study in France with Nadia Boulanger, among others. Returning to the United States, he was given an opportunity when Ms. Boulanger asked him to write a piece for her upcoming tour as organ soloist. He complied with *Symphony for Organ and Orchestra,* played by the New York Symphony Society in 1925. Copland would go on to great critical acclaim with works such as *Fanfare for the Common Man* and the ballets *Billy the Kid* and *Rodeo.* Copland ceased composing in 1970, devoting his time instead to lecturing and conducting.

1946

Leo Sowerby   846

Birth: May 1, 1895; Grand Rapids, MI. **Death:** July 7, 1968. **Education:** American Conservatory of Music, IL: MusM.

Prize: *Music,* 1946: *The Canticle of the Sun.*

Career: Guest pianist and artist, recitals and orchestras, beginning in 1913; Performer and Band Master, U.S. Army, WWI, 1917-1918; Composer, American Academy, Rome, Italy, 1921-1924; Organ soloist, St. James Episcopal Cathedral, Chicago, IL, 1927-1962; Faculty and Head of Department of Music, American Conservatory of Music, Chicago, IL, 1932-1962; Founder and Dean, College of Church Musicians, Washington, DC, 1963-1968.

Selected Works: *The Sorrow of Mydath* (Orchestra), 1915. *Rhapsody on British Folk Tunes* (Orchestra), 1915. *A Liturgy of Hope* (Vocal), 1917. *Comes Autumn Time* (Orchestra), 1917. *Money Musk* (Orchestra), 1917. *The Irish Washerwoman* (Orchestra), 1917. *A Set of 4: Suite of Ironics* (Orchestra), 1918. *King Estmere* (Orchestra), 1923. *Rhapsody* (Orchestra), 1922. *Synconata and Monata* (Orchestra), 1925. *The Vision of Sir Launfal* (Vocal), 1925. *Medieval Poem* (Orchestra), 1926. *Pop Goes the Weasel* (Chamber), 1927. *Florida* (Piano), 1929. *Prairie* (Orchestra), 1929. *Passacaglia, Interlude and Fugue* (Orchestra), 1929-1934. *Great Is the Lord* (Vocal), 1933. *Theme in Yellow* (Orchestra), 1937. *Chaconne* (Chamber), 1936. *Forsaken of Man* (Vocal), 1939. *Concert Overture* (Orchestra), 1941. *Poem* (Orchestra), 1941. *Poem* (Chamber), 1941. *Song for America* (Vocal), 1942. *Fantasy on Hymn Tunes* (Orchestra), 1943. *Portrait: Fantasy in Triptych* (Orchestra), 1943. *Classic Concerto* (Orchestra), 1944. *Fantasy Sonata* (Chamber), 1944. *Ballade* (Chamber), 1949. *Concert Piece* (Orchestra), 1951. *All on a Summer's Day* (Orchestra), 1954. *Church Sonata* (Organ), 1956. *The Throne of God* (Vocal), 1956. *Suite* (Piano), 1959. *The Ark and the Covenant* (Vocal), 1959. *Fantasy* (Cham-

ber), 1962. *Triptych for Diverisions* (Chamber), 1962. *Solomon's Garden* (Vocal), 1964. *Sinfonia Brevis* (Organ), 1965. *Dialog* (Chamber), 1967. *La Corona* (Vocal), 1967. *Bright, Blithe and Brisk* (Organ), 1967. *Passacaglia* (Organ), 1967.

Other Awards: First Recipient, American Prix de Rome, 1921. Society for the Publication of American Music Award, Four-time Winner, 1916, 1917, 1924, 1943. Honorary Fellow, Trinity College, London, England, 1957. Honorary Fellow, Royal School of Church Music, Croydon, England, 1963. Honorary MusD, University of Rochester, NY.

For More Information: von Rhein, John, "Recordings: Sowerby Undergoes a Revival," *Chicago Tribune,* May 20, 1990.

Commentary: The 1946 Pulitzer Prize in Music was awarded to Leo Sowerby for *The Canticle of the Sun,* a cantata of chorus and orchestra commissioned by the Alice M. Ditson Fund and premiered on April 16, 1945 in New York City by the Schola Cantorum.

Leo Sowerby was born in Grand Rapids, Michigan. He was only 18 years old when his first work was performed, *Concerto for Violin and Orchestra.* His style was varied from abstract to ecclesiatical to romantic. His other notable works include *Pop Goes the Weasel, Clarinet Sonata,* and *The Throne of God.*

1947

Charles Ives   847

Birth: October 20, 1874; Danbury, CT. **Death:** May 19, 1959. **Parents:** George E. and Mary (Parmalee) Ives. **Education:** Yale University, CT: BA. **Spouse:** Harmony Twichell (m. 1908). **Children:** One daughter.

Prize: *Music,* 1947: *Symphony No. 3.*

Career: Composer; Church Pianist, Danbury, Connecticut, 1887; Clerk, Mutual Life Insurance Company, 1898-1906; Organist, First Presbyterian Church, Bloomfield, NJ, beginning in 1900; Founder, Ives and Company, 1906-1907; Co-Founder, Ives and Myrick Insurance Company, 1910-1930.

Selected Works: *114 Songs* (Vocal), 1884-1921. *Central Park in the Dark* (Orchestra), 1889-1907. *A Revival Service* (Chamber), 1896. *Symphony No. 1* (Orchestra), 1896-1898. *Symphony No. 2* (Orchestra), 1897-1902. *Calcium Light Night* (Orchestra), 1898-1907. *3 Harvest Home Chorales* (Vocal), 1898-1912. *General William Booth Enters into Heaven* (Vocal), 1898-1912. *Psalm 67* (Vocal), 1898. *The Celestial Country* (Vocal), 1899. *Symphony No. 3* (Orchestra), 1901-1904. *3 Places in New England (Orchestral Set No. 1)* (Orchestra), 1903-1904. *Thanksgiving and/or Forefathers' Day* (Orchestra), 1904. *Theater Orchestra Set: In the Cage, in the Inn, in the Night* (Orchestra), 1904-1911. *3-Page Sonata* (Piano), 1905. *The*

Pond (Orchestra), 1906. *Space and Duration* (Chamber), 1907. *All the Way around and Back* (Chamber), 1907. *Some Southpaw Pitching* (Piano), 1908. *The Anti-Abolitionist Riots* (Piano), 1908. *The Innate* (Chamber), 1908. *The Unanswered Question* (Orchestra), 1908. *Sonata No. 2* (Piano), 1909-1915. *Adagio Sostenuto* (Chamber), 1910. *Symphony No. 4* (Orchestra), 1910-1916. *Universe Symphony* (Orchestra), 1911-1916. *Browning Overture* (Orchestra), 1911. *The Gong on the Hook and the Ladder; or, Fireman's Parade on Main Street* (Orchestra), 1911. *Tone Roads* (Orchestra), 1911-1915. *Lincoln the Great Commoner* (Orchestra), 1912. *Decoration Day* (Orchestra), 1912. *4th of July* (Orchestra), 1913. *Over the Pavements* (Orchestra), 1913. *Washington's Birthday* (Orchestra), 1913. *3 Protests for Piano 3 Quartertone Piano Pieces* (Piano), 1914. *Children's Day at the Camp Meeting* (Chamber), 1915. *Orchestral Set No. 2* (Orchestra), 1915. *Orchestral Set No. 3* (Orchestra), 1919-1927. *Memos* (Book), 1972. **Films:** *Life, Love & Celluloid,* Rainer Werner Fassbinder Foundation, 1998.

Other Awards: Member, National Institute of Arts and Letters, 1947.

For More Information: Pollack, Howard, *Harvard Composers: Walter Piston and His Students, From Elliott Carter to Frederic Rzewski,* Metuchen, NJ: Scarecrow Press, 1992; Block, Geoffrey and Peter Burkholder, J., *Charles Ives and the Classical Tradition,* New Haven, CT: Yale University, 1996; Swafford, Jan, *Charles Ives: A Life With Music,* New York: Norton, 1996; Burkholder, J. Peter, ed., *Charles Ives and His World,* Princeton, NJ: Princeton University, 1996; Lambert, Philip, *The Music of Charles Ives,* New Haven, CT: Yale University, 1997.

Commentary: Charles Edward Ives was awarded the 1947 Pulitzer Prize in Music for *Symphony No. 3,* which premiered on April 5, 1946 by the New York Little Symphony conducted by Lou Harrison.

Charles Edward Ives was born in Danbury, Connecticut. He was the son of George Ives, bandmaster of the First Connecticut Heavy Artillery of the Army of General Ulysses S. Grant. Charles was encouraged by his father to write music utilizing discordant sounds, and his first compositions were played by his father's band. Ives spent his life working as an insurance salesman by day and composing after hours, weekends, and holidays. Privately published or published not at all, his music would find its audience many years after it was first composed. *From the Steeples and the Mountains* was written in 1901 and was first performed in 1965, after Ives's death. His masterpieces *Concord Sonata* and *3 Places in New England* were not performed until 20 to 30 years after they were composed. He suffered a heart attack in 1919. This and other health complications led to the end of his composing in 1928 and his retiring from business in 1930. Ives stayed out of the limelight, choosing to be a recluse.

1948

Walter Piston 848

Birth: January 20, 1894; Rockland, ME. **Death:** November 12, 1976. **Parents:** Walter Hamor Piston and Leona (Stover). **Education:** Harvard University, MA: BA, summa cum laude. **Spouse:** Kathryn Nason (dec. 1976).

Prize: *Music,* 1948: *Symphony No. 3.* **Music,** 1961: *Symphony No. 7.*

Career: Composer and educator; Assistant Professor of Music, Harvard University, MA, 1926-1938; Associate Professor, Harvard University, 1938-1944; Professor, Harvard University, 1945-1959; Walter W. Naumberg Professor of Music, 1951-1960.

Selected Works: *Symphonic Piece* (Orchestra), 1927. *Suite* (Chamber), 1931. *Principles of Harmonic Analysis* (Book), 1933. *Prelude and Fugue* (Orchestra), 1934. *Symphony No. 1* (Orchestra), 1937. *Carnival Song* (Vocal), 1938. *The Incredible Flutist* (Stage), 1938. *Chromatic Studies* (Organ), 1940. *Improvisation* (Piano), 1940. *Fanfare for the Fighting French* (Orchestra), 1942. *Interlude* (Chamber), 1942. *Passacaglia* (Piano), 1943. *Prelude and Allegro* (Orchestra), 1943. *Symphony No. 2* (Orchestra), 1943. *Fugue on a Victory Tune* (Orchestra), 1944. *Variation on a Theme by Eugene Goosens* (Orchestra), 1944. *Partita* (Chamber), 1944. *Divertimento* (Chamber), 1946. *Counterpoint* (Book), 1947. *Symphony No. 3* (Orchestra), 1947. *Symphony No. 4* (Orchestra), 1950. *Tunbridge Fair: Intermezzo* (Orchestra), 1950. *Symphony No. 5* (Orchestra), 1954.

Orchestration (Book), 1955. *Symphony No. 6* (Orchestra), 1955. *Serenata* (Orchestra), 1956. *Psalm and Prayer of David* (Vocal), 1958. *3 New England Sketches* (Orchestra), 1959. *Symphony No. 7* (Orchestra), 1960. *Symphonic Prelude* (Orchestra), 1961. *Lincoln Center Festival Overture* (Orchestra), 1962. *Variations on a Theme by Edward Burlingame Hill* (Orchestra), 1963. *Capriccio* (Orchestra), 1964. *Symphony No. 8* (Orchestra), 1964-1965. *Pine Tree Fantasy* (Orchestra), 1965. *Fantasia* (Orchestra), 1967. *Ricercare* (Orchestra), 1967. *Souvenirs* (Chamber), 1967. *Variations* (Orchestra), 1967. *Ceremonial Fanfare* (Orchestra), 1969. *Bicentennial Fanfare* (Orchestra), 1971. *3 Counterparts* (Chamber), 1972.

Other Awards: Phi Beta Kappa, 1924. John Paine Knowles Traveling Fellowship, 1924-1926. Guggenheim Fellow, Guggenheim Foundation, 1935. Member, National Institute of Arts and Letters and American Academy of Arts and Sciences, 1940. New York Music Critics Award, 1944, 1957. Dickinson College Arts Award for Outstanding Achievement, 1966. Officer dans l'Ordre des Arts et Lettres, 1969. Excellence in the Arts Award, State Government of Vermont, 1971. MacDowell Award, 1974. Honorary MusD, Harvard University, MA, 1952.

For More Information: Pollack, Howard, *Walter Piston,* Ann Arbor: UMI Research, 1982.

Commentary: Walter Piston won two Pulitzer Prizes in Music. He was awarded the 1948 prize for *Symphony No. 3,* which was commissioned by the Koussevitsky Music Foundation and premiered on January 9, 1948 by the Boston Symphony. He won his second prize for *Symphony No. 7,* which was commissioned by the Philadelphia Orchestra Association and premiered on February 10, 1961 by the Philadelphia Orchestra.

Walter Hamor Piston was born in Rockland, Maine. At first he studied architectural drawing, and then he turned to piano and violin at the Boston Normal School. He studied in Paris under Nadia Boulanger. He was influenced by Serge Koussevitsky to compose for the orchestra. His teaching career was as successful as his music, with students such as Leonard Bernstein.

1949

Virgil Thomson   849
Birth: November 25, 1896; Kansas City, MO. **Death:** September 30, 1989. **Parents:** Quincy A. and May (Gaines) Thomson. **Education:** Kansas City Polytechnic Institute and Junior College. Harvard University, MA.

Prize: *Music,* 1949: *Louisiana Story.*

Career: Composer and Critic; Organist, Methodist Church, Westport, KS, 1915-1916; Served in Na-

tional Guard and Military Aviation, WWI, 1917-1918; Student and Instructor, Harvard University, MA, 1918-1921; Harvard Glee Club Member, touring Europe, 1921; Student, Nadia Boulanger, Paris, 1922; Student, Rosario Scalero, David Mannes School of Music, NY, 1923; Naumberg Fellow, Harvard University, 1924-1925; Music Critic, *New York Herald-Tribune,* 1941-1954; Conductor, Europe, 1954; Guggenheim Fellow, 1960; Visiting Slee Professor of Music, University of Buffalo, NY, 1963; Regents Professor at the University of California, Los Angeles, 1965; Visiting Mellon Professor of Music at Carnegie Institute of Technology in Pittsburgh, 1966-1967; Visiting Dorrance Professor at Trinity College in Hartford, CT, 1973; Visiting Professor, Claremont College, CA, 1974; Visiting Professor, Otterheim College, OH, 1975; Artist-in-Residence, California State University, Fullerton, 1975; Visiting Professor, University of California, Los Angeles, 1976.

Selected Works: *Sonata da Chiesa* (Chamber), 1926. *Four Saints in Three Acts* (Opera), 1927-1928. *8 Portraits for Violin Alone* (Chamber), 1928-1940. *Symphony on a Hymn Tune* (Orchestra), 1928. *Five Portraits for Two Clarinets* (Chamber), 1929. *Le Bains-Bar* (Chamber), 1929. *Portraits for Violin and Piano* (Chamber), 1930-1940. *Serenade* (Chamber), 1931. *Meditation: Portrait of Jere Abbott* (Orchestra), 1935. *The Plow That Broke the Plains* (Orchestra), 1936. *Filling Station* (Ballet), 1937. *Filling Station* (Orchestra), 1937. *The River* (Orchestra), 1937. *The State of Music* (Book), 1939. *Bugles and Birds: Portrait of Pablo Picasso* (Orchestra), 1940. *Cantabile for Strings: Portrait of Nicolas de Chatelain* (Orchestra), 1940. *Fanfare for France: Portrait of Max Kahn* (Orchestra), 1940. *Fugue: Portrait of Alexander Smallens* (Orchestra), 1940. *Tango Lullaby: Portrait of Mlle. Alvarex* (Orchestra), 1940. *Percussion Piece: Portrait of Jesse K. Lasell* (Orchestra), 1941. *Aaron Copland: Persistently Pastoral* (Orchestra), 1942. *Canons for Dorothy Thompson* (Orchestra), 1942. *The Musical Scene* (Book), 1945. *The Major LaGuardia Waltzes* (Orchestra), 1942. *Sonata for Flute Alone* (Chamber), 1943. *Barcarolle for Woodwinds: A Portrait of Georges Hugnet* (Chamber), 1944. *Fugue and Chorale on Yankee Doodle* (Orchestra), 1945. *The Mother of Us All* (Opera), 1947. *The Art of Judging Music* (Book), 1948. *Acadian Songs and Dances* (Orchestra), 1948. *Wheat Field at Noon* (Orchestra), 1948. *At the Beach* (Orchestra), 1949. *A Solemn Music* (Orchestra), 1949. *The Mother of Us All* (Orchestra), 1949. *Music Left and Right* (Book), 1951. *The Harvest According* (Ballet), 1952. *Sea Piece with Birds* (Orchestra), 1952. *Concerto: Portrait of Roger Baker* (Orchestra), 1954. *Eleven Choral Preludes* (Orchestra), 1956. *The Lively Arts Fugue* (Orchestra), 1957. *Lamentations: Etude for Accordian* (Chamber), 1959. *Fugues and Cantilenas* (Orchestra), 1959. *Lord Byron* (Opera), 1961-1968. *A Joyful Fugue* (Orchestra), 1963. *Autumn* (Orchestra), 1964.

Pilgrims and Pioneers (Orchestra), 1964. *Ode to the Wonders of Nature* (Orchestra), 1965. *Etude for Cello and Piano: Portrait of Frederic James* (Chamber), 1966. *Fantasy in Homage to an Earlier England* (Orchestra), 1966. *Edges: Portrait of Robert Indiana* (Orchestra), 1966. *Virgil Thomson* (Book), 1966. *Music Reviewed, 1940-1954* (Book), 1967. *Study Piece: Portrait of a Lady* (Orchestra), 1969. *Metropolitan Museum Fanfare: Portrait of an American Artist* (Orchestra), 1969. *American Music since 1910* (Book), 1971. *Family Portrait* (Chamber), 1974. *Parson Weems and the Cherry Tree* (Ballet), 1975. *Loyal, Steady, and Persistent: Noah Creshevsky* (Orchestra), 1981. *Something of a Beauty: Ann-Marie Soulliere* (Orchestra), 1981. *Thoughts for Strings* (Orchestra), 1981. *A Virgil Thomson Reader* (Book), 1981. *A Love Scene* (Orchestra), 1982. *Intensely Two: Karen Brown Waltuck* (Orchestra), 1982. *David Dubal in Flight* (Orchestra), 1982. *For Lou Harrison and His Jolly Games of 16 Measures (Count 'Em)* (Chamber), 1981. *A Short Fanfare* (Chamber), 1981. *Bell Piece* (Chamber), 1983. *Cynthia Kemper: A Fanfare* (Chamber), 1983. *Lili Hasings* (Chamber), 1983. *A Portrait of Two* (Chamber), 1984. *Jay Rosen: Portrait and Fugue* (Chamber), 1984-1985. *Stockton Fanfare* (Chamber), 1985. *Music with Words: A Composer's View* (Book), 1989. **Films:** *The Plow That Broke the Plains* (Film Score), 1936; *The River* (Film Score), Paramount, 1937; *The Spanish Earth* (Film Score), Contemporary Historians, 1937; *Tuesday in November* (Film Score), Paramount, 1945; *The Goddess* (Film Score), Columbia, 1957; *Power among Men* (Film Score), 1958; *Journey to America* (Film Score), 1964; *The Day After* (TV Film Score), ABC, 1983.

Other Awards: John Knowles Paine Traveling Fellowship, 1920. Elkan Naumburg Fellowship, Harvard University, MA, 1921, 1924. Juilliard Fellowship. French Legion of Honor, 1947. Member, National Institute of Arts and Letters, 1949. Member, American Academy of Arts and Letters, 1959. Guggenhiem Fellow, Guggenheim Foundation, 1960. National Institute of Arts and Letters Gold Medal, 1966. Creative Arts Award, Brandeis University, 1968. Henry Hadley Medal of the National Association for American Composers and Conductors, 1972. Edward MacDowell Medallion, 1977. Handel Medallion of the City of New York, 1977. Virgil Thomson Festival, Kansas City, MO, October, 1980. Honorary DFAs: Syracuse University, NY, 1949; Roosevelt University, IL, 1968; University of Missouri at Columbia, MO, 1971. Honorary DLetters, Rutgers University, NJ, 1956. Honorary DMus: New York University, 1971; Columbia University, NY, 1978; Kansas City Conservatory, KS, 1980. Honorary DHL, Johns Hopkins University, MD, 1978.

For More Information: Rozen, Jay and Benjamin J. Outen, eds., *The Virgil Thomson Papers: Yale University Music Library (archival collection MSS 29),* New Haven, CT: Yale Library, 1985; Tommasini, Anthony C., *Virgil Thomson's Musical Portraits,* New York: Pendragon, 1986; Rockwell, John, "Virgil Thomson, Composer, Critic, and Collaborator with Stein, Dies at 92," *New York Times,* October 1, 1989; Rorem, Ned, "Virgil Thomson, 1896-1989," *Christopher Street,* February 1990; Toll, Seymour I., "A Sunday Afternoon with Virgil Thomson," *American Scholar,* Autumn 1990; Tommasini, Anthony, *Virgil Thomson: Composer on the Aisle,* New York: Norton, 1997.

Commentary: The 1949 Pulitzer Prize in Music was awarded to Virgil Thomson for *Louisiana Story,* the film score for a documentary about a French-speaking Louisiana family and their experience in an oil development project. The film was produced by Robert Flaherty and told from the point of view of a 12-year-old boy.

Virgil Garnett Thomson was born in Kansas City, Missouri. His music career began with piano lessons at the age of 12, followed by organ lessons. During high school, he worked as an organist and accompanist. After serving in World War I, he decided he wanted to study music at Harvard University. He was a student of Nadia Boulanger in Paris in 1923 and would return to that city two years later to live. It was there that he composed his most famous work, the opera, *Four Saints in Three Acts.* The opera's libretto was written by Gertrude Stein, who was among Thomson's circle of Paris friends while he lived in Paris. He made New York's famed Chelsea Hotel his home after 15 years spent in Paris. Thomson was also a noted music critic for the *New York Herald Tribune.*

1950

Gian-Carlo Menotti   850

Birth: July 7, 1911; Cadegliano, Italy. **Parents:** Alfonso and Ines (Pellini) Menotti. **Education:** Curtis Institute of Music, PA: BMusComposition.

Prize: *Music,* 1950: *The Consul. Music,* 1955: *The Saint of Bleecker Street.*

Career: Composer and librettist; Teacher, Curtis Institute of Music, PA, 1941-1945; Founder, Festival of Two Worlds (later known as the Spoleto Festival), Spoleto, Italy, 1951; Commissioned composer, opera and ballet pieces.

Selected Works: *Trio for a House Warming Party* (Piano), 1936. *Amelia Goes to the Ball* (Opera), 1937. *The Old Maid and the Thief* (Opera), 1939. *The Island God* (Opera), 1942. *Sebastian* (Ballet), 1944. *The Medium* (Opera), 1946. *Errand into the Maze* (Ballet), 1947. *The Telephone* (Opera), 1947. *Amahl and the Night Visitors* (Opera), 1951. *Apocalypse* (Piano), 1951. *The Saint of Bleecker Street* (Opera), 1954. *The Unicorn, the Gorgon and the Manticore* (Opera), 1956. *Maria Golovin* (Opera), 1958. *Vanessa* (Libretto) (with Samuel Barber), 1958. *A Hand of Bridge* (Libretto) (with Samuel Barber), 1959. *Labyrinth* (Opera), 1963. *Death of the Bishop of Brindisi* (Opera), 1963. *Le Dernier Sauvage* (Opera), 1963. *Martin's Lie* (Opera), 1964. *Help, Help, the Globolinks!* (Opera), 1968. *The Leper* (Play), 1970. *Triplo Concerto a Tre* (Piano), 1970. *The Most Important Man* (Opera), 1971. *First Symphony* (Piano), 1976. *Landscapes and Remembrances* (Piano), 1976. *The Hero* (Opera), 1976. *The Egg* (Opera), 1976. *The Trial of the Gypsy* (Opera), 1978. *Miracles* (Opera), 1979. *A Bride from Pluto* (Opera), 1982. *Nocturne* (Piano), 1982. *For the Death of Orpheus* (Piano), 1990. **Films:** *Il Medium* (Italian Film Score), Transfilm, 1951.

Other Awards: Guggenheim Fellow, Guggenheim Foundation, 1946, 1947. New York Drama Critics Circle Award, 1950: *The Consul.* Honorary New York City Mayor's Liberty Award, 1986. George Peabody Medal, Johns Hopkins University, MD, 1987. Musician of the Year, Musica America, 1991. Member, ASCAP.

For More Information: Gruen, John, *Menotti: A Biography,* New York, NY: Macmillan, 1978; Menotti, Gian Carlo, "The Maestro Lists a Few of His Least Favorite Things," *New York Times,* May 26, 1991; Gagnard, Frank, "At 81, Opera Composer Menotti Is Just Getting Started," *Times-Picayune,* November 22, 1992; Kozinn, Allan, "Menotti Leaves Spoleto U.S.A.," *New York Times,* October 26, 1993.

Commentary: Gian-Carlo Menotti won two Pulitzer Prizes in Music. He won the first award in 1950 for *The Consul,* an opera which premiered on March 1, 1950 in tryouts in Philadelphia before moving to Broadway's Barrymore Theatre on March 15. Menotti won a second award in 1955 for *The Saint of Bleecker Street,* which premiered on December 27,

1954 at New York City's Broadway Theatre.

Gian-Carlo Menotti was born in Cadegliano, Italy. He exhibited musical talent at an early age, but did not apply his efforts at first. After the death of his father, Menotti's mother brought Gian-Carlo to the United States and successfully gained a place for him at the Curtis Institute of Music. Most of Menotti's career was filled with commissions for ballet and opera. Menotti's libretto for Samuel Barber's *Vanessa* was highly acclaimed. He was the founder of the Spoleto Festival in Italy and associated with it up until the early 1990s. His other works include *The Medium* and *Amahl and the Night Visitors.*

1951

Douglas Stuart Moore   851

Birth: August 10, 1893; Cutchogue, NY. **Death:** July 25, 1969. **Parents:** Stuart Hull and Myra (Drake) Moore. **Education:** Yale University, CT: BA, Mus. Cleveland Institute of Music, OH. **Spouse:** Emily Bailey (m. 1920).

Prize: *Music,* 1951: *Giants in the Earth.*

Career: Served in U.S. Navy, 1917-1919; Organist, Lecturer and Musical Director, Art Museum of Cleveland, 1921-1922; Organist, Adelbert College, Western Reserve University, 1923-1925; Composer, American Laboratory Theater, NY, 1925; Music Instructor and Assistant Professor, Columbia University, NY, 1926-28; Associate Professor of Music, Columbia Unversity, 1928-1940; Head, Music Department, Columbia University, 1940-1962; MacDowell Professor of Music, Columbia University, 1943-1962; Professor Emeritus, Columbia University, 1962-1969; President, National Institute of Arts and Letters, 1945-1953; Member, Board of Directors, American Academy in Rome, beginning in 1946; Director, American Society for Composers, Authors and Publishers; Member, Board of Directors, American Academy in Rome.

Selected Works: *The Pageant of P.T. Barnum* (Orchestra), 1924. *Moby Dick* (Orchestra), 1927. *Violin Sonata* (Chamber), 1929. *A Symphony of Autumn* (Orchestra), 1930. *Overture on an American Tune* (Orchestra), 1932. *String Quartet* (Chamber), 1933. *White Wings* (Opera), 1935. *The Headless Horseman* (Opera), 1936. *The Devil and Daniel Webster* (Opera), 1938. *A Mirror for the Sky* (Stage), 1939. *Village Music* (Orchestra), 1941. *Wind Quartet* (Chamber), 1942. *In Memoriam* (Orchestra), 1943. *Clarinet Quartet* (Chamber), 1946. *Frankie and Johnnie* (Stage), 1946. *Farm Journal* (Orchestra), 1947. *The Emperor's New Clothes* (Opera), 1948. *Giants in the Earth* (Opera), 1949. *Cotillion* (Orchestra), 1952. *Boston Baked Beans* (Stage), 1952. *Piano Trio* (Chamber), 1953. *The Ballad of Baby Doe* (Opera),

1956. *Gallantry* (Opera), 1958. *The Wings of the Dove* (Opera), 1961. *The Greenfield Christmas Tree* (Opera), 1962. *Carrie Nation* (Opera), 1966. **Films:** *Power and the Land* (Film Score), United States Film Service, 1940.

Other Awards: Member, National Institute of Arts and Letters. Guggenheim Fellow, Guggenheim Foundation, 1934. Great Teacher Citation, Society of Older Graduates, Columbia University, NY, 1960. Honorary MusDs: Cincinnati Conservatory, OH, 1946; University of Rochester, NY, 1947. Honorary DHL, Yale University, CT, 1955.

For More Information: Reagan, D.J. *Dougals Moore and His Orchestral Works,* Washington, DC: 1972; "Obituary," *New York Times,* July 28, 1969.

Commentary: *Giants in the Earth* won the 1951 Pulitzer Prize in Music for Douglas S. Moore. The opera, with a libretto by Arnold Sundgaard, was based on the novel by O.E. Rolvaag about Norwegians settling in the Dakotas and premiered on March 28, 1951 at Columbia University in New York City. It was sponsored by the Columbia Theater Associates.

Douglas Stuart Moore was born in Cutchogue, New York. On his father's side, he was a descendent of Thomas Moore, one of the original settlers of Long Island, who founded Southold in 1640. Moore studied with Ernst Bloch at the Cleveland Institute. On his mother's side, his forebears included Miles Standish and John Alden. Moore's first attempt at musical composition was setting some of the poems of his school friend, Archibald MacLeish, to music. Another poet, Vachel Lindsay, would later influence Moore to make his compositions tell the story of American life and history. Composed in 1956, Moore's most popular opera was *The Ballad of Baby Doe,* a tragic tale of a silver baron who loses his wealth in the Panic of 1893 and leaves his beautiful wife to die alone in a shack outside the silver mine.

1952

Gail Kubik 852

Birth: September 5, 1914; South Coffeeville, OK. **Death:** July 20, 1989. **Parents:** Henry H. and Eva O. Kubik. **Education:** Eastman School of Music, NY. University of Rochester, NY. American Conservatory of Music, IL: MusM, cum laude. Harvard University, MA. **Spouse:** Jesse Louise Mayer (m. 1938; div.); Joyce Mary Scott-Prine (m. 1946; div.); Mary Gibbs Tyler (m. 1952; div.); Joan Allred Sanders (m. 1970; div.).

Prize: *Music,* 1952: *Symphony Concertante.*

Career: Composer and conductor; Instructor of Violin and Conductor of Orchestra, Monmouth College, IL, 1934-1936; Instructor, Violin and Conducting, Dakota Wesleyan University, SD, 1936-1937;

Music faculty member, Columbia Teachers College, NY, 1938-1940; Staff Composer and Music Program Advisor, National Broadcasting Company, 1940-1943; Staff Sergeant and Composer, U.S. Air Force, WWII, 1943-1946; Professor of Music, University of Southern California, summer, 1946; Guest Lecturer, Accademia di Santa Cecilia, Rome, 1952; Guest Lecturer, Oxford University, England, 1966; Guest Lecturer, UNESCO, Paris and Budapest, 1966; Visiting Professor, Kansas State University, 1969; Visiting Professor, Gettysburg College, PA, 1970; Visiting Professor, Mount San Antonio Junior College, CA, 1970; Composer-in-Residence, Scripps College, Claremont, CA, beginning 1970; Visiting Professor, Claremont Graduate School, CA, 1970; Visiting Professor, California State University, Fullerton, 1975-1976; Member: ASCAP, American Music Center, Century Club, Honorary Life Member: Delta Omicron, Phi Mu Alpha Sinfonia.

Selected Works: *Trivialities* (Chamber), 1934. *American Caprice* (Orchestra), 1936. *Choral Profiles, Folk Song Sketches* (Vocal), 1938. *In Praise of Johnny Appleseed* (Vocal), 1938. *Sherzo* (Orchestra), 1940. *A Legend of Bethlehem* (Vocal), 1940. *Suite* (Chamber), 1941. *Litany and Prayer* (Vocal), 1943-1945. *Toccata* (Chamber), 1946. *Little Suite* (Chamber), 1947. *Spring Valley Overture* (Orchestra), 1947. *Soliloquy and Dance* (Chamber), 1948. *Fables and Song* (Vocal), 1950-1959. *Symphonie Concertante* (Orchestra), 1952. *Thunderbolt Overture* (Orchestra), 1953. *Scenario* (Orchestra), 1957. *A Christmas Set* (Vocal), 1968. *Prayer and Toccata* (Chamber), 1968. *A Record of Our Time* (Vocal), 1970. *Scholastics* (Vocal), 1972. *5 Birthday Pieces* (Chamber), 1974. *Magic, Magic, Magic* (Vocal), 1976. **Films:** *The World at War* (Film Score), 1942; *Memphis Belle* (Film Score), Paramount, 1943; *Gerald McBoing-Boing* (Film Score), United Productions of America, 1950; *The Miner's Daughter* (Film Score), Columbia, 1950; *Two Gals and a Guy* (Film Score), 1951; *Translantic* (Film Score), 1952; *The Desperate Hours* (Film Score), Paramount, 1955; *Down to Earth* (Film Score), 1959.

Other Awards: Sinfonia National Competition for Trio, Violin and Cello, 1934. Golden Jubilee Award, Chicago Symphony, 1941. First Prize, Jascha Heifetz Competition, 1941. Society of Publication of American Music Award, 1943. Citation for Documentary Film Score, *World at War,* National Association of American Composers and Conductors, 1943. New York Music Critics Award, 1944. Guggenheim Fellow, Guggenheim Foundation, 1944, 1965. Prix de Rome Award, 1950, 1951.

For More Information: Lyall, Max, *The Piano Music of Gail Kubik,* Ann Arbor, MI: University Microfilms International, 1980.

Commentary: The 1952 Pulitzer Prize in Music was awarded to Gail Kubik for *Symphony Concertante,* for piano, viola, trumpet, and orchestra, which premiered on January 7, 1952 at New York City's Town Hall by its commissioner, the Little Orchestra Society. At that time Kubik was, at age 38, the youngest winner of the Pulitzer Prize in Music.

Gail Thompson Kubik was born in South Coffeyville, Oklahoma. He was given piano lessons as a child and received a four-year scholarship to the Eastman School of Music when he was just fifteen. At Eastman, Kubik trained in violin, theory and composition. He became the first serious composer to have a staff position on a national radio network, NBC. Kubik spent most of the years from 1950 to 1967 living in Europe, composing and developing his style. His scores have been the background for numerous films and ballets, such as *The Desperate Hours* and *Frankie and Johnny.*

1953
No award

1954

Quincy William Porter   853
Birth: February 7, 1897; New Haven, CT. **Death:** November 12, 1966. **Parents:** Rev. Frank Chamberlin and Mrs. Porter. **Education:** Yale University, CT: BA, BMus. Cleveland Institute of Music, OH. **Spouse:** Louise Brown (m. 1926). **Children:** Two children.

Prize: *Music,* 1954: *Concerto for Two Pianos and Orchestra.*

Career: Composer and educator; Violinist, Capitol Theater Orchestra, NY, 1921; Instructor, Music Theory, Cleveland Institute of Music, 1923-1928, 1930-1931; Student of music in Paris, 1928-1930, 1931-1932; Professor of Music, Vassar College, NY, 1932-1938; Dean, New England Conservatory of Music, Boston, MA, 1938-1946; Co-Founder, American Music Center, 1939; Vice-President, National Association of Schools of Music, 1941; Member, Commission on Curricula, National Association of Schools of Music, 1942-1947; Professor of Music, Yale University, CT, 1946-1965; Chairman, Board of Directors, American Music Center, 1958; Treasurer, National Institute of Arts and Letters, 1954-1966; Master, Pierson College, Yale University, 1958-1965; Battel Professor of Theory and Music, Yale University, 1960-1965; Professor Emeritus, Yale University, 1965-1966.

Selected Works: *Ukranian Suite* (Orchestra), 1925. *In Monasterio* (Chamber), 1927. *Little Trio* (Chamber), 1928. *Poem and Dance* (Orchestra),

1932. *Dance in Three-Time* (Orchestra), 1937. *Quintet on a Childhood Theme* (Chamber), 1937. *8 Pieces for Bill* (Piano), 1941-1942. *Music for Strings* (Orchestra), 1941. *Fantasy on Pastoral Theme* (Orchestra), 1942. *6 Miniatures* (Piano), 1943. *The Moving Tide* (Orchestra), 1944. *String Sextet on Slavic Folk Tunes* (Chamber), 1947. *Fantasy* (Orchestra), 1950. *Concerto Concertante* (Orchestra), 1952-1953. *Day Dreams* (Piano), 1957. *New England Episodes* (Orchestra), 1958. *Ohio* (Orchestra), 1963.

Other Awards: Osborne Prize in Composition, 1920. Steinert Prize in Composition, 1920. Honorable Mention, Prix de Rome, 1921. Honorable Mention, American Composer Awards, 1936. Elizabeth Sprague Coolidge Medal, 1943. Member, National Institute of Arts and Letters, 1943-1944. Honorary DMus, University of Rochester, 1943.

For More Information: *The Porter Papers: The John Herrick Jackson Music Library, Yale University, Archival Collection MSS15,* New Haven, CT: Library, 1976.

Commentary: Quincy William Porter was awarded the 1954 Pulitzer Prize in Music for *Concerto for Two Pianos and Orchestra,* which was commissioned through a Rockefeller Foundation grant for new American compositions and premiered on March 17, 1954 by the Louisville Symphony Orchestra.

Quincy Porter was born in Bethany, Connecticut. He was from a family of theologians, a descendant of the colonial preacher Jonathan Edwards and son of a minister. Porter learned to play the violin as a child. He continued playing under the tutelage of Lucien Capet and studied composition under Vincent d'Indy at Yale University. After Yale, he continued composition under the instruction of Ernst Bloch. His critically-noted works include *String Quartet No. 7* and *String Quartet No 8.*

1955

Gian-Carlo Menotti
Full entry appears as **#850** under "Music," 1950.

1956

Ernst Toch   854
Birth: December 7, 1887; Vienna, Austria. **Death:** October 1, 1964. **Education:** University of Vienna, Austria. Frankfurt Conservatory of Music, Germany. University of Heidelberg, Germany: PhD. **Spouse:** Alice Babette Lilly Zwack (m. 1916). **Children:** One daughter.

Prize: *Music,* 1956: *Symphony No. 3.*

Career: Composer and teacher; Professor of Music, Academy of Music, Mannheim, Germany, 1913-

1915, 1921-1928; Served in Austrian Infantry, WWI; Moved to Berlin, composition performed at Berlin Festival of New Music, 1929-1930; Member of American Pro Musica Society, touring U.S., 1932; Performer in Italy, 1933; Resident of Paris, 1933-1934; Resident of the U.S., beginning in 1934; Instructor, New School for Social Research, 1934-1935; Film score composer for Paramount Studios, California, 1936-1946; Professor of Music, University of California at Los Angeles, 1940-1948; Guest Lecturer, Harvard University, 1944; Composer of works for major symphony orchestras, 1945-1964; Visiting Composer, Berkshire Music Festival, Tanglewood, MA, 1954; Member, National Institute of Arts and Letters, 1957.

Selected Works: *Melodische Skizzen* (Piano), 1903. *3 Preludes* (Piano), 1903. *Sherzo* (Orchestra), 1904. *Capriccio* (Piano), 1905. *Stammbuchverse* (Piano), 1905. *Kammersymphonie* (Chamber), 1906. *Begegnung* (Piano), 1908. *Reminiszenzen* (Piano), 1909. *An mein Vaterland* (Vocal), 1913. *4 Klavierstucke* (Piano), 1914. *Canon* (Piano), 1914. *"Spitzweg" Serenade* (Chamber), 1916. *Phantastiche Nachtmusik* (Orchestra), 1920. *Der Wald* (Chamber), 1923. *Die cinesische Flote* (Vocal), 1923. *Tanz Suite* (Chamber), 1923. *Tanz Suite* (Orchestra), 1923. *3 Burlesken* (Piano), 1923. *5 Pieces* (Orchestra), 1924. *3 Klavierstucke* (Piano), 1924. *5 Capriccetti* (Piano), 1925. *Wegwende* (Opera), 1925. *Divertimenti* (Chamber), 1926. *Spiel fur Blasorchester* (Orchestra), 1926. *3 Originalstucke fur das Welte-Mignon Klavier* (Piano), 1926. *Tanz und Spielstucke* (Piano), 1926. *Die Prinzessauf der Erbse* (Opera), 1927. *Komodie fur Orchester* (Orchestra), 1927. *Narziss* (Orchestra), 1927. *Vorspiel zu einem Marchen* (Orchestra), 1927. *Bunte Suite* (Orchestra), 1928. *Fanal* (Orchestra), 1928. *2 Etudes* (Chamber), 1930. *Der Facher* (Opera), 1930. *Der Tierkreis* (Vocal), 1930. *Das Wasser* (Vocal), 1930. *Gesprochene Musik* (Vocal), 1930. *Kleine Theater-Suite* (Orchestra), 1930. *Funfmal Zehn Etuden* (Piano), 1931. *Tragische Musik* (Orchestra), 1931. *Music for Orchestra and Baritone Solo on Poems by Rilke* (Vocal), 1931. *Miniature Overture* (Orchestra), 1932. *Variations on Mozart's Unser dummer Pobel meint* (Orchestra), 1932. *Big Ben* (Orchestra), 1934. *Pinocchio* (Orchestra), 1935. *Musical Short Story* (Orchestra), 1936. *Cantata of the Bitter Herbs* (Vocal), 1938. *The Idle Stroller* (Orchestra), 1938. *Poems to Martha* (Vocal), 1942. *Genesis Suite* (Orchestra), 1945. *Profiles* (Piano), 1946. *Ideas* (Piano), 1946. *Hyperion* (Orchestra), 1947. *The Inner Circle* (Vocal), 1947-1953. *Dedication* (Chamber), 1948. *The Shaping Forces,* 1948. *Adagio elegiaco* (Chamber), 1950. *There Is a Season for Everything* (Vocal), 1953. *Circus Overture* (Orchestra), 1953. *Notturno* (Orchestra), 1953. *Vanity of the Vanities, All Is Vanity* (Vocal), 1954. *Diversions* (Piano), 1956.

Peter Pan (Orchestra), 1956. *Sonatinetta* (Piano), 1956. *Phantoms* (Vocal), 1958. *Lange schon haben meine Freunde versucht* (Vocal), 1958. *Epilogue* (Orchestra), 1959. *Intermezzo* (Orchestra), 1959. *Sonatinetta* (Chamber), 1959. *The Last Tale* (Opera), 1960-1962. *Short Story* (Orchestra), 1961. *Jephta, Rhapsodic Poem* (Orchestra), 1961-1962. *3 Little Dances* (Piano), 1961. *Reflections* (Piano), 1961. *Song of Myself* (Vocal), 1961. *Valse* (Vocal), 1961. *Capriccio* (Orchestra), 1963. *Puppetshow* (Orchestra), 1963. *Enamoured Harlequin* (Orchestra), 1963. *3 Impromptus* (Chamber), 1963. *Placed as a Link in This Chain: A Medley of Observations by Ernst Toch,* 1971. **Films:** *Peter Ibbetson* (Film Score), Paramount, 1935; *Outcast* (Film Score), Paramount, 1937; *The Cat and the Canary* (Film Score), Paramount, 1939; *Dr. Cyclops* (Film Score), Paramount, 1940; *The Ghost Breakers* (Film Score), Paramount, 1940; *Ladies in Retirement* (Film Score), Columbia, 1941; *First Comes Courage* (Film Score), Columbia, 1943; *None Shall Escape* (Film Score), Columbia, 1944; *Address Unknown* (Film Score), Columbia, 1944; *The Unseen* (Film Score), Columbia, 1944.

Other Awards: Mozart Prize for Young Composers, Austria, 1909. Mendelssohn Prize, Germany, 1910, 1913. Austrian State Prize, four time winner. Cross of Honor for Science and Art, Austria, 1963.

For More Information: Jezic, Diane, *The Musical Migration and Ernst Toch,* Ames: Iowa State University, 1989.

Commentary: *Symphony No. 3* won the 1956 Pulitzer Prize in Music for Ernst Toch. It premiered on December 2, 1955 by the Pittsburgh Symphony Orchestra. The work was commissioned by the American Jewish Tercentenery Committee of Chicago. Toch introduced the "hisser" in this symphony, a tank of carbon dioxide that made a hissing sound. Its use was optional.

Ernst Toch was born in Vienna, Austria. He exhibited an ear for music early on and his interest led him to copy by hand the string quartets of Mozart. This process provided him with the best of all possible teachers in learning classical structure and style. His own style was primarily classical and romantic. The rise of the Nazis forced Toch to leave his residence in Berlin and head for the United States, which he had already visited on a music tour. His experiences are realized in his first three symphonies. Toch's *Pinocchio: A Merry Overture* is frequently performed. His other works included film scores such as *The Cat and the Canary* and *None Shall Escape.*

1957

Norman Dello Joio 855

Birth: January 24, 1913; New York, NY. **Parents:** Casimir and Antoinette (Garramone) Dello Joio. **Religion:** Roman Catholic. **Education:** City College, NY. Juilliard School of Music, NY. Yale School of Music, CT. **Spouse:** Grace Baumgold (m. 1939; div. 1969); Barbara Bolton (m. 1973). **Children:** Victor, Justin, Norman (GB).

Prize: *Music,* 1957: *Meditations on Ecclesiastes.*

Career: Teacher, Music Composition, Sarah Lawrence College, NY, 1945-1950; Teacher, Music Composition, Mannes College of Music, 1952; Commentator, Metropolitan Opera Broadcasts, NBC, New York City; Dean, School for the Arts, Boston University, MA, 1972-1978; Member, Research Advisory Council, U.S. Office of Education; Member, Advisory Council, State University of New York at Potsdam; Chairman, Policy Committee on Contemporary Music, Ford Foundation.

Selected Works: *Magnificat* (Orchestra), 1942. *The Duke of Sacramento* (Dance), 1942. *The Mystic Trumpeter* (Vocal), 1943. *To a Lone Sentry* (Orchestra), 1943. *Fantasia on a Gregorian Theme* (Chamber), 1943. *Duo concertante* (Chamber), 1945. *On Stage* (Orchestra), 1945. *Concert Music* (Orchestra), 1946. *The Assassination* (Vocal), 1947. *Diversion of Angels* (Dance), 1948. *Variations and Capriccio* (Chamber), 1948. *Variations, Chaconne and Finale* (Orchestra), 1948. *Serenade* (Orchestra), 1949. *New York Profiles* (Orchestra), 1949. *The Triumph of St. Joan* (Stage), 1950. *Seraphic Dialogue* (Dance), 1951. *The Triumph of St. Joan Symphony* (Orchestra), 1951. *Aria and Toccata* (Piano), 1952. *Song of Affirmation* (Vocal), 1952. *Song of the Open Road* (Vocal), 1952. *The Lamentation of Saul* (Vocal), 1954. *The Trial at Rouen* (Stage), 1956. *The Ruby* (Stage), 1955. *Air Power* (Orchestra), 1957. *Meditations on Ecclesiastes* (Orchestra), 1957. *Anthony and Cleopatra* (Orchestra), 1960. *Blood Moon* (Stage), 1961. *Family Album* (Piano), 1962. *Fantasy and Variations* (Orchestra), 1962. *Variants on a Medieval Tune* (Orchestra), 1963. *Colloquies* (Chamber), 1964. *From Every Horizon* (Orchestra), 1964. *Antiphonal Fantasy on a Theme of Vincenzo Albrici* (Orchestra), 1966. *5 Images* (Orchestra), 1967. *Capriccio on the Interval of a Second* (Piano), 1969. *Homage to Hadyn* (Orchestra), 1969. *Songs of Abelard* (Orchestra), 1969. *Lyric Pieces for the Young* (Piano), 1971. *Developing Flutist* (Chamber), 1972. *Lyric Fantasies* (Chamber), 1973. *Diversions* (Piano), 1975. *Satiric Dances for a Comedy by Aristophanes* (Orchestra), 1975. *Colonial Variants* (Orchestra), 1976. *As of a Dream* (Vocal), 1979. *Ballabili* (Orchestra), 1981. *East Hampton Sketches* (Orchestra), 1983. *Variants on a Bach Chorale* (Orchestra), 1985. *Concert Variations* (Piano), 1980. *Love Songs at Parting* (Vocal), 1982. *Short Intervallic Etudes* (Piano), 1986. *Nativity* (Vocal), 1987. **Films:** *The Smashing of the Reich* (Film Score), Documentary, 1962.

Other Awards: Elizabeth Sprague Coolidge Award, 1937. Town Hall Composition Award, 1941. Fellowship, Juilliard School of Music, 1939-1941. Guggenheim Fellow, Guggenheim Foundation, 1943-44. American Academy of Arts and Letters Grant, 1945. New York Music Critics Circle Award, 1949, 1958. Emmy Award, TV Score, 1957. Honorary MusDs: Colby College, ME; Lawrence College; University of Cincinnati, OH; St, Mary's College; Susquehanna University, PA.

For More Information: Bumgardner, Thomas A., *Norman Dello Joio,* Boston: Twayne, 1986.

Commentary: The 1957 Pulitzer Prize in Music was awarded to Norman Dello Joio for *Meditations on Ecclesiastes,* which premiered on April 20, 1956 at the Juilliard School of Music.

Norman Dello Joio was born in New York City. His name was originally Dello Ioio. His relatives in Italy were church musicians. Dello Joio took organ lessons from his godfather, Pietro Yon. He was later a student of Paul Hindemith at Yale University. He is associated with ecclesiatical themes, such as his separate symphony and opera, *The Triumph of St. Joan.* His many works include *Fantasy and Variations* and *Colonial Variants,* the latter piece commissioned for the U.S. bicentennial celebration.

1958

Samuel Barber 856

Birth: March 9, 1910; Westchester, PA. **Death:** January 23, 1981. **Parents:** Dr. Samuel Le Roy and Margurite McLeod (Beatty) Barber. **Education:** Curtis Institute of Music, PA.

Prize: *Music,* 1958: *Vanessa. Music,* 1963: *Piano Concerto No. 1.*

Career: Music Faculty member, Curtis Institute of Music, OH, 1939; Served in U.S. Army Air Corps, WWII, 1943-1945; Vice President, International Music Council, UNESCO, 1958.

Selected Works: *The Daisies* (Song), 1927. *With Rue My Heart Is Laden* (Song), 1928. *Serenade* (Chamber), 1930. *Dover Beach* (Vocal), 1931. *Overture to the School for Scandal* (Orchestra), 1933. *Music for a Scene from Shelley* (Orchestra), 1933. *The Virgin Martyrs* (Choral), 1935. *Adagio* (Chamber), 1936. *Chamber Music* (Song), 1936. *Let down the Bars, O Death* (Choral), 1936. *Symphony No. 1* (Orchestra), 1936. *Adagio for Strings* (Orchestra), 1938. *Essay No. 1* (Orchestra), 1938. *Sure on This Shining Night* (Vocal), 1938. *The Secrets of the Old* (Song), 1938. *A Stopwatch and an Ordnance Map* (Vocal), 1940. *Reincarnation* (Choral), 1940. *Essay No. 2* (Orchestra), 1942. *The Queen's Face on the Summery Coin* (Song), 1942. *Commando March* (Orchestra), 1943. *Monks and Raisins* (Song), 1943. *Capricorn Concerto* (Orchestra), 1944. *Excursions* (Piano Solo), 1944. *Symphony No. 2* (Orchestra), 1944. *The Serpent Heart* (Ballet), 1946. *Medea* (Orchestra), 1947. *Nuvoletta* (Song), 1947. *Knoxville: Summer of 1915* (Vocal), 1948. *A Death in the Family* (Vocal), 1948. *Melodies Passageres* (Song), 1951. *Hermit Songs* (Song), 1953. *Souvenirs* (Orchestra), 1953. *Souvenirs* (Piano Solo), 1953. *Prayers of Kierkegaard* (Vocal), 1954. *Medea's Meditation and Dance of Vengeance* (Orchestra), 1956. *Summer Music* (Chamber), 1956. *A Hand of Bridge* (Opera), 1958. *Vanessa* (Opera), 1958. *Wonderous Love* (Piano Solo), 1958. *Nocturne: Homage to John Field* (Piano Solo), 1959. *Toccata Festiva* (Orchestra), 1960. *Die Natali* (Orchestra), 1960. *Canzone* (Chamber), 1962. *Andromache's Farewell* (Vocal), 1963. *Night Flight* (Orchestra), 1964. *Antony and Cleopatra* (Opera), 1966. *Mutations from Bach* (Chamber), 1968. *Despite and Still* (Song), 1969. *Fadograph from a Yestern Scene* (Orchestra), 1971. *The Lovers* (Vocal), 1971. *3 Songs* (Song), 1974. *Ballade* (Piano Solo), 1977. *Essay No. 3* (Orchestra), 1978. *Canzonetta* (Orchestra), 1981.

Films: *The Elephant Man* (Film Score), Paramount, 1980; *Platoon* (Film Score), Hemdale, 1982; *El Norte* (Film Score), Independent Productions, 1983; *Lorenzo's Oil* (Film Score), Universal, 1992.

Other Awards: Bearns Prize, Columbia University, 1928, 1933. Pulitzer Traveling Fellowship, 1932 Prix de Rome, 1932. Guggenheim Fellow, Guggenheim Foundation, 1945. Member, American Academy of Arts and Letters, 1958. Wolf Trap Award, 1980. Honorary DMus, Harvard University, 1959.

For More Information: McLellan, Joseph, "Reviving Samuel Barber: From 'Vanessa' to 'School for Scandal'," *Washington Post,* July 28, 1991; Heyman, Barbara B., *Samuel Barber: The Composer and His Music,* New York: Oxford University, 1992; Glass, Herbert, "The Accessible, Melodic Samuel Barber," *Los Angeles Times,* June 14, 1992.

Commentary: Samuel Barber won two Pulitzer Prizes in Music. He won his first award in 1958 for *Vanessa,* an opera in four acts with a libretto by Gian-Carlo Menotti, which premiered on January 15, 1958 at Metropolitan Opera in New York City. Barber won a second prize in 1963 for *Piano Concerto No. 1,* a work commissioned by the G. Schirmer music publishing company, which premiered on September 24, 1962 with the Boston Symphony at Philharmonic Hall.

Samuel Barber was born in West Chester, Pennsylvania. He began his music studies with piano lessons at the age of six. He later attended the the Curtis Institute of Music in Cleveland at the age of 14. He studied conducting with Fritz Reiner. At the Curtis Institute he met his longtime companion Gian-Carlo Menotti. Barber was the first American composer to have his work, *Essay No. 1,* conducted by Toscanini on the National Broadcasting Company's network in 1938. Barber taught briefly at the Curtis Institute, but most of his career was spent composing commissioned works for the opera, ballet, and orchestra. His music was promoted by the artists Vladimir Horowitz and Martha Graham among others. One of his most favored works, *Adagio for Strings,* has been used frequently in concerts and in films such as *Platoon* and *Lorenzo's Oil.*

1959

John La Montaine 857

Birth: March 17, 1920; Chicago, IL. **Education:** American Conservatory of Music, IL. Eastman School of Music, NY: BMus. Juilliard School of Music, NY. American Conservatory at Fountainebleau, France.

Prize: *Music,* 1959: *Concerto for Piano and Orchestra.*

Career: Composer; Served in U.S. Navy, WWII, 1941-1946; Pianist and Cellist, NBC Symphony Orchestra, NY, 1950-1954; Visiting Professor of Composition, Eastman School of Music, 1961; Composer-in-Residence, American Academy in Rome, 1962; Visiting Professor of Composition at several universities; Nixon Chair and Nixon Distinguished Scholar, 1977.

Selected Works: *Songs of the Rose of Sharon* (Orchestra), 1956. *Fragments from the Song of Songs* (Orchestra), 1959. *From Sea to Shining Sea* (Orchestra), 1961. *Novellis, Novellis* (Opera), 1961. *Birds of Paradise* (Orchestra), 1964. *Te Deum* (Choral), 1964. *Nightwings* (Orchestra), 1966. *The Shepardes Playe* (Opera), 1967. *Erode the Great* (Opera), 1969. *Wilderness Journal* (Orchestra), 1972. *Be Glad Then, America: A Decent Entertainment from the 13 Colonies* (Opera), 1976. *Mass of Nature* (Choral), 1976. *The Whittier Service* (Choral), 1979. *Symphonic Variations* (Orchestra), 1982. *The Lessons of Advent* (Choral), 1983. *The Marshes of Glynn* (Choral), 1984. *Children's Games* (Orchestra), 1987. *Transformations* (Orchestra), 1987.

Other Awards: Guggenheim Fellow, Guggenheim Foundation, 1959. Rheta Sosland Chamber Music Competition, 1960. American Academy of Arts and Letters Grant, 1962. Distinguished Alumni Award, Eastman School of Music.

Commentary: The 1959 Pulitzer Prize in Music was awarded to John La Montaine for *Concerto for Piano and Orchestra,* which premiered on November 25, 1958 in Washington, DC by the National Symphony Orchestra.

John La Montaine was born in Chicago. He studied the piano from the age of five, but always wanted to be a composer. He later studied with Howard Hanson and Bernard Rogers at the Eastman School of Music. He regards *Wilderness Journal,* a symphony for bass-baritone, as one of his most significant works. He composed *Overture: From Sea to Shining Sea* for the inaugural concert for President and Mrs. John F. Kennedy in 1960.

1960

Elliott Carter   858

Birth: December 11, 1908; New York, NY. **Parents:** Elliott Cook and Florence (Chambers) Carter. **Education:** Harvard University, MA: AB, AM. **Spouse:** Helen Frost-Jones (m. 1939). **Children:** David.

Prize: *Music,* 1960: *Second String Quartet. Music,* 1973: *String Quartet No. 3.*

Career: Member, Board of Directors, American Composers Alliance, 1939-1952; Member, Board of Directors, League of Composers, 1939-1952; Member, Board of Directors, International Society of Contemporary Music, 1946-1952; Treasurer, American Composers Alliance, 1949-1950; President, U.S. Chapter, International Society of Contemporary Music, 1952; Member, National Institute of Arts and Letters, American Academy of Arts and Sciences; Member: Academy der Kunste, Berlin, Academy Santa Celia, Rome.

Selected Works: *Tom and Lily* (Opera), 1934. *The Ballroom Guide* (Ballet), 1937. *The Bridge* (Oratorio), 1937. *Madrigal Book* (Opera), 1937. *Pocahontas* (Ballet), 1939. *Heart Not so Heavy as Mine* (Choral), 1939. *The Defense of Corinth* (Choral), 1942. *The Harmony of Morning* (Choral), 1945. *Canonic Suite* (Orchestra), 1945. *Warble for Lilac Time* (Opera), 1946. *The Minotaur* (Ballet), 1947. *Holiday Overture* (Orchestra), 1948. *A Mirror on Which to Dwell* (Opera), 1976. *A Symphony of 3 Orchestras* (Orchestra), 1977. *Syringa* (Opera), 1978. *Night Fantasies* (Concerto), 1980. *In Sleep, in Thunder* (Song), 1981. *Triple Duo* (Chamber), 1982. *Changes* (Instrumental), 1983. *Penthode* (Chamber), 1984-1985. *A Celebration of Some 100 x 150 Notes* (Orchestra), 1987. *Remembrance* (Orchestra), 1988. *Enchanted Preludes* (Chamber), 1988.

Other Awards: American Composer's Alliance Prize, 1943. Guggenheim Fellowship, Guggenheim Foundation, 1945, 1950. Academy-Institute Award in Music, American Academy and Institute of Arts and Letters, 1950. Prix de Rome, 1953. Brandeis University Creative Arts Award, 1965. Harvard Glee Club Medal, 1967. Gold Medal, American Academy and Institute of Arts and Letters, 1971. Handel Medallion, 1978. MacDowell Medal, 1983. George Peabody Medal, 1984. National Medal of Arts, National Endowment of the Arts, 1985. Ernst von Siemens Musik-Preis, Munich, 1985. Commandeur dans l'Ordre des Arts et des Lettres, France, 1987. Commendatore in the Order of Merit of the Republic of Italy, 1991. Honorary MusDs: Harvard University, MA, 1970; Swarthmore College, PA, 1956; New England Conservatory of Music, MA, 1961; Princeton University, NJ, 1967; Boston University, MA, 1971; Yale University, CT, 1970; Oberlin College, OH, 1970.

For More Information: Bernard, Jonathan W., "An Interview With Elliott Carter," *Perspectives of New Music,* Summer 1990; Griffiths, Paul, "Elliott Carter at Eighty-Five," *New Yorker,* May 2, 1994; Bernard, Jonathan W., "Elliott Carter and the Modern Meaning of Time," *Musical Quarterly,* Winter 1995.

Commentary: Elliott Carter won two Pulitzer Prizes in Music. He won his first award in 1960 for *Second String Quartet,* which premiered on March 25, 1960 at the Juilliard School of Music. He won a second prize in 1973 for *String Quartet No. 3,* which premiered on January 23, 1973 at Alice Tully Hall at Lincoln Center in New York City.

Elliott Carter was born in New York City. A career in music was strongly opposed by Carter's businessman father. Elliott prevailed and has become noted for his principles of polyrhythm, known as "metrical modulation." Carter studied with Walter Piston and Nadia Boulanger, among others. Educated in Greek music and the classics, Carter is a scholar who has taught Greek, mathematics, and physics in addition to being a world-renowned composer. He was much admired and praised by Igor Stravinsky for his *Double Concerto,* for harpsichord, piano, and two chamber orchestras.

1961

Walter Piston
Full entry appears as **#848** under "Music," 1948.

1962

Robert Eugene Ward 859
Birth: September 13, 1917; Cleveland, OH. **Parents:** Albert and Carrie (Mollenkopf) Ward. **Education:** Eastman School of Music, NY: BMus. Juilliard School of Music, NY: Certificate. **Spouse:** Mary Benedict (m. 1945). **Children:** Melinda, Mark, Timothy, Jonathan, Johanna.

Prize: *Music,* 1962: *The Crucible.*

Career: Teacher, Juilliard School of Music, NY, 1946-1956; Managing Editor and Executive Vice President, Galaxy Music Corporation, until 1967; Director, Galaxy Music Corporation, beginning in 1967; Executive Vice President, Highgate Press, 1967; President, North Carolina School of the Arts, Winston-Salem, NC, 1967-1974; Teacher, Composition, North Carolina School of the Arts, 1974-1979; Professor, Composition, Duke University, Durham, NC, 1978-1987; Mary Duke Biddle Professor of Music, Duke University, 1978-1987; Chairman of the Board, Triangle Music Theater Associates; Member, National Academy of Arts and Letters.

Selected Works: *Fatal Interview* (Vocal), 1937. *Slow Music* (Orchestra), 1938. *Ode* (Orchestra), 1939. *Jubilation Overture* (Orchestra), 1946. *Concert Piece* (Orchestra), 1947-1948. *Concert Music* (Orchestra), 1948. *Night Music* (Orchestra), 1949. *Jonathan and the Gingery Snare* (Orchestra), 1950. *Sacred Songs for Pantheists* (Vocal), 1951. *Fantasia* (Orchestra), 1953. *Euphony* (Orchestra), 1954. *He Who Gets Stamped* (Opera), 1955. *Divertimento* (Orchestra), 1960. *Earth Shall Be Fair* (Vocal), 1960. *Night Fantasy* (Orchestra), 1962. *Invocation and Toccata* (Orchestra), 1963. *Let the Word Go Forth* (Vocal), 1965. *Sweet Freedom Songs* (Vocal), 1965. *Antiphony for Winds* (Orchestra), 1968. *Claudia Legare* (Opera), 1973. *Canticles of America* (Orchestra), 1976. *Minutes till Midnight* (Opera), 1978-1982. *Abelard and Heloise* (Opera), 1981. *Sonic Structure* (Orchestra), 1981. *Raliegh Divertimento* (Orchestra), 1986.

Other Awards: Alice M. Ditson Fellow, Columbia University, NY, 1945. Grantee, American Academy of Arts and Letters, 1946. Guggenheim Fellow, Guggenheim Foundation, 1950, 1952, 1966-1967.

Fine Arts Award, State of North Carolina, 1975. Gold Baton Award, American Symphony Orchestra League, 1991. A.I. DuPont Award of Delaware Symphony, 1995. Honorary DFAs: Duke University, NC, 1972; University of North Carolina, Greensboro, 1992. Honorary MusD, Peabody Institute, MD, 1975.

For More Information: "Ward Meets Wharton," *Opera News,* June 1993; Huband, J. Daniel, "Robert Ward's Instrumental Music," *American Music,* Fall 1995.

Commentary: *The Crucible* won the 1962 Pulitzer Prize in Music for Robert Ward. An opera in three acts based on the Arthur Miller play with a libretto by Bernard Stambler, it premiered on October 26, 1961 at New York City Center by the New York City Opera Company.

Robert Eugene Ward was born in Cleveland, Ohio. His first musical experiences were singing in the chorus at school and in church choirs. He later attended the Eastman School of Music. Ward studied composition with Bernard Rogers, Howard Hanson, and Aaron Copland. He studied conducting with Albert Stoessel and Edgar Schenkman. He has been greatly influenced by American folk music and jazz in his compositions. This is evident not only in *The Crucible,* but also in his symphony *Canticles of America,* which uses the poems of Walt Whitman and Henry Wadsworth Longfellow along with segments on American history and biography.

1963

Samuel Barber
Full entry appears as **#856** under "Music," 1958.

1964
No award

1965
No award

1966

Leslie Raymond Bassett 860
Birth: January 22, 1923; Hanford, CA. **Parents:** Archibald Leslie and Vera (Starr) Bassett. **Religion:** Methodist. **Education:** Fresno State College, CA: BA. University of Michigan: MMusComp, AMusD. **Spouse:** Anita Elizabeth Dinniston (m. 1949). **Children:** Wendy Lynn, Noel Leslie Ralph.

Prize: *Music,* 1966: *Variations for Orchestra.*

Career: Served in U.S. Army, 1942-1946; Fulbright Fellow, 1950-1951; Student, Ecole Normale de Musique, France, 1950-1951; Music Teacher, public schools, Fresno, CA, 1951-1952; Professor of Music, University of Michigan, beginning in 1952; Chairman, Composition Department, University of Michigan, 1970; Guest Composer, Berkshire Music Center, Tanglewood, MA, beginning in 1973; Albert A. Stanley Distinguished University Professor, University of Michigan, beginning in 1977; Henry Roussel Lecturer, University of Michigan, beginning in 1984; Henry Roussel Lecturer Emeritus, University of Michigan, beginning in 1992; Member: American Composers Alliance, Michigan Society of Fellows, American Academy of Arts and Letters, Pi Kappa Lambda, Phi Kappa Phi, Phi Mu Alpha.

Selected Works: *5 Movements* (Orchestra), 1961. *Variations for Orchestra* (Orchestra), 1963. *Designs Images and Textures* (Band and Wind), 1964. *Colloquy* (Orchestra), 1969. *Forces* (Orchestra), 1972. *Sounds Remembered* (Chamber), 1972. *Echoes from an Invisible World* (Orchestra), 1974-1975. *Wind Music* (Chamber), 1975. *Sounds, Shapes and Symbols* (Band and Wind), 1977. *Concerto grosso* (Band and Wind), 1982. *Concerto da camera* (Chamber), 1981. *Concerto Lirico* (Orchestra), 1983. *From a Source Evolving* (Orchestra), 1985. *Dialogues* (Chamber), 1987. *Duo-Interventions* (Chamber), 1988.

Other Awards: Grantee, Society of Publishers of American Music, 1960. Rome Prize, American Academy in Rome, 1961-1963. National Institute of Arts and Letters, 1964. Citation, University of Michigan Regents, 1966. Guggenheim Fellow, Guggenheim Foundation, 1973-1974, 1980-1981. Walter Naumberg Foundation Recording Award for Sextet, 1974. Distinguished Alumnus Award, California State University, Fresno, CA, 1978. Citation of Merit, University of Michigan Music Alumni, 1980. Distinguished Artist Award, Michigan Council of the Arts, 1981.

For More Information: Guinn, John, "Teaching Ends, But Not Career," *Detroit News* and *Detroit Free Press,* April 7, 1991; Johnson, Lawrence B., "Music Preview: Honored Local Composer Won't Be Defined by Any 'ism' But His Own," *Detroit News,* February 27, 1997.

Commentary: Leslie Bassett won the 1966 Pulitzer Prize in Music for *Variation for Orchestra,* which premiered on October 22, 1965 at the Academy of Music in Philadelphia by the Philadelphia Orchestra conducted by Eugene Ormandy.

Leslie Raymond Bassett was born in Hanford, California. He began piano lessons at age five. He later studied the trombone and favored this as his instrument. He studied in Paris with Nadia Boulanger while on a Fulbright scholarship. Bassett was one of the six composers requested by the National Endowment for the Arts to compose pieces in celebration of the American bicentennial. His contribution was *Echoes from an Invisible World,* a piece for orchestra. Bassett taught composition and lectured at the University of Michigan from 1952 to 1992.

1967

Leon Kirchner   861
Birth: January 24, 1919; Brooklyn, NY. **Death:** 1967. **Spouse:** Gertrude Schoenberg (m. 1949). **Children:** Two children.

Prize: *Music,* 1967: *Quartet No. 3.*

Career: Second Lieutenant, U.S. Army Signal Corps, 1943-1946; Lecturer, University of Southern California, 1950-1954; Associate Professor, University of Southern California, 1954; Luther Brusie Marchant Professor of Music, Mills College, CA, 1954; Visiting Slee Professor, State University at Buffalo, NY, 1958; Composition Instructor, Berkshire Music Center, Tanglewood, MA, summers, 1959 and 1960; Professor of Music, Harvard University, 1961-1965; Walter Bigelow Rosen Professor, Harvard University, beginning in 1965; Composer-in-Residence, American Academy in Rome, 1973; Senior Resident Fellow, American Academy, 1975; Fellow, Institute of Advanced Musical Studies, Stanford University, CA, 1977.

Selected Works: *Piano Sonata* (Chamber/vocal /solo), 1948. *Little Suite* (Chamber/vocal/solo), 1949. *String Quartet No. 1* (Chamber / vocal / solo), 1949. *Sinfonia* (Orchestra), 1951. *Sonata Concertante* (Chamber/vocal/solo), 1952. *Concerto for Piano No. 1* (Orchestra), 1953. *Trio* (Chamber/vocal/solo), 1954. *Toccata* (Orchestra), 1955. *String Quartet No. 2* (Chamber / vocal / solo), 1958. *Concerto for Violin, Violoncello, 10 Winds, and Percussion* (Orchestra), 1960. *Concerto for Piano No. 2* (Orchestra), 1963. *Fanfare* (Chamber/vocal/solo), 1965. *String Quartet No. 3* (Chamber / vocal / solo), 1966. *Words from Wordsworth* (Chamber/vocal/solo), 1966. *Music for Orchestra* (Orchestra), 1969. *Lily* (Chamber / vocal / solo), 1973. *Flutings for Paula* (Chamber/vocal/solo), 1973. *Fanfare II* (Chamber / vocal / solo), 1977. *Lily* (Opera), 1977. *Music for Flute and Orchestra* (Orchestra), 1978. *The Twilight Stood* (Chamber/vocal/ solo), 1982. *Music for Twelve* (Chamber/vocal/solo), 1985. *For Cello Solo* (Chamber / vocal / solo), 1986. *For Violin Solo* (Chamber/vocal/solo), 1986. *Illuminations* (Chamber/vocal/solo), 1986. *5 Pieces* (Chamber/vocal/solo), 1987. *For Violin Solo II* (Chamber/ vocal / solo), 1988. *2 Duos* (Chamber / vocal / solo), 1988. *Triptych* (Chamber/vocal/solo), 1988. *Interlude* (Chamber/vocal/solo), 1989. *Orchestra Piece (Music for II),* 1990. *Music for Cello and Orchestra* (Orchestra), 1992. *Trio II* (Chamber/vocal/solo), 1993.

Other Awards: George Ladd Traveling Fellowship (Prix de Paris), 1942. Guggenheim Fellow, Guggenheim Foundation, 1948. New York Music Critics Award, 1950, 1959. Fromm Music Foundation Recording Grant, 1954. Fromm Music Foundation Grant, 1955. Member, National Institute of Arts and Letters, 1962. Member, American Academy of Arts and Letters, 1962. New York City Opera Grant, 1973. National Music Award, 1976. Creative Arts Award, Brandeis University, 1977.

For More Information: Tommasini, Anthony, "Kirchner Shows His Mastery of Musical Clarity," *Boston Globe,* July 21, 1992; Shapiro, Alexander, "Kirchner's Cello Music Earns Top Friedheim Award," *Washington Post,* October 3, 1994; Buell, Richard, "Led by Kirchner, Gardner Orchestra Cheers Soul," *Boston Globe,* November 25, 1997.

Commentary: The 1967 Pulitzer Prize in Music was awarded to Leon Kirchner for *Quartet No. 3,* which premiered on January 27, 1967 at Town Hall in New York City by the Beaux Arts Quartet.

Leon Kirchner was born in Brooklyn, New York, the child of Russian immigrants. He began piano lessons at age six. His family moved to Los Angeles when Leon was nine. His lessons were interrupted for three years upon their arrival in Los Angeles due to the Depression. Later, Kirchner would be a student of Arnold Schoenberg at UCLA and with Ernst Bloch at the University of California at Berkeley. Kirchner's style used 12-tone music with other techniques. He was also noted for his opera, *Lily,* which was based upon the Saul Bellow novel, *Henderson the Rain King.*

1968

George Crumb   862

Birth: October 24, 1929; Charleston, WV. **Parents:** George Henry and Vivian (Reed) Crumb. **Education:** Mason College of Music, SC: BMus. University of Illinois: MA. University of Michigan. **Spouse:** Elizabeth May Brown (m. 1949). **Children:** Elizabeth Ann, David Reed, Peter Stanley.

Prize: *Music,* 1968: *Echoes of Time and the River.*

Career: Teacher, Theory and Analysis, Hollins College, Virginia; Instructor and Assistant Professor, Piano and Composition, University of Colorado, Boulder, 1958-1963; Creative Associate and Composer-in-Residence, Buffalo Center for the Creative and Performing Arts, State University of New York, University of Pennsylvania, Philadelphia, 1965-1982; Member, National Institute of Arts and Letters, 1975; Annenberg Professor of the Humanities, 1983-1997; Retired, May 1997; Honorary Member: Deutsche Akademie de Kunste, International Cultural Society

of Korea; Member, American Academy of Arts and Letters.

Selected Works: *Variazioni* (Orchestra), 1959. *5 Pieces for Piano,* 1962. *Night Music I,* 1963. *4 Nocturnes (Night Music II),* 1963. *Madrigals, Book I,* 1965. *Madrigals, Book II,* 1965. *11 Echoes of Autumn,* 1966. *Songs, Drones, and the Refrains of Death,* 1968. *Madrigals, Book III,* 1969. *Madrigals, Book IV,* 1969. *Night of the 4 Moons,* 1969. *Black Angels (13 Images from the Dark Land: Images I),* 1970. *Lux aeterna for 5 Masked Players,* 1971. *Vox Balanae for 3 Masked Players,* 1971. *Makrokosmos, Volume I,* 1972. *Makrokosmos, Volume II,* 1973. *Music for a Summer Evening (Makrokosmos III),* 1974. *Dream Sequence (Images II),* 1976. *Star-Child,* 1977. *Celestial Mechanics (Makrokosmos IV),* 1979. *A Little Suite for Christmas,* 1980. *Gnomic Variations,* 1982. *Pastoral Drone,* 1982. *A Haunted Landscape,* 1984. *An Idyll for the Misbegotten,* 1985. *Federico's Little Songs,* 1986. *Zeitgeist,* 1988.

Other Awards: Elizabeth Croft Fellowship for Study, Berkshire Music Centre, 1955. Fulbright Scholarship, 1955-1956. BMI Student Award, 1956. Rockefeller Grant, 1964. National Institute of Arts and Letters Grant, 1967. Guggenheim Grant, 1967 and 1973. UNESCO International Rostrum of Composers Award, 1971. Koussevitzky Recording Award, 1971. Fromm Grant, 1973. Ford Foundation Grant, 1976. Prince Pierre de Monaco Gold Medal, 1989. MacDowell Colony Medal, 1995. Brandeis University Creative Arts Award.

For More Information: Gillespie, Don C., ed., *George Crumb: Profile of a Composer,* New York: Peters, 1986; Henahan, Donal, "Helping George Crumb Celebrate His Birthday," *New York Times,* October 26, 1989; Giffin, Glenn, "What Composer Crumb Did in the '60s Is Now 'Normal'," *Denver Post,* October 9, 1992; Smith, Ken, "Voices' of Crumb Still Being Heard: Music," *Los Angeles Times,* April 18, 1997.

Commentary: George Crumb was awarded the 1968 Pulitzer Prize in Music for *Echoes of Time and the River.* Commissioned by the University of Chicago for its 75th anniversary, this orchestral suite premiered on May 26, 1967 at the university's Mandel Hall by the Chicago Symphony.

George Henry Crumb was born in Charleston, West Virginia. Music was a big part of Crumb's growing-up. His mother was a cellist and his father a clarinetist and bandmaster. George played piano by ear at the age of nine. He began composing without formal training. He would later study with Eugene Weigel at the University of Illinois at Urbana-Champaign and with Boris Balcher in Berlin. His major influences were Debussy, Mahler and Bartok. His other works include *Madrigals* and *Ancient Voices of*

Children; both use words from the poems of Frederico Garcia Lorca.

1969

Karel Husa   863

Birth: August 7, 1921; Prague, Czechoslovakia. **Parents:** Karel, Sr. and Bozena Husoua Dongresova. **Education:** Prague Conservatory of Music, CZ, magna summa cum laude. Prague Academy of Musical Arts, CZ, magna summa cum laude. Ecole Normale de Music, France: License, Conducting and Compostion. Paris Conservatory of Music, France. **Spouse:** Simone Perault (m. 1952). **Children:** Catherine, Anne Marie, Elizabeth, Caroline.

> **Prize:** *Music,* 1969: *String Quartet No. 3.*

Career: Guest Conductor, Czechoslovak Radio, Prague, Czechoslavakia, 1945-1946; Guest Conductor, orchestras in Hamburg, Brussels, Paris, Zurich, London, Manchester, Prague, Stockholm, Hong Kong, Singapore, Japan, Cincinnati, Buffalo, New York, Boston, Rochester, Baltimore, San Diego, Syracuse; Professor of Music, Cornell University, NY, beginning in 1954; Director, University Symposium and Chamber Orchestras, Cornell University, 1972-1992; Kappa Alpha Professor of Music Emeritus, Cornell University, beginning in 1992; Member: International Institute of Arts and Letters, American Academy of Arts and Letters, Belgian Royal Academy of Arts and Sciences, International Society of Contemporary Music, French Society of Composers; Honorary Member: Omicron, Phi Mu Alpha.

Selected Works: *3 Fresques* (Orchestra), 1949. *Evocations of Slovakia* (Chamber), 1952. *Musique d'amateurs* (Orchestra), 1953. *Portrait* (Orchestra), 1953. *12 Moravian Songs* (Chamber), 1956. *Fantasies for Orchestra* (Orchestra), 1957. *Mosaiques for Orchestra* (Orchestra), 1961. *Elegie et Rondeau* (Orchestra), 1962. *Festive Ode* (Orchestra), 1965. *2 Preludes* (Chamber), 1966. *Music for Prague 1968* (Orchestra), 1969. *Apotheosis of This Earth* (Orchestra), 1971. *2 Sonnets from Michaelangelo* (Orchestra), 1972. *The Steadfast Tin Soldier* (Orchestra), 1975. *Monodrama* (Orchestra), 1976. *An American Te Deum* (Orchestra), 1976. *3 Dance Sketches* (Chamber), 1980. *Intradas and Interludes* (Chamber), 1980. *3 Moravian Songs* (Chamber), 1981. *Every Day* (Chamber), 1981. *The Trojan Women* (Orchestra), 1981. *Recollections* (Chamber), 1982. *Reflections* (Orchestra), 1983. *Intrada* (Chamber), 1984. *Smetana Fanfare* (Orchestra), 1984. *Symphonic Suite* (Orchestra), 1984. *Variations* (Chamber), 1984.

Other Awards: French Government Award, 1946-1947. Prague Academy of the Arts Prize, Czechoslovakia, 1948. L. Boulanger Award, 1952. Guggenheim Fellow, Guggenheim Foundation, 1964-

1965. Academy Institute of Arts and Letters Award, 1989. Grawmeyer Award, University of Louisville, KY, 1993. Serge Koussevitsky Music Foundation Award, 1993. Czech Republic Medal of Merit of First Degree Presented by Vaclav Havel, 1995. Honorary MusDs: Coe College, IA, 1976; Cleveland Institute, OH, 1985; Ithaca College, NY, 1986; Baldwin-Wallace Conservatory, OH, 1991; Hartwicke College, NY, 1997. Honorary DHL, College of Mount St. Vincent, NY, 1996.

For More Information: Perlis, Vivian, "Karel Husa Is Home Again," *Musical America,* September 1990; McLellan, Joseph, "Neo-Romantic Composers, Straight from the Heart," *Washington Post,* March 22, 1992; Phillips, Harvey, "Musician from Prague," *The Instrumentalist,* September 1992.

Commentary: *String Quartet No. 3* won the 1969 Pulitzer Prize in Music for Karel Husa. It premiered on October 14, 1968 at the Goodman Theatre in Chicago by the Fine Arts Quartet.

Karel Husa was born in Prague in the former Czechoslavakia. He began violin lessons at age eight followed by piano lessons several years later. Husa was encouraged by his parents to pursue an engineering career, but the Nazi occupation of Czechoslavakia closed the universities in 1939. Music schools and conservatories were allowed to reopen a short time later, and Husa was able to attend the Prague Conservatory. He studied with Arthur Honegger and Nadia Boulanger in Paris and immigrated to the United States in 1954. His style is romantic and he is frequently played. His other works include *Music for Prague 1968* and *Apotheosis of This Earth.*

1970

Charles Wuorinen   864

Birth: June 9, 1938; New York, NY. **Parents:** John Henry Wuorinen and Alfhild (Kalijarvi) Wuorinen. **Education:** Columbia University, NY: BA, MA.

> **Prize:** *Music,* 1970: *Time's Encomium.*

Career: Founder, Group for Contemporary Music, 1962; Composer; Music Instructor, Columbia University, NY, 1964-1971; Professor, Manhattan School of Music, 1972-1979; Composer-in-Residence, San Francisco Symphony, 1985-1989; Professor of Music, Rutgers University, NJ; Faculty member of Princeton, Yale, the University of Iowa, University of California (San Diego), New England Conservatory and State University of New York at Buffalo; Recipient of numerous commissions and grants; Member: American Academy of Arts and Letters, American Academy of Arts and Sciences.

Selected Works: *Alternating Currents* (Chamber), 1957. *Concertante* (Orchestra), 1957-1959. *Dr. Faustus Lights the Lights* (Chamber), 1957. *Triptych*

(Chamber), 1957. *3 Pieces* (Chamber), 1958. *Trio concertante* (Chamber), 1959. *Musica duarum partum ecclesiastica* (Chamber), 1959. *Madrigali spirituale* (Vocal), 1960. *Turetzky Pieces* (Chamber), 1960. *Consort from Instruments and Voices* (Electronic), 1961. *Elovutio transcripta* (Orchestra), 1961. *Symphonia sacra* (Vocal), 1961. *Tiento sobre cabeza* (Chamber), 1961. *The Prayer of Jonah* (Vocal), 1962. *Composition* (Chamber), 1964. *Super salutem* (Vocal), 1964. *Orchestral and Electronic Exchanges* (Orchestra), 1965. *Janissary Music* (Chamber), 1966. *John Bull: Salve Regina versus Septum* (Chamber), 1966. *The Politics* (Stage), 1967. *Time's Encomium* (Electronic), 1969. *A Message to Denmark Hill* (Vocal), 1970. *A Song to the Lute* (Vocal), 1970. *Ringing Changes* (Chamber), 1970. *Canzona* (Chamber), 1971. *On Alligators* (Chamber), 1972. *Speculum speculi* (Chamber), 1972. *Arabia felix* (Chamber), 1973. *Grand Union* (Chamber), 1973. *Mannheim, 87.87.87* (Vocal), 1973. *An Anthem for Epiphany* (Vocal), 1974. *A Reliquary for Igor Stravinsky* (Orchestra), 1975. *The W. of Babylon* (Stage), 1975. *Hyperion* (Chamber), 1976. *Tashi Concerto* (Orchestra), 1976. *Percussion Symphony* (Orchestra), 1976. *Ancestors* (Chamber), 1977. *Arcangel* (Chamber), 1977. *Fast Fantasy* (Chamber), 1977. *The Winds* (Chamber), 1977. *Two-Part Symphony* (Orchestra), 1978. *The Celestial Sphere* (Vocal), 1979. *Archaeoteryx* (Chamber), 1980. *Joan's* (Chamber), 1980. *Bamboula Squared* (Orchestra), 1984. *Movers and Shakers* (Orchestra), 1984. *Winds of Parnassus* (Chamber), 1984. *Crossfire* (Orchestra), 1985.

Other Awards: New York Philharmonic's Young Composers Award, 1954. Bennington Composers Conference Scholarship, 1956-1960. Bearns Prize, 1958, 1959, 1961. Alice M. Ditson Fellowship, 1959. BMI-SCA Award, 1959, 1961, 1962, 1963. Arthur Rose Teaching Fellowship, 1960. MacDowell Colony Fellowship, 1960. Phi Beta Kappa, 1960. Evans Traveling Fellowship, 1961. Lili Boulanger Memorial Award, 1961, 1962. Regents College Teaching Fellowship, 1961-1962. Santa Fe Opera, Festival Fellow, 1962. World's Fair of Music and Sound, 1962. American Academy and Institute of Arts and Letters Award, 1967. Guggenheim Fellowship, 1968, 1972. Ingram Merrill Fellowship, 1969. Brandeis University, Creative Arts Awards Citation, 1970. Koussevitsky International Recording Award, 1970. Phoebe Ketchum Thorne Honorary Award, 1973. Arts and Letters Award, Finlandia Foundation, 1976. Creative Artists Public Service Award, 1976. MacArthur Foundation Fellowship, 1986-1991. Rockefeller Foundation Fellowship, 1979, 1981, 1982.

For More Information: Commanday, Robert, "S.F. Finale for Wuorinen in New Music," *San Francisco Chronicle,* May 8, 1989; Cunningham, Carl,

"Wuorinen in Spotlight," *Houston Post,* May 6, 1990; Paul Griffiths, "A Composer's 60th, Quirks and All," *New York Times,* June 9, 1998.

Commentary: Charles Wuorinen won the 1970 Pulitzer Prize in Music for *Time's Encomium,* an electronic work which premiered on August 16, 1969 at the Berkshire Music Festival at Tanglewood in Masschussetts.

Charles Wuorinen was born in New York City. His parents were both of Finnish descent. His father, Charles Peter, was at one time chairman of Columbia University's history department. The young Charles composed his first piece of music at age five without any training. He received the Young Composer's Award from the New York Philharmonic at age 15. He later became interested in electronic music, combining orchestra with recorded electronic music which he used in Orchestral and Electronic Exchanges in 1965. His opera, *The W. of Babylon,* was greeted with controversy.

1971

Mario Davidovsky   865

Birth: March 4, 1934; Buenos Aires, Brazil. **Parents:** Natalio and Perla (Bulanska) Davidovsky. **Religion:** Jewish. **Education:** Columbia-Princeton Electronic Music Center, NJ. **Spouse:** Elaine Blaustein (m. 1961). **Children:** Matias Gabriel, Adriana.

Prize: *Music,* 1971: *Synchromiums No. 6 for Piano and Electronic Sound (1970).*

Career: Director, Electronic Music Center, Princeton and Columbia Universities, 1964-1994; Visiting Lecturer, School of Music, University of Michigan, 1964; Guest Professor, Institut di tella, Buenos Aires, Argentina, 1965; Professor of Music, City College, City University of NY, 1968-1980; Professor of Music, Columbia University, NY, 1981-1994; McDowell Professor of Music, Columbia University, NY, 1989-1994; Fanny Peabody Mason Professor of Music, Harvard University, NY, beginning in 1994; Director, Composer's Conference, Wellesley College, MA; Member, Board of Directors, Koussevitsky Foundation; Member, Board of Directors, Fromm Foundation, Harvard University, MA; Founder and Member, Board of Directors, Robert M. Miller Fund for Music.

Selected Works: *Suite sinfonica para "El payaso,"* 1955. *3 Pieces,* 1956. *Noneto,* 1956. *Serie sinfonica,* 1959. *Contrastes,* 1960. *Pianos,* 1961. *Synchonisms,* 1963. *Inflexions,* 1965. *Junctures,* 1966. *Music,* 1968. *Chacona,* 1971. *Transientes,* 1972. *Scenes from Shir-ha-shirim,* 1975. *Pennplay,* 1978. *Consorts,* 1980. *Romancero,* 1983. *Capriccio,* 1985.

Other Awards: Guggenheim Fellow, Guggenheim Foundation, 1961-1962, 1962-1963. Koussevitsky Foundation Award, 1964. Library of Congress Award, 1964. Rockefeller Fellow, Rockefeller Foundation, 1964-1965. National Institute of Arts and Letters, 1965. Creative Arts Award, Brandeis University, 1965. Aaron Copland Award, Tanglewood, MA, 1966. Naumberg Award, 1971. Seamus National Award, 1994. Cristoph and Stephen Kaske Music Prize, Munich, 1997. Member, American Academy of Arts and Letters.

For More Information: Gagnard, Frank, "Composers Discuss Their Winning Ways," *Times-Picayune,* April 23, 1989; Kerner, Leighton, "The Refinery of the New," *Village Voice,* April 10, 1990.

Commentary: The 1971 Pulitzer Prize in Music was awarded to Mario Davidovsky for *Synchromiums No. 6 for Piano and Electronic Sound,* which premiered on August 19, 1970 at Tanglewood's Berkshire Music Festival.

Mario Davidovsky was born in Medanos, Buenos Aries, Argentina. He was from a Jewish family with a religious music background. He began violin lessons at age seven. He studied composition with Guillermo Graetzer,who was the biggest influence on the young composer. Davidovsky visited the United States in 1958 on the invitation of Aaron Copland. He was already part of the new music scene in Argentina. His interest in electronic music increased with news of the planned Columbia-Princeton Electronic Music Center. Davidovsky returned to the U.S. to study at the new center and eventually became its director. His electronic works include *3 Electronic Studies* and *Contrasts.*

1972

Jacob Druckman 866

Birth: June 26, 1928; New Haven, CT. **Death:** May 24, 1996. **Parents:** Samuel and Miriam (Golder) Druckman. **Education:** Juilliard School of Music, NY: BS, MS. **Spouse:** Murial Helen Topaz (m. 1954). **Children:** Two children.

Prize: *Music,* 1972: *Windows.*

Career: Violinist, Boston Symphony Orchestra, Berkshire Music Festival, summer, 1948; Faculty member, Juilliard School of Music, NY, 1956-1972; Adjunct Faculty, Bard College, NY, 1961-1967; Director, Electronic Music Center, Yale University, 1971-1972; Director, Electronic Music Center, Brooklyn College, NY, 1972-1976; Professor of Music, Brooklyn College, NY, 1972-1976; President, Koussevitsky Foundation, beginning in 1972; Member, Music Advisory Panel, New York State Council on the Arts, 1975-1978; Board of Directors, ASCAP, 1976; Professor of Music and Director of Electronic Music Studio, Yale University School of Music, be-

ginning in 1977; Chairman, Composer Librettist Pael, National Endowment of the Arts, 1980.

Selected Works: *Music for the Dance* (Orchestra), 1949. *Spell* (Instrumental), 1951. *Volpone Overture* (Orchestra), 1953. *Interlude* (Instrumental), 1953. *Suite* (Ballet), 1953. *Performance* (Ballet), 1956. *Animus I* (Instrumental), 1966. *Odds and Evens: A Game* (Orchestra), 1966. *Animus II* (Instrumental), 1968. *Incenters* (Instrumental), 1968. *Animus III* (Instrumental), 1969. *Synapse* (Instrumental), 1971. *Windows* (Orchestra), 1972. *Delizie contente che l'alme beate* (Instrumental), 1973. *Mirage* (Orchestra), 1976. *Bo* (Instrumental), 1977. *Chiaroscuro* (Orchestra), 1977. *Aureole* (Orchestra), 1979. *Tromba marina* (Instrumental), 1981. *Athanor* (Orchestra), 1986. *In Memoriam Vincent Perischetti* (Orchestra), 1987. *Brangle* (Orchestra), 1989.

Other Awards: Fulbright Fellow, 1954-1955. Guggenheim Fellow, Guggenheim Foundation, 1957, 1968. Society of Publications of Music Award, 1967. National Institute of Arts and Letters Grant, 1969. Creative Arts Award, Brandeis University, 1975. Member, American Academy of Arts and Letters, 1978.

For More Information: Tommasini, Anthony, "Jacob Druckman, 67, Dies: A Composer and Teacher," *New York Times,* May 27, 1996; Kerner, Leighton, "Jacob Druckman, 1928-1996," *Village Voice,* June 18, 1996; "Obituaries: Druckman, Jacob," *Current Biography,* August 1996.

Commentary: Jacob Druckman was awarded the 1972 Pulitzer Prize in Music for *Windows,* a work which premiered on March 16, 1972 at Orchestra Hall in Chicago by the Chicago Symphony.

Jacob Raphael Druckman was born in Philadelphia, Pennsylvania. He father was a skilled amateur musician. Jacob began playing piano when he was three, followed three years later by violin lessons. He studied with Louis Gesensway, who introduced him to composition, and later with Aaron Copland at the Berkshire Music Center. Druckman was composer-in-residence at the New York Philharmonic from 1982 to 1986. He has included a varied assortment of percussion instruments in his works, such as *Chiascuro* and *Aureole.*

1973

Elliott Carter

Full entry appears as **#858** under "Music," 1960.

1974

Donald Martino 867

Birth: May 16, 1931; Plainfield, NJ. **Parents:** James E. and Alma Ida (Renz) Martino. **Religion:** Roman Catholic. **Education:** Syracuse University, NY: BMus. Princeton University, NJ: MFA. **Spouse:** Mari Rice (m. 1953; div. 1967); Lora Harvey (m. 1969). **Children:** Anna Maria (MR); Christopher (LH).

Prize: *Music,* 1974: *Notturno.*

Career: Instructor, Music, Princeton University, NJ, 1957-1959; Assistant Professor, Music Theory, Yale University, CT, 1959-1966; Teacher, Composition and Theory, Yale University, CT, summers, 1960-1963; Teacher, Composition, Berkshire Music Center, MA, summers, 1965-1967, 1969; Associate Professor, Yale University, 1966-1969; Chairman, Composition Department, New England Conservatory of Music, Boston, MA, 1969-1980; Composer-in-Residence, Berkshire Music Center, MA, 1973; Visiting Lecturer, Harvard University, MA, 1979; Irving Fine Professor of Music, Brandeis University, 1980-1982; Professor of Music, Harvard University, MA, 1983; Walter Bigelow Rosen Professor Emeritus, beginning in 1993; Member: American Academy of Arts and Letters, American Academy of Arts and Sciences, College Music Society, International Composer's Alliance, American Music Center, International Society of Contemporary Music; Founder, New Haven Chapter, International Society of Contemporary Music, 1964; Director, U.S. Section, International Society of Contemporary Music, 1961-1964; Trustee, International Society of Contemporary Music, 1965; Board of Trustees, International Clarinet Society.

Selected Works: *Portraits: A Secular Cantata* (Vocal), 1954. *Quodlibets* (Chamber), 1954. *Sette canoni enigmatici* (Chamber), 1955-1956. *Contemplations* (Orchestra), 1956. *Cinque frammenti* (Chamber), 1961. *Fantasy — Variations* (Chamber), 1962. *Parisonatina al'dodecafonia* (Chamber), 1964. *Mosaic for Grand Orchestra* (Orchestra), 1965. *Strata* (Chamber), 1966. *Fantasy* (Piano), 1958. *Pianississimo* (Piano), 1970. *7 Pious Pieces* (Vocal), 1972. *Augenmusik: A Mixed Mediacritique* (Vocal), 1972. *Notturno* (Chamber), 1973. *Paradiso Choruses* (Vocal), 1974. *Ritorno* (Orchestra), 1975. *Fantasies and Impromptus* (Piano), 1978. *Quodlibets II* (Chamber), 1980. *Divertissements* (Orchestra), 1981. *Suite in Old Form: Parody Suite* (Piano), 1982. *Canzone e Tarantella sul nome Petrassi* (Chamber), 1984. *The White Island* (Vocal), 1985. *From the Other Side* (Chamber), 1988.

Other Awards: BMI Student Composer Award, 1952, 1953. Bonsall Fellow, 1953-1954. Kosciuszko Scholar, 1953-1954. National Federation of Music Clubs Award, 1953. Kate Neal Kindy Fellow, University of Illinois, 1954-1955. Fulbright Grantee, Florence, Italy, 1954-1956. Pacifica Foundation Award, 1961. Creative Arts Citation, Brandeis University, 1963. Morse Academy Fellow, 1965. Grantee, National Institute of Arts and Letters, 1967. Guggenheim Fellow, Guggenheim Foundation, 1967-1968, 1973-1974, 1982-1983. National Endowment of the Arts Grantee, 1973, 1976, 1979, 1989. Massachussetts Council on the Arts Grantee, 1973, 1979, 1989. Kennedy Center, Freidheim Awards, 1st Prize, 1985. Mark M. Harblit Award, Boston Symphony Orchestra, 1987. Paul Revere Award for Music Autography, Music Publishers Association, 1990, 1991, 1992. Honorary MA, Harvard University, MA, 1983.

For More Information: Kyr, Robert, "Point / Counter-Point: Donald Martino's Radical Statement of Mind and Soul," *Perspectives of New Music,* Summer 1991; Rhodes, Phillip, "A Tribute to Donald Martino on the Occasion of His Sixtieth Birthday (A Memoir)," *Perspectives of New Music,* Summer 1991; Boros, James, "A Conversation with Donald Martino," *Perspectives of New Music,* Summer 1991.

Commentary: *Notturno* won the 1974 Pulitzer Prize in Music for Donald Martino. Commissioned by the Walter W. Naumberg Foundation, this chamber music piece had its premiere on May 15, 1973 at Alice Tully Hall at Lincoln Center in New York City.

Donald Martino was born in Plainfield, New Jersey. He played clarinet in the school band and the experience of playing a march made him consider becoming a professional musician. He played clarinet with several bands. He received a scholarship to attend Syracuse University and he studied composition there with Ernst Bacon. He went on to Princeton University to study with Milton Babitt and Roger Sessions. His first major work was *Contemplations for Orchestra,* written in 1957 and not performed until 1965.

1975

Dominick Argento 868

Birth: October 27, 1927; York, PA. **Parents:** Michael and Nicolina (Amato) Argento. **Education:** Peabody Conservatory, MD: BA. Eastman School of Music, NY. **Spouse:** Carolyn Bailey (m. 1954).

Prize: *Music,* 1975: *From the Diary of Virginia Woolf.*

Career: Composer and educator; Cryptographer, U.S. Army, 1945-1947; Co-Founder, Hilltop Opera of Baltimore, MD; Instructor, Hampton Institute in Hampton, VA; Member, National Academy of Arts and Letters; Instructor, Yale University, the New England Conservatory, Brandeis; Walter Bigelow Rosen Professor of Composition at Harvard; Member: AS-

CAP, American Academy and Institute of Arts and Letters.

Selected Works: *Song about Spring* (Vocal), 1950. *Sicilian Limes* (Opera), 1954. *Ode to the West Wind* (Vocal), 1956. *Resurrection of Don Juan* (Ballet), 1956. *The Boor* (Opera), 1957. *Colonel Jonathan the Saint* (Opera), 1958-1961. *Divertimento* (Chamber), 1958. *6 Elizabethan Songs* (Vocal), 1962. *Christopher Sly* (Opera), 1963. *The Masque of Angels* (Opera), 1963. *Royal Invitation* (Chamber), 1964. *The Revelation of St. John the Divine* (Vocal), 1966. *Variations* (Chamber), 1966. *Shoemakers Holiday* (Opera), 1967. *A Nation of Cowslips* (Vocal), 1968. *Letters from Composers* (Vocal), 1968. *Bravo Mozart!* (Chamber), 1969. *Tria carmina paschalia* (Vocal), 1970. *Postcard from Morocco* (Opera), 1971. *A Ring of Time* (Orchestra), 1972. *To Be Sung upon the Water* (Vocal), 1973. *A Water Bird Talk* (Vocal), 1974. *From the Diary of Virginia Woolf* (Vocal), 1974. *Jonah and the Whale* (Vocal), 1974. *The Voyage of Edgar Allen Poe* (Opera), 1976. *In Praise of Music* (Vocal), 1977. *Miss Havisham's Fire* (Opera), 1978. *Casonova's Homecoming* (Opera), 1985. *Le Tombeau d'Edgar Poe* (Orchestra), 1985. *Rossini in Paris* (Orchestra), 1986. *The Aspern Papers* (Opera), 1988.

Other Awards: Fulbright Fellow, Italy, 1951. Annual Composition Prize, Peabody Conservatory. York High School Hall of Fame. American Academy of Arts and Letters Grant. Honorary DHL, York College.

For More Information: *New York Times,* November 4, 1972, p22; *New York Times,* May 6, 1975, p. 34; Davis, Peter G., "The Browning Version," *New York,* February 25, 1985, p. 62-63.

Commentary: The 1975 Pulitzer Prize for Music was won by Dominick Argento for *From the Diary of Virginia Woolf,* a piece for medium voice and piano commissioned by the Schubert Club of St. Paul. Argento composed the piece for the British mezzo-soprano Janet Baker. Accompanied by pianist Martin Isepp, Baker sang for the first time at Orchestra Hall in Minneapolis, Minnesota on January 5, 1975.

Dominick Argento was born in York, Pennsylvania. He excelled at the piano and studied textbooks on harmony and composition that he borrowed from the public library after reading about the lives of George Gershwin and other musicians. He availed himself of the GI Bill and attended the Peabody Conservatory in Baltimore. He received a Fulbright scholarship allowing him to travel to Italy and study with Pietro Scarpini at the Conservatorio Cherubini in Florence. In the view of many critics, his opera *The Voyage of Edgar Allan Poe* was a critical milestone for American opera.

1976

Ned Rorem   869

Birth: October 23, 1923; Richmond, IN. **Parents:** Dr. Clarence Rufus and Gladys (Miller) Rorem. **Religion:** Quaker. **Education:** Northwestern University, IL. Curtis Institute of Music, PA: BA. Juilliard School of Music, NY: MA.

Prize: *Music,* 1976: *Air Music.*

Career: Professor, Composer-in-Residence, University of Buffalo, NY, 1959-1961; Professor, Composition, University of Utah, 1965-1967; Professor, Curtis Institute, 1980-1984; Author of articles on music for newspapers and magazines.

Selected Works: *A Quiet Afternoon* (Piano), 1948. *Barcarolles* (Piano), 1949. *Mountain Song* (Chamber), 1949. *A Childhood Miracle* (Opera), 1952. *Design* (Orchestra), 1953. *Sicilienne* (Piano), 1950. *The Robbers* (Opera), 1956. *Slow Waltz* (Piano), 1956. *Sinfonia* (Orchestra), 1957. *Eagles* (Orchestra), 1958. *Pilgrims* (Orchestra), 1958. *Ideas for Easy Orchestra* (Orchestra), 1961. *Lions* (Orchestra), 1963. *Lovers* (Chamber), 1964. *Miss Julie* (Opera), 1965. *The Paris Diary of Ned Rorem* (Writings), 1966. *Water Music* (Orchestra), 1966. *Music from Inside Out* (Writings), 1967. *The New York Diary* (Writings), 1967. *3 Sisters Who Are Not Sisters* (Opera), 1968. *Bertha* (Opera), 1968. *Concerto in 6 Movements* (Orchestra), 1969. *Music and People* (Writings), 1969. *Critical Affairs: A Composer's Journal* (Writings), 1970. *Fables* (Opera), 1970. *Day Music* (Chamber), 1971. *Night Music* (Chamber), 1972. *Solemn Prelude* (Orchestra), 1973. *Pure Contraption* (Writings), 1973. *The Nantucket Diary* (Writings), 1973-1985. *Air Music* (Orchestra), 1974. *The Final Diary* (Writings), 1974. *Assembly and Fall* (Orchestra), 1975. *Book of Hours* (Chamber), 1975. *Hearing* (Opera), 1976. *A Quaker Reader* (Organ), 1976. *Romeo and Juliet* (Chamber), 1977. *Sunday Morning* (Orchestra), 1977. *3 Slow Pieces* (Chamber), 1978. *An Absolute Gift* (Writings), 1978. *Remembering Tommy* (Orchestra), 1979. *After Reading Shakespeare* (Chamber), 1980. *Double Concerto in 10 Movements* (Orchestra), 1981. *Views from the Oldest House* (Organ), 1981. *Winter Pages* (Chamber), 1981. *An American Oratorio* (Vocal), 1983. *Dances* (Chamber), 1983. *Picnic on the Marne* (Chamber), 1983. *Setting the Tone: Essays and a Diary* (Writings), 1983. *Paul's Blues* (Writings), 1984. *The End of Summer* (Chamber), 1985. *Scenes from Childhood* (Chamber), 1985. *Song and Dance* (Piano), 1986. *Te Deum* (Vocal), 1987. *Bright Music* (Chamber), 1988. *A Quaker Reader* (Orchestra), 1988. *Setting the Score: Essays on Music* (Writings), 1988.

Other Awards: Music Libraries Association Award, Song, 1948:"Lordly Hudson." Gershwin

Memorial Award, 1949. Lili Boulanger Award, 1950. Fulbright Fellow, Paris, France, 1951-1952. Guggenheim Fellow, Guggenheim Foundation, 1957-1958, 1977-1978. National Institute of Arts and Letters Award, 1968. Grammy Award, Best Orchestral Recording, 1989. Honorary DFA, Northwestern University, IL, 1977.

For More Information: Von Rhein, John, "A Golden Boy," *Chicago Tribune,* November 4, 1990; Beck, Eleonora M., "Ned Rorem on Music and Politics: An Interview in Celebration of the Composer's Seventieth Birthday," *Current Musicology,* 1993; Rorem, Ned, *Knowing When To Stop: A Memoir,* New York: Simon & Schuster, 1994; Smith J. Patrick, "Diamond Ned Rorem," *Opera News,* March 28, 1998.

Commentary: The 1976 Pulitzer Prize in Music was awarded to Ned Rorem for *Air Music,* which premiered on December 5, 1975 in a performance by the Cincinnati Symphony Orchestra. It is subtitled *Ten Etudes for Orchestra.*

Ned Rorem was born in Richmond, Indiana. He began piano lessons at an early age. His formal music education began when he was 15, at the American Conservatory in Chicago, studying harmony under Leo Sowerby. Later he would study composition and orchestration with Gian-Carlo Menotti and composition with Aaron Copland and Virgil Thomson. He attended the Juilliard School of Music. He is adept at songwriting, finding poetry and literature inspirational. His other works include *Five Prayers for the Young,* and *Poems of Love and the Rain.*

1977

Richard Wernick   870

Birth: January 16, 1934; Boston, MA. **Parents:** Louis and Irene (Prince) Wernick. **Education:** Brandeis University, MA: BA. **Spouse:** Beatrice Messina (m. 1956). **Children:** Lewis, Adam, Peter.

Prize: Music, 1977: *Visions of Terror and Wonder.*

Career: Music Director, Royal Winnipeg Ballet, Canada, 1957-1958; Music Instructor, University of Buffalo, NY, 1964-1965; Assistant Professor of Music and Director of University Symposium, University of Chicago, 1965-1968; Conductor, Pennsylvania Contemporary Players, 1968-1993; Professor of Music, University of Pennsylvania, 1968-1996; Professor Emeritus, University of Pennsylvania, 1996; Co-Founder, Committtee on Youth Orchestra of Delaware County, PA; Member of Conservatory of Contemporary Music, The Philadelphia Orchestra, 1983-1993; Member: Board of Directors, Theodore Presser Company; Member: ASCAP.

Selected Works: *Hexagrams,* 1962. *Stretti,* 1965. *Lyrics from IXI,* 1966. *Haiku of Basho,* 1968. *Moonsongs from the Japanese,* 1969. *A Prayer for Jerusalem,* 1971. *Kaddish Requiem,* 1971. *Songs of Rembrance,* 1973. *Visions of Terror and Wonder,* 1976. *Contemplations of the Tenth Muse Books I-II,* 1977. *Introits and Canons,* 1977. *A Poison Tree,* 1979. *Portraits of Antiquity,* 1981. *The Oracle for Shimon Bar Yochai,* 1982. *Musica Ptolemeica,* 1982. *Oracle II,* 1986.

Other Awards: Music Award, National Institute of Arts and Letters, 1976. National Endowment for the Arts Grantee, 1975, 1979, 1982. Ford Foundation Fellow, 1962-1964. Guggenheim Fellow, Guggenheim Foundation, 1976.

For More Information: McLellan, Joseph, "Friendships on a High Note," *Washington Post,* February 9, 1991; McCardell, Charles, "Wernick Wins Friedheim: Finally, No Tie in Composing Competition," *Washington Post,* November 11, 1991.

Commentary: Richard Wernick was awarded the 1977 Pulitzer Prize in Music for *Visions of Terror and Wonder,* a work for mezzo-soprano and orchestra which premiered on July 19, 1976 at the Aspen Music Festival. It was commissioned by the Festival's Conference on Contemporary Music through a grant from the National Endowment for the Arts.

Richard Frank Wernick was born in Boston, Massachussetts. He was inspired to follow a career in music after hearing Bartok's *Concerto for Orchestra* when he was age 11. He attended Brandeis University and studied music composition. He later attended the Berkshire Music Center over two successive summers and studied composition with Aaron Copland, Ernst Toch, and Boris Blacher. While at the Center, he also received instruction on conducting from Leonard Bernstein and Seymour Lipkin. His other works include *A Prayer for Jerusalem* and *Kaddish Requiem, A Secular Service for the Victims of Indo-China.*

1978

Michael Colgrass   871

Birth: April 22, 1932; Chicago, IL. **Parents:** Michael Clement and Ann (H.) Colgrass. **Education:** University of Illinois: MusB. **Spouse:** Ulla Damgaard (m. 1966). **Children:** Neal.

Prize: Music, 1978: *Deja Vu for Percussion Quartet and Orchestra.*

Career: Scholar, Tanglewood, MA, 1952-1954; Scholar, Aspen, CO, 1953; Served in U.S. Army, 1954-1956; Freelance sole percussionist, major New York music organizations, beginning in 1956; Narrator, Boston Symphony, 1969; Narrator, Philadelphia Orchestra, 1970; Director, *Virgil's Dream,* Brighton Festival; Soloist, Danish Radio Orchestra, 1965; Director, Opera Nightingale Incorporated, University of Illinois Contemporary Music Festival, 1975; Author, poet, composer of theatre works, beginning in 1966; Contributor of articles, music publications; Columnist, *Music* magazine.

Selected Works: *Chamber Music*, 1954. *Light Spirit*, 1963. *Sea Shadow*, 1966. *New People*, 1969. *The Earth's a Baked Apple*, 1969. *Letter from Mozart*, 1976. *Best Wishes*, 1976. *Concertmasters*, 1976. *Chaconne*, 1984. *Winds of Magual: A Musical Fable*, 1985.

Other Awards: Guggenheim Fellow, Guggenheim Foundation, 1964-1965, 1968-1969. Fromm Award, 1966. Rockefeller Grantee, 1967-1969. Chemical Bank Award, 1971. Ford Foundation Grantee, 1972. Emmy Award, Best Documentary, 1982: WGBH TV Film, *Soundings: The Music of Michael Colgrass.* Winner, Louis N. Sudler International Wind Band Composers Competition, 1985:"Winds of Magua." DeMoulin Prize, National Band Association, 1985. Barlow International Prize, 1986.

For More Information: *New York Times,* May 28, 1972; *High Fidelity/Musical America,* November 1978.

Commentary: The 1978 Pulitzer Prize in Music was awarded to Michael Colgrass for *Deja Vu for Percussion Quartet and Orchestra,* a work which premiered on October 20, 1977 by its commissioning orchestra, the New York Philharmonic.

Michael Charles Colgrass was born in Chicago. He began to play the drums when he was 10 years old. Colgrass attended the University of Illinois at Urbana and studied music with Paul Price and Eugene Weigel. He later attended the Berkshire Music Center, studying composition under Lukas Foss. His music career seemed destined to be that of a performer, but a loss of memory after performing at Carnegie Hall left him feeling that he was doing too much physically and mentally. He then decided to focus on composing. His other works include *Concertmasters* and *Flashbacks.*

1979

Joseph Schwantner   872

Birth: March 22, 1943; Chicago, IL. **Education:** Chicago Conservatory College, IL: BA. Northwestern University, IL: MusM, MusD. **Spouse:** Janet Elaine Rossate (m. 1965). **Children:** Two children.

Prize: *Music,* 1979: *Aftertones for Infinity.*

Career: Composer and educator; Instructor, Music Theory and Composition, Chicago Conservatory College, 1968-1969; Instructor, Music Theory and Composition, Pacific Lutheran University, Tacoma, WA, 1968-1969; Assistant Professor of Theory, Ball State University, IN, 1969-1970; Assistant Professor

of Composition and Theory, Eastman School of Music, 1970-1973; Assistant Professor of Composition, Eastman School of Music, 1975-1980; Lecturer in Music, University of Texas at Austin, 1975; Guest Composer and Lecturer, Yale University, CT, 1979; Guest Composer and Lecturer, University of Michigan, Ann Arbor, 1979; Professor of Composition, Eastman School of Music, beginning in 1980.

Selected Works: *Diaphonia Intervallum* (Chamber), 1965. *Chronicon* (Chamber), 1968. *Consortium I* (Chamber), 1970. *Consortium II* (Chamber), 1971. *Modus Caelestis* (Orchestra), 1973. *Autumn Canticles* (Chamber), 1974. *Elixir* (Chamber), 1974. *Canticle of the Evening Bells* (Chamber), 1976. *In Aeternum* (Chamber), 1976. *And the Mountains Rising Nowhere* (Orchestra), 1977. *Wild Angels of the Open Hills* (Chamber), 1977. *Aftertones of Infinity* (Orchestra), 1978. *Wind Willow, Whisper* (Chamber), 1980. *Music of Amber* (Chamber), 1981. *Through Interior Worlds* (Chamber), 1981. *2 Poems of Agueda Izarro* (Chamber), 1981. *New Morning for the World* (Orchestra), 1982. *Magabunda* (Orchestra), 1983. *Distant Runes and Incantations* (Orchestra), 1984. *Dreamcaller* (Orchestra), 1984. *A Sudden Rainbow* (Orchestra), 1984. *Toward Light* (Orchestra), 1986. *From Afar* (Orchestra), 1988. *Freeflight* (Orchestra), 1989. *A Play of Shadows* (Orchestra), 1990.

Other Awards: Broadcast Music Incorporated Student Composers Award, 1965, 1966, 1967. Bearns Prize, Columbia University, 1967. William T. Faricy Award for Creative Music, 1967. National Endowment of the Arts Grant, 1977. Guggenheim Fellow, Guggenheim Foundation, 1978.

For More Information: Rothstein, Edward, "A Meditation on Death With Drums and Gongs," *New York Times,* January 9, 1995; Harris, Paul A, "Poetry Without Words," *St. Louis Post-Dispatch,* November 19, 1995.

Commentary: *Aftertones for Infinity* won the 1973 Pulitzer Prize in Music for Joseph Schwantner. It premiered on January 29, 1979 at Alice Tully Hall at Lincoln Center in New York City by American Composers Orchestra.

Joseph Schwantner was born in Chicago. He studied the tuba in grade school and played in the school band. He took private guitar lessons and studied theory and composition in high school. He won numerous awards as his music education advanced, including three B.M.I. Young Composer Awards. Schwantner joined the faculty of the Eastman School of Music in 1970, becoming a professor in 1980. His other works include *Diaphonia Intervallum* and *Music of Amber.*

1980

David Del Tredici   873

Birth: March 16, 1932; Cloverdale, CA. **Education:** University of California, Berkeley: BA. Aspen School, CO. Princeton University, NJ: MFA.

Prize: *Music,* 1980: *In Memory of a Summer Day.*

Career: Pianist, Fromm Fellowship Players, Tanglewood, MA, summers, 1964 and 1965; Resident Composer, Marlboro Festival, VT, 1966-1967; Assistant Professor of Music, Harvard University, MA, 1967-1971; Teaching Associate, Boston University, 1971; Commissioned composer of musical works, beginning in 1971; Composer-in-Residence, Aspen Music Festival, 1975.

Selected Works: *4 Songs* (Voice and Piano), 1958-1960. *Soliloquy* (Piano), 1958. *2 Songs,* 1959. *Fantasy Pieces* (Piano), 1959-1960. *Scherzo,* 1960. *I Hear an Army,* 1963-1964. *Night Conjure-Verse,* 1965. *Syzygy,* 1966. *The Last Gospel,* 1967. *Poppourri,* 1968. *An Alice Symphony,* 1969-1976. *Adventures Underground,* 1975. *Vintage Alice: Fantascene on a Mad Tea Party,* 1972. *Final Alice,* 1976. *March to Tonality,* 1983-1985. *Haddock's Eyes,* 1985-1986. *Steps,* 1990.

Other Awards: Guggenheim Fellow, Guggenheim Foundation, 1966.

For More Information: Crabb, Michael, "Uncovering Alice: Canada's National Ballet Hosts a Tetley Tea Party," *Dance Magazine,* July 1986, p. 36-41; Kerner, Leighton, "The Refinery of the New," *Village Voice,* April 10, 1990; Schwarz, K. Robert, "A Composer Caught in Alice's Web," *New York Times,* May 24, 1998.

Commentary: David Del Tredici was awarded the 1980 Pulitzer Prize in Music for *In Memory of a Summer Day.* A work for soprano solo and orchestra, it was commissioned by the St. Louis Symphony for its 100th anniversary and premiered on February 23, 1980. This work was followed by *Happy Voices,* and both were part of a larger work titled *Child Alice.*

David Del Tredici was born in Cloverdale, California. He studied the piano from the age of 12. He was a talented musician and recitals were numerous. At 16, he was guest artist with the San Francisco Symphony. Del Tredici attended the University of California at Berkeley, studying with Seymour Shifrin, Andrew Imbrie, and Arnold Elston. His first critically acclaimed work, *I Hear An Army,* was based on a poem by James Joyce. This placed him in the spotlight which the *Child Alice* series illuminated all the more brightly.

1981
No award

1982

Roger Sessions   874

Birth: December 28, 1896; Brooklyn, NY. **Death:** March 16, 1985. **Parents:** Ruth (Huntington) Sessions. **Education:** Harvard University, MA: BA. Yale University, CT: BMus. **Spouse:** Barbara Foster (m.1920); Elizabeth Franck (m.1936). **Children:** Two children.

Prize: *Music,* 1982: *Concerto for Orchestra. Special Awards and Citations: Music,* 1974, "Life's work as a distinguished American Composer."

Career: Assistant, Music Department, Smith College, MA, 1917-1921; Resident of and student in Europe, 1919-1933, 1925-1928; Assistant Director and Instructor of Theory, Cleveland Institute of Music, OH, 1921-1925; Co-Founder, Copland-Sessions concerts in Contemporary Music, 1928; Instructor, Malkin School of Music, MA, 1933; Instructor, Boston University College of Music, 1933; Instructor, Dalcroze School, NY, 1933-1934; Instructor, New Jersey College for Women, 1935-1937; Instructor, Princeton University, NJ, 1935-1936; Assistant Professor, Princeton University, 1937-1940; Instructor of Composition, University of California, Berkeley, summers, 1935, 1936, 1938. Associate Professor, Princeton University, 1940-1944; Professor of Composition, University of California, Berkeley, 1945-1953; Fulbright Fellow, Academia Luigi Cherubini, Florence, Italy, 1952-1953; William Shubael Conant Professor of Music, Princeton University, NJ, 1953-1965; Instructor, Composition, Juilliard School of Music, NY, beginning in 1965; Ernest Bloch Professor, University of California, Berkeley, 1966-1967; Charles Eliot Norton Professor, Harvard University, 1968-1969; Visiting Professor of Composition, University of Iowa, 1971.

Selected Works: *Lancelot and Elaine* (Opera), 1910. *Nocturne* (Orchestra), 1921-1923. *The Black Maskers* (Incidental), 1923. *Romualdo's Song* (Vocal), 1923. *The Fall of the House of Usher* (Opera), 1925. *Turandot* (Incidental), 1925. *3 Chorale Preludes* (Organ), 1924-1926. *On the Beach* (Vocal), 1930. *3 Dirges* (Orchestra), 1933. *4 Pieces for Children* (Piano), 1935-1939. *From My Diary* (Piano), 1937-1939. *Chorale* (Organ), 1938. *Montezuma* (Opera), 1941-1963. *Turn, O Libertad* (Vocal), 1944. *The Trial of Lucullus* (Opera), 1947. *Mass for Unison Chair* (Vocal), 1955. *Divertimento* (Orchestra), 1959-1960. *When Lilacs Last in the Dooryard Bloom'd* (Vocal), 1964-1970. *Rhapsody* (Orchestra), 1970. *Canons* (Chamber), 1971. *3 Choruses on Biblical Tests* (Vocal), 1971-1972. *Concerto for Orchestra* (Orchestra), 1979-1981.

Other Awards: Guggenheim Fellow, Guggenheim Foundation, 1926, 1927. Walter Damrosch Fellowship, 1928-1931. Carnegie Fellowship, 1931-1932. Fulbright Fellowship, 1952-1953. Creative Arts Award, Brandeis University, 1958. Honorary Life Member, International Society of Contemporary Music, 1959. Member, Academy of Arts in West Berlin, Germany, 1960. Academy of Fine Arts in Buenos Aires, Argentina, 1965. Gold Medal, MacDowell Association, 1968. Honorary Life Member, National Institute of Arts and Letters, 1938. Honorary MusMs: Wesleyan University, CT, 1958; Rutgers University, NJ, 1962; Harvard University, MA, 1964; Brandeis University, MA, 1965; University of Pennsylvania, 1966; New England Conservatory, MA, 1967; University of California at Berkeley, 1967; Cleveland Institute of Music, OH, 1975.

For More Information: Olmstead, Andrea, ed., *Olmstead: Conversations with Roger Sessions,* Boston: Northeastern University, 1987; Nott, Michael, "Roger Sessions's Fugal Studies with Ernest Bloch: A Glimpse into the Workshop," *American Music,* Fall 1989; Lochhead, Judy, "A Question of Technique: The Second and Third Piano Sonatas of Roger Sessions," *The Journal of Musicology,* Fall 1996.

Commentary: Roger Sessions won the 1982 Pulitzer Prize in Music for *Concerto for Orchestra,* a work which premiered on October 23, 1981 by the Boston Symphony Orchestra conducted by Seiji Ozawa. Sessions was also awarded Special Award and Citation in Music in 1974 for his "life's work as a distinguished American composer."

Roger Sessions was born in Brooklyn, New York. His mother was a trained pianist who was educated in Leipzig, Germany. Sessions is said to have had perfect pitch as an infant. He studied piano from age five. After hearing a performance of Wagner's *Die Meistersinger,* Sessions made up his mind to become a composer. He attended Yale University and was a student of Horatio Parker. He took private lessons with Ernst Bloch and continued with him at the Cleveland Institute of Music. He worked with Aaron Copland to present the Copland-Sessions Concerts in New York City from 1928-1931. He served as co-director of the Columbia-Princeton Electronic Music Center in 1959. Many composers studied under him at the Juilliard School of Music from 1965 to 1985. *When Lilacs Last in the Dooryard Bloom'd* is one of his most important works.

1983

Ellen Taaffe Zwilich   875

Birth: April 3, 1939; Miami, FL. **Parents:** Edward Porter and Ruth (Howard) Taaffe. **Education:** Florida State University: MusB, MusM. Juilliard School of Music, NY: DMusArts. **Spouse:** Joseph Zwilich (m. 1965; dec.1979).

Prize: *Music,* 1983: *Symphony No. 1.*

Career: Violinist, American Symposium, 1965-1973; Premiere, Symphony for Orchestra, Pierre Boulez, NY, 1975; Composer of Chamber Symposium and Passages, Boston Musica Viva, Richard Pittman, 1979, 1982; Composer of Symphony 1, Gunther Schuller, American Composers Orchestra, 1982; Vice President, American Music Center, 1982-1984; Composer-in-Residence, Santa Fe Chamber Music Festival, 1990; Composer-in-Residence, American Academy, Rome, Italy, 1990; Member: American Academy of Arts and Letters; Honorary Lifetime Member, American Federation of Musicians; Member: Board of Directors, American Music Center, BMI Foundation, Board of Directors, MacDowell Colony, Florida Artists Hall of Fame, Carnegie Hall Composers Chair.

Selected Works: *Einsame Nacht* (Vocal), 1971. *Im Nebel* (Vocal), 1972. *Sonata in 3 Movements* (Chamber), 1973-1974. *Symposium* (Orchestra), 1973. *Trompeten* (Vocal), 1974. *Clarino Quartet* (Chamber), 1977. *Emlekezat* (Vocal), 1978. *Chamber Symphony* (Chamber), 1979. *Passages* (Vocal), 1981. *Passages* (Orchestra), 1982. *Divertemento* (Chamber), 1983. *Intrada* (Chamber), 1983. *Prologue and Variations* (Orchestra), 1983. *Celebrations* (Orchestra), 1984. *Concerto Grosso 1985* (Orchestra), 1985. *Cello Symphony* (Orchestra), 1985. *Images* (Orchestra), 1987. *Tanzspiel* (Stage), 1987. *Symbolon* (Orchestra), 1988. *Praeludium* (Chamber), 1988.

Other Awards: Elizabeth Sprague Coolidge Chamber Music Prize, 1974. Gold Medal, G.B. Viotti, Vercelli, Italy, 1975. Martha Baird Rockefeller Fund Grantee, 1977, 1979, 1982. Citation, Ernst von Dohnanyi, 1981. Composer's Award, Lancaster Symphony Orchestra, 1987. Arturo Toscanini Music Critics Award, 1987. Alfred I. DuPont Award, 1991. Honorary LHDs: Manhattanville College, NY, 1991; Marymount College, NY, 1994; Mannes College of Music, New York, NY, 1995. Honorary MusDs: Oberlin College, OH, 1987. Converse College, SC, 1994.

For More Information: Moor, Paul, "Ellen Taaffe Zwilich," *Musical America,* March 1989; Elliott, Susan, "They're Playing Her Song," *Savvy Woman,* April 1990; Schwarz, K. Robert, "A Composer Who Actually Earns a Living Composing," *New York Times,* March 22, 1998.

Commentary: Ellen Taaffe Zwilich was awarded the 1983 Pulitzer Prize in Music for *Symphony No. 1,* a work in three movements for orchestra. Commissioned by the American Composers Orchestra, it premiered and was performed by that orchestra on May 5, 1982 at Alice Tully Hall at Lincoln Center in New York City.

Ellen Taaffe Zwilich was born in Miami, Florida. She began piano lessons at an early age and her first compositions were done at age 10. She studied violin with Richard Burgin and Ivan Galamian and composition with John Boda. She attended the Juilliard School of Music and became the first woman to receive a DMusArts in composition from that institution. While there she studied with Elliott Carter and Roger Sessions. She is quite successful, with commissions and awards accumulating.

1984

Bernard Rands   876
Birth: March 2, 1935; Sheffield, England. **Education:** University of Bangor, Wales: MusB, MusM.

Prize: *Music,* 1984: *"Canti del Sole" for Tenor and Orchestra.*

Career: Private student, composition, 1958-1962; Former concert performer, Europe, Australia and the U.S.; Co-founding Artistic Director, Contemporary Music Festival, California Institute of the Arts; Lecturer, University of Wales, 1960-1966; Visiting Fellow, Princeton University, NJ, 1966-1967; Music Faculty member, Princeton University; Professor of Music, University of California, San Diego, 1975-1985; Professor of Music, Boston University, 1985-1989; Professor of Music, Harvard University, beginning in 1989; Composer-in-Residence, Philadelphia Orchestra, 1989-1996.

Selected Works: *Tre expressioni* (Instrumental Ensemble), 1960. *Actions for 6* (Instrumental Ensemble), 1962-1963. *Formants 1—Les Gestes* (Instrumental Ensemble), 1965. *Sound Patterns 1* (Voices and Instruments), 1967. *Per esempio* (Orchestra), 1968. *Wildtrack 1 and 2* (Orchestra), 1973. *Agenda* (Orchestra), 1969-1970. *Formants 2—Labyrinthe* (Instrumental Ensemble), 1969-1970. *Ballad 1* (Voices and Instruments), 1970. *Tableau* (Instrumental Ensemble), 1970. *Memo 1* (Instrumental Ensemble), 1971. *"As All Get Out"* (Instrumental Ensemble), 1972. *deja* (Instrumental Ensemble), 1972. *Mesalliance* (Orchestra), 1972. *Response—Memo 1B* (Instrumental Ensemble), 1973. *Aum* (Orchestra), 1974. *Cuaderno* (Instrumental Ensemble), 1974. *Scherzi* (Instrumental Ensemble), 1974. *Serenata 75* (Instrumental Ensemble), 1976. *Madrigali* (Orchestra), 1977. *Memo 2B* (Theater), 1980. *Memo 2D* (Theater), 1980. *Obbligato — Memo 2C* (Instrumental Ensemble), 1980. *Canti del sole* (Orchestra), 1983-1984. *Flickering Shadows* (Voices and Instruments), 1983-1984. *Le Tambourin* (Orchestra), 1984. *Ceremonial 1* (Orchestra), 1985. *Requiescant* (Orchestra), 1985-1986. *Serenata 85,* 1986. *Hiraeth* (Orchestra), 1987. *Body and Shadow* (Orchestra), 1988. *Among the Voices* (Voices and Instruments), 1988. *In the Receding Mist,* 1988.

Other Awards: Granada Fellow, Creative Arts, York University, 1968-1975. California Arts Council Award, 1978, 1992. Koussevitsky Award, 1984, 1994. Barlow Award, 1994. Honorary MusD, University of Sheffield, England, 1996.

For More Information: Dyer, Richard, "Two Premieres, Two Composers, a Husband and Wife," *Boston Globe,* March 30, 1997; Griffiths, Paul, "For a Couple of Composers, the Same Soloist, the Same Stage, the Same Night," *New York Times,* April 2, 1997.

Commentary: Bernard Rands won the 1984 Pulitzer Prize in Music for *"Canti del Sole" for Tenor and Orchestra,* a work which premiered on June 8, 1983 by the New York Philharmonic Orchestra.

Bernard Rands was born in Sheffield, England. He studied piano and organ at home and music and Celtic cultures at the University of Wales. His interest took him to Rome to study musicology with Roman Vlad and to Pierre Boulez for conducting. He has been an educator and a composer. Rands's influences have been religious as well as mathematical and sonoristic. His many works include *Canti lunatici* and *Aum.*

1985

Stephen Albert   877
Birth: February 6, 1941; New York, NY. **Death:** December 27, 1992. **Education:** Eastman School of Music, NY. Philadelphia Musical Academy. **Spouse:** Blanche Silagy (m. 1965). **Children:** One son, one daughter.

Prize: *Music,* 1985: *Symphony, RiverRun.*

Career: Composer of commissioned works throughout career; Faculty member, Philadelphia Music Academy, PA, 1970; Guest Lecturer, Stanford University, CA, 1970-1971.

Selected Works: *Illuminations* (Orchestra), 1962. *Supernatural Songs* (Orchestra), 1963. *Imitations* (Orchestra), 1964. *Wedding Songs* (Orchestra), 1965. *Bacchae* (Orchestra), 1967-1968. *Wolf Time* (Orchestra), 1968. *Letters from the Golden Notebook* (Orchestra), 1971. *Cathedral Music* (Orchestra), 1972. *Voices Within* (Orchestra), 1975. *To Wake the Dead* (Chamber), 1979. *Winterfire* (Chamber), 1979. *Music from the Stone Harp* (Chamber), 1980. *Into Eclipse* (Chamber), 1983-1984. *RiverRun* (Orchestra), 1983-1984. *TreeStone* (Chamber), 1983-1984. *Flower of the Mountain* (Orchestra), 1986. *Concerto in 1 Mountain* (Orchestra), 1986. *Anthem and Processionals* (Orchestra), 1987.

Other Awards: First Prize, BMI Hemispheric Competition, 1962. Bearns Prize, Columbia University, NY. Huntington Hartford Fellowship, 1965. Margaret Baird Rockefeller Grant, 1965. Prix de Rome, 1965-1967. Ford Foundation Grant, 1967-

1968. Guggenheim Fellow, Guggenhiem Foundation, 1968-1969.

For More Information: Dyer, Richard, "The 'Unknown' Pulitzer Winner," *Boston Globe,* August 20, 1989; Kozinn, Allan, "Stephen J. Albert, 51, Composer: Won a Pulitzer for His 'Riverrun,'" *New York Times,* December 29, 1992; Siegel, Ed, "The Sudden Stilling of a Melodic Voice," *Boston Globe,* December 29, 1992.

Commentary: The 1985 Pulitzer Prize in Music was awarded to Stephen Albert for *Symphony, River-Run,* a work which premiered on January 17, 1985 by the National Symphony Orchestra.

Stephen Albert was born in New York City. His mother played the piano by ear and often played recordings. He began playing trumpet while in the third grade. He added French horn and piano to his repertoire in the sixth grade. Albert attended the Eastman School of Music and studied composition with Bernard Rogers. He transferred to the Philadelphia Musical Academy and studied with Roy Harris and Joseph Castaldo. Albert received a grant from the National Endowment for the Arts (NEA) to help him in writing *To Wake The Dead,* derived from a verse found in James Joyce's *Finnegan's Wake.*

1986

George Perle   878

Birth: May 6, 1915; Bayonne, NJ. **Parents:** Joseph and Mary (Sanders) Perlman. **Education:** DePaul University, IL: MusB. American Conservatory of Music, IL: MusM. New York University: PhD. **Spouse:** Laura Slobe (m. 1940); Barbara Philips (m. 1958; dec.); Shirley Gobis Rhoades (m. 1982). **Children:** Kathy, Annette (LS); Max Massey, Paul Rhoads, Daisy Rhoads (SGR).

Prize: *Music,* 1986: *Wind Quintet IV.*

Career: Faculty member, University of Louisville, 1949-1957; Faculty member, University of California, Davis, 1957-1961; Assistant and Associate Professor, City University of New York, 1961-1985; Faculty member, Juilliard School of Music, 1963; Faculty member, Yale University, CT, 1965-1966; Faculty member, University of Southern California, summer, 1965; Faculty member, Tanglewood, summers, 1967, 1980, 1987; Visiting Bing Cary Professor of Music, Professor of Music, University of Buffalo, State University of New York, 1971-1972; Visiting Professor, University of Pennsylvania, 1976, 1980; Visiting Professor, Columbia University, NY, 1979, 1983; Professor Emeritus, City University of New York, beginning in 1985; Visiting Ernst Bloch Professor of Music, University of California, Berkeley, 1989; Composer-in-Residence, San Francisco Symposium, 1989-1991; Visiting Distinguished Professor

of Music, New York University, 1994; Member: American Musicology Society, ASCAP, American Academy of Arts and Letters.

Selected Works: *Interlude and Fugue* (Piano), 1937. *Hebrew Melodies* (Solo Instrumental), 1945. *Piano Piece* (Piano), 1945. *6 Preludes* (Piano), 1946. *Solemn Procession* (Chamber), 1947. *Interrupted Story* (Piano), 1956. *3 Interventions* (Piano), 1957. *The Birds* (Vocal), 1961. *Short Sonata* (Piano), 1964. *6 Bagatelles* (Chamber), 1965. *Toccata* (Piano), 1969. *Suite in C: Dodecatonal Suite* (Piano), 1970. *Fantasy—Variations* (Piano), 1971. *6 Etudes* (Piano), 1973-1976. *Sonnets of Praise and Lamentation: From the 18th Psalm* (Vocal), 1974. *A Short Symphony* (Chamber), 1980. *Ballade* (Piano), 1981. *An Anniversary Rondo for Paul* (Chamber), 1982. *6 New Etudes* (Piano), 1984. *Lyric Intermezzo* (Chamber), 1987. *Dance Overture* (Chamber), 1987. *Windows of Order* (Chamber), 1988. *Sonata a quatrro* (Chamber), 1982. *Sonata a cinque* (Chamber), 1987.

Other Awards: National Institute of Arts and Letters Award, 1977. Guggenheim Fellow, Guggenheim Foundation, 1966-1967, 1974-1975. Grantee, American Council of Learned Societies, 1968-1969. National Endowment for the Arts, 1978-1979, 1985. Macarthur Fellow, 1986. Fellow, American Academy of Arts and Letters.

For More Information: Swed, Mark, "Finally, a Composer's Music Catches Up to His Words," *New York Times,* March 19, 1989; Kosman, Joshua, "Notes on a Musical Explorer," *San Francisco Chronicle,* April 30, 1989; Moor, Paul, "A Salute to George Perle," *Musical America,* July 1991.

Commentary: *Wind Quintet IV* won the 1986 Pulitzer Prize in Music for George Perle. It premiered on October 2, 1985 at Merkin Concert Hall.

George Perle was born in Bayonne, New Jersey. His parents were Russian immigrants. He began playing the piano at age six, after listening to a relative play Chopin and Liszt. Though he was self-taught at first, he was interested in composition. He had his first formal instruction when he attended the Chicago School of Music. His other works include *String Quartet No. 7* and *Thirteen Dickinson Songs,* which were written with the help of a grant from the National Endowment for the Arts (NEA) in 1978.

1987

John Harbison   879

Birth: December 20, 1938; Orange, NJ. **Education:** Harvard University, MA: BA. Princeton University, NJ: MFA. **Spouse:** Rosemary Pederson (m. 1963).

Prize: *Music,* 1987: *The Flight into Egypt.*

Career: Instructor, MIT, MA, 1969-1982; Conductor, Contata Singers, 1969-1973, 1980-1982;

Composer-in-Residence, Pittsburgh Symphony Orchestra, 1982-1984; Conductor, Los Angeles Philharmonic, Boston Symphony, Speculum Musicae; Composer-in-Residence, Tanglewood, Santa Fe Chamber Festivals, American Academy in Rome, Aspen Music Festival, Ojai Music Festival; Instructor, California Institute of the Arts, and Boston University; Principal Guest Conductor, Emmanuel Music; Member, American Academy and Institute of Arts and Letters, 1992; Composer of commissioned works from the Baltimore Symphony and Juilliard String Quartet.

Selected Works: *Sinfonia* (Orchestra), 1963. *Autumnal* (Vocal), 1965. *Serenade* (Chamber), 1968. *Bermuda Triangle* (Chamber), 1970. *Elegiac Songs* (Vocal), 1973. *The Winter's Tale* (Opera), 1974. *Book of Hours and Seasons* (Vocal), 1975. *Moments of Vision* (Vocal), 1975. *Descant-Nocturne* (Orchestra), 1976. *Diotima* (Orchestra), 1976. *The Flower-Fed Buffaloes* (Vocal), 1976. *Full Moon in March* (Opera), 1977. *Samuel Chapter* (Vocal), 1978. *Mottetti di Montale* (Vocal), 1980. *Mirabai Songs* (Vocal), 1982. *Ulysses' Bow* (Ballet), 1983. *Ulysses' Raft* (Ballet), 1983. *Variations* (Chamber), 1985. *Music for 18 Wind Instruments* (Chamber), 1986. *The Flight into Egypt* (Vocal), 1986. *Remembering Gatsby* (Orchestra), 1986. *The Natural World* (Vocal), 1989.

Other Awards: Paine Travelling Fellow, Harvard University, MA. Guggenheim Fellow, Guggenheim Foundation, 1978. Kennedy Center, Friedheim Award, 1980. MacArthur Award, 1989. Honorary Degree, New England Conservatory of Music, MA, 1995.

For More Information: Altman, Rachel, "Composer Wins $305,000 Award," *Los Angeles Times,* July 19, 1989; Dyer, Richard, "John Harbison, Local Hero," *Boston Globe,* April 3, 1994.

Commentary: John Harbison was awarded the 1987 Pulitzer Prize in Music for *The Flight into Egypt,* a work which premiered on November 21, 1986 at the New England Conservatory of Music in Boston, Massachussetts by the Cantata Singers and Ensemble.

John Harbison was born in Orange, New Jersey. His father was a professor of history at Princeton University and played piano. His mother also played piano, often show tunes. John began improvising before he could read music. He has studied with Boris Blocher in Berlin and with Roger Sessions and Earl Kim Choth at Princeton. His first important work was an opera, *Winter's Tale,* written with the help of a grant from the National Endowment for the Arts (NEA). His other works include *The Natural World.* He was the recipient of a MacArthur Foundation "genius" award in 1989.

1988

William Bolcom 880

Birth: May 26, 1938; Seattle, WA. **Parents:** Robert Samuel and Virginia (Lauerman) Bolcom. **Education:** University of Washington: BA. Mills College, CA: MA. Paris Conservatory of Music, France. Stanford University, CA. **Spouse:** Fay Levine (m. 1963; div. 1967); Katherine Agee Ling (m. 1968; div. 1969); Joan Claire Morris (m. 1975).

Prize: *Music,* 1988: *12 New Etudes for Piano.*

Career: Student of Berthe Poncy Jacobson, 1949-1958, of John Verall, 1951-1958, of Leland Smith, 1961-1964, of Darius Millhand, 1957-1961, of George Rochberg, 1966; Acting Assistant Professor of Music, University of Washington, Seattle, 1965-1966; Lecturer and Assistant Professor of Music, Queens College, City University of New York, 1966-1968; Visiting Critic and Music Teacher, Yale Drama School, 1968-1969; Composer-in-Residence, Theater Arts Program, New York University, 1969-1971; Assistant Professor, University of Michigan, School of Music, Ann Arbor, 1973-1978; Jury Member, National Endowment for the Arts, 1976-1977, 1984, 1985; Professor, University of Michigan, 1977-1983; Ross Lee Finney Distinguished Professor of Composition, beginning in 1983; Member: American Academy of Arts and Letters, American Music Center, American Composers Alliance, Board of Directors: American Repertory Theatre, Grant Park Concerts (Chicago), Charles Ives Society, Century Club; National Patron, Delta Omicron.

Selected Works: *Songs of Innocence and of Experience* (Chamber), 1956-1981. *Decalage* (Chamber), 1961. *Dynamite Tonite* (Stage), 1963. *Concerto-Serenade* (Orchestra), 1964. *Dream Music No. 2* (Chamber), 1966. *Greatshot* (Stage), 1969. *Theatre of the Absurd* (Stage), 1970. *Commedia* (Orchestra), 1971. *Frescoes* (Chamber), 1971. *Whisper Moon* (Chamber), 1971. *Summer Divertimento* (Orchestra), 1973. *12 New Etudes* (Chamber), 1977-1986. *The Beggar's Opera* (Stage), 1978. *Humoresk* (Orchestra), 1979. *Symphony for Chamber Orchestra* (Orchestra), 1979. *3 Gospel Preludes* (Chamber), 1979-1981. *Ragomania* (Orchestra), 1982. *Aubade* (Chamber), 1982. *Capriccio* (Chamber), 1985. *Fantasia concertante* (Orchestra), 1985. *Seattle Slew* (Orchestra), 1985-1986. *Spring Concertino* (Orchestra), 1986-1987. *Afternoon* (Chamber), 1979. *5 Fold 5* (Chamber), 1987. **Films:** *Hester Street* (Film Score), Midwest, 1975; *Illuminata Greenstreet* (Film Score), 1998.

Other Awards: Kurt Weill Award, 1961. William and Nora Copley Award, 1960. Guggenheim Fellow, Guggenhiem Foundation, 1964, 1968. Marc Blitz Stein Award for Excellence, American Academy of Arts and Letters, 1965. Rockefeller Foundation Grantee, 1965, 1969, 1972. New York State Council Award, 1971. Koussevitsky Foundation Award, 1974, 1993. National Endowment for the Arts Award, 1974, 1979, 1982-1984. Henry Roussel Award, 1977. Michigan Arts Council Award, 1986. Governor's Arts Award, Michigan, 1986. Citation of Merit, University of Michigan Alumni Association, 1989. Distinguished Achievement Award, University of Washington, 1993. Alfred I. DuPont Award, 1994. Henry Roussel Lecturer, 1997. Honorary MusDs: San Francisco Conservatory, 1994; Albion College, MI, 1995.

For More Information: Tommasini, Anthony, "Music at the Service of American Poetry," *New York Times,* December 4, 1997; Ruhe, Pierre, "Bolcom's Harmonic Diversions: The Composer's Works Reveal His Eclectic Interests," *Washington Post,* February 22, 1998.

Commentary: The 1988 Pulitzer Prize in Music was awarded to William Bolcom for *12 New Etudes for Piano,* a work performed by pianist Marc-Andre Hamelin on March 30, 1987 at Temple University in Philadelphia, Pennsylvania.

William Bolcom was born in Seattle, Washington. His earliest exposure to music came while he was still in his mother's womb. He began piano lessons at age five and he would later study at the University of Washington with Berthe Poncy Jacobson, who was head of the piano department, and with John Verrall. He studied advanced composition at Stanford University. He has been the composer-in-residence for the Detroit Symphony Orchestra. He and his wife, Joan Morris, who is a singer, give concerts of popular American songs. He has a strong interest in ragtime music.

1989

Roger Reynolds   881

Birth: July 18, 1934; Detroit, MI. **Parents:** George Arthur and Katherine Adelaide (Butler). **Education:** University of Michigan: BSE, BM, MM. **Spouse:** Karen Jeanne Hill (m.1964). **Children:** Wendy Clair, Erika Lynn.

Prize: *Music,* 1989: *Whispers Out of Time.*

Career: Associate Professor, University of California, San Diego, 1969-1973; George Miller Professor, University of Illinois, beginning in 1971; Founding Director, Center for Music; Professor of Music, University of California, San Diego, beginning in 1973; Visiting Professor, Yale University, New Haven, CT, 1981; Senior Research Fellow, ISAM, Brooklyn College, 1985; Rothschild Valentine Professor, Amherst College, 1988; Composer-in-

Residence, Peabody Conservatory of Music, 1992-1993.

Selected Works: *Emperor of Ice Cream* (Stage), 1962. *A Portrait of Vanzetti* (Vocal), 1962-1963. *Graffiti* (Orchestra), 1964. *Quick Are the Mouths of the Earth* (Chamber), 1964-1965. *Gathering* (Chamber), 1965. *Blind Men* (Vocal), 1966. *Threshold* (Orchestra), 1967. *Between* (Orchestra), 1968. *Traces* (Chamber), 1968. *Ping* (Tape), 1969. *I/O: A Ritual for 23 Performers* (Stage), 1970. *From behind the Unreasoning Mask* (Chamber), 1975. *The Promises of Darkness: I,* 1975. *A Merciful Coincidence: II* (Tape), 1975. *Only Now, and Again* (Chamber), 1976. *Less than 2* (Chamber), 1977. *Shadowed Narrative* (Chamber), 1977-1979. *Eclipse: III* (Tape), 1977-1982. *The Serpent-Snapping Eye* (Chamber), 1979-1980. *Fiery Wind* (Orchestra), 1979. *The Tempest* (Stage), 1978. *Archipelago* (Orchestra), 1980. *Transfigured Wind II* (Orchestra), 1982. *Whispers out of Time* (Orchestra), 1984. *"Coconino...A Shattered Landscape"* (Chamber), 1988. *Islands from Archpelago: I Summer Island* (Chamber), 1985. *Mistral* (Chamber), 1985. *The Palace: IV* (Chamber), 1985. *Sketchbook* (Vocal), 1980.

Other Awards: Koussevitsky International Recording Award, 1970. Citation, National Endowment for the Arts Awards, 1975, 1978, 1979, 1986. Senior Fellow, Institute for Studies in American Music, 1985. Fellow, International Studies in American Music, 1985. Fellow, Institute of Current World Affairs. Fellow, Rockefeller Foundation. Guggenheim Fellow, Guggenheim Foundation. Fulbright Scholar.

For More Information: Kozinn, Allan, "Composer Considers His Pulitzer, and Then Gets Back to Work," *New York Times,* April 10, 1989; Willett, John, "Roger Reynolds," *Musical America,* November 1990.

Commentary: *Whispers Out of Time,* a work which premiered at Buckley Recital Hall in Amherst, Massachusetts on December 11, 1988, won a Pulitzer Prize in Music for Roger Reynolds in 1989.

Roger Lee Reynolds was born in Detroit. He studied engineering and music at the University of Michigan. A Fulbright scholarship to pursue electronic music sent him to Cologne, Germany in 1962. He was a founder of the avant garde festival, ONCE, in Ann Arbor, Michigan. While on the faculty of music at the University of California, he founded the Center for Music Experiment in 1971. He has traveled around the world lecturing on electronic music and held composer-in-residence positions at various universities.

1990

Mel Powell   882

Birth: February 12, 1923; New York, NY. **Death:** April 24, 1998. **Education:** Yale University, CT: MusB. **Spouse:** Martha Scott. **Children:** Kati Powell, Mary Harpel, Scott Alsop.

Prize: *Music,* 1990: *"Duplicates": A Concerto for Two Pianos and Orchestra.*

Career: Chairman, Music Composition Faculty, Yale University, CT, 1957-1969; Head of Music Composition Faculty, California Institute of the Arts, Valencia, CA, 1972-1976; Roy E. Disney Chair in Music Composition, California Institute of the Arts.

Selected Works: *Cantilena* (Orchestra), 1948. *Beethoven Analogs* (Chamber), 1949. *Symphonic Suite* (Orchestra), 1949. *Capriccio* (Orchestra), 1950. *6 Choral Songs* (Vocal), 1950. *Sweet Lovers Love the Spring* (Vocal), 1953. *Divertimento—Strings* (Chamber), 1954. *Divertimento — Wind* (Chamber), 1955. *Intrada and Variants* (Orchestra), 1956. *Etude* (Piano), 1957. *Stanzas* (Orchestra), 1957. *Miniatures for Baroque Ensemble* (Chamber), 1958. *Filigree Setting* (Chamber), 1959. *Electronic Setting* (Electronic), 1958. *Haiku Settings* (Vocal), 1961. *2nd Electronic Setting* (Electronic), 1961. *Improvisation* (Chamber), 1962. *Analogs I-IV* (Electronic), 1963. *Events* (Electronic), 1963. *2 Prayer Settings* (Vocal), 1963. *Immobiles I-IV* (Orchestra), 1965. *Cantilena* (Vocal), 1967. *3 Synthesizer Settings* (Electronic), 1969. *Inscape* (Electronic), 1970-1980. *Variations* (Electronic), 1976. *Little Companion Pieces* (Vocal), 1976. *Settings* (Vocal), 1979. *Cantilena* (Chamber), 1979. *Setting* (Orchestra), 1981. *Settings* (Orchestra), 1982. *String Quartet 1982* (Chamber), 1982. *Strand Settings: Darker* (Vocal), 1982. *Modules* (Orchestra), 1983. *Setting* (Chamber), 1985. *Amy-abilities* (Chamber), 1986. *Die Violene* (Vocal), 1987. *Invocation* (Chamber), 1987. *Letter to a Young Composer* (Vocal), 1987. *Piano Preludes* (Piano), 1987. *Computer Prelude* (Electronic), 1987. *3 Madrigals* (Chamber), 1988. *Duplicates* (Orchestra), 1988.

Other Awards: Creative Arts Medal, Brandeis University, MA, 1989. Guggenheim Fellow, Guggenheim Foundation. National Institute of Arts and Letters Grant. Honorary Life Award, Memorial Arnold Schoenberg Institute.

For More Information: Kozinn, Allan, "Mel Powell, Atonal Composer Who Won Pulitzer, Dies at 75," *New York Times,* April 27, 1998.

Commentary: Mel Powell was awarded the 1990 Pulitzer Prize in Music for *"Duplicates": A Concerto for Two Pianos and Orchestra,* a work which premiered on January 26, 1990 by the Los Angeles Philharmonic.

Mel Powell was born Melvin Epstein in New York City. He began playing piano at age four. He would later study with Ernst Toch and Paul Hindemith. His classical musical style was described as compact and atonal. Powell was a widely known jazz pianist in the 1940s, belonging to Benny Goodman's band as a pianist and arranger (at this time he changed his name) and Glenn Miller's Army Air Force Band. He also recorded piano music for *Tom and Jerry* cartoons. He was stricken with muscular dystrophy while at the height of his jazz fame. In 1948, Powell entered Yale School of Music and changed his style toward atonal music. He was the founding dean of the school of music at the California Institute of the Arts.

1991

Shulamit Ran   883

Birth: October 2, 1949; Tel Aviv, Israel. **Education:** Mannes College, New School, NY. **Spouse:** Abraham Lotam.

Prize: *Music,* 1991: *Symphony.*

Career: Music Department Faculty member, University of Chicago, beginning in 1973; William H. Colvin Professor of Music, University of Chicago; Composer-in Residence, Chicago Symphony Orchestra, 1990-1997; Lyric Opera of Chicago, 1994-1997.

Selected Works: *Capriccio* (Orchestra), 1963. *Symphonic Poem* (Orchestra), 1967. *Hatzvi Israel Eulogie* (Vocal), 1968. *Structures* (Piano), 1968. *7 Japanese Love Poems* (Vocal), 1968. *O the Chimineys* (Vocal), 1969. *10 Children's Scenes* (Orchestra), 1970. *Concert Piece* (Orchestra), 1971. *Ensembles for 17* (Vocal), 1975. *Double Vision* (Chamber), 1976. *Hyperbolae* (Piano), 1976. *Apprehensions* (Vocal), 1979. *A Prayer* (Chamber), 1981. *Sonata Waltzer* (Piano), 1981-1982. *Verticals* (Piano), 1982. *Amichai Songs* (Vocal), 1985. *Adonai Malach* (Vocal), 1985. *Concerto da camera I and II* (Chamber), 1985, 1987.

Other Awards: Guggenheim Fellow, Guggenheim Foundation, 1977, 1990. American Academy and Institute of Arts and Letters Award, 1989. Freidheim Award, Orchestral Music, Kennedy Center, 1992.

For More Information: Buell, Richard, "Shulamit Ran—Composing with a Firm Grip," *Boston Globe,* August 14, 1990; Kozinn, Allan, "Composer's Pulitzer Makes the Telephone Her New Instrument," *New York Times,* April 11, 1991; Rothstein, Edward, "The Melodic Energy and the Textures of Shulamit Ran," *New York Times,* April 23, 1992.

Commentary: *Symphony* won the 1991 Pulitzer Prize in Music for Shulamit Ran. It was commissioned and performed by the Philadelphia Orchestra on October 19, 1990.

Shulamit Ran was born in Tel Aviv, Israel. She studied with Paul Ben-Haim, Norman Dello Joio, and

Ralph Shapey. She has been on the faculty of the music department at the University of Chicago since 1973. She is currently the Chicago Symphony's composer-in-residence. Her other works include *10 Children's Scenes* and *Adonai Malach.*

1992

Wayne Turner Peterson   884

Birth: September 3, 1927; Albert Lea, MN. **Parents:** Leslie Jules Peterson and Irma Thelma (Turner) Peterson. **Education:** University of Minnesota: BA, MA, PhD. Royal Academy of Music, London, England. **Spouse:** Harriet Christiansen (m. 1948; div. 1974). **Children:** Alan, Craig, Drew, Grant.

    Prize: *Music,* 1992: *The Face of the Night, The Heart of the Dark.*

    Career: Music Instructor, University of Minnesota, 1955-1959; Assistant Professor of Music, Chico State University, CA, 1959-1960; Professor of Music, San Francisco State University, beginning in 1960; Artist-in-Residence, Briarcombe Foundation, Bolinas, CA, 1983; Visiting Professor of Composition, University of Indiana, Bloomington, 1992; Visiting Professor, Stanford University, CA, 1992-1994.

    Selected Works: *Introduction and Allegro* (Orchestra), 1953. *Free Variations* (Orchestra), 1954-1958. *Exaltation, Dithyramb and Caprice* (Orchestra), 1959-1960. *Metamorphosis* (Chamber), 1967. *Cataclysms* (Orchestra), 1968. *Phantasmagoria* (Chamber), 1968. *Clusters and Fragments* (Orchestra), 1969. *Capriccio* (Chamber), 1973. *Transformations* (Chamber), 1974. *Encounters* (Chamber), 1976. *An Interrupted Serenade* (Chamber), 1978. *Sextet* (Chamber), 1982. *Ariadne's Thread* (Chamber), 1985. *Transformations II* (Orchestra), 1985. *Duodecaphony* (Chamber), 1986-1987. *Trilogy* (Orchestra), 1987. *The Widening Gyre* (Orchestra), 1990. *The Face of the Night* (Orchestra), 1990-1991.

    Other Awards: Fulbright Scholar, Royal Academy of Music, England, 1953-1954. National Endowment for the Arts Grant, 1976. 11th Annual Norman Fromm Composer's Award, 1982. Meritorious Service Award, California State University System, 1984. Top Award American Harp Society, 1985. Composer's Award, American Academy and Institute of Arts and Letters, 1986. Guggenheim Fellow, Guggenheim Foundation, 1989-1990. Djerassi Foundation Fellow, 1989-1991.

    For More Information: Rothstein, Edward, "In the Fracas Over a Prize, No One Won," *New York Times,* April 19, 1992.

    Commentary: The 1992 Pulitzer Prize in Music was awarded to Wayne Peterson for *The Face of the Night, The Heart of the Dark,* a work which premiered on October 17, 1991 by the San Francisco Symphony.

Wayne Peterson was born in Albert Lea, Minnesota. He studied with Lennox Berkeley and Howard Ferguson at London's Royal Academy of Music. His premier work *Free Variations* was performed and recorded by the Minnesota Orchestra under Antal Dorati in 1958. His most recent works include *And The Winds Shall Blow, Vicissitudes,* and *Peregrinations.*

1993

Christopher Chapman Rouse III   885

Birth: February 15, 1949; Baltimore, MD. **Parents:** Christopher Chapman and Margery (Harper) Rouse. **Education:** Oberlin College, OH: BMus. Cornell University, NY: MFA, DMA. **Spouse:** Ann Jensen (m. 1983). **Children:** Adrian Christopher, Alexandra Elizabeth, Jillian Kathleen, Angela Therese Burg.

    Prize: *Music,* 1993: *Trombone Concerto.*

    Career: Assistant Professor of Composition, University of Michigan, Ann Arbor, MI, 1978-1981; Assistant Professor of Composition, Eastman School of Music, Rochester, NYU, 1981-1985; Associate Professor of Composition, Eastman School of Music, 1985-1991; Composer-in-Residence, Baltimore Symphony Orchestra, 1986-1989; Composer-in-Residence, Schleswer Holstein Festival, 1989; Professor of Composition, Eastman School of Music, beginning in 1991; Composer-in-Residence, Helsinki Biennale, 1997; Composer-in-Residence, Tanglewood Music Center, 1997; Faculty member, Juilliard School of Music, beginning in 1997; Commissioned composer for the Alberta Symphony, Philadelphia Symphony Orchestra, New York Philharmonic Orchestra, Los Angeles Philharmonic Orchestra, Cleveland Philharmonic Orchestra, Detroit Symphony Orchestra, St. Louis Symphony Orchestra, Rochester Philharmonic Orchestra.

    Selected Works: *Mitternachlieder,* 1979. *Liber Daemonum,* 1980. *The Infernal Machine,* 1981. *Rotae passionis,* 1982. *Gorgon,* 1984. *Phantasmata,* 1985. *Phaeton,* 1986. *Jagannath,* 1987. *Iscariot,* 1989. *Concert per Corde,* 1990. *Karolju,* 1990.

    Other Awards: Guggenheim Fellow, Guggenheim Foundation. Award, League of Composers. National Endowment for the Arts Award. Rockefeller Foundation Grant. Pitney Bowes Award. Freidheim Award, Kennedy Center, 1988. American Academy of Arts and Letters, 1993. Honorary DMus, Oberlin College, OH, 1996.

    For More Information: Rothstein, Edward, "A Mournful But Thunderous Trombone Concerto," *New York Times,* January 1, 1993; Dyer, Richard, "Affable

Composer of Tragic Works Listening to Christopher Rouse," *Boston Globe,* August 10, 1997.

Commentary: Christopher Rouse was awarded the 1993 Pulitzer Prize in Music for *Trombone Concerto,* a work which premiered on December 30, 1992 by the New York Philharmonic. This work has been recorded by Christian Lindberg on trombone and the BBC Orchestra of Wales with Grant Llewellyn conducting, and also by Joseph Alessi on trombone with the Colorado Symphony conducted by Artin Alsop.

Christopher Chapman Rouse was born in Baltimore, Maryland. He studied with Richard Hoffman, Karel Husa, Robert Palmer, and George Crumb. He has taught at the Eastman School of Music since 1981. He has been composer-in-residence for symphonies around the world. His other works include *Phantasmata* and *Karolju.*

1994

Gunther Alexander Schuller   886

Birth: November 22, 1925; New York, NY. **Parents:** Arthur Erns Schuller and Elsie (Bernartz) Schuller. **Education:** Manhattan School of Music, NY. **Spouse:** Marjorie Black (m. 1947). **Children:** Edwin, George, Gunther.

Prize: *Music,* 1994: *Of Reminiscences and Reflections.*

Career: French Horn Player, New York Philharmonic and Ballet Theater, 1942-1943; Principal French Horn Player, Cincinnati Symphony, beginning in 1943; French horn player, Miles Davis Ensemble, 1950; Staff member, Cleveland Institute of Music, 1950-1963; Head, Music Composition Department, Tangelwood, MA, 1963-1984; President, New England Conservatory of Music, 1967-1977; Artistic Director, Berkshire Music Center, Tanglewood, 1969-1984; Founder and President, Margun Music Incorporated, 1975; Founder and President, GM Records, 1980; Member, Festival of Sandpoint, beginning in 1985; Member, National Academy of Arts and Letters, National Academy of Arts and Sciences.

Selected Works: *Romantic Sonata* (Chamber), 1941. *O Lamb of God* (Vocal), 1941. *O Spirit of the Living* (Vocal), 1942. *3 Hommages* (Chamber), 1942-1946. *Suite* (Chamber), 1945. *Suite* (Orchestra), 1945. *Vertige d'Eros* (Orchestra), 1945. *Fantasia concertante No. 1* (Chamber), 1947. *Symphonic Study* (Orchestra), 1947-1948. *Perpetuum mobile* (Chamber), 1948. *Recitative and Rondo* (Orchestra), 1953. *Symphonic Tribute to Duke Ellington* (Orchestra), 1955. *Little Fantasy* (Orchestra), 1957. *Contours* (Orchestra), 1958. *Spectra* (Orchestra), 1958. *Concertino* (Orchestra), 1959. *7 Studies on Themes of Paul Klee* (Orchestra), 1959. *Fantasy* (Chamber), 1951. *Recita-tive and Rondo* (Chamber), 1953. *Fantasy Quartet* (Chamber), 1959. *Fantasy* (Chamber), 1959. *Contrasts* (Orchestra), 1960. *Lines and Contrasts* (Chamber), 1960. *Variants* (Ballet), 1960. *Music* (Chamber), 1961. *Fanfare* (Chamber), 1962. *Journey into Jazz* (Orchestra), 1962. *Journey to the Stars* (Orchestra), 1962. *Music* (Chamber), 1962. *Studies* (Chamber), 1962. *Movements* (Orchestra), 1962. *6 Renaissance Lyrics* (Vocal), 1962. *Composition in 3 Parts* (Orchestra), 1963. *Diptych* (Orchestra), 1963. *Little Brass Music* (Chamber), 1963. *Meditation* (Orchestra), 1963. *Threnos* (Orchestra), 1963. *Episodes* (Chamber), 1964. *5 Bagatelles* (Orchestra), 1964. *5 Shakespearean Songs* (Vocal), 1964. *American Triptych: 3 Studies in Textures* (Orchestra), 1965. *Gala Music* (Orchestra), 1966. *Tear Drop* (Television Score), 1966. *The Visitation* (Opera), 1966. *5 Etudes* (Orchestra), 1966. *Aphorisms* (Chamber), 1967. *The 5 Senses* (Televison Score), 1967. *Triplum I and II* (Orchestra), 1975. *Colloquy* (Orchestra), 1968. *Fanfare for St. Louis* (Orchestra), 1968. *Shapes and Designs* (Orchestra), 1969. *Consequents* (Orchestra), 1969. *Museum Piece* (Orchestra), 1970. *The Fisherman and His Wife* (Opera), 1970. *Concerto da camera* (Orchestra), 1971. *The Power within Us* (Vocal), 1971. *Capriccio stravagante* (Orchestra), 1972. *Poems of Time and Eternity* (Vocal), 1972. *3 Nocturnes* (Orchestra), 1972. *5 Moods* (Chamber), 1973. *4 Soundscapes — Hudson Valley Reminiscences* (Orchestra), 1974. *Deai—Encounters* (Orchestra), 1978. *Sonata serenata* (Chamber), 1978. *Eine kleine Posaunenmusik* (Orchestra), 1980. *Farbenspiel* (Orchestra), 1985. *Music for a Celebration* (Orchestra), 1980. *In Praise of Winds* (Orchestra), 1981. *Concerto quarternio* (Orchestra), 1984. *Jubilee Musik* (Orchestra), 1984. *On Light Wings* (Chamber), 1984. *The Sandpoint Rag* (Chamber), 1986. *Thou Art the Son of God* (Vocal), 1987. *A Bouquet for Collage* (Chamber), 1988. *Chimeric Images* (Chamber), 1988. *On Winged Flight* (Orchestra), 1989. *Chamber Symphony* (Orchestra), 1989. *Concerto for Piano 3 Hands* (Orchestra), 1989. *A Question of Taste* (Opera), 1989. *5 Impromptus* (Chamber), 1989. **Films:** *Automation* (Film Score), 1962; *Journey to the Stars* (Film Score), 1962; *Yesterday in Fact / Naprawde wczoraj* (Film Score), 1963; *Face Down* (TV Film Score), Hallmark Entertainment, 1997.

Other Awards: Guggenheim Fellow, Guggenheim Foundation, 1962. MacArthur Fellow, 1991. Creative Arts Award, Brandeis University, 1960. Deems Taylor Award, ASCAP, 1970. Alice M. Ditson Conducting Award, 1970. Rodgers & Hammerstein Award, 1971. Freidheim Award, Kennedy Center, 1988. William Schuman Award, Columbia University, 1989. Genius Award, MacArthur Foundation, 1991. Downbeat Lifetime Achievement Award, 1993. BMI Lifetime Achievement Award, 1994.

Composer of the Year Award, 1995. Gold Medal, American Academy of Arts and Letters, 1997. Order of Merit Cross, Federation of the Republic of Germany, 1997. Honorary MusDs: Northeastern University, MA, 1967; University of Illinois, 1968; Colby College, ME, 1969; Manhattan School of Music, NY, 1987; Williams College, MA, 1995.

For More Information: Dyer, Richard, "Schuller's 'Genius' Award Buttresses His Reputation," *Boston Globe,* June 18, 1991; McLellan, Joseph, "Gunther Schuller: A Prize Long Before His Pulitzer," *Washington Post,* May 1, 1994; Dyer, Richard, "Celebrating Gunther Schuller," *Boston Globe,* December 3, 1995.

Commentary: The 1994 Pulitzer Prize in Music was awarded to Gunther Schuller for *Of Reminiscences and Reflections,* a work which was commissioned and performed by the Louisville Orchestra on December 2, 1993. It was composed in memory of Schuller's late wife, Marjorie.

Gunther Schuller was born in New York City. His family were professional musicians in Germany and his father was a violinist with the New York Philharmonic. Gunther was sent to boarding school in Erfurt, Germany, where, at age 12, he studied harmony and counterpoint and flute and later, the French horn. His musical debut came at 16, with the New York Philharmonic, when he filled in for a French horn player. Schuller coined the phrase "third stream" music which combines contemporary classical with jazz improvisation, vocabulary, and instruments. He has played jazz with musicians such as Duke Ellington and Miles Davis, playing French horn on Davis's *Birth of the Cool* recording.

1995

Morton Gould   887

Birth: December 10, 1913; Richmond Hill, NY. **Death:** February 21, 1996. **Education:** New York University. **Spouse:** Shirley Bank (m. 1944). **Children:** Two sons, two daughters.

Prize: *Music,* 1995: *Stringmusic.*

Career: Pianist, motion pictures and vaudeville, 1930; Staff Pianist, Radio City Music Hall, 1931-1932; Pianist and Composer, WOR Radio, 1934; Musical Director, Cresta Blanca Carnaval and Chrysler Hour, CBS Radio, 1943; Composer of works played by many orchestras and symphonies across the United States, beginning in 1943; Member, Board of Directors, American Society of Composers, Authors and Publishers (ASCAP); Member: American Symphony League, American Music Center.

Selected Works: *3 American Symphonettes* (Orchestra), 1937. *Chorale and Fugue in Jazz* (Orchestra), 1934. *Stephen Foster Gallery* (Orchestra), 1940. *Spirituals* (Orchestra), 1941. *Latin-American Symphonette* (Orchestra), 1941. *Lincoln Legend* (Orchestra), 1942. *Cowboy Rhapsody* (Orchestra), 1942. *American Salute* (Orchestra), 1943. *Boogie Woogie Etude* (Piano), 1943. *Symphony on Marching Tunes* (Orchestra), 1944. *Billion Dollar Baby* (Stage), 1945. *Harvest* (Orchestra), 1945. *Interplay* (Stage), 1945. *Minstrel Show* (Orchestra), 1946. *Fall River Legend* (Stage), 1947. *Holiday Music* (Orchestra), 1947. *Philharmonic Waltzes* (Orchestra), 1948. *Serenade of Carols* (Orchestra), 1949. *Arms and the Girl* (Stage), 1950. *Dance Gallery* (Piano), 1952. *Dance Variations* (Orchestra), 1952. *Showpiece* (Orchestra), 1954. *Cinerama Holiday* (Film Score), 1955. *Fiesta* (Stage), 1957. *Jekyll and Hyde Variations* (Orchestra), 1957. *Dialogues* (Orchestra), 1958. *Festive Music* (Orchestra), 1965. *Abby Variations* (Piano), 1964. *At the Piano* (Piano), 1964. *World War I* (Television Score), 1964-1965. *10 for Deborah* (Piano), 1965. *Columbia: Broadsides for Orchestra* (Orchestra), 1967. *Venice* (Orchestra), 1967. *Vivaldi* (Orchestra), 1968. *Soundings* (Orchestra), 1969. *Troubadour Music* (Orchestra), 1969. *Symphony of Spirituals* (Orchestra), 1976. *American Ballads* (Orchestra), 1976. *Holocaust* (Television Score), 1978. *Cheers* (Orchestra), 1979. *Burchfield Gallery* (Orchestra), 1981. *Celebration '81* (Television Score), 1981. *Housewarming* (Orchestra), 1982. *Apple Waltzes* (Orchestra), 1983. *Concerto Concertante* (Chamber), 1983. *Flourishes and Galop* (Orchestra), 1983. *I'm Old Fashioned* (Stage), 1983. *Patterns* (Piano), 1985. *Classical Variations on Colonial Themes* (Orchestra), 1986. *2 Pianos* (Piano), 1987. *Chorales and Rags* (Orchestra), 1988. **Films:** *Delightfully Dangerous* (Film Score), United Artists, 1945; *Windjammer* (Film Score), 1958; *Holocaust* (TV Score), 1978.

Other Awards: Grammy Award, Best Recording: Charles Ives's *Symphony No. 1.* Henry Hadley Medal, National Association for American Composers and Conductors, 1967. Outstanding Service to American Music. Honored at Kennedy Center, Washington, DC, 1994.

For More Information: Holland, Bernard, "Morton Gould, Composer and Conductor, Dies at 82," *New York Times,* February 22, 1996; *Current Biography,* New York: Wilson, 1996.

Commentary: The 1995 Pulitzer Prize in Music was awarded to Morton Gould for *Stringmusic,* which premiered on March 10, 1994 at the John F. Kennedy Center in Washington, DC by the National Symphony Orchestra.

Morton Gould was born in the Richmond Hill section of Queens, New York. He began playing the piano at age four and published his first musical piece, *Just Six,* a waltz, when he was only six years old. As a student at New York University, he presented a concert of his works there at the age of 16. At age 19 in 1932, Gould was hired as the staff pianist at Radio City Music Hall. He would later conduct the popular Cresta Blanca programs on the CBS network. His major works have been performed by conductors such as Stokowski, Reiner, and Toscanini. His works included *Fall River Legend,* and *Symphony of Spirituals,* the latter written for the American bicentennial.

1996

George Walker   888

Birth: June 27, 1922; Washington, DC. **Parents:** George Theophilus and Rosa (King) Walker. **Religion:** Protestant. **Education:** Oberlin College, OH: MusB. Curtis Institute of Music, PA: Artist Diploma.

Eastman School of Music, NY: DMA. **Children:** Gregory, Ian.

Prize: *Music,* 1996: *Lilacs.*

Career: Instructor, Dillard University, LA, 1953; Instructor, New School for Social Research, NY, 1961; Instructor, Smith College, 1961-1968; Instructor, University of Colorado, 1968; Professor, Rutgers, State University of New Jersey, 1969; Chairman, Composition Department, Rutgers University, 1974; Distinguished Professor, University of Delaware, 1975; Adjunct Professor, Peabody Institute, MD, 1975; Member, American Academy of Arts and Letters.

Selected Works: *3 Lyrics* (Chamber), 1958. *Address* (Orchestra), 1959. *Perimeters* (Chamber), 1966. *Antiphonys* (Orchestra), 1968. *Music for 3* (Chamber), 1970. *Variations* (Orchestra), 1971. *5 Fancies* (Chamber), 1974. *Spirituals* (Orchestra), 1974. *Music —Sacred and Profane* (Chamber), 1975. *Dialogues* (Orchestra), 1975-1976. *Mass* (Orchestra), 1976. *Mass* (Chamber), 1978. *Overture: In Praise of Folly* (Orchestra), 1980. *An Eastman Overture* (Orchestra), 1983. *Serenata* (Orchestra), 1983. *Sinfonia No. 1* (Orchestra), 1984. *Poem* (Solo), 1987. *Folksongs* (Orchestra), 1990. *Sinfonia No. 2* (Orchestra), 1990. *Poeme* (Solo), 1991. *Orpheus* (Orchestra), 1994.

Other Awards: Fulbright Fellowship, France, 1957. Guggenheim Fellowship, 1969. Rockefeller Fellowship, Italy, 1971, 1975. Rutgers University Research Council Grants, 1970, 1971, 1973.

For More Information: Malitz, Nancy, "Black Composer Charges Tokenism," *Detroit News,* February 20, 1992; Blumenthal, Ralph, "A Pulitzer Winner's Overnight Success of 60 Years," *New York Times,* April 11, 1996; Joseph McLellan, "Hometown Homage To a D.C. Composer: Trailblazer Returns for His Day in The District," *Washington Post,* June 8, 1997.

Commentary: George Walker was awarded the 1996 Pulitzer Prize in Music for *Lilacs,* a work for voice and orchestra which premiered on February 1, 1996 by the Boston Symphony Orchestra in Boston, Massachusetts. It employs the poetry of Walt Whitman.

George Walker was born in Washington, DC. He began piano lessons at age five. He studied piano with Rudolf Serkin and Robert Casadesus, composition with Rosario Scalero, Gian-Carlo Menotti, and Nadia Boulanger, and chamber music with Gregor Piatigorsky and William Primrose. He was the first black pianist to obtain major management under the aegis of the National Concert Artists and Columbia Artists Management. Walker's music often makes use of black folk idioms. His many works include *Piano Concert,* composed in 1975, and the more recent *Orpheus.*

1997

Wynton Marsalis   889

Birth: October 18, 1961; Kenner, LA. **Parents:** Ellis and Dolores Marsalis. **Education:** New Orleans Center for Performing Arts, LA. Berkshire Music Center, MA. Juilliard School of Music, NY.

Prize: *Music,* 1997: *Blood on the Fields.*

Career: Trumpet Soloist, New Orleans Philharmonic Orchestra, 1975; Recitalist, New Orleans Center for Creative Arts, 1979; Trumpeter, New Orleans and New York Orchestras, Art Blakey's Jazz Messengers, 1980-1981, Herbie Hancock's USOP Quartet; Founder of own group, 1981; Co-Founder and Artistic Director of the Jazz at Lincoln Center Program, 1987.

Selected Works: *Wynton Marsalis* (Jazz), 1982. *Haydn/Hummel/L. Mozart Trumpet Concertos 1983* (Classical), 1983. *Think of One...* (Jazz), 1983. *Handel, Purcell, Torelli, Fasch, Molter 1984* (Classical), 1984. *Hot House Flowers* (Jazz), 1984. *Black Codes (From the Underground)* (Jazz), 1985. *Three Favorite Concertos (with Yo Yo Ma, C-L. Lin)* (Classical), 1985. *J Mood* (Jazz), 1986. *Tomasi/Jolivet: Trumpet Concertos, January* (Classical), 1986. *Carnaval* (Classical), 1987. *Marsalis Standard Time, Volume 1* (Jazz), 1987. *Baroque Music for Trumpets* (Classical), 1988. *Portrait of Wynton Marsalis* (Classical), 1988. *Wynton Marsalis Quartet Live at Blues Alley* (Jazz), 1988. *Crescent City Christmas Card* (Jazz), 1989. *The Majesty of the Blues* (Jazz), 1989. *Standard Time Volume 3: The Resolution of Romance* (Jazz), 1990. *"Tune in Tomorrow"* (Jazz), 1990. *Standard Time Volume 2: Intimacy Calling, 1991* (Jazz), 1991. *Soul Gestures in Southern Blue: Volume I—Thick in the South, Volume II—Uptown Ruler, Volume III—Levee Low Moan* (Jazz), 1991. *Blue Interlude* (Jazz), 1992. *Baroque Duet* (with Kathleen Battle), 1992. *Citi Movement (Griot New York)* (Jazz), 1993. *On the Twentieth Century* (Classical), 1993. *In This House, on This Morning* (Jazz), 1994. *Sweet Swing Blues on the Road* (Book), 1994. *The London Concert* (Classical), 1994. *Joe Cool's Blues (with Ellis Marsalis)* (Jazz) (with Ellis Marsalis), 1995. *Marsalis on Music* (Book) (Hoffman, Elizabeth, ed.), 1995. *"Wynton Marsalis: Teaching Music and Bridging Gaps," Music Educators Journal / Teaching Music* (Nolan, Evonne, ed.), 1995. *In Gabriel's Garden* (Classical), 1996. *"Wynton Marsalis: On Playing with Soul," Instrumentalist,* 1996. *The Midnight Blues: Standard Time Volume V* (Jazz), 1998. **Films:** *Shannon's Deal* (TV Film Score), 1989; *Shannon's Deal* (TV Series Score), 1990; *Tune in Tomorrow...* (Film Score), Polar Entertainment, 1990; *Night Falls on Manhattan* (Film Score), Paramount, 1997.

Other Awards: Harvey Shapiro Award, Most Gifted Brass Player, Berkshire Music Center at Tan-

glewood, 1968. Grammy Award, Best Solo Classical Performance with an Orchestra, 1983: *Hummel / Hadyn / L. Mozart Trumpet Concertos.* Grammy Award, Best Jazz Solo Instrumental, 1983: *Think of One...* Grammy Award, Best Jazz Instrumental Performance, 1985: *Black Codes from the Underground.* Grammy Award, Best Jazz Instrumentalist with a Group, 1985: *Black Codes from the Underground.* Grammy Award, Best Jazz Recording, 1987: *Marsalis Standard Time, Volume I.* Grammy Award, Best Musician of the Year, 1987. Grand Prix du Disque, France. Edison Award, The Netherlands. Honorary Member, Royal Academy of Music, England.

For More Information: Andrews, Laura, "Wynton Marsalis Awarded Pulitzer Prize Denied Duke Ellington 32 Years Ago," *Amsterdam News,* May 10, 1997; Peterson, V.R., "Horn of Plenty," *People Weekly,* May 12, 1997; Reich, Howard, "Jazz Musician of the Year: Wynton Marsalis," *Down Beat,* December 1997.

Commentary: The 1997 Pulitzer Prize in Music was awarded to Wynton Marsalis for *Blood on the Fields,* a work which premiered on January 28, 1997 at Woolsey Hall, Yale University in New Haven, Connecticut.

Wynton Marsalis was born in Kenner, Louisiana into a prominent musical family. He is the son of Ellis, the noted jazz trumpeter and brother to Branford, the saxophonist, and Defaeyo, the trombonist. All have collaborated with each other at one time or another. Wynton began trumpet lessons at age six and later studied classical trumpet at the Juilliard School of Music. He was a member of Art Blakey's Jazz Messengers and has played with Miles Davis. He began his own jazz group in 1981 with a debut album, *Wynton Marsalis,* in 1982. Marsalis has achieved renown in both the classical and jazz fields.

1998

Aaron Jay Kernis   890

Birth: January 15, 1960; Philadelphia, PA. **Education:** San Francisco Conservatory, CA. Manhattan School of Music, NY: BM. Yale University, CT. **Spouse:** Evelyne Luest (m. 1996).

Prize: *Music,* 1998: *String Quartet No. 2.*

Career: Faculty member, Manhattan School of Music, 1992 to present; Composer-in-Residence, St. Paul Chamber Orchestra, Minnesota Public Radio, and the Minnesota Composers Forum, MN, 1993-Present; MSM Faculty member since 1992; Composer of commissioned works for orchestra, chamber, voice and keyboard.

Selected Works: *Cycle II* (Chamber), 1979. *Cycle II* (Keyboard), 1979. *Six Fragments of Gertrude Stein* (Vocal), 1979. *Selections from "Stein Times*

Seven" (Vocal), 1980. *Stein Times Seven* (Choral), 1980. *Cycle III* (Chamber), 1981. *Cycle III* (Vocal), 1981. *Death Fugue* (Chamber), 1981. *Death Fugue* (Vocal), 1981. *Meditation (in Memory of John Lennon)* (Chamber), 1981. *Partita* (Solo Instrumental), 1981-1995. *The Blue Animals* (Vocal), 1982. *Dream of the Morning Sky* (Vocal), 1982-1983. *Morningsongs* (Vocal), 1982-1983. *Nocturne* (Vocal), 1982. *Dream of the Morning Sky* (Orchestra), 1982-1983. *Morningsongs* (Orchestra), 1982-1983. *Music for Trio* (Chamber), 1982. *Nocturne* (Chamber), 1982. *Suite in Three Parts* (Keyboard), 1982. *Suite in Three Parts* (Solo Instrumental), 1982. *Teach Me Thy Way, O Lord* (Choral), 1982. *America(n) (Day)dreams* (Chamber), 1984. *America(n) (Day)dreams* (Vocal), 1984. *Praise Ye the Lord* (Choral), 1984. *I Will Lie Down* (Choral), 1985. *Passacaglia — Variations* (Chamber), 1985. *Passacaglia—Variations* (Solo Instrumental), 1985. *Invisible Mosaic I* (Chamber), 1986-1987. *Love Scenes* (Vocal), 1986-1987. *Lullaby (from Before Sleep and Dreams)* (Keyboard), 1987. *Phantom Polka* (Keyboard), 1987. *Barbara Allen* (Orchestra), 1988. *Barbara Allen* (Vocal), 1988. *Delicate Songs* (Chamber), 1988. *Invisible Mosaic II* (Chamber), 1988. *Invisible Mosaic II* (Orchestra), 1988. *Invisible Mosaic III* (Orchestra), 1988. *Songs of Innocents, Book I* (Vocal), 1989. *Symphony in Waves* (Orchestra), 1989. *Before Sleep and Dreams* (Keyboard), 1990. *Brilliant Sky, Infinite Sky* (Chamber), 1990. *Brilliant Sky, Infinite Sky* (Vocal), 1990. *Musica Celestis* (Orchestra), 1990. *String Quartet, "Musica Celestis"* (Chamber), 1990. *Le Quattro Stagioni dalla Cucina Futurismo* (Chamber), 1991. *Mozart en Route: "A Little Traveling Music"* (Chamber), 1991. *Second Symphony* (Orchestra), 1991. *Simple Songs* (Orchestra), 1991. *Songs of Innocents, Book II* (Vocal), 1991. *Aria—Lament* (Solo Instrumental), 1992. *Superstar Etude No. 1* (Keyboard), 1992. *New Era Dance* (Orchestra), 1992. *Harlem River Reveille* (Chamber), 1993. *Hymn* (Keyboard), 1993. *100 Greatest Dance Hits* (Chamber), 1993. *Still Movement with Hymn* (Chamber), 1993. *Colored Field* (Concerto for English Horn and Orchestra), 1994. *Air* (Chamber), 1995. *Air* (Solo Instrumental), 1995. *Goblin Market* (Theater), 1995. *Goblin Market* (Vocal), 1995. *Lament and Prayer* (Orchestra), 1995. *Simple Songs* (Vocal), 1991, revised 1995. *Air* (Orchestra), 1996. *Salsa Pasada* (Orchestra), 1996. *Too Hot Toccata* (Orchestra), 1996. *Double Concerto for Guitar and Violin* (Orchestra), 1997.

Other Awards: National Endowment for the Arts Grant. Rome Prize Fellowship, 1984-1985. Bearns Prize, Columbia University, NY, 1985. Guggenheim Fellow, Guggenheim Foundation, 1985, 1986. New York Foundation for the Arts Fellowship, 1988. ASCAP Award. BMI Student Composer Award. Stoger Prize from Chamber Music Society of Lincoln Center. Tippett Award.

For More Information: Schwarz, K. Robert, "How Does a Young Composer Spell Success? S-e-c-u-r-i-t-y," *New York Times,* October 23, 1994; Schwarz, K Robert, "A Young Musician and His Dilemma," *New York Times,* June 27, 1993; Anthony Michael, "Aaron Jay Kernis: At 36, An Intense and Imaginative Composer," *American Record Guide,* May/June 1997; Whitaker, Barbara, "Halls Are Alive With Pulitzer-Winning Music," *New York Times,* June 7, 1998.

Commentary: The 1998 Pulitzer Prize in Music was awarded to *String Quartet No. 2,* composed by Aaron Jay Kernis. A chamber piece, also called *musica instrumentalis,* it premiered on January 10, 1998 at Merkin Concert Hall, performed by The Lark Quartet.

Aaron Jay Kernis was born in Philadelphia, Pennsylvania. Kernis took violin lessons at an early age, and taught himself piano beginning at age 12. He started composing at 13. He studied music at the San Francisco Conservatory and the Manhattan School of Music, where he is currently on the faculty. Kernis counts among his teachers three Pulitzer Prize winners: Jacob Druckman, Bernard Rands, and Charles Wuorinen. He received national acclaim for *Dream of the Morning Sky,* his first orchestral work, premiered by the New York Philharmonic at the 1983 Horizons Festival.

National Reporting

1948

Bert Andrews 891

Birth: June 2, 1901; Colorado Springs, CO. **Death:** August 21, 1953. **Parents:** Bertrand A. Andrews and Laura (Whitaker). **Education:** Stanford University, CA. **Spouse:** Martha Nadine Wright. **Children:** John Wright, Peter Ferguson.

Prize: *National Reporting,* 1948: *New York Herald-Tribune,* New York: New York Herald-Tribune, 1947.

Career: Reporter, *Sacramento (CA) Star,* 1924-25; Reporter, City Editor, Columnist, *San Diego (CA) Sun,* 1925-27; Reporter, *Chicago Herald Examiner,* 1927-28; Staff member, *Detroit Times,* 1928-29; Staff member, *Paris (France) Herald,* 1929; Staff member, *New York American,* 1930-37; Staff member, *New York Herald-Tribune,* 1937-; Washington (DC) Bureau Chief, *New York Herald-Tribune,* 1941-53; War Correspondent, *New York Herald-Tribune,* 1943-44.

Selected Works: *Washington Witch Hunt,* 1948. *A Tragedy of History: A Journalist's Confidential Role in the Hiss-Chambers Case* (with Peter Andrews), 1962.

Other Awards: National Headliners Club Award, 1945. Raymond Clapper Memorial Award, 1946. Page One Award, New York Newspaper Guild, 1947. Sigma Delta Chi Award, 1947. Heywood Broun Award, 1948.

For More Information: *New York Times,* 4 May (1948): 22; *New York Times,* 22 August (1953): 15.

Commentary: Bert Andrews won a Pulitzer Prize for his series of stories on the State Department "loyalty checks." His reporting enabled several dismissed officials to resign without prejudice rather than on unnamed charges. Andrews was a well-respected newspaperman. He traveled to the Pacific area as a war correspondent in 1944. He covered the United Nations conferences in 1945 and 1946. He died unexpectedly of a heart ailment while in New York to cover President Eisenhower's visit. The President expressed his personal condolences upon hearing of Andrews's death.

Nathaniel Solon Finney 892

Birth: October 10, 1903; Stewartsville, MN. **Death:** December 19, 1982. **Parents:** Ross Lee Finney and Caroline (Mitchell). **Education:** University of Minnesota: BA. **Spouse:** Flora Edwards (m. 1930, died 1971).

Prize: *National Reporting,* 1948: *New York Herald-Tribune,* New York: New York Herald-Tribune, 1947.

Career: Reporter, *Minneapolis (MN) Star,* 1925-29; Staff member, Harcourt, Brace & Company Publishers, 1929-30; Editor, Building Trade Publication, 1930-33; Reporter, *Minneapolis (MN) Star,* 1933-35; City Editor, *Minneapolis (MN) Star Journal,* 1935-39; Feature Editor, *Minneapolis (MN) Star Journal,* 1939-41; Washington (DC) Correspondent, *Minneapolis (MN) Star and Tribune* and *Look* magazine, 1941-50; Editorial Page Editor, *Minneapolis (MN) Star,* 1950-53; Washington (DC) Bureau Chief, *Buffalo (NY) Evening News,* 1953-68.

Selected Works: *Headlines and By-Lines: Journalism for High Schools* (with William Naill Otto), 1946.

Other Awards: Raymond Clapper Memorial Award, 1947. Outstanding Achievement Award, University of Minnesota, 1957. Hall of Fame, Sigma Delta Chi, 1975.

For More Information: *New York Times,* 22 December (1982): B12; *Washington Post,* 22 December (1982): B10.

Commentary: Nat S. Finney's exclusive reports on the Truman administration's plan to impose secrecy on the ordinary operations of federal agencies during peacetime won him a Pulitzer Prize. It also led to an amendment to an executive order.

Finney covered Washington for a number of years. He was one of the first reporters admitted to the Los Alamos Laboratory in 1945 and he witnessed the atomic bomb tests on Bikini Island in 1946. He is believed to be the first journalist to report the presence of Russian missiles in Cuba in 1962. He wrote his story on the buildup on August 16, 1962. He retired from the *Buffalo Evening News* in 1968.

1949

Charles Prescott Trussel 893

Birth: August 3, 1892; Chicago, IL. **Death:** October 2, 1968. **Parents:** Homer Milton Trussel and Margaret (Shuck). **Spouse:** Beatrice W. Tait (m. 1923). **Children:** Charles, Galen.

Prize: *National Reporting,* 1949: *New York Times,* New York: New York Times, 1948.

Career: Baltimore and Ohio Railroad worker; Owner, lumber business; Reporter, *Baltimore (MD) American,* 1916-17; Reporter, *Baltimore (MD) News,* 1917; Reporter, *Baltimore (MD) Sun,* 1917-19; Served in U.S. Army, 1918-1919; Copyreader, *Baltimore (MD) Sun,* 1919-22; Assistant City Editor, *Baltimore (MD) Sun,* 1922-25; City Editor, *Baltimore (MD) Sun,* 1925-32; Staff member, Washington (DC) Bureau, *Baltimore (MD) Sun,* 1932-41; Staff member, Washington (DC) Bureau, *New York Times,* 1941-65.

For More Information: *New York Times,* 3 October (1968): 47.

Commentary: C.P. Trussel began his career as a newspaperman in 1916 after working in the railroad, lumber, and automobile tire businesses. His continually excellent coverage of Washington, DC won him a Pulitzer Prize. He wrote about Congress, the Inter-American Defense Pact at Rio, and various presidential trips during his career.

1950

Edwin Otto Guthman 894

Birth: August 11, 1919; Seattle, WA. **Parents:** Otto Guthman and Hilda (Leiser). **Religion:** Jewish. **Education:** University of Washington: BS. **Spouse:** Jo Ann Cheim (m. 1947). **Children:** Lester, Edwin H., Gary, Diane.

Prize: *National Reporting,* 1950: *Seattle Times,* October 21, Seattle, WA: Seattle Times, 1949.

Career: Editor, college paper; Sports and General Assignment Reporter, *Seattle (WA) Star,* 1941; Served in U.S. Army, 1941-45; Sports and General Assignment Reporter, *Seattle (WA) Star,* 1945-47; General Assignment Reporter, *Seattle (WA) Times,* 1947-61; Director of Public Information, U.S. Department of Justice, 1961-64; Press Secretary, Attorney General Robert F. Kennedy, 1964-65; National News Editor, *Los Angeles Times,* 1965-77; Editor, *Philadel-*

phia (PA) Inquirer, 1977-87; Professor, University of Southern California School of Journalism, 1987-.

Selected Works: *We Band of Brothers,* 1971. *Robert Kennedy, in His Own Words: The Unpublished Recollections of the Kennedy Years* (with others), 1988. *RFK: Collected Speeches* (with others), 1993.

Other Awards: Purple Heart. Silver Star. Nieman Fellow, Harvard University, MA, 1950-51. Alumnus Summa Laude Dignatus, University of Washington, Seattle, 1975. Washington State Hall of Journalism Achievement, Washington State University, 1992. Distinguished Achievement in Journalism Award, University of Southern California School of Journalism, 1993. Honorary Degree, Holy Family College, PA, 1986.

For More Information: *Current Biography Yearbook, 1950,* New York: H. W. Wilson Company, 1950: 211-212; Hohenberg, John, *The Pulitzer Prize Story,* New York: Columbia University Press, 1959: 317-320; Rothmyer, Karen, *Winning Pulitzers: The Stories Behind Some of the Best News Coverage of Our Time,* New York: Columbia University Press, 1991: 71-83.

Commentary: Edwin O. Guthman investigated the accusation that Dr. Melvin R. Rader was a Communist. Dr. Rader, a professor of philosophy at the University of Washington, denied the accusation. Guthman checked out the professor's story, and in six months, he had the information that confirmed Dr. Rader's innocence. He story was printed on page one of the *Seattle Times* on October 21, 1949.

1951
No award

1952

Anthony Harry Leviero 895

Birth: November 24, 1905; Brooklyn, NY. **Death:** September 3, 1956. **Parents:** Anthony Faustino Leviero and Thomasina (Lepore). **Education:** Columbia University, NY. City College, NY. **Spouse:** Fay Harrison (m. 1936). **Children:** Toni.

Prize: *National Reporting,* 1952: *New York Times,* New York: New York Times, 1951.

Career: Auditor, maritime insurance and steamship firms, 1925-26; Copyboy, *New York (NY) American,* 1926; Police Reporter, *New York (NY) American,* 1926-28; General Assignment Reporter, *Bronx (NY) Home News,* 1928; Reporter, *New York Times,* 1929-41; Served in U.S. Army, 1941-46; Correspondent, Washington (DC), *New York Times,* 1946-.

For More Information: *New York Times,* 4 September (1956): 29.

Commentary: Anthony Leviero won a Pulitzer Prize for his exclusive article in April 1951 on the conversations between President Truman and General MacArthur when they were at Wake Island in October 1950. Another story he covered that year was the assassination attempt by two members of the Puerto Rican Nationalists Army on President Truman on November 1, 1950.

1953

Don Ford Whitehead
Full entry appears as **#616** under "International Reporting," 1951.

1954

Richard Lawson Wilson   896
Birth: September 3, 1905; Galesburg, IL. **Death:** January 18, 1981. **Parents:** Frank Wilson and Emily E. (McCord). **Education:** Iowa State College. University of Iowa. **Spouse:** Katherine Young Macy (m. 1928). **Children:** Susan, Katherine.

Prize: *National Reporting,* 1954: *Des Moines Register and Tribune,* Des Moines, IA: Des Moines Register and Tribune, 1953.

Career: Police Reporter, *Des Moines (IA) Register,* 1926-28; Reporter, *St. Louis (MO) Globe-Democrat,* 1928; City Political Reporter, *Des Moines (IA) Register,* 1928-30; City Editor, *Des Moines (IA) Register,* 1930-33; Washington (DC) Correspondent, *Des Moines (IA) Register and Tribune,* 1933-37; Washington (DC) Bureau Chief, Cowles Publishing, 1938-70; President of National Press Building Corporation, Washington, 1962-72.

Selected Works: *Setting the Course,* 1970. *A New Road for America: Major Policy Statements* (with Richard Nixon), 1972.

Other Awards: Sigma Delta Chi Award, 1954. National Headliners Club Award, 1954. Golden Plate Award, American Academy Achievements, 1966. Honorary Degrees: Drake University, IA, 1956; Iowa Wesleyan College, 1958; Dakota Wesleyan University, 1967.

For More Information: *New York Times,* 19 January (1981): D11.

Commentary: Richard L. Wilson's exclusive three-part series published in November 1953 gave a detailed account of the Federal Bureau of Investigation's report on the late Harry Dexter White while at the same time withholding "sensitive" aspects of the report. White was appointed as the United States director of the International Monetary Fund by President Truman. The U.S. Attorney General asserted that Truman had known about White's link to Soviet es-

pionage because of the FBI report.

Wilson was a longtime Washington reporter. He covered every national political campaign from 1932-1972.

1955

Joseph Anthony Lewis   897

Birth: March 27, 1927; New York, NY. **Parents:** Kassel Lewis and Sylvia (Surut). **Religion:** Jewish. **Education:** Harvard University, MA: BA, With Honors. **Spouse:** Linda Rannells (m. 1951, div. 1982); Margaret H. Marshall (m. 1984). **Children:** Eliza, David, Mia (LR).

Prize: *National Reporting,* 1955: *Washington Daily News,* Washington, DC: Washington Daily News, 1954. *National Reporting,* 1963: *New York Times,* New York: New York Times, 1962.

Career: Served in U.S. Navy; Reporter, Executive Editor, Managing Editor, college paper, *Harvard Crimson;* Copyboy, *New York Times,* 1946; Writer, "News of the Week in Review" Section, *New York Times,* 1948-52; Member, Democratic National Committee, 1952; General Assignment Reporter, *Washington (DC) Daily News,* 1952-55; Supreme Court Reporter, *New York Times,* 1955-63; Foreign Correspondent, London (England) Bureau, *New York Times,* 1963-65; London (England) Bureau Chief, *New York Times,* 1965-72; Columnist, "Abroad At Home," *New York Times,* 1969-; Law Lecturer, Harvard University (MA), 1974-89; James Madison Visiting Professor, Columbia University (NY), 1983-.

Selected Works: *The Supreme Court: Process and Change; John F. Murray Endowment Lecture,* 1963. *Gideon's Trumpet,* 1964. *Portrait of a Decade: The Second American Revolution,* 1964. *The Supreme*

Court and How It Works: The Story of the Gideon Case; American Birthright Books, 1966. *Gideon's Trumpet: The Legal Classics Library,* 1991. *Make No Law: The Sullivan Case and the First Amendment,* 1991.

Other Awards: Heywood Broun Award, 1955. Nieman Fellow, Harvard University, MA, 1956-57.

For More Information: *Boston Globe,* 18 May (1989): 85; *San Diego Union-Tribune,* 7 April (1996): G5; *Boston Globe,* 1 April (1997): 13:1.

Commentary: Anthony Lewis won his Pulitzer Prizes for work he did at different newspapers. The 1955 prize was for articles about a victim of the Loyalty-Security program, a longtime Federal civil servant, who was restored to his job as a result of the articles. The 1963 prize was for coverage of the Supreme Court, in particular of the decisions holding that legislative districts must be roughly equal in population. Lewis's examination of the decision on reapportionment and the consequences for the states was specifically cited by the Pulitzer board.

1956

Charles Leffingwell Bartlett   898

Birth: August 14, 1921; Chicago, IL. **Parents:** Valentine C. Bartlett and Marie (Frost). **Religion:** Roman Catholic. **Education:** Yale University, CT: BA. **Spouse:** Josephine Martha Buck (m. 1950). **Children:** Peter Buck, Michael Valentine, Robert Shubael, Helen Buck.

Prize: *National Reporting,* 1956: *Chattanooga Times,* Chattanooga, TN: Chattanooga Times, 1955.

Career: Associate Editor, college paper, *Yale Daily News;* Summer Staff member, *Winston-Salem (NC) Journal,* 1942; Member of Intelligence, U.S. Navy, 1943-46; Staff member, *Chattanooga (TN) Times,* 1946-48; Correspondent, Washington (DC), *Chattanooga Times,* 1948-62; Columnist, *Chicago Sun-Times,* 1963-75; Columnist, *Chicago Daily News,* 1975-78; Columnist, Field Syndicate, 1978-81; President, Jefferson Foundation, 1982-; Editor, *Coleman/Bartlett's Washington Focus,* 1988-.

Selected Works: *Facing the Brink: An Intimate Study of Crisis Diplomacy* (with Edward Weintral), 1967.

Commentary: Charles L. Bartlett investigated and discovered that the secretary of the Air Force had a conflict of interest with his New York City business management company, which had obtained fees from companies holding government contracts. The secretary resigned, and the United States Senate started investigation hearings into the matter.

1957

James Barrett Reston   899

Birth: November 3, 1909; Clydebank, Scotland. **Death:** December 6, 1995. **Parents:** James Reston and Johanna (Irving). **Education:** University of Illinois: BS. **Spouse:** Sarah June Fulton (m. 1935). **Children:** Richard, James, Thomas.

Prize: *Telegraphic Reporting (National),* 1945: *New York Times,* New York: New York Times, 1944. *National Reporting,* 1957: *New York Times,* New York: New York Times, 1956.

Career: Staff member, *Springfield (OH) Daily News,* 1932-33; Publicity Department Member, Ohio State University, 1933; Publicity Director, Cincinnati Baseball Club, 1934; Sportswriter, theatre columnist; Reporter, New York (NY), Associated Press, 1934-37; London (England), Associated Press, 1937-39; Reporter, London (England), *New York Times,* 1939-41; Reporter, Washington (DC), *New York Times,* 1941-89; Chief Washington (DC) Correspondent, Bureau Chief, *New York Times,* 1953-64; Associate Editor, *New York Times,* 1964-68; Executive Editor, *New York Times,* 1968-69; Vice President, *New York Times,* 1969-74; Columnist, Consultant, *New York Times,* 1974-89; Director, *New York Times* Company, 1989; Co-Chairman of the Board, *The Vineyard Gazette,* 1968-95.

Selected Works: *Prelude to Victory,* 1943. *Walter Lippmann and His Times* (with Marquis William Childs), 1959. *Artillery of the Press: Elihu Root Lectures, 1965-66,* 1967. *Sketches in the Sand,* 1967. *Washington,* 1986. *Deadline: A Memoir,* 1991.

Other Awards: Overseas Press Club Award, 1949, 1951, 1953. George Polk Memorial Award, Long Island University, NY, 1954. University of Missouri Medal, 1961. John Peter Zenger Award, 1964. Elijah Parish Lovejoy Award, Colby College, ME,

1974. Fourth Estate Award, National Press Club, 1974. Presidential Medal of Liberty, 1986. Helen B. Bernstein Excellence in Journalism Award, 1988. Chevalier, Legion d'Honneur, France. Ordre National du Merit, Chile. Commander, Order of the British Empire. Order of St. Olav, Norway. Order of Leopold, Belgium. Honorary Degrees: Colgate University, NY, 1951; Oberlin College, OH, 1955; Rutgers University, NJ, 1957; Dartmouth University, NH, 1959; New York University, 1961; Kenyon College, OH, 1962; Columbia University, NY, 1963; Boston College, 1963; Brandeis University, MA, 1964; University of Michigan, 1965; University of North Carolina, 1968; Williams College, MA, 1968; Harvard University, MA, 1970; Stanford University, CA, 1972; University of Utah, 1973; Kent State University, OH, 1974; Colby College, ME, 1975; Yale University, CT, 1977; Miami University, OH; University of Maryland; Northeastern University, MA, 1976; University of Glasgow, Scotland, 1983.

For More Information: *Akron Beacon Journal,* 4 November (1973); *Los Angeles Times,* 7 December (1995): A28; *New York Times,* 8 December (1995): A1+.

Commentary: James "Scotty" Reston joined the staff of the *New York Times* on the very day that war broke out in 1939. He won his first Pulitzer Prize for chronicling the birth of the United Nations at the Dumbarton Oaks Conference. His second was for his reporting and interpretive writing throughout the year. The example of his work that was cited in his award was the effect of President's Eisenhower's illness on the Executive branch of the government.

1958

Clark Raymond Mollenhoff   900

Birth: April 16, 1921; Burnside, IA. **Death:** March 2, 1991. **Parents:** Raymond Eldon Mollenhoff and Margaret Genevieve (Clark). **Religion:** Roman Catholic. **Education:** Webster City Junior College, IA. Drake University, IA: LLB. **Spouse:** Georgia Giles Osmundson (m. 1939, div. 1978); Jane Cook Schurz (m. 1981). **Children:** Gjore Jean, Jacquelin Sue, Clark Raymond Jr. (GO); Stepchildren: James, Jay, Robert, Susan (JS).

Prize: *National Reporting,* 1958: Associated Press, 1957.

Career: Police, Municipal Court Reporter, *Des Moines (IA) Register and Tribune,* 1941-44; Served in U.S. Navy, 1944-46; County Courthouse and Statehouse Reporter, *Des Moines (IA) Register and Tribune,* 1946-49; Reporter, Washington (DC), Cowles Publications, 1950-61; Member, U.S. Advisory Commission on Information Policy, 1962-65; Special Counsel, President Richard Nixon, 1969-70; Washington (DC) Bureau Chief, *Des Moines (IA) Register and Tribune,* 1970-; Journalism Professor, Washington and Lee University, 1976-90.

Selected Works: *Deadly Dilemma: Defense and Democracy: John Peter Zenger Award Series, 1961, 1962. Washington Cover-up, 1962. Life Line of Democracy; William Allen White Memorial Lecture, Number 15, 1964. Tentacles of Power: The Story of Jimmy Hoffa, 1965. Despoilers of Democracy, 1965. The Pentagon: Politics, Profits, and Plunder, 1967. George Romney, Mormon in Politics, 1968. Game Plan for Disaster, 1976. The Man Who Pardoned Nixon, 1976. The President Who Failed: Carter out of Control, 1980. Investigative Reporting: From Courthouse to White House, 1981. Atanasoff: Forgotten Father of the Computer, 1988. Ballad to an Iowa Farmer and Other Reflections, 1991.*

Other Awards: Nieman Fellow, Harvard University, MA, 1949-50. Sigma Delta Chi Award, 1952, 1954, 1958. Raymond Clapper Memorial Award, 1955. Heywood Broun Memorial Award, 1955. Distinguished Alumni Award, Drake University, IA, 1956. National Headliners Club Award, 1960. Eisenhower Exchange Fellowship, 1960-61. William Allen White Foundation Award, 1964. Washington Correspondents Hall of Fame, Society of Professional Journalists, 1979. George Mason Award, Sigma Delta Chi, Richmond Chapter, VA, 1987. Honorary Degrees: Colby College, ME, 1959; Cornell College, IA, 1960; Drake University, IA, 1961; Iowa Wesleyan College, 1966.

For More Information: Hohenberg, John, *The Pulitzer Prize Story,* New York: Columbia University Press, 1959: 39-44; *New Republic,* 8 April (1967); *Contemporary Authors, 1st Revision, Volumes 17-20,* Detroit: Gale Research Company, 1976: 284; *Chicago Tribune,* 3 March (1991): C6; *New York Times,*

3 March (1991): 1; *New York Times,* 4 March (1991): D9.

Commentary: Clark Mollenhoff's winning articles in 1957 capped a five-year campaign to have "racketeering in some labor unions revealed, stopped, and punished." His reporting resulted in the McCellan Senate hearings where wrongdoing was admitted by several labor leaders. Many other labor leaders took the Fifth Amendment.

Relman George Morin

Full entry appears as **#614** under "International Reporting," 1951.

1959

Howard Van Smith   901

Birth: April 6, 1909; Forest Hill, NJ. **Death:** August 14, 1986. **Parents:** Arthur Lockwood Van Smith and Florence (Garrettson). **Spouse:** Anne McCarron (m. 1938, div. 1965); Micheline Mathews (m. 1965). **Children:** Garrett, Parris, Antony, William (AM).

Prize: *National Reporting,* 1959: *Miami News,* Miami, FL: Miami News, 1958.

Career: Staff Reporter, *New York Times,* 1930-32; Freelance writer, 1933-35; Heating and Hydraulics Engineer, 1935-42; Civilian Engineer, U.S. Air Force, 1942-44; Reporter, *Orlando (FL) Sentinel,* 1944; Sunday Editor, *Miami (FL) News,* 1945-57; Lecturer, University of Miami (FL), 1948-54; Writer, *Miami (FL) News,* 1957-65; Reporter, *Ft. Lauderdale (FL) News,* 1965-77; Administrative Assistant, Florida Department of Agriculture, 1978-80; Editor, *Florida Nurseryman,* 1981-86; Gardening Columnist, *Miami (FL) News,* ?-1986.

Selected Works: *The New Speech-O-Gram Technique for Persuasive Public Speaking* (with C. Raymond Van Dusen), 1962. *Juan Can Read and How!,* 1976.

Other Awards: Meritorious Award, Florida Public Health Association, 1959. Service to Mankind Award, 1961. Horticulture Hall of Fame, 1976. Foremost Gardening Writer in America and Canada, American Association of Nurserymen, 1978. New York State Center for Migrant Studies Fellow, New York State University, Geneseo.

For More Information: *Chicago Tribune,* 18 August (1986): Chicagoland, 7.

Commentary: Howard Van Smith wrote a series of articles on the deplorable conditions in a migrant workers' camp. His articles brought in $100,000 in contributions and raised the consciousness of people to the plight of migratory workers.

1960

Vance Henry Trimble   902

Birth: July 6, 1913; Harrison, AR. **Parents:** Guy Lee Trimble and Josephine (Crump). **Religion:** Southern Baptist. **Spouse:** Elzene Miller (m. 1932). **Children:** Carol Ann.

Prize: *National Reporting,* 1960: Scripps-Howard Newspaper Alliance, 1959.

Career: Reporter, *Okemah (OK) Daily Leader,* 1927; Cub Reporter, *Wewoka (OK) Times-Democrat,* 1928-31; News Editor, *Maud (OK) Daily Enterprise,* 1931-32; Deskman, *Seminole (OK) Morning News,* 1932; Staff member, *Seminole (OK) Producer;* Staff member, *Seminole Reporter;* Staff member, *Wewoka (OK) Morning News;* Staff member, *Shawnee (OK) Morning News;* Staff member, *Muskogee (OK) Times-Democrat and Phoenix;* News Editor, *Okmulgee (OK) Times,* 1936; Deskman and Financial Writer, *Tulsa (OK) Tribune,* 1937; Reporter and Deskman, *Beaumont (TX) Enterprise,* 1937; Telegraph Editor, *Port Arthur (TX) News,* 1938-39; Copy Editor, *Houston (TX) Press,* 1939; Special Writer and City Editor, *Houston (TX) Press,* 1939-50; Managing Editor, *Houston (TX) Press,* 1950-55; News Editor, Washington (DC) Bureau, Scripps-Howard Newspaper Alliance, 1955-63; Editor, *Covington (KY) Kentucky Post and Times-Star,* 1963-79.

Selected Works: *Scripps-Howard Handbook,* 1948. *The Uncertain Miracle,* 1974. *Reagan, the Man from Main Street USA,* 1980. *Heroes, Plain Folks, and Skunks: The Life and Times of Happy Chandler, an Autobiography,* 1989. *Sam Walton: The Inside Story of America's Richest Man,* 1990. *The Astonishing Mr. Scripps: The Turbulent Life of America's Penny Press Land,* 1992. *Overnight Success: Federal Express and Frederick Smith, Its Renegade Creator,* 1993. *An Empire Undone: The Wild Rise and Hard Fall of Chris Whittle,* 1995.

Other Awards: Sigma Delta Chi Award, 1960. Raymond Clapper Memorial Award, 1960. Oklahoma Journalism Hall of Fame, 1974. Frank Luther Mott Award, 1993.

For More Information: *Contemporary Authors, Volumes 49-52,* Detroit: Gale Research Company, 1975.

Commentary: Vance Trimble won a Pulitzer Prize for his series of articles that exposed nepotism on the Congressional payroll. After his series was published, the Senate adopted a resolution to make the salaries of all its employees public information.

1961

Edward Roger Cony   903

Birth: March 15, 1923; Augusta, ME. **Parents:** Daniel William Cony and Mary (Doyle). **Religion:** Roman Catholic. **Education:** Colby College, ME. Reed College, OR: BA. Stanford University, CA: MA. **Spouse:** Susan Wheat (m. 1954). **Children:** Ann, Daniel, Elizabeth, Katharine, Marilyn, Lauren.

Prize: *National Reporting,* 1961: *Wall Street Journal,* New York: Dow Jones, 1960.

Career: Served in U.S. Army, 1943-46; Reporter, *Portland (OR) Oregonian,* 1951-52; Freelance writer, magazines, 1952-53; Staff member, San Francisco (CA) Bureau, *Wall Street Journal,* 1953-55; Los Angeles (CA) Bureau Manager, *Wall Street Journal,* 1955-57; Head, Jacksonville (FL) Bureau, *Wall Street Journal,* 1957-59; Staff member, New York, *Wall Street Journal,* 1959-60; News Editor, *Wall Street Journal,* 1960-64; Assisting Managing Editor, Pacific Coast Edition, *Wall Street Journal,* 1964-65; Managing Editor, *Wall Street Journal,* 1965-70; Executive Editor, *Wall Street Journal,* 1970; Vice President, *Wall Street Journal,* 1972-86; President, Dow Jones Publishing Company, Asia, 1976-80; Vice President, News, Dow Jones, 1977-; Director, Ottaway Nespapers, Inc., 1980-88.

For More Information: Taft, William H., *Encyclopedia of Twentieth-Century Journalists,* New York: Garland Publishing, Inc., 1986; *New York Times,* 15 April (1988): C34.

Commentary: Edward R. Cony won a Pulitzer Prize for exploring the issue of business ethics. He examined a timber transaction between Georgia-Pacific Corporation, the nation's number-one plywood producer, and Carrol Shanks, a director of Georgia-Pacific and also President of the Prudential Insurance Company.

Cony spent all but six months of his career at the *Wall Street Journal* or some part of its parent company, Dow Jones. He retired in 1988 after 35 years with the company.

1962

Nathan Green Caldwell   904

Birth: July 16, 1912; St. Charles, MO. **Death:** February 11, 1985. **Parents:** Albert Green Caldwell and Sara (Jetton). **Education:** Southwestern College, CA. Cumberland University, KY. **Spouse:** Camilla Frances Jonston (m. 1936). **Children:** John Sam.

Prize: *National Reporting,* 1962: *Nashville Tennessean,* Nashville, TN: Nashville Tennessean, 1961.

Career: Reporter, *Trenton (TN) Herald-Democrat,* 1931-33; Staff, General Assignment Reporter,

Political Reporter, Labor Relations Reporter, Economics Reporter, *Nashville (TN) Tennessean,* 1934-85.

Selected Works: *The Cotton Picker Moves People,* 1947. *Nashville Tennessean,* "TVA and Crisis" (with others), 1956. *The Strange Romance of John L. Lewis and Cyrus Eaton,* 1961.

Other Awards: Nieman Fellow, Harvard University, MA, 1940-41. Rosenwald Fellowship, Study of Migration of Negroes Out of the South, 1946.

For More Information: *New York Times,* May 8, 1962: 32; Crawford, Charles Wann, *Oral History of the Tennessee Valley Authority: Interviews With Nat Caldwell, September 30, 1979,* Memphis, TN: Oral History Research Office, Memphis State University, 1979.

Commentary: Nat Caldwell and Gene Graham won a Pulitzer Prize "for their exclusive disclosure and six years of detailed reporting, under great difficulties, of the undercover cooperation between management interests in the coal industry and the United Mine Workers." The union was adjudged guilty on May 20, 1961 of violating Federal anti-trust laws.

Gene Swann Graham   905

Birth: August 26, 1924; Murray, KY. **Death:** May 24, 1982. **Parents:** Carmon McWade Graham and Opal (Swann). **Religion:** Disciples of Christ Christian Church. **Education:** Murray State College, KY: BS. **Spouse:** Martha Fentress (m. 1945). **Children:** Susan Marie, Betty Jane, Philip Gene.

Prize: *National Reporting,* 1962: *Nashville Tennessean,* Nashville, TN: Nashville Tennessean, 1961.

Career: Pilot, U.S. Navy, 1943-45; Reporter, Government Beats—City, County, State and Federal, *Nashville (TN) Tennessean,* 1948-64; Visiting Lecturer, University of Illinois, Urbana-Champaign, 1964-65; Associate Professor of Journalism, University of Illinois, Urbana-Champaign, 1965-71; Training Consultant, *Boston Globe,* 1966-70; Communications Consultant, Middle Tennessee State University, 1969-70; Campaign Press Aide, U.S. Senator Albert Gore, 1969; Seminar Leader, America Press Institute, Columbia University (NY), 1969-70; Professor of Journalism, University of Illinois, Urbana-Champaign, 1972-75; Columnist.

Selected Works: *Nieman Reports,* September 3, 1966. *Nieman Reports,* September 3, 1967. *Quill,* February 2, 1968. *One Man, One Vote,* 1972.

Other Awards: Nieman Fellow, Harvard University, MA, 1962-63. Distinguished Alumni Award, Murray State University, KY, 1962.

For More Information: *Nashville Tennessean,* 25 May (1982): 4.

Commentary: Gene S. Graham and Nat Caldwell were cited for their efforts in exposing the secret relationship between management and the

United Mine Workers union. They spent six years covering the story.

Gene Graham was a visiting lecturer at the University of Illinois, becoming a professor. He taught and had research interests in mass media and its impact on society and on the ethical problems of the news media. He wrote and illustrated a column for the *Tennessean* while he was in Illinois.

He battled cancer and then fought brain tumors for 10 years prior to his death in 1982.

1963

Joseph Anthony Lewis
Full entry appears as **#897** under "National Reporting," 1955.

1964

A. Merriman Smith   906

Birth: February 10, 1913; Savannah, GA. **Death:** April 13, 1970. **Parents:** Albert C. Smith and Juliet Worth (Merriman). **Education:** Oglethorpe University, GA. **Spouse:** Eleanor Doyle Ball (m. 1937, div. 1966); Gailey L. Johnson (m. 1966). **Children:** Merriman, Timothy, Allison (EB); Gaillean (GJ).

Prize: *National Reporting,* 1964: United Press International, 1963.

Career: Sportswriter, *Atlanta (GA) Georgian;* Staff member, Sunday magazine, *Atlanta (GA) Journal,* 1934-35; Managing Editor, *Athens (GA) Daily Times,* 1935-36; Staff Correspondent, United Press International, 1936-41; White House Correspondent, United Press International, 1941-70.

Selected Works: *Thank You, Mr. President: A White House Notebook,* 1946. *A President Is Many Men,* 1948. *Meet Mister Eisenhower,* 1955. *A President's Odyssey,* 1961. *The Good News Day: A Not Entirely Reverent Study of Native Habits and Customs in Modern Washington,* 1962. *The Murder of the Young President,* 1963. *Merriman Smith's Book of Presidents: A White House Memoir,* 1972.

Other Awards: National Headliners Club Award, 1945. Distinguished Service in Journalism Award, University of Missouri, 1963. Presidential Medal of Freedom, 1969. Honorary Degrees: Oglethorpe University, GA, 1964; Knox College, IL, 1968.

For More Information: *New York Times,* 5 May (1964): 39; *New York Times,* 14 April (1970): 47.

Commentary: Merriman Smith's thorough and timely coverage of the assassination of John F. Kennedy won him a Pulitzer Prize in 1964. He reported on every president from Roosevelt to Johnson. He traveled with all and covered their various trips, conferences, and summit meetings in the United States, Europe, and Asia. The White House Correspondents Association named their annual award for outstanding presidential coverage the Merriman Smith Award.

1965

Louis Martin Kohlmeier Jr.   907
Birth: February 17, 1926; St. Louis, MO. **Parents:** Louis Martin Kohlmeier and Anita (Werling). **Education:** University of Missouri: BA. **Spouse:** Barbara Ann Wilson (m. 1958). **Children:** Daniel Kimbrell, Ann Werling.

Prize: *National Reporting,* 1965: *Wall Street Journal,* New York: Dow Jones, 1964.

Career: Served in U.S. Army, 1950-52; Staff Writer, Chicago (IL) and St. Louis (MO) Bureaus, *Wall Street Journal,* 1952-57; Staff Writer, *St. Louis (MO) Globe-Democrat,* 1958-59; Staff Writer, Washington (DC), *Wall Street Journal,* 1960-; Washington (DC) Editor, *Financier Magazine,* 1977-, American University, Washington (DC).

Selected Works: *The Regulators: Watchdog Agencies and the Public Interest,* 1969. *God Save This Honorable Court,* 1972. *Conflicts of Interest,* 1976. *Reporting on Business and the Economy* (with others), 1981.

Other Awards: National Headliners Club Award, 1959. Sigma Delta Chi Award, 1964.

Commentary: Louis M. Kohlmeier won a Pulitzer Prize for his investigation into and reporting on the growing wealth of President Lyndon B. Johnson and his family. After Kohlmeier published his findings, the President disclosed a detailed audit of his finances on August 19, 1964. Kohlmeier visited over a dozen Texas towns and used records from the Federal Communications Commission, the *Congressional Record,* the Senate Commerce Committee, and a number of other government organizations to tally the fortune of the President.

1966

Haynes Bonner Johnson   908

Birth: July 9, 1931; New York, NY. **Parents:** Malcolm Malone Johnson and Ludie (Adams). **Religion:** Episcopalian. **Education:** University of Missouri: BJ. University of Wisconsin: MA. **Spouse:** Julia Ann Erwin (m. 1954, div.). **Children:** Katherine Adams, David Malone, Stephen Holmes, Sarah Brooks, Elizabeth Haynes.

Prize: *National Reporting,* 1966: *Washington Evening Star,* "Selma Revisited," July 26, Washington, DC: Washington Evening Star, 1965.

Career: Copyboy, *New York Sun,* through high school; Served in U.S. Army, 1952-55; Reporter, *Wilmington (DE) News-Journal;* General Assignment Reporter, City Reporter, National Desk Rewriteman, Copy Reader, Assistant City Editor, Night Editor, Special Projects, *Washington (DC) Star,* 1957-69; National Correspondent, *Washington (DC) Post,* 1969-73; Assistant Managing Editor, *Washington (DC) Post,* 1973-77; Ferris Professor of Journalism and Public Affairs, Princeton (NJ) University, 1975-78; Columnist, *Washington (DC) Post,* 1977-94; Professional-in-Residence, Annenberg School of Journalism, Northwestern University (IL), 1993; Political Commentary and Journalism Professor, George Washington University (Washington, DC), 1994-96.

Selected Works: *Dusk at the Mountain,* 1963. *The Bay of Pigs: The Leaders' Story of Brigade 2506,*

1964. *Ku Klux Klan: The Invisible Empire* (with David Lowe), 1967. *Fulbright: The Dissenter* (with Bernard M. Gwertzman), 1968. *The Unions: The Washington Post National Report* (with Nick Kotz), 1972. *Army in Anguish: The Washington Post National Report* (with George C. Wilson), 1972. *Lyndon* (with Richard Harwood), 1973. *The Working White House* (with Frank Johnston), 1975. *In the Absence of Power: Governing America,* 1980. *Evolution and Revolutions: The World in Change; M.L. Seidman Memorial Town Hall Lecture Series, Number 24* (with others), 1990. *Sleepwalking through History: America in the Reagan Years,* 1991. *Divided We Fall: Gambling with History in the Nineties,* 1994. *The System: The American Way of Politics at the Breaking Point* (with David S. Broder), 1996. *Contemporary Views of American Journalism: The Goldstein Program in Public Affairs* (with James M. Perry), 1997.

Other Awards: Public Service Award, Washington Newspaper Guild, 1962, 1968. Grand Award for Reporting, Washington Newspaper Guild, 1962, 1968. Interpretive Reporting Award, 1965. National Headliners Club Award, 1968. Sigma Delta Chi Award, 1969. Communications Fellow, Duke University, NC, 1973-74.

For More Information: *Contemporary Authors, New Revision Series, Volume 48,* Detroit: Gale Research Company, 1995; Riley, Sam G., *Biographical Dictionary of American Newspaper Columnists,* Westport, CT: Greenwood Press, 1995.

Commentary: Haynes Johnson covered the civil rights struggle in Selma, Alabama. His reporting on the marches in the South won him a Pulitzer Prize. His father, Malcolm Johnson, won a Local Reporting Pulitzer Prize in 1949. (Two other father-son winners were the Berrymans, who were cartoonists.)

Johnson covered almost all of the major news since the 1950s. He has reported on every president from Eisenhower to Clinton. Johnson was a finalist for a Pulitzer Prize in 1983 for a study of the impact of the recession on communities across America.

1967

Monroe William Karmin   909

Birth: September 2, 1929; Mineola, NY. **Parents:** Stanley Albert Karmin and Phyllis Rae (Appelbaum). **Education:** University of Illinois: BS. Columbia University, NY: MS. **Spouse:** Maryanne Sherman (m. 1955). **Children:** Paul Nance, Elizabeth Anne.

Prize: *National Reporting,* 1967: *Wall Street Journal,* New York: Dow Jones, 1966.

Career: Served in U.S. Air Force, 1951-52; News Staff member, Washington (DC) Bureau, *Wall Street Journal,* 1953-74; Professional Staff member, U.S. House Committee on Banking, Currency & Housing,

1974-76; Staff member, Washington (DC) Bureau, *Chicago Daily News,* 1977-78; National Economic Correspondent, Knight-Ridder Newspapers, 1978-81; Senior Economic Editor, *U.S. News & World Report* Magazine, 1981-91; Editor-at-Large, *Bloomberg Business News,* 1991-.

Selected Works: *Consumers Look at Federal Protective Services: Consumer Pamphlet, Number 10,* 1959.

For More Information: *Contemporary Authors, Volume 101,* Detroit: Gale Research Company, 1981.

Commentary: Monroe W. Karmin and Stanley W. Penn exposed the connection between American criminals and gambling in the Bahamas. Karmin left a desk job at the *Wall Street Journal* to go back to reporting full time. He also has written about high finance at the United States Treasury, the legal doctrine of the Supreme Court, and civil rights.

Stanley William Penn   910

Birth: January 12, 1928; New York, NY. **Parents:** Murray Penn and Lillian (Richman). **Education:** Brooklyn College, NY. University of Missouri: BA. **Spouse:** Esther Aronson (m. 1952). **Children:** Michael, Laurel.

Prize: *National Reporting,* 1967: *Wall Street Journal,* New York: Dow Jones, 1966.

Career: Reporter, Chicago (IL) and Detroit (MI) Bureaus, *Wall Street Journal,* 1952-57; Investigative Reporter, *Wall Street Journal,* 1957-90.

Selected Works: *Have I Got a Tip for You—and Other Tales of Dirty Secrets, Political Payoffs, and Corporate Scams: A Guide to Investigative Reporting,* 1994.

For More Information: Behrens, John C., *The Typewriter Guerrillas: Closeups of 20 Top Investigative Reporters,* Chicago: Nelson-Hall, 1977: 189-99; *Contemporary Authors, Volume 101,* Detroit: Gale Research Company, 1981.

Commentary: Stanley W. Penn and his colleague Monroe W. Karmin's reporting on the connection between American criminals and gambling in the Bahamas won them a Pulitzer Prize in 1967.

1968

Howard Anthony James Jr.   911

Birth: May 28, 1935; Iowa City, IA. **Parents:** Howard Anthony James and Catherine (Richey). **Education:** Michigan State University: BA. Michigan State University: LLD. **Spouse:** Dorothy Spear Fontaine (m. 1956, div. 1971); Judith Ray Vogel Munro (m. 1972). **Children:** Paul, Heidi (DF); Jonathan (JM); Stepchildren: Mark, Eric, Katherine, Stevenson (JM).

Prize: *National Reporting,* 1968: *Christian Science Monitor,* "Crisis in the Courts," Boston: Christian Science Monitor, 1967.

Career: Radio, television news reporter, Michigan; Correspondent, Midwestern (Chicago, IL) Bureau, *Christian Science Monitor,* 1964-65; Bureau Chief, Chicago (IL), *Christian Science Monitor,* 1965-70; President, Norway (ME) Howard James Company, Inc.; Publisher, *Portland Maine Business Journal;* Editor, Publisher, *Berlin (NH) Reporter;* Editor, Publisher, *Norway (ME) Advertiser-Democrat;* Editor, Publisher, *Rumford (ME) Falls Times;* President, Skowhegan (ME) Reporter Company; President, The Oxford Group; Publisher, *North Conway (NH) Irregular;* Publisher, *North Windham (ME) 302-Times,*.

Selected Works: *Crisis in the Courts,* 1968. *Children in Trouble: A National Scandal; World News in Focus,* 1969. *The Little Victims: How America Treats Its Children,* 1975. *Knock on Our Door: A Home for Troubled Girls* (with Riccarda Moseley), 1979.

Other Awards: Sidney Hillman Foundation Award, 1968. Public Service Award, American Trial Lawyers' Association, 1968. Silver Gavel Award, American Bar Association, 1968, 1970. Michigan Mental Health Man of the Year, 1970.

For More Information: *New York Times,* 7 May (1968): 34.

Commentary: Howard James and Nick Kotz were both awarded Pulitzer Prizes in the National Reporting category in 1968. Howard James won the award for his series of 13 articles on the nation's court systems. He researched and investigated the topic for more than six months. He traveled throughout the United States and uncovered abuses of justice and outdated procedures and policies. His series assessed the strong and the weak points of the judicial system as well as its role in society.

Nathan Kallison Kotz   912

Birth: September 16, 1932; San Antonio, TX. **Parents:** Jacob Kotz and Tybe (Kallison). **Education:** Dartmouth College, NH: AB, magna cum laude, Phi Beta Kappa. London School of Economics, England. **Spouse:** Mary Lynn Booth (m. 1960). **Children:** Jack Mitchell.

Prize: *National Reporting,* 1968: *Christian Science Monitor,* Boston: Christian Science Monitor, 1967.

Career: Served in U.S. Marine Corps, 1956-58; Reporter, *Des Moines (IA) Register,* 1958-64; Correspondent, Washington (DC), *Des Moines (IA) Register,* 1964-70; National Correspondent, *Washington (DC) Post,* 1970-73; Freelance writer, 1973-; Adjunct Professor, American University School of Communications, Washington, DC, 1978-86; Farmer, 1980;

Senior Journalist-in-Residence, Duke University, NC, 1983; Correspondent, PBS *Frontline,* 1992.

Selected Works: *Let Them Eat Promises: The Politics of Hunger in America,* 1969. *The Unions: Washington Post National Report* (with Haynes Bonner Johnson), 1972. *A Passion for Equality: George A. Wiley and the Movement* (with Mary Lynn Kotz), 1977. *Hunger in America: The Federal Response,* 1979. *Wild Blue Yonder: Money, Politics, and the B-1 Bomber,* 1988.

Other Awards: Reynolds Scholarship, London School of Economics, England, 1955-56. Sigma Delta Chi Award, 1966. Raymond Clapper Memorial Award, 1966, 1968. Robert F. Kennedy Journalism Award, 1968. Special Merit Award, American University, Washington, DC, 1981. National Magazine Award, 1985. Adjunct Faculty Award, American University, Washington, DC, 1985. Olive Branch Award, New York University Center for War, Peace and News Media, 1989.

For More Information: *New York Times,* 7 May (1968): 34.

Commentary: In 1968, two awards were given in the National Reporting category. One was given to Howard James and another awarded to Nick Kotz. Kotz's exposure of unsanitary conditions in the meat processing industry led to the Federal Wholesome Meat Act of 1967.

1969

Robert Cahn   913

Birth: March 9, 1917; Seattle, WA. **Death:** October 24, 1997. **Parents:** Adolph Cahen and Edna (May). **Religion:** Christian Scientist. **Education:** University of Washington: BA. **Spouse:** Patricia Lovelady (m. 1951).

Prize: *National Reporting,* 1969: *Christian Science Monitor,* Boston: Christian Science Monitor, 1968.

Career: Staff Reporter, *Seattle (WA) Star,* 1939-41; Served in U.S. Army, 1942-46; Reporter, *Pasadena (CA) Star-News,* 1946-48; Correspondent, Los Angeles (CA) Bureau, *Life* magazine, 1948-51; Associate Editor, Senior Editor, *Collier's* magazine, 1951-56; Los Angeles (CA) Bureau Chief, *Collier's* magazine, 1954-56; Freelance writer, 1957-60; Midwestern Editor, Chicago (IL) Bureau, *Saturday Evening Post,* 1961-62; White House Reporter, *U.S. Information Agency Wire Service,* 1963-64; Correspondent, Washington (DC) Bureau, *Christian Science Monitor,* 1965-70; Member, Presidential Council on Environmental Quality, 1970-72; Environmental Editor, *Christian Science Monitor,* 1973-74; Freelance writer, 1975-77; Field Editor, *Audubon Magazine,* 1978-82; Horace M. Albright Lecturer,

University of California at Berkeley, 1980; Special Assistant, U.S. President, Advising on National Parks, 1981-.

Selected Works: *Perle: My Story* (with Perle Mesta), 1959. *Will Success Spoil the National Parks? A Series Reprinted from the Christian Science Monitor,* 1968. *Where Do We Grow from Here?,* 1973. *Footprints on the Planet: A Search for an Environmental Ethic,* 1978. *American Photographers and the National Parks* (with Robert Glenn Ketchum), 1981. *Birth of the National Park Service: The Founding Years; Institute of the American West Books, Volume 2* (with Horace M. Albright), 1981. *The Fight to Save Wild Alaska,* 1982. *An Environmental Agenda for the Future* (with John H. Adams), 1985.

Other Awards: Conservation Service Award, United States Department of Interior, 1969. Honorary Degree, Allegheny College, PA, 1970. National Literary Award, National Recreation and Park Association. Distinguished Service Award, National Wildlife Federation.

For More Information: *New York Times,* 6 May (1969): 34; *Washington Post,* 28 October (1997): B6.

Commentary: Robert Cahn, along with photographer Norman Matheny, traveled over 20,000 miles and visited more than 20 national parks in his quest to answer the question, "How are the United States national parks going to survive the pressures of increased public use and still retain the values that made them worth preserving as a national heritage?" His series of articles on that topic concluded that the parks were generally in good shape but there could be cause for concern in the future. The series won him a Pulitzer Prize in National Reporting.

1970

William James Eaton   914

Birth: December 9, 1930; Chicago, IL. **Parents:** William Miller Eaton and Rose (Ellenbast). **Education:** Northwestern University, IL: BA, MA. **Spouse:** Marilynn Myers (m. 1952, div. 1980). **Children:** Susan, Sally Ann.

Prize: *National Reporting,* 1970: *Chicago Daily News,* Chicago: Chicago Daily News, 1969.

Career: Part-Time Reporter, *Evanston (IL) Review;* Staff member, *Chicago (IL) City News Bureau,* 1952-53; Served in U.S. Army, 1953-55; Washington (DC) Bureau, Staff member, United Press International, 1955-66; Washington (DC) Correspondent, *Chicago Daily News,* 1966-76; Knight-Ridder Newspapers Staff member, 1977-78; Congressional Correspondent, *Los Angeles Times,* 1978-, *Philadelphia (PA) Inquirer;* Curator, Hubert H. Humphrey Journalism Fellowship Program, University of Maryland; Hearst Visiting Professional, University of Maryland.

Selected Works: *Reuther* (with Frank Cormier), 1970.

Other Awards: Nieman Fellow, Harvard University, MA, 1962-63. Sidney Hillman Award, 1970.

For More Information: *New York Times,* 5 May (1970): 48.

Commentary: William J. Eaton won a Pulitzer Prize for his investigation of Judge Clement F. Haynesworth Jr.'s qualifications for the United States Supreme Court. His examination came after his paper, the *Chicago Daily News,* had come out editorially in support of Haynesworth's candidacy. Haynesworth was not confirmed by the Senate after disclosures of conflicts of interest.

1971

Lucinda Laura Franks   915

Birth: July 16, 1946; Chicago, IL. **Parents:** Thomas Edward Franks and Lorraine Lois (Leavitt). **Education:** Vassar College, NY: BA. **Spouse:** Robert M. Morgenthau (m. 1977). **Children:** Joshua, Amy Elinor.

Prize: *National Reporting,* 1971: United Press International, "The Story of Diana—The Making of a Terrorist," 1970.

Career: Staff member, London (England), United Press International, 1968-73; Reporter, Northern Ireland, *New York Times,* 1974-77; Visiting Professor, Vassar College (NY), 1977-82; Freelance writer, 1977-; Ferris Professor of Journalism, Princeton University (NJ), 1983.

Selected Works: *Waiting Out a War: The Exile of Private John Picciano,* 1974. *Wild Apples,* 1991.

Other Awards: New York Newspaper Writers Association Award, 1971. National Headliners Club Award, 1976. Society of Silurians Award, 1976.

Commentary: Lucinda Franks and Thomas Powers reconstructed the life of Diana Oughton, who died March 6, 1970 in a "bomb factory" in New York's Greenwich Village. The two worked for weeks investigating Oughton and her connections to the Students for a Democratic Society, and its violent fringe group, the Weathermen.

Franks became a freelance writer after working for the *New York Times* in Northern Ireland. She has written several articles about traveling with her family.

Thomas Moore Powers   916

Birth: December 12, 1940; New York, NY. **Parents:** Joshua Bryant Powers and Susan (Moore). **Education:** Yale University, CT: BA. **Spouse:** Candace Molloy (m. 1965). **Children:** Amanda, Susan, Cassandra.

Prize: *National Reporting,* 1971: United Press International, "The Story of Diana—The Making of a Terrorist," 1970.

Career: General Assignment Reporter, *New Haven (CT) Journal-Courier;* Reporter, *Rome (Italy) Daily American,* 1965-67; Freelance Reporter, London (England) *Observer;* New York (NY), United Press International, 1967-70; Freelance writer, 1970-; Founder, Co-editor, Publisher, *Steerforth Press,* 1993-.

Selected Works: *Diana: The Making of a Terrorist,* 1971. *The War at Home: Vietnam and the American People, 1964-68,* 1973. *The Man Who Kept the Secrets: Richard Helms & the CIA,* 1979. *Thinking about the Next War,* 1982. *Total War: What It Is, How It Got That Way* (with Ruthven Tremain), 1988. *Heisenberg's War: The Secret History of the German Bomb,* 1993.

For More Information: *Boston Globe,* 15 August (1996): E1.

Commentary: Thomas Powers and Lucinda Franks investigated the life and death of Diana Oughton. Oughton, an upper-middle-class young woman, had joined the group Students for a Democratic Society (SDS). She died in what was called a "bomb factory" in an apartment in New York's Greenwich Village. Powers and Franks penetrated SDS's militant faction, the Weathermen, and interviewed Oughton's family and friends to produce a five-article, 12,000-word series on "the making of a terrorist."

1972

Jack Anderson   917

Birth: October 19, 1922; Long Beach, CA. **Parents:** Orlando N. Anderson and Agnes (Mortensen). **Religion:** Church of Jesus Christ of Latter-Day Saints. **Education:** University of Utah. Georgetown University, Washington, DC. George Washington University, Washington, DC. **Spouse:** Olivia Farley (m. 1949). **Children:** Cheri, Lance, Laurie, Tina, Kevin, Randy, Tanya, Rodney, Bryan.

Prize: *National Reporting,* 1972.

Career: Editor, Boy Scout Page, *Deseret News;* Staff member, *Murray (UT) Eagle;* Staff member, *Salt Lake City (UT) Tribune,* 1939-41; Missionary, 1941-43; Cadet Officer, Merchant Marines, 1943; Foreign Correspondent, China, *Deseret News;* Served in U.S. Army, 1945; Quartermaster Corps, 1945-47; Staff member, Columnist Drew Pearson "Washington Merry-Go-Round," 1947-69; Editor, Washington (DC), *Parade* Magazine, 1954-68; Washington (DC) Bureau Chief, *Parade* Magazine, 1968-; Columnist, "Washington Merry-Go-Round," *Washington (DC) Post,* 1969-.

Selected Works: *McCarthy: The Man, the Senator, the Ism* (with Ronald W. May), 1952. *Washington Expose,* 1967. *Case against Congress* (with Drew Pearson), 1968. *American Government — Like It Is* (with Carl Kalvelage), 1972. *The Anderson Papers* (with George Clifford), 1974. *Confessions of a Muckraker: The Inside Story of Life in Washington during the Truman, Eisenhower, Kennedy, and Johnson Years* (with James Boyd), 1979. *The Cambodia File* (with Bill Pronzini), 1981. *Alice in Blunderland* (with John Kidner), 1983. *Fiasco* (with James Boyd), 1983. *Oil: The Real Story behind the World Energy Crisis* (with James Boyd), 1983. *Control: A Novel,* 1988. *Zero Time,* 1990. *Stormin' Norman: An American Hero* (with Dale Van Atta), 1991. *The Japan Conspiracy,* 1993. *Millennium,* 1994. *Inside the NRA: Armed and Dangerous: An Expose,* 1996. *Washington Money-Go-Round,* 1997.

Other Awards: Service to Journalism Award, Society of Professional Journalists, 1987.

For More Information: *New York Times,* 6 May (1969): 34; *Current Biography Yearbook, 1972,* New York: H.W. Wilson Company, 1972: 9-12; Hume, Brit, *Inside Story,* Garden City, NY: Doubleday & Company, Inc., 1974; Downie Jr., Leonard, *The New Muckrakers,* Washington, D.C.: New Republic Book Company, Incorporated, 1976: 134-174; Behrens, John C., *The Typewriter Guerrillas: Closeups of 20 Top Investigative Reporters,* Chicago: Nelson-Hall, 1977: 1-12; Anderson, Douglas A., *A "Washington Merry-Go-Round" of Libel Actions,* Chicago: Nelson-Hall, 1980; Grauer, Neil A., *Wits and Sages,* Baltimore, MD: John Hopkins University Press, 1984:15-34.

Commentary: Jackson Northman Anderson, an investigative reporter, wrote the syndicated column "Washington Merry-Go-Round" for a number of years. It was in his column that he wrote about the United States policy decision-making in the Indo-Pakistan War, for which he won a Pulitzer Prize.

1973

Robert S. Boyd   918
Birth: January 11, 1928; Chicago, IL. **Parents:** Alden W. Boyd and Mary A. (Skinner). **Religion:** Episcopalian. **Education:** Harvard University, MA: BA. **Spouse:** Gloria L. Paulsen (m. 1949). **Children:** Peter, Susan, Andrew, Timothy.

Prize: *National Reporting,* 1973: Knight Newspapers, 1972.

Career: Served in U.S. Army, 1946-47; U.S. State Department Staff member, 1950-53; Reporter, *Lafayette (LA) Daily Advertiser,* 1953-54; State Editor, *Benton Harbor (MI) News-Palladium,* 1954-57; Reporter, *Detroit Free Press / Knight Newspaper*

Group, 1957-60; Correspondent, Washington (DC) Bureau, *Knight Newspaper Group,* 1960-67; Washington (DC) Bureau Chief, *Knight Newspaper Group,* 1967-87; Chief Correspondent, Washington (DC) Bureau, *Knight-Ridder,* 1987-.

Selected Works: *A Certain Little Evil* (with David Kraslow), 1964. *The Decline, but Not Yet the Fall, of the Russian Empire: The Lewis Cass Lectures, 1969,* 1969.

Commentary: Robert Boyd and Clark Hoyt, acting on an anonymous tip, began investigating the psychiatric history of United States Senator Thomas Eagleton, then the Democratic nominee for vice president. They provided their information to Frank Mankiewicz, the top advisor to Senator George McGovern, the Democratic nominee for President. Two days later on July 25, 1972, Senator Eagleton held a press conference and made his own disclosure and acknowledged the two reporters from the *Detroit Free Press* as the reason he divulged the information at that time. He later withdrew from the Democratic ticket.

Clark Hoyt   919
Birth: November 20, 1942; Providence, RI. **Parents:** Charles Freeland Hoyt and Maude Leslie (King). **Education:** Columbia University, NY: BA. **Spouse:** Jane Ann Hauser (m. 1967, div. 1978); Linda Kauss (m. 1988).

Prize: *National Reporting,* 1973: Knight Newspapers, 1972.

Career: Research Assistant, Senator George Smathers, 1964-66; Reporter, *Lakeland (FL) Ledger,* 1966-68; Press Secretary, LeRoy Collins, U.S. Senate Campaign, 1968; Political Writer, *Detroit (MI) Free Press,* 1969-70; Washington (DC) Correspondent, *Miami (FL) Herald,* 1970-73; National Correspondent, *Miami (FL) Herald,* 1973-75; News Editor, Washington (DC), *Miami (FL) Herald,* 1975-77; Business Editor, *Detroit (MI) Free Press,* 1977-79; Convention Editor, *Detroit (MI) Free Press,* 1979-80; Assistant, Executive Editor, *Detroit (MI) Free Press,* 1980-81; Managing Editor, *Wichita (KS) Eagle-Beacon,* 1981-85; News Editor, Washington (DC) Bureau, Knight-Ridder, 1985-87; Washington (DC) Bureau Chief, Knight-Ridder, 1987-93; Vice President for News, Knight-Ridder, 1993-.

For More Information: *Contemporary Authors, Volumes 69-72,* Detroit: Gale Research Company, 1978: 334.

Commentary: Clark Hoyt and Robert Boyd were the team that uncovered the psychiatric history of Senator Thomas Eagleton, then Democratic nominee for vice president. They did not publish the information immediately but allowed Eagleton to respond to their findings. Eagleton revealed his mental health history at a press conference. He later withdrew from the Democratic ticket.

Hoyt entered into journalism after working as a United States Senate aide. He has managed newspapers in the Knight-Ridder chain as well as headed its Washington, DC bureau.

1974

James Ray Polk 920

Birth: September 12, 1937; Oaktown, Indiana. **Parents:** Raymond S. Polk and Oeta (Fleener). **Education:** Indiana University: AB. **Spouse:** Bonnie Becker (m. 1962, d.); Cara Bryn Saylor (m. 1980). **Children:** Geoffrey, Amy (BB); Abigail (CS).

Prize: *National Reporting,* 1974: *Washington Star-News,* Washington, DC: Washington Star-News, 1973.

Career: Political Writer, *Bloomington (IN) Herald-Telephone;* Madison (WI) Bureau Chief, Associated Press, 1962-67; Washington (DC) Bureau, Associated Press, 1967-71; Investigative Reporter, *Washington (DC) Star-News,* 1972-74; Correspondent, NBC News, 1975-92; Special Assignment Reporter, CNN, 1992-.

Other Awards: American Political Science Association Award, 1961. Raymond Clapper Memorial Award, 1971-72, 1974. Sigma Delta Chi Award, 1974. Indiana Journalism Hall of Fame, 1994. Emmy Award, 1996. Distinguished Alumni Award, Indiana University.

For More Information: *New York Times,* 7 May (1974): 40; Behrens, John C., *The Typewriter Guerrillas: Closeups of 20 Top Investigative Reporters,* Nelson-Hall, 1977: 200-207; *Contemporary Authors, Volumes 69-72,* Detroit: Gale Research Company, 1978: 477.

Commentary: James R. Polk's series of articles on the improprieties of the re-election campaign financing for then-President Nixon won him a Pulitzer Prize in 1974. He broke the stories of secret fund raisers as well as the contributions of Ruth L. Farkas, who was later appointed ambassador to Luxembourg.

John Aloysius White III 921

Birth: September 16, 1942; Providence, RI. **Parents:** John Aloysius White Jr. and Margaret Catherine (Dougherty). **Education:** Boston University, MA. **Spouse:** Elizabeth Ann Finerty (m. 1966). **Children:** John Aloysius, Patrick Michael, Timothy Jason.

Prize: *National Reporting,* 1974: *Washington Star-News,* Washington, DC: Washington Star-News, 1973.

Career: Reporter, *Newport (RI) Daily News,* 1967-68; Reporter, *Providence (RI) Journal-Evening Bulletin,* 1968; Newport (RI) Bureau Chief, *Providence (RI) Journal-Evening Gazette,* 1969-73; Head,

Investigative Team, *Providence (RI) Journal-Bulletin,* 1974-78; Reporter, WBZ-TV Boston, (MA), 1978-; Freelance Writer, Columnist, Reporter, *Cape Cod (MA) Times;* Investigative Reporter, WPRI-TV, 1985-.

Other Awards: Newsman of the Year, National Association of Government Employees, 1973. Emmy Award, 1993.

For More Information: Behrens, John C., *The Typewriter Guerrillas: Closeups of 20 Top Investigative Reporters,* Chicago: Nelson-Hall, 1977: 208-18; *Providence Journal-Bulletin,* 13 April (1994): 11A; *Providence Journal-Bulletin,* 17 April (1994): 2B.

Commentary: Jack White received a tip to investigate President Richard Nixon's tax returns. He discovered that Nixon paid $792.81 in federal income taxes in 1970 and $864 for the following year on his annual income of $200,000. White's story forced the President to disclose his tax situation and to pay $500,000 in back taxes.

1975

Donald Leon Barlett 922

Birth: July 17, 1936; DuBois, PA. **Parents:** James L. Barlett and Mary V. (Wineberg). **Education:** Pennsylvania State University. **Spouse:** Shirley A. Jones (m., div.). **Children:** Matthew.

Prize: *National Reporting,* 1975: *Philadelphia Inquirer,* "Auditing the Internal Revenue System,," Philadelphia, PA: Philadelphia Inquirer, April, 1974. *National Reporting,* 1989: *Philadelphia Inquirer,* Philadelphia, PA: Philadelphia Inquirer, 1988.

Career: General Assignment Reporter, *Reading (PA) Times,* 1956-58; Served in U.S. Army, Counterintelligence, 1958-61; General Assignment Reporter, *Reading (PA) Times,* 1961-62; General Assignment Reporter, *Akron (OH) Beacon Journal,* 1962-64; Investigative Reporter, *Cleveland (OH) Plain Dealer,* 1965-66; Investigative Reporter, *Chicago Daily News,* 1967-68; Investigative Reporter, *Cleveland (OH) Plain Dealer,* 1969-70; Investigative Reporter, *Philadelphia (PA) Inquirer,* 1970-97; Staff member, *Time* magazine, 1997-.

Selected Works: *Empire: The Life, Legend, and Madness of Howard Hughes* (with James B. Steele), 1979. *Forevermore: Nuclear Waste in America* (with James B. Steele), 1983. *America: What Went Wrong?* (with James B. Steele), 1991. *America: Who Really Pays the Taxes?* (with James B. Steele), 1994.

Other Awards: George Polk Memorial Award, Long Island University, NY, 1971, 1973. Distinguished Service in Journalism Award, Sigma Delta Chi, 1971, 1974. Heywood Broun Award, 1973. Sidney Hillman Foundation, 1973. Overseas Press Club Award, 1974. Silver Gavel Award, American Bar

Association, 1974, 1989. Honor Medal for Distinguished Service to Journalism, University of Missouri, 1983. George Orwell Award, National Council of Teachers of English, 1988, 1992.

For More Information: Downie Jr., Leonard, *The New Muckrakers: An Inside Look at America's Investigative Reporters,* Washington, D.C.: New Republic Book Company, 1976; Dygert, James H., *The Investigative Journalist: Folk Heroes of a New Era,* Englewood Cliff, NJ: Prentice Hall, 1976: 93-111; *Contemporary Authors, Volume 115,* Detroit: Gale Research Company, 1985.

Commentary: Donald L. Barlett and James B. Steele have worked together since 1971. In 1975, their investigation into the federal tax system and its differing treatment of rich and poor taxpayers led to a seven-part series. They were awarded a Pulitzer Prize for their series, "Auditing the Internal Revenue Service." In 1989, the two reporters won a second Pulitzer Prize for their examination of provisions in the 1986 tax law that would give tax advantages to well-connected individuals and businesses. The pair were finalists for a Pulitzer Prize in 1992 and 1997.

James Bruce Steele Jr.   923

Birth: January 3, 1943; Hutchinson, KS. **Parents:** James Bruce Steele and Mary (Peoples). **Education:** University of Missouri, Kansas City: BA. **Spouse:** Nancy Saunders (m. 1966). **Children:** Allison.

Prize: *National Reporting,* 1975: *Philadelphia Inquirer,* "Auditing the Internal Revenue System," , Philadelphia, PA: Philadelphia Inquirer, April, 1974. *National Reporting,* 1989: *Philadelphia Inquirer,* Philadelphia, PA: Philadelphia Inquirer, 1988.

Career: Copyboy, *Kansas City (MO) Times,* 1961; Reporter-Labor, Urban Affairs, Politics, *Kansas City (MO) Star,* 1962-67; Director of Information, Laborers' International Union of North America, 1967-70; Staff Writer, Urban Affairs Specialist, Investigative Reporter, *Philadelphia (PA) Inquirer,* 1970-97; Staff member, *Time* magazine, 1997-.

Selected Works: *Empire: The Life, Legend, and Madness of Howard Hughes* (with Donald L. Barlett), 1979. *Forevermore: Nuclear Waste in America* (with Donald L. Barlett), 1983. *America: What Went Wrong?* (with Donald L. Barlett), 1991. *America: Who Really Pays the Taxes?* (with Donald L. Barlett), 1994. *America: Who Stole the Dream?* (with Donald L. Barlett), 1996.

Other Awards: Award, American Political Science Association, 1971. George Polk Memorial Award, Long Island University, NY, 1971, 1973. Distinguished Service in Journalism Award, Sigma Delta Chi, 1971, 1983. Heywood Broun Award, 1973. Sidney Hillman Foundation Award, 1973. John Hancock Award, 1973. Business Journalism Award, University of Missouri, 1973. Gavel Award, American Bar Association, 1973.

For More Information: Downie Jr., Leonard, *The New Muckrakers: An Inside Look at America's Investigative Reporters,* Washington, D.C.: New Republic Book Company, 1976: 93-111; Dygert, James H., *The Investigative Journalist: Folk Heroes of a New Era,* Englewood Cliff, NJ: Prentice Hall, 1976; *Contemporary Authors, Volume 110,* Detroit: Gale Research Company, 1985.

Commentary: James B. Steele and Donald L. Barlett have won two Pulitzer Prizes for their investigative collaborations. Their investigation in 1974 showed the inequities in the federal tax system that caused the Internal Revenue Service to deal severely with poor and middle-income taxpayers. In 1988, the duo reported on beneficial provisions in the 1986 tax law for well-connected individuals and businesses. They won a second Pulitzer for that investigation. They were also finalists for the award in 1992 and 1997.

1976

James Vaulx Risser Jr.   924

Birth: May 8, 1938; Lincoln, NE. **Parents:** James Vaulx Risser and Ella Caroline (Schacht). **Religion:** Unitarian. **Education:** University of Nebraska: BA. San Francisco University, CA: JD. University of Nebraska: MA. **Spouse:** Sandra Elizabeth Laaker (m. 1961). **Children:** David, John.

Prize: *National Reporting,* 1976: *Des Moines Register,* Des Moines, IA: Des Moines Register, 1975. *National Reporting,* 1979: *Des Moines Register,* Des Moines, IA: Des Moines Register, September 10, 1978.

Career: Lawyer, Perry, Witthoff, and Guthery, 1962-64; Staff member, *Des Moines (IA) Register,* 1964-69; Correspondent, Washington (DC) Bureau, *Des Moines (IA) Register and Tribune,* 1969-76; Washington (DC) Bureau Chief, *Des Moines (IA) Register and Tribune,* 1976-85; Director, John S. Knight Fellowship Program, Stanford University (CA), 1985-.

Selected Works: *Nebraska's "Honest Mistake" Law: Studies in Nebraska Journalism, Number 9,* 1964.

Other Awards: Thomas L. Stokes Award for Conservation and Environmental Reporting, 1971, 1979. American Political Science Award for Reporting of Public Affairs. Outstanding Professional Journalist of the Year, University of Nebraska, 1973. Knight Fellow, Stanford University, CA, 1973-74. Distinguished Service Award, Sigma Delta Chi, 1976. Raymond Clapper Memorial Award, 1976, 1978.

Farm Editor of the Year, 1979. Worth Bingham Prize, 1976. Edward J. Meeman Award, 1985.

For More Information: *Des Moines Register,* May 4, 1976: 1+; *Des Moines Register,* April 17, 1979: 1+; *Editor & Publisher,* 129:27 (July 6, 1996): 14.

Commentary: James Risser's revealing articles in 1976 on the corruption in American grain exports led to 50 convictions of individuals and companies on the charges of bribery and theft. It also led to a Congressional inquiry and an increase in the government's grain inspection staff. In 1979, he was again awarded a Pulitzer Prize for a seven-part series about the environmental impact of farming. He spent six months researching the series that examined the damage to land, water, and air caused by current farming practices.

1977

Walter Robert Mears   925

Birth: January 11, 1935; Lynn, MA. **Parents:** Edward Lewis Mears and Edythe Emily (Campbell). **Education:** Middlebury College, VT: BA, Phi Beta Kappa. **Spouse:** Sally Danton (m. 1956, died 1962); Joyce Marie Lund (m. 1963, div. 1983); Caroll Ann Rambo (m. 1986, div. 1995). **Children:** Pamela, Walter Robert, Jr. (SD); Stephanie Joy, Susan Marie (JL).

Prize: *National Reporting,* 1977: Associated Press, 1976.

Career: Boston (MA), Associated Press, 1956; Correspondent, Montpelier (VT), Associated Press, 1956-60; State House Correspondent, Boston (MA), Associated Press, 1960-61; Chief Correspondent, U.S. Senate, Associated Press, 1961-62, Chief Political Writer, Associated Press, 1962-72; Assistant Washington (DC) Bureau Chief, Associated Press, 1973-74; Washington (DC) Bureau Chief, *Detroit News,* 1974-75; Special Correspondent, Associated Press, 1975-76; Washington (DC) Bureau Chief, Associated Press, 1977-83; Vice President, Associated Press, 1978-; Executive Editor, Associated Press, 1984-88; Political Columnist, Associated Press, 1989-; Vice President, Associated Press, 1989-.

Selected Works: *The News Business* (with John Chancellor), 1983.

Other Awards: Honorary Degree, Middlebury College, VT, 1977.

For More Information: Crouse, Tim, *The Boys on the Bus,* New York: Random House, 1973; *New York Times,* 19 April (1977): 44; Rigsby, Gwendolyn Gezelle, A History of Associated Press Pulitzer Prizes (thesis), University of South Carolina, 1993.

Commentary: Walter Mears has been with the Associated Press for over 40 years. In 1976, he covered 32 presidential primaries, the campaigns, and

elections. He wrote up to 18 new leads on breaking developments and he followed up on those with analyses for the next day's papers. One of the few political stories he did not cover that year was the vice presidential debate, because he was a questioner at that forum.

1978

Gaylord D. Shaw   926

Birth: July 22, 1942; El Reno, OK. **Parents:** Charley Shaw and Ruth. **Education:** Cameron College, OK. University of Oklahoma. **Spouse:** Judith Howard (m. 1960). **Children:** Randall, Kristine, Kelly.

Prize: *National Reporting,* 1978: *Los Angeles Times,* Los Angeles, CA: Los Angeles Times, 1977.

Career: Sports Writer, *El Reno (OK) American,* 1955; Police Reporter, *Lawton (OK) Constitution-Press,* 1960-62; Statehouse Correspondent, Oklahoma City (OK), Associated Press, 1962-66; Deskman, Washington (DC), Associated Press, 1966-67; Special Assignment Team Member, Associated Press, 1967-71; White House Correspondent, Associated Press, 1971-75; Staff Writer, Washington (DC) Bureau, *Los Angeles Times,* 1975-78; Denver (CO) Bureau Chief, *Los Angeles Times,* 1978-81; Assistant Managing Editor/News, *Dallas (TX) Times-Herald,* 1981-82; Managing Editor-News, *Dallas (TX) Times-Herald,* 1982-83; Editor-in-Chief, Charlotte (NC) Shaw Communications, 1983-85; Correspondent, Washington (DC) Bureau, *Los Angeles Times,* 1985-88; Washington (DC) Bureau Chief, *Newsday (NY),* 1988-95; Senior Correspondent, *Newsday,* 1995-.

Selected Works: *How to Get Your Share of Government Treasure: A Guide to Valuable Benefits and Services; U.S. News & World Report Money Management Library,* 1975.

Other Awards: Worth Bingham Award, 1968. Merriman Smith Award, White House Correspondents Association, 1974. Distinguished Service Award, Sigma Delta Chi, 1978. Gerald Loeb Award, 1978. National Press Club Award, 1991.

For More Information: *New York Times,* 18 April (1978): 28.

Commentary: Gaylord Shaw began investigation the state of the country's dams after the failure of the Teton Dam in 1976. His reporting on the structural "time bombs" that many dams had deteriorated into had Congress and President Carter releasing funds for federal inspection of the dams.

1979

James Vaulx Risser Jr.

Full entry appears as **#924** under "National Reporting," 1976.

1980

Bette Swenson Orsini   927

Birth: December 2, 1925; St. Petersburg, FL. **Education:** University of Florida: BA.

Prize: *National Reporting,* 1980: *St. Petersburg Times,* St. Petersburg, FL: St. Petersburg Times, 1979.

Career: Staff member, *St. Petersburg (FL) Times;* Staff member, *Arkansas Democrat;* Staff member, *Richmond (VA) News-Leader.*

Other Awards: American Political Science Association Public Affairs Reporting, 1967. National Headliners Club Award, 1970. First Prize, Investigative Reporting in Education, Charles Stewart Mott Competition, 1978. Kappa Tau Alpha Hall of Fame, University of South Florida School of Mass Communications.

Commentary: Bette Swenson Orsini and Charles Stafford won a Pulitzer Prize for their 14-part series that examined the Church of Scientology, its business practices, and its move into Florida.

Charles Stafford   928

Birth: October 5, 1923; Grafton, WV. **Education:** West Virginia University: BS. **Spouse:** Married. **Children:** Three children.

Prize: *National Reporting,* 1980: *St. Petersburg Times,* St. Petersburg, FL: St. Petersburg Times, 1979..

Career: *Beckley (WV) Raleigh Register,* 1949-51; Reporter, Huntington (WV), Baltimore (MD), New York (NY), Tampa (FL), Associated Press, 1951-66; Correspondent, Washington (DC), *Tampa (FL) Tribune,* 1966-68; Correspondent, Washington (DC) Bureau, *St. Petersburg (FL) Times,* 1968-89.

Commentary: Charles Stafford and Bette Swenson Orsini wrote a 14-part series on the Church of Scientology, its business practices, and its move into Clearwater, Florida. Stafford retired from the *St. Petersburg Times* in 1989.

1981

John Mark Crewdson   929

Birth: December 15, 1945; San Francisco, CA. **Parents:** Mark Guy Crewdson and Eva Rebecca (Doane). **Education:** University of California, Berkeley: BA, Great Distinction. Queens' College of Cambridge University, Cambridge, England: Postgraduate. **Spouse:** Prudence Gray Tillotson (m. 1969). **Children:** Anders, Oliver.

Prize: *National Reporting,* 1981: *New York Times,* New York: New York Times, 1980.

Career: Part-Time Correspondent, *New York Times,* 1969; Copyboy, *New York Times,* 1970; News clerk; News Assistant, Writing Intern, *New York Times,* 1972; Staff Reporter, Washington (DC) Bureau, *New York Times,* 1973-77; National Correspondent, Houston (TX), *New York Times,* 1977-82; National News Editor, *Chicago Tribune,* 1982-83; Metropolitan News Editor, *Chicago Tribune,* 1983-84; West Coast Correspondent, *Chicago Tribune,* 1984-90; Senior National Correspondent, *Chicago Tribune,* 1990-96; Senior Writer, *Chicago Tribune,* 1996-.

Selected Works: *Slavery in Texas, Illegal Aliens, Seafood and Coyotes,* 1980. *The Tarnished Door: The New Immigrants and the Transformation of America,* 1983. *By Silence Betrayed: Sexual Abuse of Children in America,* 1988.

Other Awards: Undergraduate Prize in Economics, University of California, Berkeley, 1970. Sigma Delta Chi Award, 1973. James Wright Brown Award, New York Deadline Club, 1976. Special Achievement Award, New York Press Club, 1977. Page One Award, Newspaper Guild of New York, 1977. George Polk Memorial Award, Long Island University, NY, 1977, 1990. William H. Jones Award, 1990, 1995, 1997. Peter Lisagor Award, Sigma Delta Chi, Chicago Chapter, IL, 1997.

Commentary: John M. Crewdson wrote over 40 articles in 1980 on illegal aliens and immigration problems. He spoke with Mexicans, Cuban-Americans, and Haitians during their trips and after their arrival in the United States. He spent a year on his investigation of the system, discovering the smuggling of human contraband, corruption among United States immigration authorities, and mistreatment of migrant workers. After he published his reports, the United States Justice Department began its own investigation.

1982

Rick Atkinson   930

Birth: November 16, 1952; Munich, Germany. **Parents:** Larry Atkinson and Margaret (Howe). **Education:** East Carolina University, NC. University of Chicago, IL: MA. **Spouse:** Jane Chestnut (m. 1979). **Children:** Rush, Sarah.

Prize: *National Reporting,* 1982: *Kansas City Times,* Kansas City, MO: Kansas City Times, 1981.

Career: Reporter, *Pittsburg (KS) Morning Sun,* 1976-77; Suburban Reporter, General Assignment

Reporter, City Desk Reporter, National Reporter, *Kansas City (MO) Times,* 1977-83; General Assignments Reporter, *Washington (DC) Post,* 1983-85; Deputy National Editor, *Washington Post,* 1985-89; Investigative Reporter, *Washington Post,* 1989-91; Berlin (Germany) Bureau Chief, *Washington Post,* 1993-96; Assistant Managing Editor for Projects, *Washington Post,* 1996-.

Selected Works: *The Long Gray Line: The American Journey of West Point's Class of 1966,* 1989. *Crusade: The Untold Story of the Persian Gulf War,* 1993.

Other Awards: Livingston Award, University of Michigan. George Polk Memorial Award, Long Island University, NY. John Hancock Award, John Hancock Mutual Life Insurance Company.

For More Information: *Washington Post,* 10 August (1996): A11.

Commentary: Rick Atkinson won a Pulitzer Prize for a series of articles examining the country's "chaotic management of its water resources." He also reported on the United States Army officer corps by looking at the West Point class of 1966 reunion.

1983

Boston Globe

Full entry appears as **#823** under "Meritorious Public Service," 1966.

1984

John Noble Wilford   931

Birth: October 4, 1933; Murray, KY. **Parents:** John Noble Wilford Sr. and Pauline (Hendricks). **Religion:** Protestant. **Education:** Lambuth College, TN. University of Tennessee: BS, magna cum laude. Syracuse University, NY: MA. **Spouse:** Nancy Watts Paschal (m. 1966). **Children:** Nona.

Prize: *National Reporting,* 1984: *New York Times,* New York: New York Times, 1983.

Career: Summer Reporter, *Paris (TN) Parisian,* 1952, 1953; Reporter, *Memphis (TN) Commercial Appeal,* 1954-55; Reporter, *Wall Street Journal,* 1956; Served in U.S. Army, 1957-59; Reporter, *Wall Street Journal,* 1959-61; Contributing Editor, *Time* magazine, 1962-65; Science Reporter, *New York Times,* 1965-73; Assistant National Editor, *New York Times,* 1973-75; Director, Science News, *New York Times,* 1975-79; Science Correspondent, *New York Times,* 1979-90; Visiting Journalist, Duke University (NC), 1984; McGraw Professor of Writing, Princeton University (NJ), 1985; Daily Commentator, WQXR-Radio Station, 1987-92; Chair of Excellence in Science Journalism, University of Tennessee, Knoxville,

1989-90; Science Correspondent and Senior Writer, *New York Times,* 1990-; Reporter, commentator, instructor, consultant.

Selected Works: *We Reach the Moon: The New York Times Story of Man's Greatest Adventure; a Bantam Extra,* 1969. *Scientists at Work: The Creative Process of Scientific Research,* 1979. *The Mapmakers,* 1981. *Spaceliner: The New York Times Report on the Columbia's Voyage into Tomorrow* (with W. Stockton), 1981. *New York Times Guide to the Return of Halley's Comet* (with others), 1985. *The Riddle of the Dinosaur,* 1985. *Mars Beckons: The Mysteries, the Challenges, the Expectations of Our Next Great Adventure in Space,* 1990. *The Mysterious History of Columbus: An Exploration of the Man, the Myth, the Legacy,* 1991.

Other Awards: International Reporting Fellow, Columbia University Graduate School of Journalism, NY, 1961-62. Book Award, Aviation/Space Writers Association, 1970: *We Reach the Moon: The New York Times Story of Man's Greatest Adventure,* New York: Bantam Books, 1969. National Space Club Press Award, 1974. AAAS / Westinghouse Science Journalism Award, 1983. Chancellor's Medal, Syracuse University, NY, 1983. Honorary Degree, Rhode Island College, 1987. Distinguished Alumnus Award, Columbia University, NY, 1988. Alumni Academic Hall of Fame, University of Tennessee, 1994. Ralph Coats Roe Medal, American Society of Mechanical Engineers, 1995. Honorary Degree, Middlebury College, VT, 1991.

For More Information: *New York Times,* 17 April (1984): B4.

Commentary: John Noble Wilford won a Pulitzer Prize for his articles in 1983 that discussed the efforts by the United States and the Soviet Union to develop "space weapons." He also wrote about the American space shuttle program and various topics in astronomy.

Wilford was the first Western correspondent to visit Star City, the Soviet cosmonaut training center, in March 1972. He has covered nearly all the major missions of the United States space program. He was selected in 1986 as a finalist in the Journalist-in-Space project by NASA. (That project has since been postponed indefinitely.) He has also written about the restoration of Bikini Island, which had been a nuclear test site.

1985

Thomas Jeffrey Knudson   932

Birth: July 6, 1953; Manning, IA. **Parents:** Melvin Jake Knudson and Coreen Rose (Nickum). **Education:** Iowa State University: BA.

Prize: *National Reporting,* 1985: *Des Moines Register,* "A Harvest of Harm: The Farm Health Crisis," Des Moines, IA: Des Moines Register, 1984.

Career: Intern, *Des Moines (IA) Register,* 1978; Intern, Chicago (IL), *Wall Street Journal,* 1979; Staff Writer, *Des Moines (IA) Register,* 1980-; Head, Iowa City (IA) News Bureau, *Des Moines (IA) Register;* Reporter, Metropolitan Staff, *New York Times,* 1986; Denver (CO) Bureau Chief, *New York Times,* 1987; Staff member, *Sacramento (CA) Bee,* 1988-.

Other Awards: General News Writing Award, William Randolph Hearst Foundation, 1978. Sigma Delta Chi Award, 1980. Carl Johnson Feature Writing Award, Iowa State University, 1980. James W. Schwartz Award, Iowa State University, 1985. World Hunger Media Award, 1985. Outstanding Young Alumnus Award, Iowa State University, 1986. Enterprise Reporting Award, Society of Professional Journalists, Central California Chapter, 1991. Robert L. Kozik Award, National Press Club, 1992, 1996. Edward J. Meeman Award, Scripps-Howard Foundation, 1998.

For More Information: *New York Times,* 25 April (1985): B10; *New York Times,* 8 April (1992): B6.

Commentary: Thomas J. Knudson examined the occupation of farming and wrote a series of articles on its dangers. Two of the topics he wrote about were machine injuries and the high rate of cancer.

Knudson also reported on the Sierra Nevada Mountains in 1991. His five-part series, "Majesty and Tragedy: The Sierra in Peril," won the Meritorious Public Service Pulitzer Prize for the *Sacramento Bee* in 1992.

1986

John Craig Flournoy   933

Birth: June 26, 1951; Shreveport, LA. **Parents:** Camp Rogers Flournoy and Carolyn (Clay). **Education:** University of New Orleans, LA: BA. Southern Methodist University, TX: MA. **Spouse:** Nina Planchard (m. 1977). **Children:** Kathryn Helene, Louise, Emma.

Prize: *National Reporting,* 1986: *Dallas Morning News,* Dallas: Dallas Morning News, 1985.

Career: Freelance Reporter, weekly paper, *New Orleans (LA) Courier;* Reporter, *Houma (LA) Daily Courier,* 1976; City Hall Reporter, Political Columnist, Investigative Reporter, *Shreveport (LA) Journal,* 1977-78; Investigative Reporter, *Dallas (TX) Morning News,* 1978-.

Other Awards: Investigative Reporting Award, Louisiana Press Association, 1976. Investigative Reporting Award, Dallas Press Club, 1981. Outstanding Investigative Reporting Award, Investigative Report-

ers and Editors, 1989. Worth Bingham Prize, 1993. Edward Meeman Award for Environmental Reporting, 1993.

Commentary: Craig Flournoy and George Rodrigue's exposure of patterns of discrimination and segregation led to reforms in subsidized housing in East Texas. Flournoy was also a finalist for the Beat Reporting Pulitzer Prize in 1997.

Flournoy has also won awards for his investigation of a prescription drug ring within the Paris (Texas) Parish prison and the brutalization of a Parish prisoner.

Arthur W. Howe IV   934

Birth Place: Cleveland, OH. **Parents:** Arthur Howe. **Education:** University of Pennsylvania. Boston University, MA: MA. University of Pennsylvania: MBA. **Spouse:** Lisa H. **Children:** Three children.

Prize: *National Reporting,* 1986: *Philadelphia Inquirer,* Philadelphia, PA: Philadelphia Inquirer, 1985.

Career: Reporter, *Wilmington (DE) News Journal,* 1975-80; Staff member, *Philadelphia (PA) Inquirer,* 1980-82; Head, Wall Street (NY) Bureau, *Philadelphia (PA) Inquirer,* 1982-84; Circulation Marketing Director, *Philadelphia (PA) Inquirer;* Finance Director, *Philadelphia (PA) Inquirer;* President, Publisher, Fort Washington (PA) Montgomery Publishing Company, 1989-.

Other Awards: Investigative Reporting Award, Associated Press Managing Editors. Roy W. Howard Public Service Award, Scripps-Howard Foundation.

Commentary: There were two Pulitzer Prizes awarded for National Reporting in 1986. Arthur Howe won for his "enterprising and indefatigable" reporting on how the Internal Revenue Service processed income tax returns. His reporting led to an official apology by the Internal Revenue Service to the American taxpayers as well as reforms in its processing procedures. Howe currently is the president and publisher of Montgomery Publishing Company, which owns and operates 24 publications. He was 36 years old when he was awarded the Pulitzer Prize.

George Pierre Rodrigue III   935

Birth: May 5, 1956; Boston, MA. **Parents:** George Pierre Rodrigue Jr. and Mary (Merritt). **Education:** University of Virginia: BA.

Prize: *National Reporting,* 1986: *Dallas Morning News,* Dallas, TX: Dallas Morning News, 1985.

Career: Editor, college paper; County Courthouse and City Hall Reporter, *Atlanta (GA) Constitution,* 1978-81; Associate Editor, *Dallas (TX) D Magazine,* 1981-83; Urban Affairs Reporter, *Dallas (TX) Morning News,* 1983-.

Other Awards: Associated Press Managing Editors Award, 1985.

Commentary: George Rodrigue and Craig Flournoy won a Pulitzer Prize for their exposure of discrimination and segregation in subsidized housing in East Texas. Their series led to reforms in the system. Rodrigue was also a member of the *Dallas Morning News* team that won the International Reporting Pulitzer Prize in 1994.

1987

Miami Herald
Full entry appears as #357 under "Editorial Writing," 1983.

New York Times
Full entry appears as #375 under "Explanatory Journalism," 1986.

1988

Timothy Emlyn Weiner   936
Birth: June 20, 1956; White Plains, NY. **Parents:** Herbert Weiner and Dr. Dora (Bierer). **Education:** Columbia University, NY: BA. Columbia University, NY: MS. **Spouse:** Katharine Temple Lapsley Doyle (m. 1994).

Prize: *National Reporting,* 1988: *Philadelphia Inquirer,* Philadelphia, PA: Philadelphia Inquirer, 1987.

Career: Reporter, Fairchild News Service; Reporter, *Soho News;* Reporter, Associated Press; Staff member, *Kansas City (MO) Times,* 1981-82; Reporter, *Philadelphia (PA) Inquirer,* 1982-93; Philippines Correspondent, *Philadelphia (PA) Inquirer,* 1986; Reporter, Washington (DC) Bureau, *New York Times,* 1993-; Hearst Visiting Professional, University of Maryland, College Park.

Selected Works: *Blank Check: The Pentagon's Black Budget,* 1990. *Betrayal: The Story of Aldrich Ames, an American Spy* (with others), 1995.

For More Information: *New York Times,* 12 April (1988): C20; *New York Times,* 15 May (1994): section 9, 8.

Commentary: For six months, Tim Weiner worked exclusively investigating the "Pentagon's so-called 'black budget.'" He first heard about the story from a government source that told him to look into the secret budget. His three-part series, published in February 1987, examined the budget, which had no congressional oversight and was used to finance military research and to purchase weapons.

After the announcement of the Pulitzer to Weiner, the *National Journal* claimed that it had published an earlier article on the subject. The Pulitzer Board rejected the claims that Weiner's articles lacked originality and it "found no cause" to revoke Weiner's prize.

1989

Donald Leon Barlett
Full entry appears as #922 under "National Reporting," 1975.

James Bruce Steele Jr.
Full entry appears as #923 under "National Reporting," 1975.

1990

Ross Anderson   937
Birth Place: San Francisco, CA. **Education:** Whitworth College, WA. University of Edinburgh, Scotland. **Spouse:** Mary Rothschild. **Children:** Three children.

Prize: *National Reporting,* 1990: *Seattle Times,* Seattle, WA: *Seattle Times,* 1989.

Career: Assistant City Editor, *Seattle (WA) Times;* Staff Writer, Sunday Magazine, *Seattle Times;* Correspondent, Washington (DC), *Seattle Times;* Chief Political Reporter, *Seattle Times;* Editorial Writer, *Seattle Times.*

Other Awards: Journalism Fellow, Stanford University, CA, 1978-79.

For More Information: *Seattle Times,* 13 April (1990): B1, B2.

Commentary: Ross Anderson, along with Bill Dietrich, Mary Ann Gwinn, and Eric Nalder, won a Pulitzer Prize for their coverage of the 1989 Exxon Valdez oil spill and a series on tanker safety. Each played an unique role on the team, Anderson with his deep respect for Alaska and fishermen; Dietrich, the environmental reporter, who could make the most complex situations "meaningful and significant"; Gwinn for her way with words; and Nalder, for his ability to isolate useful information within thousands of pages of documents.

Anderson has been with the *Seattle Times* since 1971 and was 42 years old when he won the award.

William Dietrich   938
Birth: September 29, 1951; Tacoma, WA. **Parents:** William Richard Dietrich and Janice Lenore (Pooler) Anderson. **Education:** Western Washington University: BA. **Spouse:** Holly Susan Roberts (m. 1970). **Children:** Lisa Nicole, Heidi Renee.

Prize: *National Reporting,* 1990: *Seattle Times,* Seattle, WA: Seattle Times, 1989.

Career: Political Reporter, *Bellingham (WA) Herald,* 1973-76; Reporter, Gannett News Service, 1976-78; Reporter and Columnist, *Vancouver (WA) Columbian,* 1978-82; Science Reporter, *Seattle (WA) Times,* 1982-.

Selected Works: *The Final Forest: The Battle for the Last Great Trees of the Pacific Northwest,* 1992. *Northwest Passage: The Great Columbia River,* 1995. *Ice Reich,* 1998.

Other Awards: Paul Tobenkin Award, Columbia University, NY, 1986. Nieman Fellow, Harvard University, MA, 1987-88. Washington Governor's Writers Award, 1992: *The Final Forest: The Battle for the Last Great Trees of the Pacific Northwest,* New York: Simon & Schuster, 1992. Pacific Northwest Booksellers Award, 1992: *The Final Forest: The Battle for the Last Great Trees of the Pacific Northwest.*

For More Information: *Seattle Times,* 13 April (1990): B1, B2.

Commentary: Bill Dietrich, Ross Anderson, Mary Ann Gwinn, and Eric Nalder made up the team of reporters from the *Seattle Times,* which won a Pulitzer Prize for its coverage of the Exxon Valdez oil spill and a series on oil tanker safety. Dietrich, the *Seattle Times* science reporter, was the first to go to Alaska after the spill occurred. He left the day of the accident and arrived at Valdez by 8:30 a.m.

Mary Ann Gwinn   939
Birth: December 29, 1951; Forrest City, AR. **Parents:** Lawrence Baird Gwinn and Frances Evelyn (Jones). **Education:** Hendrix College, AR: BA. Georgia State University: MEd. University of Missouri: MA. **Spouse:** Richard A. King (m. 1973, div. 1981); Stephen E. Dunnington (m. 1990). **Children:** Samuel, Jackson (SD).

Prize: *National Reporting,* 1990: *Seattle Times,* Seattle, WA: Seattle Times, 1989.

Career: Special Education Teaching Aide, DeKalb County (GA) Schools, 1973-74; Special Education Teacher, DeKalb County (GA) Schools, 1975-78; Teaching Assistant, University of Missouri, News-Editorial Department, 1978-79; Reporter, *Columbia (MO) Daily Tribune,* 1979-83; Reporter, *Seattle (WA) Times,* 1983-96; Teacher, University of Washington Extension Division, 1990; Instructor, Seattle University (WA), 1994; Assistant City Editor, *Seattle (WA) Times,* 1996-.

Other Awards: C.B. Blethen Award, 1989. Award, Sigma Delta Chi, Northwest Chapter, 1986, 1988.

For More Information: *Seattle Times,* 13 April (1990): B1, B2.

Commentary: Mary Ann Gwinn, Ross Anderson, Bill Dietrich, and Eric Nalder's coverage of the

Exxon Valdez oil spill and a series on tanker safety won a Pulitzer Prize in 1990. The four were part of a group of more than 30 staff members who worked on the series of articles.

Gwinn has the ability to write and bring the reader to the scene. In one story, she described the oil spill and its tragic effect on area wildlife.

Eric Christopher Nalder
Full entry appears as **#698** under "Investigative Reporting," 1997.

1991

Marjorie Eleanor Lundstrom   940
Birth: October 9, 1956; Springfield, MO. **Parents:** Max Lundstrom and Margaret (Gowans). **Education:** University of Nebraska: BS, High Distinction, Phi Beta Kappa. **Spouse:** Sam Stanton (m. 1991). **Children:** Nicholas.

Prize: *National Reporting,* 1991: *Gannett News Service, 1990.*

Career: Reporter, *Fort Collins (CO) Coloradoan,* 1978-79; Managing Editor, *Denver (CO) Monthly* magazine, 1979-81; Features Columnist, General Assignment Reporter, *Denver (CO) Post,* 1981-87; National Correspondent, *Denver (CO) Post,* 1987-88; Visiting faculty member, Guest Lecturer, Poynter Institute for Media Studies, 1988; Assistant City Editor, *Denver (CO) Post,* 1988-89; Senior Writer, *Sacramento (CA) Bee,* 1989-90; National Correspondent, Gannett News Service, 1990; Senior Writer, *Sacramento (CA) Bee,* 1991; City Editor, *Sacramento (CA) Bee,* 1991-93; Metro Editor, *Sacramento (CA) Bee,* 1993-95; Assistant Managing Editor, *Sacramento (CA) Bee,* 1995-.

Other Awards: Outstanding Journalism Graduate, Sigma Delta Chi, 1978. National Associated Press Citation, 1979. Investigative Story of the Year, Sigma Delta Chi, Colorado Chapter, 1981. National Journalist of the Year, National Federation of Press Women, 1983. Best News Story of the Year, Colorado Press Association, 1984. Best Feature Story, Colorado Press Association, 1987. Best Spot News Reporting, Colorado Associated Press, 1986, 1987. Deadline Reporting Award, Sigma Delta Chi, Colorado Chapter, 1987. Best of Colorado Award, 1987. California Associated Press Competition, 1989. Best of the West, 1990. Master's Week Alum, University of Nebraska, Lincoln, 1992. Oustanding Journalism Alum, University of Nebraska, Lincoln, 1992. Edgar Allen Poe Award, White House Correspondents' Association, 1992. Commencement Speaker, California State University, 1991.

Commentary: Marjie Lundstrom and Rochelle Sharpe were awarded a Pulitzer Prize for their investigation into child abuse as a national issue. Their four-part series included analysis of all the deaths in the United States of children under the age of nine in 1987. Lundstrom comments on the impact of the story for her: "The subject of unexplained children's deaths haunts me still. Since writing this series—and becoming an editor—I prod my reporters to take critical looks at all child deaths and how the system did (or didn't) respond. We must keep the spotlight on these tragedies and not let them slip away, unnoticed."

Rochelle Phyllis Sharpe 941

Birth: April 27, 1956; Gary, IN. **Parents:** Norman Nathaniel Sharpe and Shirley (Kaplan). **Education:** Yale University, CT: BA.

Prize: *National Reporting,* 1991: Gannett News Service, 1990.

Career: Staff member, Columnist Jack Anderson; Reporter, *Concord (NH) Monitor,* 1979-81; Statehouse Reporter, *Wilmington (DE) News-Journal,* 1982-85; Albany (NY) Correspondent, Gannett News Service, 1985-87; National Correspondent, Washington (DC), Gannett News Service; Staff Reporter, *Wall Street Journal,* 1993-.

Selected Works: *Baby M and the Facts of Life: The Complete Inside Story,* 1988.

Other Awards: Pulliam Journalism Fellow. Fellowship, Hiroshima Cultural Foundation, 1983.

Commentary: Rochelle Sharpe and Marjie Lundstrom used a computer to analyze the deaths of children under the age of nine in 1987. Their four-part series revealed how hundreds of deaths each year are not reported as child abuse. Their series made child abuse a national issue, not just a local, isolated one.

In 1983, Sharpe obtained a fellowship to interview survivors of the atomic bombing in Japan.

1992

Mike McGraw 942

Birth: April 26, 1948; Kansas City, MO. **Education:** University of Missouri: BS. University of Missouri: MS. **Spouse:** Married. **Children:** Two children.

Prize: *National Reporting,* 1992: Kansas City Star, Kansas City, MO: Kansas City Star, 1991.

Career: Staff member, *Kansas City (MO) Star;* Business and Labor Writer, *Des Moines (IA) Register;* Labor Editor, *Hartford (CT) Courant;* Special Projects Reporter, *Kansas City (MO) Star,* 1989-.

Other Awards: Sigma Delta Chi Award, 1992. George Polk Memorial Award, Long Island University, NY, 1992. Kansas City Press Club Award, 1994.

For More Information: *Quill,* 80:6 (July 1992): 31; *Vegetarian Times,* 179 (July 1992): 14.

Commentary: Mike McGraw and Jeff Taylor's examination into the United States Department of

Agriculture won them a Pulitzer Prize. The pair spent 16 months investigating the workings of the agency. Their seven-part series was published in December 1991. Three months later, the United States Senate's Agriculture Committee began its own investigation, aimed at cutting waste.

Jeff Taylor 943

Birth: January 19, 1962; Wichita, KS. **Education:** University of Kansas: BA. **Spouse:** Married. **Children:** One child.

Prize: *National Reporting,* 1992: *Kansas City Star,* Kansas City, MO: Kansas City Star, 1991.

Career: General Assignment Reporter, *Kansas City (MO) Times,* 1984-90; Special Projects Reporter, *Kansas City (MO) Star,* 1990-93; National Correspondent, *Kansas City (MO) Star,* 1993-.

Other Awards: George Polk Memorial Award, Long Island University, NY, 1993. Sigma Delta Chi Award, 1992, 1994. Kansas City Press Club, 1994.

For More Information: *Quill,* 80:6 (July 1992): 31; *Vegetarian Times,* 179 (July 1992): 14.

Commentary: Jeff Taylor and Mike McGraw's seven-part series of articles took a critical look at the United States Department of Agriculture. They worked 16 months on the series, filing 70 requests under the Freedom of Information Act. The series, published in December 1991, examined how the agency works as well as where the money goes.

1993

David Adair Maraniss 944

Birth: August 9, 1949; Detroit, MI. **Parents:** Elliott Maraniss and Mary (Cummins). **Education:** University of Wisconsin. **Spouse:** Linda Porter (m. 1969). **Children:** Andrew, Sarah.

Prize: *National Reporting,* 1993: *Washington Post,* Washington, DC: Washington Post, 1992.

Career: *Madison (WI) Capitol Times;* News Reporter, Madison (WI), WIBA-Radio, 1972-75; Staff member, *Trenton (NJ) Times,* 1975-77; Reporter, *Washington (DC) Post,* 1977-79 ; Maryland Editor, *Washington (DC) Post,* 1979-80; Deputy Metro Editor, *Washington (DC) Post,* 1980-; Deputy Projects Editor, *Washington (DC) Post;* Metro Editor, *Washington (DC) Post;* Southwest Bureau Chief, *Washington (DC) Post,* 1985-93; National Political Reporter, *Washington (DC) Post,* 1993-.

Selected Works: *First in His Class: A Biography of Bill Clinton,* 1995. *Tell Newt to Shut Up! Prizewinning Washington Post Journalists Reveal How Reality Gagged the Gingrich Revolution* (with Michael Weisskopf), 1996.

Other Awards: Madison (WI) Reporter of the Year, 1972. New Jersey Press Association Award,

1976. John Hancock Prize, 1989. Grand Medal, National Conference of Christians and Jews, 1990. Everett McKinley Dirksen Award, 1996. George Polk Memorial Award, Long Island University, NY, 1996. Jesse Laventhol Prize, American Society of Newspaper Editors, 1997.

For More Information: *Washington Post,* 14 April (1993): A1; *Madison Capitol Times,* 6 February (1995): 1D; *Milwaukee Journal Sentinel,* 25 May (1997): Cue 1.

Commentary: David Maraniss won a Pulitzer Prize for his articles chronicling the rise of Democratic Presidential nominee Bill Clinton. He explored the forces that formed Clinton's character and affected his life. He later researched his topic further and wrote a biography in 1995 about President Clinton.

Maraniss grew up in a publishing family. His father was the editor of the *Madison Capitol Times* and his mother was an editor at the *University Press* in Madison. He was a finalist for a Pulitzer Prize in 1996.

1994

Eileen Welsome 945

Birth: March 12, 1951; New York, NY. **Parents:** Richard H. Welsome and Jane M. (Garity). **Education:** University of Texas: BA, With Honors. **Spouse:** James R. Martin (m. 1983).

Prize: *National Reporting,* 1994: *Albuquerque Tribune,* Albuquerque, NM: Albuquerque Tribune, 1993.

Career: Reporter, *Beaumont (TX) Enterprise,* 1980-82; Reporter, *San Antonio (TX) Light,* 1982-83; Reporter, *San Antonio (TX) Express-News,* 1983-86; Reporter, *Albuquerque (NM) Tribune,* 1987-95.

Selected Works: *Albuquerque Tribune,* "The Plutonium Experiment," 1993.

Other Awards: Clarion Award, 1989. National Headliners Club Award, 1989, 1994. John Hancock Award, 1991. Knight Fellow, Stanford University, CA, 1991-92. Public Service Award, Associated Press Managing Editors, 1991, 1994. Sigma Delta Chi Award, 1994. Selden Ring Award, 1994. Heywood Broun Award, 1994. George Polk Memorial Award, Long Island University, NY, 1994. Sidney Hillman Foundation Award, 1994. James Aronson Award for Social Justice Journalism, 1994.

For More Information: *Working Woman,* 19:6 (June 1994): 16; *Baltimore Sun,* 1 February (1994): 1D.

Commentary: Eileen Welsome spent more than six years working on the story of the United States government using humans as guinea pigs and injecting them with plutonium. The majority of that time was spent trying to track down the 18 people that she

had found referenced in a footnote. The difficult part was unearthing the names of the people, as they were classified "Top Secret" in the documents she had located.

1995

Anthony Lander Horwitz 946

Birth: June 9, 1958; Washington, DC. **Parents:** Norman Harold Horwitz and Elinor (Lander). **Education:** Brown University, RI: BA, magna cum laude, Phi Beta Kappa. Columbia University, NY: MA, Rick Baker Prize. **Spouse:** Geraldine Brooks (m. 1984).

Prize: *National Reporting,* 1995: *Wall Street Journal,* "Nine to Nowhere," New York: Dow Jones, 1994.

Career: Labor Organizer, United Woodcutters Association, 1982-83; Television Producer, *Mississippi Wood,* 1983; Education Reporter, *Fort Wayne (IN) News-Sentinel,* 1983-84; General Assignment Reporter, *Sydney (Australia) Morning Herald,* 1985-87; Freelance journalist, Cairo (Egypt), 1987-90; Contributor, *Wall Street Journal,* 1987-90; Reporter, London (England) Bureau, *Wall Street Journal,* 1990-93; Reporter, Pittsburgh (PA) Bureau, *Wall Street Journal,* 1993-.

Selected Works: *One for the Road: A Hitch-hiker's Outback,* 1987. *Baghdad without a Map, and Other Misadventures in Arabia,* 1991. *Confederates in the Attic: Dispatches from America's Unfinished Civil War,* 1998.

Other Awards: Best Independent Video Award, Indiana Focus, 1984: *Mississippi Wood.* Hal Boyle Award, Overseas Press Club, 1991. Overseas Press Club Award, 1992. John Hancock Award, 1994.

For More Information: *Wall Street Journal,* 19 April (1995): A2.

Commentary: Tony Horwitz examined the working conditions of people in low-paying, low-skill jobs. His series, "Nine to Nowhere," looked at the conditions in a poultry slaughterhouse, garbage plants, and clerical "sweatshops." His articles revealed the dangerous and demoralizing working conditions of low-paid and low-skilled employees.

Horwitz has worked as a union organizer and a television producer, and has reported from the Middle East.

1996

Alix M. Freedman 947

Birth: November 25, 1957; New York. **Parents:** Emanuel R. Freedman and Eva (Magyar). **Education:** Harvard University, MA: BA.

Prize: *National Reporting,* 1996: *Wall Street Journal,* "'Impact Booster': Tobacco Firm Shows How Ammonia Spurs Delivery of Nicotine," October 18, A1," New York: Dow Jones, 1995.

Career: News Assistant, *New York Times,* 1979-82; Staff Reporter, *Business Week* Magazine, 1983-84; Reporter, Philadelphia (PA) Bureau, *Wall Street Journal,* 1984-87; Reporter, New York (NY) Bureau, *Wall Street Journal,* 1987-91; Senior Special Writer, New York (NY) Bureau, *Wall Street Journal,* 1991-.

Other Awards: Gerald Loeb Award, 1993. Front Page Award, 1993.

For More Information: *Wall Street Journal,* April 10, 1996: A2.

Commentary: Alix M. Freedman, who had covered the food and tobacco industries for almost a decade, spent two months examining confidential tobacco industry documents. Her winning article disclosed the tobacco industry's regulation of nicotine delivery. Freedman was 38 when she won the award in 1996.

1997

Wall Street Journal 948

Founded: July 8, 1889; New York, NY. **Founder(s):** Charles Bergstresser, Charles Henry Dow, Edward Davis Jones.

Prize: *National Reporting,* 1997: *Wall Street Journal,* New York: Dow Jones, 1996.

Other Awards: Individual staff members of the *Wall Street Journal* have won 18 Pulitzer Prizes.

For More Information: *The Wall Street Journal in Its Beginnings,* New York: The Journal, 1923; Feemster, Robert M., *The Wall Street Journal, Purveyor of News to Business America, Newcomen Address, 1954,* New York: Newcomen Society in North America, 1954; *From Wall Street to Main Street: A Story of Publishing Progress,* New York: Dow Jones & Company, Inc., 1964; Neilson, Winthrop and Frances Fullerton Neilson, *What's News — Dow Jones: Story of the Wall Street Journal,* Radnor, PA: Chilton Book Co., 1973; Kerby, William F., *A Proud Profession: Memoirs of a Wall Street Journal Reporter, Editor, and Publisher,* Homewood, IL: Dow Jones-Irwin, 1981; Rosenberg, Jerry Martin, *Inside the Wall Street Journal: The History and the Power of Dow Jones & Company and America's Most Influential Newspaper,* New York: Macmillan, 1982; Wendt, Lloyd, *The Wall Street Journal: The Story of Dow Jones & the Nation's Business Newspaper,* Chicago: Rand McNally & Company, 1982; Scharff, Edward E., *Worldly Power: The Making of the Wall Street Journal,* New York: Beaufort Books, 1986; Winans, R. Foster, *Trading Secrets: Seduction and Scandal at the Wall Street Journal,* New York: St.

Martin's Press, 1987; *The Wall Street Journal: The First 100 Years,* New York: Dow Jones, 1989; Dealy, Francis X., *The Power and the Money: Inside the Wall Street Journal,* Secaucus, NJ: Carol Pub. Group, 1993; *Wall Street Journal,* 8 April (1997): A2.

Commentary: For their in-depth research on the new drug therapies available to combat AIDS, the staff of the *Wall Street Journal* won a National Reporting Pulitzer Prize in 1997. The staff also looked into how the pharmaceutical and medical industries had to change their fundamental understanding of treatment and long-term survival. Michael Waldholz, science writer, wrote five of the ten articles included in the winning entry. David Sanford, a senior special writer, wrote a firsthand account of his own experience with AIDS in November 1996. Amanda Bennett, Anita Sharpe, Elyse Tanouye, George Anders, and Laurie McGinley contributed articles in the series.

Dow Jones & Company, the owner of the *Wall Street Journal,* was formed in 1882, and seven years later the newspaper was officially launched. Although named for a small area on Manhattan Island in New York, the newspaper had a national scope and assured readers that it would search for and report the news in the United States, Canada, and Europe. In January 1899, unexpectedly, and with no public reason given, Edward D. Jones retired from the firm of Dow Jones & Company. The remaining owners at the time — Charles H. Dow, Charles M. Bergstresser, Thomas F. Woodlock, and Frank M. Brady—assumed all assets and liabilities of the firm and retained the name. In 1902, the four individuals sold their interest in Dow Jones and Company to Clarence Walker Barron, who was the owner of the Boston News Bureau. (He later published *Barron's, The National Financial Weekly.*) After C.W. Barron's death in October 1928, the bulk of his estate was inherited by his adopted daughter, Jane Bancroft. Descendants of Barron own stock in Dow Jones & Company today.

1998

Russell Carollo 949

Birth: March 16, 1955; Lacombe, LA. **Parents:** Victor Carollo and Norma. **Education:** Southeastern Louisiana University. Louisiana State University.

Prize: *National Reporting,* 1998: *Dayton Daily News,* "Unnecessary Danger," October 5 - 11, Dayton, OH: *Dayton Daily News,* 1997.

Career: General Assignment Reporter, Military Projects *Spokane (WA) Spokesman-Review,* 1986-90; Special Projects Reporter and Computer Assisted Reporting, *Dayton (OH) Daily News,* 1990-93; Military and Projects Reporter, *Tacoma (WA) News Tribune,* 1993-94; Special Projects Reporter and Computer Assisted Reporting, *Dayton (OH) Daily News,* 1994-.

Other Awards: Journalism Fellowship, University of Michigan, 1989-90. Investigative Reporters and Editors Award, 1992, 1995, 1996. John Hancock Award, 1992. Edgar A. Poe Award, White House Correspondents Association, 1995. Society of Professional Journalists Award, 1995. Goldsmith Award, Harvard University, MA, 1996. Fellow, International Center for Journalists, 1997. George Polk Memorial Award, Long Island University, NY, 1998. National Headliners Club Award, 1998.

For More Information: *New Orleans Times-Picayune,* June 7, 1998: H2.

Commentary: Russell Carollo and Jeff Nesmith were awarded a Pulitzer Prize for "their reporting that disclosed dangerous flaws and mismanagement in the military health care system and prompted reforms." In a follow-up article on October 27, the Department of Defense acknowledged serious problems in its health care system.

Carollo has worked at papers in Mississippi, Louisiana, Washington, and Ohio. He has covered both domestic and foreign assignments in his career. He was a Pulitzer finalist in 1992 for a five-part series on worker safety in America. In 1996, he was a Pulitzer finalist for his reporting on the lenient handling of sexual misconduct cases by the military.

Jeff Nesmith   950

Birth: June 28, 1940; Hillsborough County, FL. **Parents:** Hollis Jefferson Nesmith and Thetis. **Education:** University of Florida. **Spouse:** Achsah Posey (m. 1966). **Children:** Susannah, Jeff.

Prize: *National Reporting,* 1998: *Dayton Daily News,* "Unnecessary Danger," October 5 - 11, Dayton, OH: *Dayton Daily News,* 1997.

Career: Part-Time Reporter, *Plant City (FL) Courier;* Teacher, *Howey Academy (FL),* 1963-64; Obituary Writer, *Atlanta (GA) Constitution,* 1964; Police, City Government, State Politics, Investigative Reporter, *Atlanta (GA) Constitution;* Investigative Reporter, *Philadelphia (PA) Evening Bulletin;* Correspondent, Washington (DC), *Atlanta (GA) Constitution;* Reporter, Washington (DC) Bureau, Cox Newspapers, 1977-.

Other Awards: Gold Medal, Investigative Reporters and Editors. Goldsmith Award, Harvard University, MA. George Polk Memorial Award, Long Island University, NY, 1998. National Headliners Club Award, 1998.

For More Information: *Tampa Tribune,* May 2, 1998: 2.

Commentary: Jeff Nesmith (Hollis Jefferson Nesmith Jr.) and Russell Carollo were awarded a Pulitzer Prize for their reporting of the United States military health care system and the serious flaws within the system.

After graduating from college, Nesmith was a teacher for one year. He then turned to journalism and began his new career as an obituary writer. He was a finalist for a Pulitzer Prize in 1996 for reporting on the lenient handling of sexual misconduct cases by the United States military.

Newspaper History Award

1918

Henry Beetle Hough 951

Birth: November 8, 1896; New Bedford, MA. **Death:** June 6, 1985. **Parents:** George Anthony Hough and Abby Louise (Beetle). **Education:** Columbia University, NY: BLitt. **Spouse:** Elizabeth Wilson Bowie (m. 1920, died 1965); Edith Sands Graham Blake (m. 1979).

Prize: *Newspaper History Award,* 1918: *A History of the Service Rendered to the Public by the American Press During the Year 1917,* New York: Columbia University Press, 1918.

Career: Served in U.S. Naval Reserve, 1918-1919; Public Relations Staff member, Institute of American Meat Packers, 1919-1920; Owner, Publisher, Editor, *Edgartown (MA) Vineyard Gazette,* 1920-1968; Newspaper Publicity Staff member, Western Electric Company, 1923-1926; Bergen Lecturer, Yale University (CT), 1952-53; Editor, *Edgartown (MA) Vineyard Gazette,* 1968-1985.

Selected Works: *The Heath Hen's Journey to Extinction, 1792-1933,* 1933. *Martha's Vineyard, Summer Resort, 1835-1935,* 1936 (2nd ed. 1966, 3rd ed. 1982). *Country Editor,* 1940. *That Lofty Sky,* 1941. *All Things Are Yours: A Novel,* 1942. *At Christmas All Bells Say the Same,* 1942. *Roosters Crow in Town,* 1945. *Long Anchorage: A New Bedford Story,* 1947. *Once More the Thunderer,* 1950. *Singing in the Morning, and Other Essays about Martha's Vineyard,* 1951. *Whaling Wives,* 1952. *An Alcoholic to His Sons* (with Emma Whiting), 1954. *Thoreau of Walden: The Man and His Eventful Life,* 1956. *Great Days of Sailing: North Star Books, 1,* 1958. *The New England Story: A Novel,* 1958. *Lament for a City,* 1960. *Melville in the South Pacific,* 1960. *The Port,* 1963. *Vineyard Gazette Reader,* 1967. *The Road,* 1970. *Martha's Vineyard,* 1970. *Tuesday Will Be Different: Letters in the Sheriff's Lane* (with Alfred Eisenstaedt), 1971. *Mostly on Martha's Vineyard: A Personal Record,* 1975. *To the Harbor Light,* 1976. *To the Vineyard and the Sea: Poems,* 1977. *Soundings at Sea Level* (with Charles Wharton Stork), 1980. *Remembrances and Light: Images of Martha's Vineyard,* 1984. *Far Out the Coils: A Personal View of Life and Culture on Martha's Vineyard* (with Alison Shaw), 1985.

Other Awards: Medal for Excellence, Columbia University, NY, 1942. Yankee Quill Award, Academy of New England Journalism. Elijah Parish Lovejoy Award, Southern Illinois University, 1974. Honorary Degrees: Yale University, CT, 1958; Simmons College, MA, 1977; Southeastern Massachusetts University, 1977; Columbia University, NY, 1978.

For More Information: *Contemporary Authors, New Revision Series, Volume 2,* Detroit: Gale Research Company, 1981; *Los Angeles Times,* 8 June (1985): part 4, 7; *New York Times,* 7 June (1985): D17.

Commentary: Henry Beetle Hough and Minna Lewinson were awarded the first and only Pulitzer Prize given in the Newspaper History category. Hough was an editor of the Edgartown *Vineyard Gazette* on Martha's Vineyard for over 60 years. The paper was a wedding gift from Hough's father in 1920. Hough was a prolific writer and, besides running the newspaper, he wrote over 25 books.

Minna Lewinson 952

Birth: June 28, 1897; New York, NY. **Education:** Barnard College, NY. Columbia University, NY: BLitt.

Prize: *Newspaper History Award,* 1918: *A History of the Service Rendered to the Public by the American Press During the Year 1917,* New York: Columbia University Press, 1918.

Career: Copy Writer, Arnold Constable; Reporter, Columnist, *Daily Investment News;* Reporter, *Women's Wear;* Copy Reader, *Wall Street Journal.*

Commentary: Minna Lewinson and Henry Beetle Hough were awarded the first and only prize given in the Newspaper History category. They both were students at Columbia University, graduating in 1918.

Novel

1917

No award

1918

Ernest Poole 953

Birth: January 23, 1878; Chicago, IL. **Death:** January 10, 1950. **Parents:** Abram and Mary (Howl) Poole. **Education:** Princeton University, NJ: AB. **Spouse:** Margaret Winterbottom (m. 1907). **Children:** William Morris, Nicholas, Mrs. Robert Henry Lancaster.

Prize: *Novel,* 1918: *His Family,* New York: Macmillan, 1917.

Career: Reporter, *The Outlook;* Union Press Agent; Contributor, *The Call, Saturday Evening Post, Collier's, The New York American;* Reporter and Correspondent, *McClure's.*

Selected Works: *The Avalanche,* 1924. *The Hunter's Moon,* 1925. *With Eastern Eye,* 1926. *Silent Storms,* 1927. *The Car of Croesus,* 1930. *The Destroyer,* 1931. *Great Winds,* 1933. *The Bridge: My Own Story,* 1940. *Giants Gone: Men Who Made Chicago,* 1943. *The Great White Hills of New Hampshire,* 1946. *The Nancy Flyer,* 1949. *The Voice of the Street,* 1906. *The Harbor,* 1915. *His Second Wife,* 1918. *The Village: Russian Impressions,* 1918. *Blind: A Story of These Times,* 1920. *Beggars' Gold,* 1921. *Millions,* 1922. *Danger,* 1923.

For More Information: Keefer, Truman Frederick, *Ernest Poole,* New Haven, CT: College & University Press, 1966.

Commentary: Ernest Poole won the Pulitzer Prize for Novel for *His Family,* an immigrant's story. He wrote about the changing pace of American life in the 20th century and the problems arising from these changes.

Poole was a staunch advocate for the abolition of child labor and slum conditions, calling for improvement in living and working conditions. He assisted Upton Sinclair in gathering information for *The Jungle.* He was also a reporter who is remembered for his dispatches from Russia during the revolutions of 1905 and 1917. Poole experienced success for a series of novels published in the 1940s and set in New England.

1919

Booth Tarkington 954

Birth: July 29, 1869; Indianapolis, IN. **Death:** May 19, 1946. **Parents:** John Stevenson and Elizabeth (Booth) Tarkington. **Education:** Purdue University, IN. Princeton University, NJ. **Spouse:** Laurel Louis Thatcher (m. 1902; div. 1911); Susanah Robinson (m. 1912).

Prize: *Novel,* 1919: *The Magnificent Ambersons,* Garden City, NY: Doubleday, 1918. *Novel,* 1922: *Alice Adams,* Garden City, NY: Doubleday, 1921.

Career: Novelist, essayist.

Selected Works: *The Gentleman from Indiana,* 1899. *Poe's Run, and Other Poems,* 1904. *Monsieur Beaucaire,* 1900. *The Two Vanrevels,* 1902. *Cherry,* 1903. *In the Arena: Stories of Political Life,* 1905. *The Beautiful Lady,* 1905. *The Conquest of Canaan,* 1905. *His Own People,* 1907. *The Guest of Quesnay,* 1908. *Beasley's Christmas Party,* 1909. *Beauty and the Jacobin,* 1912. *The Flirt,* 1913. *Penrod,* 1914. *Seventeen,* 1916. *Destroyers of Nuremberg,* 1917. *The Gibson Upright,* 1919. *Ramsey Milholland,* 1919. *Harlequin and Columbine,* 1921. *Gentle Julia,* 1922. *The Fascinating Stranger, and Other Stories,* 1923. *The Midlander,* 1923. *Looking Forward,* 1926. *Growth,* 1927. *The Plutocrat,* 1927. *Claire Ambler,* 1928. *The World Does Move,* 1928. *Young Mrs. Greeley,* 1929. *Mary's Neck,* 1932. *Wanton Mally,* 1932. *Presenting Lily Mars,* 1933. *Little Orvie,* 1934. *Mr. White, The Red Barn, Hell, and Bridewater,* 1935. *The Lorenzo Bunch,* 1936. *The Fighting Littles,* 1941. *The Heritage of Hatcher Ide,* 1941. *Kate Fennigate,* 1943. *Image of Josephine,* 1945. *The Show Piece,* 1947. *Three Selected Short Novels,* 1947. **Films:** *Alice Adams,* RKO, 1933; *Seventeen,* Paramount, 1940; *The Magnificent Ambersons,* RKO, 1942; *Presenting Lily Mars,* MGM, 1943; *Monsieur Beaucaire,* Paramount, 1946; *On Moonlight Bay,* Warner Bros., 1951; *By the Light of the Silvery Moon,* Warner Bros., 1953.

Other Awards: Gold Medal, National Institute of Arts and Letters, 1933. Roosevelt Distinguished Service Medal, 1942. Howells Medal, American Academy of Arts and Letters, 1945. Honorary Degrees: DePauw University, IN, 1923; Columbia University, NY, 1924. Honorary MA, Princeton University, NJ, 1918. Honorary LHDs: Princeton University, NJ, 1918; Purdue University, IN, 1939.

For More Information: Holliday, Robert Cortes, *Booth Tarkington,* Garden City, NY: Doubleday, Page, 1918; Woodress, James Leslie, *Booth*

Tarkington: Gentleman from Indiana, New York: Lippincott, 1955; Fennimore, Keith J., *Booth Tarkington,* New York: Twayne, 1974; Mayberry, Susanah, *My Amiable Uncle: Recollections About Booth Tarkington,* West Lafayette, IN: Purdue, 1983.

Commentary: Booth Tarkington won two Pulitzer Prizes. He was awarded the 1919 prize for Novel for *The Magnificent Ambersons,* which followed the life of a snob who eventually suffers the consequences of his condescendence. He won the 1920 prize for Novel for *Alice Adams,* a story that many critics regarded as his best work. Alice, the daughter in a middle-class family in the Midwest, tries very hard to be attractive and appealing, but is really a wallflower at social events. Alice's only hope in life was a college education.

Tarkington enjoyed much success, especially from *Penrod,* a novel about a 12-year-old boy living in small-town America during World War I. *Penrod* in its time rivaled *The Adventures of Tom Sawyer* in popularity. Tarkington was also a playwright and the founder of the Princeton Triangle Club. He had a keen interest in politics and went on to serve in the Indiana House of Representatives, which led him to write *In the Arena,* a tale of corruption in politics.

1920
No award

1921

Edith Newbold Wharton   955
Birth: January 24, 1862; New York, NY. **Death:** August 11, 1937. **Parents:** George Frederic and Lucretia Stevens (Rhinelander) Jones. **Education:** Privately educated. **Spouse:** Edward Wharton (m. 1885; div. 1912).

Prize: *Novel,* 1921: *The Age of Innocence,* New York: Appleton, 1920.

Career: Short story writer, novelist; Member, National Institute of Arts and Letters, 1930-37; Member, American Academy of Arts and Letters, 1934-37.

Selected Works: *Stories of New York,* 1893. *The Greater Inclination,* 1899. *The Touchstone,* 1900. *A Gift from the Grave,* 1901. *Crucial Instances,* 1901. *The Valley of Decision,* 1902. *Sanctuary,* 1903. *The Descent of Man: And Other Stories,* 1904. *The House of Mirth,* 1905. *The Fruit of the Tree,* 1907. *Italian Backgrounds,* 1907. *Madame de Treymes,* 1907. *A Motor-Flight through France,* 1908. *Artemis to Actaeon, and Other Verse,* 1909. *Tales of Men and Ghosts,* 1910. *Ethan Frome,* 1911. *The Reef,* 1912. *The Custom of the Country,* 1913. *Fighting France, from Dunkerque to Belfort,* 1915. *The Book of the Homeless,* 1916. *Xingu: And Other Stories,* 1916.

Summer, 1917. *The Marne,* 1918. *French Ways and Their Meaning,* 1919. *In Morocco,* 1920. *The Glimpses of the Moon,* 1922. *A Son at the Front,* 1923. *New Year's Day,* 1924. *False Dawn,* 1924. *The Old Maid,* 1924. *The Spark,* 1924. *The Mother's Recompense,* 1925. *The Writing of Fiction,* 1925. *Here and Beyond,* 1926. *Twilight Sleep,* 1927. *The Children,* 1928. *The Marriage Playground,* 1928. *Hudson River Bracketed,* 1929. *Certain People,* 1930. *The Gods Arrive,* 1932. *Human Nature,* 1933. *A Backward Glance,* 1934. *The World Over,* 1936. *Ghosts,* 1937. *The Buccaneers,* 1938. **Films:** *The Children* (based on *The Marriage Playground*), Paramount, 1929; *The Age of Innocence,* RKO, 1934; *The Old Maid,* Warner Bros., 1939; *The Age of Innocence,* Columbia, 1993.

Other Awards: Gold Medal, National Institute of Arts and Letters. Cross, Legion of Honor, France, WWI. Chevalier of the Order of Leopold, Belgium, WWI. Monteyn Prize, French Academy. Honorary DLitt, Yale University, CT.

For More Information: Vita-Finzi, Penelope, *Edith Wharton and the Art of Fiction,* London, England: Pinter, 1990; Wolff, Cynthia Griffin, *A Feast of Words: The Triumph of Edith Wharton,* Reading, MA: Addison-Wesley, 1995; Bell, Millicent, ed., *The Cambridge Companion to Edith Wharton,* New York: Cambridge University Press, 1995; Craig, Theresa, *Edith Wharton: A House Full of Rooms, Architecture, Interiors, and Gardens,* New York: Monacelli, 1996; Dwight, Eleanor, *The Gilded Age: Edith Wharton and Her Contemporaries,* New York: Universe, 1996; Price, Alan, *The End of the Age of Innocence: Edith Wharton and the First World War,* New York: St. Martin's, 1996.

Commentary: Edith Wharton's *The Age of Innocence* won the Pulitzer Prize for its depiction of the complex social relationships among New York society's elite in the 1870s. Wharton's understanding of the social mores which governed the lives and behavior of this caste was a result of her own upbringing and exposure.

Wharton had a prolific career in writing, but she experienced problems in her personal life. Enduring a difficult marriage, she focused her mind on the moral questions and situations which interested her and made them the subjects of her novels. A close friendship with Henry James is said to have influenced her, and many critics drew comparisons both of their subject matter and their styles.

1922

Booth Tarkington
Full entry appears as **#954** under "Novel," 1919.

1923

Willa Cather   956

Birth: December 7, 1873; Back Creek Valley, VA.
Death: April 24, 1947. **Parents:** Charles F. and Mary
Virginia (Boak) Cather. **Education:** University of
Nebraska.

Prize: *Novel,* 1923: *One of Ours,* New York:
Knopf, 1922.

Career: Reporter and Critic, *Nebraska State
Journal;* Editor, *Home Monthly;* Journalist; Managing Editor, *McClure's.*

Selected Works: *April Twilights: Poems,* 1903.
Alexander's Bridge, 1912. *O Pioneers!,* 1913. *My
Autobiography,* 1914. *The Song of the Lark,* 1915. *My
Antonia,* 1918. *Youth and the Bright Medusa,* 1920.
One of Ours, 1922. *A Lost Lady,* 1923. *April Twilights
and Other Poems,* 1923. *The Professor's House,*
1925. *My Mortal Enemy,* 1926. *Death Comes for the
Archbishop,* 1927. *The Song of the Lark,* 1929. *Youth
and the Bright Medusa,* 1929. *Shadows on the Rock,*
1931. *Obscure Destinies,* 1932. *Lucy Gayheart,* 1935.
Not under Forty, 1936. *Shadows on the Rock,* 1937.
Sapphira and the Slave Girl, 1940. *The Old Beauty,
and Others,* 1948. *On Writing: Critical Studies on
Writing as an Art,* 1949. **Films:** *A Lost Lady,* Warner
Bros., 1934; *O Pioneers!* Lorimar (TV), 1992.

Other Awards: Howells Medal, 1930: *Death
Comes to the Archbishop.* New York: Knopf, 1927.
Prix Femina Americaine, Distinguished Literary Accomplishment, 1932. Gold Medal, National Institute
of Arts and Letters, 1944. Honorary Degrees:
Creighton University, NE; University of Michigan;
University of Nebraska; University of California.

For More Information: Ambrose, Jamie, *Willa
Cather: Writing at the Frontier,* New York: St. Martin's, 1988; March, John, *A Reader's Companion to*
the Fiction of Willa Cather, Westport, CT: Greenwood, 1993; Meyering, Sheryl L., *A Reader's Guide
to the Short Stories of Willa Cather,* New York: G.K.
Hall, 1994; Urgo, Joseph R., *Willa Cather and the
Myth of American Migration,* Urbana: University of
Illinois Press, 1995; Gerber, Philip L., *Willa Cather,*
New York: Twayne, 1995; Reynolds, Guy, *Willa
Cather in Context: Progress, Race, Empire,* Basingstoke, England: Macmillan, 1996.

Commentary: The 1923 Pulitzer Prize for Novel
went to Willa Cather for *One of Ours,* the story of a
young man dismayed by the unstoppable changes
taking place around his Nebraska hometown. He enlists in the army during World War I and dies in battle.
The story puts in perspective the diminution of frontier life at the beginning of the 20th century.

Cather's many works highlight the appeal of a
simpler, slower, and quieter time and place. She left
Nebraska for Pittsburgh, where she wrote for a magazine. She then went on to New York to work for S.S.
McClure as the editor of *McClure's.* She left that
position to write fulltime and at close to 40 years of
age, she published her first novel, *Alexander's Bridge.*

1924

Margaret Wilson   957

Birth: January 16, 1882; Iowa. **Death:** 1973. **Education:** University of Chicago, IL. **Spouse:** Colonel
G.D. Turner (m. 1923).

Prize: *Novel,* 1924: *The Able McLaughlins,* New
York: Harper, 1923.

Career: Missionary, teacher, novelist.

Selected Works: *The Kenworthys,* 1925. *The
Painted Room,* 1926. *Daughters of India,* 1928. *Trousers of Taffeta: Child Mothers of India,* 1929. *The
Crime of Punishment,* 1931. *One Came Out,* 1932.
The Valiant Wife, 1934. *The Law and the McLaughlins,* 1936.

Other Awards: Harper Prize, 1923: *The Able
McLaughlins.* New York: Harper, 1923.

For More Information: *Oxford Companion to
American Literature,* New York: Oxford University
Press, 1965; *Dictionary of Literary Biography,* Detroit: Gale, 1981; *Feminist Companion to Literature
in English,* New Haven, CT: Yale University Press,
1990.

Commentary: Margaret Wilson's first novel,
The Able McLaughlins, the story of Scottish pioneers
making a life on a farm in Iowa, won the Pulitzer Prize.
Wilson wrote a sequel, *The Law and the McLaughlins,*
that was also very popular. She stated that she wrote
for women readers from a woman's point of view.

Wilson considered herself "the most Middle
Western of Middle Westerners." Raised on a farm in
Iowa, she went to the University of Chicago and

studied English. After college she traveled to India as a missionary. Once there, her compassionate nature was not able to handle the poverty and misery she witnessed. Her experiences there were the subject of several of her novels. Returning to the United States, she met and married a Englishman. They moved to his country and she lived there for the rest of her life.

1925

Edna Ferber   958

Birth: August 15, 1887; Kalamazoo, MI. **Death:** April 16, 1968. **Parents:** Jacob Charles and Julia (Neuman) Ferber. **Religion:** Jewish. **Spouse:** Single.

Prize: *Novel,* 1925: *So Big,* Garden City, NY: Doubleday, Page, 1924.

Career: Reporter, *Appleton Daily Crescent,* Appleton, WI; Writer and Reporter, *Milwaukee Journal,* Milwaukee, WI; War Correspondent, U.S. Army Air Forces, WWI.

Selected Works: *Dawn O'Hara: The Girl Who Laughed,* 1911. *Roast Beef, Medium: The Business Adventures of Emma McChesney,* 1913. *Personality Plus: Some Experiences of Emma McChesney and Her Son, Jock,* 1914. *Fanny Herself,* 1917. *Cheerful, By Request,* 1918. *Half Portions,* 1920. *$1200 a Year: A Comedy in Three Acts* (Play) (with Newman Levy), 1920. *Gigolo,* 1922. *The Girls,* 1923. *So Big,* 1924. *Show Boat,* 1926. *Mother Knows Best,* 1927. *The Royal Family: A Comedy in Three Acts,* Garden City, NY: (Play) (with George S. Kaufman), 1928. *Cimarron,* 1930. *American Beauty,* 1931. *Dinner at Eight* (Play) (with George S. Kaufman), 1932. *They Brought Their Women: A Book of Short Stories,* 1933. *Come and Get It,* 1935. *Stage Door: A Play* (Play) (with George S. Kaufman), 1936. *Nobody's in Town,* 1938.

A Peculiar Treasure, 1939. *No Room at the Inn,* 1941. *Saratoga Trunk,* 1941. *The Land Is Bright* (Play), 1941. *Great Son,* 1945. *One Basket: Thirty-One Short Stories,* 1947. *Giant,* 1952. *Ice Palace,* 1958. *A Kind of Magic,* 1963. **Films:** *Cimmaron,* RKO, 1930; *So Big,* Warner Bros., 1932, 1953; *Dinner at Eight,* MGM, 1933; *Stage Door,* RKO, 1937.

Other Awards: Honorary LittDs: Columbia University; Adelphi College, NY.

For More Information: Shaughnessy, Mary Rose, *Women and Success in American Society in the Works of Edna Ferber,* New York: Gordon, 1977; Gilbert, Julie Goldsmith, *Ferber, A Biography,* Garden City, NY: Doubleday, 1978.

Commentary: Edna Ferber was awarded the Pulitzer Prize for Novel in 1925 for *So Big,* the touching story of a penniless young widow who struggles to make a living and raise her baby son. Ferber wrote about the lower and middle classes in Midwestern America. Her work was greatly respected and admired by the journalist and historian, William Allen White, as an accurate depiction of American life in the early part of the 20th century.

Ferber's career began in journalism. She then turned her efforts to short stories, novels, and drama. Her novel, *Showboat,* was adapted to the musical theater with music by Oscar Hammerstein II and lyrics by Jerome Kern. One of her last works, *Giant,* an epic story of oil and a Texas family, became a blockbuster Hollywood film.

1926

Sinclair Lewis   959

Birth: February 7, 1885; Sauk Centre, MN. **Death:** January 10, 1951. **Parents:** Edward J. and Emma

(Kermott) Lewis. **Education:** Yale University, CT. **Spouse:** Grace Hegger (m.1914, div.1928); Dorothy Thompson (m.1928, div. 1943). **Children:** Well (GH); Michael (DT).

Prize: *Novel,* 1926: *Arrowsmith,* New York: Harcourt Brace, 1927.

Career: Janitor, Helicon Home (Upton Sinclair's socialist community), Englewood, NJ, 1906-1907; Assistant Editor, *Transatlantic Tales,* NY, 1907; Reporter, *Daily Courier,* Waterloo, IA, 1908; Charity worker, New York City, 1908; Secretary to Alice MacGowan and Grace MacGowan Cooke in Carmel, CA, 1909; Staff writer, *Evening Bulletin,* San Francisco, CA, 1909; Staff writer, Associated Press, San Francisco, 1909-1910; Staff member, *Volta Review,* Washington, DC, 1910; Manuscript Reader, Frederick A. Stokes, NY, 1910-1912; Assistant Editor, *Adventure,* New York City, 1912; Editor, Publisher's Newspaper Syndicate, New York City, 1913-1914; Editorial Assistant and Advertising Manager, George H. Doran, NY, 1914-1915; Writer-in-Residence, University of Wisconsin, Madison, 1942; Vice President, National Institute of Arts and Letters, 1944.

Selected Works: *Our Mr. Wrenn,* 1914. *The Trail of the Hawk: A Comedy of the Seriousness of Life,* 1915. *The Innocents: A Story for Lovers,* 1917. *The Job: An American Novel,* 1917. *Free Air,* 1919. *Main Street: The Story of Carol Kennicott,* 1920. *Arrowsmith,* 1925. *Babbitt,* 1922. *Elmer Gantry,* 1927. *Mantrap,* 1926. *The Man Who Knew Coolidge: Being the Soul of Lowell Schmaltz, Constructive and Nordic Citizen,* 1928. *Ann Vickers,* 1933. *Dodsworth,* 1929. *The Trail of the Hawk: A Comedy of the Seriousness of Life,* 1933. *Work of Art,* 1934. *It Can't Happen Here: A Novel,* 1935. *Jayhawker: Play in Three Acts* (with Lloyd Lewis), 1935. *Selected Short Stories of Sinclair Lewis,* 1935. *The Prodigal Parents,* 1938. *Bethel Merriday,* 1940. *Gideon Planish,* 1943. *Cass Timberlane: A Novel of Husbands and Wives,* 1945. *Kingsblood Royal,* 1947. *The God-Seeker,* 1949. *World So Wide,* 1951. **Films:** *Arrowsmith,* United Artists, 1931; *Ann Vickers,* RKO, 1933; *Babbitt,* Warner Bros., 1934; *Dodsworth,* United Artists, 1936; *Main Street* (based on *I Married a Doctor*), Warner Bros., 1936; *Mantrap* (based on *Untamed*), Paramount, 1940; *Cass Timberlane,* MGM, 1947; *Elmer Gantry,* United Artists, 1960; *Sparrers Can't Sing,* Warner Bros., 1962.

Other Awards: Nobel Prize, Literature, 1930. *Ebony* Magazine Award, Promoting Racial Harmony: *Kingsblood Royal.* New York: Random House, 1947. Honorary LittD, Yale University, CT, 1936.

For More Information: Lewis, Grace Hegger, *With Love From Gracie: Sinclair Lewis, 1912-1925,* New York: Harcourt, Brace, 1955; Schorer, Mark, *Sinclair Lewis: An American Life,* New York:

McGraw-Hill, 1961; Grebstein, Sheldon Norman, *Sinclair Lewis:* New York: Twayne, 1962; Griffin, Robert J., ed., *Twentieth Century Interpretations of Arrowsmith, A Collection of Critical Essays,* Englewood Cliffs, NJ: Prentice Hall, 1968; Fleming, Robert E., *Sinclair Lewis, A Reference Guide,* Boston: Hall, 1980; Bloom, Harold, ed., *Sinclair Lewis,* New York: Chelsea House, 1987; Hutchisson, James M., *The Rise of Sinclair Lewis, 1920-1930,* University Park, PA: Pennsylvania State University Press, 1996.

Commentary: Sinclair Lewis won the Pulitzer Prize for Novel in 1930 for *Arrowsmith,* the story of a young doctor who has devoted his life to the study of bacteria, only to discover that the "search for truth" is neither aided nor encouraged by the American establishment.

Lewis's most important works, *Main Street, Arrowsmith, Babbitt,* and *Elmer Gantry,* were critical of the American small town. Lewis conveyed this criticism with humor while holding fast to his beliefs. (American writers heretofore had lauded American simplicity and idealism.) He also wrote under the pseudonym Tom Graham.

1927

Louis Bromfield   960

Birth: December 27, 1896; Mansfield, OH. **Death:** March 18, 1956. **Parents:** Charles and Annette Maria (Coulter) Bromfield. **Education:** School of Agriculture, Cornell University, NY. School of Journalism, Columbia University, NY. **Spouse:** Mary Appleton Wood (m. 1921). **Children:** Hope, Anne, Ellen.

Prize: *Novel,* 1927: *Early Autumn,* London, England: Cape, 1926.

Career: Ambulance driver, French Army, WWI; Writer, New York News Association, Associated Press and *Musical America.*

Selected Works: *Possession,* 1925. *The Green Bay Tree,* 1927. *A Good Woman,* 1927. *The Strange Case of Miss Annie Spragg,* 1928. *The House of Women* (Play), 1928. *Awake and Rehearse,* 1929. *Twenty-Four Hours,* 1930. *A Modern Hero,* 1932. *The Farm,* 1933. *Deluxe* (Play), 1935. *Times Have Changed* (Play), 1935. *It Had to Happen,* 1936. *The Rains Came,* 1937. *It Takes All Kinds,* 1939. *Night in Bombay,* 1940. *Until the Day Break,* 1942. *Mrs. Parkington,* 1943. *What Became of Anna Bolton,* 1944. *Colorado,* 1947. *Kenny,* 1947. *Malabar Farm,* 1948. *The Wild Country,* 1948. *Mr. Smith,* 1951. **Films:** *The Rains Came,* Fox, 1939; *Better Than Life* (based on *It All Came True*), Warner Bros., 1940; *A Modern Hero,* Warner Bros., 1940; *McLeod's Folly* (based on *Johnny Come Lately*), Cagney, 1943; *Mrs. Parkington,* MGM, 1944; *The Rains of Rainchipur,* Fox, 1955.

Other Awards: Croix de Guerre, Legion of Honor, France, 1939. Honorary Degree, Ohio Northern University.

For More Information: Brown, Morrison, *Louis Bromfield and His Books,* London, England: Cassell, 1956; Geld, Ellen Bromfield, *The Heritage: A Daughter's Memories of Louis Bromfield,* New York: Harper, 1962; Anderson, David D., *Louis Bromfield,* New York: Twayne, 1964.

Commentary: Louis Bromfield was awarded the Pulitzer Prize for Novel in 1927 for *Early Autumn,* one of four novels in a Bromfield series. The Escape series was a collection that depicted a changing America in which going against the norm had strong implications for the individual.

Bromfield enjoyed a successful career as a novelist and an even more successful and lucrative career as a screenwriter. He traveled to India, which became the subject of some of his works. There he observed the destruction of traditional agrarian values, a mirror of what he saw occurring in the United States. Later he established Malabar Farm, a cooperative in Ohio for agricultural experimentation. He continued to produce novels while living and working on the farm.

1928

Thornton Wilder
Full entry appears as **#185** under "Drama," 1938.

1929

Julia Peterkin   961
Birth: October 31, 1880; Laurence County, SC. **Death:** August 10,1963. **Parents:** Julius Andrew and Alma (Archer) Mood. **Education:** Converse College, SC: BA. **Spouse:** William George Peterkin (m.1903). **Children:** William George.

Prize: *Novel,* 1929: *Scarlet Sister Mary,* Indianapolis, IN: Bobbs-Merrill, 1928.

Career: Country school teacher; Freelance writer.

Selected Works: *Green Thursday,* 1924. *Black April,* 1927. *Scarlet Sister Mary,* 1928. *Bright Skin,* 1932. *A Plantation Christmas,* 1934. *The World We Live In,* 1944.

For More Information: Shealy, Ann, *The Passionate Mind: Four Studies,* Philadelphia, PA: Dorrance, 1976; Landess, Thomas H., *Julia Peterkin,* Boston: Twayne, 1976; Williams, Susan Millar, *A Devil and a Good Woman, Too: The Lives of Julia Peterkin,* Athens, GA: University of Georgia Press, 1997.

Commentary: *Scarlet Sister Mary* is a novel about the area of coastal South Carolina known as the Gullah. Its heroine is a black woman and it presents a picture of the black Gullah culture, and its language and customs.

Peterkin was raised by a Gullah nurse on a South Carolina plantation. She married a plantation owner and was able to continue her immersion in the Gullah culture through her writing.

1930

Oliver La Farge   962
Birth: December 19, 1901; New York, NY. **Death:** August 2, 1963. **Parents:** Christopher Grant and Florence Bayard (Lockwood) La Farge. **Religion:** Roman Catholic. **Education:** Harvard University, MA: BA. **Spouse:** Wanden E. Mathews (m. 1929, div. 1937); Consuelo Odil Baca (m. 1939). **Children:** Povy, Oliver Albee (WEM); John Pendaries (COB).

Prize: *Novel,* 1930: *Laughing Boy,* Boston: Houghton Mifflin, 1929.

Career: President, *The Advocate,* Harvard University, MA; Editor, *Lampoon,* Harvard University, MA; Assistant, Department of Ethnology, Tulane University, LA, 1926-1928; Research Associate, Department of Anthropology, Columbia University, NY, 1931-1933; President, National Association of Indian Affairs, 1933-1937; President, American Association of Indian Affairs, 1937-1942 and 1946-1963; Member, Advisory Board, Laboratory of Anthropology at Santa Fe, NM; Director, International Exhibition of

Indian Art; Member: American Anthropological Association, American Association for the Advancement of Science, PEN.

Selected Works: *Sparks Fly Upward,* 1931. *Long Pennant,* 1933. *The Enemy Gods,* 1937. *All the Young Men,* 1935. *As Long as the Grass Shall Grow,* 1940. *The Changing Indian,* 1942. *The Copper Pot,* 1942. *Raw Material,* 1945. *Santa Eulalia: The Religion of a Cuchumat in Indian Town,* 1947. *The Eagle in the Egg,* 1949. *Cochise of Arizona: The Pipe of Peace is Broken,* 1953. *Behind the Mountains,* 1956. *A Pictorial History of the American Indian,* 1956. *A Pause in the Desert: A Collection of Short Stories,* 1957. *The Door in the Wall,* 1965.

Other Awards: Hemmenway Fellow, 1924-26. O. Henry Memorial Prize Award, 1931: *Haunted Ground.* Guggenheim Fellowship, 1941. Honorary Degree, Brown University, MA. 1932.

For More Information: Gillis, Everett A., *Oliver La Farge,* Austin, TX: Steck-Vaughn, 1967; McNickle, D'Arcy, *Indian Man: A Life of Oliver La Farge,* Bloomington: Indiana University Press, 1971; Pearce, T.M., *Oliver La Farge,* New York: Twayne, 1972; Caffey, David L., ed., *Yellow Sun, Bright Sky: The Indian Country Stories of Oliver La Farge,* Albuquerque: University of New Mexico Press, 1988; Hecht, Robert A., *Oliver La Farge and the American Indian: A Biography,* Metuchen, NJ: Scarecrow, 1991.

Commentary: Oliver La Farge wrote about the Native American. His novel, *Laughing Boy,* is the story of a Navajo who elopes with his cherished love only to discover that she has another lover. Dishonored and betrayed, he unsuccessfully attempts to kill both.

La Farge was a respected anthropologist as well as a novelist and short-story writer. He traveled throughout the American Southwest and Central America on archaeological digs and had a thorough knowledge of the Native American cultures he wrote about. He served as President of the American Association on Indian Affairs and was at one time a special advisor to the Hopi Nation.

1931

Margaret Ayer Barnes   963

Birth: April 8, 1886; Chicago, IL. **Death:** October 2, 1967. **Parents:** Benjamin F. and Janet (Hopkins) Ayer. **Education:** Bryn Mawr College, PA. **Spouse:** Cecil Barnes (m. 1910). **Children:** Three sons.

Prize: *Novel,* 1931: *Years of Grace,* New York: Houghton Mifflin, 1930.

Career: Author, wife, mother.

Selected Works: *Prevailing Winds,* 1928. *Years of Grace,* 1930. *Westward Passage,* 1931. *Within This Present,* 1933. *Edna, His Wife, An American Idyll,* 1935. *Wisdom's Gate,* 1938. **Films:** *Letty Lynton* (based on *Dishonored Lady*), MGM, 1932; *Westward Passage,* RKO, 1932; *Murder in Coweta County,* Telecom (TV), 1983.

For More Information: Taylor, Lloyd C., *Margaret Ayer Barnes,* New York: Twayne, 1973.

Commentary: *Years of Grace,* Barnes's novel, won the Pulitzer Prize in 1931. Barnes wrote mostly about America's upper-middle class and focused on the narrower roles of women in that segment of society.

Barnes's writing career began after an automobile accident left her bedridden for several months. Lately, she has come to be viewed as a feminist for calling attention to the economic inequalities between the sexes.

1932

Pearl S. Buck   964

Birth: June 26, 1892; Hillsboro, WV. **Death:** March 6, 1973. **Parents:** Absalom Sydenstricker and Caroline (Stulting). **Education:** Randolph-Macon Woman's College, VA: BA. Cornell University, NY: MA. **Spouse:** John Lossing Buck (m. 1915, div. 1935); Richard John Walsh (m. 1935, died 1960). **Children:** Carol, Janice (JLB); Richard, John, Edgar, Jean C., Henriette, Theresa, Chieko, Johanna (RJW— All adopted except Carol.).

Prize: *Novel,* 1932: *The Good Earth,* New York: Grossett & Dunlap, 1931.

Career: Writer; Teacher, Randolph-Macon Woman's College, VA, 1914; Teacher, University of Nanking, China, 1921-1931; Teacher, Southeastern University, Nanking, China, 1925-1927; Teacher, Chung Yang University, Nanking, China, 1928-1930; Founder and Director, East and West Association, 1941-1951; Founder, Welcome House, (adoption agency for Asian-American children), 1949; Founder and Director, Pearl S. Buck Foundation, 1964; Board of Directors, Weather Engineering, 1966; Member: American Academy of Arts and Letters, Cosmopolitan Club (NY), Kappa Delta, National Institute of Arts and Letters, Phi Beta Kappa.

Selected Works: *East Wind: West Wind,* 1930. *Is There a Case for Foreign Missions?,* 1932. *Sons,* 1932. *The Young Revolutionist,* 1932. *The First Wife and Other Stories,* 1933. *The Mother,* 1934. *A House Divided,* 1935. *Fighting Angel: Portrait of a Soul,* 1936. *The Exile,* 1936. *The Patriot,* 1939. *Other Gods: An American Legend,* 1940. *Stories for Little Children,* 1940. *Of Men and Women,* 1941. *Today and Forever: Stories of China,* 1941. *American Unity and Asia,* 1942. *The Chinese Children Next Door,* 1942.

Dragon Seed, 1942. *Pearl Buck Speaks for Democracy,* 1942. *Asia and Democracy,* 1943. *China Sky,* 1943. *What America Means to Me,* 1943. *Yu Lan, Flying Boy of China,* 1945. *Portrait of a Marriage,* 1945. *Talk about Russia with Masha Scott,* 1945. *Tell the People: Talks with James Yen about the Mass Education Movement,* 1945. *The Townsman* (Sedges, John, pseudonym), 1945. *Pavilion of Women,* 1946. *The Angry Wife,* 1947. *Far and Near: Stories of Japan, China, and America,* 1947. *How It Happens,* 1947. *The Big Wave,* 1948. *Peony,* 1948. *American Argument,* 1949. *Kinfolk,* 1949. *The Long Love* (Sedges, John, pseudonym), 1949. *One Bright Day,* 1950. *Bright Procession* (Sedges, John, pseudonym), 1952. *The Hidden Flower,* 1952. *Come, My Beloved,* 1953. *The Man Who Changed China: The Story of Sun Yat-Sen,* 1953. *The Beech Tree,* 1954. *My Several Worlds,* 1954. *Imperial Woman,* 1956. *Christmas Miniature,* 1957. *Letter from Peking,* 1957. *Command the Morning,* 1959. *The Christmas Ghost,* 1960. *Fourteen Stories,* 1961. *A Bridge for Passing,* 1962. *The Living Reed,* 1963. *Children for Adoption,* 1964. *The Joy of Children,* 1964. *Death in the Castle,* 1965. *The Gifts They Bring: Our Debt to the Mentally Retarded,* 1965. *For Spacious Skies: Journey in Dialogue,* 1966. *The People of Japan,* 1966. *The Time is Noon,* 1966. *To My Daughters, with Love,* 1967. *New Year,* 1968. *Good Deed, and Other Stories of Asia, Past and Present,* 1969. *The Three Daughters of Madame Liang,* 1969. *Mandala,* 1970. *China as I See It,* 1970. *The Chinese Story Teller,* 1971. *Pearl Buck's America,* 1971. *Of Men and Women,* 1971. *The Goddess Abides,* 1972. *Oriental Cookbook,* 1972. *All under Heaven,* 1973. *The Rainbow,* 1974. *Words of Love,* 1974. *East and West: Stories,* 1975. *Secrets of the Heart: Stories,* 1976. *The Lovers and Other Stories,* 1977. *The Woman Who Was Changed, and Other Stories,* 1979. **Films:** *The Good Earth,* MGM, 1937; *Dragon Seed,* MGM, 1944; *The China Story,* RKO, 1945; *The Devil Never Sleeps,* Fox, 1962.

Other Awards: William Dean Howells Medal, Most Distinguished Work of American Fiction, 1930-1935, 1935: *The Good Earth,* New York: Grossett & Dunlap, 1931. Nobel Prize for Literature, 1938. Women's National Book Association Skinner Award, 1960. Pennsylvania Governor's Award for Excellence, 1968. Philadelphia Club of Advertising Women Award, 1969. Honorary MA, Yale University, CT, 1933. Honorary DLitts: University of West Virginia, 1940; St. Lawrence University, 1942; Delaware Valley College, NY, 1965. Honorary LLDs:, Howard University, Washington, DC, 1942; Muhlenberg College, PA, 1966. Honorary LHDs: Lincoln University, 1953; Woman's Medical College of Philadelphia, 1954; Rutgers University, NJ, 1969. Honorary DHLs: University of Pittsburgh, 1960; Bethany College, 1963; Hahnemann Hospital, 1966. Honorary

DMus, Combs College of Music, 1962. Honorary HHD, West Virginia State College, 1963. President's Committee on Employment of Physically Handicapped Citation, 1958. Big Brothers of America Citation.

For More Information: Harris, Theodore F., *Pearl S. Buck: A Biography,* New York: John Day, 1969-1971; Conn, Peter, *Pearl S. Buck: A Cultural Biography,* New York: Cambridge University Press, 1996; Liao, Kang, *Pearl S. Buck: A Cultural Bridge Across the Pacific,* Westport, CT: Greenwood, 1997.

Commentary: *The Good Earth,* the story of a Chinese peasant family, was Buck's second novel. Buck was raised in China by her American missionary parents and she learned the Chinese language before she learned English. She attended college in the States, then immediately returned to China to teach. It is then that she began her long writing career.

Buck is the only American woman to win the Nobel Prize for Literature (1938). The Nobel Committee cited her "for rich and genuine epic portrayals of Chinese peasants and masterpieces of biography." Buck was a tireless worker for the handicapped and for democracy. Buck was very active in a great number of organizations for child welfare and retarded children's services and was the recipient of over 300 humanitarian awards. She also wrote under the pseudonym John Sedges.

1933

T.S. Stribling 965

Birth: March 4, 1881; Clifton, TN. **Death:** July 8, 1965. **Parents:** Christopher Columbus and Amelia Annie (Waits) Stribling. **Education:** University of Alabama: LLB. **Spouse:** Louella Kloss (m. 1932).

Prize: *Novel,* 1933: *The Store,* Garden City, NY: Doubleday, Doran, 1932.

Career: Novelist.

Selected Works: *The Cruise of the Dry Dock,* 1919. *Birthright,* 1922. *Fombombo,* 1923. *Red Sand,* 1924. *Teeftallow,* 1926. *East is East,* 1928. *Bright Metal,* 1928. *Clues of the Caribbees: Being Certain Criminal Investigations of Henry Poggiolo,* 1929. *Strange Moon,* 1929. *Backwater,* 1930. *The Forge,* 1931. *The Store,* 1932. *Unfinished Cathedral,* 1934. *The Sound Wagon,* 1935. *These Bars of Flesh,* 1938. *Laughing Stock: The Posthumous Autobiography of T.S. Stribling,* 1982.

For More Information: Eckley, Wilton, *T. S. Stribling,* Boston: Twayne, 1975.

Commentary: *The Store* was the second novel of a Civil War trilogy which began with *The Forge* and ended with *Unfinished Cathedral.* The trilogy followed the rising fortunes of an Alabama family.

Stribling trained as a teacher but quickly found that he was not suited to the profession. He then turned his energies to law, and soon dropped that as well. Writing was an activity he turned to slowly. His early stories were published in a Sunday School magazine. His first novel, *Birthright,* dealt with race relations and was published in 1922.

1934

Caroline Pafford Miller 966

Birth: August 26, 1903; Waycross, GA. **Death:** July 12, 1992. **Children:** Three sons.

Prize: *Novel,* 1934: *Lamb in His Bosom,* New York: Harper, 1933.

Career: Author, editor.

Selected Works: *Lebanon,* 1944.

For More Information: Sibley, Celestine, "Obituary," *Atlanta Constitution,* July 15, 1992, Section B, P.1, Col. 1; "Obituary," *Washington Times,* July 15, 1992, Section B, P.8, Col.2.

Commentary: *Lamb in His Bosom* is a tale about life in back-country Georgia just before the Civil War, and was Miller's first novel. She gathered material for the story from her own experiences, those of family members, and local stories from the area around Waycross, Georgia.

Miller was born in Waycross and lived most of her life there. She married her high school English teacher, raised a family, then divorced. She continued her writing, mostly short stories. She was working on her third novel, *Pray, Love, Remember,* at the time of her death in 1992.

1935

Josephine Winslow Johnson 967

Birth: June 20, 1910; Kirkwood, MO. **Death:** October 3, 1990. **Parents:** Benjamin and Ethel (Franklin) Johnson. **Religion:** Society of Friends. **Education:** Washington University, MO. **Spouse:** Grant C. Cannon (m. 1942). **Children:** Terence, Ann, Carol.

Prize: *Novel,* 1935: *Now in November,* New York: Simon and Schuster, 1934.

Career: Teacher, freelance writer.

Selected Works: *Winter Orchard, and Other Stories,* 1935. *Year's End,* 1937. *Jordanstown,* 1937. *Wildwood,* 1946. *The Dark Traveler,* 1963. *The Sorcerer's Son, and Other Stories,* 1965. *The Inland Island,* 1969.

Other Awards: Sarah Chapman Francis Medal, Garden Club of America, 1970. Honorary Doctor, Humane Letters, Washington University, 1970.

For More Information: *Kirkwood Historical Review,* December, 1968; *Saturday Review,* February 15, 1969; *New York Times,* February 21, 1969; *New*

York Times Book Review, March 2, 1969; *Atlantic Monthly,* May, 1969.

Commentary: *Now In November,* a poetic story of life on a Midwestern farm, was Josephine Johnson's first novel. That same year, Johnson won an O. Henry Memorial Award for her short story, "Park."

Johnson, who trained as a writer and a painter, also wrote poetry. Farm life and country living were what satisfied Johnson. She especially admired the simple beauty of ordinary things. She was very much interested in social work and cooperatives, serving as president of the Consumers' Cooperative in 1938. She married a lawyer from the regional office of the National Labor Relations Board. The marriage fit well with her social and political activism.

1936

Harold Lenoir Davis   968

Birth: October 18, 1896; Yonoalla, OR. **Death:** October 30, 1960. **Parents:** James Alexander and Ruth (Bridges) Davis.

Prize: *Novel,* 1936: *Honey in the Horn,* New York: Harper, 1935.

Career: Cattle herder, sheriff, writer.

Selected Works: *Harp of a Thousand Strings,* 1947. *Beulah Land,* 1949. *Winds of Morning,* 1952. *Team Bells Woke Me, and Other Stories,* 1953. *The Distant Music,* 1957.

Other Awards: Guggenheim Fellowship, 1932.

For More Information: Bryant, Paul T. *H. L. Davis,* Boston: Twayne, 1978.

Commentary: *Honey In The Horn* is a story about frontier life in early Oregon. The story also won a Harper Prize, which was accompanied by $7,500. Davis was both a novelist and a poet.

Davis was a man who seemed to have done everything. He is said to have worked as both cattle and sheep herder, sheriff, surveyor, novelist, and poet. He won a prize for *Poetry,* published in 1919, and also a Guggenheim Fellowship in 1932.

1937

Margaret Mitchell   969

Birth: November 8, 1900; Atlanta, GA. **Death:** August 16, 1949. **Parents:** Eugene and Maybelle (Stephen). **Religion:** Roman Catholic. **Education:** Smith College, MA: MA. **Spouse:** Berrien Kinnard Upshaw (m. 1922, div. 1924) John Robert Marsh (m. 1925).

Prize: *Novel,* 1937: *Gone with the Wind,* New York: Macmillan, 1936.

Career: Author.

Selected Works: *Margaret Mitchell's Gone with the Wind Letters, 1936-1949,* 1976. **Films:** *Gone with the Wind,* MGM, 1939; *Warning to Wantons,* Aquila, 1949.

Other Awards: Academy Award, Best Picture, 1939: *Gone with the Wind.*

For More Information: Farr, Finis, *Margaret Mitchell of Atlanta, the Author of Gone With the Wind,* New York: Morrow, 1965; Edwards, Anne, *Road to Tara: The Life of Margaret Mitchell,* New Haven, CT: Ticknor & Fields, 1983; Bridges, Herb, *Gone With the Wind: the Definitive Illustrated History of the Book, the Movie, and the Legend,* New York: Simon & Schuster, 1989; Hanson, Elizabeth I, *Margaret Mitchell,* New York: Macmillan, 1990; Pyron, Darden Asbury, *Southern Daughter: The Life of Margaret Mitchell,* New York: Oxford University Press, 1991; Freer, Debra, *Lost Laysen/Margaret Mitchell,* New York: Scribners, 1996.

Commentary: The Pulitzer Prize winning *Gone With the Wind* was Margaret Mitchell's first and only novel. It is the second-best selling book in history (surpassed only by the Bible) and the basis of a Hollywood classic film (Howard Sidney Coe wrote the screenplay for MGM). It is the story of Georgia before, during, and immediately following the Civil

War.

It is thought that the book's huge success was an impediment to Mitchell's ability to equal or surpass it with a follow-up. Mitchell experienced a premonition about her own death in an automobile crash. Eerily, she *was* struck by a car, dying five days later at the age of 48.

1938

John Phillips Marquand   970

Birth: November 10, 1893; Wilmington, DE. **Death:** July 1, 1960. **Parents:** Philip and Margaret (Fuller) Marquand. **Education:** Harvard College, MA: BA. **Spouse:** Christine Davenport Sedgwick (m. 1922, div. 1935); Adelaide F. Hooker (m. 1937). **Children:** John P., Jr., Christine (CDS); Blanche Ferry, Timothy Fuller, Elon Huntington Hooker (AFH).

Prize: *Novel,* 1938: *The Late George Apley,* Boston: Little, Brown, 1937.

Career: Reporter, Writer, *Boston Transcript,* 1916; First Lieutenant, Artillery, U.S. Army, 1916-1917; Magazine Feature Writer, *New York Herald-Tribune,* 1919-1920; Copywriter, J. Walter Thompson Advertising, 1921-1922; Writer, 1922-1960; Special Consultant to the U.S. Secretary of War, 1944-1945.

Selected Works: *The Unspeakable Gentleman,* 1922. *Four of a Kind,* 1923. *The Black Cargo,* 1925. *Lord Timothy Dexter of Newburyport, Massachusetts, First in the East, First in the West, and the Greatest Philosopher in the Western World,* 1925. *Thank You, Mr. Moto,* 1936. *Wickford Point,* 1939. *H.M. Pulham, Esquire,* 1941. *Last Laugh, Mr. Moto,* 1942. *So Little Time,* 1944. *Repent in Haste,* 1945. *B.F.'s Daughter,* 1946. *Point of No Return,* 1949. *Melville Goodwin, USA,* 1951. *Thirty Years,* 1954. *Sincerely, Willis Wayde,* 1955. *Life at Happy Knoll,* 1957. *Stopover: Tokyo,* 1957. *Women and Thomas Harrow,* 1958. *Timothy Dexter Revisited,* 1960. **Films:** *Thank You, Mr. Moto,* Fox, 1937; *H.M. Pulham, Esquire,* MGM, 1940; *Within the Tides* (based on *The Late George Apley*), Fox, 1946; *B.F.'s Daughter,* MGM, 1948; *Melville Goodwin, USA* (based on *Top Secret Affair*), Warner Bros., 1957; *Stopover Tokyo,* Fox, 1957.

For More Information: Hamburger, Philip Paul, *J.P. Marquand, Esquire, a Portrait in the Form of a Novel,* Boston: Houghton Mifflin, 1952; Gross, John J, *John P. Marquand,* New York: Twayne, 1963; Birmingham, Stephen, *The Late John Marquand: A Biography,* Philadelphia, PA: Lippincott, 1972; Bell, Millicent, *Marquand: An American Life,* Boston: Little, Brown, 1979; Wires, Richard, *John P. Marquand and Mr. Moto: Spy Adventures and Detective Films,* Muncie, IN: Ball State University Press, 1990.

Commentary: *The Late George Apley,* written as the memoir of a self-satisfied Bostonian, is an ironic picture of a Boston family. It was first published in a serialized version. After winning the Pulitzer Prize, it was issued in book form.

Marquand was descended from a New England blueblood family. He secured a job as a reporter for the *Boston Transcript* before leaving to fight in World War I. After the war, he became a writer in the magazine department of the *New York Tribune.* He traveled to many parts of the world, including China and Japan, where he created the character of *Mr. Moto.*

1939

Marjorie Kinnan Rawlings   971

Birth: August 8, 1896; Washington, DC. **Death:** December 15, 1953. **Parents:** Arthur Frank and Ida May (Traphagen) Rawlings. **Education:** University of Wisconsin: BA. **Spouse:** Charles Rawlings (m. 1919, div. 1933); Norton Baskin (m. 1941).

Prize: *Novel,* 1939: *The Yearling,* New York: Scribners, 1938.

Career: Publicist, Young Women's Christian Association National Headquarters, New York City, 1918-1919; Assistant Service Editor, *Home Sector,* 1919; Writer, *Louisville Courier-Journal,* Louisville, KY, and Journalist, *Rochester Journal,* Rochester, NY, 1919-1923; Verse writer, United Features Syndicate, 1925-1927; Author, 1931-1953; Owner and manager of an orange grove in Florida.

Selected Works: *South Moon Under,* 1933. *Golden Apples,* 1935. *When the Whippoorwill,* 1940. *Cross Creek,* 1942. *Jacob's Ladder,* 1950. *The Sojourner,* 1953. *The Secret River,* 1955. *Poems by Marjorie Kinnan Rawlings: Songs of a Housewife*

(Tarr, Rodger L., ed.), 1997. **Films:** *The Yearling,* MGM, 1946; *Cross Creek,* United Artists, 1983.

Other Awards: Second Place, Scribner Prize Contest, 1931: *Jacob's Ladder,* Coral Gables, FL: University of Miami, 1950. O. Henry Memorial Award, 1933: "Gal Young Un." O. Henry Memorial Award, 1946: "Black Secret." Newbery Medal Honor Book, 1956: *The Secret River,* New York: Scribners, 1955. Lewis Carroll Shelf Award, 1963: *The Yearling,* New York: Scribners, 1938. Honorary LLD, Rollins College, FL. Honorary LHD, University of Florida. Honorary Degree, University of Tampa.

For More Information: Bigelow, Gordon E., *Frontier Eden: The Literary Career of Marjorie Kinnan Rawlings,* Gainesville: University of Florida, 1966; Bellman, Samuel Irving, *Marjorie Kinnan Rawlings,* New York: Twayne, 1974; Silverthorne, Elizabeth, *Marjorie Kinnan Rawlings: Sojourner at Cross Creek,* Woodstock, NY: Overlook, 1988; Parker, Idella, *Idella: Marjorie Rawlings' "Perfect Maid,"* Gainesville: University of Florida Press, 1992; Tarr, Rodger L., *Marjorie Kinnan Rawlings: A Descriptive Bibliography,* Pittsburgh, PA: University of Pittsburgh Press, 1996.

Commentary: *The Yearling* is the story of a year in the lives of a backwoods Florida man, his wife, and their son. The son learns some of life's bigger lessons through his relationship with an orphaned fawn.

Rawlings's career began as a reporter. She almost gave up fiction writing due to failed attempts at getting published. She won an O. Henry Memorial Prize for her short story, "Gal Young Un," in the same year that her novel won the Pulitzer Prize.

1940

John Steinbeck   972
Birth: February 27, 1902; Salinas, CA. **Death:** December 20, 1968. **Parents:** John Ernst and Olive (Hamilton) Steinbeck. **Education:** Stanford University, CA. **Spouse:** Carol Henning (m. 1930, div. 1943); Gwyn Conger (m. 1943, div. 1948); Elaine Scott (m. 1950). **Children:** Tom, John (ES).

Prize: *Novel,* 1940: *The Grapes of Wrath,* New York: Viking, 1939.

Career: Fruit-picker, painter, laboratory assistant, caretaker, surveyor, and reporter; Writer; Foreign Correspondent, *New York Herald-Tribune,* 1943; Writer, U.S. Army Air Forces, WWII; Foreign Correspondent, Vietnam, *Newsday,* 1966-1967.

Selected Works: *The Pastures of Heaven,* 1932. *To a God Unknown,* 1933. *Tortilla Flat,* 1935. *Cup of Gold: A Life of Sir Henry Morgan, Buccaneer, with Occasional Reference to History,* 1936. *In Dubious Battle,* 1936. *Of Mice and Men,* 1937. *Of Mice and Men* (Play) (with George S. Kaufman), 1937. *The*

Long Valley, 1938. *The Grapes of Wrath,* 1939. *The Moon Is Down,* 1942. *The Moon Is Down* (Play), 1942. *Cannery Row,* 1945. *The Pearl,* 1947. *The Wayward Bus,* 1947. *Burning Bright: A Play in Story Form,* 1950. *A Russian Journal,* 1948. *Burning Bright* (Play), 1951. *East of Eden,* 1952. *Sweet Thursday,* 1954. *The Short Reign of Pippin IV: A Fabrication,* 1957. *Once There Was a War,* 1958. *The Winter of Our Discontent,* 1961. *Travels with Charley in Search of America,* 1962. *America and Americans,* 1966. *Steinbeck: A Life in Letters,* 1975. *Letters to Elizabeth: A Selection of Letters from John Steinbeck to Elizabeth Otis,* 1978. *Your Only Weapon is Your Work: A Letter by John Steinbeck to Dennis Murphy,* 1985. *Working Days: The Journals of the Grapes of Wrath, 1938-1941,* 1989. **Films:** *Of Mice and Men,* United Artists, 1939; *The Grapes of Wrath,* Fox, 1940; *Tortilla Flat,* MGM, 1942; *The Moon Is Down,* Fox, 1943; *The Pearl,* RKO, 1949; *The Red Pony,* BL, 1949; *East of Eden,* Warner Bros., 1954; *The Wayward Bus,* Fox, 1957; *Cannery Row,* MGM, 1982; *The Winter of Our Discontent,* MAR, 1983.

Other Awards: General Literature Gold Medal, Commonwealth Club of California, 1936: *Tortilla Flat,* New York: Viking, 1935. General Literature Gold Medal, Commonwealth Club of California, 1937: *Of Mice and Men,* New York: Covici-Friede, 1937. New York Drama Critics Circle Award, 1938: *Of Mice and Men.* General Literature Gold Medal, Commonwealth Club of California, 1940: *The Grapes of Wrath,* New York: Viking, 1939. Nobel Prize for Literature, 1962. Paperback of the Year Award, Best Sellers, 1964: *Travels with Charley: In Search of America,* New York: Viking, 1962.

For More Information: Hayashi, Tetsumaro, *John Steinbeck, a Dictionary of His Fictional Characters,* Metuchen, NJ: Scarecrow, 1976; St. Pierre, Brian, *John Steinbeck: The California Years,* Literary West, San Francisco: Chronicle, 1983; Millichap, Joseph R., *Steinbeck and Film,* New York: Ungar, 1983; Benson, Jackson J., *The True Adventures of John Steinbeck, Writer: A Biography,* New York: Viking, 1984; Timmerman, John H., *John Steinbeck's Fiction: The Aesthetics of the Road Taken,* Norman: University of Oklahoma Press, 1986; Bloom, Harold, ed., *John Steinbeck, Modern Critical Views,* New York: Chelsea House, 1987; Timmerman, John H., *The Dramatic Landscape of Steinbeck's Short Stories,* Norman: University of Oklahoma, 1990; Wyatt, David, ed., *New Essays on The Grapes of Wrath,* New York: Cambridge University Press, 1990; Hayashi, Tetsumaro, ed., *A New Study Guide to Steinbeck's Major Works, with Critical Explications,* Metuchen, NJ: Scarecrow, 1993; Parini, Jay, *John Steinbeck: A Biography,* London, England: Heinemann, 1994.

Commentary: *The Grapes Of Wrath* is the epic story of the Joad family, forced by drought, foreclosure, and hunger to uproot from the Oklahoma dust-bowl during the Depression. The family travels to the orange groves of California, where an oversupply of migrant workers allows for their exploitation. The story captures the grave circumstances and violent social upheaval that gripped America at that time.

Steinbeck is one of America's most renowned novelists. He wrote many stories about the Salinas area of California where he was born and raised, such as *Cannery Row, Tortilla Flat,* and *East of Eden.* He was awarded the Nobel Prize for Literature in 1962.

1941
No award

1942

Ellen Anderson Gholson Glasgow   973

Birth: April 22, 1874; Richmond, VA. **Death:** November 21, 1945. **Parents:** Francis Thomas and Anne Jane (Gholson) Glasgow. **Religion:** Calvinist. **Education:** Self-educated. **Spouse:** Single.

Prize: *Novel,* 1942: *In This Our Life,* New York: Harcourt, Brace, 1941.

Career: Writer.

Selected Works: *The Descendant,* 1897. *Phases of An Inferior Planet,* 1898. *The Voice of the People,* 1900. *The Battle-Ground,* 1902. *The Freeman, and Other Poems,* 1902. *The Deliverance: A Romance of the Virginia Tobacco Fields,* 1904. *The Wheel of Life,* 1906. *The Ancient Law,* 1908. *The Romance of a Plain Man,* 1909. *The Miller of Old Church,* 1911. *Virginia,* 1913. *A Little Lane,* 1914. *Life and Gabriella: The Story of a Woman's Courage,* 1916. *The Builders,* 1919. *One Man in His Time,* 1922. *The Shadowy Third, and Other Stories,* 1923. *Barren Ground,* 1925. *The Romantic Comedians,* 1926. *They Stooped to Folly: A Comedy of Morals,* 1929. *Vein of Iron,* 1935. *A Certain Measure: An Interpretation of Prose Fiction,* 1943. *The Woman Within: An Autobiography,* 1954. **Films:** *In This Our Life,* Warner Bros., 1942.

Other Awards: William Dean Howells Medal, American Academy of Arts and Letters, 1941.

For More Information: Thiebaux, Marcelle, *Ellen Glasgow,* New York: Ungar, 1982; Saunders, Catherine E., *Writing the Margins: Edith Wharton, Ellen Glasgow, and the Literary Tradition of the Ruined Woman,* Cambridge, MA: Harvard University Press, 1987; Scura, Dorothy M., *Ellen Glasgow: The Contemporary Reviews,* New York: Cambridge University Press, 1992; Matthews, Pamela R., *Ellen Glasgow and a Woman's Traditions,* Charlottesville: University Press of Virginia, 1994; Scura, Dorothy

M., *Ellen Glasgow: New Perspectives,* Knoxville: University of Tennessee Press, 1995.

Commentary: *In This Our Life* won Ellen Anderson Gholson Glasgow the Pulitzer Prize in 1942. Glasgow wrote stories about the South from an ivy-covered house in Richmond where she felt she belonged. She is viewed as a feminist.

Glasgow was self-educated through books in her father's library. Her family was unaware of her interest in writing until her novel, *The Descendent,* published anonymously, was attributed to her. She served as president of the Richmond Society for the Prevention of Cruelty to Animals, and counted the American Academy of Arts and Letters as one of her memberships.

1943

Upton Sinclair   974

Birth: September 20, 1878; Baltimore, MD. **Death:** November 20, 1968. **Parents:** Upton B. and Priscilla (Harden) Sinclair. **Education:** City College, NY: AB. Columbia University, NY. **Spouse:** Meta Fuller (m. 1900, div. 1911); Mary Craig Kimbraugh (m. 1913, died 1961); Mary Elizabeth Willis (m. 1961, died 1967). **Children:** David (MF).

Prize: *Novel,* 1943: *Dragon's Teeth,* New York: Viking, 1942.

Career: Comic writer, newspapers and adventure magazines during college; Founder, Intercollegiate Socialist Society (now League for Industrial Democracy), 1906; Founder, Helicon Home Colony, Englewood, NJ, 1906; Assisted U.S. Government investigation of Chicago stockyards, 1906; Socialist candidate for U.S. House of Representatives from New Jersey, 1906; Established theater company for performance of socialist plays, 1908; Socialist candidate for U.S. House of Representatives from California, 1920; Socialist candidate for U.S. Senate from California, 1922; Socialist candidate for governor of California, 1926 and 1930; Democratic candidate for governor of California, 1934; Founder, End Poverty in California (EPIC) League, 1934; Lecturer; Founder, Authors League of America; Member, American Institute of Arts and Letters; Founder, Southern California Chapter, American Civil Liberties Union.

Selected Works: *Springtime and Harvest: A Romance,* 1901. *King Midas: A Romance,* 1901. *The Jungle,* 1906. *The Overman,* 1907. *The Metropolis,* 1908. *Samuel the Seeker,* 1910. *Love's Pilgrimage,* 1911. *Plays of Protest: The Naturewoman, The Machine, The Second-Story Man, Prince Hagen* (Play), 1912. *Sylvia: A Novel,* 1913. *Sylvia's Marriage,* 1914. *King Coal,* 1917. *100%: The Story of a Patriot,* 1920. *They Call Me Carpenter: A Tale of the Second Coming,* 1922. *Manassas: A Novel of the War,* 1923.

Letters to Judd, an American Workingman, 1926. *The Spokesman's Secretary: Being the Letters of Mame to Mom*, 1926. *The Book of Life: Mind and Body*, 1926. *Money Writes!*, 1927. *Oil! A Novel*, 1927. *Boston: A Novel*, 1928. *The Millennium: A Comedy of the Year 2000*, 1929. *Mountain City*, 1930. *Roman Holiday*, 1931. *The Wet Parade*, 1931. *American Outpost: A Book of Reminiscences*, 1932. *Co-op: A Novel of Living Together*, 1936. *The Gnomobile: A Nice Gnew Gnarrative with Gnonsense, but Gnothing Gnaughty*, 1936. *What God Means to Me: An Attempt at a Working Religion*, 1936. *The Flivver King: A Story of Ford-America*, 1937. *Our Lady*, 1938. *Little Steel*, 1938. *Marie Antoinette* (Play), 1939. *World's End*, 1940. *Between Two Worlds*, 1941. *Wide Is the Gate*, 1943. *Presidential Agent*, 1944. *Dragon Harvest*, 1945. *A World to Win*, 1946. *Presidential Mission*, 1947. *One Clear Call*, 1948. *A Giant's Strength* (Play), 1948. *O Shepherd, Speak!*, 1949. *Another Pamela, or, Virtue Still Rewarded*, 1950. *The Enemy Had It Too* (Play), 1950. *A Personal Jesus: Portrait and Interpretation*, 1952. *What Didymus Did*, 1954. *My Lifetime in Letters*, 1960. *Affectionately, Eve: A Novel*, 1961. *The Autobiography of Upton*, 1963. *The Cry for Justice: An Anthology of the Literature of Social Protest*, 1963. **Films:** *The Wet Parade*, MGM, 1932; *The Gnome Mobile*, Disney, 1967.

Other Awards: New York Newspaper Guild Page One Award, 1962. United Auto Workers Social Justice Award, 1962.

For More Information: Dell, Floyd, *Upton Sinclair: A Study in Social Protest*, New York: AMS Press, 1970. Blinderman, Abraham, *Critics on Upton Sinclair: Readings in Literary Criticism*, Coral Gables, FL: University of Miami Press, 1975; Bloodworth, William A., *Upton Sinclair*, Boston: Twayne, 1977.

Commentary: *Dragon's Teeth*, the story of American anti-Nazi activities in the early 1930s, won the Pulitzer Prize in 1943. Sinclair was a socialist best remembered for his expose of the Chicago meatpacking industry, *The Jungle*, published in 1906. A classic on the reform bookshelf, it is still popular and is internationally read.

Sinclair wrote close to 100 "dime novels" under several pseudonyms while attending graduate school. His socialist leanings led to his developing a cooperative community, the Helion Home Colony, in Englewood, New Jersey. He made several unsuccessful bids for public office, including a run for California governor. His campaigns successfully raised issues important to the average working man. His prolific pen found him using the pseudonyms Clarke Fitch, Frederick Garrison, and Arthur Stirling.

1944

Martin Flavin 975

Birth: November 2, 1883; San Francisco, CA. **Death:** December 27, 1967. **Parents:** Martin J. and Louise (Archer) Flavin. **Spouse:** Daphne Virginia Springer (m. 1914; div. 1917); Sarah Keese Arnold (m. 1919; died 1937); Cornelia Clampett (m.1949). **Children:** Flavia (DVS); Martin, Sean (SKA).

Prize: *Novel*, 1944: *Journey in the Dark*, New York: Harper's, 1943.

Career: Executive, manufacturing, Chicago, 1906-1926; Officer candidate, U.S. Army, Field Artillery, 1918; Writer, *Harper's;* Scriptwriter, MGM and Paramount, 1930-1934; Member: Dutch Treat Club (NY), Players Club (NY), Old Capitol Club (CA).

Selected Works: *The Children of the Moon* (Play), 1924. *Lady of the Rose* (Play), 1925. *Brains, and Other One Act Plays* (Play), 1926. *Service for Two* (Play), 1927. *The Criminal Code* (Play), 1930. *Spendthrift* (Play), 1930. *Broken Dishes* (Play), 1930. *Amaco* (Play), 1933. *The Cock Crowed* (Play), 1935. *Achilles Had a Heel* (Play), 1936. *Tapestry in Gray* (Play), 1937. *Around the Corner* (Play), 1937. *Mr. Littlejohn*, 1940. *Corporal Cat, the Story of a German Parachute Soldier*, 1941. *The Enchanted*, 1947. *Black and White: From the Cape to the Congo*, 1950. *Red Poppies and White Marble: A Journey on the Riviera of Antiquity*, 1962. **Films:** *One Way Out* (based on *Convicted*), Columbia, 1950.

Other Awards: Harper Prize, 1943: *Journey in the Dark*, New York: Harper's, 1943.

For More Information: *Dictionary of Literary Biography*, Detroit: Gale, 1981; *Concise Oxford Companion to American Theater*, New York: Oxford University Press, 1987.

Commentary: *Journey In The Dark* won Flavin a Pulitzer Prize for Novel in 1944. A small-town boy at an early age equates wealth with equality. He grows up, goes to the big city, makes his fortune, and returns to the town he grew up in to build a monument to himself. He has changed in the process. Now rich, his old friends don't fit with his new image.

Flavin was born in San Francisco. He was vice-president of a wallpaper company when he produced his first play on Broadway. Its success led to others and he was able to quit his business and devote all his time to writing. His plays include *Children of the Moon, The Criminal Code,* and *Cross Roads*.

1945

John Hersey   976

Birth: June 17, 1914; Tientsin, China. **Death:** March 24, 1993. **Parents:** Roscoe Monroe and Grace (Baird) Hersey. **Education:** Yale University, CT. Clare College of Cambridge University, England. **Spouse:** Frances Ann Cannon (m. 1940, div. 1958); Barbara Day Addams Kaufman (m. 1958). **Children:** Martin, John Ann, Baird (FAC); Brook (BDAK).

Prize: *Novel,* 1945: *A Bell for Adano,* New York: Knopf, 1944.

Career: Private secretary, Sinclair Lewis, 1937; Writer, Editor, and Correspondent, *Time,* 1937-1944; Editor and Correspondent, *Life,* 1944-1945; Correspondent, China and Japan, *Life* and *The New Yorker,* 1945-1946; Writer, *The New Yorker* and other magazines, 1945-1993; Member of Council, Authors League of America, 1946-1970, 1975-1993; Editor and Director, *Writers' Co-Operative* Magazine, 1947; Vice-President, Authors League of America, 1949-1955; Fellow, Berkeley College, Yale University, 1950-1965; Chairman, Connecticut Volunteers for Stevenson, 1952; Delegate, White House Conference on Education, 1955; Member, Adlai Stevenson's Campaign Staff, 1956; Trustee, National Citizens' Council for the Public Schools, 1956-1958; Member, Yale University Council Committee on Yale College, 1959-1961; Member, Visiting Committee, Harvard Graduate School of Education, 1960-1965; Secretary, National Institute of Arts and Letters, American Academy of Arts and Letters, 1961-1978; Trustee, National Committee for Support of the Public Schools, 1962-1968; Chairman, Yale University Council Committee on Yale College, 1964-1969; Master, Pierson College, Yale University, 1965-1970; Fellow, Pierson College, Yale University, 1965-1993;

Writer-in-Residence, American Academy in Rome, 1970-1971; Lecturer, Yale University, 1971-1975; President, Authors League of America, 1975-1980; Professor, Yale University, 1975-1984; Member, Loeb Theater Center, 1980-1993; Chancellor, National Institute of Arts and Letters, 1981-1984; Professor Emeritus, Yale University, 1984-1993; Member of Council, Authors Guild; Member, PEN.

Selected Works: *Into the Valley,* 1943. *Men on Bataan,* 1943. *Hiroshima,* 1946. *The Wall,* 1950. *The Marmot Drive,* 1953. *A Single Pebble,* 1956. *The War Lover,* 1959. *The Child Buyer,* 1960. *Here to Stay,* 1962. *White Lotus,* 1965. *Too Far to Walk,* 1966. *Under the Eye of the Storm,* 1967. *The Algiers Motel Incident,* 1968. *Letter to the Alumni,* 1970. *The Conspiracy,* 1972. *Ralph Ellison: A Collection of Critical Essays; Twentieth Century Views Series* (Hersey, John, ed.), 1974. *My Petition for More Space,* 1974. *The Writer's Craft* (Hersey, John, ed.), 1974. *The President,* 1975. *The Walnut Door,* 1977. *Aspects of the Presidency,* 1980. *The Call,* 1985. *Blues,* 1987. *Life Sketches,* 1989. *Fling and Other Stories,* 1990. *Antonietta: A Novel,* 1991. *Key West Tales,* 1994.

Films: *The War Lover,* Columbia, 1962; *A Bell for Adano,* Fox, 1945 and Hayward (TV), 1967; *The Wall,* Time-Life, 1982.

Other Awards: Anisfield-Wolf Award, 1950: *The Wall,* New York: Knopf, 1950. Daroff Memorial Fiction Award, Jewish Book Council of America, 1950: *The Wall.* Sidney Hillman Foundation Award, 1951: *The Wall.* Howland Medal, Yale University, 1952. National Association of Independent Schools Award, 1957: *A Single Pebble,* New York: Knopf, 1956. Sarah Josepha Hale Award, 1963. Honorary Fellow, Clare College, Cambridge University, England. Honorary MA, Yale University, CT. Honorary LHDs: New School for Social Research, NY. Honorary LHD, Syracuse University, NY. Honorary LLD, Washington and Jefferson College, PA. Honorary LittD, Wesleyan University, CT. Honorary Degrees: Albertus Magnus College, CT; Bridgeport University, CT; Clarkson College of Technology; Monmouth College, NJ; University of New Haven, CT; William and Mary College, VA; Yale University, CT.

For More Information: Sanders, David, *John Hersey,* New York: Twayne, 1967; Huse, Nancy L., *The Survival Tales of John Hersey,* Troy, NY: Whitston, 1983; Sanders, David, *John Hersey Revisited,* Boston: Twayne, 1990.

Commentary: *A Bell For Adano* is a novel about Hersey's observations of Italy during the American occupation in World War II. Hersey was a war correspondent, reporting for *Time, Life,* and *The New Yorker.* His first novels were based on his experiences at different trouble spots around the globe.

Born in China, Hersey spoke Chinese before he spoke English. While on assignment in China, Hersey visited Japan to see Hiroshima firsthand after the war. His novel *Hiroshima* brought home the devastation and inhumanity of atomic weapons to the American public. He was at one time secretary to Sinclair Lewis. Hersey published many works right up until his death in 1993.

1946
No award

1947

Robert Penn Warren   977

Birth: April 24, 1905; Guthrie, KY. **Death:** September 15, 1989. **Parents:** Robert Franklin and Anna Ruth (Penn) Warren. **Education:** Vanderbilt University, TN: BA, summa cum laude. University of California, Berkeley. Yale University, CT. Oxford University, England: BLitt. **Spouse:** Emma Brescia (m. 1930, div. 1950); Eleanor Clark (m. 1952). **Children:** Rosanna Phelps, Gabriel Penn (EC).

Prize: *Novel,* 1947: *All the King's Men,* New York: Harcourt, Brace, 1946. *Poetry,* 1958: *Promises: Poems, 1954-1956,* New York: Random House, 1957. *Poetry,* 1979: *Now and Then: Poems, 1976-1978,* New York: Random House, 1978.

Career: Poet, novelist, playwright, educator; Assistant Professor, English, Southwestern Presbyterian University, Memphis, TN, 1930-1931; Acting Assistant Professor, Vanderbilt University, Nashville, TN, 1931-1934; Assistant Professor, Louisiana State University, Baton Rouge, 1936-1942; Professor, English, University of Minnesota, Minneapolis, 1942-1950; Consultant in Poetry, Library of Congress, 1944-1945; Professor, Playwrighting in School of Drama, Yale University, New Haven, CT, 1950-1956; Professor of English, Yale University, New Haven, CT, 1961-1973; Professor Emeritus, Yale University, New Haven, CT, 1973-1989; Jefferson Lecturer, National Endowment for the Humanities, 1974; Board Member, American Academy of Arts and Letters; Chancellor, Academy of American Poets; Honorary Fellow, Modern Language Association; Member: American Academy of Arts and Sciences, American Philosophical Society, Century Club.

Selected Works: *John Brown: The Making of a Martyr,* 1929. *Night Rider,* 1939. *At Heaven's Gate,* 1943. *Selected Poems, 1923-1943,* 1944. *The Rime of the Ancient Mariner,* 1946. *The Circus in the Attic, and Other Stories,* 1947. *World Enough and Time: A Romantic Novel,* 1950. *Brother To Dragons: A Tale in Verse and Voices,* 1953. *Band of Angels,* 1955. *Remember the Alamo!,* 1958. *How Texas Won Her Freedom: The Story of Sam Houston & the Battle of San Jacinto,* 1958. *The Gods of Mount Olympus,*

1959. *The Cave,* 1959. *You, Emperors, and Others: Poems, 1957-1960,* 1960. *The Legacy of the Civil War: Meditations on the Centennial,* 1961. *Wilderness: A Tale of the Civil War,* 1961. *Flood: A Romance of Our Time,* 1964. *Who Speaks for the Negro?,* 1965. *Selected Poems, New and Old, 1923-1966,* 1966. *Incarnations: Poems, 1966-1968,* 1968. *Audubon: A Vision,* 1969. *Meet Me in the Green Glen,* 1971. *Or Else — Poem / Poems, 1968-1974,* 1974. *Democracy and Poetry,* 1975. *Selected Poems, 1923-1975,* 1976. *Rumor Verified: Poems, 1979-1980,* 1981. *Chief Joseph of the Nez Perce, Who Called Themselves the Nimipu,* 1983. *New and Selected Poems, 1923-1985,* 1985. *Portrait of a Father,* 1988. *New and Selected Essays,* 1989. **Films:** *All the King's Men,* Columbia, 1949.

Other Awards: Rhodes Scholar, Oxford University, England, 1928-1930. Levinson Prize, 1936. Houghton Mifflin Literary Fellowship, 1936. Guggenheim Fellowship, 1939-1940, 1947-48. Shelley Memorial Prize, 1942 : *Eleven Poems on the Same Theme,* Norfolk, CT: New Directions, 1942. Southern Prize, 1947. Robert Meltzer Award, Screen Writers Guild, 1949. Union League Civic and Arts Foundation Prize, *Poetry* magazine, 1953. Edna St. Vincent Millay Memorial Award, American Poetry Society, 1958. National Book Award, 1958. Irita Van Doren Award, *New York Herald-Tribune,* 1965: *Who Speaks for the Negro?,* New York: Random House, 1964. Bollingen Prize in Poetry, Yale University, 1967: *Selected Poems: New and Old, 1923-1966,* New York: Random House, 1966. National Endowment for the Arts Grant, 1968. Van Wyck Brooks Award for Poetry, 1970: *Audubon: A Vision,* New York: Random House, 1969. National Medal for Literature, 1970: *Audubon: A Vision,* Henry A. Bellaman Prize, 1970: *Audubon: A Vision.* Award for Literature, University of Southern California, 1973. Golden Rose Trophy, New England Poetry Club, 1975. Emerson-Thoreau Medal, American Academy of Arts and Sciences, 1975. Copernicus Prize, American Academy of Poets, 1976. Wilma and Robert Messing Award, 1977. Harriet Monroe Award for Poetry, 1979: *Selected Poems: 1923-1975,* New York: Random House, 1976. Commonwealth Award for Literature, 1980. Connecticut Arts Council Award, 1980. Hubbell Memorial Award, Modern Language Association, 1980. MacArthur Foundation Fellowship, 1980. Presidential Medal of Freedom, 1980. Creative Arts Award, Brandeis University, 1984. First Poet Laureate of the United States, 1986. National Medal of Arts, 1987. Honorary Degrees: Bridgeport University, CT; Colby College, ME; Fairfield University, CT; Harvard University, MA; Johns Hopkins University, MD; Kenyon College, OH; Monmouth College, Oxford University, England; Southwestern at Memphis, TN; Swarthmore College, PA; University of Kentucky;

University of Louisville, KY; University of New Haven, CT; University of the South, TN; Wesleyan University, CT; Yale University, CT.

For More Information: Bloom, Harold, ed., *Robert Penn Warren, Modern Critical Views,* New York: Chelsea House, 1986; Burt, John, *Robert Penn Warren and American Idealism,* New Haven, CT: Yale University Press, 1988; Weeks, Dennis L., *To Love So Well the World: A Festschrift in Honor of Robert Penn Warren,* New York: Peter Lang, 1992; Blotner, Joseph Leo, *Robert Penn Warren: A Biography,* New York: Random House, 1997.

Commentary: *All The King's Men* is a novel about Willie Stark, a fictional governor of Louisiana and his political machine. It drew comparisons to Huey Long, who served as governor of Louisiana in the 1930s. Warren won two Pulitzer Prizes for Poetry, in 1958 for *Promises: Poems 1954-1956,* and in 1979 for *Now And Then.*

Warren was a novelist, poet, short story writer, Rhodes Scholar, educator, and critic. He was named America's first poet laureate in 1986. He regarded himself as poet first, as novelist and critic second.

Photography

1942

Milton E. Brooks   978

Birth: August 29, 1901; St. Louis, MO. **Death:** September 3, 1956. **Parents:** James W. Brooks.

Prize: *Photography,* 1942: *Detroit News,* "Ford Strikers Riot," April 3, Detroit, MI: The Detroit News, 1941.

Career: Photographer,*Chicago (IL) Herald Examiner, Chicago (IL) Daily News,* Paramount News Reel, *New York (NY) Daily News;* Photographer, *Detroit (MI) News,* 1928-1953; Commercial photographer, 1953-.

Other Awards: *Editor and Publisher* Award. Michigan State/Associated Press Photo Award. Inland Daily Press Association Award.

For More Information: Leekley, Sheryle and John Leekley, *Moments: The Pulitzer Prize Photographs, Updated Version: 1942-1982,* New York: Crown Publishers, Inc., 1982: 12-13.

Commentary: Milton E. "Pete" Brooks's winning photograph shows rioting United Auto Workers at the Ford Motor Company in Detroit.

1943

Frank E. Noel   979

Birth: 1905; Dalhart, TX. **Death:** November 29, 1966. **Spouse:** Evelyn G.

Prize: *Photography,* 1943: Associated Press, "Water!," 1942.

Career: Staff Photographer,*Chicago (IL) Daily Tribune,* 1925-; Freelance photographer; Aerial Photography Instructor, U.S. Army Air Corps; Photographer *Washington (DC) Post, Wichita (KS) Eagle, Kansas City (MO) Star, Oklahoma City (OK) News;* Photographer, Associated Press, 1937-66; Freelance photographer, 1966-.

Other Awards: Overseas Press Club Award, 1952. Special Citation Award, National Press Photographers Association, 1952.

For More Information: *AP World,* Winter (1966-67): 34; Leekley, Sheryle and John Leekley, *Moments: The Pulitzer Prize Photographs, Updated Version: 1942-1982,* New York: Crown Publishers, Inc., 1982: 50-51; Rigsby, Gwendolyn Gezelle, "A History of Associated Press Pulitzer Prizes" (thesis), University of South Carolina, 1993.

Commentary: Frank "Pappy" Noel, a photographer for over 40 years, won a Pulitzer Prize for his photograph of a man in a lifeboat appealing for water to drink. (During the war Noel himself was in a lifeboat after the ship he was on had been sunk.) His work took him to four continents, covering three wars, and he spent three years as a prisoner in a Communist prison camp.

1944

Earle L. Bunker   980

Birth: September 4, 1912. **Death:** January 29, 1975. **Parents:** Doris A. **Spouse:** Helen E. (m., died 1977). **Children:** Barbara.

Prize: *Photography,* 1944: *Omaha World-Herald,* "Homecoming," July 16, Omaha, ME: World-Herald, 1943.

Career: *Omaha (NE) Bee-News,* 1929-1937; *Omaha (NE) World-Herald,* 1937-75.

For More Information: *Editor & Publisher,* 77:19 (6 May 1944): 44; Leekley, Sheryle and John Leekley, *Moments: The Pulitzer Prize Photographs, Updated Version: 1942-1982,* New York: Crown Publishers, Inc., 1982: 18-19; *Omaha World-Herald,* November 9, 1997: 1.

Commentary: Earle "Buddy" Bunker's winning photograph of Lieutenant Colonel Robert Moore's homecoming is unique in that not a face shows in the picture. However, the joy of the moment is evident. The same photograph was reprinted in *Life* magazine as its Picture of the Week and was chosen by Kodak in 1956 as the best human interest photo of the past 25 years.

Frank Filan   981

Birth: 1905; Brooklyn, NY. **Death:** July 23, 1952. **Parents:** Marcella. **Spouse:** Katherine Tyler (m. 1940). **Children:** Sheila.

Prize: *Photography,* 1944: Associated Press, "Tarawa Island," 1943.

Career: *Los Angeles (CA) Times;* War Cameraman, Associated Press, 1930-52; Photographer.

For More Information: Leekley, Sheryle and John Leekley, *Moments: The Pulitzer Prize Photographs, Updated Version: 1942-1982,* New York: Crown Publishers, Inc., 1982: 16-17; Rigsby, Gwendolyn Gezelle, "A History of Associated Press Pulitzer Prizes" (thesis), University of South Carolina, 1993.

Commentary: With a borrowed camera, Frank Filan captured the image of Tarawa, the entrenched stronghold of the Japanese that United States Marines battled over and won during World War II. All his equipment had been destroyed in the landing. He borrowed a camera from a Coast Guard photographer. Out of 3,000 assault forces, only a few hundred came out alive or unwounded.

1945

Joseph J. Rosenthal   982

Birth: November 9, 1911; Washington, DC. **Parents:** David Rosenthal and Lena. **Religion:** Roman Catholic. **Education:** University of San Francisco, CA. **Spouse:** Lee Walch (m. 1947, div.). **Children:** Joe, Anne.

Prize: *Photography,* 1945: Associated Press, 1945.

Career: Officeboy, Newspaper Enterprise Association, 1930-32; Reporter, Photographer, *San Francisco (CA) News,* 1932-35; Chief Photographer, San Francisco (CA) Bureau, Acme News Service, 1935-36; Bureau Manager, World Wide Photos, 1936-41; Photographer, Associated Press, 1941-46; Photographer, *San Francisco (CA) Chronicle,* 1946-81; Photojournalism Instructor, City College of San Francisco (CA), 1949-51.

Other Awards: *Editor & Publisher* Award, 1936. *U.S. Camera Magazine* Award. Medal of Merit, International News Service, 1945. Press Photographers of New York Award, 1947. Photography Award, San Francisco Press Club, CA, 1958.

For More Information: Leekley, Sheryle and John Leekley, *Moments: The Pulitzer Prize Photographs, Updated Version: 1942-1982,* New York: Crown Publishers, Inc., 1982: 20-21; Rigsby, Gwendolyn Gezelle, "A History of Associated Press Pulitzer Prizes" (thesis), University of South Carolina, 1993; Thomey, Tedd, *Immortal Images: A Personal History of Two Photographers and the Flag Raising on Iwo Jima,* Annapolis, MD: Naval Institute Press, 1996.

Commentary: Joe Rosenthal captured a classic image of World War II when he snapped a photograph of five Marines and one Navy corpsman raising the United States flag on Mount Suribachi on Iwo Jima. His photograph caused some controversy; as this flag was the second one raised, some thought he had staged the scene. He did not; he just captured it for posterity. Since the photograph was taken in February of 1945 and not in 1944, it was technically not eligible for the 1945 Pulitzer, but the rule was suspended "for this distinguished example." The United States Marine Memorial in Washington, DC is modeled on his photograph.

1946
No award

1947

Arnold Hardy   983

Birth Place: Shreveport, LA. **Parents:** Clarence S. **Education:** Centenary College, LA: BS. Georgia School of Technology.

Prize: *Photography,* 1947.

Career: Served in U.S. Army Air Corps, 1943-45; Research Assistant, Physics Department, Georgia School of Technology, 1947.

For More Information: *Atlanta Constitution,* 6 May (1947): 1+; *New York Times,* 6 May (1947): 1, 20; Leekley, Sheryle and John Leekley, *Moments: The Pulitzer Prize Photographs, Updated Version: 1942-1982,* New York: Crown Publishers, Inc., 1982: 22-24.

Commentary: Arnold Hardy was the first amateur photographer to win a Pulitzer Prize. He was 25 years old and a student at Georgia Tech when the prize was awarded. His photo shows a girl falling to her death. She had crawled out of the window at the Winecoff Hotel in Atlanta to escape a fire. 119 people died in the blaze.

1948

Francis W. Cushing   984

Birth: August 10, 1915. **Death:** March 17, 1975. **Spouse:** Mary E. Broderick. **Children:** Michael F., Peter, Ann M.

Prize: *Photography,* 1948: *Boston Traveler,* "Boy Gunman and Hostage," Boston: Boston Traveler, 1947.

Career: Aerial Photographer, U.S. Army Air Corps, WWII; Messenger, Staff Photographer, *Boston (MA) Traveler,* 1932-68; Painter, Fore River Shipyard.

For More Information: *New York Times,* 18 March (1975): 40; Leekley, Sheryle and John Leekley, *Moments: The Pulitzer Prize Photographs, Updated Version: 1942-1982,* New York: Crown Publishers, Inc., 1982: 24-25; *Boston Evening Globe,* 17 March (1975): 35.

Commentary: Frank Cushing's award-winning photograph shows a 15-year-old boy using another teenager as a shield while police are being held back by the boy at gunpoint.

Cushing had to take his photographs from odd positions, one by holding his camera above his head and another from the roof of a nearby building.

1949

Nathaniel Fein 985

Birth: August 7, 1914; Indianapolis, IN. **Parents:** Herman Fein and Francis (Werth). **Spouse:** Lois Arnold (m. 1938). **Children:** David.

Prize: *Photography,* 1949: *New York Herald-Tribune,* "Babe Ruth Bows Out," New York: New York Herald-Tribune, 1948.

Career: Advertising Copy Retoucher, *New York (NY) Journal-American;* Copyboy, *New York (NY) Herald-Tribune,* 1933; Photofile Clerk, *New York (NY) Herald-Tribune;* Staff Photographer, *New York (NY) Herald- Tribune,* 1939-66; Served in U.S. Army Air Forces, 1943-46; Freelance Photographer, Orange and Rockland Utility Company, 1971-; Freelance photographer.

Other Awards: New York Press Photographers Association Award. Diamond Graflex Award, 1950. TWA Aviation Award, 1950. William Randolph Hearst Trophy, 1960.

For More Information: Leekley, Sheryle and John Leekley, *Moments: The Pulitzer Prize Photographs, Updated Version: 1942-1982,* New York: Crown Publishers, Inc., 1982: 26-27; *Newsday,* 13 December (1992): 43; *New York Times,* 27 November (1992): C8.

Commentary: Nat Fein's photograph of Babe Ruth in Yankee Field on the day his uniform number was retired is unique in that the photograph is of Ruth's back with the number showing.

Fein has taken over 50,000 photographs in his career and is known for his success in photographing both children and animals. He prepared in advance for every photo, carrying props with him to help capture a moment or to aid in the composition of a shot.

1950

Bill Crouch 986

Birth: 1915; Missouri. **Death:** December 27, 1997. **Spouse:** Doris C. (m. 1946, died 1990). **Children:** Janice, Carolyn, Betty Ann, Dorothy.

Prize: *Photography,* 1950: *Oakland Tribune,* "Near Collision at Air Show," Oakland, CA: Oakland Tribune, 1949.

Career: Photographer, Associated Press, ?-1941; Served in U.S. Marine Corps, 1941-45; Photographer, *Oakland (CA) Tribune,* 1941-84.

Other Awards: National Press Photographers Award.

For More Information: Leekley, Sheryle and John Leekley, *Moments: The Pulitzer Prize Photographs, Updated Version: 1942-1982,* New York:

Crown Publishers, Inc., 1982: 28-29; *Oakland Tribune,* 31 December (1997).

Commentary: Bill Crouch was off duty at an air show when he captured the photo of the near collision between an upside-down biplane and a military aircraft. Crouch was "never one to carry around a camera just looking for a picture," but he happened to have one with him on October 2, 1949, when he captured his winning photograph.

1951

Max Desfor 987

Birth: November 8, 1913; Bronx, NY. **Parents:** Benjamin Desfor and Anna (Bick). **Education:** Brooklyn College, NY. **Spouse:** Clara Mehl (m. 1934). **Children:** Barry David.

Prize: *Photography,* 1951: Associated Press, "The Bridge at Pyongyang," 1950.

Career: Darkroom Assistant, Associated Press, 1933-; Staff Photographer, Associated Press, 1938-; Supervising Editor, Wide World Photos, 1954-78; Photo Editor, Photo Director, *U.S. News and World Report,* 1979-.

Other Awards: Graflex Diamond Honor, 1951.

For More Information: Leekley, Sheryle and John Leekley, *Moments: The Pulitzer Prize Photographs, Updated Version: 1942-1982,* New York: Crown Publishers, Inc., 1982: 30-31; Taft, William H., *Encyclopedia of Twentieth-Century Journalists,* New York: Garland Publishing Incorporated, 1986.

Commentary: Max Desfor captured the desperate nature of the retreat of the Korean people with his photograph of thousands of refugees crawling over the bombed-out bridge across the Taedong River. Desfor took the photo while wearing two pairs of gloves against the freezing wind coming down from Siberia. He perched on a jagged piece of the bridge that had a 50-foot drop.

1952

John R. Robinson 988

Birth: June 19, 1907; Des Moines, IA. **Death:** September 28, 1972. **Spouse:** Dorothy R.

Prize: *Photography,* 1952: *Des Moines Register and Tribune,* Des Moines, IA: Des Moines Register and Tribune, 1951.

Career: Served in U.S. Army Signal Corps, WWII; Photographer, *Des Moines (IA) Register and Tribune,* 1927-72.

Other Awards: Honorary Lifetime Member, National Press Photographers Association. Graflex Diamond Award, 1952. Kappa Alpha Mu Award, 1952.

For More Information: *New York Times,* 9 September (1972): 34; Leekley, Sheryle and John Leekley, *Moments: The Pulitzer Prize Photographs, Updated Version: 1942-1982,* New York: Crown Publishers, Inc., 1982: 32-33.

Commentary: John Robinson and Don Ultang captured on film the attack on the football field on Johnny Bright, a black All-American halfback. Bright was punched and his jaw broken, but he stayed in the game. Two plays later, players piled on top of him and he was carried off the field.

Donald Theodore Ultang   989

Birth: March 23, 1917; Fort Dodge, IA. **Education:** Iowa State University. University of Iowa: BA. **Spouse:** Veda U. (m., died 1985). **Children:** Linda, Ellen, Joanne.

Prize: *Photography,* 1952: *Des Moines Register and Tribune,* Des Moines, IA: Des Moines Register and Tribune, 1951.

Career: Photographer, commercial photographic company; Staff Photographer and Company Pilot, *Des Moines (IA) Register and Tribune,* 1946-59; News Photography Manager, *Des Moines (IA) Register and Tribune,* 1953-59; Insurance executive, 1959-79; Photojournalism Lecturer, Drake University (IA), 1979-; Freelance photographer.

Selected Works: *Holding the Moment: Mid-America at Mid-Century,* 1991.

Other Awards: Feature Award, *Detroit Times,* 1949. "Great Pictures" Award, University of Missouri-National Photographer, 1951, 1954. Photographer of the Year, *Photography Annual,* 1954.

For More Information: Leekley, Sheryle and John Leekley, *Moments: The Pulitzer Prize Photographs, Updated Version: 1942-1982,* New York: Crown Publishers, Inc., 1982: 32-33.

Commentary: Don Ultang and John Robinson's series of photographs of the Drake University/Oklahoma A&M football game show the deliberate attacks on Johnny Bright. Bright was a black All-American halfback. While on the playing field he was punched on the first play of the game. His jaw was broken, but he did not leave the field. On Drake's next possession, Bright handed off the football and was punched a second time. The next play, he was down and players piled on top of him. He was carried off the field.

1953

William M. Gallagher   990

Birth: February 26, 1923; Hiawatha, KS. **Death:** September 28, 1975. **Parents:** George P. Gallagher and Anna Marie (Bowmaker). **Religion:** Roman Catholic.

Prize: *Photography,* 1953: *Flint Journal,* Flint, MI: Flint Journal, 1952.

Career: Served in U.S. Army, 1943-45; Staff member, *Flint (MI) Sporting Digest,* 1946; Wirephoto Operator, *Flint (MI) Journal,* 1947; Staff Photographer, *Flint (MI) Journal,* 1947-75.

Other Awards: Best in Show, Michigan Associated Press, 1953. First Place, Michigan Associated Press, 1953. First Place, Michigan Press Photography, 1953.

For More Information: *Current Biography Yearbook, 1953,* New York: H.W. Wilson Company, 1953; *New York Times,* 29 September (1975): 34; Leekley, Sheryle and John Leekley, *Moments: The Pulitzer Prize Photographs, Updated Version: 1942-1982,* New York: Crown Publishers, Inc., 1982: 34-35.

Commentary: William M. Gallagher won his first camera by selling magazines in high school. His Pulizer Prize-winning photograph captured a rare sight. His photograph is of Adlai Stevenson, who became the Democratic nominee for president in 1954. When Stevenson crossed his legs, he revealed a hole in the sole of his shoe. Gallagher circumspectly placed his camera on the platform where the candidate was sitting to snap the photo.

1954

Virginia Schau   991

Birth: February 23, 1915; North Sacramento, CA. **Death:** May 28, 1989. **Education:** University of the Pacific, CA: BMusic. University of the Pacific, CA: BA. **Spouse:** Walter Schau (m., died 1984). **Children:** Kurt.

Prize: *Photography,* 1954.

Career: Amateur Photographer; Homemaker.

For More Information: Leekley, Sheryle and John Leekley, *Moments: The Pulitzer Prize Photographs, Updated Version: 1942-1982,* New York: Crown Publishers, Inc., 1982: 36-37; *San Francisco Chronicle,* 3 June (1989): C11.

Commentary: Virginia Schau was the first woman and the second amateur to win a Pulitzer Prize for Photography. Her 1953 photograph showed the dramatic rescue of two men from the cab of a semi-trailer truck as it dangled over the side of a bridge. Schau was on a fishing trip with her husband when she took the photograph with two exposures left on a roll of film that was past the developing expiration date by over a year.

1955

John L. Gaunt Jr. 992

Birth: June 4, 1924; Syracuse, NY. **Education:** Compton Junior College, CA. University of Southern California. **Spouse:** Married.

Prize: *Photography,* 1955: *Los Angeles Times,* "Tragedy by the Sea," Los Angeles, CA: The Los Angeles Times, 1954.

Career: Served in U.S. Air Force, WWII; Staff member, *Redondo Beach (CA) South Bay Daily Breeze; Los Angeles (CA) Times,* 1950-; Commercial fisherman.

For More Information: Leekley, Sheryle and John Leekley, *Moments: The Pulitzer Prize Photographs, Updated Version: 1942-1982,* New York: Crown Publishers, Inc., 1982: 38-39.

Commentary: Jack Gaunt was at his house on the beach when he captured the photograph showing the tragic despair a young couple experienced when they realized their infant son had been swept out to sea.

1956

New York Daily News 993

Founded: June 26, 1919; New York, NY. **Founder(s):** Robert Rutherford McCormick and Joseph Medill Patterson.

Prize: *Photography,* 1956: *New York Daily News,* New York, 1955.

Other Awards: Staff members of the *New York Daily News* have won six individual Pulitzer Prizes.

For More Information: Bessie, Simon Michael, *Jazz Journalism: The Story of the Tabloid Newspapers,* New York: Dutton, 1938; Tebbel, John William, *An American Dynasty,* Garden City, N.Y.: Doubleday & Company, Inc., 1947; Chapman, John Arthur, *Tell It to Sweeney: The Informal History of the New York Daily News,* Garden City, NY: Doubleday, 1961; Vigilante, Richard, *Strike: The Daily News War and The Future of American Labor,* New York: Simon & Schuster, 1994.

Commentary: The entire photographic staff of the *New York Daily News* won a Pulitzer Prize for its coverage of life in New York City. George Mattson's photograph was deemed representative. The staff members were Al Amy, Paul Bernius, Ed Clarity, Jack Clarity, Tom Cunningham, Jack Eckhart, Albert Fougel, Tom Gallagher, Ed Giorandino, Phil Greitzer, Charles Hoff, Frank Hurley, Walter Kelleher, Bob Koller, Hal Mathewson, George Mattson, Fred Morgan, Charles Payne, Ed Peters, Joe Petrella, Sam Platnick, Al Pucci, Gordon Rynders, Nick Sorrentino, Paul Thayer, and Seymour Wally.

The founders of the *New York Daily News,* R.R. McCormick and J.M. Patterson, were related to the publishers of the *Chicago Tribune.* They were the expansion team into the New York newspaper market.

1957

Harry Albert Trask 994

Birth: April 15, 1928; Roxbury, MA. **Parents:** Harry S. Trask and Bertha (Muise). **Education:** Eastern School of Photography, MA. University of Massachusetts: BA. Bridgewater State College, MA: MEd. **Spouse:** Joan Mueller (m. 1955). **Children:** Mark, Matthew, Peter, Claire, Andrew, Philip, Sarah.

Prize: *Photography,* 1957: *Boston Traveler,* Boston: Boston Traveler, 1956.

Career: Mail Clerk, *Boston (MA) Herald and Traveler,* 1944-51; Radarman, U.S. Navy, 1946-48; Officeboy, Photography Department, *Boston (MA) Herald and Traveler,* 1951-55; Staff Photographer, *Boston (MA) Traveler,* 1955-73; History Teacher, Jeremiah E. Burke High School, 1973-.

Other Awards: Graflex Diamond Award, 1957.

For More Information: *Editor & Publisher,* 4 August (1956): 10; Leekley, Sheryle and John Leekley, *Moments: The Pulitzer Prize Photographs, Updated Version: 1942-1982,* New York: Crown Publishers, Inc., 1982: 42-43.

Commentary: Harry Trask flew out over the crash site of the *Andrea Doria,* a luxury ocean liner, and captured on film its last heave and then its disappearance into the depths. The *Andrea Doria* collided with the *Stockholm,* a smaller liner. Only 46 people out of the 1706 passengers lost their lives.

1958

William Charles Beall   995

Birth: February 6, 1911; Washington, DC. **Death:** March 27, 1994. **Parents:** Frank Beall and Zula (Walters). **Spouse:** Mildred Watson (m. 1929, div. 1939); Anna Mahoney Norman (m. 1941). **Children:** Betty Jane (MW); Dennis Wade, March Ann, Louise Mahoney, Janet Evelyn (AN).

Prize: *Photography,* 1958: *Washington Daily News,* "Faith and Confidence," September 11, Washington, DC: Washington Daily News, 1957.

Career: Photographic Printer, Underwood and Underwood, 1927-32; Photographer, *Washington (DC) Post,* 1933-35; Photographer, *Washington (DC) Daily News,* 1935-39; Chief Photographer, *Washington DC Daily News,* 1940-; Combat Photographer, U.S. Marine Corps, 1944-46.

Other Awards: Air Medal, 1945.

For More Information: *Washington Daily News,* September 13, 1957: 3; Leekley, Sheryle and John Leekley, *Moments: The Pulitzer Prize Photographs, Updated Version: 1942-1982,* New York: Crown Publishers, Inc., 1982: 88-89.

Commentary: William C. Beall's photo of Allen Weaver, age 2, and his encounter with police officer Cullinane is a touching photograph of trust and respect. Officer Cullinane was warning the child to be careful of the firecrackers being lit in a celebration by local Chinese. The picture was reprinted in *Life* magazine at the request of readers.

1959

William Casper Seaman   996

Birth: January 19, 1925; Grand Island, NE. **Death:** December 6, 1997. **Parents:** William H. Seaman and Minnie (Cords). **Spouse:** Ruth Witwer (m. 1945). **Children:** Lawrence William.

Prize: *Photography,* 1959: *Minneapolis Star,* Minneapolis, MN: Minneapolis Star, 1958.

Career: Photographer, Leschinsky Studio; Photograher, *Minneapolis (MN) Star,* 1945-82.

Other Awards: National Headliners Club Award, 1956. Award, Kent State University, OH. Silver Anniversary Award, Honeywell Photographers Products, 1975.

For More Information: Leekley, Sheryle and John Leekley, *Moments: The Pulitzer Prize Photographs, Updated Version: 1942-1982,* New York: Crown Publishers, Inc., 1982: 46-47; *Minneapolis Star Tribune,* 8 December (1997): 4B.

Commentary: Bill Seaman worked for the *Minneapolis Star* his entire career and retired when the *Star* merged with the *Minneapolis Tribune.* He was

known for his action photography, especially his sports photographs. His Pulitzer Prize-winning photograph was of a small boy with a wagon who had been hit by an automobile. He took the photograph on May 15, 1958.

1960

Andrew Lopez   997

Birth: May 10, 1910; Burgos, Spain. **Death:** October 30, 1986. **Parents:** Santiago Lopez and Petra (Gomez). **Spouse:** Amy Weyrauch (m. 1936). **Children:** Joan, Andrew.

Prize: *Photography,* 1960: United Press International, 1959.

Career: Photographer, Acme Newspix, 1942-57; Photographer, United Press International, 1957-83.

Other Awards: Medal of Freedom, 1944.

For More Information: Leekley, Sheryle and John Leekley, *Moments: The Pulitzer Prize Photographs, Updated Version: 1942-1982,* New York: Crown Publishers, Inc., 1982: 48-49; *Chicago Tribune,* 31 October (1986): 10; *New York Times,* 31 October (1986): A20; *Los Angeles Times,* 1 November (1986): part 4, 7.

Commentary: Andy Lopez covered the war crimes tribunal after the Cuban Civil War. His photograph shows Jose Rodriguez, nicknamed "Pepe Caliente," receiving last rites from a priest. His firing squad is in the background. Lopez took the photograph on January 17, 1959.

Lopez came to the United States in 1915 and became a naturalized citizen in 1937. He was a war correspondent in Europe and the Pacific during World War II. He was on hand to photograph the Japanese surrender on the USS *Missouri* as well as the atomic bomb tests at Bikini Island.

1961

Yasushi Nagao   998

Birth: May 20, 1930; Tokyo, Japan. **Education:** Chiba University, Japan.

Prize: *Photography,* 1961: "Tokyo Stabbing," 1960.

Career: Staff Photographer, *Tokyo (Japan) Mainichi.*

For More Information: Leekley, Sheryle and John Leekley, *Moments: The Pulitzer Prize Photographs, Updated Version: 1942-1982,* New York: Crown Publishers, Inc., 1982: 50-51.

Commentary: Yasushi Nagao had one frame of film left after taking photographs of a three-party political debate. He captured the assassination by sword of Socialist Party Chairman Inejiro Asanuma.

Otoya Yamaguchi, the assassin, was a 17-year-old ultra-nationalist, who later committed suicide.

Nagao was the first foreign photographer to win a Pulitzer Prize.

1962

Paul Vathis 999

Birth: October 18, 1925; Jim Thorpe, PA. **Parents:** Peter G. Vathis and Pauline A. (Kachoulieris). **Religion:** Episcopalian. **Spouse:** Barbara Gay Gardiner (m. 1949). **Children:** Victoria Elizabeth, Randall Carl, Stephanie Ellen.

Prize: *Photography,* 1962: Associated Press, "Serious Steps," 1961.

Career: Served in U.S. Marine Corps, WWII; Copyboy, Associated Press, 1946; Photographer, Pennsylvania, Associated Press, 1949-.

For More Information: Leekley, Sheryle and John Leekley, *Moments: The Pulitzer Prize Photographs, Updated Version: 1942-1982,* New York: Crown Publishers, Inc., 1982: 52-53; Rigsby, Gwendolyn Gezelle, "A History of Associated Press Pulitzer Prizes" (thesis), University of South Carolina, 1993.

Commentary: Paul Vathis captured a Pulitzer Prize with his photograph of President John F. Kennedy and former President Dwight D. Eisenhower. The photograph was captioned "Serious Steps." It is the first photograph to win with the subjects' backs to the camera since 1949 when Nat Fein won with his photograph of "Babe Ruth Bows Out." Vathis was a finalist for a Pulitzer Prize in 1988.

1963

Hector Rondon 1000

Prize: *Photography,* 1963: "Aid From the Padre," 1962.

Career: Glass factory employee, Los Togues, Venezuela; Corporal, Communications Unit, Venezuelan Army, 1952-59; Taxi driver, 1954; Photographer, city and state governments; Technical photographer, police department; Photographer, *Caracas (Venezuela) La Republica.*

Other Awards: George Polk Memorial Award, Long Island University, NY, 1963.

For More Information: *New York Times,* 7 May (1963): 35; Leekley, Sheryle and John Leekley, *Moments: The Pulitzer Prize Photographs, Updated Version: 1942-1982,* New York: Crown Publishers, Inc., 1982: 54-55.

Commentary: Hector Rondon was the second foreign photographer to win a Pulitzer Prize. His

photograph of a priest helping a wounded soldier in Venezuela was distributed worldwide by the Associated Press. Rondon took the photograph while under fire during a two-day revolt in June 1962.

1964

Robert Hill Jackson 1001

Birth: April 8, 1934; Dallas, TX. **Parents:** William C.H. Jackson and Anna (Bridges). **Education:** Southern Methodist University, TX. **Spouse:** Margaret Ann Looney (m. 1962, div. 1972). **Children:** Carol Lynn, Anne E., Kelly.

Prize: *Photography,* 1964: *Dallas Times-Herald,* Dallas: Dallas Times-Herald, 1963.

Career: Served in U.S. Army, 1958-59; Official Photographer, Texas Region of the Sports Car Club of America; News Photographer, *Dallas (TX) Times-Herald,* 1960-68; Photographer, *Denver (CO) Post,* 1968-69; Photographer, *Dallas (TX) Times-Herald,* 1969-74; Freelance photographer, 1974-80; Photographer, *Colorado Springs (CO) Gazette-Telegraph,* 1981-.

Other Awards: Texas Headliners Club Award, 1964. Best Spot News Picture Award, Associated Press, 1964. Sweepstakes Award, Associated Press, 1964. Sigma Delta Chi Award, 1964. News Photography Award, University of Missouri/National Press Photographers Association, 1964.

For More Information: *New York Times,* 5 May (1964): 39; Leekley, Sheryle and John Leekley, *Moments: The Pulitzer Prize Photographs, Updated Version: 1942-1982,* New York: Crown Publishers, Inc., 1982: 58-59; *News Photographer,* 50:4 (1995): F1.

Commentary: Robert H. Jackson began his professional career as a photographer, taking photos of stock car races. He won a Pulitzer Prize for his photograph of Jack Ruby fatally shooting Lee Harvey Oswald.

1965

Horst Faas   1002

Birth: April 28, 1933; Berlin, Germany. **Parents:** Adalbert Faas and Gerda (Schulz). **Education:** Munich University, Germany. **Spouse:** Ursula Gerienne (m. 1965).

Prize: *Photography,* 1965: Associated Press, 1964. *Spot News Photography,* 1972: Associated Press, "Death in Dacca," 1971.

Career: Photography salesman, Dusseldorf, Germany; Photographer, Germany Keystone Agency, 1952-56; Photographer, Germany, Associated Press, 1956-60; Photographer, Congo, Algeria, Associated Press, 1960-62; Photographer, Vietnam, Associated Press, 1962-70; Roving Photographer, Southeast Asia, Associated Press, 1970-77; Photographer, London, Associated Press, 1977-78; European Photography Editor, Associated Press, 1978-90; Senior Photo Editor-Operations, Associated Press, 1990-.

Selected Works: *Requiem: By the Photographers Who Died in Vietnam and Indochina* (with others), 1997.

Other Awards: Overseas Press Club Award, 1963-64, 1970, 1972. Robert Capa Award, Overseas Press Club, 1965. Associated Press Managing Editors Award, 1965. National Headliners Club Award, 1967, 1972. George Polk Memorial Award, Long Island University, NY, 1967, 1970, 1972. Sigma Delta Chi Award, 1970. Best Spot News and Best News Picture Story, University of Missouri/National Press Photographers Association, 1972.

For More Information: Leekley, Sheryle and John Leekley, *Moments: The Pulitzer Prize Photographs, Updated Version: 1942-1982,* New York: Crown Publishers, Inc., 1982: 58-59, 84-85; Rigsby, Gwendolyn Gezelle, "A History of Associated Press Pulitzer Prizes" (thesis), University of South Carolina, 1993.

Commentary: Horst Faas, a photographer with the Associated Press for over 40 years, is a two-time winner of a Pulitzer Prize. Both of his awards were of photos taken in Southeast Asia. The first was for photographs taken in Vietnam and the second was for photos taken, with Michel Laurent, titled "Death in Dacca," of retaliating Bangladesh soldiers executing turncoats.

1966

Kyoichi Sawada   1003

Birth: February 22, 1936; Aomori, Japan. **Death:** October 28, 1970. **Parents:** Naoyoshi Sawada and Maki (Aoyama). **Spouse:** Sata Tazawa (m. 1956).

Prize: *Photography,* 1966: United Press International, "Flee to Safety," 1965.

Career: Staff Photographer, United Press International, 1961-70; Staff Photographer, Saigon (Vietnam), United Press International, 1965-70.

Selected Works: *Senjo: Sawada Kyoichi Shashinshu,* 1971. *Betonamu Senso,* 1989. *Sawada: Nokosareta 30,000 — Mai No Nega Kara: Aomari, Betonamu, Kanbojia: Sawada Kyoichi Shashinshu,* 1990.

Other Awards: First Prize News Photography, World Press Photo Exhibition, 1965. Grand Prize, World Press Photo Exhibition, 1965. American Award, Overseas Press Club, 1966-67. Achievement Award, *U.S. Camera Magazine,* 1966. First and Second Prizes News Photography, World Press Photo Exhibition, 1966. Grand Prize, World Press Photo Exhibition, 1966. Robert Capa Award, Overseas Press Club, 1971.

For More Information: Leekley, Sheryle and John Leekley, *Moments: The Pulitzer Prize Photographs, Updated Version: 1942-1982,* New York: Crown Publishers, Inc., 1982: 58-61; Browne, Turner and Elaine Partnow, *Macmillan Biographical Encyclopedia of Photographic Artists & Innovators,* New York: Macmillan Publishing Co., 1983; Aoki, Fukiko, *Raika de Guddobai, Bunshun Bunko, 375-1,* Tokyo, Japan: Bungei Shunju, 1985.

Commentary: Kyoichi Sawada won a Pulitzer Prize for his coverage of the Vietnam War. He captured the desolate nature of the war with his photography. Sawada was killed while on assignment in Cambodia.

1967

Jack Randolph Thornell   1004

Birth: August 29, 1939; Vicksburg, MS. **Parents:** Benjamin O. Thornell and Myrtice (Jones). **Spouse:** Carolyn Wilson (m. 1964). **Children:** Candice, Jay Randolph.

Prize: *Photography,* 1967: Associated Press, 1966.

Career: Served in Signal Corps, U.S. Army, 1957-60; Photographer, *Jackson (MS) Daily News,* 1960-64; Photographer, Associated Press, 1964-; Photographer, Dominican Republic, Associated Press, 1965; Photographer, Selma, Alabama, Associated Press, 1965.

Other Awards: National Headliners Club Award, 1967.

For More Information: *New York Times,* 2 May (1967): 40; Leekley, Sheryle and John Leekley, *Moments: The Pulitzer Prize Photographs, Updated Version: 1942-1982,* New York: Crown Publishers, Inc., 1982: 62-63; Rigsby, Gwendolyn Gezelle, "A History of Associated Press Pulitzer Prizes" (thesis), University of South Carolina, 1993.

Commentary: Jack R. Thornell was awarded a Pulitzer Prize for his photograph of the shooting of James Meredith by a sniper near Hernando, Mississippi. Meredith was wounded while marching from Memphis to encourage voter registration in the South.

Poetry

1918

Sara Teasdale   1005

Birth: August 8, 1884; St. Louis, MO. **Death:** 1933.
Parents: John Warren and Mary Elizabeth (Villard)
Teasdale. **Spouse:** Ernest R. Filsinger (m. 1914; div.
1929).

Prize: *Poetry,* 1918: *Love Songs,* New York:
Macmillan, 1917.

Career: Poet; Traveled to Europe and the Near
East.

Selected Works: *Sonnets to Duse, and Other
Poems,* 1907. *Helen of Troy, and Other Poems,* 1911.
Rivers to the Sea, 1915. *The Answering Voice: One
Hundred Love Lyrics by Women* (Teasdale, Sara, ed.),
1917. *Flame and Shadow,* 1920. *Rainbow Gold: Po-
ems Old and New Selected for Boys and Girls,* 1922.
Dark of the Moon, 1926. *Stars To-Night, Verses New
and Old for Boys and Girls,* 1930. *Strange Victory,*
1933. *The Collected Poems of Sara Teasdale,* 1937.
Mirror of the Heart: Poems of Sara Teasdale (Drake,
William, ed.), 1984.

For More Information: Carpenter, Margaret
Haley, *Sara Teasdale, A Biography,* New York: Schulte,
1960; Drake, William D., *Sara Teasdale, Woman &
Poet,* New York: Harper & Row, 1979; Schoen, Carol,
Sara Teasdale, Boston: Twayne, 1986.

Commentary: Sara Teasdale was awarded the
1918 Pulitzer Prize in Poetry for *Love Songs,* a volume
of poetry which went into a fifth printing during its
first year of publication.

Teasdale was born in St. Louis, Missouri and
educated privately. She was a peripheral member of
the literary group connected with *Poetry* magazine in
Chicago. Her first poems were published privately in
1907, *Sonnets to Duse, and Other Poems.* She attracted attention with *Helen of Troy, and Other Poems*
and *Rivers to the Sea.* She committed suicide in 1933,
precipitated by the suicide of her longtime love,
Vachel Lindsay.

1919

Carl Sandburg

Full entry appears as **#555** under "History," 1940.

Margaret Widdemer   1006

Birth: 1890; Doylestown, PA.. **Death:** July 14, 1978.
Parents: Howard Taylor and Alice (de Witt) Widde-
mer. **Education:** Drexel Institute Library School, DE.
Spouse: R. H. Schaufler (m. 1919; div.).

Prize: *Poetry,* 1919: *The Old Road to Paradise,*
New York: Holt, 1918.

Career: Poet, novelist, short story writer; Lecturer, the Art of Fiction, New York University, NY,
1943-1944; Assistant Director, Chautauqua Writers'
Conference, 1950-1965; Chairman, National Unity
Committee of Writers' War Board, WWII; Vice President, Poetry Society of America; Executive Board
Member, Christodora House; Executive Board Member, Pen and Brush; Former Executive Board Member, Authors Guild; Honorary Member, Browning
Society; Member: PEN, Query Club.

Selected Works: *Why Not?,* 1915. *The Rose-Gar-
den Husband,* 1915. *The Factories, with Other Lyrics,*
1915. *Winona of the Camp Fire,* 1915. *The Wishing-
Ring Man,* 1917. *Factories, Poems,* 1917. *Winona of
Camp Karonya,* 1917. *You're Only Young Once,* 1918.
Winona's Way: A Story of Reconstruction, 1919. *The
Haunted Hour: An Anthology* (Widdemer, Margaret,
ed.), 1920. *The Year of Delight,* 1921. *Cross-Currents,*
1921. *Winona on Her Own,* 1922. *Winona's Dreams
Come True,* 1923. *Graven Image,* 1923. *Charis Sees It
Through,* 1924. *Ballads and Lyrics,* 1925. *Gallant
Lady,* 1926. *The Singing Wood,* 1926. *Collected Poems
of Margaret Widdemer,* 1928. *Rhinestones: A Ro-
mance,* 1929. *Loyal Lover,* 1930. *All the King's
Horses,* 1930. *Pre-War Lady,* 1932. *The Best Ameri-
can Love Stories of the Year,* 1932. *The Years of Love,*
1933. *The Other Lovers,* 1934. *Eve's Orchard,* 1935.
This Isn't the End, 1936. *Hill Garden: New Poems,*
1936. *Hand on Her Shoulder,* 1938. *Marriage Is Pos-
sible,* 1939. *Someday I'll Find You,* 1940. *Constancia
Herself,* 1945. *Lani,* 1948. *Red Cloak Flying,* 1950.
Lady of the Mohawks, 1951. *Prince in Buckskin: A
Story of Joseph Brant at Lake George,* 1952. *Basic
Principles of Fiction Writing,* 1953. *The Great Pine's
Son: A Story of the Pontiac War,* 1954. *The Golden
Wildcat,* 1954. *The Dark Cavalier: The Collected Po-
ems of Margaret Widdemer,* 1958. *Golden Friends I
Had: Unrevised Memories of Margaret Widdemer,*
1964. *Jessie Rittenhouse: A Centenary Memoir-An-
thology* (Widdemer, Margaret, ed.), 1969.

Other Awards: Trimmed Lamp Prize, Best Lyric
of Year, 1917. American Poetry Society Prize, 1919:
The Old Road to Paradise, New York: Holt, 1918.
Saturday Review of Literature Award, Best Satire,
1922: "Tree with a Bird in It." Lyric West Prize, 1922:
"Hill Sunset." English Poetry Society Prize, Best Ballad, 1926: "Fiddler's Green." Lyric Award, Distin-

guished Services to Poetry, 1960. Honorary LittD, Bucknell University, PA, 1931. Honorary MA, Middlebury University, VT, 1933.*Child Life* Award, Best Poem of the Year, 1937, "Lullaby."

For More Information: *Twentieth-Century Authors,* New York: Wilson, 1942; *American Women Playwrights, 1900-1930,* Westport, CT: Greenwood, 1992.

Commentary: Margaret Widdemer was a co-winner of the 1919 Pulitzer Prize in Poetry for *Old Road to Paradise.*

Widdemer was born in Pennsylvania and educated at Middlebury College in Vermont. Her career as a poet received a boost when she was dismissed from her job at the University of Pennsylvania library for lack of accuracy in copying catalog cards. Her first poem *The Factories,* published in 1915, was about child labor and won her instant recognition. She taught and lectured on creative writing in addition to publishing verse, lyrics, and light romantic fiction. She is known not only as a poet but also for her Winona series of books for girls, for the novels *The Rose-Garden Husband* and *Red Cloak Flying,* and for several plays.

1920
No award

1921
No award

1922

Edwin Arlington Robinson   1007

Birth: December 22, 1869; Head Tide, Maine. **Death:** April 6, 1935. **Parents:** Edward and Mary Elizabeth (Palmer) Robinson. **Education:** Harvard University, MA. Yale University, CT: DLitt. Bowdoin College, ME: DLitt.

Prize: *Poetry,* 1922: *Collected Poems,* New York: Macmillan, 1921. *Poetry,* 1925: *The Man Who Died Twice,* New York: Macmillan, 1924. *Poetry,* 1928: *Tristram,* New York: Macmillan, 1927.

Career: Poet; New York Customs House employee, 1905-1909; Guest writer, MacDowell Colony, Peterborough, NH, 1911-1935.

Selected Works: *The Torrent and The Night before, Gardiner, Maine: 1889-1896,* 1896. *The Children of the Night: A Book of Poems,* 1897. *Captain Craig: A Book of Poems,* 1902. *The Town Down the River: A Book of Poems,* 1910. *Van Zorn: A Comedy in Three Acts,* 1914. *The Porcupine: A Drama in Three Acts,* 1915. *Merlin: A Poem,* 1917. *Tendencies in Modern American Poetry,* 1917. *The Three Taverns: A Book of Poems,* 1920. *Lancelot: A Poem,* 1920. *The Man against the Sky: A Book of Poems,* 1921. *Avon's Harvest,* 1921. *Roman Bartholow,* 1923. *Dionysus in Doubt: A Book of Poems,* 1925. *Cavender's House,* 1929. *Sonnets, 1889-1927,* 1928. *Selections from the Letters of Thomas Sergeant Perry* (Robinson, Edwin A., ed.), 1929. *Collected Poems of Edwin Arlington Robinson,* 1929. *The Glory of the Nightingales,* 1930. *Poems, Selected,* 1931. *Matthias at the Door,* 1931. *Nicodemus: A Book of Poems,* 1932. *Talifer,* 1933. *Amaranth,* 1934. *King Jasper: A Poem,* 1935. *Selected Letters of Edwin Arlington Robinson,* 1940. *Letters of Edwin Arlington Robinson to Howard George Schmitt* (Weber, Carl J., ed.), 1943. *Untriangulated Stars; Letters of Edwin Arlington Robinson to Harry de Forest Smith 1890-1905* (Sutcliffe, Denham, ed.), 1947. *Tilbury Town,* 1953. *Edwin Arlington Robinson's Letters to Edith Brower* (Cary, Richard, ed.), 1968.

Other Awards: Levinson Prize, 1923. Gold Medal, National Institute and American Academy of Arts and Letters, 1929.

For More Information: Fussell, Edwin S., *Edwin Arlington Robinson: The Literary Background of a Traditional Poet,* Berkeley: University of California Press, 1954; Robinson William R., *Edwin Arlington Robinson: A Poetry of the Act,* Cleveland, OH: Western Reserve University Press, 1967; Murphy, Francis E., ed., *Edwin Arlington Robinson: A Collection of Critical Essays,* Englewood Cliffs, NJ: Prentice Hall, 1970; Joyner, Nancy, *Edwin Arlington Robinson: A Reference Guide,* Boston: Hall, 1978; Burton, David Henry, *Edwin Arlington Robinson: Stages in a New England Poet's Search,* Lewiston, ME: Mellen, 1987; Boswell, Jeanetta, *Edwin Arlington Robinson and the Critics: A Bibliography,* Metuchen, NJ: Scarecrow, 1988.

Commentary: Edward Arlington Robinson won three Pulitzer Prizes, all in Poetry. He won in 1922 for *Collected Poems,* in 1925 for *The Man Who Died Twice,* and in 1928 for *Tristram.*

Robinson was born in Head Tide, Maine. He was educated at Harvard University but left before completing his degree. He wrote verse from the age of 11. He spent many years working at any job, including subway conductor in New York City, to support himself and allow him to write poetry. He published several volumes himself without gaining much notice. Theodore Roosevelt did take note of Robinson's work and offered him a job at the United States Customs House. He finally bloomed after age 50 when he visited the MacDowell Colony, a creative retreat in Peterborough, New Hampshire. He found it inspirational and spent much of the rest of his life there. He published many volumes of verse and was considered by many to be, along with Robert Frost, one of America's greatest poets.

1923

Edna St. Vincent Millay   1008

Birth: February 22, 1892; Rockland, ME. **Death:** October 19, 1950. **Parents:** Henry Tolman Millay and Cora (Buzzelle). **Education:** Barnard College, NY. Vassar College, NY: AB. **Spouse:** Eugene Jan Boissevain (m. 1923; died 1949).

Prize: *Poetry,* 1923: *The Ballad of the Harp-Weaver; A Few Figs From Thistles; Eight Sonnets in American Poetry, 1922, A Miscellany,* New York: Shay, 1922.

Career: Poet, dramatist, lyricist, lecturer, translator, and short story writer; Actor, Provincetown Players, 1917-1919; Freelance writer, 1919-1920;

Traveled Europe, 1921-1923; Traveled Orient, 1924; Participant in poetry reading tours, beginning in 1925; National radio broadcaster, 1932-1933; President and Presenter, Prix Femina Committee, 1930s; Propaganda verse writer, Writers' War Board, 1940s.

Selected Works: *Renascence,* 1917. *Aria da Capo: A Play in One Act,* 1920. *Second April,* 1921. *The Lamp and the Bell: A Drama in Five Acts,* 1921. *Three Plays: Two Slatterns and a King, Aria de Capo, The Lamp and the Bell,* 1926. *The King's Henchman,* 1927. *The Buck in the Snow, & Other Poems,* 1928. *Fatal Interview: Sonnets,* 1931. *The Princess Marries the Page: A Play in One Act,* 1932. *Wine from These Grapes,* 1934. *Conversation at Midnight,* 1937. *Huntsman, What Quarry?,* 1939. *"There Are No Islands, Any More,"* 1940. *Make Bright the Arrows: 1940 Notebook,* 1940. *Mine the Harvest: A Collection of New Poems,* 1954. *Collected Poems* (Millay, Norma, ed.), 1956. *Take Up the Song: Poems,* 1986.

Other Awards: Prize from Poetry, 1920. "The Beanstalk." Helen Haire Levinson Prize, *Sonnets,* 1931: *Poetry* Laureate of General Federation of Women's Clubs, 1933. Gold Medal of the Poetry Society of America, 1943. Honorary LittDs: Tufts College, MA, 1925; University of Wisconsin, 1933; Russell Sage College, NY, 1933; Colby College, ME, 1937. Honorary LHD, New York University, 1937.

For More Information: Gould, Jean, *The Poet and Her Book: A Biography of Edna St. Vincent Millay,* New York: Dodd, Mead, 1969; Cheney, Anne, *Millay in Greenwich Village,* Tuscaloosa: University of Alabama Press, 1975; Nierman, Judith, *Edna St. Vincent Millay: A Reference Guide,* Boston: Hall, 1977; Brittin, Norman A., *Edna St. Vincent Millay,* Boston: Twayne, 1982; Thesing, William B., ed., *Critical Essays on Edna St. Vincent Millay,* New York: Hall, 1993; Freedman, Diane P., ed., *Millay at 100: A Critical Reappraisal,* Carbondale: Southern Illinois University Press, 1995.

Commentary: *The Ballad of the Harp-Weaver; A Few Figs from Thistles; Sonnets in American Poetry, 1922, A Miscellany* won the 1923 Pulitzer Prize in Poetry for Edna St. Vincent Millay.

Millay was born in Rockland, Maine. She was educated at Barnard and Vassar Colleges. Upon graduation from Vassar, she joined the literary community in Greenwich Village and enjoyed the moral support of other writers before publishing poetry and plays that captured the public's interest. She published her first volume of poetry, *Renascence and Other Poems,* in 1917. Her other works include the play *The King's Henchmen* and *The Buck in the Snow and Other Poems.*

1924

Robert Frost   1009

Birth: March 26, 1874; San Francisco, CA. **Death:** January 29, 1963. **Parents:** William Prescott and Isabel (Moodie) Frost. **Education:** Dartmouth College, NH. Harvard University, MA. **Spouse:** Elinor Miriam White (m. 1895; died 1938). **Children:** Elliott, Lesley (daughter), Carol (son), Irma, Marjorie, Elinor Bettina.

Prize: *Poetry,* 1924: *New Hampshire: A Poem With Notes and Grace Notes,* New York: Holt, 1923. *Poetry,* 1931: *Collected Poems,* New York: Holt, 1930. *Poetry,* 1937: *A Further Range,* New York: Holt, 1936. *Poetry,* 1943: *A Witness Tree,* New York: Holt, 1942.

Career: Poet; Phi Beta Kappa Poet, Tufts College, Medford, MA, 1915 and 1940; Professor of English and Poet-in-Residence, Amherst College, MA, 1916-1920, 1923-1925, and 1926-1928; Phi Beta Kappa Poet, Harvard University, Cambridge, MA, 1916 and 1941; Co-Founder, Bread-Loaf School and Conference of English, Middlebury College, Middlebury, VT, 1920; Annual Lecturer, Bread-Loaf School and Conference of English, Middlebury College, Middlebury, VT, beginning in 1920; Professor and Poet-in-Residence, University of Michigan, Ann Arbor, 1921-1923; Fellow in Letters, University of Michigan, Ann Arbor, 1925-1926; Phi Beta Kappa Poet, Columbia University, New York City, 1932; Associate Fellow, Yale University, New Haven, CT, beginning in 1933; Charles Eliot Norton Professor of Poetry, Harvard University, 1936; Board Overseer, Harvard University, 1938-1939; Ralph Waldo Emerson Fellow, Harvard University, 1939-1941; Associate of Adams House, Fellow in American Civilization, Harvard University, 1941-1942; Honorary Fellow,

Harvard University, 1942-1943; George Ticknor Fellow in Humanities Visiting Lecturer, Dartmouth College, Hanover, NH, 1943-1949; Member: American Academy of Arts and Letters, American Philosophical Society, International PEN, National Institute of Arts and Letters.

Selected Works: *A Boy's Will,* 1915. *North of Boston,* 1915. *Mountain Interval,* 1921. *Selected Poems,* 1923. *West-Running Brook,* 1928. *Selected Poems,* 1928. *Two Tramps in Mud-Time: A New Poem,* 1934. *Neither Out Far Nor in Deep: A Poem,* 1935. *From Snow to Snow,* 1936. *To a Young Wretch,* 1937. *Triple Plate,* 1939. *The Wood-Pile,* 1939. *I Could Give All to Time,* 1941. *Come In, and Other Poems,* 1943. *Collected Poems of Robert Frost, 1939,* 1943. *An Unstamped Letter in Our Rural Letter Box,* 1944. *A Masque of Reason,* 1945. *A Masque of Mercy,* 1947. *Steeple Bush,* 1947. *A House in Chicago,* 1947. *Complete Poems of Robert Frost, 1949,* 1949. *On a Tree Fallen across the Road (To Hear Us Talk),* 1949. *The Road Not Taken,* 1951. *A Cabin in the Clearing,* 1951. *Does No One But Me At All Ever Feel This Way in the Least,* 1952. *One More Brevity: A New Poem,* 1953. *From a Milkweed Pod,* 1954. *Some Science Fiction,* 1955. *Away!,* 1958. *In the Clearing,* 1962. *The Prophets Really Prophesy as Mystics, the Commentators Merely by Statistics: A New Poem,* 1962. *A Pocket Book of Robert Frost's Poems,* 1962. *The Letters of Robert Frost to Louis Untermeyer,* 1963. *Robert Frost: Farm-Poultryman* (Lathem, Edward C. and Thompson, Lawrence eds.), 1963. *Selected Poems,* 1963. *Family Letters of Robert and Elinor Frost* (Grade, Arnold, ed.), 1972. *Robert Frost on Writing* (Harry, Elaine, ed.), 1973. *Stories for Lesley (Eighteen Stories Written by Robert Frost for His Children on Their New England Farm between the Years 1899 and 1907 or 1908),* 1984. *Birches,* 1988.

Other Awards: Levinson Prize, *Poetry,* 1922. Golden Rose Trophy, New England Poetry Club, 1928. Russell Loines Prize for Poetry, National Institute of Arts and Letters, 1931. Mark Twain Medal, 1937. Gold Medal of the National Institute of Arts and Letters, 1939. Gold Medal of the Poetry Society of America, 1941, 1958. Gold Medal, Limited Editions Club, 1949. Unanimous Resolution in His Honor and Gold Medal, United States Senate, March 24, 1950. American Academy of Poets Award, 1953. Medal of Honor, New York University, 1956. Huntington Hartford Foundation Award, 1958. Emerson-Thoreau Medal, American Academy of Arts and Sciences, 1958. Participant, Inauguration Ceremonies for President John F. Kennedy, 1961, read his poems "Dedication" and "The Gift Outright." Congressional Gold Medal, 1962. Edward MacDowell Medal, 1962. Bollingen Prize in Poetry, 1963. Induction, American Poet's Corner at Cathedral of St. John the Divine,

1986. Poet Laureate of Vermont, State League of Women's Clubs.

For More Information: Thompson, Lawrance Roger, *Robert Frost,* New York: Holt, Rinehart and Winston, 1966-1976; Rotella, Guy L., *Reading & Writing Nature: The Poetry of Robert Frost, Wallace Stevens, Marianne Moore, and Elizabeth Bishop,* Boston: Northeastern University Press, 1991; Brodsky, Joseph, Seamus Heaney, and Derek Walcott, *Homage to Frost,* New York: Farrar, Straus & Giroux, 1996; Cramer, Jeffrey S., *Robert Frost Among His Poems: A Literary Companion to the Poet's Own Biographical Contexts and Associations,* Jefferson, NC: McFarland, 1996; Meyers, Jeffrey, *Robert Frost: A Biography,* Boston: Houghton Mifflin, 1996; Faggen, Robert, *Robert Frost and the Challenge of Darwin,* Ann Arbor: University of Michigan Press, 1997; Richardson, Mark, *The Ordeal of Robert Frost: The Poet and His Poetics,* Urbana: University of Illinois Press, 1997.

Commentary: Robert Frost won four Pulitzer Prizes, all in Poetry. He won in 1924 for *New Hampshire: A Poem with Notes and Grace Notes,* in 1931 for *Collected Poems,* in 1937 for *A Further Range* and in 1943 for *A Witness Tree.*

Frost was born in San Francisco, California. He was educated at Dartmouth College and Harvard University. He knew from an early age that he wanted to be a poet and he succeeded in becoming one of America's most celebrated ones. He worked at many different occupations, including farmer, and didn't do very well at any—except that of poet. At his wife's suggestion, he sailed to England with his family and there succeeded in publishing two volumes of poetry and capturing the attention of other poets. Upon his return to the United States, his name as a poet was secured. His subject matter was New England. He stated that "a complete poem is one where an emotion has found its thought and the thought has found its words."

1925

Edwin Arlington Robinson
Full entry appears as #**1007** under "Poetry," 1922.

1926

Amy Lowell   1010
Birth: February 9, 1874; Brookline, MA. **Death:** May 12, 1925. **Parents:** Augustus and Katherine Bigelow (Lawrence) Lowell. **Religion:** Episcopalian. **Education:** Brooklyn Institute of Arts and Sciences, NY. Tufts University, MA. Columbia University, NY. Baylor University, TX: LittD. **Spouse:** Ada Dwyer Russell.

Prize: *Poetry,* 1926: *What's O'Clock,* Boston: Houghton Mifflin, 1925.

Career: Poet and essayist; Francis Bergen Foundation Lecturer, Yale University, New Haven, CT, 1921; Marshall Woods Lecturer, Brown University, Providence, RI, 1921; Member, Phi Beta Kappa.

Selected Works: *A Dome of Many-Coloured Glass,* 1912. *Sword Blades and Poppy Seed,* 1914. *Men, Women and Ghosts,* 1916. *Tendencies in Modern American Poetry,* 1917. *Can Grande's Castle,* 1918. *Pictures of the Floating World,* 1919. *Development: A Novel,* 1920. *Legends,* 1921. *Six French Poets: Studies in Contemporary Literature,* 1921. *A Critical Fable: A Sequel to the Fable for Critics, by a Poker of Fun,* 1922. *John Keats,* 1925. *East Wind,* 1926. *Ballads for Sale,* 1927. *Selected Poems of Amy Lowell* (Lowes, John L., ed.), 1928. *Poetry and Poets: Essays,* 1930. *A Shard of Silence: Selected Poems* (Ruihley, G.R., ed.), 1957.

For More Information: Wood, Clement, *Amy Lowell,* New York: Harold Vinal, 1926; Gould, Jean, *Amy: The World of Amy Lowell and the Imagist Movement,* New York: Dodd, Mead, 1975; Ruihley, Glenn Richard, *The Thorn of a Rose: Amy Lowell Reconsidered,* Hamden, CT: Archon, 1975; Heymann, C. David, *American Aristocracy: The Lives and Times of James Russell, Amy, and Robert Lowell,* New York: Dodd, Mead, 1980.

Commentary: Amy Lowell was awarded the 1926 Pulitzer Prize in Poetry posthumously for *What's O'Clock.*

Lowell was born in Brookline, Massachusetts into a wealthy family. She was not educated formally; instead, she was steered toward marriage and family. Lowell found herself drawn to poetry, especially of the free imagist variety. Her interest led to her traveling to England to meet with the poets of this school and to her sponsoring several imagist anthologies, a complete break from traditional verse. It was the beginning of a 20th-century style and she was a proponent, as exhibited in *Modern American Poetry,* published in 1917. She is most noted for *A Dome of Many-Coloured Glass, Sword Blades and Poppy Seed, Pictures of the Floating World,* and her last effort, a scholarly biography, *John Keats.*

1927

Leonora Speyer   1011
Birth: 1872; Washington, DC. **Parents:** Ferdinand and Julia (Thompson) von Stosch. **Religion:** Episcopalian. **Education:** Brussels Conservatory, Belgium. **Spouse:** Edgar Speyer (m. 1902). **Children:** Mrs. Robert J. Hewitt, Pamela Moy, Leonora, Vivian.

Prize: *Poetry,* 1927: *Fiddler's Farewell,* New York: Knopf, 1926.

Selected Works: *A Canopic Jar,* 1921. *Naked Heel,* 1931. *Slow Wall: Poems Together with Nor without Music,* 1946.

For More Information: *Benet's Reader's Encyclopedia of American Literature,* New York: Harper-Collins, 1991.

Commentary: Leonora Speyer was awarded the 1927 Pulitzer Prize in Poetry for *Fiddler's Farewell,* a volume noted for its wit and understanding of the feminine character.

Speyer was born in Washington, DC. She was a trained concert violinist as well as a poet. Her subject matter was personal and was presented with great skill. Her other works include *Naked Heel* and *Slow Wall.*

1928

Edwin Arlington Robinson

Full entry appears as **#1007** under "Poetry," 1922.

1929

Stephen Vincent Benet   1012

Birth: July 22, 1898; Bethlehem, PA. **Death:** March 13, 1943. **Parents:** James Walker and Frances Neill (Rose) Benet. **Education:** Yale University, CT. Sorbonne University, France. **Spouse:** Rosemary Carr (m. 1921). **Children:** One son and two daughters.

Prize: *Poetry,* 1929: *John Brown's Body,* New York: Rinehart, 1928. *Poetry,* 1944: *Western Star,* New York: Farrar & Rinehart, 1943.

Career: Staff member of State Department, Washington, DC, 1918; Advertising, NY, 1919; Vice President, National Institute of Arts and Letters.

Selected Works: *Young Adventure,* 1920. *Heavens and Earth,* 1920. *The Beginning of Wisdom,* 1921. *Young People's Pride: A Novel,* 1922. *Jean Huguenot,* 1923. *The Ballad of William Sycamore, 1790-1880,* 1923. *Tiger Joy: A Book of Poems,* 1925. *Spanish Bayonet,* 1926. *Ballads and Poems, 1915-1930,* 1931. *A Book of Americans* (with Rosemary Benet), 1933. *James Shore's Daughter,* 1934. *Burning City, New Poems,* 1936. *Thirteen O'Clock: Stories of Several Worlds,* 1937. *The Devil and Daniel Webster,* 1937. *Johnny Pye & the Fool-Killer,* 1938. *Letter to a Comrade,* 1938. *Tales before Midnight,* 1939. *"Dear Adolf," Letter from a Farmer,* 1942. *They Burned the Books,* 1942. *Selected Works of Stephen Vincent Benet,* 1942. *Twenty-Five Short Stories,* 1943. *Western Star,* 1943. *America,* 1944. *We Stand United, and Other Radio Scripts,* 1945. *The Last Circle, Stories and Poems,* 1946. *Selected Letters* (with Charles A. Fenton), 1960. *Stephen Vincent*

Benet on Writing: A Great Writer's Letters of Advice to a Young Beginner (with George Abbe), 1964.

Other Awards: Poetry Society of America Prize, 1921. Guggenheim Fellowship, 1926. O. Henry Award, 1932, 1937, 1940. Mary Shelley Memorial Award, 1933. American Academy Gold Medal, 1943.

For More Information: Stroud, Parry Edmund, *Stephen Vincent Benet,* New York: Twayne, 1962; *Stephen Vincent Benet: The Life and Times of an American Man of Letters, 1898-1943,* New Haven, CT: Yale University, 1958.

Commentary: Stephen Vincent Benet was awarded two Pulitzer Prizes, both in Poetry. He won in 1929 for *John Brown's Body,* a collection about the Civil War which he completed while in Paris on a Guggenheim scholarship. He won again in 1944 for *Western Star,* the first book of an epic left unfinished at his death.

Benet was born in Bethlehem, Pennsylvania and educated at Yale University. He was a lecturer and radio propagandist for the liberal cause during the 1930s and 1940s. Benet also wrote prose fiction, most notably *The Devil and Daniel Webster,* published in 1937. His brother, William Rose Benet, was also a poet and Pulitzer Prize winner.

1930

Conrad Aiken   1013

Birth: August 5, 1889; Savannah, GA. **Death:** August 17, 1973. **Parents:** William Ford and Anna (Potter) Aiken. **Education:** Harvard University, MA: AB. **Spouse:** Jessie McDonald (m. 1912; div. 1930); Clarice Lorenz, (m. 1930; div. 1937); Mary Augusta Hoover (m. 1937). **Children:** John Kempton, Jane Kempton (Mrs. Alan Hodge), Joan Delano (JM).

Prize: *Poetry,* 1930: *Selected Poems,* New York: Scribners, 1929.

Career: Poet, essayist, novelist, and short-story writer; President, *Advocate,* Harvard University, MA; Reviewer, *New Republic, Poetry, Chicago Daily News, Poetry Journal,* and *Dial;* Contributing Editor, *Dial,* 1917-1918; Writer, "Letters from America" to *Athenaeum* and *London Mercury;* English Tutor, Harvard University, 1925-1926; London Correspondent, *New Yorker,* under pseudonym Samuel Jeake, Jr.,1934-1936; Consultant in Poetry, Library of Congress, 1950-1952; Poet Laureate of Georgia, 1973; Member: American Academy of Arts and Letters, Harvard Club, MA.

Selected Works: *Turns and Movies and Other Tales in Verse,* 1916. *The Jig of Forslin: A Symphony,* 1916. *Looking Pegasus in the Mouth,* 1916. *Nocturne of Remembered Spring and Other Poems,* 1917. *The Charnel Rose. Senlin: Biography and Other Poems,* 1918. *Scepticisms, Notes on Contemporary Poetry,* 1919. *The House of Dust: A Symphony,* 1920. *Punch: The Immortal Liar, Documents in His History,* 1921. *The Pilgrimage of Festus,* 1923. *Bring! Bring! and Other Stories,* 1925. *Blue Voyage,* 1927. *Modern American Poets* (Aiken, Conrad, ed.), 1927. *Costumes by Eros,* 1928. *American Poetry 1671-1928: A Comprehensive Anthology* (Aiken, Conrad, ed.), 1929. *John Deth, a Metaphysical Legend, and Other Poems,* 1930. *Preludes for Memnon,* 1931. *The Coming Forth by Day of Osiris Jones,* 1931. *Great Circle,* 1933. *Among the Lost People,* 1934. *King Coffin,* 1935. *Landscape West of Eden,* 1935. *Time in the Rock: Preludes to Definition,* 1936. *A Heart for the Gods of Mexico,* 1939. *Conversation, or, Pilgrim's Progress,* 1940. *And in the Human Heart,* 1940. *Brownstone Eclogues, and Other Poems,* 1942. *The Kid,* 1947. *Skylight One, Fifteen Poems,* 1949. *The Short Stories of Conrad Aiken,* 1950. *Ushant, an Essay,* 1952. *Collected Poems,* 1953. *Mr. Arcularis. A Play,* 1957. *Sheepfold Hill: Fifteen Poems,* 1958. *Selected Poems,* 1961. *The Morning Song of Lord Zero, Poems Old and New,* 1963. *A Seizure of Limericks,* 1964. *Cats and Bats and Things with Wings: Poems,* 1965. *Scepticisms: Notes on Contemporary Poetry,* 1967. *Thee: A Poem,* 1967. *Ushant: An Essay,* 1971. *Selected Letters of Conrad Aiken* (with Joseph Killorin), 1978. *The Letters of Conrad Aiken and Malcolm Lowry, 1929-1954* (Sugars, Cynthia C., ed.), 1992.

Other Awards: Shelley Memorial Award, 1930. Guggenheim Fellowship, 1934. Fellow in American Letters, 1947. Bryher Award, 1952. National Book Award, 1954: *Collected Poems.* Bollingen Prize in Poetry, 1956. Academy of American Poets Fellowship, 1957. Gold Medal of the National Institute of Arts and Letters, 1958. Huntington Hartford Foundation Award, 1961. St. Botolph Award, 1965. Gold Medal of Achievement, Brandeis University Creative Awards Commission, 1967. National Medal for Literature, 1969.

For More Information: Hoffman, Frederick John, *Conrad Aiken,* New York: Twayne, 1962; Martin, Jay, *Conrad Aiken, A Life of His Art,* Princeton, NJ: Princeton University Press, 1962; Killorin, Joseph, *Selected Letters of Conrad Aiken,* New Haven, CT: Yale University Press, 1978; Lorenz, Clarissa M., *Lorelei Two: My Life With Conrad Aiken,* Athens, GA: University of Georgia Press, 1983; Spivey, Ted Ray, *The Writer As Shaman: The Pilgrimages of Conrad Aiken and Walker Percy,* Macon, GA: Mercer University Press, 1986; Marten, Harry, *The Art of Knowing: The Poetry and Prose of Conrad Aiken,* Columbia: University of Missouri Press, 1988; Spivey, Ted Ray, and Arthur Waterman, *Conrad Aiken: A Priest of Consciousness,* New York: AMS, 1989; Spivey, Ted Ray, *Time's Stop in Savannah: Conrad Aiken's Inner Journey,* Macon, GA: Mercer University Press, 1997.

Commentary: *Selected Poems* won the 1930 Pulitzer Prize in Poetry for Conrad Aiken.

Aiken was born in Savannah, Georgia. When he was 10 years old, Aiken's mother was murdered by his father, who then committed suicide. He was taken in by relatives and later attended Harvard University. He published his first book of verse, *Earth Triumphant,* in 1914. He was influenced initially by Edgar Allan Poe, and later by the French Symbolists and the Imagists, and especially by Freud. Some of his most noted works were prose, such as the autobiographical novel, *Ushant: An Essay,* published in 1952. He was named poet laureate of Georgia in 1973.

1931

Robert Frost
Full entry appears as **#1009** under "Poetry," 1924.

1932

George Dillon   1014
Birth: November 12, 1906; Jacksonville, FL. **Death:** 1968?. **Education:** Yale University, CT: BA. University of California, Berkeley: MA, PhD. **Spouse:** Judith D.

Prize: *Poetry,* 1932: *The Flowering Stone,* New York: Viking, 1931.

Career: Staff member, *Poetry* magazine, 1925-1949; Served in U.S. Army Signal Corps, 1942-1945.

Selected Works: *Boy in the Wind,* 1927. *Flowers of Evil, from the French of Charles Baudelaire* (with Edna St. Vincent Millay), 1936. *Three Plays: An-*

dromache, Britannicus and Phaedra (Translation), 1961.

Other Awards: Guggenheim Fellowship, 1932, 1933.

For More Information: *Benet's Reader's Encyclopedia of American Literature,* New York: Harper-Collins, 1991; *Contemporary Authors,* Detroit: Gale, 1997.

Commentary: George Dillon was awarded the 1932 Pulitzer Prize in Poetry for *The Flowering Stone,* his second collection of poems.

Dillon was born in Jacksonville, Florida. While attending the University of Chicago, he became editor of *Poetry* magazine. His first poetry collection, *Boy in the Wind,* was published in 1927, the year he graduated. He was also known for translating the poetry of Racine and collaborating with Edna St. Vincent Millay on a translation of Baudelaire's *Flowers of Evil.*

1933

Archibald MacLeish
Full entry appears as #**201** under "Drama," 1959.

1934

Robert Hillyer   1015
Birth: June 3, 1895; Orange, NJ. **Death:** 1961. **Education:** Harvard University, MA. University of Copenhagen, The Netherlands. **Spouse:** Dorothy Hancock Tilton (m. 1926; div. 1943). **Children:** One son.

Prize: *Poetry,* 1934: *The Collected Verse of Robert Hillyer,* New York: Knopf, 1933.

Career: Ambulance driver, WWI; Professor, Harvard University, MA, 1919-1944; Assistant Professor, Trinity College, 1926-1928; Chancellor, Academy of American Poets, 1942; Boylston Professor of Rhetoric and Oratory, Harvard University; President, Poetry Society of America, 1949.

Selected Works: *The Five Books of Youth,* 1920. *Alchemy: A Symphonic Poem,* 1920. *The Hills Give Promise,* 1923. *The Halt in the Garden,* 1925. *The Seventh Hill,* 1928. *The Gates of the Compass: A Poem in Four Parts, Together with Twenty-Two Shorter Pieces,* 1930. *Riverhead,* 1932. *Some Roots of English Poetry,* 1933. *A Letter to Robert Frost and Others,* 1937. *First Principles of Verse,* 1938. *In Time of Mistrust,* 1939. *Pattern of a Day,* 1940. *My Heart for Hostage,* 1942. *Poems for Music, 1917-1947,* 1947. *The Death of Captain Nemo: A Narrative Poem,* 1949. *First Principles of Verse,* 1950. *The Suburb by the Sea, New Poems,* 1952. *The Relic & Other Poems,* 1957. *In Pursuit of Poetry,* 1960. *Collected Poems,* 1961.

Other Awards: Garrison Prize for Poetry, 1919. Bollingen Prize, 1948. Honorary MA, Trinity College, 1928.

For More Information: *Benet's Reader's Encyclopedia of American Literature,* New York: Harper-Collins, 1991.

Commentary: Robert Silliman Hillyer was awarded the 1934 Pulitzer Prize in Poetry for *Collected Verse.*

Hillyer was born in New Jersey. He was educated at Harvard University and served in World War I. After the war, he returned to Harvard as a professor. He published many volumes of poetry, mostly in the romanticist style, as well as several novels. He is said to have started a war of words by criticizing the "elitism" of expatriate poets such as Ezra Pound and T.S. Eliot. His other works include *The Death of Captain Nemo* and *Riverhead.*

1935

Audrey Wurdemann   1016
Birth: January 1, 1911; Seattle, WA. **Death:** 1960. **Parents:** Harry and Mary Audrey (Flynn) Wurdemann. **Education:** University of Washington. **Spouse:** Joseph Auslander (m. 1933).

Prize: *Poetry,* 1935: *Bright Ambush,* New York: Day, 1934.

Career: Author; Collaborator with husband on two novels and on poetry series about heroism in WWII.

Selected Works: *The House of Silk,* 1927. *The Seven Sins,* 1935. *Splendor in the Grass,* 1936. *Testament of Love,* 1938. *My Uncle Jan: A Novel* (with Joseph Auslander), 1948. *The Islanders* (with Joseph Auslander), 1951.

For More Information: *Benet's Reader's Encyclopedia of American Literature,* New York: Harper-Collins, 1991.

Commentary: *Bright Ambush* won the 1935 Pulitzer Prize in Poetry for Audrey Wurdemann. It was only her second collection of poetry and she was at the time the youngest winner of a Pulitzer Prize.

Wurdemann was born in Seattle, Washington and attended the University of Washington. She wrote poetry from an early age. Her first collection, *The House of Silk,* was published in 1926. She is also known for another poetry collection, *Splendor in the Grass.* She and her husband, Joseph Auslander, collaborated on several novels, such as *The Islanders.* Wurdemann was a great-great-granddaughter of Percy Bysshe Shelley.

1936

Robert P. Tristram Coffin   1017

Birth: 1892; Brunswick, ME. **Death:** 1955. **Parents:** James W. and Alice M. (Coomb) Coffin. **Education:** Bowdoin College, ME. Princeton University, NJ. Oxford University, England: Rhodes Scholar. **Spouse:** Ruth Neal Philip (m. 1918). **Children:** Mary Alice, Margaret Rollins, Robert Peter Tristram, Richard Neal Coffin.

    Prize: *Poetry,* 1936: *Strange Holiness,* New York, The Macmillan Company, 1935.

    Career: Poet.

    Selected Works: *Christchurch,* 1924. *Book of Crowns and Cottages,* 1925. *Dew and Bronze,* 1927. *An Attic Room,* 1929. *Golden Falcon,* 1929. *Laud, Storm Center of Stuart England,* 1930. *Portrait of an American,* 1931. *The Dukes of Buckingham: Playboys of the Stuart World,* 1931. *The Yoke of Thunder,* 1932. *Ballads of Square-Toed Americans,* 1933. *Lost Paradise: A Boyhood on a Maine Coast Farm,* 1934. *Red Sky in the Morning,* 1935. *John Dawn,* 1936. *Saltwater Farm,* 1937. *Kennebec, Cradle of Americans,* 1937. *Maine Ballads,* 1938. *New Poetry of New England: Frost and Robinson,* 1938. *Collected Poems of Robert P. Tristram Coffin,* 1939. *Captain Abby and Captain John: An Around-the-World Biography,* 1939. *Thomas-Thomas-Ancil-Thomas,* 1941. *Christmas in Maine,* 1942. *There Will Be Bread and Love,* 1942. *The Substance That Is Poetry,* 1942. *Book of Uncles,* 1942. *Primer for America,* 1943. *Mainstays of Maine,* 1944. *Poems for a Son with Wings,* 1945. *People Behave Like Ballads,* 1946. *Yankee Coast,* 1947. *Collected Poems,* 1948. *One-Horse Farm: Down-East Georgics,* 1949. *The Third Hunger, & The Poem Aloud,* 1949. *Apples by Ocean,* 1950. *Maine Doings,* 1950. *On the Green Carpet,* 1951. *New England,* 1951. *Selected Poems,* 1955.

    For More Information: Sanborn, Annie Coffin, *The Life of Robert Peter Tristram Coffin and Family,* Alton, NH: 1963; Swain, Raymond Charles, *A Breath of Maine: Portrait of Robert P. Tristram Coffin,* Boston: Branden, 1967.

    Commentary: Robert P. Tristram Coffin was awarded the 1936 Pulitzer Prize in Poetry for *Strange Holiness,* his third volume of verse.

    Coffin was born in Brunswick, Maine. He was educated at Bowdoin College and Princeton University, and was a Rhodes Scholar at Oxford University in England. He later taught at Wells and Bowdoin colleges. He ran two farms in addition to publishing poetry and prose. He also created drawings for his books. He was a New Englander in his verse and lifestyle. His other works included *Ballads of Square-Toed Americans* and *Mainstays of Maine.*

1937

Robert Frost

Full entry appears as **#1009** under "Poetry," 1924.

1938

Marya Zaturenska   1018

Birth: September 12, 1902; Kiev, Russia. **Death:** January 19, 1982. **Parents:** Avram Alexander and Johanna (Lupovska) Zaturensky. **Education:** Valparaiso University, IN. University of Wisconsin. **Spouse:** Horace Gregory (m. 1925). **Children:** Joanna (Mrs. Samuel Howell Zeigler), Patrick.

    Prize: *Poetry,* 1938: *Cold Morning Sky,* New York: Macmillan, 1937.

    Career: Writer, 1919-1982.

    Selected Works: *Threshold and Hearth,* 1934. *The Listening Landscape,* 1941. *The Golden Mirror,* 1944. *A History of American Poetry, 1900-1940* (with Horace Gregory), 1946. *Christina Rossetti: A Portrait with Background,* 1949. *Selected Poems,* 1954. *Collected Poems,* 1965. *The Silver Swan: Poems of Romance and Mystery* (with Horace Gregory), 1966. *Selected Poems of Christina Rossetti* (Zaturenska, Marya, ed.), 1970. *The Hidden Waterfall: Poems,* 1974.

    Other Awards: John Reed Memorial Award, *Poetry* magazine, 1922. Shelley Memorial Award, 1935. Guarantors Award, *Poetry* magazine, 1937. Honorary PhD, University of Wisconsin, 1977.

    For More Information: *Benet's Reader's Encyclopedia of American Literature,* New York: HarperCollins, 1991.

    Commentary: Marya Zaturenska was awarded the 1938 Pulitzer Prize in Poetry for *Cold Morning Sky.*

    Zaturenska was born in Kiev, Russia. She immigrated with her family to the United States in 1909 and was naturalized in 1912. She married a poet and a critic, Horace Gregory. Zaturenska wrote a biography of Christina Rosetti (1834-1890), the pre-Raphaelite British poet. She and her husband collaborated on *A History of American Poetry, 1900-1940* which was published in 1946.

1939

John Gould Fletcher   1019

Birth: January 3, 1886; Little Rock, AR. **Death:** May 20, 1950. **Parents:** John Gould and Adolphone (Krause) Fletcher. **Spouse:** Florence Emily Arbuthnot (m. 1916); Charlie May Hogie (m. 1936).

Prize: *Poetry,* 1939: *Selected Poems,* New York: Farrar & Rinehart, 1938.

Career: Author and poet.

Selected Works: *Irradiations, Sand and Spray,* 1915. *Goblins and Pagodas,* 1916. *Tendencies in Modern American Poetry,* 1917. *Japanese Prints,* 1918. *The Tree of Life,* 1918. *Breakers and Granite,* 1921. *Preludes and Symphonies,* 1922. *Parables,* 1925. *The Black Rock,* 1928. *John Smith—Also Pocahontas,* 1928. *Preludes and Symphonies,* 1930. *The Two Frontiers: A Study in Historical Psychology,* 1930. *XXIV Elegies,* 1935. *Life Is My Song: The Autobiography of John Gould Fletcher,* 1937. *South Star,* 1941. *The Burning Mountain,* 1946. *Arkansas,* 1947. *The Autobiography of John Gould Fletcher: Originally Life Is My Song* (Carpenter, Lucas, ed.), 1988.

For More Information: Simon, Charlie May Hogue, *Johnswood,* New York: Dutton, 1953; Stephens, Edna B., *John Gould Fletcher,* New York: Twayne, 1967; Carpenter, Lucas, *John Gould Fletcher and Southern Modernism,* Fayetteville: University of Arkansas Press, 1990. Johnson, Ben F., *Fierce Solitude: A Life of John Gould Fletcher,* Fayetteville: University of Arkansas Press, 1994.

Commentary: *Selected Poems* won the 1939 Pulitzer Prize in Poetry for John Gould Fletcher.

Fletcher was born in Little Rock, Arkansas and he attended Harvard University. After he left the university, he lived in London and was influenced in several directions, but became associated with the imagist school of poetry and Amy Lowell, developing a style known as polyphonic prose. This style contained many poetic devices employed with a rhythm that was not strictly metered. Lowell helped him to find an American publisher for his first book of verse *Irradiations: Sand and Spray.* Fletcher returned to Arkansas in 1933. Included in his many works are a biography (published while still in England) of Paul Gauguin, and a history of his home state, *Arkansas.*

1940

Mark Van Doren   1020

Birth: June 13, 1894; Hope, IL. **Death:** December 10, 1972. **Parents:** Charles Lucius and Dora Ann (Butz) Van Doren. **Education:** University of Illinois: AB, AM. Columbia University, NY: PhD. **Spouse:** Dorothy Graffe (m. 1922). **Children:** Charles, John.

Prize: *Poetry,* 1940: *Collected Poems, 1922-1938,* New York: Holt, 1939.

Career: Served as member of Infantry, U.S. Army, WWI; Instructor, Columbia University, NY, 1920-1924; Assistant Professor, Columbia University, NY, 1924-1935; Associate Professor, Columbia University, NY, 1935-1942; Lecturer, St. John's College, MD, 1937-1957; Participant, "Invitation to Learning," CBS radio talk show, 1940-1942; Professor of English, Columbia University, NY, 1942-1959; Visiting Professor of English, Harvard University, MA, 1963; Member: American Academy of Arts and Letters, National Institute of Arts and Letters.

Selected Works: *Henry David Thoreau: A Critical Study,* 1916. *The Poetry of John Dryden,* 1920. *Spring Thunder, and Other Poems,* 1924. *American and British Literature Since 1890* (with Carl Van Doren), 1925. *7 p.m. and Other Poems,* 1926. *Edwin Arlington Robinson,* 1927. *An Anthology of English and American Poetry* (Van Doren, Mark, ed.), 1928. *Now the Sky, & Other Poems,* 1928. *Correspondence of Aaron Burr and His Daughter Theodosia* (Van Doren, Mark, ed.), 1929. *An Anthology of World Poetry* (Van Doren, Mark, ed.), 1929. *A Junior Anthology of World Poetry* (Van Doren, Mark, ed.), 1929. *The Life of Sir William Phips, by Cotton Mather* (Van Doren, Mark, ed.), 1929. *An Autobiography of America,* 1929. *Jonathan Gentry,* 1931. *American Poets, 1630-1930* (Van Doren, Mark, ed.), 1932. *The Transients,* 1935. *A Winter Diary and Other Poems,* 1935. *Windless Cabins,* 1940. *The Transparent Tree,* 1940. *The Travels of William Bartram,* 1940. *The Mayfield Deer,* 1941. *The Private Reader: Selected Articles & Reviews,* 1942. *Our Lady Peace: And Other War Poems,* 1942. *Liberal Education,* 1943. *Tilda,* 1943. *Dick and Tom, Tales of Two Ponies,* 1943. *The Seven Sleepers, and Other Poems,* 1944. *Walt Whitman* (Van Doren, Mark, ed.), 1945. *The Portable Emerson* (Van Doren, Mark, ed.), 1946. *The Country Year: Poems,* 1946. *The Noble Voice: A Study of Ten Great Poems,* 1946. *The Careless Clock: Poems about Children in the Family,* 1947. *The World's Best Poems* (Van Doren, Mark, and Lapolla, Garibaldi M., eds.), 1947. *New Poems,* 1948. *Nathaniel Hawthorne,* 1949. *Short Stories,* 1950. *Introduction to Poetry,* 1951. *Nobody Say a Word, and Other Stories,* 1953. *Spring Birth, and Other Poems,* 1953. *Mortal Summer,* 1953. *Man's Right to Knowledge and the Free Use Thereof,* 1954. *Selected Poems,* 1954. *Home with Hazel, and Other Stories,* 1957. *Autobiography,* 1958. *Don Quixote's Profession,* 1958. *The Mayfield Deer,* 1959. *The Last Days of Lincoln: A Play in Six Scenes,* 1959. *Morning Worship, and Other Poems,* 1960. *The Happy Critic, and Other Essays,* 1961. *Samuel Sewall's Diary* (Van Doren, Mark, ed.), 1963. *Narrative Poems,* 1964. *The Dialogues of Archibald MacLeish and Mark Van Doren* (Bush, Warren V., ed.), 1964. *Somebody Came,* 1966. *Three Plays: Never, Never Ask His Name; A Little Night Music; The Weekend That Was,* 1966. *That Shining Place,* 1969. *Good Morning: Last Poems,* 1973. *The Selected Letters of Mark Van Doren* (Hendrick, George, ed.), 1987. *Collected Stories,* 1962-1968.

Other Awards: St. John's College Fellowship, 1959. Alexander Hamilton Medal, Columbia College, 1959. Sarah Josepha Hale Award, Richards Free Library, Newport, NH, 1960. Golden Rose Award, New England Poetry Society, 1960. Brotherhood Award, National Conference of Christians and Jews, 1960. Creativity Award, Huntington Hartford Foundation, 1962. Emerson-Thoreau Award, American Academy of Arts and Sciences, 1963. Academy of American Poets Fellowship, 1967. Honorary LittDs: Bowdoin College, ME, 1944; University of Illinois, 1958; Columbia University, NY, 1960; Knox College, MA, 1966; Harvard University, MA, 1966; Jewish Theological Seminary of America, NY, 1970. Honorary LHDs: Adelphi University, NY, 1957; Mount Mary College, WI, 1965. Honorary MD, Connecticut State Medical Society, 1966.

For More Information: *Benet's Reader's Encyclopedia of American Literature,* New York: Harper-Collins, 1991.

Commentary: Mark Van Doren was awarded the 1940 Pulitzer Prize in Poetry for *Collected Poems.*

Van Doren was born in Hope, Illinois. He was the brother of the Pulitzer Prize-winning author, Carl Van Doren. He was educated at the University of Illinois and at Columbia University. He was a poet, a teacher, a critic, and an editor. He was literary editor and film critic for the *Nation* during the 1920s. As a critic, he wrote insightful biographies of Shakespeare, Henry David Thoreau, and Nathaniel Hawthorne. He also produced a collection of short stories, *Nobody Say a Word.*

1941

Leonard Bacon   1021

Birth: May 26, 1887; Solvay, NY. **Death:** January 1, 1954. **Parents:** N.T. and Helen (Hazard) Bacon. **Education:** Yale University, CT: BA. **Children:** Three children.

Prize: *Poetry,* 1941: *Sunderland Capture, and Other Poems,* New York: Harper & Brothers, 1940.

Career: English Teacher, University of California, 1910-1923.

Selected Works: *The Scrannel Pipe: A Book of Verse,* 1909. *Ulug Beg: An Epic Poem, Comic in Intention, in VII Cantos; Being the History of the Origin, Progress, and Explosion of a Superstition. By Autolycus, a Snapper-Up of Unconsidered Trifles,* 1923. *Ph.D.s, Male and Female Created He Them,* 1925. *Guinea-Fowl and Other Poultry,* 1927. *The Legend of Quincibald,* 1928. *Lost Buffalo, and Other Poems,* 1930. *The Furioso,* 1932. *Dream and Action,* 1934. *The Voyage of Autoleon: A Fantastic Epic,* 1935. *Rhyme and Punishment,* 1936. *The Goose on the Capitol,* 1936. *Bullinger Bound and Other Poems,* 1938. *Day of Fire,* 1943. *The Lusiads* (Translation), 1950.

For More Information: *Benet's Reader's Encyclopedia of American Literature,* New York: Harper-Collins, 1991.

Commentary: Leonard Bacon was awarded the 1941 Pulitzer Prize in Poetry for *Sunderland Capture.*

Bacon was born in Solvay, New York and attended Yale University. He began his career teaching at the University of California. He left teaching in 1923 to write full time. He published many works of poetry, most noted for a satiric style, including *The Legend of Quincibald* and *Rhyme and Punishment.* He wrote an autobiography, *Semi-centennial, Some of the Life and Part of the Opinions of Leonard Bacon.*

1942

William Rose Benet   1022

Birth: February 2, 1889; Fort Hamilton, NY. **Death:** May 4, 1950. **Parents:** James Walker and Frances Neill (Rose) Benet. **Education:** Yale University, CT. **Spouse:** Teresa Frances Thompson (m. 1912; died 1919); Elinor Wylie (m. 1923; died 1928); Lora Baxter (m. 1932; div. 1937); Marjorie Flack (m. 1941). **Children:** Three children.

Prize: *Poetry,* 1942: *The Dust Which Is God,* New York: Dodd, Mead, 1941.

Career: Office boy, *Century,* NY, 1911-1914; Assistant Editor, *Century,* NY, 1914-1918; Writer, advertising, NY, 1919; Staff, *Nation's Business,* Washington, DC, 1920; Co-Founder, *Literary Review,* 1920; Co-Founder, *Saturday Review of Literature,* NY, 1924; Associate Editor, *Saturday Review of Literature,* 1924-1929; Contributing Editor and Columnist, "The Phoenix Nest," *Saturday Review of Literature,* 1929-1950.

Selected Works: *Merchants from Cathay,* 1913. *The Falconer of God: And Other Poems,* 1914. *The East I Know, by Paul Claudel* (Translation) (with Teresa Frances), 1914. *The Burglar of the Zodiac, and Other Poems,* 1918. *Perpetual Light: A Memorial,* 1919. *Moons of Grandeur: A Book of Poems,* 1920. *The First Person Singular,* 1922. *Poems for Youth: An American Anthology,* 1925. *The Flying King of Kurio: A Story for Children,* 1926. *Wild Goslings: A Selection of Fugitive Pieces,* 1927. *Man Possessed,* 1927. *Rip Tide: A Novel in Verse,* 1932. *Starry Harness,* 1933. *Fifty Poets: An American Auto-Anthology* (Benet, William Rose, ed.), 1933. *Golden Fleece: A Collection of Poems and Ballads Old and New,* 1935. *Harlem and Other Poems,* 1935. *Poems for Modern Youth* (Benet, William Rose, and Gillis, Adolph, eds.), 1938. *The Oxford Anthology of American Literature* (Benet, William Rose, ed.), 1938. *With Wings as Eagles: Poems and Ballads of the Air,* 1940. *Day of Deliverance: A Book of Poems in Wartime,* 1944. *The Poetry of Freedom* (Benet, William Rose, and Cousins, Norman, eds.), 1945. *The Reader's Encyclopedia: An Encyclopedia of World Literature and the Arts* (Benet, William Rose, ed.), 1948. *The Spirit of the Scene,* 1951. *The Reader's Encyclopedia,* 1965. *Benet's Reader's Encyclopedia,* 1987.

For More Information: *Benet's Reader's Encyclopedia of American Literature,* New York: HarperCollins,1991; *Cambridge Biographical Encyclopedia,* New York: Cambridge University Press, 1995; *Contemporary Authors,* Detroit: Gale, 1997.

Commentary: *The Dust Which Is God,* an autobiographical novel in verse, won the 1942 Pulitzer Prize in Poetry for Willliam Rose Benet.

Benet was born in Fort Hamilton, New York. He was the brother of Stephen Vincent Benet, who was also a Pulitzer Prize-winning poet. William was educated at Yale University. He was married to the poet and novelist, Elinor Wylie. Benet was known for an exuberant and romantic style. His works include *Merchants of Cathay* and *Moons of Grandeur.* He is well-known for his *Reader's Encyclopedia of American Literature.*

1943

Robert Frost

Full entry appears as **#1009** under "Poetry," 1924.

1944

Stephen Vincent Benet

Full entry appears as **#1012** under "Poetry," 1929.

1945

Karl Shapiro   1023

Birth: November 10, 1913; Baltimore, MD. **Parents:** Joseph and Sarah (Omansky) Shapiro. **Education:** University of Virginia. Johns Hopkins University, MD. Enoch Pratt Library School, MD. **Spouse:** Evalyn Katz (m. 1945; div. 1967); Teri Kovach (m. 1967; div. 1982); Sophie Wilkins (m. 1985). **Children:** Katharine, John Jacob, Elizabeth (EK).

Prize: *Poetry,* 1945: *V-Letter, and Other Poems,* New York: Reynal & Hitchcock, 1944.

Career: Served in U.S. Army, 1941-1945; Consultant in Poetry, Library of Congress, Washington, DC, 1946-1947; Associate Professor of Writing, Johns Hopkins University, MD, 1947-1950; Visiting Professor, University of Wisconsin, 1948; Member, Bollingen Prize Committee, 1949; Editor, *Poetry,* Chicago, 1950-1956; Visiting Professor, Loyola University, 1951-1952; Visiting Professor, Salzburg Seminar in American Studies, 1952; U.S. Department of State Lecturer, India, summer, 1955; Visiting Professor, University of California, 1955-1956; Visiting Professor, University of Indiana, 1956-1957; Professor of English, University of Nebraska, Lincoln, 1956-1966; Professor of English, University of Illinois at Chicago Circle, 1966-1968; Professor of English, University of California, Davis, 1968-1985; Honorary Member, American Academy of Arts and Sciences; Member: National Institute of Arts and Letters, Phi Beta Kappa, PEN.

Selected Works: *Person, Place and Thing,* 1942. *Essay on Rime,* 1945. *Trial of a Poet: And Other Poems,* 1947. *A Bibliography of Modern Prosody,* 1948. *Poems, 1940-1953,* 1953. *A Primer for Poets,* 1953. *Poems of a Jew,* 1958. *American Poetry,* 1960. *In Defense of Ignorance,* 1960. *Prose Keys to Modern Poetry,* 1962. *The Bourgeois Poet,* 1964. *A Prosody Handbook* (with Robert Beum), 1965. *To Abolish Children, and Other Essays,* 1968. *Selected Poems,* 1968. *White-Haired Lover,* 1968. *Edsel,* 1971. *The Poetry Wreck: Selected Essays, 1950-1970,* 1975. *Adult Bookstore,* 1976. *Collected Poems, 1940-1978,* 1978. *Adam & Eve,* 1986. *New & Selected Poems, 1940-1986,* 1987. *Poet: An Autobiography in Three Parts,* 1988. *The Old Horsefly,* 1992.

Other Awards: Fellow in American Letters, Library of Congress. Jeanette S. Davis Prize, 1942. Levinson Prize, 1942. *Contemporary Poetry* Prize, 1943. American Academy of Arts and Letters Grant, 1944. Shelley Memorial Prize, 1946. Guggenheim Fellowship, 1944, 1953. Kenyon School of Letters Fellowship, 1956-1957. Eunice Tietjens Memorial Prize, 1961. Oscar Blumenthal Prize, Poetry, 1963. Bollingen Prize, 1968. Robert Kirsch Award, *Los Angeles Times,* 1989. Charity Randall Citation, 1990.

For More Information: White, William, *Karl Shapiro: A Bibliography,* Detroit: Wayne State University, 1960; Reino, Joseph, *Karl Shapiro,* Boston: Twayne, 1981.

Commentary: Karl Shapiro was awarded the 1945 Pulitzer Prize in Poetry for *V-Letter and Other Poems,* a collection written while he served in the Pacific during World War II.

Shapiro was born in Baltimore, Maryland. He was educated at the University of Virginia and Johns Hopkins University, and also attended library school. His first poetry collection was published in 1935, *Poems.* Early in his career he wrote in rhymed stanzas. Later he employed a free prose verse style. Besides poetry, Shapiro wrote a number of essays and criticisms including *Prose Keys to Modern Poetry* and *The Poetry Wreck: Selected Essays 1950-1970.*

1946
No award

1947

Robert Lowell   1024

Birth: March 1, 1917; Boston, MA. **Death:** September 12, 1977. **Parents:** Robert Traill Spence and Charlotte (Winslow) Lowell. **Education:** Harvard University, MA. Kenyon College, OH: AB, summa cum laude. Louisiana State University. **Spouse:** Jean Stafford (m. 1940; div. 1948); Elizabeth Hardwick (m. 1949; div. 1972); Caroline Blackwood (m. 1972). **Children:** Harriet Winslow (EH); Robert Sheridan (CB).

Prize: *Poetry,* 1947: *Lord Weary's Castle,* New York: Harcourt, Brace, 1946. *Poetry,* 1974: *The Dolphin,* New York: Farrar, Straus and Giroux, 1973.

Career: Poet, writer, and translator; Editorial Assistant, Sheed & Ward, NY, 1941-1942; Conscientious objector, WWII, served prison term as a result, 1943-1945; Consultant in Poetry, Library of Congress, Washington, DC, 1947-1948; Instructor, State University of Iowa, 1950 and 1953; Instructor, Kenyon School of Letters, 1950 and 1953; Instructor, Salzburg Seminar on American Studies (Salzburg, Austria), 1952; Instructor, University of Cincinnati, 1954; Instructor, Boston University, 1956; Instructor, Harvard University, 1958, 1963-70, 1975, and 1977; Instructor, New School for Social Research, 1961-1962; Writer-in-Residence, Yale University, 1967; Instructor, University of Essex (Wivenhoe, Colchester, England), 1970-1972; Instructor, Kent University (Canterbury, England), 1970-1975; Visiting Fellow, All Souls College, Oxford, 1970; Member: American Academy of Arts and Letters, National Academy and Institute of Arts and Letters, Phi Beta Kappa.

Selected Works: *Prelude to Summer, Two Poems,* 1939. *Poems, 1938-1949,* 1950. *The Mills of the Kavanaughs,* 1951. *Life Studies,* 1959. *Imitations,*

1961. *For the Union Dead,* 1964. *The Old Glory,* 1965. *The Old Glory* (Play), 1965. *Near the Ocean,* 1967. *The Voyage, and Other Versions of Poems by Baudelaire,* 1968. *Prometheus Bound. Derived from Aeschylus,* 1969. *For Lizzie and Harriet,* 1973. *The Dolphin,* 1973. *History,* 1973. *Selected Poems,* 1976. *Day by Day,* 1977. *The Oresteia of Aeschylus* (Translation), 1978. *Collected Prose* (Giroux, Robert, ed.), 1987.

Other Awards: National Institute of Arts and Letters Award, 1947. Guggenheim Fellowship, 1947. Harriet Monroe Poetry Award, University of Chicago, 1952. Co-Winner, Guinness Poetry Award, Ireland, 1959: "Skunk Hour." National Book Award, 1960: *Life Studies,* New York: Farrar, Straus and Cudahy, 1959. Boston Arts Festival Poet, 1960. Harriet Monroe Memorial Prize, Poetry, 1961. Bollingen Prize in Poetry Translation, Yale University Library, 1962: *Imitations.* New York: Farrar, Straus and Cudahy, 1961. Levinson Prize, 1963. Golden Rose Trophy, New England Poetry Club, 1964. Obie Award, Best New Play, *Village Voice,* 1965: *The Old Glory,* New York: Farrar, Straus & Giroux, 1965. Sarah Josepha Hale Award, Friends of the Richards Library, 1966. National Council on the Arts Grant, 1967: *Prometheus Bound,* New York: Farrar, Straus & Giroux, 1969. Copernicus Award, Academy of American Poets, 1974. National Medal for Literature, National Academy and Institute of Arts and Letters, 1977. National Book Critics Circle Award, 1978: *Day by Day,* New York: Farrar, Straus and Giroux, 1977. Honorary LittDs: Williams College, MA, 1965; Yale University, CT, 1968. Honorary Degree, Columbia University, NY, 1969.

For More Information: Kunitz, Stanley, ed., *Robert Lowell, Poet of Terribilit,* New York: Pierpont Morgan Library, 1974; Axelrod, Steven Gould, *Robert Lowell: Life and Art,* Princeton, NJ: Princeton University Press, 1978; Hamilton, Ian, *Robert Lowell: A Biography,* New York: Random House, 1982; Rudman, Mark, *Robert Lowell: An Introduction to the Poetry,* New York: Columbia University Press, 1983; Bell, Vereen M., *Robert Lowell, Nihilist as Hero,* Cambridge, MA: Harvard University Press, 1983; Meyers, Jeffrey, ed., *Robert Lowell, Interviews and Memoirs,* Ann Arbor: University of Michigan Press, 1988; Doreski, William, *The Years of Our Friendship: Robert Lowell and Allen Tate,* Jackson: University Press of Mississippi, 1990; Tillinghast, Richard, *Robert Lowell's Life and Work: Damaged Grandeur,* Ann Arbor: University of Michigan, 1995; Hart, Henry, *Robert Lowell and the Sublime,* Syracuse, NY: Syracuse University Press, 1995.

Commentary: Robert Lowell was awarded two Pulitzer Prizes, both in Poetry. He won in 1947 for his first published volume, *Lord Weary's Castle,* which contains the much-acclaimed poem "The Quaker

Graveyard in Nantucket." He won again in 1974 for *The Dolphin,* an autobiographical verse collection.

Lowell was born in Boston into the distinguished Lowell family whose members included Amy Lowell, James Russell Lowell, and Robert's grandfather, Robert Traill Spence Lowell. He was educated at Harvard University, Kenyon College, and Louisiana State University. During his time at the latter two schools, Lowell befriended John Crowe Ransom, Cleanth Brooks, and Robert Penn Warren and he met and married the novelist Jean Stafford. He was a conscientious objector during World War II and served a prison term as a result from 1943 to 1944. Lowell was influenced by many of the leading modernist poets and he in turn left an indelible mark on his own generation. His poetry spanned three marriages, various teaching positions and trips to and from Europe, and reflects his personal life, moods, and psychological themes.

1948

W. H. Auden 1025

Birth: February 21, 1907; York, England. **Death:** September 28, 1973. **Parents:** George Augustus and Constance Rosalie (Bicknell) Auden. **Religion:** Episcopalian. **Education:** Oxford University, England. **Spouse:** Erika Mann (m. 1935; div).

Prize: *Poetry,* 1948: *The Age of Anxiety,* New York: Random House, 1947.

Career: Poet, playwright, librettist, critic, editor, and translator; Schoolmaster, Larchfield Academy, Helensburgh, Scotland and Downs School, Colwall near Malvern, England, 1930-1935; Co-Founder, The Group Theatre, 1932; General Post Office Film Unit Member, 1935; Stretcher-bearer, Loyalists, Spanish Revolution, 1937; Teacher, St. Mark's School, Southborough, MA, 1939-1940; Faculty member, American Writers League Writers School, 1939; Instructor, New School for Social Research, 1940-1941 and 1946-1947; Faculty member, University of Michigan, 1941-1942; Faculty member, Swarthmore College, 1942-1945; Faculty member, Bryn Mawr College, 1943-1945; Faculty member, Bennington College, 1946; Faculty member, Barnard College, 1947; Co-Founder, Reader's Subscription Book Club, 1951; Contributor, *The Griffin,* Reader's Subscription Book Club, 1951-1958; W. A. Neilson Research Professor, Smith College, MA, 1953; Professor of Poetry, Oxford University, Oxford, England, 1956-1961; Co-Founder, Mid-Century Book Society, 1959; Contributor, *The Mid-Century,* Mid-Century Book Society, 1959-1963; Member, American Academy of Arts and Letters.

Selected Works: *The Orators: An English Study,* 1932. *The Dance of Death,* 1933. *Poems,* 1933. *The Orators: An English Study,* 1934. *A Tragedy in Two Acts: The Ascent of F6,* 1936. *Look, Stranger!,* 1936. *Letters from Iceland* (with Louis MacNiece), 1937. *On This Island,* 1937. *Spain,* 1937. *Poems,* 1934. *On the Frontier: A Melodrama in Three Acts* (with Christopher Isherwood), 1938. *Selected Poems,* 1938. *The Oxford Book of Light Verse* (Auden, W. H., ed.), 1938. *The Poet's Tongue: An Anthology* (with John Garrett), 1938. *Journey to a War* (with Christopher Isherwood), 1939. *Love Letter,* 1939. *On the Frontier: A Melodrama in Three Acts* (with Christopher Isherwood), 1938. *Another Time: Poems,* 1940. *Some Poems,* 1940. *New Year Letter,* 1941. *The Double Man,* 1941. *For the Time Being,* 1945. *The Collected Poetry of W.H. Auden,* 1945. *The Portable Greek Reader* (Auden, W. H., ed.), 1948. *Collected Shorter Poems, 1930-1944,* 1950. *Poets of the English Language* (Auden, W. H., and Pearson, Norman H., eds.), 1950. *The Enchafd Flood; or, The Romantic Iconography of the Sea,* 1950. *Keats in His Letters,* 1951. *The Living Thoughts of Kierkegaard,* 1952. *The Shield of Achilles,* 1955. *The Criterion Book of Modern American Verse,* 1956. *Selected Writings* (Auden, W. H., ed.), 1956. *The Poet's Tongue: An Anthology* (with John Garrett), 1957. *Thinking What We Are Doing,* 1959. *Homage to Clio,* 1960. *The Viking Book of Aphorisms* (with Louis Kronenberger), 1962. *The Dyer's Hand, and Other Essays,* 1962. *On Goethe: For a New Translation,* 1962. *Strachey's Cry,* 1962. *A Change of Air,* 1962. *Going into Europe,* 1963. *Iceland Revisited,* 1964. *About the House,* 1965. *Since,* 1965. *19th Century British Minor Poets* (Auden, W.H., ed.), 1966. *Collected Shorter Poems, 1927-1957,* 1966. *Insignificant Elephants,* 1966. *A Cobble Poem, Snatched from the Notebooks of W. H. Auden & Now Believed to Be in the Morgan Library,* 1967. *Selected Poems,* 1968. *Two Songs,* 1968. *City without Walls, and Other Poems,* 1969. *Collected Longer Poems,* 1969. *G. K. Chesterton: A Selection from His Non-Fictional Prose* (Auden, W.H., ed.), 1970. *Academic Graffiti,* 1971. *Epistle to a Godson, and Other Poems,* 1972. *Wystan Hugh Auden, 1907-1973: Memorial Service, Wednesday, October 3, 1973, 8:00 p.m.,* 1973. *Forewords and Afterwords,* 1973. *A Choice of Dryden's Verse* (Auden, W.H., ed.), 1973. *Thank You, Fog: Last Poems,* 1974. *That Night When Joy,* 1982. *What's in Your Mind,* 1982. *To You Simply,* 1982. *Let the Florid Music,* 1982. *Three Unpublished Poems,* 1986. *The Language of Learning and the Language of Love: Uncollected Writing, New Interpretations* (Bucknell, Katherine, and Jenkins, Nicholas, eds.), 1994. *In Solitude, for Company: W.H. Auden after 1940; Unpublished Prose and Recent Criticism* (Bucknell, Katherine, and Jenkins, Nicholas, eds.), 1995. *Prose and Travel Books in Prose and Verse,* 1996.

Other Awards: King's Gold Medal for Poetry, 1937. Guggenheim Fellowship, 1942, 1945. Award of Merit Medal, American Academy of Arts and Letters, 1945. Bollingen Prize in Poetry, 1954. National Book Award, 1956: *The Shield of Achilles*. Feltrinelli Prize, Rome, 1957. Alexander Droutzkoy Memorial Award, 1959. Co-Recipient, Guinness Poetry Award, Ireland, 1959 Chicago Poetry Day, Honored, 1960. Honorary Fellow, Christ College, Oxford University, 1962-1973. Austrian State Prize for European Literature, 1966. National Medal for Literature, National Book Committee, 1967. Gold Medal, National Institute of Arts and Letters, 1968.

For More Information: Spender, Stephen, *Wystan Hugh Auden, 1907-1973,* New York: American Academy of Arts and Letters and The National Institute of Arts and Letters, 1974; Spender, ed., *W.H. Auden: A Tribute,* London, England: Weidenfeld and Nicolson, 1975; Gingerich, Martin E., *W.H. Auden: A Reference Guide,* Boston: Hall, 1977; Miller, Charles H., *Auden, An American Friendship,* New York: Scribners, 1983; Farnan, Dorothy J., *Auden in Love,* New York: Simon & Schuster, 1984; Rowse, A. L., *The Poet Auden: A Personal Memoir,* London, England: Methuen, 1987; Boly, John R., *Reading Auden: The Returns of Caliban,* Ithaca, NY: Cornell University Press, 1991; Hecht, Anthony, *The Hidden Law: The Poetry of W.H. Auden,* Cambridge, MA: Harvard University Press, 1993; Davenport-Hines, R.P.T., *Auden,* New York: Pantheon, 1995; Smith, Stan, *W.H. Auden,* Plymouth, England: Northcote House, 1997.

Commentary: Wystan Hugh Auden was awarded the 1948 Pulitzer Prize in Poetry for *The Age of Anxiety: A Baroque Eclogue.*

Auden was born in York, North Yorkshire, England. He was educated at Christ Church, Oxford, England. He married Erika Mann, the daughter of Thomas Mann, in 1935 to secure a passport for her out of Nazi Germany. He was a leftist who fought on the Republican side in the Spanish Civil War, and wrote *Spain.* He had an enduring relationship with Christopher Isherwood, with whom he collaborated on three plays. He and Isherwood travelled to China and together wrote *Journey to a War,* published in 1939. They immigrated together to New York in 1939 and Auden was naturalized in 1946. His Anglo-Catholic faith grew more devout as he grew older. He taught poetry at American colleges and was professor of poetry at Oxford from 1956 to 1961. He is most noted for his collections, *Another Time* and *The Shield of Achilles.* Auden also wrote opera librettos for the composer Chester Kallman, with whom he lived for over 20 years.

1949

Peter Viereck   1026

Birth: August 5, 1916; New York, NY. **Parents:** George Sylvester and Margaret (Hein) Viereck. **Education:** Harvard University, MA: BS, summa cum laude: MA, PhD. Christ Church, Oxford University, England: Henry Fellow. **Spouse:** Anya de Markov (m. 1945; div. 1970); Betty Martin Falkenberg (m. 1972). **Children:** John-Alexis, Valerie Edwina (Mrs. John Gibbs) (ADM).

Prize: *Poetry,* 1949: *Terror and Decorum: Poems, 1940-1948,* New York: Scribners, 1948.

Career: Served in the U.S. Army, Psychological Warfare, 1943-1945; History Teacher, U.S. Army University, Florence, Italy, 1945; Instructor in German Literature, Tutor in History and Literature, Harvard University, MA, 1946-1947; Assistant Professor of History, Smith College, MA, 1947-1948; Visiting Lecturer in Russian History, Smith College, MA, 1948-49; Mount Holyoke College, South Hadley, MA, Associate Professor, 1948-1955; Whittal Lecturer in Poetry, Library of Congress, 1954, 1963; Fulbright Professor in American Poetry and Civilization, University of Florence, 1955; Professor, Modern European and Russian History, 1955-1965; Elliston Chair, Poetry Lecturer, University of Cincinnati, 1956; Visiting Lecturer, University of California, Berkeley, 1957, 1964; Researcher of History, Rockefeller Foundation, Germany, summer, 1958; U.S. State Department Cultural Exchange, Russia, 1961; Visiting Research Scholar in Russia for Twentieth Century Fund, 1962-1963; Visiting Lecturer, City College of the City University of New York, 1964; Director of Poetry Workshop, New York Writers Conference, 1965-1967; Mount Holyoke Alumnae Foundation Chair of Interpretive Studies, 1965-1979; William R. Kenan Chair of History, Mount Holyoke College, beginning in 1979; Member of Executive Committee, American Committee for Cultural Freedom; Charter Member, Committee for Basic Education; Member: American Historical Association, Oxford Society, PEN, Poetry Society of America, Phi Beta Kappa, Harvard Club (NY), Harvard Club (London, England), Bryce Club (Oxford, England).

Selected Works: *Metapolitics: From the Romantics to Hitler,* 1941. *Conservatism Revisited: The Revolt against Revolt, 1815-1949,* 1949. *Strike through the Mask! New Lyrical Poems,* 1950. *The First Morning, New Poems,* 1952. *Shame and Glory of the Intellectuals: Babbitt Jr. vs. the Rediscovery of Values,* 1953. *Dream and Responsibility: Four Test Cases of the Tension between Poetry and Society,* 1953. *The Unadjusted Man, a New Hero for Americans: Reflections on the Distinction between Conforming and Conserving,* 1956. *Inner Liberty: The Stubborn Grit* *in the Machine,* 1957. *The Tree Witch: A Poem and Play,* 1961. *Metapolitics: The Roots of the Nazi Mind (Revised and Updated),* 1961. *Conservatism Revisited (Revised and Enlarged),* 1962. *New and Selected Poems, 1932-1967,* 1967. *Tide and Continuities: Last and First Poems, 1995-1938,* 1995.

Other Awards: Two Battle Stars, WWII. Eunice Tietjens Prize for Poetry, 1948. Guggenheim Fellowship, Rome, 1949-1950. Most Distinguished Alumnus Award, Horace Mann School for Boys, 1958. National Endowment for the Humanities Senior Research Fellow, 1969. Poetry Award of the Massachusetts Artists Foundation, 1978. Sadin Prize, Lyrical Poetry, *New York Quarterly,* 1980. Golden Rose Award of the New England Poetry Club, 1981. Varoujan Poetry Prize of the New England Poetry Club, 1983. Ingram Merrill Foundation Fellow in Poetry, 1985. Poetry Translation Award, Columbia University Translation Center: *Transplantings.* Honorary LHD, Olivet College, MI, 1959.

For More Information: Henault, Marie, *Peter Viereck,* New York: Twayne, 1969.

Commentary: Peter Viereck was awarded the 1949 Pulitzer Prize in Poetry for *Terror and Decorum,* his first book of poems.

Viereck was born in New York City. He was educated at Harvard University, where he later would teach. He also taught at Radcliffe, Smith, and Mount Holyoke colleges. He is a poet and a historian. He first gained notice for *Metapolitics,* published in 1941, which he termed "a psychoanalysis of Nazism." He became known as a liberal conservative. He revised the 1941 book and published it as *Metapolitics: The Roots of the Nazi Mind* in 1961. His other poetry collections include *Strike Though the Mask!, The Tree Witch,* and *Archer in the Marrow.* The last work was hailed by the late poet Joseph Brodsky as a major event in American poetry.

1950

Gwendolyn Brooks 1027

Birth: June 7, 1917; Topeka, KS. **Parents:** David Anderson Brooks and Keziah Corinne (Wims). **Education:** Wilson Junior College, NC. **Spouse:** Henry Lowington Blakely. **Children:** Henry III, Nora.

Prize: *Poetry,* 1950: *Annie Allen,* New York: Harper, 1949.

Career: Poet and novelist; Publicity Director, NAACP, 1930s; Instructor, Northern Illinois State College; Professor, Columbia College, IL; Professor, Elmhurst College, IL; Distinguished Professor of the Arts, City College, CUNY, NY, 1971 to present.

Selected Works: *A Street in Bronzeville,* 1945. *Maud Martha,* 1953. *Bronzeville Boys and Girls,* 1956. *The Bean Eaters,* 1960. *Selected Poems,* 1963. *A Portion of That Field: The Centennial of the Burial of Lincoln,* 1967. *In the Mecca,* 1968. *Riot,* 1969. *Family Pictures,* 1970. *Aloneness,* 1971. *The World of Gwendolyn Brooks,* 1971. *Jump Bad: A New Chicago Anthology,* 1971. *A Broadside Treasury,* 1971. *The World of Gwendolyn Brooks,* 1971. *Report from Part One,* 1972. *The Tiger Who Wore White Gloves, or, What You Are You Are,* 1974. *Beckonings,* 1975. *Primer for Blacks,* 1980. *Young Poet's Primer,* 1980. *To Disembark,* 1981. *Black Love,* 1982. *Mayor Harold Washington; and, Chicago, the I Will City,* 1983. *Very Young Poets,* 1983. *Children Coming Home,* 1991.

Other Awards: Guggenheim Fellowship, 1946-1947. Grant, National Institute of Arts and Letters, 1946. Eunice Tietjens Memorial Prize, 1949. Anisfield Wolf Award, 1968. Shelley Memorial Award, 1976. Poet Laureate of Illinois, 1969. Honorary LLD, Columbia College, 1964. Honorary DLitts: Lake Forest University, IL, 1965; Brown University, RI, 1974.

For More Information: Miller, R. Baxter, *Langston Hughes and Gwendolyn Brooks: A Reference Guide,* Boston: Hall, 1978; Shaw, Harry B., *Gwendolyn Brooks,* Boston: Twayne, 1980; Kent, George E., *A Life of Gwendolyn Brooks,* Lexington, KY: University Press of Kentucky, 1990; Caldwell, Stephen, ed., *On Gwendolyn Brooks: Reliant Contemplation,* Ann Arbor: University of Michigan Press, 1996.

Commentary: *Annie Allen,* poetic portraits of ordinary African Americans leaving the South and living in the city, won the 1950 Pulitzer Prize in Poetry for Gwendolyn Brooks.

Brooks was born in Topeka, Kansas, but has lived most of her life in Chicago. Her character depictions and use of terza rima and blues meter have gained wide praise. Brooks achieved several "firsts." She was the first African American recipient of a Pulitzer Prize. Brooks was named poet laureate of Illinois in 1968 and was the first African American woman admitted to the National Institute of Arts and Letters in 1976. She was also the first African American woman to serve as poetry consultant to the Library of Congress, from 1985 to 1986. Her other works include *Maud Martha,* a novel, *The Bean Eaters, Riot,* and *Family Pictures.* She published an autobiography in 1972, *Report from Part One.*

1951

Carl Sandburg

Full entry appears as **#555** under "History," 1940.

1952

Marianne Moore   1028

Birth: November 15, 1887; Kirkwood, MO. **Death:** February 5, 1972. **Parents:** John Milton and Mary (Warner) Moore. **Religion:** Presbyterian. **Education:** Bryn Mawr College, PA: AB. Carlisle Commercial College, PA.

Prize: *Poetry,* 1952: *Collected Poems,* New York: Macmillan, 1951.

Career: Author and poet; Teacher, U.S. Indian School, Carlisle, PA, 1911-1915; Assistant, New York Public Library, NY, 1921-1925; Member: American Academy of Arts and Letters, Bryn Mawr Club, National Institute of Arts and Letters.

Selected Works: *Observations,* 1924. *Selected Poems,* 1935. *What Are Years,* 1941. *Nevertheless,* 1944. *The Fables of La Fontaine* (Translation), 1954. *Predilections,* 1955. *Like a Bulwark,* 1956. *O to Be a Dragon,* 1959. *A Marianne Moore Reader,* 1961. *The Arctic Ox,* 1964. *Dress and Kindred Subjects,* 1965. *Tell Me, Tell Me: Granite, Steel, and Other Topics,*

1966. *The Complete Poems of Marianne Moore,* 1982. *The Complete Prose of Marianne Moore,* 1986.

Other Awards: Dial Award, 1924. Helen Haire Levinson Prize, 1932. Ernest Hartsock Memorial Prize, 1935. Shelley Memorial Award, 1941. Contemporary Poetry's Patrons Prize, 1944. Harriet Monroe Poetry Award, 1944. Guggenheim Memorial Fellowship, 1945. National Institute of Arts and Letters, Grant in Literature, 1946. National Book Award for Poetry, 1952: *Collected Poems,* New York: Macmillan, 1951. National Institute of Arts and Letters, Gold Medal, 1953. Bollingen Prize in Poetry, Yale University, 1953: *Collected Poems.* M. Carey Thomas Award, 1953. Poetry Society of America Gold Medal Award, 1960, 1967. Brandeis Award for Poetry, 1963. Academy of American Poets Fellowship, 1965: Distinguished Poetic Achievement over a Period of More than Four Decades. MacDowell Medal, 1967. Chevalier of the Legion of Honor, Order of Arts and Letters. Woman of Achievement, American Association of University Women, 1968. Honorary LittDs: Wilson College, PA, 1949; Mount Holyoke College, MA, 1950; University of Rochester, NY, 1951; Dickinson College, PA, 1952; Long Island University, NY, 1953; New York University, 1967; St. John's University, NY 1968; Princeton University, NJ, 1968. Honorary LHDs: Rutgers University, NY, 1955; Smith College, MA, 1955; Pratt Institute, NY, 1958.

For More Information: Molesworth, Charles, *Marianne Moore: A Literary Life,* New York: Atheneum, 1990; Parisi, Joseph, ed., *Marianne Moore: The Art of a Modernist,* Ann Arbor: UMI Research, 1990; Rotella, Guy L., *Reading & Writing Nature: The Poetry of Robert Frost, Wallace Stevens, Marianne Moore, and Elizabeth Bishop,* Boston: Northeastern University Press, 1991; Diehl, Joanne Feit, *Elizabeth Bishop and Marianne Moore: The Psychodynamics of Creativity,* Princeton, NJ: Princeton University Press, 1993; Leavell, Linda, *Marianne Moore and the Visual Arts: Prismatic Color,* Baton Rouge: Louisiana State University Press, 1995; Miller, Cristanne, *Marianne Moore: Questions of Authority,* Cambridge, MA: Harvard University Press, 1995; Schulze, Robin G., *The Web of Friendship: Marianne Moore and Wallace Stevens,* Ann Arbor: University of Michigan Press, 1995.

Commentary: Marianne Moore was awarded the 1952 Pulitzer Prize in Poetry for *Collected Poems,* a volume which also received the National Book Award, the Bollingen Prize, and the Gold Medal from the American Academy of Arts and Letters.

Moore was born in Kirkwood, Missouri and educated at Bryn Mawr College. She was first published in the campus literary magazine. She moved with her mother to New York City in 1918 and fell into the literary movement of the time. She left a strong and positive impression on many of the other writers she met. Her first collection *Poems,* was published in 1921 by friends, without her knowledge. She edited *The Dial* journal from 1925 to 1929. Moore was the first female recipient of the Bollingen Prize for Poetry from Yale University Library in 1951. Her other works include *What Are Years, Nevertheless,* and *The Complete Poems of Marianne Moore.*

1953

Archibald MacLeish

Full entry appears as **#201** under "Drama," 1959.

1954

Theodore Roethke   1029

Birth: May 25, 1908; Saginaw, MI. **Death:** August 1, 1963. **Parents:** Otto Theodore and Helen Marie (Huebner) Roethke. **Education:** University of Michigan: AB, magna cum laude: MA. Harvard University, MA. **Spouse:** Beatrice Heath O'Connell (m.1953; died 1963).

Prize: *Poetry,* 1954: *The Waking: Poems: 1933-1953,* Garden City, NY: Doubleday, 1953.

Career: Instructor of English, Lafayette College, PA, 1931-1935; Director of Public Relations and varsity tennis coach, Lafayette College, PA, 1934-1935; Instructor of English, Michigan State College (now University), East Lansing, 1935; Instructor, Pennsylvania State University, University Park, 1936-1939; Assistant Professor of English and varsity tennis coach, 1939-1943, 1947; Assistant professor of English, Bennington College, VT, 1943-1946; Associate Professor, University of Washington, Seattle, 1947-1948; Professor of English, University of Washington, Seattle, 1948-1962; Fulbright Lecturer, Italy, 1955; Poet-in-Residence, University of Washington, Seattle, 1962-1963; Member: Chi Phi, National Institute of Arts and Letters, Phi Beta Kappa, Phi Kappa Phi.

Selected Works: *Open House,* 1941. *The Lost Son, and Other Poems,* 1948. *Praise to the End!,* 1951. *Words for the Wind,* 1958. *I Am! Says the Lamb,* 1961. *Party at the Zoo,* 1963. *The Far Field,* 1964. *On the Poet and His Craft: Selected Prose* (Mills, Ralph J., Jr., ed.), 1965. *The Achievement of Theodore Roethke* (Martz, William J., ed.), 1966. *Selected Letters* (Mills, Ralph J., Jr., ed.), 1968. *Straw for the Fire, from the Notebooks of Theodore Roethke, 1943-63* (Wagoner, David, ed.), 1972. *Dirty Dinky and Other Creatures: Poems for Children* (Roethke, Beatrice and Lushington, Stephen, eds.), 1973.

Other Awards: Guggenheim Fellowship, 1945, 1950. Eunice Tietjens Memorial Prize, 1947. Levinson Prize, 1951. National Institute of Arts and Letters

Grant, 1952. Ford Foundation Grant, 1952, 1959. Borestone Mountain Award, 1958. Bollingen Prize in Poetry, Yale University Library, 1958: *Words for the Wind,* Garden City, NY: Doubleday, 1958. National Book Award, 1959: *Words for the Wind.* Edna St. Vincent Millay Award, 1959. Longview Award, 1959. Pacific Northwest Writers Award, 1959. Shelley Memorial Award for Poetry, 1962. Poetry Society of America Prize, 1962. National Book Award, 1965: *The Far Field,* Garden City, NY: Doubleday, 1964, Garden City, NY: Doubleday, 1964. Honorary DLitt, University of Michigan, 1969.

For More Information: Stiffler, Randall, *Theodore Roethke: The Poet and His Critics,* Chicago: American Library Association, 1986; Kalaidjian, Walter B., *Understanding Theodore Roethke,* Columbia: University of South Carolina Press, 1987; Balakian, Peter, *Theodore Roethke's Far Fields: The Evolution of His Poetry,* Baton Rouge: Louisiana State University Press, 1989; Bogen, Don, *Theodore Roethke and the Writing Process,* Athens: Ohio University Press, 1991.

Commentary: Theodore Roethke was awarded the 1954 Pulitzer Prize in Poetry for *The Waking,* a volume marked by traditional elegance.

Roethke was born in Saginaw, Michigan and educated at the University of Michigan. He taught at the University of Washington at Seattle from 1947 until his death in 1963. Roethke achieved increased acclaim with each new publication. Although he suffered from psychological problems, his artistry seemed not to be diminished. His most noted works were *The Lost Son, and Other Poems* which included greenhouse imagery, and *Words for the Wind,* which was published in 1958 and won both the Bollingen Award and the National Book Award.

1955

Wallace Stevens   1030

Birth: October 2, 1879; Reading, PA. **Death:** August 2, 1955. **Parents:** Garret Barcalow and Margaretha Catherine (Zeller) Stevens. **Religion:** Roman Catholic. **Education:** Harvard University, MA. **Spouse:** Elsie Viola Kachel (m. 1909). **Children:** Holly Bright.

Prize: *Poetry,* 1955: *Collected Poems,* New York: Knopf, 1954.

Career: Poet; New York *Tribune* Reporter; Insurance lawyer.

Selected Works: *Harmonium,* 1923. *The Man with the Blue Guitar & Other Poems,* 1937. *Parts of a World,* 1942. *Transport to Summer,* 1947. *The Necessary Angel: Essays on Reality and the Imagination,* 1951. *Opus Posthumous* (Morse, Samuel F., ed.), 1957. *Letters of Wallace Stevens* (Stevens, Holly, ed.),

1966. *The Palm at the End of the Mind* (Stevens, Holly, ed.), 1971.

Other Awards: Bollingen Prize, 1949. National Book Award, 1951: *The Auroras of Autumn,* New York: Knopf, 1950. National Book Award, 1955: *Collected Poems,* New York: Knopf, 1954.

For More Information: Richardson, Joan, *Wallace Stevens: The Early Years, 1879-1923,* New York: Morrow, 1986; Rehder, Robert, *The Poetry of Wallace Stevens,* New York: St. Martin's, 1988; Grey, Thomas C., *The Wallace Stevens Case: Law and the Practice of Poetry,* Cambridge, MA: Harvard University Press, 1991; Schwarz, Daniel R., *Narrative and Representation in the Poetry of Wallace Stevens: "A Tune Beyond Us, Yet Ourselves,"* New York: St. Martin's, 1993; Schulze, Robin G., *The Web of Friendship: Marianne Moore and Wallace Stevens,* Ann Arbor: University of Michigan Press, 1995; Whiting, Anthony, *The Never-Resting Mind: Wallace Stevens' Romantic Irony,* Ann Arbor: University of Michigan Press, 1996; Voros, Gyorgyi, *Notations of the Wild: Ecology in the Poetry of Wallace Stevens,* Iowa City: University of Iowa Press, 1997.

Commentary: *Collected Poems* won the 1955 Pulitzer Prize in Poetry for Wallace Stevens.

Stevens was born in Reading, Pennsylvania. He attended Harvard University and New York Law School. Stevens worked for the Hartford Accident and Indemnity Company from 1916 until his death in 1955. Initially, his poems appeared in the *Harvard Advocate,* a campus literary magazine of which he was editor, and in *Poetry* magazine between 1914 and 1922. His first collection, *Harmonium,* was published in 1923. His poetry has been called exotic and seems somewhat out of character with his occupation as a lawyer. He received the Bollingen Prize in 1949 and was the recipient of two National Book Awards, in 1951 for *The Auroras of Autumn* and in 1955 for *Collected Poems.*

1956

Elizabeth Bishop   1031
Birth: February 8, 1911; Worcester, MA. **Death:** October 6, 1979. **Parents:** William Thomas and Gertrude (Bulmer) Bishop. **Education:** Vassar College, NY: AB.

Prize: *Poetry,* 1956: *Poems: North & South,* Boston: Houghton Mifflin, 1955.

Career: Poet and translator; Consultant in Poetry, Library of Congress, Washington, DC, 1949-1950; Honorary Consultant in American Letters, beginning in 1958; Poet-in-Residence, University of Washington, Seattle, 1966; Teacher, Harvard University; Teacher, Massachusetts Institute of Technology; Member, National Institute of Arts and Letters; Chan-

cellor, Academy of American Poets, beginning in 1966.

Selected Works: *The Diary of "Helena Morley"* (Translation), 1957. *Questions of Travel,* 1965. *Selected Poems,* 1967. *The Ballad of the Burglar of Babylon,* 1968. *An Anthology of Twentieth-Century Brazilian Poetry* (Bishop, Elizabeth, ed.), 1972. *Poem,* 1973. *The Complete Poems, 1927-1979,* 1983. *The Collected Prose,* 1984. *One Art: Letters* (Giroux, Robert, ed.), 1994. *Exchanging Hats: Paintings,* 1996.

Other Awards: Houghton Mifflin Poetry Award, 1946: *North & South.* Guggenheim Fellowship, 1947. American Academy of Arts and Letters Grant, 1951. First Lucy Martin Donnelly Fellowship, Bryn Mawr College, 1951. Shelley Memorial Award, 1952. Academy of American Poets Award, 1955. Partisan Review Fellowship, 1956. Amy Lowell Traveling Fellowship, 1957. Chapelbrook Fellowship, 1962. Academy of American Poets Fellowship, 1964. Rockefeller Foundation Grant, 1967. Merrill Foundation Award, 1969. National Book Award in Poetry, 1970: *The Complete Poems,* New York: Farrar, Straus & Giroux, 1983. Order Rio Branco, Brazil, 1971. Harriet Monroe Award for Poetry, 1974. Neustadt International Prize for Literature, 1976. National Book Critics Circle Award in Poetry, 1977: *Geography.* Honorary LLDs: Rutgers University, NJ, 1972; Brown University, RI, 1972.

For More Information: Wilbur, Richard, *Elizabeth Bishop: A Memorial Tribute,* New York: Albodocani, 1980; Rotella, Guy L., *Reading & Writing Nature: The Poetry of Robert Frost, Wallace Stevens, Marianne Moore, and Elizabeth Bishop,* Boston: Northeastern University Press, 1991; Diehl, Joanne Feit, *Elizabeth Bishop and Marianne Moore: The Psychodynamics of Creativity,* Princeton, NJ: Princeton University Press, 1993; Harrison, Victoria, *Elizabeth Bishop's Poetics of Intimacy,* Cambridge, MA: Cambridge University Press, 1993; Fountain, Gary, *Remembering Elizabeth Bishop: An Oral Biography,* Amherst: University of Massachusetts Press, 1994; Monteiro, George, ed., *Conversations With Elizabeth Bishop,* Jackson: University Press of Mississippi Press, 1996; Colwell, Anne, *Inscrutable Houses: Metaphors of the Body in the Poems of Elizabeth Bishop,* Tuscaloosa: University of Alabama Press, 1997.

Commentary: Elizabeth Bishop was awarded the 1956 Pulitzer Prize in Poetry for *Poems: North & South,* her first published collection.

Bishop was born in Worcester, Massachusetts. Her father died when Elizabeth was eight months old, and her mother was institutionalized when she was five. Bishop was raised by relatives in Boston and Nova Scotia. She was educated at Vassar College where she befriended the writer Mary McCarthy, and the poet Muriel Rukeyser. Her friendships with the poets and Pulitzer Prize winners Marianne Moore, who became Bishop's mentor, and Robert Lowell were strong. Lowell acknowledged Bishop's influence on his *Life Studies.* She lived for a time in Brazil and published *Questions of Travel* in 1965. Her last published work, *Geography III,* was considered her best. She died of a cerebral aneurysm in 1979.

1957

Richard Wilbur   1032

Birth: March 1, 1921; New York, NY. **Parents:** Lawrence Lazear and Helen Ruth (Purdy) Wilbur. **Religion:** Episcopalian. **Education:** Amherst College, MA: AB. Harvard University, MA: AM. **Spouse:** Mary Charlotte Hayes Ward (m. 1942). **Children:** Ellen Dickinson, Christopher Hayes, Nathan Lord, Aaron Hammond.

Prize: *Poetry,* 1957: *Things of This World,* New York: Harcourt, Brace, 1956. *Poetry,* 1989: *New and Collected Poems,* San Diego: Harcourt Brace Jovanovich, 1988.

Career: Poet and educator; Staff Sergeant, U.S. Army, Infantry, 1943-1945; Junior Fellow, Society of Fellows, Harvard University, MA, 1947-1950; Assistant Professor of English, Harvard University, MA, 1950-1954; Associate Professor of English, Wellesley College, Wellesley, MA, 1955-1957; Professor of English, Wesleyan University, Middletown, CT, 1957-1977; Cultural Exchange Representative to the USSR, U.S. State Department, 1961; President, American Academy and Institute of Arts and Letters, 1974-1976; Chancellor, American Academy and Institute of Arts and Letters, 1976-1978; Writer-in-Residence, Smith College, Northampton, MA, 1977-1986; Poet Laureate of the U.S., Library of Congress, Washington, DC, 1987-1988; Chancellor, Academy of American Poets; Honorary Fellow, Modern Language Association; Member: American Academy of Arts and Sciences, ASCAP, Authors League of America, Dramatists Guild, Century Club, Chi Psi, PEN.

Selected Works: *Ceremony, and Other Poems,* 1950. *The Misanthrope: Comedy in Five Acts, 1666, Done into English Verse,* 1955. *Digging for China,* 1956. *Advice to a Prophet, and Other Poems,* 1961. *Tartuffe: Comedy in Five Acts, 1669* (Translation), 1963. *Walking to Sleep: New Poems and Translations,* 1969. *Opposites,* 1973. *Responses: Prose Pieces, 1953-1976,* 1976. *Elizabeth Bishop: A Memorial Tribute,* 1980. *More Opposites,* 1988. *New and Collected Poems,* 1988. *Runaway Opposites,* 1995. *The Catbird's Song: Prose Pieces, 1963-1995,* 1997.

Other Awards: Harriet Monroe Memorial Prize, 1948, 1978. Oscar Blumenthal Prize, 1950. Guggenheim Fellowship, 1952-1953, 1963. Prix de Roma Fellowship, American Academy of Arts and Letters, 1954. Edna St. Vincent Millay Memorial Award, 1957. National Book Award, Poetry, 1957: *Things of This World,* New York: Harcourt, Brace, 1956. Boston Festival Award, 1959. Ford Foundation Fellowship, Drama, 1960. Melville Cane Award, 1962. Co-Recipient, Bollingen Prize for Translation, Yale University Library, 1963: *Tartuffe,* New York: Harcourt, Brace & World, 1963. Sarah Josepha Hale Award, 1968. Co-Recipient, Bollingen Prize for Poetry, 1971: *Walking to Sleep,* New York: Harcourt, Brace & World, 1969. Creative Arts Award, Brandeis University, 1971. Prix Henri Desfueilles, 1971. Shelley Memorial Award, 1973. Book World's Children's Spring Book Festival Award, 1973: *Opposites: Poems and Drawings,* New York: Harcourt Brace Jovanovich, 1973. PEN Translation Prize, 1983: *Moliere: Four Comedies.* St. Botolph's Club Foundation Award, 1983. Drama Desk Award, 1983. Chevalier, Ordre des Palmes Academiques, 1983. Poet Laureate of the United States, Library of Congress, 1987-1988. Taylor Poetry Award, *Sewanee Review,* University Press of the South, 1988. Bunn Award, 1988. Washington College Literature Award, 1988. *Los Angeles Times* Book Prize, 1988: *New and Collected Poems,* San Diego, CA: Harcourt Brace Jovanovich, 1988. St. Louis Literature Award, 1988. Gold Medal for Poetry, American Academy and Institute of Arts and Letters, 1991. Edward MacDowell Medal, 1992. National Arts Club Medal of Honor for Literature, 1994. PEN/Manheim Medal for Translation, 1994. Milton Center Prize, 1995. Academy American Achievement Award, 1995. Honorary LHDs: Lawrence College (now Lawrence University, WI), 1960; Washington University, MO, 1964. Williams College, MA, 1975; University of Rochester, NY, 1976; Carnegie-Mellon University, PA, 1980; State University of New York, Potsdam, 1986; Skidmore College, NY, 1987. University of Lowell, MA, 1990. Honorary LittDs: Amherst College, MA, 1967; Clark University, MA, 1970; American International College, MA, 1974; Marquette University, WI, 1977; Wesleyan University, CT, 1977; Lake Forest College, IL, 1982. Honorary MA, Amherst College, 1952.

For More Information: Butts, William, ed., *Conversations With Richard Wilbur,* Jackson: University Press of Mississippi, 1990; Bixler, Frances, *Richard Wilbur: A Reference Guide,* Boston: Hall, 1991; Edgecombe, Rodney Stenning, *A Reader's Guide to the Poetry of Richard Wilbur,* Tuscaloosa: University of Alabama Press, 1995.

Commentary: Richard Wilbur was awarded two Pulitzer Prizes, both in Poetry. He won in 1957 for *Things of This World,* his third book and a National Book Award winner. He won again in 1989 for *New and Collected Poems,* which also won the *Los Angeles Times* Book Prize for Poetry.

Wilbur was born in New York City and educated at Amherst College and at Harvard University. He taught at Wesleyan University from 1955 to 1977. He was named the second poet laureate of the United States in 1987, following Robert Penn Warren. He is also known for his translations of Moliere. His many works include *The Pelican from a Bestiary of 1120, Complaint, Pedestrian Flight: Twenty-One Clerihews for the Telephone,* and *Runaway Opposites.*

1958

Robert Penn Warren
Full entry appears as **#977** under "Novel," 1947.

1959

Stanley Kunitz   1033
Birth: July 29, 1905; Worcester, MA. **Parents:** Solomon Z. and Yetta Helen (Jasspon) Kunitz. **Education:** Harvard University, MA: AB, summa cum laude: AM. **Spouse:** Helen Pearce (m. 1930; div. 1937); Eleanor Evans (m. 1939; div. 1958); Elise Asher (m. 1958). **Children:** Gretchen (EE).

Prize: *Poetry,* 1959: *Selected Poems, 1928-1958,* Boston: Little, Brown, 1958.

Career: Poet; Editor, *Wilson Library Bulletin,* NY, 1928-1943; Staff Sergeant, U.S. Army, Air Transport Command, 1943-1945; Professor of English, Bennington College, Bennington, VT, 1946-1949; Professor of English, Potsdam State Teachers College (now State University of New York College at Potsdam), Potsdam, NY, 1949-1950; Director of Seminar, Potsdam Summer Workshop in Creative Arts, 1949-1953; Lecturer of English, New School for Social Research, New York City, 1950-1957; Poet-in-Residence, University of Washington, 1955-1956; Poet-in-Residence, Queens College (now Queens College of the City University of New York), 1956-1957; Poet-in-Residence, Brandeis University, 1958-1959; Director of Poetry Workshop, Poetry Center, Young Men's Hebrew Association (YMHA), NY, 1958-1962; Danforth Visiting Lecturer, U.S. Colleges and Universities, 1961-1963; Lecturer, Columbia University, NY, 1963-1966; Cultural Exchange Program, USSR and Poland, 1967; Adjunct Professor of Writing, School of the Arts, Columbia University, 1967-1985; Staff, Writing Division, Fine Arts Work Center, Provincetown, MA, beginning in 1968; Fellow, Yale University, beginning in 1969; Chancellor, Academy of American Poets beginning in 1970; Visiting Professor, Yale University, 1972, and Rutgers University, 1974; Consultant on Poetry, Library of Congress, Washington, DC, 1974-1976; Cultural Exchange Program, Senegal and Ghana, 1976; Honorary

Consultant in American Letters, Library of Congress, DC, 1976-1983; Visiting Senior Fellow, Council of the Humanities, and Old Dominion Fellow in Creative Writing, Princeton University, 1978-1979; Poet-in-Residence, and Princeton University, 1979; Cultural Exchange Program, in Israel and Egypt, 1980; Secretary, American Academy and Institute of Arts and Letters, 1985-1988; Founding President, Poets House, 1985-1990; Member, Phi Beta Kappa.

Selected Works: *Intellectual Things,* 1930. *Authors Today and Yesterday: A Companion Volume to Living Authors* (Kunitz, Stanley and Haycraft, Howard, eds.), 1933. *The Junior Book of Authors: An Introduction to the Lives of Writers and Illustrators for Younger Readers, from Lewis Carroll and Louisa Alcott to the Present Day* (Kunitz, Stanley and Haycraft, Howard, eds.), 1934. *Twentieth Century Authors: A Biographical Dictionary of Modern Literature* (Kunitz, Stanley and Haycraft, Howard, eds.), 1942. *Passport to the War,* 1944. *Twentieth Century Authors: A Biographical Dictionary of Modern Literature. First Supplement* (Kunitz, Stanley, ed.), 1955. *Poems of John Keats* (Kunitz, Stanley, ed.), 1964. *The Testing-Tree,* 1971. *Poems of Akhmatova* (Kunitz, Stanley, ed.), 1973. *Robert Lowell, Poet of Terribilit,* 1974. *The Coat without a Seam: Sixty Poems, 1930-1972,* 1974. *A Kind of Order, a Kind of Folly: Essays and Conversations,* 1975. *The Lincoln Relics: A Poem,* 1978. *The Poems of Stanley Kunitz, 1928-1978,* 1979. *The Wellfleet Whale and Companion Poems,* 1983. *American Authors, 1600-1900: A Biographical Dictionary of American Literature* (Kunitz, Stanley and Haycraft, Howard, eds.), 1966.

Other Awards: Garrison Medal for Poetry, Harvard University, 1926. Oscar Blumenthal Prize, 1941. Guggenheim Fellowship, 1945-1946. Amy Lowell Traveling Fellowship, 1953-1954. Levinson Prize, *Poetry* magazine, 1956. *Saturday Review* Award, 1957. Harriet Monroe Poetry Award, University of Chicago, 1958. Ford Foundation Grant, 1958-1959. National Institute of Arts and Letters Award, 1959. Brandeis University Creative Arts Award Medal, 1964. Academy of American Poets Fellowship, 1968. New England Poetry Club Golden Rose Trophy, 1970. American Library Association Notable Book Citation, 1979: *The Poems of Stanley Kunitz, 1928-1978,* Boston: Little, Brown, 1979. Lenore Marshall Award for Poetry, 1980. National Endowment for the Arts Senior Fellowship, 1984. Bollingen Prize in Poetry, Yale University Library, 1987. State Poet of New York, Walt Whitman Award Citation of Merit, 1987. Montgomery Fellow, Dartmouth College, 1991. Centennial Medal, Harvard University, 1992. National Medal of Arts, 1993. National Book Award, 1995: *Passing Through: Later Poems, New and Selected,* New York: Norton, 1995. Shelley Memorial Award, 1995. Honorary LittDs: Clark University, MA, 1961;

Anna Maria College, MA, 1977. Honorary LHDs: Worcester State College, MA, 1980; SUNY, Brockport, 1987.

For More Information: Henault, Marie, *Stanley Kunitz,* Boston: Twayne, 1980; Orr, Gregory, *Stanley Kunitz: An Introduction to the Poetry,* New York: Columbia University Press, 1985; *A Celebration for Stanley Kunitz: On His Eightieth Birthday,* Riverdale-on-Hudson, NY: Sheep Meadow, 1986; Moss, Stanley, ed., *Interviews and Encounters with Stanley Kunitz,* Riverdale-on-Hudson, NY: Sheep Meadow, 1993, *Passing Through: Later Poems, New and Selected,* New York: Norton, 1995.

Commentary: *Selected Poems 1928-1958* won the 1958 Pulitzer Prize in Poetry for Stanley Jasspon Kunitz. It was a volume that was difficult for Kunitz to get published.

Kunitz was born in Worcester, Pennsylvania and educated at Harvard University. His first volume of poetry, *Intellectual Things* was published in 1930. He didn't publish again until 1944 with *Passport to the War.* His work has been called intellectual, intelligent, and graceful. He achieved a simpler style in his later work which brought praise from Robert Lowell. His other works include *The Testing Tree* and *The Wellfleet Whale and Companion Poems.* Kunitz was editor of the H.W. Wilson series of author biographies which includes *Twentieth Century Authors.*

1960

W. D. Snodgrass   1034
Birth: January 5, 1926; Wilkinsburg, PA. **Parents:** Bruce DeWitt and Jesse Helen (Murchie) Snodgrass. **Education:** Geneva College, NY. University of Iowa: BA, MA, MFA. **Spouse:** Lila Jean Hank (m. 1946; div. 1953); Janice Marie Ferguson Wilson (m. 1954; div. 1966); Camille Rykowski (m. 1967; div. 1978); Kathleen Ann Brown (m. 1985). **Children:** Cynthia Jean (LJH); Kathy Ann Wilson (stepdaughter), Russell Bruce (JMF).

Prize: *Poetry,* 1960: *Heart's Needle,* New York: Knopf, 1959.

Career: Served in U.S. Navy, 1944-1946; Instructor of English, Cornell University, Ithaca, NY, 1955-1957; Leader, Morehead Writers' Conference Poetry Workshop, 1955; Instructor, University of Rochester, NY, 1957-1958; Leader, Antioch Writers' Poetry Workshop Conference, 1958, 1959; Assistant Professor of English, Wayne State University, Detroit, MI, 1959-1968; Professor of English and Speech, Syracuse University, NY, 1968-1977; Leader, Narrative Poetry Workshop, State University of New York at Binghamton, 1977; Visiting Professor, Old Dominion University, Norfolk, VA, 1978-1979; Distinguished Professor, University of Delaware, Newark, DE, 1979-1980; Distinguished Professor of Creative Writing and Contemporary Poetry, 1980-1994; Lecturer and performer of poetry readings; Fellow, Academy of American Poets; Member: Dramatists Guild, National Institute of Arts and Letters, PEN.

Selected Works: *Gallows Songs* (Translation), 1967. *After Experience: Poems and Translations,* 1968. *The Fuehrer Bunker: A Cycle of Poems in Progress,* 1977. *If Birds Build with Your Hair,* 1979. *These Trees Stand,* 1981. *Heinrich Himmler: Platoons and Files,* 1982. *Six Minnesinger Songs,* 1983. *The Kinder Capers: Poems,* 1986. *Lullaby: The Comforting of Cock Robin,* 1988. *The Death of Cock Robin,* 1989. *Autumn Variations,* 1990. *Each in His Season: Poems,* 1993. *The Fuehrer Bunker: The Complete Cycle,* 1995.

Other Awards: Ingram Merrill Foundation Award, 1958. Hudson Review Fellowship in Poetry, 1958-1959. Longview Foundation Literary Award, 1959. Poetry Society of America Citation, 1960. National Institute of Arts and Letters Grant, 1960: *Heart's Needle.* British Guinness Award, 1961: *Heart's Needle.* Yaddo Resident Award, 1960, 1961, 1965. Ford Foundation Grant, 1963-1964. Miles Poetry Award, 1966. National Endowment for the Arts Grant, 1966-1967. Guggenheim Fellowship, 1972. Bicentennial Medal, College of William and Mary, 1976. Centennial Medal, Romania, 1977. Honorary Doctorate of Letters, Allegheny College, PA, 1991.

For More Information: Gaston, Paul, *W. D. Snodgrass,* Boston: Twayne, 1978; Haven, Stephen, ed., *The Poetry of W.D. Snodgrass: Everything Human,* Ann Arbor: University of Michigan Press, 1993.

Commentary: William DeWitt Snodgrass was awarded the 1960 Pulitzer Prize in Poetry for *Heart's Needle,* a collection in the style of "confessional poetry" or autobiographical. The poems found here were dedicated to a child who grew up to become an Episcopalian priest and married her father to his present wife.

Snodgrass was born in Wilkensburg, Pennsylvania. He was educated at Geneva College and at the University of Iowa under Robert Lowell. He is said to have inaugurated the vogue of confessional poetry as the style for the 1960s. His other works include *The Remains, The Death of Cock Robin,* and *The Fuhrer Bunker: The Complete Cycle.*

1961

Phyllis McGinley   1035
Birth: March 21, 1905; Ontario, OR. **Death:** February 22, 1978. **Parents:** Daniel and Julia (Kiesel) McGinley. **Religion:** Roman Catholic. **Education:** University of Southern California. University of Utah.

Spouse: Charles L. Hayden (m. 1937; died 1972).
Children: Julia Elizabeth, Phyllis Louise.

Prize: *Poetry,* 1961: *Times Three; Selected Verse from Three Decades, With Seventy New Poems,* New York: Viking, 1960.

Career: Poet and writer; Teacher in Utah, 1928; English Teacher, junior high school, New Rochelle, NY, 1929-1934; Copywriter, advertising, NY, 1930s; Writer, *Town and Country,* NY, 1937.

Selected Works: *On the Contrary,* 1934. *One More Manhattan,* 1937. *A Pocketful of Wry,* 1940. *Husbands Are Difficult, or, the Book of Oliver Ames,* 1941. *Stones from a Glass House: New Poems,* 1946. *A Short Walk from the Station,* 1951. *The Make-Believe Twins,* 1951. *The Horse Who Had His Picture in the Paper,* 1951. *Blunderbus,* 1951. *Love Letters,* 1954. *The Year without a Santa Claus,* 1957. *Merry Christmas, Happy New Year,* 1958. *Lucy McLockett,* 1959. *The Province of the Heart,* 1959. *Mince Pie and Mistletoe,* 1961. *Sixpence in Her Shoe,* 1964. *Wonderful Time,* 1966. *A Wreath of Christmas Legends,* 1967. *Saint-Watching,* 1969.

Other Awards: Catholic Writers Guild Award, 1955. Christopher Medal, 1955. Edna St. Vincent Millay Memorial Award, Poetry Society of America, 1955. St. Catherine de Siena Medal, Theta Phi Alpha, 1956. Catholic Institute of the Press Award, 1960. National Association of Independent Schools Award, 1961: *Times Three: Selected Verse from Three Decades with Seventy New Poems.* Spirit Gold Medal, Catholic Poetry Society of America, 1962. Laetare Medal, University of Notre Dame, 1964. Among the Best Children's Books of the Year, *New York Times,* 1966: *Wonderful Time,* Philadelphia, PA: Lippincott, 1960. Campion Award, 1967. Golden Book Award. Honorary DLitts: Wheaton College, MA, 1956; St. Mary's College, IN, 1958; Marquette University, WI, 1960; Dartmouth College, NH, 1961; Boston College, MA, 1962; Wilson College, PA, 1964; Smith College, MA, 1964; St. John's University, NY, 1964.

For More Information: Wagner-Martin, Linda, *Phyllis McGinley,* New York: Twayne, 1971.

Commentary: Phyllis McGinley was awarded the 1961 Pulitzer Prize in Poetry for *Times Three: Selected Verse From Three Decades,* which included many of her poems first published in newspapers and magazines.

McGinley was born in Ontario, Oregon. She was educated at the University of Southern California and the University of Utah. McGinley's poetry had broad appeal for its humorous view of contemporary life. Her poetry first appeared in the Franklin P. Adams column, "The Conning Tower," in the *New York Herald-Tribune* and later in the *New Yorker* and other magazines. She also wrote children's books including *The Make-Believe Twins* (1953) and *Boys Are Awful.* Her other works include *A Wreath of Christmas Leg-*

ends. She also wrote under the pseudonym S. S. Gardons.

1962

Alan Dugan   1036

Birth: February 12, 1923; Brooklyn, NY. **Education:** Queens College, NY. Olivet College, IL. Mexico City College, Mexico: BA. **Spouse:** Judith Shahn.

Prize: *Poetry,* 1962: *Poems,* New Haven, CT: Yale University, 1961.

Career: Poet; Served in U.S. Army Air Forces, WWII; Staff member in advertising, publishing; Model maker, medical supply house, NY; Faculty member, Sarah Lawrence College, NY, 1967-1971; Faculty member, Fine Arts Work Center, MA, beginning in 1971.

Selected Works: *Poems 2,* 1963. *Poems 3,* 1967. *Collected Poems,* 1969. *Poems 4,* 1974. *Sequence,* 1976. *New and Collected Poems, 1961-1983,* 1983.

Other Awards: Award, *Poetry* magazine, 1946. Yale Series of Younger Poets Award, 1961. National Book Award, 1961: *Poems.* New Haven, CT: Yale University, 1961. Rome Fellowship, American Academy of Arts and Letters, 1962-1963. Guggenheim Fellow, 1963-1964. Rockefeller Foundation Fellow, 1966-1967. Levinson Poetry Prize, *Poetry* magazine, 1967.

For More Information: *Current Biography,* New York: Wilson, 1990; Ellefson, J.C. and Belle Waring, "Alan Dugan: An Interview," *American Poetry Review,* May 1990.

Commentary: *Poems* won the 1962 Pulitzer Prize in Poetry for Alan Dugan as well as a National Book Award and the Yale Younger Poets Award.

Dugan has been known to use everyday language in his imagery. His other works include *Collected Poems* and *New and Collected Poems.*

1963

William Carlos Williams   1037

Birth: September 17, 1883; Rutherford, NJ. **Death:** March 4, 1963. **Parents:** William George and Raquel Helene (Hoheb) Williams. **Education:** University of Pennsylvania: MD. University of Leipzig, Germany. **Spouse:** Florence Herman (m. 1912). **Children:** William, Eric, Paul Herman.

Prize: *Poetry,* 1963: *Pictures from Breughel, and Other Poems,* New York: New Directions, 1962.

Career: Poet, playwright, novelist, essayist, and physician; Intern, French Hospital and Nursery and Child's Hospital, NY, 1906-1909; Private physician, Rutherford, New Jersey, 1910-1951; Visiting Professor of English, University of Washington, Seattle,

1948; Member: Academy of American Poets, Bergen County, NJ Medical Association, American Academy of Arts and Letters, National Institute of Arts and Letters.

Selected Works: *A Book of Poems, Al Que Quiere!,* 1917. *Kora in Hell: Improvisations,* 1920. *Sour Grapes: A Book of Poems,* 1921. *The Great American Novel,* 1923. *In the American Grain,* 1925. *A Voyage to Pagany,* 1928. *The Knife of the Times and Other Stories,* 1932. *Collected Poems, 1921-1931,* 1934. *An Early Martyr and Other Poems,* 1935. *White Mule: A Novel,* 1937. *Life along the Passaic River,* 1938. *The Complete Collected Poems of William Carlos Williams, 1906-1938,* 1938. *In the American Grain,* 1939. *The Broken Span,* 1941. *Selected Poems,* 1949. *Make Light of It: Collected Stories,* 1950. *Collected Later Poems,* 1950. *Collected Earlier Poems,* 1951. *The Autobiography of William Carlos Williams,* 1951. *The Build-Up: A Novel,* 1952. *The Desert Music, and Other Poems,* 1954. *Selected Essays,* 1954. *Journey to Love,* 1955. *Selected Letters,* 1957. *I Wanted to Write a Poem: The Autobiography of the Works of a Poet* (Heal, Edith, ed.), 1958. *To Be Recited to Flossie on Her Birthday,* 1959. *The Farmers' Daughters: The Collected Stories of William Carlos Williams,* 1961. *The Collected Later Poems,* 1963. *Paterson,* 1963. *The William Carlos Williams Reader* (Rosenthal, M.L., ed.), 1966. *Selected Poems* (Tomlinson, Charles, ed.), 1976. *A Recognizable Image: William Carlos Williams on Art and Artists* (Dijkstra, Bram, ed.), 1978. *Yes, Mrs. Williams: A Personal Record of My Mother,* 1982. *Flowers of August,* 1983. *The Doctor Stories* (Coles, Robert, ed.), 1984. *Selected Poems* (Tomlinson, Charles, ed.), 1985. *Something to Say: William Carlos Williams on Younger Poets* (Breslin, James E.B., ed.), 1985. *The Collected Poems of William Carlos Williams* (Walton, Litz A., and MacGowan, Christopher, eds.), 1986. *Asphodel, That Greeny Flower & Other Love Poems,* 1994. *The Lost Works of William Carlos Williams: The Volumes of Collected Poetry as Lyrical Sequences* (Cirasa, Robert J., ed.), 1995.

Other Awards: Dial Award, Distinguished Service to American Literature, 1926. Guarantors Prize from Poetry, 1931. Russell Loines Memorial Award for Poetry, National Institute of Arts and Letters, 1948. Chair of Poetry, Library of Congress, 1949. National Book Award for Poetry, 1950: *Selected Poems and Paterson, Book III.* Bollingen Prize in Poetry, Yale University Library, 1952. Levinson Prize, 1954, for poems published in *Poetry.* Oscar Blumenthal Prize, 1955, for poems published in *Poetry.* Academy of American Poets Fellowship, 1956. Brandeis University Creative Arts Medal, Lifetime of Distinguished Achievement, Poetry-Fiction-Nonfiction, 1957-1958. American Academy of Arts and Letters Gold Medal for Poetry, National Institute of Arts and

Letters, 1963. Honorary LLDs: University of Buffalo, NY, 1946; Fairleigh Dickinson University, NJ, 1959; Honorary LittDs: Rutgers University, NJ, 1948; Bard College, NY, 1948; University of Pennsylvania, 1952.

For More Information: Mariani, Paul L., *William Carlos Williams: A New World Naked,* New York: McGraw-Hill, 1981; Baldwin, Neil, *To All Gentleness: William Carlos Williams, the Doctor Poet,* New York: Atheneum, 1984; Williams and Sanford, John, *A Correspondence,* Santa Barbara, CA: Oyster, 1984; Witemeyer, Hugh, ed., *William Carlos Williams and James Laughlin: Selected Letters,* New York: Norton, 1989; Bremen, Brian A., *William Carlos Williams and the Diagnostics of Culture,* New York: Oxford University Press, 1993; Ahearn, Barry, *William Carlos Williams and Alterity: The Early Poetry,* Cambridge, England: Cambridge, 1994; O'Neil, Elizabeth Murrie, ed., *The Last Word: Letters Between Marcia Nardi and William Carlos Williams,* Iowa City: University of Iowa Press, 1994; Axelrod, Steven G. and Helen Deese, eds., *Critical Essays on William Carlos Williams,* New York: G.K. Hall, 1995; Lowney, John, *The American Avant-Garde Tradition: William Carlos Williams, Postmodern Poetry, and the Politics of Cultural Memory,* Lewisburg, PA: Bucknell University Press, 1997.

Commentary: William Carlos Williams was awarded the 1963 Pulitzer Prize in Poetry posthumously for *Pictures from Brueghel, and Other Poems.* He passed away a month before the prize was announced.

Williams was born in Rutherford, New Jersey. He was educated at the University of Pennsylvania, where he became a medical doctor, and at the University of Leipzig. Williams was a doctor in Rutherford for over 40 years and took his inspiration from his patients and his surroundings. He published 45 books in the course of his lifetime while ministering to the health of his patients. He is most noted for his five-volume epic poem *Paterson.* His other writings include *Selected Essays* and *The Selected Letters of William Carlos Williams.*

1964

Louis Simpson   1038

Birth: March 27, 1923; Kingston, Jamaica, British West Indies. **Parents:** Aston and Rosalind (Marantz) Simpson. **Education:** Columbia University, NY: BS, MA, PhD. **Spouse:** Jeanne Rogers (m. 1949; div. 1954); Dorothy Roochvarg (m. 1955; div. 1979); Miriam Butensky Bachner (m. 1985). **Children:** Matthew (JR); Anne, Anthony (DR).

Prize: *Poetry,* 1964: *At the End of the Open Road: Poems,* Middletown, CT: Wesleyan University Press, 1963.

Career: Sergeant, U.S. Army, 1943-1946; Editor, Bobbs-Merrill Publishing, NY, 1950-1955; Instructor of English, Columbia University, NY, 1955-1959; Assistant Professor and Professor of English, University of California, Berkeley, 1959-1967; Professor of English and Comparative Literature, State University of New York at Stony Brook, 1967-91; Distinguished Professor, State University of New York at Stony Brook, beginning in 1991; Member, American Academy in Rome.

Selected Works: *The Arrivistes: Poems, 1940-1949,* 1949. *A Dream of Governors: Poems,* 1959. *James Hogg: A Critical Study,* 1962. *Riverside Drive,* 1962. *Selected Poems,* 1965. *An Introduction to Poetry,* 1967. *North of Jamaica,* 1972. *Three on the Tower: The Lives and Works of Ezra Pound, T. S. Eliot, and William Carlos Williams,* 1975. *Searching for the Ox,* 1976. *A Revolution in Taste: Studies of Dylan Thomas, Allen Ginsburg, Sylvia Plath, and Robert Lowell,* 1978. *Armidale,* 1979. *Caviare at the Funeral: Poems,* 1980. *A Company of Poets,* 1981. *People Live Here: Selected Poems 1949-1983,* 1983. *The Best Hour of the Night: Poems,* 1983. *The Character of the Poet,* 1986. *Selected Prose,* 1989. *In the Room We Share,* 1990. *Ships Going into the Blue: Essays and Notes on Poetry,* 1994. *There You Are: Poems,* 1995.

Other Awards: Bronze Star with Oak Leaf Cluster. Presidential Unit Citation. Two Purple Hearts. Prix de Rome, American Academy in Rome, 1957. Hudson Review Fellowship, 1957. Distinguished Alumni Award, Columbia University, 1960. Edna St. Vincent Millay Award, 1960. Guggenheim Fellowship, 1962, 1970. American Council of Learned Societies Grant, 1963. Medal for Excellence, 1965. American Academy of Arts and Letters Award in Literature, 1976. Institute of Jamaica, Centenary Medal. 1980. Jewish Book Council, Award for Poetry, 1981. Elmer Holmes Bobst Award, 1987. Honorary DHL, Eastern Michigan University, 1977. Honorary DLitt, Hampden Sydney College, VA, 1990.

For More Information: Moran, Ronald, *Louis Simpson,* New York: Twayne, 1972; *A Company of Poets,* Ann Arbor: University of Michigan Press, 1981; *The Character of the Poet,* Ann Arbor: University of Michigan Press, 1986; Lazer, Hank, ed., *On Louis Simpson: Depths Beyond Happiness,* Ann Arbor: University of Michigan Press, 1988.

Commentary: Louis Aston Marantz Simpson was awarded the 1964 Pulitzer Prize in Poetry for *At the End of the Open Road,* a collection composed in free verse with surreal imagery.

Simpson was born in Kingston, Jamaica in the British West Indies and educated at Columbia University. He came to the United States at the age of 17. His style has been divided into two distinct stages, using traditional meter in the first half of his career and then moving to free verse in the second half. His other works include *Riverside Drive, The Character of the Poet,* and *There You Are: Poems.*

1965

John Berryman   1039

Birth: October 25, 1914; McAlester, OK. **Death:** January 7, 1972. **Parents:** John Allyn and Martha (Little) Smith. **Education:** Columbia University, NY: AB. Clare College at Cambridge University, England: BA. **Spouse:** Eileen Mulligan (m. 1942; div. 1953); Ann Levine (m. 1956; div. 1959); Kate Donahue (m. 1961). **Children:** Paul (AL); Martha, Sara (KD).

Prize: *Poetry,* 1965: *77 Dream Songs,* New York: Farrar, Straus, 1964.

Career: Instructor of English, Wayne University (now Wayne State), Detroit, MI, 1939-1940; Instructor, Harvard University, MA, 1940-1943; Fellow, Princeton University, NJ, 1943-1944; Lecturer in Creative Writing, Princeton University, 1946-1949; Hodder Fellow, Princeton University, 1950-1951; Elliston Lecturer in Poetry, University of Cincinnati, OH, 1951-1952; Lecturer and later Regents Professor of Humanities, University of Minnesota, Minneapolis, 1955-1972; Poet-in-Residence, Trinity College, 1967; Poetry Reader, U.S. State Department Tour, India; Member: American Academy of Arts and Sciences, National Institute of Arts and Letters, Phi Beta Kappa.

Selected Works: *Poems,* 1942. *The Dispossessed,* 1948. *Stephen Crane,* 1950. *Homage to Mistress Bradstreet,* 1956. *Berryman's Sonnets,* 1967. *Short Poems,* 1967. *His Toy, His Dream, His Rest: 308 Dream Songs,* 1969. *Love & Fame,* 1970. *Delusions, Etc.,* 1972. *Recovery,* 1973. *A Tumult for John Berryman* (Harris, Marguerite, ed.), 1976. *A Dream Song,* 1976. *The Freedom of the Poet,* 1976. *Henry's Fate & Other Poems, 1967-1972,* 1977. *One Answer to a Question,* 1981. *We Dream of Honour: John Berryman's Letters to His Mother* (Kelly, Richard J., ed.), 1987. *Collected Poems, 1937-1971,* 1989.

Other Awards: Kellett Fellowship to Clare College, Oxford, England, 1936-1938. Oldham Shakespeare Scholar, Clare College, 1937. Rockefeller Fellow, 1944-1946. Kenyon Review-Doubleday Short Story Award, 1945: "The Imaginary Jew." Shelley Memorial Award, Poetry Society of America, 1949. Levinson Prize, 1950. National Institute of Arts and Letters Grant in Literature, 1950. Guggenheim Fellow, 1952-1953, 1966. Partisan Review Fellowship, 1957. Harriet Monroe Poetry Award, University of Chicago, 1957. Brandeis University Creative Arts Award, 1959-1960. Loines Award, National Institute of Arts and Letters, 1964. Academy of American

Poets Fellowship, 1966. National Endowment for the Arts Award, 1967. Emily Clark Balch Award, *Virginia Quarterly Review,* 1968. Bollingen Prize, 1969: *His Toy, His Dream, His Rest,* New York: Farrar, Straus and Giroux, 1969. National Book Award, 1969: *His Toy, His Dream, His Rest.*

For More Information: Arpin, Gary Q., *John Berryman: A Reference Guide,* Boston: G.K. Hall, 1976; Conarroe, Joel, *John Berryman: An Introduction to the Poetry,* New York: Columbia University Press, 1977; Haffenden, John, *The Life of John Berryman,* Boston: Routledge & K. Paul, 1982; Thomas, Harry, ed., *Berryman's Understanding: Reflections on the Poetry of John Berryman,* Boston: Northeastern University Press, 1988; Bloom, Harold, ed., *John Berryman,* New York: Chelsea House, 1989.

Commentary: *77 Dream Songs* won the 1965 Pulitzer Prize in Poetry for John Berryman. It was his major work, begun in 1955 and published in successive volumes.

John Berryman's original surname was Smith. It was changed to Berryman upon his adoption by his mother's second husband, John A. Berryman, after the suicide of his father. The suicide was constantly reflected in his poetry. He was a student of Mark Van Doren and Allen Tate while at Columbia. His first volume, *Poems,* was published in 1942. He pursued a career as poet and Shakespearean scholar, primarily teaching at the University of Minnesota. His other works include *Stephen Crane,* a critical biography, and *Recovery,* a novel about his lifelong struggle with alcoholism. He committed suicide in 1972 by jumping off a bridge in Minneapolis, Minnesota.

1966

Richard Eberhart   1040

Birth: April 5, 1904; Austin, MN. **Parents:** Alpha La Rue and Lena (Lowenstein) Eberhart. **Religion:** Episcopalian. **Education:** University of Minnesota. Dartmouth College, NH: BA. St. John's College, Cambridge, England: BA, MA. Harvard University, MA. **Spouse:** Helen Elizabeth Butcher (m. 1941). **Children:** Richard, Gretchen.

Prize: *Poetry,* 1966: *Selected Poems, 1930-1965,* New York: New Directions, 1965.

Career: Private tutor to son of King Prajadhipok of Siam, 1930-1931; Master in English, St. Mark's School, Southboro, MA, 1933-1941; Phi Beta Kappa Poet, Tufts University, 1941; English teacher, Cambridge School, Kendal Green, MA, 1941-1942; Lieutenant Commander, U.S. Naval Reserve, 1942-1946; Assistant Manager to Vice-President, Butcher Polish Company, MA, 1946-1952; Founder and President, The Poets' Theatre, 1950; Poet-in-Residence, University of Washington, Seattle, 1952-1953; Professor of English, University of Connecticut, Storrs, 1953-1954; Visiting Professor, Wheaton College, 1954-1955; Professor of English and Poet-in-Residence, Wheaton College, MA, 1954-1955; Christian Gauss Lecturer and Resident Fellow, Princeton University, NJ, 1955-1956; Member, Yaddo Corporation, beginning in 1955; Professor of English and Poet-in-Residence, Dartmouth College, NH, 1956-1968; Phi Beta Kappa Poet, Brown University, MA, 1957; Member of Advisory Committee on the Arts, John F. Kennedy Memorial Theatre, beginning in 1959; Consultant in Poetry, Library of Congress, Washington, DC, 1959-1961; Phi Beta Kappa Poet, College of William and Mary, VA, 1963; Phi Beta Kappa Poet, Swarthmore College, PA, 1963; Phi Beta Kappa Poet, Trinity College, CT, 1963; Honorary Consultant in American Letters, Library of Congress, 1963-1969; Director, Yaddo Corporation,1964; Phi Beta Kappa Poet, University of New Hampshire, 1964; Phi Beta Kappa Poet, Harvard University, MA, 1967; Professor Emeritus, Class of 1925, Dartmouth College, NH, 1968-1971; Professor, Dartmouth College, NH, beginning 1970; Honorary President, Poetry Society of America, 1972; Visiting Professor, University of Florida, 1974-1980; Adjunct Professor, Columbia University, 1975; Regents Professor, University of California, Davis, 1975; Fellow, Academy of American Poets; Member: American Academy of Arts and Sciences, American Academy and Institute of Arts and Letters, Bucks Harbor Yacht Club (ME), Century Club (NY), Phi Beta Kappa, Signet Club.

Selected Works: *Reading the Spirit,* 1936. *Song and Idea,* 1940. *Poems, New and Selected,* 1944. *War and the Poet: An Anthology of Poetry Expressing Man's Attitudes to War from Ancient Times to the Present* (Eberhart, Richard, and Rodman, Seldon, eds.), 1945. *Burr Oaks,* 1947. *Selected Poems,* 1951. *Undercliff: Poems, 1946-1953,* 1953. *Great Praises,* 1957. *Collected Poems, 1930-1960: Including 51 New Poems,* 1960. *Collected Verse Plays,* 1962. *The Quarry, New Poems,* 1964. *Thirty One Sonnets,* 1967. *Shifts of Being: Poems,* 1968. *Two Poems,* 1975. *Poems to Poets,* 1976. *Collected Poems, 1930-1976: Including 43 New Poems,* 1976. *Survivors,* 1979. *Of Poetry and Poets,* 1979. *Ways of Light: Poems, 1972-1980,* 1980. *Chocorua,* 1981. *The Long Reach: New & Uncollected Poems, 1948-1984,* 1984. *Collected Poems, 1930-1986,* 1987. *Maine Poems,* 1989.

Other Awards: Harriet Monroe Memorial Prize, 1950. New England Poetry Club Award, 1950. Shelley Memorial Award, 1952. Harriet Monroe Poetry Award, 1955. National Institute of Arts and Letters Grant in Literature, 1955. Co-Recipient, Bollingen Prize in Poetry, Yale University, 1962. Academy of American Poets Fellowship, 1969. National Book Award, 1977: *Collected Poems, 1930-1976,* New York: Oxford University Press, 1976.

President's Medallion, University of Florida, 1977. Poet Laureate of the State of New Hampshire, 1979-1984. Sarah Josepha Hale Award, Newport Library, NH, 1982. American Academy of Arts and Letters, 1982. Richard Eberhart Day Declared, Governor of Rhode Island, 1982. Richard Eberhart Day Declared, Dartmouth College, 1982. Florida Ambassador of Arts, 1984. St. John's College Honorary Fellow, 1986. Poetry Society of America, Robert Frost Medal, 1986. Presidential Medal for Outstanding Leadership and Achievement, Dartmouth College, 1990. Gold Medal for Poetry, Dartmouth College, 1992. Honorary DLitts: Dartmouth College, NH, 1954; Skidmore College, NY, 1966; College of Wooster, OH, 1969; Colgate University, NY, 1974. Honorary DHLs: Franklin Pierce College, NY, 1978; St. Lawrence University, NH, 1985; Plymouth State College, NH, 1987.

For More Information: Engel, Bernard F., *Richard Eberhart,* New York: Twayne, 1971.

Commentary: Richard Eberhart was awarded the 1966 Pulitzer Prize in Poetry for *Selected Poems.*

Eberhart was born in Austin, Minnesota. He was educated at the University of Minnesota, Dartmouth College, St. Johns at Cambridge in England, and at Harvard University. He served in the naval reserve as a lieutenant commander during World War II. He was appointed consultant in poetry to the Library of Congress from 1959 to 1961. His inspiration has come primarily from nature and the cycles of life. His first volume, *A Bravery of Earth,* was published in 1930. His other works include *Of Poetry and Poets* and *Maine Poems.*

1967

Anne Sexton   1041

Birth: November 9, 1928; Newton, MA. **Death:** October 4, 1974. **Parents:** Ralph Churchill and Mary Grab (Staples) Harvey. **Spouse:** Alfred M. Sexton II (m. 1948; div. 1974). **Children:** Linda Gray, Joyce Ladd.

Prize: *Poetry,* 1967: *Live or Die,* Boston: Houghton Mifflin, 1966.

Career: Model, Boston, MA, 1950-1951; Scholar, Radcliffe Institute for Independent Study, 1961-1963; Teacher, Wayland High School, MA,1967-1968; Lecturer of Creative Writing, Boston University, Boston, 1970-1971; Crawshaw Professor of Literature, Colgate University, NY, 1972; Professor of Creative Writing, Boston University, 1972-1974; Fellow, Royal Society of Literature; Honorary Member, Phi Beta Kappa; Member: New England Poetry Club, Poetry Society of America.

Selected Works: *To Bedlam and Part Way Back,* 1960. *All My Pretty Ones,* 1962. *Selected Poems,*

1964. *Love Poems,* 1969. *Transformations,* 1971. *The Book of Folly,* 1972. *The Death Notebooks,* 1974. *The Wizard's Tears* (with Maxine Kumin), 1975. *The Awful Rowing toward God,* 1975. *Anne Sexton: A Self-Portrait in Letters* (Sexton, Linda G. and Ames, Lois, eds.), 1977. *Words for Dr. Y: Uncollected Poems with Three Stories* (Sexton, Linda G., ed.), 1978. *Anne Sexton: The Artist and Her Critics* (McClatchy, J.D., ed.), 1978. *The Complete Poems,* 1981. *No Evil Star: Selected Essays, Interviews, and Prose* (Colburn, Steven E., ed.), 1985. *Selected Poems of Anne Sexton* (Middlebrook, Diane W. and George, Diana H., eds.), 1988.

Other Awards: Audience Poetry Prize, 1958-1959. Robert Frost Fellowship, Bread Loaf Writers Conference, 1959. Levinson Prize, Poetry, 1962. Traveling Fellowship, American Academy of Arts and Letters, 1963-1964. Ford Foundation Grant, 1964-1965. *First Literary* Magazine Travel Grant, Congress for Cultural Freedom, 1965-1966. Shelley Memorial Award, 1967. Guggenheim Fellowship, 1969. Honorary LittDs: Tufts University, MA, 1970; Regis College, MA, 1971; Fairfield University, CT, 1971.

For More Information: Northouse, Cameron, and Thomas P. Walsh, *Sylvia Plath and Anne Sexton: A Reference Guide,* Boston, G. K. Hall, 1974; George, Diana Hume, *Oedipus Anne: The Poetry of Anne Sexton,* Urbana: University of Illinois Press, 1987; *Sexton: Selected Criticism,* Urbana: University of Illinois Press, 1988; Wagner-Martin, Linda, ed., *Critical Essays on Anne Sexton,* Boston: G.K. Hall, 1989; Sexton, Linda Gray, *Searching for Mercy Street: My Journey Back to My Mother, Anne Sexton,* Boston: Little, Brown, 1994.

Commentary: Anne Sexton was awarded the 1967 Pulitzer Prize in Poetry for *Live or Die,* a telling collection of poems which indicate the precarious state of mind of the poet.

Sexton was born in Newton, Massachusetts and educated at Garland School, a finishing school in Massachusetts. She married at 19 and suffered a severe depression and attempted suicide after the birth of her second child. While hospitalized, her psychiatrist advised her to write poetry as therapy. She later won a scholarship to the Antioch Writers' Conference where she came under the tutelage of W.D. Snodgrass. It was his suggestion that she take a writing course with Robert Lowell. This led to a friendship with Sylvia Plath. Sexton took up the confessional style to relate her experiences in the mental hospital. She attempted suicide several more times and was successful in 1974, inhaling carbon monoxide. Her other works include *To Bedlam and Part Way Back, All My Pretty Ones,* and her last, *The Awful Rowing Toward God.*

1968

Anthony Hecht   1042

Birth: January 16, 1923; New York, NY. **Parents:** Melvyn Hahlo and Dorothea (Holzman) Hecht. **Education:** Bard College, NY: BA. Columbia University, NY: MA. **Spouse:** Patricia Harris (div.); Helen D'Alessandro (m. 1971). **Children:** Jason, Adam (PH); Evan Alexander (HD).

Prize: *Poetry,* 1968: *The Hard Hours: Poems,* New York: Atheneum, 1967.

Career: Served in Europe and Japan, U.S. Army; Instructor, Kenyon College, State University of Iowa, New York University, Smith College, and Washington University; Associate Professor of English, Bard College, NY, 1962-1967; John H. Deane Professor of Poetry and Rhetoric, University of Rochester, NY, 1967-1985; Chancellor, Academy of American Poets, 1971-1975; Visiting Professor, Harvard University, MA, 1973; Visiting Professor, Yale University, CT, 1977; Consultant in Poetry, Library of Congress, 1982-1984; Trustee, American Academy, Rome, beginning in 1983; University Professor, Georgetown University, Washington, DC, 1985-1993; Andrew Mellon Lecturer in the Fine Arts, National Gallery of Art, 1992; Rockefeller Foundation Resident, Villa Serbelloni, Bellagio, Italy, 1993; Fellow, American Academy of Arts and Sciences; Member: Century Association, National Institute of Arts and Letters, Phi Beta Kappa.

Selected Works: *A Summoning of Stones,* 1954. *Jiggery-Pokery: A Compendium of Double Dactyls* (Hecht, Anthony and Hollander, John eds.), 1966. *Seven against Thebes* (Translation) (with Helen. H. Bacon), 1973. *Obbligati: Essays in Criticism,* 1986. *Collected Earlier Poems: The Complete Texts of "The Hard Hours," "Millions of Strange Shadows," "The Venetian Vespers,"* 1990. *The Hidden Law: The Poetry of W.H. Auden,* 1993. *On the Laws of the Poetic Art,* 1995. *Flight among the Tombs: Poems,* 1996.

Other Awards: Prix de Rome Fellowship, 1951. Guggenheim Fellowships, 1954, 1959. Hudson Review Fellowship, 1958. Ford Foundation Fellowship, 1960. Brandeis University Creative Arts Award in Poetry, 1965. Rockefeller Foundation Fellowship, 1967. Russell Loines Award, 1968: *The Hard Hours.* Miles Poetry Prize, 1968: *The Hard Hours.* Academy of American Poets Fellowship, 1969. Fulbright Professor, Brazil, 1971. English-Speaking Union Award, 1981. Charles Kellogg Award, Bard College, 1982. Bollingen Prize, 1983. Eugenio Montale Award for Poetry, 1983. Harriet Monroe Award, 1987. Ruth B. Lilly Award, 1988. Aiken Taylor Award, *Sewanee Review,* 1989. National Education Association Grant, 1989. Honorary PhDs: Bard College; NY, Georgetown University, Washington, DC; Towson State

University, NY; University of Rochester, NY; St. John Fisher College, NY.

For More Information: German, Norman, *Anthony Hecht,* New York: Lang, 1989; Lea, Sydney, ed., *The Burdens of Formality: Essays on the Poetry of Anthony Hecht,* Athens, GA: University of Georgia Press, 1989.

Commentary: *The Hard Hours* won the 1968 Pulitzer Prize in Poetry for Anthony Evan Hecht.

Hecht was born in New York City and educated at Bard College and at Columbia University. His style has been termed erudite and ornate. His other works include *Millions of Strange Shadows, The Transparent Man, The Hidden Law: The Poetry of W.H. Auden,* and *Flight Among the Tombs: Poems.* His poems appear regularly in such magazines as the *New Yorker* and *Harper's.*

1969

George Oppen   1043

Birth: April 24, 1908; New Rochelle, NY. **Death:** July 7, 1984. **Parents:** George A. and Elsie (Rothfeld) Oppen. **Spouse:** Mary Colby (m. 1928). **Children:** Linda.

Prize: *Poetry,* 1969: *Of Being Numerous,* New York: New Directions, 1968.

Career: Poet; Publisher, Paris, France, 1930-1933; Member, Objectivist Press Co-Op, NY, 1934-1936; Organizer, Workers Alliance, Brooklyn, NY, and Utica, NY, beginning in 1935; Combat soldier, U.S. Army, 1942-1945; Cabinet maker and contractor, Los Angeles, CA, late 1940s; Operator of furniture factory, Mexico City, Mexico, 1950s; Poet, U.S., 1958-.

Selected Works: *Discrete Series,* 1934. *The Materials,* 1962. *The Collected Poems of George Oppen,* 1975. *Primitive,* 1978. *The Selected Letters of George Oppen* (DuPlessis, Rachel B., ed.), 1990. *Poems of George Oppen, 1908-1984* (Tomlinson, Charles, ed.), 1990.

Other Awards: American Academy and Institute of Arts and Letters Award, 1980.

For More Information: Oppen, Mary, *Meaning a Life: An Autobiography,* Santa Barbara, CA: Black Sparrow, 1978; Hatlen, Burton, ed., *George Oppen, Man and Poet,* Orono, ME: National Poetry Foundation, 1981; *Not Comforts, But Vision: Essays on the Poetry of George Oppen,* Budleigh Salterton, Devon, England: Interim, 1985.

Commentary: George Oppen was awarded the 1969 Pulitzer Prize in Poetry for *Of Being Numerous.*

Oppen was born in New Rochelle, New York. While living in France, Oppen and his wife Mary published *An Objectivist Anthology* in 1932. They returned to New York and he founded the Objectivist

Press in New York, which published his first collection of poems, *Discrete Series,* in 1934. He was an active Communist who organized the unemployed in the late 1930s. Despite having fought in World War II, he came under investigation by Senator Joseph McCarthy and the House Committee on Un-American Activities and fled to Mexico to avoid prosecution. He returned to the United States following the death of Senator McCarthy. His other works include *Poems of George Oppen, 1908-1984.*

1970

Richard Howard   1044
Birth: October 13, 1929; Cleveland, OH. **Education:** Columbia University, NY: BA, MA. Sorbonne University, France.

Prize: *Poetry,* 1970: *Untitled Subjects: Poems,* New York: Atheneum, 1969.

Career: Poet, critic, and translator; Lexicographer, World Publishing Company, 1953-1957; President, PEN American Center, 1977-1979; Rhodes Professor of Comparative Literature, University of Cincinnati, Ohio, beginning in 1988; Fellow, Yale University, CT; Member, American Institute of Arts and Letters.

Selected Works: *Quantities: Poems,* 1962. *The Damages: Poems,* 1967. *Alone with America: Essays on the Art of Poetry in the United States since 1950,* 1969. *Findings: Poems,* 1971. *Two-Part Inventions: Poems,* 1974. *Fellow Feelings: Poems,* 1976. *Lining Up: Poems,* 1984. *Quantities/Damages: Early Poems,* 1984. *No Traveller: Poems,* 1989. *Like Most Revelations: New Poems,* 1994.

Other Awards: Guggenheim Fellow, 1966-1967. Harriet Monroe Memorial Prize, 1969. National Institute of Arts and Letters Grant, 1970. Levinson Prize, *Poetry* magazine, 1973. Cleveland Arts Prize, 1974. American Academy and Institute of Arts and Letters Medal for Poetry, 1980. American Book Award, 1984. Translation of *Les Fleurs du Mal* by Charles Baudelaire. PEN American Center Medal for Translation, 1986. National Endowment for the Arts Fellow, 1987. France-America Foundation Award for Translation, 1987.

For More Information: Biemiller, Lawrence, "Elegant Interjections and Learnedly Raunchy Humor From Richard Howard," *Chronicle of Higher Education,* January 13, 1995; Longenbach, James, "Richard Howard's Modern World," *Salmagundi,* Fall 1995.

Commentary: Richard Howard was awarded the 1970 Pulitzer Prize in Poetry for *Untitled Subjects,* a series of 15 dramatic monologues.

Howard was born in Cleveland, Ohio and educated at Columbia University and the Sorbonne in France. He has done many translations of works by

French writers. His other works include *Two-Part Inventions, Like Most Revelations: New Poems,* and the recent translation of Jules Verne's *Paris in the Twentieth Century.*

1971

William S. Merwin   1045
Birth: September 30, 1927; New York, NY. **Education:** Princeton University, NJ: AB. **Spouse:** Dorothy Jeanne Ferry; Dido Milroy; Paula Schwartz.

Prize: *Poetry,* 1971: *The Carrier of Ladders,* New York: Atheneum, 1970.

Career: Tutor, France and Portugal, 1949; Tutor, Spain, 1950; Spanish and French Literary Translator, British Broadcasting Corporation Third Programme, London, England, 1951-1954; Playwright, Poets' Theatre, Cambridge, MA, 1956; Member, National Institute of Arts and Letters.

Selected Works: *A Mask for Janus,* 1952. *The Dancing Bears,* 1954. *Green with Beasts,* 1956. *The Drunk in the Furnace,* 1960. *The Moving Target,* 1963. *Transparence of the World,* 1969. *The Lice,* 1969. *Animae,* 1969. *The Miner's Pale Children,* 1970. *Darling Bender,* 1971. *Signs* (with A. D. Moore), 1971. *Chinese Figures,* 1971. *Japanese Figures,* 1971. *Asian Figures,* 1973. *Writings to an Unfinished Accompaniment,* 1973. *For a Coming Extinction,* 1974. *The First Four Books of Poems,* 1975. *Three Poems,* 1975. *Houses and Travellers,* 1977. *The Compass Flower,* 1977. *Sanskrit Love Poetry* (Translation) (with J. Moussaieff Masson), 1977. *Feathers from the Hill,* 1978. *Unframed Original,* 1982. *Finding the Islands,* 1982. *Opening the Hand,* 1983. *The Lost Upland,* 1992. *Unframed Originals: Recollections,* 1994. *The Miner's Pale Children,* 1994. *The Vixen: Poems,* 1996. *Flower & Hand: Poems, 1977-1983,* 1997.

Other Awards: Kenyon Review Fellowship in Poetry, 1954. Rockefeller Fellowship, 1956. National Institute of Arts and Letters Grant, 1957. Playwriting Bursary, Arts Council of Great Britain, 1957. Rabinowitz Foundation Grant, 1961. Bess Hokin Prize, *Poetry* magazine, 1962. Ford Foundation Grant, 1964-1965. Chapelbrook Foundation Fellowship, 1966. Harriet Monroe Memorial Prize, *Poetry,* 1967. Rockefeller Foundation Grant, 1969. Academy of American Poets Fellowship, 1973. Guggenheim Fellowship, 1973, 1983. Shelley Memorial Award, 1974. Bollingen Prize for Poetry, Yale University Library, 1979. Lenore Marshall Poetry Prize, 1994: "Travels." Tanning Prize for Poetry, 1994. Lila Wallace/Reader's Digest Fellowship, 1994.

For More Information: Davis, Cheri, *W.S. Merwin,* Boston: Twayne, 1981; Christhilf, Mark, *W.S. Merwin, the Mythmaker,* Columbia: University of

Missouri Press, 1986; Brunner, Edward, *Poetry as Labor and Privilege: The Writings of W.S. Merwin,* Urbana: University of Illinois Press, 1991; *Unframed Originals: Recollections,* New York: Holt, 1994; Hix, H.L., *Understanding W.S. Merwin,* Columbia: University of South Carolina Press, 1997.

Commentary: *The Carrier of Ladders* won the 1971 Pulitzer Prize in Poetry for William Stanley Merwin.

Merwin was born in New York City and was educated at Princeton University. He is known for a surrealistic style and an obsession with the meaning of America. He has also done translations, prose, and drama. His first volume, *A Mask for Janus,* was published in 1952 and received critical acclaim.

1972

James Wright   1046
Birth: December 13, 1927; Martins Ferry, OH. **Death:** March 25, 1980. **Education:** Kenyon College, OH: BA. University of Washington: MA, PhD. **Spouse:** Second marriage, Edith Anne Runk (m. 1967). **Children:** Franz Paul, Marshall John (first wife).

Prize: *Poetry,* 1972: *Collected Poems,* Middletown, CT: Wesleyan University Press, 1971.

Career: Poet and translator; Served in U.S. Army, WW II; English Instructor, University of Minnesota, Minneapolis, 1957-1964; English Instructor, Macalester College, MN, 1963-1965; Professor of English, Hunter College, City University of NY, 1966-1980; Visiting Lecturer, State University of New York at Buffalo, 1974; Fellow, Academy of American Poets.

Selected Works: *The Green Wall,* 1957. *Saint Judas,* 1959. *The Branch Will Not Break,* 1963. *Shall We Gather at the River,* 1968. *Two Citizens,* 1973. *Moments of the Italian Summer,* 1976. *To a Blossoming Pear Tree,* 1977. *A Reply to Matthew Arnold,* 1981. *Leave It to the Sunlight,* 1981. *Fresh Wind in Venice: A Poem,* 1982. *The Temple in Nimes,* 1982. *This Journey,* 1982. *Collected Prose,* 1983. *The Heart of the Light,* 1990.

Other Awards: Fulbright Fellow, Austria, 1952-1953. Eunice Tietjens Memorial Prize, 1955. Oscar Blumenthal Award, 1968. Yale Series of Younger Poets Award, 1957: *The Green Wall.* New Haven, CT: Yale University Press, 1957. *Kenyon Review* Fellowship in Poetry, 1958. National Institute of Arts and Letters Grant in Literature, 1959. Ohiona Book Award, 1960: *Saint Judas,* Middletown, CT: Wesleyan University Press, 1959. Guggenheim Fellowship, 1964, 1978. Creative Arts Award, Brandeis University, 1970. Academy of American Poets Fellowship, 1971. Melville Cane Award, Poetry Society of America, 1972.

For More Information: Saunders, William S., *James Wright, An Introduction,* Columbus: State Library of Ohio, 1979; Smith, Dave, ed., *The Pure Clear Word: Essays on the Poetry of James Wright,* Urbana: University of Illinois Press, 1982; Dougherty, David C., *James Wright,* Boston: Twayne, 1987; Stein, Kevin, *James Wright: The Poetry of a Grown Man: Constancy and Transition in the Work of James Wright,* Athens: Ohio University Press, 1989; Elkins, Andrew, *The Poetry of James Wright,* Tuscaloosa: University of Alabama Press, 1991.

Commentary: James Arlington Wright was awarded the 1972 Pulitzer Prize in Poetry for *Collected Poems,* which contained much of his earlier volumes.

Wright was born in Martins Ferry, Ohio and educated at Kenyon College and the University of Washington. He studied with John Crowe Ransom and Theodore Roethke. Wright was known for his ability to experiment with language and style. His first collection, *The Green Wall,* was published in 1957. His other works include *Saint Judas, Moments of the Italian Summer,* and *The Heart of the Light,* which was published posthumously.

1973

Maxine Kumin   1047
Birth: June 6, 1925; Philadelphia, PA. **Parents:** Peter and Doll (Simon) Winokur. **Education:** Radcliffe College, MA: AB, AM. **Spouse:** Victor Montwid Kumin (m. 1946). **Children:** Jane Simon, Judith Montwid, Daniel David.

Prize: *Poetry,* 1973: *Up Country: Poems of New England, New and Selected,* New York: Harper & Row, 1972.

Career: Poet, children's author, and fiction writer; Instructor, Tufts University, MA, 1958-1961; Scholar of Radcliffe Institute for Independent Study, Radcliffe College, MA, 1961-1963; Lecturer of English, Tufts University, MA, 1965-1968; Visiting Lecturer of English, University of Massachusetts, Amherst, 1973; Adjunct Professor of Writing, Columbia University, NY, 1975; Fannie Hurst Professor of Literature, Brandeis University, MA, 1975; Visiting Senior Fellow and Lecturer, Princeton University, NJ, 1977; Carolyn Wilkerson Bell Visiting Scholar, Randolph-Macon Woman's College, VA, 1978; Woodrow Wilson Visiting Fellow, 1979; Visiting Lecturer, Princeton University, NJ, 1979 and 1981-1982; Poet-in-Residence, Bucknell University, Lewisburg, PA, 1983; Visiting Professor, Massachusetts Institute of Technology, MA, 1984; Master Artist, Atlantic Center for the Arts, New Smyrna Beach, FL, 1984; Member of staff, Bread Loaf Writers' Conference, 1969-71, 1973, 1975, 1977; Poetry Consultant, Library of Congress, 1981-1982; Arts America Tour member, traveled with the U.S. Information Agency, 1983; Elector, The Poet's Corner, The Cathedral of St. John the Divine, beginning in 1990; Member: Authors Guild, PEN, Radcliffe Alumnae Association, Writers Union.

Selected Works: *Halfway,* 1961. *Through Dooms of Love,* 1965. *The Privilege,* 1965. *The Passions of Uxport: A Novel,* 1968. *The Nightmare Factory,* 1970. *The Abduction,* 1971. *The Wizard's Tears* (with Anne Sexton), 1975. *House, Bridge, Fountain, Gate,* 1975. *What Color Is Caesar?,* 1978. *The Retrieval System,* 1978. *To Make a Prairie: Essays on Poets, Poetry, and Country Living,* 1979. *Why Can't We Live Together Like Civilized Human Beings?,* 1982. *Our Ground Time Here Will Be Brief,* 1982. *Closing the Ring,* 1984. *The Long Approach: Poems,* 1985. *In Deep: Country Essays,* 1987. *Nurture: Poems,* 1989. *Connecting the Dots: Poems,* 1996. *Selected Poems, 1960-1990,* 1997.

Other Awards: Lowell Mason Palmer Award, 1960. National Endowment for the Arts Grant, 1966. National Council on the Arts and Humanities Fellow, 1967-1968. William Marion Reedy Award, 1968. Eunice Tietjens Memorial Prize, *Poetry,* 1972. Borestone Mountain Award, 1976. Radcliffe College Alumnae Recognition Award, 1978. Woodrow Wilson Fellowship, 1979-1980 and 1991-1993. American Academy and Institute of Arts and Letters, Excellence in Literature Award, 1980. Academy of American Poets Fellowship, 1986. Honorary DHL: Centre College, 1976; Davis and Elkins College, 1977; Regis College, 1979. Honorary DHumLett: New England College, 1982; Claremont Graduate School, 1983; and University of New Hampshire, 1984.

For More Information: *To Make a Prairie: Essays on Poets, Poetry, and Country Living,* Ann Arbor: University of Michigan Press, 1979; Grosholz, Emily, ed., *Telling the Barn Swallow: Poets on the Poetry of Maxine Kumin,* Hanover, NH: University Press of New England, 1997.

Commentary: Maxine Kumin was awarded the 1973 Pulitzer Prize in Poetry for *Up Country: The Poems of New England,* inspired by Kumin's life on a New Hampshire farm.

Kumin was born in Philadelphia, Pennsylvania and educated at Radcliffe College. She writes verse in a traditional style. She has held numerous teaching positions and is currently the chancellor at the Academy of American Poets. She has been the elector at Poet's Corner at the Cathedral of St. John the Divine since 1990. Her first collection, *Halfway,* was published in 1961. Her other works include *Looking for Luck,* the novel *The Designated Heir,* a collection of short

stories, *Why Can't We Live Together Like Civilized Human Beings?* and *Selected Poems: 1960-1990.*

1974

Robert Lowell
Full entry appears as **#1024** under "Poetry," 1947.

1975

Gary Snyder   1048
Birth: May 8, 1930; San Francisco, CA. **Parents:** Harold Alton and Lois (Wilkie) Snyder. **Religion:** Mahayana-Vajrayana Buddhist. **Education:** Reed College, OR: BA. Indiana University. University of California, Berkeley. **Spouse:** Alison Gass (m. 1950; div. 1951); Joanne Kyger (m. 1960; div. 1964); Masa Uehara (m. 1967; div.); Carole Koda (m.1991). **Children:** Kai, Gen (MU).

Prize: *Poetry,* 1975: *Turtle Island,* New York: New Directions, 1974.

Career: Poet and translator; Seaman, logger, and forest lookout, 1948-1956; Lecturer, University of California, Berkeley, 1964-65; Member, United Nations Conference on the Human Environment, 1972; Professor, University of California, Davis, beginning in 1985; Former Chair, California Arts Council; Member, American Academy and Institute of Arts and Letters.

Selected Works: *Riprap,* 1959. *Myths & Texts,* 1960. *The Wooden Fish: Basic Sutras & Gathas of Rinzai Zen* (with Kanetsuki Gutetsu), 1961. *Six Sections from Mountains and Rivers without End,* 1965. *Riprap, & Cold Mountain Poems,* 1965. *A Range of Poems,* 1966. *The Back Country,* 1968. *Manzanita,* 1972. *Myths & Texts,* 1978. *Songs for Gaia,* 1979. *He Who Hunted Birds in His Father's Village: Dimensions of a Haida Myth,* 1979. *Passage through India,* 1983. *Axe Handles: Poems,* 1983. *Tree Song,* 1986. *Left out in the Rain: New Poems, 1947-1985,* 1986. *The Practice of the Wild: Essays,* 1990. *A Place in Space: Ethics, Aesthetics, and Watersheds; New and Selected Prose,* 1995.

Other Awards: First Zen Institute of America Scholarship, 1956. National Institute and American Academy Poetry Award, 1966. Bollingen Foundation Grant, 1966-1967. Frank O'Hara Prize, 1967. Levinson Prize, 1968. Guggenheim Fellowship, 1968-1969.

For More Information: Kherdian, David, *Six Poets of the San Francisco Renaissance: Portraits and Checklists,* Fresno, CA: Giligia,1967; Halper, Jon, ed., *Gary Snyder: Dimensions of a Life,* San Francisco, CA: Sierra Club, 1991; Dean, Tim, *Gary Snyder and the American Unconscious: Inhabiting* *the Ground,* Houndmills, England: Macmillan, 1991; Murphy, Patrick D. *Understanding Gary Snyder,* Columbia: University of South Carolina Press, 1992.

Commentary: *Turtle Island* won the 1975 Pulitzer Prize in Poetry for Gary Snyder. It is a collection of poems which explore the need for community and cultural renewal.

Snyder was born in San Francisco. He was educated at Reed College, Indiana University, and the University of California at Berkeley, where he studied Oriental languages. Snyder has worked as a merchant seaman, logger, and forest lookout. He was a part of the Beat movement and was the basis for Kerouac's character Japhy Ryder in the novel *The Dharma Bums.* Snyder is noted for his knowledge of geology, anthropology, and evolutionary biology, which comes out in his poetry. He has taught at the University of California at Davis. His works include *Passage Through India, Tree Song,* and *A Place in Space: Ethics, Aesthetics, and Watersheds: New and Selected Prose.*

1976

John Ashbery   1049

Birth: July 28, 1927; Rochester, NY. **Parents:** Chester Frederick and Helen (Lawrence) Ashbery. **Education:** Harvard University, MA: BA. Columbia University, NY: MA. New York University.

Prize: *Poetry,* 1976: *Self-Portrait in a Convex Mirror: Poems,* New York: Viking, 1975.

Career: Writer, critic, and editor; Reference Librarian, Brooklyn Public Library, NY; Copywriter, Oxford University Press, New York City, 1951-1954; Copywriter, McGraw-Hill Book Co., New York City, 1954-1955; Instructor, Elementary French, New York University, NY, 1957-1958; Editor, *Locus Solus,* Lans-en-Vercors, France,1960-1962; Art Critic, *New York Herald-Tribune,* European Edition, Paris, France, 1960-1965; Art Critic, *Art International,* Lugano Switzerland, 1961-1964; Editor, *Art and Literature,* Paris, 1963-1966; Paris Correspondent, *Art News,* NY, 1964-1965; Executive Editor, *Art News,* NY, 1966-1972; Staff member, Brooklyn College, City University of NY, 1974-1990; Poetry Editor, *Partisan Review,* 1976-80; Art Critic, *Art International,* Switzerland, 1961-1964 and New York, 1978-1980; Art Critic, *New York Magazine,* 1978-1980; Art Critic, *Newsweek,* NY, 1980-1985; Member, American Academy and Institute of Arts and Letters, beginning in 1980; Professor of English and Co-Director of Master of Fine Arts Program in Creative Writing, Brooklyn College, NY, 1980-1990; Chancellor, Academy of American Poets, beginning in 1988; Charles Eliot Norton Professor of Poetry, Harvard University, MA, 1989-1990; Distinguished Emeritus

Professor, Brooklyn College, NY, 1990; Bard College, Annandale-on-Hudson, NY, beginning in 1990; Member, American Academy of Arts and Sciences.

Selected Works: *Some Trees,* 1956. *The Poems,* 1960. *The Tennis Court Oath: A Book of Poems,* 1962. *Fragment: Poem,* 1966. *Rivers and Mountains,* 1966. *A Nest of Ninnies* (with James Schuyler), 1969. *The Double Dream of Spring,* 1970. *Three Poems,* 1972. *The Vermont Notebook,* 1975. *Houseboat Days: Poems,* 1977. *Three Plays: "The Heroes," "The Compromise," "The Philosopher,"* 1978. *Shadow Train: Poems,* 1981. *Kitaj Paintings, Drawings, Pastels,* 1983. *A Wave: Poems,* 1984. *Selected Poems,* 1985. *Not a First,* 1987. *Reported Sightings: Art Chronicles, 1957-1987,* 1989. *Flow Chart,* 1991. *Hotel Lautramont,* 1992. *Three Books: Poems,* 1993. *And the Stars Were Shining,* 1994. *Pistils/Mapplethorpe,* 1996.

Other Awards: Co-Winner, Discovery Prize, Young Men's Hebrew Association, 1952. Fulbright Scholarships, France, 1955-1956, 1956-1957. Yale Series of Younger Poets Prize, 1956: *Some Trees.* Poets' Foundation Grants, 1960, 1964. Ingram-Merrill Foundation Grants, 1962, 1972. Harriet Monroe Poetry Award, 1963. Union League Civic and Arts Foundation Prize, 1966. Guggenheim Fellowships, 1967, 1973. National Endowment for the Arts Grants, 1968, 1969. National Institute of Arts and Letters Award, 1969. Shelley Memorial Award, Poetry Society of America, 1973: *Three Poems,* New York: Viking, 1972. Frank O'Hara Prize, Modern Poetry Association, 1974. Harriet Monroe Poetry Award, University of Chicago, 1976: *Self-Portrait in a Convex Mirror,* New York: Viking, 1975. National Book Award, 1976: *Self-Portrait in a Convex Mirror.* National Book Critics Circle Award, 1976: *Self-Portrait in a Convex Mirror.* Levinson Prize, 1977. Rockefeller Foundation Grant, Playwriting, 1978. Phi Beta Kappa Poet, Harvard University, 1979. English-Speaking Union Poetry Award, 1979. Academy of American Poets Fellowship, 1982. The Mayor's Award of Honor for Arts and Culture, New York City, 1983. Charles Flint Kellogg Award in Arts and Letters, Bard College, 1983. Poet of the Year, Pasadena City College, 1984. Co-Winner, Bollingen Prize, 1985, for the body of his work. Wallace Stevens Fellowship, Yale University, 1985. MacArthur Foundation Fellowship, 1985-1990. Common Wealth Award, 1986. Lenore Marshall Award, *Nation,* 1986: *A Wave,* New York: Viking, 1984. Creative Arts Award in Poetry, Brandeis University, 1989. Ruth Lilly Poetry Prize, *Poetry* magazine, 1992. Robert Frost Medal, Poetry Society of America, 1995. Grand Prix des Biennales Internationales de Poesie, 1996. D.Litt., Southampton College of Long Island University, 1979.

For More Information: Shapiro, David, *John Ashbery, An Introduction to the Poetry,* New York:

Columbia University Press, 1979; Lehman, David, ed., *Beyond Amazement: New Essays on John Ashbery,* Ithaca, NY: Cornell University Press, 1980; Ward, Geoff, *Statutes of Liberty: The New York School of Poets,* New York: St. Martin's, 1993; Schultz, Susan, ed., *The Tribe of John: Ashbery and Contemporary Poetry,* Tuscaloosa: University of Alabama Press, 1995.

Commentary: John Ashbery was awarded the 1976 Pulitzer Prize in Poetry for *Self-Portrait in a Convex Mirror,* a collection which Ashbery said was successful due to "the essayistic thrust" of its title poem.

Ashbery was born in Rochester, New York. He was educated at Harvard, Columbia, and New York Universities. He was art critic for the *Herald Tribune* and *Art News* in the 1950s and 1960s before joining the creative writing faculty at Brooklyn College. He has long been associated with avant-garde and experimental art and poetry. His first volume, *Some Trees,* was published in 1956. His other works include *Shadow Train, April Galleons,* and *And the Stars Were Shining.* He has also published under the pseudonym Jonas Berry. Ashbery has conducted special research on the life and work of Raymond Roussel.

1977

James Merrill   1050

Birth: April 25, 1920; Los Angeles, CA. **Death:** February 6, 1995. **Parents:** Clarence Mercer and Helen (Hillman) Merrill. **Religion:** Episcopalian. **Education:** Pomona College, CA: BA. Claremont Graduate School, CA: MA. University of California, Los Angeles: PhD. **Spouse:** Ann McIntosh (m. 1945). **Children:** Eugenia Louise, James McIntosh.

Prize: *Poetry,* 1977: *Divine Comedies: Poems,* New York: Atheneum, 1976.

Career: Lieutenant, U.S. Naval Reserve, 1942-1946; Assistant Professor, Whittier College, CA, 1952-1958; Associate Professor of History, Whittier College, CA, 1958-1966; Professor of History, University of Delaware, Newark, beginning in 1966; Member: American Historical Association, Southern Historical Association.

Selected Works: *First Poems,* 1950. *The Seraglio,* 1957. *The Country of a Thousand Years of Peace, and Other Poems,* 1958. *Selected Poems,* 1961. *Water Street, Poems,* 1962. *The (Diblos) Notebook,* 1965. *Nights and Days: Poems,* 1966. *The Fire Screen: Poems,* 1969. *Yannina,* 1972. *Braving the Elements: Poems,* 1972. *The Yellow Pages: 59 Poems,* 1974. *Metamorphosis of 741,* 1977. *Ideas, Etc.,* 1980. *Scripts for the Pageant,* 1980. *Santorini: Stopping the Leak,* 1982. *Marbled Paper,* 1982. *Peter,* 1982. *From the First Nine: Poems, 1946-1976,* 1982. *The Chang-*

ing Light at Sandover, 1982. *Bronze,* 1984. *Souvenirs,* 1984. *Late Settings: Poems,* 1985. *The Image Maker: A Play in One Act,* 1986. *Recitative: Prose,* 1986. *The Inner Room: Poems,* 1988. *Overdue Pilgrimage to Nova Scotia,* 1990. *Selected Poems, 1946-1985,* 1992. *A Different Person: A Memoir,* 1993. *A Scattering of Salts: Poems,* 1995.

Other Awards: Pacific Ribbon, Three Battle Stars, U.S. Naval Reserve, 1942-1946. Guggenheim Research Fellowship, 1958-1959. Mershon National Security Research Fellowship, 1961-1962.

For More Information: Lehman, David and Charles Berger, eds., *James Merrill: Essays in Criticism,* Ithaca, NY: Cornell University Press, 1983; Rotella, Guy, ed., *Critical Essays on James Merrill,* New York: G.K. Hall, 1996; Adams, Don, *James Merrill's Poetic Quest,* Westport, CT: Greenwood, 1997.

Commentary: James Merrill was awarded the 1977 Pulitzer Prize in Poetry for *Divine Comedies,* a book of occult poetry.

Merrill was born in Los Angeles and was educated at Pomona College, Claremont Graduate School, and the University of California at Los Angeles. Merrill grew up in a wealthy family. His work has been described as mixing different stanzaic patterns with blank verse and even prose. His first collection, *First Poems,* was published in 1951. His other works include *Water Street, The Inner Room,* and *A Scattering of Salts.*

1978

Howard Nemerov   1051

Birth: March 1, 1920; New York, NY. **Death:** July 5, 1991. **Parents:** David and Gertrude (Russek) Nemerov. **Education:** Harvard University, MA: AB. **Spouse:** Margaret Russell (m. 1944). **Children:** David, Alexander Michael, Jeremy Seth.

Prize: *Poetry,* 1978: *The Collected Poems of Howard Nemerov,* Chicago: University of Chicago Press, 1977.

Career: Flying Officer, Royal Canadian Air Force, 1942-1944; First Lieutenant, U.S. Army Air Forces, 1944-1945; Instructor, Hamilton College, NY, 1946-1948; Member of Faculty in Literature, Bennington College, VT, 1948-1966; Visiting Lecturer in English, University of Minnesota, 1958-1959; Writer-in-Residence, Hollins College, 1962-1964; Consultant in Poetry, Library of Congress, 1963-1964; Professor of English, Brandeis University, MA, 1966-1969; Visiting Hurst Professor of English, Washington University, MO, 1969-1970; Professor of English, Washington University, MO, 1970-1976; Edward Mallinckrodt Distinguished University Professor of English, Washington University, MO, 1976-

1990; Chancellor, American Academy of Poets, beginning in 1976.

Selected Works: *The Image and the Law,* 1947. *The Melodramatists,* 1949. *Guide to the Ruins: Poems,* 1950. *The Salt Garden: Poems,* 1955. *Mirrors & Windows, Poems,* 1958. *New & Selected Poems,* 1960. *The Next Room of the Dream: Poem and Two Plays,* 1962. *Poetry and Fiction: Essays,* 1963. *Journal of the Fictive Life,* 1965. *Poets on Poetry,* 1966. *Dangers of Reasoning by Analogy,* 1966. *The Blue Swallows: Poems,* 1967. *The Winter Lightning: Selected Poems of Howard Nemerov,* 1968. *Stories, Fables & Other Diversions,* 1971. *Reflexions on Poetry & Poetics,* 1972. *The Western Approaches: Poems, 1973-75,* 1975. *Figures of Thought: Speculations on the Meaning of Poetry & Other Essays,* 1978. *Sentences,* 1980. *Inside the Onion,* 1984. *New & Selected Essays,* 1985. *War Stories: Poems about Long Ago and Now,* 1987. *The Oak in the Acorn: On Remembrance of Things Past, and on Teaching Proust, Who Will Never Learn,* 1987. *Trying Conclusions: New and Selected Poems, 1961-1991,* 1991.

Other Awards: Bowdoin Prize, Harvard University, 1940. Kenyon Review Fellowship in Fiction, 1955. Oscar Blumenthal Prize, 1958. Harriet Monroe Memorial Prize, 1959. Frank O'Hara Memorial Prize, 1971. Levinson Prize, 1975. Second Prize, Virginia Quarterly Review Short Story Competition, 1958. National Institute of Arts and Letters Grant, 1961. Golden Rose Trophy, New England Poetry Club, 1962. Brandeis Creative Arts Award, 1963. National Endowment for the Arts Grant, 1966-1967. First Theodore Roethke Memorial Award, 1968. *The Blue Swallows.* Prize for Poetry, St. Botolph's Club, Boston, 1968. Guggenheim Fellow, 1968-1969. Academy of American Poets Fellowship, 1970. O'Hara Prize, 1971. National Book Award, 1978: *The Collected Poems of Howard Nemerov.* Chicago, IL: University of Chicago Press, 1977. Bollingen Prize, Yale University Press, 1981: *The Collected Poems of Howard Nemerov.* First Aiken Taylor Award for Modern Poetry, *Sewanee Review,* University Press of the South, 1987. National Medal of the Arts, 1987. Poet Laureate of the United States, 1988-1990. Honorary Degree, Washington and Lee University,VA.

For More Information: Mills, William, *The Stillness in Moving Things: The World of Howard Nemerov,* Memphis, TN: Memphis State University Press, 1975; Labrie, Ross, *Howard Nemerov,* Boston: Twayne, 1980; Potts, Donna L., *Howard Nemerov and Objective Idealism: The Influence of Owen Barfield,* Columbia: University of Missouri Press, 1994.

Commentary: *Collected Poems* won the 1978 Pulitzer Prize in Poetry for Howard Nemerov. It contained many of his earliest poems.

Nemerov was born in New York City and edu-

cated at Harvard University. He served as a pilot during World War II. He began work as editor of a literary magazine and started teaching in 1946. He published his first collection, *The Image and the Law,* in 1947. He published his second book in 1949, a novel called *The Melodramatists.* His poems have been described as witty, ironic, and philosophical. He was named poet laureate of the United States in 1988. His other works include *The Painter Dreaming at the Scholar's House, Inside the Onion,* and *War Stories: Poems About Long Ago and Now.*

1979

Robert Penn Warren
Full entry appears as **#977** under "Novel," 1947.

1980

Donald Justice   1052
Birth: August 12, 1925; Miami, FL. **Parents:** Vascoe J. and Mary Ethel (Cook) Justice. **Education:** University of Miami, FL: BA. University of North Carolina: MA. Stanford University, CA. University of Iowa: PhD. **Spouse:** Jean Catherine Ross (m. 1947). **Children:** Nathaniel Ross.

Prize: *Poetry,* 1980: *Selected Poems,* New York: Atheneum, 1979.

Career: Visiting Assistant Professor of English, University of Missouri, Columbia, 1955-1956; Assistant Professor of English, Hamline University, St. Paul, MN, 1956-1957; Visiting Lecturer, State University of Iowa (now University of Iowa), Iowa City, 1957-1959; Assistant Professor, State University of Iowa, 1959-1963; Associate Professor of English, 1963-1966; Associate Professor, Syracuse University, Syracuse, NY, 1966-1967; Professor of English, Syracuse University, Syracuse, 1967-1970; Visiting Professor of English, University of California, Irvine, 1970-1971; Professor of English, University of Iowa, 1971-1982; Bain-Swiggett Lecturer, Princeton University, 1976; Visiting Professor, University of Virginia, Charlotte, 1980; Professor of English, University of Florida, Gainesville, 1982-1992; Member, American Academy and Institute of Arts and Letters.

Selected Works: *The Summer Anniversaries,* 1960. *Night Light,* 1967. *From a Notebook,* 1972. *Departures,* 1973. *Platonic Scripts,* 1984. *Tremayne: Four Poems,* 1984. *The Sunset Maker: Poems, Stories, a Memoir,* 1987. *A Donald Justice Reader: Selected Poetry and Prose,* 1991. *New & Selected Poems,* 1995.

Other Awards: Rockefeller Foundation Fellow in Poetry, 1954-1955. Lamont Poetry Selection,

Academy of American Poets, 1959: *The Summer Anniversaries.* Middletown, CT: Wesleyan University Press, 1960. Inez Boulton Prize, *Poetry* magazine, 1960. Ford Foundation Fellowship in Theater, 1964-1965. National Endowment for the Arts Grant, 1967, 1973, 1980, 1989. Guggenheim Fellowship in Poetry, 1976-1977. Harriet Monroe Award, University of Chicago, 1984. American Academy of Poets Fellow, 1988. Bollingen Prize for Poetry, 1991. Lannan Literary Award for Poetry, 1996.

For More Information: Gioia, Dana and William Logan, *Certain Solitudes: On the Poetry of Donald Justice,* Fayetteville: University of Arkansas Press, 1997.

Commentary: Donald Justice was awarded the 1980 Pulitzer Prize in Poetry for *Selected Poems.*

Justice was born in Miami, Florida. He was educated at the University of Miami, the University of North Carolina, and Stanford University. Justice published his first collection, *The Summer Anniversaries,* in 1960 and received the Lamont Poetry Selection of the Academy of American Poets in 1959. His verse has been described as gentle and controlled. He has held teaching positions at the University of Florida, the University of Miami, the University of Iowa, and Syracuse University, among other institutions. He currently lives in Iowa City, Iowa. His other works include *The Sunset Maker, Platonic Scripts,* a book of essays, and his latest, *Orpheus Hesitated Beside the Black River.*

1981

James Schuyler   1053

Birth: November 9, 1923; Chicago, IL. **Death:** April 12, 1991. **Parents:** Marcus James and Margaret (Connor) Schuyler. **Education:** Bethany College, WV. University of Florence, Italy.

Prize: *Poetry,* 1981: *The Morning of the Poem: Poems,* New York: Farrar, Straus and Giroux, 1980.

Career: Poet, novelist, and playwright; Staff, Museum of Modern Art, NY, 1955-1961; Art Critic, *Art News.*

Selected Works: *Salute,* 1960. *May 24th or So,* 1966. *A Nest of Ninnies* (with John Ashbery), 1969. *Hymn to Life: Poems,* 1974. *The Home Book: Prose and Poems, 1951-1970,* 1977. *What's for Dinner?,* 1978. *Broadway, a Poets' and Painters' Anthology* (with Charles North), 1979. *Early in 71,* 1982. *A Few Days: Poems,* 1985. *Broadway 2: A Poets' and Painters' Anthology* (with Charles North), 1989. *Two Journals* (with Darragh Park), 1995. *The Diary of James Schuyler* (Kernan, Nathan, ed.), 1997.

Other Awards: Longview Foundation Award, 1961. Frank O'Hara Prize for Poetry, 1969: *Freely Espousing: Poems.* National Endowment for the Arts

Grant, 1971, 1972. National Institute of Arts and Letters Award, 1976. Guggenheim Fellowship, 1981. Academy of American Poets Fellowship, 1983. Whiting Award, 1985.

For More Information: Auslander, Philip, *The New York School Poets As Playwrights: O'Hara, Ashbery, Koch, Schuyler, and the Visual Arts,* New York: Lang, 1989; Corbett, William and Geoffrey Young, eds., *That Various Field for James Schuyler (1923-1991),* Great Barrington, MA: Figures, 1991; Ward, Geoff, *Statutes of Liberty: The New York School of Poets,* New York: St. Martin's, 1993.

Commentary: James Schuyler was awarded the 1981 Pulitzer Prize in Poetry for *The Morning of the Poem.*

Schuyler was born in Chicago. He was educated at Bethany College and at the University of Florence in Italy. He joined the Navy in 1943 and spent two years on a destroyer in the North Atlantic. Schuyler moved to the Isle of Ischia in Italy for two years in 1947. He lived there with W.H. Auden, whom he had met in New York. Schuyler served as Auden's secretary, typing the manuscript for Auden's book *Gnomes* and Auden's translation of Jean Cocteau's "Les Chevaliers de la Table Ronde." Schuyler returned to New York and became a member of the New York School of Poets. A group formed in the early 1950s, they were experimental and had close ties with the New York abstract expressionist painters. John Ashbery and Frank O'Hara were also members. Schuyler's first collection, *Salute,* was published in 1960. He co-authored *A Nest of Ninnies* with John Ashbery in 1969. His other works include *The Crystal Lithium, What's for Dinner,* and *A Few Days: Poems.*

1982

Sylvia Plath   1054

Birth: October 27, 1932; Boston, MA. **Death:** February 11, 1963. **Parents:** Otto Emil and Aurelia (Schober) Plath. **Religion:** Unitarian Universalist. **Education:** Smith College, MA: BA, summa cum laude. Harvard University, MA. Newnham College, Cambridge, England: Fulbright Scholar, MA. **Spouse:** Ted Hughes (m. 1956; sep. 1962). **Children:** Frieda Rebecca, Nicholas Farrar.

Prize: *Poetry,* 1982: *The Collected Poems,* Boston: Faber and Faber, 1981.

Career: Volunteer Art Teacher, People's Institute, Northampton, MA; Guest Editor, *Mademoiselle,* summer, 1953; Instructor of English, Smith College, 1957-1958; Member, Phi Beta Kappa.

Selected Works: *Ariel,* 1965. *The Bell Jar,* 1966. *The Colossus & Other Poems,* 1968. *Million Dollar Month,* 1971. *Winter Trees,* 1971. *Lyonnesse: Poems,* 1971. *Fiesta Melons,* 1971. *Crossing the Water: Tran-*

sitional Poems, 1971. *Pursuit,* 1973. *Letters Home: Correspondence, 1950-1963* (Plath, Aurelia Schober, ed.), 1975. *The Bed Book,* 1976. *The Journals of Sylvia Plath,* 1982. *Sylvia Plath's Selected Poems* (Hughes, Ted, ed.), 1985.

Other Awards: *Mademoiselle* College Board Contest Winner in Fiction, 1953. Irene Glascock Poetry Prize, Mount Holyoke College, 1955. Bess Hokin Award, *Poetry* magazine, 1957. First Prize in Cheltenham Festival, 1961. Eugene F. Saxon Fellowship, 1961.

For More Information: Newman, Charles, ed., *The Art of Sylvia Plath,* Boston: Faber, 1970; Bundtzen, Lynda K., *Plath's Incarnations: Woman and the Creative Process,* Ann Arbor: University of Michigan Press, 1983; Alexander, Paul, ed., *Ariel Ascending: Writings About Sylvia Plath,* New York: Harper & Row, 1985; Wagner-Martin, Linda, *Sylvia Plath: A Biography,* New York: Simon & Schuster, 1987; Annas, Pamela J., *A Disturbance in Mirrors: The Poetry of Sylvia Plath,* New York: Greenwood, 1988; Stevenson, Anne, *Bitter Fame: A Life of Sylvia Plath,* London, England: Viking, 1989; Malcolm, Janet, *The Silent Woman: Sylvia Plath and Ted Hughes,* New York: Knopf, 1994.

Commentary: *The Collected Poems* won the 1982 Pulitzer Prize in Poetry posthumously for Sylvia Plath. The volume consisted of, for the most part, previously unpublished poems.

Plath was born in Boston and she was educated at Smith College and at Harvard University. She was seen as a model student and considered "a super-normal, All-American girl" at school. In England on a Fulbright scholarship, Plath met the poet Ted Hughes, who would later become poet laureate of England, and they soon married. She was the student of Robert Lowell. Her first collection, *The Colossus and Other Poems,* was published in 1960. She is perhaps best known for the novel *The Bell Jar.* Published under the pseudonym Victoria Lucas, the novel's plot was autobiographical in its story of a young woman's depression, attempted suicide, and recovery. Plath's mental health would fail her again, and she committed suicide after she and Hughes separated in 1963. Her other works, published posthumously, include *Ariel, Crossing the Water,* and *Johnny Panic and the Bible of Dreams and Other Prose Writings.*

1983

Galway Kinnell 1055

Birth: February 1, 1927; Providence, RI. **Parents:** James Scott and Elizabeth (Mills) Kinnell. **Education:** Princeton University, NJ: AB: summa cum laude. University of Rochester, NY: MA. **Spouse:** Ines Delgado de Torres. **Children:** Maud, Fergus, Natasha.

Prize: *Poetry,* 1983: *Selected Poems,* Boston: Houghton Mifflin, 1982.

Career: Served in U.S. Navy, 1944-1946; Poet and translator, beginning in 1949; Instructor in English, Alfred University, Alfred, NY, 1949-1951; Supervisor, Liberal Arts Program, Downtown Campus, University of Chicago, IL, 1951-1955; American Lecturer,University of Grenoble, Grenoble, France, 1956-1957; Lecturer, Summer Session, University of Nice, Nice, France, 1957; Fulbright Lecturer, University of Iran, Teheran, 1959-1960; Field Worker, Congress of Racial Equality (CORE), 1963; Poet-in-Residence, Juniata College, 1964; Poet-in-Residence, Reed College, 1966-1967; Poet-in-Residence, Colorado State University, 1968; Poet-in-Residence, University of Washington, 1968; Poet-in-Residence, University of California, Irvine, 1968-1969; Resident Writer, Deya Institute, Mallorca, Spain, 1969-1970; Poet-in-Residence, University of Iowa, 1970; Visiting Professor, Queens College, City University of New York, 1971; Visiting Professor, Pittsburgh Poetry Forum, 1971; Adjunct Associate Professor, Columbia University, NY, 1972; Visiting Poet, Sarah Lawrence College, 1972-1978; Visiting Professor, Brandeis University, 1974; Adjunct Professor, Columbia University, NY, 1974, 1976; Visiting Professor, Skidmore College, 1975; Visiting Poet, Princeton University, 1976; Poet-in-Residence, Holy Cross College, 1977; Visiting Poet, University of Hawaii; Visiting Professor, University of Delaware, 1978; Visiting Writer, Macquarie University, Sydney, Australia, 1979; Director, Squaw Valley Community of Writers, beginning in 1979; Citizens' Professor, University of Hawaii at Manoa, Honolulu, 1979-1981; Director of Writing Program, New York University, NY, 1981-1984; Samuel F.B. Morse Professor of Arts and Sciences, New York University, NY, beginning in 1985; Member: Corporation of Yaddo, National Academy and Institute of Arts and Letters, PEN.

Selected Works: *What a Kingdom It Was,* 1960. *Flower Herding on Mount Monadnock,* 1964. *Body Rags,* 1967. *Poems of Night,* 1968. *First Poems, 1946-1954,* 1970. *The Shoes of Wandering,* 1971. *The Book of Nightmares,* 1971. *Three Poems,* 1976. *Little Children's Prayer,* 1978. *Two Poems,* 1979. *Fergus Falling,* 1979. *"Angling," "A Day," and Other Poems,* 1980. *Two Poems* (with Diane Wakoski), 1980. *The Last Hiding Places of Snow,* 1980. *Black Light: A Novel,* 1980. *Thoughts Occasioned by the Most Insignificant of All Human Events,* 1982. *The Fundamental Project of Technology,* 1983. *The Music Box,* 1983. *The Mind,* 1984. *The Past,* 1985. *Three Books: "Body Rags"; "Mortal Acts, Mortal Words"; "The Past,"* 1993. *Imperfect Thirst,* 1994.

Other Awards: Ford Foundation Grant, 1955. Fulbright Scholarship, 1955-1956. Guggenheim Fellowships, 1961-1962, 1974-1975. National Institute of Arts and Letters Grant, 1962. Longview Foundation Award, 1962. Rockefeller Foundation Grants, 1962-1963, 1968. Bess Hokin Prize, 1965. Eunice Tietjens Prize, 1966. Cecil Hemley Poetry Prize, Ohio University Press, 1968, for translation of Yves Bonnefoy's work. Special Mention, National Book Awards for Poetry, 1969: *Body Rags,* London, England: Rapp & Whiting, 1967. Ingram Merrill Foundation Award, 1969. Amy Lowell Travelling Fellowship, 1969-1970. National Endowment for the Arts Grant, 1969-1970. Brandeis University Creative Arts Award, 1969. Shelley Prize from Poetry Society of America, 1974. Medal of Merit, National Institute of Arts and Letters, 1975. London Translation Prize, 1979. Co-Recipient, American Book Award for Poetry, 1983: *Selected Poems.* MacArthur Fellow, 1984. National Book Award for Poetry, 1984: *Selected Poems.* National Book Critics Circle Award, 1986: *The Past,* Boston: Houghton, Mifflin, 1985. Vermont State Poet, 1989-1993.

For More Information: Zimmerman, Lee, *Intricate and Simple Things: The Poetry of Galway Kinnell,* Urbana: University of Illinois Press, 1987; Calhoun, Richard James, *Galway Kinnell,* New York: Twayne, 1992; Tuten, Nancy Lewis, ed., *Critical Essays on Galway Kinnell,* New York: G.K. Hall, 1996.

Commentary: Galway Kinnell was awarded the 1983 Pulitzer Prize in Poetry for *Selected Poems,* a collection which covered Kinnell's poems from the 1940s to the 1980s.

Kinnell was born in Providence, Rhode Island and educated at Princeton University and the University of Rochester. His first collection, *What a Kingdom It Was,* was published in 1960. Kinnell's themes have often been aloneness, selfhood, and the confrontation with death, which is universal. He has taught at many universities and has also done translations of French novels and poetry. His other works include *Flower Herding on Mount Monadnock, Body Rags,* and *The Book of Nightmares.*

1984

Mary Oliver   1056

Birth: September 10, 1935; Cleveland, OH. **Parents:** Edward William and Helen M. (Vlasak) Oliver. **Education:** Ohio State University. Vassar College, NY.

Prize: *Poetry,* 1984 : *American Primitive: Poems,* Boston: Little, Brown, 1983.

Career: Mather Visiting Professor, Case Western Reserve University, Cleveland, OH, 1980, 1982; Poet-in-Residence, Bucknell University, PA, 1986;

Elliston Visiting Professor, University of Cincinnati, OH, 1986; Margaret Banister Writer-in-Residence, Sweet Briar College, Sweet Briar, VA, beginning in 1991; Member: PEN, Poetry Society of America.

Selected Works: *No Voyage, and Other Poems,* 1965. *The River Styx, Ohio, and Other Poems,* 1972. *Dream Work,* 1986. *New and Selected Poems,* 1992. *White Pine: Poems and Prose Poems,* 1994. *Blue Pastures,* 1995.

Other Awards: First Prize, Poetry Society of America, 1962: "No Voyage." Devil's Advocate Award, 1968: "Christmas, 1966." Shelley Memorial Award, 1972. National Endowment for the Arts Fellow, 1972-1973. Alice Fay di Castagnola Award, 1973. Guggenheim Fellow, 1980-1981. Award in Literature, American Academy and Institution of Arts and Letters, 1983. Christopher Award, 1991. L. L. Winship Award, 1991: *House of Light,* Boston: Beacon, 1991. National Book Award for Poetry, 1992: *New and Selected Poems.* Boston: Beacon, 1992.

For More Information: Graham, Vicki, "Into the Body of Another": Mary Oliver and the Poetics of Becoming Other," *Papers on Language and Literature,* Fall 1994; Burton-Christie, Douglas, "Nature, Spirit, and Imagination in the Poetry of Mary Oliver," *Cross Currents,* Spring 1996.

Commentary: Mary Oliver was awarded the 1984 Pulitzer Prize in Poetry for *American Primitive,* a passionate collection dedicated to the poet James Wright.

Oliver was born in Cleveland, Ohio and educated at Ohio State University. Her first collection, *No Voyage, and Other Poems,* was published in 1965. Oliver's focus on nature is evident in her verse, which has been described as "leaving human consciousness." She won the National Book Award in 1992 for *New and Selected Poems.* Her other works include *Dream Work* and *Blue Pastures.*

1985

Carolyn Kizer   1057

Birth: December 10, 1925; Spokane, WA. **Parents:** Benjamin Hamilton and M. (Ashley) Kizer. **Religion:** Episcopalian. **Education:** Sarah Lawrence College, NY: BA. Columbia University, NY. University of Washington. **Spouse:** Charles Stimson Bullitt (m. 1948; div. 1954); John Marshall Woodbridge (m. 1975). **Children:** Ashley Ann, Scott, Jill Hamilton (CSB).

Prize: *Poetry,* 1985: *Yin: New Poems,* Brockport, NY: Boa Editions, 1984.

Career: Poet and educator; Student of Theodore Roethke, University of Washington, Seattle, 1953-1954; Founder and Editor, *Poetry Northwest,* Seattle, WA, 1959-1965; Volunteer Worker, American

Friends Service Committee, 1960; Specialist in Literature, U.S. State Department in Pakistan, 1964-1965; First Director of Literary Programs, National Endowment for the Arts, Washington, DC, 1966-1970; Poet-in-Residence, University of North Carolina at Chapel Hill, 1970-1974; Hurst Professor of Literature, Washington University, MO, 1971; Lecturer, spring, Barnard College, 1972; Acting Director, Graduate Writing Program, Columbia University, 1972; McGuffey Lecturer and Poet-in-Residence, Ohio University, Athens, 1975; Professor of Poetry, Iowa Writer's Workshop, University of Iowa, Iowa City, 1976; Professor, University of Maryland, College Park, 1976-1977; Professor of Poetry, spring, Stanford University, CA, 1986; Senior Fellow in the Humanities, Fall, Princeton University, NJ, 1986; Visiting Professor of Writing, University of Arizona, 1989 and 1990; Visiting Professor of Writing, University of California, Davis, 1991; Coal Royalty Chair, University of Alabama, 1995; Chancellor, Academy of American Poets; Founding Member, Association of Literary Magazines of America; Member: American Civil Liberties Union, Amnesty International, Founding Board of Directors, Seattle Community Psychiatric Clinic, International PEN, Poetry Society of America, Poets and Writers.

Selected Works: *The Ungrateful Garden,* 1961. *Knock upon Silence: Poems,* 1965. *Midnight Was My Cry: New and Selected Poems,* 1971. *Mermaids in the Basement: Poems for Women,* 1984. *The Nearness of You: Poems,* 1986. *Proses: On Poems & Poets,* 1993. *Picking and Choosing: Essays on Prose,* 1995. *100 Great Poems by Women: A Golden Ecco Anthology,* 1995. *Harping On: Poems 1985-1995,* 1996.

Other Awards: Masefield Prize, Poetry Society of America, 1983. Award in Literature, American Academy and Institute of Arts and Letters, 1985. Governors Award, State of Washington: *Mermaids in the Basement: Poems for Women.* Port Townsend, WA: Copper Canyon, 1984. San Francisco Arts Commission Award: *Mermaids in the Basement: Poems for Women.* Frost Medal, Poetry Society of America, 1988. President's Medal, Eastern Washington University, 1988. Honorary DLitts: Whitman College, WA, 1986; St. Andrew's College, NC, 1989; Mills College, CA, 1990; Washington State University, 1991.

For More Information: Phillips, Robert, "Collections Prove Range of Poet," *Houston Chronicle,* March 9, 1997.

Commentary: *Yin* won the 1985 Pulitzer Prize in Poetry for Carolyn Kizer.

Kizer was born in Spokane, Washington and educated at Sarah Lawrence College, Columbia University, and the University of Washington. Her first collection, *The Ungrateful Garden,* was published in 1961. She was the first director of the literature pro-

gram at the National Endowment for the Arts. Her other works include *Mermaids in the Basement: Poems for Women,* and her most recent, *Harping On: Poems 1985-1995.*

1986

Henry Taylor   1058
Birth: June 21, 1942; Loudoun County, VA. **Parents:** Thomas Edward and Mary (Splawn) Taylor. **Religion:** Society of Friends. **Education:** University of Virginia: BA. Hollins College, VA: MA. **Spouse:** Second marriage, Frances Ferguson Carney (m. 1968). **Children:** Thomas Edward, Richard Carney (FFC).

Prize: *Poetry,* 1986: *The Flying Change: Poems,* Baton Rouge, LA: Louisiana State University Press, 1985.

Career: Instructor of English, Roanoke College, VA, 1966-1968; Assistant Professor of English, University of Utah, Salt Lake City, 1968-1971; Director, University of Utah Writers' Conference, 1969-1972; Writer-in- Residence, Hollins College, 1978; Associate Professor of Literature, Washington, DC, 1971-1976; Professor of Literature, American University, beginning in 1976; Co-Director of Creative Writing Program, beginning in 1982; Director of American Studies program, 1983-1985; Member, Agricultural History Society.

Selected Works: *The Horse Show at Midnight: Poems,* 1966. *Poetry: Points of Departure,* 1974. *An Afternoon of Pocket Billiards: Poems,* 1975. *The Water of Light: A Miscellany in Honor of Brewster Ghiselin,* 1976. *Compulsory Figures: Essays on Recent American Poets,* 1992. *Understanding Fiction: Poems, 1986-1996,* 1996.

Other Awards: Academy of American Poets Prize, University of Virginia, 1962, 1964. Utah State Institute of Fine Arts Poetry Prize, 1969, 1971. Creative Writing Fellowships, National Endowment of the Arts, 1978-1987. Research Grant, National Endowment for the Humanities, 1980-1981. Witter Bynner Prize for Poetry, American Academy and Institute of Arts and Letters, 1984.

For More Information: Bowers, Neal, "Taylor's Essays Bring Rhyme and Reason to U.S. Poetry," *Washington Times,* November 15, 1992.

Commentary: Henry Taylor was awarded the 1986 Pulitzer Prize in Poetry for *The Flying Change,* his third collection of verse.

Taylor was born in Loudoun County, Virginia. He was educated at the University of Virginia and at Hollins College. Taylor's first collection, *The Horse Show at Midnight,* was published in 1966. Taylor's translations from Bulgarian, French, Hebrew, Italian, and Russian have appeared in many periodicals and anthologies; he has also published translations from Greek and Roman classical drama. He is currently professor of literature and co-director of the Master of Fine Arts Program in Creative Writing at American University in Washington, DC. His other works include *An Afternoon of Pocket Billiards* and his most recent collection, *Understanding Fiction: Poems 1986-1996,* published in 1996.

1987

Rita Dove   1059

Birth: August 28, 1952; Akron, OH. **Parents:** Ray A. and Elvira E. (Hord) Dove. **Education:** Miami University, OH: BA, summa cum laude. Universitaet Tuebingen, West Germany. University of Iowa: MFA. **Spouse:** Fred Viebahn (m. 1979). **Children:** Aviva Chantal Tamu Dove-Viebahn.

Prize: *Poetry,* 1987: *Thomas and Beulah: Poems,* Pittsburgh, PA: Carnegie-Mellon University Press, 1986.

Career: Assistant Professor, Arizona State University, Tempe, 1981-1984; Writer-in-Residence, Tuskegee Institute, 1982; Member of Literature Panel, National Endowment for the Arts, 1984-1986; Associate Professor, Arizona State University, 1984-1987; Chair of Poetry Grants Panel, National Endowment for the Arts, 1985; Member, Board of Directors, Associated Writing Programs, 1985-1988; President, Board of Directors, Associated Writing Programs, 1986-1987; Professor of English, Arizona State University, 1987-1989; Commissioner, Schomburg Center for the Preservation of Black Culture, New York Public Library, beginning in 1987; Professor of English, University of Virginia, Charlottesville, 1989-1993; Judge, Walt Whitman Award, Academy of American Poets, 1990; Judge, Poetry, National Book Award, 1991; Judge, Poetry, Pulitzer Prizes, 1991; Judge, Ruth Lilly Prize, 1991; Judge, Anisfield-Wolf Book Awards, beginning in 1992; U.S. Poet Laureate, 1993-1995; Commonwealth Professor of English, University of Virginia, beginning in 1993; Member: Academy of American Poets, PEN, Phi Beta Kappa, Phi Kappa Phi, Poetry Society of America, Poets and Writers.

Selected Works: *The Yellow House on the Corner: Poems,* 1980. *Museum: Poems,* 1983. *Fifth Sunday: Stories,* 1985. *The Other Side of the House* (with Tamarra Kaida), 1988. *Grace Notes: Poems,* 1989. *Through the Ivory Gate: A Novel,* 1992. *Selected Poems,* 1993. *The Darker Face of the Earth: A Verse Play in Fourteen Scenes,* 1994. *Mother Love,* 1995.

Other Awards: Fulbright Fellow, 1974-1975. National Endowment for the Arts Grant, 1978. Ohio Arts Council Grant, 1979. Portia Pittman Fellow, Tuskegee Institute from National Endowment for the Humanities, 1982. John Simon Guggenheim Fellow, 1983. Peter I. B. Lavan Younger Poets Award, Academy of American Poets, 1986. General Electric Foundation Award for Younger Writers, 1987. Bellagio Residency, Italy, Rockefeller Foundation, 1988. Ohio Governor's Award, 1988. Mellon Fellow, National Humanities Center, 1988-1989. Ohioana Award, 1991: *Grace Notes,* New York: Norton, 1989. Literary Lion Citation, New York Public Libraries, 1991. Ohio Hall of Fame, 1991. Women of the Year Award, *Glamour* magazine, 1993. NAACP Great American Artist Award, 1993. Harvard University Phi Beta Kappa Poetry Award, 1993. Distinguished Achievement Medal, Miami University Alumni Association, 1994. Renaissance Forum Award for Leadership in the Literary Arts, Folger Shakespeare Library, 1994. Carl Sandburg Award, International Platform Association, 1994. Poet Laureate of the United States, 1994-1995. National Medal of Arts. Charles Frankel Prize in Humanities. Honorary DLitts: Miami University, OH, 1988; Knox College, IL, 1989; Tuskegee University, AL, 1994; University of Miami, FL, 1994; Washington University, MO, 1994; Case Western Reserve University, OH, 1994; University of Akron, OH, 1994; Arizona State University, 1995; Boston College, 1995; Dartmouth College, NH, 1995.

For More Information: Vendler, Helen Hennessy, *The Given and the Made: Strategies of Poetic Redefinition,* Cambridge, MA: Harvard University Press, 1995.

Commentary: Rita Frances Dove was awarded the 1987 Pulitzer Prize in Poetry for *Thomas and Beulah,* poems involving two characters who speak of their lives in the South and their current surroundings in Akron, Ohio.

Dove was born in Akron, Ohio. She was educated at Miami University, Ohio, and the University of Iowa. She is an African-American writer and teacher. Her poetry speaks of the experiences of her race. Her first collection, *The Yellow House on the Corner,* was published in 1980. She was poet laureate of the United States from 1993 to 1995. Her other works include *Fifth Sunday, The Darker Face of Earth,* and *Mother Love.*

1988

William Meredith   1060

Birth: January 9, 1919; New York, NY. **Parents:** William Morris and Nelley Atkin (Keyser) Meredith. **Education:** Princeton University, NJ: AB, magna cum laude.

Prize: *Poetry,* 1988: *Partial Accounts: New and Selected Poems,* New York: Knopf, 1987.

Career: Copyboy and Reporter, *New York Times,* NY, 1940-1941; Served in U.S. Army Air Forces,

1941-1942; Lieutenant, Pacific Theater, Naval Aviation, U.S. Navy, 1942-1946; Instructor of English and Woodrow Wilson Fellow in Writing, Princeton University, NJ, 1946-1950; Associate Professor of English, University of Hawaii, Honolulu, 1950-1951; Lieutenant Commander, Naval Aviator, Korean War, U.S. Naval Reserve, 1952-1954; Associate Professor, Connecticut College, CT, 1955-1965; Instructor at Bread Loaf School of English, Middlebury College, VT, 1958-1962; Member, Connecticut Commission on the Arts, 1963-1965; Director of the Humanities, Upward Bound Program, 1964-1968; Professor of English, Connecticut College, CT, 1965-1983; Poetry Consultant, Library of Congress, 1978-1980; Chancellor, Academy of American Poets; Member, National Institute of Arts and Letters; Second Vice President, American Choral Society.

Selected Works: *Love Letter from an Impossible Land,* 1944. *Ships and Other Figures,* 1948. *The Open Sea, and Other Poems,* 1957. *Alcools: Poems, 1898-1913. The Wreck of the Thresher, and Other Poems* (with Guillaume Apollinaire), 1964. *Earth Walk: New and Selected Poems,* 1970. *Hazard, the Painter,* 1975. *The Cheer,* 1980. *Poems Are Hard to Read Series,* 1991. *Effort at Speech: New and Selected Poems,* 1997. *Window on the Black Sea: Bulgarian Poetry in Translation,* 1992.

Other Awards: Yale Series of Younger Poets Award, 1943. *Love Letter from an Impossible Land.* Harriet Monroe Memorial Prize, 1944. Oscar Blumenthal Prize, 1953. Woodrow Wilson Fellowship, Princeton University, 1946-1947. Rockefeller Grant, 1948, 1968. Two Air Medals, Korean War. *Hudson Review* Fellow, 1956. National Institute of Arts and Letters Grant in Literature, 1958. Ford Foundation Fellowship for Drama, 1959-1960. Loines Prize, National Institute of Arts and Letters, 1966. Van Wyck Brooks Award, 1971. National Endowment for the Arts Grant, 1972. Guggenheim Fellow, 1975-1976. International Vaptsarov Prize for Literature, Bulgaria, 1979. National Endowment for the Arts Fellow, 1984. *Los Angeles Times* Prize, 1987. Academy of American Poets Fellowship, 1990. National Book Award, 1997: *Effort at Speech: New and Selected Poems,* Boston: Triquarterly Books/Northwestern University Press, 1997.

For More Information: Kastor, Elizabeth, "The Poet & His Brave New Journey," *Washington Post,* January 2, 1990.

Commentary: *Partial Accounts* won the 1988 Pulitzer Prize in Poetry for William Meredith.

Meredith was born in New York City and educated at Princeton University. His first collection, *Love Letter from an Impossible Land,* was published in 1944 and was chosen by Archibald MacLeish to receive the Yale Younger Poets Award. His other works include *The Cheer, The Open Sea, and Other*

Poems and his most recent, *Effort at Speech: New and Selected Poems.*

1989

Richard Wilbur
Full entry appears as #**1032** under "Poetry," 1957.

1990

Charles Simic   1061
Birth: May 9, 1938; Belgrade, Yugoslavia. **Parents:** George and Helen (Matijevic) Simic. **Religion:** Eastern Orthodox. **Education:** New York University: BA. **Spouse:** Helene Dubin (m. 1965). **Children:** Anna, Philip.

Prize: *Poetry,* 1990: *The World Doesn't End: Prose Poems,* San Diego, CA: Harcourt Brace Jovanovich, 1989.

Career: Served in U.S. Army, 1961-1963; Editorial Assistant, *Aperture,* New York City, 1966-1969; Visiting Assistant Professor of English, State University of California, Hayward, beginning in 1970-1973; Associate Professor of English, University of New Hampshire, Durham, beginning in 1974; Visiting Assistant Professor of English, Boston University, MA, 1975; Visiting Assistant Professor of English, Columbia University, NY, 1979.

Selected Works: *What the Grass Says: Poems,* 1967. *Dismantling the Silence,* 1971. *White,* 1972. *Return to a Place Lit by a Glass of Milk,* 1974. *Another Republic: 17 European and South American Writers* (Simic, Charles, and Strand, Mark, eds.), 1976. *Biography and a Lament: Poems 1961-1967,* 1976. *Charon's Cosmology: Poems,* 1977. *White,* 1980. *Austerities,* 1982. *Shaving at Night,* 1982. *Weather Forecast for Utopia & Vicinity: Poems 1967-1982,* 1983. *Selected Poems, 1963-1983,* 1985. *The Uncertain Certainty: Interviews, Essays, and Notes on Poetry,* 1985. *Nine Poems: A Childhood Story,* 1989. *Walking the Black Cat: Selected Poems, 1963-1983,* 1990. *Wonderful Words, Silent Truth: Essays on Poetry and a Memoir,* 1990. *Evening Walk,* 1991. *The Unemployed Fortune-Teller: Essays and Memoirs,* 1994. *A Wedding in Hell: Poems,* 1994.

Other Awards: PEN International Award for Translation, 1970. Guggenheim Fellowship, 1972-1973. National Endowment for the Arts Fellowship, 1974-1975, 1979-1980. Edgar Allan Poe Award, American Academy of Poets, 1975. National Institute of Arts and Letters and American Academy of Arts and Letters Award, 1976. Harriet Monroe Poetry Award, University of Chicago, 1980. Di Castignola Award, Poetry Society of America, 1980. PEN Translation Award, 1980. Fulbright Travelling Fellowship,

1982. Ingram Merrill Fellowship, 1983-1984. Mac-Arthur Foundation Fellowship, 1984-1989.

For More Information: Weigl, Bruce, ed., *Charles Simic: Essays on the Poetry,* Ann Arbor: University of Michigan Press, 1996; Stitt, Peter, *Uncertainty & Plenitude: Five Contemporary Poets,* Iowa City: University of Iowa Press, 1997.

Commentary: Charles Simic was awarded the 1990 Pulitzer Prize in Poetry for *The World Doesn't End,* a collection of prose poems.

Simic was born in Belgrade, Yugoslavia. His family emigrated from Serbia to the United States in 1954. He was educated at New York University. His style is autobiographical and sometimes surreal. His first collection, *What the Grass Says,* was published in 1967. He has taught for many years at the University of New Hampshire. Simic won a MacArthur Fellowship award for 1984-1985.

1991

Mona Van Duyn   1062
Birth: May 9, 1921; Waterloo, IA. **Parents:** Earl George and Lora G. (Kramer) Van Duyn. **Education:** Iowa State Teachers College (now University of Northern Iowa): BA. University of Iowa: MA. **Spouse:** Jarvis A. Thurston (m. 1943).

Prize: *Poetry,* 1991: *Near Changes: Poems,* New York: Knopf, 1990.

Career: Poet; Instructor of English, State University of Iowa, Iowa City, 1943-1946; Instructor of English, University of Louisville, KY 1946-1950; Lecturer of English, Washington University, MO, 1950-1967; Lecturer, Salzburg Seminar in American Studies, Salzburg, Austria, 1973; Poet-in-Residence, Bread Loaf Writing Conference, MA, 1974 and 1976; Adjunct Professor, Washington University, MO,1983; Chancellor, Academy of American Poets, 1985; Visiting Fannie Hurst Professor, Washington University, MO, 1987; Lecturer, Sewanee Writing Conference, Tennessee, 1990 and 1991; Poetry Consultant, Olin Library Modern Literature Collection; Member: American Academy of Arts and Sciences, National Academy of Arts and Letters.

Selected Works: *A Time of Bees,* 1964. *To See, to Take: Poems,* 1970. *Merciful Disguises: Published and Unpublished Poems,* 1973. *Letters from a Father, and Other Poems,* 1982. *If It Be Not I: Collected Poems, 1959-1982,* 1993.

Other Awards: Eunice Tietjens Memorial Prize, Poetry, 1956: *Three Valentines to the Wide World.* Helen Bullis Prize, 1964: *Poetry Northwest.* National Endowment for the Arts Grants, 1966-1967, 1985. Harriet Monroe Memorial Prize, Poetry, 1968. Hart Crane Memorial Award, American Weave Press, 1968. First Prize, Borestone Mountain Awards, 1968.

Bollingen Prize, Yale University, 1970. National Book Award for Poetry, 1971: *To See, To Take,* New York: Atheneum, 1970. John Simon Guggenheim Memorial Fellowship, 1972-1973. Loines Prize, National Institute of Arts and Letters, 1976. Academy of American Poets Fellow, 1981. Sandburg Prize, Cornell College, 1982. Shelley Memorial Award, Poetry Society of America, 1987. Ruth Lilly Poetry Prize, Modern Poetry Association, 1989. Missouri Arts Award, 1990. Golden Plate Award, American Academy of Achievement, 1992. St. Louis Award, Arts and Education Council, 1994. Poet Laureate of the United States, 1992-1993. Honorary DLitts: Washington University, MO, 1971; Cornell College, IA, 1972; University of Northern Iowa, 1991; University of the South, TN, 1993; George Washington University, Washington, DC, 1993; Georgetown University, Washington, DC, 1993.

For More Information: *Discovery and Reminiscence: Essays on the Poetry of Mona Van Duyn,* Fayetteville: University of Arkansas Press, 1998.

Commentary: *Near Changes* won the 1991 Pulitzer Prize in Poetry for Mona Van Duyn.

Van Duyn was born in Waterloo, Iowa. She was educated at Iowa State Teachers College and at the State University of Iowa. She and her husband, Jarvis Thurston, founded the journal *Perspective: A Quarterly of Literature* in 1947. Her first collection, *Valentines to the World,* was published in 1959. Van Duyn won the National Book Award for *To See, To Take* in 1971. She was poet laureate of the United States in 1992. Her other works include *Bedtime Stories* and her most recent, *Firefall.*

1992

James Tate   1063
Birth: December 8, 1943; Kansas City, MO. **Parents:** Samuel Vincent Appleby Tate and Betty Jean Whitsitt. **Education:** University of Missouri. Kansas State College: BA. University of Iowa: MFA.

Prize: *Poetry,* 1992: *Selected Poems,* Middletown, CT: Wesleyan University Press, 1991.

Career: Instructor of Creative Writing, University of Iowa, Iowa City, 1966-1967; University of California, Berkeley, Visiting Lecturer, 1967-1968; Columbia University, NY, Assistant Professor of English, 1969-1971; Poet-in-Residence, Emerson College, 1970-1971; Associate Professor and Professor of English, University of Massachusetts, Amherst, beginning in 1971; Consultant, Coordinating Council of Literary Magazines, 1971-74; Member, Bollingen Prize Committee, Yale University Library, 1974-1975; Consultant, Kentucky Arts Commission, 1979; Member, PEN.

Selected Works: *The Lost Pilot,* 1967. *The Torches,* 1968. *The Oblivion Ha-Ha: Sixty Poems,* 1970. *Hints to Pilgrims,* 1971. *Apology for Eating Geoffrey Movius' Hyacinth,* 1972. *Absences: New Poems,* 1972. *Hottentot Ossuary,* 1974. *Viper Jazz,* 1976. *Lucky Darryl: A Novel* (with Bill Knott), 1977. *The Lost Pilot: Poems,* 1978. *Riven Doggeries,* 1979. *Land of Little Sticks,* 1981. *Hints to Pilgrims,* 1982. *Constant Defender: Poems,* 1983. *The Worshipful Company of Fletchers: Poems,* 1994.

Other Awards: Yale Younger Poets Award, 1966: *The Lost Pilot,* New Haven, CT: Yale University Press, 1967. Poet of the Year, Phi Beta Kappa, 1972. National Institute of Arts and Letters Award for Poetry, 1974. Massachusetts Arts and Humanities Fellow, 1975. Guggenheim Fellow, 1976. National Endowment for the Arts Fellow, 1980. National Book Award for Poetry, 1994: *Worshipful Company of Fletchers,* Hopewell, NJ: Ecco, 1994. Tanning Prize, Academy of American Poets, 1995.

For More Information: Caldwell, Jean, "For UMass' Tate, Life's Work Crowned," *Boston Globe,* April 8, 1992; Mehegan, David, "Mass Poet Wins National Book Award," *Boston Globe,* November 17, 1994; "Three Prize-Winning Poems," *Wall Street Journal,* January 19, 1995.

Commentary: James Tate was awarded the 1992 Pulitzer Prize in Poetry for *Selected Poems.*

Tate was born in Kansas City, Missouri. He was educated at the University of Missouri, Kansas State College, and the University of Iowa. He is known for a poetry style which uses surreal imagery and ironic stance. He taught at the University of Massachusetts at Amherst starting in 1967. His collection, *The Worshipful Company of Fletchers* received the National Book Award in 1994. His other works include *The Oblivion Ha-Ha: Sixty Poems* and *Viper Jazz.*

1993

Louise Gluck   1064
Birth: April 22, 1943; New York, NY. **Parents:** Daniel and Beatrice (Grosby) Gluck. **Education:** Sarah Lawrence College, NY. Columbia University, NY. **Spouse:** Charles Hertz (div); John Dranow (m. 1977). **Children:** Noah Benjamin.

Prize: *Poetry,* 1993: *The Wild Iris,* New York: Ecco, 1992.

Career: Poet; Visiting Teacher, Fine Arts Work Center, Provincetown, MA, 1970; Artist-in-Residence, Goddard College, VT, 1971-1972; Faculty, Goddard College, VT, 1973-1974; Poet-in-Residence, University of North Carolina, Greensboro, spring, 1973; Visiting Professor, University of Iowa, 1976-1977; Faculty and Board Member, M.F.A. Writing Program, Goddard College, VT, 1976-1980; El-

lison Professor of Poetry, spring, University of Cincinnati, OH, 1978; Visiting Professor, Columbia University, NY, 1979; Poet-in-Residence, Writer's Community, 1979; Visiting Professor, University of California, Davis, 1983; Faculty and Board Member, M.F.A. Program for Writers, Warren Wilson College, NC, 1980-1984; Holloway Lecturer, University of California, Berkeley, 1982; Scott Professor of Poetry, Williams College, MA, 1983; Senior Lecturer of English, Williams College, MA, beginning in 1984; Phi Beta Kappa Poet, Harvard University, 1990; Board Member, PEN, beginning in 1988.

Selected Works: *Firstborn,* 1969. *The House on Marshland,* 1975. *The Garden,* 1976. *Descending Figure,* 1980. *The Triumph of Achilles,* 1985. *Ararat,* 1990. *Proofs & Theories: Essays on Poetry,* 1994.

Other Awards: Academy of American Poets Prize, Columbia University, 1967. Rockefeller Foundation Grant in Poetry, 1968-1969. National Endowment for the Arts Creative Writing Fellowships, 1969-1970, 1979-1980, 1988-1989. Eunice Tietjens Memorial Prize, 1971. John Simon Guggenheim Memorial Fellowship in Poetry, 1975-1976, 1987-1988. Vermont Council for the Arts Individual Artist Grant, 1978-1979. American Academy and Institute of Arts and Letters Award in Literature, 1981. National Book Critics Circle Award for Poetry, 1985: *The Triumph of Achilles,* New York: Ecco, 1985. Melville Cane Award, Poetry Society of America, 1985. Sara Teasdale Memorial Prize, Wellesley College, 1986. Co-Recipient, Bobbitt National Prize, 1992.

For More Information: Dodd, Elizabeth Caroline, *The Veiled Mirror and the Woman Poet: H.D., Louise Bogan, Elizabeth Bishop, and Louise Gluck,* Columbia: University of Missouri Press, 1992.

Commentary: Louise Gluck was awarded the 1993 Pulitzer Prize in Poetry for *The Wild Iris,* a collection which explored life and death as seen through attitudes towards religion.

Gluck was born in New York City. She was educated at Sarah Lawrence College and at Columbia University. Her first collection, *Firstborn,* was published in 1968. She won the National Book Critics Circle Award for *The Triumph of Achilles* in 1985. Her other works include *The House on the Marshland* and *Ararat.*

1994

Yusef Komunyakaa   1065
Birth: April 29, 1947; Bogalusa, LA. **Education:** University of Colorado: BA. Colorado State University, CO: MA. University of California, Irvine: MFA. **Spouse:** Mandy Sayer (m. 1985).

Prize: *Poetry,* 1994: *Neon Vernacular: New and Selected Poems,* Middletown, CT: Wesleyan University Press, 1993.

Career: Information Specialist and Editor, *Southern Cross* military newspaper, U.S. Army, 1965-1967; Elementary Teacher, New Orleans Public Schools; Instructor of English and Poetry, University of New Orleans, Lakefront, LA; Associate Professor, Arts and Sciences, Indiana University, Bloomington, IN, 1985; Ruth Lilly Professor, Indiana University, Bloomington, 1989-1990.

Selected Works: *Lost in the Bonewheel Factory: Poems,* 1978. *Copacetic,* 1984. *Dien Cai Dau,* 1988. *The Jazz Poetry Anthology* (Komunyakaa, Yusef and Feinstein, Sascha, eds.), 1991. *Magic City,* 1992. *The Second Set: The Jazz Poetry Anthology, Volume 2,* 1996. *Thieves of Paradise,* 1998.

Other Awards: Bronze Star, Vietnam. Kingsley Tufts Poetry Award, Claremont Graduate School, CA, 1994: *Neon Vernacular: New and Selected Poems.* Middletown, CT: Wesleyan University, 1993.

For More Information: Weber, Bruce, "A Poet's Values: It's the Words Over the Man," *New York Times,* May 2, 1994; Stein, Kevin, "Vietnam and the 'Voice Within': Public and Private History in Yusef Komunyakaa's *Dien Cai Dau,*" *Massachusetts Review,* Winter 1995; Washington, Durthy A. "Seeking Surprises: An Interview with Yusef Komunyakaa," *Black Scholar,* Spring 1997; Conley, Susan, "About Yusef Komunyakaa," *Ploughshares,* Spring 1997.

Commentary: *Neon Vernacular: New and Selected Poems* won the 1994 Pulitzer Prize in Poetry for Yusef Komunyakaa.

Komunyakaa was born in Bogalusa, Louisiana and educated at the University of Colorado, Colorado State University, and the University of California at Irvine. He served in the Vietnam War and was awarded the Bronze Star. His poetry has been shaped by his experience there. His first collection, *Lost in the Bonewheel Factory* was published in 1978. He was co-editor of *The Jazz Poetry Anthology,* which is now in two volumes. He currently teaches at Princeton University. His other works include *Magic City, Dien Cai Dau* (the title is Vietnamese for "crazy"), and his most recent *Thieves of Paradise.*

1995

Philip Levine   1066

Birth: January 10, 1928; Detroit, MI. **Parents:** A. Harry and Esther Gertrude (Priscoll) Levine. **Education:** Wayne State University, MI: AB, AM. University of Iowa: MFA. **Spouse:** Frances Artley (m. 1954). **Children:** Mark, John, Theodore Henri.

Prize: *Poetry,* 1995: *The Simple Truth: Poems,* New York: Knopf, 1994.

Career: Poet; Industrial Worker, Detroit, MI, early 1950s; Faculty, University of Iowa, Iowa City, 1955-1957; Professor of English, California State University, Fresno, 1958-1992; Elliston Professor of Poetry, University of Cincinnati, 1976; Poet-in-Residence, National University of Australia, Canberra, summer, 1978; Visiting Professor of Poetry, Columbia University, 1978, 1981, 1984; Professor of English, Tufts University, Medford, MA, 1981-1988; New York University, 1984 and 1991, and Brown University, 1985; Teacher, Princeton University, Columbia University, Squaw Valley Writers Community, Bread Loaf, and Midnight Sun; Poet-in-Residence, National University of Australia and Vassar College; Chair of Literature Board, National Endowment for the Arts, 1984-1985.

Selected Works: *On the Edge,* 1963. *Not This Pig: Poems,* 1968. *5 Detroits,* 1970. *Red Dust: Poems,* 1971. *Pili's Wall,* 1971. *They Feed the Lion,* 1972. *1933: Poems,* 1974. *The Names of the Lost,* 1976. *Ashes: Poems New & Old,* 1979. *One for the Rose: Poems,* 1981. *Don't Ask,* 1981. *Selected Poems,* 1984. *Sweet Will: Poems,* 1985. *Blue,* 1989. *What Work Is: Poems,* 1991. *New Selected Poems,* 1991. *The Bread of Time: Toward an Autobiography,* 1994. *Unselected Poems,* 1997.

Other Awards: Stanford University Poetry Fellowship, 1957. Joseph Henry Jackson Award, San Francisco Foundation, 1961: *Berenda Slough and Other Poems.* (Published as *On the Edge,* Iowa City, IA: Second Press, 1963). Chaplebrook Foundation Grant, 1969. National Endowment for the Arts Grant, 1969, 1970, 1976, 1981, 1987. Outstanding Lecturer, California State University, Fresno, 1971. Outstanding Professor, California State University System, 1972. Frank O'Hara Prize, Poetry, 1973. National Institute of Arts and Letters Grant, 1973. Award of Merit, American Academy of Arts and Letters, 1974. Frank O'Hara Prize, Poetry, 1974. Levinson Prize, Poetry, 1974. Guggenheim Fellowship, 1974, 1981. Harriet Monroe Memorial Prize for Poetry, University of Chicago, 1976. Lenore Marshall Award for Best American Book of Poems, 1976: *The Names of the Lost,* Iowa City, IA: Windhover, 1976. National Book Award for Poetry, 1979: *Ashes: Poems New and Old,* Port Townsend, WA: Graywolf, 1979. National Book Critics Circle Prize, 1979: *Ashes: Poems New and Old* and *7 Years from Somewhere.* New York: Atheneum, 1979. Notable Book Award, American Library Association, 1979: *7 Years from Somewhere,* Golden Rose Award, New England Poetry Society, 1985. Ruth Lilly Award, 1987. Elmer Holmes Bobst Award, New York University, 1990. *Los Angeles Times* Book Prize, 1991: *What Work Is,* New York: Knopf, 1991.

National Book Award for Poetry, 1991: *What Work Is.*

For More Information: Buckley, Christopher, ed., *On the Poetry of Philip Levine: Stranger to Nothing,* Ann Arbor: University of Michigan Press, 1991; Skenazy, Paul, "Philip Levine's Poems Plumb Memory and Metaphor," *San Francisco Chronicle,* January 1, 1995.

Commentary: Philip Levine was awarded the 1995 Pulitzer Prize in Poetry for *The Simple Truth.*

Levine was born in Detroit and educated at Wayne State University and the University of Iowa. His verse is strongly autobiographical and lyrical and he is a self-described "anarchist." He taught for many years at California State University at Fresno. Levine won the National Book Award for *What Work Is,* in 1991. His other works include *Poetry, Somewhere,* and his most recent, *Unselected Poems.*

1996

Jorie Graham   1067
Birth: May 9, 1951; New York, NY. **Parents:** Curtis Bill and Beverly (Stoll) Pepper. **Education:** New York University: BFA. University of Iowa: MFA. **Spouse:** James Galvin.

Prize: *Poetry,* 1996: *The Dream of the Unified Field: Selected Poems, 1974-1994,* Hopewell, NJ: Ecco, 1995.

Career: Assistant Professor of English, Murray State University, KY, 1978-1979; Assistant Professor of English, Humboldt State University, CA, beginning in 1979; Workshop Instructor, Writers Community, 1982; Workshop Instructor, Columbia University, 1982-1983; Workshop Instructor, University of Iowa, beginning in 1983.

Selected Works: *Hybrids of Plants and of Ghosts,* 1980. *Erosion,* 1983. *The End of Beauty,* 1987. *Region of Unlikeness,* 1991. *Materialism: Poems,* 1993. *The Errancy: Poems,* 1997.

Other Awards: Academy of American Poets Prize, 1977. Young Poet Prize, 1980: *Poetry Northwest.* Pushcart Prize, Pushcart Press, 1980 "I Was Taught Three." Award from Great Lakes Colleges Association, 1981: *Hybrids of Plants and of Ghosts,* Princeton, NJ: Princeton University Press, 1980. Ingram-Merrill Foundation Grant, 1981. Pushcart Prize, Pushcart Press, 1982: "My Garden, My Daylight". Bunting Fellow, Radcliffe Institute, 1982. *American Poetry Review* Prize, 1982: *The Age of Reason and Other Poems.* Guggenheim Fellow, 1983.

For More Information: Vendler, Helen Hennessy, *The Given and the Made: Strategies of Poetic Redefinition,* Cambridge, MA: Harvard University Press, 1995; Schiff, Stephen, "Big Poetry," *New Yorker,* July 14, 1997; *Current Biography,* New York: Wilson, 1997.

Commentary: Jorie Graham was awarded the 1996 Pulitzer Prize in Poetry for *The Dream of the Unified Field,* a collection that draws on her love of gardening.

Graham was born in New York City and educated at New York University and the University of Iowa. Her first collection, *Hybrids of Plants and Ghosts,* was published in 1980. She was elected a Chancellor of The Academy of American Poets in 1997. She is on the faculty of the University of Iowa's Creative Writers' Workshop. She gives poetry readings frequently. Her other works include *The End of Beauty* and a recent anthology which she edited, *Earth Took of Earth: 100 Great Poems of the English Language.*

1997

Lisel Mueller   1068
Birth: February 8, 1924; Hamburg, Germany; came to United States in 1939, naturalized in 1945. **Parents:** Fritz C. and Ilse (Burmester) Neumann. **Education:** University of Evansville, IL: BA. Indiana University. **Spouse:** Paul E. Mueller (m. 1943). **Children:** Lucy, Jenny.

Prize: *Poetry,* 1997: *Alive Together: New and Selected Poems,* Baton Rouge, LA: Louisiana State University Press, 1996.

Career: Social Worker, writer and reviewer; Instructor of Poetry Writing, Elmhurst College, 1969-1972; Participating poet, Poets In The Schools, 1972-1977; Instructor, MFA Writing Program, Goddard College, VT, beginning in 1977.

Selected Works: *Dependencies,* 1965. *Life of a Queen,* 1970. *The Private Life: Poems,* 1976. *Voices from the Forest,* 1977. *Second Language: Poems,* 1986. *Waving from Shore: Poems,* 1989. *Learning to Play by Ear: Essays and Early Poems,* 1990.

Other Awards: Robert M. Ferguson Memorial Award, Friends of Literature, 1966: *Dependencies,* Chapel Hill, NC: University of North Carolina Press, 1965. Helen Bullis Award, 1974, 1977. Lamont Poetry Selection, 1975: *The Private Life,* Baton Rouge, LA: Louisiana State University Press, 1976. Emily Clark Balch Award, 1976.

For More Information: Schwartz, Amy E., "Lisel Mueller's Monet," *Washington Post,* April 13, 1997; Murphy, Meg, "Lake Forest-Area Poet Wins Pulitzer," *Chicago Tribune,* April 8, 1997.

Commentary: *Alive Together: New and Selected Poems* won the 1997 Pulitzer Prize in Poetry for Lisel Mueller.

Mueller was born in Hamburg, Germany. She immigrated with her family to the United States in 1939. She was educated at the University of Evansville and at Indiana University. She said that her first poem was sparked by the death of her mother and writing allowed her to grieve. Her first publication was a collection of essays, *Dependencies,* published in 1965. She worked as a book reviewer for the *Chicago Daily News.* Mueller is a founding member of the Poetry Center of Chicago. Her other works include *Waving from Shore* and *Learning to Play by Ear.*

1998

Charles Wright   1069

Birth: August 25, 1935; Pickwick Dam, TN. **Parents:** Charles Penzel and Mary Castleman (Winter) Wright. **Religion:** Episcopalian. **Education:** Davidson College, NC: BA. University of Iowa: MFA. University of Rome, Italy. **Spouse:** Holly McIntire Wright (m. 1969). **Children:** Luke Savin Herrick.

Prize: *Poetry,* 1998: *Black Zodiac,* Farrar, Straus and Giroux, 1997.

Career: Faculty member, University of California, Irvine, 1966-1983; Fulbright Lecturer, University of Padua, Italy, 1968-1969; Professor, University of Virginia, 1983-1987; Souder Family Professor of English, University of Virginia, 1988-Present; Distinguished Visiting Professor, Universia Degli Studi, Florence, Italy, 1992; Member, Fellowship of Southern Writers; Visiting Professor, University of Iowa, Princeton University, and Columbia University.

Selected Works: *The Dream Animal,* 1968. *The Grave of the Right Hand,* 1970. *The Venice Notebook,* 1971. *Hard Freight,* 1973. *Bloodlines,* 1975. *Colophons: Poems,* 1977. *China Trace,* 1977. *The Storm and Other Poems* (Translation) (with Eugenio Montale), 1978. *Wright: A Profile,* 1979. *Dead Color: Poems,* 1980. *The Southern Cross,* 1981. *Country Music: Selected Early Poems,* 1982. *The Other Side of the River Poems,* 1984. *Five Journals,* 1986. *Halflife: Improvisations and Interviews, 1977-87,* 1988. *A Journal of the Year of the Ox: A Poem,* 1988.

Xionia: Poems, 1990. *Country Music: Selected Early Poems,* 1991. *Quarter Notes: Improvisations and Interviews,* 1995. *Chickamauga,* 1995.

Other Awards: Eunice Tietjans Award, 1969. National Endowment of the Arts Grant, 1974. Guggenheim Fellow, Guggenheim Foundation, 1975. Poetry Society of America Melville Cone Award, 1976. American Academy Grant, 1977. PEN Translation Prize, 1979. Ingram Merrill Fellow, 1980. American Book Award, 1984. Brandeis Creative Arts Award, 1987. Award of Merit Medal, American Academy of Arts and Letters, 1992. Distinguished Contribution to Letters Award, Ingram Merrill Foundation, 1993. Ruth Lilly Poetry Prize, 1993. Member, American Academy of Arts and Letters, 1995. The Lenore Marshall Poetry Prize, 1996: *Chicamauga,* New York: Farrar, Straus and Giroux, 1995. *Los Angeles Times Book Prize,* 1997. National Book Critics Circle Prize, Poetry, 1997. Ambassador Book Award, Poetry, 1998.

For More Information: Meeks, Kenneth, "Charles Wright: Almost Victim to Censorship of Black Writers," *Amsterdam News,* April 17, 1993; Bond, Bruce, "Metaphysics of the Image in Charles Wright and Paul Cezanne," *Southern Review,* Winter 1994; Gussow, Mel, "A Good Ear For the Music of His Own Life," *New York Times,* April 16, 1998.

Commentary: The 1998 Pulitzer Prize in Poetry was awarded to *Black Zodiac* written by Charles P. Wright Jr. This is an autobiographical volume, as are many of Wright's collections.

Charles Penzel Wright Jr. was born in Pickwick Dam, Tennessee. His first work, *The Grave of the Right Hand,* was published in 1970. Wright has been influenced by both Dante and Eugenio Montale. He has done several translations of Montale's work. He has taught at the Universities of California and Iowa; currently, he is a professor of English at the University of Virginia at Charlottesville. His style has been called one of non-emphasis.

Reporting

1917

Herbert Bayard Swope 1070

Birth: January 5, 1882; St. Louis, MO. **Death:** June 20, 1958. **Parents:** Isaac Swope and Ida (Cohn). **Spouse:** Margaret Pearl Honeyman Powell (m. 1912, died 1967). **Children:** Jane Marion, Herbert Bayard.

Prize: *Reporting,* 1917: *New York World,* New York: New York World, 1916.

Career: Cub Reporter, *St. Louis (MO) Post-Dispatch;* Reporter, *St. Louis (MO) Post-Dispatch,* 1909-; Reporter, *New York Times;* Reporter, *New York World,* ?-1913; War Correspondent with German Armies, *New York (NY) World* and *St. Louis (MO) Post-Dispatch,* 1914-16; Served in U.S. Navy, WWI; Served on U.S. War Industries Board; Assistant to B.M. Baruch, City Editor, *New York (NY) World,* 1915; Chief Correspondent, Paris Peace Conference, *New York (NY) World;* Executive Editor, *New York (NY) World,* 1920-29.

Selected Works: *Inside the German Empire in the Third Year of the War,* 1917.

Other Awards: Poor Richard Medal, Philadelphia, PA. United States Medal for Merit by President. United States Gold Medal, Interfaith in Action, 1950. Knight Commander, Republic of Liberia, 1954. Honorary Degrees: Hobart College, NY, 1924; Colgate University, NY, 1927.

For More Information: Drewry, John E., *Post Biographies of Famous Journalists,* Athens, GA: The University of Georgia Press, 1942: 411-430; *New York Times,* 21 June (1958): 1; Kahn, E.J., *The World of Swope,* New York: Simon & Schuster, 1965; Lewis, Alfred Allan, *Man of the World: Herbert Bayard Swope, a Charmed Life of Pulitzer Prizes, Poker and Politics,* Indianapolis, IN: Bobbs-Merrill, 1978; Fischer, Erika J., *American Reporter at the International Political Stage: Herbert Bayard Swope and His Pulitzer Prize-Winning Articles from Germany in 1916, Studies in International Communication, Volume 2,* Bachum, Germany: Studienverlag Brockmeyer, 1982; *Dictionary of Literary Biography, Volume 25,* Detroit: Gale Research Company, 1984: 280-290.

Commentary: Herbert Bayard Swope was awarded the first Pulitzer Prize for Reporting. His series of articles explored the German Empire prior to the United States' involvement in World War I. His stories examined Germany, the peoples of Germany, and their feelings on the war. His stories were published on October 10, 15, and November 4-22, 1916. Swope's descriptive writing and aggressive reporting style drew people into his stories.

Swope retired from the *New York World* in 1929. He was a founder of the American Society of Newspaper Editors as well as the Overseas News Agency. He was a personal consultant to the United States Secretary of War during World War II.

1918

Harold Aylmer Littledale 1071

Birth: 1885; Wales. **Death:** August 11, 1957. **Spouse:** Clara Savage (m., died 1956). **Children:** Harold, Irene, Rosemary.

Prize: *Reporting,* 1918: *New York Evening Post,* New York: New York Evening Post, 1917.

Career: Rancher in Canada; Reporter, Chicago, 1906; Ship News Reporter, *New York (NY) Evening Mail;* Assistant Cable Editor, *New York (NY) Evening Post,* 1913; Staff member, *New York (NY) Evening Post;* Served with British Tank Forces, WWI; Suburban Editor, *New York Times,* 1928-; Assistant Managing Editor, *New York Times.*

Selected Works: *Mastering Your Disability,* 1952.

For More Information: *New York Times,* 12 August (1957): 19.

Commentary: Harold A. Littledale was the second New York reporter to win a Pulitzer Prize. His award was for exposing abuses in the New Jersey penal system which led to significant reforms. He visited all the prisons in New Jersey and was even incarcerated in one to get the whole story. His reporting several years later about the treatment of disabled veterans led to the creation of the United States Veterans Administration.

1919
No award

1920

John Joseph Leary Jr. 1072

Birth: February 2, 1874; Lynn, MA. **Death:** January 4, 1944. **Parents:** John J. Leary and Mary Ann (Cronin). **Spouse:** Alice Ruth Dwyer (m. 1896, died 1942). **Children:** One child.

Prize: *Reporting,* 1920: *New York World,* New York: New York World, 1919.

Career: Staff member, *Lynn (MA) Press,* 1893; Reporter, *Boston (MA) Advertiser and Record,* 1893; Reporter, *Denver (CO) Times,* 1894; Night Editor, *Boston (MA) Post,* 1895-1903; Night City Editor, *Boston (MA) Journal,* 1904; City Editor, *Boston (MA) Herald,* 1904-07; Associate Editor, *New York (NY) Herald,* 1907-12; Special European Correspondent and Editorial Advisor in Paris to James Gordon Bennett, 1912-13; Reporter, *New York (NY) World,* 1913; Labor and Economics Reporter, *New York (NY) Tribune,* 1914-19; Labor and Economics Reporter, *New York (NY) World,* 1919-31; Surveyor of employment exchange system of Europe, 1931, delegated by President Hoover.

Selected Works: *Talks with Theodore Roosevelt, from the Diaries of John J. Leary Jr.,* 1920. *Hoover's Fight for Labor,* 1932.

Other Awards: Gold Watch, American Federation of Labor. Silver Button of Honorary Membership, "Mutual Welfare League" by the 1,600 Convicts of SingSing Prison for his Interest in Their Welfare.

For More Information: *New York Times,* 5 January (1944): 17.

Commentary: John J. Leary prepared to practice law but instead went into the newspaper business. His reporting on the labor problems of the coal industry in West Virginia won him a Pulitzer Prize in 1920. He stayed with the *New York World* until its suspension in 1931. He then went to Europe, at the request of President Hoover, to study the labor conditions there.

1921

Louis Seibold   1073

Birth: October 10, 1863; Washington, DC. **Death:** May 10, 1945. **Parents:** Louis Philip Siebold and Josephine Burrows (Dawson). **Spouse:** Jennie Lind Hopkins (m. 1891, died 1925). **Children:** Martin.

Prize: *Reporting,* 1921: *New York World,* New York: New York World, 1920.

Career: Officeboy, *Washington (DC) Post;* Reporter, *Washington (DC) Post,* 1886-; Staff member, Denver (CO), St. Louis (MO), Chicago (IL), San Francisco (CA), Pendleton (OR) Newspapers; Staff member, *New York (NY) World,* 1894-1902; Corresponent, Albany (NY), *New York (NY) World,* 1905-21; War Correspondent, *New York (NY) World;* Head, Washington (DC) Bureau, *New York (NY) World,* 1916-17; Correspondent, Japan, *New York (NY) Herald,* 1921; Correspondent, *New York (NY) Evening Post.*

Selected Works: *The Loyalty of Wisconsin,* 1918. *Japan and Its Expansion: A Series of Articles,* 1921.

For More Information: *New York Times,* 11 May (1945): 19; *Dictionary of American Biography,*

Supplement Three, 1941-1945, New York: Charles Scribner's Sons, 1973.

Commentary: Louis Seibold's interview of President Woodrow Wilson won him a Pulitzer Prize. He covered many of the major news stories of his time. He reported on every national party convention from 1896-1920. He was the first journalist to arrive on the scene after the volcanic explosion of Mount Pelee on Martinique in which 30,000 people were killed.

1922

Kirke Larue Simpson   1074

Birth: August 14, 1881; San Francisco, CA. **Death:** June 16, 1971. **Parents:** Sylvester C. Simpson and Frances Marion (McFarland). **Spouse:** Ella May Field (m. 1945, died 1952); Irene L. (m. 1953).

Prize: *Reporting,* 1922: Associated Press, "The Unknown Soldier," 1921.

Career: Editor, *Tonapah (NV) Daily Sun;* Night Reporter, San Francisco (CA), 1906; Washington (DC), Associated Press, 1908-45.

Selected Works: *The Unknown Soldier: Complete Texts of the Service of the Associated Press on "The Unknown Soldier," as Sent from Washington, D.C., on Wednesday, Thursday, and Friday, November 9, 10, and 11, 1921,* 1928.

For More Information: *AP World,* Spring (1970): 34-36; *New York Times,* 17 June (1972): 36; Rigsby, Gwendolyn Gezelle, "A History of Associated Press Pulitzer Prizes" (thesis), University of South Carolina, 1993.

Commentary: Kirke L. Simpson was the first reporter for the Associated Press to have a byline, for his winning story on the burial of the unknown soldier of World War I. His was the first Pulitzer Prize for the Associated Press.

Simpson served in the Spanish American War and the Philippine Insurrection of 1898. He was with military intelligence in 1921. Some of the stories he covered for the Associated Press included Theodore Roosevelt's Presidential bid and Vera Cruz's campaign in Mexico. He was the first writer to use the wording "smoke-filled room" with regard to politics.

1923

Alva Johnston   1075

Birth: August 1, 1888; Sacramento, CA. **Death:** November 23, 1950. **Parents:** Alfred John Johnston and Luella (Buckminster). **Spouse:** Evelyn Colgan (m. 1914). **Children:** Elizabeth, Margaret.

Prize: *Reporting,* 1923: *New York Times,* December 27-30, New York: New York Times, 1922.

Career: Reporter, *Sacramento (CA) Bee,* 1906; Staff member, *New York Times,* 1912-28; Staff member, *New York (NY) Herald-Tribune,* 1928-32; Magazine Writer, *New Yorker* and *Saturday Evening Post,* 1932-.

Selected Works: *Wilson Mizner: A New Yorker Profile,* 1933. *The Great Goldwyn,* 1937. *The Case of Erle Stanley Gardner,* 1947. *Hot Documents,* 1947. *The Legendary Mizners,* 1953.

For More Information: *The New York Times,* 24 November (1950): 35; *National Cyclopaedia of American Biography, Volume 38,* New York: James T. White & Company, 1953: 413; Applegate, Ed, *Literary Journalists,* Westport, CT: Greenwood Press, 1996.

Commentary: Alva Johnston won a Pulitzer Prize for his dispatches from the convention of the American Association for the Advancement of Science. Johnston was known for his ability to translate difficult topics into understandable language.

1924

Magner White   1076

Birth: July 31, 1894; McKinney, TX. **Parents:** Rev. Henry Oliver White and Charlotte (Magner). **Spouse:** Laura Irene Batey (m. 1914, div. 1940); Pauline Ristow (m. 1941, died 1951). **Children:** Evelyn Grace, Breton Rayfield, Magner, Phyllis, Patricia Irene, Charlotte Ada (LB); Paul, Magdala, Michael (PR).

Prize: *Reporting,* 1924: *San Diego Sun,* "The Eclipse of the Sun," September 10, San Diego, CA: San Diego Sun, 1923.

Career: Printer's Devil, Oklahoma, Washington, and Idaho newspapers, 1910-14; Staff member, *Spokane (WA) Chronicle,* 1916; City Editor, *Moscow (ID) Daily Star Mirror;* State Capital Reporter, Assistant City Editor, *Boise (ID) Daily Statesman,* 1917, State Capital Reporter, Assistant City Editor, *Boise (ID) Evening Capital News;* News Editor, *Chico (CA) Enterprise;* City Hall Reporter, *San Diego (CA) Sun,* 1920; Assistant to Editor, *San Diego (CA) Sun,* ?-1925; Magazine writer, 1925-29; Managing Editor, *El Paso (TX) Times,* 1930-31; Sunday Magazine Editor, *Los Angeles (CA) Times,* 1932-33; Assistant Editor, *San Diego (CA) Sun,* 1933-35; Editor, *San Diego (CA) Sun,* 1935-38; Writer, *Saturday Evening Post* Magazine, 1939-41; Publicist, Metro-Goldwyn-Mayer, 1943-47; Writer, *Look* Magazine, 1946; Editor and Reporter, *Los Angeles (CA) Examiner.*

Selected Works: *Our Great Water Problem,* 1957.

For More Information: *The Fourth Estate,* March 24, 1924; *Los Angeles Times,* September 8, 1989: Metro 1.

Commentary: Magner White won the 1924 Pulitzer Prize for his reporting on the eclipse of the sun. He wrote the story from the newsroom. Other reporters had been assigned to see how animals at the zoo reacted to the event. But White, without those distractions, wrote the more memorable article. His award was the first given to a reporter or newspaper on the West Coast.

1925

Alvin H. Goldstein   1077

Birth: 1902; Chattanooga, TN. **Death:** May 7, 1972. **Education:** University of Chicago, IL. **Spouse:** Willmett Geist. **Children:** Alvin, Peter.

Prize: *Reporting,* 1925: *Chicago Daily News,* Chicago: Chicago Daily News, 1924.

Career: Cub Reporter, *Chicago (IL) Daily News,* 1924-25; Staff member, *St. Louis (MO) Post-Dispatch,* 1925-65.

Selected Works: *The Unquiet Death of Julius and Ethel Rosenberg,* 1975.

For More Information: *Chicago Daily News,* 27 April (1925): 1, 4; *St. Louis Post-Dispatch,* 7 May (1972): 7A; *New York Times,* 8 May (1972): 40; *Contemporary Authors, First Revision, Volumes 33-36,* Detroit: Gale Research Company, 1978; Rothmeyer, Karen, *Winning Pulitzers: The Stories Behind Some of the Best News Coverage of Our Times,* New York: Columbia University Press, 1991: 26-31.

Commentary: Alvin Goldstein and James Mulroy were just one year out of college when they reported several key stories that led to an arrest in the investigation of Leopold and Loeb for the murder of Bobby Franks. They were the first to confirm the identity of a murder victim as the kidnapped Franks and the ones to locate the typewriter that had been used to type the ransom note.

James W. Mulroy   1078

Birth Place: Chicago, IL. **Death:** April 29, 1952. **Parents:** James Robert Mulroy. **Education:** University of Chicago, IL. **Spouse:** Fayette Krum (m., died); Helen M. **Children:** Fayette Krum Mulroy (FK).

Prize: *Reporting,* 1925: *Chicago Daily News,* Chicago: Chicago Daily News, 1924.

Career: Campus Correspondent, *Chicago (IL) Daily News;* Cub Reporter, *Chicago (IL) Daily,* 1924; Staff member, *New York (NY) World;* Executive Secretary, National Outboard Association; Staff member, *Chicago (IL) Sun,* 1941; Promotion Manager, *Chicago (IL) Sun;* Managing Editor, *Chicago (IL) Sun,* ?-48; Campaign Manager, Adlai L. Stevenson, 1948; Executive Secretary, Illinois Governor Adlai E. Stevenson, 1949-51.

For More Information: *Chicago Daily News,* 27 April (1925): 1, 4; *New York Times,* 3 May (1925): 11; *New York Times,* 30 April (1952): 27; *Chicago Daily Tribune,* 30 April (1952): 10; Rothmeyer, Karen, *Winning Pulitzers: The Stories Behind Some of the Best News Coverage of Our Time,* New York: Columbia University Press, 1991: 26-31.

Commentary: James Mulroy and Alvin Goldstein, fraternity brothers at the University of Chicago and cub reporters at the *Chicago Daily News* wrote the key stories in the Leopold-Loeb investigation for the murder of Bobby Franks. Mulroy was 25 years old when he won the award in 1925.

Mulroy was part of the start-up team for the *Chicago Sun* when it began publication in 1941. He left to become campaign manager for Adlai Stevenson in his race for the Illinois governorship.

1926

William Burke Miller   1079
Spouse: Madge M.

Prize: *Reporting,* 1926: *Louisville Courier-Journal,* Louisville, KY: Louisville Courier-Journal, 1925.

Career: Reporter, *Louisville (KY) Courier-Journal,* 1925-26; ice cream manufacturer, 1926; Special events reporter, radio; Night Executive Officer, NBC; Staff member, *Rutland Herald.*

For More Information: *Newsweek,* 13 May (1963): 20.

Commentary: William Burke Miller won a Pulitzer Prize for his reporting on Floyd Collins. Collins was trapped in Sand Cave, Kentucky. Because of Miller's small physical stature, he was the only person able to reach the place where Collins was trapped. He brought Collins food and placed electric lights close to him. His narratives of the story were published nationwide. Collins, who was trapped for 17 days, died before rescuers could reach him.

Miller left the newspaper business and went into ice cream manufacturing. Later, he worked for NBC-TV.

1927

John T. Rogers   1080
Birth: April 19, 1881; Louisville, KY. **Death:** March 2, 1937. **Parents:** Mrs. Alice Welch. **Spouse:** Missie R. (m. 1903). **Children:** Mrs. P.S. Chamberlain.

Prize: *Reporting,* 1927: *St. Louis Post-Dispatch,* St. Louis: St. Louis Post-Dispatch, 1926.

Career: Telegraph Operator, 1896; Reporter, *Louisville (KY) Times;* Reporter, *Louisville (KY) Courier-Journal;* Reporter, *Kansas City (MO) Post;* Cor-

respondent and Contributor, *New York (NY) World;* Served in Tanks Corps, U.S. Army, WWI; Reporter, *St. Louis (MO) Post-Dispatch,* 1916-.

Selected Works: *The Murders of Mer Rouge,* 1923.

For More Information: *St. Louis Post-Dispatch,* 3 March (1937): 1, 3; *New York Times,* 4 March (1937): 23.

Commentary: John T. Rogers, who was well known for his ability to gain the trust of all types of people, was the recipient of many confessions to crimes, including murder and kidnapping. He received a Pulitzer Prize for his work that led to the impeachment of United States District Judge George W. English.

1928
No award

1929

Paul Yewell Anderson   1081
Birth: August 29, 1893; Knoxville, TN. **Death:** December 6, 1938. **Parents:** William Holston Anderson and Elizabeth Dill Haynes. **Education:** Washington University, MO. **Spouse:** Beatrice Wright (m. 1914, div. 1919); Anna Alberta Fritschle (m. 1928, div. 1936); Katherine Lane (m. 1937). **Children:** Paul Webster, Kenneth Paine (BW).

Prize: *Reporting,* 1929: *St. Louis Post-Dispatch,* "How a Bullfighter's Painful Experience Helped a Tree Fall and Sinclair;" "Bonds, Bonds, Who's Got Bonds?" St. Louis: St. Louis Post Dispatch, 1928.

Career: Reporter, *Knoxville (KY) Journal,* 1911; Staff member, *St. Louis (MO) Times,* 1912; Staff member, *St. Louis Star,* 1912; Reporter, *St. Louis Post-Dispatch,* 1914-38; Editorial writer, 1921-23; Freelance Reporter, *Omaha (NE) World-Herald;* Staff member, *Raleigh (NC) News and Observer,* and *St. Louis Post-Dispatch;* Correspondent, Washington (DC), *St. Louis Post-Dispatch,* 1923-28; Columnist, *Nation,* 1929-34; Washington (DC) Bureau, *St. Louis Star-Times,* 1938.

Other Awards: Headliners Club Award, 1937.

For More Information: *American Mercury,* 22 (April 1931): 403-406; *Quill,* April (1935): 8-10; *St. Louis Post-Dispatch,* 6 December (1938): 1, 10; *New York Times,* 8 December (1938): 27; Kirchway, Freda, and Oswald Garrison Villard, and Maruerite Young, *Where is There Another? A Memorial to Paul Y. Anderson,* Norman, OK: Cooperative Books, 1939; *Esquire,* 29 March (1948): 101-105; *Dictionary of American Biography, Supplement 2,* New York: Charles Scribner's Sons, 1958; *Dictionary of Literary*

Biography, Volume 29, Detroit: Gale Research Company, 1984.

Commentary: Paul Y. Anderson was considered one of the most brilliant reporters of his time. He attacked corruption and dishonesty in government. His persistent reporting led to the United States Senate reopening the investigation into the Teapot Dome Scandal. He was awarded a Pulitzer Prize for his reporting on the subject.

Other stories that he covered included the Leopold and Loeb trial in Chicago and the Scopes trial in Dayton, Tennessee. He took his own life at the end of 1938.

1930

Russell D. Owen   1082

Birth: January 8, 1889; Chicago, IL. **Death:** April 3, 1952. **Parents:** William Owen and Annie R. (Brown). **Spouse:** Ethel J. McGregor (m. 1913, died 1948). **Children:** Jean.

Prize: *Reporting,* 1930: *New York Times,* New York: New York Times, 1929.

Career: Stenographer, 1904; Linotype Operator, Reporter, *New York (NY) Sun,* 1906-20; Reporter, Canandaigua (NY); Reporter, *Syracuse (NY) Herald;* Staff member, *New York Times,* 1921-24; Head, News Bureau, General Electric Company, 1924-26; Reporter, *New York Times,* 1926-.

Selected Works: *The Barque "City of New York," the Heroic Flagship of the Byrd Antarctic Expedition,* 1930. *South of the Sun,* 1934. *We Saw It Happen: The News behind the News That's Fit to Print* (with others), 1938. *The Antarctic Ocean: Oceans of the World,* 1941. *The Conquest of the North and South Poles: Adventures of the Peary and Byrd Exhibitions; Landmark Books, 27,* 1952.

Other Awards: Medal for First Antarctic Expedition, United States Congress.

For More Information: *New York Times,* 4 April (1952): 25.

Commentary: Russell Owen won a Pulitzer Prize for his year-long reporting on the Byrd expedition to the Antarctic. Most of the stories he sent back by radio were published on the front page of the *New York Times.*

He was a fan of aviation and covered Lindbergh's transatlantic flight. In 1925, he was chosen to cover the Scopes Trial in Dayton, Tennessee. Twenty years later he went back to Tennessee to write about the atomic bomb factory at Oak Ridge.

1931

Alexander Black MacDonald   1083

Birth: May 6, 1861; New Brunswick, Canada. **Death:** April 9, 1942. **Parents:** Rev. Alexander Black MacDonald and Jemina (McDonald). **Religion:** Baptist. **Spouse:** Mary Larkin (m. 1893). **Children:** Donald, Frank, Mary, Arthur, Malcolm.

Prize: *Reporting,* 1931: *Kansas City Star,* Kansas City, MO: Kansas City Star, 1930.

Career: Staff Reporter, *Kansas City (MO) World,* 1893; Staff Reporter, *Kansas City (MO) Star,* 1894-1920; Staff Writer, *Country Gentleman* and *Ladies' Home Journal,* 1920-28; Staff Reporter, *Kansas City (MO) Star,* 1928-.

Selected Works: *What Family Religion Does for One Church: The Story of the Mennonite Church of Berne, Indiana,* 1922. *Can We Trust the Brewers? Here Is Their Record, It Should Speak for Itself, to Congress and to the People,* 1924. *Hands Up! Stories of the Six-Gun Fighters of the Old Wild West* (with Fred Ellsworth Sutton), 1927.

For More Information: *New York Times,* 10 April (1942): 17.

Commentary: A.B. MacDonald's reporting and solution of a Texas murder won him a Pulitzer Prize in 1931. He came to the United States in 1890 and became a naturalized citizen in 1896. He worked as a circus press agent before he began his career in journalism.

1932

Douglas DeVeny Martin   1084

Birth: September 9, 1885; Benton Harbor, MI. **Death:** September 26, 1963. **Parents:** William Samuel Martin and Mary Morrison (McKellar). **Spouse:** Cecelia Cleora Wilcox (m. 1913). **Children:** Mary Isabella.

Prize: *Reporting,* 1932: *Detroit Free Press,* "The Legion Marched," September 23, Detroit, MI: Detroit Free Press, 1931.

Career: Writer, *Detroit (MI) News,* 1918; Manager, *Masonic News;* Staff member, Publishers Advertising Agency, 1930-; Associate Editor, *Detroit (MI) Free Press;* Managing Editor, *Detroit (MI) Free Press,* 1939-45; Professor of Journalism, University of Arizona, 1946-56.

Selected Works: *Tombstone's Epitaph,* 1951. *Yuma Crossing,* 1954. *The Earps of Tombstone: The Truth about the OK Corral Gun Fight and Other Events in Which Wyatt Earp and His Brothers Participated,* 1959. *The Lamp in the Desert: The Story of the University of Arizona,* 1960. *Silver, Sex and Six Guns: Tombstone Saga of the Life of Buckskin Frank*

Leslie, a Story of Tombstone's Early Gunmen (with Frank Nashville Leslie), 1962. *An Arizona Chronology: The Territorial Years 1846-1912,* 1963. *An Arizona Chronology: Statehood, 1913-1936,* 1966.

For More Information: *New York Times,* May 30, 1932: 15.

Commentary: Douglas D. Martin, along with four of his colleagues, wrote about the massive American Legion Parade in Detroit in 1931. He worked briefly with an advertising agency before joining the *Detroit Free Press.* He went on to become managing editor, then taught journalism in the warmer climate of Arizona.

James S. Pooler   1085

Birth: 1905; Sheboygan, WI. **Death:** February 18, 1967. **Parents:** Suzanne. **Religion:** Roman Catholic. **Education:** University of Detroit, MI: BS. **Spouse:** Marie H. LaLonde (m. 1932). **Children:** Patrick, Susan, Mary Ann, Sheila.

Prize: *Reporting,* 1932: *Detroit Free Press,* "The Legion Marched," September 23, Detroit, MI: Detroit Free Press, 1931.

Career: Office boy, Reporter, *Detroit (MI) Free Press,* 1923-67; Columnist, *Detroit Free Press.*

Other Awards: Junior Chamber of Commerce. First Michigan Humane Society Award, 1960.

For More Information: *New York Times,* May 30, 1932: 15; *Detroit Free Press,* 19 February (1967): A3, A6.

Commentary: James S. Pooler, along with four of his colleagues, won a Pulitzer Prize in 1932 for their reporting of the large American Legion Parade in Detroit. Pooler also contributed to the Pulitzer Prize won by his paper in 1945. For eight years he wrote the column "Sunnyside." He was known for his offbeat stories and was a charter member of the Detroit Press Club.

William C. Richards   1086

Birth Place: Rochester, NY. **Death:** November 29, 1956. **Education:** University of Michigan. **Spouse:** Rosemary R. (m. 1926).

Prize: *Reporting,* 1932: *Detroit Free Press,* "The Legion Marched," September 23, Detroit, MI: Detroit Free Press, 1931.

Career: Reporter, upstate New York papers; Reporter, Columnist, Associate Editor, *Detroit (MI) Free Press,* 1916-35; Freelance writer; Michigan Director of the Office of Government Reports, 1940; Account Executive, Campbell-Ewald Advertising Agency; Director of Publicity, Detroit Community Fund, 10 Years.

Selected Works: *The Last Billionaire, Henry Ford,* 1948. *Biography of a Foundation: The Story of*

the Children's Fund of Michigan, 1929-1954 (with William John Norton), 1957.

Other Awards: American Social Work Publicity Council Award, 1930.

For More Information: *New York Times,* May 30, 1932: 15; *Detroit Free Press,* 30 November (1956): 28; *New York Times,* November 30, 1956: 23.

Commentary: William C. Richards, along with four other staff members of the *Detroit Free Press,* won a Pulitzer Prize for their reporting on the American Legion Parade in December 1931. He was 46 years old when he won the award.

Richards left newspaper work to work in the private sector and, for a time, for the state of Michigan. He wrote a bestselling biography of Henry Ford.

John N.W. Sloan   1087

Education: Columbia University, NY: BA. **Spouse:** Margaret K.

Prize: *Reporting,* 1932: *Detroit Free Press,* "The Legion Marched," September 23, Detroit, MI: Detroit Free Press, 1931.

Career: Staff member, *Detroit (MI) Free Press,* 1926-; Assistant Real Estate Editor, *Detroit (MI) Free Press,* ?-1930; Real Estate Editor, *Detroit (MI) Free Press,* 1930-.

For More Information: *New York Times,* May 30, 1932: 15.

Commentary: John N.W. Sloan, along with four other staff members of the *Detroit Free Press,* won a Pulitzer Prize for their reporting of the American Legion Parade in December 1931. Sloan was 33 years old when he won the award in 1932.

Frank D. Webb   1088

Death: August 10, 1964. **Education:** University of Michigan. **Spouse:** Anna Belle.

Prize: *Reporting,* 1932: *Detroit Free Press,* "The Legion Marched," September 23, Detroit, MI: Detroit Free Press, 1931.

Career: Staff member, *Detroit (MI) Free Press,* 1924-; Automobile Editor, *Detroit (MI) Free Press;* Public relations counselor.

For More Information: *New York Times,* May 30, 1932: 15.

Commentary: Frank Webb won a Pulitzer Prize with four fellow journalists for their coverage of the American Legion Parade in Detroit in 1931. He was 34 years old when he was awarded the Prize in 1932. He later became a public relations counselor and worked in advertising.

1933

Francis Anthony Jamieson 1089

Birth: November 8, 1904; Trenton, NJ. **Death:** January 30, 1960. **Parents:** William Michael Jamieson and Mary Ellen (Crawford). **Spouse:** Charlotte Wiggin (m. 1933, div.); Linda Eder (m. 1940). **Children:** Joan Ellen (CW); Margaret, Frances (LE).

Prize: *Reporting,* 1933: Associated Press, 1932.

Career: Legislative Correspondent, Kelly News Bureau, 1922-28; Correspondent, *Hoboken (NJ) Jersey Observer,* 1924-28; Reporter, Trenton (NJ) and New York (NY), Associated Press, 1929-35; Public Relations Member, John Price Jones Corporation, 1935-40; Publicity Advisor, Election Campaign of Governor Charles Edison (NJ), 1940; Office Coordinator of Inter-American Affairs, 1940-46; Acting Director, Inter-American Affairs, 1945-46; Associate, Rockefeller Brothers; Director, Government Affairs Foundation, Inc.; Director, International Basic Economy Corporation; Director, American International Association; Chief Public Relations Advisor, Rockefeller, 1946-.

For More Information: *New York Times,* 2 May (1933): 15; *The Reminiscences of Francis Jamieson, Columbia University Oral History Collection, Part 4, Number 114,* 1959; *New York Times,* 31 January (1960): 94; *National Cyclopaedia of American Biography, Volume 43,* New York: James T. White & Company, 1961: 594; Rigsby, Gwendolyn Gezelle, "A History of Associated Press Pulitzer Prizes" (thesis), University of South Carolina, 1993.

Commentary: A reporter turned public relations executive, Francis Jamieson was an advisor to New York governor Nelson Rockefeller and an associate of Rockefeller for over 20 years. Jamieson was awarded a Pulitzer Prize for his reporting on the Lindbergh kidnapping and the recovery of the infant's body.

1934

Royce Brier 1090

Birth: April 18, 1894; River Falls, WI. **Death:** January 10, 1975. **Parents:** Warren Judson Brier and Marion (Royce). **Education:** University of Washington. **Spouse:** Monica Doonan (m. 1926, died 1949); Crystal Smith (m. 1949, died 1970). **Children:** Susan, Judith (MD); Royce (CS).

Prize: *Reporting,* 1934: *San Francisco Chronicle,* San Francisco: San Francisco Chronicle, 1933.

Career: Short story writer, 1920-25; Reporter, *San Francisco (CA) Chronicle,* 1926-36; Interpretive News Columnist, *San Francisco (CA) Chronicle,*

1937-75; Editorial Director, *San Francisco (CA) Chronicle,* 1942-75.

Selected Works: *Crusade,* 1931. *Reach for the Moon,* 1934. *Bay in Blue,* 1937. *No More Dreams,* 1938. *Last Boat from Beyrouth,* 1943. *Western World: A Study of the Forces Shaping Our Time,* 1946.

Other Awards: Literary Gold Medal, Commonwealth Club of California, 1947.

For More Information: *New York Times,* 8 May (1934): 20; *Contemporary Authors, Volumes 93-96,* Detroit: Gale Research Company, 1980.

Commentary: Royce Brier and four assistants worked for 16 straight hours dispatching stories on the San Jose kidnapping and lynching of Brooke Hart, the son of an area merchant.

Brier was also a novelist. He traveled around the world in 1925 and used his trip to provide "local color about China and Arabia."

1935

William Howland Taylor 1091

Birth: May 31, 1901; New Bedford, MA. **Death:** January 6, 1966. **Parents:** Stephen Hickmott Taylor and Martha Ellen (Williams). **Education:** Dartmouth College, NH: BS. **Spouse:** Anne Kay Hocking (m. 1927). **Children:** Stephen Howland, William Hocking.

Prize: *Reporting,* 1935: *New York Herald-Tribune,* New York: New York Herald-Tribune, 1934.

Career: Reporter, *New Bedford (MA) Standard,* 1923-24; Staff member, manufacturer of oil burners, 1924; Reporter, *Fall Rivers (MA) News,* 1924-25; Reporter, *Boston (MA) Herald,* 1925-27; Sportswriter, *New York (NY) Herald-Tribune,* 1927-63; Managing Editor, Vice-President, *Yacht Magazine,* Served in U.S. Navy, 1942-45.

Selected Works: *Just Cruising,* 1949. *On and off Soundings,* 1951. *The America's Cup Races* (with Herbert Lawrence Stone), 1958. *Outboards at Work,* 1958. *The Story of American Yachting* (with others), 1958.

For More Information: *New York Times,* 7 May (1935): 20; *New York Times,* 8 January (1966): 25.

Commentary: William Taylor was the first sportswriter to win a Pulitzer Prize. His reporting on the America's Cup races of 1934 introduced yachting to the everyday reader.

1936

Lauren Dwight Lyman 1092

Birth: April 24, 1891; Easthampton, MA. **Death:** December 17, 1971. **Parents:** Henry Lauren Lyman and Annie (McMahon). **Education:** Yale University,

CT. **Spouse:** Mabel Styring (m. 1921, died 1947); Bertha H. Williams (m. 1949). **Children:** Ellen, Elizabeth, Philip Henry, Anne, Mary.

Prize: *Reporting,* 1936: *New York Times,* "Lindbergh Family Sails for England to Seek a Safe, Secluded Residence," New York: New York Times, 1935.

Career: Served in U.S. Army, 1917-19; Vacation Substitute, *Northampton (MA) Daily Hampshire Gazette and Easthampton (MA) News;* Staff member, Dodge Reports, Inc., 1919; Assistant Real Estate Editor, *New York Times,* 1919-20; General Assignment Reporter, *New York Times,* 1920-38; Assistant to President, United Aircraft Corporation, 1938-43, Assistant to Chairman, United Aircraft Corporation, 1943-46, Vice President, United Aircraft Corporation, 1946-.

Selected Works: *The Wonder Book of the Air* (with Carl B. Allen), 1930.

For More Information: *Editor & Publisher,* 28 December (1935): 10; *Contemporary Authors, Volumes 89-92,* Detroit: Gale Research Company, 1980.

Commentary: Lauren D. Lyman's exclusive story of the Lindbergh family's move to England in December 1935 won him a Pulitzer Prize. Lyman first met and wrote about Lindbergh in Spring 1927 at Roosevelt Field prior to Lindbergh's transatlantic flight. Lyman also covered the kidnapping of Lindbergh's son and the trial and execution of the infant's kidnapper.

1937

Howard Walter Blakeslee   1093

Birth: March 21, 1880; New Dungeness, WA. **Death:** May 2, 1952. **Parents:** Jesse Walter Blakeslee and Jennie (Howard). **Education:** University of Michigan. **Spouse:** Marguerite Fortune (m. 1906, d.); Rosamund Robinson (m. 1936). **Children:** John Herbert, Merlys, Alton Lauren, Carol (MF); Howard Jr., Rosamund, Alan Robinson (RR).

Prize: *Reporting,* 1937: Associated Press, 1936.

Career: News writer, 1901; Feature Writer, *Detroit (MI) Journal,* 1901-02; Sports Reporter, Chicago (IL) and Detroit (MI) newspapers, 1903-05; Bureau Chief, New Orleans (LA), Atlanta (GA), Dallas (TX), Associated Press, 1906-16; News Editor, Chicago (IL), Associated Press, 1916-26; News Editor, Eastern Division, New York (NY), Associated Press, 1926-28; Photo Service Editor, Associated Press, 1928; Science Editor, Associated Press, 1928-.

Selected Works: *Miracle of Atomics* (with Bernard R. Gray), 1945. *The Atomic Future,* 1946. *Genshiryoku No Shorai* (with Saburo Yamaya), 1947. *Know Your Heart: Public Affairs Pamphlet, No. 137,* 1948. *Atomic Progress: The Hydrogen Race,* 1951.

Other Awards: Wilson L. Fairbanks Award, American College Publicity Association, District II, 1940. Award for Distinguished Achievement in Interpretation of Higher Education. National Headliners Club Award, 1940. George Westinghouse Science Writers Award, American Association for the Advancement of Science, 1946. Medal, School of Journalism, Syracuse University, NY, 1946. Fellow, Sigma Delta Chi, 1950.

For More Information: *New York Times,* 4 May (1937): 20-21; *Dictionary of American Biography, Supplement 5,* New York: Charles Scribner's Sons, 1977; McKerns, Joseph P., *Biographical Dictionary of American Journalism,* New York: Greenwood Press, 1989; Rigsby, Gwendolyn Gezelle, "A History of Associated Press Pulitzer Prizes" (thesis), University of South Carolina, 1993.

Commentary: Howard Blakeslee, along with four other journalists, won the Pulitzer Prize for his reporting from the tercentenary conference at Harvard University.

David Henry Dietz   1094

Birth: October 6, 1897; Cleveland, OH. **Death:** December 9, 1984. **Parents:** Henry William Dietz and Hannah (Levy). **Education:** Western Reserve University, OH: BA. **Spouse:** Dorothy B. Cohen (m. 1918). **Children:** Doris Jean, Patricia Ann, David H. Jr.

Prize: *Reporting,* 1937: *New York Herald-Tribune,* New York: New York Herald-Tribune, 1936.

Career: Editorial Staff member, *Cleveland (OH) Press,* 1915-77; Science Editor, Scripps-Howard Newspapers, 1921-77; Science and Medicine Columnist, Scripps-Howard Newspapers, 1923-77; Lecturer, Western Reserve University (OH), 1927-50; Science Correspondent, United Press International, 1933-; Science Correspondent, *NBC News,* 1940-50; Consultant to Surgeon General, U.S. Army, WWII.

Selected Works: *The Story of Science,* 1931. *Medical Magic,* 1937. *Atomic Energy in the Coming Era,* 1945. *Atomic Science, Bombs and Power,* 1954. *Harvest of Research: The Story of the Goodyear Chemical Division,* 1955. *Science in Hawaii: Observations of a Globetrotting Newspaperman in the Pacific,* 1968. *Stars and the Universe: Random House Science Library, No. 3,* 1968. *The New Outline of Science,* 1972.

Other Awards: B.F. Goodrich Award for Distinguished Public Service, 1940. Westinghouse Distinguished Science Writers Award, 1946. Lasker Medical Journalism Award, 1954. Ohioana Career Medal, 1958. Grady Medal, American Chemical Society, 1961. Honorary Degrees: Western Reserve University, OH, 1948; Bowling Green State University, OH, 1954.

For More Information: *Current Biography Yearbook, 1940,* New York: H.W. Wilson, 1940; *Contemporary Authors, First Revision, Volume 2,* Detroit: Gale Research Company, 1981: 173; *New York Times,* 11 December (1984): B14.

Commentary: David Dietz was one of five journalists to win a Pultizer Prize in 1937 for Reporting. They won for their coverage of the tercentenary celebration at Harvard University in 1936. Dietz was a pioneer in science reporting, being the first American journalist to be named a science editor.

He was the first president of the American Association of Science Writers and he wrote the article on atomic energy in the 1946 *Encyclopaedia Brittanica.*

Gobind Behari Lal 1095

Birth: October 9, 1889; Delhi, India. **Death:** April 1, 1982. **Parents:** Bishan Lal and Jagge (Devi). **Education:** University of Punjab, India: BSc. University of Punjab, India: MA. University of California: Postgrad. Columbia University, NY: Postgrad.

Prize: *Reporting,* 1937: Universal Service, 1936.

Career: Assistant Professor, University of Punjab (India), 1909-12; Editor, Indian language newspaper; *San Francisco (CA) Examiner,* 1925-30; Science Editor, *New York (NY) American;* Science Editor, Universal Service, 1954-82.

Selected Works: *Joseph Mazzini as a Social Reformer,* 1915. *Science and Polity in India,* 1920. *Chemistry of Personality,* 1932.

Other Awards: Research Fellow, University of California, Berkeley, 1912. George Westinghouse Award, American Association for the Advancement of Science, 1946. Watumill Foundation Research Fellow, Columbia University, NY, 1946-48. Guggenheim Fellowship, 1956. Distinguished Service Award, American Medical Association, 1958. Padma Bushar, 1969. Tamra Patra, 1973.

For More Information: *New York Times,* 4 May (1937): 20; *New York Times,* 3 April (1982): 18.

Commentary: Gobind Behari Lal, the son of the Governor of the Indian State of Bikaner, won a Pulitzer Prize, along with four other reporters, for his coverage of the tercentenary celebration at Harvard University.

Lal worked for Indian independence and won two of his native land's highest honors in 1969 and 1973. He wrote on a variety of subjects and interviewed some of the preeminent thinkers of this century, including Albert Einstein, Mahatma Gandhi, H.L. Mencken, Edna St. Vincent Millay, Enrico Fermi, and Max Planck.

Lal was the first journalist to use the term "science writer" with his byline. He was a founder and the 1940 president of the National Association of Science Writers. He died of cancer in 1982 at the age of 92.

William Leonard Laurence 1096

Birth: March 7, 1888; Salantai, Lithuania. **Death:** March 19, 1977. **Parents:** Lipman Siew and Sarah (Preuss). **Religion:** Jewish. **Education:** Harvard University, MA. University of Besancon, France. Harvard University, MA, cum laude. Boston University, MA: LLB. **Spouse:** Florence Davidow (m. 1931).

Prize: *Reporting,* 1937: *New York Times,* New York: New York Times, 1936. *Reporting,* 1946: *New York Times,* New York: New York Times, 1945.

Career: Staff member, *Boston (MA) American,* 1914; Instructor of Philosophy, Roxbury Tutoring School, 1915-17; Served in U.S. Army, 1917-19; Director and Instructor in Philosophy, Mt. Auburn Tutoring School, 1919-21; Freelance writer and play adapter, 1921-26; General Reporter, *New York (NY) World,* 1926; Associate Aviation Editor, *New York (NY) World,* 1927-30; Science News Reporter, *New York Times,* 1930-56; Science Editor, *New York Times,* 1956-64; Science Editor Emeritus, *New York Times,* 1964-77; Consultant of Science Affairs, Natural Foundation-March of Dimes, 1964-66; Science Consultant, New York World's Fair, 1965; Secretary of Board of Trustees of Hall Science City, NY, 1966-.

Selected Works: *Eye Witness Account: Atomic Bomb over Nagasaki, 1945,* 1945. *The Story of the Atomic Bomb: A Series of Articles Reprinted from the New York Times,* 1945. *Dawn over Zero: The Story of the Atomic Bomb,* 1946. *The Hell Bomb,* 1950. *We Are Not Helpless: How We Can Defend Ourselves against Atomic Weapons,* 1950. *Science in Israel: Herzl Institute Pamphlet, Number 4,* 1958. *Men and Atoms: The Discovery, the Uses, and the Future of Atomic Energy,* 1959. *Science at the Fair,* 1964. *New Frontiers of Science: Bantam Pathfinder Editions,* 1964. *Let Us Reason Together* (with William Berkowitz), 1970. *Survival or Suicide: A Summons to Old and Young to Build a United, Peaceful World; With Chapters from the Writings of William L. Laurence. Essay Index Reprint Series* (with others), 1971.

Other Awards: Award, Society of Silurians, 1946. George Washington Distinguished Science Writer's Award, American Association for the Advancement of Science, 1946. Distinguished Service to Journalism Medal, University of Missouri, 1947. Lasker Award, 1950. George Polk Memorial Award, Long Island University, NY, 1950. Page One Award, 1950. Grady Gold Medal, American Chemical Society, 1958. Wisdom Award of Honor. Honorary Degrees: Boston University, MA, 1946; Grinnell College, IA, 1951; Stevens Institute of Technology, NJ, 1951; Yeshiva University, NY, 1957.

For More Information: *The Reminiscences of William L. Laurence, Columbia University Oral History Collection, Part 1, Number 113,* 1972; *New York Times,* 19 March (1977): 1, 7; *Contemporary Authors, Volumes 77-80,* Detroit: Gale Research Company,

1979; McKerns, Joseph P., *Biographical Dictionary of American Journalism,* New York: Greenwood Press, 1989; *Dictionary of American Biography, Supplement 10,* New York: Charles Scribner's Sons, 1995.

Commentary: William L. Laurence is a two-time winner of the Pulitzer Prize. His first was for his coverage of the tercentenary conference at Harvard University. He was cited along with four other journalists who covered the conference. His second was for his coverage of the bombing of Nagasaki and his subsequent series of 10 articles, published between September 26 and October 9, 1945, that included the development, production, and the significance of the atomic bomb.

He first wrote about atomic power in 1940 with the discovery of uranium fission. He was the only journalist to witness the testing of the bomb in Alamogordo, New Mexico in 1945. He witnessed the bombing on Bikini Island in 1946, the atomic tests in Nevada in 1952, 1953, and 1955, and he was in the reporting pool which witnessed the hydrogen bomb tests in 1956. Laurence had the nickname "Atomic Bill."

He came to the United States in 1905, changed his name from Siew to Laurence in 1906, and became a naturalized citizen in 1913. He and David Dietz created the National Association of Science Writers.

John Joseph O'Neill   1097

Birth: June 21, 1889; New York, NY. **Death:** August 30, 1953. **Parents:** James O'Neill and Catherine (Kelleher). **Spouse:** Marie Bock (m. 1912). **Children:** Kenneth, Peggy Theresa.

Prize: *Reporting,* 1937: *New York Herald-Tribune,* New York: New York Herald-Tribune, 1936.

Career: Printer, 1903-04; Electrician, 1905-06; Staff member, New York (Astor) Public Library, 1906-07; Staff member, New York Herald Library, 1907-08; Reporter, 1908-15; Reporter, *Brooklyn (NY) Daily Eagle,* 1915-17; Feature Editor, *Brooklyn (NY) Daily Eagle,* 1918-22; Radio Editor, *Brooklyn (NY) Daily Eagle,* 1922-25; Automobile and Aviation Editor, *Brooklyn (NY) Daily Eagle,* 1925-26; Science Editor, *Brooklyn (NY) Daily Eagle,* 1926-32; Supervisor, construction of new building and plant, *Brooklyn (NY) Daily Eagle,* 1929-30; Science Editor, *New York Herald-Tribune,* 1933-.

Selected Works: *Prodigal Genius: The Life of Nikola Tesla,* 1944. *Almighty Atom: The Real Story of Atomic Energy,* 1945. *You and the Universe: What Science Reveals,* 1946. *Engineering the New Age,* 1949.

Other Awards: Best Science Story of the Year, University of Kansas, 1938. Clement Cleveland Award, New York Cancer Society, 1938. Westinghouse Distinguished Science Writing Medal, Ameri-

can Association for the Advancement of Science, 1946.

For More Information: *New York Times,* 4 May (1937): 20; *New York Times,* 31 August (1953): 17.

Commentary: John J. O'Neill shared the 1937 Pulitzer Prize with four other journalists. They won for their science coverage at the Harvard University conference in 1936.

O'Neill was a self-taught man whose formal education did not go beyond public schooling. He was a founding member of both the American Newspaper Guild and the National Association of Science Writers.

1938

Martin Raymond Sprigle   1098

Birth: August 14, 1886; Akron, OH. **Death:** December 22, 1957. **Parents:** Emanuel Peter Sprigle and Sarah Ann (Hoover). **Education:** Ohio State University. **Spouse:** Agnes Marie Trimmer (m. 1922). **Children:** Rae Jean.

Prize: *Reporting,* 1938: *Pittsburgh Post-Gazette,* September 13-19, Pittsburgh, PA: Pittsburgh Post-Gazette, 1937.

Career: Served in U.S. Army, WWI; Reporter, *Columbus (OH) Sun,* 1906; Staff member, Akron (OH), Canton (OH), Lansing (MI), Chicago (IL), St. Louis (MO), and Little Rock (AR) newspapers, ?-1916; Police Reporter, General Assignment Reporter, *Pittsburgh (PA) Post,* 1911; Assistant City Editor, *Pittsburgh (PA) Post;* City Editor, *Pittsburgh (PA) Post,* 1912-; Staff member, *Pittsburgh Press;* Staff member, *Pittsburgh (PA) Dispatch;* Staff member, *Chicago (IL) Examiner;* Staff member, New Orleans (LA) newspaper; Reporter, *Pittsburgh (PA) Post Gazette,* 1916; Editor, Camp Humphreys (VA) Newspaper, U.S. Army, 1917-18; Reporter, *Pittsburgh (PA) Post,* 1918-; City Editor, *Pittsburgh (PA) Post,* 1927; City Editor, *Pittsburgh (PA) Post-Gazette,* 1927-32; Allegheny County Director, Property and Supplies, 1933-35; Special Investigative Reporter, *Pittsburgh (PA) Post-Gazette,* 1935-57; Correspondent, London (England), *Pittsburgh (PA) Post-Gazette,* 1940.

Selected Works: *In the Land of Jim Crow,* 1949.

Other Awards: National Headliners Club Award, 1945. Posthumously Awarded National Mental Health Association Award, 1958.

For More Information: *New York Times,* December 23, 1957: 13; *Pittsburgh Post-Gazette,* December 23, 1957: 1, 7, 10; Sheffer, Alan Guy, "Investigative Reporter: Ray Springle of Pittsburgh" (thesis), Carnegie-Mellon University, 1973.

Commentary: Ray Sprigle won a Pulitzer Prize for his exposure of Supreme Court Justice Hugo L. Black as a member of the Ku Klux Klan.

He went undercover several times to report on stories, once as a butcher. On another occasion, he darkened his skin to obtain information for a series, "I Was a Negro in the South for Thirty Days." He died from injuries from an automobile accident in 1957.

1939

Thomas Lunsford Stokes Jr. 1099

Birth: November 1, 1898; Atlanta, GA. **Death:** May 14, 1958. **Parents:** Thomas Lunsford Stokes and Emma (Layton). **Education:** University of Georgia: AB, Phi Beta Kappa. **Spouse:** Hannah Hunt (m. 1924). **Children:** Thomas Lunsford III, Layton.

Prize: *Reporting,* 1939: Scripps-Howard Newspaper Alliance, 1938.

Career: Writer, college paper, *Red and Black;* Sports and College News Correspondent, *Atlanta (GA) Constitution* and *Atlanta (GA) Georgian;* Reporter, *Savannah (GA) Press,* 1920; Staff member, *Macon (GA) News,* 1920-21; Staff member, *Athens (GA) Herald,* 1921; Correspondent, Washington (DC), United Press International, 1921-33; Correspondent, Washington (DC), *New York (NY) World-Telegram,* 1933-36; Correspondent, Washington (DC), Scripps-Howard Newspaper Alliance, 1936-44; Political Columnist, United Features Syndicate, 1944-.

Selected Works: *Carpetbaggers of Industry,* 1937. *Chip off My Shoulder,* 1940. *The Savannah: Rivers of America,* 1951.

Other Awards: Saturday Review of Literature Award, 1944. Raymond Clapper Memorial Award, 1947. Special Citation for Journalistic Achievement, 1958.

For More Information: *Current Biography Yearbook, 1947,* New York: H.W. Wilson, 1947: 611-612; *New York Times,* 15 May (1958): 29.

Commentary: Thomas L. Stokes's articles on the political corruption of the Works Progress Administration in Kentucky won him a Pulitzer Prize. He exposed the work relief program as a mechanism for buying votes.

Stokes was a Southerner who worked for several Georgia newspapers before borrowing funds from his father to try to make his way to New York City and the New York newspaper industry. He found his niche, however, in Washington, DC.

1940

S. Burton Heath 1100

Birth: December 20, 1898; West Lynn, MA. **Death:** July 12, 1949. **Parents:** Horace Burton Heath and Ida Victoria (Marine). **Religion:** Methodist. **Education:** University of Vermont: PhB, Phi Beta Kappa. **Spouse:** Emily J. Dodge (m. 1923). **Children:** Nancy Emily, Burton Dodge.

Prize: *Reporting,* 1940: *New York World-Telegram,* New York: New York World-Telegram, 1939.

Career: Served in U.S. Army, American Expeditionary Force, WWI; Apprentice Printer, *Bradford (VT) Opinion,* 1913; Editor, *Groton (VT) Times,* 1917-21; Owner, *Groton (VT) Times,* 1920-21; Assistant Campaign Manager, U.S. Senator P.H. Dale, 1926; Reporter, New Haven (CT), Associated Press, 1926-28; Reporter, *New York Telegram,* 1928-30; Secretary, St. Lawrence Power Development Community, 1930-32; Reporter, *New York Telegram,* 1932-40; Editor and Columnist, *McClure Newspaper Syndicate,* 1941; Writer, Newspaper Enterprise Association, 1942; Publicity consultant, political campaigns, political campaign manager.

Selected Works: *Burial Insurance,* 1939. *Yankee Reporter,* 1940. *Last Testimony: An American Document,* 1949.

For More Information: *New York Times,* 7 May (1940): 20; *Current Biography Yearbook, 1940,* New York: H.W. Wilson Company, 1940: 373-374; *New York Times,* 13 July (1949): 3.

Commentary: S. Burton Heath's investigation into Federal Judge Martin T. Manton led to the judge's resignation, indictment, and conviction. Heath's reporting showed that the judge had participated, while on the Court of Appeals, in cases in which his business concerns had profited. Heath was killed along with several other journalists in an airplane crash while returning from a trip to Indonesia in 1949.

1941

James Westbrook Pegler   1101

Birth: August 2, 1894; Minneapolis, MN. **Death:** June 24, 1969. **Parents:** Arthur James Pegler and Frances (Nicholson). **Religion:** Catholic. **Spouse:** Julia Harpman (m. 1922, died 1955); Pearl Doane (m. 1959, div. 1961); Maud Toward (m. 1961).

Prize: *Reporting,* 1941: *New York World-Telegram,* New York: New York World-Telegram, 1940.

Career: Office Boy, United Press International, 1910; Staff member, International News Service, 1912; Des Moines (IA), New York (NY), St. Louis (MO), Dallas (TX), United Press International, 1913-16; Correspondent, Europe, United Press International, 1916-18; Correspondent, European Staff, American Expeditionary Force, 1917-18; Served in U.S. Navy, 1918-19; Sports Editor, United News, New York, 1919-25; Eastern Sports Correspondent, *Chicago (IL) Tribune,* 1925-33; Staff member, *New York (NY) World-Telegram;* Columnist, *Chicago (IL) Daily News* 1933-44; Syndicated Columnist, King Features Syndicate, 1944-62; Freelance writer, journalist, 1962-69.

Selected Works: *Tain't Right,* 1936. *The Dissenting Opinions of Mister Westbrook Pegler,* 1938. *George Spelvin, American, and Fireside Chats,* 1942. *Lady I.,* 1942. *Thirty-Eighth Anniversary of the Dutch Treat Club* (with Will Irwin), 1943.

Other Awards: Gold Medal, Nassau County Bar Association, 1944. American Legion Award. National Headliners Club Award.

For More Information: Alexander, Jack, *Post Biographies of Famous Journalists,* Athens, GA: The University of Georgia Press, 1942: 364-90; Pilat, Oliver Ramsey, *Pegler, Angry Man of the Press,* Boston: Beacon Press, 1963; *New York Times,* 25 June (1969): 1+; Farr, Finis, *Fair Enough: The Life of Westbrook Pegler,* New Rochelle, NY: Arlington House Publishers, 1975.

Commentary: Westbrook Pegler spent most of his career as a columnist. He wrote "Fair Enough" for the *New York World* for 11 years. When he moved to King Features Syndicate, his column name changed to "As Pegler Sees It." He did not hold back in his column and his comments could be rather caustic.

He won a Pulitzer Prize for his articles on organized labor, which led to the investigation and conviction of George Scalise.

1942

Stanton Hill Delaplane   1102

Birth: October 12, 1907; Chicago, IL. **Death:** April 18, 1988. **Parents:** Frank Hugh Delaplane and Marion Stella (Hill). **Spouse:** Miriam Moore (m. 1940, div. 1958); Susan Aven (m. 1961, div. 1973); Laddie Marshack (m. 1979). **Children:** Kristen Moore, Thomas Scott (MM); Andrea Aven, John Berry Hill (SA).

Prize: *Reporting,* 1942: *San Francisco Chronicle,* San Francisco: San Francisco Chronicle, 1941.

Career: Editor, *Apertif Magazine,* 1933-36; Editor, *The Young Democrat,* 1933-34; Reporter and Rewriteman, *San Francisco (CA) Chronicle,* 1936-53; Served in U.S. Marine Corps, 1942-44; War Correspondent, Pacific Area, *San Francisco (CA) Chronicle,* 1944-45, Syndicated Humor Travel Columnist, *San Francisco (CA) Chronicle,* 1953-88.

Selected Works: *Postcards from Delaplane,* 1953. *The Little World of Stanton Delaplane, Being Stanton Delaplane's Observations of the Lighter Side of Life on Our Small Planet,* 1959. *Delaplane in Mexico: A Short Happy Guide* (with Robert William de Roos), 1960. *And How She Grew,* 1961. *The City: San Francisco in Pictures; with an Introduction by Stanton Delaplane; a Chronicle Classic,* 1961. *Pacific Pathways,* 1963. *In the Gold Mines in '50, '51, and '52; El Dorado County Historical Society, Publication Number 3* (with others), 1966. *Stan Delaplane's Mexico* (with Stuart Nixon), 1976. *Bicycle Touring in Europe,* 1975.

Other Awards: National Headliners Club Award, 1946, 1959. First Annual Writers Award, Transpacific Passenger Conference.

For More Information: *Contemporary Authors, First Revision, Volumes 25-28,* Detroit: Gale Research Company, 1977; *Los Angeles Times,* 19 April (1988): part 1, 25; Riley, Sam G., *Biographical Dictionary of American Newspaper Columnists,* Westport, CT: Greenwood Press, 1995.

Commentary: Stanton Delaplane wrote a wry and humorous column for the *San Francisco Chronicle.* His last column appeared on April 19, 1988, one day after his death. He was awarded a Pulitzer Prize for reporting on the "Free State of Jefferson," a group of four northern California counties and one Oregon county that wished to secede and become the 49th state.

Delaplane is credited with popularizing the recipe for Irish coffee in the United States.

1943

George Anthony Weller   1103

Birth: July 13, 1907; Boston, MA. **Parents:** George Joseph Weller and Matilda B. (McAleer). **Education:** Harvard University, MA: AB, Phi Beta Kappa. University of Vienna, Austria. **Spouse:** Katherine Deupree (m. 1932, div. 1944); Charlotte Ebener (m. 1948). **Children:** Ann (KD); Anthony (CE).

Prize: *Reporting,* 1943: *Chicago Daily News,* December 14, Chicago: Chicago Daily News, 1942.

Career: Teacher, Evans Ranch School, Tucson (AZ), 1929-30; Correspondent, Greece and Balkans, *New York Times,* 1932-35; Director, New York Homeland Foundation, 1937-40; Foreign Correspondent, *Chicago (IL) Daily News,* 1940-72; War Correspondent in Balkans, Belgian Congo, Abyssinia, Singapore, Java, New Guinea, Solomon Islands.

Selected Works: *Not to Eat, Not for Love,* 1933. *Fontamara* (with Ignazio Silone), 1934. *Clutch and Differential,* 1936. *The Belgium Campaign in Ethiopia: A Trek of 2,500 Miles through Jungle Swamps and Desert Wastes,* 1941. *Singapore Is Silent,* 1943. *Bases Overseas,* 1944. *The Crack in the Column,* 1949. *The Story of the Paratroops,* 1958. *Story of the Submarine,* 1962.

Other Awards: Nieman Fellow, Harvard University, MA, 1947-48. George Polk Memorial Award, Long Island University, NY, 1955. British Drama Contest Award, 1960. Public Service Citation, United States Navy, 1968. Scarfoglio Prize for Journalism, Italy, 1984.

Commentary: George Weller's compelling human interest story contrasts with the other awards given to journalists covering the war. His winning article was on the surgery performed by a United States Navy pharmacist's mate in a submarine in enemy waters. The surgery for emergency appendicitis saved the sailor's life.

1944

Paul Schoenstein   1104

Birth: June 10, 1902; New York, NY. **Death:** April 14, 1974. **Parents:** Rudolf Schoenstein and Kornel (Grossman). **Education:** City College, NY. University of California. **Spouse:** Miriam Laura Stahl (m. 1929). **Children:** Ralph, Carol.

Prize: *Reporting,* 1944: *New York Journal-American,* New York: New York Journal-American, 1943.

Career: Reporter, *Bronx (NY) Home News,* 1922; Staff member, *New York (NY) Herald and Tribune,* 1923-25; Staff member, *Los Angeles (CA) Record,* 1925; Staff member, *Bronx (NY) Home News,* 1926;

Staff member, *New York Journal-American,* 1926-66; City Editor, *New York Journal-American,* 1938-56; Assistant Managing Editor, *New York Journal-American,* 1956-61; Managing Editor, *New York Journal-American,* 1961-66; Managing Editor, *New York World-Journal-Tribune,* 1966-67; Special Projects Department, Hearst Newspapers.

For More Information: *New York Times,* 15 April (1974): 34.

Commentary: Paul Schoenstein's day was generally spent on the telephone from 6:30 a.m. to 4:00 p.m. directing his staff in the gathering and publishing of the news. He and his associates won a Pulitzer Prize for their efforts in locating penicillin for a sick child.

1945

Jack Sherman McDowell   1105

Birth: February 23, 1914; Alameda, CA. **Death:** May 9, 1998. **Parents:** John Sherman McDowell and Myra Lorraine (Frierson). **Education:** San Jose College (now San Jose State University), CA. **Spouse:** Jeanette California Ofelth (m. 1938). **Children:** Nancy Lynn, Peggy Joanne, Judy.

Prize: *Reporting,* 1945: *San Francisco Call-Bulletin,* "Reporter, with S.F. Blood, Flies to Wounded in Pacific," December 5; "How Blood Flown from S.F. Saved Nip Sniper's Victim," December 6; "Reporter's Saga of Flight with Blood to Pacific Wounded," December 6; "McDowell Sees S.F. Blood in Use at Front," December 7; "S.F. Blood Aids Romance of Yank Hero in Pacific," December 9, San Francisco: San Francisco Call-Bulletin, 1944.

Career: Officeboy, Cub Reporter, *Alameda (CA) Times-Star,* 1926-31; Staff member, *San Jose (CA) Evening News,* 1932; Owner, Operator, *Turlock (CA) Daily Journal,* 1933-40; Staff member, *Eugene (OR) Daily News,* 1941-42; Reporter, *San Francisco (CA) Call-Bulletin,* 1942-; War Correspondent, *San Francisco (CA) Call-Bulletin,* WWII; Columnist, *San Francisco (CA) Call-Bulletin,* 1946-; Partner of Political Consulting Firm, Woodward and McDowell, Burlingame (CA).

Selected Works: *"And Pass the Ammunition"* (with Howell M. Forgy), 1944.

Other Awards: Best News Photo Award, California Newspaper Publishers Association, 1939.

Commentary: After the Navy announced a new program to fly whole human blood from San Francisco to the Pacific theater, Jack S. McDowell conceived the idea of donating blood, then traveling with it to the front. When he returned, his five-part series was published and blood donations increased sharply, even at a time of the year when they normally decline.

1946

William Leonard Laurence

Full entry appears as **#1096** under "Reporting," 1937.

1947

Frederick Enos Woltman   1106

Birth: March 16, 1905; York, PA. **Death:** March 5, 1970. **Parents:** Enos Frederick Woltman and Ella (Strayer). **Education:** University of Pittsburgh, PA: BA, magna cum laude. University of Pittsburgh, PA: MA. University of Pittsburgh, PA: Postgraduate. **Spouse:** Virginia Russell (m. 1940, died 1952); Nancy Winslow Jackson (m. 1952, d.); Myra Lehman.

Prize: *Reporting,* 1947: *New York World-Telegram,* New York: New York World-Telegram, 1946.

Career: Graduate Assistant, Department of Philosophy, University of Pittsburgh (PA), 1928-29; Reporter, *New York (NY) Telegram,* 1929-31; Reporter, *New York (NY) World-Telegram,* 1931-59.

Selected Works: *The Facts,* 1948. *The Shocking Story of the Amerasia Case,* 1950. *The McCarthy Balance Sheet,* 1954.

Other Awards: Page One Award, Newspaper Guild of New York, 1943. Heywood Broun Award, 1943. Award, Society of Silurians, 1946. Special Citation, AMVETS, 1950.

For More Information: *Current Biography Yearbook, 1947,* New York: H.W. Wilson, 1947; Reeves, Jo A.W. "A Study of a Pulitzer Prize Winning Journalist: Frederick Enos Woltman, 1929-1954" (thesis), East Tennessee State University, 1967; *New York Times,* 6 March (1970): 39; *Contemporary Authors, Volumes 89-92,* Detroit: Gale Research Company, 1980; Hamm, Bradley Jay, 'Freddie the Fink': Investigative Reporting by the *New York World-Telegram's* Frederick Woltman" (thesis), University of South Carolina, 1990.

Commentary: Frederick Woltman's award in 1947 was actually his second Pulitzer citation. The first was an honorable mention in 1934 for his clear writing on the status of local banks after the national bank holiday in 1933. He won a Pulitzer Prize in 1947 for his exposure of Communist influence into United States labor and political organizations. His series, which numbered 107 stories, articles, and editorials from January 7 to December 17, 1946, identified Gerhart Eisler as a principal Kremlin agent. Eisler was indicted but posted bond and fled the country, eventually ending up in East Germany.

Special Awards and Citations: Journalism

1930

William Osborne Dapping   1107

Birth: June 21, 1880; New York, NY. **Death:** August 1, 1969. **Parents:** William Dapping and Mathilda (Lauterbach). **Religion:** Universalist. **Education:** Harvard University, MA: AB. **Spouse:** Ina May Fairchild (m. 1911, died 1965).

    Prize: *Special Awards and Citations: Journalism,* 1930: *Auburn Citizen,* Auburn, NY: Auburn Citizen, 1929.

    Career: Reporter for college paper, *Crimson;* Reporter, Editorial Writer, Managing Editor, Publisher, *Auburn (NY) Citizen-Advertiser;* Presidential Elector, Democratic National Convention, 1932-64; Secretary and Treasurer, Auburn Publishing Company, 1938-60.

    Other Awards: Gold Watch, Associated Press, 1930.

    For More Information: *New York Times,* 13 May (1930): 12; *New York Times,* 3 August (1969): 65; *Contemporary Authors, Volume 115,* Detroit: Gale Research Company, 1985.

    Commentary: William O. Dapping obtained an exclusive interview from Warden Edgar S. Jennings from his hospital bed. The warden had been held hostage in an inmate uprising at the Auburn, NY prison.

1938

Edmonton Journal   1108

Founded: October 2, 1911.

    Prize: *Special Awards and Citations: Journalism,* 1938: *Edmonton Journal,* Edmonton, Canada, 1937.

    For More Information: Uluschak, Edd, *The World of Uluschak: Cartoons from the Pages of the Edmonton Journal,* Edmonton, Canada: *Edmonton Journal,* 1974; Fisher, Heinz Dietrich, *Struggle for Press Freedom in Canada: A Case Study From the Province of Alberta and the Key Role Played by the Edmonton Journal in 1938: Based on a Pulitzer Prize Winning Exhibit, Canada-Communication; Volume 1,* Bochum: Universitatsverlag Dr. N. Brockmeyer, 1992.

    Commentary: The *Edmonton Journal* was given a special citation for its defense of freedom of the press in Canada. In 1937, the legislature of Alberta passed the "Alberta Press Act of 1937." The *Edmonton Journal* campaigned against government control of the press and its managing director, John M. Imrie, was chairman of a special committee to aid solicitors in their argument before the Supreme Court of Canada about the Alberta Press Act of 1937.

1941

New York Times

Full entry appears as **#375** under "Explanatory Journalism," 1986.

1944

Byron Price   1109

Birth: March 25, 1891; Topeka, IN. **Death:** August 6, 1981. **Parents:** John Price and Emaline (Barnes). **Religion:** Methodist. **Education:** Wabash College, IN: AB, Phi Beta Kappa. **Spouse:** Priscilla Alden (m. 1920).

    Prize: *Special Awards and Citations: Journalism,* 1944.

    Career: Newspaper staff member, Crawfordsville and Indianapolis, 1909-12; Reporter and Editor, Chicago (IL), Omaha (NE), United Press International, 1912; Associated Press, 1912-; Served in U.S. Army, 1917-19; News Editor, Washington (DC), Associated Press, 1922-27; Washington (DC) Bureau Chief, Associated Press, 1927-37; Executive News Editor, Associated Press, 1937-; News Censor, President Roosevelt, 1941.

    For More Information: *Contemporary Authors, Volume 104,* Detroit: Gale Research Company, 1982; Paneth, Donald, *Encyclopedia of American Journalism,* New York: Facts on File Publications, 1983; McKerns, Joseph P., *Biographical Dictionary of American Journalism,* New York: Greenwood Press, 1989; Sweeney, Michael Steven, "Bryon Price and the Office of Censorship's Press and Broadcasting Divisions in World War II" (thesis), Ohio University, 1996.

Commentary: Byron Price, director of the Office of Censorship during World War II, won a special Pulitzer Prize in 1944 for his outstanding job in running that office. He wrote no stories, but he was a force fighting for the printing of information on the war.

William Allen White

Full entry appears as **#41** under "Biography or Autobiography," 1947.

1945

Cartographers 1110

Prize: *Special Awards and Citations: Journalism,* 1945.

Commentary: A collective award was given to the cartographers of the press for their excellent maps of World War II. They kept the American people informed of the war and the progress of the armies and navies.

1947

Columbia University and the Graduate School of Journalism 1111

Prize: *Special Awards and Citations: Journalism,* 1947.

For More Information: Baker, Richard Terrill, *A History of the Graduate School of Journalism, Columbia University,* New York: Columbia University Press, 1954.

Commentary: In the centennial year of Joseph Pulitzer's birth, the School of Journalism was given an award for "its efforts to maintain and advance the high standards governing the Pulitzer Prizes."

St. Louis Post-Dispatch

Full entry appears as **#802** under "Meritorious Public Service," 1937.

1948

Frank Diehl Fackenthal 1112

Birth: February 22, 1883; Hellertown, PA. **Death:** September 5, 1968. **Parents:** Michael Fackenthal and Mary Jane (Diehl). **Religion:** Congregationalist. **Education:** Columbia University, NY: AB.

Prize: *Special Awards and Citations: Journalism,* 1948.

Career: Chief Clerk, Columbia University (NY), 1906-10; Secretary, Columbia University (NY),

1910-37; Member of University Committee on Student Organizations, 1914-45; Secretary, University Council, Columbia University (NY), 1925-45; Provost, Columbia University (NY), 1937-45; Acting President, Columbia University (NY), 1945-48; President, Associated Universities, Incorporated, 1948-50; Consultant, Carnegie Corporation, 1948-52; Member of Committee on Financing Higher Education, 1949-52; President, Columbia University Press, 1953-58; Chairman, Columbia University Press, 1958-.

Selected Works: *The Great Power: And Other Addresses,* 1949.

Other Awards: Chevalier, Legion of Honor. Honorary Degrees: Columbia Unversity, NY, 1920; Franklin and Marshall College, PA, 1929; Princeton University, NJ, 1947; Rutgers University, NJ, 1947; Syracuse University, NY, 1947; New York University, 1948; Union College, NY, 1948; Trinity College, 1955.

For More Information: *Current Biography Yearbook, 1949,* New York: H.W. Wilson Company, 1949; *New York Times,* 6 September (1968): 43.

Commentary: Frank Fackenthal was acting President of Columbia University when he retired in 1948. From 1945 until his retirement, he was a member of the Pulitzer Prize board. After his retirement, he was given a scroll in appreciation of his interest and service.

1951

Arthur Krock

Full entry appears as **#127** under "Correspondence," 1935.

Cyrus Leo Sulzberger 1113

Birth: October 27, 1912; New York, NY. **Death:** September 20, 1993. **Parents:** Leo Sulzberger and Beatrice (Josephi). **Education:** Harvard University, MA: BS, magna cum laude. **Spouse:** Marina Tatiana Lada (m. 1942, died 1976). **Children:** Marina, David.

Prize: *Special Awards and Citations: Journalism,* 1951: *New York Times,* "Stepinac in Cell Interview Says His Fate is Up to Pope," November 13, New York: New York Times, 1950.

Career: Reporter and Rewriteman, *Pittsburgh (PA) Press,* 1934-35; Reporter, Washington (DC), United Press International, 1935-38; Foreign Correspondent, *London (England) Evening Standard,* 1938-39; Foreign Correspondent, *New York Times,* 1939-; Chief Foreign Correspondent, *New York Times,* 1944-54; Columnist, *New York Times,* 1954-78.

Selected Works: *Sit Down with John L. Lewis,* 1938. *Tito's Yugoslav Partisan Movement,* 1944. *The*

Big Thaw: A Personal Exploration of the "New" Russia and the Orbit Countries, 1956. What's Wrong with U.S. Foreign Policy, 1959. *My Brother Death,* 1961. *The Resistentialists,* 1962. *The Test: De Gaulle and Algeria,* 1962. *Unfinished Revolution: America and the Third World,* 1965. *The American Heritage Picture History of World War II,* 1966. *A Long Row of Candles: Memoirs and Diaries, 1934-1954,* 1969. *The Last of the Giants,* 1970. *The Tooth Merchant: A Novel,* 1973. *An Age of Mediocrity: Memoirs and Diaries, 1963-1972,* 1973. *The Coldest War: Russia's Game in China,* 1974. *Go Gentle into the Night,* 1976. *Seven Continents, and Forty Years: A Concentration of Memoirs,* 1977. *The Fall of Eagles,* 1977. *The Tallest Liar,* 1977. *Marina: Letters and Diaries of Marina* (with Marina Sulzberger), 1978. *How I Committed Suicide: A Reverie,* 1982. *Such a Peace: The Roots and Ashes of Yalta,* 1982. *The World and Richard Nixon,* 1987. *Fathers and Children,* 1987. *Paradise Regained: Memoir of a Rebel,* 1989.

Other Awards: Overseas Press Club Award, 1951, 1957, 1970.

For More Information: *Contemporary Authors, New Revision Series, Volume 7,* Detroit: Gale Research Company, 1982; *New York Times,* 21 September (1993): B9; *Los Angeles Times,* 22 September (1993): A14.

Commentary: C.L. Sulzberger's exclusive interview in Yugoslavia with Archbishop Alojzije Stepinac won him a special Pulitzer Prize. In his first three years with the *New York Times* he traveled over 100,000 miles and to over 30 countries. He began his column "Foreign Affairs" in 1954. It appeared three times weekly, first on the editorial page and then on the Op-Ed page. He retired in 1978.

1952

Kansas City Star
Full entry appears as #**306** under "Editorial Writing," 1933.

Max Kase   1114
Birth: July 21, 1898; New York, NY. **Death:** March 19, 1974. **Spouse:** Kathleen K. (m., died 1979).
Prize: *Special Awards and Citations: Journalism,* 1952: *New York Journal-American,* New York: New York Journal-American, 1951.
Career: Staff member, International News Service, 1917-23; Sports Editor, *Havana Telegram,* 1923-25; International News Service, 1925-34; Sports Editor, *Boston (MA) American,* 1934-38; Sports Editor, *New York (NY) Journal-American,* 1938-66.
For More Information: *New York Times,* 20 March (1974): 44.

Commentary: Max Kase exposed the college basketball scandal of 1951. His exclusive story was of several members of the City College of New York basketball team being questioned by the District Attorney. Several team members confessed to "shaving" points. The scandal spread to Long Island University, the University of Kentucky, and Bradley University, all strong basketball schools at the time. Kase worked for the *New York Journal-American* until it closed in 1966. He wrote a column, "Brief Kase," for a number of years.

1953

Lester Markel   1115
Birth: January 9, 1894; New York, NY. **Death:** October 23, 1977. **Parents:** Jacob Leo Markel and Lillian (Hecht). **Religion:** Jewish. **Education:** City College, NY. Columbia University, NY: LittB. **Spouse:** Meta Edman (m. 1917). **Children:** Helen.
Prize: *Special Awards and Citations: Journalism,* 1953: *New York Times,* New York: New York Times, 1952.
Career: Reporter, Rewriteman, Copy Reader, Telegraph Editor, Cable Editor, City Editor, *New York (NY) Tribune,* 1914-15; Night Editor, *New York (NY) Tribune,* 1915-19; Assistant Managing Editor, *New York (NY) Tribune,* 1919-23; Sunday Editor, *New York Times,* 1923-65; Associate Editor, *New York Times,* 1965-69; Freelance writer and consultant, 1969-77; Distinguished Visiting Professor, Fairleigh Dickinson University, 1969-77.
Selected Works: *Public Opinion and Foreign Policy,* 1949. *Background and Foreground,* 1963. *What You Don't Know Can Hurt You: A Study of Public Opinion and Public Emotion,* 1973. *Global Challenges to the United States* (with Audrey March), 1976.
Other Awards: Honorary Degrees: Bates College, ME, 1953; New School for Social Research, NY, 1953.
For More Information: *New York Times,* 5 May (1953): 24; *Contemporary Authors, Volumes 73-76,* Detroit: Gale Research Company, 1978; *Current Biography Yearbook, 1978,* New York: H.W. Wilson Company, 1978; Taft, William H., *Encyclopedia of Twentieth-Century Journalists,* New York: Garland Publishing, 1986.
Commentary: Lester Markel founded the "Review of the Week" section of the Sunday *New York Times* in 1935. The section won a special citation for the "enlightenment and intelligent commentary" it brought to readers. He developed the section when he reorganized the Sunday supplements. During the 1960s, he moderated a television program, "News in Perspective."

1958

Walter Lippmann

Full entry appears as **#629** under "International Reporting," 1962.

1964

Gannett News Service

Full entry appears as **#830** under "Meritorious Public Service," 1980.

1976

John Hohenberg   1116

Birth: February 17, 1906; New York, NY. **Parents:** Louis Hohenberg and Jettchen (Scheuermann). **Education:** University of Washington. Columbia University, NY: BLitt. University of Vienna, Austria: Postgrad. **Spouse:** Dorothy Lannuier (m. 1928, died 1977); JoAnn Fogarty (m. 1979). **Children:** Pamela Jo, Eric.

Prize: *Special Awards and Citations: Journalism,* 1976.

Career: Reporter, *Seattle (WA) Star,* 1923; *New York (NY) World;* Correspondent, United Press International, 1927-28; Assistant City Editor, *New York Evening Post,* 1928-33; Political Writer, *New York Journal-American,* 1933-42; Served in U.S. Army, 1942-46; United Nations Correspondent, *New York Post,* 1946-50; Part-Time Instructor, Columbia University (NY), 1948-50; Journalism Faculty, Columbia University, 1950-74; Pulitzer Prize Administrator, Columbia University, 1954-76; Visiting Lecturer,

Chinese University of Hong Kong, 1970-71; Edward Meeman Distinguished Professor of Journalism, University of Tennessee, 1976-79; Faculty member, University of Kansas; Gannett Distinguished Professor of Journalism, University of Florida, 1981-82.

Selected Works: *The Pulitzer Prize Story,* 1959. *The Professional Journalist,* 1960. *Foreign Correspondence: The Great Reporters and Their Times,* 1964. *The New Front Page,* 1966. *Between Two Worlds: Press Policy and Public Opinion in Asian-American Relations,* 1967. *The News Media,* 1968. *Free Press/Free People,* 1971. *New Era in the Pacific,* 1972. *The Pulitzer Prizes: A History, 1917-1974,* 1974. *A Crisis for the American Press,* 1978. *The Pulitzer Prize Story II, 1949-1980,* 1980. *The Parisian Girl,* 1986. *Concise Newswriting,* 1987. *The Bill Clinton Story: Winning the Presidency,* 1994. *John Hohenburg: The Pursuit of Excellence,* 1995. *The Pulitzer Diaries,* 1997. *Re-Electing Bill Clinton,* 1997. *Israel at 50: A Journalist's Perspective.*

Other Awards: Pulitzer Traveling Scholarship, 1927-28. Distinguished Service Award, Sigma Delta Chi, 1965. Distinguished Service to Journalism Award, Columbia University Journalism Alumni Association, 1966. 50th Anniversary Medal, Columbia University Graduate School of Journalism, 1966. Sigma Delta Chi Award, 1968, 1974. Hall of Fame, New York City Deadline Club, 1981. Honorary Degree, Wilkes College, PA, 1971.

For More Information: *Contemporary Authors, New Revision Series, Volume 106,* Detroit: Gale Research Company, 1982; Taft, William H., *Encyclopedia of Twentieth-Century Journalists,* New York: Garland Publishing, 1986.

Commentary: John Hohenberg received a special citation for his excellent service in the administration of the Pulitzer Prizes for 22 years.

1978

Richard Lee Strout   1117

Birth: March 4, 1898; Cohoes, NY. **Death:** August 19, 1990. **Parents:** George Morris Strout and Mary Susan (Lang). **Education:** Harvard University, MA: AB. Harvard University, MA: MA. **Spouse:** Edith R. Mayne (m. 1924, died 1932); Ernestine Wilke (m. 1939). **Children:** Alan, Phyllis (EM); Nancy, Elizabeth, Mary (EW).

Prize: *Special Awards and Citations: Journalism,* 1978.

Career: Served in U.S. Army, WWI; Staff member, *Sheffield (England) Independent,* 1919; Staff member, *London (England) Starmore Press;* Reporter, *Boston (MA) Post,* 1921; Reporter, *Christian Science Monitor,* 1921-25; Correspondent, Washington (DC), *Christian Science Monitor,* 1925-; Columnist, *New Republic,* 1943-83.

Selected Works: *Farewell to Model T* (with E.B. White), 1936. *Maud,* 1939. *America's Founding Fathers: The Christian Science Monitor,* 1975. *TRB: Views and Perspectives on the Presidency,* 1979.

Other Awards: George Polk Memorial Award, Long Island University, NY, 1958. Sidney Hillman Foundation Award, 1974. University of Missouri School of Journalism Award, 1974. Fourth Estate Award, National Press Club, 1975.

For More Information: *New York Times,* 18 April (1978): 28; McKerns, Joseph P., *Biographical Dictionary of American Journalism,* New York: Greenwood Press, 1989; *New York Times,* 21 August (1990): B11; *Christian Science Monitor,* 22 (1990): 19; Riley, Sam G., *Biographical Dictionary of American Newspaper Columnists,* Westport, CT: Greenwood Press, 1995.

Commentary: Richard L. Stout knew every president since Harding. He was known for his commentary and his accurate reporting for over 60 years.

1987

Joseph Pulitzer Jr. 1118

Birth: May 13, 1913; St. Louis, MO. **Death:** May 26, 1993. **Parents:** Joseph Pulitzer and Elinor (Wickham). **Education:** Harvard University, MA: BA. **Spouse:** Louise Vauclain (m. 1939, died 1968); Emily S. Rauh (m. 1973). **Children:** Joseph IV (LV).

Prize: *Special Awards and Citations: Journalism,* 1987.

Career: Reporter, *San Francisco (CA) News,* 1935; Staff member, *St. Louis (MO) Post-Dispatch,* 1936-48; Served in U.S. Naval Reserve, 1942-45;

Associate Editor, *St. Louis (MO) Post-Dispatch,* 1948-55; Editor and Publisher, *St. Louis (MO) Post-Dispatch,* 1955-86; Chairman, Pulitzer Prize Board, 1955-86; Chairman, Pulitzer Publishing Company, 1986-93.

Selected Works: *A Tradition of Conscience, Proposals for Journalism* (with Leonard Baskin), 1965. *Pulitzer Publishing Company: Newspapers and Broadcasting in the Public Interest; Newcomen Publication, No. 1322* (with Michael E. Pulitzer), 1988.

For More Information: Pfaff, Daniel W., *Joseph Pulitzer II and Advertising Censorship, 1929-1939, Journalism Monographs, No. 77,* Columbia: Association of Education in Journalism, University of South Carolina, College of Journalism, 1982; *New York Times,* 27 May (1993): D27; *St. Louis Post-Dispatch,* 27 May (1993): A1; *St. Louis Post-Dispatch,* 27 May (1993): A19.

Commentary: The Pulitzer Prize board gave Joseph Pulitzer Jr. a special award after his retirement from the board. It was for his extraordinary service to American journalism and for his accomplishments as an editor and publisher.

1996

Herbert Eugene Caen 1119

Birth: April 3, 1916; Sacramento, CA. **Death:** February 1, 1997. **Parents:** Lucien Caen and Augusta (Gross). **Education:** Sacramento Junior College, CA. **Spouse:** Sally Gilbert (m. 1952, div. 1959); Maria Theresa Shaw (m. 1963, div. 1983); Ann Moller (m. 1996). **Children:** Stepchild: Deborah (SG); Christopher (MS); Stepchildren: Stephen, Catherine (AM).

Prize: *Special Awards and Citations: Journalism,* 1996: *San Francisco Chronicle,* San Francisco: *San Francisco Chronicle,* 1995.

Career: Sports Reporter, *Sacramento (CA) Union,* 1932; Radio Columnist, *San Francisco (CA) Chronicle,* 1936; Daily Columnist, *It's News To Me,* 1938; Served in U.S. Air Force, 1942; Captain, Air Force, 1945; Staff member, *San Francisco (CA) Chronicle,* 1949; Staff member, *San Francisco (CA) Examiner,* 1950-58; Staff member, *San Francisco (CA) Chronicle,* 1955-97.

Selected Works: *The San Francisco Book,* 1948. *Baghdad-by-the-Bay* (with Howard Brodie), 1949. *Baghdad '51,* 1950. *Don't Call It Frisco,* 1953. *Herb Caen's Guide to San Francisco,* 1957. *Only in San Francisco,* 1960. *City on Golden Hills* (with Dong Kingman), 1967. *The Cable Car and the Dragon* (with Barbara Ninde Byfield), 1972. *Bennie Goodman: An Album,* 1976. *One Man's San Francisco,* 1976. *The Best of Herb Caen 1960-1975,* 1991. *The World of Herb Caen: San Francisco: 1938-1997* (with others), 1997.

For More Information: *Contemporary Authors, New Revision Series, Volume 1,* Detroit: Gale Research Company, 1981; Taft, William H., *Encyclopedia of Twentieth-Century Journalists,* New York: Garland Publishing, 1986; *San Francisco Chronicle,* 2 (1997): A1; *San Francisco Chronicle,* 3 (1997): A1.

Commentary: Herb Caen chronicled the history of San Francisco for over 58 years. He first wrote a column in his high school paper titled "Raisin' Caen." He was known for his writing about the prominent people, politicians as well as celebrities, and the common man. Many people read his column that began with his traditional "..." before turning to the front page. In tribute, the San Francisco Board of Supervisors named a waterfront promenade for him — The Herb Caen Way ...—in 1996.

Special Awards and Citations: Letters

1944

Richard Rodgers

Full entry appears as **#194** under "Drama," 1950.

1957

Kenneth Roberts   1120

Birth: December 8, 1885; Kennebunk, ME. **Death:** July 21, 1957.

Prize: *Special Awards and Citations: Letters,* 1957, His Historical Novels.

Career: Staff Writer, *Boston Post,* Boston, MA, 1909-1917; Staff Writer, *Life* and *Puck* magazines; Captain, Intelligence Section, Siberian Expeditionary Force, 1918-1919; Staff Correspondent, *Saturday Evening Post,* 1919-1928.

Selected Works: *Europe's Morning After,* 1921. *Why Europe Leaves Home,* 1922. *Sun Hunting: Adventures and Observations among the Native and Migratory Tribes of Florida...,* 1922. *Black Magic,* 1924. *Concentrated New England: A Sketch of Calvin Coolidge,* 1924. *Florida Loafing,* 1925. *Arundel: A Chronicle of the Province of Maine and of the Secret Expedition against Quebec,* 1933. *Rabble in Arms: A Chronicle of Arundel and the Burgoyne Invasion,* 1933. *For Authors Only, and Other Gloomy Essays,* 1935. *It Must Be Your Tonsils,* 1936. *Captain Caution: A Chronicle of Arundel,* 1937. *Northwest Passage,* 1938. *March to Quebec,* 1938. *Trending into Maine,* 1938. *Oliver Wiswell,* 1940. *The Kenneth Roberts Reader,* 1945. *Moreau de St.-Mery's American Journey, 1793-1798* (Translation), 1947. *Lydia Bailey,* 1947. *Voyage aux Etats-Unis de l'Amerique, 1793-1798* (Translation), 1947. *The Lively Lady,* 1948. *I Wanted to Write,* 1949. *Henry Gross and His Dowsing Rod,* 1951. *Boon Island,* 1955. *The Battle of Cowpens: The Great Morale-Builder,* 1957. *Water Unlimited,* 1957. *The Lively Lady and Captain Caution (Two Novels),* 1958. **Films:** *The Shell Game,* Metro, 1918; *Captain Caution,* Hal Roach, 1940; *Northwest Passage,* MGM, 1940; *Frontier Rangers,* MGM, 1959.

Other Awards: Honorary PhDs: Dartmouth College, NH; Colby College, ME; Middlebury College, VT.

For More Information: Bales, Jack, *Kenneth Roberts: The Man and His Works,* Metuchen, NJ: Scarecrow, 1989; Whitman, Sylvia, "The West of a Down Easterner: Kenneth Roberts and The Saturday Evening Post, 1924-1928," *Journal of the West,* January 1992.

Commentary: A special award and citation was given to Kenneth Lewis Roberts for his historical novels which have long contributed to the creation of greater interest in our early American history.

Kenneth Lewis Roberts was a journalist and novelist whose fictional works, most notably *Arundel,* published in 1930, were primarily based on the American Revolution. His best-known work is *Northwest Passage.* He was called a stickler for accuracy. Many of his novels were serialized in the *Saturday Evening Post.* He and Booth Tarkington were close friends.

1960

Garrett Mattingly   1121

Birth: May 6, 1900; Washington, DC. **Death:** December 8, 1962. **Parents:** Leonard Howard and Ida Roselle (Garrett) Mattingly. **Religion:** Episcopalian. **Education:** Harvard University, MA: BA, MA, PhD. **Spouse:** Gertrude McCollum (m. 1928).

Prize: *Special Awards and Citations: Letters,* 1960: *Armada,* Boston: Houghton Mifflin, 1959.

Career: Served in 43rd Infantry Division, U.S. Army, WWI, 1918-1919; Student in Europe on a Guggenheim Fellowship, 1922-1924; Teacher, Northwestern University, IL, 1926-1927; Faculty member, Long Island University, NY, 1928-1942; U.S. Navy, WWII, 1942-1945; Faculty member, Cooper Union, NY, 1946-1949; Faculty member, Columbia University, 1949-1962; William R. Shepherd Professor of History, Columbia University, NY, 1960-1962; Member: American Historical Society, Phi Beta Kappa.

Selected Works: *Catherine of Aragon,* 1941. *Renaissance Diplomacy,* 1955. *The Invincible Armada and Elizabethan England,* 1963.

Other Awards: Sheldon Traveling Fellowship, 1922. Guggenheim Fellow, Guggenheim Foundation, 1936, 1946, 1960. Literary Guild Book Selection,

1942: *Catherine of Aragon,* Boston: Little, Brown, 1941. Fulbright Scholar.

For More Information: *New York Post,* February 1, 1960; *Thinkers of the Twentieth Century,* Detroit: Gale, 1983.

Commentary: A special citation was given to Garrett Mattingly for *The Armada,* a critically acclaimed work of history which detailed the events of the year 1588.

Garrett Mattingly was born in Washington, DC. He was considered the leading authority on early diplomatic history. Each of his four books received critical praise. *Catherine of Aragon,* published in 1942, is the standard biography on its subject. *Renaissance Diplomacy,* published in 1955, provided a keen analysis of the origins of modern diplomacy. He was named George Eastman Visiting Professor at Oxford University for the 1962-1963 term.

1961

American Heritage Picture History   1122

Founded: 1954; Washington, D.C.. **Founder(s):** James Parton, Joseph J. Thorndike Jr., and Oliver Jenson.

Prize: *Special Awards and Citations: Letters,* 1961: *The American Heritage Picture History of the Civil War,* New York: American Heritage, 1960.

Commentary: A special citation was given to *The American Heritage Picture History of the Civil War* in 1961 as a distinguished example of American book publishing. The one-volume history was written by Civil War historian and Pulitzer prize-winner (History, 1954) Bruce Catton and includes illustrations and color photographs of the battlefields.

American Heritage Publishing Company was founded in 1954. Founding editor, Bruce Catton, stated in the magazine's first issue, "Our beat is anything that ever happened in America." The bimonthly magazine's editors had left *Life* magazine to create an illustrated history magazine with articles written by historians. It was sponsored by the American Association for State & Local History (AASLH) and the Society of American Historians. The company bought the title from the AASLH and enlisted the aid of Bruce Catton and Allan Nevins. Over the years, the company has changed ownership many times and is now published by Forbes, Inc.

1973

James Thomas Flexner   1123

Birth: 1908; New York, NY. **Parents:** Simon and Helen (Thomas) Flexner. **Education:** Harvard University, MA: BS, magna cum laude. Lincoln School of Teachers College, Columbia University, NY. Eastern Illinois University, IL: LHD. **Spouse:** Beatrice Hudson (m. 1950). **Children:** Helen Hudson.

Prize: *Special Awards and Citations: Letters,* 1973: *George Washington, Volumes I-IV,* Boston: Little, Brown, 1965-1972.

Career: Reporter, *New York Herald-Tribune,* 1929-1931; Executive Secretary, Noise Abatement Commission, New York City Department of Health, NY, 1931-1932; President, PEN, 1954-1955; Conservator, Colonial Williamsburg, 1956-1957; Honorary Vice President, PEN, 1963-1966; Conservator, Amon Carter Museum of Western Art, 1974-1975; Lecturer on founding fathers and history of American art and civilization; President, Society of American Historians, 1975-1977; Vice President for Literature, American Academy Institute of Arts and Sciences, 1981-1985; Member: Authors League of America, Century Association, Phi Beta Kappa; Honorary Member, Century Club.

Selected Works: *Doctors on Horseback: Pioneers of American Medicine,* 1937. *William Henry Welch and the Heroic Age of American Medicine* (Flexner and Simon), 1941. *Steamboats Come True: American Inventors in Action,* 1944. *John Singleton Copley,* 1948. *The Pocket History of American Painting,* 1950. *The Traitor and the Spy: Benedict Arnold and John Andre,* 1953. *The World of Winslow Homer, 1836-1910,* 1966. *George Washington and the New Nation, 1783-1793,* 1970. *The Face of Liberty,* 1975. *The Young Hamilton: A Biography,* 1978. *Lord of the Mohawks: A Biography of Sir William Johnson,* 1979. *America's Old Masters,* 1980. *States Dyckman, American Loyalist,* 1980. *An American Saga: The Story of Helen Thomas and Simon Flexner,* 1984. *On Desperate Seas: A Biography of Gilbert Stuart,* 1995. *Maverick's Progress: An Autobiography,* 1996. **Films:** *George Washington* (TV Mini Series), USA, 1984; *George Washington II: The Forging of a Nation* (TV Mini Series), USA, 1986.

Other Awards: Archives of American Art Award, Smithsonian Institute, 1979. Gold Medal, American Academy and Institute of Arts and Letters, 1988.

For More Information: Speer, Glenn, "In the American Grain," *Washington Post,* March 10, 1996; Hartle, Terry, "The Wide, Humorous Reach of a 'Public Intellectual,'" *Christian Science Monitor,* August 29, 1996.

Commentary: A special citation was awarded in 1973 to *George Washington, Volumes I-IV,* written by James Thomas Flexner. These four volumes cover the Forge of Experience, 1732-1775; the American Revolution, 1775-1783; the New Nation, 1783-1793; and the Anguish and Farewell, 1793-1799.

James Thomas Flexner was born in New York City. He was the son of Simon Flexner. (Simon, the son of immigrant German Jews, was a pathologist who created the "Flexner serum" which helped those afflicted with cerebrospinal meningitis.) His mother's family arrived in America in 1651. James, influenced greatly by his parents' experience as Americans, became a biographer and historian. His autobiograhy, *Maverick's Progress,* was published in 1996.

1977

Alex Haley   1124

Birth: Aug. 11, 1921; Ithaca, NY. **Death:** February 10, 1992. **Parents:** Sinmon and Bertha (Palmer) Haley. **Education:** Elizabeth City Teachers College, NC. **Spouse:** Nannie Branch (m. 1941; div. 1964); Juliette Collins (m. 1964). **Children:** Lydia Ann, William Alexander (NB); Cynthia Gertrude (JC).

Prize: *Special Awards and Citations: Letters,* 1977: *Roots,* Garden City, NY: Doubleday, 1976.

Career: Writer, Cook, and Journalist, U.S. Coast Guard, 1939-1959; Freelance Writer, *Reader's Digest* and *Playboy* Magazines, 1960-1991; Steward, Hope Methodist Church, Henning, TN.

Selected Works: *A Different Kind of Christmas,* 1988. *Alex Haley's Queen: The Story of an American Family* (with David Stevens), 1993. *The Playboy Interviews,* 1993. **Films:** *Roots* (TV Mini Series), ABC, 1977; *Roots: The Next Generations* (TV Mini Series), ABC, 1979; *Roots: The Gift* (TV Mini Series), ABC, 1988; *Malcolm X,* 40 Acres & A Mule Filmworks, 1992; *Queen* (TV Mini Series), 1993; *Mama Flora's Family* (TV Movie), 1998.

For More Information: "Alex Haley, Illuminator," Obituary, *New York Times,* February 12, 1992; Fisher, Murray, "In Memoriam: Alex Haley," *Playboy,* July 1992; Henneberger, Melinda, "The Tangled Roots of Alex Haley," *New York Times,* February 14, 1993; Bloom, Harold, *Alex Haley & Malcolm X's the Autobiography of Malcolm X, (Bloom's Notes Series),* New York: Chelsea House, 1996.

Commentary: A special award was given to Alex Haley in 1977 for *Roots,* the story of a black family from its origins in Africa through seven generations to the present day in America. *Roots* was the result of Haley's perseverance and commitment to tracing his race's history from Africa via slave ships to the United States and up to the present. This was accomplished through writing advances from *Dou-*

bleday and the *Reader's Digest,* and extensive travel and research conducted in archives, libraries, and ships' records on three continents. Haley booked passage on a freighter from Africa to the United States and over a 10-day period reenacted for himself the experience of a slave held in shackles in the ship's lower hold.

Alex Palmer Haley was born in Ithaca, New York. He grew up in Tennessee where his mother's family owned a lumber business near Memphis. After a career in the United States Coast Guard, where he had already started writing, Haley began submitting articles and stories to magazines. After receiving "hundreds of rejections," he finally sold some sea stories. In 1962, *Reader's Digest* gave him some biographical assignments. His big break came with a recording he made of an interview he conducted with Malcolm X. This became the first of the *Playboy* interviews and later formed the basis for the book *The Autobiography of Malcolm X* and the Spike Lee film *Malcolm X.* Haley would create the Kinte Foundation in 1972 dedicated to storing records which would aid in tracing black genealogy. His papers are archived at the Schomberg Collection of the New York Public Library.

1978

E.B. White   1125

Birth: July 11, 1899; Mount Vernon, NY. **Death:** October 1, 1977. **Spouse:** Katherine Sergeant Angell (m. 1929, died 1977). **Children:** Joel McCoun.

Prize: *Special Awards and Citations: Letters,* 1978, Letters, Essays and Full Body of His Work.

Career: Journalist and writer; Reporter, *Seattle Times,* beginning in 1921; Mess boy, ship bound for Alaska; Advertising copywriter; Editor and Writer, the *New Yorker,* NY, 1929-1985; Contributor, *Harper's* Magazine, 1938-1943; Author.

Selected Works: *The Lady Is Cold,* 1929. *Is Sex Necessary? or, Why You Feel the Way You Do* (with James Thurber), 1929. *Everyday Is Saturday,* 1934. *Quo Vadimus? or, The Case for the Bicycle,* 1938. *A Subtreasury of American Humor: E. B. White and Katharine S. White,* 1941. *One Man's Meat,* 1942. *Stuart Little in the Schoolroom,* 1945. *The Wild Flag,* 1946. *Here Is New York,* 1949. *Charlotte's Web,* 1952. *The Second Tree from the Corner,* 1954. *The Elements of Style by William Strunk, Jr.* (E. B. White, ed.), 1959. *The Points of My Compass: Letters from the East, the West, the North, the South,* 1962. *The Trumpet of the Swan,* 1970. *Writings from the New Yorker 1927-1976* (Dale, Rebecca M. ed.), 1990. **Films:** *The Family That Dwelt Apart,* National Film Board of Canada, 1974.

Other Awards: President's Medal of Freedom, 1963. Limited Editions Club Gold Medal, 1945: *One Man's Meat,* New York: Harper, 1942.

For More Information: Elledge, Scott, *E.B. White, A Biography,* New York: Norton, 1984. Russell, Isabel, *Katharine and E.B. White: An Affectionate Memoir,* New York: Norton, 1988; Davis, Linda H., "The Man on the Swing," *New Yorker,* December 27, 1993.

Commentary: A special citation was awarded to E.B. White in 1978 for his letters, essays, and the full body of his work.

Elwyn Brooks White was born in Mount Vernon, New York. He was an editor at the *New Yorker* throughout most of his life. He collaborated with James Thurber in 1929 on a spoof of the current crop of sex manuals coming to publication at the time. Their version, *Is Sex Necessary?* was an immediate hit. White revised and updated William Strunk Jr.'s *Elements of Style* in 1959, and again in 1972 and 1979. His children's books, *Stuart Little, The Trumpet of the Swan,* and *Charlotte's Web,* are classics. He was the essence of the 20th century urbane literary stylist. He also wrote poetry. He was an advocate of world government based on international law, described in *The Wild Flag,* as the best route for survival of the human race.

1984

Theodore Seuss Geisel   1126

Birth: March 2, 1904; Springfield, MA. **Death:** September 24, 1991. **Parents:** Theodor Robert and Henrietta (Seuss) Geisel. **Education:** Dartmouth College, NH. Lincoln College, Oxford University, England. **Spouse:** Helen Marion Palmer (m. 1927; died 1967); Audrey G.

Prize: *Special Awards and Citations: Letters,* 1984: His special contribution over nearly a century to the education and enjoyment of America's children and their parents.

Career: Cartoonist, illustrator and author of children's books; Freelance cartoonist, 1927-1931; Illustrator, Viking Press, 1931; Political Cartoonist, *PM* Magazine, NY, 1940-1942; Writer and Director, Film Unit, Information and Education Division, U.S. Army Signal Corps, 1943-1946; Founder, Beginner Books, Incorporated, 1958.

Selected Works: *And to Think That I Saw It on Mulberry Street,* 1937. *The 500 Hats of Bartholomew Cubbins,* 1938. *The Seven Lady Godivas,* 1939. *McElligot's Pool,* 1947. *The Cat in the Hat,* 1957. *The Butter Battle Book,* 1984. *You're Only Old Once!,* 1986. *The Tough Coughs as He Ploughs the Dough: Early Writings and Cartoons by Dr. Seuss,* 1987. *Oh, the Places You'll Go!,* 1990. *The Secret Art of Dr. Seuss,* 1995. **Films:** *Gerald McBoing-Boing's Symphony,* Columbia, 1953; *The 5,000 Fingers of Dr. T.,* Columbia, 1953; *How the Grinch Stole Christmas* (TV), Metro Goldwyn Mayer, 1966.

Other Awards: Academy Award, Best Documentary Feature, 1947: *Design for Death.* Academy Award, Best Cartoon, 1952: *Gerald McBoing-Boing.*

For More Information: MacDonald, Ruth K., *Dr. Seuss,* Boston: Twayne, 1988; Pace, Eric, "Dr. Seuss, Modern Mother Goose, Dies at 87," *New York Times,* September 26, 1991; *Current Biography,* New York: November, 1991; Morgan, Judith and Neil Morgan, *Dr. Seuss & Mr. Geisel: A Biography,* New York: Random House, 1995; Agee, Jon, "The 500 Cats of Theodor Geisel," *Los Angeles Times,* December 3, 1995.

Commentary: In 1984, a special citation was awarded to Theodore Seuss Geisel, more widely known as Dr. Seuss, for his special contribution over nearly half a century to the education and enjoyment of America's children and their parents.

Theodore Seuss Geisel was born in Springfield, Massachusetts. He began his career as a cartoonist, moved on to illustrator, and found a very successful outlet for his sense of humor when he became the creator of the *Cat in the Hat* series of children's books. These books, full of new phrases and nonsense words, were considered not only humorous but also educational. They have been enjoyed by several generations of children ever since. The annual television broadcast of his *How the Grinch Stole Christmas,* has been viewed by millions. Several of his works have been translated to film. He lived most of his life in La Jolla, California.

1992

Art Spiegelman   1127

Birth: February 15, 1948; Stockholm, Sweden. **Parents:** Vladek and Anja (Zylerberg) Spiegelman. **Religion:** Jewish. **Education:** Harpur College (now State University of New York, Binghampton). **Spouse:** Francoise Mouly (m. 1977). **Children:** Nadja Dashiell.

Prize: *Special Awards and Citations: Letters,* 1992: *Maus: A Survivor's Tale (Volume 1 & 2),* New York: Pantheon, 1986, 1991.

Career: Artist, designer, editor and writer, Topps Chewing Gum, 1966-1988; Editor, Douglas Comix, 1972; Instructor, San Francisco Academy of Art, 1974-1975; New York School of Visual Arts, 1979-1987; Contributing Editor, *New Yorker,* 1992-Present.

Selected Works: *Work and Turn,* 1979. *Open Me I'm a Dog!,* 1997. **Films:** *Comic Book Confidential,* Sphinx, 1988.

Other Awards: Playboy Editorial Award, Best Comic Strip, 1982. Yellow Kid Award, Best Comic Strip Author, 1982. Regional Design Award, *Print* magazine, 1983, 1984, 1985. Inkpot Award, San Diego Comics Convention, 1987. Strips Chappening Award, Best Foreign Comic Album, 1987. Alpha Art Award, France, 1993.

For More Information: Witek, Joseph, *Comic Books as History: The Narrative Art of Jack Jackson, Art Spiegelman, and Harvey Pekar,* Jackson: University Press of Mississippi, 1989; Fein, Esther B., "Holocaust as a Cartoonist's Way of Getting to Know His Father," *New York Times,* December 10, 1991; Hess, Elizabeth, "Meet the Spiegelmans," *Village Voice,* January 14, 1992; "The Orphaned Voice in Art Spiegelman's Maus I & II," *Literature and Psychology Providence,* Volume 44, Issue: 1/2, pages 1-22, 1998.

Commentary: A monetary award of $3,000 was given to Art Spiegelman for *Maus: A Survivor's Tale* It is an autobiographical two-volume work. The first volume, *My Father Bleeds History,* was published in 1986 in the form of a comic strip which tells the story of the Jews and Germans in Poland in the 1930s and 1940s. In the comic strip, the faces of the Jews are depicted as mice, the Germans as cats who hunt the mice, and the Poles as pigs who are victimizers. The second volume, *And Here My Troubles Began,* was published in 1991. This volume is about Spiegelman's relationship with his father Vladek, a survivor of Auschwitz, as a result of all that has gone before, including the suicide of his mother Anja, who was a survivor of the Birkenau death camp.

Art Spiegelman was born in Stockholm, Sweden. He has been a comic strip illustrator and writer, a design teacher, and an author. He is currently a contributing editor to the *New Yorker* magazine.

Special Awards and Citations: Music

1974

Roger Sessions
Full entry appears as **#874** under "Music," 1982.

1976

Scott Joplin   1128
Birth: November 24, 1868; Texarkana, TX. **Death:** April 1, 1917. **Parents:** Giles and Florence (Givens) Joplin. **Education:** George R. Smith College for Negroes, MO.

    Prize: *Special Awards and Citations: Music,* 1976.

    Career: Piano player and composer, "King of Ragtime."

    Selected Works: *Maple Leaf Rag,* 1899. *The Ragtime Dance,* 1902. *A Guest of Honor,* 1903. *Sycamore,* 1904. *Chrysanthemum,* 1904. *Sugar Cane,* 1908. *Fig Leaf Rag,* 1908. *Treemonisha,* 1911. *Reflection Rag,* 1917. **Films:** *The Sting,* Universal, 1973.

    For More Information: Gammond, Peter, *Scott Joplin and the Ragtime Era,* New York: St. Martin's Press, 1975; Haskins, James, *Scott Joplin,* Garden City, NY: Doubleday, 1978; Curtis, Susan, *Dancing to a Black Man's Tune: A Life of Scott Joplin,* Columbia: University of Missouri Press, 1994.

    Commentary: A special citation was given to Scott Joplin in the Bicentennial Year of 1976, for his contributions to American music. He composed and performed "ragtime" music, which is a rhythm with accompaniment in strict two-four time and a melody that is in steady syncopation with improvised embellishments.

    Scott Joplin was born in Texarkana, Texas. A self-taught musician, he played piano to make a living and performed throughout the Midwest, living for a time in Chicago and St. Louis. He settled in Sedalia, Missouri in 1896. There, he attended college and wrote music. His *Maple Leaf Rag* is believed to have been written for the Maple Leaf Club, where a group of black performers in Sedalia appeared. Ragtime took the nation by storm and became the popular music of its day. Joplin's music was made popular again when his composition *The Entertainer* was used as the theme song and as background for the film, *The Sting.* Joplin also wrote an opera, *Treemonisha.* The

Scott Joplin International Ragtime Foundation is located in Sedalia. It is dedicated to preserving and promoting an understanding of ragtime music and Joplin's contribution.

1982

Milton Babbitt   1129
Birth: May 10, 1916; Philadelphia, PA. **Parents:** Albert E. and Sara (Potamkin) Babbitt. **Education:** New York University: BA, Phi Beta Kappa. Princeton University, NJ: MFA. **Spouse:** Sylvia Miller (m. 1939). **Children:** Betty Ann.

    Prize: *Special Awards and Citations: Music,* 1982.

    Career: Instructor, Princeton University, NJ, 1938; Math Instructor, Princeton, 1943-1945; Participant, Salzburg Seminar in American Studies, 1952; Faculty member, Berkshire Music Center, summers, 1957, 1958; Faculty member, Advanced Musical Studies, Princeton University, 1959-1960; Director, Electronic Music Center, Princeton University, beginning in 1959; Instructor, Juilliard School of Music, NY, beginning in 1973; Lecturer in music; Commissioned creator of musical works; Member, Board of Directors, League of Composers, beginning in 1954; Member: Acoustical Society of America, American Institute of Physics, American Music Center, American Musicological Society, Audio Engineering Center, International Society of Contemporary Music, League of Composers.

    Selected Works: *Three Compositions for Piano,* 1947. *Composition for 4 Instruments,* 1948. *Composition for 12 Instruments,* 1948. *Composition for Viola and Piano,* 1950. *The Widow's Lament in Springtime,* 1950. *Du,* 1951. *2 Sonnets,* 1955. *Semisimple Variations,* 1956. *All Set,* 1957. *Sounds and Words,* 1958. *Composition for Voice and 6 Instruments,* 1960. *Vision and Prayer,* 1961. *Philomel,* 1964. *Ensemble,* 1964. *Relata I,* 1965. *Post-Partitions,* 1966. *Sextets,* 1966. *Relata II,* 1968. *Occasional Variations,* 1969. *Phonemena,* 1970. *Aria de Capa,* 1974. *Reflections,* 1975. *Paraphrases,* 1979. *A Solo Requiem,* 1979. *Dual,* 1980. *Elizabethan Sextette,* 1986. *Transfigured Notes,* 1986. *Beaten Paths,* 1988. *The Crowded Air,* 1988. *Consortini,* 1989. **Films:** *Babbitt: Portrait of a Serial Composer,* Robert Hilferty, 1998.

Other Awards: Guggenheim Fellow, Guggenheim Foundation, 1961.

For More Information: Brody, Martin, "Music for the Masses: Milton Babbitt's Cold War Music Theory," *Musical Quarterly,* Summer 1993; Dubiel, Joseph, "Three Essays on Milton Babbitt," *Perspectives of New Music,* Summer 1990, Winter 1991, Winter 1992; Mead, Andrew Washburn, *An Introduction to the Music of Milton Babbitt,* Princeton, NJ: Princeton University Press, 1994; Griffiths, Paul, "Babbitt Redux," *New Yorker,* July 8, 1996.

Commentary: A special citation was presented to Milton Babbitt for his life's work as a distinguished and seminal American composer. He composed many works for the electronic synthesizer.

Milton Byron Babbitt was born in Philadelphia, Pennsylvania. He grew up in Jackson, Mississippi, where he received his early musical training. He was adept at mathematics and eventually would teach it at Princeton University. This proved to be very useful in his formulation of musical theories. He studied with Pulitzer Prize winner Roger Sessions and has become an influential electronic composer. Babbitt as a composer and theorist advocates "tonal serialism" which is musical composition based on prior arrangements including all twelve pitches of the chromatic scale, dynamic, duration, timbre, and register. This has been very popular among young American composers. His works include *Composition for Synthesizer* and *All Set.*

1985

William Schuman

Full entry appears as **#843** under "Music," 1943.

1998

George Gershwin   1130

Birth: September 26, 1898; Brooklyn, New York. **Death:** July 11, 1937. **Parents:** Morris and Rose Gershwin. **Religion:** Jewish.

Prize: *Special Awards and Citations: Music,* 1998.

Career: Composer and pianist.

Selected Works: *Swanee,* 1917. *Lullaby,* 1920. *Our Nell,* 1922. *Sweet Little Devil,* 1924. *Lady Be Good!,* 1924. *Primrose,* 1924. *Rhapsody in Blue,* 1924. *Tip-Toes,* 1925. *Oh Kay!,* 1926. *Strike Up the Band,* 1927. *Funny Face,* 1927. *Rosalie,* 1928. *Treasure Girl,* 1928. *An American in Paris,* 1928. *Show Girl,* 1929. *Girl Crazy,* 1930. *Of Thee I Sing,* 1931. *Rhapsody No. 2,* 1932. *Cuban Overture,* 1932. *Pardon My English,* 1933. *Let 'Em Eat Cake,* 1933. *I Got Rhythm,* 1934. *Porgy and Bess,* 1935. **Films:** *The King of Jazz,* Universal, 1930; *Delicious,* Fox, 1931; *Girl Crazy,* RKO, 1932; *Shall We Dance,* RKO, 1937; *A Damsel in Distress,* RKO, 1937; *The Goldwyn Follies,* United Artists, 1938.

For More Information: Peyser, Joan, *The Memory of All That: The Life of George Gershwin,* New York: Simon & Schuster, 1993; Gilbert, Steven E., *The Music of Gershwin,* New Haven, CT: Yale University Press, 1995; Schiff, David Gershwin, *Rhapsody in Blue,* New York: Cambridge University Press, 1997; McLellan, Joseph, "Rhapsody in Review: Musicologist Reconsiders Gershwin for '98 Centennial," *Washington Post,* April 20, 1997.

Commentary: A special citation was awarded to George Gershwin posthumously, commemorating the centennial year of his birth, for his distinguished and enduring contributions to American music.

George Gershwin was born "Jacob Gershvin" in New York City, brother to Pulitzer Prize winner Ira Gershwin. He began playing piano at the age of 12 and played professionally when he was 16. *Swanee,* composed when he was 19, was the first of many hit songs Gershwin would write. Others included *Fascinating Rhythm* and *I've Got Rhythm.* He and brother Ira composed music for the Broadway musical theatre and for films, including the Broadway hit and Pulitzer Prize-winning musical, *Of Thee I Sing.* His extended concert works were *Rhapsody in Blue, An American in Paris,* and *Porgy and Bess.* He died at the age of 38 after unsuccessful surgery revealed he was suffering from a brain tumor. He was at the height of his success when he died.

Specialized Reporting

1985

Jacqueline Garton Crosby   1131

Birth: May 13, 1961; Jacksonville, FL. **Parents:** James Ellis Crosby and Marianne (Garton). **Religion:** Episcopalian. **Education:** University of Georgia: ABJ. University of Central Florida: MBA. **Spouse:** Robert Edward Legge Jr. (m. 1985).

Prize: *Specialized Reporting,* 1985: *Macon Telegraph and News,* Macon, GA: Macon Telegraph and News, 1984.

Career: Staff Writer, *Macon (GA) Telegraph and News,* 1980-84; Copy Editor, *Orlando (FL) Sentinel,* 1984-85; Writer, 1985; Special Projects Director, Orlando (FL) Ivanhoe Communications, 1987-89; Special Projects Producer, Minneapolis (MN), KSTP-TV, 1989-94; Assistant News Editor, *Minneapolis (MN) Star Tribune Online,* 1994-.

Other Awards: Best Sports Story Award, Georgia Press Association, 1982. Best Series of the Year, Associated Press, 1985.

For More Information: *Sports Illustrated,* 6 May (1985): 9.

Commentary: Jackie Crosby and Randall Savage delved into the athletic world at the University of Georgia and Georgia Institute of Technology. They discovered that athletes were receiving preferential treatment. Crosby won the award four months after leaving the *Macon Telegraph and News* to return to graduate school.

Randall Ernest Savage   1132

Birth: March 3, 1939; Commerce, GA. **Parents:** Ernest Kyle Savage and Sara Beatrice (Collins). **Religion:** Baptist. **Education:** University of Maryland. University of Georgia: BA. **Spouse:** Joyce Carol Martin (m. 1964, div. 1984); Mary Elizabeth Hallmark (m. 1984). **Children:** Kimberly, Bradley (JM); Brook, Laura, Shaw (MH).

Prize: *Specialized Reporting,* 1985: *Macon Telegraph and Journal,* Macon, GA: Macon Telegraph and Journal, 1984.

Career: Service station worker, Commerce (GA), Collins (GA), 1958; Billing Clerk, Atlanta (GA) Benton Rapid Express, 1958-61; Served in U.S. Army, 1961-64; Truck Driver, Highpoint (NC) Southern Oil Company, 1964-65; Served in U.S. Air Force, 1966-69; Reporter, *Commerce (GA) News,* 1972; Senior Special Projects Reporter, *Macon (GA) Telegraph and News,* 1972-.

Other Awards: Outstanding Alumnus Award, Henry Grady College of Journalism and Mass Communication, University of Georgia, 1989.

For More Information: *Sports Illustrated,* 6 May (1985): 9.

Commentary: Randall Savage and Jackie Crosby won a Pulitzer Prize for their investigation into the world of academics and athletics at two of Georgia's institutions of higher learning. They discovered and exposed the preferential treatment that athletes received.

1986

Mary Pat Flaherty   1133

Birth: May 7, 1955; Pittsburgh, PA. **Parents:** Patrick Flaherty and Mary (Lydon). **Education:** Northwestern University, IL: BSJ.

Prize: *Specialized Reporting,* 1986: *Pittsburgh Press,* "The Challenge of a Miracle," Pittsburgh, PA: Pittsburgh Press, 1985.

Career: Intern, *Pittsburgh (PA) Press,* 1975; Reporter, Editor, *Pittsburgh (PA) Press,* 1977-1992; Metro Projects Editor, Staff Writer, *Washington (DC) Post,* 1993-.

Selected Works: *The Challenge of a Miracle: Selling the Gift* (with Andrew Schneider), 1985. *Presumed Guilty: The Law's Victims in the War on Drugs* (with Andrew Schneider), 1991.

Other Awards: Golden Quill Award, Western Pennsylvania Newspaper Association. Keystone Press Newspaper Publishers' Association. George Polk Memorial Award, Long Island University, NY, 1992. Sigma Delta Chi Award, 1992. Series Reporting Award, Maryland-Delaware-DC Press Association, 1995.

For More Information: *Contemporary Authors, Volume 127,* Detroit: Gale Research Company, 1989; *Quill,* 80:6 (July 1992): 35.

Commentary: Mary Pat Flaherty and Andrew Schneider's 13-part series, "The Challenge of a Miracle," explored the scientific and ethical questions raised by organ donation and organ transplants. She joined the Pittsburgh Press upon her graduation from college and specializes in human interest and in-depth features. She and a colleague were finalists for a Pulitzer Prize in 1995 for a series of articles on the hiring practices of the Washington, DC police force.

Andrew J. Schneider   1134
Birth: November 13, 1942; New York, NY. **Parents:** Jack Schneider and Frances (Roder). **Education:** University of Maryland. University of Miami, FL. San Antonio College, TX. University of Lowell, MA. **Children:** Patrick, Kelly.

Prize: *Specialized Reporting,* 1986: *Pittsburgh Press,* "The Challenge of a Miracle," Pittsburgh, PA: Pittsburgh Press, 1985.

Career: Writer and Photographer, U.S. Army, 1960-63; Freelance Writer and Photographer, Far East and Miami (FL), United Press International, 1963-67; Chief Photographer, Washington (DC), Sentinel Newspapers, 1967-71; Associate Editor, *Family Magazine,* 1971-73; Managing Editor, Journal Newspapers, 1973-75; Freelance writer and photographer, 1975-76; Special Projects Reporter, Concord (NH), Associated Press, 1976-82; Director of Research, Technology Hazards Research Group, University of Lowell (MA), 1982-84; National Correspondent, Special Projects Leader, Medical Editor, *Pittsburgh (PA) Press,* 1984-; Founder, Director, Riley Professor of Journalism, Indiana University National Institute for Advanced Reporting, 1989-90; Assistant Managing Editor/Investigations, Assistant Managing Editor /Projects, Scripps-Howard News Service.

Selected Works: *The Challenge of a Miracle: Selling the Gift* (with Mary Pat Flaherty), 1985. *Presumed Guilty: The Law's Victims in the War on Drugs* (with Mary Pat Flaherty), 1991.

Other Awards: National Journalism Award of Excellence, American College of Physicians, 1986-88. Roy Howard Award, Scripps-Howard Foundation, 1987. Liberty Bell Award, National Mental Health Association. Environmental Merit Award, Federal Environmental Protection Agency. George Polk Award, Long Island University, NY, 1992. Sigma Delta Chi Award, 1992.

For More Information: *Contemporary Authors, Volume 127,* Detroit: Gale Research Company, 1989.

Commentary: Andrew Schneider and Mary Pat Flaherty's winning series of 13 articles explored the scientific and ethical questions raised by organ donation and organ transplants. Schneider (along with Matthew Brelis) also helped the *Pittsburgh Press* win the Meritorious Public Service Pulitzer Prize for its series, "Danger in the Cockpit."

1987

Alex S. Jones   1135
Birth: November 19, 1946; Greeneville, TN. **Parents:** John M. Jones and Arnold (Susong). **Religion:** Episcopalian. **Education:** Washington and Lee University, VA: BA. **Spouse:** Susan E. Tifft (m. 1985).

Prize: *Specialized Reporting,* 1987: *New York Times,* "The Fall of the House of Bingham," January 19, New York: New York Times, 1986.

Career: Served in United States Naval Reserve, active duty, 1968-71; Managing Editor, *Athens (TN) Daily Post-Athenian,* 1974-78; Editor, *Greenville (TN) Sun,* 1978-83; Business Reporter, *New York Times,* 1983-92; Host of "On the Media," WNYC-AM New York Public Radio, 1993-; Host, Executive Editor, *Media Matters,* PBS, 1995-; Eugene C. Patterson Professor of the Practice of Public Policy and Journalism, Duke University (NC), 1996-.

Selected Works: *The Patriarch: The Rise and Fall of the Bingham Dynasty* (with Susan E. Tifft), 1991.

Other Awards: Nieman Fellow, Harvard University, MA, 1981-82.

Commentary: Alex S. Jones's reporting on the Bingham newspaper family of Kentucky and their internal disagreements about the family's holdings won him a Pulitzer Prize. He continued to cover the family throughout the year as they sold their newspaper, television, and radio holdings.

1988

Walt Bogdanich   1136

Birth: October 10, 1950; Chicago, IL. **Parents:** Walter Bogdanich and Helen (Chabraja). **Education:** University of Wisconsin: BS. Ohio State University: MA. **Spouse:** Stephanie Saul (m. 1982). **Children:** Nicholas Walter, Peter Eric.

Prize: *Specialized Reporting,* 1988: *Wall Street Journal,* New York: Dow Jones, 1987.

Career: Reporter, *Hammond (IN) Compass,* 1974-75; Managing Editor, *Hammond (IN) Compass,*

1975-77; Reporter, *Dayton (OH) Daily News,* 1977; Reporter, *Cleveland (OH) Press,* 1977-79; Reporter, *Cleveland (OH) Plain Dealer,* 1979-84; Reporter, New York (NY), *Wall Street Journal,* 1984-88; Reporter, Washington (DC), *Wall Street Journal,* 1989-93; Television Producer, *Day One,* ABC-TV, 1993-96; Television Producer, *60 Minutes,* CBS-TV, 1996-.

Selected Works: *The Great White Lie: How America's Hospitals Betray Our Trust and Endanger Our Lives,* 1991.

Other Awards: Kiplinger Fellow, Ohio State University, 1976. George Polk Memorial Award, Long Island University, NY, 1980. Overseas Press Club Award, 1983. Penney-Missouri Award.

For More Information: *Wall Street Journal,* 1 April (1988): A2.

Commentary: Walt Bogdanich interviewed more than 500 people for his stories on faulty testing by medical laboratories. His series of articles led to an investigation by the American Medical Association and various government agencies. Bogdanich left the *Wall Street Journal* to join ABC Television. He was the producer for *Day One*'s tobacco-spiking story, the story which prompted a $10 billion lawsuit against the network by Philip Morris and the R.J. Reynolds tobacco companies. ABC settled the case with a fairly weak apology. Bogdanich refused to sign the settlement and has since moved to the CBS network.

1989

Edward Humes   1137

Birth: April 27, 1957; Philadelphia, PA. **Education:** Hampshire College, MA. **Spouse:** Donna H. **Children:** Gabrielle.

Prize: *Specialized Reporting,* 1989: *Orange County Register,* Orange County, CA: Orange County Register, 1988.

Career: *Austin (TX) Texas Observer;* Staff member, *Pine Bluff (AR) Commercial,* 1980-81; Reporter, *Tucson (AZ) Citizen,* 1981-85; General Assignment Reporter, *Orange County (CA) Register,* 1985-90; Writer, 1990-.

Selected Works: *Buried Secrets: A True Story of Serial Murder, Black Magic, and Drug-Running on the U.S. Border,* 1991. *Murderer with a Badge: The Secret Life of a Rogue Cop,* 1992. *Mississippi Mud: A True Story from a Corner of the Deep South,* 1994. *No Matter How Loud I Shout: A Year in the Life of Juvenile Court,* 1996.

Other Awards: Investigative Reporting Award, Orange County Press Club, 1989. Beat Reporting Award, Orange County Press Club, 1986, 1989. Research Nonfiction Award, PEN Center USA West Literary Competition, 1997: *No Matter How Loud I*

Shout: A Year in the Life of Juvenile Court, New York: Simon and Schuster, 1996.

For More Information: *Orange County Register,* 31 March (1989): A1; *Orange County Register,* 8 November (1992): H23.

Commentary: Edward Humes covered military affairs for the *Orange County Register* during 1988. While investigating a series of military helicopter crashes, he discovered that the use of defective night vision goggles, not pilot error, was the true cause of the accidents. He also wrote about military war games, the attempt by the military to use whales and dolphins for warfare, and an Orange County man's effort to overturn his uncle's murder conviction from World War II.

Humes left the *Orange County Register* in 1990 and currently writes nonfiction.

1990

Tamar Stieber   1138

Birth: September 15, 1956; Brooklyn, NY. **Parents:** Alfred Stieber and Freidele (Spector). **Education:** Rockland Community College, NY. Columbia University, NY. University of California, Berkeley: BA, cum laude, Phi Beta Kappa. Police Reserve Academy, cum laude.

Prize: *Specialized Reporting,* 1990: *Albuquerque Journal,* "Three N.M. Women Contract Unusual Medical Symptoms," November 7, Albuquerque, NM: Albuquerque Journal, 1989.

Career: Secretary, San Francisco (CA), Associated Press, 1981-83; Intern, *San Francisco (CA) Examiner,* 1984; Reporter, *Sonoma (CA) Index-Tribune,* 1987-88; City Hall Reporter, *Vallejo Times-Herald,* 1988-89; General Assignment and Special Projects Reporter, *Albuquerque (NM) Journal,* 1989-94; Freelance writer, 1994-.

Other Awards: Public Service Award, New Mexico Press Association, 1990. Public Service Award, Albuquerque Press Club, 1990. Newswriting Award, New Mexico Press Association, 1991.

For More Information: Wills, Kendall J., *The Pulitzer Prizes 1990,* New York: Simon & Schuster, 1990; Bates, Douglas, *The Pulitzer Prize: The Inside Story of America's Most Prestigious Award,* New York: Carol Publishing Group, 1991.

Commentary: Tamar Stieber connected the development of a rare blood disorder and the non-prescription drug, L-Tryptophan. Two weeks after she broke the story, there were 287 cases in 37 states and one death. The Federal government then recalled the drug. Stieber continued working on the aftermath of the story. Three months after the story, there were reports of 21 deaths and 1,500 cases nationwide.

Spot News Photography

1968

Rocco Morabito   1139

Birth: November 2, 1920; Port Chester, NY. **Parents:** Frank Morabito and Fortunata (Famma). **Religion:** Roman Catholic. **Spouse:** Sophia B. Rio (m. 1952). **Children:** Tina, Anne.

Prize: *Spot News Photography,* 1968: *Jacksonville Journal,* "The Kiss of Life," Jacksonville, FL: Jacksonville Journal, 1967.

Career: Newsboy, *Jacksonville (FL) Journal,* 1930; Staff member, Circulation Department, *Jacksonville (FL) Journal,* 1939-43; Served in U.S. Army Air Forces, 1943-45; Staff member, *Jacksonville (FL) Journal,* 1945-49; Church Column and Sports Reporter, *Jacksonville (FL) Journal,* 1949-52; Staff Photographer, *Jacksonville (FL) Journal,* 1952-82; Owner, Landmark Art, Incorporated, Jacksonville, FL, 1984-.

For More Information: Leekley, Sheryle and John Leekley, *Moments: The Pulitzer Prize Photographs, Updated Version: 1942-1982,* New York: Crown Publishers, Inc., 1982: 64-65; *Florida Times-Union,* 4 August (1997).

Commentary: Rocco Morabito was out on assignment when he passed several men working on power lines. Suddenly one of the workmen touched a live wire. He was left hanging upside down and turning blue. A co-worker scrambled up the pole and gave him "The Kiss of Life"—mouth to mouth resuscitation. The worker, R.G. Champion, started to breathe again.

1969

Edward Thomas Adams   1140

Birth: June 12, 1933; New Kensington, PA. **Parents:** Edward I. Adams and Adelaide (Suprano). **Spouse:** Ann Fedorchak; Alyssa Ann Adkins. **Children:** Susan, Edward, Amy Marie (AF); August (AA).

Prize: *Spot News Photography,* 1969: Associated Press, "Saigon Execution," 1968.

Career: *New Kensington (PA) Daily Dispatch,* 1950-51; Combat Photographer, U.S. Marine Corps, 1951-54; Staff Photographer, *New Kensington (PA) Daily Dispatch,* 1954-58; Staff Photographer, *Battle Creek (MI) Enquirer & News,* 1958; Staff Photographer, *Philadelphia (PA) Evening Bulletin,* 1958-62; Photographer, Associated Press, 1962-72; Photographer, *Time* Magazine, 1972-76; Special Correspondent, Associated Press, 1976-80; Freelance photographer, 1980-; Faculty member, Daytona Beach (FL) Community College, 1984.

Other Awards: Photographer of the Year, New York Press Photographers Association, 1966, 1967, 1970, 1972. Associated Press Managing Editors Award, 1968, 1979. National Press Photographer Award, 1969. Sigma Delta Chi, 1969-71. World Press Photography Award, 1969, 1972, 1974-85. Overseas Press Club, 1969, 1974-75. George Polk Memorial Award, Long Island University, NY. National Headliners Club Award, 1973. Magazine Photographer of the Year, University of Missouri/National Press Photographers Association, 1975. Joseph Sprague Memorial Award, National Press Photographers Association, 1976. Robert Cape Memorial Award, Overseas Press Club, 1978. American Society of Magazine Photographers Anniversary Award, 1980. Professional Photographer of the Year, Photographic Manufacturers and Dealers Association, 1996.

For More Information: Leekley, Sheryle and John Leekley, *Moments: The Pulitzer Prize Photographs, Updated Version: 1942-1982,* New York: Crown Publishers, Inc., 1982: 68-69; *Washington Post,* 12 September (1982): G1; Taft, William H., *Encyclopedia of Twentieth-Century Journalists,* New York: Garland Publishing, Inc., 1986; Rigsby, Gwendolyn Gezelle, "A History of Associated Press Pulitzer Prizes" (thesis), University of South Carolina, 1993.

Commentary: Eddie Adams has photographed over 50 heads of state as well as superstars of film, television, sports, and fashion.

He has photographed thirteen wars and has won over 500 awards. His Pulitzer Prize-winning photograph was of a Vietnamese general who shot a member of the Viet Cong at point blank range.

1970

Steven Dawson Starr   1141

Birth: September 6, 1944; Albuquerque, NM. **Parents:** Richard Vernon Starr and Carol (Harley). **Education:** Antioch College, OH. Bethel College, MN. San Jose State University, CA: BA. **Spouse:** Marilynne Sue Anderson (m. 1965). **Children:** Stephen.

Prize: *Spot News Photography,* 1970: Associated Press, "Campus Guns," 1969.

Career: Photographer, *San Jose (CA) Mercury News,* 1966-67; Photographer, Picture Editor, Associated Press, 1970-; Freelance photographer, 1974-.

Other Awards: National Headliners Club Award, 1970. George Polk Memorial Award, Long Island University, NY, 1970.

For More Information: *AP World,* 26:1 (1970): 2; Leekley, Sheryle and John Leekley, *Moments: The Pulitzer Prize Photographs, Updated Version: 1942-1982,* New York: Crown Publishers, Inc., 1982: 72-73; Rigsby, Gwendolyn Gezelle, "A History of Associated Press Pulitzer Prizes" (thesis), University of South Carolina, 1993.

Commentary: Steve Starr spent hours waiting to take the photograph that won him a Pulitzer Prize. His photograph shows armed students at Cornell University leaving a building that they had taken over and held for 36 hours.

1971

John Paul Filo   1142
Birth: August 21, 1948; Natrona Heights, PA. **Parents:** John Paul Filo and Mary Jane (Micholas). **Education:** Kent State University, OH: BS. **Spouse:** Margaret Jane Emerson (m. 1970, div.).

Prize: *Spot News Photography,* 1971: *Tarentum Valley Daily News,* Tarentum, PA: 1970, and *New Kensington Daily Dispatch,* New Kensington, PA: 1970.

Career: Photographer, Kansas City (MO), Associated Press, 1971; Photographer, Springfield (KS), Associated Press, 1974; Photographer, *Philadelphia (PA) Inquirer;* Photo Editor, *Baltimore (MD) Evening Sun;* Deputy Picture Editor, *Sports Illustrated,* 1990-; Assistant Managing Editor/Photo and Graphics, *Camden (NJ) Courier-Post;* Deputy Picture Editor, *Newsweek* Magazine, 1995-.

Other Awards: George Polk Memorial Award, Long Island University, NY, 1971. Sigma Delta Chi Award, 1971.

For More Information: Leekley, Sheryle and John Leekley, *Moments: The Pulitzer Prize Photographs, Updated Version: 1942-1982,* New York: Crown Publishers, Inc., 1982: 78-79; *Washington Post,* 12 September (1982): G1; *News Photographer,* 50:5 (May 1995): 16; *New York Times,* 11 October (1995): B1.

Commentary: John Filo's photograph of Mary Ann Vecchio screaming over the lifeless body of a student at Kent State University captured the horror that the nation felt over the incident. Filo, a journalism student at the time, snapped the photograph, then, fearing that the National Guard might confiscate his film, he drove to Pennsylvania to have it developed.

1972

Horst Faas
Full entry appears as **#1002** under "Photography," 1965.

Michel Laurent   1143
Birth: 1945; Paris, France. **Death:** April 28, 1975.

Prize: *Spot News Photography,* 1972: Associated Press, "Death in Dacca," 1971.

Career: Photographer, Associated Press, 1962-75.

Selected Works: *Je Pense a Vous,* 1994.

Other Awards: World Press Photo Award, 1972. George Polk Memorial Award, Long Island University, NY.

For More Information: *New York Times,* 5 May (1975): 15; *New York Times,* 8 May (1975): 16; Rigsby, Gwendolyn Gezelle, "A History of Associated Press Pulitzer Prizes" (thesis), University of South Carolina, 1993.

Commentary: Michel Laurent and Horst Faas, working for the Associated Press, captured the brutality of the reprisals of those in Bangladesh toward suspected Pakistani collaborators or soldiers. Their photographs show four prisoners being tortured while a mob watches. They shipped their photographs back to London in a disguised package as they had been refused transmission as "detrimental to the national interests."

Laurent was the last journalist or photographer to be killed in Vietnam, on April 28, 1975.

1973

Huynh Cong Ut   1144

Birth: March 29, 1951; Long An Province, Vietnam.
Spouse: Married. **Children:** Michael, Bettina.

Prize: *Spot News Photography,* 1973: Associated Press, "Terror of War," 1972.

Career: Darkroom Technician, Photographer, Reporter, Vietnam, Associated Press, 1965-75; Photographer, Tokyo (Japan), Associated Press, 1975-77; Photographer, Associated Press, 1977-93; Head, Hanoi (Vietnam) Bureau, Associated Press, 1993; Photographer, Los Angeles (CA), Associated Press.

Other Awards: World Press Photo Award. George Polk Memorial Award, Long Island University, NY, 1973. Overseas Press Club Award. National Press Club Award. Sigma Delta Chi Award.

For More Information: Leekley, Sheryle and John Leekley, *Moments: The Pulitzer Prize Photographs, Updated Version: 1942-1982,* New York: Crown Publishers, Inc., 1982: 88-89; *Los Angeles Times Magazine,* 20 August (1989): 12; Rigsby, Gwendolyn Gezelle, "A History of Associated Press Pulitzer Prizes" (thesis), University of South Carolina, 1993.

Commentary: Huynh Cong "Nick" Ut won a Pulitzer Prize for his photograph of Vietnamese children fleeing after Napalm bombs had been dropped on their village. His photograph captures the "sheer horror" and abject pain on the face of Phan Thi Kim Phuc, a nine-year-old girl. She had torn off her burning clothes, but her skin had already been badly burned.

Ut's older brother, Huynh Thanh My, who had been an Associated Press photographer, was killed earlier in the war. Ut, himself, was injured several times. He evacuated with the Associated Press staff in 1975 and worked in Toyko and Los Angeles for the Associated Press. In 1993, he went back to Vietnam to establish a bureau for the Associated Press.

1974

Anthony K. Roberts   1145
Birth Place: Hawaii. **Education:** University of California, Los Angeles. **Spouse:** Gloria R.

Prize: *Spot News Photography,* 1974, "Fatal Hollywood Drama," 1973.

Career: Script department member, film company; Freelance photographer.

Other Awards: Sigma Delta Chi Award, 1974.

For More Information: *New York Times,* 7 May (1974): 40; Leekley, Sheryle and John Leekley, *Moments: The Pulitzer Prize Photographs, Updated Version: 1942-1982,* New York: Crown Publishers, Inc., 1982: 94-95; Rigsby, Gwendolyn Gezelle, "A History of Associated Press Pulitzer Prizes" (thesis), University of South Carolina, 1993.

Commentary: Anthony K. Roberts, a freelance photographer, literally shot his prize-winning photograph while out shopping. It was his first news photograph as he usually worked for record companies and magazines. His photograph is of a kidnapper holding a young woman hostage at knifepoint.

1975

Gerald Harry Gay   1146
Birth: October 30, 1946; Seattle, WA. **Parents:** Fred N. Gay and Doma H. (Westman). **Education:** Brooks Institute of Photography, CA. **Spouse:** Charlanne Dunn (m. 1975, div.). **Children:** Amy, Ellen, Dharma, Demian, Matthew, Eric.

Prize: *Spot News Photography,* 1975: *Seattle Times,* "Lull in the Battle," Seattle, WA: Seattle Times, 1974.

Career: Photographer, *Everett (WA) Herald,* 1968-; Photographer, *Seattle (WA) Times,* 1972-, *Los Angeles (CA) Times;* Publisher, *Picture Magazine;* Photographer, independent projects.

Other Awards: Sweepstake Award, Washington-Oregon Associated Press, 1974. Award, Sigma Delta Chi, Washington Chapter.

For More Information: *Washington Post,* 12 September (1982): G1; Leekley, Sheryle and John Leekley, *Moments: The Pulitzer Prize Photographs, Updated Version: 1942-1982,* New York: Crown Publishers, Inc., 1982: 98-99.

Commentary: Jerry Gay captured the exhaustion of four firefighters after five hours of battling a house fire. They sat on a muddy hillside resting before going back to work. His photograph showed dedicated men exhausted after hard labor.

1976

Stanley Joseph Forman   1147
Birth: July 10, 1945; Winthrop, MA. **Parents:** David Forman and Gertrude (Levy). **Education:** Franklin Institute, MA. **Spouse:** Debbie F. (m. 1983). **Children:** Two children.

Prize: *Spot News Photography,* 1976: *Boston Herald American,* Boston: Boston Herald American, 1975. *Spot News Photography,* 1977: *Boston Herald American,* "The Soiling of Old Glory," Boston: Boston Herald American, 1976.

Career: Campaign Photographer, Attorney General Edward W. Brooke campaign for United States Senate, 1966; News Photographer, *Boston (MA) Herald American,* 1966-82; News Photographer, WCVB-TV, 1982-.

Other Awards: Best Press Photos, World Press Photo Foundation, Amsterdam, Netherlands, 1976-

78. Picture of the Year, National Headliners Club, 1976-77. Picture of the Year Trophy, University of Missouri/National Press Photographers Association, 1976-77. The International Firefighters Association, 1976-77. Nieman Fellow, Harvard University, MA, 1979-80. Joseph A. Sprague Memorial Award, 1980. Picture of the Year, World Press Photographers Association. Sigma Delta Chi Plaque for Distinguished Service to Journalism. United Press International Award. Boston Press Association, Five Awards.

For More Information: *Boston Herald-American,* 4 May (1976): 1+; Leekley, Sheryle and John Leekley, *Moments: The Pulitzer Prize Photographs, Updated Version: 1942-1982,* New York: Crown Publishers, Inc., 1982: 104-107; Rothmeyer, Karen, *Winning Pulitzers: The Stories Behind Some of the Best News Coverage of Our Time,* New York: Columbia University Press, 1991: 148-158.

Commentary: Stanley Forman is one of only three people to win back-to-back Pulitzer Prizes.

His first winning photograph was of a woman and child falling to the ground when a fire escape gave away. The photo was circulated worldwide and led to tougher and more frequent inspections of fire escapes in Boston.

His second winning photograph captured the raw racism by white students at an anti-busing demonstration. A student holding a steel pole with an American flag attacked a black lawyer who happened to be walking by.

1977

Stanley Joseph Forman
Full entry appears as #1147 under "Spot News Photography," 1976.

Neal Hirsch Ulevich　　　　　　　1148
Birth: June 18, 1946; Milwaukee, WI. **Parents:** Ben Ulevich and Leah (Klitsner). **Religion:** Jewish. **Education:** University of Wisconsin: BA. **Spouse:** Maureen Vaughan (m. 1974). **Children:** Jacob, Sarah.

Prize: *Spot News Photography,* 1977: Associated Press, 1976.

Career: Writer, Wisconsin, Associated Press, 1966-68; Reporter, St. Louis (MO), Associated Press, 1968-69; Freelance photographer, Far East, 1969-70; Photographer and Reporter, Saigon (Vietnam), Associated Press, 1970-75; Photographer and Reporter, Bangkok (Thailand), Associated Press, 1975-79; Head, Photo Coverage, Asia, Associated Press, 1979-83; Photo Technology Team, Denver (CO), Associated Press.

Other Awards: Journalism Fellow, University of Wisconsin, Madison, 1971-72. Ralph O. Nafziger

Award, School of Journalism and Mass Communication, University of Wisconsin, Madison, 1981.

For More Information: Leekley, Sheryle and John Leekley, *Moments: The Pulitzer Prize Photographs, Updated Version: 1942-1982,* New York: Crown Publishers, Inc., 1982: 112-113; Rigsby, Gwendolyn Gezelle, "A History of Associated Press Pulitzer Prizes" (thesis), University of South Carolina, 1993.

Commentary: In a rare occurrence, two Pulitzer Prizes were given in Spot News Photography in 1977, one to Neal Ulevich and another to Stanley Forman. Neal Ulevich's photographs of a Thai rightist about to strike the body of a hanged student showed clearly that the situation in Southeast Asia was still unstable.

1978

John H. Blair　　　　　　　　　1149
Birth: 1942; Des Moines, IA. **Education:** Parsons College, IA. Drake University, IA: BA. **Spouse:** Married.

Prize: *Spot News Photography,* 1978: United Press International, 1977.

Career: Night Newsman, United Press International, 1963-67; Photographer, Des Moines (IA), United Press International, 1967-68; Chief of News Pictures, Indianapolis (IN), United Press International, 1968-; United Press International.

Commentary: John Blair was awarded a Pulitzer Prize on April 20, 1978, three days after the winners were announced by Columbia University. His winning photograph had been misattributed to another staff photographer of United Press International. The winning photo is of a bank robber holding an Indianapolis brokerage employee hostage with a shotgun.

1979

Thomas J. Kelly III　　　　　　1150
Birth: August 8, 1947; Hackensack, NJ. **Parents:** Thomas J. Kelly and Severina (Augenti). **Spouse:** Patricia Lee Moulder (m. 1975). **Children:** Danielle, Devon, Thomas IV, Taylor.

Prize: *Spot News Photography,* 1979: *Pottstown Mercury,* "Tragedy on Sanatoga Road," Pottstown, PA: Pottstown Mercury, 1978.

Career: Salesman; Draftsman; Volunteer Fireman, Norriton Fire Company; Part-time Staff member, *Norristown (PA) Montgomery Post,* 1969-71; Photographer, *Valley Forge (PA) Today's Post,* 1971-74; Photography Supervisor, *Pottstown (PA) Mercury,* 1974-89; Chief Photographer, *Pottstown (PA) Mercury;* Freelance photographer; Director of Photography, *Trenton (NJ) Trentonian,* 1990-96.

Other Awards: Region III Newspaper Photographer of the Year, National Press Photographers Association, 1975-1976, 1979. Pennsylvania Photographer of the Year, 1976. Robert F. Kennedy Journalism Award, 1980.

For More Information: Leekley, Sheryle and John Leekley, *Moments: The Pulitzer Prize Photographs, Updated Version: 1942-1982,* New York: Crown Publishers, Inc., 1982: 124-127.

Commentary: Tom Kelly's photographs of the "Tragedy on Sanatoga Road" won him a Pulitzer Prize. His photographs are of Richard Greist holding members of his family hostage. Greist's young daughter walked out the front door covered in blood after being stabbed in the face and eyes with a screwdriver. Police stormed the house because of fear for Janice Greist, Richard's pregnant wife. They captured Greist, but not before he stabbed and killed his wife.

1980

Anonymous   1151

Prize: *Spot News Photography,* 1980: United Press International, 1979.

Commentary: This was the first time a Pulitzer Prize went to an anonymous person. The winning photographs were of an Iranian firing squad killing Kurd rebels and former police officials of the deposed Shah. United Press International withheld the name of the photographer because of fear of reprisals from those who supported the Iranians.

1981

Larry C. Price

Full entry appears as **#414** under "Feature Photography," 1985.

1982

Ronald Edmonds   1152
Birth: June 16, 1946; Richmond, CA. **Parents:** Ernest Clifford Edmonds and Dorothy (Theis). **Spouse:** Grace Feliciano (m. 1979).

Prize: *Spot News Photography,* 1982: Associated Press, 1981.

Career: Freelance photographer, Sacramento (CA); Staff Photographer, *Honolulu (HI) Star-Bulletin,* 1972-76, Chief Photographer, *Honolulu (HI) Star-Bulletin,* 1977-78; Sacramento (CA) Bureau Chief, United Press International Newspictures,

1978-81; Photographer, Washington (DC), Associated Press, 1981-.

Other Awards: National Headliners Club Award, 1982.

For More Information: Leekley, Sheryle and John Leekley, *Moments: The Pulitzer Prize Photographs, Updated Version: 1942-1982,* New York: Crown Publishers, Inc., 1982: 150-151; Rigsby, Gwendolyn Gezelle, "A History of Associated Press Pulitzer Prizes" (thesis), University of South Carolina, 1993.

Commentary: Ron Edmonds's series of photographs show frame-by-frame the shooting of President Ronald Reagan by John Hinckley. Edmonds was using a motor-driven camera which took about five photos a second. (President Reagan recovered and John Hinckley was found not guilty by reason of insanity.) Edmonds has covered the Olympic Games and the eruption of Mount St. Helens. He spent nine months following and chronicling Reagan on the campaign trail.

1983

Bill Foley   1153
Birth: December 12, 1954; Chicago, IL. **Parents:** William Robert Foley and Sara (Sloan). **Education:** Indiana University.

Prize: *Spot News Photography,* 1983: Associated Press, 1982.

Career: Photographer, Louisville (KY) *Courier Journal;* Photographer, Cairo (Egypt), Associated Press, 1978; Photographer, Middle East, Cairo (Egypt), Syria, Jordan, Iraq, Beirut (Lebanon), Associated Press; Photographer, *Time* magazine.

Selected Works: *Renewing a Block in Harlem: The Children's Aid Society-Carmel Hill Project: Year 1-4* (with Terry Quinn), 1996.

For More Information: *Popular Photography* 93 (January 1986): 18, 22; *Boston Globe,* 23 July (1989): 68; Rigsby, Gwendolyn Gezelle, "A History of Associated Press Pulitzer Prizes" (thesis), University of South Carolina, 1993.

Commentary: Bill Foley, one of the first photographers to reach the Sabra Camp in West Beirut, recorded the massacre of Palestinian refugees there. Foley has covered assignments throughout the Middle East, including Cairo, Syria, Jordan, and Iraq. He was a finalist for a Pulitzer Prize in 1984.

1984

Stan Grossfeld

Full entry appears as **#413** under "Feature Photography," 1985.

1985

Santa Ana Register   1154
Founded: 1905.

Prize: *Spot News Photography,* 1985: *Santa Ana Register,* Santa Ana, CA, 1984.

Commentary: For their "exceptional coverage" of the 1984 Olympic Games, the staff of the *Santa Ana Register* was awarded a Pulitzer Prize. In 1985, the paper changed its name to the *Orange County Register.*

1986

Michel duCille
Full entry appears as **#417** under "Feature Photography," 1988.

Carol Guzy   1155

Birth: March 7, 1956; Bethlehem, PA. **Parents:** John Guzy and Julia (Mulzet) Pammer. **Education:** Northhampton County Area Community College, PA: AA. Art Institute of Fort Lauderdale, FL: Applied Science Associate Degree.

Prize: *Spot News Photography,* 1986: *Miami Herald,* Miami, FL: Miami Herald, 1985. *Spot News Photography,* 1995: *Washington Post,* Washington, DC: Washington Post, 1994.

Career: Intern, Broward Bureau, *Miami (FL) Herald;* Staff Photographer, *Miami (FL) Herald,* 1980-88; Staff Photographer, *Washington (DC) Post,* 1988-.

Other Awards: Feature Photography Award, Atlanta Press Photographers Association, 1982. Best Portfolio Award, Atlanta Press Photographers Asso-

ciation, 1982, 1985, 1990. General News Photography Award, Atlanta Press Photographers Association, 1984. News Picture Story Award, Atlanta Press Photographers Association, 1985, 1990-91. Best in Show Award, Atlanta Press Photographers Association, 1990. Feature Picture Story Award, Atlanta Press Photographers Association, 1990. Newspaper Photographer of the Year, University of Missouri / National Press Photographers Association, 1990, 1993, 1997. Photographer of the Year, White House News Photographers Association, 1991, 1993-94 1996-98. Feature Photography Award, White House News Photographers Association, 1996-97. Global News Award, University of Missouri/National Press Photographers Association, 1997. International Photojournalism Award. Robert F. Kennedy Journalism Award, 1997.

For More Information: *Miami Herald,* 18 April (1986): A1. *News Photographer* 53: 2 (February 1998): 22.

Commentary: Carol Guzy, a two-time winner of a Pulitzer Prize, won her first prize with Michel DuCille, covering the mudslides in Colombia that followed the eruption of the Nevado del Ruiz volcano. Her second Pulitzer was for her coverage of the crisis in Haiti.

Guzy has been named newspaper photographer of the year three times and photographer of the year by the White House News Photographers six times. She was 28 years old when she was awarded her first Pulitzer Prize. She was a finalist for a Pulitzer Prize in 1988.

1987

Kim Komenich   1156
Birth: October 15, 1956; Laramie, WY. **Parents:** Milo Komenich and Juanita Mary (Beggs). **Education:** San Jose State University, CA: BA.

Prize: *Spot News Photography,* 1987: *San Francisco Examiner,* San Francisco: San Francisco Examiner, 1986.

Career: Reporter/Photographer, *Manteca (CA) Bull,* 1976-77; Staff Photographer, *Walnut Creek (CA) Contra Costa Times,* 1979-82; Staff Photographer, *San Francisco (CA) Examiner,* 1982-; Instructor, San Francisco (CA) Academy of Art College.

Selected Works: *Day in the Life of California,* 1988. *Christmas in America. Power to Heal. 15 Seconds: The 1989 San Francisco Earthquake,* 1989. *The Mission: Inside the Church of Jesus Christ of Latter-Day Saints,* 1995.

Other Awards: Photographer of the Year, San Francisco Bay Area Press Photographers Association, 1982, 1984. National Headliners Club Award, 1982, 1988. World Press Photo Award, 1983. Distinguished

Service Award, Society of Professional Journalists, 1987. John S. Knight Journalism Fellow, Stanford University, CA, 1993-94. National Press Photographers Association Awards.

For More Information: Leekley, Sheryle and John Leekley, *Moments: The Pulitzer Prize Photographs, Updated Version: 1942-1982,* New York: Crown Publishers, Inc., 1982: 84-85; Wills, Kendall J., *The Pulitzer Prizes Volume 1, 1987,* New York: Simon & Schuster, 1987.

Commentary: Kim Komenich's winning series of photographs were of Philippine President Ferdinand E. Marcos's last days in office, the brief uprising of the people against his government, and the new President Corazon Aquino.

1988

## Scott Alan Shaw									1157

Birth: September 17, 1963; Danville, IL. **Parents:** Ron Shaw and Carol (Bonebrake). **Education:** Southern Illinois University: BS. **Spouse:** Brynne Solowinski. **Children:** Carson.

Prize: *Spot News Photography,* 1988: *Odessa American,* Odessa, TX: Odessa American, 1987.

Career: Staff member, *Danville (IL) Commercial News;* Staff member, college paper, *Daily Egyptian;* Staff member, *Carbondale (IL) Southern Illinoisan;* Staff member, *Paragould (AR) Daily Press,* 1985-86; Staff Photographer, *Odessa (TX) American,* 1986-89; Staff Photographer, *Cleveland (OH) Plain Dealer,* 1990-.

Other Awards: Region 4 Photographer of the Year, National Press Photographers Association, 1993.

For More Information: *New York Times,* 1 April (1988): B4.

Commentary: Scott Shaw's photographs of toddler Jessica McClure as she was taken to an ambulance won him a Pulitzer Prize. McClure had fallen down an abandoned well and the entire nation followed the rescue operation. Shaw spent 22 hours waiting for the photograph with dozens of more seasoned photographers. He was 24 years old when he won the award in 1988. Shaw has won over 200 awards for his work in various local and regional press contests.

1989

## Ron Olshwanger									1158

Birth: November 30, 1936; St. Louis, MO. **Education:** University of Missouri. Washington University, MO. **Spouse:** Sally O. **Children:** Son.

Prize: *Spot News Photography,* 1989: *St. Louis Post-Dispatch,* St. Louis: St. Louis Post-Dispatch, 1988.

Career: Volunteer Assistant Chief, Red Cross Disaster Service; Co-Owner, MMI Wholesale Furniture Showroom, St. Louis, MO; Amateur photographer.

For More Information: *New York Times,* 22 May (1989): B3; *Editor & Publisher,* 128:16 (22 April 1995): 30-32.

Commentary: Ron Olshwanger, an amateur photographer, won a Pulitzer Prize for his picture of a firefighter giving mouth-to-mouth resuscitation to a child he has just pulled from a burning building. The photograph was first published in the *St. Louis Post-Dispatch.*

1990

## Oakland Tribune									1159

Founded: February 21, 1874.

Prize: *Spot News Photography,* 1990: *Oakland Tribune,* Oakland, CA, 1989.

Other Awards: Bill Crouch won a photography Pulitzer Prize in 1950 while at the *Oakland Tribune.*

For More Information: *Journalism Quarterly,* 45:3 (Autumn 1968): 487-495; *Washington Journalism Review,* 13:8 (October 1991): 20-24; *Washington Journalism Review,* 14:10 (October 1992).

Commentary: For the photographic coverage of the devastating effect to the Bay Area of the earthquake on October 17, 1989, the entire photographic staff of the *Oakland Tribune* won a Pulitzer Prize. Their photographs made the front page of newspapers around the world. Tom Faupl, graphics and photography director, coordinated the coverage. Other members of the staff included Tom Duncan, Pat Greenhouse, Steve Hotvedt, Matthew Lee, Michael Macor, Paul Miller, Angela Pancrazio, Reginald Pearman, Gary Reyes, Ron Riesterer, and Roy H. Williams.

The *Oakland Tribune* was started in 1874 as the *Oakland Daily Tribune.* Later in the same year it changed its name to the *Oakland Daily Evening Tribune* and then to the *Oakland Evening Tribune.* The following year it took the name *Oakland Daily Evening Tribune,* which it kept until 1891 when the name *Oakland Tribune* was first used on August 28. Between 1978 and 1979 and between 1982 and 1991 the paper went under the name *The Tribune,* but otherwise from 1891 to the present it has used the name *Oakland Tribune.*

1991

Greg Marinovich   1160

Birth Place: Springs, South Africa.

Prize: *Spot News Photography,* 1991: Associated Press, 1990.

Career: Photographer, *Newsweek;* Chief Photographer in Jerusalem, Associated Press.

Other Awards: Leica Award. Overseas Press Club Award.

For More Information: Rigsby, Gwendolyn Gezelle, "A History of Associated Press Pulitzer Prizes" (thesis), University of South Carolina, 1993.

Commentary: Greg Marinovich's winning series of photographs show the brutal murder of a man believed to be a Zulu spy by a mob of supporters of the African National Congress. At the time, Marinovich was a freelance photographer working in South Africa. The Associated Press distributed the photos to its 950 member newspapers.

In 1994, he was caught in the turmoil of the region. He was shot in the chest, hand, and buttocks. He survived, although a colleague of his, Ken Oosterbroek, died.

1992

Associated Press

Full entry appears as **#421** under "Feature Photography," 1993.

1993

Ken Geiger   1161

Birth: 1957. **Parents:** George Geiger and Carol (Welzenbach). **Education:** Rochester Institute of Technology, NY. **Spouse:** Kristen Koenig (m. 1994). **Children:** Ruby, Cory.

Prize: *Spot News Photography,* 1993: *Dallas Morning News,* Dallas: Dallas Morning News, 1992.

Career: Welder; Intern, *Baltimore (MD) Sun;* Photo Editor, college paper; Photographer, *Austin (TX) American-Statesman,* 1980-83; General Assignment Photographer, *Dallas (TX) Morning News,* 1983-; Senior Staff Photographer, *Dallas (TX) Morning News.* Deputy Director of Photography, Dallas (TX) *Morning News,* 1997-.

Other Awards: Sports Action Award, Atlanta Photojournalism Seminar, 1986. National Headliners Club Award. Associated Press Managing Editors Award. Dallas Press Club. National Press Photographers Association Award. Texas Headliner Club Award. Society of Newspaper Design Award.

For More Information: *Dallas Morning News,* 14 April (1993): A1, B8.

Commentary: Ken Geiger and William Snyder's photographs from Barcelona capture the spirit of the Olympic Games. They worked 16- to 20-hour days for three weeks. Their entry included 20 photographs. Geiger was 36 when he won the award in 1993.

William D. Snyder

Full entry appears as **#382** under "Explanatory Journalism," 1989.

1994

Paul Watson   1162

Birth: July 13, 1959; Weston, Canada. **Education:** Carleton University, Canada: BA. Columbia University: MA. **Spouse:** Zelda Shun Sai Hung.

Prize: *Spot News Photography,* 1994: *Toronto Star,* Toronto, Canada: Toronto Star, 1993.

Career: General Assignment Reporter, London (England) Free Press, 1980; Feature Writer and General Assignment Reporter, *Vancouver (Canada) Sun,* 1981-82; Reporter, *Toronto (Canada) Star,* 1987-92; Africa Bureau Chief, *Toronto (Canada) Star,* 1992-95; Asia Bureau Chief, *Toronto (Canada) Star,* 1995-98; Vienna (Austria) Bureau Chief, *Los Angeles Times,* 1998-.

Other Awards: Canadian National Newspaper Award, 1991-94, 1996; Robert Capa Gold Medal, Overseas Press Club of America, 1993

For More Information: *Maclean's,* 107 (25 April 1994): 56-57.

Commentary: Paul Richard Watson is the first Canadian to win a photography Pulitzer Prize. His photograph shows a dead American serviceman being dragged through the streets of Mogadishu, Somalia. The Associated Press picked up the photograph and it was published in several United States newspapers. Watson uses an auto-focus camera because, due to a congenital defect, he has no fingers on his left hand.

1995

Carol Guzy

Full entry appears as **#1155** under "Spot News Photography," 1986.

1996

Charles H. Porter IV   1163

Education: University of Central Oklahoma. **Spouse:** Sherylynn P.

Prize: *Spot News Photography,* 1996.

Career: Bank credit specialist; Amateur photographer.

Other Awards: Outstanding Spot News Photography, National Headliners Club Award, 1996. Spot News Photography Award, University of Missouri/National Press Photographers Association, 1996. British Picture Editors Award.

For More Information: *USA Today,* 8 April 1996.

Commentary: Charles H. Porter IV's 1995 photograph of firefighter Chris Fields cradling one-year-old Baylee Almon in his arms dramatically told the tale of the wanton destruction of the bombing of the Murrah building in Oklahoma City. The infant died at the scene. Porter is an amateur photographer. He was 25 years old when he took the photograph. The photo was distributed by the Associated Press.

1997

Annie Wells   1164

Birth: March 24, 1954; Fairfax, VA. **Parents:** Claude Wells and Elizabeth. **Education:** University of California, Santa Cruz: BA. San Francisco State University, CA.

Prize: *Spot News Photography,* 1997: *Press Democrat,* Santa Rosa, CA: Press Democrat, 1996.

Career: Scientific/Technical Photographer, Letterman Army Institute of Research; Part-time Staff member, law firm; Design and Production Editor, college paper, *Golden Gator;* Photographer, *Logan (UT) Herald Journal;* Photographer, *Greeley (CO) Tribune;* Photographic Intern, San Francisco (CA) Associated Press; Photographer, *Santa Rosa (CA) The Press Democrat;* Photographer, *Los Angeles Times,* 1997-.

Selected Works: *News Photographer,* July 7, 1996.

For More Information: *News Photographer,* 52:10 (October 1997): 36, 37, 39.

Commentary: Ann Justice Wells's winning photograph is of the rescue of a young woman from a flooded creek in Santa Rosa, California. After the photo appeared, not a day passed for two months without someone mentioning it to her. Wells's background is in science writing and she went back to school to take courses in photography.

1998

Martha Rial   1165

Birth Place: Murrysville, PA. **Education:** Art Institute of Pittsburgh, PA. Ohio University.

Prize: *Spot News Photography,* 1998: *Pittsburgh Post-Gazette,* "Trek of Tears," January 26, Pittsburgh, PA: *Pittsburgh Post-Gazette,* 1997.

Career: Staff Photographer, *Fort Pierce (FL) Tribune;* Staff Photographer, *Alexandria (VA) Journal Newspapers;* Staff Photographer, *Pittsburgh (PA) Post-Gazette,* 1994-.

Other Awards: Hall of Fame Award, Pennsylvania Association of Private School Adminstrations, 1998. National Headliners Club Award, 1998. National Journalism Award, Scripps-Howard Foundation Award, 1998.

For More Information: *Pittsburgh Post-Gazette,* April 15, 1998: A1.

Commentary: Martha Rial won a Pulitzer Prize for her "life-affirming portraits of survivors of the conflicts in Rwanda and Burundi." In December 1996, Rial, on a visit to her sister, a public health nurse at the Mtendeli Refugee Camp in Tanzania, spent some of her time photographing the plight of the refugees. Her photographs captured the essence of their lives.

Spot News Reporting

1991

Miami Herald
Full entry appears as **#357** under "Editorial Writing," 1983.

1992

Newsday
Full entry appears as **#722** under "Local General Spot News Reporting," 1984.

1993

Los Angeles Times
Full entry appears as **#91** under "Breaking News Reporting," 1998.

1994

New York Times
Full entry appears as **#375** under "Explanatory Journalism," 1986.

1995

Los Angeles Times
Full entry appears as **#91** under "Breaking News Reporting," 1998.

1996

Robert Dennis McFadden   1166

Birth: February 11, 1937; Milwaukee, WI. **Parents:** Frank Joseph McFadden and Violet (Charleston). **Education:** University of Wisconsin, Eau Claire. University of Wisconsin: BS. **Spouse:** Elizabeth Hathaway (m. 1963, div. 1968); Judith Silverman (m. 1971). **Children:** Nolan (JS).

Prize: *Spot News Reporting,* 1996: *New York Times,* New York: New York Times, 1995.

Career: Reporter, *Wisconsin Rapids (WI) Daily Tribune,* 1957-58; Reporter, *Wisconsin State Journal,* 1958-59; Reporter, *Cincinnati (OH) Enquirer,* 1960-61; Copyboy, *New York Times,* 1961-62; Police and General Assignment Reporter, *New York Times,* 1962-67; Rewriteman, *New York Times,* 1967-; Senior Writer, *New York Times,* 1990-.

Selected Works: *No Hiding Place: The New York Times Inside Report on the Hostage Crisis* (with others), 1981. *Outrage: The Story behind the Tawana Brawley Hoax,* 1990.

Other Awards: Distinguished Service to Journalism Award and Mass Communication, University of Wisconsin, Madison, 1987. Byline Award, New York Press Club, 1973-74, 1980, 1987, 1989. Peter Kinss Award, New York Society of Silurians, 1977. Page One Award, Newspaper Guild of New York, 1978. Spot News Award, Long Island Press Club, NY, 1984.

For More Information: *New York Times,* 10 April (1996): B6.

Commentary: Robert D. McFadden's "highly skilled writing" won him a Pulitzer Prize in 1996. He is known within the *New York Times* for his ability to write effective prose after receiving reports from many journalists. He has written about the 1977 New York City blackout; the 1986 suicide of Donald Manes, the Queens (NY) borough president; and other events of the 20th century including natural disasters, crime, education, and the environment. He began with the *New York Times* as a copyboy in 1960. His winning articles were published throughout the year from February 6 to December 9, 1995. He was a finalist in the same category for a Pulitzer Prize in 1994.

1997

Newsday

Full entry appears as **#722** under "Local General Spot News Reporting," 1984.

Telegraphic Reporting (International)

1942

Laurence Edmund Allen 1167

Birth: October 19, 1908; Mt. Savage, MD. **Death:** May 12, 1975. **Parents:** Laurence Bernard Allen and Mary Caroline (Crowe). **Spouse:** Helen Fazakerley Quisenberry (died 1963). **Children:** Stepchildren: Mrs. Frank Trammel, Mrs. Philip Miner Jr.

Prize: *Telegraphic Reporting (International),* 1942: Associated Press, 1941.

Career: Staff member, *Baltimore (MD) News,* 1926; Staff member, *Washington (DC) Herald* and *Huntington (WV) Evening Herald;* Reporter, Telegraph Editor, *Charleston (WV) Daily Mail,* 1927-33; Reporter and State Editor, Charleston Bureau, Associated Press, 1933-35; Reporter, Washington (DC) Bureau, Associated Press, 1935-37; Foreign Cables Deskman, New York, Associated Press, 1937-38; War Correspondent, Europe, Associated Press, 1938-44; Correspondent, Poland, Associated Press, 1945, 1947, 1949; Moscow (Russia) Bureau Chief, Associated Press, 1949; Correspondent, Tel Aviv (Israel), Associated Press, 1950; War Correspondent, Southeast Asia, Singapore, Associated Press, 1951, Correspondent, French Vietnam, Indochina, Associated Press, 1951-55; Correspondent, Malay, Thailand, Burma, Associated Press, 1956; Correspondent, Caribbean Area, Associated Press, 1957-61.

Other Awards: First Annual National Headliners Club Award, 1941. Bronze Star for Defending Freedom Press as Prisoner of War, 1945. Order of British Empire by King George VI, England, 1947. Croix de Guerre French High Command, Indochina, for Frontline Reporting, 1952.

For More Information: *New York Times,* 13 May (1975): 38:1; Taft, William H., *Encyclopedia of Twentieth-Century Journalists,* New York: Garland Publishing, Inc., 1986.

Commentary: Larry Allen won a Pulitzer Prize for his combat correspondence during World War II. He lived dangerously, especially during war situations. He survived eight sinkings from torpedoes and bombs, was held prisoner twice during World War II, and was caught in a riot in Singapore in 1950 and left for dead. He went on to cover Vietnam and South America.

1943

Ira Wolfert 1168

Birth: November 1, 1908; New York, NY. **Death:** November 24, 1997. **Education:** Columbia University, NY: BA. **Spouse:** Helen Herschdorfer (m. 1928, died 1985). **Children:** Ruth, Michael.

Prize: *Telegraphic Reporting (International),* 1943: *North American Newspaper Alliance, Inc.,* "How the Japs Were Caught with Their Kimonos Down," *Boston Evening Globe,* November 27; "Wolfert Discloses Pacific Drama of Unsinkable Ship," *Atlanta Constitution,* December 1; "Jap Warships Deserted 8 Transports in Battle," *Syracuse Post-Standard,* December 3, 1942.

Career: Correspondent, North American Newspaper Alliance, ?-1945; Writer.

Selected Works: *Tucker's People,* 1943. *Battle for the Solomons,* 1943. *Torpedo 8: The Story of Swede Larsen's Bomber Squadron,* 1943. *One-Man Air Force* (with D.S. Gentile), 1944. *American Guerrilla in the Philippines,* 1945. *Battle for Solomons,* 1945. *The Epic of Tarawa* (with W. Richardson), 1945. *An Act of Love,* 1948. *Married Men: Eagle Books/125-31,* 1953. *An Act of Love: A Completely Retold Tale of the Novel,* 1954. *An Epidemic of Genius,* 1960. **Films:** *Force of Evil* (movie with Abraham Polonsky), Robert's Production, 1948.

For More Information: *New York Times,* 27 November (1997): B15.

Commentary: Ira Wolfert's three articles on the fifth battle of the Solomon Islands won him a Pulitzer Prize. They were published in North American Newspaper Alliance papers in late November and early December, 1942.

1944

Daniel De Luce 1169

Birth: June 8, 1911; Yuma, AZ. **Parents:** Robert De Luce and Myrtle (Hickey). **Education:** University of California, Los Angeles: BA, Phi Beta Kappa. **Spouse:** Alma Chalupnik (m. 1936).

Prize: *Telegraphic Reporting (International),* 1944: Associated Press, 1943.

Career: Staff member, San Francisco (CA), Associated Press, 1929; Staff member, Los Angeles

(CA), Associated Press; Reporter, *Los Angeles (CA) Examiner,* 1934-35; Correspondent, Balkan Bureau, Associated Press, 1935-; Germany Bureau Chief, Associated Press, 1950-56; General Executive, Associated Press, 1956-65; Assistant General Manager, Associated Press, 1965-.

Other Awards: National Headliners Club Award, 1948.

For More Information: *New York Times,* 2 May (1944): 16; Rothmeyer, Karen, *Winning Pulitzers: The Stories Behind Some of the Best News Coverage of Our Time,* New York: Columbia University Press, 1991: 51-60; Rigsby, Gwendolyn Gezelle, "A History of Associated Press Pulitzer Prizes" (thesis), University of South Carolina, 1993.

Commentary: Daniel De Luce was the first Allied journalist inside Yugoslavia after Germany invaded the country in 1941. He crossed the Adriatic Sea in a small boat in September, 1943. His series of articles told the story of the Balkans and the Partisan Army and its objectives.

1945

Mark Skinner Watson   1170

Birth: June 24, 1887; Plattsburgh, NY. **Death:** March 25, 1966. **Parents:** Winslow Charles Watson and Ella (Barnes). **Religion:** Presbyterian. **Education:** Union College, NY: AB. **Spouse:** Susan Elizabeth Owens (m. 1921). **Children:** Ellen Brashears, Susan Barnes.

Prize: *Telegraphic Reporting (International),* 1945: *Baltimore Sun,* Baltimore, MD: Baltimore Sun, 1944.

Career: Staff member, *Plattsburgh (NY) Press,* 1908-09; Reporter, Traveling Correspondent, *Chicago (IL) Tribune,* 1909-14; Director of Publicity, San Diego Exposition, 1914-15; Reporter, Traveling Correspondent, *Chicago (IL) Tribune,* 1915-17; Served in U.S. Army, 1917-19; Managing Editor, *Ladies' Home Journal,* 1920; Assistant Managing Editor, *Baltimore (MD) Sun,* 1920-27; Sunday Editor, *Baltimore (MD) Sun,* 1927-41; Military Correspondent, *Baltimore (MD) Sun,* 1941-; Served in U.S. Army, 1946-50; Reporter, U.S. Department of Defense, *Baltimore (MD) Sun.*

Selected Works: *The U.S. and Armaments: Headline Series, Number 143,* 1960. *The Chief of Staff: Prewar Plans and Preperations; United States Army in World War II; History of the War Department,* 1950.

Other Awards: Medal of Freedom, United States Army, 1946. Citation, Department of Defense, 1961. Distinguished Public Service Award, United States Navy, 1962. Presidential Medal of Freedom, 1963. Arts and Letters Trophy, Air Force Association, 1964. Honorary Degree, Union College, NY, 1948.

For More Information: *New York Times,* 26 March (1966): 29.

Commentary: Mark S. Watson's reporting from London, Washington, DC, and the battlefronts in Italy, Sicily, and France won him a Pulitzer Prize. In 1944, he entered Paris with the American Fourth Divisions. A lieutenant colonel summoned him to the head of the entering forces to interpret the French directions. After the war, he covered the demobilization of the United States and the problems with war surplus.

1946

Homer William Bigart

Full entry appears as **#612** under "International Reporting," 1951.

1947

Eddy Lanier King Gilmore   1171

Birth: May 28, 1907; Selma, AL. **Death:** October 6, 1967. **Parents:** Edwin Luther Gilmore and Evelyn (King). **Education:** Washington and Lee University, VA. Carnegie Institute of Technology, PA. **Spouse:** Tamara Adamovna Chernashova (m. 1943). **Children:** Christopher, Vicki, Susanna, Natasha.

Prize: *Telegraphic Reporting (International),* 1947: Associated Press, 1946.

Career: Newspaperman, *Atlanta (GA) Journal,* 1929-32; Staff member, *Washington (DC) Daily News,* 1932-35; Reporter, Washington (DC) Bureau, Associated Press, 1936-40; Correspondent, London (England) Bureau, Associated Press, 1940-41; Moscow (Russia) Bureau Chief, Associated Press, 1945-54; London (England) Bureau, Associated Press, 1954-67.

Selected Works: *Me and My Russian Wife,* 1954. *Troika,* 1961. *After the Cossacks Burned Down the "Y,"* 1964.

Other Awards: Sigma Delta Chi Award, 1947. National Headliners Club Award, 1947.

For More Information: *New York Times,* 7 October (1967): 30; Gilmore, Tamara, *Me and My American Husband,* Garden City, NY: Doubleday, 1968; Rigsby, Gwendolyn Gezelle, "A History of Associated Press Pulitzer Prizes" (thesis), University of South Carolina, 1993.

Commentary: Eddy Gilmore, whose Southern accent stayed with him all his life, won a Pulitzer Prize for his interview with Stalin. He sent his questions to the Soviet leader by mail and the replies were the basis of his story. The *New York Times* carried the interview on its first page under a four-column headline on March 23, 1946.

Telegraphic Reporting (National)

1942

Louis Stark   1172
Birth: May 1, 1888; Tibold Daracz, Hungary. **Death:** May 17, 1954. **Parents:** Adolph Stark and Rose (Kohn). **Education:** New York Training School for Teachers. **Spouse:** Jennie S. House (m. 1916). **Children:** Arthur.

Prize: *Telegraphic Reporting (National),* 1942: *New York Times,* New York: New York Times, 1941.

Career: Teacher, New York City public schools, 1909; Book agent, New York publisher, 1909; Publishing and advertising, 1909-13; Advertising Department, *New York Times,* 1911; Reporter, New York City News Association, 1913-17; Staff member, *New York (NY) Evening Sun,* 1917; Staff member, *New York Times,* 1917-22; Reporter, Economic Affairs, Labor News, Washington (DC) Bureau, *New York Times,* 1923-51; Editorial Department Staff member, *New York Times,* 1951-54.

Selected Works: *Labor and the New Deal: Public Affairs Pamphlets, Number 2,* 1936.

Other Awards: Honorary Degree, Reed College, OR, 1937.

For More Information: *Current Biography Yearbook, 1945,* New York: H.W. Wilson Company, 1945; *New York Times,* 18 May (1954): 29; *Dictionary of American Biography, Supplement 5,* New York: Charles Scribner's Sons, 1977.

Commentary: In 1923, Louis Stark began to specialize in reporting on business and economics and, specifically, issues related to labor. He covered all topics that have a connection to employment and the workforce including strikes, international conventions of labor organizations, and the organization of labor, as well as national legislation and its impact on labor. He had a reputation for his "accuracy and impartiality." He was awarded a Pulitzer Prize in 1942 "for his distinguished reporting of important labor stories during the year."

1943
No award

1944

Dewey Lee Fleming   1173
Birth: July 19, 1898; Whitmer, WV. **Death:** May 18, 1955. **Parents:** Sidney Albert Fleming and Hattie Alice (Bowers). **Religion:** Presbyterian. **Education:** Davis and Elkins College, WV: BA. Columbia University, NY. **Spouse:** Elizabeth Walker (m. 1932, died 1938).

Prize: *Telegraphic Reporting (National),* 1944: *Baltimore Sun,* Baltimore, MD: Baltimore Sun, 1943.

Career: Reporter, *Elkins (WV) Inter-Mountain,* 1917-19; Staff member, *Baltimore (MD) American,* 1922-23; Reporter, Staff member, *Baltimore (MD) Sun,* 1923-26; Reporter, Washington (DC), *Baltimore (MD) Sun,* 1926-27; Correspondent, New York (NY), *Baltimore (MD) Sun,* 1927-28; Correspondent, Chicago (IL), *Baltimore (MD) Sun,* 1928-29; London (England) Bureau Chief, *Baltimore (MD) Sun,* 1929-31; Washington (DC) Bureau Staff member, *Baltimore (MD) Sun,* 1931-; Washington (DC) Bureau Chief, *Baltimore (MD) Sun,* 1941-; London (England) Bureau Chief, *Baltimore (MD) Sun,* 1949-53; Washington (DC) Bureau Chief, *Baltimore (MD) Sun,* 1953-54.

Other Awards: Honorary Degree, Davis and Elkins College, WV, 1944.

For More Information: *Editor & Publisher,* 77:19 (6 May 1944): 7-8, 60; *New York Times,* 19 May (1955): 29.

Commentary: Dewey Fleming was awarded a Pulitzer Prize for his "consistently outstanding work" throughout 1943 on national issues. He started reporting on Washington, DC in 1931 and became the head of the Washington, DC bureau in 1941. He then specialized in covering the White House and the State Department.

1945

James Barrett Reston
Full entry appears as **#899** under "National Reporting," 1957.

1946

Edward Arnold Harris   1174
Birth: October 20, 1910; St. Louis, MO. **Death:** March 14, 1976. **Parents:** Nathan Harris and Rose (Goldman). **Education:** Washington University, MO: AB. University of California, Los Angeles: MS. **Spouse:** Miriam Sima Levy (m. 1938). **Children:** Linda Gail, Mark Geoffrey, Robert Nathaniel.

Prize: *Telegraphic Reporting (National),* 1946: *St. Louis Post-Dispatch,* St. Louis: St. Louis Post-Dispatch, 1945.

Career: Campus Correspondent, *St. Louis (MO) Star-Times,* 1931-33; Columnist, General Reporter, *St. Louis (MO) Star-Times,* 1933-40; Correspondent, St. Louis (MO), *Fortune* magazine, *Life* magazine, and *Time* magazine, 1936-43; City Hall Reporter, *St. Louis (MO) Post-Dispatch,* 1940; Rewrite Specialist, Reporter, Local Political Writer, *St. Louis (MO) Post-Dispatch,* 1940-43; Correspondent, Washington (DC), *St. Louis (MO) Post-Dispatch,* 1943-54; West Coast Bureau Chief, *St. Louis (MO) Post-Dispatch,* 1954-58; Syndicated columnist, 1960-63; President, Edward A. Harris & Associates, 1963-76.

Selected Works: *Public Men, in and out of Office* (Salter, J.T., ed.), 1946. *Love Thy Neighbor,* 1958.

Other Awards: Journalism Award, Fontbonne College, MO, 1947. Alumni Citation, Washington University, MO, 1957. Award of Distinction, University of California, Los Angeles Department of Journalism, 1958. Agricultural Writers' Award, 1961.

For More Information: *New York Times,* 17 March (1976): 44.

Commentary: Edward A. Harris's expose on the Tidewater Oil situation and Ed Pauley's involvement won him a Pulitzer Prize. Ed Pauley had stated in 1940 that he could get several hundred thousand dollars for campaign contributions from several California oil men. Harris's story led the nation to oppose the confirmation of Pauley as Undersecretary of the Navy.

1947

Edward Thomas Folliard   1175

Birth: May 14, 1899; Washington, DC. **Death:** November 25, 1976. **Parents:** Thomas Folliard and Rose (Greene). **Religion:** Roman Catholic. **Education:** George Washington University, Washington, DC. **Spouse:** Helen Liston (m. 1933). **Children:** Nancy, Michael.

Prize: *Telegraphic Reporting (National),* 1947: *Washington Post,* Washington, DC: Washington Post, 1946.

Career: Staff member, *Washington (DC) Herald,* 1922; *Washington (DC) Post and Times Herald,* 1923-76.

Selected Works: *Washington: Stepchild of the Union,* 1933. *The Byrd Machine,* 1957.

Other Awards: National Headliners Club Award, 1948. Hall of Fame, Sigma Delta Chi, Washington, DC Chapter.

For More Information: *New York Times,* 26 November (1976): 22; *Contemporary Authors, Volumes 69-72,* Detroit: Gale Research Company, 1978: 241.

Commentary: Edward T. Folliard's series of articles on the Columbians, Inc., a hate group, won him a Pulitzer Prize. Other stories he covered in his career include the Canadian tour of King George and Queen Elizabeth in 1930, the Roosevelt-Churchill war conferences in Quebec in 1943-44, and national political campaigns since 1928.

INDEXES

Index of Newspaper and Organization Winners

Numbers refer to profile entries, not page numbers.

Index of Individual Winners

Numbers refer to profile entries, not page numbers.

Index of Education Institutions

This index lists the prize winners under the educational institutions they attended for both graduate and postgraduate studies. Numbers refer to profile entries, not page numbers.

Chronology of Prizes Awarded

Numbers refer to profile entries, not page numbers.

1917

Biography or Autobiography
Elliott, Maud Howe, 11
Hall, Florence Marion Howe, 12
Richards, Laura E., 13

Drama
No award

Editorial Writing
New York Tribune, 294

History
Jusserand, Jean Adrien Antoine Jules, 534

Meritorious Public Service
No award

Novel
No award

Reporting
Swope, Herbert Bayard, 1070

1918

Biography or Autobiography
Bruce, William Cabell, 14

Drama
Williams, Jesse Lynch, 167

Editorial Writing
Louisville Courier-Journal, 295

History
Rhodes, James Ford, 535

Meritorious Public Service
New York Times, 375

Newspaper History Award
Hough, Henry Beetle, 951
Lewinson, Minna, 952

Novel
Poole, Ernest, 953

Poetry
Teasdale, Sara, 1005

Reporting
Littledale, Harold Aylmer, 1071

1919

Biography or Autobiography
Adams, Henry, 15

Drama
No award

Editorial Writing
No award

History
No award

Meritorious Public Service
Milwaukee Journal, 788

Novel
Tarkington, Booth, 954

Poetry
Sandburg, Carl, 555
Widdemer, Margaret, 1006

Reporting
No award

1920

Biography or Autobiography
Beveridge, Albert Jeremiah, 16

Drama
O'Neill, Eugene, 168

Editorial Writing
Newbranch, Harvey Ellsworth, 296

History
Smith, Justin Harvey, 536

Meritorious Public Service
No award

Novel
No award

Poetry
No award

Reporting
Leary Jr., John Joseph, 1072

1921

Biography or Autobiography
Bok, Edward, 17

Drama
Gale, Zona, 169

Editorial Writing
No award

History
Hendrick, Burton Jesse, 19
Sims, William Sowden, 537

Meritorious Public Service
Boston Post, 789

Novel
Wharton, Edith Newbold, 955

Poetry
No award

Reporting
Seibold, Louis, 1073

1922

Biography or Autobiography
Garland, Hamlin, 18

Drama
O'Neill, Eugene, 168

Editorial Cartooning
Kirby, Rollin, 239

Editorial Writing
O'Brien, Frank Michael, 297

History
Adams, James Truslow, 538

Meritorious Public Service
New York World, 790

Novel
Tarkington, Booth, 954

Poetry
Robinson, Edwin Arlington, 1007

Reporting
Simpson, Kirke Larue, 1074

1923

Biography or Autobiography
Hendrick, Burton Jesse, 19

Drama
Davis, Owen, 170

Editorial Cartooning
No award

Editorial Writing
White, William Allen, 41

History
Warren, Charles, 539

Meritorious Public Service
Memphis Commercial Appeal, 791

Novel
Cather, Willa, 956

Poetry
Millay, Edna St. Vincent, 1008

Reporting
Johnston, Alva, 1075

1924

Biography or Autobiography
Pupin, Michael Idvorsky, 20

Drama
Hughes, Hatcher, 171

Editorial Cartooning
Darling, Jay Norwood, 240

Editorial Writing
Boston Herald, 298
Cobb, Frank Irving, 299

History
McIlwain, Charles Howard, 540

Meritorious Public Service
New York World, 790

Novel
Wilson, Margaret, 957

Poetry
Frost, Robert, 1009

Reporting
White, Magner, 1076

1925

Biography or Autobiography
Howe, Mark Antony Dewolfe, 21

Drama
Howard, Sidney, 172

Editorial Cartooning
Kirby, Rollin, 239

Editorial Writing
Lathan, Robert, 300

History
Paxson, Frederic Logan, 541

Meritorious Public Service
No award

Novel
Ferber, Edna, 958

Poetry
Robinson, Edwin Arlington, 1007

Reporting
Goldstein, Alvin H., 1077
Mulroy, James W., 1078

1926

Biography or Autobiography
Cushing, Harvey Williams, 22

Drama
Kelly, George, 173

Editorial Cartooning
Fitzpatrick, Daniel Robert, 241

Editorial Writing
Kingsbury, Edward Martin, 301

History
Channing, Edward, 542

Meritorious Public Service
Columbus Enquirer Sun, 792

Novel
Lewis, Sinclair, 959

Poetry
Lowell, Amy, 1010

Reporting
Miller, William Burke, 1079

1927

Biography or Autobiography
Holloway, Emory, 23

Drama
Green, Paul, 174

Editorial Cartooning
Harding, Nelson, 242

Editorial Writing
Bullard, Frederic Lauriston, 302

History
Bemis, Samuel Flagg, 44

Meritorious Public Service
Canton Daily News, 793

Novel
Bromfield, Louis, 960

Poetry
Speyer, Leonora, 1011

Reporting
Rogers, John T., 1080

1928

Biography or Autobiography
Russell, Charles, 24

Drama
O'Neill, Eugene, 168

Editorial Cartooning
Harding, Nelson, 242

Editorial Writing
Hall, Grover Cleveland, 303

History
Parrington, Vernon Louis, 543

Meritorious Public Service
Indianapolis Times, 794

Novel
Wilder, Thornton, 185

Poetry
Robinson, Edwin Arlington, 1007

Reporting
No award

1929

Biography or Autobiography
Hendrick, Burton Jesse, 19

Correspondence
Mowrer, Paul Scott, 120

Drama
Rice, Elmer L., 175

Editorial Cartooning
Kirby, Rollin, 239

Editorial Writing
Jaffe, Louis Isaac, 304

History
Shannon, Fred Albert, 544

Meritorious Public Service
New York Evening World, 795

Novel
Peterkin, Julia, 961

Poetry
Benet, Stephen Vincent, 1012

Reporting
Anderson, Paul Yewell, 1081

1930

Biography or Autobiography
James, Marquis, 25

Correspondence
Stowe, Leland, 121

Drama
Connelly, Marc, 176

Editorial Cartooning
Macauley, Charles Raymond, 243

Editorial Writing
No award

History
Van Tyne, Claude H., 545

Meritorious Public Service
No award

Novel
La Farge, Oliver, 962

Poetry
Aiken, Conrad, 1013

Reporting
Owen, Russell D., 1082

Special Awards and Citations: Journalism
Dapping, William Osborne, 1107

1931

Biography or Autobiography
James, Henry, 26

Correspondence
Knickerbocker, Hubert Renfro, 122

Drama
Glaspell, Susan, 177

Editorial Cartooning
Duffy, Edmund, 244

Editorial Writing
Ryckman, Charles Silcott, 305

History
Schmitt, Bernadotte Everly, 546

Meritorious Public Service
Atlanta Constitution, 796

Novel
Barnes, Margaret Ayer, 963

Poetry
Frost, Robert, 1009

Reporting
MacDonald, Alexander Black, 1083

1932

Biography or Autobiography
Pringle, Henry F., 27

Correspondence
Duranty, Walter, 123
Ross, Charles Griffith, 124

Drama
Gershwin, Ira, 178

Kaufman, George S., 179
Ryskind, Morrie, 180

Editorial Cartooning
McCutcheon, John Tinney, 245

Editorial Writing
No award

History
Pershing, John J., 547

Meritorious Public Service
Indianapolis News, 797

Novel
Buck, Pearl S., 964

Poetry
Dillon, George, 1014

Reporting
Martin, Douglas DeVeny, 1084
Pooler, James S., 1085
Richards, William C., 1086
Sloan, John N.W., 1087
Webb, Frank D., 1088

1933

Biography or Autobiography
Nevins, Allan, 28

Correspondence
Mowrer, Edgar Ansel, 125

Drama
Anderson, Maxwell, 181

Editorial Cartooning
Talburt, Harold M., 246

Editorial Writing
Kansas City Star, 306

History
Turner, Frederick J., 548

Meritorious Public Service
New York World-Telegram, 798

Novel
Stribling, T.S., 965

Poetry
MacLeish, Archibald, 201

Reporting
Jamieson, Francis Anthony, 1089

1934

Biography or Autobiography
Dennett, Tyler, 29

Correspondence
Birchall, Frederick T., 126

Drama
Kingsley, Sidney, 182

Editorial Cartooning
Duffy, Edmund, 244

Editorial Writing
Chase, Edwin Percy, 307

History
Agar, Herbert, 549

Meritorious Public Service
Medford Mail Tribune, 799

Novel
Miller, Caroline Pafford, 966

Poetry
Hillyer, Robert, 1015

Reporting
Brier, Royce, 1090

1935

Biography or Autobiography
Freeman, Douglas Southall, 30

Correspondence
Krock, Arthur, 127

Drama
Akins, Zoe, 183

Editorial Cartooning
Lewis, Ross Aubrey, 247

Editorial Writing
No award

History
Andrews, Charles McLean, 550

Meritorious Public Service
Sacramento Bee, 800

Novel
Johnson, Josephine Winslow, 967

Poetry
Wurdemann, Audrey, 1016

Reporting
Taylor, William Howland, 1091

1936

Biography or Autobiography
Perry, Ralph Barton, 31

Correspondence
Barber, Wilfred Courtenay, 128

Drama
Sherwood, Robert E., 43

Editorial Cartooning
No award

Editorial Writing
Morley, Felix Muskett, 308
Parker, George B., 309

History
McLaughlin, Andrew C., 551

Meritorious Public Service
Cedar Rapids Gazette, 801

Novel
Davis, Harold Lenoir, 968

Poetry
Coffin, Robert P. Tristram, 1017

Reporting
Lyman, Lauren Dwight, 1092

1937

Biography or Autobiography
Nevins, Allan, 28

Correspondence
McCormick, Anne Elizabeth O'Hare, 129

Drama
Hart, Moss, 184
Kaufman, George S., 179

Editorial Cartooning
Batchelor, Clarence Daniel, 248

Editorial Writing
Owens, John Whitefield, 310

History
Brooks, Van Wyck, 552

Meritorious Public Service
St. Louis Post-Dispatch, 802

Novel
Mitchell, Margaret, 969

Poetry
Frost, Robert, 1009

Reporting
Blakeslee, Howard Walter, 1093
Dietz, David Henry, 1094
Lal, Gobind Behari, 1095
Laurence, William Leonard, 1096
O'Neill, John Joseph, 1097

1938

Biography or Autobiography
James, Marquis, 25
Shepard, Odell, 32

Correspondence
Krock, Arthur, 127

Drama
Wilder, Thornton, 185

Editorial Cartooning
Shoemaker, Vaughn Richard, 249

Editorial Writing
Waymack, William Wesley, 311

History
Buck, Paul Herman, 553

Meritorious Public Service
Bismarck Tribune, 803

Novel
Marquand, John Phillips, 970

Poetry
Zaturenska, Marya, 1018

Reporting
Sprigle, Martin Raymond, 1098

Special Awards and Citations: Journalism
Edmonton Journal, 1108

1939

Biography or Autobiography
Van Doren, Carl, 33

Correspondence
Lochner, Louis Paul, 130

Drama
Sherwood, Robert E., 43

Editorial Cartooning
Werner, Charles George, 250

Editorial Writing
Callvert, Ronald Glenn, 312

History
Mott, Frank Luther, 554

Meritorious Public Service
Miami Daily News, 804

Novel
Rawlings, Marjorie Kinnan, 971

Poetry
Fletcher, John Gould, 1019

Reporting
Stokes Jr., Thomas Lunsford, 1099

1940

Biography or Autobiography
Baker, Ray Stannard, 34

Correspondence
Tolischus, Otto David, 131

Drama
Saroyan, William, 186

Editorial Cartooning
Duffy, Edmund, 244

Editorial Writing
Howard, Bart S., 313

History
Sandburg, Carl, 555

Meritorious Public Service
Waterbury Republican & American, 805

Novel
Steinbeck, John, 972

Poetry
Van Doren, Mark, 1020

Reporting
Heath, S. Burton, 1100

1941

Biography or Autobiography
Winslow, Ola Elizabeth, 35

Correspondence
Group award, 132

Drama
Sherwood, Robert E., 43

Editorial Cartooning
Burck, Jacob, 251

Editorial Writing
Maury, Reuben, 314

History
Hansen, Marcus Lee, 556

Meritorious Public Service
St. Louis Post-Dispatch, 802

Novel
No award

Poetry
Bacon, Leonard, 1021

Reporting
Pegler, James Westbrook, 1101

Special Awards and Citations: Journalism
New York Times, 375

1942

Biography or Autobiography
Wilson, Robert Forrest, 36

Correspondence
Romulo, Carlos Pena, 133

Drama
No award

Editorial Cartooning
Block, Herbert Lawrence, 252

Editorial Writing
Parsons, Geoffrey, 315

History
Leech, Margaret, 557

Meritorious Public Service
Los Angeles Times, 91

Novel
Glasgow, Ellen Anderson Gholson, 973

Photography
Brooks, Milton E., 978

Poetry
Benet, William Rose, 1022

Reporting
Delaplane, Stanton Hill, 1102

Telegraphic Reporting (International)
Allen, Laurence Edmund, 1167

Telegraphic Reporting (National)
Stark, Louis, 1172

1943

Biography or Autobiography
Morison, Samuel Eliot, 37

Correspondence
Baldwin, Hanson Weightman, 134

Drama
Wilder, Thornton, 185

Editorial Cartooning
Darling, Jay Norwood, 240

Editorial Writing
Seymour, Forrest W., 316

History
Forbes, Esther, 558

Meritorious Public Service
Omaha World-Herald, 806

Music
Schuman, William, 843

Novel
Sinclair, Upton, 974

Photography
Noel, Frank E., 979

Poetry
Frost, Robert, 1009

Reporting
Weller, George Anthony, 1103

Telegraphic Reporting (International)
Wolfert, Ira, 1168

Telegraphic Reporting (National)
No award

1944

Biography or Autobiography
Mabee, Carleton, 38

Correspondence
Pyle, Ernest Taylor, 135

Drama
No award

Editorial Cartooning
Berryman, Clifford Kennedy, 253

Editorial Writing
Haskell, Henry Joseph, 317

History
Curti, Merle, 559

Meritorious Public Service
New York Times, 375

Music
Hanson, Howard, 844

Novel
Flavin, Martin, 975

Photography
Bunker, Earle L., 980
Filan, Frank, 981

Poetry
Benet, Stephen Vincent, 1012

Reporting
Schoenstein, Paul, 1104

Special Awards and Citations: Journalism
Price, Byron, 1109
White, William Allen, 41

Special Awards and Citations: Letters
Rodgers, Richard, 194

Telegraphic Reporting (International)
De Luce, Daniel, 1169

Telegraphic Reporting (National)
Fleming, Dewey Lee, 1173

1945

Biography or Autobiography
Nye, Russell Blaine, 39

Correspondence
Boyle, Harold Vincent, 136

Drama
Chase, Mary Coyle, 187

Editorial Cartooning
Mauldin, William Henry, 254

Editorial Writing
Potter, George W., 318

History
Bonsal, Stephen, 560

Meritorious Public Service
Detroit Free Press, 328

Music
Copland, Aaron, 845

Novel
Hersey, John, 976

Photography
Rosenthal, Joseph J., 982

Poetry
Shapiro, Karl, 1023

Reporting
McDowell, Jack Sherman, 1105

Special Awards and Citations: Journalism
Cartographers, 1110

Telegraphic Reporting (International)
Watson, Mark Skinner, 1170

Telegraphic Reporting (National)
Reston, James Barrett, 899

1946

Biography or Autobiography
Wolfe, Linnie Marsh, 40

Correspondence
Cortesi, Arnaldo, 137

Drama
Crouse, Russel, 188
Lindsay, Howard, 189

Editorial Cartooning
Russell, Bruce Alexander, 255

Editorial Writing
Carter Jr., William Hodding, 319

History
Schlesinger Jr., Arthur Meier, 59

Meritorious Public Service
Scranton Times, 807

Music
Sowerby, Leo, 846

Novel
No award

Photography
No award

Poetry
No award

Reporting
Laurence, William Leonard, 1096

Telegraphic Reporting (International)
Bigart, Homer William, 612

Telegraphic Reporting (National)
Harris, Edward Arnold, 1174

1947

Biography or Autobiography
White, William Allen, 41

Correspondence
Atkinson, Justin Brooks, 138

Drama
No award

Editorial Cartooning
Shoemaker, Vaughn Richard, 249

Editorial Writing
Grimes, William Henry, 320

History
Baxter III, James Phinney, 561

Meritorious Public Service
Baltimore Sun, 808

Music
Ives, Charles, 847

Novel
Warren, Robert Penn, 977

Photography
Hardy, Arnold, 983

Poetry
Lowell, Robert, 1024

Reporting
Woltman, Frederick Enos, 1106

Special Awards and Citations: Journalism
Columbia University and the Graduate School of
  Journalism, 1111
St. Louis Post-Dispatch, 802

Telegraphic Reporting (International)
Gilmore, Eddy Lanier King, 1171

Telegraphic Reporting (National)
Folliard, Edward Thomas, 1175

1948

Biography or Autobiography
Clapp, Margaret Antoinette, 42

Drama
Williams, Tennessee, 190

Editorial Cartooning
Goldberg, Reuben Lucius, 256

Editorial Writing
Dabney, Virginius, 321

Fiction
Michener, James Albert, 445

History
De Voto, Bernard, 562

International Reporting
Ward, Paul William, 608

Local Reporting
Goodwin, George Evans, 759

Meritorious Public Service
St. Louis Post-Dispatch, 802

Music
Piston, Walter, 848

National Reporting
Andrews, Bert, 891
Finney, Nathaniel Solon, 892

Photography
Cushing, Francis W., 984

Poetry
Auden, W. H., 1025

Special Awards and Citations: Journalism
Fackenthal, Frank Diehl, 1112

1949

Biography or Autobiography
Sherwood, Robert E., 43

Drama
Miller, Arthur, 191

Editorial Cartooning
Pease, Lucius Curtis, 257

Editorial Writing
Crider, John Henshaw, 322
Elliston, Herbert Berridge, 323

Fiction
Cozzens, James Gould, 446

History
Nichols, Roy Franklin, 563

International Reporting
Day, Price, 609

Local Reporting
Johnson, Malcolm Malone, 760

Meritorious Public Service
Nebraska State Journal, 809

Music
Thomson, Virgil, 849

National Reporting
Trussel, Charles Prescott, 893

Photography
Fein, Nathaniel, 985

Poetry
Viereck, Peter, 1026

1950

Biography or Autobiography
Bemis, Samuel Flagg, 44

Drama
Hammerstein II, Oscar, 192
Logan, Joshua, 193
Rodgers, Richard, 194

Editorial Cartooning
Berryman, James T., 258

Editorial Writing
Saunders, Carl Maxon, 324

Fiction
Guthrie Jr., A.B., 447

History
Larkin, Oliver W., 564

International Reporting
Stevens, Edmund William, 610

Local Reporting
Berger, Meyer, 761

Meritorious Public Service
Chicago Daily News, 810
St. Louis Post-Dispatch, 802

Music
Menotti, Gian-Carlo, 850

National Reporting
Guthman, Edwin Otto, 894

Photography
Crouch, Bill, 986

Poetry
Brooks, Gwendolyn, 1027

1951

Biography or Autobiography
Coit, Margaret Louise, 45

Drama
No award

Editorial Cartooning
Manning, Reginald West, 259

Editorial Writing
Fitzpatrick, William Henry Walter, 325

Fiction
Richter, Conrad, 448

History
Buley, R. Carlyle, 565

International Reporting
Beech, Keyes, 611
Bigart, Homer William, 612
Higgins, Marguerite, 613
Morin, Relman George, 614
Sparks, Fred, 615
Whitehead, Don Ford, 616

Local Reporting
Montgomery, Edward Samuel, 762

Meritorious Public Service
Brooklyn Eagle, 811
Miami Herald, 357

Music
Moore, Douglas Stuart, 851

National Reporting
No award

Photography
Desfor, Max, 987

Poetry
Sandburg, Carl, 555

Special Awards and Citations: Journalism
Krock, Arthur, 127
Sulzberger, Cyrus Leo, 1113

1952

Biography or Autobiography
Pusey, Merlo John, 46

Drama
Kramm, Joseph, 195

Editorial Cartooning
Packer, Fred Little, 260

Editorial Writing
La Coss, Louis, 326

Fiction
Wouk, Herman, 449

History
Handlin, Oscar, 566

International Reporting
Hightower, John Murmann, 617

Local Reporting
De Carvalho, George, 763

Meritorious Public Service
St. Louis Post-Dispatch, 802

Music
Kubik, Gail, 852

National Reporting
Leviero, Anthony Harry, 895

Photography
Robinson, John R., 988
Ultang, Donald Theodore, 989

Poetry
Moore, Marianne, 1028

Special Awards and Citations: Journalism
Kansas City Star, 306
Kase, Max, 1114

1953

Biography or Autobiography
Mays, David John, 47

Drama
Inge, William, 196

Editorial Cartooning
Kuekes, Edward D., 261

Editorial Writing
Royster, Vermont Connecticut, 105

Fiction
Hemingway, Ernest, 450

History
Dangerfield, George, 567

International Reporting
Wehrwein, Austin Carl, 618

Local Reporting, Edition Time
Providence Journal-Bulletin, 694

Local Reporting, No Edition Time
Mowery, Edward Joseph, 776

Meritorious Public Service
Tabor City Tribune, 812
Whiteville News Reporter, 813

Music
No award

National Reporting
Whitehead, Don Ford, 616

Photography
Gallagher, William M., 990

Poetry
MacLeish, Archibald, 201

Special Awards and Citations: Journalism
Markel, Lester, 1115

1954

Biography or Autobiography
Lindbergh, Charles A., 48

Drama
Patrick, John, 197

Editorial Cartooning
Block, Herbert Lawrence, 252

Editorial Writing
Murray, Donald Morison, 327

Fiction
No award

History
Catton, Bruce, 568

International Reporting
Lucas, Jim Griffing, 619

Local Reporting, Edition Time
Vicksburg Post-Herald, 764

Local Reporting, No Edition Time
McCoy, Alvin Scott, 777

Meritorious Public Service
Newsday, 722

Music
Porter, Quincy William, 853

National Reporting
Wilson, Richard Lawson, 896

Photography
Schau, Virginia, 991

Poetry
Roethke, Theodore, 1029

1955

Biography or Autobiography
White, William S., 49

Drama
Williams, Tennessee, 190

Editorial Cartooning
Fitzpatrick, Daniel Robert, 241

Editorial Writing
Detroit Free Press, 328

Fiction
Faulkner, William, 451

History
Horgan, Paul, 569

International Reporting
Salisbury, Harrison Evans, 620

Local Reporting, Edition Time
Brown, Caro, 765

Local Reporting, No Edition Time
Towery, Roland Kenneth, 778

Meritorious Public Service
Columbus Ledger and Sunday Ledger-Enquirer,
   814

Music
Menotti, Gian-Carlo, 850

National Reporting
Lewis, Joseph Anthony, 897

Photography
Gaunt Jr., John L., 992

Poetry
Stevens, Wallace, 1030

1956

Biography or Autobiography
Hamlin, Talbot Faulkner, 50

Drama
Goodrich, Frances, 198
Hackett, Albert, 199

Editorial Cartooning
York, Robert, 262

Editorial Writing
Soth, Lauren Kephart, 329

Fiction
Kantor, MacKinlay, 452

History
Hofstadter, Richard, 496

International Reporting
Conniff, Frank, 621
Hearst Jr., William Randolph, 622
Kingsbury-Smith, Joseph, 623

Local Reporting, Edition Time
Hills, Lee, 766

Local Reporting, No Edition Time
Daley, Arthur John, 779

Meritorious Public Service
Watsonville Register-Pajaronian, 815

Music
Toch, Ernst, 854

National Reporting
Bartlett, Charles Leffingwell, 898

Photography
New York Daily News, 993

Poetry
Bishop, Elizabeth, 1031

1957

Biography or Autobiography
Kennedy, John Fitzgerald, 51

Drama
O'Neill, Eugene, 168

Editorial Cartooning
Little, Tom, 263

Editorial Writing
Boone Sr., James Buford, 330

Fiction
No award

History
Kennan, George F., 61

International Reporting
Jones, Russell, 624

Local Reporting, Edition Time
Salt Lake Tribune, 767

Local Reporting, No Edition Time
Lambert, William G., 780
Turner, Wallace L., 781

Meritorious Public Service
Chicago Daily News, 810

Music
Dello Joio, Norman, 855

National Reporting
Reston, James Barrett, 899

Photography
Trask, Harry Albert, 994

Poetry
Wilbur, Richard, 1032

Special Awards and Citations: Letters
Roberts, Kenneth, 1120

1958

Biography or Autobiography
Ashworth, Mary Wells, 52
Carroll, John Alexander, 53
Freeman, Douglas Southall, 30

Drama
Frings, Ketti, 200

Editorial Cartooning
Shanks, Bruce McKinley, 264

Editorial Writing
Ashmore, Harry Scott, 331

Fiction
Agee, James, 453

History
Hammond, Bray, 570

International Reporting
New York Times, 375

Local Reporting, Edition Time
Fargo Forum, 768

Local Reporting, No Edition Time
Beveridge Jr., George David, 782

Meritorious Public Service
Arkansas Gazette, 816

Music
Barber, Samuel, 856

National Reporting
Mollenhoff, Clark Raymond, 900
Morin, Relman George, 614

Photography
Beall, William Charles, 995

Poetry
Warren, Robert Penn, 977

Special Awards and Citations: Journalism
Lippmann, Walter, 629

1959

Biography or Autobiography
Walworth, Arthur Clarence, 54

Drama
MacLeish, Archibald, 201

Editorial Cartooning
Mauldin, William Henry, 254

Editorial Writing
McGill, Ralph Emerson, 332

Fiction
Taylor, Robert Lewis, 454

History
Schneider, Jean, 571
White, Leonard Dupee, 572

International Reporting
Martin, Joseph George, 625
Santora, Philip Joseph, 626

Local Reporting, Edition Time
Werner, Mary Lou, 769

Local Reporting, No Edition Time
Brislin, John Harold, 783

Meritorious Public Service
Utica Daily Press, 817
Utica Observer-Dispatch, 818

Music
La Montaine, John, 857

National Reporting
Van Smith, Howard, 901

Photography
Seaman, William Casper, 996

Poetry
Kunitz, Stanley, 1033

1960

Biography or Autobiography
Morison, Samuel Eliot, 37

Drama
Abbott, George, 202
Bock, Jerry, 203
Harnick, Sheldon, 204
Weidman, Jerome, 205

Editorial Cartooning
No award

Editorial Writing
Chambers, Lenoir, 333

Fiction
Drury, Allen Stuart, 455

History
Leech, Margaret, 557

International Reporting
Rosenthal, Abraham Michael, 627

Local Reporting, Edition Time
Nelson, John Howard, 770

Local Reporting, No Edition Time
Ottenberg, Miriam, 784

Meritorious Public Service
Los Angeles Times, 91

Music
Carter, Elliott, 858

National Reporting
Trimble, Vance Henry, 902

Photography
Lopez, Andrew, 997

Poetry
Snodgrass, W. D., 1034

Special Awards and Citations: Letters
Mattingly, Garrett, 1121

1961

Biography or Autobiography
Donald, David Herbert, 55

Drama
Mosel, Tad, 206

Editorial Cartooning
Orr, Carey, 265

Editorial Writing
Dorvillier, William Joseph, 334

Fiction
Lee, Harper, 456

History
Feis, Herbert, 573

International Reporting
Heinzerling, Lynn Louis, 628

Local Reporting, Edition Time
De Gramont, Sanche, 771

Local Reporting, No Edition Time
May, Edgar, 785

Meritorious Public Service
Amarillo Globe-Times, 819

Music
Piston, Walter, 848

National Reporting
Cony, Edward Roger, 903

Photography
Nagao, Yasushi, 998

Poetry
McGinley, Phyllis, 1035

Special Awards and Citations: Letters
American Heritage Picture History, 1122

1962

Biography or Autobiography
No award

Drama
Burrows, Abe, 207
Loesser, Frank, 208

Editorial Cartooning
Valtman, Edmund Siegfried, 266

Editorial Writing
Storke, Thomas More, 335

Fiction
O'Connor, Edwin Greene, 457

General Non-Fiction
White, Theodore H., 494

History
Gipson, Lawrence Henry, 574

International Reporting
Lippmann, Walter, 629

Local Reporting, Edition Time
Mullins, Robert D., 772

Local Reporting, No Edition Time
Bliss, George William, 786

Meritorious Public Service
Panama City News-Herald, 820

Music
Ward, Robert Eugene, 859

National Reporting
Caldwell, Nathan Green, 904
Graham, Gene Swann, 905

Photography
Vathis, Paul, 999

Poetry
Dugan, Alan, 1036

1963

Biography or Autobiography
Edel, Leon, 56

Drama
No award

Editorial Cartooning
Miller, Frank, 267

Editorial Writing
Harkey Jr., Ira Brown, 336

Fiction
Faulkner, William, 451

General Non-Fiction
Tuchman, Barbara W., 495

History
Green, Constance McLaughlin, 575

International Reporting
Hendrix, Harold Victor, 630

Local Reporting, Edition Time
Fox, Sylvan, 773
Longgood, William Frank, 774
Shannon, Anthony F., 775

Local Reporting, No Edition Time
Griffin Jr., Oscar O'Neal, 787

Meritorious Public Service
Chicago Daily News, 810

Music
Barber, Samuel, 856

National Reporting
Lewis, Joseph Anthony, 897

Photography
Rondon, Hector, 1000

Poetry
Williams, William Carlos, 1037

1964

Biography or Autobiography
Bate, Walter Jackson, 57

Drama
No award

Editorial Cartooning
Conrad, Paul Francis, 268

Editorial Writing
Smith, Hazel Brannon, 337

Fiction
No award

General Non-Fiction
Hofstadter, Richard, 496

History
Powell, Sumner Chilton, 576

International Reporting
Browne, Malcolm Wilde, 631
Halberstam, David, 632

Local General Spot News Reporting
Miller Jr., Norman Charles, 703

Local Investigative Specialized Reporting
Gaudiosi, Albert V., 723
Magee, James V., 724
Meyer, Frederick A., 725

Meritorious Public Service
St. Petersburg Times, 821

Music
No award

National Reporting
Smith, A. Merriman, 906

Photography
Jackson, Robert Hill, 1001

Poetry
Simpson, Louis, 1038

Special Awards and Citations: Journalism
Gannett News Service, 830

1965

Biography or Autobiography
Samuels, Ernest, 58

Drama
Gilroy, Frank D., 209

Editorial Cartooning
No award

Editorial Writing
Harrison, John Raymond, 338

Fiction
Grau, Shirley Ann, 458

General Non-Fiction
Jones, Howard Mumford, 497

History
Unger, Irwin, 577

International Reporting
Livingston, Joseph Arnold, 633

Local General Spot News Reporting
Ruder, Melvin Harvey, 704

Local Investigative Specialized Reporting
Goltz, Eugene Francis, 726

Meritorious Public Service
Hutchinson News, 822

Music
No award

National Reporting
Kohlmeier Jr., Louis Martin, 907

Photography
Faas, Horst, 1002

Poetry
Berryman, John, 1039

1966

Biography or Autobiography
Schlesinger Jr., Arthur Meier, 59

Drama
No award

Editorial Cartooning
Wright, Donald Conway, 269

Editorial Writing
Lasch, Robert N., 339

Fiction
Porter, Katherine Anne, 459

General Non-Fiction
Teale, Edwin Way, 498

History
Miller, Perry Gilbert Eddy, 578

International Reporting
Arnett, Peter Gregg, 634

Local General Spot News Reporting
Los Angeles Times, 91

Local Investigative Specialized Reporting
Frasca, John Anthony, 727

Meritorious Public Service
Boston Globe, 823

Music
Bassett, Leslie Raymond, 860

National Reporting
Johnson, Haynes Bonner, 908

Photography
Sawada, Kyoichi, 1003

Poetry
Eberhart, Richard, 1040

1967

Biography or Autobiography
Kaplan, Justin, 60

Drama
Albee, Edward Franklin, 210

Editorial Cartooning
Oliphant, Patrick Bruce, 270

Editorial Writing
Patterson, Eugene Corbett, 340

Fiction
Malamud, Bernard, 460

General Non-Fiction
Davis, David Brion, 499

History
Goetzmann, William Henry, 579

International Reporting
Hughes, Robert John, 635

Local General Spot News Reporting
Cox, Robert Vernon, 705

Local Investigative Specialized Reporting
Miller, Gene Edward, 714

Meritorious Public Service
Louisville Courier-Journal, 295
Milwaukee Journal, 788

Music
Kirchner, Leon, 861

National Reporting
Karmin, Monroe William, 909
Penn, Stanley William, 910

Photography
Thornell, Jack Randolph, 1004

Poetry
Sexton, Anne, 1041

1968

Biography or Autobiography
Kennan, George F., 61

Drama
No award

Editorial Cartooning
Payne, Eugene Gray, 271

Editorial Writing
Knight, John Shively, 341

Feature Photography
Sakai, Toshio, 397

Fiction
Styron, William, 461

General Non-Fiction
Durant, Ariel, 500
Durant, William James, 501

History
Bailyn, Bernard, 580

International Reporting
Friendly, Alfred, 636

Local General Spot News Reporting
Detroit Free Press, 328

Local Investigative Specialized Reporting
Lukas, J. Anthony, 520

Meritorious Public Service
Riverside Press-Enterprise, 824

Music
Crumb, George, 862

National Reporting
James Jr., Howard Anthony, 911
Kotz, Nathan Kallison, 912

Poetry
Hecht, Anthony, 1042

Spot News Photography
Morabito, Rocco, 1139

1969

Biography or Autobiography
Reid, Benjamin Lawrence, 62

Drama
Sackler, Howard, 211

Editorial Cartooning
Fischetti, John R., 272

Editorial Writing
Greenberg, Paul, 342

Feature Photography
Sleet Jr., Moneta J., 398

Fiction
Momaday, N. Scott, 462

General Non-Fiction
Dubos, Rene Jules, 502
Mailer, Norman, 470

History
Levy, Leonard W., 581

International Reporting
Tuohy, William Klaus, 637

Local General Spot News Reporting
Fetterman, John Davis, 706

Local Investigative Specialized Reporting
Delugach, Albert Lawrence, 728
Walsh, Denny Jay, 729

Meritorious Public Service
Los Angeles Times, 91

Music
Husa, Karel, 863

National Reporting
Cahn, Robert, 913

Poetry
Oppen, George, 1043

Spot News Photography
Adams, Edward Thomas, 1140

1970

Biography or Autobiography
Williams, T. Harry, 63

Commentary
Childs, Marquis William, 92

Criticism
Huxtable, Ada Louise, 139

Drama
Gordone, Charles, 212

Editorial Cartooning
Darcy, Thomas Francis, 273

Editorial Writing
Geyelin, Philip Laussat, 343

Feature Photography
Kinney, Dallas, 399

Fiction
Stafford, Jean, 463

General Non-Fiction
Erikson, Erik H., 503

History
Acheson, Dean, 582

International Reporting
Hersh, Seymour Myron, 638

Local General Spot News Reporting
Fitzpatrick, Thomas, 707

Local Investigative Specialized Reporting
Martin, Harold Eugene, 730

Meritorious Public Service
Newsday, 722

Music
Wuorinen, Charles, 864

National Reporting
Eaton, William James, 914

Poetry
Howard, Richard, 1044

Spot News Photography
Starr, Steven Dawson, 1141

1971

Biography or Autobiography
Thompson, Lawrance, 64

Commentary
Caldwell, William Anthony, 93

Criticism
Schonberg, Harold Charles, 140

Drama
Zindel, Paul, 213

Editorial Cartooning
Conrad, Paul Francis, 268

Editorial Writing
Davis Jr., Horance Gibbs, 344

Feature Photography
Dykinga, Jack William, 400

Fiction
No award

General Non-Fiction
Toland, John, 504

History
Burns, James MacGregor, 583

International Reporting
Hoagland, Jimmie Lee, 112

Local General Spot News Reporting
Akron Beacon Journal, 490

Local Investigative Specialized Reporting
Jones, William Hugh, 731

Meritorious Public Service
Winston-Salem Journal and Sentinel, 825

Music
Davidovsky, Mario, 865

National Reporting
Franks, Lucinda Laura, 915

Powers, Thomas Moore, 916

Poetry
Merwin, William S., 1045

Spot News Photography
Filo, John Paul, 1142

1972

Biography or Autobiography
Lash, Joseph P., 65

Commentary
Royko, Michael, 94

Criticism
Peters Jr., Frank Lewis, 141

Drama
No award

Editorial Cartooning
MacNelly, Jeffrey Kenneth, 274

Editorial Writing
Strohmeyer, John, 345

Feature Photography
Kennerly, David Hume, 401

Fiction
Stegner, Wallace, 464

General Non-Fiction
Tuchman, Barbara W., 495

History
Degler, Carl N., 584

International Reporting
Kann, Peter Robert, 639

Local General Spot News Reporting
Cooper, Richard Lee, 708
Machacek, John W., 709

Local Investigative Specialized Reporting
DeSantis, Ann, 732
Kurkjian, Stephen Anoosh, 733
Leland, Timothy, 734
O'Neill, Gerard Michael, 735

Meritorious Public Service
New York Times, 375

Music
Druckman, Jacob, 866

National Reporting
Anderson, Jack, 917

Poetry
Wright, James, 1046

Spot News Photography
Faas, Horst, 1002
Laurent, Michel, 1143

1973

Biography or Autobiography
Swanberg, W.A., 66

Commentary
Broder, David Salzer, 95

Criticism
Powers, Ronald D., 142

Drama
Miller, Jason, 214

Editorial Cartooning
No award

Editorial Writing
Linscott, Roger Bourne, 346

Feature Photography
Lanker, Brian Timothy, 402

Fiction
Welty, Eudora, 465

General Non-Fiction
Coles, Robert, 505
Fitzgerald, Frances, 506

History
Kammen, Michael, 585

International Reporting
Frankel, Max, 640

Local General Spot News Reporting
Chicago Tribune, 710

Local Investigative Specialized Reporting
Sun Newspapers of Omaha, 736

Meritorious Public Service
Washington Post, 826

Music
Carter, Elliott, 858

National Reporting
Boyd, Robert S., 918
Hoyt, Clark, 919

Poetry
Kumin, Maxine, 1047

Special Awards and Citations: Letters
Flexner, James Thomas, 1123

Spot News Photography
Ut, Huynh Cong, 1144

1974

Biography or Autobiography
Sheaffer, Louis, 67

Commentary
Roberts Jr., Edwin Albert, 96

Criticism
Genauer, Emily, 143

Drama
No award

Editorial Cartooning
Szep, Paul Michael, 275

Editorial Writing
Spencer, Frederick Gilman, 347

Feature Photography
Veder, Slava, 403

Fiction
No award

General Non-Fiction
Becker, Ernest, 507

History
Boorstin, Daniel J., 586

International Reporting
Smith, Hedrick Laurence, 641

Local General Spot News Reporting
Hough, Hugh Frederick, 711
Petacque, Arthur Martin, 712

Local Investigative Specialized Reporting
Sherman, William, 737

Meritorious Public Service
Newsday, 722

Music
Martino, Donald, 867

National Reporting
Polk, James Ray, 920
White III, John Aloysius, 921

Poetry
Lowell, Robert, 1024

Special Awards and Citations: Music
Sessions, Roger, 874

Spot News Photography
Roberts, Anthony K., 1145

1975

Biography or Autobiography
Caro, Robert, 68

Commentary
McGrory, Mary, 97

Criticism
Ebert, Roger Joseph, 144

Drama
Albee, Edward Franklin, 210

Editorial Cartooning
Trudeau, Garretson Beekman, 276

Editorial Writing
Maurice, John Daniell, 348

Feature Photography
Lewis, Matthew, 404

Fiction
Shaara, Michael, 466

General Non-Fiction
Dillard, Annie, 508

History
Malone, Dumas, 587

International Reporting
Carter, Ovie, 642
Mullen, William Charles, 643

Local General Spot News Reporting
Xenia Daily Gazette, 713

Local Investigative Specialized Reporting
Indianapolis Star, 738

Meritorious Public Service
Boston Globe, 823

Music
Argento, Dominick, 868

National Reporting
Barlett, Donald Leon, 922
Steele Jr., James Bruce, 923

Poetry
Snyder, Gary, 1048

Spot News Photography
Gay, Gerald Harry, 1146

1976

Biography or Autobiography
Lewis, R.W.B. (Richard Warrington Baldwin), 69

Commentary
Smith, Walter Wellesley, 98

Criticism
Kriegsman, Alan Mortimer, 145

Drama
Bennett, Michael, 215
Dante, Nicholas, 216
Hamlisch, Marvin, 217
Kirkwood, James, 218
Kleban, Edward, 219

Editorial Cartooning
Auth Jr., William Anthony, 277

Editorial Writing
Kerby, Philip Pearce, 349

Feature Photography
Louisville Courier-Journal, 295

Fiction
Bellow, Saul, 467

General Non-Fiction
Butler, Robert Neil, 509

History
Horgan, Paul, 569

International Reporting
Schanberg, Sydney Hillel, 644

Local General Spot News Reporting
Miller, Gene Edward, 714

Local Investigative Specialized Reporting
Chicago Tribune, 710

Meritorious Public Service
Anchorage Daily News, 827

Music
Rorem, Ned, 869

National Reporting
Risser Jr., James Vaulx, 924

Poetry
Ashbery, John, 1049

Special Awards and Citations: Journalism
Hohenberg, John, 1116

Special Awards and Citations: Music
Joplin, Scott, 1128

Spot News Photography
Forman, Stanley Joseph, 1147

1977

Biography or Autobiography
Mack, John E., 70

Commentary
Will, George Frederick, 99

Criticism
McPherson, William Alexander, 146

Drama
Cristofer, Michael, 220

Editorial Cartooning
Szep, Paul Michael, 275

Editorial Writing
Cardoza, Norman Francis, 350
Church, Foster, 351
Lerude, Warren Leslie, 352

Feature Photography
Hood, Robin Lee, 405

Fiction
No award

General Non-Fiction
Warner, William Whitesides, 510

Spot News Photography
Price, Larry C., 414

1982

Biography or Autobiography
McFeely, William Shield, 74

Commentary
Buchwald, Arthur, 103

Criticism
Bernheimer, Martin, 151

Drama
Fuller, Charles, 225

Editorial Cartooning
Sargent, Ben, 279

Editorial Writing
Rosenthal, Jacob, 356

Feature Photography
White, John Henry, 410

Feature Writing
Pett, Saul, 428

Fiction
Updike, John Hoyer, 472

General Non-Fiction
Kidder, John Tracy, 515

History
Woodward, Comer Vann, 593

International Reporting
Darnton, John Townsend, 650

Local General Spot News Reporting
Kansas City Star, 306
Kansas City Times, 720

Local Investigative Specialized Reporting
Henderson III, Paul, 750

Meritorious Public Service
Detroit News, 832

Music
Sessions, Roger, 874

National Reporting
Atkinson, Rick, 930

Poetry
Plath, Sylvia, 1054

Special Awards and Citations: Music
Babbitt, Milton, 1129

Spot News Photography
Edmonds, Ronald, 1152

1983

Biography or Autobiography
Baker, Russell Wayne, 75

Commentary
Sitton, Claude Fox, 104

Criticism
Hoelterhoff, Manuela Vali, 152

Drama
Norman, Marsha, 226

Editorial Cartooning
Locher, Richard Earl, 280

Editorial Writing
Miami Herald, 357

Feature Photography
Dickman, James Bruce, 411

Feature Writing
Robertson, Nan, 429

Fiction
Walker, Alice, 473

General Non-Fiction
Sheehan, Susan, 516

History
Isaac, Rhys Llywelyn, 594

International Reporting
Friedman, Thomas Loren, 651
Jenkins, Loren B., 652

Local General Spot News Reporting
Fort Wayne News-Sentinel, 721

Local Investigative Specialized Reporting
Tofani, Loretta A., 751

Meritorious Public Service
Jackson Clarion-Ledger, 833

Music
Zwilich, Ellen Taaffe, 875

National Reporting
Boston Globe, 823

Poetry
Kinnell, Galway, 1055

Spot News Photography
Foley, Bill, 1153

1984

Biography or Autobiography
Harlan, Louis R., 76

Commentary
Royster, Vermont Connecticut, 105

1985

1986

Biography or Autobiography
Frank, Elizabeth, 78

Commentary
Breslin, Jimmy, 107

Criticism
Henahan, Donal Joseph, 155

Drama
No award

Editorial Cartooning
Feiffer, Jules Ralph, 281

Editorial Writing
Fuller, Jack William, 360

Explanatory Journalism
New York Times, 375

Feature Photography
Gralish, Tom, 415

Feature Writing
Camp, John Roswell, 432

Fiction
McMurtry, Larry, 476

General News Reporting
Buchanan, Edna, 489

General Non-Fiction
Lelyveld, Joseph, 519
Lukas, J. Anthony, 520

History
McDougall, Walter Allen, 596

International Reporting
Carey, Peter Kevin, 657
Ellison, Katherine, 658
Simons, Lewis Martin, 659

Investigative Reporting
Marx, Jeffrey A., 676
York, Michael M., 677

Meritorious Public Service
Denver Post, 835

Music
Perle, George, 878

National Reporting
Flournoy, John Craig, 933
Howe IV, Arthur W., 934
Rodrigue III, George Pierre, 935

Poetry
Taylor, Henry, 1058

Specialized Reporting
Flaherty, Mary Pat, 1133
Schneider, Andrew J., 1134

Spot News Photography
duCille, Michel, 417
Guzy, Carol, 1155

1987

Biography or Autobiography
Garrow, David J., 79

Commentary
Krauthammer, Charles, 108

Criticism
Eder, Richard Gray, 156

Drama
Wilson, August, 230

Editorial Cartooning
Breathed, Guy Berkeley, 282

Editorial Writing
Freedman, Jonathan, 361

Explanatory Journalism
Gorner, Peter, 376
Lyon, Jeffrey R., 377

Feature Photography
Peterson, David Charles, 416

Feature Writing
Twomey, Stephen M., 433

Fiction
Taylor, Peter Hillsman, 477

General News Reporting
Akron Beacon Journal, 490

General Non-Fiction
Shipler, David K., 521

History
Bailyn, Bernard, 580

International Reporting
Parks, Michael Christopher, 660

Investigative Reporting
Biddle, Daniel R., 678
Bissinger III, Henry Gerald, 679
Tulsky, Fredric Neal, 680
Woestendiek, John William, 681

Meritorious Public Service
Pittsburgh Press, 836

Music
Harbison, John, 879

National Reporting
Miami Herald, 357
New York Times, 375

Poetry
Dove, Rita, 1059

Special Awards and Citations: Journalism
Pulitzer Jr., Joseph, 1118

Specialized Reporting
Jones, Alex S., 1135

Spot News Photography
Komenich, Kim, 1156

Poetry
Meredith, William, 1060

Specialized Reporting
Bogdanich, Walt, 1136

Spot News Photography
Shaw, Scott Alan, 1157

1988

Biography or Autobiography
Donald, David Herbert, 55

Commentary
Barry, David M., 109

Criticism
Shales, Thomas W., 157

Drama
Uhry, Alfred, 231

Editorial Cartooning
Marlette, Douglas Nigel, 283

Editorial Writing
Healy, Jane Elizabeth, 362

Explanatory Journalism
Hertzberg, Daniel, 378
Stewart, James B., 379

Feature Photography
duCille, Michel, 417

Feature Writing
Banaszynski, Jacqueline Marie, 434

Fiction
Morrison, Toni, 478

General News Reporting
Alabama Journal, 491
Lawrence Eagle-Tribune, 492

General Non-Fiction
Rhodes, Richard, 522

History
Bruce, Robert V., 597

International Reporting
Friedman, Thomas Loren, 651

Investigative Reporting
Baquet, Dean Paul, 682
Gaines, William Chester, 683
Lipinski, Ann Marie, 684

Meritorious Public Service
Charlotte Observer, 831

Music
Bolcom, William, 880

National Reporting
Weiner, Timothy Emlyn, 936

1989

Biography or Autobiography
Ellmann, Richard, 80

Commentary
Page, Clarence Eugene, 110

Criticism
Skube, Michael, 158

Drama
Wasserstein, Wendy, 232

Editorial Cartooning
Higgins, Jack, 284

Editorial Writing
Wille, Lois Jean, 363

Explanatory Journalism
Blessen, Karen Alyce, 380
Hanners, David, 381
Snyder, William D., 382

Feature Photography
Crisostomo, Manny, 418

Feature Writing
Zucchino, David Alan, 435

Fiction
Tyler, Anne, 479

General News Reporting
Louisville Courier-Journal, 295

General Non-Fiction
Sheehan, Neil, 523

History
Branch, Taylor, 598
McPherson, James M., 599

International Reporting
Frankel, Glenn, 661
Keller, Bill, 662

Investigative Reporting
Dedman, Bill, 685

Meritorious Public Service
Anchorage Daily News, 827

Music
Reynolds, Roger, 881

National Reporting
Barlett, Donald Leon, 922

Steele Jr., James Bruce, 923

Poetry
Wilbur, Richard, 1032

Specialized Reporting
Humes, Edward, 1137

Spot News Photography
Olshwanger, Ron, 1158

1990

Biography or Autobiography
De Grazia, Sebastian, 81

Commentary
Murray, James Patrick, 111

Criticism
Temko, Allan Bernard, 159

Drama
Wilson, August, 230

Editorial Cartooning
Toles, Thomas G., 285

Editorial Writing
Hylton, Thomas James, 364

Explanatory Journalism
Coll, Stephen Wilson, 383
Vise, David Allan, 384

Feature Photography
Turnley, David Carl, 419

Feature Writing
Curtin, David Stephen, 436

Fiction
Hijuelos, Oscar, 480

General News Reporting
San Jose Mercury News, 493

General Non-Fiction
Maharidge, Dale Dmitro, 524
Williamson, Michael, 525

History
Karnow, Stanley, 600

International Reporting
Kristof, Nicholas D., 663
WuDunn, Sheryl, 664

Investigative Reporting
Ison, Christopher John, 686
Kilzer, Louis Charles, 687

Meritorious Public Service
Philadelphia Inquirer, 718
Washington (NC) Daily News, 837

Music
Powell, Mel, 882

National Reporting
Anderson, Ross, 937
Dietrich, William, 938
Gwinn, Mary Ann, 939
Nalder, Eric Christopher, 698

Poetry
Simic, Charles, 1061

Specialized Reporting
Stieber, Tamar, 1138

Spot News Photography
Oakland Tribune, 1159

1991

Beat Reporting
Angier, Natalie, 1

Biography or Autobiography
Naifeh, Steven Woodward, 82
Smith, Gregory White, 83

Commentary
Hoagland, Jimmie Lee, 112

Criticism
Shaw, David Lyle, 160

Drama
Simon, Neil, 233

Editorial Cartooning
Borgman, James Mark, 286

Editorial Writing
Casey, Ronald Bruce, 365
Jackson, Harold, 366
Kennedy Jr., Joey David, 367

Explanatory Journalism
Faludi, Susan C., 385

Feature Photography
Snyder, William D., 382

Feature Writing
James, Sheryl Teresa, 437

Fiction
Updike, John Hoyer, 472

General Non-Fiction
Holldobler, Bert, 526
Wilson, Edward Osbourne, 512

History
Ulrich, Laurel Thatcher, 601

International Reporting
Murphy, Caryle Marie, 665
Schmemann, Serge, 666

Investigative Reporting
Hallinan, Joseph Thomas, 688
Headden, Susan M., 689

Meritorious Public Service
Des Moines Register, 838

Music
Ran, Shulamit, 883

National Reporting
Lundstrom, Marjorie Eleanor, 940
Sharpe, Rochelle Phyllis, 941

Poetry
Van Duyn, Mona, 1062

Spot News Photography
Marinovich, Greg, 1160

Spot News Reporting
Miami Herald, 357

1992

Beat Reporting
Blum, Deborah Leigh, 2

Biography or Autobiography
Puller Jr., Lewis B., 84

Commentary
Quindlen, Anna, 113

Criticism
No award

Drama
Schenkkan, Robert, 234

Editorial Cartooning
Wilkinson, Signe, 287

Editorial Writing
Henson, Glenda Maria, 368

Explanatory Journalism
Capers, Robert S., 386
Lipton, Eric S., 387

Feature Photography
Kaplan, John, 420

Feature Writing
Raines, Howell Hiram, 438

Fiction
Smiley, Jane Graves, 481

General Non-Fiction
Yergin, Daniel, 527

History
Neeley Jr., Mark E., 602

International Reporting
Sloyan, Patrick Joseph, 667

Investigative Reporting
Adams, Lorraine, 690
Malone, Dan F., 691

Meritorious Public Service
Sacramento Bee, 800

Music
Peterson, Wayne Turner, 884

National Reporting
McGraw, Mike, 942
Taylor, Jeff, 943

Poetry
Tate, James, 1063

Special Awards and Citations: Letters
Spiegelman, Art, 1127

Spot News Photography
Associated Press, 421

Spot News Reporting
Newsday, 722

1993

Beat Reporting
Ingrassia, Paul Joseph, 3
White, Joseph B., 4

Biography or Autobiography
McCullough, David, 85

Commentary
Balmaseda, Elizabeth R., 114

Criticism
Dirda, Michael, 161

Drama
Kushner, Tony, 235

Editorial Cartooning
Benson, Stephen Reed, 288

Editorial Writing
No award

Explanatory Journalism
Toner, Michael F., 388

Feature Photography
Associated Press, 421

Feature Writing
Lardner Jr., George, 439

Fiction
Butler, Robert Olen, 482

General Non-Fiction
Wills, Garry, 528

History
Wood, Gordon Stewart, 603

International Reporting
Burns, John Fisher, 668
Gutman, Roy William, 669

Investigative Reporting
Berry, Steve, 692
Brazil, Jeff, 693

Meritorious Public Service
Miami Herald, 357

Music
Rouse III, Christopher Chapman, 885

National Reporting
Maraniss, David Adair, 944

Poetry
Gluck, Louise, 1064

Spot News Photography
Geiger, Ken, 1161
Snyder, William D., 382

Spot News Reporting
Los Angeles Times, 91

1994

Beat Reporting
Freedman, Eric, 5
Mitzelfeld, Jim, 6

Biography or Autobiography
Lewis, David Levering, 86

Commentary
Raspberry, William James, 115

Criticism
Schwartz, Lloyd, 162

Drama
Albee, Edward Franklin, 210

Editorial Cartooning
Ramirez, Michael Patrick, 289

Editorial Writing
Dold, Robert Bruce, 369

Explanatory Journalism
Kotulak, Ronald, 389

Feature Photography
Carter, Kevin, 422

Feature Writing
Wilkerson, Isabel Alexis, 440

Fiction
Proulx, E. Annie, 483

General Non-Fiction
Remnick, David, 529

History
No award

International Reporting
Dallas Morning News, 670

Investigative Reporting
Providence Journal-Bulletin, 694

Meritorious Public Service
Akron Beacon Journal, 490

Music
Schuller, Gunther Alexander, 886

National Reporting
Welsome, Eileen, 945

Poetry
Komunyakaa, Yusef, 1065

Spot News Photography
Watson, Paul, 1162

Spot News Reporting
New York Times, 375

1995

Beat Reporting
Shribman, David M., 7

Biography or Autobiography
Hedrick, Joan D., 87

Commentary
Dwyer, James, 116

Criticism
Jefferson, Margo L., 163

Drama
Foote, Horton, 236

Editorial Cartooning
Luckovich, Mike, 290

Editorial Writing
Good, Jeffrey, 370

Explanatory Journalism
Dash Jr., Leon DeCosta, 390
Perkins, Lucian, 391

Feature Photography
Associated Press, 421

Feature Writing
Suskind, Ronald Steven, 441

Fiction
Shields, Carol, 484

General Non-Fiction
Weiner, Jonathan, 530

History
Goodwin, Doris Kearns, 604

International Reporting
Fritz, Mark, 671

Investigative Reporting
Donovan, Brian R., 695
Saul, Stephanie, 696

Meritorious Public Service
Virgin Islands Daily News, 839

Music
Gould, Morton, 887

National Reporting
Horwitz, Anthony Lander, 946

Poetry
Levine, Philip, 1066

Spot News Photography
Guzy, Carol, 1155

Spot News Reporting
Los Angeles Times, 91

1996

Beat Reporting
Keeler, Robert F., 8

Biography or Autobiography
Miles, Jack, 88

Commentary
Shipp, E.R., 117

Criticism
Campbell, Robert, 164

Drama
Larson, Jonathan, 237

Editorial Cartooning
Morin, James, 291

Editorial Writing
Semple Jr., Robert Baylor, 371

Explanatory Journalism
Garrett, Laurie, 392

Feature Photography
Welsh, Stephanie, 423

Feature Writing
Bragg, Ricky Edward, 442

Fiction
Ford, Richard, 485

General Non-Fiction
Rosenberg, Tina, 531

History
Taylor, Alan, 605

International Reporting
Rohde, David, 672

Investigative Reporting
Orange County Register, 697

Meritorious Public Service
News & Observer, 840

Music
Walker, George, 888

National Reporting
Freedman, Alix M., 947

Poetry
Graham, Jorie, 1067

Special Awards and Citations: Journalism
Caen, Herbert Eugene, 1119

Spot News Photography
Porter IV, Charles H., 1163

Spot News Reporting
McFadden, Robert Dennis, 1166

1997

Beat Reporting
Acohido, Byron, 9

Biography or Autobiography
McCourt, Frank, 89

Commentary
McNamara, Eileen, 118

Criticism
Page, Tim, 165

Drama
No award

Editorial Cartooning
Handelsman, Walt, 292

Editorial Writing
Gartner, Michael Gay, 372

Explanatory Journalism
Cortes, Ron, 393
Saul, April, 394
Vitez, Michael, 395

Feature Photography
Zemlianichenko, Alexander Vadimovich, 424

Feature Writing
Pollak, Lisa K., 443

Fiction
Millhauser, Steven, 486

General Non-Fiction
Kluger, Richard, 532

History
Rakove, Jack N., 606

International Reporting
Burns, John Fisher, 668

Investigative Reporting
Nalder, Eric Christopher, 698
Nelson, Deborah, 699
Tizon, Alex, 700

Meritorious Public Service
Times-Picayune, 841

Music
Marsalis, Wynton, 889

National Reporting
Wall Street Journal, 948

Poetry
Mueller, Lisel, 1068

Spot News Photography
Wells, Annie, 1164

Spot News Reporting
Newsday, 722

1998

Beat Reporting
Greenhouse, Linda Joyce, 10

Biography or Autobiography
Graham, Katharine, 90

Breaking News Reporting
Los Angeles Times, 91

Commentary
McAlary, Michael, 119

Criticism
Kakutani, Michiko, 166

Drama
Vogel, Paula, 238

Editorial Cartooning
Breen, Stephen P., 293

Editorial Writing
Stein, Bernard L., 373

Explanatory Journalism
Salopek, Paul F., 396

Feature Photography
Williams, Clarence, 425

Feature Writing
French, Thomas, 444

Fiction
Roth, Philip, 487

General Non-Fiction
Diamond, Jared Mason, 533

History
Larson, Edward John, 607

International Reporting
New York Times, 375

Investigative Reporting
Cohn, Gary, 701
Englund, Will, 702

Meritorious Public Service
Grand Forks Herald, 842

Music
Kernis, Aaron Jay, 890

National Reporting
Carollo, Russell, 949
Nesmith, Jeff, 950

Poetry
Wright, Charles, 1069

Special Awards and Citations: Music
Gershwin, George, 1130

Spot News Photography
Rial, Martha, 1165